The Stanford Companion
to Victorian Fiction

The Stanford Companion to Victorian Fiction

John Sutherland

Stanford University Press
Stanford, California

Stanford University Press,
Stanford, California

First published as *The Longman Companion to Victorian Fiction* by Longman Group UK Ltd

First published in the United States of America by Stanford University Press, 1989

LC 88-61462

ISBN 0-8047-1528-9

Printed in Singapore

Preface

There are two ways of existing for ever, as a living creature
or as a mummy. Now in these days of literary activity the
continuation of a large number of literary mummies is certain. They will be preserved in their hundreds by biographies,
dictionaries, etc. We shall know their names, but how many
writers of the Victorian era will remain alive through the
ages? Half a dozen?

— Maarten Maartens, 1889

LIBRARIANS will shelve this volume under 'Reference'. The designation
properly reflects the *Companion*'s main duty as a source of ready factual
information about Victorian fiction and its immediate context. The lack of
such a source (equivalent in nature, say, to *Jane's All The World's Aircraft*)
has often added weary time to my own research. The following 1,606 entries
aim, above all, to be useful and timesaving.

There is another aim. Over the last 88 years, our map of nineteenth-
century fiction has shrunk to Lilliputian dimensions. The tiny working areas of the 'canon', the 'syllabus' and the paperbacked 'classics' are poor
reflections of what the Victorian novel actually meant to Victorians. Generations of students have left their academies thinking that this richest
of literary fields comprises half-a-shelf's length of works by Dickens, two
Brontës, George Eliot and Hardy. (Add a handful of titles from Fielding,
Woolf and Lawrence and you can call it for most academic purposes 'the
English novel'.) And within the academy, scholars have similarly pared the
subject area to exclusive first and second divisions. Thus the authoritative
NCBEL confidently lists eighteen 'major' and 190 'minor' authors as consti-
tuting the field. Both categories seriously underrate the range and depth of
the Victorian novel which has effectively become a lost continent of English
literature.

It is one of the larger lost continents. Annual statistics in the *Publisher's Circular* suggest that there were somewhere around 60,000 works
of adult and juvenile fiction published 1837–1901 (i.e. around 20 percent of
total book production in the period). Non-book tract fiction produced by
evangelical organisations like the Religious Tract Society and short stories in
magazines might well double this figure. There were, at an educated guess,
around 7,000 Victorians who could legitimately title themselves 'novelist'.

I would not condemn anyone to the lower reaches of Victorian fiction.
Life is too short and eternity scarcely long enough to read the 197-strong
output of Annie S. Swan or all the 251 works of L. T. Meade deposited in the
British Library. But not all the Victorian novels we neglect are worthless.
One of the questions often asked me during the five years' preparation of
this *Companion* was: 'what unread masterpieces have you discovered?'. Very

1

few, as it happens. (Although I would propose Ella Hepworth Dixon's *Story Of A Modern Woman* as the greatest unread novel of female struggle in the century.) In general, the best of Victorian fiction is fairly represented in the few novels we revere, read and re-read, adapt for television, set for examination and discuss in learned journals. But below this *corps d'élite* there is a quantity of first-rate and consistently worthwhile achievement which has been let go into oblivion; wrongly so, I would maintain. For this reason, I hope that in addition to being used, the *Companion* will be browsed in and that it may inspire readers of the Victorian novel, professional and lay, to cast their nets wider than is nowadays normal.

The following material is arranged alphabetically. There are several categories of entry. The bulk, 878, are on individual Victorian novelists (distinguished in the text by upper-case bold lettering for surname). Of these, 566 are men, 312 women. The per-author lifetime total of novels published by these writers breaks down to 17.6; 21 for the female and 15.7 titles for the male. (One of the interesting statistical facts to be derived from this gathering of facts is that 5 per cent of novelists acounted for just under a third of all the 15,490 works produced by the 878 authors.) Among the men, no less than 110 had law as either a concurrent or previous vocation. (Journalism comes second with 82.) Among the women, the vast bulk had no other recorded activity than being wives (167), or spinsters (113). Not surprisingly, perhaps, the Victorian spinster was the most productive single category of novelist, with an average lifetime output of 24 titles.

Some 554 Victorian novels are synopsised in the *Companion*. Arrangement is alphabetically by the first key word in the title: thus *The History Of Henry Esmond* will be found in the 'H' section, under 'Henry Esmond' not 'History'. Following the title and author (usually styled according to the title page, not the birth certificate) the date, publisher and details of the first volume and serial issues of the work are given. In using this information, the reader should bear in mind that the principal form of publication for Victorian fiction was the three-volume novel (or 'three-decker') costing 31s.6d. and designed for distribution by the circulating libraries (notably Mudie's and W. H. Smith's). The three-decker remained the main form of new fiction until 1894, when the libraries finally embargoed multi-volume novels. The single-volume novel at 6s. subsequently took over, its reign lasting until the 1930s.

Following Dickens's example with the epoch making *Pickwick Papers* (1836–37), a number of mid-Victorian novels were serialised in 32-page monthly numbers (usually from twelve to twenty) at 1s. per instalment. These novels in parts were normally in a larger format than the three-decker and illustrated, often with distinction, by artists of the calibre of George Cruikshank, Thackeray, Du Maurier, or John Leech. But in general, the novel in monthly numbers was a bow of Ulysses which only Dickens could draw with consistent success. After his death in 1870 (during the triumphant serialisation of *Edwin Drood*) it was seldom used. The last example I have found is William Black's *Sunrise*, in 1880. George Eliot's serialisation of her last novels in bi-monthly or monthly 5s. 'books' (unillustrated) is one among several variants of this Dickensian mode of part-issue.

The serialisation of novels in magazines began with Frederick Marryat's *Metropolitan* in the 1830s. The practice was boosted by the successful launch of *Bentley's Miscellany* (initially edited by Dickens) in 1837 and even more by George Smith's lavish *Cornhill Magazine* (1860, initially edited by Thackeray). Such monthly magazines costing as little as 1s. or less and carrying two illustrated serials and a wealth of other material were clearly a better bargain than the novel in numbers, and continued triumphantly with Newnes's *Strand Magazine* well into the 1890s.

Serialisation in newspapers was never as strong in Britain as in France. But the fiction-carrying *Chambers's Edinburgh Journal*, costing a penny-halfpenny a weekly issue and launched in 1832 paved the way for Dickens's 2d. weeklies *Household Words* and *All The Year Round*. For the literate masses, the *Sunday Times* had serialised novels in the 1840s, an innovation which was seized on by the Salisbury Square, or slum publishers, like Edward Lloyd and G. W. M. Reynolds, whose *Miscellany* is supposed to have had at its peak circulation of a quarter of a million among the semi-literate urban population. Juvenile fiction at the end of the century routinely came out in newspaper-format 'comics' like the 1d. *Boy's Own Paper*, aimed at a reading public newly enfranchised into literacy by the 1870 Education Act.

The *Companion* contains some 47 entries on Victorian magazines and periodicals. Several kinds of journal are covered: fiction-carrying miscellanies (often affiliated to publishing houses); major reviews and opinion-forming journals; booktrade magazines. These organs also provided a main vehicle for the advertising of Victorian books. The remaining entries deal with the major publishers of Victorian fiction (63) the dominant schools of novel-writing and such miscellaneous items as 'the yellowback' (38 entries) and major illustrators (26). Cross-references between entries in the text are indicated by an asterisk.

The widespread use of pseudonyms by Victorian novelists and the double use by women writers of maiden and married names create some difficulties. To reduce clutter, two indexes of variant names are given as appendices. They should be referred to when an author cannot be immediately located. Asterisks indicate the name under which the entry will be found. Within the text, novelists are normally entered according to the name by which they were primarily known to their contemporaries. (Thus 'Ouida', not 'Marie Louise de la Ramée'.)

There are two approved ways of writing a companion to literature of this kind. Team composition, while it divides the workload, can produce a certain deadness of presentation. Single authorship risks a higher degree of error and bias, but sometimes results in a zestier book. At least I hope it does, since I have undertaken to prepare this *Companion* single-handed. Among the many debts I have nevertheless accumulated, I wish to acknowledge those to Betsy Arbuckle, Rosemary Ashton, Robert A. and Vineta Colby, Philip Collins, Kate Flint, N. John Hall, Jenijoy La Belle, Bettina Lehmbeck, Susan Navarette, Patrick Scott, Michael Slater, Patricia Srebrnik, and Michael Wheeler. Over many years I have had the constant practical help and the scholarly example of Ken Fielding to whom I am particularly grateful. My colleague (and amateur Trollopian) Mac Pigman gave expert and unstinted assistance with typesetting the manuscript.

Abbreviations and Short Titles

BL   Indicates number of fiction titles listed in the *British Museum Catalogue of Printed Books* (263 vols, London: Trustees of the British Museum, 1965-66).

BLM   Indicates a main entry in *British Literary Magazines* (3 vols, ed. Alvin Sullivan, 1984, London: Greenwood Press).

Boase   Indicates a principal directory entry in Frederic Boase's *Modern English Biography* (6 vols, Truro: privately printed, 1892–1928).

DNB   Indicates a principal directory entry in the *Dictionary Of National Biography* (eds L. Stephen and S. Lee, 22 vols, London: Smith, Elder, 1908-09, and supplements).

Hou   Indicates a main entry in Simon Houfe's *The Dictionary Of British Book Illustrators And Caricaturists, 1800–1914* (London: The Antique Collectors' Club, 1978).

NCBEL   Indicates a main bibliographical entry in the *New Cambridge Bibliography Of English Literature* (5 vols, ed. George Watson, Cambridge University Press, 1969–77).

RLF   Indicates the author was an applicant to the Royal Literary Fund (archive by World Microfilms, 145 reels, 1984).

RM   Indicates the author has an entry in *A Dictionary Of Literature In The English Language, Vol I, From Chaucer To 1940* (Compiled and Edited by Robin Myers, London: Pergamon, 1970).

Sad   Indicates the author has title(s) listed in Michael Sadleir's *XIX Century Fiction* (2 vols, Cambridge University Press, 1951).

WI   Indicates a main entry in the *Wellesley Index To Victorian Periodicals* (4 vols, eds Walter E. and E. R. Houghton, and J. H. Slingerland, 1966–87, Toronto and London: University of Toronto Press, Routledge).

Wol   Indicates the author has title(s) listed in *Nineteenth-Century Fiction; A Bibliographical Catalogue Based On The Collection Formed By Robert Lee Wolff* (5 vols, New York: Garland, 1981–86).

WW   Indicates a principal directory entry in the semi-annual volumes of *Who's Who*, published from 1897 by A. and C. Black.

4

A

Aaron The Jew, Benjamin L. Farjeon, 1894, 3 vols, Hutchinson. Usually reckoned to be Farjeon's best novel incorporating as it does a mature examination of Victorian racial prejudice with a highly theatrical plot. The story begins in Portsmouth in the early 1870s. The philanthropic Doctor Spenlove saves an unwed mother, Mary Turner, from suicide. With the help of a benevolent Jewish pawnbroker the doctor contrives to have the unfortunate woman taken back by her former fiancé. Turner goes to Australia, leaving her bastard daughter to be adopted by a Gosport shopkeeper, Aaron Cohen. Aaron's wife, Rachel, is struck blind while delivering a stillborn baby daughter of her own. To preserve his wife's will to live, Aaron deludes her into thinking Mary Turner's child is theirs. The Cohens subsequently move to the south of France, where Aaron prospers as an engineer and has a son Joseph. He returns to England in 1893, enriched. But he is ruined by a rival, Poynter (in fact Mary Turner's original seducer), who publicises the true parentage of Ruth 'Cohen'. Ruth, meanwhile, has made a happy marriage with a young aristocratic gentile, Percy Storndale, having been told the secret of her past. At the end of the novel, Aaron is rescued by Mary, now a respectable woman, who reveals how honestly he has always acted. Despite wild narrative improbabilities, *Aaron The Jew* has numerous scenes reflective of the mean-minded persecution inflicted on the Victorian Jew.

à'BECKETT, Arthur [William] (1844–1909). Like his somewhat better-known father Gilbert Abbott and his brother Gilbert Arthur, à'Beckett is primarily remembered for the family association with *Punch**. Born in Fulham (where his father was a JP, as well as a prominent man of letters) he was sent to Felsted public school in Essex. But when in 1856 à'Beckett's father died the family income dwindled from £3,000 per annum to almost nothing and the subsequent years were difficult. After a half-hearted stab at clerking in the Post and War Offices (1862–64), the young man left the Civil Service for full-time work in periodical literature, around 1865. He subsequently edited a monthly magazine, *Britannia*, in the later 1860s and covered the Franco-Prussian War for the *Globe* in 1870. He was converted to Catholicism in 1874 (an act which may have been preparatory to his marriage two years later). In 1875 à'Beckett joined the staff of *Punch*, the paper which his father had helped found thirty years earlier. Unusually late in life, he determined to become a lawyer and was called to the Bar in 1882, at the advanced age of thirty-eight. But he never practised, returning instead to full-time journalism. At the high-point of his career, he edited the *Sunday Times*, 1891–95. On the side à'Beckett wrote half a dozen novels. *Fallen Among Thieves* (1870, hopefully subtitled 'A Novel Of Interest') is an early country-house murder story, featuring the detective* feats of John Barman. *The Ghost Of Greystone Grange* (1877) and *The Mystery Of Mostyn Manor* (1878) are routine thrillers. The author gives an amusing account of writing the second of these around some spare woodcuts which his publisher had.

An active and convivial man, à'Beckett entered his recreation for *Who's Who* as 'amateur soldiering' and was an active organiser for the profession of journalism. He died prematurely after an unsuccessful leg amputation. BL 7. *DNB*. Wol. RLF.

ABELL, F[rank] (i.e. Charles Butler Greatrex, 1832?–98). Greatrex, who also used the pseudonyms 'Lindon Meadows' and 'Abel Log', was born in Birmingham, the son of a lieutenant in the Royal Marines. On graduation from King's College, London he took orders in 1855 after which he held a succession of livings, mostly in the West Country. A writing parson of the hearty Charles Kingsley* stamp, he published a number of volumes of humorous sketches, random tales and boisterous verse. He also wrote (and himself competently illustrated) a successful novel, *The Adventures Of Maurice Drummore* (1884). This rollicking story of a Royal Marine evidently drew on his father's experiences. BL 3. Boase.

The Academy (1869–1916). A review founded on Arnoldian principles by Charles Appleton, an Oxford don, assisted by Mark Pattison and a coterie of university intellectuals. For its first year, the journal was published by the firm of Murray*. But Appleton quarrelled with him on the subject of advertisements. Thereafter, the financial base of the paper was precarious. Uncertain of its market, the *Academy* was monthly until 1871, then a fortnightly and after 1874 a weekly costing initially 6d. The paper's novel reviewers (who signed their pieces) are reckoned among the best in the period. (Edith Simcox writing as 'H. Lawrenny' stands out.) After 1874, the journal began the practice of group fiction reviews by Andrew Lang*, George Saintsbury and W. E. Henley. They were severe on fatuous stories and bad English and embody a systematic intention to raise the general 'trashy' and 'coarse' level of the English novel (as they saw it) to that of the French. Edmund Gosse* and (late in the century) Arnold Bennett were also *Academy* fiction reviewers of note. The paper shook off some of its Oxford academicism in 1896, when it was acquired by the rich American John Morgan Richards. But its later career was erratic, and dogged by poor sales. The *Academy* was a principal model for the twentieth-century *TLS* which took over its format and style. *BLM*.

ACKWORTH, John (i.e. the Rev. Frederick R. Smith, 1845–1919?). A Methodist minister, Smith wrote tales dealing with the lives of Lancashire mill hands, prominently featuring dialect humour. His most popular work in this vein was *The Clogshop Chronicles* (1896). Its success inspired a sequel, *Doxie Dent* (1899), whose heroine is an enterprising mill lass of the kind that Gracie Fields was later to immortalise on film. Smith gathered together other of his Lancashire stories as *The Scowcroft Critics* (1898) and *The Mangle House* (1902). *The Coming Of The Preachers* (1901) and *The Minder* (1900) chronicle the rise of Methodism. The last, subtitled: 'The Story Of The Courtship, Call And Conflicts Of John Ledger, Minder And Minister' probably contains autobiographical material. Otherwise, not much is known about Smith's life. By the end of the century, there was no objection to nonconformist ministers writing novels though pseudonyms were apparently prudent. BL 10. Wol.

Adam Bede, George Eliot, 1859, 3 vols, Blackwood. Eliot's first full-length novel. A runaway success, it provoked intense curiosity about the mysteriously pseudonymous author. *Adam Bede* is set in 1799–1807, in rural 'Hayslope' which is recognisably a village in Eliot's native Warwickshire. The Methodist revival is historically central in the narrative which opens with a scene introducing the carpenters Adam and Seth Bede. Adam, the harder and more interesting of the brothers, loves Hetty Sorrel who lives with her aunt and uncle Poyser at Hall Farm. Hetty is beautiful but shallow. Her cousin, Dinah Morris (also an orphan), is a Methodist evangelist, and has the moral depth Hetty lacks. Seth loves Dinah, but his adoration is returned only as friendship. The naïvely well-intentioned squire, Arthur Donnithorne, who has just come of age, sees Hetty in the dairy, and is captivated. Neglecting the counsels of his mentor, the Rev. Adolphus Irwine, Arthur seduces Hetty. Adam discovers what he thinks is mere flirtation, and thrashes the young squire whom previously he idolised. Arthur leaves in shame to join the militia, crushing Hetty with a farewell note. Listlessly, she agrees to marry Adam. But discovering she is pregnant, she follows the unwitting Arthur to Windsor. On the way, she lets her new-born child die for which she is arrested and condemned to hang. There is a moving episode on the eve of the execution in which Hetty is consoled by Dinah, and Arthur forgives the man who has wronged him. Hetty is reprieved on the scaffold and her sentence commuted to transportation. Adam marries Dinah. Arthur devotes his life to unspectacular reparation abroad. The novel, which is sternly moral, bears out Eliot's maxim that 'our deeds determine us as much as we determine our deeds'. But *Adam Bede*'s tone is lightened by the pastoral mood of its early sections, 'full of the breath of cows and the scent of hay'.

ADAM, G[raeme] M[ercer] (1839–1912). Adam was born near Edinburgh, and educated in the city. He went to Toronto in 1858 as an overseas publisher's representative and remained some years in Canada where he founded and edited various magazines, including the *Canadian Monthly*. In 1892, he moved to the USA. Adam wrote a number of books on Canadian history and with A. E. Wetherald co-authored the much reprinted historical romance, *An Algonquin Maiden* (1887). Set in 1820s Canada, the work's tone is chauvinistically hostile to the English colonial rulers for whom Adam seems to have retained a Scot's antipathy. BL 1. RM. Wol.

ADAMS, Mrs [Bertha Jane] Leith (née Grundy, 1850?–1912). Mrs Leith-Adams (as she was professionally known) worked on the staff of *All The Year Round**, from 1878, and as one of the earliest English women journalists must have been unusually resourceful. Born in Cheshire, the daughter of a solicitor, her first marriage was in 1859 to Surgeon-General Leith-Adams. It would seem from the far-flung backgrounds to her stories that the couple travelled extensively in the course of his military duty and Adams went on to introduce army settings into some of her later fiction, such as *A Garrison Romance* (1892). In 1882 Leith-Adams died, and a year later his widow married the Rev. Robert Stuart De Courcy Laffan, Rector of St Stephen Walbrook. An active educationalist, Laffan took a particular interest in higher education for the working classes. Mrs Leith-Adams (as she still was authorially) continued to write a vast quantity of fiction, of which the novel *Geoffrey Stirling* (1883) was the most popular. This story of a wife's ruthless revenge on the man who killed her husband is fashionably melodramatic. Like all Adams's fiction, it is written in a choppy, breathless style that jerks the reader along. Her other novels show some skill in ringing the changes on the galloping serials favoured by *All The Year Round*. They include wholesomely jaunty fiction targeted at the adolescent, like *Aunt Hepsy's Foundling* (1881); a new woman* novel about post-marital conflict, *Bonnie Kate* (1891); a patriotic military tale, *Colour Sergeant No.1 Company* (1894), which went into six editions; and simple moral pieces for the young like *Nancy's Work, A Church Story* (1876). Among other worthy causes, Mrs Leith-Adams interested herself actively in the promotion of women's and working-class education. BL 25. *WW*. Wol.

ADAMS, Francis [William Lauderdale] (1862–93). Remembered principally as a poet and essayist of Australian life, Adams was born as a member of the British garrison community in Malta. His paternal grandfather (also called Francis Adams) was a scholarly physician who gained fame as an authority on ancient Greek medicine. His father, Andrew Leith-Adams, a Scot, was an eminent military surgeon and later a professor in zoology at Queen's College, Cork and his mother was the successful novelist, Mrs Leith-Adams* (see above). Francis Adams went to school at Shrewsbury and spent the years 1878–80 as a student in Paris. He married and in 1882 emigrated to Australia having struggled unsuccessfully at school teaching. In Australia Adams joined the staff of the *Sydney Bulletin* and began to write extensively. He was by the early 1880s, estranged from his family. His candid autobiographical novel *Leicester* appeared in 1885 and its 'unnecessary realism' affronted some reviewers. (Adams rewrote the novel as *A Child Of The Age*, 1894.) In Sydney he had by now made a name for himself with his vigorous socialist poems *Songs Of The Army Of The Night* (1888). He was also writing on Australian topics for such English journals as the *Fortnightly Review*. By this time his first wife had died and he remarried Edith Goldstone, a former actress, in 1887. His writing had meanwhile won some popularity in England, where he returned in 1889. By now, Adams was seriously ill with consumption and he spent the winter of 1892–93 in Alexandria, Egypt. On returning to Margate he shot himself dead at the age of thirty-one after a particularly distressing haemorrhage. Adams's fiction is notable for its treatment of loneliness. Particularly effective are the early chapters of *Leicester*, which find the dreamy young hero adrift in London. *John Webb's End* (1891) is a vigorous study of bush life in Australia. Adams followed it with *Australian Life* (1892). *The Melbournians* (1892) deals with Australian urban life and has as its hero a young journalist who defeats an English earl for the heroine's love. As this plot suggests, Adams was politically radical and hated what he called English 'religious liberalism'. At the time of his suicide he was writing against British colonialism in the Middle East and his fiercely anti-aristocratic play *Tiberius* (1894) was published posthumously. BL 5. *DNB*. RM. Wol.

ADAMS, the Rev. H[enry] C[adwallader] (1817–99). Adams was born in London where his father was a judge. The family had its roots in the landowning Warwickshire gentry and Adams's childhood was materially comfortable. He was educated at Winchester public school (whose history he later wrote). After graduating from Oxford, where he took a first-class degree in classics, he was ordained in 1846 and served as a clergyman in Berkshire until 1878, later moving to a living in Sussex. As clergymen could, Adams also taught in various schools and wrote textbooks on classics. In later life he was a prolific producer of stories for boys and it was his quirk to introduce the word 'boy' into titles wherever he could. Hence, for instance: *Schoolboy Honour: A Tale Of Halminster College* (1861) and *The Boy Cavaliers* (1869). As a novelist Adams's main line was in adventure stories (e.g. *For James Or George?*, 1880), and mildly improving fiction for juvenile 'Sunday reading'. As an educationalist he strongly advocated the monitorial system by which boys taught boys. BL 42. Boase. Wol.

ADAMS-ACTON, Marion ('Jeanie Hering', née Hamilton, 1846–1928). Little is known of her life. Marion Hamilton was born on the island of Arran, and around 1865 married the sculptor, John Adams-Acton (1830–1910). As an author she wrote numerous novels under the Scottish-sounding pseudonym, 'Jeanie Hering'. (She is also sometimes listed by her publishers as Mrs Jeanie Acton.) Her writing career began with tales for juveniles such as: *Garry, A Holiday Story* (1867) and *Little Pickles* (1872). Her *Golden Days, A Tale Of A Girl's School Life In Germany* (1873) was widely reprinted. Other of her fiction is more obviously for adults, although a maternal vein of moralising runs through all her published work. Adams-Acton had stopped writing well before her death. BL 20. (JAA) *WW*.

ADCOCK, A[rthur] St John (1864–1930). Born in London, Adcock abandoned his career in law for literature in 1893. His first book, *An Unfinished Martyrdom And Other Stories* appeared the following year. In 1897, he brought out his *East End Idylls* and in 1898, the follow-up, *In The Image Of God*. Both portray London slum life in the graphically authentic style of Arthur Morrison* and the cockney* school of fiction. In 1900, Adcock published two topical Boer War novels: *In The Wake Of The War* (set on the home front) and the more jingoistic *The Luck Of Private Foster*. Adcock later became editor of the *Bookman** and lived comfortably in Hampstead as a leading man of twentieth-century letters. BL 14. *WW*. Wol.

ADDERLEY, the Hon. and Rev. James [Granville] (1861–1942). A son of the first Baron Norton (a Tory minister), Adderley was educated in the style of a young aristocrat at Eton and Oxford. He graduated in 1883 and took orders in 1888. As a pastor he interested himself particularly in the missions and settlements set up to help the working classes of London. He was director of Oxford House at Bethnal Green (1885–86) and for fifteen years thereafter ran the St Phillips Mission at Plaistow in east London. This first-hand experience inspired his fiercely Christian Socialist novels, *Stephen Remarx, A Religious Novelette* (1893) and *Paul Mercer* (1897). The first, subtitled 'The Story Of A Venture In Ethics', concerns a clergyman (the younger son of a lord) who tries to set up a commune in Hoxton, northeast London, and is closely reminiscent of Mrs Humphry Ward's* better-known *Robert Elsmere** (1888). It went into four editions in its first year selling over 20,000 copies in a pamphlet format. (It was one of the first novels published by Edward Arnold* and evidently helped set the house up.) The hero of *Paul Mercer* is a young millionaire who immerses himself in the slums of London's East End. The plot bears out Adderley's aggressive doctrine that 'work is worship' and in its details strongly recalls Walter Besant's* *All Sorts And Conditions Of Men** (1882) and is subtitled: 'A Story Of Repentance Among Millions'. Adderley wrote an introduction to his friend A. St John Adcock's* *East End Idylls* (1897). But novel writing was evidently a youthful and idealistic phase of his life which he soon gave up for more practical philanthropy. After 1904, he was a vicar in Saltley, the working-class area of Birmingham. BL 3. *WW.*

ADDISON, [Lt.-Col.] Henry Robert (1805–76). Addison was born in Calcutta and was commissioned into the 2nd Dragoon Guards in 1827. He rose to the rank of lieutenant-colonel, and was evidently mainly stationed overseas in Ireland and India. In 1833, he went on half pay. In retirement he took to writing and turned out around sixty dramas and farces, much journalism and some fiction. He was also for a time editor of *Who's Who.* Addison's most successful novel was *Behind The Curtain* (1865) whose sub-Wilkie Collins* sensation* plot was declared by the *Athenaeum** reviewer to be the most foolish he had ever read. *Traits And Stories Of Anglo-Indian Life* (1858) is the rag-bag its title suggests. Better is the semi-fictional *Recollections Of An Irish Police Magistrate* (1862), an early depiction of Victorian criminal detective* work. BL 4. Boase. Wol.

The Adventures Of Sherlock Holmes, Arthur Conan Doyle, 1892, 1 vol, Newnes. (Illustrated by Sidney Paget*.) The first book collection of Holmes stories, reprinted from the *Strand Magazine**. The volume contained a dozen of the amateur sleuth's earliest cases including: 'The Five Orange Pips', 'The Speckled Band' and 'The Man With A Twisted Lip'. Doyle began the Holmes saga speculatively, with 'A Case Of Identity'. Thereafter, the stories followed a set formula: the Baker Street detective and his confidant Dr Watson would be presented a fiendishly complex mystery which the inscrutable Holmes would solve by the application of pure intellect, usually keeping the gullible Watson (and the reader) in the dark until the very last moment. Much of the physical appearance of Holmes (his hatchet profile and deerstalker, for instance) was supplied by Sidney Paget. Doyle underrated the Holmes stories, thinking them inferior to his historical* romances. But the public adored 'the unofficial detective' and Holmes became a literary cult object. Some 20,000 copies of the *Adventures* were sold within the year. Doyle was constrained to write a sequel, *The Memoirs Of Sherlock Holmes* (1894), which ends with the hero apparently plunging to his death in the Reichenbach Falls grappling with his great adversary Professor Moriarty on 4 May 1891. American publishers induced Doyle to revive the detective for yet another series, *The Return Of Sherlock Holmes*, in 1905.

After London, Richard Jefferies, 1885, 1 vol, Cassell. (Subtitled 'Or Wild England'). A novel about post-catastrophe England, set in the vague distant future. After a mysterious environmental disaster ('the event'), society has 'relapsed into barbarism' and the countryside has reverted to idyllic wilderness. In the centre of Britain, a vast crystalline lake has formed. The hero, Felix Aquila, sets out on a canoe voyage of discovery and finds London 'utterly extinct' surviving only as a pestilential swamp. In a later section of the narrative he settles for a while with a community of shepherds, but the end of the novel finds him 'still moving rapidly westwards toward the sunset'. Felix's determined quest for his idealised lover, Aurora Thyma, supplies romantic interest, but the work is principally interesting for the author's enlightened attitudes to nature and its conservation. The novel was published during a severe period of agricultural distress which may account for some of its apocalyptic gloom.

Agatha's Husband, Dinah Mulock [Craik], 1853, 3 vols, Chapman and Hall. The Agatha Bowen of the title is an orphan and an heiress. She marries Nathanael Harper, the younger brother of her trustee. Courtship occupies most of the first volume and the subsequent two deal with marital problems. Nathanael discovers that his brother, Major Harper, has embezzled Agatha's (now his) fortune. But honour requires him to keep the theft secret from his young wife. Meanwhile, he has come to suspect Agatha of misconduct. She is perplexed by his coldness to her and when she forms ungrounded suspicions of her own the marriage almost breaks down. The second volume ends with Agatha crying wildly. But in the third, the truth emerges, and the Harpers are happily reconciled. The plot is one of Mulock's many variations on the love and property theme.

Agincourt, G. P. R. James, 1844, 3 vols, Bentley. Set in the early fifteenth century, this is a routine historical* romance. The hero, Richard of Woodville, meets a benighted Prince Hal in the wilds of Hampshire and conducts him in disguise to his home. Richard is later rebuffed in love, calumniated by a vile foe, and goes to seek his fortune in the Court of Burgundy. The narrative climaxes at Agincourt, where Richard (disguised as 'the black knight') vanquishes his rival and shares in the English glory. James's borrowings from Scott's *Ivanhoe* are painfully obvious.

Agnes Grey, Acton Bell (i.e. Anne Brontë), 1847, 3 vols, Newby. (Newby bound the story in with *Wuthering Heights**.) A novel told in the first person as a 'true history', *Agnes Grey* deals with familiar Brontëan themes. Mrs Grey, a squire's daughter, marries a poor north of England parson and is as a result estranged from her family. Only two of her six children survive, Mary and the much younger Agnes. After her father is ruined by speculating, the eighteen-year-old Agnes takes up work as a governess. Her first position is at Wellwood, with the odious Bloomfield family. Agnes stops Tom, the young son of the house, torturing animals and is unfairly dismissed. Her next post is with the slightly more civilised Murrays, at Horton Lodge. Her main charge is Rosalie, a flighty sixteen-year-old and her duller sister Matilda. Agnes meanwhile is drawn to the curate at Horton, Edward Weston, whom she meets while visiting the poor and sick. Rosalie throws herself at Weston, but eventually marries Sir Thomas Ashby, a brute. Agnes's father dies. She and Mrs Grey set up a school (Mary Grey meanwhile having married). By happy chance, Weston moves to the district. He proposes to Agnes and the school prospers. The narrative tails off with a complacent: 'And now I think I have said enough.' By comparison with Charlotte's Jane Eyre* Agnes is a passive creature.

AGNUS, Orme (i.e. John C. Higginbotham, d. 1919). Higginbotham was born in Cheshire, and at the age of eighteen moved to Wareham, Dorset, where he worked as a schoolteacher until his death. He is usually classed as a disciple of Thomas Hardy*, but with a more optimistic view of life. Agnus specialised in the rural sketches ('idylls') which were popular at the turn of the century. His best-received work in the genre was *Jan Oxber* (1900), which gathered together Dorset stories, with plentiful dialect colouring. The setting is the village of 'Barleigh' (or 'The Quiet Elsewhere') as described by a happy refugee from London, forced into country retirement for his health. *Love In Our Village* (1900) is a mild Wessex* tale. BL 11. RLF.

AGUILAR, Grace (1816–47). Well known in her lifetime as a writer on Judaism, Aguilar was the author of seven works of fiction, most published posthumously by her mother. Born in Hackney, London, the eldest child of Spanish-Jewish parents she was educated by her mother at home which after 1828 was in rural Devon where her consumptive father (formerly a merchant) was obliged to retire. Grace Aguilar displayed strikingly precocious literary ability (writing her first work of literature, a play, at the age of twelve) and an engaging personality. But she was never strong, being under constant medical care from the age of three. In 1835 she fell ill with measles and was thereafter a chronic invalid with drastically limited marriage prospects. Moreover, her father's death obliged her to write to help support the family. Her writing on Jewish subjects (for which she remains read) argued against doctrinal rigidity. Aguilar died in 1847 on a visit to a brother in Frankfurt, a trip partly undertaken to recover her health at the baths of Schwalbach. Of her novels, only the homiletic (and very popular) *Home Influence: A Tale For Mothers And Daughters* (1847) appeared in her lifetime with an apologetic preface for suspicious Christian matrons. The Devon setting of the narrative evokes Aguilar's childhood in the West Country. Exactly why her very innocuous fiction was held back is not clear. *A Mother's Recompense* (a sequel to *Home Influence*) was published in 1850 and *Woman's Friendship* in 1851. Both are stories of domestic life which centre on family relationships (particularly those between mother and daughter) which were the author's favourite concern. Some of Aguilar's other fiction has Jewish themes. *Records Of Israel* (1844), for example, was written to correct 'vulgar errors concerning Jewish feelings, faith and character' and her *Home Scenes And Heart Studies* (1853) contains tales of Jewish life. Aguilar's historical* novel, *The Vale Of Cedars, Or The Martyr* (written 1831–35, published in 1850) is set in Spain, in the reign of Ferdinand and Isabella. Its heroine, Marie Morales, is a Sephardic Jewess beloved by the Englishman Arthur Stanley. She refuses to convert and is tortured to death by Torquemada's Inquisition. Marie's last words to her lover are: 'In heaven I feel there is no distinction of creed or faith. We shall all love God and one another there.' Aguilar's other historical novel, *The Days Of Bruce, A Story From Scottish History* (1852), is a routine costume melodrama of feminine heroism under the stress of war which was widely reprinted through the century and is still frequently found in second-hand bookshops. BL 10. *DNB*. RM.

AIDÉ, [Charles] Hamilton (1826–1906). Aidé (whose name was sometimes printed as it was evidently pronounced, 'Aïdé') was born in Paris, the son of a Graeco-Armenian merchant father and an aristocratic English mother, the daughter of Sir George Collier. Aidé's father was killed in a duel in 1830, and the family moved to England. Educated at Greenwich and at the

University of Bonn he went on to take a commission in the British army in which he served until 1853. On selling out and still a young man of striking good looks he travelled widely, living while in England with his mother at Lyndhurst, in the New Forest. When she died, in 1875, he moved to London, where he entertained lavishly. Multilingual and highly accomplished, Aidé composed music, painted and wrote poetry. His first novel, *Rita** (a Parisian tale) came out anonymously in 1856, and was a huge success. His grand narrative poem *Eleonore* (also published in 1856) was not a huge success. In all, he wrote some fifteen novels, many with settings drawing on his cosmopolitan knowledge of the world. *The Marstons* (1868) recounts the vicissitudes of a London merchant's family after he loses his fortune. *In That State Of Life* (1871), has a young girl of wealthy background, who refuses her guardian's selection of husband and goes instead into domestic service. *Penruddock* (1873) is an autobiographical novel drawing on the author's early history (the army sections and the hero's vexed relation with his mother are particularly revealing). *A Voyage Of Discovery* (1892) is 'A Novel Of American Society' which upset some transatlantic readers. It chronicles a visit to the United States by Grace Ballinger and her brother Sir Mordaunt. Having travelled overland to the West Coast (witnessing en route such sights as Barnum's Circus and a whole range of Yankee vulgarity), Grace is finally reconciled with her lover, he meanwhile having been acquitted of altering his uncle's will. In *Elizabeth's Pretenders* (1895), the heroine is a rich heiress who eludes her importunate suitors by going to Paris as a needy art student. Aidé's preference for heroines and 'I narration' misled early reviewers into thinking him a female writer. He wrote some competent society verse, collected as *Songs Without Music* (1882) and *Past And Present* (1903). He never married, and died in London. BL 15. *DNB*. Wol.

AINSWORTH, William Harrison (1805–82). Following Scott, the leading historical* novelist of the nineteenth century. Ainsworth was born in Manchester and went to school at the local grammar school (commemorated in *Mervyn Clitheroe**, 1858). His father, Thomas Ainsworth, was a solicitor, and at sixteen the young Harrison was articled to the same profession. While working in his father's office, he wrote gothic* melodramas and befriended a fellow clerk, James Crossley, who encouraged both his literary and his antiquarian enthusiasm. When his father died in 1824, Ainsworth travelled south to London, ostensibly to continue studying law at the Inner Temple. He was soon drawn away into the writing and publishing world. He founded unsuccessful journals, did pastiches of 'old drama', wrote juvenile poetry and in 1826 John Ebers (among other things, manager of the Opera House) brought out Ainsworth's first novel (written in collaboration with J. P. Aston) *Sir John Chiverton*. In the same year, Ainsworth married Ebers's daughter, Fanny. This marriage, like his second (in the 1870s), was to end unhappily. After *Chiverton*, Ainsworth dabbled for a while in publishing. But the period from 1826 to 1831 was unsettled for the ambitious young man and his main fame was as a Byronic dandy, sporting 'the chest of Apollo and the waist of a gnat'. In 1831, inspired by a visit to Chesterfield, he began *Rookwood**. Following the French model, he introduced into his gothic tale (which features the highway exploits of Dick Turpin) *chansons d'argot*, and 'flash', or low slang. Bentley* brought the novel out in 1834 to huge sales success. On its strength, Ainsworth was widely compared by reviewers with Scott. The comparison unduly flatters him. Essentially derivative, he was at his most creative when paired with a more original mind than his own such as the illustrator George Cruikshank's* in the period 1836–45. Cruikshank directed Ainsworth into populism and connected him with the tradition of Hogarthian satire which is his strength. He is at his best (and all too seldom, taking his career as a whole) the chronicler of law-breakers, street scenes, 'old' and 'low' London. Left to himself, Ainsworth (like G. P. R. James*) had a fatal weakness for stereotyped historical 'romances'. Never the less, readers of the late 1830s and early 1840s relished Ainsworth's fiction and during this period his star was higher than even Dickens's*. He set up a splendid literary salon at his new London home, Kensal Manor House, and was editor of *Bentley's Miscellany** from March 1839 to December 1841. *Jack Sheppard** (1839), the tale of an eighteenth-century cracksman, enjoyed an immense success. There were at least eight (pirated) dramatic versions put on the London stage. But for all its popularity, Ainsworth was alarmed by the moral fury stirred up by the work which was accused of condoning murder. He subsequently gave up Newgate* subject-matter and followed Victor Hugo's example, making places rather than notorious historical figures the centre of his work. There followed such topographic bestsellers as: *The Tower Of London** (1840), *Old Saint Paul's** (1841) and the floridly illustrated *Windsor Castle** (1843). During this hectically busy phase Ainsworth also turned out *Guy Fawkes** (1841); *The Miser's Daughter** (1842) and *Modern Chivalry** (co-authored with Mrs Gore*, 1843). A new phase began in his career in February 1842, when he founded the immodestly entitled *Ainsworth's Magazine**. Ainsworth went on to acquire the *New Monthly Magazine** in 1845 and in 1854, he bought as his own property *Bentley's Miscellany*. With proprietorship, there is a palpable deterioration in his writing. After *Saint James's, Or The Court Of Queen Anne* (1844) a crude pro-Tory line appears in his fiction. His previous densely descriptive mode with its genuinely effective set pieces (such as the storm in *Jack Sheppard*) gives way to short, skeletal paragraphs, stagey dialogue and intrigue plotting. In 1853 he moved to Brighton and his career fell into its final phase of decline. His payment descended from the £2,000 which Bentley had given for *The Tower Of London* (1840) to the paltry £100 which William Tinsley* paid for the last novels. Ainsworth attempted a tale of contemporary life with *Hilary St Ives* (1870) but otherwise he was locked into the historical romance, even though that commodity was bringing ever diminishing returns. Between 1860 and his death in 1882, he brought out twenty-five novels, with titles such as *The Lord Mayor Of London, Or City Life In The Last Century* (1862): *The Spanish Match, Or Charles Stuart At Madrid* (1865): *The South Sea Bubble, A Tale Of The Year 1720* (1871); *Merry England, Or Nobles And Serfs* (1874); *Beau Nash, Or Bath In The Eighteenth Century* (1880). The most readable are those centred on his native Lancashire, to which Ainsworth returned in his later years (e.g. *The Good Old Times, The Story Of The Manchester Rebels Of The Fatal '45*, 1873). The end of his life found Ainsworth virtually destitute and sadly declined from the dandy who had lorded it in London in the 1840s. In 1881, by way of consolation, he was honoured by the city and mayor of Manchester with a banquet, 'as an expression of the high esteem in which he is held by his fellow townsmen'. Taking a long view, Ainsworth's career reveals first-rate business instinct, yoked to a second-rate literary talent which could only raise itself in the company of a gifted collaborator like Cruikshank. BL 39. *DNB. NCBEL. RM.* Wol. Sad.

Ainsworth's Magazine (1842–54). Ainsworth founded his magazine in opposition to *Bentley's Miscellany**, which he had previously edited. Subtitled 'A Miscellany Of Romance, General Literature And Art', the journal appeared monthly and cost 1s.6d. (Eventually the price rose to 2s.6d.) Its early circulation peak was around 7,000 copies per issue. Ainsworth devised the magazine strictly as a vehicle for his own historical romances, as illustrated by George Cruikshank*, although the most impressive work to appear in the magazine was *Windsor Castle** (1843), on which the French artist Tony Johannot and W. Alfred Delamotte* shared with the illustrations. In July 1844, Hablôt K. Browne (better known under his pseudonym Phiz*) took over as main illustrator from Cruikshank. William Maginn* contributed the novel *John Manesty** to the journal but he died before finishing it, and the story was concluded haphazardly by one of Ainsworth's sub-editors. Otherwise no fiction of interest is to be found in the journal's pages. In 1843, Ainsworth sold the magazine to the publisher John Mortimer but remained himself editor. In 1845, he repurchased it. Thereafter Ainsworth used the magazine principally to reprint his popular fiction of earlier years. Illustrations disappeared in 1850, and *Ainsworth's* finally expired in December 1854, a sad relic of what it once had been. *WI. BLM.*

ALCOCK, [Miss] Deborah (1835–1913). Born in Kilkenny, Ireland, she was the daughter of the Venerable John Alcock, Archdeacon of Waterford. Deborah Alcock never married and lived with her father until his death in 1886. In addition to a memoir of her distinguished parent, she wrote improving and adventure stories for children many of which were published under the auspices of the RTS* in the 1870s–1880s. Her works include *The Spanish Brothers* (1870), 'A Tale Of The Sixteenth Century' dealing with Protestant martyrdom; *The Czar* (1882), a story of Napoleon's invasion of Russia; *Archie's Chances* (1886). BL 15. (JA)Boase.

ALDIN, Cecil Charles Windsor (1870–1935). An illustrator in the John Leech* style, strong on sporting and animal subjects. Aldin was born in Slough and studied animal painting under the rather more distinguished artist, Frank W. Calderon. Much of his mature work was reproduced in *Good Words** and the *Boy's Own Paper**. Aldin also illustrated reprints of Kipling's* *Jungle Books** (1894–95) and R. S. Surtees's* horsey fiction. He did some famous Cadbury posters and in later life was Master of Fox Hounds for the South Berkshire Hunt. *WW.* Hou.

Aldine Publishing Company. The firm flourished in the last two decades of the nineteenth century specialising in reprints of American dime novels, penny dreadfuls* and boys' adventure literature. Among its series were the *Aldine Cheerful Library* (1894–95), and the *Aldine Half-Holiday Library* (1893–1910).

Alec Forbes Of Howglen, George MacDonald, 1865, 3 vols, Hurst and Blackett. The story recounts the hero's birth and education among his own folk in the Highland village of Glamerton and at Glasgow University. The whole of the first volume of the novel is taken up with his schooldays, which culminate in the bursary that is to be his passport to the outer world and a future beyond his family's Howglen croft. Alec is tempted in the city, falls and is redeemed by the combined influence of his pure-hearted village lover Annie Anderson, his widow mother and loyal friends such as the scholarly but alcoholic and eccentric librarian Cosmo Cupples. The theme of self-improvement via education is peculiarly Scottish but MacDonald had no time for strict Calvinist doctrines on sin. The novel's tone is pastoral, and the narrative is interspersed with verse and dialect.

ALEXANDER, Mrs [Annie] Hector (née French, 1825–1902). The only daughter of a Dublin solicitor, Annie French was related on her mother's side to the divine Jeremy Taylor (1613–67) and the author Edmund Malone (1741–1812). She was educated at home by a governess and as a child was encouraged to read widely. In 1844, her father lost most of his money and the family moved to Liverpool, eventually settling in reduced circumstances in London. Annie French visited Ireland only once again in her lifetime. In London, she was helped by her countrywoman Mrs S. C. Hall* and was befriended by Mrs Lynn Linton*, the eccentric novelist, and by W. H. Wills, Dickens's* co-editor on *Household Words** (in whose pages she made her literary début). A couple of early novels, published anonymously in 1854–55, sank without trace. In 1858, she married Alexander Hector, the explorer and bore him four children. His health collapsed shortly after marriage obliging his wife to shoulder the main burden of providing the family income. In 1865, she published *Look Before You Leap*, the romance of an officer who elopes with a supposed heiress, finds her penniless, treats her harshly, but is later tenderly reconciled. The novel was popular, and set the author up as a professional writer. *Which Shall It Be?* (1866) has a heroine, Madeline Digby, who is left in the charge of her grandmother and resourcefully sets herself up independently as a governess. After nearly being abducted on a train by a love-maddened Frenchman, Madeline finally makes a decent middle-class marriage to a tall Englishman (the happy ending of all the author's fiction). French's best-known novel, *The Wooing O't**, came out in 1873 (after serialisation in *Temple Bar**). Partly set in Paris, it follows the love affairs of an engaging heroine, Maggie Grey, who has a vulgar aunt and an affection for an unsuitably worldly man. French's husband died in 1875 and as a widow she continued to support herself and her family by writing over forty more novels. He, apparently, had disapproved of her fiction and while he lived she wrote in her maiden name. After 1875, she took her deceased husband's Christian name, and wrote as 'Mrs Alexander'. *Her Dearest Foe* (1876), which must have been written during mourning, is one of the novelist's best works. The work opens with a vivid death scene in which Mrs Kate Travers is shown newly widowed. The novel's subsequent setting moves between London and the suburbs following the heroine's indefatigable attempts to recover an inheritance. In the end, this entails marrying a rival heir, her dearest foe. *The Freres* (1882), records the misfortunes of a genteel family in a cheap London lodging house. *The Admiral's Ward* (1883) again deals with loss of inheritance. As one reviewer enthusiastically noted about this work, 'everyday life is transformed to something like poetry by the patience of the heroine in her humble duties'. *A Choice Of Evils* (1894) nods towards the fashionable new woman* novel. It has a married couple who rationally decide to divorce, when a 'dead' former spouse comes back from the grave. *Barbara, Lady's Maid And Peeress* (1898) is an inheritance romance. In *Through Fire To Fortune* (1900) the heroine escapes her drudging destiny as a milliner's apprentice when she is thought killed in a fire. But by the end of the century, even Alexander's superabundant energies were exhausted. The last ten years of her life were moreover made miserable by chronic neuritis. Nevertheless, in the months before she died she completed a revealing autobiographical novel, *Kitty Costello* (1904), the story of an ingenuous Irish girl's introduction to English society in the 1840s. Alexander's fiction typically revolves around a young girl torn between money, family and love (often complicated by legacy). A strong conviction of an eventually benevolent providence pervades her work. BL 46. *DNB*. Wol. Sad. RLF.

ALEXANDER, William (1826–94). Alexander was born in Aberdeenshire into a farm labouring family. He began working life as a herdboy and at manhood rose to be a ploughman. But an accident cost him his right leg, and disabled him from further work on the land. In his convalescence, he read widely and went on to win a prize for an essay as a result of which, he was invited to contribute to local newspapers. A natural writer, Alexander joined the staff of the *North Of Scotland Gazette* in 1852 at 6s. a week, eventually becoming the paper's editor. In 1871, he brought out his very popular and frequently reprinted dialect work, *Johnny Gibb Of Gushetneuk*, a story of Aberdeenshire parochial life in the 1840s. (The work opens: 'Heely, heely, Tam, ye glaiket stirk – ye hinna on the hin shelvin' o' the cairt!') This was followed up by *Sketches Of Life Among My Ain Folk* (1875) which like its predecessor artfully mixes fiction and local history. Alexander was widely respected by his contemporaries and received an honorary doctorate from Aberdeen University in 1886. BL 2. Boase.

Alice Lorraine, A Tale Of The South Downs, R. D. Blackmore, 1875, 3 vols, Sampson Low. (Serialised in *Blackwood's Magazine**, March 1874– April 1875.) Set in the period of the Napoleonic Wars, the hero of the story is Hilary, a scion of the old Lorraine family of Coombe Lorraine. In addition to betraying his lover, Mabel Lovejoy, Hilary loses £50,000 of Wellington's army funds which have been entrusted to him. The House of Lorraine is saved from consequent shame and disaster by the daughter Alice's offering to marry Captain Stephen Chapman for money. Blackmore originally intended a tragic ending, but after some wrestling with his artistic conscience softened it. A cache of lost family jewels is turned up which enriches the Lorraines and allows Hilary to settle his debt of honour. The novel resembles Hardy's* *The Trumpet Major**, and has a charming regional* flavour.

Alice's Adventures In Wonderland, Lewis Carroll, 1865, 1 vol, Macmillan. (The first edition was illustrated by John Tenniel*.) This best known of children's stories began as a tale told by Charles Dodgson (a mathematics don at Oxford) to Alice Liddell and her sisters, in July 1862. Having written the full-scale *Alice*, Dodgson was not sure whether to publish it. He sent the manuscript to George MacDonald* who warmly recommended publication.

Dodgson first intended to print the work through Oxford University Press, with illustrations by himself. In 1863, he was introduced to Macmillans* who had just published Kingsley's* *The Water-Babies* (1863). They undertook to distribute *Alice*. Dodgson eventually decided to have a professional illustrator, and selected Tenniel who specialised in animal subjects. The first edition appeared in June 1865. But Tenniel was displeased with the execution of his designs, and the 2,000 copies were withdrawn. The book finally went on sale in November 1865, under the author's pen name, Lewis Carroll. In 1871, Dodgson produced a cleverer but less satisfying sequel, *Through The Looking Glass*. The *Alice* books are unusual in children's literature in appealing equally to adult readers and the nonsense, especially in *Through The Looking Glass*, verges on playful philosophy. Nevertheless, both books have gripping narratives. In *Alice's Adventures In Wonderland*, the heroine, while reading, sees a white rabbit rush by, feverishly consulting a watch. She follows him down a hole in the ground, encounters various locked doors, eats and drinks substances which enlarge and shrink her, encounters mythical creatures like the Gryphon, extinct creatures like the Dodo, cartoon creatures like the Cheshire Cat, breaks in on the Mad-Hatter's tea party and is sentenced to be beheaded by the irascible Queen of Hearts. As the playing card entourage falls on her, Alice wakes with dead leaves brushing her face.

All In The Dark, J. Sheridan Le Fanu, 1866, 2 vols, Bentley. The central character is an old aunt, Miss Dinah Perfect of Gilroyd Hall, given to table rapping. Under the influence of a spiritual adviser, 'Henbane', she interferes in the lives of her niece Violet Darkwell (choosing marriage partners for her) and her orphaned nephew William (choosing a career for him). After various comic complications the young people marry happily. The work is lighter in tone than the author's better-known ghost* stories. There are some interesting descriptions of the Victorian spiritualist seance.

All Sorts And Conditions Of Men, Walter Besant, 1882, 3 vols, Chatto and Windus. (Serialised in *Belgravia*, January–December 1882, illustrated by Fred Barnard*. The work has a dedication to Besant's recently dead collaborator, James Rice*.) The story opens with two young women discussing their future, at Newnham College. Angela Messenger, heiress to a Stepney brewery fortune, determines to do something useful. This means spinsterhood ('marriage spoils a woman's career'), changing her name to Kennedy and setting up a dressmakers' cooperative association in Stepney, complete with gymnasium and tennis court. In another part of the story, Harry Goslet discovers that he is not, as he supposed, a blue-blooded aristocrat ('Harry Le Breton') but the son of an army sergeant. He too plunges into the 'marvellous unknown country which we call East London', as a cabinet maker. He and Angela meet at Mrs Bormalack's lodging house, and fall in love. He tells her his dream of a Ruskinian People's Palace of Delight for the Eastenders and Angela (now the richest woman in England) secretly sinks her wealth into the project. They marry, and he discovers the pleasant truth. Besant subtitled the novel 'An Impossible Story' because a friend told him that his 'Palace' would never materialise. It did, partly due to the author's efforts, in 1887, although it did not as in the novel transform Stepney into an earthly paradise.

All The Year Round (1859–95). A weekly paper, costing 2d. and started in April 1859 by Charles Dickens* as the successor to *Household Words*. Dickens had broken with Bradbury and Evans*, over their objection to printing in *Punch* a notice explaining to the English public his reasons for separating from Mrs Dickens. *All The Year Round*, while retaining the general appearance and format of its predecessor, differed in important respects. It was, for instance, independent of any publisher. And, unlike *Household Words*, *All The Year Round* invariably featured long continuous fiction as its lead item. (Its subtitle was, 'The Story Of Our Lives From Year To Year'). The paper kicked off with *A Tale Of Two Cities*, and there followed over the succeeding years *Great Expectations*, Collins's* *The Woman In White* and *The Moonstone*, Reade's* *Hard Cash*, Gaskell's* *A Dark Night's Work*, Bulwer-Lytton's* *A Strange Story*. Under Dickens's editorship, the journal also published some distinguished reportage (notably the editor's own *Uncommercial Traveller* papers). Dickens personally conducted the magazine (with the help until 1868 of W. H. Wills, his former assistant on *Household Words*) until his death in 1870. During this period, circulation was very high, starting at 120,000 a week for normal issues, rising to as much as 300,000 for the larger fourpenny Christmas numbers, which featured specially commissioned short fiction from star writers. Charles Dickens Jr* succeeded his father as editor. As early as the mid-1860s, the journal had begun to lose ground, tending to serialise increasingly minor fiction by writers like Percy Fitzgerald*, Rosa Mulholland*, G. A. Sala* and Miss Braddon*. It did, however, publish three of Trollope's* best late works: *Is He Popenjoy?*, *The Duke's Children* and *Mr Scarborough's Family*. In its last year, the journal serialised *Prisoners Of Silence* by its founder's novel-writing descendant, Mary Angela Dickens*, appropriately enough. *BLM*.

Allan Quatermain, H. Rider Haggard, 1887, 1 vol, Longman. (Serialised in *Longman's Magazine*, January–August 1887. The book edition had twenty illustrations by C. H. M. Kerr.) The 'Allan Quatermain' saga began with *King Solomon's Mines* (1885). Its success led to this sequel. Fourteen more episodes in Quatermain's life were eventually called for, until the last, *Allan And The Ice Gods*, in 1927. All the stories hinge on the African explorer of the title. Various companions share in his adventures: Sir Henry Curtis, the fair-haired Anglo-Saxon warrior; Umslopogaas, the gigantic Zulu with his fearsome axe Inkosi-kaas (he dies in this novel); the doughty seaman, Commander John Good RN. Haggard resolved, unsuccessfully, to kill his hero off at the end of *Allan Quatermain*. But the character was too popular and the author was obliged to write *Allan's Wife* (1889), which returns to the great hunter's youth in Africa. Most of the stories have the same outline as these 'further adventures and discoveries' of *Allan Quatermain*. At the beginning, 'Hunter' Quatermain is rich, sixty-three years old and unhappy. His doctor son Harry has died and to relieve his misery Curtis and Good suggest an expedition to Mount Kenya. In Africa, the white men pick up with their old comrade Umslopogaas. An underground river leads them to a mysterious city in the centre of Africa. Its white skinned people (the Zu-Vendis) are ruled by two sister queens: Nyleptha (fair) and Sorais (dark). After various intrigues, the story climaxes bloodily with the kind of 'kingly fray' Haggard excelled in. At the end of the novel Quatermain dies and

Curtis survives, the consort of Nyleptha and benign ruler of the Zu-Vendis. The novel's motto is 'Ex Africa semper aliquid novi'.

ALLARDYCE, Alexander (1846–96). Allardyce's father was an Aberdeenshire farmer. After attending the University of Aberdeen, he went to Bengal, where he edited the *Friend Of India* newspaper from 1868. His best novel, *The City Of Sunshine* (1877), reflects this formative period of the author's life. Set in the Bengal village of Dhupnagar it offers a sympathetic account of Hindu society and its exotic mores (child marriage, caste, money-lending). In 1877, Allardyce returned to Edinburgh, where he worked on *Blackwood's Magazine** as an assistant editor until his death. His other novels are *Balmoral* (1893), a Stevensonian* story of the 1715 rebellion, and *Earlscourt: A Novel Of Provincial Life* (1894). BL 3. *DNB*. Wol. RLF.

ALLEN,[Charles] Grant[Blairfindie]('J. Arbuthnot Wilson', 'Cecil Power', 'Olive Pratt Rayner', 1848–99). Author and scientist. Grant Allen was born in Ontario, Canada, where his father was a clergyman of the Irish Church, who had emigrated in 1840. His mother was Scottish (the author was to make much of his Celtic blood in later life). Allen spent his first thirteen years very happily in rural Canada. In 1861, the family moved to Connecticut, in the USA where the sons were taught by a tutor from Yale. After a year broadening his mind in France, Allen went as a prize scholar to Merton College, Oxford in 1867, graduating in 1871. Allen had meanwhile made the mistake of marrying early and for love, which prevented him from pursuing the academic career which his abilities would otherwise have opened to him. When his wife died prematurely he supported himself in some financial difficulty, by schoolteaching. The work was beneath him and in 1873 he took up a chair of philosophy at a newly founded Government College in Jamaica, intended to provide higher education for West Indian blacks (this was seven years after a fierce rebellion in the colony). The scheme was an utter failure, although his years in the Caribbean had a formative effect on Allen. (Among other things, he developed a fanatical hatred of all forms of human exploitation.) On returning to England in 1876 he made writing his profession. For the next seven years his publications were principally in science. A child of the 1860s and a disciple of Herbert Spencer, Allen dedicated himself to disseminating enlightenment about evolution. But technical scientific writing was only moderately profitable and in 1884 Allen gathered into a volume several 'Strange Stories' he had contributed to magazines under the pseudonym J. Arbuthnot Wilson. A preface relates how the author 'by trade a psychologist and scientific journeyman' had strayed into the 'flowery fields of pure fiction'. Chatto* published the work, which was well received. In the same year, 1884, Allen put out his first full-length novel, *Philistia* (under the *nom de plume*, Cecil Power), a satire on socialism and modern journalism. *Babylon* followed a year later. Like much of Allen's fiction, it takes emancipation as its theme, following the twinned careers of a farmer's boy from America and a peasant boy from England, both with artistic genius. In Rome they transcend their limiting backgrounds, develop their talents for painting and sculpture thus winning themselves fame, money and the love of beautiful women. Allen went on to produce some thirty works of fiction over the next fifteen years under his own name and various pseudonyms. They were popular and remunerative. His story *What's Bred In The Bone*, for instance, won a £1,000 prize from *Tit Bits*, in 1891, which was probably the largest windfall of its kind received by any Victorian writer. The work has a striking opening with a scene in which a young man in a train captivates a female fellow-passenger with a snake he happens to have about him. This is promptly followed by a catastrophic tunnel collapse in which he nobly performs prodigies of chivalrous valour. Most of Allen's writing is perfunctory, although the plots of his novels are often arresting. *In All Shades* (1886) is set in Jamaica, and deals frankly with love and race. *The Devil's Die* (1888) features a young doctor (an enlightened Hindu) given to fatal experiments on his patients. *The Tents Of Shem* (1891) utilises the author's Algerian travels in an exciting tale of Arab Jihad. *A Splendid Sin* (1896) is a Shavian satire on conventional genetic morality. *The Type-Writer Girl* (1897, by 'Olive Pratt Rayner') is an interesting novelty written in the form of a journal by a 'Girton girl' who resolves to support herself as an office stenographer. *Miss Cayley's Adventures* (1899) gaily mixes the detective* and the 'Girton girl' novel. *The Scallywag* (1893), *An African Millionaire* (1897) and *Hilda Wade, Hospital Nurse* (1900) are more straightforward detective novels. *Linnet* (1898) is set partly in the Tyrol, and features two young English tourists captivated by primitivism (the heroine of the title is a Trilby-like untutored songstress who goes on to conquer Europe). Allen's most important works are: *The British Barbarians* (1895; subtitled 'A Hill-Top* Novel'), a satire on English society from the standpoint of the twenty-fifth century and the notorious *The Woman Who Did** (1895, another 'Hill-Top' novel) whose massive sales helped set up the firm of John Lane*. *The Woman Who Did* chronicles the career of Herminia Barton who refuses to marry, on ethical principles, and nobly lives in sin. She comes to a tragic (but 'stainless') end. It offended middle-class readers and helped make notorious the new woman* novel as a genre. (Among many take-offs was *The Woman Who Didn't*, by 'Victoria Crosse', i.e. Vivian Cory, later a successful twentieth-century romancer.) Allen provocatively dedicated the work to his (second) wife. Always prey to bronchitis, his health was chronically poor, and after 1881 he lived quietly at Dorking, wintering in the south of France as he could now well afford to do. As a scientific philosopher, his early *Physiological Aesthetics* (1877) is the only work which remains read and cited. In his own day, Allen was much admired, Andrew Lang* calling his genius 'the most versatile, beyond comparison, of any man in our age'. He wrote delightful light verse, collected as *The Lower Slopes* (1894). BL 32. *DNB*. *NCBEL*. RM. Wol.

ALLHUSEN, Beatrice May (née Butt, 1850?–1918). Born in Scotland the daughter of an army officer, Beatrice Butt married William Hutt Allhusen, a sportsman and traveller, around 1875. As Beatrice May Butt, she began writing short stories for *Blackwood's Magazine**, graduating eventually to full-length fiction. Butt's novels are mainly tender studies of feminine psychology under romantic stress. *Miss Molly* (1876) is a tale of patient devotion in which the heroine waits five years for her lover to be released from prison. Her other works in much the same mould include: *Eugénie* (1877); *Geraldine Hawthorne* (1882); *Alison* (1883); *Ingelheim* (1892). She died at Kensington Palace Gardens, in London. BL 12. *WW*. Wol.

ALLINGHAM, Helen (née Paterson, 1848–1926). Illustrator. The daughter of a doctor, Helen Paterson studied art at the Birmingham School of Design and later at the Royal Academy Schools in London. Her subsequent style of illustration was influenced by that of Fred Barnard*. Allingham worked for the *Cornhill**, and illustrated Thomas Hardy's* *Far From The Madding Crowd** (1874) for that magazine. Also in 1874 she married the Irish poet William Allingham. *WW*. Hou.

ALLISON, William ('Blinkhoolie', 1851–1923?). A noted sportsman and man of the turf, Allison was educated at Oxford. In later life he wrote extensively about hunting and horses. Under the pseudonym 'Blinkhoolie', Allison also threw off such sprightly novels as: *Angram: The Tale Of A Wasted Horse* (1880); *Blair Athol* (1881); *The Tale Of A Horse* (1884); *A Tory Lordling* (1887). The last is a satire on the radical doctrines disseminated by 'Mugby' (i.e. Rugby) school. Virtually nothing is known of Allison's life. BL 5. Wol.

ALMA-TADEMA, Laurence (d. 1940). A daughter of the distinguished Victorian artist, Sir Lawrence Alma-Tadema, she apparently never married and lived most of her life in Kent. In the 1880s and 1890s she contributed verse and prose to various magazines, notably the *Yellow Book** in whose success she played a significant part. In fiction Alma-Tadema wrote among other things *Love's Martyr* (1886), a passionate and morbid story of extra-marital passion; *The Wings of Icarus* (1894), described as 'being the life of one Emilia Fletcher as revealed by herself in thirty-five letters', with a fragmentary journal and postscript; and *The Crucifix* (1895), comprising three long short stories, the title piece being a 'Venetian Phantasy'. Her novels are self-consciously idealistic specialising in fashionably 'neurotic' heroines and semi-documentary modes of narration. Alma-Tadema worked for Polish refugees during the First World War and was awarded a CBE in 1918. BL 4. *WW*. Wol.

Altiora Peto, Laurence Oliphant, 1883, 2 vols, Blackwood. (Serialised in four 5s. parts, June–September 1883.) The main line of the story follows the exploits of two lively American girls, the heiress Stella Walton and her friend Mattie Terrill. Their New World emancipation is set off by the comic prejudices of their chaperone Hannah. The heroines change places and cut a swathe through European society. They take up with Altiora, a nineteen-year-old bluestocking, rescuing her from a tangle of love and money problems. Oliphant's philosophical interests invade the narrative as long dialogues. The heroine's name echoes an Oliphant family motto ('I seek the higher thing'). The novel was very successful and as the *Athenaeum** reviewer noted: 'It contains enough to equip a score of ordinary novelists for the production of a score of extraordinary novels.' It was first serialised in the form pioneered by George Eliot's* *Middlemarch**.

Alton Locke, Charles Kingsley, 1850, 2 vols, Chapman and Hall. (Subtitled 'Tailor And Poet'.) Arguably the finest of the social problem* novels produced by the hungry 1840s, *Alton Locke* is told autobiographically. The hero is born into a working-class ('I am a Cockney') and strict Baptist household of the 1830s. Barely grown, he is put into a sweat shop in Piccadilly, to make 'cheap clothes and nasty' (on which, as 'Parson Lot', Kingsley wrote an accompanying pamphlet). Alton is subsequently introduced by his fellow tailor John Crossthwaite to physical-force Chartism. (The so-called 'People's Charter' demanded: universal suffrage, the ballot, annual parliamentary elections, rational electoral districts, abolition of property qualifications for voters, salaried MPs.) When his zealot mother turns him out, Alton takes shelter with Sandy Mackaye, a Scottish bookseller (modelled on Thomas Carlyle). Under Mackaye's tutelage, the hero educates himself. During an expedition to Dulwich art gallery, he also falls hopelessly in love with Lillian, daughter of Dean Winnstay of Cambridge. Mackaye encourages his literary genius, and Alton becomes a famous working-class poet. He walks to Cambridge, where he has a rich cousin George Locke, who turns out to be a Newmanite and selfishly unhelpful. Lord Lynedale, however, is sympathetic and introduces him to Lillian's father. At the Dean's house, Alton makes friends with Eleanor Staunton (a Carlylean). The Dean agrees to help Alton, if he purges his poems of radicalism. Lord Lynedale marries Eleanor. Cousin George gets a double first, and asks for Lillian's hand. After the publication of his poems, Alton is attacked by the Chartist leader Fergus O'Flynn (i.e. Fergus O'Connor) and provoked into taking part in a riot in Norfolk for which he is jailed for three years. He is released in 1848, the year of the great Chartist petition. After the petition's débâcle in which he is soaked to the skin, Alton sickens. In a feverish reverie ('Dream Land') he recapitulates all the stages of man's evolution from primeval slime to *homo sapiens*. He is nursed by Eleanor (Lynedale has meanwhile been killed in a fall from a horse). She is now a moral-force Chartist, organising needlewomen into cooperatives. George dies of typhus, caught from a fine new coat. Alton and Crossthwaite (also chastened) prepare for a purifying pilgrimage to the New World on the proceeds of Mackaye's will. Off the coast of America, Alton dies.

The Amalgamated Press (1893–1960). A late Victorian industrial-scale publishing firm which put out vast quantities of weekly fiction costing 6d. or less. The firm took over such magazines as *Bow Bells* (1862–97, a weekly at one point edited by Ainsworth*) and *Horner's Penny Novels*. In the twentieth century the Amalgamated Press had a huge success with *Peg's Paper*, a story magazine for young working-class girls.

Amaryllis At The Fair, Richard Jefferies, 1887, 1 vol, Sampson Low. Jefferies' last published book and one of his most effective studies of country life. The narrative centres on Farmer Iden of Coombe Oaks, his wife and his young daughter Amaryllis. Iden, a man of powerful intellectual powers, is on the brink of bankruptcy and the novel gives an exact picture of his spring labours. His wife is embittered and broken down. But Amaryllis is young, vital and possessed of latent artistic talent. In the way of Jefferies' fiction, nothing much happens. Amaryllis antagonises her wealthy grandfather by spurning the local landowner's son. In the last chapters, Coombe Oaks is visited by the bohemian Flamma side of the family, including the dissolute engraver Alere Flamma and the tubercular Amadis whom Amaryllis loves. The couple are last seen idyllically framed in the orchard. The book is memorable for its portrait of Iden, 'the Man of the Land'.

The Amazing Marriage, George Meredith, 1895, 2 vols, Constable. (Serialised in *Scribner's Magazine*, January–December 1895.) The story follows the career of Carinthia Jane Kirby, a beautiful but innocent heroine who has bloomed in the Austrian mountains. The daughter of an amazing marriage (her father eloped with a bride fifty years his junior), Carinthia is left an orphan with her brother Chillon. They come into the custody of a mean uncle, Lord Levellier. Lord Fleetwood impulsively proposes to the twenty-one-year-old Carinthia on first seeing her in her native woods. He immediately regrets his offer, but is held to it by Lord Levellier. On his wedding day Fleetwood attends a prize fight, and subsequently deserts his bride, returning only one night to impregnate her. She takes refuge with the family of a Welsh shoemaker and dissenting preacher in Whitechapel, and finds a true friend in the son of the house, Gower Woodseer, who tries to reconcile the couple. But now Carinthia spurns Fleetwood. She goes as a nurse to Spain, where Chillon is soldiering with the English contingent (the date being the early 1840s). Fleetwood becomes a Roman Catholic monk, and dies. Carinthia survives to make a less amazing marriage. The work is written in Meredith's impenetrable style full of 'the meanderings of Dame Gossip', and the plot is fantastic. But the depiction of Carinthia's noble masochism is psychologically convincing.

An American Girl In London, Mrs Everard Cotes, 1891, 1 vol, Chatto. (First published under the author's maiden name, Sara Jeannette Duncan, with over 100 illustrations by F. H. Townsend, the novel was serialised in *The Ladies' Pictorial*.) The story is autobiographical in form, and opens: 'I am an American girl.' Cotes had herself been a Canadian girl in London, and the novel is sharp in its national observations. Mamie Wick (her 'poppa' is a politician, her 'momma' an invalid) comes to England, only to be oppressed by the conventionality of English womanhood, frozen by the civility of her English relatives, and repelled by the standoffish attentions of an English gentleman, Charles Mafferton. She flees back to America. In the sequel, *A Voyage Of Consolation* (1899), Mamie eventually reconciles herself to the Old World. Much of the first novel is given over to a tour of London sights (Westminster, Tussaud's, etc.). Despite its hostility to many of the forms of English life, the novel was extremely popular in England. It was very heavily illustrated in the late *Punch** style by Frederick Henry Townsend (1868–1920), who also embellished other of Cotes's books.

The American Senator, Anthony Trollope, 1877, 3 vols, Chapman and Hall. (Serialised in *Temple Bar**, May 1876–July 1877.) The husband-hunting heroine, Arabella Trefoil, goes to Washington where (managed by her predatory mother Lady Augustus) she catches the English Secretary of Legation, John Morton. The affianced pair return to England, where Morton has inherited the Bragton Park estate. The bulk of the novel chronicles a hectic month's events in the country. Morton has brought with him an American Senator, Elias Gotobed, who is chronically perplexed by such things as the Anglican Church, fox-hunting and the subtleties of the English electoral system. Arabella attempts to jilt Morton for the better-off Lord Rufford. This leads to threats of a breach-of-promise action when he refuses to be caught. John Morton dies, and nobly leaves Arabella a £5,000 bequest. Thus enriched she is taken off the marriage market by Mounser Green, a minor diplomat recently dispatched by the Foreign Office to Patagonia. Gotobed's Yankee provocations climax in a lecture at St James's Hall on

'English Irrationality' which ends in a riot. Gotobed reappears briefly as the American ambassador to London in *The Duke's Children** (1880). A subplot deals with the charming daughter of a local attorney, Mary Masters, who staunchly resists the marriage proposals of a young farmer, Lawrence Twentyman. She is finally rewarded for her courage and obstinacy when the new squire, Reginald Morton, marries her. The novel is a fine example of late Trollope comedy.

Anonyma. The corporate pseudonym for the syndicate who produced a licentious series of books in the 1860s. The *Anonyma* novels were first published by Vickers as 2s. pocketbooks and some were reprinted in the 1880s, as yellowbacks*, by C. H. Clarke. They may not have been copyright-protected. Typical titles are: *Fair But Frail*, a story of West End life; *Annie*; *Cora Pearl*; *Delilah, Or The Little House In Piccadilly*; *Lola Montez*; *The Soiled Dove*. As Michael Sadleir records, the authorship of 'Anonyma' has been variously attributed to Bracebridge Hemyng*, W. Stephens Hayward and E. L. Blanchard. Hemyng is the most likely candidate, though joint composition is probably involved. Sad.

ANSTEY, F. (i.e. Thomas Anstey Guthrie, 1856–1934). A gifted author of miscellaneous humorous works, Guthrie was born in London of 'frankly plebeian' stock. His father was a prosperous West End military tailor who could afford to send his son to good private schools and to Cambridge University (where he scraped a third-class degree). On graduating, Guthrie first applied himself to law. But although called to the Bar in 1880, he never practised. Instead, he began sending stories to the journals. In 1882, Anstey had a hit with the novel *Vice Versa, Or A Lesson To Fathers*, the fable of a stuffy widower (Bultitude Sr) and his schoolboy son (Bultitude Jr) who with the aid of a magic stone from the East change bodies for a week. The book was revised in 1883 and republished with additions in 1894. In 1886, Anstey began a long association with *Punch**, to which he contributed the column of 'overheard conversations', *Voces Populi*, shrewdly illustrated by J. Bernard Partridge. Guthrie's longer fiction tends to employ extravagant plot devices. In *The Tinted Venus* (1885), for instance, a statue of Aphrodite is brought to life by a London hairdresser, Leander Tweddle. *A Fallen Idol* (1886) has an English artist, Ronald Campion, vexed by interference from the astral plane. *The Man From Blankley's* (1893) is a 'story in dialogue'. *Baboo Jabberjee, B. A.* (1897) recounts the adventures of an innocent Indian lawyer in his comic progress through London society and the Inns of Court. *The Brass Bottle** (1900) is a modern-day genie story. *Tourmalin's Time Cheques* (1891) is an early time-travel fantasy and *The Statement Of Stella Maberly* (1896) is a split personality story with an insane narrator. Anstey also wrote some serious fiction, notably: *The Giant's Robe* (1884) and *The Pariah* (1889). The first (which was serialised in *Cornhill**) is the more interesting. Its hero is Mark Ashburn, a schoolteacher and failed novelist, who assumes ownership of the manuscript of a more gifted friend, supposed dead at sea. When the friend returns, Mark is disgraced but lives to redeem himself as a drudging lawyer. The novel was accused of having been plagiarised from Follett Synge's* earlier published *Tom Singleton*. *The Pariah* is more tragic in design. The unfortunate hero, Allen Chadwick, is a parvenu youth who tries to buy himself into higher society, and earns only scorn for his efforts.

The complicated plot ends with nemesis, death and general gloom. Critics received the work badly, and advised Anstey 'to give free rein to his humour'. Although he ruefully felt he had outlived his time, Anstey continued writing until well into the twentieth century. His autobiography, *A Long Retrospect*, came out in 1936. BL 22. *DNB*. RM. *NCBEL*. Wol. Sad.

Antonina, Or The Fall Of Rome, Wilkie Collins, 1850, 3 vols, Bentley. Collins's first published novel, a historical* romance set in the fifth-century Rome of the Emperor Honorius as the destroying Gothic hordes close in. The heroine is a beautiful Roman maiden, the daughter of Numerian, a Christian. Antonina captures the heart of Hermanric, a Gothic chieftain, the enemy of her people. The fall of Rome provides a lurid backdrop and such tremendous setpieces as the Banquet of Famine given by the libertine patrician Vetranio, in which the tables are laden not with food but treasure. Hermanric is killed (after being first hamstrung) but with Vetranio's help Antonina survives to care for her father in peaceful seclusion despite the implacable enmity of a sadistic Gothic matron, Goisvintha (who is resolved to stab the heroine with the same knife that maimed her brother, Hermanric). Antonina also has to escape a pagan votary, Ulpius, who intends to offer her up as a virgin sacrifice to Serapis. *Antonina* (which in places is ultra-violent) successfully inaugurated Collins's career.

ARCHDEACON, Matthew (1800–63). An Irish novelist, specialising in Connaught settings. Archdeacon was born at Castlebar in Co. Mayo, and taught at the academy there. His works include: *Connaught, A Tale Of 1798* (1830); *Everard* (1835); *Legends Of Connaught* (1839); *The Priest Hunter* (1844). Little is known of Archdeacon's life, other than the fact that he died utterly destitute. BL 3. Boase. Sad. RLF.

ARCHER, Thomas (1830–93). Archer's father worked in the corporation of the City of London where, after a private education, his son followed him for a while. He subsequently turned to literature, specialising in stories and sketches of the lower classes in the metropolis. A Fellow of the Royal Historical Society, Archer wrote several multi-volume novels. *Wayfe Summers* (1863) tells the story of a London 'waif'. *A Fool's Paradise* (1870) follows four generations of the Fairhoe family through various trials and tribulations. Later in his career, Archer wrote fiction for the younger reader often drawing on his historical knowledge: e.g., *By Fire And Sword, A Story Of The Huguenots* (1885); *Little Tottie* (1885). BL 10. Boase. Wol. RLF.

Ardath, Marie Corelli, 1889, 3 vols, Bentley. (Subtitled 'The Story Of A Dead Self'.) A tale of the occult. It opens with a typical Corelli flourish: 'Deep in the heart of the Caucasus mountains a wild storm was gathering.' Theos Alwyn travels to the monastery of Lars to consult the magician Heliobas (previously encountered in *A Romance Of Two Worlds**, 1886), who will, he hopes, restore his lost poetic genius. Time travel ensues, in which Theos is transported to Al-Kyris ('The Magnificent') 5,000 BC, a city on the later site of Babylon. Here he meets the beautiful Edris and the seductive Lysia ('the unvirgined virgin') whose priesthood possesses the secret knowledge of electricity. He also meets his previous incarnation Sah-Lûma. Al-Kyris is eventually destroyed by earthquake and Theos returns to his own time, his poetic genius and his faith in God restored. The action ends with exaltation in Cologne Cathedral. The novel is even more chaotic in its fantasies than usual with Corelli but it remained her favourite work.

The Argosy (1865–1901). A monthly magazine, *Argosy* was started by Alexander Strahan* with Isa Craig* as its first editor. Subtitled 'A Magazine Of Tales, Travels, Essays And Poems', it sold for 6d. and offered 100 pages of text with two illustrations. The journal was launched with Charles Reade's* *Griffith Gaunt*, a tale of bigamy*. Strahan (a very strait-laced publisher) was mortified by the fuss the story provoked and promptly sold *Argosy* to Mrs Henry Wood* in October 1867. She patterned it as a rival to Elizabeth Braddon's* *Belgravia*, using it primarily as a vehicle for her own fiction. Wood's best contributions to the magazine are generally thought to be her 'Johnny Ludlow' stories. She remained editor until her death in 1887, at which point her assistant C. W. Wood took over. Other novelists featured in *Argosy* are Sarah Doudney* and Rosa Nouchette Carey*. The magazine had various imprints until 1871, when Bentley* adopted it though apparently not as his sole property. In 1898, just before extinction, it was bought by Macmillan*.

Ariadne, The Story Of A Dream, Ouida, 1877, 3 vols, Chatto and Chapman and Hall. The story is told by an old Roman cobbler, Crispin of the Ponte Sisto, who has adopted Gioja (whom he calls Ariadne, after his favourite statue), a beautiful and amazingly ingenuous sixteen-year-old orphan. Ariadne's father, it emerges, was a sculptor of genius and she herself develops as a natural artist. The melodramatic and slow-moving plot involves a poetic half-Greek villain, Hilarion, and a heroic French sculptor Germain Maryx. Hilarion seduces Ariadne and takes her to Paris where he heartlessly abandons her. Crispin follows his ward and brings her back to Rome where she revives sufficiently to create a magnificent statue of Hilarion. Ariadne's two lovers fight a duel, and Maryx is killed. Hilarion finally realises that he loves the girl he has wronged. But she dies and the novel ends with the gloomy observation that 'All things come too late.' There are numerous high-flown conversations about art in Ouida's usual manner.

Armadale, Wilkie Collins, 1866, 2 vols, Smith, Elder. (Serialised in *Cornhill*, November 1864–June 1866 with illustrations by George H. Thomas*.) In this highly regarded sensation* novel Collins deliberately denies the reader suspense, concentrating instead on situation and the psychology of crime. The story is divided into six books and narrated from time to time by characters' diaries and personal testimony. It begins in 1832 with the father of one young man confessing on his deathbed to the murder of the father of another young man. The murderer's son (a creole) adopts the name Ozias Midwinter. The victim's son takes the name and inheritance (to which Ozias is really entitled) of Allan Armadale. But Ozias is loyal to Allan, who has saved his life in a yachting accident. The story becomes immensely complicated with no less than five characters called Allan Armadale. (Thus, at one point, Allan Armadale disowns his son Allan Armadale and adopts another young man on condition he takes the name Allan Armadale. Both young Allan Armadales have sons called Allan Armadale.) Much of the novel's interest attaches to Lydia Gwilt, a fiendish villainess. The former maid of

Ozias's mother and a convicted adulteress and murderer, Gwilt returns after a life of crime to entangle the Armadale heirs. In a tremendous final episode, she plots to suffocate Allan while he sleeps in a sanatorium in Hampstead. But by mistake, she almost kills Ozias, whom she loves ('her last weakness'). In a fit of remorse, Gwilt uses the contents of her sinister purple flask on herself to commit suicide. Dreams and prophecy feature centrally in the narrative. Midwinter survives to become a writer. Allan marries happily.

ARMITAGE, Robert (1805–52). The Rector of Easthope in Salop (now Shropshire) from 1843 until his death, Armitage wrote and anonymously published *Doctor Hookwell, Or The Anglo-Catholic Family* (1842). The novel was enormously successful, in the context of the 1840s Oxford movement and so-called Catholic aggression. Armitage also wrote a second work of fiction, *Ernest Singleton* (1847), a theological work on animals' souls, and a study of Samuel Johnson. BL 2. Boase. Wol.

Armorel Of Lyonesse, Walter Besant, 1890, 3 vols, Chatto. Subtitled a 'Romance Of Today', the most effective parts of the narrative are set in the Scilly Isles (or 'Lyonesse'). The hero Roland Lee (an artist) is almost drowned there in a rowing boat. As a result he meets Armorel, a stunning peasant girl. They have an idyllic love affair. But there is a long history of seduction and abandonment in Armorel's family; in fact, 130 years before, Roland's great-grandfather deserted one of Armorel's ancestors. He repeats the pattern by returning to the mainland without her. In London, Roland falls into the clutches of a villain who fraudulently acquires inexperienced artists' work and passes it off as his own. Armorel who has £10,000 in family treasure comes to England as an heiress and rescues her lover. They return to Lyonesse as man and wife. The novel throws a melodramatic sidelight on Besant's concurrent work for the Society of Authors* and Armorel is one version of the fashionably strong new woman*.

Edward Arnold (1890–). One of the new generation of publishers in the 1890s, Arnold was a grandson of Dr Thomas Arnold of Rugby School and a cousin of Mrs Humphry Ward*. His firm came to specialise in school books, but also published some bestselling novels (mainly in the new one-volume 6s. form) in the 1890s, including: James Adderley's* *Stephen Remarx* (1893), a work which sold over 20,000 copies in its first year; M. E. Coleridge's* *The King With Two Faces* (1897); Mary Cholmondeley's* *Red Pottage* (1899).

ARNOLD, Edwin Lester [Linden] (1857–1935). The eldest son of the poet and orientalist, Sir Edwin Arnold, he was educated privately and at Cheltenham College. Thereafter, as he records, he took up cattle-breeding 'on the wildest part of the Scottish border'. Arnold then went to India, where he attempted to cultivate virgin forest without much success. On his return to England, Arnold took up literature and journalism. His major work is the fantasy, *Phra The Phoenician* (1890). A tale of reincarnation, it has a hero who is sacrificed by the Druids and wakes to find himself in the England of Julius Caesar. The work was very popular in its day, and has found some favour with twentieth-century science fiction* enthusiasts. Arnold used the same time-travel idea less successfully in *Lepidus The Centurion: A Roman*

Of Today (1901). He also wrote the conventionally historical* *The Constable Of St Nicholas* (1894) about the knights of Rhodes. BL 5. *WW*. Wol.

ARNOLD, the Rev. Frederick (1832–91). The son of a clergyman, Arnold was born at Cheltenham, and graduated from Oxford in 1860. (A recollection of his college experience is given in *Christ Church Days*, 1867.) He was ordained on graduation and served as a curate until 1884. But he also had a strong literary vocation, and for a while edited the *Literary Gazette*. Arnold wrote books and articles for the papers on diverse topics. His *Reminiscences Of A Literary And Clerical Life* were published in 1889. Apart from *Christ Church Days*, Arnold wrote the novel *Alfred Leslie, A Story Of Glasgow Life* (1856), based on a year he spent in the city before going to Oxford. BL 2. Boase. Wol. Sad. RLF.

ARNOLD, Sir [Robert] Arthur (1833–1902). He was born at Gravesend, the son of a JP and brother of Edwin, later Sir Edwin Arnold, poet and orientalist. Arthur Arnold is principally remembered as a political radical. He served as an Assistant Commissioner under the Public Works Act during the Lancashire 'cotton famine' in 1863–64, and wrote an account of the episode. In his leisure time, while occcupied as a surveyor and land agent, he turned out two successful sensation* novels, *Ralph, Or St Sepulchre's And St Stephen's* (1863) and *Hever Court* (1867; serialised in *Once A Week**). Arnold's connection with fiction was brief. He was elected MP for Salford in 1880 and went on to pursue a successful career in public life. BL 2. *DNB*.

ARNOLD, William Delafield (1828–59). William was the second son of Thomas Arnold and the younger brother of Matthew. Educated at Rugby and Christ Church, Oxford, he chose a military career (he is recorded as having 'a determined and sometimes aggressive temper') and in 1848 was posted to India as an army officer. Arnold subsequently transferred to the civilian administration of the Punjab where as an educationalist he refused to allow the Bible as a class book in Indian schools. Under the pseudonym 'Punjabee' he wrote *Oakfield, Or Fellowship In the East** (1853). The novel represents a deliberate attempt to raise the level of Anglo-Indian society. In form, the narrative is the autobiography of an earnest young Oxford graduate, Edward Oakfield, who goes to India as an army officer and is revolted by the dissipation of his comrades and fellow English civilians. *Oakfield* also chronicles the Second Sikh War, and has a vivid description of the battle of Chillianwallah in January 1849. It was generally received as an attack on the East India Company in whose commercial care the colony was entrusted until after the Mutiny of 1857, when its sovereignty was reluctantly handed over to the crown. Arnold was taken sick in 1859, and died at Gibraltar on the journey home to England. BL 1. *DNB*. Wol.

J. W. Arrowsmith. A Bristol publisher, who flourished from the 1880s to the end of the century, Arrowsmith specialised in cheap 1s. reprint volumes of fiction commonly called 'shilling shockers'. The firm's major success was with Hugh Conway's (i.e. F. J. Fargus's*) thriller, *Called Back**.

Arthur O'Leary, Charles Lever, 1844, 3 vols, Colburn. (Serialised in the *Dublin University Magazine**, January–December 1843. The three-volume edition was illustrated by George Cruikshank*.) The subtitle 'His Wanderings And Ponderings In Many Lands' indicates the random conception of this work, which Lever personally claimed to 'detest'. Nor have his readers ever much liked it. The narrative follows the travels and comic misadventures of a Pickwickian Irish gentleman (an acquaintance of Lever's more likeable hero Harry Lorrequer) in Belgium, France and finally Germany. At the end of the narrative, O'Leary is supposed to be setting off for Africa. There is no plot, and several inset travellers' tales.

As It Was Written, Henry Harland, 1885, 1 vol, Cassell. A psychological thriller. Subtitled 'A Jewish Musician's Story', the story is set in New York, and told autobiographically. Ernest Neumann, a promising but temperamental Jewish violinist, is suspected of stabbing to death his singer fiancée, Veronika Pathzuol. He is tried for the crime, but acquitted. For two years, Ernest lives in a state of vague, moral unease. Then he discovers that Veronika's father was the seducer of his mother and that subconsciously he has revenged his family dishonour by murder. He recollects the crime in a music-induced trance and finally kills himself.

ASHBY-STERRY, J[oseph] (1838–1917). Ashby-Sterry was born in London, and educated privately. He wanted, above all else, to be a painter. But, as he put it, circumstances forced him to abandon the pencil for the pen. In the 1860s he was drawn into the *Punch** orbit, and began writing comic pieces, many of them based on his vast and curious knowledge of London and the Thames. *Nutshell Novels* (1891), *A Naughty Girl* (1893) and *A Tale Of The Thames* (1896) classify as fiction. In 1895, Ashby-Sterry published the conservative polemic: *The New Fiction, A Protest Against Sex Mania*. BL 3. *WW*. Wol.

ASHFORD Daisy (i.e. Margaret Devlin, formerly Mrs George Norman, 1881–1972). The youngest novelist ever to achieve world wide fame, Daisy Ashford was born at Lewes in Sussex, into a prosperous and numerous Catholic family. As a nine-year-old girl, she wrote novels after tea for the delectation of her father (a Civil Servant), who copied them out for her. They included *The Hangman's Daughter*, *Where Love Lies Deepest*, and the piece on which her fame rests, *The Young Visiters*. The work was published by Chatto and Windus* as a curiosity in 1919, with an introduction by the writer J. M. Barrie*, vouching for its authenticity. A mish-mash of late Victorian romance, filtered through the naive sensibility of a clever little girl, the work is historically interesting and delightful. It follows the amorous adventures of Mr Salteena ('an elderly man of 42') in his luckless pursuit of the beautiful Ethel Monticue. Ethel marries Bernard Clark and they live happily ever after, since he loves his wife 'to the bitter end'. So good is the tale, that it was widely considered a forgery. But the author was publicly revealed, at the end of a long life in 1972. She wrote nothing after thirteen, at which age she was sent to convent school. She worked in the British Legation at Berne during the First World War, marrying James Patrick Devlin in 1920. Thereafter the couple lived in Norfolk, where he farmed. Daisy's musical sister, Angela, also wrote the juvenile tale *The Jealous Governes*, aged eight. (An obituary of Mrs Devlin was published in *The Times*, 17 January 1972.) (DA) BL 4. RM. *NCBEL*.

ASHWORTH, John (1813–75). Ashworth was born at Cutgate, near Rochdale. Both his parents were weavers, and the boy received minimal education. Nevertheless, by strenuous self-improvement, Ashworth rose in life. In 1858, he founded a chapel for destitutes at Rochdale, and in later years made a name for himself as a lay preacher and successful manufacturer. His *Strange Tales From Humble Life* (initially published in pamphlet form, three series, 1863–76) had an immense circulation. Ashworth did other short tales-cum-tracts with strong Lancashire local colouring. BL 5. *DNB*.

ASHWORTH, [the Rev.] John H[arvey] (1795–1882) Ashworth was born in Elland, Yorkshire and educated at Manchester Grammar School and at Oxford. He took orders in 1820. A keen antiquarian, he not only wrote on history but acquired a castle in Co. Clare which he restored. Ashworth wrote the popular historical* work, *The Saxon In Ireland* (1851) and the novels *The Young Curate, Or The Quicksands Of Life* (1859), and *Rathlynn* (1864). BL 2. Boase. Wol.

At His Gates, Mrs Oliphant, 1872, 3 vols, Tinsley. The story reflects the financial scandals which rocked England at the beginning of the 1870s (which Trollope* also drew on for *The Way We Live Now**, 1875). The millionaire Reginald Burton inveigles investors into putting money into his bank which he knows will fail. Robert Drummond, a successful genre painter, is married to Helen, the woman who earlier rejected Burton (her cousin) as a suitor. Drummond becomes one of Burton's victims, is ruined and falsely suspected of fraud. He fakes his death by a staged drowning in the Thames (such watery 'deaths' were a favourite device of the sensation* novel). Burton is eventually brought down, when Drummond reappears after seven years from America. In the interim his name has been cleared. Drummond forgoes his revenge and Burton, now a ruined man, flies abroad in disgrace 'to make a miserable new beginning'. The plot has echoes of Mrs Gaskell's* *Sylvia's Lovers** (1863) and Tennyson's pathetic narrative poem about a husband returned from the dead, *Enoch Arden* (1864).

At Odds, Baroness Von Tautphoeus, 1863, 2 vols, Bentley. The novel is set in Bavaria in the Napoleonic era, beginning with the battle of Hohenlinden (1800) and ending climactically with Hofer's insurrection nine years later. In the foreground is a pallid love plot in which (for reasons of protocol and a promise made when the girl was twelve) the aristocratic soldier hero, Sigmund Waldering, is obliged to marry the sister of the woman he really loves. Although the *Athenaeum** reviewer complained that 'this is an insipid work', Von Tautphoeus's novels and their popularity reflect the growing international perspective of British fiction after the 1860s. The novel has an interesting autobiographical preface, describing the importance of Napoleon in the memory of living Bavarians.

At The Back Of The North Wind, George MacDonald, 1871, 1 vol, Strahan. (Serialised in *Good Words For The Young*, with illustrations by Arthur Hughes*, November 1868–October 1869.) Diamond is the son of a coachman, named after his father's horse, 'big Diamond'. At night, the boy is visited by the North Wind, in the shape of a beautiful maiden with long hair (entrancingly pictured by Hughes). She carries Diamond in her arms to London, the city which she purifies by night. She also transports him to a paradisal country at the back of the North Wind. The same wind sinks a ship which ruins the employer of Diamond's father's who becomes a cab driver (with the four-legged Diamond) in London. After various adventures and mystic encounters, the young hero dies, haunted by his sense of the mysterious country at the back of the North Wind. The story is one of MacDonald's more inscrutable fantasies*, suggestively rich and finally rather gloomy.

At The Red Glove, Katharine S. MacQuoid, 1885, 3 vols, Ward and Downey. The title refers to the lodging house (and glove shop) of Mme Bobineau in Berne. Two of its lodgers, the bank clerk Rudolf Engemann and the less prepossessing Captain Loigerot (favoured by Mme Bobineau), woo Marie Peyrolles, recently arrived from a convent. Rudolf is also loved by Mme Elvire Carouge, proprietress of the fashionable Hotel Beauregard and a widow 'as indolent as she was by nature luxurious'. On this slight 'spider and the fly' plot (which finishes with Marie and Rudolf conventionally united and the Captain having his ears boxed by the furious Carouge) MacQuoid hangs a series of pleasant character studies, foreign scenery and episodes of mild domestic comedy. The novel began as short sketches in *Temple Bar** and *Harper's Magazine*.

Atalanta (1887–98). Subtitled 'Every Girl's Magazine' it was published monthly, under a succession of publishers. Among its editors was for six years (1887–93) the indefatigable L. T. Meade*. The journal specialised in fiction of high quality and serialised works by H. Rider Haggard* and R. L. Stevenson* including, notably, the latter's rather desultory sequel to *Kidnapped**, *Catriona* (1892–93).

The Athenaeum (1828–1921). The most influential of the Victorian literary reviews, the *Athenaeum* was founded as a weekly (costing 8d.) largely as the brainchild of Henry Colburn*, who had earlier set up the rival *Literary Gazette*. The early years of the journal were difficult. It took on its distinctive character under the editorship of Charles Wentworth Dilke (1830–46). Dilke inaugurated strict independence (particularly from 'puffing' publishers like Colburn) and widened the scope of the journal so that it became, in Leslie Marchand's description, a 'mirror of Victorian culture'. Circulation approached 20,000 at its peak, and the price dropped to 3d. in 1861. The *Athenaeum*'s reviewers of fiction were very strong, Henry Chorley standing out in the 1840s. Geraldine Jewsbury*, G. H. Lewes*, J. Westland Marston and T. K. Hervey were other novel reviewers of note. Under the editorship of Norman MacColl (1871–1900), the paper undertook more group reviews of novels, and quality dropped somewhat. The *Athenaeum* was the main vehicle for book advertising in the Victorian period. *BLM.*

ATHERSTONE, Edwin (1788–1872). Atherstone was born in Nottingham, and devoted the major part of his adult life to the production of verse epic. His great work, *The Fall Of Nineveh*, had six books published in 1828, but was not completed in its thirty-book entirety until 1868. Atherstone also wrote the prose romances *The Sea-Kings In England* (1830) and *The Handwriting On The Wall* (1858), which is set in biblical Babylon, 538 BC. Of the last, the *Saturday Review** tartly noted: 'whatever faults the book may have, it is certainly free from the sin of being light reading'. Among the few details known about Atherstone it is recorded that he was a friend of the post-Blakean painter John Martin. In 1860 he was awarded a Civil List pension of £100 and evidently spent most of his later life in some poverty. BL 2. *DNB*. Wol. RLF.

Aunt Judy's Magazine (1866–85). A magazine 'for young people' founded and originally edited by Mrs Alfred Gatty*, the mother of Juliana Horatia Ewing*. It was published by Bell and Daldy, publishers with a pronounced interest in evangelicalism. The journal was discreetly educational (running competitions on readers' knowledge of Scott's fiction, for instance). It also sponsored practical philanthropy, setting up such things as 'Aunt Judy's Jackanapes* Work Societies'. Each number featured an 'emblem', demonstrating an allegorical or parabolic truth. But, as its opening editorial stressed, 'stories will form a staple commodity in our bill of fare'. Many of Ewing's stories duly appeared in the magazine, as did Lewis Carroll's* *Bruno's Revenge* (1862). George Cruikshank*, Randolph Caldecott* and Gordon Browne (son of Phiz*) did pictorial work for the magazine. After Mrs Gatty's death in October 1873 (aged sixty-four), the editorship was taken over by another daughter, Mrs Horatia Eden, who kept the journal going until 1885. In its later years, *Aunt Judy's* aimed at a slightly older juvenile readership. In the year of its close, it featured serials and shorter stories by K. S. MacQuoid* and F. Anstey*. (MG) *DNB*.

Auriol, W. H. Ainsworth, 1850, 1 vol, Chapman and Hall. Ainsworth began serialising *Auriol* as *Revelations Of London* in *Ainsworth's Magazine**, from October 1844, with illustrations by Phiz*. Following the novelist's break with his publisher, Mortimer, *Auriol* was suspended in May 1845. In August 1845, Ainsworth picked it up again in the *New Monthly Magazine**, now entitled *Auriol, Or The Elixir Of Life*. It ran until January 1846 but was not published in book form until 1850. The story opens with an Elizabethan prelude in which Dr Lamb is seen discovering the elixir of life. (Ainsworth borrowed this theme from Bulwer-Lytton's* *Zanoni**, 1842.) Dying in Lamb's chamber is Auriol Darcy, who seizes the potion and drinks it just as the new year 1600 breaks. The scene flashes forward to 1830, and the London 'Rookery' (Ainsworth here borrows from *Oliver Twist**). Auriol, now immortal, becomes doubly involved with a woman he loves, Ebba Thorneycroft an ironmaster's daughter, and a mysterious Rosicrucian foe, Cyprian de Rougemont who imprisons the heroine in a 'chamber of mystery'. As is usual in *elixir vitae* stories, the hero's dilemma is that to consummate his love he must sacrifice his immortality. Ainsworth clearly had no strong incentive to develop his initial conception and the cobbled together narrative ends with a return to Dr Lamb's cell by London Bridge, the preceding events being dismissed as nothing more than a hallucinatory vision.

Aurora Floyd, M. E. Braddon, 1863, 3 vols, Tinsley. (Serialised in *Temple Bar**, January 1862–January 1863). A follow-up to *Lady Audley's Secret**, which uses the same 'dead but not dead' device beloved by sensation* novelists. The novel's setting is horsey, and its plot is succinctly described by a contemporary reviewer: 'before Aurora is twenty she has eloped with one groom [James Conyers] and horsewhipped another, fallen violently in love with an ultra-refined young gentleman [Talbot Bulstrode] and, after being brought to death's door by his desertion has consoled herself within the year by marrying an honest but rough Yorkshire squire [John Mellish], exactly his opposite'. Aurora's second marriage is threatened by the reappearance of her brutish first husband whom she thought dead in a racing accident. When, after blackmailing her, he is murdered, suspicion automatically falls on Aurora and the subsequent narrative revolves around the discovery of the real culprit, the degenerate groom Stephen Hargraves whom she earlier horsewhipped (for mistreating her dog).

AUSTIN, Alfred (1835–1913). The Poet Laureate who succeeded Lord Tennyson, Austin was born in Headingley, where his father was a timber merchant. A Catholic, Austin was educated at Stonyhurst and called to the Bar in 1857. In 1858, enriched by inheritance, he gave up law for literature having already published a verse tale and a novel. Austin turned out poetry, higher journalism and was leader writer for the *Evening Standard*, 1866–96. It was as reward for political services that his undistinguished talent was dignified with the laureateship in 1896, a post to which he brought no lustre. Austin considered *The Human Tragedy* (1862), a narrative poem, his great work. But he also has some early novels in the wordy Bulwerian-Disraelian* style ('of the more serious sort', as he pompously called them) to his name: *Five Years Of It* (1858), the story of a young lawyer's growth to maturity; *An Artist's Proof* (1864); *Won By A Head* (1866); *The Lord Of All* (1867). As Michael Sadleir surmises, Austin continued to write fiction in later life anonymously and pseudonymously. In 1867, for instance, he produced *Jessie's Expiation*, under the pen name 'Oswald Boyle'. It features an evil nobleman who is foiled in his seduction of a rustic maid (Jessica) and as 'expiation' makes a man who owes him gambling debts marry her. The *Athenaeum** reviewer took the novel to be an amateurish first effort and pronounced it 'improbable nonsense'. BL 4. *DNB*. RM. *NCBEL*. Wol. Sad.

The Author (1890–). The journal founded by Walter Besant* as the official organ of the Society of Authors* (itself officially founded in 1884). Issued monthly, the *Author* concentrated on informing its readers on questions of contract and other professional matters. Besant edited the journal until 1901. Under him the *Author* adopted a consistently aggressive attitude towards the publishing industry, and paraded the grievances of authors incessantly. *BLM*.

The Autobiography Of A Slander, Edna Lyall, 1887, 1 vol, Longman. A novel with a purpose, aimed to rectify the slanderous wrong which Lyall felt had been done her personally by her contemporaries. In the country town of Muddleton, a vicious old gossip, Mrs O'Reilly, tells a friend (falsely) that a newcomer to the area, the young Polish merchant Sigismund Zaluski, 'is nothing less than a Nihilist'. The slander is repeated, travels to London and eventually to Russia. (Lyall handles the canard's migrations with sarcastic deftness.) On a trip to St. Petersburg, Zaluski is arrested on suspicion of being involved in the Tsar's assassination and dies in prison.

The Autobiography Of Christopher Kirkland, Mrs Lynn Linton, 1885, 3 vols, Bentley. Linton's most autobiographical novel. Christopher is born in the early nineteenth century and brought up in a Lake District parsonage ('Braeghyll') where he is generally unhappy and awkward with his vicar father. A new clergyman, Henry Grahame (very different from other degenerate clerics of the period), introduces Christopher to the work of Coleridge, which has a formative influence. Ainsworth* accepts one of his poems for *Ainsworth's Magazine*＊ and Christopher moves to London, where he becomes a journalist and novelist. In this main section of the novel, Linton portrays a gallery of Victorian literary figures under thin disguise, or in their own persons and the narrative breaks down into unvarnished reminiscence (although the transposed sexuality is awkward when dealing with 'Christopher's' marriage). A late and interestingly candid work by an underrated writer.

The Autobiography Of Mark Rutherford, William Hale White, 1881, 1 vol, Trübner. A spiritual autobiography of a 'commonplace life' formed in religious nonconformity which closely follows the author's own. Rutherford's childhood is passed in the austere surroundings of provincial congregationalism ('the Independents') in the English Midlands. At fourteen, he is perfunctorily 'converted', and goes on to prepare for the ministry. The narrow world of his college life is shattered by the discovery of Wordsworth's poetry. He takes up his first ministry in an unnamed town. With his new sense of God Mark tries to live rather than merely preach Christianity. This brings him into conflict with a hypocritical co-religionist, Mr Snale. Mark is also unsettled by an agnostic acquaintance, Mardon. After a religious crisis, crippling hypochondria and an unhappy love affair with Mardon's daughter, Mark resigns his ministry. He goes to London, where he works for a free-thinking bookseller, Wollaston, and falls in love with Wollaston's niece Theresa (a character based on George Eliot*). This comes to nothing and Mary Mardon, to whom he has remained faithful, dies. The narrative which is edited by a 'friend' (Reuben Shapcott) fades out inconclusively with Mark having become a newspaper reporter. The work had a sequel, *Mark Rutherford's Deliverance*＊, in which the hero dies of a stroke.

AVERY, [Charles] Harold (1867–1943). Avery was born at Headless Cross, Worcestershire, the son of a local JP, and was educated at New College, a boarding school in Eastbourne. He subsequently wrote numerous tales of schoolboy pluck on sports- and battle-field, from the 1890s onwards, in the Talbot Baines Reed* style. *Frank's First Term: Or Making A Man Of Him*, (1896) is a typical offering. From 1897 he was a regular contributor to the *Boy's Own Paper*＊. Although then in his fifties, Avery contrived to join the army in the First World War. BL 70. *WW*.

Ayala's Angel, Anthony Trollope, 1881, 3 vols, Chapman and Hall. The orphaned daughter of an artist, Ayala Dormer, is sent to live with her Aunt Emmeline (the wife of a rich financier, Sir Thomas Tringle). Her quieter sister Lucy Dormer goes to live more humbly in the family of Reginald Dosett, a £900-a-year Admiralty clerk. Ayala is unhappy with her rich relations, more so as the coltish Tom Tringle insists on proposing marriage to her. She has an ideal vision of the man she will love to which Tom does not conform. The sisters change places, which causes the charmingly selfish Ayala some discomfort. The main part of the subsequent narrative concerns the two sisters' eventual choice of husbands. After Tom Tringle, Ayala receives an offer from a bluff hunting man, Captain Batsby. But eventually, she marries Jonathan Stubbs, the youngest colonel in the British army. He is not her ideal 'Angel of Light', but will do. The less demanding Lucy marries a sculptor, Isadore Hamel. The work is late, and rather routine Trollope, although it has its modern admirers.

Aylwin, Theodore Watts-Dunton, 1898, 1 vol, Hurst and Blackett. Watts-Dunton's romance (originally entitled 'The Renascence Of Wonder') was long-awaited. The florid narrative centres on Henry Aylwin's search for Winifred Wynne, who has disappeared on Snowdon (the outcome of a curse, laid on her father, for stealing an amulet from the tomb of Aylwin's father). The couple were betrothed in childhood; he being a cripple (and likely heir to an earldom), she the mystical daughter of a drunken organist. In his quest, and with the help of the gypsy Sinfi Lovell, Aylwin is cured of his 'materialism'. The story has a remarkable climax in which Winifred's curse is lifted by means of the latest psychological techniques from Salpêtrière in which hysteria is exorcised with powerful magnets. *Aylwin* was extraordinarily successful, selling 16,000 copies in a few months.

AYTOUN, W[illiam] E[dmonstoune] (1813–65). Aytoun was born and raised in Scotland, in whose history his family had occupied a famous place. After university at Edinburgh, duty directed him towards the law (his father's profession), but he had a strong inclination to write. In 1836 he began what was to be a lifelong connection with *Blackwood's Magazine**. It was not interrupted when in 1845 he was appointed to the Regius Chair of Rhetoric and Belles Lettres at Edinburgh University. In 1845, together with Theodore Martin, he brought out his most popular work, *The Bon Gaultier Ballads*. Aytoun's only novel, *Norman Sinclair*, was published from January 1860 to August 1861 in *Blackwood's Magazine*. It tells the story of a young man, born in Scotland in the second decade of the century. The early autobiographical chapters (especially those dealing with George IV's visit to Edinburgh) are excellent. The work ends on the eve of the Reform Bill, with Norman refusing the offer of his patron, Lord Windermere, to place him in Parliament. Aytoun also wrote some charmingly light-hearted stories for *Blackwood's*, such as 'The Emerald Studs, A Reminiscence Of The Circuit' (1847). His satiric parody of the 'Spasmodics', *Firmilian, A Tragedy*, was published in 1854. BL 1. *DNB*. RM. *NCBEL*. Wol. Sad.

B

BADDELEY, R[ichard] Whieldon (1840–76). The eldest son of a Staffordshire solicitor, Baddeley had a classical education and co-authored a volume of Greek exercises for schools in 1870. He began seriously writing for a living in his early twenties, bringing out his first novel, *The Fortunes Of Fairstone* in 1866. The Fairstone of the title is an estate out of which the hero is defrauded. The plot was stale, but critics rather liked Baddeley's quirky rural comedy. He followed with two other bucolic novels, *The Village Of The West* (1870) and *The Last Of The Lythams* (1873). In the second of these, Baddeley's comedy had begun to pall on reviewers, who complained about his tiresome 'troupe of jokers'. There was also an ugly accusation of plagiarism from *Middlemarch**. Baddeley was a poet of promise and a collection of his verse, *The Golden Lute* (1876), was published after his premature death. BL 3. *DNB*. Wol.

BAGOT, Richard (1860–1921). The son of a Guards officer, Bagot was closely related to the Dukes of Northumberland. He was educated privately, and from 1882 to 1883 was private secretary to the governor of Western Australia. Created a Knight of the Sovereign Order of Malta, he resigned the honour in 1901, after publishing articles critical of the Vatican. Bagot began writing fiction relatively late in his career. He was (for at least part of his life) a Catholic, but temperamentally disobedient. His fiction embodies prominent anti-Catholic themes and Italian settings. *A Roman Mystery* (1899) is readable principally for a flamboyant hereditary madness (or *lupomanoro*) plot in which the hero conceives himself a werewolf. *Casting Of Nets* (1901) is propaganda attacking Roman snares set for the English aristocracy. Its hero, Lord Redman, is lured into a mixed marriage with a Catholic with predictable melodramatic consequences. The novel was much reprinted. *The Just And The Unjust* (1902) is along the same religio-melodramatic lines as its predecessors. It opens with the memorable question from Lady Heversham, 'I wonder whether God has any sense of humour?'. Bagot lived his later life largely in Italy and wrote well into the twentieth century, often on his adoptive country's place in the modern world. BL 11. *WW*.

BAKER, James (1847–1920). Baker was born in Somerset, where he was educated by his father who was a schoolmaster and local publisher. His adult life was occupied in constant travel and he was a fellow of both the Royal Geographical and Royal Historical societies. In addition to books of foreign travel, Baker wrote at length about the town of Clifton, Bristol, where he resided when in England. He also produced several novels. Most interesting is *By The Western Sea* (1889). A 'summer idyll', set in Lynmouth and dedicated to R. D. Blackmore*, it recounts a love affair in which the man, Lovatt, is an artist and a hunchback. Otherwise, Baker's fiction is routine melodrama which reviewers generally found tame for the 1890s. It includes: *John Westacott* (1886); *Mark Tillotson* (1892); *A Double Choice* (1901). James Baker also wrote historical* romance for the juvenile market such as: *The Gleaming Dawn* (1896) and *The Cardinal's Page* (1898). BL 7. *WW*. Wol. RLF.

BAKER, Mrs Louie [Louisa] Alice ('Alien', née Dawson, 1858–1903?). Louisa Dawson was born in New Zealand. The subsequent facts of her life are obscure, although it is known that as a young woman she contributed to the *Otago Witness* as 'Alice'. In 1884 she came to England, and presumably married Mr Baker. Under the resonant pseudonym 'Alien', she wrote grim romances set in New Zealand, evidently inspired by the example of Olive Schreiner* ('Ralph Iron'). *The Untold Half* (1899) follows the complicated sexual relationships of a quartet of characters in the colony. (The 'untold half' is left to the reader's imagination.) *The Devil's Half Acre* (1900) deals powerfully with religious fanaticism and murder in the New Zealand goldfields. *Another Woman's Territory* (1901) is another tale of passion under Australasian skies. 'Alien' wrote other fiction with more conventional European settings such as *The Majesty Of Man* (1895) and *Wheat In The Ear* (1898). In 1899, she collaborated on the novel *Looking Glass Hours* with 'Rita' (i.e. E. M. J. von Booth*, later Mrs Desmond Humphreys). BL 16.

BALDWIN, Mrs Alfred L[ouisa] (née Macdonald, 1845–1925). One of the remarkable daughters of the Rev. George B. Macdonald. Her sister, Alice, was the mother of Rudyard Kipling*; another sister, Georgiana, became the wife of the artist Edward Burne-Jones. Louisa married Alfred Baldwin, Worcestershire ironmaster and MP. Their only child, Stanley Baldwin, later became Prime Minister of England. In her early married life, Louisa Baldwin wrote books for children and half a dozen novels for adults which found little favour with the reviewers. *A Martyr To Mammon* (1886) was called 'well intentioned and tiresome'. *The Story Of A Marriage* (1889) has an upper-class hero who marries a working-class girl, both of whom were criticised as 'sawdust' characters. In a gloomy climax the heroine, Bessie, dies of scarlet fever after deserting her worthy husband. *Richard Dare* (1894) has a hero who runs away from his drunken blacksmith father to become a famous surgeon. In later life, he operates on his mother, who does not know him. Baldwin's ghost* stories, first published in the *Argosy**, *Cornhill** and *Longman's* magazines were collected as *The Shadow On The Blind* (1895) and are thought superior to her long fiction. The volume was published by John Lane* and dedicated to 'my friend and kinsman Rudyard Kipling'. She also published poetry. BL 5. (SB) *DNB*. Wol.

BALFOUR, [Sir] Andrew (1873–1931). The son of a doctor, Balfour was born in Edinburgh. After studying medicine there, he travelled the world as a ship's surgeon. In the later 1890s, Balfour carried out medical research at Cambridge, where he also found time to win a blue in rugby. From 1900 to 1901 he served with distinction as a field surgeon in the Boer War. He married in 1902 and spent the following three years in Khartoum, developing what was to be a lifelong interest in tropical medicine. In 1914–18 he again served in the armed forces after which he was appointed director of the London School of Hygiene and Tropical Medicine, from 1923 until his death. He is regarded as a pioneer of preventive medicine. Early in his career, Balfour gained some incidental fame as the author of belligerent, Stevensonian* historical* romances such as: *By Stroke Of Sword* (1897), *To Arms* (1898), and *Vengeance Is Mine* (1899). *Gentleman Jerry* (1899) and *Cashiered* (1902), a collection of 'war tales' first published in *Chambers's Journal**, were inspired by the Boer campaign. Interestingly, actual experience of war seems subsequently to have extinguished Balfour's interest in writing fiction about it. BL 6. *DNB*.

BALFOUR, Mrs C[lara] L[ucas] (née Liddell, 1808–78). Clara Liddell was born in the New Forest, Hampshire. An only child, her father died during her childhood and she moved to London with her mother, who educated her. In 1827, she met and married James Balfour of the Ways and Means Office, in the House of Commons. The couple subsequently lived in Chelsea, where Mrs Balfour was a close friend of the neighbouring Carlyles. In 1841, she began to lecture on temperance and devoted the main energies of her later life to promoting teetotalism. Balfour also interested herself in the cause of feminism and lectured on literary topics to women's classes. Her stories and tracts (e.g. *Moral Heroism*, 1846) enjoyed a large sale and were mostly aimed at the lower-class juvenile public. In 1854, she wrote a useful sketch of the novelist Charlotte Elizabeth [Tonna*]. Representative examples of her other fiction are: *'Scrub', Or The Workhouse Boy's First Start In Life* (1860); *The Victim, Or An Evening's Amusement At The Vulture Tavern* (1860); *Drift, A Story Of Waifs And Strays* (1861). BL 18. *DNB*. *NCBEL*. Wol.

BALLANTINE, James (1808–77). Ballantine was born in Edinburgh of working-class parents. A self-made man, he began working life as a house painter. He subsequently established himself as an artist and after the 1840s was famous as one of the Victorian revivers of the art of stained glass. In this capacity he created the illuminated window panes for the restored House of Lords. Ballantine also wrote poems, and a two-part work of fiction, *The Gaberlunzie's Wallet* (1843) and its continuation, *The Miller Of Deanhaugh* (1844). His prose and poetry are firmly in the Scottish vernacular tradition. BL 2. *DNB*. Wol.

BALLANTYNE, R[obert] M[ichael] (1825–94). Like other Victorian authors of simple tales for children, Ballantyne was a complex man. The youngest of nine children, he was born in Edinburgh, where his family's fortunes were ruined with Sir Walter Scott's bankruptcy in 1826. (His uncle James was the great novelist's printer.) Ballantyne had virtually no formal education, and at sixteen he shipped out of the country as an apprentice clerk in the Hudson's Bay Company, at £20 annual salary. He spent six tough years in Rupert's Land and in northern Canada buying furs from Eskimos, often finding himself in sole charge of remote trading posts. His mother kept his letters home, and when her son followed them to work as a printer in Scotland, they were privately put out as *Hudson's Bay* (1848) a story of 'Every-day Life In The Wilds Of North America'. The volume brought Ballantyne to the notice of William Nelson* the publisher who suggested a children's* tale, and in 1856, Ballantyne produced (for a mere £50) *The Young Fur Traders*. Its success set Ballantyne on a productive career in adventure fiction. In 1858, he produced three of his finest works: *Ungava, A Tale Of Esquimeaux Land**; *The Coral Island**; and *Martin Rattler, Or A Boy's Adventures In The Forests Of Brazil*. (The publisher paid some £60 apiece for the entire copyrights: this abysmal rate of payment for juvenile fiction explains the astounding productivity of authors like Ballantyne, G. A. Henty* and W. H. G. Kingston*). Ballantyne had considerable creative ability (he was able, for instance, to illustrate his own work). He was, more importantly, a shameless self publiciser and exploiter of his own mystique. He specialised in lectures, which he would open by stalking on stage in buckskin, and shooting a stuffed eagle. In later life, 'research' led him to disguise himself as an Arab in the native quarter of Algiers in order to write *Pirate City* (1874). He also submersed himself with nearly fatal results in a diving suit and marooned himself in a lighthouse as preparation for other tales. Lighthouses and lifeboats were, in fact, a passion of Ballantyne's. So successful was his 1864 novel *The Lifeboat* in raising money for the National Lifeboat Institution that the first Edinburgh vessel was named after him.

In 1864 he also spent a month making the journey from London to Edinburgh by foot. He married in 1866. After much travelling abroad, he settled at Harrow in 1883 with his wife and six children. Harrow School appropriately led the subscription to raise a monument to his name after he died in Rome, where he had gone in a vain attempt to mend his failing health, having suffered from Ménière's disease for several years. Ballantyne did for the English schoolboy's geography what Henty did for his history. But some of his domestic tales of heroism also deserve attention; for instance, *Fighting The Flames, A Tale Of The London Fire Brigade* (1867). *The Dog Crusoe* (1861) was one of his most popular items, and shows a gentler side to Ballantyne's code of manliness. *Ballantyne's Miscellany* (1863–86) was an attempt to inculcate learning and virtue into the lower-class juvenile reader by using the attractions of the adventure story. It was not successful. Between 1884 and 1890 Ballantyne continued producing two books a year, his last adventure story being *The Walrus Hunters* (1892). BL 60. *DNB*. RM. *NCBEL*. Sad. RLF.

BANIM, John (1798–1842) and **BANIM**, Michael (1796–1874). Michael and John Banim were born in Kilkenny, sons of a prosperous farmer and sporting outfitter who furnished them with a good education. Michael was initially destined for law, although family difficulties prevented him from entering the profession. John (the cleverer of the two) showed artistic ability. At some financial sacrifice, the family sent him to the Protestant St John's College at Kilkenny where Congreve and Swift had earlier been pupils. From 1813, he studied art at the academy of the Royal Dublin Society and had his heart broken when a girl he loved in Kilkenny died of tuberculosis. Already in poor health himself, John Banim abandoned this vocation in 1820, married in 1822 and moved to London where he lived until the early 1830s. Together, under the pseudonym 'The O'Hara Family', the brothers went on to publish a succession of 'Irish* National Tales' which set out to do for Ireland what Scott had done for Scotland. The first series came out in 1825, and was an immediate success. But John (always the dominant partner) had suffered a severe attack of cholera in 1826 and was chronically ill until his premature death. Michael survived him, to become (in 1852) postmaster at Kilkenny having married in 1840. His health failed latterly and like his brother his last years were eased by grants from the Royal Literary Fund*. Two of his works, *Clough Fion* (1852) and *The Town Of The Cascades* (1864) overlap the Victorian period, and jointly the brothers in John's last year of life published the interesting psychological study *Father Connell* (1842), a novel which despite its artificial murder plot has vivid pictures of suffering Irish humanity. The Banims claim attention as folklorists, Irish Nationalists and pioneers of regional authenticity in early nineteenth-century fiction. BL 14. *DNB*. RM. *NCBEL*. Wol. Sad. RLF.

BANKS, Mrs G[eorge] Linnaeus [Isabella] (née Varley, 1821–97). The daughter of a Manchester chemist (and amateur artist), Isabella Varley had her eyesight injured as a child by a smoky chimney. Her father subsequently lost £10,000 in a Chancery suit, defending a bleaching process he had invented. Isabella showed early literary ability, having some of her poetry published at the age of sixteen in the *Manchester Guardian*. Before her marriage in 1846 to George L. Banks (1821–81), she was a schoolteacher, at Cheetham in Lancashire. George Banks was a journalist and poet with strong Methodist affiliations and a charismatic lecturing style. The couple went to live in Birmingham, and Isabella contributed to various of the journals put out by her husband. It would seem that he was either mentally unstable or drunken and his financial problems induced her to write novels to supplement the family income. There were other misfortunes; by 1864, five of her eight children had died. The couple moved to London at this troubled period and Banks's first effort in fiction, *God's Providence House*, appeared in 1865. Set in 1790s Chester, it has a rather Brontëan* gothic* plot, and touches on slave emancipation and its consequences for local trade. It was followed by *Stung To The Quick, A North Country Story* (1867). Banks went on to gain some fame as 'The Lancashire Novelist'. Her best work in this character is *The Manchester Man** (1876) which elaborately reconstructs the city at the turn of the century, and has a chapter on the Peterloo massacre. Its hero, the textile worker Jabez Clegg, expresses the author's faith in the ultimate virtue of passive working-class suffering. A foundling, Jabez marries his employer's daughter and ends the novel himself a prosperous and enlightened master. Banks's views were nonconformist Christian, although she also supported some degree of women's rights. In the early 1870s her health broke down, but she continued to write. (Her husband meanwhile was a total invalid, drinking heavily, and finally died of cancer in 1881.) In 1891, she was awarded a Civil List pension. Other of her Mancunian novels are *Bond Slaves* (1893), a story of the Luddite riots, and *Forbidden To Marry* (1883), a manufacturing melodrama set in the Napoleonic War period. Wretchedly ill, she wrote a host of romances of various kinds up to her death, and established a loyal readership. Her work is notable for its well-researched and observed local detail, and its reliance on pacey dialogue. BL 14. *DNB*. Wol. Sad. RLF.

Barabbas, Marie Corelli, 1893, 3 vols, Methuen. Subtitled 'A Dream Of The World's Tragedy', this extravagant novel deals with Christ's last three days on earth. It opens with Barabbas, in prison, awaiting punishment for the murder of a Pharisee. As in the Gospel account, the Jews perversely choose him as the beneficiary of their Passover right of reprieve. In Corelli's account, Barabbas subsequently becomes involved with 'Judith Iscariot', the evil, high-born genius who prompted her brother Judas to betray Christ. The high priest Caiaphas is Barabbas's rival for Judith's love. She eventually goes mad with remorse and Barabbas is once more imprisoned for attempted murder (of Caiaphas) and the theft of Christ's body. He is converted to Christianity having witnessed the resurrection and dies peacefully in jail, redeemed. Reviewers found the novel absurd and tasteless. Even for Corelli, the dialogue is grotesquely unconvincing. By 1951, the work was in its fifty-ninth English printing.

Barbara's History, Amelia B[lanford] Edwards, 1864, 3 vols, Hurst and Blackett. Strongly influenced by *David Copperfield**, Edwards's novel is told autobiographically. Barbara Churchill is the daughter of a selfish widower. Clever, shy and physically unprepossessing she visits and is taken under the wing of a kindly aunt, Mrs Shandyshaft of Stoneycroft Hall in Suffolk. Under this eccentric relative's benevolence, Barbara blooms. She also meets the man of her life, Hugh Farquhar, much older than her at twenty-seven and heir to the neighbouring Broomhill estate. The couple are temporarily separated when Barbara goes to college in Germany where her father frustrates her ambition to become a painter. The lovers subsequently marry, but problems arise to trouble the heroine. There is a strange Italian woman secreted in their mansion at Broomhill whom Barbara comes to believe is Hugh's legal wife. She runs away to Rome. But Hugh joins her to explain that he is not a bigamist, nor even the seducer of the mysterious Maddalena. He merely took her into his protection as an act of chivalry when she threw herself at him. Hugh and Barbara are reconciled. Maddalena fortuitously dies. The novel was a hit and established Edwards as a popular author.

BARBER, Margaret Fairless ('Michael Fairless', 1869–1901). Margaret Barber was born in Yorkshire, the youngest daughter of a lawyer with antiquarian tastes. Brought up devoutly in the Church of England, she never married. Early in her life she travelled in Germany, an experience with mystical overtones which profoundly influenced her. Her parents both having died early, she took up nursing as 'The Fighting Sister' in the East End of London in 1890, but ill health prevented her continuing. In later life she evidently suffered a severe spinal injury which left her an invalid and she lived by herself in a country cottage, with an adopted half-witted girl. As 'Michael Fairless', Barber subsequently wrote some fiction, notably the eccentric novella *The Gathering Of Brother Hilarius* (1897), the story of a monk in the Middle Ages who goes on travels and eventually becomes a prior. It contains a powerful Black Death episode. Rather more effective was Fairless's deathbed work of popular philosophy, *The Roadmender* (1902) whose main character (i.e. Fairless herself) watches the highway of life tranquilly from the sidelines. Her pseudonym was a composite of her father's Scottish family name (Fairless) and the Christian name of the man she evidently loved in her youth. BL 2. *WW*. RM. *NCBEL*.

Barchester Towers, Anthony Trollope, 1857, 3 vols, Longman. The novel is a sequel to *The Warden**, although somewhat more ambitious in its narrative scope. It opens with the Bishop dying, and his son, Archdeacon Theophilus Grantly, mourning by his bedside. But his grief is contaminated by ambition. If his father dies quickly, the son will inherit the bishopric. If the old man lingers, there will be a change of government, and the new administration will prefer its own candidate. Grantly is disappointed, and Bishop Proudie descends on Barchester with an evangelical new broom. In-fighting between the reform and reactionary Barchester factions constitutes most of the novel's comedy. Proudie is dominated by his wife, and his odious domestic chaplain, Obadiah Slope. Eleanor Bold, the heroine of *The Warden*, is now a widow, and Slope, coveting her £1,200 per annum, sets out to win her. But he has a rival in the dilettante Bertie Stanhope. Bertie appears on the scene when Proudie recalls his prebendary father, Dr Stanhope, from a luxurious absentee life in Italy. Dr Stanhope's daughter, Signora Madeline Vesey Neroni, also returns with the household entourage. A *femme fatale* with a mysterious past and crippled, the Signora none the less exercises a bewitching power over men. Slope becomes entangled, and is dismissed. Eleanor eventually marries Francis Arabin, the amiable (and High Church) new Dean of Barchester. In the long-running Barsetshire* series, many of this novel's characters were to be called out again.

BARCLAY, Florence [Louisa] ('Brandon Roy', née Charlesworth, 1862–1920). Florence Charlesworth was born in Limpsfield, Surrey, a clergyman's daughter. When she was seven, the family moved to London, where the Rev. Charlesworth took up work in an unfashionable East End parish in Limehouse. Florence was educated by a governess and in 1881 married the Rev. Charles W. Barclay. The honeymoon took the form of a tour to Palestine, an experience which touched the young woman profoundly. On their return the couple took up a living near Hertford, and she bore five children in as many years. In the early 1890s, she suffered a severe illness and evidently began serious writing during convalescence. Barclay thereafter wrote a dozen novels, beginning with *Guy Mervyn* (1891) written under the male pseudonym 'Brandon Roy'. Her most successful work was *The Rosary* (1909) which sold 150,000 copies in under a year, and which expresses her fervently spiritualist and erotic brand of Christianity. BL 12. *WW*. RM. Wol. Sad.

BARING-GOULD, S[abine] (1834–1924). The most fluently productive of late Victorian dilettante novelists, Sabine Baring-Gould's family were rich Devon landowners and with a patrimony of 3,000 acres he was himself never obliged to labour for his living. His father was a retired East India Company lieutenant, his mother an admiral's daughter. Baring-Gould was born at Dix's Fields, Exeter. A delicate child, he was educated partly abroad, and developed the remarkable sensitivity to place which distinguishes his later writing. (See his *Early Reminiscences 1834–64*, 1923.) After leaving Clare College, Cambridge, in 1856, Baring-Gould taught for seven years before taking orders in 1864. His Anglicanism was very high and is reflected in his later historical* novels, such as *Perpetua* (1897) which chronicles the persecutions of Christians in second-century Nimes. But Baring-Gould's interests were far from dry and academic. Two of his early publications are *The Book Of Werewolves* (1865) and *Curious Myths Of The Middle Ages* (1866) both of which display a lively turn of mind. Taking up a curacy in Yorkshire in 1865, Baring-Gould fell in love with, educated and married (happily) a mill girl, Grace Taylor, in 1868. The episode is closely recalled in his first novel, *Through Flood And Flame* (1868). Working-class heroines were to recur frequently in the author's later fiction. The couple eventually went on to have fourteen children. In 1871, Baring-Gould began a ten years' stint as a clergyman at East Mersea, on the Essex coast. The sojourn is commemorated in *Richard Cable The Lightshipman** (1888) whose plot has a low-born Essex man marrying an heiress. In 1872, he inherited his father's vast estate, Lew-Trenchard. In 1881 he returned there, having presented himself with the local living. He resided in north Devon until his death. In the ample leisure which his duties as parson-cum-squire allowed him, he turned out a torrent of writing on religion (notably a massive *Lives Of The British Saints*), travel, history and fiction. Baring-Gould produced a total of 159 books, of which a quarter are novels. As a novelist, he is principally interesting as a connoisseur of British locality, in its recent historical past. His strongest setting, unsurprisingly, is that of the West Country. A selection of his works dealing with this region are: *John Herring* (1883), a pessimistic story of village life on the borders of Devon and Cornwall; *Red Spider* (1887), a realistic reconstruction of village life on the Devon and Cornwall border in the mid-nineteenth century; *The Gaverocks* (1888), a story of wife murder among the peasant class in bygone Cornwall; *Urith* (1891), a historical romance, set in Dartmoor at the time of the Monmouth uprising; *In The Roar Of The Sea** (1892), a wild melodrama set on the Cornish coast; *Guavas The Tinner* (1897), a primitive romance of mining in Cornwall in the Elizabethan era; *Winefred* (1900), a smuggling adventure set on the Devonshire coast. Baring-Gould also used other English settings effectively in, for instance: *Mehalah** (1880), set in the East Coast salt marshes near Mersea; *Cheap Jack Zita* (1893), set on the Ely fens, around 1815; *Bladys Of The Stewponey* (1897), a story of eighteenth-century highwaymen and rock dwellers in Shropshire; *The Frobishers* (1901), a saga of working life in the pottery district of north Staffordshire. All Baring-Gould's regional stories have galloping pace and vivid colour. His historical novels are stodgier. Among them are: *Noémi* (1895), set in fourteenth-century France and *Domitia* (1898) which rather woodenly reconstructs Roman court life during the terror under Domitian. As a painter of English rural life in its regional variety Baring-Gould belongs with Hardy*. But his plots are paper-thin melodrama, and his tone often that of the condescending tourist. He wrote the hymn, 'Onward Christian Soldiers' which is probably his most enduring claim to fame. Despite the frail health of his childhood and his Herculean writing labours, he lived a remarkably long life. In his two-volume autobiography, he makes no reference to himself as a novelist. BL 49. *DNB*. RM. *NCBEL*. Wol. Sad.

BARKER, M[atthew] H[enry] (1790–1846). Barker was born in Deptford, the son of a dissenting minister. He joined an East Indiaman, while still a boy, and went on to serve in the Royal Navy. He rose no further than master's mate after which he freebooted in the merchant marine for some years, seeing action in the Napoleonic Wars. After retirement ashore in 1825, Barker wrote extensively in the magazines as 'The Old Sailor'. He was naval editor of *The United Service Gazette*, and he took advantage of the 1830s vogue for nautical* yarns with works such as: *Land And Sea Tales* (1836); *Topsail Sheet Blocks* (1838) and *Hamilton King* (1839). Much of Barker's nautical fiction was finely illustrated by his friend George Cruikshank*. BL 11. *DNB*. Wol. Sad. RLF.

BARLOW, Jane (1857–1917). Barlow was born in Dublin, the daughter of a clergyman who later became the Vice-Provost of Trinity College. She was educated at home, and lived all her life in or near the Irish capital, never marrying. As a writer of fiction, Barlow specialised in delicate sketches, ballads and tales of western Irish peasant life which were much admired by Swinburne and Victorian readers generally. Her first published volumes were collections: *Bogland Studies* (1892) and *Irish Idylls* (1893). *Kerrigan's Quality* (1893) is a full-length series of linked episodes. Its quirky hero Martin Kerrigan returns to Ireland from Australia after twenty years and buys the 'big house' at Glenore which he then lets out to tenants of 'quality'. She returned to the short pieces and versifying which suited her better with *A Creel Of Irish Stories* (1897) and *From The Land Of The Shamrock* (1901). Jane Barlow had a strong following among the Irish community in America. BL 15. *WW*. RM. *NCBEL*. Wol.

Barnaby Rudge, Charles Dickens, 1841, 1 vol, Chapman and Hall. (The novel was illustrated by Phiz* and George Cattermole*, and serialised in *Master Humphrey's Clock**, February–November 1841.) Dickens's fifth published and first historical* novel. The story begins in 1775, at landlord John Willet's Maypole Inn, Chigwell, Essex. A mysterious stranger is told the story of the murder of Reuben Haredale at the Warren twenty-two years before. Haredale's brother Geoffrey was suspected, but nothing could be proved. A steward, Rudge, was somewhat later found stabbed dead. Barnaby, his son, was born the day after the crime and has grown up simple-minded but endowed with visionary power. His constant companion is a tame raven, Grip. Geoffrey Haredale's niece, Emma, loves Edward, the son of the haughty Sir John Chester. The match is broken off by the two parents. The love affair between Joe Willet (son of the Maypole's landlord) and Dolly Varden (the daughter of the London locksmith Gabriel Varden) is also forbidden. Joe goes off to be a soldier, and Dolly enters service as Emma's companion. She is persecuted by the attentions of a brutish ostler, Hugh. Varden's apprentice, the absurdly vain Sim Tappertit, is loved by the household maid Miggs, but he too has ambitious designs on Dolly. The action climaxes with the 'No Popery!' Gordon riots of 1780 in which Hugh takes a major part. The Maypole is looted and the Warren is destroyed. Emma and Dolly are kidnapped by Sim. Old Rudge, the original murderer, is discovered not to have died after all (a gardener's body was mistaken for his) and is hanged after the riots. Barnaby, who has innocently participated in the disorder, is reprieved. Sim's legs, of which he was inordinately proud, are crushed and he becomes a shoeblack. Sir John Chester is revealed to be the father of Hugh, and is killed in a duel with Geoffrey Haredale. The novel is rich in its thematic workings out of the father–son relationship and makes a powerful plea against capital punishment.

BARNARD, Fred[erick] (1846–96). Illustrator. The youngest son of a silversmith, Barnard was born in London and later studied art and figure drawing both there and in Paris. He began contributing drawings to the *Illustrated London News** in 1863 and at the same period became associated with *Punch** and *Once A Week**. His best-known illustrations of fiction are the designs for the 'Household Edition' of Dickens's* novels (1871–79). He also illustrated some of the later reissued fiction of Thackeray* and Besant's* *All Sorts And Conditions Of Men** (1882). Barnard's style is vigorous, and exploits the mid-century preference for naturalistic woodcuts. He died prematurely, accidentally burned to death in a friend's house in Wimbledon. *DNB*. Hou. Wol.

BARR, Amelia [Edith] (née Huddleston, 1831–1919). Born at Ulverston in Lancashire, Huddleston's father was a clergyman with a substantial private income which he lost (by a friend's fraud) when his daughter was sixteen. After qualifying herself at the Normal School in Glasgow, she took up work teaching. In Glasgow, where she found employment, she met and married a merchant, Robert Barr, in 1850. Harriet Beecher Stowe, then visiting Britain, suggested that the Barrs come to America. In 1853, when Robert Barr in his turn went bankrupt, they took her advice and emigrated. After landing at New York the family settled in Chicago until Barr's political activities forced them to leave. They moved on to Galveston, Texas, then a new state. Misfortune continued to dog the Barrs. Robert and three children died in the yellow fever epidemic of 1867. Now a widow, Amelia travelled north to New York, arriving with only $5 in her purse and three daughters to support. From 1868 onwards, she supported herself by writing. Some years later, in her fifties, she began writing novels. *Jan Vedder's Wife* (1885), a story of the Shetland Isles in the 1830s, caught the public taste and she followed it with other stories of humble life in Scottish fishing communities: *A Daughter Of Fife* (1886); *A Knight Of The Nets* (1894). These melodramatic narratives deal mainly with marriages gone wrong and contain scenes of heavy pathos. Yorkshire settings also featured prominently in Barr's fiction as in *Between Two Loves*, (1886), a tale of the West Riding; *Master Of His Fate* (1888). The best of her novels, however, are those dealing with historical New York, such as: *A Bow Of Orange Ribbon* (1886), a story of Dutch New York, just before the War of Independence, and its sequel *The Maid Of Maiden Lane* (1900). Barr also wrote a successful patriotic American historical* novel, *Remember The Alamo* (1888), which survived to inspire a John Wayne movie in the 1960s. An energetic old lady, Barr wrote scores of potboilers up to the year of her death. Her very last novels, such as *Joan, A Romance Of An English Mining Village* (1917), suggest that the strong vein of religious conscience found in her early fiction had become more political. Barr was one of the admirable band of Victorian ladies who wrote fiction of a respectable standard primarily to keep bread on their families' tables. Her daughter, Miss Lillie Barr, wrote tales for juveniles in the 1870s and 1880s. BL 64. *Dictionary Of American Biography*. RM.

BARR, Robert ('Luke Sharp', 1850–1912). Born in Glasgow, Barr was educated and brought up in Toronto, Canada where his family moved in 1854. He remained there as a schoolteacher until 1876, when he moved to Detroit to work as a journalist rising to a senior position on the *Detroit Free Press*. In 1881, he returned to England (nominally to launch an English edition of his paper), where he settled down in Surrey and supported himself by his pen. (Barr continued to travel to and fro across the Atlantic, writing a book on the subject, *In A Steamer Chair*, 1892.) In 1892, he founded *The Idler** magazine, with Jerome K. Jerome*. (The two men were later to fall out in 1895, with a quarrel arising from a libel action.) Barr was popular for his spoofs (often written under the facetious pseudonym 'Luke Sharp') such as *The Adventures Of Sherlaw Kombs* (1892). His best novels proper are: *In The Midst Of Alarms* (1894), a story set in rural Canada, at the time of the threatened 1867 Fenian invasion from the USA and *The Countess Tekla* (1898), a Zendaish romance of medieval Germany with a heroine who is wooed by the emperor in disguise. A strongly promoted Methuen* author, Barr wrote much short fiction, and had a strong line in ghost* and detective* stories. His novella *From Whose Bourne* (1893) combines the two, with a corpse who ingeniously solves his own murder in the spirit world. *The Mutable Many* (1896) is a contemporary story of London strikes and socialism which is as reactionary as its title (a quotation from Shakespeare's *Coriolanus*) suggests. *Jennie Baxter Journalist* (1898) is a lively new woman* romance. BL 20. *WW*. Wol.

BARRETT, A[lfred] W[alter] ('R. Andom', 1869–1920). Barrett was born in London, and as an adult worked there mainly as a journalist. He was for some years assistant editor of the *Literary World* and in 1900 became editor of the comic 1d.-weekly paper, *Scraps*. He wrote jolly, heavily illustrated, lightweight fiction under the pseudonym 'R. Andom', and enjoyed some succcess in the 1890s with his 'Troddles' series of tales of London life. *The Strange Adventure Of Roger Wilkins* (1895) is Wellsian* scientific romance about migrant personality, a theme Barrett also used in *The Identity Exchange* (1902). *Side Slips* (1898) recounts comic 'misadventures on a bicycle'. BL 23. *WW*. Wol.

BARRETT, Frank (1848–1926). According to his own account, Barrett began his working life as a journalist at eighteen, writing literary and dramatic criticism. He turned to pottery and sculpture, but gave up when a kiln collapsed, destroying two years' work. Literary friends (including the publisher Bentley*) induced him in the early 1880s to take up fiction in which line he had produced some forty volumes by 1901. His novels are sensational, episodic, and their settings usually historical. Typical titles are: *Fettered For Life* (1889); *Between Life And Death* (1890), a melodramatic treatment of adultery; *Out Of The Jaws Of Death* (1892). The last is a crime story set in a seedily portrayed London dockland. Written in the author's habitual rat-a-tat paragraphs, it has a heroine who escapes various threatened disasters to become, ultimately, a Russian princess. Barrett's most popular works seem to have been *A Set Of Rogues* (1895), the story of a company of strolling players, driven from seventeenth-century London by the plague and *Breaking The Shackles* (1900), a detective* story with some strong prison scenes. Barrett liked pacey action and autobiographical narration in his novels. He evidently made a comfortable income from his writing and spent his later years in Norfolk living in a converted rectory. His wife, Joan Barrett, also wrote three volumes of fiction including (in the Victorian period), *Monte Carlo Stories* (1896). BL 39. (JB) BL 3. *WW*. Wol.

BARRETT, Wilson [William Henry] (1846–1904). Barrett is principally remembered as a man of the theatre. Brought up in Essex, the son of a farmer, he was educated privately, but family misfortune led to his leaving school early. After working briefly as a printer he began his acting career in 1864 and was followed by two of his siblings who later worked with him on the stage. In 1866, Barrett married one of his leading ladies, Caroline Heath (1835–87). He became manager of the London Court Theatre in 1879 and made a name for himself in Britain and America with lavishly spectacular productions. In the 1890s, he successfully adapted a number of Hall Caine's* florid melodramas for the stage and himself wrote novelisations of his own plays of which the most popular were: *The Sign Of The Cross* (1896); *The Daughters Of Babylon* (1899), co-authored with Robert Hichens*; *In Old New York* (1900), co-authored with E. A. Barron. BL 3. *DNB*. Wol.

BARRIE, [Sir] J[ames] M[atthew] (1860–1937). Barrie was born in Kirriemuir, Forfarshire, the ninth child of a handloom weaver and a strict Presbyterian mother. At thirteen, he went to school in Dumfries and from there he progressed to Edinburgh University, graduating in 1882. From early youth (when he was addicted to penny dreadfuls*) Barrie was determined on a career in literature and in 1883 he secured a post as leader writer to the *Nottingham Journal*. At around the same period, he was writing semifictional sketches set in 'Thrums' (i.e. Kirriemuir). Barrie moved to London in 1885 and began the round of writing for the magazines. At this stage of his career, he was encouraged by the influential editor, Frederick Greenwood*. Barrie's first efforts in fiction parallel the miscellaneous nature of his early employment. *Better Dead* (1887, published at the author's own expense) is a 'murder as a fine art' joke. The young Scottish hero, Andrew Riach, newly arrived in London, evidently reflects some of the author's recent experience. *Auld Licht Idylls* (1888) is a collection of Barrie's 'Thrums' pieces, centred around his mother's austere religious sect. In 1888, he produced the more substantial *When A Man's Single* (by 'Gavin Ogilvy', his mother's maiden name). The history of a self-educated Scot, Rob Angus, who goes to London to make his way as a leader writer, this work is transparently autobiographical. There followed *A Window In Thrums* (1889) and *My Lady Nicotine* (1890), a set of smoking club stories. Success came in 1891, with *The Little Minister*. First serialised in *Good Words*, this story of a Presbyterian minister in love with a beautiful 'Egyptian' was the most connected of Barrie's narratives hitherto and caught the public fancy. In 1894, Barrie married a young actress, Mary Ansell. The Barries' marriage was childless, wretched and embittered his subsequent fiction. (The couple eventually divorced in 1909.) In 1895, Barrie was profoundly affected by the death of his mother. *Sentimental Tommy* (1896) and *Tommy And Grizel* (1900) chronicle the progress of a raw Thrums lad, Tommy Sandys. The first deals with Tommy's early days in working-class London and his relocation in his native Scotland. The narrative reveals Barrie's fascination with formative childhood experience. *Tommy And Grizel* jumps to the hero at nineteen. Tommy now returns to London to make his fortune. He succeeds in material terms, but his love life goes wrong and he dies, climbing the iron railings of the house of Lady Pippinworth, who has seduced him. ('His last reflection before he passed into unconsciousness was – serves me right!'.) These novels embody details of the author's own unhappy marriage. Barrie wrote one other major piece of biographical fiction, *Margaret Ogilvy* (1896), an intimate portrait of his mother. Although he was acknowledged as the leader of the kailyard* school, Barrie now gave up novels altogether. Finance was a main reason. There was infinitely more money to be made on the stage. His dramatic adaptation of *The Little Minister*, for instance, earned him almost £90,000 in British and American box-office receipts; many times what the novel had brought its author as a serial and a volume for Cassell*. In the twentieth century, Barrie gained world-wide fame as a playwright, and (after 1904) was immortalised as the creator of Peter Pan. But, as Michael Sadleir observes, fiction represents 'the vital phase of Barrie's literary career'. His last decades were loaded with public honours and he was created a baronet in 1913, given the Order of Merit in 1922 and made Chancellor of Edinburgh University in 1930. At his own wish he was buried in Kirriemuir alongside his mother. BL 13. *DNB*. RM. *NCBEL*. Wol. Sad.

Barrington, Charles Lever, 1863, 1 vol, Chapman and Hall. (Serialised in monthly parts, February 1862–January 1863, illustrated by Phiz*.) One of Lever's last novels in monthly numbers. The story loosely follows the fortunes, misfortunes and mended fortunes of a landed Irish family. Peter Barrington loses his inheritance by gambling and is forced (together with his maiden sister, Dinah) to live in genteel squalor. Eventually he is enriched again by an inheritance from India. The novel is clear evidence of Lever's declining powers in his later career as he began to over-produce, in an attempt to regain his hold on the public.

BARRINGTON, Mrs Russell [Emilie Isabel] (née Wilson, 1842–1933). The daughter of James Wilson MP, she was educated privately at home by governesses. As a young woman she was a professional artist and married in 1868 into the family of Viscount Barrington. In later life she served on the council of the National Trust and wrote some substantial art criticism. She also published some less substantial fiction. *Lena's Picture* (1892) is a 'Story Of Love' in which the heroine has to decide whether her family's taint of insanity should prevent her marrying. The work is heavily laced with poetic epigraphs from the Brownings. *Helen's Ordeal* (1894), another 'beautiful tragedy', is the story of a woman who marries a selfish artist and probably transcribes some of the author's early bohemian experience. BL 2. *WW. Wol.*

BARROWCLIFFE, A. J. (i.e. Albert Julius Mott, *fl.* 1850–70). A miscellaneous man of letters whose background is mysterious, Mott wrote on various subjects from alcoholism to local history. He evidently lived in Liverpool and wrote fiction for a short period of his life, under the pseudonym 'A. J. Barrowcliffe' which may have had some regional reference. *Amberhill* (1856) and *Trust For Trust* (1859) were both published by Smith, Elder* and were both popular works. They were evidently inspired by *Cranford**, being small parochial sagas, centred on village intrigues and squabbles. After scathing reviews for his last effort in fiction, *Normanton* (1862), Mott apparently lost heart as a novelist. Ironically, *Normanton* was rediscovered as a 'masterpiece' in the 1930s. As Michael Sadleir puts it, the novel 'is a fine period specimen, with a stern father who drives two erring daughters out of his house and so to suicide by drowning. It is told with a delicacy, with a sense of landscape, which raise it to a high level of achievement.' BL 3. *NCBEL. Wol. Sad.*

BARRY, John Arthur (1850–1911). Barry was born in Torquay and went to sea at thirteen, in the merchant service. After twelve years, he left with a chief mate's certificate. In 1875, he travelled to the Australian gold diggings, settling after various adventurous occupations in Sydney where he spent the rest of his life. He never married. Barry was a foreign correspondent for *The Times* and wrote several adventure stories with pioneer Australian or lusty nautical* settings. They include: *Steve Brown's Bunyip* (1893); *In The Great Deep* (1895); *A Son Of The Sea* (1899); *Against The Tides Of Fate* (1899). He died in Sydney. BL 8. *WW.*

BARRY, [the Right Rev. Mgr] William [Francis] (1849–1930). Barry was born in London, of Irish parents and educated at Oscott College near Birmingham and at the Gregorian University in Rome. He entered the priesthood in 1873 and returned to England to take up the chair of philosophy at the new theological college at Olton. As 'Canon Barry' he wrote articles for the *Dublin Review* and the *Contemporary.* As a theological historian, his published work on the medieval popes was censured by his Catholic superiors. By nature controversial, Barry also wrote provocative novels. His *The New*

Antigone* (1887) mounted a broadside and often witty attack on free thinking, free love, atheism, socialism and the new woman* cult. His work, which
parades a wide range of literary allusion and learning, was published by
the new firm of T. Fisher Unwin who specialised in intellectual books for
the 1890s. *The Two Standards* (1898) is a more overtly Catholic work, with
an artist hero based on Wagner and satire on modern high finance. *Arden
Massiter* (1900) has as its hero a young English socialist involved in Italian
revolutionary politics. *The Wizard's Knot* (1901) is comic at the expense of
the Celtic revival. Barry's ghost* stories (which are not reckoned good of
their kind) were gathered as *The Place Of Dreams* (1893), and published
under the imprint of the Catholic Truth Society. BL 5. *WW*. Wol.

Barry Lyndon, W. M. Thackeray, 1856, 1 vol, Bradbury and Evans.
(As *The Luck Of Barry Lyndon, By Fitz-Boodle*, the story was serialised
irregularly in *Fraser's Magazine**, January–December 1844.) This Irish*
picaresque tale is an early and not entirely successful effort by Thackeray.
The story is told in the first person by the vain, bullying hero, Redmond
Barry. The darling of his widowed mother he is absurdly indulged as a child.
At the age of fifteen, he falls in love with his older cousin Nora Brady and
fights a duel with her more desirable English suitor. Redmond is deluded into
thinking he has killed his man, and takes flight. After various adventures, he
enlists as a soldier during the Seven Years War and eventually deserts the
English army (having fought at Minden) to serve as an infantryman for the
Prussians. Frederick the Great sends him to spy on the Chevalier Balibari
who turns out to be the hero's uncle, Cornelius. Redmond deserts again,
and he and his uncle become professional gamblers. In Dresden, Redmond
almost cardsharps and bullies his way to a rich marriage, but is foiled. At
a fashionable watering place, he falls in with Sir Charles and Lady Honoria
Lyndon. The husband dies, and Redmond forces himself on the widow.
Married to her, he changes his name to Barry Lyndon. He mistreats his
stepson, Viscount Bullingdon, who finally runs away to fight in America,
where he is reported killed. Barry presumptuously sets up his young son,
Bryan, as heir. But the boy is killed in a riding accident. Barry's persecution
of his wife becomes so gross that her friends conspire to free her. Bullingdon
returns, and publicly horsewhips Barry. The hero's luck finally runs out, and
he dies of delirium tremens in the Fleet Prison, a debtor and with only his
faithful old crone of a mother to care for him. The novel is a *tour de force*
of ironic narration but so bitter in tone as to make even Thackeray wonder
if it was worth writing.

The Barsetshire [Barchester] Novels. A loosely linked sequence of
stories by Anthony Trollope*, centred on the cathedral city of Barchester in
the imaginary county of Barsetshire. Although clergymen and ecclesiastical
reform figure prominently, religion does not. Trollope scrupulously made
it difficult to identify the original of his cathedral city but it supposedly
amalgamates features of Salisbury and Winchester. The series, which grew
accidentally, comprises: *The Warden** (1855); *Barchester Towers** (1857);
Doctor Thorne* (1858); *Framley Parsonage** (1861); *The Small House At
Allington** (1864) and *The Last Chronicle Of Barset** (1867).

BARWELL, Louisa Mary (née Bacon, 1800–85). Born in Norwich the
daughter of a journalist, Louisa Bacon's family was strongly musical, and

she was gifted in this direction herself. As a young woman, she helped her father edit his *Quarterly Musical Magazine And Review*. After her marriage to wine merchant John Barwell, she devoted herself to educational books and philanthropic work with the young. As a married woman Louisa Barwell continued to live in Norwich where she was a pillar of the local literary society. Foremost among her improving tales for juveniles are: *The Elder Brother* (1835); *The Nursery Maid* (1839) and *Gilbert Harland, Or Good In Everything* (1850) BL 11. DND.

Basil, Wilkie Collins, 1852, 3 vols, Bentley. (The work was revised and reissued in 1862.) Collins's second novel, and unlike his first (*Antonina**) a 'Story Of Modern Life'. Basil (his surname is withheld, 'for reasons of honour') is high-born, but falls in love with Margaret Sherwin, a linen-draper's daughter, with whom, for unlikely reasons, he contracts a secret (and for a year, unconsummated) marriage. She is subsequently seduced by her father's confidential clerk, Mannion, the son of a forger. The guilty couple are discovered in a sordid hotel by the wronged husband who hears them copulating through a thin wall (the scene infuriated contemporary reviewers). In the ensuing struggle, Mannion is thrown on a newly macadamised road, horribly disfigured and dedicates himself to revenge. Margaret dies of typhus and remorse. The rivals bring their conflict to a climax in Cornwall whose landscape is vividly described by Collins. (By this stage, the narrative is in the form of the hero's diary.) In a cliff-face struggle, Mannion is finally hurled into the boiling sea. The story is told autobiographically at a lively pace and was moderately successful for its young author.

The Battle Of Dorking, Colonel G. T. Chesney, 1871, 1 vol, Blackwoods. (Originally published in *Blackwood's Magazine**, May 1871. A 6d. edition, put out by the publisher in June 1871, sold 80,000 copies.) Chesney was an army engineer who decided to alert the English people with an invasion fable. It takes the form of a volunteer addressing his grandchildren fifty years after a victorious German blitzkrieg on British soil. The shambolic British forces are routed at Dorking. Prussia had overrun France in 1870, which made the fantasy horribly plausible. England is stripped of her colonies and forced to pay massive reparations to the Hun. The work's effect was sensational and Gladstone himself was obliged to warn the population against 'alarmism'. Chesney's fiction inspired a host of imitators, including the invasion-phobia stories of William Le Queux* and Wells's* *The War Of The Worlds**.

The Battle Of Life, Charles Dickens, 1846, 1 vol, Bradbury and Evans. (A Christmas Book*, lavishly illustrated by D. Maclise*, C. Stanfield*, R. Doyle* and J. Leech*.) A love story, centred on the two daughters of a cheerful philosopher, Dr Anthony Jeddler. On the eve of her wedding, Marion runs away, leaving her elder sister, Grace, to marry the intended groom, Alfred Heathfield, a medical student. Marion returns six years later to reveal that it was an altruistic act, knowing as she did the pair's love for each other. She has meanwhile been in hiding with her aunt Martha. The story (one of the world's 'thousand bloodless battles') is set in the eighteenth century and the title comes from the Jeddlers' tranquil house, located on one of the former battlefields of the Civil War.

BAYLY, Ada Ellen ('Edna Lyall', 1857–1903). She was born in Brighton, the youngest of three daughters of a barrister who died when she was eleven. Her mother followed three years after. Delicate in health, she was partly educated at home, partly by an uncle who took over the role of guardian and partly at boarding school. As an adult Ada Bayly lived with her sisters (both of whom had married clergymen) in London, Lincoln and Eastbourne. A lifelong spinster and deeply religious, she supported the women's suffrage movement from its early days. Her first book (written under her invariable pseudonym, Edna Lyall) was *Won By Waiting* (1879). In 1882, she brought out *Donovan*. This melodrama, with a redeemed agnostic ('A Modern Englishman') as its hero, only sold 320 copies of its first edition. But it attracted the admiration of Gladstone and led to a connection with the notorious free-thinker, Charles Bradlaugh, with whom Bayly was (religion apart) sympathetic. In the sequel, *We Two*, (1884), Bradlaugh's influence can be seen in the novel's secularist preoccupations, and in the character of Luke Raeburn, 'public agitator'. Raeburn's daughter Erica is finally weaned from parental atheism. *In The Golden Days* (1885), a historical* novel set in the reign of Charles II, established Lyall as a popular author. In 1886, 'Edna Lyall' was libelled by the allegation that the mysteriously pseudonymous authoress was in a lunatic asylum. She defended herself in her novel, *The Autobiography Of A Slander** (1887). *Derrick Vaughan: Novelist* (1889), though brief, contains revealing autobiographical material. The sexual transposition apart, the pacifist writer Derrick is clearly the young Lyall. Lyall's novels are most interesting when they deal with questions of faith and freedom, as in *To Right The Wrong* (1893), where she offers a sympathetic portrait of John Hampden, in the context of the Civil War. *Doreen** (1894) is a pro-Home Rule Irish novel. The heroine is the daughter of a Fenian who loses her singing voice after mistreatment in prison. *The Autobiography Of A Truth* (1896) champions the Armenian people against their Turkish oppressor. And the author's fierce opposition to the Boer War is conveyed in *The Hinderers* (1902). The title alludes to the enigmatic accusation in St. Luke, 'Ye hindered'. Lyall's point in the book is that the 'awful war' could have been averted if England had had the courage of its 'best convictions'. Lyall's apolitical historical and present-day romances were probably more to her contemporaries' taste. They include: *Wayfaring Men* (1897); *Hope The Hermit* (1898); *In Spite Of All* (1901). Lyall suffered from heart trouble after 1889, and passed her last years as a semi-invalid. Childless, she had three bells named after characters in her books at her church, St Saviour's Eastbourne. BL 18. *DNB*. RM. *NCBEL*. Wol. Sad.

The Beach of Falesá, R. L. Stevenson, 1892, 1 vol, Cassell. (Serialised as *Uma* in the *Illustrated London News**, July–August 1892, illustrated by Gordon Browne.) The tale is told by a South Seas trader, John Wiltshire, who has been transferred to the island of Falesá. There he is met with apparent friendliness by a rival trader, Case, who arranges a bogus marriage for Wiltshire with a trusting native beauty, Uma. Wiltshire subsequently realises that he has been tricked, for Uma is tabooed and none of the natives will deal with him. But now he finds that he loves his concubine, and arranges for a proper Christian marriage ceremony by the visiting missionary, Tarleton. Wiltshire later discovers that Case has been playing on the superstitions of Falesá's natives, with a supposedly haunted jungle shrine. The two traders fight it out hand to hand and Case is killed. The novella ran into various censorship problems, initially from the *ILN*. It was not printed in its original unexpurgated form until 1984.

BEARDSLEY, Aubrey [Vincent] (1872–98). Artist and writer. A precocious genius, Beardsley was born at Brighton, and educated at the grammar school there. His mother was a dominant influence in his early boyhood and one that he never properly outgrew. On leaving school, Beardsley was for a short time a clerk in London. His artistic efforts were encouraged by Burne-Jones, and his striking style was strongly influenced by the posters of Toulouse Lautrec. (Beardsley visited Paris in 1892.) In 1893 the young artist sprang into notoriety and fame with his highly mannered and erotic drawings. He was art editor of the *Yellow Book** from 1894 to 1895, his tenure being cut short by the Oscar Wilde* scandal. Subsequently he was art editor of the *Savoy** during its short existence in 1896. At the same period, Beardsley wrote (and published in expurgated form) his libidinous fantasy, based loosely on Wagner's *Tannhäuser, Under The Hill*. In 1897 he entered the Catholic Church, and before dying of consumption at Mentone a year later requested (unsuccessfully) that all his obscene drawings be destroyed. Beardsley was as much a book designer as an illustrator. He furnished the frontis and tailpieces for John Lane's* *Keynotes** series supplying its unique physical appearance. BL 2. *DNB*. RM. *NCBEL*. Hou.

Beauchamp's Career, George Meredith, 1875, 3 vols, Chapman and Hall. (Serialised in the *Fortnightly Review**, August 1874–December 1875.) Nevil Beauchamp is a well-born British naval officer, obsessed with noble ideals of self-sacrifice and honour. Having been wounded in the Crimean War, he goes to Venice to recuperate. There he falls in love and tries to elope with Renée de Croisnel, the sister of a French officer, Roland, whose life he earlier saved. Renée is betrothed to a French aristocrat, however, and the elopement is foiled. Nevil returns for a while to sea. In the seaport of Bevisham, he next comes under the influence of a radical Liberal, Dr Shrapnel, and stands unsuccessfully for Parliament. This leads to complications. Cecilia Halkett, a beautiful Tory, falls in love with him. And his uncle Everard Romfrey ('a fighting earl') enraged by Nevil's new political doctrines, horsewhips the luckless eighty-six-year-old Shrapnel. Renée reappears, having fled from her husband, but Nevil contrives to reunite the couple. By a series of misadventures, Cecilia rejects Nevil's proposal. He falls ill, is reconciled with his uncle, and eventually makes a loveless but friendly marriage with Jenny Denham, Shrapnel's ward. Nevil finally dies in the act of saving a drowning working-class child. The novel ends sardonically with the mud-spattered 'urchin' and the reflection: 'This is what we have in exchange for Beauchamp!'. Nevil's unlucky enthusiasms and idealism draw on Meredith's recently evolved theory of comedy. The character of the hero is probably based on the novelist's friend, Frederick Augustus Maxse (1833–1900), a naval captain whom Meredith assisted in his campaign to win Southampton as a radical MP in 1868.

BECKE, [George Lewis] Louis (1855–1913). 'The Rudyard Kipling* of the Pacific.' Becke was born in Port Macquarie, New South Wales, the youngest son of an English trader in the South Seas and local magistrate (the town then being a penal colony). The family moved to Sydney in the mid-1860s. At fourteen, young Becke was sent to learn the family business on one of his father's boats. His subsequent adventures at sea supplied material for much of his later fiction and resulted in his being tried on one occasion for piracy together with the American buccaneer, Captain Bully Hayes. Becke returned to Australia and married in 1886. Having worked as a journalist in Sydney, Becke came to Britain in 1896, where he continued to write successful novels with South Seas settings and rousing adventure plots. At this period of his life he was a literary celebrity. Representative titles are: *By Reef And Palm* (1894), his first book; *His Native Wife* (1896); *Edward Barry, South Sea Pearler* (1900). In collaboration with Walter Jeffery, an Australian journalist, Becke also wrote two interesting colonial historical* novels: *A First Fleet Family* (1895), the story in authentic journal form of the settlement of New South Wales in the eighteenth century, and *The Mutineer* (1898), a romance based on the *Bounty* episode following the vessel's return journey from Tahiti and the mutineers' ultimate settlement on Pitcairn Island. It is on Becke's account that twentieth-century movie treatments of the subject are partly based. His fiction is liberally encrusted with documentary apparatus and, often, maps. In his last years, Becke was afflicted with chronic malaria and alcoholism. He died, alone, of cancer of the throat in Sydney. BL 27. (WJ and LB) 4. *WW*. RM. Wol. RLF.

Beeton (1850?–66). A publisher, based in Fleet Street, Samuel Orchart Beeton (1831–77) rushed out the first English pirated edition of *Uncle Tom's Cabin* in 1852. He later took a gratuity of £100 to Harriet Beecher Stowe, in partial recompense for the millions of copies which the British book trade printed, without permission, of her unprecedented bestseller. The widower of the famous cook-book author, Beeton specialised in Christmas annuals. In 1866 he suffered in the widespread financial collapse and sold out his business to Ward, Lock and Tyler* for £400 and a sixth share of future profits. Boase.

BELCHER, Captain Sir Edward (1799–1877). Belcher entered the Royal Navy in 1812, and saw action as a boy late in the Napoleonic Wars. He rose in the service, was knighted in 1843, and became an admiral in 1872. As a captain, he commanded the unlucky expedition to the Arctic to search for Sir John Franklin in 1852. Belcher wrote many books, including the three-volume nautical* novel set in the early century, *Horatio Howard Brenton* (1856). Wolff notes: 'apparently he was both unpopular and inefficient and perhaps also cowardly'. BL 1. *DNB*. Wol.

A Beleaguered City, Mrs Oliphant, 1880, 1 vol, Macmillan. Subtitled 'A Story Of The Seen And The Unseen', this is Oliphant's most successful supernatural tale. Set in the French town of Semur, the story records, via the mayor Martin Dupin's *procés verbal*, 'certain recent events'. Following public blasphemy by the town atheist, Semur is shrouded by a strange mist. There follow strange phenomena: the cathedral's bells ring and its lights blaze. A visionary, Paul Lecamus, explains that benevolent spirits are making contact. The mayor and priest venture into the gloomy and deserted town, to celebrate mass. Sunlight reappears, and the citizens return. The novel has an ironic epilogue, recording the transitory effect of the episode: 'the wonderful manifestation which interrupted our existence has passed absolutely as if it had never been'.

Belgravia (1866–99). Subtitled *A London Magazine*, it was begun by the publisher John Maxwell*, largely as a vehicle for the fiction of his consort Mary Elizabeth Braddon* who was also the journal's first editor, or 'conductor'. In format and name, *Belgravia* followed the trail blazed by *Cornhill** in 1860. Issue was monthly, the cost was 1s. and the circulation peaked (in the 1860s) at around 18,000. Moderately good artists, such as M. E. Edwards*, supplied illustrations. G. A. Sala* and J. S. Le Fanu* contributed in the period that Braddon was editor. In March 1876, Chatto and Windus* acquired and revamped the magazine. Illustrations became more prominent, and a more famous class of novelist contributed. They included: Charles Reade*, Wilkie Collins*, Mark Twain and Thomas Hardy*. Like most fiction-carrying journals, *Belgravia* was quickly upstaged by newer and more fashionable publications. In 1889, Chatto sold it to F. V. White and Co. Under this lesser publisher, it went downhill, dropping its price and its illustrations, and featuring the work of second-rank novelists like Mrs Lovett Cameron* and Annie Thomas (i.e. Mrs Pender Cudlip*). *BLM*.

Belinda, Rhoda Broughton, 1883, 3 vols, Bentley. (Serialised in *Temple Bar**, January 1883–January 1884.) The sharpest of Broughton's smart romances. The story is divided into four periods. The first and brightest introduces the reader to the Churchill sisters, Belinda and Sarah. Parentless, this vivacious couple are deposited in the care of their grandmother while wintering at Dresden. Sarah is a flirt. Belinda, more serious and given to chilling sarcasm, falls in love with a northerner, David Rivers. Mysteriously, he leaves Dresden, merely informing Belinda that a 'catastrophe' has befallen him. After some months waiting in ignorance, Belinda makes a *mariage de raison* with an aged Oxbridge don, Professor James Forth. On her wedding day, she receives a letter from Rivers. His father, an ironmaster, was ruined and committed suicide. But now he has made his fortune again and still loves her. Yoked to Forth, who callously employs her as an unpaid secretary, Belinda withers. On holiday in the Lake District she meets Rivers again and after a terrible moral struggle decides to elope with him. But just at the moment she leaves, Forth dies. The novel has a number of points of biographical interest. Forth is a malicious portrait of Mark Pattison (husband of Emilia Strong, later Lady Dilke*) also claimed to be the original of Casaubon in *Middlemarch** and Squire Wendover in *Robert Elsmere**.

BELL, Lady Florence [Mrs Hugh] [Isabel Eveleen Eleanore] (née Olliffe, 1851–1930). The daughter of Sir Joseph Olliffe, MD, she was born in Paris, where her father was physician to the British Embassy. In 1876 she married Hugh Bell (after 1885 Sir Hugh), an ironmaster and colliery owner in the North Riding of Yorkshire. In later life, Mrs Bell wrote plays and some lightweight works of fiction for adults and children. *The Story Of Ursula* (1895) has a new woman* heroine, a promiscuous governess who spends a night in a hotel with a former lover. Reviewers complained at the immorality of the scene. *Miss Tod And The Prophets* (1898) is lighter in tone. The heroine is an old maid who eats drinks and is merry on learning that the earth is about to be destroyed by a comet. The catastrophe does not come, and she is left penniless. *The Arbiter* (1901) is a self-consciously 'modern' treatment of marital breakup and reconciliation. BL 6. (HB) *WW*.

BELL, Mrs Mary Letitia (née Martin, 1815–50). Born at Ballinahinch Castle, Co. Galway, Martin's was a landowning and parliamentary family. As the only child she inherited 200,000 acres in 1847. In the same year she married Arthur Gonne Bell. He was evidently a poor man and on marriage changed his name to hers. This was the period of the Irish famine and Mrs Bell Martin (as she was known) devoted herself to the relief of her father's tenants. In so doing, she ruined her family and was gratefully termed 'The Princess of Connemara' by her people. Thereafter penniless and landless, she emigrated to Belgium where she supported herself writing romances. The Bells sailed for America in 1850 and she died in childbirth on board ship. In the year of her death, Bell published the novel *Julia Howard* (1850), a sensitive study of Irish peasantry clearly inspired by the Banims*. Bell's grandfather, Richard Martin (1754–1834), married twice. By his second wife he had a daughter, Harriet Letitia Martin (1801–91) who also wrote some Banim-inspired fiction, notably *The Changeling* (1848). BL 8. (HLM) BL 2. *DNB*. Wol.

BELL, Robert (1800–67). Bell was born at Cork, the son of an Irish magistrate who died while his son was still at school. Friends of the family secured him a Civil Service post, but he gave it up to attend Trinity College, Dublin. Here he had his introduction to the lively world of 1820s Dublin journalism and wrote two successful plays. In 1828, Bell moved to the larger literary world of London, where he became editor of the *Atlas* weekly paper. Bell turned out a quantity of miscellaneous works, including a life of Canning in 1846. He also produced an annotated twenty-four-volume edition of the English poets (1854–57), for which his contemporaries most respected him. By the 1840s, he was a leading British man of letters although he never enjoyed an income to match that rank. In later life, Bell wrote two works of fiction. *The Ladder Of Gold* (1850), subtitled 'An Englishman's Story' follows the rise and fall of a clerk, Richard Rawlings. Rawlings marries his former employer's widow, Mrs Raggles, and finds himself rich. He turns to railway speculation, makes himself even richer and aspires to a seat in Parliament. Finally, his wealth evaporates (the third volume opens with a vivid description of the railway panic of 1845) and having tumbled down the ladder of gold all Richard has left is the love of his family. *The Ladder Of Gold* (serialised in *Bentley's Miscellany**) was extraordinarily well reviewed and has been unfairly forgotten by posterity. The author's second work of fiction was the collection of tales *Hearts And Altars* (1852). Bell was a close friend of Thackeray* and of Anthony Trollope* who ruefully observed after Bell's death that 'he never made that mark which his industry and talents would seem to ensure'. BL 2. *DNB*.

BELL, Robert Stanley Warren (1871–1921). Bell was born at Long Preston, Yorkshire, the son of a clergyman and was educated at Leatherhead School, near London. In later life he became the first editor (1899–1910) of the *Captain, A Magazine For Boys And Old Boys*. His fiction is comic and insubstantial. It includes: *The Cub In Love* (1897), *The Papa Papers*

(1897), *Bachelorland* (1899). *Love The Laggard* (1901) is a comedy in which a gay young thing jilts a millionaire. Most of his later writing is directed to the juvenile market and features school tales. BL 15. *WW*. RLF.

The Bell Of St Paul's, Walter Besant, 1889, 3 vols, Chatto and Windus. (Serialised in *Longman's Magazine*, January–December 1889.) Laurence Waller, a handsome, rich, young Australian, comes to England as a tourist in the late 1860s. He lodges in the Thames-side house of Lucius Outtle (later found to be a relative). In a June sunset scene, Laurence sees Althea Indagine rowing on the river and falls in love. Althea, it emerges, is the daughter of an unsuccessful poet, Clement Indagine. Her uncle, Dr Luttrel, has adopted a gypsy boy, Oliver, and brought him up as a wholly rational scientist. Laurence and Oliver become rivals for Althea. But Oliver's bad blood asserts itself, and he is exposed as a will forger and flies the country in disgrace. At the end of the action the principal characters are all happily transported back to Australia.

The Belton Estate, Anthony Trollope, 1866, 3 vols, Chapman and Hall. (Serialised in the *Fortnightly Review**, May 1865–January 1866.) The Belton estate, in Somerset, is entailed to Charles Amedroz, a wastrel. He commits suicide, and the inheritance passes to Will Belton, a rough and ready Norfolk farmer. Will falls in love with Clara Amedroz; but it has been decided she will marry the more eligible Captain Frederic Aylmer, MP. Aylmer's family snubs Clara who by a complex series of legal twists is now penniless, and the engagement with Aylmer is broken off. Will proposes again, and is successful. A sub-plot follows the problems of Colonel Askerton and his wife Mary, who live on the Belton estate. Trollope did not regard this effort as one of his successes and declared 'it will add nothing to my reputation as a novelist'. Most readers concur and the work has seldom been reprinted and is rarely written about. The novel launched the *Fortnightly Review* on its first, not very successful, phase of existence.

BENSON, E[dward] F[rederic] (1867–1940). Benson was born at Wellington College, the son of a clergyman (Edward White Benson) who in 1882 became Archbishop of Canterbury. His mother, Mary Sidgwick, was renowned for her cleverness and in later life her eccentricity. After graduating from King's College, Cambridge with high honours, Benson worked for a while as an archaeologist in Egypt and Greece. This experience feeds into his two novels dealing with the Greek Civil War in the early nineteenth century: *Vintage* (1898) and *The Capsina* (1899). Benson's circumstances were always comfortable, and he never married. For many years he lived in what had been Henry James's house, and was the mayor of Rye, 1934–37. As a novelist, Benson was productive. His first published story, *Dodo, A Detail Of The Day* (1893) had a considerable vogue. He repeated its witty view of modern society in *The Babe, B.A.* (1897), a Cambridge University novel whose undergraduate hero is 'a cynical old gentleman of twenty years of age who plays the banjo charmingly'. The story features up-to-date slang and the mannerisms of contemporary gilded youth. There is some sharp satire against the older Victorian earnestness of Mrs Humphry Ward's* *Robert Elsmere**. *Mammon And Co* (1899) is a satire which mockingly exposes swindles among the smart set. Benson wrote three 'Dodo' novels in all; the fatally fascinating Dodo herself is supposed to have been based on Margot Tennant, later Lady Oxford. Benson continued writing well into the twentieth century, though his Victorian fiction has a distinct feel of the brittle 1890s about it. In *Limitations* (1896), the hero is a sculptor with great Hellenic ideals, reduced to carving trumpery statuettes. (The theme has some similarities to *Jude The Obscure**). In *The Princess Sophia* (1900), Benson created a Zendaish territory, Rhodope, whose ruling princess converts it into a free-for-all gambling haven. There were two other writing Benson brothers, Arthur Christopher (1862–1925) and Robert Hugh (1871–1914). The second wrote fiction published mainly between 1906 and 1912, having become a Catholic priest in 1903. All four surviving Benson sons remained lifelong bachelors. Benson published an autobiography (*As We Were*) in the year of his death. BL 59. *DNB*. RM. *NCBEL*. Wol.

Richard Bentley and Son (1829–98). The house of Bentley was the leading producer of multi-volume fiction for the libraries for most of the nineteenth century. Richard Bentley (1794–1871) began working life as a printer with his brother Samuel, in 1819. Their trade involved the brothers with Henry Colburn*. In 1829 (partly to write off debts) Richard Bentley became Colburn's publishing partner. The alliance was a failure, and at considerable expense and vexation, Bentley released himself in 1832 to set up independently. His publishing habits, however, and most of his clientele were inherited from Colburn. In the 1830s (a difficult period for business), Bentley published novels by Bulwer [-Lytton*], John Galt, G. P. R. James*, and W. H. Ainsworth*. During their brief partnership, Colburn and Bentley pioneered the so-called Standard Novel*, the 6s. one-volume reprint. This set the pattern for second-form novel publishing for most of the century. In January 1837, there appeared the first issue of *Bentley's Miscellany**, which soon teamed Dickens* and Cruikshank* on *Oliver Twist**. But Bentley could not hold Dickens, despite desperate attempts to fence him in with various contracts. The publisher's attempt to launch a weekly newspaper in 1845, *Young England*, was one of several business failures which led to the setting up of an 'Inspectorate' governing the affairs of the firm. This lasted from 1855 to 1858. In 1859, George Bentley (1828–95) began to take a larger part in the firm's affairs, especially after his father's injury in a rail crash in 1867. After this date George went on to edit Bentley's main journal, *Temple Bar**. From the mid-century onward, Bentley's handled the fiction of a number of circulating library favourites: Wilkie Collins*, Charles Reade*, Ouida*, Rhoda Broughton*, Ellen Wood*, Marie Corelli*. In 1895 (shortly after the disappearance of the three-decker in which they had specialised) George Bentley died, and the firm was finally bought by Macmillan* for £8,000 in 1898. (RB and GB) *DNB*.

Bentley's Miscellany (1837–68). Richard Bentley originally intended his illustrated monthly magazine to be entitled the *Wits' Miscellany* (about which his rivals made merry). On its launch, the new venture had an immense success. This was largely due to its being edited by Dickens* who contributed *Oliver Twist** to the early issues. After stormy disagreements with Bentley, Dickens was succeeded as editor and lead contributor in 1839 by W. H. Ainsworth*. Ainsworth's *Jack Sheppard** was, if anything, even more popular than *Oliver Twist* and drove circulation up to near the 10,000 mark. Both novels were illustrated by George Cruikshank*, another of the magazine's principal attractions. As an editor, Ainsworth, like Dickens, only lasted two years. His successor Richard Bentley represented a distinct decline in quality. The main achievement of the journal in its first five years was its popularisation of the long, serialised and handsomely illustrated novel. It borrowed something from the *Dublin University Magazine**, and contributed much to the idea of George Smith's *Cornhill Magazine** in 1860. From tho mid 1840s the magazine was only a shadow of its original self. Bentley actually parted with it in 1854, when it was taken over by Ainsworth and Chapman and Hall*. George Bentley recovered the *Miscellany* in 1868, only to submerge it in *Temple Bar**. *WI. BLM.*

BERKELEY, the Hon. [George Charles] Grantley F[itzhardinge] (1800–81). 'A fantastic blackguard', as R. L. Wolff calls him. For seventy years, Berkeley was the heir presumptive to an earldom. His godfather, the Prince Regent, presented him at sixteen with a commission in the Coldstream Guards from which the young man retired at twenty-one, thereafter to live the life of a British sportsman. From 1832 to 1852 he was MP for Gloucestershire West. In 1836, he published the novel *Berkeley Castle*, based on private family records. The self-glorifying work invited satire, and was duly reviewed savagely in *Fraser's Magazine**. Berkeley went with his bullies, and horsewhipped the frail proprietor of the journal, James Fraser, who gallantly refused to name the reviewer, William Maginn*. Maginn later challenged Berkeley to a duel. A court case was brought against Berkeley for assault, and Fraser was awarded £100. He died four years later. In a countersuit for slander, the aggrieved nobleman was awarded a paltry 40s. Berkeley wrote miscellaneous books on various topics, and two other derided works of fiction: *Sandron Hall, Or The Days Of Queen Anne* (1840) and *Tales Of Life And Death* (1870). BL 3. *DNB*. Wol.

The Bertrams, Anthony Trollope, 1859, 3 vols, Chapman and Hall. George Bertram is the son of a soldier of fortune, Lt.-Col. Sir Lionel Bertram, serving in Persia. A lax father, he entrusts the welfare of George to a rich merchant uncle, also called George Bertram. Young George, although intelligent and well educated (Winchester and Oxford), does not know what to do with his life. Toying with the Church as a career, he visits Jerusalem. There he meets and falls in love with his uncle's granddaughter, Caroline Waddington. She will not marry him until he finds some worthwhile work. George has a moment of truth at the Mount of Olives and thereafter resolves to study law. After three years' waiting, Caroline accepts the proposal of Sir Henry Harcourt, MP. But when his parliamentary career crashes, he commits suicide. George finally marries the widowed Caroline. There is a busy sub-plot level to the novel involving other troubled courtships, notably that between George's friend the Rev. Arthur Wilkinson and Adela Gauntlet. Trollope came to think ill of this novel, which he called 'more than ordinarily bad'. Under the motto 'Vae Victis', however, it offers a close examination of the theme of failure in Victorian middle-class life.

BESANT, Walter (1836–1901). Besant was born the fifth child of a family of ten in Portsea where his father was a not very successful merchant. One of his brothers, William Henry, went on to become a famous mathematician, and his sister-in-law Annie (the wife of his brother Frank) was later a noted theosophist. A bookish child, Besant gives a picture of his early background in *The Holy Rose* (1890) and in his *Autobiography* (1902). From 1851 he attended successively Stockwell Grammar School, King's College, London (for a year) and Christ's College Cambridge, where he was a moderately successful mathematics student, graduating in 1859 with a healthy contempt for the 'dullness, the incapacity, the stupidity of the dons'. In his *Autobiography*, Besant notes the impact which the rigorously critical *Saturday Review** had on him at this period of his life. Despite his mathematical training Besant was well read, especially in French and German. (In later life he was one of the main popularisers of Rabelais in England.) He was also, from an early age, an authority on London. (His great 'Survey Of London', begun in 1894, was unfinished at his death, for all the author's prodigious labour on it.) Having decided against going into the Church, Besant took up teaching. In 1861, he accepted a post at the Royal College in Mauritius. Ill health and boredom forced his return in 1867, when he settled in London as a tyro man of letters to 'begin life again'. His first book was on early French poetry, and he published articles on similarly high-toned subjects. But, as he calculated, it took him six months research to write a piece on *The Romance Of The Rose*, and it earned him a measly £37. (Besant invariably measured literary success by money, rather than esteem.) In 1868, he was appointed secretary of the Palestine Exploration Fund. (Besant was, throughout his life, an organiser and fund-raiser of genius.) He held this post eighteen years, and the £200–£300 stipend paid, as he said, for his bread and cheese. Through James Rice*, the editor of *Once A Week**, Besant was drawn into writing fiction. Rice had good ideas for novels, but could not write them up. He and Besant joined forces on *Ready Money Mortiboy** (1872), the story of a larger than life miser, and they remained a fiction writing team until Rice's premature death from cancer in 1882, normally producing at least one novel a year. Not much was expected from their first work, and they had to pay Tinsley* themselves to publish an edition of 600 copies. But the story was to the public's taste, as were its successors. Their biggest hit was with the racy comedy of an American millionaire's vulgarity, *The Golden Butterfly** (1876). Besant's own favourite of the collaborative novels was *The Chaplain Of The Fleet** (1881). Other of their works were: *This Son Of Vulcan* (1876), a story of steelworkers; *The Monks of Thelema* (1878) an obscure satire on modern communitarianism; *By Celia's Arbour* (1878), a 'tale of Portsmouth Town' set in the Crimean upheaval of 1854. As he records in his *Autobiography*, Besant was endowed with 'untiring industry', and he continued turning out his annual novel for the eighteen years he survived Rice. His staple product was the historical* romance, of which the best is the charming *Dorothy Forster** (1884), a tale of the Jacobite uprising. But he also turned out anti-feminist dystopian fantasy such as *The Revolt Of Man** (1882). *For Faith And Freedom* (1889) is a story of Monmouth's rebellion, told from the unusual viewpoint of a young Puritan heroine. *The Ivory Gate* (1892) features a sober Conservative solicitor, Edmund Dering, who under the influence of brain disease becomes Edmund Gray, a rabid socialist. *The Rebel Queen* (1893) focuses on modern Judaism. Besant himself thought his 'most serious' work was *The Fourth Generation** (1900) a complex Ibsenite tale, dealing with the intricate consequences of parental crime on children. But his most popular works were novels set in 'the great and marvellous country which we call East London'. Of these, *All Sorts And Conditions Of Men** (1882) and *Children Of Gibeon** (1886) stand out. The first deals with the setting up of a People's Palace in Stepney, an impossible dream, the author was told. Nevertheless, he helped draw the donations to found just such a institute in the Mile End Road for the recreation and cultivation of East-enders in 1887. (The premises were opened by Queen Victoria herself, in the year of her Jubilee.) In addition to his philanthropic work, Besant was instrumental in establishing the Society of Authors in 1883 and was its moving spirit until his death. Through the society and its organ (*The Author**) he successfully professionalised British letters. Besant married Mary Forster-Barham in 1874, had four children by her, was elected to the Athenaeum in 1887 and was knighted in 1895. Among his later novels, *The Alabaster Box* (1900) which deals with settlements in London, is unusually interesting. Its hero is a wealthy young man who conscientiously makes amends for his father's unscrupulousness as a moneylender. Besant's dates render him a perfect Victorian. He was also the avatar of the versatile man of letters in the century: scholar, novelist, philanthropist, translator, journalist, historian and organiser of his fellow writers. His novels are lively, fresh and often enriched by his profound topographic knowledge of London. (JR and WB) BL 14. (WB) BL 31. *DNB*. RM. *NCBEL*. Wol. Sad. RLF.

Beside The Bonnie Brier Bush, Ian Maclaren (i.e. the Rev. John Watson), 1894, 1 vol, Hodder and Stoughton. The classic text of the kail-yard* school. A very popular collection of short sketches of Scottish life in 'Drumtochty', Perthshire, this volume sold 4,000 copies in its first year of publication. The opening episodes centre on 'Domsie', Mr Jamieson, the teacher at the 'auld schule'. In the first sketch, a 'lad o' pairts', Geordie Howe, wins all the prizes at Edinburgh University but sickens and dies. His pathetic death serves to strengthen the community. Other episodes centre on the village physician Maclure, 'a doctor of the old school' and Lachlan Campbell, a 'Wee Free' puritan from the Highlands who falls into dispute with the Rev. Davidson. A joint expedition to save Lachlan's daughter Flora from moral destruction in London brings the religious opponents together. The tone of Maclaren's narration is overwhelmingly sentimental.

The Beth Book, Sarah Grand (i.e. Frances Elizabeth McFall), 1897, 1 vol, Heinemann. The most thoroughgoing portrait of the new woman* in fiction. The novel's subtitle is 'Being A Study From The Life Of Elizabeth Caldwell Maclure, a Woman of Genius' and its defiant epigraph (from Shakespeare) 'yet I'll speak'. The larger part of the 300-page narrative dwells on Elizabeth's childhood. She is brought up in shabby gentility in Northern Ireland where her father is a coastguard official (but also 'a gentleman'). Elizabeth is neglected while attention is lavished on her brother; her father is unfaithful to her mother and dies prematurely from a brain tumour. Elizabeth and her mother then move to Yorkshire to live with an unpleasant relative, Uncle James Patten. Amidst this domestic upheaval, Elizabeth grows up poorly educated and at sixteen marries a doctor, Dan Maclure. He is unfaithful to her with a female patient and is secretly employed at a Lock hospital for the forcible treatment of women prostitutes (a discriminatory practice which had enraged earlier feminists). He is also, Beth discovers, a sadistic vivisectionist. She cannot surrender to him sexually and leaves to become a novelist. In the boarding house where she takes up residence Elizabeth meets an American artist, Arthur Brock, and nurses him through illness. She turns down the proposal of a decadent modernist writer that she become his mistress. In the course of her tribulations Beth is politicised and becomes a speaker on women's rights. At the end of the novel, Beth and Arthur are mystically united at harvest time in the countryside. A violently polemical novel, *The Beth Book* contains much thinly veiled autobiography.

BETHAM-EDWARDS, Matilda [Barbara] (1836–1919). With Richard Cobbold*, Edwards is Suffolk's most famous novelist. She was born a farmer's daughter at Westerfield (her father's name was Edwards, Betham her mother's maiden name) and was educated at schools in Ipswich and Peckham, London. From early youth she was an enthusiastic tourist in France, a country which figures frequently in her later writing and for whose republicanism she had a lifelong admiration. When Edwards's father died in 1864, she carried on the family farm for a while with the aid of a sister. But when the sister died in 1865, she moved to London where she became a prominent member of the literary world and a friend of George Eliot* (who records her addiction to chloral in the mid-1870s). Her subsequent writing career was mostly divided between factual books about France (for which she was honoured by the French government), and fiction about Suffolk. According to Elaine Showalter, she was 'a Christian free-thinker, interested in anti-vivisection and cremation'. Her first novel was *The White House By The Sea* (1857), a love story written from the heroine's autobiographical viewpoint. Edwards came to have a strong line in impulsive young heroines, such as those in *Kitty* (1869), a story of artistic Bohemia, and *Bridget* (1878). Her best Suffolk novel is *The Lord Of The Harvest* (1899), a novella-length work set in the 1840s before the repeal of the Corn Laws. The narrative contains lyrical descriptions of the East Anglian landscape and commemorates the folklore of the traditional (and pagan) harvest festivals in which 'when Queen Victoria was a maiden, harvest men of East Anglia chose for their chief the best among them'. Also impressive is *A Suffolk Courtship* (1900), which tells the story of four orphaned daughters of a farmer, whose struggles recall the author's own in 1864. 'Farming folk', the narrator observes, 'did not cosset themselves in those days'. Edwards's other fiction includes: *Dr Jacob* (1868), a story set in Frankfurt whose sixty-year-old hero seduces a young girl; *Brother Gabriel* (1878), the story of a young Irish monk in France, who falls in love with an English girl, Zoë and becomes involved with the Commune; *A Romance Of Dijon* (1894), set in pre-Revolution France; *The Dream Charlotte* (1896), set in Normandy, during the Revolution. Betham-Edwards was a cousin of Amelia Blanford Edwards* and died at Hastings. BL 11. *DNB. NCBEL.* Wol. Sad. RLF.

Bevis, The Story Of A Boy, Richard Jefferies, 1882, 3 vols, Sampson Low. The idealised chronicle of the author's boyhood in Wiltshire. The narrative follows a few weeks' adventure of ten-year-old Bevis and his friend Mark around a reservoir which they fancifully call 'the New Sea'. They explore, fight battles and relive all the hardships of colonial pioneers. The few events in the novel centre on the boys learning to swim and their building a boat. Nature is keenly observed and the adult world is prominently absent. The work ends with the boys resolving one day to conquer the 'great [i.e. real] sea'.

BICKERDYKE, John (born Charles Henry Cook, 1858–1933). Charles Cook was born in London and educated in Germany and at Trinity Hall, Cambridge. (His novel, *With The Best Intentions*, 1884, a tale of undergraduate life, recalls his college experiences.) For a while he read for the law at the Inner Temple, before becoming an author by profession. In later life, Bickerdyke developed a lifelong passion for freshwater angling and worked both to advance the sport and to protect the Thames. An early pioneer of cinematography, he spent much of his later life in South Africa. In addition to numerous works on fishing, Bickerdyke produced the novels *Lady Val's Elopement* (1896); *Daughters Of Thespis* (1897), a story of the 'Green Room'; *Her Wild Oats* (1898), a story of 'The Stage And Thames Life', later dramatised. BL 5. *WW.*

Bigamy Novels. Bigamy was a favourite complication throughout the century's fiction. (It figures as an imminent disaster in Jane Eyre's* adventures, for instance.) The bigamous marriage was taken up as a vogue by the sensation* novel, however, after the much-publicised Yelverton trial, in 1861–64. The high-born Major [William] Charles Yelverton (1824–83) had gone through a marriage ceremony with Theresa Longworth (1832–81), which he later repudiated to marry another woman. The resulting court case (in which a verdict in the injured first wife's favour was set aside by the House of Lords) had the whole country agog. The bigamy device was spectacularly exploited by Mary Braddon in *Lady Audley's Secret** (1862), *Aurora Floyd** (1863) and *John Marchmont's Legacy** (1863). Wilkie Collins* alludes to the case (particularly the anomalies in Scottish law which it revealed) in *Man And Wife** (1870). The 'Hon. Mrs Yelverton', as she termed herself, also wrote a novel, *Martyrs To Circumstance* (1861) and hired herself out for readings in the 1860s. Direct recollections of the Yelverton case are found in J. R. O'Flanagan's* *Gentle Blood, Or The Secret Marriage* (1861) and Cyrus Redding's* *A Wife And Not A Wife* (1867). A large number of novels in the 1860s and 1870s introduce the bigamy motif. By the end of the century (in Hardy's* fiction, notably) the plot device was incorporated into general agitation for divorce law reform. (WCY)*DNB.*

Bildungsroman. This term, from German, applies to novels dealing with the youth and moral growth of a hero(ine), usually identifiable with the novelist. The genre was inspired by Goethe's *Wilhelm Meister* (1786–1830), a novel in which the hero's main aspiration was his own self-fulfilment, or *Bildung. Entwicklungsroman* (development novel) is an alternative label. In England, the *Bildungsroman* was in vogue during the 1840s and 1850s. Famous examples are Thackeray's* *Pendennis**; Dickens's* *David Copperfield**; George Eliot's* *Mill On The Floss**; Amelia Edwards's* *Barbara's History**; J. A. Froude's* *Nemesis Of Faith**. A remark by the hero of the last that 'I have nothing but myself to write about' could serve as a motto for the whole genre. As developed by the English novelists, the *Bildungsroman* habitually displayed an ironic attitude towards the innocent *foibles* of youth and a strong emphasis on moral education through ordeal.

Birch Dene, William Westall, 1889, 3 vols, Ward and Downey. An industrial novel set in the England of George IV. A young gentlewoman comes to London to meet her officer husband who is due to return from military service abroad. She does not find him and is later arrested for stealing a cloak for her freezing child. The crime is capital, but she escapes the rope by dying of shock at court in the Old Bailey. Her son Robin cannot remember his father's name and his mother refused to give it. He is brought up by an amiable bookseller, Mr Bartlett. When this patron dies leaving no will the nineteen-year-old Robin is apprenticed to a cotton spinner in Birch Dene, Lancs. In the working out of the plot there is an industrial riot and the hero discovers his identity as a close relative of his employer, Colonel Dene. The story's first volume contains Hogarthian pictures of London and its second and third volumes a powerful evocation of the early Industrial Revolution in the north.

BIRCHENOUGH, Mabel C. (née Bradley, 1860–1936). Mabel Bradley was the third daughter of the Dean of Westminster, later the Master of University College, Oxford. She married Henry (after 1920 Sir Henry) Birchenough, a silk manufacturer, of Macclesfield. The novels which she subsequently wrote are slight. *Disturbing Elements* (1896) is a collection of sketches and character studies in the 1890s manner centred on a group of girl students in the oddly named 'Brontë Hall'. *Potsherds* (1898) is a story of love in the Staffordshire potteries which ends in violence and suicide. BL 3. *WW*. Wol.

BLACK, Clementina (1855?–1923). Black was born the daughter of a solicitor and brought up in Brighton as one of eight children. She taught French and German to her younger sisters, one of whom went on to become Constance Garnett (1862–1946), the well known translator from the Russian. Clementina Black began writing early with *A Sussex Idyll* in 1877, a tame 'autobiography' of which the *Athenaeum** wryly commented that it was 'in every sense what its title implies'. Although she received little encouragement from publishers, she persisted with fiction. *Orlando* (1880) is a tale of unhappy love (Black herself never married). In the early 1880s, she moved to London to live with her sisters in Bloomsbury. In this phase of her life she worked at the British Museum and became actively involved with the Fabian Society. For a while she lived abroad with the writer Amy Levy*, and when in England helped organise women workers in the East End. In the 1880s, Black founded the Women's Labour Bureau, with Frances Hicks. This led to the Women's Industrial Council, in 1894. In the early twentieth century, Black led the struggle against 'sweating' and for working-women's rights. At an early stage of her radicalisation, Black wrote some interesting, politically tinged fiction. *An Agitator* (1894) is the story of a socialist strike leader, Christopher Brand, who is falsely imprisoned and finally redeemed from fanaticism. *The Princess Desirée* (1896) has a heroine who rejects the marriage of state convenience arranged for her. *The Pursuit Of Camilla* (1899) is more melodramatic. Set in Italy, the plot has an Anglo-Italian heroine abducted by a villainous marquis and saved by the teamwork of an Englishman and a Polish artist. BL 7. Wol.

BLACK, William (1841–98). Black was born and brought up in Scotland, and his best fiction is set there and energetically promotes 'Celtic' consciousness. The son of a small businessman (d. 1855) with bookish tastes, he left school at sixteen, and studied art for a while in Glasgow (which may account for the extensive landscape description in his later novels). Black soon switched from art (in which he had taste but no talent) to journalism, emigrating to London in 1864 where he was befriended by his countryman, Robert Buchanan*, and became a successful newspaperman. Black married in 1865, his wife dying of a fever barely a year later. He worked initially for the radical *Morning Star* and the *Examiner* and hacked out freelance pieces for the magazines after a false start as a business clerk. His first novel, *James Merle, An Autobiography* was published in 1864. The story of a young boy growing up among the severities of Scottish puritanism, it sank without trace. It was followed by *In Silk Attire* in 1869 and *Kilmeny* (a story of artistic life) in 1870. In 1870 Black was also promoted to the assistant editorship of the *Daily News*. As a foreign correspondent, he covered the Franco-Prussian War (his sympathies were strongly with Germany and German scenes figure strongly in his early fiction). His only child, Martin, died in 1871. Black was by now a prominent writer but made little impact with his fiction until *A Daughter Of Heth** (1871). This quiet story of a French girl, 'Coquette', transplanted into a dour Scottish home with tragic results, was a terrific success. *The Strange Adventures Of A Phaeton* (1872) was equally popular. The account of a coaching trip from London to Edinburgh, the narrative is little more than a pretext for the landscape descriptions in which Black excelled. He followed up with another Scottish novel, *A Princess Of Thule** (1874), whose heroine is a beautiful Hebridean girl who pines in the oppressive atmosphere of London society. 'Maiden' heroines were to become Black's speciality. He had, as the *Spectator* put it, 'a true chivalric feeling towards women' in his novels. *Madcap Violet* (1876) has a tomboy heroine who comes to the tragic end normal in Black's fiction. *Macleod Of Dare** (1878) tells the story of proud young Highland chief who comes to fatal mischief in the fleshpots of London. Black was now established as a Macmillan* author, and was immensely popular and well thought of by the critics. The *Athenaeum** claimed in 1877 that 'His genius resembles that of Mr Trollope*, but his taste is better.' Black remarried in 1876 and was sufficiently wealthy from his fiction to live in style at Brighton after 1878, indulging in his favourite pastime of yachting. (See *White Wings, A Yachting Romance*, 1880.) *Judith Shakespeare* (1883) fantasises a romance around the dramatist's daughter and was regarded by the author himself as his great work. The most controversial novel of his later period was *Sunrise* (1880) which deals with international socialism and political secret societies. By this stage in his life, Black was suffering from the obscure nervous ailments which were to make his last ten years miserable. In these last years, Black enjoyed the status of respected (and by his friends loved) man of letters both in Britain and America. It was sometimes objected that his fiction was merely travelogue, with a thin layer of plot. Nor did he much change his successful formula. *Briseis* (1896), for instance, has a Greek heroine who comes to Deeside in Scotland, in much the same fashion as Coquette did, twenty-five years before. BL 33. *DNB*. RM. *NCBEL*. Wol. Sad.

The Black Arrow, R. L. Stevenson, 1888, 1 vol, Cassell. (Serialised in *Young Folks*, June–October 1883, by 'Captain George North'.) A historical* tale set in the fifteenth century which became a favourite with the Victorian juvenile reader. The narrative is closely involved with the seesawing progress of the Wars of the Roses. It begins on the eve of battle with Sir Daniel Brackley mustering men. Sir Daniel is a sinister figure, of a kind common in Stevenson's novels. He systematically makes himself the guardian of rich and noble orphans. The young hero, Master Dick Shelton, is Sir Daniel's ward and it is suspected the nobleman may have killed Dick's father. Subsequent interest centres on the mysterious avenger, John Amendall, who sets out to assassinate Sir Daniel and his henchmen with distinctive black arrows. Dick escapes and has various adventures with the outlaw, Lawless. He also falls in with another of Sir Daniel's young victims, the heiress Joanna Sedley. Sir Daniel has prospered by attaching himself to the House of Lancaster, and schemes to marry Joanna to Lord Shoreby. But his plans are foiled, his party is defeated by Richard Crookback and while trying to escape to France he is confronted by Dick in the forest near Holywood. Richard refuses Sir Daniel sanctuary and he is shot with a black arrow by the outlaw Ellis Duckworth, who is revealed to be Amendall. Joanna and Richard marry and live in the forest away from the great affairs of history. The novel has a notably lively action and carries a mocking dedication to the 'critic on the hearth'.

Black Beauty, Anna Sewell, 1877, 1 vol, Jarrold. (Subtitled, 'The Autobiography Of A Horse, Translated From The Original Equine'.) The most famous animal story of the century. The novelty of the work is that it is told autobiographically by a horse (apparently sexless) miraculously able to talk like a well brought-up Victorian servant. He tells his life story from foal to colt to broken-in mount and finally to broken-down hack. The work is strongly marked by Sewell's passionate hatred of cruelty to animals and her campaign against the use of the 'bearing rein'. The early part of the narrative deals with Beauty's training and his dialogues on the equine condition with his partner Ginger. He is sold to the Birtwick household where he returns kindness for kindness by saving his master's life. At Earlshall, by contrast, Beauty is subjected to the cruelty of the bearing rein. He is unfairly blamed for a fatal accident and is sold first as a job horse, later as a cab horse. He ends up a degraded cart-horse, the lowest of the equine low. Finally he is returned to Birtwick and lives out a comfortable retirement, his final message being: 'We horses do not mind hard work if we are treated reasonably.'

Black Sheep!, Edmund Yates, 1867, 3 vols, Tinsley. (Serialised in *All The Year Round**, August 1866–March 1867). George Dallas is the black sheep of the title. His mother, a widow, marries a wealthy snob, Capel Carruthers. George rebels against his stepfather by becoming a wild scapegrace. Disowned, he plunges into wilful dissipation. George subsequently takes up journalism as his profession and falls in with the swindling Stewart Routh and his wife Harriet. On Routh's behalf George goes to Amsterdam, with stolen jewellery. Eventually, under the saintly influence of his mother, the hero reforms. Meanwhile Stewart Routh frames him for murder. As a result of Harriet's remorse, the ruse is discovered and Routh kills himself in prison. At the end of the story, George is reconciled with his family and engaged to a beautiful heiress. The best scene in the novel is the first, in which the black sheep returns by night train to his parents' house, Poynings. According to William Tinsley*, its publisher, 'quite two-thirds' of the work was written by the unacknowledged Mrs Cashel Hoey* and palmed off on Charles Dickens*, the unsuspecting editor of *All The Year Round* as all Yates's original composition.

BLACKBURNE, E[lizabeth] Owens (i.e. Elizabeth O'B. Casey, 1848–94). Born at Slane, near the Boyne, Co. Meath she lost her sight at some point in 1859 and recovered it around 1866. She subsequently attended Trinity College, Dublin, where she was a prize-winning student. In 1874, she moved to London where she supported herself by writing. She remained a spinster, Blackburne being her pen name. Her novels have Irish settings and conventional melodramatic love plots. They include: *A Woman Scorned* (1876); *Molly Carew* (1876); *The Way Women Love* (1877); *A Bunch Of Shamrocks* (1879). BL 8. Boase. Wol. RLF.

BLACKMORE, R[ichard] D[oddridge] (1825–1900). Blackmore is mainly remembered as the author of *Lorna Doone**, the most reprinted of Victorian regional-historical* novels. Blackmore was born in Longworth, Berkshire, the third son of a clergyman of cultivated literary tastes. The family roots were in Devon where 'Blackmore' is an old established name. A distant ancestor was Philip Doddridge, the non-conformist divine and hymn-writer. Richard's mother died in a typhus epidemic four months after the boy's birth and he was initially brought up by his grandmother in Glamorgan, as the prelude to a generally unsettled childhood. It was further troubled by the first manifestations of what was to be a lifelong affliction of epilepsy. At eleven, Blackmore went to school at Tiverton. This and other childhood locations, especially those in the West Country, were to haunt his later fiction. At Oxford (where he went in 1843) he proved himself a clever student, a gifted chess-player and dabbled in poetry as he was to do for the rest of his life, without much success. In 1847, he took a second-class degree in classics. Having resolved not to go into the Church, Blackmore took to the law on graduation and was called to the Bar in 1852. But his fear of an epileptic attack in open court made him nervous of barristry, and he applied himself to conveyancing. But a proper professional start in life was made difficult by an imprudent and concealed marriage in 1853 to Lucy Maguire, whose Irish Catholic origins made her unacceptable to his family. (This situation was transmuted melodramatically into the plot of *Lorna Doone*.) Blackmore thereafter tried teaching, at which he scraped a bare living for two years. In 1857, a legacy from an uncle enabled him to buy sixteen acres of orchard land and Gomer House (named after a favourite dog) at Teddington. Blackmore loved farming, but always lost money at it. He had begun writing for publication as early as 1854 and in 1862, he tried Edward Marston of Sampson Low* with a translation of Virgil. Having broken the ice, two years later he published (anonymously) his first novel, *Clara Vaughan**. *Cradock Nowell** (1866, 'A Tale Of The New Forest') followed. *Lorna Doone* (1869) was Blackmore's third effort, and after a shaky start, this romance of lawless Exmoor in Stuart times became a hit. It has been argued that the work caught on with the library reading public because of its supposed connection with the Marquis of Lorne, who was engaged to Queen Victoria's daughter in 1870. Whatever the reason,

Lorna Doone went on to be a perennial bestseller and its mixture of closely observed regional setting and wild theatrical plot was reproduced in the author's later works. Like Marryat* and Scott, Blackmore loved his land. He was a passionate horticulturist, and sank much of the revenue of his profitable writing into his chronically unprofitable smallholding. By the 1880s, he was earning up to £2,000 for a novel, although high critical acclaim persistently eluded him during his lifetime. Nor were his last years always personally happy. In 1875, Blackmore's estranged and eccentric brother Henry Turberville died in suspicious circumstances, and the novelist made some injudicious allegations about poisoning which involved him in libel difficulties. Blackmore's mode of life was very retired, although he travelled frequently to the west of England, which remained his favourite fictional setting, and conducted a number of literary friendships by correspondence. Like Scott, he was obsessed by historical eras transitionally placed between romantic barbarism and modern civilisation. Despite the pre-eminence successive publics have given *Lorna Doone*, *The Maid Of Sker** (1872) remained Blackmore's own favourite novel. It follows the adventures of the foundling daughter of an old Devon family, and is narrated by a garrulous fisherman with great art. *Alice Lorraine** (1875) is a full-blooded romance set in the early years of the century. *Cripps The Carrier** (1876) is a story of abduction, set in Oxfordshire and is fashionably sensational*. *Erema* is set in the USA (although Blackmore never in his life left England's shores) and *Mary Anerly* (1880) in Yorkshire. The first of these damaged his reputation as a novelist, the second somewhat repaired it. The public preferred Blackmore as a historically nostalgic chronicler of the English countryside, and he obliged them with *Christowell* (1881), a Dartmoor idyll of the 1840s and *Springhaven** (1887), set in Sussex during the Napoleonic Wars. (A patriotic theme was appropriate for the Queen's Golden Jubilee year.) In 1888, Blackmore's wife Lucy died of pneumonia. Their marriage had been childless but happy and grief permeates his last three novels: *Kit And Kitty* (1889), *Perlycross** (1894) and the oddly mystical *Dariel* (1897). Blackmore's writing is more diverse than his reputation as the author of one blockbuster romance* would suggest. His fiction is energetic and regularly experiments with fresh themes while at the same time reworking classical myth in a more subtle way than any other Victorian novelist. His influence as a regionalist was an inspiration to disciples like the West Country novelist Eden Phillpotts*. Blackmore epitomises the late-nineteenth-century fondness for rural idyll and romantic pastoralism. Politically, he was deeply conservative and hated the bustle of Victorian industrial change. BL 14. *DNB*. RM. *NCBEL*. Wol. Sad.

Blackwood and Sons (1804–). The principal Scottish publishers of fiction in the nineteenth and twentieth centuries. The house was founded by William Blackwood (1776–1834) who in 1804 set up in business in Edinburgh as a dealer in second-hand books. Blackwood gradually moved into jobbing printing, publishing and agency work (notably for the London publisher, Murray*, for whom he published some of Scott's tales). In 1817, he set up *Blackwood's Magazine**. William was succeeded as head of the firm by his son Alexander (who died in 1845) and by John (1818–79). Under John, the house became a dominant force in British publishing. Although the *Magazine* was overtaken by such publications as *Bentley's Miscellany** and *Cornhill** Blackwood consistently managed to recruit top rank novelists such as George Eliot*, Bulwer-Lytton* and Margaret Oliphant*. The character of the firm was paternal, conservative and fostered long alliances. (Eliot, for instance, published all but one of her major novels with John Blackwood in spite of tempting offers from rival houses.) The firm set up a prosperous London branch in 1840. (WB) *DNB*.

Blackwood's Magazine (1817–1980). *Blackwood's Edinburgh Magazine* (familiarly known to its contributors as 'Maga') was initially conceived as a Tory opponent for the Whig *Edinburgh Review* (1802–1929). But the monthly issue and miscellaneous format of the new journal made it much more a vehicle for creative literature than its ponderous quarterly rivals. From the first, William Blackwood and his editors gathered a distinguished coterie of co-ideological contributors: De Quincey, John Lockhart, James Hogg. And fiction figured early in the magazine's menu, with John Galt's *Annals Of The Parish*, in 1821. From then until 1900 (when Conrad's *Lord Jim* was appearing in its pages) the journal serialised major novels by Samuel Warren* (*Ten Thousand A Year**), Bulwer-Lytton* (*The Caxtons**, *What Will He Do With It?*), George Eliot* (*Scenes Of Clerical Life**), Anthony Trollope* (five novels), and Margaret Oliphant*, most of whose serialised novels appeared in its pages. Especially after the appearance of *Cornhill** in 1860, the unillustrated *Maga* tended to look dull, and its circulation after the 1860s dropped from a high point of 10,000 to a humble 3,000 or so. But its stamina was remarkable, and in mere longevity it is the outstanding magazine vehicle for fiction in the nineteenth century. In its criticism of literature, *Blackwood's* sustained a consistently indignant moral tone, whether against Keats and the 'Cockney School' of poets in 1817, or against 'low' novelists like Dickens* in the 1840s, or Hardy* and the 'anti-marriage' league of modern novelists in the 1890s. The *Blackwood's* formula was taken over by William Maginn* for *Fraser's Magazine**. WI. BLM.

BLAGDEN, Isa[bella] (1817?–73). As Gordon Haight observes in his biography of George Eliot*, 'nothing is known of Isabella Blagden's origins. Rumour had her the illegitimate daughter of an English father and an East Indian mother.' Blagden, who never apparently married, settled in Florence in 1849, where she was intimate with the Brownings, T. A. Trollope* and George Eliot. Her novels include *Agnes Tremorne* (1861), *The Cost Of A Secret* (1863), and *The Crown Of A Life* (1869). BL 5.

BLAKE, Lady [Elizabeth] (née Lock, 1801–77?). Born in Norbury, Surrey, Elizabeth Lock married Joseph Henry Blake, the third Lord Wallscourt in 1822. He died prematurely in 1849 at the age of fifty-four. Widowed, Blake wrote numerous three-deckers for Hurst and Blackett*, from the mid-1860s to the late 1870s. They include *My Stepfather's Home* (1864); *Claude* (1870); *Mrs Grey's Reminiscences* (1878). The last is a typical story of quiet doings in 'Castleford', a country town, told by a doctor's wife whose life has been 'very uneventful as regards outward circumstance'. The Blakes were a wealthy Northern Irish Ascendancy family, and it is unlikely that Lady Elizabeth was obliged to write for money. She suppressed her first name so effectively, that even the *British Library Catalogue* remains ignorant of it. BL 11. Wol.

BLAND, Edith (née Nesbit, 1858–1924). Edith Nesbit was born in London, the sixth child of an agricultural chemist and teacher, who died prematurely when she was only four. The young girl was subsequently convent educated, partly abroad and partly (after 1870) in Kent, whose landscape features in her later fiction. Nesbit's first poem (on 'Dawn') was published when she was seventeen. In 1880 she married (probably to the disapproval of her mother) the socialist author, Hubert Bland, by whom she was to have four children. She was herself actively political, and a founder member of the Fabian Society. (See her 'Ballads And Lyrics Of Socialism', 1908.) The failure of Bland's brush-making business and his catching smallpox shortly after marriage threw the early burden of household support on the wife. He gradually established himself as a journalist, however, and by 1886 was editor of *To-Day* in which G. B. Shaw's* early fiction appeared. Husband and wife (under the pseudonym 'Fabian Bland') collaborated on the novel *The Prophet's Mantle* (1885). As E[dith] Nesbit, she began writing professionally in the 1890s with such titles as: *Grim Tales* (1893); *Something Wrong* (1893); *The Butler In Bohemia* (1894). Fame came with her novels for children, beginning with *The Story Of The Treasure Seekers* (1899), expressively subtitled: 'Being The Adventures Of The Bastable Children, In Search Of A Fortune'. (*The Secret Of Kyriels*, a mystery published also in 1899, did not do well.) Her best-known work, *The Railway Children*, was published in 1906. Nesbit also wrote novels for grown-ups, such as *The Red House* (1902), the humorous story of a young couple's stress and strain on moving into a new home. Among other real stresses Bland was obliged to undergo at this period was looking after her husband's second bastard child. And in 1900 her sixteen-year-old son Fabian died under a routine operation. His death coincided with her complete withdrawal from active politics. Her children's books contrive to be adventurous while at the same time celebrating the cosy camaraderie of intra-family relationships. Hubert Bland died in 1914, she was awarded a Civil List pension in 1915 and remarried (another socialist, T. T. Tucker) in 1917. The author's reputation has steadily grown throughout the twentieth century. BL 32. *DNB*. RM. *NCBEL*. RLF.

BLATCHFORD, Robert [Peel Glanville] (1851–1943). Blatchford was born at Maidstone, into a theatrical family. His father died before Robert was two. His mother was an actress and half-Italian. According to his own account, he was educated 'nowhere'. At the age of fourteen, young Robert was apprenticed to a Halifax brushmaker, in which employment he met the woman he was later to marry. But he was not yet ready to settle down and at twenty, he enlisted in the Dublin Fusiliers, being honourably discharged in 1877, with the rank of sergeant. Military service had a formative effect on his personality but gave him no clear idea of what career to follow. On his release, Blatchford married in 1880 and drifted into journalism around 1883. Investigation of the Manchester slums in 1887 for the *Sunday Chronicle*, converted him to socialism. He gave up his highly paid reporter's post in London, to settle in the North and start the *Clarion*, a socialist weekly, in 1891. A collection of his contributions to the paper, reprinted as *Merrie*

England (1893) sold in the millions, and made the *Clarion* a major organ of the British labour movement which found its expression in the Independent Labour Party of 1892. But Blatchford's political views were not always orthodox. At the end of the 1890s, he found himself at odds with the socialist establishment ('anti-British Reds', as he contemptuously called them) over his old soldier's instinctive support for the Boer War. Blatchford wrote some fiction, among his many books. *A Son Of The Forge* (1894), tells the story of a waif from the Black Country, who goes to fight in the Crimean War, is invalided, and struggles for his existence in an inhospitable London. *Tommy Atkins Of The Ramchunders* (1895) is a realistic, and Kiplingesque* story of life in the ranks. The best of Blatchford's books is probably his Utopia, or 'impossible romance', *The Sorcery Shop* (1907). He published his autobiography, *My Eighty Years*, in 1931. BL 6. *DNB*. Wol.

BLAZE DE BURY, Baroness [Marie Pauline Rose] (née Stuart, 1813–94). Born in Oban, Scotland, she was brought up as the daughter of an army officer, William Stuart, but is supposed actually to have been the illegitimate child of Lord Brougham*. Around 1840, Marie Stuart met Henri Blaze de Bury (1813–88), a French writer. They married in 1844 and she lived most of her subsequent life in Paris where she presided over a literary salon and corresponded with such notables as Bismarck. She is reported to have been strikingly beautiful and was an enthusiastic promoter of Anglo-European friendship. Her novels include: *All For Greed* (1868) and *Love The Avenger* (1869). Blaze De Bury wrote extensively for *Blackwood's Magazine** and the *Revue Des Deux Mondes*. BL 2. Boase. Wol. RLF.

Bleak House, Charles Dickens, 1853, 1 vol, Bradbury and Evans. (The novel was first published in monthly parts, March 1852–September 1853, with illustrations by Phiz*.) The novel is narrated partly autobiographically by Esther Summerson, partly in the third person (present tense). The action opens in the Court of Chancery, which is interminably hearing the suit of *Jarndyce* and *Jarndyce*. The lawyer Tulkinghorn reports on some recent developments to Sir Leicester Dedlock and his frigidly beautiful wife, Lady Dedlock, recognises a former lover's handwriting among the lawyer's documents. This lover, Nemo, is now an opium-addicted scrivener, near death in the lodging house of Krook, a drunken rag and bottle merchant. Nemo has befriended the illiterate young crossing sweeper, Jo, who is later visited by a disguised Lady Dedlock, after her lover's death. Tulkinghorn has noted Lady Dedlock's consternation, and will later blackmail her. The other line of the narrative centres on Esther, a parentless child. (In fact, Esther is the daughter of Nemo and Lady Dedlock.) After a strict, unhappy childhood, Esther is taken into the household of her guardian, the amiable John Jarndyce, who lives at Bleak House, near St Albans. Here she is the companion of two other wards of Jarndyce, Richard Carstone and Ada Clare. Jarndyce has also taken under his protection the hypocritically innocent Harold Skimpole. On the fringe of the great law suit, the young people encounter various victims of Chancery such as the demented Miss Flite, who has an aviary of birds symbolic of the captives of the English legal system. Less likeable is Mrs Jellyby who in her 'telescopic philanthropy' for Africa neglects the care of her own family. Esther establishes herself as housekeeper at Bleak House. Ada and Richard fall in love, but infatuated as he is with his

Jarndyce prospects, he can settle down to no employment. William Guppy, a lawyer's clerk, suspects Esther's parentage, and proposes to her, but she refuses him. Esther instead falls in love with Allan Woodcourt, a doctor, whom she meets through Miss Flite. But she catches smallpox from Jo, loses her beauty and gives up all hope of marrying. Guppy, pursuing proof of Esther's parentage, witnesses the spontaneous combustion of Krook, from an explosive excess of gin. Tulkinghorn, also investigating Lady Dedlock's secret, is found shot dead. George Rouncewell is arrested. Rouncewell is the proprietor of a shooting gallery and an associate of Nemo, in his former identity of Captain Hawdon. Lady Dedlock, another suspect, flees and her recently dead body is discovered by Esther, whom earlier she had encountered and acknowledged as her daughter. Inspector Bucket eventually discovers the true culprit, Hortense, Lady Dedlock's French maid. Jo dies. Richard, who has drifted in and out of various professions, marries Ada. But the great Jarndyce case finally consumes all the estate in legal costs, and he faces a ruined future. Jarndyce proposes to Esther, who agrees to marry him, but Woodcourt returns to England after service overseas and the older man releases her. Esther later recovers her looks. The work is notable for its symbolic play with the London fog, for its detective* plot, and for its satire of the lumbering apparatus of English law.

BLESSINGTON, Countess of [Marguerite] (née Power, 1789–1849). The most fashionable of fashionable novelists, Blessington's fiction is scarcely more romantic than her own life. She was born into the penurious Irish squirearchy in Clonmel. Her father Edmund Power (a Catholic won over to the English side after 1798) was a hated magistrate, a dandy and a drunken bully. Marguerite picked up what education she could from female friends of the family and was virtually sold into marriage with a brutal Irish army officer, Captain Farmer, at fifteen. After three months, she fled. She took refuge with another army officer, with whom she lived for ten years. During this period she read widely and largely cultivated herself. Her husband was eventually killed in 1817 in a drunken brawl in debtor's prison, and at twenty-eight years old, Marguerite was for the first time in her life a free woman. In 1818 she married the Earl of Blessington, who compensated her former protector, Captain Jenkins, with £10,000. Blessington, who was seven years older than his wife, showered her with wealth. She became a leading hostess in London society, although the taint of scandal never left her. In the early 1820s, she published some poetry, travelled extensively in Europe, and consorted with Byron. In 1829, her husband died at the age of forty-six, from a stroke. His wife's income was suddenly reduced from over £20,000 to a mere £2,000 a year. Blessington thereafter lived with Alfred Count D'Orsay, the estranged husband of her stepdaughter. With this dandy, she re-established her London salon in 1831. Financial pressure drove her to write her best-known work, the *Journal Of Conversations With Lord Byron* (1834). She also turned out various silver fork* and Irish* novels, beginning with *Grace Cassidy, Or The Repealers* (1833). Her subsequent fiction includes: *The Confessions Of An Elderly Gentleman* (1836); *The Victims Of Society* (1837); *The Governess* (1839), probably the first Victorian novel on this interesting theme; *The Lottery Of Life* (1842); *Strathern** (1845); *Country Quarters* (1850). Her literary career (masterminded by Colburn*) was remunerative, but her income was cut into by the 1845 Irish famine and in May 1849 she went bankrupt. Gore House and her goods were sold off and she died of apoplexy a month later in Paris. Blessington's fiction is facile, and chronicles a milieu soon eclipsed by Victorian decency. Her niece Margaret Power* also wrote fiction. BL 12. *DNB*. RM. *NCBEL*. Wol. Sad.

Blind Love, Wilkie Collins and Walter Besant, 1890, 3 vols, Chatto. (Serialised in the *Illustrated London News*, July–December 1889 with illustrations by Amedée Forestier.) In August 1889, on his deathbed, Collins commissioned the finishing of this novel to his friend Besant: 'Tell him I would do the same for him if he were in my place.' He left a remarkably full 'scenario' for Besant to work from and the resulting narrative was competently done. *Blind Love* deals topically with Fenian outrages and is largely set in Ireland. The central figure of the early story is Sir Giles Mountjoy, a banker. His god-daughter, Iris Henley, refuses his respectable nephew Hugh in favour of the wild Irishman, Lord Harry Norland. Harry is implicated in the political murder of Hugh's brother Arthur, but Iris shields him. After their marriage, Harry uses photographic evidence to fake his death, for insurance gain. Iris thinks herself a widow. Harry meanwhile joins a rabid Nationalist cell in America. Eventually he is killed on a terrorist mission and Iris marries Hugh retaining, however, a lock of Harry's hair as a memento of her 'blind love'.

BLUNDELL, Mrs Francis [Mary] ('M. E. Francis', née Sweetman, 1859–1930). Born a Catholic in Dublin Sweetman was educated at home by governesses, and abroad in Belgium. After marriage to Francis Blundell in 1879, she settled in Crosby, near Liverpool, the setting for many of her subsequent stories. They include: *A Daughter Of The Soil* (1895), a tearful bigamy* novel set in Lancashire; *Frieze And Fustian* (1896), sketches and stories arranged in two parts so as to contrast Irish ('frieze') and northern English ('fustian') manners; *In A North Country Village* (1897); *The Duenna Of A Genius* (1898), the story of two Hungarian musicians in London; *Miss Erin* (1898), whose heroine aspires to be the Irish Joan of Arc. BL 13. *WW*. Wol.

BODKIN, M[atthias] M'Donnell (1850–1933). Bodkin was born in Galway, Ireland, the son of a doctor. He was educated at a Jesuit college, and the Catholic University after which he studied for the law. Bodkin later became Nationalist MP for North Roscommon and later still, in 1907, a judge. He produced some fiction, with a fiery patriotic content such as his two tales of the 1798 rebellion, *Lord Edward Fitzgerald* (1896) and *The Rebels* (1897). In lighter vein, he wrote detective* stories such as *Dora Myrl, The Lady Detective* (1900) and *Paul Beck, The Rule Of Thumb Detective* (1899). BL 24. *WW*. Wol.

Bogue (1843–56). Publisher. David Bogue (1812–56) began in business as a bookseller in Edinburgh. He then became assistant to the London publisher, Charles Tilt, from 1836 to 1840. He remained Tilt's partner until 1843, after which he started up his own independent publishing business at 86 Fleet Street. He specialised in cheap, often illustrated books, for mass readership and pirated American fiction quite extensively. After 1847 he was for some years George Cruikshank's* preferred publisher and put out the illustrator's fine collaborations in fiction with the Mayhew* brothers. On Bogue's death his business was taken over by W. Kent and Co. (DB)Boase.

BOHN, Henry George (1796–1884). The son of a Soho bookbinder, Bohn began in the book trade as an assistant to his father in Covent Garden. As a young independent bookseller, he was largely responsible for the development of the Victorian 'remainder' booktrade by which reduced-price new books were made available to the public. Although his main lines as a publisher were non-fiction, Bohn pirated the work of American novelists such as Cooper and Hawthorne in the 1840s and 1850s, profiting from the boom in 1s. railway* novels. (He was closely followed in this by George Routledge*). A connoisseur and learned bibliophile, Bohn sold his stock to Bell and Daldy for £40,000 in 1864. His copyrights and plates he sold to Chatto and Windus* for £20,000 in 1874. In retirement, Bohn lived the life of a rich connoisseur. *DNB*.

BOLDREWOOD, Rolf (i.e. Thomas Alexander Browne, born 'Brown', 1826–1915). Brown was born in London, the son of a naval officer who emigrated in 1830. He was educated in Australia where his enterprising father, now retired, helped found Melbourne in 1838. But the family's fortunes were ruined in the 1841–45 slump, and the young Thomas Brown was denied the gentlemanly start in life he might otherwise have expected. At the age of seventeen he set up as a squatter and supported his mother and six unmarried sisters on his 32,000-acre cattle station in the western district. He married in 1861 and rose to the rank of police magistrate, a post which he held until 1895 (in 1862, he added the final 'e' to his surname). In 1865, having suffered some financial reverses and being lamed temporarily by a kick from a horse, Browne began to write. His first publication was 'A Kangaroo Drive', accepted by *Cornhill** in 1866. In 1869, fierce drought ruined him as a farmer and he returned to Sydney with his family. In the 1890s he helped administer the law in the goldfields. The novels which Browne wrote, as Rolf Boldrewood, celebrate the hardy virtues and material rewards of emigrant life in the colony, and doubtless inspired many young Victorians to follow him. From 1873 to 1878 he turned out a serial novel every year. *Robbery Under Arms** (1883), is his best-known work, and when it was published in England in 1888 brought Browne international fame. The narrative takes the form of a bushranger recounting his escapades the night before he is due to hang. It was followed by *The Miner's Right* (1890); *A Colonial Reformer* (1890); *Nevermore* (1892), a reconstruction of Ballarat and the goldfields in the 1850s; *A Modern Buccaneer* (1894, co-authored with Louis Becke*); *War To The Knife* (1899), a novel dealing with the Maori Wars, in the 1860s; *Babes In The Bush* (1900). BL 19. *WW*. RM. Wol. Sad.

The Bondman, Hall Caine, 1890, 3 vols, Heinemann. A tale of revenge, and one of the biggest Victorian bestsellers. The action is set in the late eighteenth century. Stephen Orry, a dissolute seaman, seduces and marries Rachel, the daughter of Iceland's Danish Governor-General, only to desert her before the birth of their son Jason. Twenty years later, Jason dedicates himself to vengeance. Orry, meanwhile, has settled on the Isle of Man, has bigamously remarried a peasant woman, and has a second son, Michael Sunlocks, who wins the love of the Manx Governor's daughter, Greeba Fairbrother. Trying to wreck the ship bringing Jason to the Isle of Man, Orry is fatally injured, though rescued from drowning by the son who has sworn to kill him. There follows a complicated unravelling of the plot. Michael crosses the sea to make his peace with his half-brother and, frustrated in this intention, goes on to become Governor of an independent Iceland. Meanwhile, Jason has fallen in love with Greeba, and tries to murder Michael. After his trial, Jason is condemned to the sulphur mines. And when Denmark reconquers Iceland, Michael joins him there. The half-brothers are physically yoked together, and after much suffering are reconciled. They escape and after a tremendous climax on Iceland's Mount of Laws Jason is executed. Michael and Greeba are finally united. The novel drew much of its appeal from the vogue for highly coloured regional fiction at the end of the century and is notable for what Hall Caine grandly called: 'the clash of passions as bracing as a black thunderstorm'.

The Bookman (1891–1934). The brainchild of William Robertson Nicoll (who was its editor for thirty-two years), *The Bookman* gives the best picture of late Victorian authorship in its social aspect. Issued monthly at 6d. by Hodder and Stoughton, the tone of the journal was resolutely middlebrow. It profiled popular authors, circulated the latest literary intelligence, and featured belletristic essays on books and the book world including 'Novel Notes', chatty discussions on fiction of the day. With its glossy photographic and cartoon illustration *The Bookman* took over from the drably newspaper-like *Athenaeum** as the premier advertising spot for late Victorian fiction. Its American edition launched the first ever bestseller lists in 1895. *BLM.*

BOOTH, Mrs [Eliza Margaret J.] Otto Von ('Rita', later Mrs Desmond Humphreys, née Gollan, 1860?–1938). Margaret Gollan was born in Inverness, Scotland, where her father was a landowner, having formerly been a businessman in India. Her parents' marriage was violent and unhappy. In her young girlhood Margaret followed her father to Sydney, Australia. He did not, as hoped, make his fortune and around 1874 the Gollans returned to England. By this time, her mother was a chronic invalid. Margaret Gollan had her education largely at second hand from her brother's tutor and began writing in her late teens, after a broken engagement. She took her pen name Rita as a conscious homage to her idol, Ouida*, whose novels she had been forbidden to read in her childhood. Gollan's first marriage was to the popular music composer, Otto von Booth. The son of a German baron and an English mother, he was regarded as an unsuitable match by Gollan's parents. The marriage was, in fact, wretched and she describes aspects of it in her later novel *Sâba Macdonald* (1906). After divorce she made a second marriage with an Irishman of no fixed employment, Desmond Humphreys. As his wife, she became knowledgeable about Ireland and the couple lived for many years at Youghal. Rita wrote numerous romantic novels, aimed at female library subscribers. Although her principal model was Ouida, reviewers noted that she lacked the other novelist's irresistible 'badness'. Rita was particularly fond of journal and diary novels. Her stories feature 'willowy forms, flashing eyes, long, long embraces and clinging kisses'. Her best, and probably autobiographical work, is *Sheba** (1889), the story of a wild Australian girl whose childhood (if not her passionate sexual progress) parallels the author's own. Rita's other novels include: *Vivienne* (1877); *Fragoletta* (1881); *My Lady Coquette* (1881); *Two Bad Blue Eyes* (1884); *Corinna* (1888). *A Husband Of No Importance* (1894) is an anti-new woman* novel, with a heroine who neglects home and husband to write novels. Her years in Ireland inspired the popular *Peg, The Rake* (1894) and she had a late hit with the social satire, *Souls* (1903). In later life she was a devotee of theosophy and knew Madame Blavatsky. In her *Recollections Of A Literary Life* (1936) Rita records herself as having been 'robbed unmercifully' by publishers during her long career. BL 65. *WW.* Wol. Sad. RLF.

BOOTHBY, Guy [Newell] (1867–1905). Born in Adelaide, the son of an Australian politician, Boothby was educated in England. He returned to Australia in 1883, staying there eleven years, employed as secretary to the mayor of Adelaide. During this period, he tried his hand at some unsuccessful plays. In 1891, he undertook an arduous cross-continental trip across Australia. In 1894, he returned to England, and threw himself into the writing of fiction. Over the eleven years of life that remained to him, Boothby turned out a mass of adventure romances and other popular genre fiction. They include some detective* novels (e.g. *The Mystery Of The Clasped Hands*, 1901) and a number of tales drawing on his early Australian experience. Most successful were the 'Nikola' books based on the exploits of a ruthless mastermind. The series began with *A Bid For Fortune, Or Dr Nikola's Vendetta* (1895; Nikola is introduced as an immaculate dinner host, with a black cat perched inscrutably on his shoulder. The wizard motif is sustained throughout the saga). It was followed by *Dr Nikola* (1896), *Dr Nikola's Experiment* (1899) and *Farewell Nikola* (1901). A typical Boothby romp is *A Maker Of Nations* (1900), where the hero plans a revolution in a South American republic, falls in love with the President's daughter, and changes sides. Boothby died young from influenza at Boscombe, a prosperous and successful author. He was also an amateur farmer and dog-breeder. BL 53. *WW.* Wol.

Born In Exile, George Gissing, 1892, 3 vols, A. and C. Black. Gissing's mordant study of the social consequences of agnosticism. The hero, Godwin Peak, is first encountered as a prize philosophy student at a provincial college (an institution clearly based on Owens College, where Gissing himself was educated). The antics of his vulgar cockney uncle Andrew lead him to give up his studies to work as a scientist at the Royal School of Mines. A decade later in 1882, Godwin is discovered a successful scientist in London. On a visit to Exeter, he meets the Warricombe family and falls in love with the daughter Sidwell. She is rich, well bred and devout. To win her, Godwin pretends to have a religious vocation. In fact he is the author of a currently notorious anti-religious article, 'The New Sophistry', and is unmasked by Buckland Warricombe who remembers him as an atheist at college. But Sidwell now loves Godwin, and a legacy allows him to propose. At the last moment, she will not surrender all the values of her class and Peak travels to Vienna, where he dies 'in exile' of a fever, his last words, 'ill again, and alone'.

BORROW, George [Henry] (1803–81). Borrow was born in Norfolk, the son of a maltster turned army NCO and a Norfolk actress of French Protestant descent. There was also a Cornish strain in his father's background, which may account for Borrow's subsequent fascination with the Celtic race. His father's occupation as a recruiting officer for the West Norfolk Militia involved the young George's travelling extensively around Britain (vividly recorded in *Lavengro**) anticipating the vagrant existence of his later life. Until the age of thirteen he received little formal education. The longest residence he experienced in his youth was from 1816 until his father's death in 1824, when the family were stationed in Norwich. At seventeen, George was articled to a solicitor in that city. Norwich had a famously literary community and Borrow became associated with William Taylor, who was to exercise a profound influence on him. Taylor, a scholar, introduced the young Borrow to German literature and philosophy and encouraged his remarkable facility in languages. Physically, Borrow was striking, being very tall, white-haired from his youth and subject to fits. Also from his earliest life he had shown an instinctive kinship with social outsiders, notably gypsies. When Borrow went to London in 1824 to make his way in the literary world, Taylor provided him with introductions to the leading men of letters. Despite his contacts, Borrow's entry into successful authorship was not easy nor is much known of this so-called 'veiled period' of his life. From 1825 to 1832, he travelled (probably) gathering at first hand the experience later worked up into *Lavengro* and *The Romany Rye**. He also translated and possibly wrote gothic* fiction and poetry. In 1833, Borrow was commissioned by the British and Foreign Bible Society to translate the New Testament into Manchu. With one of the linguistic feats for which he was famous, he made himself competent in the language in less than a month. He was, in fact, to work seven years in all for the society. He spent two years in Russia, (1833–35) and then travelled to Portugal, spending four years in the Iberian Peninsula, furnishing himself with experience for later books. In 1840, he returned to England, married a widow and settled on his wife's estate in the Norfolk Broads near Lowestoft. His *The Zincali, Or The Gypsies In Spain* (1841) and *The Bible in Spain* (1843, bought by some under the misapprehension it was an evangelical book) sold well. His masterpiece, *Lavengro* (1851, the title means 'he who is expert with words'), was less to the public taste. Nevertheless, Borrow produced a sequel, *The Romany Rye* (1857, 'Man of the Gypsies'). *Wild Wales* was published in 1862. Until his seventies, Borrow was an extraordinary hale and vigorous man, swimming daily in the sea, and he continued to walk huge distances. His wife died in 1869, and in his later years the author was regarded locally as eccentric and cantankerous. Borrow's writing is situated on the ambiguous borders of fiction, reportage and autobiography. (Defoe was clearly a major influence.) His remarkable cultural adaptiveness qualifies him as a lay anthropologist. At the very least, he is the greatest of English writers about gypsy life. He also did a vast amount of translation, of which no residue remains. He died at Oulton. BL 2. *DNB*. RM. *NCBEL*. Wol.

BOULGER, Mrs George Simonds [Dorothy Henrietta, also called on occasion 'Theodora' and 'Dora'] ('Theo Gift', née Havers, 1847–1923). Dorothy Havers's father was a colonial administrator, and although she was born in Norfolk, much of her youth (after 1854) was spent in the Falklands and South America. She came to England when her father died in 1870 and began to publish her work in *Once A Week**. She also worked for ten years on the staff of *All The Year Round** (Dickens's* magazine) and for two on *Cassell's Magazine* (with G. Manville Fenn*). In the early 1870s, she married George Simonds Boulger (1853–1922), a distinguished botanist. Dorothy Boulger wrote heroine-centred fiction directed at women readers such as: *True To Her Trust, Or Womanly Past Question* (1874) and *A Matter Of Fact Girl* (1881). *Lil Lorimer* (1885) is the semi-autobiographical account of a girl brought up in South America. *Dishonoured* (1890) describes at three volume length the agonies of a young woman who unexpectedly discovers herself illegitimate. For much of her writing, Boulger used the pseudonym 'Theo Gift' which led early reviewers to think her a man. Among much else, she wrote a number of children's stories, some in collaboration with Edith Nesbit (née Bland*). BL 22. *WW*. Wol. Sad.

The Boy Slaves, Captain Mayne Reid, 1865, 1 vol, C. H. Clarke. (Serialised in *The Boy's Journal*, 1864.) One of Mayne Reid's most powerful stories for boys. Three young midshipmen, Terence, Harry and Colin, are shipwrecked in North Africa, together with a canny old tar, 'Sailor Bill'. They are saved from drowning only to be captured by Arab slave traders. They pass through the hands of a number of sheiks in the Sahara, before being ransomed by a British consul. In the process, they discover Bill's brother, also a slave. In later life, we are told, the three heroes 'rose to rank and distinction in the naval service of their country'.

BOYD, Alexander Stuart (1854–1930). Illustrator. Boyd was born in Glasgow where his father was a muslin manufacturer. For six years, he worked in a bank. In his twenties Boyd moved to London where he illustrated for various magazines, including *Punch**. One of the *Graphic* school of artists, he specialised in pseudo-photographic work. In the 1890s, he did effective illustrations for the fiction of Israel Zangwill*, R. L. Stevenson* and Jerome K. Jerome*. In 1880 he married Mary Stuart Kirkwood (1860–1937). As 'J. Colne Dacre' Mary Boyd wrote a number of novels, which appeared serially in the magazines (e.g. *Our Stolen Summer*, 1900, illustrated by Alexander Boyd). In later life, she moved with her husband to New Zealand, where she was politically active and became first President of the League of New Zealand Penwomen. BL 11. *WW*. Hou.

BOYLE, [R] Fred[erick] (1841–93). Boyle was born at Wolstanton, Staffs, and educated at Cheltenham College and Oxford University. On graduating he studied law and was called to the Bar in 1866. But he soon transferred to free-lance journalism and travelled in this capacity to Borneo, Central America and Australia. As a correspondent for the English papers he covered most of the big wars of the 1870s (the Franco-Prussian, Ashantee, Afghan). As a literary sideline Boyle also wrote novels of action and foreign adventure for Chapman and Hall* such as: *Fools Of Fortune* (1876); *Legends Of My Bungalow* (1881), reminiscences written, as the author says, 'at that time of life when a man gets drowsy after dinner'; *The Golden Prime* (1882); *A Good Hater* (1885), a romance incorporating Afghan adventures; *An English Vendetta* (1887). Among his many miscellaneous interests Boyle was a leading expert on the cultivation of orchids, about which he wrote voluminously. BL 14.

BOYLE, the Hon. Mary Louisa (1810–90). A granddaughter of the seventh Earl of Cork and Orrery and a daughter of Sir Courtney Boyle, a vice admiral, there is little else recorded of her life. She lived in the West End of London and never married. Her pious poem, 'My Father's At The Helm', was very popular with her contemporaries and she wrote a number of less successful novels including the historical* romances: *The State Prisoner* (1837), a tale of the French Regency; *The Forester, A Tale Of 1688* (1839); *The Tangled Weft* (1866). BL 3. Boase. Wol.

The Boy's Own Paper (1879–1967). The *BOP* (as it was familiarly known) was founded in 1879, as a boys' weekly. Its publisher was the RTS* and the paper was intended principally to counteract the pernicious effects of the penny dreadful* class of literature with 'pure and entertaining reading'. Also costing a penny it courageously (for an evangelical journal) made secular fiction its main element; the opening item of the first issue, for instance, was Talbot Baines Reed's* story 'My First Football Match'. The *BOP* in this way fought the secular juvenile publishers on their own ground, even taking its name from other popular papers with the 'Boys' prefix such as E. J. Brett's* *Boys Of England.* Under its gifted first editor George Hutchison (1841–1913) the *BOP* featured stories by G. A. Henty*, R. M. Ballantyne*, Conan Doyle*, 'Captain' Charles Gibson and W. H. G. Kingston*. Large graphic illustrations and witty vignettes were part of the layout. Among the artists who worked for the paper were: Frank Brangwyn and Jack Nettleship. *BOP* quickly became the market leader among boys' magazines of the late nineteenth century, with a circulation approaching a quarter of a million and annual profits of over £4,000 a year. The paper specialised in tales of adventure, sport and of public school life and left an indelible mark on generations of 'lads' of all classes. The *BOP* survived in attenuated form until the 1960s. In 1880, a *Girl's Own Paper** was begun as a sister publication.

BOZ. The pseudonym under which Charles Dickens* published his early journalism and fiction. It was, as he explained in an 1847 preface to *The Pickwick Papers**, a corruption of the nickname 'Moses' given to his small brother Augustus (b. 1827). In a desperate attempt to cash in on his success, a spate of would-be Dickenses in the late 1830s came up with such authorial sobriquets as 'Pos', 'Bos' and 'Poz'. Dickens himself dropped the pen name with *Dombey And Son** in 1847, after which date he appeared before the public in his own identity.

Bradbury and Evans (1830–). Publishers and printers. William Bradbury and Frederick Mullet Evans became partners in 1830. For the first ten years of their professional association they were exclusively printers, based originally in Bouverie Street, then in Lombard Street, Whitefriars. As printers they worked for Edward Moxon and Chapman and Hall*, Dickens's* publishers. When Dickens parted from Chapman and Hall in 1844, Bradbury and Evans became the publisher of his serials. In 1847, they also published Thackeray's* *Vanity Fair** in its monthly parts, and went on to bring out most of the novelist's mature fiction. In 1841, they became proprietors of

*Punch**, and in 1859 (after their break with Dickens) founded *Once A Week**, the finest of the illustrated fiction-carrying magazines of the mid-century. Both magazines provided them with popular novelist clients such as R. S. Surtees*, Shirley Brooks* and Charles Reade*. Bradbury and Evans, almost accidentally, became a major Victorian fiction publisher. Perhaps it was because they were famously good-natured, but a more probable reason is that they came to terms early with the new technologies of industrial-scale printing and distribution.

BRADDON, M[ary] E[lizabeth] (1835–1915). The 'Queen of the Circulating Libraries' and the most consistent of Victorian bestseller novelists. Mary Braddon was born in Soho, London, the youngest daughter of a Cornish solicitor and sports writer. Her father, Henry Braddon, was a feckless man and her mother deserted him when Mary was only four, taking her three children to the Sussex coast. The family returned to London four years later, at which point (aged eight) the young girl began to write. Among the continuous parental disturbance, she was educated mainly at home by her mother. She began producing material for the magazines in 1856 to help support her family. When this failed, Braddon went onto the stage in 1857 as 'Mary Seyton', to support herself and her mother. This theatrical experience feeds into some of the later novels (e.g., *A Strange World*, 1875). In 1860 a Yorkshire squire, John Gilby, gave her money to write an epic on Garibaldi. Instead she wrote a novel, *Three Times Dead* (later published in London as *The Trail Of The Serpent*, 1861). In 1860, she quit the stage and became acquainted with the Irish publisher John Maxwell*, for whose magazine, the *Welcome Guest*, she provided stories. Her first success came with *Lady Audley's Secret** (1862), the serial rights for which were bought by Maxwell. Maxwell was, as it turned out, to be the most important man in Braddon's life and shortly after their first meeting she went to live with him. Her first child by him, Gerald, was born in 1862. *Lady Audley's Secret* began inauspiciously as a serial in Maxwell's ailing paper *Robin Goodfellow**. Nor did Braddon labour over it, writing the third volume in less than a fortnight. But republished in volume form (by William Tinsley*) the work became immensely successful and set Braddon up for life. (It also set up Tinsley, who built a villa at Barnes called 'Audley Lodge' on the profits.) The plot is succinctly summarised by Elaine Showalter: 'Braddon's bigamous heroine deserts her child, pushes husband number one down a well, thinks about poisoning husband number two and sets fire to a hotel in which her other male acquaintances are residing.' Braddon's own marital problems were not as easily managed. Maxwell had five children and a wife in an Irish lunatic asylum. He was also deeply in debt to another publisher, Ward, Lock and Tyler* and much of the money from Braddon's 1860s bestsellers was probably swallowed up in the effort to clear him, which was finally managed in 1871. Thereafter, things were easier. In 1874, when the first Mrs Maxwell died, Braddon was free to marry her publisher, and bore him another six children, as well as continuing to be the principal family breadwinner. The actual marriage of Braddon to Maxwell was ugly, however, requiring public confirmation that the previous union was irregular (all their servants promptly gave notice). But the couple rode the scandal out. In the mid-1860s, her price peaked at £2,000 a novel.

Her output was prodigious, and in addition to her other labours she edited or 'conducted' several magazines, including *Temple Bar** (up to 1866) and *Belgravia** (after 1866). Many of Braddon's novels were dramatised, and she wrote plays herself. As the *DNB* puts it: 'prolific vitality was not a rare quality among Victorian novelists, but Miss Braddon's indefatigable zest is unrivalled.' She was a top favourite with the circulating library subscriber; with the railway reader (by 1899, fifty-seven of her novels had appeared in yellowbacks*); and with the lower-class market for whom she wrote in such journals as Ward and Lock's *Sixpenny Magazine* and Maxwell's *Halfpenny Journal*. Her many works of fiction include: *Aurora Floyd** (1863), a fashionable bigamy* tale which Henry James admired; *Eleanor's Victory* (1863), the story of a resourceful heroine who traps her father's murderer; *Henry Dunbar* (1864); *John Marchmont's Legacy** (1863); *Birds Of Prey* (1867); *Dead Sea Fruit* (1868), in which a fifty-year-old man falls in love with a young girl also loved by his own son; *Joshua Haggard's Daughter* (1876), the story of a Methodist minister who marries a girl many years his junior; *An Open Verdict* (1878), the melodrama of an heiress, falsely suspected of her father's death; *Under The Red Flag* (1883), a story of the Paris Commune; *The Golden Calf* (1883), a convincingly low-keyed English version of Zola's novel of alcoholism, *L'Assommoir*, whose accurate depictions suggest that Braddon had painful first-hand acquaintance with the disease; *Gerard, Or The World, The Flesh And The Devil* (1891), a Victorian reworking of Goethe's *Faust*; *The Infidel* (1900), a story of the Methodist revival (Braddon having become religious in her later years). Despite the treadmill speed and regularity of her composition, Braddon's fiction is frequently clever, sharp and well written. She profited as an artist from the advice of Bulwer-Lytton* early in her career. (He invariably instructed her, vainly, to take more time over her writing). Her later work is notably less sensational* and more psychological in its concerns. Two of Braddon's children, W. B. and Gerald Maxwell, went on to write novels. In later life she was as R. L. Wolff puts it: 'an admired and beloved member of the London literary, theatrical, artistic and social world'. BL 71. *DNB*. *NCBEL*. RM. Wol. Sad.

BRADLEY, Edward ('Cuthbert Bede, MA', 1827–89). Bradley was born at Kidderminster, the son of a surgeon. After graduating in 1848 from Durham (then a 'new' university, founded in 1832), he seems to have spent a year in Oxford, evidently the most influential period of his life. He was ordained in 1850. From 1859 to 1871 he held a series of rural incumbencies. He eventually moved to Stretton, Rutlandshire, where he officiated from 1871 to 1883. Finally, he took up the post of Vicar of Lenton, near Grantham, where he remained until his death. In addition to his clerical duties, Bradley was a humorous writer (principally for *Bentley's Miscellany** and *Punch**) and lecturer. As 'Cuthbert Bede' (the patron saints of Durham being St Cuthbert and the Venerable Bede) he had a strong line in comic stories of school and (particularly) of Oxford life, although he had never been a registered student or a don at the university. Like Thackeray*, he illustrated his own work in a pleasantly amateurish fashion. The best known of his books is *The Adventures Of Mr Verdant Green, An Oxford Freshman* (1853). This *ingénu*'s career and that of his friend Mr Bouncer extend over subsequent sequels. Further *Adventures* (1854) find Verdant a more knowing undergraduate. *Married And Done For* (1857) brings him to graduation and the altar. In 1873 Bede brought out the inferior *Little Mr Bouncer, And His Friend, Verdant Green.* An example of Bradley's juvenile fiction is *Nearer And Dearer, A Tale Out Of School* (1857), the story of a young fellow who sets out by various ruses to circumvent the formidable security of a local academy for young ladies. Among Bradley's other novels and novelettes are: *Mattins And Muttons, Or The Beauty of Brighton* (1866) and *Tales Of College Life* (1856). In later life the author gave popular public lectures in which capacity he earned many thousands of pounds for church repair. He was throughout his adult life a close friend of the *Punch* coterie. BL 13. *DNB.* RM. *NCBEL.* Wol.

BRANDT, Francis Frederick (1819–74). Brandt was born at Gawsworth, Cheshire, the son of a clergyman, and educated at Macclesfield Grammar School. He was called to the Bar in 1847. Always interested in sport (he contributed regularly to *Bell's Life*) Brandt helped bring about important changes in the English law as it affects sports. He also produced a novel with a legal background, *Frank Marland's Manuscripts, Or The Memoirs Of A Modern Templar* (1859). BL 1. Boase.

The Brass Bottle, F. Anstey (i.e. Thomas A. Guthrie), 1900, 1 vol, Smith, Elder. A light fantasy, very popular in its time. Horace Ventimore, a young architect, impulsively buys a brass jug at a public auction for a guinea. It is found to contain a singularly bad-tempered genie called Fakrash-el-Aamash, whose attempts to assist Ventimore's architectural commissions go comically awry. A murderous feud develops between master and superhuman servant. Horace finally tricks his antagonist back into the bottle which he throws into the Thames. The genie spends the rest of eternity in river sludge while the hero returns to his bourgeois destiny. The story was turned into a popular Victorian stage farce and in the twentieth century into a film.

BRAY, Anna Eliza (née Kempe, 1790–1883). Born in Newington, Surrey, she was the daughter of a bullion porter in the Royal Mint. One of her early ambitions was to go on the stage. Instead she married Charles Stothard, an artist, in 1818. He died falling from a ladder while working at a church in Devon, three years later. She subsequently married the Rev. Edward Atkyns Bray, settled in Tavistock and began to write. In 1857, she was widowed again and went to London, where she moved in the best literary circles. Between 1826 and 1874 Bray turned out a dozen novels, despite chronically poor health. Her fiction comprises historical* romance and tales for children. She also gathered West Country folklore and devised romances around the legends of Devon and Cornwall families (e.g. *Courtenay Of Warbreddon*, 1844). Particularly in the 1840s, she was a popular writer. But after this decade her output was very small. An *Autobiography* (taking her life to 1843) was published in 1884. Some of her letters to the poet Robert Southey (whom she hero-worshipped) were published in 1836. She was also the cousin of Christina Rossetti's mother. Bray's last years were embittered by the false accusation that she had stolen a fragment of the Bayeux tapestry in her youth. BL 14. *DNB.* RM. *NCBEL.* Wol. RLF.

BRAY, Mrs Caroline [Cara] (née Hennell, 1814–1905). The eighth and youngest daughter of a Manchester merchant, she was educated at home (on Unitarian principles) after which she worked for a while as a governess. Her brother was Charles Hennell, author of *An Inquiry Into The Origins Of Christianity* (1838). In 1836 she married Charles Bray, a prosperous ribbon manufacturer in Coventry. He was also a philosophical writer and philanthropist. The Brays and Hennells were after 1841 intimate with George Eliot* and the Brays ran something of a literary salon at their home, Rosehill. Mrs Bray interested herself particularly in the welfare of animals, and wrote, to promote sympathy for animal suffering, *Paul Bradley, A Village Tale Inculcating Kindness To Animals* (1876) and *Richard Barton, Or The Wounded Bird* (1871). She also wrote a number of instructional books for children whom she continued to teach after her marriage. Eliot called Bray 'the most religious person I know'. BL 3. *DNB.*

BRENT, John (1808–82). Brent was born at Rotherhithe, Kent, where his father was a shipbuilder. The family moved to Canterbury, around 1820. The senior Brent went on to become mayor of the city, and his son devoted himself to chronicling Canterbury's past. In addition to much local history and archaeology, Brent wrote tales for magazines and such historical* romances as: *The Sea Wolf* (1834); *The Battle Cross* (1845), a romance of the fourteenth century; *Ellie Forestere* (1850). His publisher was the disreputable Newby*. BL 2. Boase.

Brett (1855?–95). Publisher. E[dwin] J[ohn] Brett (1828–95) was was born in Canterbury, the son of an army officer. He began working life as an illustrator but soon moved into bookselling and publishing, initially in partnership with Ebenezer Landells. In 1860 he joined the Newsagents' Publishing Company, a firm which put out penny dreadfuls* for boys, notably the 'Wild Boys' series. The firm was temporarily shut down in 1877 by the police, urged on by public moralists. Indirectly, this panic about boys' literature led to the founding by the RTS* of the *Boy's Own Paper** in 1879. Brett had formed his own firm in Fleet Street as early as 1868. He went on to edit a stream of popular juvenile publications such as *The Boys' Comic Journal* (1883–98) and the weekly, *Boys Of England* (1866–99). This last periodical featured Jack Harkaway*, one of the most renowned heroes of boys' fiction in the century and claimed a circulation of a quarter of a million in the early 1870s. Brett became in later life a wealthy man, collected ancient armour and endowed a lifeboat, the *Edwin J. Brett*, at Southend. Boase.

A Bride From The Bush, E. W. Hornung, 1890, 1 vol, Smith, Elder. (Serialised in *Cornhill**, July–November 1890.) Alfred Bligh brings home a bride from Australia whom his aristocratic parents in England have never met. Gladys is unconventional ('typically Australian') and upsets Sir James (an English judge) and Lady Bligh. In mortification 'the Bride', as she is called, flees back to Australia, intending to preserve her husband's reputation in English society. Alfred pursues her, and there is a dramatic reunion set against a sandstorm in the outback. The reconciled couple settle on Gladys's sheep station, free from stifling English conventionality.

BRIERLEY, Ben[jamin] ('Ab o' the Yate', 1825–96). Brierley was born at Failsworth, near Manchester, the son of a handloom weaver. He left school, before he was six years old, to work as a bobbin winder. Brierley subsequently gained some education at Sunday school and helped organise a mutual improvement society in Failsworth at the age of fifteen. In the 1850s, he began publishing tales, verse and sketches of Lancashire life under the pseudonym 'Ab o' the Yate'. In 1863 he abandoned silk warping to become sub-editor of the *Oldham Times*. Brierley's published volumes include the collections: *Tales And Sketches Of Lancashire Life* (1862–63), and *The Chronicles Of Waverlow* (1863). *The Layrock Of Langleyside* (1864) was his first long narrative. In 1869, he started the popular *Ben Brierley's Journal*, a weekly which ran until 1891. In later life he was in demand as a dialect reciter of his tales. In this capacity he visited America in 1884. In the same year, Brierley lost his capital in a building society failure. His fellow Lancastrians, among whom he was a much-loved figure, raised over £600 by subscription for him. A statue of Brierley was erected in Manchester's Queen Park in 1898. BL 7. *DNB*. Wol.

The Broadway (1868–73). An unsuccessful attempt by Routledge* to emulate Smith, Elder's* *Cornhill*. Like the other magazine, *Broadway* was an illustrated monthly with serialised fiction as its main element. It began auspiciously enough with stories by Henry Kingsley* and Annie Thomas (i.e. Pender Cudlip*), but soon deteriorated and quickly expired. The title (like *Cornhill*) is derived from its publisher's London address.

BROCK, Charles E[dmund] (1870–1938). Illustrator. Brock was born at Holloway in London but soon after his birth the family moved to Cambridge where his father had taken the post of Reader in Oriental Languages. Charles continued to live there very privately most of his working life. Brock studied under the sculptor Henry Wiles and by the age of twenty-one was an established book illustrator. Like his younger brother, H[enry] M[atthew] Brock (1875–1960), he specialised in period illustrations for the classics of fiction (many of them Victorian). Brock also did lively illustrations for the horsey fiction of Whyte-Melville* in the 1890s. His style is economical in its line and naturalistic. *WW*. Hou.

BRONTË, Anne ('Acton Bell', 1820–49); Charlotte ('Currer Bell', 1816–55); Emily [Jane] ('Ellis Bell', 1818–48). The Brontës comprise a writing family, three of whom rank as major Victorian novelists. Their father, Patrick Brontë, was born in 1777, in Co. Down, Ireland. His family background was poor and he began working life as a blacksmith's labourer. But by dint of intellectual ability and determination he graduated from Cambridge University in 1806, and entered the Church of England, holding curacies in Essex, Shropshire and Yorkshire. Between 1811 and 1818 he published various volumes of verse and tales. In 1812, he married Maria Branwell, the daughter of a Cornish parson. After nine years of marriage (in which she bore six children) Mrs Brontë died in 1821, aged thirty-seven. Charlotte was born in 1816, Emily Jane in 1818 and Anne in 1820. In the year of Anne's birth the Rev. Brontë moved to the perpetual curacy of Haworth, a small mill town in the West Riding of Yorkshire. After being widowed, he tried unsuccessfully to remarry. Eventually the running of the household was taken over by his sister-in-law, Miss Elizabeth Branwell (an unloved figure in the young girls' childhood). Charlotte and Emily had an unhappy short spell at the Cowan Bridge Clergy Daughters' School, which inspired the hellish Lowood in *Jane Eyre**. Two elder sisters, Maria and Elizabeth, died in 1825 of consumption, a disease which was to rage through the family on an epidemic scale. After this the Rev. Brontë decided to educate the surviving children himself. If nothing else, they were free to read widely in the parsonage library and in the collection of books circulated by a nearby Mechanics Institute. Around 1826, the three sisters, together with their gifted but wayward brother Branwell (1817–48), began secretively to write long romantic serials about imaginary worlds. (At least one of the serials, that involving the fantastic kingdom of Gondal, was kept going until 1845 by Anne and Emily; Charlotte evidently gave up her parallel Angria saga in 1839.) In 1831, Charlotte went for eighteen months to a more congenial school at Roe Head, where she made friends with Ellen Nussey (who was later to be the main source of biographical information about the family). Emily and Anne followed her to Roe Head (at which Charlotte was briefly a teacher in 1835), which supplied the girls with elements of a respectable English education. In 1837 Emily became a governess at a school near Halifax, and in 1839 Anne and Charlotte went as governesses to private families. Charlotte's first two positions were short and unhappy. She had, meanwhile, received and rejected two proposals of marriage. Anne, the most docile of the sisters, was the most successful governess. Her second post with the Robinson family at Thorp Green near York lasted from 1840 to 1845. In 1843 she was joined by Branwell as tutor. But his sexual involvement with the Rev. Robinson's wife turned out disastrously and in 1845 the four Brontë children were together again at Haworth. Branwell worked for a while as a railway clerk, but was already a slave to drink and died soon after. The sisters made various unsuccessful attempts to publish their writing, and had hopeful plans with the financial assistance of an aunt to establish a school of their own (a dream which expresses itself frequently in their later fiction). As training, Charlotte and Emily went to Brussels in 1842 to study and teach at a boarding school. Charlotte, now twenty-six, fell hopelessly in love with the proprietor, M. Constantin Heger, whom she later portrayed as the exemplarily correct Paul Emmanuel, in *Villette**. The sisters returned to Haworth in 1842 and only Charlotte returned for a second year in 1843. Emily, the most poetic Brontë sister, was most rooted to Haworth and Yorkshire and seems to have hated leaving it. For Charlotte the Belgian experience was extraordinarily stimulating emotionally and intellectually, although clearly she disliked Brussels, despised Catholics and suffered horribly from her unrequited love for the incorrigibly proper Heger. In 1844, the Brontës' school venture fell through. At Charlotte's initiative, *Poems* by 'Currer, Ellis and Acton Bell' were published in 1846. They made no impression on the reading world. In 1847, Emily's *Wuthering Heights** and Anne's *Agnes Grey** were accepted by the dubious London publisher Thomas Newby*, who brought them out lumped all together as a single three-decker in 1847. They were indifferently received. Charlotte's *The Professor** was turned down by Smith, Elder* but *Jane Eyre** was eagerly accepted. On publication in October 1847, it was a terrific success. Newby, encouraged by this success, published Anne's *The Tenant Of Wildfell Hall** in 1848, with the implication that it was actually the work of the mysterious 'Currer Bell' (i.e. Charlotte, who disliked the book for its graphic depiction of Branwell's alcoholism). Anne and Charlotte proved their existence by going to London, meeting George

Smith and other members of the literary world. (Thackeray* on this occasion met Charlotte, whom he admired immensely. She, on her part, dedicated the second edition of *Jane Eyre* to him.) It was Anne's only trip outside Yorkshire. In 1848, consumption claimed Emily (who is supposed to have refused medical attention) and drink Branwell. Meanwhile, Charlotte was writing *Shirley*, her novel of industrial Yorkshire in 1812. The work was published in 1849, and in the same year Anne died of consumption after a rapid decline. She was aged twenty-nine and had never, as far as is known, even had a suitor. At thirty-three, Charlotte was the only child left alive. In 1850, she became acquainted with Mrs Gaskell* (later her biographer) and turned down a third proposal of marriage. In 1853, she published her most autobiographical work, *Villette*. The following year, she married the Rev. Arthur Bell Nicholls, her father's curate since 1845. Though not loveless, the marriage was certainly not passionate. Charlotte died of complications arising from pregnancy (abetted apparently by the family pulmonary weakness) in 1855. Her previously unwanted novel, *The Professor*, was published posthumously in 1857. In the same year, partly to put down scandalous rumours, Mrs Gaskell's *Life Of Charlotte Brontë* was published. But Gaskell's pro-Charlotte bias led to libel problems, and the work was heavily revised in subsequent editions and, if anything, fanned the aura of scandal hanging over the doomed family. (AB) BL 2. (CB) BL 4. (EJB) BL 1. *DNB. NCBEL.* Wol. Sad.

BROOKE, E[mma] F[rances] ('E. Fairfax Byrrne', 1859?–1926). One of the most successful of the new woman* novelists. She was born in Cheshire in the north of England where her father was a rich industrialist (or 'capitalist' as she later described him). Brooke subsequently attended Newnham College Cambridge, and came to London in 1879 where she lived the rest of her life in Hampstead. She was converted to socialism and belonged to the Fabian Society from its inception, serving for a while on its executive committee. She was also associated with the London School of Economics and herself published economic analyses of the working conditions of women in Britain and Europe. Brooke never married. Under the mystifying pseudonym E. Fairfax Byrrne (which retained her initials) she wrote a number of novels. The early *A Fair Country Maid* (1883), *Entangled* (1885) and *An Heir Without A Heritage* (1887) were apolitical and made little impact. They were, one condescending reviewer wrote, 'the kind of stories which ladies delight in on a summer afternoon'. But the more feminist *A Superfluous Woman** (1894) attracted more notice. Its heroine, Jessamine, dies in childbirth, victimised by society and a callous husband. Jessamine's story is painted (as the *Athenaeum** noted) with 'lurid lights and coal black shadows'. It was followed by *Transition* (1895). Its heroine, Honora Kemball, is a Girton girl who leaves the stuffiness of her father's rectory to work as a socialist in London. *Life The Accuser* (1896) gathers the stories of three women. Rosalie is too emancipated for her own good; Eliza is too conventional and Constantia is afflicted with an unfaithful husband, Norman, to whom she remains true out of motives not of religious duty but sexual appetite. In *The Confession Of Stephen Whapshare* (1898) the hero's wife is so self-denying that when he gives her an overdose of narcotic (so as to free himself for another woman) she nobly writes an exonerating suicide note before expiring. *The Engrafted Rose* (1900), a modern changeling fable, is similarly militant in its sexual politics. A sharply intelligent woman, Brooke archly listed her recreations in *Who's Who* as bird-watching and 'listening to clever people talk'. BL 10. *WW*. Wol.

BROOKFIELD, Mrs Jane Octavia (née Elton, 1821–96). The eighth and youngest daughter of Sir Charles Elton (1778–1853, in early life a writer) Jane Elton was born at Clevedon. In 1841, she married the Rev. W. H. Brookfield (1809–74), the close friend from Cambridge days of Tennyson and Thackeray* (with the second of whom Jane was to have a destructive love affair around 1850). The Brookfields ran an influential literary salon. He had a moderately successful career in the Church (becoming an honorary chaplain to the Queen) and in educational administration. But his life was shadowed by the sense that he had never fulfilled the brilliant promise he had shown at university. In later life, she wrote the novels: *Only George* (1868); *Not Too Late* (1868), a story of crossed love and ill-assorted marriage; *Influence* (1871) and *Not A Heroine* (1873). Some critics have seen echoes of the Thackeray affair in these works. (It is only too clearly reflected in the other novelist's *Henry Esmond**, 1852.) Brookfield's fiction is stilted in tone and dwells on the educative 'trials' of middle-class marriage. The Brookfields had three children. A son, Arthur [Montagu] Brookfield (1853–1940), was educated at Rugby and Cambridge and gave up an army career in India to become a Unionist MP (1885–1902). Arthur Brookfield wrote five novels in the Victorian period, including *Simiocracy* (1884), a polemical fable about a Liberal Party which enfranchises orang-utans and then imports them by the million to vote for the cause. Brookfield went on to pursue a successful diplomatic career in the twentieth century. (JOB)BL 4. (AMB)BL 5. (WHB)*DNB*. Wol.

BROOKS, [Charles William] Shirley (1816–74). Editor of *Punch** and versatile bohemian man of letters. Brooks was born in London, the oldest son of a noted architect. Virtually nothing is known of his boyhood although it seems the Brooks home was strongly nonconformist. After a false start in his uncle's law firm at Oswestry in 1832, he turned to journalism around 1835 and by 1843 was a full-time man of letters. He subsequently worked on the *Illustrated London News**, reported on Parliament for the *Morning Chronicle* and joined the staff of *Punch* (as 'Epicurus Rotundus') in 1851, still in the journal's early days. In 1870, he succeeded Mark Lemon* to the editorship. Among many other things, Brooks wrote a number of fluent, comic and easy-going novels whose 'airy satire' found favour with the reviewers. The best of them is *Aspen Court* (1855), 'A Story Of Our Own Time', dedicated to Charles Dickens*. Other of Brooks's novels (as interesting for their illustration as their texts) are: *The Gordian Knot** (1860) which was published in 1s. numbers, with illustrations by John Tenniel*; *The Silver Cord* (1861), again illustrated by Tenniel, and *Sooner Or Later* (1868), illustrated by Du Maurier*. The last offers an interesting picture of London legal, newspaper and club life, set against a conventional romance plot. Brooks also wrote plays, and a quantity of occasional journalism on politics and current affairs. He was a talented conversationalist among a coterie that valued the skill above all things. His assumption of the *Punch* editorship in 1870 coincided with the collapse of his physical health, and his short tenure of the post was unmemorable. His widow was awarded a Civil List pension in 1876 but Brooks himself seems to have remained to the end of his life reasonably prosperous, leaving an estate valued at £6,000. BL 5. *DNB*. RM. *NCBEL*. Wol. Sad. RLF.

Brother Jacob, George Eliot, July 1864, *Cornhill*. (First reprinted by Blackwood in a collective cheap edition of Eliot's fiction in 1878.) A mordant moral 'parable'. David Faux steals twenty guineas from his mother before running away from home to set up in the new world as a confectioner. He is observed by his idiot brother Jacob, whom he distracts with gifts of sweetmeats. Some years later David sets up shop in a nearby town, pretending to be Edward Freely, a Jamaica plantation owner's nephew. But he is exposed for the fraud he is by the now grown-up Jacob, who in his simple-mindedness remembers the one kindness his mean-spirited brother did him, years earlier. 'An admirable instance', Eliot notes, 'of the unexpected forms in which the great Nemesis hides herself.'

BROUGH, Robert B[arnabas] (1828–60). Brough was born in London, the son of an unsuccessful brewer. He worked for some time as a clerk in Manchester and before he was twenty-one, had started with his brother William a satirical magazine, the *Liverpool Lion*. In the early 1850s, he had some success with a burlesque version of Shakespeare's *Tempest*, which was put on in London and with his brother he went on to write more works of the same kind. In later life, Brough edited Maxwell's* *Welcome Guest*, wrote for all the leading comic papers and was an admired associate of the influential men of letters G. A. Sala* and Edmund Yates*. A radical in politics and a bohemian in lifestyle, he wrote some fiction such as: *Miss Brown* (1860) and *Which Is Which?* (1860). His most interesting novel is *Marston Lynch*, an autobiographical work which recounts Brough's early experiences in the Liverpool and London literary worlds. The work was begun in 1856, partly serialised in Yates's journal the *Train* and finished after the author's death in 1860 by Sala. Brough's most enduring contributions to literature are the radical and satirical *Songs Of The Governing Classes* (1855), published by the congenially anti-establishment Henry Vizetelly*. In 1859, Brough appeared in debtors' court for an unsettled drinks bill of £13. Never in good health and given to dissipation, he died prematurely of 'neuralgia' leaving his wife and children penniless. BL 4. *DNB*. *NCBEL*. Wol. RLF.

BROUGHAM, Lord Henry (1778–1868). The famous politician was the author of a fiction curiosity, *Albert Lunel, Or The Chateau Of Languedoc*. This 'philosophical romance' is supposed to have been printed by the author for private circulation among a few friends. Michael Sadleir notes: 'It would appear that Brougham genuinely believed the authorship of this novel, a novel à clef about an intimate circle, actually staged in the Chateau at Cannes built in his daughter's memory in 1840 but ostensibly a tale of pre-Revolutionary France, to be known only to five friends; also that he thought to have secured its complete suppression.' In fact the work was published in three volumes anonymously in 1844 and evidently had a much wider circulation than Sadleir imagined. BL 1. *DNB*. RM. *NCBEL*. Wol. Sad.

BROUGHTON, Rhoda (1840–1920). A top Victorian bestseller. Rhoda Broughton was one of three daughters of a widowed clergyman in North

Wales, the granddaughter of an English baronet and distantly the niece of the novelist, Joseph Sheridan Le Fanu* who later serialised her fiction in his *Dublin University Magazine**. Broughton's childhood was spent in an Elizabethan manor house in Staffordshire, which supplied the setting for much of her fiction. Its library made her better read than most women writers of her time. And her father taught her classics and modern languages, learning which she ostentatiously parades in her later fiction. Left an orphan in 1863, Broughton lived with a sister in Wales and (after 1878) in Oxford. Following her sister's death in 1894, she lived with a cousin at Headington Hill. A confirmed spinster she began to write in emulation of Anne Thackeray's, *The Story Of Elizabeth** (1863). Michael Sadleir plausibly supposes that she suffered a catastrophic disappointment in love about this time. In later life in Oxford, she was a well-known figure and was friendly with Mark Pattison, a scholar whom she spitefully portrayed as Professor Forth in *Belinda**. In London, where she always spent part of her year, Broughton was by this time a friend of Anne Thackeray Ritchie* (now married) and of Henry James. Herself a renowned conversationalist, she made witty dialogue the main component in her fiction. As a writer, Broughton quickly established a reputation for fast, and sexually provocative novels, a reputation which was astutely exploited by her publisher Bentley*. Broughton's fictional stock-in-trade was the dilemma of love and duty. In *Cometh Up As A Flower** (1867), the heroine, Nell Le Strange (who tells her own story), has to make a marriage of convenience with a rich aristocrat in order to repair her family fortunes. She finally dies pathetically of a convenient consumption. This work put Broughton in the top, £1,000-a-novel, bracket of her profession. In *Not Wisely But Too Well* (1867), the heroine almost stoops to folly with a bounder, holds back at the brink, but ultimately expires in the agony of virtuous self-control. *Red As A Rose Is She** (1870), has another love and virtue dilemma plot. In *Goodbye, Sweetheart* (1872), unwise love ends in picturesquely lingering death for the heroine Lenore Herrick. *Nancy* (1873) is a showcase for one of Broughton's many tomboy heroines and bubbling family life. Nancy Grey, nineteen years old, marries Mr Tempest, twenty years her senior. After difficulties, illness and the pathetic death of a sister, Barbara, the couple are finally reconciled to each other. Broughton turned out fiction ceaselessly and very fast. (A novel in six weeks was usual.) But after the decease of the three-decker in 1894 she found that the new shorter format suited her epigrammatic, dialogue-based fiction better. Three interesting later works by her are *Dr Cupid* (1886) which contrasts the development of a bunch of love affairs; *A Beginner* (1894), where the young heroine writes a novel which (like the young Broughton's) is attacked, and brings shame to her family; and *Foes In Law* (1900) which offers a jaundiced look at the Victorian family. Broughton noted her own inevitable *embourgeoisement* with the wry comment: 'I began my career as Zola. I finish it as Miss Yonge*.' BL 26. *DNB*. RM. *NCBEL*. Wol. Sad.

BROWN, George Douglas ('George Douglas', 'Kennedy King', 1869–1902). Author of *The House With The Green Shutters** (1901), the best realistic novel of Scottish small-town life to emerge in the nineteenth century. Brown was born at Ochiltree, Ayrshire, the illegitimate son of a farmer. From Ayr Academy (which he attended 1884–87) he went to Glasgow University

(1887–91) on a bursary, to study classics and history. He proceeded from there as a prize student to Balliol College, Oxford to finish his university education. He was poor as a young man and always in bad health. Brown remained at Oxford until 1895, when he moved to London, intending to live by his pen. At this period of his life (having always loved 'trashy novels') he wrote a boys' adventure novel, *Love And A Sword* (1899), under the pen name Kennedy King. He also turned out periodical work for *Blackwood's Magazine**. Brown had a major success with his *The House With The Green Shutters*, a narrative which in its depiction of the rural community of Barbie pungently contradicts the bucolic sentimentality of the kailyard* school (i.e. the fiction of Ian Maclaren*, S. R. Crockett*, James Barrie*). Brown's novel shows the strong influence of Hardy*, and like Hardy, he aimed to recreate the lofty power of Greek tragedy with regional* materials. More effectively, in the downfall of the central figure, Brown conveys a sense of the claustrophobic and morally venomous atmosphere of a small Scottish community. Brown's health collapsed and he died of pneumonia the year following the novel's publication which remains his single significant achievement. Notes for two other novels have survived which suggest a major career in fiction was cut short with his death. BL 2. *DNB*. RM. *NCBEL*. Wol.

BROWN, Oliver Madox (1855–74). Son of the Pre-Raphaelite painter, Ford Madox Brown, precocious novelist, artist and poet who sold his first painting at fourteen and published his first novel four years later. Brown was educated mainly at home spending two years in the junior classes of University College, London (1863–65). He also attended life classes at art school in Chelsea in 1871. Otherwise his skills were entirely developed by exposure to the artistic and intellectual milieu in which his family lived. He began writing fiction at fifteen, published his first story, *Gabriel Denver* (1873), at the age of eighteen and died of an obscure blood disorder a year later, leaving two unfinished novels (*The Dwale Bluth*, *Hebditch's Legacy*) and a quantity of shorter fiction. *Gabriel Denver* is a story of violently unhappy love, set on board the *Black Swan* (which was the original title) sailing from Hobart Bay to England. It takes in betrayal, vengeful arson, and lifeboat melodrama. The action passages in the narrative are handled with remarkable maturity. BL 1. *DNB*. *NCBEL*. Wol.

BROWN[E], Frances (1816–79). Born in Stranorlar, Northern Ireland, the daughter of the village postmaster, she was blinded in babyhood by small-pox. Unusually adaptive, she taught herself by listening to other children recite their lessons. Twenty-one years old and virtually self-educated, Browne left home to support herself by writing, living first in Edinburgh, then (after 1852) in London where she became known as 'the blind poetess of Donegal'. Helped by her sister, she turned out articles for various magazines (including, after 1841, the *Athenaeum**), and was a regular contributor to *Leisure Hour* for over twenty years. Browne's first novel was *The Ericksons* (1852). Her subsequent work was principally for the RTS*. Of the eighteen books she wrote, her story for children, *Granny's Wonderful Chair* (1857), was the most successful. Among her other novels are: *My Share Of The World, An Autobiography* (1861) and *The Hidden Sin* (1866). Browne was awarded a

Civil List pension in 1863 and died of an apoplectic seizure aged sixty-three at Richmond. BL 13. Boase. RM. *NCBEL*. Wol. RLF.

BRYDEN, Henry Anderson (1854–1937). Bryden was born in Surbiton, the son of a solicitor. After attending school at Cheltenham he was articled himself, but eventually took up writing as his profession. A talented sportsman, Bryden played rugby for England in 1874 and was a noted athlete. (In 1875 he held the English amateur mile record.) He moved to South Africa in the 1890s and his subsequent fiction draws on this colonial experience. Representative titles are: *Tales Of South Africa* (1896); *An Exiled Scot* (1899), the exile being a Jacobite, in eighteenth-century Capetown; *From Veldt Camp Fires* (1900). This last work, which deals with pioneer life in the Cape, was boosted by the Boer War. BL 3. *WW*. RLF.

BUCHAN, John (later Baron Tweedsmuir, 1875–1940). Buchan was born in Perth, the eldest son of a Free Church minister. The family moved to Fife in 1876 and Glasgow in 1888, where John went to grammar school. In 1892, he won a bursary to Glasgow University and three years later a scholarship to Brasenose College, Oxford. Buchan led a brilliant student career (1895–99). He took a first-class degree in Greats, read manuscripts for the publisher John Lane*, was elected President of the Union and contributed to the *Yellow Book*. While a student, Buchan also wrote fiction which chronologically and in its spirit is Victorian. *Scholar Gypsies* (1896) celebrates the scenery and people of the author's beloved Tweedside. *John Burnet Of Barns* (1898) is a Stevensonian* romance, set in the 1680s, portraying the struggles of the Covenanters. (The hero, initially hostile to the rebels' cause, is eventually won round to sympathy with it.) *A Lost Lady Of Old Years* (1899) is a novel of the '45. *The Half-Hearted* (1900) is a story of modern life, set in Scotland and India. It shows the latent heroism in a seeming dilettante, brought out by crisis. On graduation, Buchan read for the Bar as a prelude to a distinguished career in public life which culminated with his being appointed Governor-General of Canada in 1935 (as Baron Tweedsmuir). His famous spy* thriller, *The Thirty-Nine Steps* (1915), was written during one of his rare periods of relaxation from public affairs, convalescing from an illness. BL 32. *DNB*. RM. *NCBEL*. Wol.

BUCHANAN, Robert [Williams] (1841–1901). Best remembered as a poet, and most successful in his lifetime as a playwright, Buchanan was born at Caverswall in Staffordshire but educated at Glasgow High School and University. His father, also Robert Buchanan, was a Scottish tailor who later became a noted socialist journalist and disciple of Robert Owen. The family lived an unsettled life and in his youth Buchanan, the only surviving child, was steeped in politics. In 1859, his father having been ruined by newspaper speculation, young Robert went to London, to pursue a literary career and was taken on the staff of the *Athenaeum* by Hepworth Dixon*, who admired the young man's verse. Buchanan has been called, 'probably the most quarrelsome author of his day' and was aggressively reactionary and hostile to what he took to be 'decadence'. He soon earned notoriety (and a libel action) with his attack in the *Contemporary Review* on the Pre-Raphaelites and their 'Fleshly School of Poetry' (October, 1871). Buchanan made a lot of money from his writing (particularly his wordy plays) and from public readings of his poetry which he later lost by imprudent speculation. In 1874 he turned to fiction with the conscious intention of writing bestsellers ('with his left hand', as one of his biographers puts it). His first novel, *The Shadow Of The Sword* (1876), has as its hero a Breton conscientious objector in the Napoleonic Wars. It has a powerful final chapter, describing the tormented sleeping hours of the exiled emperor. His finest work is usually judged to be *God And The Man** (1881), a study in the futile psychology of hatred with a terrific action climax in the polar wastelands. *The Martyrdom Of Madeline* (1882) follows the fortunes of a resourceful heroine after she is betrayed in love by her French music master. *Foxglove Manor* (1884) has a ritualist clergyman who seduces and abandons a young girl, and goes on to various acts of Romish apostasy. *The Master Of The Mine* (1885) has a Cornish mining setting. *The Heir Of Linne* (1888) is a conventional inheritance melodrama with an 1840s Scottish setting. *Effie Hetherington* (1896) is a story of ill-assorted marriage and justified desertion with some similarity to Hardy's* *Jude The Obscure**. Some of Buchanan's poems (e.g. 'The Ballad Of Judas Iscariot') survive in modern anthologies of verse. He had no children (his wife whom he married in 1861 died prematurely of cancer in 1882) and was declared bankrupt in 1900, a year before dying miserably of a stroke. BL 26. *DNB*. RM. *NCBEL*. Wol. Sad. RLF.

BULLEN, Frank T[homas] (1857–1915). Bullen was born at Paddington, of London working-class parents and was probably illegitimate. His parents separated and deserted him as a baby. He was brought up by an aunt, and when she died 'was flung on to the street'. He left school very young to work as an errand boy in an oil shop and for a bootmaker. At the age of twelve, he went to sea as cabin boy in a ship commanded by an uncle. Fifteen years later (having risen to the position of chief mate), he went to work as a clerk at the London Meteorological Office. In later life, he wrote a number of sea yarns, such as *Idylls Of The Sea* (1899); *The Log Of A Sea Waif* (1899), 'the recollections of the first four years of my sea life'; *Deep Sea Plundering* (1901). A confessed 'Kipling* worshipper', Bullen was renowned as a public lecturer in later life. BL 26. *WW*. Wol. RLF.

BULLOCK, Shan F. (1865–1935). Bullock was born at Crom, Co. Fermanagh, the eldest of eleven children of a wealthy Protestant landowner. Showing no aptitude for the family business of farming, he was educated at King's College, London, and on graduation settled in the capital, working for a while as a clerk. He married in 1889, thereafter spending most of his life resident in Surrey. Bullock's subsequent novels are nevertheless set in Ireland, and are graphically detailed. He was particularly drawn to the borderland Fermanagh area, between the Protestant North and Catholic South of the country. Bullock's fiction lacks narrative coherence and comes across as rather wispy gatherings of Irish sketches rich in quiet comedy, pathos and dialect, which were classified as Hibernian kailyard*, equivalent to J. M. Barrie's* Scottish 'Thrums' idylls. His main titles are *The Awkward Squads* (1893); *By Thrasna River* (1895); *Ring O' Rushes* (1897); *The Barrys* (1899); *Irish Pastorals* (1901). His best novel is generally taken to be the very late *The Loughsiders* (1924). Bullock was a friend of C. K. Shorter, who shared his enthusiasm for things Celtic. In 1931, he put out an autobiography, *After Sixty Years*, dealing with his childhood in the 'autocracy' (as

he called it) of Anglo-Ireland. In 1913, he collaborated with Emily Lawless*
on the novel *The Race Of Castlebar*. BL 20. *WW*. Wol.

BULWER, Rosina [Doyle] ('Lady Lytton Bulwer', 'Lady Bulwer-Lytton',
née Wheeler, 1802–82). Born in Limerick, Rosina Doyle Wheeler was a
niece of Sir John Doyle (Governor of Guernsey). In her youth she was a
famous Irish beauty and witty, but poor. The young Rosina attracted the
attention of Edward Bulwer [-Lytton*], in his most Byronic phase. Against
his mother's wishes, they married in 1827. After a furious episode in Naples
in 1833 the couple returned to England, separating in 1836. The two children
of the marriage were forcibly taken from their mother in 1838. She fought
back with bitter lawsuits and public defamation of their father, culminating
in the public interruption of his election campaign at Hertford in 1858.
Bulwer-Lytton (as he now was) had her temporarily locked up on grounds
of insanity. As Leslie Stephen put it, 'Bulwer must be counted among the
eminent authors who have not made and not deserved success in married
life'. Rosina commemorated his failure as a husband with a number of novels,
most pungently *Cheveley, Or The Man Of Honour** (1839). A success (for
reasons other than its small literary merit), it put her in the rank of novelists
earning £500 a work. Over the years, she sank to a £100-a-novel hack. And
her husband, ever vindictive, succeeded in frightening the better class of
publisher from taking her work. Rosina Bulwer's novels include: *The Budget
Of The Bubble Family* (1840); *Behind The Scenes* (1854); *Very Successful*
(1856); *The World And His Wife, A Photographic Novel* (1858). BL 7. *DNB*.
NCBEL. Wol. Sad.

BUNBURY, Selina (1802–82). One of the fifteen children of a Methodist
clergyman in Co. Louth, Ireland, Selina Bunbury had a distant family
connection with Fanny Burney on whom the young woman seems to have
modelled herself. Her father's bankruptcy obliged the family to move to
Dublin in 1819 and around 1830 the Bunburys moved on to Liverpool. After
this date, Selina Bunbury kept house for her twin brother and subsidised her
family's finances by her writing. Following her brother's marriage in 1845 she
began to travel extensively. She was subsequently the author of numerous
travel books (on which her literary reputation largely rests) and some slight
romances written in an unattractively wooden style. Her fiction includes:
Tales Of My Country (1833); *The Star Of The Court, A Story Of Anne
Boleyn* (1844); *Coombe Abbey* (1844), a Guy Fawkes tale overshadowed
by Harrison Ainsworth's* bestselling romance about the Jacobite terrorist;
Evelyn (1849), a novel-cum-travel book, describing a trip from Stockholm
to Rome; *Our Own Story* (1856), 'the history of Magdalene and Basil St
Pierre'; *Florence Manvers* (1865). Bunbury also wrote evangelical fiction for
both the RTS* and SPCK*. BL 24. *NCBEL*. Wol. RLF.

BURGIN, G[eorge] B[rown] (1856–1944). Burgin was born in Croydon,
the son of a barrister. He was educated at public school and first took up
employment as private secretary to Baker Pasha (i.e. General Valentine
Baker, 1827–87). This entailed extensive travel in Asia Minor. After his
return to England in 1885 Burgin went into journalism. He wrote and
sub-edited for Jerome's* the *Idler**, the *Bookseller*, and eventually became
literary editor of the *Daily Express*. A versatile man of letters, he was

secretary of the Authors' Club and general editor of the 'New Vagabond' fiction series. His own novels include: *His Lordship And Others* (1894); *The Dance At The Four Corners* (1896); *Tuxter's Little Maid* (1895); *The Judge Of The Four Corners* (1896); *Gascoigne's Ghost* (1896); *Tomalyn's Quest* (1896) and *The Hermits Of Gray's Inn* (1899). The last is the story of a Masonic society of lawyers who make ingenious use of the newly invented phonograph. Burgin's tales were found 'wholesome and witty' by reviewers and many were serialised first in *Pearson's Magazine**. He wrote torrents of fiction in the twentieth century. BL 81. *WW*. Wol.

BURNETT, Frances Eliza (née Hodgson 1849–1924). Author of the best-selling children's tale, *Little Lord Fauntleroy**. Frances Hodgson was born in Manchester, the daughter of a prosperous furniture dealer. But her father, Edwin Hodgson, died in 1853 and the family circumstances were impoverished over the following ten years. In 1865, the surviving Hodgsons emigrated to Tennessee to live with an uncle. This too was an impecunious existence although the American South was more to the young girl's taste than the English North. (A vivid account of the author's youth is given in *The One I Knew Best Of All*, 1893.) From 1866, Hodgson supported herself by writing stories. In 1870 her mother died and two years later she married a childhood sweetheart, Dr Swan M. Burnett. Frances continued to write, to supplement the family income, despite the birth of a son in 1874. Burnett's first full-length novel (aimed at the adult reader), *That Lass O' Lowries** (1877) was set in coalmining Lancashire. It enjoyed great success, selling 30,000 copies straight off in the American market. She followed it with another work in the same vein dealing with industrial manufacturing in the North, *Haworth's* (1879). Burnett then turned to American settings and heroines with *Louisiana* (1880) and *A Fair Barbarian* (1881). In the last of these, Octavia Bassett of Nevada is transported to Stowbridge and the house of her English aunt. *Through One Administration* (1883) is probably the outstanding achievement of this phase of her career, an ambitious depiction of American political life. By this stage, the Burnetts had settled in Washington and although she did not naturalise herself until 1905 she was now a thoroughly Americanised writer. It was as a writer of children's stories that Burnett achieved her greatest success. *Little Lord Fauntleroy* (1886) and *The Secret Garden* (1911) are works which made her famous in her lifetime and have kept her a published author to the present day. But for all its popularity, *Fauntleroy* was too saccharine for some tastes. As Mrs Elizabeth Riddell* tartly noted, the story was a 'cross between a tract and a play. It appeals to mothers'. As a play, starring Elsie Leslie in the juvenile lead, *Little Lord Fauntleroy* made £20,000 for its author and her main income in the following years was from stage adaptations of her work. Despite prosperity, Burnett's personal life was increasingly unhappy. In 1890, her son Lionel died and her own health deteriorated into chronic invalidism. In 1898 the Burnetts divorced. Two years later she married her secretary, Stephen Townesend, who was ten years younger than her. The marriage lasted only two years. Thereafter, Burnett lived alternately in England and America dying at Long Island, NJ. BL 52. *DNB*. RM. *NCBEL*.

Burns (1832–71). Publisher. James Burns (1808–71) opened a bookshop at Manchester Square in 1832. By the 1840s (when he had moved to Portman

Square) he had an important list of books under his imprint including 'Burns's Fireside Library'. It comprised thirty-five titles, published at prices ranging from 6d. to 2s. 6d. and advertised itself as 'a series of cheap books for popular reading, suited for the fireside, the lending library, the steamboat or the railway carriage'. J. H. Newman* and his sister Harriet Mozley* published with Burns who was also a major publisher of children's books. Boase.

BURY, Lady [Charlotte Susan Maria] (née Campbell, 1775–1861). Belle, courtier, diarist and novelist. She was born the youngest daughter of the Duke of Argyll. At twenty-one, she married Colonel John Campbell, who died in 1809, leaving her with nine children. For nine years, she was lady in waiting to Queen Caroline and later (1838) published an indiscreet diary of her experiences in the royal household. In 1818, she married Edward Bury (d. 1832), Rector of Lichfield, and bore him two more children. She wrote lively silver fork* novels, which did well for her and Colburn*, her publisher. As Sadleir puts it, 'she was not a good novelist, but she contrived to introduce a vein of thoughtfulness even into the most conventional of her many silver fork fictions'. They include: *The Exclusives* (1830); *The Disinherited And The Ensnared* (1834); *The Devoted* (1836); *The Divorced* (1837); *Family Records* (1841); *The Manoeuvring Mother* (1842); *The Lady Of Fashion* (1856). BL 16. *DNB*. RM. *NCBEL*. Wol. Sad.

BUSS, Robert William (1804–75). Illustrator. Born into a family of engravers, Buss was apprenticed to his father. As a young man he worked for Charles Knight and helped illustrate the *Penny Cyclopaedia*. He was tried out by Dickens* for *Pickwick Papers** after the death of Robert Seymour, but his designs were so inept that Phiz* was recruited to replace him. Buss illustrated Frances Trollope's* *The Widow Barnaby** (1839) and various novels by Ainsworth* and Marryat*. But his work rarely rises above the competent and often even fails to reach that minimal level. *DNB*. Hou.

BUTLER, Samuel (1835–1902). Philosopher, Victorian rebel and author of two of the most remarkable quasi-novels of the period. Butler was born the eldest son of the Rector of Langar (later Canon of Lincoln) and a grandson of Dr Samuel Butler, Bishop of Lichfield. His high Victorian childhood and its patriarchal tyrannies are acidly recalled in *The Way Of All Flesh** (1903). Butler went to school at Shrewsbury, and formed there two of the great loves of his life: Italy (which he first visited in 1843) and the music of Handel. He graduated from Cambridge in 1858 with a degree in classics. It was assumed that like his forebears, Samuel would enter the church. He refused, and instead pursued his passions for music and drawing while working among the poor of London. To save the family reputation, he was set up with £4,000 as a sheep-farmer in New Zealand. In the five years (1859–64) that he was there, Butler was a resourceful emigrant and he returned having doubled his capital. (The interlude also furnished the narrative framework of *Erewhon**.) Pastoral leisure also enabled Butler to pursue his reading. Darwin was a particular interest, and in this period he seems to have worked out the heterodox philosophical views that he was later to expound in his writing. (Influencing, thereby, G. B. Shaw* among others.) His letters home to his father were published in 1863. Butler returned to London in 1864, rich enough to support himself independently. He took up bachelor rooms at Clifford's Inn, in Fleet Street, and remained there for the rest of his life. In his maturity Butler dedicated himself to painting, music and writing. In 1865, he published a typically provocative pamphlet, suggesting that Jesus had not died on the cross, but merely fainted. His Swiftian reflections on the hypocrisies and contradictions of Victorian England were published at his own expense as *Erewhon, Or Over The Range*, in 1872. (A sequel appeared in 1901.) He produced a stream of works with a rationalist tendency, and one superbly eccentric novel, *The Way Of All Flesh*. Begun in 1873, this work, which flays the uncongenial age in which Butler found himself, was not published until the year after his death. In 1877, Butler finally gave up his ambition to paint, and his last twenty years were passed as a higher journalist active in the furious end-of-century debate on evolution and ethics. Butler's versatile mind had a lasting impression on the thought of his time and he can be credited with dismantling much of the idealism and false consciousness by which the Victorian bourgeoisie sustained itself. BL 3. *DNB*. RM. *NCBEL*. Wol. Sad.

BUXTON, B[ertha] H[enry] ('Auntie Bee', née Leopold, 1844–81). Bertha Leopold, the daughter of a London merchant, was educated at Queen's College, London. As a young woman she travelled extensively in Holland, Germany and America. In 1860 she married Henry Buxton, a club manager and author. On being widowed in early life, she went on the stage. Buxton subsequently wrote fiction, some of it with a theatrical and international background, e.g. *Jennie Of The Prince's* (1876); *Won!* (1877); *Nell, On And Off The Stage* (1878), a work written as the author proclaimed to redeem the image of the stage as a career for 'right-minded women'. Buxton also wrote children's books as 'Auntie Bee'. BL 9. Boase. Wol.

By Proxy, James Payn, 1878, 2 vols, Chatto and Windus. (Serialised in *Belgravia**, May 1877–May 1878, with illustrations by Arthur Hopkins.) An unusual variant on the sensation* novelist's beloved 'dead but not dead' formula. The action opens in northern China. Two Englishmen, Captain Arthur Conway and Ralph Pennicuik, are found journeying together. Former college friends, they are very different in character. Conway is decent and something of a failure. Pennicuik is rich, selfish and ruthless. (Unknown to his comrade, he has even tried to seduce Mrs Conway, to that respectable lady's disgust.) Pennicuik recklessly steals from its holy shrine one of the 'tears of Buddha', a priceless jewel. He is caught and sentenced to the death of 10,000 cuts. To provide for his beloved daughter Nelly, Conway offers himself as a proxy victim. But Pennicuik, once returned to England, destroys Conway's will and does not hand over the £20,000 he promised to give Conway's family. Meanwhile, Pennicuik's son Raymond and Nelly Conway fall in love. But her mother dies and as a penniless orphan Pennicuik forbids his son to think of marrying her. The orphaned Nelly is looked after by an eccentric couple, the Wardlaws. Pennicuik is elected to Parliament but is haunted by mysterious rumours about his conduct in China. He takes to brandy and on his deathbed confesses all. Arthur Conway finally emerges, having escaped execution with the help of a friendly Chinese official. It is he who has been blighting Pennicuik's public career. Before he too dies,

Conway sees his daughter and Raymond happily married. The vivid Chinese settings are well handled and created something of a vogue in popular fiction. The work has always been Payn's most highly regarded.

BYRON, Henry James (1834–84). Playwright and actor-manager. Byron was born in Manchester, the son of a British diplomat. Educated in London, he went into medicine, the law and journalism before turning to the stage. He was manager of the Prince of Wales Theatre from 1865, and also wrote over a hundred burlesques and farces. His most successful venture was the play *Our Boys*, which ran from 1875 to 1879 at the Vaudeville Theatre, London. Byron wrote one novel, *Paid In Full* (1865) which was in a third edition by 1868. The work is a florid melodrama, featuring a peer who has 'ruined simple girls by the score'. The novel was thought by the *Athenaeum*** reviewer to 'give promise of better things in the future'. But Byron seems never to have produced those better things. BL 1. *DNB*.

C

CAFFYN, [Stephen] Mannington (1851–96). Iota's* husband. Caffyn was born at Salehurst, Sussex and qualified as a surgeon at Edinburgh in 1876. Three years later he married Kathleen Hunt, who later gained fame as the novelist Iota. The couple and their one child went to Australia in 1880, remaining there until 1892. Caffyn held various medical posts in the country, and contributed to journals as a miscellaneous writer. He also invented a process for preserving raw meat known as Liquor Carnis. A man of many parts, he wrote two popular novels just prior to his return to England: *Miss Milne And I* (1889), the story of a doctor and his woman mental patient; and *A Poppy's Tears* (1890), a study of opium addiction. BL 2. Boase. Wol.

CAINE, [Sir Thomas Henry] Hall (1853–1931). Hall Caine was born at Runcorn, Cheshire, the eldest son of a ship's smith and, more importantly, a Manxman by ancestry. Hall was his mother's name. She came from Cumberland, another regional influence on his later writing. Some formative years of his childhood were spent in the Isle of Man, a location with whose 'primitive, patriarchal life' he later aggressively identified himself. Hall Caine's family had been dispossessed (on account of the father's 'extravagant living') from their sixty-acre island smallholding, and he went to school in Liverpool, leaving at fourteen to study architecture. Ill health three years later led to a sojourn in the Isle of Man, where he taught for a year. His salary was only £40 but the experience renewed his sense of Manx identity. He then returned to Liverpool, to work in the building trade. He was meanwhile writing on architecture, and a lecture brought him to the notice of the poet and artist, D. G. Rossetti, in 1879. In 1881, Caine resolved to devote himself entirely to literature and went to live with Rossetti, whom he hero-worshipped, until the poet's death in 1882. This was also the year in which Hall Caine married his London-born wife, Mary. They were to have two children. He was subsequently employed as leader writer on the *Liverpool*

Mercury by John Lovell, an editor who took an interest in the young man's career. As London correspondent for the paper (on a salary of £150 a year) Caine attended what he later called the 'university' of the capital's streets. The *Mercury* subsequently serialised Caine's first novel, *The Shadow Of A Crime* (1885). Set during the Civil War in Cumberland, and fiercely anti-royalist, it has as its main character Ralph Ray, who undergoes the *peine forte et dure* rather than surrender his family's inheritance. The story was made the vehicle for 'a mass of Cumbrian folk-lore and folk-talk' and earned the author a welcome £100 from Lovell who read the manuscript in the train from Liverpool to London. Caine followed with *A Son Of Hagar* (1886), a romance of fraternal villainy set in modern Cumberland (his mother's native county). The novel features the supercharged melodrama that was to be Caine's stock in trade. One scene, for instance, has a young mother temporarily blinded who must either risk permanent loss of sight or never see the new-born child dying in her arms. At this point in his career, Caine resolved to give up journalism and settle in the Isle of Man and his writing thereafter is steeped in Manx themes, lore and local history (this was partly at Rossetti's earlier urging). In 1887, with *The Deemster**, he made himself a bestselling author (sarcastic contemporaries thereafter labelled Caine 'the Boomster'). *The Deemster* is set on Man in the eighteenth century. Its hero is a killer who is tried according to age-old custom by the Bishop (his father) and is condemned to live in desolate solitude. The description of his years-long misery and redemption owes much to Victor Hugo's *Les Misérables*. Although Chatto and Windus* only gave £150 for the entire copyright, Caine had £1,000 for the dramatic rights from Wilson Barrett*. And like many of the bestselling authors of the end of the century, subsidiary rights were subsequently to be the main element in his literary income. Caine's next major work, *The Bondman** (1890), is a 'new saga' set in the Isle of Man and Iceland during the Napoleonic Wars. The narrative brings in blood feud, murder and tremendous scenic descriptions. Again, Caine had a smash hit with the reading public and Gladstone himself wrote to congratulate the author. By the early 1890s, with his new publisher Heinemann* (who used modern advertising techniques to promote him) Caine had established the 6s. single-volume novel as a standard format, against the soon to be superseded three-decker. *The Scapegoat** (1891), describes Jewish life in Morocco (sympathetically), and features the author's favourite themes of guilt and atonement. In 1892, Hall Caine was commissioned to investigate the pogroms against the Jewish population in Poland. Now a public figure of some eminence, he helped negotiate international copyright protection for authors in 1895. From 1901 to 1908, Hall Caine was a Liberal member of the Manx Parliament, the House of Keys. Appropriately, his finest novel is *The Manxman** (1894), a work which by the end of the century had sold half a million copies in Britain. *The Christian** (1897) deals with the contradictions of life and religion in London, and marks Hall Caine's entry into a more tendentious phase of his writing career. (But still a prosperous phase: the work earned the author £6,000 for serial and dramatic rights alone.) This novel, however, marks the decline of the author's critical reputation with the more discriminating contemporary reviewers. In 1901, he brought out his most ambitious novel, *The Eternal City**. Set in Rome and covering seven decades, the highly congested plot follows the twin careers of the Tolstoyan socialist Rossi and the more spiritual Roma. (Narrative dualism of this kind was a favourite device in Caine's novels.) A prophetic section moves forward to 1950, foreseeing a republic, whose charter is the Lord's Prayer. As one reviewer put it: 'to enter Mr Caine's city is rather like plunging into a vast cauldron of primitive hotch-potch'. Nevertheless, *The Eternal City* was immensely popular and was probably the first million-selling novel in Britain. In the USA it had a strong influence on early film makers such as D. W. Griffith. *The Prodigal Son* (1904) like *The Bondman* is set in Iceland. During the First World War, Caine was a correspondent for the *New York Times* and wrote a stream of articles urging America to join the war. These patriotic efforts earned him a knighthood. (And lost him, as he reckoned, $150,000 in literary earnings.) Hall Caine died in Greeba Castle (which he had bought for £1,000) on the Isle of Man, universally respected and the wealthiest of Victorian novelists, leaving just under £250,000. This fortune is the more remarkable since he wrote relatively few major novels. But he benefited from the fact that the Isle of Man then (as now) was a tax haven. Caine was not much liked by his fellow Manxmen, who resented the tourism his fiction inspired and the steamy sexuality which he imputed to their in fact rather austere way of life. Nor did he gain much respect from literary critics of the twentieth century despite his constant reminders to posterity of how closely he resembled Shakespeare. The *Cambridge History Of English Literature* (1941) did not, for instance, rate Caine's 'numerous novelistic melodramas' as worthy of any discussion whatsoever. The author's Tolstoyan *Life Of Christ* (1938) which he began in 1893 was never completed, although evidently a million words of its text survive in typescript. BL 14. *DNB*. RM. *NCBEL*. Wol. Sad.

CAIRD, Mrs [Alice] Mona [Henryson-] ('G. Noel Hatton', née Alison, 1858–1932). One of the most aggressive of the new woman* novelists, her father was an inventor, John Alison. Part of her childhood was spent in Australia. This experience resurfaces in her first novel, *Lady Hetty* (1875), which she published anonymously at the age of seventeen. In 1877 Mona Alison married J. Alexander Henryson-Caird (d. 1921). Using the sexually neutral pen name, G. Noel Hatton, she published *Whom Nature Leadeth* in 1883. A modish melodrama, the narrative is set in the English hunting shires and on the Riviera. The work sank without trace as did its successor, *One That Wins* (1887), subtitled 'The Story Of A Holiday In Italy'. But she attracted some attention in 1889 with *The Wing Of Azrael* which has a heroine, Viola Sedley, who quite justifiably stabs her sadistic husband to death, Azrael being 'the Angel of Death'. Cursed by her dying mate ('May the gallows spare you for a more hideous fate!') Viola escapes justice by throwing herself over a cliff. But it was with the fiercely anti-marriage work, *The Daughters Of Danaus** (1894), that Caird eventually reached a wide readership. (The title refers to the mythological women eternally doomed for killing their husbands.) She followed up with a fierce treatise, *The Morality Of Marriage* (1897) and an odd fantasy set in modern and mythological Rome, *The Pathway Of The Gods* (1898). Like many late Victorian feminists, Caird was fanatically anti-vivisectionist, a theme which recurs in her fiction. An obituary in *The Times*, while adding nothing to the sparsely known facts of her life, noted: 'she was prominent and effective among the pioneer champions of the "woman's movement" but declined to join the militants.' *The Great Wave* (1931), her last published novel, is exalted and visionary, a full-blown expression of the mysticism latent in all Caird's writing. BL 6. *WW*. Wol.

CALDECOTT, Randolph (1846–86). Illustrator. Caldecott was born in Chester, the son of an accountant and himself began working life as a bank clerk in Shropshire. In 1872 he moved to London and over the next fifteen years established himself as one of the most admired of illustrators, particularly of children's books whose style he influenced (and continues to influence) strongly. His manner of illustration owes something to that of John Leech* whose affection for outdoor subjects he shares, but is generally less fussy and clean in its lines. Caldecott died prematurely of rheumatic fever in Florida. *DNB*. Hou.

CALDWELL, Mrs [Sara] Anne [Anna] Marsh (1791–1874). Born into the landed gentry (her father, James Caldwell, was a Deputy Lieutenant of Staffordshire, her mother an heiress), she married a banker, Arthur Marsh in 1817. Marsh was ruined seven years later by the notorious swindler Henry Fauntleroy. Encouraged by Harriet Martineau* (who introduced her to the publishers Saunders and Otley*), Marsh began publishing fiction in 1834, with *Two Old Men's Tales* ('The Deformed', 'The Admiral's Daughter'). Like Martineau's, her work is overpoweringly earnest. Nevertheless, it was to popular taste and a second series of tales, *Woods And Fields* (1836), was called for. Arthur Marsh died in 1849, leaving his wife with seven children to provide for. As a widow, Marsh wrote novels to support herself (which she did quite comfortably), beginning with *Lettice Arnold* (1850). In 1858, her brother died and she inherited her family estate, and changed her name to Marsh-Caldwell. As a novelist, she wrote at different times as Anne Caldwell, Mrs Marsh, and Mrs Marsh-Caldwell. The most appealing of her novels are the 'tales of country' such as *Heathside Farm* (1863) and the *Cranford*-like *Chronicles of Dartmoor* (1866), although, as contemporary critics pointed out, her narratives are often dull. Her most popular work of fiction was the early *Emilia Wyndham* (1846), whose heroine has to cope after her father is swindled out of his property by a villainous attorney, a plot which clearly reflects Arthur Marsh's earlier business misfortunes. The work is dedicated to Wordsworth, with whose moral teaching Marsh felt herself in sympathy. Her stilted romances evidently appealed to older Victorian readers and were energetically marketed by her publisher Henry Colburn*. Marsh-Caldwell also published a quantity of children's* fiction. BL 26. *DNB*. *NCBEL*. Wol.

Called Back, 'Hugh Conway' (i.e. F. J. Fargus), 1884, 1 vol, Arrowsmith. (First published in *Arrowsmith's Christmas Annual*, 1883). A hugely popular bestseller in the new (for the 1880s) 1s. paperback format of 'Arrowsmith's* Bristol Library'. *Called Back* has a startling opening situation. Gilbert Vaughan, a rich young man, has been blinded in his youth by lenticular cataracts. One midnight, walking in London, he blunders into a house where murder is under way. Gilbert senses there are three men, a woman and a body at the scene of the crime, but can identify none of them. He also hears a strange haunting tune played on the piano. The criminals drug him, and the police later will not credit his story. Two years after, an operation restores Gilbert's sight. He impulsively marries a beautiful half-Italian girl, called Pauline March who was also involved with the murder through her supposed brother, an Italian political conspirator working to overthrow the Russian government. But she cannot remember any of this, for as Gilbert discovers on their honeymoon in the Lake District, she is a total amnesiac and can recall nothing for more than a few minutes. By playing the tune Gilbert heard on the night of the murder, Pauline's memory of the terrible event in London is revived. Mystically, by touching his wife's hand, Gilbert too 'sees' the murder. Travelling to Siberia (by permission of Tsar Alexander no less), the hero finally unravels the mystery and discovers that the murder victim was in fact Pauline's real brother, Anthony. His assassins come to appropriately horrible ends. Pauline is restored to normality. Within three years, Conway's novel had sold over 350,000 copies and a dramatised version ran for a year, 1884–85.

Callista, John Henry [Cardinal] Newman, 1856, 1 vol, Burns and Lambert. Newman began writing his 'Sketch Of The Third Century' in 1848, and finished it in 1855. The story, written from a frankly 'Catholic point of view', is set in North Africa on the site of the modern Tunisia. Callista, a beautiful Greek sculptress, captivates Agellius, a Christian. He almost manages to convert her but falls ill with fever and is cared for by Cyprian, the fugitive Bishop (later canonised) of Carthage. The novel climaxes with a plague of locusts, and a slaughter of Christians. Cyprian and Agellius are captured by the mob, but escape. Callista converts wholly to Christianity, is confirmed, tortured on the rack and dies for her faith. Agellius takes a portion of her remains as a holy relic, survives to become a bishop, and is himself later martyred. The novel presumably evokes Newman's own feelings of persecution on leaving the Church of England for Rome in 1845.

CAMBRIDGE, Ada [Cross] (1844–1926). Born in a Norfolk village, Ada Cambridge began her writing career early. In 1865, she published a collection of hymns and a novel, *The Two Surplices* (1865). It was followed by another novel with a religious purpose, *The Vicar's Guest*, in 1869. Cambridge married the Rev. George Frederick Cross in 1870, and accompanied him five weeks later on his missionary work to Australia where the couple were to spend the next thirty-eight years, mainly in Melbourne. Their life is recalled in a late and mellow novel, *Materfamilias* (1898). Life abroad softened Cambridge's early evangelicalism while apparently giving her ample encouragement to continue writing. In Australia, she wrote poetry, autobiographical reminiscence and fiction with carefully documented local settings. The most interesting of her works is *Path And Goal* (1900) in which an Australian doctor, Adrian Black, travels to Ely in Cambridgeshire, and falls in love with three girls. He marries none of them, and is subsequently drowned at sea with a fourth lover. Other of Cambridge's novels are: *My Guardian* (1877), which is set in the Norfolk fen country; *In Two Years Time* (1879); *A Mere Chance* (1882); *A Marked Man* (1891); *The Three Miss Kings* (1891). The opening sentences of the last capture the essence of an Ada Cambridge novel: 'On the second of January, in the year 1880, three newly orphaned sisters, finding themselves left to their own devices, with an income of exactly £100 apiece, sat down to consult together as to the use they should make of their independence.' In 1908, following an unexpected legacy, Mrs Cross returned for the first time to England, 'an old woman'. The experience inspired a fine autobiographical reminiscence of her childhood, *The Retrospect* (1912). George Cross died in 1917. BL 24. *WW*. RM. Wol.

CAMERON, Mrs [Caroline Emily] Lovett (née Sharp, 1850?–1921). Emily Sharp was born in Walthamstow, London, into a comfortably-off family and educated in Paris. She married Henry Lovett Cameron in 1874. Three years later her first novel, *Juliet's Guardian* (1877), was serialised in *Belgravia** (as *Juliet*, 1876–77) to unusually good reviews. The story chronicles the barely legal love affair between Juliet Blair, a young girl of seventeen (subsequently a married woman), and her much older guardian, Colonel Fleming. The work is written in the abrupt, breathless style that was in vogue in the 1870s. Cameron capitalised on her success in the 1880s and 1890s, with a stream of similar love stories, aimed principally at women readers of yellowbacks*. They include: *Deceivers Ever* (1878), a story of the 'dust and ashes' left by exhausted passion; *Pure Gold* (1885); *In A Grass Country* (1885). The last is a story of love, hunting and seduction in the shires with an acknowledgement to the inspiration of G. Whyte-Melville*. A reviewer in 1885 wryly summarised the typical Lovett Cameron plot as: 'beautiful women and handsome men, all misunderstanding each other, tormenting and tempting each other, dying of broken hearts and blood vessels'. Her titles typically hint at sins her narratives dare not describe, as in: *This Wicked World* (1889); *A Sister's Sin* (1893); *A Bad Lot* (1895); *Devil's Apples* (1898). She stopped publishing fiction around 1899. According to *Who's Who*, she was 'devoted to dogs'. BL 45. *WW*. Wol.

CAMPBELL, Lady Colin [Gertrude Elizabeth] ('G. E. Brunefille', née Blood, 1861–1911). Born in Co. Clare, Ireland, Gertrude Blood was educated in Italy and France. Her marriage in 1881 with Lord Colin Campbell, a younger son of the Duke of Argyll, was ended by legal separation in 1886, on the grounds of his cruelty. In later life, she was the art critic of the *World*. Campbell's single published novel is *Darell Blake: A Study* (1889). A 'society novel', the work drew unashamedly on the publicity of the author's recent court case and has considerable naïve power. The hero is a journalist (a profession Campbell knew at first hand), but the main interest focuses on his long-suffering wife, Victoria. Darell rises in the world from provincial to London editor to radical MP. But he is led astray by the heartless beauty, Lady Alma Vereker. While dallying at Homberg with her, his virtuous wife Victoria dies in childbirth. Blake survives a shattered shell of a man. The novel was a hit, selling 5,000 copies in the course of a year under the imprint of the Hansom Cab Co. (named after Fergus Hume's* bestseller). As 'G. E. Brunefille' Campbell had earlier written a children's story, *Topo* (1878), illustrated by Kate Greenaway*. The heroine is a young 'pickle of a girl' who is forever getting into scrapes with her brother and sister. Campbell was evidently a sportswoman, and also published a study of freshwater fish called *The Book Of The Running Brook* (1886). Her estranged husband died in 1895. BL 2. *WW*.

CAMPBELL, Harriette (1817–41). Campbell was born in Stirling, Scotland. Unusually precocious, she finished her first novel, *The Only Daughter*, a domestic* tale, in 1837. It was published by Henry Colburn* two years later, well received and reprinted. *The Cardinal Virtues* followed in 1841. At this period of her life, Campbell's health broke down. *Katherine Randolph, Or Self Devotion* was written during her final illness, and was published in 1842, a year after her death, with an introduction by G. R. Gleig* who was evidently Campbell's patron. He testifies to her 'gentle spirit' and 'delicate hand'. The novel itself follows the careers of the heroine and her brother Julian from childhood in the Highlands to his eventual trial and acquittal on charges of murder. Harriette Campbell never married. The three works of fiction she completed suggest a promising if simple talent ruined by illness. BL 3. *DNB.*

CAMPBELL, James (i.e. James Campbell Reddie, d. 1878). Pornographer. Little is known of Campbell's life. According to H. S. Ashbee, a connoisseur of libertine books, he was a self-taught scholar, who 'viewed erotic literature from a philosophical point of view'. Campbell had a huge private collection of erotica, and was also a prolific author, providing the publisher William Dugdale* with numerous titles. His major work is the *The Amatory Experiences Of A Surgeon* ('Printed for the Nihilists, Moscow', 1881). Apart from its sexual narrative (in which the un-Hippocratic hero seduces a thirteen-year-old cripple girl), the work gives some insight into Victorian abortion practices. The British Library also contains the author's *Adventures Of A Schoolboy* (1866). Any record of his other pornographic fiction seems to have disappeared. Campbell lived in London until 1876, at which point he was nearly blind. He died in Crieff, Scotland. BL 2. Boase.

Can You Forgive Her?, Anthony Trollope, 1865, 2 vols, Chapman and Hall. (Serialised in monthly numbers, January 1864–August 1865, illustrated by Phiz* and E. Taylor.) The first of Trollope's Palliser* or parliamentary novels. The main heroine is Alice Vavasor whose suitors are her Byronic cousin, George Vavasor and John Grey, an honest but dull (as she thinks) country gentleman. Alice jilts Grey for George who turns out to be unworthy. His speculations go wrong, he is disinherited and when his attempt to establish himself in Parliament fails, he assaults his faithful sister Kate, blackmails Alice, tries to murder John Grey and finally skulks out of England, a disgraced man (revealing that he had a common mistress all the while). A parallel plot follows the affairs of Plantagenet Palliser, heir apparent to the Duke of Omnium, and Lady Glencora MacCluskie, heiress to a Scottish industrial fortune. Their arranged marriage is doubly threatened. First by childlessness. Secondly by Glencora's infatuation with Burgo Fitzgerald. Burgo drinks, gambles and is penniless. He arranges an elopement, which Plantagenet foils in a dramatic ballroom scene. On a comic level, Alice's aunt, Arabella Greenow, has her two suitors: one is a stolid Norfolk farmer, the other a raffish ex-military man. She chooses the latter, 'because he is better looking'. The narrative examines permutations of marriage for prudence and marriage for passion. At the end of the novel, the three heroines are happily married and Plantagenet has an heir for the duchy of Omnium. Trollope discharged the ailing Phiz as his illustrator during the course of the novel's serialisation.

CANNING, the Hon. A[lbert] S[tratford] G[eorge] (1832–1916). Canning was born in Ireland, the second son of the first Baron Garvagh. He spent most of his life in Rostrevor, Co. Down, where he was Deputy Lieutenant and a JP. Canning wrote voluminously, but without any distinction, on Irish history and politics about which he took a moderate line. He also turned out a number of Irish* historical* novels, including: *Kilsorrel Castle* (1863); *Baldearg O'Donnell* (1868), a tale of 1691; *Heir And No Heir* (1890). Critics found his writing feeble, and it is unlikely that without an inherited title, 4,500 acres and a fortune he could have lived by his pen. BL 5. *WW.* Wol.

CAPES, Bernard [Edward Joseph] (1850?–1918). Capes was a highly secretive man (his entry in *Who's Who* gives only publications and a current address). One can deduce that his main profession was journalism, and that since he edited the *Theatre* magazine in the late 1870s he was connected with the world of drama. In later life, Capes wrote novels in a precious, sub-Meredithean* mode, adding to the formula the romantic adventure episodes that Stanley Weyman* and R. L. Stevenson* had made fashionable. He also wrote competent detective* and ghost* stories for the magazines. In 1896 his mystery story, *The Mill Of Silence*, won second prize in the *Chicago Record*'s '$30,000 to Authors' competition. *The Lake Of Wine* (1898) is a brisk story of eighteenth-century skulduggery and a valuable ruby whose name gives the novel its odd title. *The Adventures Of The Comte De La Muette* (1898) is a lively autobiographical romance set in the Reign of Terror. *At A Winter's Fire* (1899) collects the author's ghost stories and is noteworthy for the much anthologised 'An Eddy On The Floor'. *Our Lady Of Darkness* (1899) has an adventure plot, again set at the period of the French Revolution. *Joan Brotherhood* (1900) tells the bleak history of a foundling girl who marries a parson, then goes on the London stage, encountering misery along the way. Capes evidently passed his later life in Winchester. BL 32. *WW. NCBEL.*

CAPES, J[ohn] M[oore] (1812–89). Capes was born at Stroud and had his education at Westminster School and Balliol College, Oxford. He took orders in 1840, and came under the influence of the Tractarians. Privately wealthy, he spent £4,000 on founding a new Anglican church at Eastover in 1843. Two years later, he converted to Catholicism. Shortly after, Capes went blind. In 1858, he returned to the Church of England, only to go over to Rome again in 1889, just before his death in Hammersmith. Capes published two three-volume novels: *The Mosaic Worker's Daughter* (1868) and *The Buckhurst Volunteers* (1869). The first tells the story of an English family in Rome and features adventures with banditti and Catholic intrigues. The other novel is a quieter study of English village life. Capes also wrote an opera, *The Druid*, which was performed in 1879. BL 2. Boase. *NCBEL.* Wol.

Captains Courageous, Rudyard Kipling, 1897, 1 vol, Macmillan. (Subtitled 'A Story Of The Grand Banks', the story was serialised in *Pearson's Magazine**, December 1896–April 1897, with illustrations by I. W. Taber and Fred T. Jane*.) Harvey Cheyne, the pampered son of an American multi-millionaire robber baron, falls overboard from an Atlantic liner in fog and is picked up by a fishing schooner aptly named *We're Here*. Harvey is made to work for a season on the Newfoundland cod banks and under the rough tutelage of skipper Disko Troop and the comradeship of young Dan Troop matures into manhood. The work has always been popular in the USA and various versions have been filmed.

The Cardinal's Snuff-Box, Henry Harland, 1900, 1 vol, John Lane. An intricate and Jamesian art novel, written in the second and more 'serious' phase of Harland's career. In Lombardy, Italy, the English novelist Peter Marchdale meets the 'double' of the heroine of his *A Man Of Words* ('Oh, what supernatural luck!'). Beatrice, the widowed Duchess of Santangiolo, subsequently embarks on a teasing relationship with Peter, affecting not to know he is the author of the work, written under the pseudonym Felix Wildmay. Finally, the couple are brought to the point of proposal by her cousin the Cardinal Udeschini, who leaves his snuff-box on Peter's copy of the novel. When he returns it, he meets Beatrice in the garden, and finally confesses his identity and his love. Lane* produced the novel as an extraordinarily handsome volume, in line with the improvements in book design in the 1890s.

CAREY, Rosa Nouchette (1840–1909). Carey was born in London, the eighth child and fourth daughter of a ship-broker. She went to school at the Ladies' Institute in St John's Wood, and retained from her girlhood strong High Church principles. As a child, Carey had entertained her seven siblings with improvised tales. This led to her first published novel, *Nellie's Memories* (1868), published in three volumes by William Tinsley*. Although reviewers sneered at this babblingly autobiographical chronicle of an elder sister ('a weak girl of one-and-twenty') heroically replacing her dead mother (and dedicated to the author's own dead mother), it sold over 50,000 copies and by 1910 was still in print as an improving schoolbook for juveniles. (Macmillan* bought the copyright in 1898 when it was in its twelfth edition; they promptly brought out seven more editions in the next decade). Carey followed up with *Wee Wifie* (1869) and some forty other domestic* melodramas, establishing herself as a solidly prosperous author of what reviewers liked to call 'wholesome' and 'harmless' tales. Carey's fictional themes revolve around the condition and anxieties of woman in her roles of mother, daughter, sister. She specialised in characters 'without a single redeeming vice', as one sarcastic commentator put it. Carey herself remained a lifelong spinster, living most of her adult years quietly in Hampstead. Her best-received novel was *Not Like Other Girls* (1884) in which three genteel daughters repair their lost fortune by dressmaking. The Challoners are unlike other girls in never flirting or indulging any feminine weaknesses. *Esther* (1887) records a ruined and widowed mother's noble struggles aided by her gallant eldest daughter. *Only The Governess* (1888) and *Lover Or Friend?* (1890) are entirely summed up in their banal titles. *Life's Trivial Round* (1900) is set in a country house, whose widowed head remarries. Like many of Carey's later works, the novel is aimed directly at schoolgirl readers. *Rue With A Difference* (1900) is a story of love in a cathedral town, 'Wycombe'; the novel has an engaging heroine, Pansy, whose life is complicated by a stepmother. Carey was a close friend of Mrs Henry Wood* and her fiction shows the clear influence of Charlotte Yonge*. As the *DNB* puts it, 'she held orthodox and conservative views of life' and many of her works came out under the tendentious auspices of the RTS*. BL 44. *DNB*. Wol.

The Carissima, 'Lucas Malet' (i.e. Mary St Leger Harrison), 1896, 1 vol, Methuen. (Subtitled 'A Modern Grotesque' and originally entitled 'The

Power Of The Dog'.) The villainous heroine of the title is Charlotte Perry, wife-to-be of Constantine Leversedge, a rich young Englishman from colonial South Africa. Leversedge is obsessed by the memory of a dog he once killed in the Veldt and has nightly hallucinations of the beast and its vile scent. After their wedding and during a leisurely European sojourn, Charlotte claims herself to have seen the dog. This is a cold-blooded ruse which when he finds out drives Leversedge to suicide by drowning, on which the Carissima inherits his fortune and blithely goes on to marry a brilliant artist. The novel has good dialogue which critics compared favourably with that of Henry James. The story is also told in a Jamesian circuitous fashion, beginning: 'Antony Hammond told me this story one wet afternoon sitting in the smoking-room of a certain country house.'

CARLETON, William (1794–1869). Carleton was born, the youngest of fourteen children of a Catholic tenant farmer, at Prillisk, Co. Tyrone, Northern Ireland. Steeped from childhood in folklore (his parents were Irish speakers), the Bible (which his father knew by heart) and in national song (his mother was a noted singer), Carleton had his early education at a hedge school. He intended to enter the priesthood but had his faith in the Church shaken by an ominous dream at the age of nineteen, an experience recalled in his *The Lough Derg Pilgrim* (1839). Carleton subsequently converted to Protestantism, and supported himself in Dublin (where he moved in 1820) as the clerk of a Sunday School Society, writing and teaching on the side. His condition in life was at this period very precarious, and he was jailed for debt. Carleton's first full-length publication, *Traits And Stories Of The Irish Peasantry* (first series 1830; second series 1833) made his name, and remains an enduring achievement. With sketches such as 'Phil Purcel The Pig Driver', Carleton popularised the stereotype Paddy. He was active in the booming Dublin magazine world of the 1830s and early 1840s, and devised (or wrote up) a large number of ethnic stories, typically drawn from the south Tyrone locality. He also wrote a quantity of fiction, inferior in literary quality to that of Samuel Lover* and Charles Lever*. But unlike them he catered less obviously for the mainland English public. Carleton's first full-length novel, *Jane Sinclair* (1836), was a love story, and a failure. It was followed by the more substantial *Fardorougha, The Miser* (1839), a grim study of avarice and Catholic family life. Critics consider it the author's finest achievement. *Valentine M'Clutchy, The Irish Agent* (1845), is a social problem* novel, written against absentee Protestant landlordship. Subtitled 'The Chronicles Of Castle Cumber, Together With The Pious Aspirations, Permissions, Vouchsafements And Other Sanctified Privileges Of Solomon M'Slime, A Religious Attorney' the work uses biting sarcasm in the Nationalist cause. Phiz's* illustrations are among the best he did. *Art Maguire* (1845) is a straightforward temperance story. *The Black Prophet, A Tale Of The Irish Famine* (1847) is possibly the most topical novel of the century and again shows Carleton's ability to interweave the chronicles of several families. The narrative also contains unbearable pictures of Irish suffering. (See Chapter 17: 'National Calamity'.) *The Emigrants Of Ahadarra* (1848) similarly describes the ravages of Irish depopulation in the wake of the famine. In the early 1850s (which saw a wholesale collapse of Dublin literary culture) Carleton made some efforts to move his base to London, and toyed with the idea of emigrating to Canada, where three of his daughters had gone. *Willy Reilly* (1855) is a story of crossed Catholic and Protestant love, more romantic and ballad-like than other of Carleton's later novels, which are generally angry and protesting in tone. The story ends happily after much harrowing ordeal with Willy safely united with his Colleen Bawn on the Continent. The author's last years were dogged by poverty and drunkenness. As one commentator puts it: 'he succeeded in offending everybody during the course of his life'. Carleton figures as a precursor of the Celtic revival. W. B. Yeats salutes him as: 'the great novelist of Ireland'. BL 16. *DNB*. RM. *NCBEL*. Wol. Sad. RLF.

Carmilla, J. S. Le Fanu, 1872, 3 vols, Bentley. (The story was first serialised in the magazine *Dark Blue** December 1871–March 1872 and published with other Le Fanu stories under the collective title *In A Glass Darkly*, supposedly all from the casebook of Dr Hesselius, a German practitioner of 'metaphysical medicine'.) *Carmilla* is generally considered the finest vampire story of the century. The narrative is set in Styria, where Laura (who tells most of the story) is befriended by the captivating Carmilla. When Laura's health fails, an old family friend diagnoses vampirism and identifies Laura's beautiful friend as the culprit. She is revealed to be Mircalla, Countess Karnstein, 'dead' for a century and a half. Exorcism by a stake through the heart by Baron Vordenburg forms the story's climax. *Carmilla*, which is as much a psychological study (with explicit lesbian overtones) as it is a gothic* tale, was published together with three other famous ghost* stories by Sheridan Le Fanu: *Green Tea**; *The Familiar*; *Mr Justice Harbottle*.

CARROLL, Lewis (i.e. Charles Lutwidge Dodgson, 1832–98). Mathematician, pioneer photographer and author of the most famous of Victorian juvenile stories. Dodgson was born at Daresbury, the eldest son among the eleven children of the Rev. Charles Dodgson. Until he was twelve years old, young Charles was educated at home by his father, and showed precocious brilliance. A shy child, he was afflicted by a severe stammer. His subsequent school and university career (Rugby, which he did not much like and Christ Church, Oxford, which he did) marked him as gifted and he remained at his college after graduation in 1854 as a lecturer in mathematics. Preparation for holy orders was a formal requirement and Dodgson was ordained deacon in 1861, although he went no further with a religious career. Restrictions on dons were relaxed in the 1850s and 1860s and Dodgson contributed to light journals, such as the *Comic Times* and Edmund Yates's* *Train*. It was in the second of these (and at the suggestion of Yates) that he initially used the pen name 'Lewis Carroll', in 1856. Dodgson was fond of children, especially little girls. In 1862, an impromptu tale for the benefit of Dean Liddell's daughters (one of whom was called Alice) resulted in *Alice's Adventures In Wonderland** (1865). The sequel, *Through The Looking Glass** (1871) shows more of Dodgson the mathematician. The *Alice* books satisfy both child and adult readers and are among the cleverest productions in fiction of the period, anticipating in many aspects modernist works of a century later. Dodgson's other works of literature comprise the nonsense poem, *The Hunting Of The Snark* (1876) and the fairy story *Sylvie And*

Bruno (1889), a work which reflects the author's growing interest in psychical phenomena. A confirmed and somewhat eccentric bachelor, resident at Christ Church from 1868 until his death, Dodgson wrote treatises on mathematics (although in 1881, he was sufficiently wealthy from his stories to resign his lectureship). A man of lively intellectual interests, he acquired his first camera in 1856 and went on to become a pioneer of British photographic portraiture. The last of his books to appear in his lifetime was *Symbolic Logic* (1896). Dodgson moved in good society and literary circles but made only one trip out of England in his life, to Russia in 1867. BL 3. *DNB*. RM. *NCBEL*. Wol.

CARTWRIGHT, the Rt Hon. [Sir] Fairfax L[eighton] (1857–1928). Born into a wealthy county family, Cartwright pursued a distinguished career in the Foreign Office after leaving university. He was ambassador to Austria, 1908–13, and was knighted in 1908. An amateur author of verse and drama under the masked name, 'F. L. Cartwright', he also published a three-volume novel, *Olga Zanelli* (1890), satirically depicting Berlin high society and low life of the period. The work was not admired by the critics. BL 1. *WW*. Wol.

Cashel Byron's Profession, George Bernard Shaw, 1886, 1 vol, The Modern Press. (Serialised in *To-Day*, April 1885–March 1886.) The fourth of Shaw's novels, written in the unsuccessful early phase of his literary career. The son of an actress, Cashel Byron goes to school at Moncrief House, where he proves to be the best fighter among the boys there. When he finds his mother intends to keep him there, he runs away to Australia, where he goes into training with Ned Skene, former boxing champion of England. Thereafter, Cashel himself becomes a professional pugilist. Preparing for a fight, he meets Lydia Carew in the grounds of Wiltstoken Castle. The young heiress is immediately entranced by the godlike athlete but does not apprehend what he does for a living. When she discovers he is a prizefighter, she asks him to take up some nobler profession, which he will not. By accident Lydia attends Cashel's bout with 'William Paradise' and is disgusted by the violence. But she gives him refuge when he flees the police (boxing being unlawful). Improbably, Cashel discovers he is heir to a fortune, and is finally free to marry Lydia. In respectable later life he becomes an MP (Conservative). The boxing scenes are lively and the idea of the novel more interesting than its execution. Shaw later wrote: 'I never think of *Cashel Byron's Profession* without a shudder at the narrowness of my escape from becoming a successful novelist.'

Cassell and Co. (1850–). Publishers. The firm was founded by John Cassell (1817–65). The son of a Manchester publican, Cassell originally went to work as a carpenter. In his early youth he was converted to teetotalism, and evangelised on the subject. Cassell moved to London in 1836 and by 1845, he was the proprietor of a grocer's shop. In the early 1850s, he began publishing books from the Belle Sauvage, Ludgate Hill. From the first, he specialised in works of popular instruction often in cheap part instalments. Having weathered a financial crisis in 1855 the firm expanded steadily. In the 1860s, Cassell's moved into the publication of fiction, largely via the magazines which came out under their imprint. The *Quiver** (begun in 1861) was the best known, and gave Mrs Henry Wood* her start in authorship. After John Cassell's death, the business grew dramatically with the growing literacy of the English working class. By 1888, it had seven large circulation journals, and 1,200 staff. Notable among the firm's many publications was *Cassell's Magazine* begun in 1867. Aiming at a 'family readership', the heavily illustrated magazine published name novelists such as R. L. Stevenson*, A. Quiller Couch*, Rider Haggard*, Charles Reade*, Wilkie Collins*, and J. M. Barrie*. After 1874 the journal was retitled *Cassell's Family Magazine* and its featured novelists sank to the second rank (authors such as Mrs G. Linnaeus Banks*, J. Berwick Harwood and Theo Gift). By the late 1890s, the journal had been increasingly influenced by the *Tit-Bits* genre of miscellaneous journalism, and the new pictorial techniques pioneered in Newnes's *Strand Magazine*. The magazine survived into the twentieth century. Cassell and Co. prospered as a major British publisher until the mid 1970s. (JC)*DNB*.

CASTLE, Egerton (1858–1920). Castle was born in London. His namesake grandfather was a well-known philanthropist and founded the *Liverpool Mercury*, a paper in which Castle inherited an interest. He had his education at the universities of Paris, Cambridge and Glasgow. (His mastery of French subsequently enabled him to translate the novels of R. L. Stevenson* into that language.) After a brief try at the law in London, Castle enrolled at the military academy Sandhurst. He went on to serve in the Royal Engineers, specialising in submarine mining, and in later life was on the staff of the *Saturday Review** (1885–94). He wrote plays, some authoritative books on fencing and a few novels, among which were *Consequences* (1891) and *Young April* (1899). In the second of these, the hero, Edward Warrender, unexpectedly wakes up to discover himself to be the Duke of Rochester and devotes himself to a month's glorious hedonism. The end of the narrative finds him sadly crumbling a dried flower and contemplating his love letters: 'Life had given the man no more than this – an April month, a memory of folly and frolic, of joy and of the bitterness which paid for it, a kiss from an idealized woman under a starlit sky – and these relics.' *Marshfield The Observer* (1900) collects his short stories through the person of a choric narrator. With his Irish wife Agnes (née Sweetman) Castle, (sister to Mrs Francis Blundell*) he wrote a large quantity of fiction, much of it stylish and heavily mannered eighteenth-century historical* romance. The Castles' joint productions include: *The Pride Of Jennico* (1898), in which an English aristocrat, Captain Basil Jennico, inherits a princedom in 'Moravia' ('an odd turn of fortune's wheel') and *The Bath Comedy* (1900) which reconstructs the watering place in its Beau Nash era. The work was popular enough to warrant a sequel, *Incomparable Bellairs* (1904). Castle was one of the literary élite who belonged to the Athenaeum Club and until 1901 was on the managing committee of the Society of Authors*. He was also a Fellow of the Society of Antiquaries. Agnes Castle survived her husband by two years. (EC) BL 4. (EC and AC) BL 39. *WW*. Wol.

The Castle Of Ehrenstein, G. P. R. James, 1847, 3 vols, Smith, Elder. A gothic* romance. Ehrenstein castle is haunted by strange inhabitants, 'earthly and unearthly', ghastly voices and ominous happenings. Ferdinand of Altenburg, the young hero, loves Adelaide, but the match is opposed by her father, the Count of Ehrenstein, who has usurped his brother's title while the latter is away fighting in the Crusades. After marrying secretly with the aid of a friendly hermit, Father George, the couple are saved by the reappearance of the legitimate Count who has disguised himself as the court jester. It was he who arranged the supernatural phenomena, by which he intended to prick his brother's conscience. In the mid-1840s, James was producing up to three novels like this a year.

Castle Richmond, Anthony Trollope, 1860, 3 vols, Chapman and Hall. This novel, which is one of Trollope's least popular, was put off for the writing of *Framley Parsonage**, traditionally one of the author's most popular works. *Castle Richmond* is a study of Irish social decay, set in the disastrous 1840s and Trollope apparently considered calling it: 'A Tale Of The Famine Year'. The plot centres on the affairs of two genteel families: the Fitzgeralds of Castle Richmond and the Desmonds of Desmond Court. Sir Thomas Fitzgerald is blackmailed by a (supposed) former husband of his wife. If the earlier marriage is exposed, the Richmond property will go to a young relative, Owen Fitzgerald. Owen is in love with Clara Desmond, but is himself passionately loved by Clara's mother, the Dowager Countess. These love, property and crime complications are finally resolved, although Sir Thomas dies of strain in the meanwhile. In a rueful prelude, Trollope notes that: 'Irish novels were once popular enough. But there is a fashion in novels as there is in colours and petticoats; and now I fear they are drugs in the market.'

Catharine Furze, 'Mark Rutherford' (i.e. William Hale White), 1893, 2 vols, Fisher Unwin. Set in 'Eastthorpe' in the English Midlands of the 1840s, the heroine Catharine is an ironmonger's daughter whose family has risen from its nonconformist origins. A philanthropist, Catharine does her best to help her father's workers (notably Mike Catchpole, who has been blinded in the factory and his son Tom who loves her). The narrative covers Catharine's schooldays at the Misses Ponsonby's 'finishing' establishment, where she falls in love with the married preacher, Mr Cardew. Their unconsummated passion purifies them, and they part without a word of illicit love having passed. On her deathbed he thanks Catharine for 'saving' him. The novel, like others by Rutherford, is effective in its reconstruction of provincial, nonconformist society.

Catherine, Ikey Solomons, Esq., Jr (i.e. W. M. Thackeray), 1869, 1 vol, Smith Elder. (Serialised in *Fraser's Magazine**, May 1839–February 1840, with illustrations by Thackeray.) A 'cathartic' written by Thackeray against the Newgate* school of crime fiction. The story is set in the early eighteenth century. Catherine Hall lives with her martinet aunt, landlady of the Bugle Inn. Count von Galgenstein and the worldly Corporal Brock stay at the inn on one of their recruiting expeditions. Catherine leaves as Galgenstein's mistress. When she later finds that he intends to discard her, she unsuccessfully tries to poison him. The story then jumps forward several years. Catherine has married her former village lover, John Hayes, a weak-spirited fellow now a modestly prosperous London moneylender. Catherine's illegitimate son by Galgenstein, Tom Billings, has grown up a lout and Brock, now known as 'Doctor Wood', lodges with the Hayes family.

Galgenstein returns to London, as the Bavarian envoy. Catherine, who still loves and hopes to be reunited with her former lover, kills Hayes. She is executed, and von Galgenstein goes mad after seeing the murdered man's head in St Margaret's churchyard. Thackeray intended to make the work wholly disgusting, but found he could not help liking his villainess.

CATTERMOLE, George (1800–68). Illustrator. Cattermole was born in Norfolk and began working life as an architectural draughtsman. As a book illustrator, he was first drawn to historical subjects and did some illustrations of Scott's novels which brought him to public notice. Cattermole subsequently illustrated Dickens's* *Barnaby Rudge**, *The Old Curiosity Shop** and *Master Humphrey's Clock**. Often hard to please, the novelist thought better of Cattermole's work than that of other illustrators who collaborated with him. The artist refused a knighthood in later life, and devoted himself to painting in oils without ever achieving the fame he desired in this line. His woodcuts for Dickens are more naturalistic than Phiz's* or George Cruikshank's* engravings. That of Barnaby Rudge asleep with his raven Grip is particularly effective. *DNB*. Hou.

The Caxtons, A Family Picture, E. G. E. L. Bulwer-Lytton, 1849, 3 vols, Blackwoods. (Serialised anonymously in *Blackwood's Magazine**, April 1848–October 1849.) The work's domestic* milieu and and easy-going narrative manner contrast with the plotted melodramas of high life and low crime for which Bulwer-Lytton had hitherto been renowned. *The Caxtons*'s chatty narrator hero Pisistratus returns to conduct *My Novel** (1853), and the Shandyan mode of narration was influential on both Thackeray* and Trollope*. In content, *The Caxtons* is a small beer chronicle. For the first half of its narrative, interest centres on family portraits: the father forever preoccupied with his *magnum opus* (a history of human error); the military uncle Captain Roland de Caxton, the veteran of Waterloo, whose hobby-horse is family honour; the speculator uncle Jack whose 'great anti-booksellers publishing company' nearly ruins his relatives. After leaving school, Pisistratus becomes secretary to a statesman, Mr Trevanion, before going on to Cambridge. Trevanion's wife, it emerges, was loved by Pisistratus's father and uncle Roland when young. Pisistratus himself falls in love with Trevanion's daughter, Fanny. Meanwhile, a Byronic stranger whom Pisistratus has befriended attempts to elope with her. The stranger turns out to be Roland's lost son Vivian (or Herbert) by a Spanish mother. The family misfortunes make university impossible, so Pisistratus and Vivian emigrate to Australia. They return after five years, enriched by sheep farming. Vivian goes off to fight and die for his country in India. Pisistratus marries not Fanny but Blanche, Roland's daughter, completing the family pattern of the work. *The Caxtons*, with its domestic tone, marks a turning-point in Bulwer-Lytton's career, and in Victorian fiction generally. It was immensely popular throughout the period.

Cecil, Mrs [Catherine Grace Frances] Gore, 1841, 3 vols, Bentley. (Published anonymously, the identity of the work's author was kept secret until 1845.) *Cecil* records the career from 1800 to 1832 of a figure whom we first meet as an 'arch-coxcomb', then as a regency dandy, a Waterloo warrior and finally as a Byronist. Cecil is introduced as an illegitimate, unloved younger son. He turns to coxcombry as an assertion of independence, is expelled from Oxford, throws himself into London society and embarks on numerous affairs. Gore gives a brilliant *tour* of the world of clubs, balls and slangy aristocratic conversation. Volume two finds the hero in Portugal, in the diplomatic corps. His love, Emily, dies of a broken heart, brought on by malicious London scandal. Cecil himself falls dangerously ill. Recovered, he is cured of dandyism, and serves in the Peninsular campaign. By 1814, he is a colonel, and fights at Waterloo. After the war, he takes to writing, and hob-nobs with Byron. The third volume finishes with the death of Byron, and Cecil restored to his family fortune and cured of his waywardness. Gore wanted a 'hit' with this novel, and succeeded. It remains the best of the silver fork* novels.

Cerise, George John Whyte-Melville, 1866, 3 vols, Chapman and Hall. One of the author's vigorous historical* romances. The narrative is set at the end of the reign of Louis XIV and during the regency of Orleans. The hero, George Hamilton, is trained as a page under the Sun King and grows up to be a captain in the Grey Musketeers. But he makes an enemy of the lecherous Regent when the latter insults the Marquise de Montmirail, the mother of George's childhood sweetheart Cerise. He flies to England and the Montmirails take refuge at their estate in the West Indies. The lovers are reunited there, and undergo various adventures, including a slave uprising. Married, they return to England where he assumes his family title. The last section is taken up with Jacobite intrigues and plots, which Sir George and his wife barely survive.

CHALLICE, Mrs Annie Emma (née Armstrong, 1821–75). Little is known of her life. Born in London, she married a West End doctor and active Liberal politician, John Challice (1815–63). Books by her on France suggest that the Challices spent time in that country. She wrote history, children's stories and some fiction for adults, namely: *The Sister Of Charity, Or From Bermondsey To Belgravia* (1857); *The Wife's Temptation, A Tale Of Belgravia* (1859). The first is a tale inspired by the heroic nurse, Florence Nightingale. The second is a mystery of marriage in high life which, as one reviewer tartly put it, 'might just as appropriately have been called a tale of Bedlam'. According to one account Annie Challice was remarkable for 'wit and graceful manners'. Another records that she died at a young age from cancer of the liver. BL 2. *DNB*. Wol.

Chambers's Journal (1832–1956). The journal began as *Chambers's Edinburgh Journal* in 1832, a weekly unillustrated paper selling at a penny-halfpenny. This format was retained until 1897, although the title was changed in 1854 to *Chambers's Journal of Popular Literature, Science and Arts*. The founders were the Scottish publishers and popular educators Robert (1802–71) and William Chambers (1800–83). Although the paper was mainly designed for the self-improving artisan, it featured from the first 'tales' and occasional serialised stories. In 1857, for instance, the journal carried Captain Mayne Reid's* *War Trail* in instalments. When James Payn* became editor in 1858 (in succession to Leitch Ritchie*), his *Lost Sir Massingberd*raised weekly circulation by some 20,000 copies. By the 1890s, the paper (still much the same in its drab appearance as it had been fifty years before) was serialising such major novelists as Grant Allen* and Walter Besant*. *Chambers's Journal* was the direct inspiration for Dickens's* *Household Words* and *All The Year Round*. *BLM.*

CHAMIER, Captain [Frederick] RN (1796–1870). Chamier was one of the novel-writing sea captains who enjoyed a vogue in the 1830s and early 1840s. He was born in India, the son of a senior administrator in the colony. Chamier's mother was an admiral's daughter and fostered his interest in the sea. At the age of thirteen he entered the Royal Navy and took part in the ill-fated Walcheren expedition. He made lieutenant in 1815, commander in 1826 and was paid off and retired in 1833. In 1832 he married Elizabeth, a granddaughter of Sir John Soane. Like others of the service, Chamier eked out his half pay writing fiction for Bentley*, who with Colburn* specialised in the nautical* novel. Chamier began his writing career with *The Life Of A Sailor* (1832) and the similarly naval *The Unfortunate Man* (1835). His works (especially those before 1840) are spirited sub-Marryat* yarns which take as their motto: 'A sailor's life's the life for me, he takes his duty merrily' and maintain a forced jollity of tone in their (generally) autobiographical narratives. But his continuation of James's *Naval History* (1837) has lasted better than his novels, which include: *Ben Brace* (1836), a narrative which climaxes with the pathetically rendered death of Nelson; *The Arethusa* (1837); *The Spitfire* (1840); *Tom Bowling* (1841), a novelisation of the ballad hero's life. Chamier's tales stress the morally uplifting effects of hardship at sea. BL 12. *DNB.* RM. *NCBEL.* Wol. Sad.

Chandos, Ouida (i.e. Marie Louise de la Ramée), 1866, 3 vols, Chapman and Hall. One of Ouida's hyper-romantic melodramas. Ernest Chandos is a young, gilded aristocrat devoted entirely to hedonistic pleasure, but withal the soul of honour and chivalry. Although he does not know it, his trusted agent, John Trevenna, is a bastard half-brother who has dedicated his life to bringing the envied Chandos down. On the eve of the hero's wedding to 'The Queen of Lilies' (a lady who promptly deserts him), Trevenna achieves the hero's total ruin. Chandos throws himself into dissipation on the Continent and is saved from death by a musician whom he earlier patronised, Guido Lulli. His estate, Clarencieux, has meanwhile been bought at auction by a noble friend, the Duc d'Orvâle. When the Duke is assassinated in Venice, Chandos reinherits. The Jewish moneylender whom Trevenna used to ruin Chandos confesses on his deathbed. The half-brothers confront each other in the House of Commons (where Trevenna is now a rising politician) and Chandos finally crushes his foe by forgiving him. Ouida's schoolgirlish adoration of *noblesse* constantly verges on the embarrassing. But the novel is written with verve.

The Channings, Mrs Henry Wood, 1862, 3 vols, Bentley. One of Wood's bestsellers. The novel is in the style of Charlotte Yonge's* family sagas and was first serialised in the *Quiver*. The Channings and the Yorkes live in the vicinity of Helstonleigh Cathedral (Wood's rival to Trollope's* Barsetshire*, but based on her native Worcester). The action opens with Mr Channing learning that the decision of the Lord Chancellor has gone against him in an inheritance case. A difficult year ensues for the family. The principal trial concerns a £20 note which goes missing from the solicitor's office where young Arthur Channing is articled. Arthur believes that his feckless brother, Hamish (who works in Mr Channing's insurance firm), has stolen the money and does not contradict sufficiently forcibly the accusation which the detective Butterby makes. But Hamish is not the culprit. On his part, Arthur is acquitted when his employer Mr Galloway declines to press charges. Charley, the youngest and most nervous of the Channings, is terrified in a graveyard by malicious school-fellows, and is thought drowned. At the end of the novel, Roland Yorke emigrates to Africa, leaving a letter confessing to the £20 theft and Charley returns, having been rescued by a passing barge. The novel ends with a marriage between William Yorke (a newly ordained clergyman) and Constance Channing. The family finally conclude that their year's tribulation since the loss of the lawsuit has actually strengthened and enriched them spiritually. *Roland Yorke* (1869) is the novel's sequel.

CHANTER, Charlotte (née Kingsley, 1828–82). One of a writing family, a younger sister of Henry and Charles Kingsley*. Her father was the Rev. C. Kingsley and she was brought up in Devon, a region for which (like Charles Kingsley) she retained a lifelong fondness and about which she later wrote. Charlotte Kingsley moved to London in 1836, and later married John Mill Chanter, the Vicar of Ilfracombe. She collaborated with her husband on a volume of children's tales in 1858 and on her own account wrote a novel, *Over The Cliffs* (1860). The story has sensational* elements evidently borrowed from Wilkie Collins*: an inheritance plot, murder in Chelsea, a woman assumed dead after a fall over the cliffs tracking down the criminal who has robbed her. Although *Over The Cliffs* was well received, Chanter published no other fiction. BL 1. Boase. Wol.

The Chaplain Of The Fleet, Walter Besant and James Rice, 1881, 3 vols, Chatto. The title alludes to the 'Rules' (or houses) of eighteenth-century London's Fleet Prison. Within these houses, debtors lived freely. Among their residents were clergymen, able (until 1753) to perform secret marriages for the law-abiding citizens of the city. The novel is in the form of an autobiography by the vivacious Kitty Pleydell. After her father dies, Kitty comes up from the country to stay with her uncle, Gregory Shovel 'Chaplain of the Fleet'. She is tricked into marriage with Lord Chudleigh. Later, in the 'polite world' of Epsom Wells, Chudleigh comes to love her in good faith and after various adventures all is finally made well. The story is interesting principally for the plucky character of the narrator-heroine and Besant's intimate knowledge of eighteenth-century low life. The foiling of Shovel, who has cruelly revenged himself on the son of an ancient enemy, takes the action into high watering-place society.

CHAPMAN, Mary Francis ('J. C[alder]Ayrton', 'Francis Meredith', 1838–84). Chapman was born in Dublin, where her father worked in the Excise. He was transferred to London while she was still a young child, and she was mainly educated at Staplehurst, Kent. Mary Chapman was a precocious author, and composed part of *Mary Bertrand* when she was just fifteen. The novel (an insipid love story) was published by her under the name 'Francis Meredith' (a scrambling of her Christian names Mary Francis) in 1860. It was followed by *Lord Bridgenorth's Niece* (1862) and *Bellasis, Or The*

Fortunes Of A Cavalier (1869). This last was written in collaboration with her father for the *Churchman's Family Magazine**. A visit to her brother in Scotland produced the first of her books to achieve any sizeable success, *A Scotch Wooing* (1875). It is the story of a pretty young girl, Arundel Fielding, 'English to the very core', forced to live with relatives in north of the border 'Lairg'. A year later, she published what is reckoned the best of her works, *Gerald Marlowe's Wife* (1876), a melodrama chronicling routine marital trials. Chapman wrote her fiction (most of which is domestic in subject-matter) under the habitual, male-seeming pseudonym J. C. Ayrton. Her last novel, *The Gift Of The Gods* (1879) was unusual in that it appeared under her own name. One reviewer summarised its plot as 'flirtation, some cross purpose arising from an undue proportion of gentlemen, three happy marriages and a baby'. Chapman remained a lifelong spinster and died, as she had largely lived, in Kent. BL 5. *DNB*.

Chapman and Hall (1830–1938). Publishers. Although famous as the publishers of Dickens*, Chapman and Hall in fact handled many major Victorian novelists, including: Ouida*, Meredith* (who also acted as the firm's literary adviser for many years, in succession to John Forster), Lever*, Anthony Trollope*, Bulwer-Lytton*. Edward Chapman and William Hall set up business at 186 the Strand in 1830, as modest booksellers. Chapman is generally thought to have had the literary taste and Hall the business acumen. In June 1830, the partners brought out an unambitious journal, *Chat Of The Week*. But the firm did nothing of note until 1836, when they launched a 'Library of Fiction' and devised a plan for a serial publication based on Robert Seymour's sporting plates. The young and unknown Charles Dickens was contracted to provide the text for what subsequently became *The Pickwick Papers**. After a shaky start (not helped by Seymour's suicide) the monthly serial was fabulously successful. Having extricated himself from his contractual involvements with Richard Bentley* and John Macrone*, Dickens made Chapman and Hall his principal publishers. Together they pioneered the illustrated novel in monthly 1s. parts. And it was through Chapman and Hall that Dickens became acquainted with John Forster, as friend, literary agent and eventually biographer. The firm published *Nicholas Nickleby**, *The Old Curiosity Shop**, *Barnaby Rudge**, *American Notes* and *Martin Chuzzlewit**. By the time of this last (1844), Dickens's payments had grown to around £150 a monthly instalment. There were, however, disagreements over money (partly to do with expenses for *A Christmas Carol**) and in 1844, Dickens petulantly appointed Bradbury and Evans* (whom he knew as Chapman and Hall's printers) as publishers of his new fiction. But he retained Chapman and Hall for his very profitable cheap reprints. Chapman and Hall had meanwhile diversified their list. In 1843, they published Thackeray's* *Irish Sketch Book*. And in the 1840s, they developed a line in social problem* literature, bringing out Mrs Gaskell's* *Mary Barton** (1848), Charles Kingsley's* *Alton Locke** (1850) and many of Carlyle's writings. William Hall died in 1847, and three years later the business moved to 193 Piccadilly. Anthony Trollope* came to Chapman and Hall in 1858, with *Doctor Thorne**. He published other major novels with them, helped found the *Fortnightly Review** under their imprint in 1865 and eventually became a director of the firm. In 1859, Chapman and Hall were appointed Dickens's principal publisher once more, when (petulant again) he broke with Bradbury and Evans. Major changes occurred to the firm in the 1860s. Frederic Chapman (1823–95) took over from his cousin Edward as head of the business in 1864. The young Chapman brought a sporty and up-to-date look to the firm's list with writers like Edmund Yates*, Whyte-Melville*, Ouida* and Hawley Smart*. He also made the most costly deal ever with Dickens, giving £7,500 advance for *Edwin Drood**. In 1870, he bought all Dickens's copyrights and in 1881, Carlyle's. Frederic Chapman was not, however, financially successful. Under some duress the firm was incorporated as a limited company in 1880, with an authorised capital of £150,000. They moved to Henrietta Street and underwent another change of character in 1895, with Frederic's death. In the early part of the twentieth century, the firm ran into financial difficulties which it barely survived. Finally, in 1938, it was taken over by Methuen*. Chapman and Hall in the mid-Victorian period stand out as a notably innovative firm. They can take much credit for the Dickensian experiment in part-issue serialisation. They were also pioneers in cheap reprints, bringing out collective reissues of the fiction of Bulwer-Lytton, Ainsworth* and Dickens in the 1840s. In the 1850s and 1860s they were in the forefront of the yellowback* fiction reprint industry. In the late 1830s, Chapman and Hall pioneered colour printing in England. They were early producers of popular children's books, bringing out Mary Howitt's* translation of Hans Christian Andersen in 1846 and the first annuals for young people in the same decade.

CHARLES, Elizabeth (née Rundle, 1828–96). She was born at Tavistock, the only child of the local MP, John Rundle. Educated at home by governesses and tutors, Elizabeth Rundle was a famously precocious writer whose juvenile literary efforts were admired by J. A. Froude* and Tennyson. Her first published tale, *Monopoly* (1847), imitated Harriet Martineau's* political science fables. A more lasting influence in her mature life was the Oxford movement. Her first book, *Tales And Sketches Of Christian Life In Different Lands And Ages* (1850) hovers between fiction and religious tract. In 1851, she married Andrew Charles, a London soap and candle manufacturer. Her best-selling (and still read) novel was *The Chronicles Of The Schönberg Cotta Family** (1863) which deals with the domestic lives of Luther and Melanchthon. *The Diary Of Mrs Kitty Trevylyan* (1864) is 'A Story Of The Times Of Whitefield And The Wesleys', and is written more simply. *The Draytons And The Davenants* (1867) is 'A Story Of The Civil Wars' and was published like much of her work by the publisher Nelson* primarily for the juvenile reader. Charles's husband died of consumption in 1868 leaving his widow impoverished. She supported herself competently by her pen for the rest of her life. Among her more successful novels (all of which were published anonymously) was *Against The Stream* (1873), a story of evangelical revival in the Napoleonic era, which proposes religion as the antidote for revolution and ends with a eulogy to William Wilberforce. *The Bertram Family* (1876) formed part of a novel sequence* of the kind popularised by Charlotte Yonge*. *Lapsed But Not Lost* (1877) is a 'Story Of Roman Carthage'. *Joan The Maid* (1879) tells the Joan of Arc story in terms of the heroine being the 'Deliverer of England and France' under the forbidding epigraph 'there is nothing fruitful but sacrifice'. Charles lived in

Hampstead (building a large house there in 1894) and travelled widely in Europe. In 1885, she founded a charitable 'home of peace' or hospice for the dying at Swiss Cottage. She was personally friendly with many of the leaders of Victorian religious thought (particularly the Clapham sect) and much of her work came out under the imprint of the SPCK*. She also wrote outright Protestant propaganda such as *The Martyrs Of Spain* (1862). BL 15. *DNB. NCBEL.* Wol.

Charles Auchester, Elizabeth Sara Sheppard, 1853, 3 vols, Hurst and Blackett. (The work was initially published anonymously, with some artificial mystery as to its authorship.) An 'art novel', dealing with the growth of the musical soul. Charles is born in England of partly Jewish descent. He is brought up by his mother and sister Millicent who recognise his musical talents. After voice training in England, where he meets the virtuoso singer Clara Benette, he goes to Germany to study the violin. At the Cecilia School he comes under the overpowering influence of Chevalier Seraphael, a genius. The second volume climaxes with a concert at which Seraphael's lover Maria (also a genius) dies conducting her symphony. The third volume 'The Crown Of Martyrdom' returns the action to England. Charles introduces Seraphael to Clara. They marry and have twins; but father and children die in an epidemic. Seraphael's music lives on. Charles survives a talented, but no more than talented musician. The novel is remarkable for its celebration of the cult of musical sensibility and its frank worship of Jewish national genius. Seraphael is based on Mendelssohn.

Charles O'Malley, Charles Lever, 1841, 2 vols, Curry. (Serialised in the *Dublin University Magazine**, March 1840–December 1841, and issued in monthly parts over the same period, with illustrations by Phiz*.) A picaresque autobiography of a lovable Irish rogue, like its bestselling predecessor, *The Confessions Of Harry Lorrequer**. Charles O'Malley is first discovered, a seventeen-year-old bravo in Galway. On an electioneering mission for his uncle, Godfrey O'Malley, he becomes enamoured of the English beauty, Lucy Dashwood. Following a duel, Charles goes to Dublin to study law but eventually enlists in the dragoons. He sees action in the Peninsular War, and rises to the rank of captain. Meanwhile, the O'Malley estates have fallen into bankruptcy, and it seems they will be bought up by General Dashwood, Lucy's father. The principals meet in Brussels, before Waterloo. As a special courier, Charles is captured by the enemy, and witnesses the battle by Napoleon's side. He contrives to save the life of General Dashwood and the marriage with Lucy is allowed to go forward. The novel has good battle scenes, and sustains a rollicking pace.

CHARLESWORTH, Maria Louisa (1819–80). Charlesworth was born in Suffolk, near Ipswich, the only child of a hard-working rector. From the age of six, she assisted her father in his parochial duties until he died in 1864. She never married, living first in her parents' home, then with her clergyman brother Samuel in Limehouse and for the last sixteen years of her life in Nutfield, Surrey. Charlesworth wrote tract-like improving fiction aimed at the young reader. She was also a conscientious female visitor to the local poor. Her outstanding and much reprinted novel is *Ministering Children* (1854), a work which, as R. L. Wolff sarcastically notes, is 'full of unconscious but unctuous snobbery'. BL 14. *DNB. NCBEL.* Wol.

CHATTERTON, Lady [Henrietta] Georgiana [Marcia Lascelles] (née Iremonger, 1806–76). Born in the West End of London, the daughter of a prebendary clergyman at Winchester Cathedral, Henrietta Iremonger was brought up in the best society and ennobled herself in 1824 by marriage to an Irish baronet, Sir William Chatterton (twelve years older than she). Until her husband's death in 1855 she lived a life of cultivated fashion, was an amateur painter of some distinction and travelled widely (although the couple's income from Irish rents was reduced by the 1845 famine). In the late 1830s Chatterton had begun to write occasional moralistic fiction, starting with *Aunt Dorothy's Tales* (1837). In 1859, a fifty-three-year-old widow, she married Edward Heneage Dering*, twenty years her junior and also an occasional novelist. The Derings lived in a country house together with her relatives Marmion and Rebecca Ferrers. Their time was spent in genteel cultivation, and it was Edward Dering's foible to dress in seventeenth-century clothing. In 1865, he was received into the Catholic Church by a no less dignitary than Cardinal Newman*. His wife eventually (after ten years of 'trial and suffering') followed in 1875, spurred by his novel *Sherborne, The House At The Four Ways* (1875). The title alludes to the four routes which may be taken to the destination of religious truth. *Sherborne* is the most interesting work of fiction either partner produced. The supposed autobiography of a heroic convert, it recalls (with an intensity verging on bigotry) the long persecution which the Catholic Church has historically suffered in England. Chatterton's output is not impressive and largely comprises what one reviewer called 'foolish fiction written with good intentions'. She was frequently accused of sermonising and dullness in her plots. *Allanston, Or The Infidel* (1844) is a routine novel of religious doubt. *Compensation, A Tale Of Real Life Thirty Years Ago* (1856) has more action. Its two heroines reject the advances of a duke because each thinks the other has romantic priority; the narrative brings in Italian brigands and all the hoary devices of gothic* fiction. Dering collaborated on some of her later fiction, such as *Grey's Court* (1865), which has a Catholic flavour. *Country Coteries* (1868), as its title implies, is one of the rural idylls popular in the 1860s. *Won At Last* (1874) is sensational*; it has a heroine abducted by Indian rebels who returns to her family as an Italian governess. Chatterton also wrote books of travel and verse. BL 11. *DNB*. Wol. Sad.

Chatto and Windus (1855–). Publishers. The firm was begun by John Camden Hotten* (1832–73) in 1855, in premises at 151 Piccadilly, which it was to occupy for most of nineteenth century. Hotten had travelled extensively in the USA, and he introduced a number of American authors (notably Mark Twain) to the English public. After his death, the firm was sold to a junior partner, Andrew Chatto, for £25,000. Chatto had as his partner (and banker) the minor poet W. E. Windus, who was relatively unimportant to the development of the firm that still bears his name. Andrew Chatto (assisted after 1876 by Percy Spalding) energised the business in the 1870s. He purchased the magazine *Belgravia* * from John Maxwell* in 1876, and acquired a large number of fiction copyrights for reissue in the 'Piccadilly Library'. These included prime works by Anthony Trollope*, Wilkie Collins*, Ouida*, and Walter Besant* and James Rice*. At this period, Chatto and Windus were, as Michael Sadleir calls them, the 'hustlers' of the book trade, 'climbing to prominence over the crumbling supremacy of Chapman and Hall*'. Together with Heinemann*, the firm helped in the overthrow of the three-volume novel system in the 1890s.

CHESNEY, General Sir George Tomkyns, KCB (1830–95). By profession a distinguished soldier and administrator, Chesney was an accomplished amateur novelist in his spare time. He was born in Devon, the youngest of four sons of an Indian army officer who died in 1830. After an ineffectual start in medicine, Chesney enrolled at the military academy of the East India Office and was commissioned into the Bengal Engineers in 1848. He served with distinction in the Indian Mutiny, and was severely wounded at the siege of Delhi in 1857. In 1867, he returned on long furlough to England, and made a number of intelligent proposals for military reorganisation. Chesney's brother, Charles Cornwallis Chesney (1826–76), was at this time a professor of military history at Sandhurst and his publications (notably his lectures on Waterloo, 1868) were having a profound effect on military thinking. In 1871, George Chesney emulated his brother with the brilliantly successful fantasy about imminent German invasion, *The Battle Of Dorking**, by a 'Volunteer'. With Bulwer-Lytton's* simultaneously published *The Coming Race**, this pamphlet-length work laid down the blueprint for English science fiction*. Encouraged by its runaway popularity, Chesney wrote *A True Reformer* (1874). Set in Simla and London this novel has as its hero Captain Charles West who while serving in India comes into an unexpected fortune of £3,500 p.a. He returns to England, enters Parliament as a technocrat MP where (in the novel's climax) he makes a powerful speech for army reform. The work is sometimes attributed to the author's uncle, Francis Rawdon Chesney (1789–1872). *The Dilemma* (1876) is Chesney's best novel. Set in the Indian up-country station of Mustaphabad, it describes a surprise attack and siege of the Residency during the Indian Mutiny (the plans of the besieged building are provided for greater authenticity). *The Private Secretary* (1881) has as its hero Robert Clifford, a philanthropist who falls in love with his vivacious secretary and induces her to become his mistress. Chesney's last novel, *The Lesters* (1893), is very odd. It centres on the discovery of a vast treasure in England which allows the hero to build a model new city, 'Lestertia'. The direct inspiration seems to have been Chesney's irritation at the jerry-builders, currently disfiguring the London suburbs where he lived. His novels were all serialised in *Blackwood's Magazine**, and he was one of the most loyal of the publisher's authors. Chesney was knighted in 1890, made the rank of general in 1892 and was elected to Parliament as a Conservative MP in the same year. BL 5. *DNB*. RM. Wol. Sad.

Cheveley, Lady Rosina Bulwer, 1839, 3 vols, Bull. *Cheveley* was written by Edward Bulwer's wife, shortly after the break-up of their marriage and the seizure of her children. The opening two volumes concentrate on the unhappy marriage of the Cliffords. Lord De Clifford ('A Man of Honour') is portrayed as a brute, a fool and the ill-bred son of a vulgar harridan. His wife is pure, long-suffering and quite innocent in the passionate love which springs up between herself and Mowbray (later to be Marquis of Cheveley). De Clifford has a 'predilection for governesses' and spawns a bastard by a village girl on his estate. He frames her father on a charge of stealing to keep him quiet during his election campaign. There is a complicated unravelling of the plot, in which the husband-villain is killed falling from his horse. The novel went through three editions, despite the mortified husband's embarrassed attempts to suppress it.

CHICHESTER, Frederick Richard ('Lord B******', 1827–53). The second son of the third Marquess of Donegal, titled by courtesy the 'Earl of Belfast'. Chichester was educated at Eton and displayed a precocious interest in art, literature and music. In adult life he was actively philanthropic, taking a particular interest in the cultural needs of the working class in Belfast. Politically, Chichester proclaimed radical tendencies at odds with his background. He wrote (as 'Lord B******') a number of social problem* novels of which the most interesting are: *Two Generations* (1851); *Masters And Workmen* (1852); *Wealth And Labour* (1853; Chichester's authorship of this last work was, however, denied by his family). *The County Magistrate* (1855) has a typically implausible plot, featuring a father who locks up evidence of his son's innocence of a murder charge in order to spare the feelings of the guilty man's family. The story is accompanied by interpolated essays on the virtues of sanitary improvement. BL 7. *DNB.* Wol.

A Child Of The Age, Francis Adams, 1894, 1 vol, John Lane. (The novel was first issued in somewhat different form as *Leicester, An Autobiography* in 1884.) Adams's autobiographical *Bildungsroman**. Bertram Leicester (who tells his own story) is first encountered a schoolboy at Glastonbury (i.e. Shrewsbury) school. An orphan he is in the care of an indifferent guardian, Colonel James. A critical episode in his youth is a fortnight which he spends in 'Seabay' with a distant relative, Mr Cholmeley, and his daughter Rayne. Some time later, Bertram is told that he must leave school, as his trust fund is now empty. Colonel James declines to help so the hero immerses himself in the London slums. He finds he cannot sell his poetry and survives by pawning his few valuables. Poor as he is, Bertram rescues from starvation a young working girl Rosy ('Rosebud') Howlet. They become lovers. Bertram eventually becomes personal secretary to a world-traveller after which he inherits a handsome legacy. Rayne meanwhile has married unhappily and is now Lady Gwatkin. Rosy suspects that Bertram loves Rayne (who is fortuitously widowed) and leaves her lover for the other woman of his own class. Bertam seeks out Rosy, finding her dying of influenza in a garret. She expires in his arms amidst protestations of mutual love. Melodramatic as the ending is, the novel's early London chapters are soberly effective.

A Child Of The Jago, Arthur Morrison, 1896, 1 vol, Methuen. A chronicle of slum life, set in 'the Jago', in the East End of London. Morrison spent eighteen months in Shoreditch, immersing himself in its actual degradation. The child of the title is Dicky, whose father Josh Perrott is eventually hanged for a murder of revenge. ('Thieves' honour' is a main theme in the novel.) Dicky is trained as a thief by the villainous fence, Aaron Weech (clearly inspired by Dickens's* Fagin). Dicky makes some feeble attempts to reform, under the influence of the saintly clergyman Father Sturt. But he dies in a street knife fight and 'honourably' will not name his killer. Scenes such as the fight between Norah Walsh and Sally Green with broken bottles shocked reviewers.

Children Of Gibeon, Walter Besant, 1886, 3 vols, Chatto. (Serialised in *Longman's Magazine*, January–December 1886.) Lady Mildred Eldridge adopts Polly Monument, the daughter of a London washerwoman and brings her up with her own daughter Beatrice. She keeps secret which of the two is her heiress until the girls are twenty-one, giving them the names Valentine and Violet. At twenty (in 1885), the girls are introduced to the impoverished Monument family, and slum life. Valentine is convinced she is the low-born Polly, and goes to live in Hoxton with her siblings. From her blind mother she discovers she is in fact Beatrice, but does not divulge the fact. Meanwhile Polly's father, a convict, returns to England and inflicts himself on Claude Monument, now a lawyer. He is fortuitously killed and all ends happily with Beatrice marrying Claude. Although the idea of the novel is artificial, the working-class scenes (as in Besant's *All Sorts And Conditions Of Men**) are persuasive as are the girls' eye-opening visits to their Hoxton 'mother'.

Children Of The Ghetto, Israel Zangwill, 1892, 3 vols, Heinemann. (Subtitled, 'A Study Of A Peculiar People', the work was first commissioned by the Jewish Publication Society of Philadelphia, who wanted the author to create a 'Jewish *Robert Elsmere**'.) Like most of Zangwill's fiction, this volume is made up of thematically linked vignettes and exemplary tales. The first half of the work is set among the Jewish ghetto population (the 'schnorrers' and shopkeeping petty bourgeois) of London's Stepney and Whitechapel district, recently swollen by an influx of Polish refugees. In the characters of the Ansell family, Zangwill depicts the dignity of Jewish poverty and in the story of accidentally married Hannah Jacobs the religious severity which is both the peculiar people's curse and their salvation. The second part, 'Grandchildren Of The Ghetto'· deals with the lives of second-generation assimilated Jews (much less sympathetic to Zangwill) who have become rich and cultivated. Through the stories of representative personages, Zangwill explores cultural idealism (in the character of the visionary journalist, Raphael Leon), fanaticism (in the Rev. Joseph Strelitski) and Anglicised vulgarity (in the Goldsmith family). The principal heroine of the work is Esther Ansell, who while rising in the world never cuts her ghetto roots. As 'Edward Armitage' she has written a definitive story of ghetto life (*Mordecai Josephs*) and when the secret of its authorship is revealed she decides to go to America. The novel ends with Raphael and Esther betrothed but not physically united as she leaves on 'the throbbing vessel that glided with its freight of hopes and dreams across the great waters towards the New World'.

The Children Of The New Forest, Frederick Marryat, 1847, 2 vols, Hurst. (Illustrated by Frank Marryat.) Marryat's last complete novel, set 200 years earlier in 1647. The Royalist cavalier, Colonel Beverley, is killed at the battle of Naseby. His wife dies shortly after, leaving their four children orphans. The Roundheads burn the Beverleys' house, Arnwood, and the children are thought dead. In fact, they are given refuge by a faithful old servant Jacob Armitage at his cottage in the New Forest. Before he dies Jacob teaches them how to survive in their new home. Growing up, the Beverleys undergo numerous adventures. In later life Edward goes to fight for Charles II in France. Humphrey becomes a farmer. The two girls go to friends in the north of England. After the Restoration, Arnwood is rebuilt. The story (Marryat's most popular) is addressed to the 'juvenile reader'.

Children Of Tomorrow, William Sharp, 1889, 1 vol, Chatto. An art novel. Felix Dane, a fashionable sculptor, is disillusioned with his current work, a figure of the goddess Hertha, and unhappily married to the beautiful but shallow Lydia. He is struck by a poem on Hertha written by a mysterious poetess, 'Sanpriel'. At a country-house party he discovers her to be the daughter of a half-mad Jewish musician-cum-prophet, Adama Acosta. The Acostas have dedicated themselves to a millenarian movement called 'the children of tomorrow'. Lydia Dane's lover, Gabriel Ford (an assimilated Jew), tries to kill Felix by sending him into an area of quicksand. Meanwhile, the hero and Sanpriel have fallen in love and he at last embarks on a sculpture worthy of his genius called *Destiny*. In a climax on board Felix's yacht, the *Lotus*, Gabriel poisons Lydia, intending to kill his rival. A month later, during a furious thunderstorm, Sanpriel agrees to live with Felix, not as his wife (which would compromise her Jewish faith) but as his lover. At this moment, they are both struck by lightning, their blasted bodies remaining 'so closely knit, that they seemed as one'. The novel is written with Sharp's wispy late romantic hypersensitivity.

Children's Fiction. The juvenile market was significant throughout the nineteenth century, but changed radically over the period. One main change was in patterns of purchase. At the beginning of the century books were bought for children. At the end, by children. Few Regency boys, for instance, can have bought Thomas Day's *Sandford And Merton* for themselves; few late Victorian parents can have presented their sons with gift copies of the *Boy's Own Paper**. A second main difference is literacy. The 1870 Universal Education Act recruited a whole new block of readers into the literary marketplace. Viewed as a whole, the period also saw a large shift from fiction for the juvenile reader with an overt evangelical purpose to secular entertainment (although often with a subtle imperial propaganda for boys, domestic indoctrination for girls). The foundation texts in the history of children's fiction are *Sandford And Merton* (1789); Mrs Sherwood's 'Rewards' (i.e. tales showing God's blessing for Christian conduct); *The Pilgrim's Progress* and *Robinson Crusoe* (the progenitor of most subsequent boy's adventure stories). The Society for the Promotion of Christian Knowledge (SPCK*) and the Religious Tract Society (RTS*) utilised fiction as a vehicle for propaganda and were, title for title, among the largest producers in the first half of the nineteenth century. Sunday schools and other church educational institutions also acted as distributors of approved fiction via prize books and lending libraries. Early publishers of fiction for the young such as James Nisbet* and Thomas Nelson* were little less strict in their evangelical tone than the RTS itself. The RTS, SPCK and the evangelical publishers had a puritanical terror of merely entertaining fiction and regularly argued in committee about what was to be done with such things as fairy-tales. (Dickens* satirises evangelical and utilitarian mutilations of imaginative children's stories in *Hard Times**.) It was not until the 1850s that a stable commercial infrastructure for children's fiction was established. This involved setting up magazines such as the RTS's *Sunday At Home* and the emergence of 'name' novelists such as George E. Sargent whose *Roland Leigh, The Story*

Of A City Arab (1857) pioneered a string of similar chronicles of ragged but indomitably virtuous heroes. The 1850s also saw the emergence of Charlotte Maria Tucker* ('ALOE'), the most gifted writer of children's fiction to date. Hesba Stretton* (i.e. Sarah Smith) represents another high point of the evangelical style (see *Jessica's First Prayer**, 1867). The 1860s saw the establishment of a number of fiction-carrying, religiously flavoured magazines for children such as Charlotte Yonge's* *The Monthly Packet** and Alexander Strahan's* *Good Words For The Young.* Other creative energies were meanwhile flowing into children's literature. Fantasy* flowered with Thackeray's* *The Rose And The Ring** (1855); Ruskin's* *The King Of The Golden River** (1851); Charles Kingsley's* *The Water-Babies* (1863)** and George MacDonald's* stories. The boys' adventure story also evolved as a direct outgrowth of Frederick Marryat's* manly nautical yarns. (It is also probable that many boys devoured the penny dreadfuls* of the 1840s, ostensibly aimed at their semi-literate elders.) Boys' literature as it developed in the mid-Victorian period propagated a code of manliness in the setting of hunting, field sports, military adventure and travel on the high seas or in exotic places. Charles Kingsley's novels for adults such as *Westward Ho!** (1855) were probably devoured by Victorian boys, as were other products of the muscular* school, such as Thomas Hughes's* *Tom Brown's School Days** (1857). George Henty* and G. Manville Fenn* put the production of boys' stories on an industrial footing. But the outstanding writer of such fiction was W. H. G. Kingston* who after his début in 1851 with *Peter The Whaler** produced a stream of juvenile adventure as well as editing such magazines as the ultra patriotic *Union Jack** (1880–83). Kingston's pattern was copied by Captain Mayne Reid* and R. M. Ballantyne*, whose *Coral Island** is the finest product of the genre. Other popular writers with the literate young were J. C. Edgar, Gordon Stables* and Talbot Baines Reed*. Books for girls developed in the 1850s as a separate category of juvenile fiction. Whereas earlier in the century the young reader was conceived as neuter, by the mid-Victorian period Harriet Mozley*, Elizabeth Sewell* and Charlotte Yonge were writing exclusively for girls, as G. A. Henty wrote exclusively for boys. Girls' fiction does not stress adventure so much as the psychological strains of growing up and of adjustment to the family group. (Judging by the quality of Yonge's novels, girls must have been more sophisticated readers than their male counterparts.) It is noticeable that the evangelical strain lasts longer in girls' fiction, although it is exhausted with the voluminous work of L. T. Meade*, late in the century.

The Chimes, Charles Dickens, 1844, 1 vol, Chapman and Hall. (Illustrated by Daniel Maclise*, Richard Doyle*, John Leech* and Clarkson Stanfield*.) A Christmas* Book. The narrative centres on Trotty (i.e. Toby) Veck, a ticket-porter who has his post outside an old church, waiting for work. In a dream vision (brought on by the spirits of the bells and an indigestible bowl of tripe) Trotty sees catastrophe for his daughter Margaret. This happily does not come to pass, and he wakes on New Year morning to a hopeful future. The story contains more direct social satire (on utilitarianism, for instance) than its predecessor, *A Christmas Carol**.

CHOLMONDELEY, Mary (1859–1925). Born at Hodnet, Shropshire, Cholmondeley was a clergyman's daughter (the eldest of five), and related to the Marquis of Cholmondeley. A lifelong victim of poor health, she was educated mainly at home by a family governess and by her father and in later life declared her youth to have been heavily 'repressed'. From the age of sixteen to thirty, Cholmondeley lived in the country, helping her father with his parochial duties, her mother having been afflicted with creeping paralysis. She never married. In 1896, when the Rev. Cholmondeley retired as Rector of Hodnet, the family moved to London to live in a flat. Mary (who wrote her first novel at seventeen) had begun to circulate her work among publishers as early as 1883. Her first published novel, *The Danvers Jewels** (1887, put out anonymously in *Temple Bar**) was an ingenious detective* story successful enough to warrant a sequel, *Sir Charles Danvers* (1889). During this period, her mother's health was failing as was Mary's own. Although she lived a retired mode of life Cholmondeley specialised in drawing-room novels, with smart Shavian dialogue. Her fiction (especially when it satirised established religion) sometimes scandalised. *Diana Tempest* (1893) shows Cholmondeley's more melodramatic tendencies with a plot centred on murder. The novel was dedicated to her sister Hester (who had died, aged twenty-two) with an apparent allusion to God, the tyrannical father: 'He put our lives so far apart, we cannot hear each other speak'. The story centres on a hidebound villainous father, Colonel Tempest, whose plots go awry and who dies in a condition of religious mania. *Diana Tempest* was the first book to appear under Cholmondeley's own name. *Red Pottage** (1899) is her best-remembered work. It has a duel, a guilty man's self-destruction and sharp satire against religious cant (this aspect of the work provoked denunciation from a London pulpit which delighted the author). Cholmondeley went on to produce five novels in the twentieth century, one of which, *Prisoners* (1906), ran into libel trouble and irritated all her acquaintance who were portrayed in the work. In later life, she lived with her sister in London and Suffolk. BL 10. *WW*. RM. *NCBEL*. Wol. Sad.

CHORLEY, Henry Fothergill ('Paul Bell', 1808–72). Chorley was born at Blackley Hurst, near Billinge in Lancashire, into a north-country Quaker family, enriched by trade. Shortly after his father's lock-making firm failed in 1816, Chorley left home and went to work in an office in Liverpool. He studied literature and music and wrote in his spare time. His amateur efforts were encouraged by the established writer Geraldine Jewsbury*. Eventually Chorley moved to London and joined the staff of the *Athenaeum** in 1833, as literary reviewer and musical editor. A versatile man of letters, he wrote verse, opera libretti, literary criticism and occasional fiction. Chorley's music reviews were rigorous but his intellectual qualities were unappreciated by his contemporaries and the later part of his life was embittered. *The Lion, A Tale Of The Coteries* (1839) is his earliest and best work of full-length fiction, a sharply observed picture of literary fashion charting the rise and fall of a 'child of genius'. Other novels by him are: *Roccabella* (1859) and *A Prodigy, A Tale of Music* (1866; dedicated to Chorley's friend, Charles Dickens*). The first, subtitled 'A Tale Of A Woman's Life', centres on Rosamond Westwood, a young woman shackled in marriage to an unsympathetic Liverpool merchant. He dies leaving her a fortune, on condition that she never remarries. She gives up the money to marry the dashing Italian, Count Roccabella. *A Prodigy* draws on Chorley's knowledge of the world of music, tracing the career (largely in Germany) of the young genius, Carl Einstern. For his fiction Chorley used the pseudonym 'Paul Bell', which he acknowledged to be an act of homage to the Brontë* sisters, who had called themselves Ellis, Currer and Acton Bell. None of his novels succeeded with the public and Chorley died disappointed and evidently alcoholic, having retired from the *Athenaeum** in 1868. BL 4. *DNB. NCBEL.* Wol.

The Christian, Hall Caine, 1897, 1 vol, Heinemann. A late Victorian superseller. The novel follows the intertwined careers of a young hero and heroine in London, 'the modern Babylon'. Glory Quayle is the beautiful, red-haired granddaughter of a gentle Manx clergyman who goes to London as a nurse but is later drawn into the world of the theatre. After hardship she wins through to worldly success playing Ibsen. John Storm is a nephew of the Prime Minister with a strong religious vocation. After dabbling with the fashionable Anglican Church as a hospital chaplain, he joins a monastic brotherhood ('The Society of the Holy Gethsemane'). But this does not fulfil him and he returns to the masses of slum London and Glory, whom he loves and whose soul he means to save. As a crusading social reformer, Storm whips the working classes into a hysterical belief that the world is coming to an end. In the ensuing riots he is mortally injured and marries a contrite Glory on his deathbed. The apocalyptic scenes in the novel are overdone but powerful.

CHRISTIE, Alexander (1841–95). Christie was born in Montrose, Scotland. He went to sea and rose to be a captain in the merchant marine. In his retirement he published three Marryat*-like tales of seafaring life: *Among Typhoons* (1891); *A Cruise In An Opium Clipper* (1891); *Allan Gordon* (1892). For these works he used the pseudonym 'Captain Lindsay Anderson', an amalgamation of his wife's and mother's maiden names. The critics were severe on Christie's efforts and it seems he did not persevere in his career as author. He died in London. BL 3. Boase.

Christie Johnstone, Charles Reade, 1853, 1 vol, Bentley. Reade's second novel. Viscount Ipsden (named after the house in which Reade was born) loves Lady Barbara Sinclair, a bluestocking who rejects him on the grounds that he has neither virtues nor vices. The young lord is stale and bored even with £18,000 a year to spend. An eccentric doctor prescribes a stay among the poor. This brings Ipsden to the fishing village of Newhaven, near Edinburgh, where Christie Johnstone is a young fishwife. Christie loves a frail artist, Charles Gatty ('the daft painter' as the irreverent locals call him). His family forbid any marriage, but are finally won over when she saves him from drowning in the Firth of Forth. All ends well for the novel's two sets of lovers. Ipsden saves Barbara from financial ruin and in gratitude she consents to marry him. It is suggested that Christie is an idealised version of an Edinburgh woman with whom Reade had a common-law marriage. In an 'autocriticism' Reade noted the work's over-reliance on dialogue and an 'arbitrary' plot.

Christmas Books. The 'Annual' and Christmas 'Giftbook' industries were started up in the 1820s. In 1843, with *A Christmas Carol**, Charles Dickens popularised the short, heavily illustrated, one-volume tale released for the holiday market, at 5s. or 6s. In the 1840s, other novelists (Thackeray* and Lever* notably) took up the form. By the 1860s, publishers like Routledge* were releasing a whole range of fiction for the Christmas reader. And in his journals *Household Words** and *All The Year Round** Dickens pioneered special Christmas issues featuring self-contained tales, often with a strong supernatural element. Dickens's other Christmas Books are *The Chimes** (1844); *The Cricket On The Hearth** (1845); *The Battle Of Life** (1846); *The Haunted Man* (1847). Thackeray's Christmas Books (which specialise in 'social zoology' rather than the supernatural) comprise: *Mrs Perkins's Ball** (1847); *Our Street** (1848); *Dr Birch And His Young Friends* (1849); *Rebecca And Rowena** (1850; a comic continuation of Scott's *Ivanhoe*); *The Kickleburys On The Rhine* (1850). Lever's most successful Christmas Book was *St Patrick's Eve* (1845).

A Christmas Carol, Charles Dickens, 1843, 1 vol, Chapman and Hall. (Illustrated by John Leech*). See above. The skinflint businessman Ebenezer Scrooge is visited on Christmas Eve by the ghost of his former partner, Marley. Scrooge is subjected to visions of Christmas Past, Christmas Present and, most affectingly, of Christmas As Yet To Come. Christmas Day finds him morally new-born. He becomes the kind patron of his clerk, Bob Cratchit and a 'second father' to Cratchit's crippled son, Tiny Tim.

The Chronicles Of Carlingford. The group title of Margaret Oliphant's* novel sequence set in the country town, Carlingford. The series traces in serio-comic detail the infighting between the community's Anglican and dissenting factions. The same characters reappear, but the novelist makes relatively little effort to knit the separate narratives together. The chronicles include: *Salem Chapel** (1863); *The Rector And The Doctor's Family* (1863); *The Perpetual Curate** (1864); *Miss Marjoribanks** (1866); *Phoebe Junior** (1876).

The Chronicles Of The Schönberg-Cotta Family, Elizabeth Rundle Charles, 1863, 1 vol, Nelson. (The work was first commissioned for £400 by the editor of the Scottish magazine, the *Family Treasury*.) Charles's documentary narrative of Martin Luther's life was one of the most popular and reprinted religious* novels of the century. Luther's reforming career is recorded through the diaries ('chronicles') of the Cotta children over the period 1503 to 1546. The offspring of a printer in Eisenach, they observe his progress from miner's son, to student at Erfurt, to Augustinian monk to heretic, to national hero finally dying where he began at Eisleben. Friedrich Cotta follows Luther as a disciple, being fellow student, fellow monk and finally fellow Protestant. He eventually marries his cousin Eva von Schönberg, whose testimony (together with that of Else and Thekla Cotta) makes up the narrative. It is the Cotta children who print Luther's texts, and the Gospels in German. The novel manages to capture the contemporary bewildered excitement of religious reform, together with such terrific historical episodes as visitations of the plague and the Peasants' Revolt.

Chums (1892–1934). A boys' paper, launched by Cassells* to compete with *The Boy's Own Paper**. It was edited by Max Pemberton* and although it never rivalled the *BOP* in sales or longevity ran well into the twentieth century, featuring in the Victorian period stories by R. L. Stevenson* and G. A. Henty* among others.

CHURCH, Professor A[lfred] J[ohn] (1829–1912). Church was born in London, one of six surviving (out of twelve) children of an impecunious solicitor. All the male children went on to achieve solid success in the legal and academic professions. Alfred was educated at King's College, London, and Lincoln College, Oxford. Mark Pattison was a strong influence on him at this period. On graduation in 1851 with a second-class degree in classics, he was ordained. After three years as a curate, Church taught at various grammar schools until 1880, when he became professor of Latin at University College, London. He retired from academic life in 1892, taking up a living at Ashley St James in Wiltshire. The Rev. Church wrote books on classical history, and historical* tales for boys. His fiction includes: *Heroes Of Chivalry And Romance* (1898); *The Chantry Priest Of Barnet* (1884), a historical tale, illustrated with mock fifteenth-century illuminations; *With The King At Oxford* (1885). His best known work is *Two Thousand Years Ago, Or The Adventures Of A Roman Boy* (1886). Neither the academic profession, the Anglican ministry nor juvenile fiction paid well, and Church's last years were impoverished. Throughout life he was an enthusiastic angler and follower of cricket. In his autobiography, *Memories Of Men And Books* (1908), Church carefully omits all reference to his own fiction. BL 12. *WW. NCBEL*. Wol. RLF.

The Churchman's Family Magazine (1863–73). Published by James Hogg, the magazine was illustrated and issued monthly. It mainly contained articles by clergymen and was evidently subscribed to by a pious, Anglican, home-based readership. As an attraction, it featured suitably uplifting fiction, including Charlotte Yonge's* tale of young female experience, *The Clever Woman Of The Family* (1864–65), illustrated by Florence Claxton.

Churton and Co (1835?–55?). Publisher. Edward Churton (1812–85) set up business first at 26 Holles Street, then in Cavendish Square. He specialised in third-rate, three-volume novels for the lending libraries, along with such other West End establishments as A. K. Newman and Edward Bull.

A City Girl, John Law (i.e. Margaret Harkness), 1887, 1 vol, Vizetelly. An English novel which Friedrich Engels greatly admired. The heroine is an East End trouser seamstress, Nelly Ambrose. Pretty and with ideas above her station, she is loved by George the stolid caretaker of Charlotte's Buildings, where she lives. On a trip to buy finery in Petticoat Lane, Nelly hears a Radical speaker, Arthur Grant. Grant, a 'gentleman', seduces the city girl, then returns to his Kensington wife and children. Nelly is turned out by her Irish Catholic parents and given refuge by the Salvation Army (sympathetically presented by Law). Her child dies in a bleak charity ward, and she bitterly returns the corpse to Arthur. At the end of the novel, George takes her back and makes an honest woman of her. The novel is notable for its stark depiction of working-class labour, play and society. But as critics note, Law's political views, though powerful, are unfocused and seem to have changed unpredictably during her writing career.

Clara Vaughan, R. D. Blackmore, 1864, 3 vols, Macmillan. (Serialised as *The Purpose Of A Life* in *Cassell's Illustrated Paper*, March–August 1864.) The father of the heroine is a rich English gentleman, living in Gloucestershire, who is murdered in his bed. His wife witnesses the crime, but cannot identify the murderer. Clara, ten years old at the time, sets out to solve the mystery. First on her list is a wicked uncle, Edgar Vaughan, whom she suspects and accuses. But in the event, it emerges that he is innocent of the crime. Her father, it transpires, was the innocent victim of Corsican revengers, actually intending to murder Edgar (who is finally reconciled with Clara, after chastening illness). The story has colourful touches such as a prominent Cuban bloodhound called Giudice who helps unravel the crime and a vividly described wrestling match. But the sensation* genre did not really suit Blackmore.

CLARKE, [Charles] (1815–70). Clarke was educated at Oxford University and graduated in 1837. He was subsequently ordained and took up a curacy at Norton-by-Daventry in 1849. In 1864, he was appointed Chaplain to the Earl of Stamford. Little else is known of Clarke's life. But in the last eight years of his clerical career, in the undemanding post of private chaplain, he wrote a string of successful sporting* novels, such as *Charlie Thornhill* (1863) and *The Flying Scud* (1867). Clarke's plots are ramshackle and the appeal of his fiction is its (evidently firsthand) depiction of gambling at Baden Baden, steeplechasing in France and turf adventures at Newmarket. He also wrote a semi-autobiographical novel, *Lord Falconberg's Heir* (1868), which attractively recalls Oxford in the 1830s. The main plot line, which revolves around a secret marriage, is typically incoherent. Clarke edited the *Wimbledon Annual* from 1868 and in later life called himself Charles Carlos Clarke. He died at Esher of a tumour of the abdomen. BL 11. Boase. *NCBEL*. Wol.

CLARKE, [Charles] Allen ('Teddy Ashton', 1863–1935). Clarke was born at Bolton, to working-class parents. After leaving school, he himself went to work in a cotton mill. By self-improvement he eventually became a journalist, and conducted *Teddy Ashton's Weekly* for fourteen years. Clarke spent his later life at Blackpool, was the founder of the Lancashire Authors' Association and made a study of the region's folklore and dialect. He wrote regional* tales (often with a frankly Marxist line) such as: *The Knobstick: A Story Of Love And Labour* (1893); *Tales Of A Deserted Village* (1894); *The Witch Of Eagle's Crag* (1895) and *Starved Into Surrender* (1904). Leo Tolstoy admired Clarke's work. *The Red Flag* (1907), 'A Tale Of The People's Woe' is probably the most explicitly communist work of fiction published in Edwardian England. Clarke was evidently unknown to London readers and catered exclusively for a local public. BL 17. *WW. NCBEL*.

CLARKE, Marcus [Andrew Hislop] (1846–81). Author of the finest Australian novel of the nineteenth century, *His Natural Life**. Clarke was born in Kensington, London, the only child of a rich Chancery lawyer and a mother who died of consumption in his infancy. He went to school in Highgate, where one of his fellows was the poet, Gerard Manley Hopkins. As a young man, Clarke was rich and, by his own account, dissipated. But on his father's insanity and death in 1863, he found himself poorer than expected.

The hoped-for career in the Foreign Office was no longer feasible and with
£750 in his pocket, he emigrated to Australia in 1863. There Clarke worked
in a Melbourne bank for a while, then tried life on a sheep station called
Dinkledoodledum. By 1867 he had returned to Melbourne. Clarke's first love
was the stage and he became a theatre critic for the *Melbourne Argus* (a
squatters' paper) at £300 a year. He himself wrote plays and pantomimes,
none of which made him anything. In 1868, he became proprietor of the
Colonial Monthly, in which he published *Long Odds* (1869). A sensation*
novel, *Long Odds* has a hero who marries secretly and is informed immediately after the ceremony that a brother's death steeplechasing has made him
heir to the family fortune. Bigamous complications ensue. Neither novel nor
journal did well. And the author apologises rather awkwardly in his preface
for 'offering to the Australian public a novel in which the plot, the sympathies, the interest, the moral are all English'. Clarke ceased to be proprietor
of the *Colonial Monthly* in 1869. In 1870, he began to serialise *His Natural
Life* in the *Australian Journal*. This melodrama of convict life in the 1840s
was not immediately popular. The *Spectator*, for instance, thought the novel
'too graphic, too powerful for general consumption'. Posterity, however, has
judged it a work equal to Victor Hugo's *Les Misérables* (1862) and superior
to Charles Reade's* more successful prison story *It Is Never Too Late To
Mend* (1856). Clarke had only £100 for the serial rights and the journal
lost readers over the story's interminable thirty-month run. Effectively, he
was discouraged from writing long fiction for the rest of his life. Clarke married Marian Dunn, an actor's daughter, in 1869, and went on to have six
children. The marriage was unhappy, and there was a hopeless affair with
his sister-in-law. Pressed for money, Clarke took up work in the public library of Victoria. He continued to supplement his income by writing for the
newspapers and produced some short stories but his third novel, *Felix And
Felicitas*, never got beyond notes. He twice went bankrupt. Clarke died at
the age of thirty-five, from pleurisy. A shortened version of his major work
was published in Australia in 1874 and in England in 1875. BL 4. *DNB.*
RM. *NCBEL.* Wol. Sad.

CLARKE, Mary [Victoria] Cowden (née Novello, 1809–98). Born in London, she was the eldest daughter of the musician Vincent Novello's eleven
children. Novello was associated with various literary and musical notables
and Mary Lamb, especially, took an interest in the young Mary. She married Charles Cowden Clarke in 1828, and began to publish her writing at
the same period. In 1829, she began to compile her massive *Concordance
To Shakespeare* which finally saw print in 1845. From 1853 to 1856, she
edited the *Musical Times*. After 1856, the Clarkes lived in Italy and both
died in that country. They are remembered principally as popularisers of
Shakespeare and as members of the Dickens* circle but both wrote novels
and tales, largely directed at the young reader. Mary Clarke's fiction includes: *Kit Bam's Adventures* (1849). A series of exemplary tales told by an
old sailor, this volume is memorable for its illustrations by George Cruikshank*. She ventured into adult fiction with *The Iron Cousin* (1854) and
(after a long interval), *A Rambling Story* (1874). The first is a moral romance, written against the vice of rigidity in personal relationships. Leigh
Hunt thought its lovemaking 'dainty and noble', but the reviewers were

unimpressed. The second story has more action; an artist woos and wins an aristocratic bride who is promptly kidnapped by a jealous lover. *Uncle Peep And I, A Child's Novel* (1886) is aimed at the very young. Shortly before her death, Clarke published an autobiography, *My Long Life* (1896). She died one year short of the ninety that her husband achieved when he predeceased her in 1877. BL 6. *DNB. NCBEL.* Wol.

The Claverings, Anthony Trollope, 1867, 2 vols, Smith, Elder. (Serialised in *Cornhill**, February 1866–May 1867, illustrated by M. E. Edwards*). Harry Clavering, a poor (if brilliant) schoolmaster, is thrown over by Julia Brabazon, who accepts instead the vicious but rich Lord Ongar. Harry determines to rise in the world and apprentices himself to the engineering firm of Beilby and Burton. He lodges with the Burton family, and despite the vulgarity of some of its members falls in love with the daughter Florence. Meanwhile, Lord Ongar has drunk himself to death and Julia, now a rich widow, throws herself at Harry who jilts Florence. After much indignation in the Burton family, he finally returns and marries her. Things are made easier when Harry's cousins are drowned on a sailing trip, leaving him an estate and a title. Trollope thought the plot of *The Claverings* was good, but that the hero was too weak.

CLAYTON, Eleanor C[reathorne] (1834–1900). Born in Dublin, she was the only daughter of Benjamin Clayton, the painter. About 1864, she came to London and made a name for herself designing cards and calendars for Rimmell's, a perfumer in the Strand. Clayton also wrote romantic novels, mainly for Tinsley*. *Cruel Fortune* (1865) is a simple-minded melodrama depicting the vices of London high society with a climactic episode based on the recent Staplehurst railway accident in which Dickens* was almost killed. *Playing For Love* (1876) is an art novel, set in the 1840s. *A Girl's Destiny* (1882) has a hero whose father's will requires him to marry a woman with whom, quite unknowingly, he has already fallen in love. In 1879, Clayton made a late-life marriage with James Needham and is sometimes listed in her married name. BL 7. Boase. Wol.

CLEEVE, Lucas (i.e. Adelina Georgina Isabella Kingscote, née Wolff, 1850?–1908). The daughter of Sir Henry Drummond Wolff, she attended Oxford University (one of the first female novelists to do so) and married Colonel Howard Kingscote. A woman of the world, Cleeve described herself for *Who's Who* as a 'great traveller and linguist'. Her fiction is smart, highly eclectic and features topical social settings and themes. It includes *Tales Of The Sun* (1890); *The Woman Who Wouldn't* (1895) a 'sex problem' story, written in support of Grant Allen's* bestselling novel about the woman who did and whose heroine, Opalia, has one of the oddest names in Victorian fiction; *Lazarus* (1896), a historical story set in biblical times recounting 'the earth's great miracle' and probably inspired by Marie Corelli's* 1893 bestseller, *Barabbas**; *Epicures* (1896), a story of modern 'neurotic' love in the *Keynotes** style. Cleeve was prolific, and published three novels typical of her range in 1901: *As The Twig Is Bent* tells the story of a decent young man, George Bowman, who is corrupted by the shady world of high finance but eventually saved by a woman's love. *What Men Call Love* is a Rider Haggard*-like story of South Africa (currently fashionable by virtue of the

Boer War) in the days of Cetewayo. The third, *Plato's Handmaiden*, is
the story of a girl, Georgie, who opens a hat shop in Oxford Street and has
various adventures preserving her virginity in her platonic relationships. The
work is consciously of the modish Hill-Top* school in its feminist concerns.
BL 57. *WW*.

Cleg Kelly, S. R. Crockett, 1896, 1 vol, Smith, Elder. (Subtitled 'An Arab
Of The City', the work was serialised in *Cornhill**, July 1895 March 1896.)
The hero is a slum child in Edinburgh, 'Cleg' being dialect for 'horsefly'.
The story opens with his defiantly denying God and being expelled from
his mission school. Cleg's father, Tim Kelly, is a drunken Irish burglar who
drives his wife Isbel to an early grave. The boy befriends Vara Kavannah,
whose mother Sal is as degenerate as Cleg's father. Cleg is given a start in
life by Celie Tennant and Donald Iverach (benefactors who also appear in
The Stickit Minister*) and succeeds as a paper boy. With his help, Vara
escapes to rural Netherby. There the climax of the story occurs when Tim
Kelly and Sally Kavannah conspire to rob the house of General Theophilus
Ruff (a madman whom Cleg has befriended). Cleg foils the crime and the
wicked parents are entombed and die in the general's strongroom. Cleg and
Vara go on to live useful lives. The novel is humorous and sordidly realistic
by turns. The later chapters in the country belong to the kailyard* genre
and the work is dedicated to the school's leader, J. M. Barrie*.

Cleopatra, H. Rider Haggard, 1889, 1 vol, Longman. (Serialised in the
Illustrated London News*, January–June 1889, with illustrations by R.
Caton Woodville.) A short work, lengthily subtitled, 'Being An Account
Of The Fall And Vengeance Of Harmachis, The Royal Egyptian, As Set
Forth By His Own Hand'. One of Haggard's more ambitious efforts, this
romance tells the story of Cleopatra through the fragmentary papyrus rolls
left by one of her priests, also a pretender to her throne. Harmachis plots
to assassinate the Queen, but falls in love with her instead. She betrays
his love, and he feigns death. As the magician Olympus, Harmachis spends
the next ten years working Cleopatra's eventual downfall, knowing it will
be his as well. Haggard chose to write in a stilted idiom and the text was
profusely illustrated. Reviewers generally felt that the author was more at
home with his stories of southern Africa. Haggard continued to experiment,
however, with a romance of the Vikings, *Eric Brighteyes* (1891), which was
also relatively unpopular.

The Clever Woman Of The Family, Charlotte M. Yonge, 1865, 2 vols,
Macmillan. (Serialised in the *Churchman's Family Magazine**, 1864–65, with
illustrations by Florence Claxton.) The clever woman of the title is Rachel
Curtis, unmarried and twenty-five years old when the story begins. Rachel
lives at Avoncester and is a daughter of the squire of Homestead. She is
in search of a mission on which to devote herself. Plot complications arise
with the arrival in England of a cousin, Fanny. The widow of an elderly
soldier and mother of a young family, Fanny is accompanied by a guardian,
Colonel Colin Keith. He is the former lover of one of Rachel's clever friends,
Ermine Williams. Ermine has been crippled in a fire, caused by her sister,
but the chivalrous Colin still loves her. Colin's brother, Alick (also a soldier,
holder of the Victoria Cross, won in the Indian Mutiny) falls in love with

and eventually marries Rachel. The story is given melodramatic interest by Rachel's philanthropic society for unemployed lace workers being embezzled by a rogue, Mauleverer (alias Maddox). He is eventually brought to justice and Rachel, cured of her unfeminine cleverness, settles down to wifehood.

CLIFFORD, [Sir] Hugh Charles (1866–1941). Clifford was born in London, the eldest son of an army general, and holder of the Victoria Cross. Educated at Woburn Park, a private school for Catholics, he joined the Malay States Civil Service in 1883. Clifford subsequently had a distinguished career as a colonial governor, became a High Commissioner in 1927 and was knighted in 1900. His fiction, which anticipates that of Joseph Conrad (a personal friend) reflects his experiences as an administrator in the Malayan Peninsula. *Since The Beginning* (1898) is an Eastern tale. *In A Corner Of Asia* (1899) is made up of eight Malayan stories. *Studies In Brown Humanity* (1898) deals with native life, *Bush Whacking And Other Stories* (1901) with the white man's life in the colonies. As one reviewer put it, this volume showed Clifford to be 'the chief recorder of the principality ruled by Mr Conrad'. By marriage, Clifford had other literary associations. His first wife was a daughter of Gilbert à'Beckett of *Punch**. She died in 1907 and in 1910 he married the novelist Mrs Henry de la Pasture*. BL 10. *DNB*. Wol.

CLIFFORD, Mrs W[illiam] K[ingdon] [Sophia Lucy] (née Lane, 1853–1929). Sophia Lane was born in the West Indies, the daughter of a colonial administrator. She showed precocious talent and as a young girl played at writing stories. In 1875, she married William Kingdon Clifford (b. 1845), an eminent Cambridge mathematician and philosopher. During their short marriage, the couple travelled widely. In 1879, Clifford died of consumption, leaving his wife with two small children. The struggle of the solitary woman was to be Clifford's staple fictional theme thereafter. She was a friend of Henry James, of George Eliot* (who was widowed around the same time) and of M. E. Braddon* who encouraged her writing. Clifford brought out *Anyhow Stories*, a volume for children, in 1882. Three years later there appeared (anonymously) her first successful novel, *Mrs Keith's Crime**. Its heroine is a dying mother who poisons her similarly afflicted child. The euthanasia theme provoked controversy. Clifford wrote with increasing fluency in the 1890s. *Love Letters Of A Worldly Woman* (1891) is a clever exercise in epistolary fiction. *Aunt Anne* (1892), has a cantankerous old heroine who falls prey to a gigolo forty years her junior. The novel caught the public's fancy, and was a sales success. *The Last Touches* (1892) is a collection of short stories which show off the terse economy of Clifford's literary style. *A Wild Proxy* (1893) is 'a tragic comedy of today', written in the author's increasingly brittle manner. *A Flash Of Summer* (1894) is a modish study of marriage problems. *A Woman Alone* (1901) is another collection of shorter pieces. The title story is the typically ironic study of a wife who kills her husband's love for her by displaying too much love for him. Clifford also wrote plays. She was granted a Civil List pension of £80 in 1880, probably in recognition of her husband's services to mathematics. Her daughter, Ethel Clifford, wrote some fiction in the early twentieth century. BL 20. *WW*. *NCBEL*. Wol. Sad. RLF.

CLIVE, Caroline Archer (née Meysey-Wigley, 1801–73). An eccentric and gifted occasional novelist. Caroline Meysey-Wigley was the daughter of an

English MP and born among the landed gentry in Worcestershire. As a child she was lamed by infantile paralysis and although no beauty ('an ugly little cripple' her biographer uncompromisingly calls her), she had a vivacious and tough personality. At the age of thirty-five she met the Rev. Archer Clive, a good-looking, wealthy and clever clergyman. In 1840, he proposed and was accepted. Despite everything, the marriage was happy, and produced two children. Her husband was happy to turn squire, and the Clives lived comfortably at Whitfield, travelling quite extensively on the Continent. Clive had begun her authorial career writing poems which she published in 1840, under the pseudonym 'V'. For her own delectation 'she filled thousands of sheets of paper with abstract ideas and snatches of dialogue and rough ideas for plots'. Great stir was caused by her first novel (published anonymously), *Paul Ferroll** (1855). She had always liked horrific crime fiction, and in Ferroll produced the most unusual criminal hero of the Victorian period. He murders his wife, and escapes punishment to live happily with his new wife and daughter. (The fourth edition added a chapter bringing him to his death.) So successful was the story that a verbena was named after it. Clive followed up with a sequel, *Why Paul Ferroll Killed His Wife* (1860) which is moralistic and inferior and confusingly changes Ferroll's name. Her last novel, *John Greswold* (1864), begins strikingly with sudden death in a London gambling casino, but tails off badly with a hero who gives up all worldly ambition at the age of twenty-three. Lack of story is a usual weakness in Clive's fiction. The novelist suffered a paralytic stroke in 1865, while travelling in France, and eight years later was burned to death in her study at Whitfield in Herefordshire when her clothes and books caught fire. BL 3. *DNB. NCBEL*. Wol. Sad.

The Cloister And The Hearth, Charles Reade, 1861, 4 vols, Trübner. (Serialised in *Once A Week**, July–October 1859 as *A Good Fight*, with illustrations by Charles Keene*. In this form, the novelist was prevailed on to shorten the work and sweeten its ending.) Reade's vast historical narrative is set in fifteenth-century Europe and takes as its hero the father of Erasmus, Gerard Eliassoen. Gerard's life is strung between two ideals: that of domestic fulfilment (the Dutch hearth) and that of devotion to religion (the Italian cloister). The younger son of a mercer at Tergou, Gerard is destined for the Church and convent-educated in penmanship. He subsequently goes to Rotterdam, falls in love and is betrothed to Margaret Brandt, the daughter of a scholar. His family oppose the match and engineer his arrest. Once escaped, Gerard determines to make his fortune. Accompanied by the amiable Burgundian Denys, he travels to Rome through Germany, France and Lombardy. In the holy city, he receives the false news that Margaret is dead, and plunges into a life of debauchery. He attempts suicide in the Tiber, is rescued and nursed back to health. After this, he enters the Dominican order as Brother Clement and returns to Rotterdam, only to meet Margaret alive and the mother of his child. Shattered again, Gerard retreats from life to become the forlorn Hermit of Gouda. Margaret lures him back to human society by leaving their son to babble in his cell. They subsequently live separate but useful lives. She then dies of plague and he follows soon after. Their son will grow up to be the famous scholar and theologian. The novel is written in Reade's abrupt, hyper-sensational* style.

CLOSE, J[ohn] (1816–91). Known (somewhat ironically) in later life as 'the Poet Close', he was born in Gunnerside, Swaledale, the son of a butcher and Wesleyan lay preacher. From 1822 to 1826 John Close assisted in his father's shop. At the age of thirty, he turned his hand to printing. Thereafter, he moved into the bookselling end of the trade, and ran a stall at Bowness in Windermere, catering principally to Lake District tourists brought by the newly opened train service. Close sold his own poems and made a name for himself as a working-class author. In 1860 a Civil List pension of £50 was awarded the Poet Close, and promptly withdrawn by Palmerston after sarcastic questions in Parliament. The loss embittered the author's last years. Close wrote some simple chapbook-style fiction, notably: *The Wise Man Of Stainmore* (1864) and *The Waddle Family* (1868). BL 3. *DNB*. Wol.

CLOUSTON, J[oseph] Storer (1870–1944). Born in Cumberland, the son of Sir Thomas Smith Clouston, MD, he was educated at Edinburgh and Oxford. A lawyer by profession, Clouston's later life as a writer was spent in Orkney where he was active in local politics. His first novel was *The Lunatic At Large* (1899), a comic series of asylum sketches. His next work, *The Duke* (1900), enjoyed more success. It is the prince-and-pauperish story of a young aristocrat who allows an eccentric Irishman to take over his dukedom for a month. Clouston's fiction is all very light reading, and he was turning out large quantities of it well into the twentieth century. BL 40. *WW.*

CLOWES, [Sir] William Laird (1856–1905). Clowes was born in Hampstead, the eldest son of a legal officer, and after attending King's College, London himself trained as a lawyer before turning to journalism in 1879. Fascinated by the sea, Clowes soon became Britain's leading naval correspondent and had a major influence on government policy. His interest over the years shifted from journalism to history, and in 1903, he produced his massive history of the Royal Navy. On the side, Clowes wrote poetry and a number of nautical tales, including: *The Great Naval War Of 1887* (1886), a prophetic fable, modelled on Chesney's* *Battle Of Dorking**. Other of Clowes's 'tales of tomorrow' are *The Captain Of The Mary Rose* (1892) and *The Great Peril, And How It Was Averted* (1893). Clowes was knighted in 1902 but his last years were passed in poverty and ill health. BL 3. *DNB.*

COBB, Thomas (1854–1932). Cobb was born at Marylebone, London, and educated privately. He began his novel-writing career with *Lucy Carter* (1887), a work which prominently features the drawing-room comedy which later became Cobb's speciality. His skill in dialogue is well displayed in *The Judgement Of Helen* (1899) in which a matchmaker is outwitted by her wards. *The Bishop's Gambit* (1901) is another comedy, this time about the 'divorce problem', an elderly Anglican cleric benignly presiding over the action. Cobb went on to write a huge number of novels in the twentieth century. BL 86. *WW.* Wol.

COBBAN, J[ames] MacLaren (1849–1903). Cobban was born in Aberdeen, and educated at a kirk school there and at New College, London, where he trained to be a Presbyterian minister. Instead he drifted into teaching, journalism and finally full-time novel writing. Cobban's main line was adventure fiction. But his first novel, *The Care Of Souls* (1879) is the story of an eccentric vicar in a country parish. *Tinted Vapours* (1885) is a sensational* 'shilling shocker', on the model of Hugh Conway's (i.e. Frederick Fargus's*) *Called Back**. *The Red Sultan* (1893) is set in Morocco in the eighteenth century and features the escapades of an improbable Scottish laird. *The Angel Of The Covenant* (1898) is a Scottish historical* novel about cavaliers and Presbyterians. *Cease Fire* (1900) is a story of the Transvaal War of 1881, from the British viewpoint; *The Golden Tooth* (1901) is a straightforward murder and detection novel. Cobban was evidently hard up in his later years and applied to the Royal Literary Fund for assistance. BL 22. *WW*. Wol. RLF.

COBBOLD, Richard (1797–1877). Cobbold was born one of twenty-one children of a rich Suffolk brewing family. His mother had cultivated literary tastes which she passed on to her son who was educated at Bury St Edmunds and at Cambridge University. After ordination Cobbold took up a post at Diss in his native East Anglia, where he was a sporting parson with a lively amateur's interest in writing and art (he often illustrated his own publications). He was also passionately philanthropic. Cobbold's great success was with the charming regional-historical novel, *The History Of Margaret Catchpole, A Suffolk Girl** (1845; Colburn* is supposed to have given £1,000 for the copyright). Cobbold's historical novels are less interesting than his first-hand depictions ('real histories' as he called them) of East Anglian life and scenery. *Mary Anne Wellington, The Soldier's Daughter, Wife And Widow* (1846) brought in donations of £600 for the unfortunate woman (a military widow, resident in Norwich) on whom the work was based. The larger philanthropic aim of the novel was to show that 'the common soldier is not a mere machine' and to protest at the flogging of servicemen. Cobbold's other fiction includes: *Jack Rattler, Or The Horrors Of Transportation* (1852), a social problem* novel, never published; *Zenon The Martyr* (1847), 'An Historical Narrative Of The Early Days Of Christianity'; *Courtland* (1852), ostensibly 'by the daughter of Mary Anne Wellington'. BL 6. *DNB*. RM. *NCBEL*. Wol. Sad.

COCHRANE, Alexander Baillie [Dundas Ross Wishart] MP (1816–90). The son of an admiral of the fleet, and later the first Baron Lamington, Cochrane (also variously titled Baillie-Cochrane and Cochrane-Baillie) was educated at Eton and Cambridge. He was a Conservative MP from 1841 to 1852 and allied himself with Disraeli's* Young England* movement. His later political career is a catalogue of missed chances, although he managed to represent the Isle of Wight in Parliament from 1870 to 1880, when he was made a peer. He married in 1844, and had one son who later went on to be Governor of Queensland. A dilettante man of letters, Cochrane among other things published four well-received, but trashy (as the reviewers thought), fashionable novels: *Lucille Belmont* (1849); *Ernest Vane* (1849); *Florence The Beautiful* (1854); *Théâtre Francais* (1879). The last cobbles together in fictional form materials that the author originally intended for a history of French theatre. The *Academy** found the idea 'very weak indeed'. BL 4. *DNB*. Wol.

The Cockney School. Cockneys feature prominently in the Victorian novel from Dickens's* Sam Weller onwards. But in the last two decades of the century a well-defined genre specialising in London slum types emerged.

Major precursors were E. J. Milliken's* popular 'Arry character (1872) and Besant's* bestselling East End novel, *All Sorts And Conditions Of Men* (1882). But the main impetus came from Charles Booth's seventeen volumes of *Life And Labour Of The People In London* (1889–1903). There followed naturalistic depictions of slum life in Arthur Morrison's* *Tales Of Mean Streets* (1894) and *A Child Of The Jago* (1896); Arthur St John Adcock's* *East End Idylls* (1897); Somerset Maugham's* *Liza Of Lambeth* (1897). At the turn of the century, Edwin Pugh* and William Pett Ridge* were established as the leaders of the cockney school. In the twentieth century depictions of low-life Londoners tended more towards bland comic stereotypes of the lovable 'Cockney sparrer'.

COCKTON, Henry (1807–53). Little is known of Cockton's life, other than that he made a lot of money with his first novel, *Valentine Vox, The Ventriloquist* (1840) and promptly lost it speculating in the East Anglian malting business. Cockton was born in London, probably illegitimate. (Even Cockton's son reported himself ignorant of his father's origins.) He married in 1841 at Bury St Edmunds and passed his later life in Suffolk, dying there of consumption at an early age. *Valentine Vox* (serialised in monthly numbers) is broadly comic (although it has some horrific lunatic asylum scenes), and may possibly have influenced Dickens*. It carried sixty illustrations by Thomas Onwhyn*. *Stanley Thorn* (serialised in *Bentley's Miscellany*, January 1840–February 1842) was illustrated by George Cruikshank*. *George St George Julian, The Prince Of Swindlers* (1841, a Newgate* influenced work) was illustrated by Onwhyn. *The Sisters* (1844; a more sentimental tale) was serialised in the *Illustrated London News* illustrated by J. Kenny Meadows* and Alfred Crowquill*. Cockton's late novel *Percy Effingham* (1853) is very poor stuff although its story may have some autobiographical reference. Effingham loses all his money (as Cockton had) and discovers who his real friends are and the emptiness of the 'world's esteem'. As is common in Cockton's work, the setting is 'horsey and houndy'. *Lady Felicia* (1852), another late work, has a setting in Sudbury, Suffolk, of some local interest. BL 9. *DNB. NCBEL.* Wol. Sad. RLF.

Colburn and Co. (1808–53). The most notorious publisher of nineteenth-century fiction. The firm was founded by Henry Colburn (d. 1855) whose origins are shrouded in mystery. Various rumours suggest that he was either a bastard of the Duke of York or of Lord Lansdowne. He began in the book trade, while still a lad, at William Earle's bookshop in Albemarle Street. By 1808, he was at the 'British and Foreign Library' in Conduit Street, and was publishing books under his own name. At some point soon thereafter, he became sole proprietor of the establishment. During the period of the Napoleonic Wars, Colburn established his publishing style. He catered exclusively for the West End carriage trade, with expensive editions (mainly available through the circulating library) and specialised in volumes of travel, biography and, above all, fashionable fiction. Colburn is the main architect of the so-called 'silver fork*' genre; that is to say, novels by aristocratic authors, depicting the life of aristocrats. Colburn had one of his early successes with the fiction and travel books of Lady Morgan (i.e. Sydney Owenson, 1776–1859). In 1824, he sold his circulating library to Saunders and Otley* (publishers who went on to model themselves on Colburn). In the

1820s, Colburn made himself the undisputed market leader in three-volume novels*, a form of fiction which he did much to standardise. He promoted his wares by energetic and often unscrupulous advertising, gaining the nickname 'Prince of Puffers'. In 1814, he founded the *New Monthly Magazine**, and in 1817, he set up England's first serious weekly review, the *Literary Gazette*. In 1828, he helped found the *Athenaeum**. The journal soon turned on Colburn, attacking his fashionable authors and his log-rolling for them. In the 1820s, Colburn introduced Disraeli*, Bulwer-Lytton*, Mrs Gore*, Captain Marryat*, and G. P. R. James* to the British public. But by 1829, he was financially overextended, and he went into partnership with the printer, Richard Bentley*. The men were temperamentally at odds, and the partnership broke up with bad feeling in 1832. For the period 1833–35, Colburn operated from Windsor in a very small way. (The terms of his separation from Bentley forbade his publishing in London.) But in 1836, he contrived to start business once again, at 13 Great Marlborough Street, Mayfair. For the next seventeen years, Colburn churned out three-deckers for the libraries (increasingly after 1842 for Mudie's* circulating library). He and Bentley were in constant rivalry and were called by Mrs Oliphant* (who had her start with Colburn) the Scylla and Charybdis of Victorian publishing. His main authors in the 1840s were Disraeli, Mrs Gore, Frances Trollope* and Mrs Marsh (née Caldwell*). In the 1840s he also published the early fiction of Anthony Trollope*, Richard Cobbold* and R. S. Surtees*. In 1853, Colburn sold his business in thriving condition to Hurst and Blackett*. He died in 1855, leaving £35,000 and a widow whom Dickens's* friend John Forster married in 1856. Colburn is a vilified publisher who in fact contributed much to the development of the Victorian fiction industry, not all of it bad. *DNB*.

COLERIDGE, C[hristabel] R[ose] (1843–1921). Born in Chelsea, she was the daughter of the Rev. Derwent Coleridge, and a granddaughter of the poet. She never married and lived her adult life privately at Torquay. Her first published novel was *Lady Betty* (1869), a tale of the early eighteenth century for juvenile readers. It was followed by a regular succession of similar works, many published by the SPCK*. They include: *An English Squire* (1881); *A Near Relation* (1886); *The Prophet's Mantle* (1897), the story of a young clergyman's apprenticeship. Coleridge had old-fashioned views on the place of women, and in 1894 published a collection of essays entitled, *The Daughters Who Have Not Revolted*. In 1893, she collaborated with Charlotte Yonge* (whose biography she was later to write) in producing *Strolling Players*, a story recounting the adventures of a genteel amateur dramatic touring company. She participated in other of the group-authored novels that were faddish at the end of the century. From 1890, Coleridge helped edit the magazines the *Monthly Packet** and *Friendly Leaves*. BL 39. *WW. NCBEL*. Wol.

COLERIDGE, M[ary] E[lizabeth] (1861–1907). Coleridge was born in London, the daughter of a legal officer, and distantly related as great-grandniece to the poet Samuel Taylor Coleridge. Educated at home, mainly by the minor poet W. J. Cory (1823–92), Coleridge displayed precocious writing and artistic talent. At twenty, she was already contributing to magazines. In 1893, she published her first novel, *The Seven Sleepers Of Ephesus*.

The plot is very extravagant, moving out from matrimonial strife to a melodramatically conceived revolution in Germany. The title refers to the name of the secret society at the centre of the story. The novel made no stir with critics or the reading public. Coleridge's reputation as a poet was, however, already considerable. She had a marked success with *The King With Two Faces** (1897), an unusually clever romance dealing with the assassination of Gustavus III of Sweden in 1792 and the French Revolution. The tale had gone through ten editions by 1908. Another superior historical* fiction is *The Fiery Dawn* (1901), whose sprightly romantic action brings in the Duchesse de Berry. Coleridge's main idea in historical fiction is expressed in the preface to her *The Shadow On The Wall* (1904): 'history is chock-full of improbabilities'. She never married. After reading Tolstoy in the mid-1890s, she became actively philanthropic and taught to university level at the Working Women's College in London. According to her biographer, 'no one so feminine can ever have longed more to be a man'. BL 5. *DNB*. RM. *NCBEL*. Wol.

COLERIDGE, Sara (1802–52). The only daughter of the poet, Samuel Taylor Coleridge, she is principally remembered as the editor of his works, notably *Biographia Literaria*. Sara Coleridge was born at Keswick. Her home life was very irregular, and she had much of her education from the poet Southey. As a girl, she was extraordinarily precocious, and at an early age had learned Latin and Greek as well as modern languages. She was also possessed of great beauty. In 1829, she married her cousin, Henry Nelson Coleridge, a barrister. The couple had five children, only two of whom survived. A poet and translator principally, Sara Coleridge also wrote children's books. In fiction, her major effort is *Phantasmion* (1837). This extraordinary work is a prose epic set in the Lake District and modelled on Spenser's *Faerie Queene*. The hero, Prince Phantasmion, inherits the fertile kingdom of Palmland and the narrative follows his various adventures in the neighbouring 'Land of Rocks' (i.e. a fabulous Lake District) across the Black Mountains. The work was highly valued by discriminating readers and influenced later Victorian fantasy*. But it was a complete failure commercially being first published anonymously in an edition of 250 copies at the high price of 9s. by the obscure publisher Pickering. In 1843, her husband died, and Sara took over his task as executor for Coleridge's literary remains. BL 1. *DNB*. RM. *NCBEL*. Wol.

COLLINGWOOD, Harry (i.e. William Joseph Cosens Lancaster, 1851–1922). Lancaster was born in Weymouth, the son of a Royal Navy captain and educated at the Naval College, Greenwich. He went to sea as a boy of fifteen but had to abandon his chosen career because of extreme short sight. He subsequently became a marine engineer, and travelled widely around the world. In 1878, Lancaster married and began to publish nautical* tales for juveniles under his Collingwood pseudonym. (Cuthbert Collingwood having been a hero of British naval history in the Napoleonic Wars.) Collingwood's fiction is Hentyesque* in tone, and much of it was published by the SPCK*. His works include: *The Yarn Of The Sands* (1879); *The Rover's Secret* (1888); *Jack Beresford's Secret* (1896). In 1878, Collingwood summed up his philosophy of writing thus: 'If my books serve but to while pleasantly away an idle hour or two for the general reader, or to convey a scrap of useful information to the young yachtsman, their purpose will be fully accomplished.' His most popular work (to judge by its many reprintings) was *The Pirate Island* (1884). BL 40. *WW*. Wol.

COLLINGWOOD, William Gershom (1854–1932). Collingwood was educated at Liverpool and at Oxford. His father was a successful water-colourist, and the son went on to study art at the Slade School in London. From 1881 to 1900 he was secretary and disciple to John Ruskin*, about whom he later wrote sympathetically. Collingwood developed a passion for the area of the Lake District around Coniston where Ruskin built his house at Brantwood. His major work of fiction is the experimental *Thorstein Of The Mere* (1895), a pastiche saga of the Norsemen in Cumberland and Westmorland in the tenth century. Collingwood did three other works in the same hybrid saganovel line including *The Bondwoman* (1896), a reconstruction of Langdale in Anglo-Saxon times. More realistic is *Dutch Agnes, Her Valentine* (1910), the fictional journal of the Curate of Coniston, 1616–23. Collingwood's very precious exercises in fiction enjoyed something of a vogue early in the twentieth century, and were quite substantially reprinted. BL 4. *WW*.

Collins and Co. (1819–). Publisher, founded by William Collins (1789–1853). Collins, a high-minded Glaswegian Scot, began the city's first Sunday school in 1816, and helped found the British and Foreign Temperance Society. He started publishing in 1819. William Collins II joined the firm in 1843, and was knighted in 1881. Collins specialised in school-books, bibles and instructional works, pioneering techniques of cheap, mass production. In 1875, the firm had some 1,300 employees, and grew in the twentieth century to become the country's largest producer of books. In the later nineteenth century, the firm published large quantities of low-price, reprint fiction, mainly for the juvenile reader. (WC)Boase.

COLLINS, Charles Allston (1828–73). A son of the painter William Collins RA, he inherited more of his father's artistic talent than his famous older brother Wilkie Collins*. Charles Collins was trained at the Royal Academy Schools, and was associated with the Pre-Raphaelites. Like that of his brother, his career was strongly influenced by Dickens*, whose daughter Kate he married in 1860. After 1858, he devoted himself to writing, producing journalism (for *All The Year Round**, particularly) and some insubstantial novels. Even more than Wilkie, he suffered poor health which hindered him making anything of his talent. His abilities as a novelist are best represented in *The Bar Sinister* (1864). A psychologically intricate narrative, it tells the story of a man who loves the natural daughter of a woman who ruined his brother. Collins was originally contracted to illustrate Dickens's last novel, *Edwin Drood**, but illness prevented him doing more than the cover. BL 2. *DNB*. *NCBEL*. Wol.

COLLINS, [Edward James] Mortimer (1827–76). Collins was born in Plymouth, the only son of a solicitor and amateur poet who died of consumption in 1839. As a boy he was privately educated and much dominated by his mother (d. 1873). To please her, he gave up his ambition to be a newspaperman taking instead a succession of respectable but dull teaching positions, latterly in Guernsey. Around 1849 he married Susannah Crump, a clergyman's widow, and in the mid-1850s he finally took the plunge and became a full-time journalist and magazine writer for *Punch**, *Tinsley's Magazine** and *Temple Bar**. His verse is pleasantly Latinate and his novels lively, mostly comic and insubstantial. Famously fluent, he could write his fiction while conducting a conversation. He also made a reputation for himself as a knowledgeable classical scholar and philhellenist. Known as 'the King of the Bohemians' Collins affected a raffish man-of-the-world pose. Privately, however, he was the most morally conventional and home-loving of men and the temper of his mind is well reflected in his ruminatively philosophical *Thoughts In My Garden* (1880). His first wife died in 1867, and a year later he remarried. Afterwards he rarely left his home at Knowl Hill, Berkshire, even for a day, restricting his social life to the local village where it was his habit to appear clad in velvet coat and straw hat, accompanied by a pair of dogs. He was not, however, a popular figure with his neighbours ('bucolic louts', as he called them). Among his literary friends was R. D. Blackmore* whose influence can be detected in Collins's fiction, the best of which is the in-its-day controversial, *Sweet Anne Page* (1868). The work has an extravagant plot, opening at 'Idlechester', where the dreamy young orphan Stephen Langton falls in love with a local heiress, Anne Page. After some not very convincing twists of plot, the action climaxes with a vendetta in Corsica and fierce love quarrels which leave Anne a hopeless imbecile, nursed by her remorseful former rival. *The Vivian Romance* (1870) has a Byronic hero who suffers a change of personality after an attack of sunstroke and becomes a pirate in the Aegean. *Two Plunges For A Pearl* (1872) features a pair of sisters who after their father's death take up divergent careers on the stage, and in domestic service. Like most of Collins's novels, its narrative is punctuated by light versifying and classical quotation. *Squire Silchester's Whim* (1873) is a digressive Devon tale. *Sweet And Twenty* (1875) is a typically slight love story. *Transmigration* (1874) is a more interesting work of science fiction* in which the hero is reincarnated after an enlightening sojourn on Mars (conceived as being like ancient Athens). Collins had a great deal of assistance in writing novels from his second wife, Frances (née Cotton, d. 1886) and some of their novels came out under joint authorship. They include the idyll *You Play Me False* (1878) which chronicles the unconventional marriage of a peer and a governess. *A Fight With Fortune* (1876) dramatises the history of the Cotton family, into which the author had married. Collins suffered poor health, and died relatively young of heart disease. After his death, his widow (as 'Mrs Mortimer Collins') brought out some inferior novels of her own, such as *A Broken Lily* (1882), the story of a squire, Thornton Meadows, who loves a young girl but marries her villainous adoptive mother. Collins was a man of wide interests, including chess, mathematics and science. A daughter of the first marriage (and the author's only child), Mabel Collins (1851–1927), subsequently wrote on occultism and anti-vivisectionism and published numerous novels of the supernatural and on modern 'sex problems', including: *In This World* (1879); *Cobwebs* (1882), a series of vignettes; *Suggestion* (1892). *Outlawed* (1908) is a novel on the woman suffrage question, written with Charlotte Despard*. Mabel Collins married the journalist Keningale Cook in 1871, but was separated around 1880 when he went mad. She subsequently became a prominent theosophist coediting the movement's monthly *Lucifer* magazine with Madame Blavatsky, from 1887. Collins's *In The Flower Of Her Youth*

(1883) contains a close record of her upbringing ('What a glorious girlhood!') with her eccentric father Mortimer portrayed as 'Brough Warrington, the King of Bohemia'. Less glowingly, it also chronicles her marriage with Cook portrayed as 'Charlie Newman'. Newman's wife, the abused heroine Lil, goes on the stage and dies pathetically in the novel's last chapter. (Mortimer Collins) BL 19. (Mabel Collins) BL 18. *DNB*. (Mabel Collins) *WW. NCBEL*. Wol. Sad. RLF.

COLLINS, [William] Wilkie (1824–89). The leading sensation* novelist of the century. Born in London, he was the eldest son of William Collins, the painter and Royal Academician. He was named after his father, and his father's friend the artist Sir David Wilkie. In his twenties, he assumed 'Wilkie' as his first name. The Collins household was bohemian and as a boy Wilkie spent some years with his father in Italy and was educated privately. William Collins (a Puseyite) hoped his son would go into the Church. But Wilkie inherited his father's poor health (both suffered obscurely from 'rheumatic gout') and he was not considered strong enough for Oxford. In 1841, he was articled to work in the establishment of a London tea merchant. This did not suit the young man, who already had clear artistic and literary inclinations. In 1846, he entered Lincoln's Inn, and was called to the Bar in 1851, but never practised. William Collins died in 1847, and in the following year Wilkie published as his first book a dutiful two-volume memoir of his father. At the same period, he was trying his hand at painting, without success. He had for some time been working on a romance of ancient Rome, *Antonina**, which was published in 1850. Although the work was successful, Collins never wrote another historical* novel. His career continued with a well-received Cornish travel book, *Rambles Beyond Railways* (1851) and 'A Story Of Modern Life', the sexually superheated melodrama *Basil** (1852). In the preface to this early novel Collins enunciated his famous doctrine that 'the Novel and the Play are twin-sisters in the Family of Fiction'. In 1851, he became acquainted with Dickens*. Both men had a passion for drama, and they collaborated on amateur theatricals. Collins also began contributing short stories and non-fiction to Dickens's weekly magazine, *Household Words**. His first contribution, the horror story, *A Terribly Strange Bed* (1852), has been widely anthologised and producing a quantity of short pieces for Dickens (collected as *After Dark*, 1856) Collins in the 1850s produced the full-length mystery novels: *Hide And Seek* (1854) and *The Dead Secret** (1857). Both used physical handicap in their plots (deaf and dumbness in the first, blindness in the second). *Hide And Seek*'s opening chapters describing Zack Thorpe's childhood Sundays plausibly recall Collins's own upbringing in his father's strictly religious household. Critics (including Dickens) approved highly of these densely plotted works, although some detected a 'close, stifling, unwholesome odour' in Collins's imagination. In 1856, Collins wrote the melodrama, *The Frozen Deep*, in which he and Dickens acted the following year. (Collins rewrote the piece as a short story in 1874.) In 1856, Collins had been struck at a court hearing by the narrative possibilities of witnesses' testimony. The reportage technique was brilliantly employed in *The Woman In White** (1860). Collins first published this, his most famous work, in Dickens's new journal, *All The Year Round**. The novel made his name and largely inspired the 1860s vogue for so-called sensation fiction. He followed up with *No Name** (1862), a work which attacked the British laws of inheritance. George Smith of the *Cornhill Magazine** paid £5,000 for his next work, *Armadale**, the most complex and melodramatic of Collins's novels. In 1868, he published *The Moonstone** (first as a serial in Dickens's journal), which is plausibly regarded as the first detective* story proper in English. By this period, Collins's health was poor, and he was chronically overdosed with laudanum to relieve the pain of his rheumatic gout. His uncontrollable screams of agony made it difficult for him to retain amanuenses. And in 1868, his friendship with Dickens cooled. Mutual jealousy may have played a part, since Collins could now regard himself as almost an equal. *Man And Wife** (1870) heralds a propagandistic phase of Collins's career. A 'fiction founded on facts', it protests the British marriage laws. The governess-heroine, Anne Silvester, is seduced and victimised by the looseness of the Scottish common-law wife statute. The novel also puts forward an anti-muscular* thesis, arguing that athleticism destroys the moral fibre. *Poor Miss Finch* (1872) has another plot drawing in the author's obsessive interest in blindness. (The heroine has her sight restored, but actually welcomes the loss of her sight again. An improbable sub-plot involving her husband's turning blue is latched onto this paradox.) Collins continued to propagandise in *The New Magdalen* (1873). This work shows Collins's knack for combining the topical and the melodramatic. Its heroine, Mercy Merrick, is a fallen woman who goes as a nurse to the Franco-Prussian War where she is shot and left for dead. Mercy recovers, and changes identities with another (supposedly) dead woman, Grace Roseberry, leading to inevitable complications and final redemption at the hands of an idealistic clergyman. The novel was successfully dramatised as were many of Collins's later works. *The Law And The Lady* (1875) is another attack on 'Mrs Grundy', English sexual hypocrisy and the Scottish 'Not Proven' verdict. Written from the viewpoint of a perplexed wife (Valeria), it is a simpler constructed narrative than many of the author's. Collins's reputation was extraordinarily high in the 1870s, although his writing showed clear signs of decline. In 1871, his stock rose with a very successful stage version of *The Woman In White*. And in 1873, he made an applauded reading tour of America (from which, like Dickens before him, his health suffered terribly). In 1875, Chatto* reissued his fiction in cheap half-crown form with great sales success. Occultism interested Collins towards the end of his life and *The Two Destinies* (1876) deals with telepathy between childhood friends (eventually husband and wife in later life). Collins's austere documentary style helps authenticate the absurd fantasy. *The Fallen Leaves* (1879), the story of a reformed prostitute (an heiress, as it emerges) and a socialist, Amelius, who courageously marries her, is generally regarded as Collins's worst novel. In it he aimed to publicise the miseries of 'the people who have drawn blanks in the lottery of life'. The novel was dedicated to his common-law wife Caroline and Collins insisted that he had treated his awkward theme with 'scrupulous delicacy'. *Jezebel's Daughter* (1880) has some macabre scenes in a German morgue. *The Black Robe* (1881) attacks the Jesuits and features the fiendishly complex legal plotting that Collins loved. *Heart And Science* (1883) caused some stir with its propaganda against vivisection, aided by some powerful descriptions of animal surgery. *The Evil Genius* (1886) is a study of modern divorce. *The*

Legacy Of Cain (1889) is a genetic mystery story, with two heroines, one of whom (the reader is not told which) is the daughter of a murderess. Collins died while his last novel, *Blind Love** (1890), was running in *The Illustrated London News** and the work was completed by Walter Besant*. Despite appalling health, Collins's writing career of forty years is one of the longest and most productive in Victorian fiction. His sexual life was irregular. In the mid-1850s he took up with Caroline Graves (an original for Anne Catherick in *The Woman In White*). She married another man in 1868 but in the early 1870s returned to Collins. From 1868 he lived with Martha Rudd, who bore him three children. His estate was divided between the two women. BL 30. *DNB*. RM. *NCBEL*. Wol. Sad.

A Comedy In Spasms, 'Iota' (i.e. Kathleen Mannington Caffyn), 1895, 1 vol, Hutchinson. A sexual cross-purpose plot by one of the new woman* novelists, written in Iota's archly elliptic manner. The story begins on the Marrables' cattle station in Australia. Elizabeth, the daughter, rejects the proposal of a noble lover. When her father is killed and the family income is reduced to £500 a year she allows herself to be wooed and won by the aged intellectual, Colonel Prynne. But in her heart she loves Tom Temple, whom she met on the voyage back to England. Ironically, in England, Mrs Marrable inherits a fortune, making Elizabeth's sacrifice meaningless. She and Tom meet, decide to run away, but at the last minute resolve on renunciation. Elizabeth survives 'only altered as flowers are by young ladies who thrust iron wires through their hearts'.

Cometh Up As A Flower, Rhoda Broughton, 1867, 2 vols, Bentley. (Serialised in shortened form in the *Dublin University Magazine**, July 1866–January 1867.) One of Broughton's early, and slightly scandalous romances. The story is told in prattling style autobiographically by the heroine Nell Le Strange. The motherless daughter of an amiable but impoverished nobleman ('dad') Nell falls 'neck and crop' in love with a handsome, penniless soldier, Major Dick M'Gregor. She is meanwhile proposed to by a rich aristocrat, Sir Hugh Lancaster. The proposal coincides with her father's bankruptcy and death. Nell's sister Dolly forges a letter jilting Dick. When the truth comes out, Nell (who has married Sir Hugh) pines and it emerges that her ostensibly gay narrative is being written from her deathbed. Dick, meanwhile has died on service in India. The pert tough-mindedness of the narrator-heroine is appealing.

The Coming Race, E. G. E. L. Bulwer-Lytton, 1871, 1 vol, Blackwood. A pioneer work of British science fiction*. The hero is a bumptious, ultra-republican American mining engineer who stumbles on a lost underground civilisation. The 'Vril-ya', as they are called, enjoy a utopian, perfectly stable social organisation based on vril, a source of infinitely renewable electrical power. (Commerce promptly invented the brand name 'Bovril', the beef essence drink.) Also present are ray guns, aerial travel, ESP and super-advanced technology. But for all its futurism, the subterra of the Vril-ya has its period charm, conceived as it is as a superior Crystal Palace, glistening with paste jewellery and electroplate. The adventure plot (love between earthling and alien princess) is suspended for many chapters of essayistic digression. There is one fine irony of plot. The hero finds the perfect static utopia of the Vril-ya insufferably boring. He is rescued at the last minute from a death sentence by Princess Zee, who flies him to safety. The novel ends with an ominous prophecy that the superior race will invade upper earth, 'the Darwinian proposition' as Bulwer-Lytton called it.

Comin' Thro' The Rye, Helen Mathers, 1875, 3 vols, Bentley. The author's first published novel, and a huge hit which remained perennially popular through the Victorian period and after. The author's style is essentially an exaggeration of Rhoda Broughton's* in *Cometh Up As A Flower** (1867). The story is narrated autobiographically by Helen ('Nell') Adair, a colonel's daughter, with a profusion of girlish archness and much literary quotation of a sententious or facetious kind. The first section of the tripartite narrative, 'Seed Time', finds the heroine a precocious fourteen-year-old at the family home Manor House in 'Silverbridge' (a name borrowed from Trollope's* Barsetshire* sequence of novels). Already Nell has a sweetheart, George Temple, who promises to marry her at eighteen. And Nell also has a rival, the sly Silvia Fleming. The second section, 'Summer', jumps four years. Nell is now of age. Her brother Jack has become a barrister and her sister Milly has married. But she cannot bring herself now to marry the faithful George, although she admires him. Instead, Nell loves Paul Vasher, whom she wrongly thinks loves Silvia. When she finds out this is not so, the lovers declare their passion, George meanwhile taking his disappointment manfully. In the third section, 'Harvest', Silvia falsely inserts an announcement of George's marriage to Nell in *The Times*. George hurries off to Italy to disabuse Paul, but too late to avert tragedy. Thinking himself betrayed, Paul has married Silvia. At the end of the novel, Paul and Nell have a final meeting in which they realise the impossibility of adultery. Nell cares for Paul's child, who dies. Paul himself goes off to the wars to die at Sedan, his last words being, 'Comin' thro' the rye – *God's Rye*, Nell!', in memory of the harvest field where they plighted their troth.

Confessions Of A Thug, Captain Meadows Taylor, 1839, 3 vols, Bentley. Until Kipling's* *Kim**, the most informed and successful Victorian novel of Indian life. The secret religious cult of Thuggee, bands of assassins committing murder and robbery in the service of the goddess Kali, first came to light in the 1820s. As Taylor wrote, 'Few who were in India at that period will ever forget the excitement which the discovery occasioned in every part of the country; it was utterly discredited by the magistrates of many districts, who could not be brought to believe that this silently destructive system could have worked without their knowledge.' The cult was broken up by the use of informants, and draconian punishment. Taylor's novel takes the form of the prison confession of a Thug, Ameer Ali, to a white 'sahib'. The story begins with the murder of Ameer's parents, and his adoption by a thug, Ismail. He is inducted into the mysteries of Thuggism, and the use of the Roomal, or strangling handkerchief. He marries, but so secret is the society of Thuggee that even his wife Azima does not know his profession. Ameer's adventures (some of them extremely bloody and violent) take him all over the sub-continent. He is finally caught by the Feringhee (British) authorities and partly to revenge the treacherous murder of his family turns queen's evidence. Apart from its virtues as a tale of adventure, the novel is a remarkable attempt to enter the colonised Indian consciousness. The work was extremely popular, and introduced the word 'thug' into general English usage.

The Confessions Of Harry Lorrequer, Charles Lever, 1839, 1 vol, Curry. (Serialised irregularly in the *Dublin University Magazine**, February 1837–June 1842 and in monthly parts, March 1839–January 1840, with illustrations by Phiz*.) Lever's first hit. The novel began accidentally with a successful short magazine tale of garrison life in Cork, narrated autobiographically by the amiable military hero. Lorrequer is an English officer posted to Ireland with his regiment. An opening episode in which the hero (after an egregiously drunken night) goes on parade unconscious of his blacked face sets the tone of the narrative. He is subsequently posted all round Ireland where he loves, duels, steeplechases, gambles, drives tandems and feasts. Harry later travels to France where he has various adventures with Arthur O'Leary* (later the subject of another much inferior novel) ending up with the latter's arrest and trial. The action winds up in Munich, where with the aid of a rich uncle, the hero finally wins the hand of his Irish love, Lady Jane Callonby. As Lever recorded: 'I wrote as I felt, sometimes in good spirits, sometimes in bad, always carelessly.'

Coningsby, Benjamin Disraeli, 1844, 3 vols, Colburn. The first of the author's Young England* trilogy together with *Sybil** (1845) and *Tancred** (1847). All three were dedicated to the youth of England. The Young England programme proposed regeneration for the Conservative Party, whose traditional ideology Disraeli thought was tired and contaminated by utilitarianism. Harry Coningsby's parents marry against the wishes of his father Lord Monmouth (a character based, like Thackeray's* Steyne in *Vanity Fair**, on the Marquis of Hertford who died in 1842). Orphaned, Harry regains his grandfather's favour and is sent to Eton. There he saves the life of Oswald Millbank (an industrialist's son, supposedly based on Gladstone) who becomes a lifelong friend. Later in life, Harry marries Edith Millbank, symbolising the union of new wealth and old rank. Coningsby goes on to Cambridge. But the main educational influence in his life comes from a chance meeting in a thunderstorm with the mysterious and omnicompetent Jew, Sidonia. Sidonia inspires Harry with new Conservative idealism and the young man falls out with his grandfather when he offers him an 'agreeably safe' seat in Parliament. On the Marquis's death, Harry discovers himself disinherited. But he sets himself to work as a barrister, eventually wins the patronage of the industrialist Millbank and successfully enters the House of Commons. He is made wealthy when Monmouth's illegitimate daughter and heiress, Flora, dies leaving him her fortune. The novel made a great impact. It inspired an anonymous squib, *The Anti-Coningsby* (1844) and Thackeray's cruel burlesque, *Codlingsby* (1847). There were a number of 'keys' supplied for the dramatis personae.

CONYBEARE, [Rev.] William John (1815–57). Born in the West Country, he was a son of the eminent geologist, the Rev. William Conybeare (1787–1857). Young Conybeare was educated at Westminster School and Cambridge, where he was for a while a fellow. In 1842, he was appointed principal of the new Liverpool Collegiate Institution. He held this post until 1848, when his health collapsed. The year before he died (of consumption)

Conybeare brought out a powerful religious novel, *Perversion, A Tale For The Times* (1856). The hero, Charles Bampton, progresses through High and Low Church and atheistic free-thought before finding a true Christian vocation. The novel contains intelligent criticism of the many varieties of belief and infidelity rampant in the mid-1850s. BL 1. *DNB*. *NCBEL*. Wol.

COOK, [Edward] Dutton (1829–83). Born the son of a prosperous London solicitor, Cook began working life articled to his father. He subsequently trained as an artist, without success. From 1867 to 1875, he was drama critic of the *Pall Mall Gazette*, and edited the *Cornhill**, 1868–71. Cook wrote books on the theatre, short stories for the magazines and a number of three-volume novels. *Paul Foster's Daughter* (1861) is a lively tale of Bohemian London, and was well received by the critics. The hero of the title is 'a historical painter, an unsuccessful great man. Perhaps on reflection we had better say, simply, unsuccessful'. The plot is sensational* in nature, and involves forgery. *Leo* (1863) is a novel of the London art world, created around the love adventures of a vivacious heroine, Leo. *Doubleday's Children* (1879) is a family saga, narrated autobiographically. Cook is particularly strong on current slang and up-to-the minute metropolitan mores. BL 11. Boase. RLF.

COOPER, Edward H[erbert] (1867–1910). Cooper was born in Staffordshire, the son of a landowning father. While at preparatory school, he developed an illness that left him crippled for life. At Oxford, where he took a mediocre degree in history, Cooper was active politically as a Liberal Unionist. After a false start in chartered accountancy, he supported himself principally by journalism. A bachelor, Cooper passed much of his adult life abroad, mainly in France. In 1896, he became *Galignani's* Paris correspondent and was later foreign correspondent for the *Daily Mail*. He began publishing novels with *Geoffory Hamilton* (1893), a rather plotless work with some good autobiographical Oxford episodes. It was followed by *Richard Escott* (1893) and the more interesting political tale, *The Enemies* (1896), which deals with Ireland after the Parnell scandal. Despite his disability, Cooper had a passion for gambling and the turf. (He was, in fact, to die, of apoplexy, at Newmarket racecourse aged only forty-three.) He successfully used his knowledge of horse-racing in *Mr Blake Of Newmarket* (1897) and *The Monk Wins* (1900). The former drew a letter of praise from Lord Rosebery and the *Sportsman* called it 'the best exposition of turf life that we know'. Less effective is the portentous plot of *The Eternal Choice* (1901) in which a devout Christian disinherits his nephew for marrying an agnostic, only to find out his new heir is a rogue. In 1899, Cooper (who had a great fondness for children) began to bring out his series of 'Wyemarke' fables for the young, Wyemarke being a pretty little rich girl who tells her own stories. The publisher, Grant Richards, prettily embellished these volumes with actual photographs of young Edwardian ladies. BL 22. *DNB*. Wol.

COOPER, Thomas ('Adam Hornbook', 1805–92). The famous Chartist and original of Charles Kingsley's* proletarian hero, Alton Locke*. Cooper was born in Leicester of working-class parents. On his father's early death, Cooper's mother took on the family dyeing business, with no great success. Cooper himself almost died of smallpox at five. He was apprenticed while still a boy to a shoemaker, and mainly educated himself. An account of Cooper's arduous course of early reading is given in his autobiographical *Life* (1872). He had his first religious conversion at fourteen and having made a name for himself as a Methodist preacher, opened a school at Gainsborough in 1827. The school did not do well, and teaching was disillusioning to the young idealist. In 1833, Cooper published an early collection of poems and embarked on a literary career. He took up journalism in 1836, moving to London soon after. In London he worked as a bookseller and was increasingly attracted to political radicalism. In 1840, he returned to his birthplace to work on the *Leicester Mercury* newspaper, associating himself at the same period with the physical force wing of the Chartist movement. He was imprisoned for two years and eleven weeks in 1843 for encouraging riot. In Stafford jail he wrote his major work, the Miltonic poem, *The Purgatory Of Suicides, A Prison Rhyme* (1845). In the face of respectable publishers' indifference, the work was touted as a masterpiece by Disraeli* and Douglas Jerrold*. In 1856, Cooper was reconverted to Christianity and towards the end of his life he published several novels, beginning with *Captain Cobler* (1850), a story of rebellion in Lincolnshire in the reign of Henry VIII. Later in life, as 'Adam Hornbook', Cooper wrote *Alderman Ralph* (1853) and *The Family Feud* (1855). Routledge* gave £100 each for these works which are whimsical in tone. *The Family Feud* (which Cooper thought the better of the two) contains apolitical portions from a Chartist novel which the author had written some years earlier. The narrative follows the misadventures of an artist whose career is blighted by family quarrels. Cooper had another novel incomplete at the time of his death. In his last years, the now repentant Chartist was helped by middle-class friends who acquired for him a clerkship at the Board of Health. BL 3. *DNB. NCBEL.* Wol. Sad. RLF.

The Coral Island, R. M. Ballantyne, 1858, 1 vol, Nelson. (The work was illustrated by the author.) The most popular boys' story of the century. It tells the adventures of Ralph Rover (the fifteen-year-old hero), Jack Martin (eighteen) and Peterkin Gay (the comic runt of the trio at fourteen). They are shipwrecked on a deserted Pacific island where they discover coconut lemonade (a geographical solecism), fish, make fire by rubbing sticks together, narrowly escape being eaten by sharks and cannibals and have various close shaves with pirates. The action ends with 'wholesale murder'. In the climax of their adventures the heroes are captured by 'savages' and expecting torture and death are rescued by a heroic English missionary. In a foreword, the author warns off any 'morose' boy reader not interested in 'fun' of this kind. As later critics have observed, the story is a fable of British imperialism, with Ballantyne's lads as romanticised colonisers. Ballantyne drew on the American James F. Bowman's *The Island Home, Or The Young Castaways* (1852). And he had only £90 as payment in full for a work that eventually sold by the million. In 1861, the author put out a sequel with the same (but older) heroes, *The Gorilla Hunters*.

CORBETT, [Sir] Julian [Stafford] (1854–1922). Corbett was born at Thames Ditton, the son of an architect. He was educated at Marlborough, and at Trinity College, Cambridge, gaining a first-class degree in law in 1875. He practised until 1882 after which, having inherited a fortune, he travelled extensively abroad, particularly in Scandinavia. Corbett wrote four novels. *The Fall Of Asgard* (1886) is an unusual historical* romance chronicling the expulsion of the Norse gods by the two Olafs who introduced Christianity to Norway. The work is uneasy in its style, like most distant reconstructions of its kind. ('Trolls take me!' one character ejaculates, in high emotion.) *For God And Gold* (1887), is a historical romp, set in the age of Elizabeth. 'Frank' Drake features centrally. (Corbett wrote a life of Drake at the same period.) *Kophetua The Thirteenth* (1889) is a utopian fantasy, set in a mythical African kingdom, 'Oneiria'. *A Business In Great Waters* (1895) is a lively tale of smuggling in late-eighteenth-century Sussex. These works make up the list of Corbett's fiction. At forty-five, he stood at the crossroads of his career. His inclination was to continue writing novels. His friends were urging him to go into Parliament. His wife, Edith (whom he married in 1899), wanted him to give up fiction for 'serious historical writing'. He acceded to her desire, and devoted himself thereafter to naval history, becoming the country's leading authority on the subject. He was knighted in 1917. BL 4. *DNB*. Wol.

CORELLI, Marie [Isabella Mary] (née Mills, later Mackay, 1855–1924). Probably the bestselling of all Victorian novelists. Corelli was born plain Mary Mills, in Bayswater, London, the daughter of Charles Mackay*, poet and journalist. (In later life, among many other absurd inventions about herself, Corelli claimed to have been adopted by Mackay.) Her mother was a servant, Mary Mills. At birth the young Mary ('Minnie') was illegitimate, although Mackay six years later married her mother, his first wife having died in 1859. During Corelli's childhood, the family lived at Box Hill, where George Meredith* was a neighbour. Apart from a brief period in a convent school, Corelli was educated privately by governesses and showed a quick and precocious intelligence. But lack of formal learning was to mar her more pretentious literary efforts in later life. In 1876, her mother (now Mrs Mackay) died and Bertha Vyver, a childhood playmate, joined the household. Initially a companion, Vyver (the daughter of a countess) became Corelli's closest and lifelong friend. Corelli devised her Italianate name with a view to a musical career (she was a gifted instrumentalist). It also reflects the self-dramatising tendencies which were to flower in the glow of her subsequent fame. She was no beauty, but vain to the point of mania. (In later life, she would never allow herself to be photographed, preferring that the public should have an idealised mental image of her.) From 1883 (when her father had a stroke) until 1889, she ran the Mackay household. As 'Rose Trevor' and 'Marie di Corelli' she gave some piano recitals. She also published some florid poems. In July 1885, Corelli began to put her writing out for publication. The following year George Bentley* (against the advice of his reader, Hall Caine*), published her novel, *A Romance Of Two Worlds** (1886). She was thirty-one and resolutely claimed to be seventeen. The story was inspired, Corelli claimed, by a 'peculiar psychic occurrence' and was designed to expound 'the gospel of electricity'. The plot revolves around a visionary dream, or cosmic voyage, in which the heroine-narrator (a pianist, of course) encounters the magician Heliobas (a figure who recurs in Corelli's later fiction). Corelli's first effort created little excitement and was generally dismissed as ungrammatical bosh. Its successor, *Vendetta, Or The Story Of One Forgotten* (1886), did little better.

This autobiographically narrated story of a vengeful Neapolitan who is buried by mistake, and returns to find his 'widow' in the arms of a lover earned its publisher only £50. But Corelli's third novel, *Thelma, A Society Novel* (1887) made an impact. The heroine is a Norse maiden who for love of a dashing English baronet ('Sir Philip Bruce-Errington') leaves her native fiords in 'the Land of the Midnight Sun' for English high society and high melodrama. *Thelma*'s narrative contains vivid descriptions of Norwegian scenery, although Corelli had never set foot there. There followed *Ardath, The Story Of A Dead Self** (1889). A sequel to *A Romance Of Two Worlds* the novel reintroduces Heliobas in the setting of Babylon, some 5,000 years before the birth of Christ. Corelli always thought *Ardath* her best work and it made her a celebrity. But by now, reviews of her fiction were an orchestrated chorus of ridicule and savagery. (In the 1890s, several journals boycotted her fiction entirely.) Nevertheless Gladstone, Queen Victoria and millions of English and American readers devoured her works as fast as they appeared. *Wormwood* (1890) is a study of absinthism and transcendentalism in Paris which ends with a terrific denunciation of French tippling. *The Soul Of Lilith* (1892) is set in modern London, and has another incarnation of Heliobas ('El Râmi'), now preaching a doctrine of androgynous divinity. *The Silver Domino* (1892) contains Corelli's pugnacious counterattack on her enemies, the reviewers. Despite them she had a sensational hit in 1893 with *Barabbas, A Dream Of The World's Tragedy**. A melodrama centred around the Crucifixion, it re-creates Judas's and Barabbas's lives in erotic detail and invents a 'Judith Iscariot' (as if 'Iscariot' were a Hebrew surname like 'Smith') to supply the love interest unaccountably left out in the Gospels. The work was written ostensibly to contradict the 'agnosticism' of Mrs Humphry Ward's* *Robert Elsmere**. Corelli hated the well-bred, well-educated and universally admired other novelist. An even bigger hit was *The Sorrows Of Satan** (1895). A story of the wicked Nineties, it features Geoffrey Tempest, a glamorous young novelist who makes a Faustian pact with the devil. Corelli introduces herself flatteringly as 'Mavis Clare' a persecuted but popular authoress who gets the better of Satan. This work, which appeared in the new one-volume 6s. form (instead of the old three-decker), established Corelli as the bestselling novelist of the English-speaking world. As usual, it was mauled by the reviewers. Corelli offered another portrait of herself as the heroine of *The Murder Of Delicia* (1896), a new woman* influenced work, dealing with unhappy marriage and unkind husbands (although the heroine has a very loving dog, Spartan). Delicia dies when her brute of a husband refuses separation. *Ziska* (1897) is an occult fantasy set in Egypt, on the theme of reincarnation. (Corelli evidently believed herself to be the reincarnation of Shakespeare.) The shorter *Jane, A Social Incident* (1897) has a rich heroine who turns her back on London society ('the Swagger Set') for more important things in her country home of Ashleigh-in-the-Dell. In this splendid phase of her literary career, Corelli was as productive as her publishers (now Methuen*) could wish. Bestseller followed bestseller. She was reputed to be earning £10,000 for each of her romances. Corelli also took herself very seriously as an artist and social theorist. *The Mighty Atom* (1896) is a story written against secular education. A boy, Lionel Valliscourt, being tutored by free-thinkers, hangs himself to find out whether God (the 'atom' in question) exists. The novel is sarcastically dedicated to the child-murdering 'Self-styled Progressivists who by Precept and Example assist the infamous Cause of Education without Religion'. *The Master Christian* (1900) is a plea for peace unashamedly directed to all the Christian churches of the world, 'in the name of Christ' whose advocate the novelist took herself to be. In 1897, Corelli's health collapsed. (Years of overtight corsets may have been the cause.) A year later, her half-brother Eric died, an event which prostrated her. In 1901, she moved to Mason Croft, Stratford upon Avon, claiming an affinity with her fellow author Shakespeare which was to bring her into ridicule and general loathing. (In 1917, malicious Stratford neighbours had her prosecuted for food hoarding.) By the time of her death, Corelli was a spent force authorially. But her romances, with their wild concoction of spiritualism, science, eroticism and religiosity are the first supersellers of the twentieth century. She never married, although in her fifties she had a passionate but largely unreciprocated affair with the artist Arthur Severn. BL 23. *DNB*. RM. *NCBEL*. Wol. Sad.

CORKRAN, Alice [Abigail] (1856?–1916). Born in Paris, her father was the journalist J. Frazer Corkran. Educated at home in France, the young Corkran moved to Bloomsbury in London as she was growing up. She was in later life the editor of *Girl's Realm* and *The Bairn's Annual*. She never married, and reported her favourite recreations as 'chess and sketching from nature'. She was afflicted by poverty at the end of her life and lived quietly and out of the way in Hampshire. Corkran wrote stories for young female readers; e.g. *Bessie Lang* (1876), a rustic love story set in the Lake District; *Latheby Towers* (1879), a story of aristocratic love; *Margery Merton's Girlhood* (1887). Corkran's short stories have some charm. Notable is 'The English Teacher At The Convent' (1887). BL 11. *WW*. *NCBEL*. RLF.

The Cornhill Magazine (1860–1975). The premier fiction-carrying magazine of the century. *Cornhill* was the brainchild of George Smith (1824–1901), of Smith, Elder and Co*. Drawing on the example of the American *Harper's Magazine*, Smith drew up plans for a high-quality monthly magazine, well illustrated, costing only 1s. His first intention was to have Thomas Hughes* as editor. But in the event, he recruited Thackeray*. The appointment was inspired. The first issue of January 1860 (which carried serials by Trollope* and Thackeray and illustrations by Millais*) was an unprecedented success, 110,000 copies being sold. Although circulation halved within three years, the magazine was established as market leader among British monthly periodicals. Charles Reade*, Wilkie Collins*, Mrs Gaskell*, Thomas Hardy*, George Eliot* and James Payn* all serialised major novels in the journal. In April 1862, Thackeray gave up the editorship (for which Smith had been paying him £2,000 a year). But his last, incomplete work, *Denis Duval* appeared in the magazine. Later editors included G. H. Lewes*, Leslie Stephen and James Payn*. *Cornhill* inspired a spate of imitations, with names derived from London topography: *Temple Bar*; *St Paul's*; *Belgravia*; *St James's*. The monthly magazine was eventually superseded by weekly or fortnightly publications costing half as much, with many more illustrations. *WI. BLM*.

CORNISH, F[rancis] Warre (1839–1916). Cornish was the son of a clergyman and former Oxford don, who presumably left his university post to marry. He was educated at Eton and Cambridge. After university, Warre-Cornish (as he was generally known) returned to Eton and eventually rose to be Vice-Provost of the school in 1893, a post he held until his death. A bibliophile, he published books on a variety of subjects, including the harmless novel *Sunningwell* (1899), a study of clerical complications, in a quiet provincial setting. Sunningwell has an imaginary cathedral which figures centrally. Reviewers found the work replete with 'wit and wisdom'. It was reprinted and inspired a sequel, *Dr Ashford And His Neighbours* (1914). Cornish married in 1866, and had eight children. His wife, Blanche (born Ritchie) was distantly related to Thackeray*, and herself wrote novels. Her *Alcestis* (1873), a dreamy 'musical novel' set in the eighteenth-century world of Dresden opera, was well received. It is dedicated discreetly to Thackeray's* lover, Jane Brookfield*. She also wrote *Northam Cloisters* (1882), a mild story of love and ecclesiastic affairs in a cathedral city apparently based on Durham. Reviewers found her fiction very amateurish. BL 3. (Blanche Cornish) BL 2. *DNB*. Wol.

Cosmopolis (1896–98). An 'International Monthly Review' published in New York by the International News Co. and in England (where it cost 2s.6d.) by T. Fisher Unwin. It was edited by F. Ortmans and the unusual feature of the journal was its simultaneously publishing the same articles in English, French and German. It contained sophisticated literary criticism by writers such as Andrew Lang*. Fiction also figured prominently. The first issue of January 1896 contained the opening instalment of Stevenson's* *The Weir Of Hermiston**. During its brief life, the *Cosmopolis* also printed fiction, long and short, by S. R. Crockett*, Israel Zangwill* and Somerset Maugham*.

COSTELLO, Dudley (1803–65). The brother of the more considerable novelist, Louisa Costello*, he was born in Sussex, of Irish descent. Costello's father was an army colonel who died when his son was eleven, and Dudley himself went to Sandhurst with a view to a military career. He was commissioned in 1821, serving mainly in the West Indies until 1828, when he went on half pay. Costello's sketching talents had been obvious as a child and while in the armed services, he began to write for the magazines. On returning to civilian life, he joined his mother and sister in Paris, hoping unsuccessfully for a government post. In Paris, Costello supported himself by copying illuminated manuscripts (as did his sister). The Costellos continued to live mainly abroad, and Dudley wrote travel books, some of which were well received. He was also foreign correspondent for the *Morning Herald* from 1838, and wrote for various other English papers and magazines. His main employer was *Bentley's Miscellany**, for whom he turned out sprightly miscellaneous articles and serial fiction that the editor (W. H. Ainsworth*) thought highly of. Costello married in 1843, but apparently still depended on his sister for financial support. In 1861, he was awarded a Civil List pension of £75. His fiction includes *Stories From A Screen* (1855); *The Joint Stock Bank* (1856); *The Millionaire Of Mincing Lane* (1858); *Faint Heart Never Won Fair Lady* (1859). His wife's premature death in 1865 precipitated a fatal collapse in his own health. BL 4. *DNB*.

COSTELLO, Louisa Stuart (1799–1870). A versatile, second-rank Victorian lady of letters, Louisa Costello was born in England the daughter of an Irish officer in the British army. On her father's death, when she was fifteen, she and her mother went to live in Paris. In 1825, she published some verses which made her known to Scott and Moore. A talented artist, she helped support her family (and put her brother Dudley Costello* through Sandhurst) by painting miniatures, governessing, and copying illuminated manuscripts. (The Costellos were instrumental in drawing official attention to the care of these important objects.) The remainder of her life was passed as a spinster, providing for her dependent mother and her brother, always less competent than she as a writer. Louisa Costello was rewarded by the French government in 1852, for her work in preserving the national heritage. She received an English Civil List pension in the same year. Louisa Costello wrote novels which drew on her cosmopolitan experience. She had a strong line in French historical settings and incorporated translations from the old poets into her narratives. *The Queen's Poisoner* (1841), set in sixteenth-century Paris, is Costello's best-regarded work. *Clara Fane, Or The Contrasts Of A Life* (1848) has a contemporary governess-heroine whose experiences probably recall the author's own. *Gabrielle* (1843) is set in France, during the reign of Louis XIV. The heroine is an innocent girl of the people who is bigamously married by a nobleman pretending to be an artist. Louisa Costello died of cancer of the mouth, presumably brought on by licking the tips of her paint brushes. BL 3. *DNB. NCBEL.* Wol. RLF.

COTES, Mrs Everard [Sara Jeannette] (née Duncan, 1861–1922). Sara Duncan was born and educated in Brantford, Canada West (later Ontario), where her father was a prosperous merchant. At nine, she recalled wanting to be a novelist. After a brief spell teaching (which she did not like), she became a successful reporter, a relatively new career for women of the 1880s, even in North America. In October 1885, Duncan went to Washington to take up a position on the *Post* as a staff writer. In 1886, she returned to Canada to work on the *Toronto Globe*, writing the 'Woman's World' daily column. In 1889 her next paper, *The Montreal Star*, sent her on a global tour with another woman journalist (Lily Lewis) which led to her sprightly first book: *A Social Departure. How Orthodocia And I Went Round The World By Ourselves* (1890). The work sold well. In 1891, she married Charles Everard Cotes, the curator of the Indian Museum at Calcutta. She met him on her global tour and he proposed at the Taj Mahal. In later life, Mrs Cotes was much travelled, but made London her principal literary base. All her novels celebrate flagrantly unconventional female behaviour and international themes. Much of her fiction vivaciously transcribes her experiences in India (which she found stuffy) and Europe. In *An American Girl In London* * (1891), the heroine Mamie Wick has various comic and romantic adventures in a hidebound England. *The Simple Adventures Of A Mem Sahib* (1893), narrated autobiographically and ironically, and the more savage *His Honour And A Lady* (1896) draw directly on the author's years in India. *A Daughter Of Today* * (1894) is one of the livelier new woman* novels with a heroine, Elfrida Bell, who travels from Illinois to study art in Paris's Latin Quarter. *On The Other Side Of The Latch* (1901) records an interlude in Simla, away from the heat and dust of Calcutta. *The Imperialist* (1904) is considered an early classic of Canadian literature. BL 22. *WW.* RM. Wol.

COUCH, [Sir] A[rthur] T[homas] Quiller ('Q', 1863–1944. The author hyphenated his surname in later life.) Quiller Couch was born at Bodmin, Cornwall, where his father was a doctor. He retained throughout his life a strong attachment to the Duchy. At the age of ten he was sent to school at Newton Abbot in Devon, where his mother's family (the Couches) lived. From there, he went to Clifton College, Bristol. In 1882 he went up to Oxford, and studied classics with some distinction. As an undergraduate he also published parodies using his later famous 'Q' pseudonym. Quiller Couch lectured at the university, staying five years in all. But in 1887 (partly motivated by his family's financial crises after his father's death in 1884) he gave up his academic career for journalism in London. His first novel, *Dead Man's Rock*, appeared in 1887. A gory Stevensonian romance, it is set in Cornwall in the 1840s. A main part of the plot (which uses diary narration extensively) concerns the quest for the 'Great Ruby of Ceylon'. Published by Cassell's* (who had recently had great success with *Treasure Island** and *King Solomon's Mines**) the novel hit the public taste. In 1888, he published *The Astonishing History Of Troy Town* (an evocation, partly humorous, of Fowey in Cornwall). His next (and most popular) novel, *The Splendid Spur** (1889), is a romance of the Civil War, set in the West Country, with a strong pro-Royalist sentiment. In 1890, Quiller Couch took over the assistant editorship of Cassell's* new Liberal journal, *The Speaker*, but continued writing novels at an unabated pace. *The Blue Pavilions* (1891), is a romance set in the 1690s which introduces William III and a young Marlborough into the narrative. While turning out these novels (a task which came relatively easily to him) Quiller Couch was writing voluminously for the magazines, and was employed by the publisher Cassell's. He had married in 1889 (his wife came from his beloved Fowey), and was supporting his widowed mother and two brothers. In 1892, his health collapsed under the strain of work. Insomnia and agoraphobia made London intolerable to him and he retired to Fowey, where he lived for twenty years in a house by the sea called 'the Haven', supporting himself as a free-lance author. Romance continued to flow from his pen: *I Saw Three Ships* (1892) is a tale of old Cornish wrecking days. *Ia* (1896) is titled after the heroine's Cornish name; a peasant girl, she falls in love with and is seduced and abandoned by a local preacher. The narrative ends with her nobly dismissing him, although he offers belatedly to make her an honest woman. *The Ship Of Stars** (1899), the autobiographical life story of Taffy Raymond, a Cornish lad, is Quiller Couch's most substantial achievement in fiction. *Hetty Wesley* (1903) is a story about the founders of Methodism designed to vindicate a heroine the author thinks 'deeply wronged' by her father, Samuel. His last novel, *Foe-Farrell*, was published in 1918. A contemporary adventure story, it touches on the World War, in a patriotic spirit. His various stories and sketches for the magazines were collected into a string of successful books: *Noughts And Crosses* (1891); *The Delectable Duchy* (1894); *Wandering Heath* (1895). But in general, Quiller Couch's shorter pieces lack originality and are less effective than his long fiction. He also wrote verse and his 'Alma Mater' (published in the *Oxford Magazine*, 1896) is frequently reprinted. In 1900, 'Q', as he was now known, brought out his *Oxford Book Of English Verse*, the most successful enterprise of its kind since F. T. Palgrave's* *Golden Treasury*. It sold half a million copies in his lifetime. In his later years,

Quiller Couch associated himself with the Liberal Party and supported all things Cornish. In 1910 he was knighted. Two years later, he was made King Edward VII Professor of English at Cambridge. It was a popular appointment in line with the middlebrow ethos of the period, and 'Q' was instrumental in establishing the School of English in 1917, so freeing the subject from its dedication to Germanic philology. In 1937, he was elected mayor of Fowey, where he died and where a monument to him was raised. BL 28. *DNB*. RM. *NCBEL*. Wol.

Cousin Henry, Anthony Trollope, 1879, 2 vols, Chapman and Hall. (Serialised in the *Manchester Weekly Times Supplement*, from March–May 1879.) The old Welshman, Indefer Jones, has the dilemma of whom to leave his wealth to: his niece Isabel Broderick or a nephew whom he does not like, Henry Jones, who nevertheless bears the family name which he wants perpetuated. Isabel has the dilemma of whether to marry Henry Jones, whom she does not like, or William Owen, a clergyman. Henry, meanwhile, has the dilemma of whether or not to disclose the existence of a will disinheriting him which he has come across in a volume of sermons. Isabel finally comes into the property and Owen changes his name to Indefer Jones, thus carrying out the old man's wishes. The story displays the psychological and legal convolutions typical of Trollope's later period.

Cousin Phillis, Mrs Gaskell, 1865, 1 vol, Smith, Elder. (Serialised in the *Cornhill Magazine**, November 1863–February 1864, with illustrations by George Du Maurier*.) A late and idyllic work. The story is narrated by Paul Manning, an eighteen-year-old engineer assisting with the laying of railway line in Lancashire. His cousin Phillis Holman lives with her father at 'Hope Farm' in the neighbourhood where he is working. Paul introduces her to his senior colleague, Edward Holdsworth. Recovering from illness at the farm, Holdsworth wins Phillis's heart. But he is offered a better position in Canada and takes it. Once there, he marries a French-Canadian girl, and Paul has to tell Phillis the heart-breaking news. She succumbs to a brain fever, but eventually recovers. Paul (who has loved Phillis from a distance) marries another. The novella is notable for its pastoral descriptions and its delicate portraiture of the heroine.

COUVREUR, Jessie Catherine ('Tasma', née Huybers, 1848–97). Jessie Huybers was born in Highgate, London, of Belgian parents. Her father was a merchant who moved to Tasmania when she was only four years old. She grew up there and in Victoria, Australia and in 1867 married a Tasmanian, Charles Forbes Fraser, thereafter moving with him to Melbourne. In 1873, she came to Europe, where she supported herself by writing and lecturing. Eventually the Frasers' marriage ended in divorce in 1883. (Public accounts at the time discreetly identify her as a widow.) Two years later, she married Auguste Couvreur (1828–94), a Belgian journalist and later a member of the country's Parliament. Jessie Couvreur started to write fiction late in life using the Australasian pseudonym 'Tasma'. *A Sydney Sovereign* (1890) is a collection of Australian tales, fashionably sombre and morbid in tone. *In Her Earliest Youth* (1890) has an Australian heroine, Pauline, who marries a drunken gambler. She deserts him, he reforms and the narrative ends uncertainly. (Bitter recollections of Couvreur's first marriage recur throughout all her fiction.) *Not Counting The Cost* (1895) has a heroine, Eila, who brings her family from Australia to Paris on the death of her father, and heroically supports them in the face of hardship (by entering a Parisian beauty competition, among other things). *A Fiery Ordeal* (1897) is another portrayal of utterly wretched marriage in Australia. Tasma's most interesting novel is *Uncle Piper Of Piper's Hill* (1889) which deals with her early Australian experiences in what is for her a relatively cheerful manner (although it should also be said that all her writing is fast-moving and lively in tone, if lugubrious in subject). After her second husband's death she worked as Belgian correspondent for *The Times*. Tasma died in Brussels. BL 7. Boase. RM. Wol.

COXWELL, Henry Tracey (1819–1900). Coxwell was born in Rochester, where his father was a clergyman. He began working life apprenticed to a dentist, and practised in London, 1840–46. Coxwell subsequently became one of the country's leading balloonists and wrote an aeronautical novel for young boys: *A Knight Of The Air* (1895). The work has up-to-date depictions of late-Victorian flying machinery. BL 1. *DNB*. Wol.

CRACKANTHORPE, Hubert Montague (born Cookson, 1870–96). A promising short story writer at a period when, as H. G. Wells* put it, 'the short story broke out everywhere'. Like others of the 1890s generation, Crackanthorpe died before his talents could fully emerge. Born Hubert Cookson (the family name was changed in 1888), he had a literary and intellectual background. His mother, Blanche Crackanthorpe, was a writer on feminist topics; his father was a QC and contributed to the serious journals on current affairs. The young Crackanthorpe was educated partly at Eton, partly in France, and was tutored by George Gissing*. During the period 1888–92 (about which little is known of his life) Crackanthorpe associated himself with the aesthetic and decadent* movements. Some accounts suggest he may have been a student at Cambridge at this time. He married in 1893, but his wife, Leila (née Macdonald), deserted him and he returned to Paris (which features in many of his stories) in 1896. There, he committed suicide by throwing himself in the Seine forestalling an ugly divorce action in which he would have been accused of infecting his wife with venereal disease. It was two months before his body was identified and the newspapers gave his disappearance considerable publicity. Crackanthorpe's fiction shows the influence of Maupassant and the continental realists. It comprises: *Wreckage* (1893), a collection of cold short stories; *Sentimental Studies* (1895), pieces which show a notable advance in technique; *Vignettes* (1896), published posthumously. A typically bleak story from *Wreckage*, 'The Struggle For Life', snapshots a working-class wife who sells herself for half-a-crown to feed her starving baby while her husband spends his wages on a prostitute in a riverside brothel. Crackanthorpe edited the *Albemarle* magazine from January to September 1892. Henry James commended Crackanthorpe's 'small, sharp, bright pictures', and 'his eye for the Bohemian panorama'. BL 4. *NCBEL*. Boase.

Cradock Nowell, R. D. Blackmore, 1866, 3 vols, Chapman and Hall. (The story was first serialised in *Macmillan's Magazine** May 1865–August 1866.) Unusually for Blackmore, the narrative is set in the New Forest and the period is contemporary. The hero believes himself to be heir to a baronetcy and Nowelhurst Hall, but on coming to age he discovers that the true heir is his twin brother Clayton. (A confused Irish nurse, Biddy O'Gaghan, is to blame.) Clayton is killed in a hunting accident, and Cradock is suspected. Although he is cleared, suspicion lingers. His father casts him out and he throws himself into London slum life as 'Charles Newman'. There follows a protracted period of degradation, taking the action as far afield as the Congo. Finally it emerges that the real culprit was an illegitimate half-brother to the baronet, enraged at Clayton's attempted seduction of his daughter. Cradock is restored to wealth and title. He marries his sweetheart Amy Rosedew and lives 'enlarged and purified by affliction, able now to understand and feel for every poor man'. The novel's most effective sections are Cradock's descent into the London underworld and the descriptions of the murderer Bull Garnet's self-flagellating moral anguish.

CRAIG, Isa (1831–1903). The only child of an Edinburgh hosier and glover, Craig was orphaned in childhood. Brought up by her grandmother, she left school at ten. Overcoming the handicaps of her background, Craig made a name for herself as a poet, and was employed by the *Scotsman* from 1853 until 1857, when she travelled to London. There she became secretary to the National Association for the Promotion of Social Science and became friendly with such literary figures as Christina Rossetti. In 1866, she married her cousin, John Knox, a London iron merchant. For a short period on its inception she was editor of the *Argosy** magazine. In addition to her well-received poetry, Craig wrote the novels *Esther West* (1870); *Tales On The Parables* (two series, 1872–73); *Deepdale Vicarage* (1881). Other of her stories were serialised in the *Quiver**. Craig died in Suffolk. BL 4. *DNB*.

CRAIK, Dinah Maria (née Mulock, 1826–87). Dinah Mulock was born at Stoke-on-Trent, the eldest child of a nonconformist and emotionally unstable Irish clergyman father who lost his chapel and moved to Newcastle under Lyme (Mrs Mulock's birthplace) in 1831. Precociously clever and literary, Dinah was able to help her mother teach school at the age of thirteen. An inheritance enabled the family to move to London in 1839. In 1844, she and her mother separated from Thomas Mulock. A year later, Mrs Mulock died. Thereafter, Dinah was responsible for the financial support of her family. (This situation is projected on to the early career of her most famous character, John Halifax.) She began her authorial career writing stories for children and contrived to scrape a living for herself and her dependants aided with another small inheritance from her mother's family. Mulock's fortunes improved with the success of her first novel, *The Ogilvies**, which came out in 1849. The novel follows the route to marriage of three girl cousins. Melodramatic and passionate in tone (there is an especially powerful death scene), the work was well received by the reviewers. Mulock had £150 from Chapman and Hall* and entered the literary world as a minor celebrity. (By this time her two brothers were independent, and she was living in lodgings with another young woman, Frances Martin.) *Olive* (1850) has a deformed, less than beautiful heroine who none the less contrives to convert an agnostic lover. *The Head Of The Family* (1852) is a family chronicle, in the fashionable style of Bulwer-Lytton's* *The Caxtons** or Thackeray's* *The Newcomes**. It tells the story of a young Edinburgh lawyer, Ninian Graeme, who inherits the responsibility of looking after a brood of English half-siblings. Mulock's reputation was enormously enhanced by her bestseller, *John Halifax Gentleman** (1856). A story of exemplary capitalist morality, it chronicles a hero who rises from poverty to business prosperity. Now wealthy herself and commanding £2,000 a novel, Mulock moved in 1859 to Hampstead, where she entertained on a modest scale. *A Life For A Life* (1859) is in some ways her most interesting work of fiction, written as it is in the form of intertwining diaries ('His Story', 'Her Story') of two sympathetically regarded 'criminals' who contrive to atone for their crimes and eventually marry. *Mistress And Maid* (1862) examines the condition of spinsterhood more realistically than usual in the Victorian novel. In 1863, Mulock's brother Ben died wretchedly, trying to escape from a lunatic asylum. She subsequently moved to Glasgow to recuperate. *A Noble Life** (1866) is a saccharine study of invalidism and moral nobility. *The Woman's Kingdom* (1868) has twin sisters, one plain, one beautiful; their contrasting narratives examine the power of women to make or mar their husbands' destinies. Written during a period of personal upheaval, the story reflects the author's reactionary convictions about her sex's place and role. In 1865 Mulock had married George Lillie Craik (a nephew of the author of the same name, 1798–1866), eleven years her junior. The couple first intended to live in Glasgow, but an offer to George Craik from Alexander Macmillan to become a partner in his publishing house kept the newly-weds in London. She was past childbearing age, and they adopted an abandoned baby, Dorothy, in 1869. Dinah Craik's heterodox views on adoption are stated in *King Arthur: Not A Love Story* (1886). After marriage, Craik continued writing at a rapid rate. *A Brave Lady* (1870) and *Hannah* (1871) are two novels with a purpose; the first argues for the married woman's property rights, the second for the right of in-laws to marry after a spouse's decease. A genuinely philanthropic woman, Mrs Craik seems to have lived by the virtues which her novels advocate. She died of heart failure during preparations for her daughter Dorothy's wedding. BL 20. *DNB. RM. NCBEL*. Wol.

CRAIK, Georgiana M[arion] (1831?–95). Craik was born in Old Brompton, London, the youngest daughter of the man of letters, George Lillie Craik (1798–1866). Her mother (née Jeanette Dempster) died around 1856. She began writing for *Household Words** as early as 1851, her first published novel being *Riverston* (1857). A carefully written work, it contains three domestic stories connected by the person of the governess narrator, Honor Haig. In 1886 Craik married the artist, Allan Walter May and continued after marriage to write voluminously. Her novels were aimed mainly at young readers and youngish women. Critics approved of their easy, undemanding narratives which mainly dealt with the problems of love from the young female's viewpoint. *Dorcas* (1879) has a heroine, Letty, who discovers, at the crucial stage of her love life, that her mother is low-born. *Godfrey Helstone* (1884) tells the story of two lovers who resume their affair after an interval of twenty years. *Patience Holt* (1891) is a fashionable (for the 1890s) study of tomboyish female personality, following the heroine from the trials of girlhood to early marriage. BL 33. Boase. Wol.

CRANE, Walter (1845–1915). Illustrator and socialist. Crane was born in Liverpool where his father was a portrait painter. As a boy he was apprenticed in 1857 to the London wood-engraver and socialist, W. J. Linton. The experience gave Crane a strong Pre-Raphaelite sense of the whole book, and directed him as much to general design as illustration. With Edmund Evans (1826–1905), Crane devised a new form of colour-illustrated children's literature, the so-called 'Toy Book'. In the 1870s, the artist travelled widely and was strongly influenced by the Paris Commune. He was subsequently a disciple of William Morris* and was influential in the development of art education in Britain. Among other works of fiction, Crane illustrated Trollope's* *Miss Mackenzie** and the juvenile stories of Mrs Molesworth* in the 1870s. *DNB.* Hou.

Cranford, Mrs Elizabeth Gaskell, 1853, 1 vol, Chapman and Hall. (The work was first serialised in *Household Words** as 'Our Society At Cranford', December 1851–May 1853.) Gaskell's idyllic reconstruction of Knutsford, where she was brought up. Cranford is a north-country village (not too far from the mill town of Manchester, or 'Drumble') mainly populated by genteel spinsters whom Gaskell playfully terms 'Amazons'. The period is vaguely the 1830s. The stories which make up *Cranford* largely revolve around two maiden sisters: the timid Miss Matty and the domineering Miss Deborah Jenkyns, now middle-aged daughters of a deceased rector. Deborah dies. Miss Matty is ruined by the failure of the Town and Country bank, and makes ineffectual but heart-warming efforts to recoup her losses by shopkeeping. Eventually, a brother thought lost returns from India to rescue her. There are other such unspectacular episodes as a series of imaginary burglaries in the district which mightily alarm the Cranford ladies. A topical and uncharacteristically violent episode is the military man Captain Brown's being run down by a train while reading Boz's* latest instalment. The narrative was written and published irregularly and its structure is correspondingly loose knit. In 1863 Gaskell latched on a late episode, 'The Cage At Cranford'. Altogether, *Cranford* represents the most successful of the Victorian 'novels of community', a thriving minor genre throughout the century.

CRAVEN, Mrs Augustus [Pauline Marie Armande Aglaé] (née de la Ferronays, 1808–91). Born in London, she was the eldest daughter of a refugee French aristocrat, the Comte de la Ferronays. In 1814, the Count returned to Paris, and was appointed French ambassador to St Petersburg. In 1827 he returned to Paris as Minister for Foreign Affairs and the next year he was posted to Rome. But with the accession of Louis-Philippe in 1830, the de la Ferronays were again forced into exile, taking up residence in Naples. In 1834, Pauline married Augustus Craven, a minor English diplomat in Germany. The match was against the wishes of her family (she was Catholic, he was not) and the next ten years were difficult. A brother, two sisters and her parents died; her husband's career in the diplomatic service was disappointing. But in 1851, he came into his father's wealth, and the Cravens settled in Naples. In this retired state of life she began writing (a close friend, Lady Georgiana Fullerton*, encouraged her). Her first novel was *Anne Severin* (1868). *A Sister's Story* (1868; non-fiction, dealing with her family history) was first written in French, and was well received in that country. In 1867 (a year of general financial instability) the Cravens lost most of their fortune and she was obliged henceforth to write for money. Craven went on to write other novels in French, which were translated by Fullerton; e.g., *The Story Of A Soul* (1875); *Natalie Narischkin* (1877); *Eliane* (1882). *Lucia* (1886). All draw on the author's cosmopolitan background and feature superheated plots of love in *grands salons* at superb fêtes and in the setting of magnificent chateaux. She died in Paris. BL 4. *DNB*. Wol. Sad.

CRAWFURD, Oswald [John Frederick] ('John Dangerfield', 1834 1909). The son of a diplomat, Crawfurd was educated at Eton and Oxford (leaving, however, without a degree). He made his career in the Foreign Office, specialising in the affairs of Portugal about whose history and geography he later wrote several books. He was British consul at Oporto 1866–90. In 1891, after witnessing the Oporto riots against the British, Crawfurd retired and devoted himself to literature and field sports. He edited over the years various magazines, including the *New Quarterly* and *Chapman's Magazine Of Fiction*. His fiction concentrated on the more 'inaccessible' regions of Britain. *The World We Live In* (1884) is a lively country house novel, set in the Scottish highlands. It evidently sold well. *Sylvia Arden* (1888), a more adventurous tale of murder and hidden treasure in the 'shilling shocker' style, was Crawfurd's most successful work. It is set on the rocky coastal landscape of 'Scarfell Chace', of which a pictorial 'bird's-eye view' is supplied. His other fiction includes: *The White Feather* (1896) and *The Mystery Of Myrtle Cottage* (1908). Crawfurd was a personal friend of Frederic Chapman, and was a director of the publishing firm Chapman and Hall* in the 1890s. As 'John Dangerfield' he published some fiction in the 1870s, including *The Fool Of The Family* (1876). BL 10. *DNB*. Wol.

CREASY, Sir Edward [Shepherd] (1812–78). Historian (author of *Fifteen Decisive Battles Of The World*, 1852), barrister and professor of history at London University, Creasy wrote one unsuccessful novel, *The Old Love And The New* (1870). Set in Athens around the period of the Peloponnesian War, the story follows the adventures of an unlucky (and eventually suicidal) heroine, Atalanta. Creasy was evidently badly off in his later years and applied to the Royal Literary Fund for assistance. BL 1. *DNB*. Wol. Sad. RLF.

CRESWICK, Paul (1866–1947). Creswick was born into a theatrical family, and privately educated. He left school at sixteen to work in an assurance firm, rising eventually to a senior managerial position in the Prudential company. He took up writing in his spare time, around 1890. His first book appeared in 1894. In 1898, he founded and edited *The Windmill Magazine*. His fiction is breezily romantic in tone, and includes: *At The Sign Of The Cross Keys* (1896); *The Temple Of Folly* (1897); *Bruising Peg* (1898). *In Alfred's Days* (1900) and *Under The Black Raven* (1901) are historical* tales for juveniles. BL 16. *WW*.

Crichton, W. H. Ainsworth, 1837, 3 vols, Bentley. Ainsworth's follow-up to his bestselling first novel, *Rookwood**. The narrative opens at the sixteenth-century University of Paris where the young Scot, James Crichton, is a non-pareil scholar and chevalier. Around the dazzling hero Ainsworth introduces a number of types later to become stereotypes in his fiction: the mysterious magician Cosmo Ruggieri, the loyal comrade Jasper Ogilvy, the Spanish rival Caravaja, the beautiful and endangered Princess Esclairmonde. The story is a catalogue of Crichton's triumphs. In the first volume he outdisputes all other students. In the second he rescues Esclairmonde. In the third he saves the King from a bull with his bare hands. The narrative is padded out with songs, verses, epigraphs and pedantic footnotes.

The Cricket On The Hearth, Charles Dickens, 1845, 1 vol, Bradbury and Evans. (Illustrated by Daniel Maclise*, Edwin Landseer, Clarkson Stanfield*, Richard Doyle* and John Leech*.) A Christmas* Book. The fairy-story plot centres on John Peerybingle, a dim but amiable carrier, and his young wife Dot. Their happiness is threatened by the misanthropic toymaker, 'Gruff and Tackleton', who sows suspicions in John's mind. These suspicions are apparently confirmed when Dot is found consorting with a disguised young man, Edward Plummer. But he is revealed to be the true lover of May Fielding, whom the odious Tackleton schemes to marry. All ends happily thanks to the benign intervention of the cricket on the hearth who guards over the Peerybingles.

Cripps The Carrier, R. D. Blackmore, 1876, 3 vols, Sampson Low. (Serialised in the *Graphic*, January–June 1876.) 'A Woodland Tale' set in the village of Beckley, near Oxford, in the late 1830s, this novel is in part a homage to Thomas Hardy's* *Under The Greenwood Tree** (1872), which also features a rural 'tranter', or carrier. Before 1839 and the national postal service, the carrier was an important link between village and outside world. The squire's daughter Grace Oglander is feared murdered. In fact, she has been abducted by a fanatically religious relative and is rescued from the woods a few months later by Cripps. Her lawyer abductor subsequently commits suicide. The interest of the novel is less in its melodramatic plot than the gritty character of Zacchary ('Zak') Cripps (particularly in his victory over Oxford's Tractarians) and the village life of Beckley with its superstitions and seasonal rituals. (See, for instance, Chapter 37, 'May-Day'.) A sub-plot concerns which of the two women in his life Zak will marry, so as to continue the dynasty of carrying Crippses. He finally lets his horse Dobbin decide for him.

CROCKETT, S[amuel] R[utherford] (1860–1914). Crockett was born in Kirkcudbrightshire. Illegitimate, he took his mother's name and in later life liked to proclaim himself 'born of the hill folk', rather than a soft lowlander. In adolescence he won a £20 bursary to Edinburgh University where he matriculated at the age of sixteen and where he largely supported himself as an undergraduate by writing for the newspapers. He graduated in 1879 with a degree in Arts. After some European travel as a tutor in Italy (which found its way into later novels such as *The Silver Skull*, 1901), Crockett entered New College, Edinburgh as a student of divinity, and in 1886 was ordained into the Church of Scotland. His first ministry was in nearby Penicuik, and he married in 1887. (The Crocketts were eventually to have four children.) He began serious writing in the early 1890s. In 1895, he resigned the ministry to write full time. Crockett soon became a leader of the so-called kailyard* ('cabbage patch') school, producing Scottish vernacular fictions, typically set in Galloway. He had a literary friendship with Stevenson*, a writer whose reputation somewhat overshadowed his own. Of Crockett's many works the title story in the early collection, *The Stickit Minister** (1893), has lasted best. The tale of a patiently consumptive student of divinity who gives all his substance to an ungrateful brother, it combines pathos and 'pawky' social realism. *The Stickit Minister's Wooing* (1900) brings him to his self-sacrificing death. Crockett's other main line was historical* romance. *The Raiders** (1894) is set in Solway Moss in the late eighteenth century, and tells the story of Patrick Heron, the young laird of Isle Rathan. (As critics noted, the abduction plot has strong resemblances to Blackmore's* *Lorna Doone**.) *The Lilac Sunbonnet* (1894) is a more sentimental tale, set in a rustically conceived Galloway redolent with 'that heather scent on which the bees grow tipsy'. *Bog Myrtle And Peat* (1894) is a collection of similarly idyllic rustic tales and sketches 'in praise of Galloway'. *The Men Of The Moss Hags* (1895) is a story of the Covenanters, under the persecution of Claverhouse, a favourite subject of Scottish historical novelists. The narrative is in the form of William Gordon of Earlstoun's autobiography, and was carefully researched. As always with Crockett, he took pains to indicate the depth of his research in a self-serving preface. *Cleg Kelly** (1896) has as its hero an Edinburgh street arab. *The Gray Man* (1896) is another story of feuding in seventeenth-century Galloway, interesting for the depiction of the legendary Scottish cannibal, Sawney Bean. *Lochinvar* (1897) features the famous hero of the ballad, here conceived as a soldier of fortune in the reign of William of Orange. *The Standard Bearer* (1898) is another tale of the Covenanters and the 'Great Killing'. *The Red Axe* (1898) is a historical romance set in Germany, during the Thirty Years War. *Kit Kennedy* (1899) is Crockett's evocation of his boyhood in Galloway. *Joan Of The Sword Hand* (1900) is a sequel to *The Red Axe*, with an amazonian Irish princess for heroine. Although he was much admired by his contemporaries, Crockett wrote too much, too fast and retold the same story too often. BL 59. *DNB*. RM. *NCBEL*.

CROKER, [Mrs] B[ithia] M[ary] (née Sheppard, 1860?–1921). The daughter of a Church of Ireland clergyman, Bithia Sheppard was born in Co. Roscommon, Ireland, but educated in Cheshire, England. In the late 1870s she married an officer in the Royal Scots, and with him spent fourteen years in India and Burma. Her fiction (which generally deals with upper-class colonial life) is marked by a keen observation of India, and a sentimental nostalgia for her native Ireland. She was unusually sympathetic to the Indian natives. As one reviewer put it in 1888: 'she does not regard the natives as "niggers" but bears eloquent testimony to their courtesy, chivalry and charity.' Croker's many novels were popular with library readers, and invariably have strong romantic interest together with heavily worked-in local description. *Proper Pride* (1882) is her first published work (for Tinsley*), a story of Anglo-Indian life with some lively military chapters set in Afghanistan. *Pretty Miss Neville* (1883) has as heroine-narrator a faithless coquette (and huntswoman) in the Indian station of Mulkapore. The novel ends inevitably with Miss Neville a miss no more. *Someone Else* (1884) chronicles the mishaps that follow from a mistaken kiss. *A Bird Of Passage* (1886) is another study of colonial flirtation, this time in the Andamans in the Indian Ocean. *Interference* (1891) begins with some lively fox-hunting in Ireland and ends with husband-hunting in India. *Beyond The Pale* (1897, first serialised in *The Times* weekly edition) features a horsey Irish heroine, 'Galloping Jerry', and is set in Munster. Croker could turn out such fiction with effortless ease, and built up a readership which remained faithful until the 1920s earning at her peak in the early twentieth century as much as £2,000 a novel. On their part, critics were unanimous in finding her novels 'fresh and wholesome as an autumn breeze'. BL 49. *WW*. Wol.

CROLY, the Rev. George (1780–1860). Croly was born in Dublin. Ordained into the Church of Ireland in 1804, he was inspired by the poetry of Byron and Moore (and dislike for his rural pastoral work) to try a literary career. Around 1810, he moved to London, and was taken up by Blackwood's*, the publisher. An all-round man of letters (always proudest of his poetry) Croly had some success in 1829 with his novel *Salathiel*, a smart work in the pre-Victorian manner about the Wandering Jew. His later fiction such as *Marston, Or The Soldier And Statesman* (1846) is somewhat out of place in the later era. A Colburn* three-decker set in the French Revolution the narrative is autobiographical in form. First serialised in *Blackwood's Magazine** the novel was held back from publication in book form for some months because of an unspecified 'severe domestic affliction'. As Rector of St Stephen's, Walbrook (after 1835), Croly enjoyed fame as preacher in his later years. But after the 1840s life was evidently hard for him. BL 3. *DNB*. RM. *NCBEL*. Wol. Sad.

CROMARTY, Deas (i.e. Elizabeth Sophia Watson, née Fletcher, 1850–1918). The daughter of a Wesleyan minister, Sophia Fletcher was born and raised in London. In 1874, she married Robert A. Watson (1845–1921), a minister of the United Free Church in Aberdeen. He wrote theology, she fiction, using the various Scottish backgrounds to which his work took them. Her novels include: *Crabtree Fold* (1881); *A High Little World* (1892); *Under God's Sky* (1895), subtitled, 'The Story Of A Cleft In Marland'. These three novels feature the wild northern landscape descriptions with much reference to 'rifts', 'scaurs', 'clefts', 'pikes', 'cloughs' and so on, which were Cromarty's speciality. *The Heart Of Babylon* (1900) is the story of a young Methodist originally trained for the ministry, who comes to London to work first in a draper's store, then for a newspaper. He is eventually rescued from the modern Babylon by his mother. The narrative presumably contains something of the Rev. Watson's early experience. She died at Newport in Fife. BL 5. (RAW) *WW*. Wol.

CROMMELIN, May [Maria Henrietta de la Cherois] (1850?–1930). She was born in Ireland, well off and a descendant of Louis Crommelin, the Huguenot founder of the Ulster linen industry. Largely educated at home, Crommelin spent most of her early life in Ireland. As an adult she travelled widely in far-flung parts of the world (travel was, in fact, listed as her only recreation in *Who's Who*). Ireland is the main setting for her fiction. But her voyages to South America and the East also find their way into her novels, of which the earliest were: *Queenie* (1874); *My Love, She's But A Lassie* (1875); *A Jewel Of A Girl* (1877); *In The West Countrie* (1883). Crommelin wrote voluminously, but her fiction is quite insubstantial and aimed at the indiscriminate female reader. BL 42. *WW*. Wol. RLF.

CROSLAND, Mrs Newton [Camilla Dufour] (née Toulmin, 1812–95). Toulmin was born in London, the daughter of a solicitor and well connected with literary society on her mother's side. She was exceptionally precocious, reading at the age of three. But her father was ruined and died when she was only eight. Toulmin was thereafter educated at home, largely by her own efforts. After 1838, she devoted herself to literature and began contributing miscellaneously to the magazines, a practice she was to keep up all her life. In 1848, she married Newton Crosland (1819–99), a London wine merchant. In the 1850s the Croslands both became enthusiastic spiritualists, a preoccupation which enters her subsequent fiction. Crosland's earliest successful novel is *Hildred, The Daughter* (1855), the story of a young girl who comes into a fortune which she does not spend, thinking it belongs to another. Her other fiction includes *Mrs Blake* (1865) and *Hubert Freeth's Prosperity* (1873), the story of a family's changes under the effect of a financial windfall. BL 13. *DNB*. Wol. RLF.

CROWE, Mrs Catherine [Ann] (née Stevens, 1790–1876). Born in Kent, Catherine Stevens was brought up in Edinburgh, where she became a disciple of the noted phrenologist, George Combe. She enjoyed a reputation as a woman of intellect, and was credited by some as the author of Chambers's anonymously published *The Vestiges of Creation* (1844). Stevens married Lt.-Col. John Crowe in 1822 and began writing novels in 1839. But fame came with *Susan Hopley, Or Circumstantial Evidence** (1841), the story of a resourceful servant who solves a mysterious crime. *Men And Women, Or Manorial Rights* (1844) is a stodgy melodrama of murder, detection and remorse with a warning in the last paragraph that readers should carefully guard the morals of their domestic servants. *Lilly Dawson* (1847) is more eventful. Its heroine is shipwrecked as a girl, and forcibly adopted by smugglers where she is forced to be 'everybody's servant, and maid-of-all work in the most emphatic sense of the term'. Her Cinderella-like return to wealthy, middle-class existence is fraught with difficulties. At the end of her adventures she disdains gentility and returns to marry a lover, Philip, from the lower orders. The last sentence of the novel informs the reader that she died happy and 'at peace with God and Man'. These two works, written as they were with unadorned simplicity, succeeded both as novels and in dramatised form on the stage. Crowe was fascinated by psychic phenomena and was a proselytising spiritualist. This is reflected in her most striking volume, *The Night Side Of Nature* (1848), which contains an assortment of weird tales, haunted houses, supernatural happenings and apparitions, all vouched for as genuine by the author. *The Adventures Of A Beauty* (1852) was written after Crowe had transferred to the publisher Colburn* and in line with his preferences is more consciously 'fashionable' than her earlier homiletic work. Crowe had a severe mental breakdown in the 1850s, and wrote little in her last years. John Crowe died in 1860. His widow lived on as an invalid at Folkestone dying, as the record puts it, 'of natural decay'. Her fiction is direct and uncomplicated in its appeal. She also wrote a number of books for children. BL 12. *DNB* (which gives her date of birth as 1800). *NCBEL*. Wol. Sad.

The Crown Of Life, George Gissing, 1899, 1 vol, Methuen. A late and surprisingly romantic novel for Gissing, written at the period when his second marriage was falling apart. The hero, Piers Otway, is illegitimate, intellectual and sensitive. His legitimate half-brothers, Daniel and Alex, exploit, cheat and humiliate him socially. Piers falls passionately in love with Irene Derwent, but drunkenly disgraces himself in her eyes. He runs off to Russia to make his fortune. After some years, he returns to find Irene now engaged to an imperialist politician, Arnold Jacks. Piers finally manages to win her and defeat the schemes of his half-brothers, the 'crown of life' being, as he discovers, love. As a political sub-plot, the novel (whose setting is studiously contemporary) explores British imperialism in the period of the Boer War from the author's increasingly pacifist standpoint.

CROWQUILL, Alfred (i.e. Alfred Henry Forrester, 1804–72). Illustrator and writer. Forrester was born in London and educated privately. After short spells in law and business, he took up illustration, caricature and comic-writing full time. Until 1843, he shared the 'Crowquill' pseudonym with his brother, Charles Robert Forrester (1803–50). Alfred was associated with *Punch** in its early years and the *Illustrated London News** and wrote for *Bentley's Miscellany**. He illustrated G. W. M. Reynolds's* *Pickwick Abroad* (1839) and various novels of Henry Cockton*. His illustrations are stylistically reminiscent of Phiz* and particularly influenced the development of Victorian children's* books. *DNB*. Hou.

CRUIKSHANK, George (1792–1878). Illustrator. The son of the satirist, Isaac Cruikshank (1756?–1811?), George began in the family's London engraving business at the age of thirteen. By the age of eighteen, he was regarded as the likely successor to Gillray, and was employed by William Hone during that satirist's most stormy phase. His first sustained illustration for fiction was with Pierce Egan's seminal *Life In London* (1821). In the 1820s and 1830s, Cruikshank turned increasingly to novel illustration, mainly for reprints of classic British and European works. But in 1836, the young and enterprising publisher John Macrone* had the bright idea of partnering Cruikshank with Ainsworth* (on *Rookwood**) and with Dickens* (on *Sketches By Boz*). Artistically (if not temperamentally) the partnerships worked wonderfully. Bentley* continued the connection by uniting Dickens with Cruikshank on *Oliver Twist** and Cruikshank with Ainsworth on *Jack Sheppard**. The high point of Cruikshank's novel illustration was reached with Ainsworth's *The Tower Of London** in 1840 for which the illustrator furnished forty full-page etchings on steel and innumerable woodcuts. Cruikshank's tableaux compositions (derived from theatrical settings and groupings) were extremely effective. In later life, Cruikshank caused some controversy by claiming (without much evidence) to have invented the plots of *Oliver Twist* and some of Ainsworth's early romances. He broke with Ainsworth in 1842, and thereafter did little worthwhile fiction illustration, apart from some work for Frank Smedley* and the Mayhew* brothers in the early 1850s. (About the same time he transferred his allegiance from the publisher Bradbury and Evans* to David Bogue*.) His influence is strongly evident in *Punch**, although he personally had nothing to do with the magazine. In the early 1840s, decades of bohemian living caught up with Cruikshank. He reformed, in 1847, and became thereafter one of the country's leading temperance propagandists, a career inaugurated by his hugely successful moral series of plates, *The

Bottle (1847) and culminating with his massive oil painting *The Worship Of Bacchus* in 1862. Cruikshank's illustrations to fiction are a small part of his total work, but they represent a high point of the alliance of pen and pencil in the century connecting prose realists like Dickens with the pictorial tradition of Hogarth. *DNB*. Hou.

A Crystal Age, W. H. Hudson, 1887, 1 vol, T. Fisher Unwin. A utopia, strongly influenced by Samuel Butler's* *Erewhon** (1872) and pervaded with Hudson's romanticised Darwinism. An Englishman falls over a cliff botanising and mysteriously wakes up eons in the future. He discovers that mankind now lives in beehive-like communes ('houses') based not on industrial production and consumption but on conservation. A suit of clothes takes a year to make and lasts a lifetime; books pass on from generation to generation; houses are regarded as eternally durable structures. Most strikingly, individual sex has been bred out of the species and only one woman in the house is sexed (like the queen bee). The work, which is lacking in either action or Butlerian comedy, ends mystically with a union between Smith and his love Yoletta, the new 'mother'.

The Cuckoo In The Nest, Mrs Oliphant, 1892, 3 vols, Hutchinson. Patty Hewitt, a village beauty and the daughter of the local inn, has two suitors: Gervase Piercey, a baronet's alcoholic son and Roger Pearson, a sturdy village lad. She marries Gervase and when he dies so ingratiates herself with his father Sir Giles that eventually she becomes an heiress, to the consternation of her aristocratic in-laws. After a number of social misadventures, Patty realises that genteel life is not what she wants. She renounces her wealth and title, and marries Roger who is now a star cricketer.

CUDLIP, Mrs Pender [Annie Hall] (née Thomas, 1838–1918). Known authorially by her maiden name, even after marriage, Annie Thomas was born in Aldborough, Suffolk, the only daughter of a Royal Navy lieutenant. She was educated at home, and in the late 1850s married Pender Hodge Cudlip, a High-Church clergyman, and amateur theological author. She began publishing her work in 1862 eventually becoming one of the more voluminous producers of romantic fiction in the second half of the century. Cudlip claimed to be able to write a three-volume novel in six weeks. William Tinsley* remembered her as a 'bright, merry light-hearted girl and a writer of bright, easy reading fiction'. In the preface to *A Narrow Escape* (1875) Thomas credited Edmund Yates's* lecture 'Good Authors At A Discount' with having inspired her with the sense that 'there was something glorious even in a non-successful literary career'. Representative works by her are: *Blotted Out* (1876); *Our Set* (1881); *That Other Woman* (1889). Some of her novels, such as *False Colours* (1865), the study of an unwed mother, were found improper by her contemporaries. In general, her novels are unpretentious but not so bad as to be wholly unenjoyable. Her trademark was the abrupt opening. Cudlip's son-in-law, Major William Price Drury*, a Royal Marine, wrote some nautical* novels at the end of the century. BL 70. *WW*. Wol. RLF.

CUNNINGHAM, Sir Henry [Stewart] (1832–1920). The son of a clergyman and a titled mother, Cunningham was educated at Harrow and Oxford. He was called to the Bar in 1859, and rose to be Advocate-General at Madras, in 1873. From 1877–87, he was a judge in India and was knighted in 1889. For someone as involved with the law, Cunningham wrote a large amount of polished fiction. *Wheat And Tares* (1860) is a love story, set in a seaside town, Westborough, on the south coast. The story ends in a vaguely melancholy way. *Late Laurels* (1864) is a more amusing chronicle of upper-class life in the shires. *The Chronicles Of Dustypore* (1875) is a panorama of Anglo-Indian life in the hill stations, and one of the best novels of its kind in the period. *The Heriots* (1889) is the story of Olivia who marries the wealthy heir, Jack Heriot, and thus gains entrance into high society. *Sibylla* (1894) is a study of 1890s womanhood, against a high society and politics setting. Cunningham's fiction is entertainingly sharp in its depiction of late Victorian mores. He chose not to list it among his literary accomplishments in *Who's Who*. BL 6. *WW*. Wol. Sad.

CURLING, Captain [Henry] (1803–64). Curling served as an infantry officer in the period following the Napoleonic Wars. He went on half pay in 1834, and retired in 1854, dying in Kensington. His novels are mainly military in subject-matter and historical* in setting. They include: *The Soldier Of Fortune* (1843); *John Of England* (1846); *Frank Beresford, Or Life In The Army* (1858); *The Self Divorced, Or The School For Wives* (1861). BL 13. *DNB*. Wol. Sad.

CURRIE, Lady [Mary Montgomerie] ('Violet Fane', née Lamb, 1843–1905). Born at Littlehampton Sussex into a distinguished and literary family, Lamb was educated privately. Her parents objected to her desire to write, hence she took from Disraeli's* *Vivian Grey* the pseudonym 'Violet Fane'. Beautiful and socially accomplished, in 1864 Lamb married an Irish landowner, Henry Sydenham Singleton. He died in 1893, leaving her with four children. She remarried Sir Philip Henry Wodehouse Currie, of the diplomatic corps. Their married life was passed in ambassadorial service at Constantinople and Rome and after his retirement (in 1903) at Hawley in Hampshire. A versatile writer, Violet Fane's works include the unusual novel in verse, *Denzil Place* (1875). The heroine Constance is married to a Tory baronet, and falls in love with the more dashing Geoffrey Denzil. Critics found the description of their adulterous affair distasteful. *Sophy, Or The Adventures Of A Savage* (1881) has an ingenuous heroine Sophy St Clair who is first encountered as a precocious eight-year-old, 'a barefooted pantheist'. By the end of the novel, after trials and tribulations (including a devastating false death report) Sophy is married to her cousin Godfrey. The narrative is overloaded with quotation and redundant literary allusion but it was to the public taste of the period and went into three editions in its first year. *Thro' Love And War* (1886) is livelier. It has a heroine who falls in love with a military man whom she meets by chance in a railway carriage, and subsequently hunts down. Again, critics found the subject mildly distasteful and their disapproval did nothing to hurt the book's sales. *The Story Of Helen Davenant* (1889) is a more tedious study of modern womanhood. *Two Moods Of A Man* (1901) contains papers and short stories. Fane is portrayed as 'Mrs Sinclair' in W. H. Mallock's* satire, *The New Republic* (1877), a work which the author dedicated to her. BL 4. *DNB*. *NCBEL*. Wol.

Curry (1830?–46). Irish Publisher. William Curry (d. 1846) published Charles Lever's* fiction, while the novelist was based in Dublin. On his death, Curry was succeeded by James McGlashan* (d. 1858), who took on the business in a run-down state caused partly by the financial consequences of the Irish famine, partly by Lever's defection to London publishers.

CURWEN, Henry (1845–92). Curwen was born in Workington, Cumberland (where the Curwens were a well-known family) the son of a clergyman. On leaving grammar school he came to London to work in the publishing world (a subject on which he was later to become an authority). For a while, he was associated with John Camden Hotten*, the founder of Chatto and Windus*. Curwen at this period published a number of literary translations from the French and wrote a critical work on Poe in 1872. In 1876, he went to India, and was assistant editor of the *Times Of India* in Bombay. In 1880 he became editor and in 1889 proprietor of the paper. Around 1892, Curwen's health collapsed, and he died during the return voyage from India. He never married. His novels are all casual efforts. His most readable work is the panorama of modern sexual behaviour in London gathered as *Within Bohemia* (1876). Curwen's other fiction includes: *Zit And Xoe* (1879), an odd utopian romance dealing with the descent of man from prehistoric times; *Lady Bluebeard* (1888), a tale of India; *Dr Hermione* (1890). His influential *History Of Booksellers* was published in 1873. BL 4. *DNB*. Wol.

CUSHING, Paul (i.e. Roland Alexander Wood-Seys, 1854–1919). Wood-Seys was born at Stourbridge in Worcestershire, and educated privately. From 1876 onwards, he travelled widely, eventually settling in southern California to grow olives and write novels. Reviewers often identified him wrongly thereafter as an American writer. His fiction, as 'Paul Cushing', includes: *The Blacksmith Of Voe* (1886), a story set in the Derbyshire Peak sheepfarming hills with a bigamy* and murder plot; *A Woman With A Secret* (1885); *Cut With His Own Diamond* (1891), set in 'Fellby' on the Scottish border; *The Shepherdess Of Treva* (1895). The last of these has as its heroine Bitha Treloare, who leaves her rustic idyll to conquer the artistic circles of upper-class London life as the society painter Meg Quin. It all ends tragically. BL 9. *WW*. Wol.

D

DAHLE, Thomas T[heodore] (1867–1910). Dahle was born in Norway of Scandinavian parents, but moved in early life to Hull, where he settled and married. After an unsuccessful attempt at law he took up journalism, became editor of the *Hull Critic* at the age of nineteen and rose to be editor of the *Sun*. He also furnished the popular column of causerie by 'The Man in the Street' for the same paper. Dahle wrote one Victorian novel, *A Tragedy Of Three* (1900). The tragedy concerns a man who marries without discarding his former mistress. Despite its gloomy subject the novel was something of a hit. BL 1. *WW*.

The Daisy Chain, Charlotte M. Yonge, 1856, 1 vol, J. W. Parker. (Subtitled 'Or Aspirations' the novel was serialised irregularly in *The Monthly Packet**, from 1853; Yonge being editor of the journal.) Yonge described *The Daisy Chain* as 'a family chronicle, a domestic record of home events during those years of early life when the character is chiefly formed'. Dr May, a warm-hearted but quick-tempered man, gave up a distinguished career in medicine by marrying early. His wife is killed when a carriage overturns, and May is left a widower with eleven children to look after. The title derives from the new-born (and motherless) Gertrude Margaret, who is nicknamed Daisy. She becomes the symbol of enduring family unity as 'mamma's precious flower, her pearl of truth'. Around the members of the May family various dramas develop as the children grow up and make their entrances into life. Most interesting is clever and impulsive Ethel, the third sister. By subduing her wayward energies (and with the help of a bequest from her sister Margaret's dead lover) she sets up a school in the quarry town of Stoneborough and builds a church in her village of Cocksmoor. (Yonge was passionately interested in the construction of new Anglican churches which is the theme of her first novel, *Abbeychurch*, 1844.) In the last paragraphs, Ethel stoically accepts useful spinsterhood as her destiny in life ('Need I dread a few short years?'). The narrative is marked by lively dialogue and a strong sense of ebullient communal energy. There was a sequel, *The Trial* (1863), in which Leonard Ward, the son of Dr May's old partner, is falsely accused of murder. The Mays are convinced of his innocence and young Tom May (a doctor and scientist) succeeds in detecting the real culprit, Francis Axworthy, who is dying in Paris. After three bitter years, Ward is released from prison and goes off to be a missionary. (Tom brings back and marries Ward's consumptive and invalid sister, Averil, who has run away to America.) In this sequel, Yonge exploits the 1860s vogue for sensation* novels of crime and detection as well as making her usual assertion that moral trial is a uniquely uplifting experience.

DALTON, William (1821–75). Dalton was born in Yorkshire. At some point he must have travelled to the Orient which furnishes the staple subject-matter for his later fiction such as *The English Boy In Japan* (1858), *The Wolf Boy Of China* (1860) and *The White Elephant* (1860). Dalton was at one point a journalist in London, and edited the *Daily Telegraph* for a while. He died destitute, the inquest finding the cause to be 'a diseased heart accelerated by cold and want'. Dalton's most successful tale was the Elizabethan tale, *Will Adams, The First Englishman In Japan* (1861), and his main readership was evidently juvenile. BL 15. Boase. Wol. RLF.

Danesbury House, Mrs Henry Wood, 1860, 1 vol, Scottish Temperance League. The author's first published novel, written in a few days for a temperance competition in which it won the first prize of a £100. Given these constraints, the story is well managed. It covers forty years in the life of the Danesbury family. John Danesbury is a manufacturer in the industrial town of Eastborough. A drunken nurse gives a baby of the family laudanum by error. In rushing back, Mrs Danesbury's coach is overturned, and she is killed. A drunken gateman is to blame. The husband marries a woman with lax views on strong liquor. The two children of the second marriage go to the bad. Robert enters the army and becomes a confirmed drunkard and finally cuts his throat. Lionel becomes a doctor and eventually dies of delirium tremens. Of the three other children, William also has the drinking disease but by the end of the novel has almost conquered it with the help of a good wife. Isabel marries Lord Temple, who is saved from alcoholic perdition after almost dying in a drink-provoked duel. Only the oldest son, Arthur, a water drinker from birth, is untouched by the epidemic boozing that ravages the Danesburys. He spreads abstinence among his workers by the benevolent construction of a temperance 'gin palace' which serves good coffee.

DANIEL, Robert Mackenzie (1814–47). Daniel was born in Inverness, and educated at the universities of Aberdeen and Edinburgh. In 1836 he gave up a career in Scottish law for literary work in London where he became editor of the *Court Journal*. In fiction, he specialised in historical three-deckers, of which the first was *The Scottish Heiress* (1843). This was followed by *The Grave Digger* (1843). Around this time, Daniel moved to Jersey. His next novel, *The Young Widow* (1844), is the story of a young wife's trials after her missionary husband is reported dead in Africa. The work was very well received. So too was its successor, *The Young Baronet* (1845), a tale of a nobleman's struggles to recover his title and property in 1830s Scotland. On the strength of these successes, his publisher (the dubious Newby*) labelled him 'The Scottish Boz*', and Daniel was favourably compared with both Galt and Marryat*, whom he sometimes resembles. But in 1846 the young author went mad and died in Bedlam the following year. Under her married name Daniel's widow began writing novels in 1846, with *The Poor Cousin* and over the next thirty years produced a three-decker a year, mainly of a domestic* romantic kind, and principally for Newby. Her last work seems to have been *The Squire's Courtship* in 1877. (RD) BL 5. (Mrs RD) BL 30. *DNB*. Wol. RLF.

Daniel Deronda, George Eliot, 1876, 4 vols, Blackwood. (Serialised in eight monthly parts, February–September 1876.) George Eliot's last novel. The story opens strikingly at a gambling casino, where the heroine Gwendolen Harleth first catches the attention of Daniel, a young aristocrat of mysterious origins who has been brought up by Sir Hugo Mallinger. Gwendolen is essentially good, but a 'spoiled child'. For money, she agrees to marry the heartless Henleigh Grandcourt (a nephew of Sir Hugo), despite the pleas of his discarded mistress Lydia Glasher. Grandcourt proves a sadistic husband. Daniel meanwhile has discovered his ancestry by a series of accidents. He saves a young Jewess, Mirah Lapidoth, from drowning herself in the Thames and places her with his friends the Meyrick family. Through Mirah and her saintly, zealous brother Mordecai (whom he tracks down) Daniel feels an affinity with Judaism. An interview with his hitherto unknown mother in Genoa reveals that he is in fact a Jew. The action of the Gwendolen plot also climaxes in Genoa. Grandcourt falls overboard while boating and his morally paralysed wife calmly lets him drown. Although they are attracted to each other, Daniel does not marry the widowed Gwendolen as the conventions of romance would require. Instead he chooses Mirah and at the end of the novel leaves with her on a Zionist pilgrimage to the middle East. A linked plot in the novel follows the career of the Jewish musician Klesmer and his eventual marriage to the heiress Catherine Arrowpoint in the face of her family's bitter prejudice. Although it has faults of construction, *Daniel Deronda* contains Eliot's most comprehensive vision of actual and ideal society and the principle of 'separateness and communication' which makes up the complex of social relationships.

The Danvers Jewels, Mary Cholmondeley, 1887, 1 vol, Bentley. (Serialised in *Temple Bar**, January–March 1887.) An early hit, by the author of *Red Pottage**. The story is told by Colonel Middleton, who to oblige a dying comrade brings from India a set of priceless jewels for the new Danvers heir, Ralph. On the voyage a young American thief called Carr, whom Middleton thinks his friend, unsuccessfully tries to rob him. At Ralph Danvers's fine country house, Stoke Moreton, Middleton takes part in some amateur theatricals. He invites Carr to join him. The jewels disappear, and Carr is suspected. But the criminal turns out to be Ralph's fiancée 'Miss Grant' (in fact Carr's wife in disguise). She is killed in a railway accident, and the jewels are found on her. The idea and plot of the work are clearly derived from Wilkie Collins*, but Cholmondeley (who published the work anonymously), brings to the style a distinctive liveliness. A sequel, *Sir Charles Danvers*, was published in 1889.

D'ARCY, [Miss] Ella (1851–1937?). D'Arcy was born in London, of an aristocratic Irish family, and educated largely on the Continent. In the mid-1890s, she was assistant editor on the *Yellow Book**, and her work reflects the aestheticist doctrines and advanced topics (e.g. unhappy marriage) which the journal specialised in. She never herself married, but reputedly had affairs with John Lane* and Henry Harland*. A half-dozen of D'Arcy's stories were collected as *Monochromes* (1895; number XIII of John Lane's* *Keynotes** series) and as *Modern Instances* (1898). *The Bishop's Dilemma* (1898) is a novel. Critics found her fiction impressive but morbid and pessimistic in tendency. The opening piece of *Monochromes*, *The Elegie*, is a typically sardonic fable of musical genius feeding on victimised womanhood. BL 3. *WW*. Wol.

Dark Blue (1871–73). A monthly magazine edited by John C[hristian] Freund, who also wrote serial fiction for the journal. As the name implies, the readership was intended to be Oxford graduates. Initially, the short-lived venture was published by Sampson Low* before being taken over by the British and Colonial Publishing Co. During its brief existence, the magazine published stories by Compton Reade and from December 1871 J. S. Le Fanu's* classic vampire story *Carmilla**. Freund is a very minor literary figure. Born in 1849 in London, the son of an Austrian doctor, he was a graduate of Exeter College, Oxford. In addition to fiction published in *Dark Blue*, he wrote *By The Roadside* (1870). *WI*.

A Dark Night's Work, Mrs Gaskell, 1863, 1 vol, Smith, Elder. (Serialised in *All The Year Round**, January–March 1863.) Edward Wilkins is an unhappy conveyancing attorney in the rural district of Hamley. Despite an education at Eton and wealth inherited from his fashionable wife he suffers from an ineradicable sense of inferiority which he solaces with drink. His daughter Ellinor is wooed by a young lawyer, Ralph Corbet. But he is repulsed by Wilkins's drunken boorishness. Wilkins conceives a maniac hatred for his assistant Dunster, and striking him accidentally kills him.

Ellinor and a faithful servant Dixon bury the body in the garden. In the following years Wilkins dies and his accomplices are consumed with remorse. Finally, the body is discovered and Dixon accused of murder. Ellinor returns from Rome to save him. The presiding judge is Corbet. All is explained, and Ellinor marries a faithful clergyman, Livingstone, who has loved her for years. The narrative projects a darker view of country life than the author's idyllic *Cranford**.

DASENT, [Sir] George Webbe (1817–96). Dasent was born in the West Indies, where his father was Attorney-General for St Vincent. He went to school at Westminster in London and graduated from Oxford in 1840. He immediately entered the foreign service and postings in Scandinavia led to his becoming the leading Norse scholar of his generation. In 1852 he was called to the Bar, but seems not to have practised and the following year he took up a professorship at King's College, London, where he remained until 1860. Dasent was also for many years an assistant editor of *The Times* and prepared (although he never completed) a biography of its famous editor, Delane. From 1870, he was a Civil Service commissioner, taking a particular interest in the preservation of historical manuscripts. Dasent was knighted in 1876 and he retired from the Civil Service in 1892 with a gratuity of £1,200. As an author he undertook a number of modern fictional versions of the Norse sagas such as: *The Story Of Gisli The Outlaw* (1866) and *The Vikings Of The Baltic* (1875). He also wrote a closely autobiographical novel, *Annals Of An Eventful Life* (1870), which was extremely popular and reprinted five times in its first year. Dasent followed with *Three To One, Or Some Passages Out Of The Life Of Amicia Lady Sweetapple* (1872) whose arch comedy about a resourcefully eligible widow did not catch on with the public or critics. More successful was *Half A Life* (1874) which has lively scenes recalling the author's early life at Westminster and Oxford. BL 5. *DNB*. Wol.

A Daughter Of Heth, William Black, 1871, 3 vols, Sampson Low. (Originally published in the *Glasgow Weekly Herald*, 1871.) The novel with which Black made his name and fortune. The heroine is 'Coquette' (i.e. Catherine Cassilis), a vivacious and Catholic French girl transplanted to her uncle's puritanical Scottish manse (a milieu Black knew at first hand). The novel shows her refining social influence on the minister's five sons at Airlie, and her love dilemma, wooed as she is by Lord Earlshope (with whom she tours the Highlands) and Tom ('the whaup'), her sturdy Scottish cousin. The successful suitor, Earlshope, eventually turns out to be already married. He emigrates to America, where he dies, still loved by Coquette. She dies, pathetically, after marrying Tom, now a doctor. The work contains effective sketches from lowland village life. But it is striking mainly for the depiction of the finely bred heroine.

A Daughter Of Today, Mrs Everard Cotes (i.e. Sara Jeannette Duncan), 1894, 2 vols, Chatto. A serious novel in the new woman* style by a normally comic writer. The doomed 'daughter of today', Elfrida Bell, comes to the Latin Quarter of Paris from 'Sparta', Illinois, buoyed up by parochial fame among her fellow Spartans. She is first an artist, then a journalist in England and finally a novelist. Her love affair with a more

171

gifted artist, John Kendal, fails. Life defeats her and she poisons herself. The inscription on her tombstone in Sparta is, 'pas femme – artiste'. The novel's ostentatious amorality offended reviewers and the author's attitude towards her monstrously egotistic heroine is not clear.

The Daughters Of Danaus, Mona Caird, 1894, 1 vol, Bliss and Sands. A thoughtful new woman* novel. The title alludes to the fifty maidens of classical antiquity doomed to an eternity of drawing water in sieves, as punishment for having killed their husbands. Caird's heroine, Hadria Fullerton, rejects dreary Scottish respectability by marrying an Englishman, Hubert Temperley. Hadria makes it a strict condition of their union that she shall have absolute freedom. She none the less finds English domestic life intolerable and after seven years escapes to Paris, where her musical talent can develop. In the third section of the novel, Hadria has an affair with the free-thinking Professor Theobald. But the relationship breaks when she discovers that he is an unprincipled seducer. The action ends with Hadria still rebellious, but effectively beaten by the tyrannous institution of marriage. The interest of Caird's novel lies in Hadria's long and lively dialogues on New Womanhood with her militant sister Agitha, the congenial writer Valeria Du Prel and the saintly Professor Fortescue.

Davenport Dunn, Charles Lever, 1859, 1 vol, Chapman and Hall. (The story was first serialised in monthly parts, July 1857–April 1859, with illustrations by Phiz*.) Davenport Dunn is a rogue, loosely based (like Merdle in *Little Dorrit**) on the notorious Irish politician and swindler John Sadleir (1814–56), who ultimately killed himself on Hampstead Heath. In Lever's novel Dunn is a tycoon banker who has enriched himself at the expense of his fellow Irishmen after the calamities of the 1840s. One of his schemes is to set up the Anglo-French alliance in the Crimean War on the lines of a limited liability company. He conquers English society, is courted by ministers and looks to an aristocratic marriage. But when his affairs begin to fail, he prepares for flight. He is killed (accidentally) by a lesser rogue, 'Grog' Davis, on his getaway train. With his death, the Dunn bubble bursts. A sub-plot deals with the restoration of a wounded Crimean hero, Charles Conway, to the title Dunn robbed him of, and his eventual marriage to the daughter of another victim, Captain Kellett. Lever handles the enigmatic character of his majestic criminal hero effectively.

DAVEY, Richard [Patrick Boyle] (1848–1915). Davey was born in Norfolk, and educated in France and Italy. From 1870, he was a journalist based in New York. A lifelong bachelor, he returned to England in 1880, where he took up work as literary and dramatic critic of the *Morning Post* and the *Saturday Review**. He was also something of an artist and was multilingual. His fiction, which is largely Stevensonian* historical* romance embellished with owlishly 'scholarly' footnotes, includes *A Royal Amour* (1882), a book on which he claimed to have been helped by the famous American poet, Henry W. Longfellow. He also claimed that 'no less than 200 volumes, many of them rare manuscripts, have been consulted in order to render what I might call the *mise-en-scène* as correctly as possible'. Yet another colourful tale about Nell Gwyn, the novel was savaged by the critics as was *Weatherleigh* (1894), 'A Romance Of Hampton Court' set in the seventeenth century. His plays were evidently more successful, *Inheritance* enjoying a long run in New York in the early 1890s. BL 4. *WW*. Wol.

David Copperfield, Charles Dickens, 1850, 1 vol, Bradbury and Evans. (The work was first published in monthly instalments, May 1849–November 1850, with illustrations by Phiz*.) The most autobiographical of Dickens's novels, and the one he claimed to 'like best'. Told by David himself as a 'personal history', the work opens with his birth in Blundorotonc, Suffolk, six months after his father's death. David's mother, Clara, remarries but pines and eventually dies under the domestic oppression of her new husband Mr Murdstone and his sadistic maiden sister. David bites Murdstone, and is sent to Salem House, the school of the equally unkind Mr Creakle at Blackheath. There he forms what are to be lifelong friendships with the brilliant James Steerforth and the stolid Tommy Traddles. After his mother's death, David is sent to work as a menial in the bottling factory of Murdstone and Grinby in London. (Dickens drew heavily on his own childhood employment in Warren's blacking factory for this episode.) He lodges with the amiable ever-indebted and ever-optimistic Mr Micawber and his family. David finally runs away from his degrading London life and, penniless, finds refuge with his good-natured great-aunt Betsey Trotwood at Dover. He is taken in, to share her protection with the friendly monomaniac Mr Dick. David is subsequently sent to school in Canterbury and lives there with the lawyer Wickfield and his daughter Agnes. On leaving school, David returns to London to study for the law in the firm of Spenlow and Jorkins. He becomes intimate again with Steerforth, whom he unwisely introduces to the family of his old nurse, Peggotty, in Great Yarmouth. Steerforth seduces and elopes with Little Em'ly, devastating the young fisherman Ham to whom she is engaged. Later Ham attempts to rescue Steerforth from a sinking ship and both men are drowned. David meanwhile has married the hopelessly feather-brained Dora Spenlow. Weakened by pregnancy she dies and eventually David turns to Agnes, whose father had earlier become entrapped by the villainous Uriah Heep. The oleaginously 'humble' Heep is exposed as a forger by Micawber (now a lawyer's clerk) aided by Traddles (now a barrister). After three years, David (set for a career of writing novels) marries Agnes. Micawber goes to Australia where he prospers and where Little Em'ly atones by a life of humble self-sacrifice.

David Grieve, Mrs Humphry Ward, 1892, 3 vols, Smith, Elder. (Full title, *The History Of David Grieve*.) The follow-up to Ward's bestselling *Robert Elsmere**. The narrative begins pastorally, with David and Louie Grieve left orphans in rural Derbyshire. They are looked after by a weak uncle and a viciously cold aunt who keep from the children the knowledge that they have a legacy. This money was left by their father, who died shortly after his French wife drowned herself. (Suicide recurs as a motif in the narrative.) David's intellectual gifts are brought on by the local minister but Louie is flighty and headstrong. David runs off to Manchester, and finds work with a bookseller. When he discovers their inheritance, he and Louie make a trip to Paris. There, David falls in love with an artist, Elise Delaunay. She rejects him, for the sake of her art. Louie takes up with M. Montjoie. In the face of these emotional catastrophes, David attempts suicide, but is nursed back to health and Christianity by his friends. He marries his former employer's daughter, Lucy Purcell. She is unworthy of him and dies of cancer, leaving a son, Sandy. David returns to Derbyshire to recover. Louie meanwhile has had a daughter who dies of diphtheria. David thinks he hears Louie calling to him, and goes to France to find her. They are reunited, but she commits suicide. David finally finds a compatible mate in the politically aware Dora, who works as a seamstress with the poor. *David Grieve* was taken as a disappointing successor to *Robert Elsmere*.

DAVIDSON, John (1857–1909). John Davidson was born in Barrhead, Renfrewshire. His father was an evangelical pastor but poverty forced young Davidson to work in a sugar factory laboratory in Greenock at the age of thirteen. He cultivated himself, and developed a lifelong interest in science. Davidson won a bursary to Edinburgh University in 1876, but was unable to complete his undergraduate courses. He then went into teaching, but in an obscure episode was dismissed from his post at Perth Academy in 1881 for 'conduct unbecoming a schoolmaster'. In 1885, he married. His first novel, *The North Wall*, was published in 1885 and represents the first of the author's satires on aestheticism. After several unhappy years teaching in Scotland, at the age of thirty-three Davidson took his family to London, determined to live henceforth by writing. He undertook various hack commissions, making a name for himself eventually with the sprightly *Fleet Street Eclogues* (1893). He wrote plays, poetry of ideas, journalism, short stories, fantasies, treatises and worked out an ambitious philosophical system (derived from Nietzsche and Ibsen), synthesising science and public morality. Davidson became a member of the Rhymers' Club and from 1893 was associated with the publishers Elkin Mathews and John Lane*, contributing to the latter's *Yellow Book**. His most interesting novel, in so far as it attaches to more important literary figures than Davidson himself, is *Earl Lavender* (1895), a burlesque on the decadents, the cult of flagellation and the creed of 'Evolution'. *Perfervid* (1890) is a historical extravaganza on the theme of megalomania (the hero, Ninian Jamieson, believes himself by divine right to be the King of England, Scotland and Ireland). Illustrated by Harry Furniss*, the work was popular. *Laura Ruthven's Widowhood* (1892) and *Baptist Lake* (1894) also feature Davidson's literary caricature and habitual ironies. *Miss Armstrong's And Other Circumstances* (1896) gathers together various shorter pieces. Despite the patronage of such literary notables as Edmund Gosse* and G. B. Shaw*, and a Civil List pension (awarded in 1906), Davidson's last years were wretched. Suspecting he was suffering from cancer, Davidson drowned himself at Penzance, leaving a destitute family and his most ambitious philosophical drama, *God And Mammon*, unfinished. Davidson's fiction is marked by an epigrammatic wit and comic manner derived from American humorists like Mark Twain. BL 6. *DNB*. RM. *NCBEL*. Wol. Sad. RLF.

DAVIES, [Rev] Dr [Charles] Maurice (1829–85). Davies graduated from Durham University and was ordained deacon in 1851, remaining a fellow until 1856. He was one of the clergymen who used fiction as a polemical outlet in the wake of the Oxford movement controversy, his most successful work in this line being *Philip Paternoster* (1858). A 'Tractarian Love Story, By An Ex-Puseyite', the novel has as its hero an Anglican clergyman pulled back from Romish seductions by a good wife. As Davies explains in the text, he too had been tempted by Rome as a young man, but had been saved in the nick of time. Davies subsequently taught at a Church of England school in London, 1861–68 and was a noted Greek scholar. His views on religion were moderate and his other fiction includes *Broad Church* (1875), a work whose story critics found 'improbable and tedious' and whose style 'slovenly and vulgar'. Nevertheless, he followed up with *Verts, Or The Three Creeds* (1876), another religious propaganda novel. BL 4. Boase. Sad.

DAVIES, Mrs Christi|an|na [Jane] (née Douglas, 1822–87). The daughter of Pringle Home Douglas, a commander in the Royal Navy, she was born in Kelso, Scotland. Christina Douglas began writing very young, and secretively (her father, who lived until 1859, evidently disapproved of her authorship). Her first novels, *Honour And Shame* (1845) and *Anne Dysart, A Story Of Everyday Life* (1850), were published with only one of her sisters knowing she had written the works. All her later novels were published in strict anonymity. In middle age, she married Charles Greenall Davies (1804–77), Vicar of Tewkesbury. After her husband's death, she moved to London in 1878 and devoted herself to writing. Her novels are all domestic in tone and subject. *Marion's Married Life* (1885) is a typical work, tracing the heroine's moderately difficult transition from the state of good daughter to good wife. BL 10. Boase. Wol.

DAWE, [William] Carlton [Lanyon] (1866–1935). Born in Adelaide, Dawe was all his life an indefatigable traveller, and evidently took a particular interest in the white man's awkward adjustment to the Far East. His fiction (mainly short stories) anticipates that of Joseph Conrad and Somerset Maugham*. Dawe lived in England after 1892. *Yellow And White* (1895) is a collection of stories and sketches notable for its frank treatment of interracial sex ('the love of the white for the yellow'). It was not, as one reviewer put it, 'a volume for those who cherish a patriotic belief in the nobility of the Englishman abroad'. *Kakemonos* (1897) is more of the same. *The Mandarin* (1899) is a travel book thinly disguised as fiction. *The Yellow Man* (1900) is a thriller, based on Chinese secret societies. *The Emu's Head* (1893) is a violent story of the Australian goldfields. (The odd title is the name of a hotel which features centrally in the narrative.) *Claudia Pole* (1901) is a modern romance set in London. Dawe wrote a vast number of novels in the twentieth century. BL 77. *WW*. Wol.

DAWSON, Major A[lec] J[ohn], ('Howard Kerr', 1872–1952). Dawson was born in Wandsworth. He left grammar school there very young to enter the merchant marine, jumping ship in Australia, after three years at sea. For a while he drifted in Australasia and along the Mediterranean coast. Eventually, he took up journalism, and became special correspondent for the *Daily Express*. In later life he wrote copious fiction as 'Major' Dawson (a rank he earned in the First World War) and under the pseudonym 'Howard Kerr'. *Bismillah* (1898) is the first of many narratives exploiting Dawson's acquaintance with North African settings (particularly Morocco, which was a speciality with him). His best works are the autobiographical *Daniel Whyte* (1899) which recalls his youthful adventures in Australia and *The Story Of Ronald Kestrel* (1900) which draws more on his subsequent literary career, ending with the hero a famous novelist settled in New

South Wales. *African Nights' Entertainments* (1900) is Kiplingesque and employs the fashionable 'photographic method' of narration. The volume is dedicated 'with all comradely regard to the Empire's adventurers'. Dawson's other Victorian fiction includes the Australian novel *Middle Greyness* (1897) and the modishly 1890s collection of short stories *Mere Sentiment* (1897). Dawson returned to England around 1907 and was a notably imperialistic journalist and editor in the period prior to 1914. BL 21. *WW. NCBEL.* Wol.

The Dead Secret, Wilkie Collins, 1857, 2 vols, Bradbury and Evans. (Serialised in *Household Words**, January–June 1857.) Collins's fourth full-length novel. The narrative depends heavily on its moody Cornwall setting, and the mysterious Porthgenna Tower which contains the secret of the title. Captain and Mrs Treverton live at Porthgenna with their daughter Rosamond and a servant, the prematurely grey-haired, and strangely distracted Sarah Leeson. As the story opens in 1829, Sarah is summoned to her mistress's deathbed, and is given a letter for the husband which she instead secretes in the Myrtle Room before vanishing. Fifteen years pass, Treverton dies at sea and Rosamond marries the blind Mr Leonard Frankland. They return to Porthgenna, as does Sarah, now masquerading as 'Mrs Jazeph'. After various adventures, Rosamond discovers herself to be the 'love child' of Sarah and a miner. Mrs Treverton (a former actress) had duped her husband. Rosamond is reconciled with her mother, who finally dies in peace. The eccentric recluse, Mr Andrew Treverton, returns the Franklands their falsely inherited fortune and all ends happily. After a superb introduction, the novel's middle sections lack suspense.

DEAN, Andrew (i.e. Cecily Sidgwick, née Ullmann, 1852–1934). Born in London, Cecily Ullmann's family was German-Jewish, and as a girl she visited that country extensively. In 1883, she married the philosopher Alfred Sidgwick and the couple thereafter lived largely in Cornwall. Cecily Sidgwick wrote mainly under her male pseudonym, 'Andrew Dean', sometimes combining her maiden and married names as 'Mrs Alfred Ullmann Sidgwick'. Her fiction specialises in the German settings which were modish in the 1880s and 1890s. *Caroline Schlegel* (1889) has a heroine with a background similar to the author's. *Isaac Eller's Money* (1889) is a frankly anti-semitic novel dealing with the community (or 'colony') of moneylending Frankfurt Jews in England. *A Splendid Cousin* (1892) features a heroine, Theodora Legh, whose selfishness has tragic consequences as she finally walks out into the foam and drowns herself. *Mrs Finch-Brassey* (1893) is a rather more amiable study of middle-aged female eccentricity in the north of England town of 'Whincliffe'. It was evidently one of the author's more popular works and was in a third edition by 1896. *Lesser's Daughter* (1894) examines Austrian anti-semitism ('a country where Jews are openly reviled'). The hero, Lesser Bremen, dies after a racial insult to his daughter. *The Grasshoppers* (1895) is a novel about intermarriage with a new woman* heroine, Hilary Frere. *A Woman With A Future* (1896) depicts the unhappy marriage of another new woman* heroine, Hesperia Madison, who runs away with an American Jewish millionaire. *The Inner Shrine* (1900) follows the moral growth of a girl in a north of England vicarage. *Cynthia's Way* (1901) opens with the millionaire heroine receiving her seventh offer of marriage in two months. Sardonic comedy ensues. As a recent critic has noted: 'All of

Dean's fiction describes the ways middle-class parents, Jewish or Christian, scheme to marry their daughters and sons to mates the parents or other relatives choose.' Dean's last novel, *Refugees* (1934), features a Jewish heroine fleeing from Nazi Germany. BL 44. *WW*.

Decadent Fiction. Decadence is a loose term for an end-of-century literary movement which took in all the arts and popularised a fashionable life-style. In fiction, the principal exponent of the decadent mood was John Lane's* *Keynotes** series which flourished in the 1890s. The *Keynotes* list featured such works as Francis Adams's* *A Child Of The Age** (1894), Ella D'Arcy's* *Monochromes* (1895) and M. P. Shiel's* *Shapes In The Fire* (1895). Ernest Dowson's* *A Comedy Of Masks* (1893) was another exemplary text. The decadent movement is associated with notable innovations in book design. (Aubrey Beardsley*, for instance, supplied uniform pictorial embellishments for the *Keynotes* series.) Novels in the style are self-consciously sensitive to atmosphere and 'tendencies'. Frequently they affect French mannerisms and deal with the contemporary problems of the so-called new woman*. Pessimism is a dominant mood and hedonism the dominant philosophy (in Pater's* motto, 'Not the fruit of experience, but experience itself is the end'). Urban decay and racial decline were favourite subject-matters. In their psychology, the decadent writers were fascinated by the dark places of the human mind. (See, for instance, the fiction of Arthur Machen* and Stevenson's* *Dr Jekyll And Mr Hyde**.) A cultish interest in diabolism was also associated with the movement. (William Sharp*, for instance, put out in 1892 what he called *The Pagan Review*.) As a flavour, decadence can be found in the work of mainstream writers of the 1880s and 1890s such as George Moore*, Gissing* and Thomas Hardy*. But the public disgrace of Oscar Wilde* in 1895 made the style distinctly unfashionable.

The Deemster, T. H. Hall Caine, 1887, 3 vols, Chatto. One of Caine's biggest bestsellers. The narrative is set on the author's native Isle of Man in the late eighteenth century. Ewan Mylrea has two sons. Thorkell, hard and selfish, becomes a Deemster, or Manx judge. Gilcrist, soft and merciful, becomes the island's Bishop. Thorkell's house and dynasty have been cursed by the mother of a girl he wronged. His wife dies, his son Ewan is a weakling. Gilcrist's son, Dan, grows up a wild seafarer. The cousins fight a savage duel with knives over a supposed wrong done Ewan's sister Mona. Ewan falls over the cliff on which they are struggling and a remorseful Dan confesses to murder. By a quirk of Manx law, he is sentenced by the Bishop, his father, to ostracism on a lonely corner of the island. His subsequent journal forms the most interesting section of the narrative. Dan finally atones by heroic service during an epidemic of sweating sickness and dies forgiven.

Deerbrook, Harriet Martineau, 1839, 3 vols, Moxon. The two orphaned Ibbetson sisters, Hester and Margaret, come from the city of Birmingham to the 'rather pretty' village of Deerbrook to live with their cousins, the Greys. (Much of the early narrative is reflected through the bright personality of sixteen-year-old Sophia Grey.) Edward Hope, the local surgeon, falls in love with Margaret. But a series of accidents makes him the husband of the younger Hester. A rival of the Grey family, Mrs Rowland, does all she can to ruin the newly married couple, spreading the rumour that the match is unhappy and poisoning the minds of Hope's gullible patients with stories of malpractice and grave robbing. Edward and Hester are brought to the brink of ruin. But during a fever epidemic, he performs prodigies of medical heroism. Margaret can finally marry a chastened Mrs Rowland's brother, Philip Enderby. Aptly called 'a poor novel with a few good pages', *Deerbrook* anticipates some plot complications of *Middlemarch** and other 'novels of community'.

DELAMOTTE, William [Alfred] (1775–1863). Artist and book illustrator. Delamotte was born at Weymouth of Huguenot descent, the son of a postal agent. He studied with the artist Benjamin West in the 1790s at which period George III took an interest in the young artist's career. In 1803, he was appointed drawing master at the Royal Military Academy, Sandhurst, holding the post until 1843. In fiction, his main contribution was as one of the illustrators on Ainsworth's* *Windsor Castle**. *DNB*. Hou.

DE LA PASTURE, Mrs Henry [Elizabeth Lydia Rosabelle] (née Bonham, 1866–1945). Elizabeth Bonham was born at Naples, the daughter of a diplomat father. She subsequently married Henry De La Pasture, the son of a Welsh marquis and a former cavalry officer. The couple were to have two daughters. Mrs De La Pasture later wrote plays and novels. Her fiction is composed largely of middle and high-society melodrama centred on the love affairs of young girls. *Deborah Of Tod's* (1897), is the story of an independent young peasant girl, who single-handedly keeps her family's West Country freehold going. Her other fiction includes: *Adam Grigson* (1899), a melodrama with a virtuous working-class hero; *Catherine Of Calais* (1901). The last is the story of a sentimental young heroine who falls in love with an elderly and prickly baronet. After his death, she refuses to be disillusioned in him and the novel ends with a sanctified vignette of her noble wifely idolatry. The work was popular enough to warrant a sequel, *Catherine's Child* (1908). Critics found De La Pasture's fiction amiable in tone and she was touted as a worthy successor to Mrs Oliphant*. Her first husband died in 1908 and in 1910 she married the diplomat and author, Sir Hugh Clifford*, continuing to write fiction and children's* books well into the twentieth century. BL 14. *WW*.

DE MORGAN, William [Frend] (1839–1917). A Victorian novelist in everything but the belated date of his publications, De Morgan was born in London, where his father was a university professor of mathematics. William was precociously clever, and attended University College, London as a boy. He went on at the age of sixteen to study art, and came under the influence of William Morris* and the arts and crafts movement. De Morgan ingeniously rediscovered medieval techniques for staining glass and set up a ceramics works at Chelsea in 1872 producing distinctive lustre and glazed ware. In 1882, he joined Morris at Merton Abbey, near Wimbledon. A few years later, De Morgan built his own factory at Fulham, having married the artist Mary Evelyn Pickering in 1887. He retired moderately prosperously in 1905, and embarked at the age of sixty-five on a new career in novel writing (partly at his wife's encouragement, she being alarmed at his depressed state of mind). His first published work of fiction was *Joseph Vance* (1906), facetiously subtitled 'An Ill-written Autobiography'. This account of growing up in

London in the mid-1850s was a hit, and De Morgan followed it with five subsequent novels and had two incomplete at the time of his death. BL 7. *DNB*. RM. *NCBEL*. Wol.

Demos, George Gissing, 1886, 3 vols, Smith, Elder. Subtitled 'A Story Of English Socialism', the work was given topicality by the politically motivated Trafalgar Square riots of 1887, and did unusually well for the author. The story begins with the Mutimer mining estate at Wanley being left to a young proletarian socialist from Hoxton, Richard Mutimer, rather than the aristocratic and aesthetic Hubert Eldon. The well-born Adela Waltham gives up Hubert for Richard, and Richard on his part jilts his working-class lover, Emma Vine. Once enriched, Mutimer betrays his former socialist principles and shows himself a brutal husband. His relatives (especially his young sister Alice, nicknamed 'The Princess') exhibit gross vulgarity in their newly elevated station at Wanley Manor. The narrative is complicated by Adela's discovery of a valid will which leaves all the mining property to Hubert, who closes down the works altogether. Richard, now on the side of the workers, loses their funds and is killed by a stone thrown from an irate mob. His brother 'Arry Mutimer takes to drink and robbery; Alice marries a criminal bigamist. The novel ends with the marriage of Hubert and Adela. The novel powerfully expresses Gissing's disillusioned political views and examines a whole spectrum of socialist ideologies from Richard's populism to the intellectualism of Mr Westlake (i.e. William Morris*).

Denis Duval, W. M. Thackeray, 1864, 1 vol, Smith, Elder. (Serialised in the *Cornhill Magazine**, from March to June 1864, illustrated by Frederick Walker*.) Thackeray's last novel, broken off after the eighth chapter. The story is told autobiographically. The descendant of French Huguenots, Denis is brought up in the 1760s at Rye and Winchelsea where his grandfather Peter Duval is a wig-maker and smuggler. As a boy Denis falls in love with Agnes, the daughter of a runaway French mother who has taken refuge in the Duval household. Agnes is persecuted by the villainous Chevalier de la Motte, who has settled in Rye to dabble in smuggling and espionage with a German henchman, Lütterloh. Denis is weaned from smuggling by his patron, the Rector Dr Barnard and has some close shaves with a pair of highwayman brothers, the Westons. After war breaks out with France, Denis discovers that de la Motte is spying, and exposes him, so making a lifelong enemy. Here the story was interrupted by Thackeray's death. Evidently as it was planned, Denis would go to sea on the *Serapis* and would eventually be captured by the American hero, Paul Jones. De la Motte would attempt to force Agnes into marriage with Lütterloh but would finally end on the gallows for his spying activities. The novel has a charming freshness of tone and a fine evocation of period and place.

J. M. Dent (1888–). Publishing firm, founded by Joseph Mallaby Dent (1849–1926). Dent was born in Darlington, Yorkshire, the tenth child of a musician. Having been apprenticed as a printer, he went to London in 1867, where he set up shop as a printer and bookbinder. In 1887, his business burned down, and from his rebuilt premises the following year Dent and Co. published their first volumes. In the 1890s, he established himself as one of the more energetic of the new generation of British publishers.

Always interested in reprints (especially of fiction), Dent in collaboration with Ernest Rhys (husband of Grace Rhys*) established the 'Everyman' library in 1904. (JMD) *WW*.

DERING, E[dward] H[eneage] (1827–92). Dering was born in Pluckley, Kent, the second son of an Anglican clergyman. He took a commission in the Coldstream Guards in 1846, but sold out in the early 1850s, after catching malaria in Italy. In 1859, Dering married Georgiana, Lady Chatterton*, a widow twenty years his senior. The couple lived in Mayfair and with Chatterton's relatives, Marmion and Rebecca Ferrers, in a country house, Baddesley Hall: 'cultivating the arts and gradually withdrawing into a communal mystical retirement'. It was Dering's habit to dress in seventeenth-century costume. He (but not she) converted to Catholicism, and was received into the Church by Newman* in 1865. Around the same turbulent period of his life, Dering wrote the novels *Lethelier* (1860); *A Great Sensation* (1862); *Florence Danby* (1868). The settings and plots of these works were fashionable and romantic, and they frequently served as vehicles for the author's religious prejudices. Reviewers generally found Dering an odious novelist. But *Sherborne, Or The House At The Four Ways* (1875), a 'metaphysico-religious dissertation on the beauties of Catholicism', was sufficiently persuasive to bring his wife across to Rome. After Chatterton's death in 1876, Dering married the widowed Rebecca Ferrers. *The Ban Of Mablethorpe* (1894), a pro-Catholic country house novel, was finished on the night Dering died and was privately published with a request that the reader pray for the author's soul. BL 7. Boase. Wol. Sad.

DESART, Earl of (born William Ulick O'Connor Cuffe, 1845–98). The eldest son of the third Earl of Desart, Cuffe was educated at Eton and Bonn. He served in the Grenadier Guards until assuming his earldom at the age of twenty. His first marriage ended in divorce in 1878. Desart wrote for the London papers, often on hunting which was his passion. He began publishing novels with the desultory *Only A Woman's Love* (1869) for Tinsley*. His other fiction includes: *Children Of Nature, A Story Of Modern London* (1878); *The Honourable Ella* (1879), a tale of 'Foxshire'; *Lord And Lady Piccadilly* (1887); *The Little Chatelaine* (1889). The author presented himself on his title pages: 'The Earl of Desart', which may have been a selling point. His most popular work was the mystery story, *Herne Lodge* (1888). Desart died aboard his yacht in Falmouth harbour. BL 12. Boase. Wol.

DESPARD, Mrs M. C[harlotte] (née French, 1844–1939). Born in London, she was the daughter of a wealthy Irishman, Captain John French. In her early childhood, her father died suddenly and her mother went insane. The young Charlotte was brought up by strict relatives, against whose discipline she rebelled. In 1870 she met and married Colonel Maximilian Despard. The marriage was childless but happy. In the 1870s, Despard wrote some high-pressured romantic novels for Tinsley* of which *Chaste As Ice, Pure As Snow* (1874) was moderately popular. The portrait of a wife wronged by her husband's groundless suspicions, the work exhibits psychological subtlety in the presentation of a woman 'face to face with the world'. Settings move between Russia and Switzerland. *A Modern Iago* (1879) is another study of modern marriage. A growing political consciousness is evident in Despard's semi-fictional *A Voice From The Dim Millions, Being The True History Of A Working Woman* (1884). Despard's husband died in 1890. She went to live among the poor at Vauxhall and thereafter became increasingly militant politically. In the twentieth century she was openly Marxist, fiercely Catholic and a supporter of Sinn Fein. BL 5. Wol.

Desperate Remedies, Thomas Hardy, 1871, 3 vols, Tinsley. Hardy's first published novel, written while he was still 'feeling his way to a method'. Sensational* in tone, the plot revolves around a wealthy woman with a mysterious past, Cytherea Aldclyffe of Knapwater House, near Casterbridge (i.e. Dorchester in Hardy's Wessex* topography). She takes as lady's maid, Cytherea Graye, the daughter, as it turns out, of one of her early suitors. The young Cytherea loves Edward Springrove, an architect. But he is poor and promised to another woman whom he does not love. This, and the needs of a sick brother, Owen, induce Cytherea to marry the handsome but ruthless Aeneas Manston, her mistress's estate manager. Manston, it emerges, is Miss Aldclyffe's bastard son, and he murders his wife, Eunice, a third-rate American actress, so as to free himself for young Cytherea. Immediately after the ceremony Edward (now a free man) discovers the truth about Manston who is hunted down, arrested and eventually hangs himself in his cell after confessing all. Cytherea and Edward are finally united. As Manston's widow, she inherits the Aldclyffe estate. The story which shows Hardy still to be an immature artist has derivative resemblances to Collins's* *The Woman In White** and Braddon's* *Lady Audley's Secret**.

Detective Fiction. The origins of the genre are obscure. But most historians see it as taking on its distinctive form in France in the 1820s, with the published reminiscences of Parisian police officers like E. F. Vidocq (whose *Memoirs* came out in 1828) and the so-called *roman policier*. Edgar Allan Poe's *The Murders In The Rue Morgue* (1843) is probably the first fully evolved detective story in English. The emergence of organised police forces in the 1830s (in Paris and London especially) was a precondition for the detective novel's catching on as a widely popular form of fiction. Eugène Sue's *Mysteries Of Paris* was published in France in 1842, and translations and imitations began to appear in Britain soon after. Among the most popular was G. W. M. Reynolds's* *The Mysteries Of The Court Of London* (1849–56). In English literature the rudimentary conventions of detective fiction made their first appearance in Newgate* novels of the 1830s. Fascination with criminal heroes like Ainsworth's* Jack Sheppard* accompanied a corresponding interest in the methodical uncovering of crime. Dickens*, the finest product of this school, introduced the first police detective into fiction with Inspector Bucket in *Bleak House** (1852–53). It was, however, the sensation* school who supplied the principal narrative techniques of detective fiction: teasing suspense, rapid tempo, ingenuity of plot. Dickens was again the dominant influence on this school of writers. But the first out-and-out detective story in English is Wilkie Collins's* *The Moonstone** (1868). It is with Collins that the uncovering of crime becomes a pseudo-scientific exercise involving the application of superior powers of intellect and deduction. (There was, again, a French predecessor; Emile Gaboriau's

L'Affaire Lerouge appeared in 1866.) Detective themes and sub-plots appear in many of the popular novels of the 1870s. Trollope*, for instance, involved a 'private detective' (probably the first so-called in fiction) in the action of *He Knew He Was Right* (1869). M. E. Braddon*, Charles Reade* and J. S. Le Fanu* introduce detectives into their fiction of the 1870s. But it was in the 1880s and 1890s that the genre was fully developed as mass entertainment. A major landmark is Conan Doyle's* first Sherlock Holmes story, *A Study In Scarlet* (1887). In 1888, H. Rider Haggard* created an early masterpiece with *Mr Meeson's Will* in which the crucial document is tattooed on the heroine's back. In 1886, *The Mystery Of A Hansom Cab* by an obscure young New Zealander, Fergus Hume*, sold a quarter of a million copies in a year. In 1899, E. W. Hornung* also introduced his gentleman burglar Raffles* in *The Amateur Cracksman.* The detective story came into its maturity in the 1890s with the work of Grant Allen* (especially his 'Hilda Wade' series), B. L. Farjeon*, Arthur Morrison* (especially in his 'Martin Hewitt*, Investigator' series), Hawley Smart*, Rudyard Kipling* and 'Dick Donovan' (i.e. J. E. P. Muddock*). Israel Zangwill* is credited with having invented the fiendishly teasing 'locked room' murder mystery. Many of these exponents of detective fiction published in the *Strand Magazine**. Newnes's* magazine first came out in January 1891, priced 6d. In July, the Holmes story 'A Scandal In Bohemia' appeared, distinctively illustrated by Sidney Paget*. By the mid-1890s, it has been estimated that of the 800 weekly papers in Britain, 240 were carrying some variety of detective story. These, together with the 'dime novel' industry in America, laid the ground for the 'pulps' of the early twentieth century.

The Devil's Chain, [John] Edward Jenkins MP, 1876, 1 vol, Strahan. A temperance tract-cum-novel which enjoyed remarkable success, selling 25,000 copies in two years. The narrative traces the universally ruinous effect of drink on all classes of the English population. It opens effectively with a mysterious (drink-induced) suicide in London's West End. As it unravels the mystery draws in the heir of a great brewing house, Henry Bighorne, his angelic sister and a secretary of state. The last is killed on a burning boat in the Channel (the captain and crew being hopelessly drunk). There is a vivid and bloody interlude in the steel-manufacturing and gin-sodden north of England. The work was attacked by the *Pall Mall Gazette* and defended vigorously by its author: 'there is not an incident which is not unhappily only possible, but probable'.

Diana Of The Crossways, George Meredith, 1885, 3 vols, Chapman and Hall. (An abbreviated twenty-six-chapter version of the novel ran in the *Fortnightly Review**, June–December 1884.) Diana Antonia Merion, a vivacious Irish orphan with something of the 'tigress' in her, makes a marriage of convenience with Augustus Warwick, a retired barrister fifteen years older than she. The pair separate on account of his groundless suspicion that she has had an affair with the political grandee, Lord Dannisburgh. Augustus brings an unsuccessful legal action for divorce against her. As a separated woman, Diana goes to her family home, Crossways. Subsequently, while travelling abroad, she is wooed by Dannisburgh's nephew, Sir Percy Dacier, a young politician. She writes a successful book (aided by a loyal friend, Thomas Redworth, who has always loved her) and Lord Dannisburgh leaves her a legacy in his will. Under continued persecution from her husband (who threatens to repossess his conjugal rights) Diana agrees to elope to Paris with Sir Percy. This recklessness is narrowly averted and Diana further alienates her lover by divulging (for money) his political secrets to the editor of *The Times*. Warwick is killed in a street accident, and Diana is finally united with her faithful admirer, Redworth. The novel is notable for its spirited depiction of female sexual adventurism. The narrative is full of obliquity and uses dialogue extensively. The heroine was based, as many contemporary readers immediately appreciated, on Caroline Norton* and the work enjoyed considerable sales success.

The Diary Of A Nobody, George and Weedon Grossmith, 1892, 1 vol, Arrowsmith. (The work was first published in shorter form in *Punch**, April 1891–July 1892, with illustrations by W. Grossmith.) The nobody is Charles Pooter, who works in a city office as a clerk under Mr Perkupp. He lives in a rented villa, The Laurels, Brickfield Terrace, Holloway, with his wife Carrie. The diary recounts his Lilliputian daily adventures at work and in his social life (in which the biggest event is an invitation to the Mansion House ball). Pooter's son, Lupin, is a source of distress. He gets engaged to a highly unsuitable girl. He joins his father to work for Perkupp, and is discharged. All ends well, however, with Pooter able to buy his own house at last, a consummation recorded as 'the happiest day of my life'. The Grossmiths' charming work was immensely popular and inspired a whole genre of pseudo-diaristic successors.

DICKENS, Charles [John Huffam] (1812–70). Dickens was born on 7 February 1812 at Portsea, the son of John Dickens an £80 a year clerk in the Navy Pay Office. Dickens's paternal grandfather had been a steward at Crewe Hall in Chester. Dickens's mother Elizabeth (née Barrow) was the daughter of a senior clerk in the Navy Pay Office who in 1810 was exposed as an embezzler. There were ten Dickens children, five of whom survived childhood, Charles being the oldest son. His early childhood was unsettled. The family moved to London in 1816, to Chatham in 1817 and back to London again in 1822 to settle in Camden Town. John Dickens's salary of £350 a year (after 1820) should have been adequate but, like Mr Micawber, he lived beyond his means. The home atmosphere seems to have been friendly, but neither parent gave the young Charles the intense love he craved. Nor were they good providers. But the early years at Chatham were a 'golden age' for the young boy. By 1824, the Dickens's financial state had deteriorated to bankruptcy. Everything in the house was pawned, and at the age of twelve Charles was put to work at a shoe blacking factory on the bank of the Thames at a wage of 6s. or 7s. a week. Although this menial labour lasted only a few months, the 'secret agony of my soul' was remembered for the rest of his life. And in February of the same year, John Dickens was imprisoned for debt in the Marshalsea. All the family, apart from Charles, lived with him there in the prison, while Charles had lodgings in Camden. A small legacy enabled the family to discharge their debts by midsummer of 1824, and Charles was sent as a day-boy to a decent London school, Wellington House Academy. In 1827, however, family finances were again precarious, and Charles was articled as a solicitor's clerk in Gray's Inn, at something under £1 a week. He hated law, and was drawn to journalism in which his father had dabbled after retiring from the Navy Office. Charles studied shorthand, and at the age of seventeen he was a free-lance reporter at the Doctors' Commons Courts. From 1831 to 1832, he took shorthand on Parliamentary debates for various London papers. Dickens was earning up to £5 in some weeks and had hopes of marrying Maria Beadnell, a banker's daughter, but her parents obstructed the relationship. Successful as his writing was, Dickens was tempted to try his luck on the stage. His future was determined, however, by the *Monthly Magazine*'s accepting his first published story, 'A Dinner At Poplar Walk', in December 1833. Soon after, Dickens began writing descriptive pieces under the pseudonym 'Boz' for the *Morning Chronicle*. In 1835, work for the new paper, the *Evening Chronicle*, led to his engagement to Catherine Hogarth, the co-editor's daughter. They married in April 1836 and set up house with Kate's younger sister, Mary. (Dickens had the tenderest feelings for Mary, and her sudden death, in May 1837, prostrated him.) *Sketches By Boz*, published by Macrone* in February 1836, was a definite success with the reading public. The pseudonym Boz was taken from the family nickname for his younger brother, Augustus. *Pickwick Papers**, which began publishing with Chapman and Hall* in monthly parts in April 1836 started poorly. But by the end of its run in November 1837, the serial was selling 40,000 an instalment. In November 1836, Richard Bentley*, offered Dickens the editorship of his new *Bentley's Miscellany**. Dickens accepted and also contributed *Oliver Twist** to the magazine (brilliantly illustrated by George Cruikshank*). The story of the parish boy who asked for more was gloomier by far than the comic adventures of Pickwick, and set a fashion for social problem* fiction which continued through the 1840s. In 1837, Dickens's first of ten children, Charles, was born. Dickens was now England's favourite and best-paid author. For *Nicholas Nickleby** Chapman and Hall paid £150 a monthly part (and an extra £1,500, eventually). But he was over-extended and in danger, as he put it, of 'busting his boiler'. He broke with Macrone in 1837 and Bentley in January 1839. Both severances were acrimonious, particularly that with Bentley, whom Dickens regarded as a publishing 'brigand'. He was helped through these difficulties by John Forster (1812–76) who was to become the novelist's closest friend, literary agent and eventually his biographer. In 1839, the Dickens family moved to a comfortable house in Devonshire Terrace, by Regent's Park, where they stayed until 1851. Dickens's career suffered its first reverse with his weekly miscellany, *Master Humphrey's Clock** (1840–41), which failed to live up to expectations, despite the serialisation in its pages of *The Old Curiosity Shop** and Dickens's first historical novel, *Barnaby Rudge**. A trip to America in 1842 produced the sharply observed *American Notes* (1842). Dickens took particular exception to American piracy of his copyrights and launched a lifelong campaign to protect the property rights of authors. *Martin Chuzzlewit** (1843–44) makes use of the American trip, but its failure to live up to sales expectations led to a break with Chapman and Hall. For the next fifteen years he transferred his new fiction to Bradbury and Evans*. In 1843, Dickens broke new ground again with his successful Christmas* Book, *A Christmas Carol**. There followed a lull in his writing during which he seems to have rethought the whole basis of his narrative art. In 1845 he travelled in Italy and in January 1846 began a newspaper, the *Daily News*, but he failed as an editor, quickly resigned and in June left with his family for Switzerland to concentrate on his fiction. In October 1846, the serialisation of *Dombey And Son** began. This was by far the most carefully plotted and thematically ambitious novel Dickens had hitherto attempted. Together with the cheap issue of his works put out by Chapman and Hall in 1847, *Dombey* confirmed Dickens's pre-eminence among British authors. He was also increasingly active as a social reformer. He put himself forward (unsuccessfully) as a London magistrate and in 1847 began an association with Angela Burdott Coutts and her Urania Cottage, a rehabilitation centre for London prostitutes, which lasted until 1858. For his own profession, he set up the charitable Guild of Literature and Art with Edward Bulwer-Lytton* in 1851 whose funding he assisted with private theatrical performances. This rival to the Royal Literary Fund* did not succeed, however. In 1849–50, the serialisation of the autobiographical novel, *David Copperfield**, earned Dickens around £7,000. It was followed by the more socially satirical *Bleak House** (1852–53). For some years Dickens had been anonymously contributing to the *Examiner* and in 1850 he started his own weekly paper *Household Words**. The serialisation in its pages of the industrial novel *Hard Times** (1854) confirmed the journal's popularity, although by this time much of the editing had been taken over by Dickens's assistant, W. H. Wills. *Little Dorrit** came out in monthly numbers (1855–57) and reached sales as high as 35,000, earning Dickens the largest reward of his writing career (around £12,000). In 1857, amateur theatricals (with which Dickens was constantly active, despite his taxing writing commitments) brought the author into contact with Ellen Ternan who probably became his mistress. The Dickens marriage (having produced ten children) had not been happy for some years, and in 1858 there was a formal separation. This period of Dickens's life was embattled. There was a bitter quarrel with Thackeray* in 1858 ('the Garrick Club affair') in which Dickens took the part of his fellow bohemian, Edmund Yates*, who had slandered Thackeray in his column in *Town Talk*. Dickens subsequently broke with Bradbury and Evans over their refusal to carry in *Punch** a notice of his separation (justified as he claimed) from Catherine. In defiance, he wound up *Household Words* which they published and started in its place *All The Year Round** in April 1859. The journal kicked off with Dickens's novel of the French Revolution, *A Tale Of Two Cities** (1859), soon followed by *Great Expectations** (1860–61). In 1858, Dickens had begun a series of immensely popular and remunerative public readings from his work which together with editing his new paper absorbed much of his creative energies in the 1860s. Only two more full-length serial novels were embarked on: *Our Mutual Friend** (1864–65) and *The Mystery Of Edwin Drood** (1870) which was cut short by death. In 1864, his health had begun to deteriorate rapidly with symptoms of gout and the early warnings of an impending cerebral stroke. In June 1865, he and Ellen Ternan were involved in a disastrous train crash at Staplehurst which shattered his nerves for months after. (His nervousness was sharpened by fear that his liaison with the young actress might become public knowledge.) Despite all this and in defiance of medical advice, Dickens continued with a gruelling schedule of readings, including a triumphant tour in America, 1867–68, which netted £19,000. But more important than the money were the emotional rewards of the readings (which were clearly hastening his death). He died in the dining room of his house at Gadshill of a cerebral aneurysm on 9 June 1870, and was buried five days later at Westminster Abbey. Dickens's achievements as a novelist are unparalleled in the English language. His extraordinary success and popularity gave a new dignity to the profession; he revived both the serialised and the illustrated forms of fiction; he invested the novel with a social mission to reform society. He can be plausibly seen as the father of both the social problem and detective* novel in English. His dense thematic compositions, striking use of imagery, rhetoric and dramatic device advanced fiction technically to the threshold of modernism. BL 15. *DNB*. RM. *NCBEL*. Wol. Sad.

DICKENS, Charles [Culliford Boz] (1837–96). First son of the novelist, and the bearer of his father's social aspirations, Charles Dickens Jr was educated at Eton and went into banking in 1855. But he left this profession in 1861, in which year he also married Bessie Evans, the daughter of his father's publisher. Young Dickens subsequently went to work in the City, but went bankrupt. In 1869, he turned to journalism and took a post in his father's journal *All The Year Round** which he went on to inherit as his sole property in 1870, incorporating it as part of the Dickens and Evans printing firm. Latterly, his career was exclusively that of Charles Dickens's son, culminating in a series of readings from his father's works given in America, 1887. He died of a paralytic seizure, impoverished, leaving a widow and five unmarried daughters. *DNB*. *NCBEL*. RLF.

DICKENS, Mary Angela (1863?–1948). Eldest grandchild of the famous novelist, she was born in London the daughter of Charles Dickens Jr* in whose *All The Year Round** her early fiction was serialised. Mary Dickens never married, and wrote novels mainly in her thirties. Her style showed the strong influence of Wilkie Collins* but she added to his sensational* formula a cloying pathos. Dickens's most successful novel was *Cross Currents* (1891), the story of Selma Malet, a young actress who is trapped in an agonised conflict between love and her art. Gloom thickens when she rejects the man she loves, and he marries another. Later, her teacher proposes to Selma, and on being rejected kills himself. The novel ends with the heroine alone in the dusk. *A Mere Cypher* (1893) has an unhappily married heroine, who redeems the emptiness of her life by saving a young man from ruin. *A Valiant Ignorance* (1894) recalls Ibsen's *Ghosts* and has as its central character a mother torn by the prospect of her son's inheriting his father's fatal passion for commercial speculation. *Prisoners Of Silence* (1895) is among the oddest and gloomiest of her tales dealing with what the author typically calls 'the ghastly riddle of our existence'. It centres on a family in which the son passes himself off as his mother's half-brother and introduces unsavoury incestuous plot complications. In *Against The Tide* (1897) a man with a hereditary disease marries, and is eventually driven to murder and suicide. *On The Edge Of A Precipice* (1899) starts with the heroine being thrown from her bicycle and suffering an amnesia which is exploited by a villainous cousin. Dickens largely ceased publishing fiction in the first decade of the twentieth century and evidently converted to Catholicism in later life. BL 9. *WW*. Wol.

DIEHL, Mrs A[lice Georgina] M[angoldt] (1844–1912). She was born at Aveley in Essex, the daughter of Carl Mangoldt, a German musician from

Darmstadt. Educated privately by tutors, she became a concert pianist herself and performed on the Continent, winning praise from Berlioz, among others. In the 1860s, she appeared in London and in the 1870s began writing fiction. Around this period, she married the minor composer Louis Diehl (d. 1910). A confirmed invalid, he was unable to support his family and afflicted his wife with 'a life of great vicissitude'. As a novelist, Diehl wrote romantic fiction mainly for the libraries. The word 'love' features in no less than eight of her titles and her other fiction includes: *A Woman's Whim* (1894), *A Woman's Cross* (1896) and *A Woman Martyr* (1904). Some of Diehl's fiction was illustrated by her son Arthur. In 1907, she published an autobiography, *The True Story Of My Life* and she died at Ingatestone in Essex, not far from where she was born. BL 33. *WW*. Wol. RLF.

DILKE, Lady [Emilia Francis] (née Strong, 1840–1904). The daughter of an Indian army officer (later a banker) she was educated by governesses at Oxford. Francis Strong showed early artistic promise and in 1859 went to London (somewhat against her family's wishes) to study art. At this period of her life she came strongly under the personal and aesthetic influence of Ruskin*. In 1861, she met Mark Pattison (1813–84) the Rector of Lincoln College. Although he was twenty-seven years her senior they married after a few months' acquaintance. At Oxford her active interest in art was stifled, and she was generally unhappy and out of place. There were no children. Mrs Pattison formed an influential salon and came into contact with, among others, George Eliot* who (it has been suggested) used her as an original for Dorothea Brooke in *Middlemarch**. After 1867, Emilia Pattison was afflicted with unspecified nervous ailments which entailed extensive convalescence abroad. In 1875, she refused to have any further sexual relations with her husband. On his part, Pattison formed a scandalous (to Oxford) liaison with Meta Bradley. In the late 1870s, she began to take an interest in women's politics and in later life was militant for the cause of female rights and education. A year after Mark Pattison's death in 1884, she married Sir Charles Wentworth Dilke (1843–1911), who had just emerged from a divorce scandal. The couple had been friendly for some years. As an author, Emilia Dilke made some mark as a critic of eighteenth-century art and as a hostess she formed another influential salon which included Browning. Her efforts in fiction are confined to two collections of mystical stories written in heavily cadenced prose and published in the period following her second marriage: *The Shrine Of Death* (1886) and *The Shrine Of Love* (1891). The title piece of the first has a heroine who marries death, personified. Many of the stories (which Dilke persisted in seeing as her most important writing) are similar allegorical treatments of woman possessed and abused. As her second husband noted, 'she wrote her stories to lay ghosts'. BL 3. *DNB*. Wol.

DISRAELI, Benjamin (1804–81). Born in London, the eldest son of Isaac D'Israeli, of Spanish Jewish descent, he was educated largely by his father, an antiquarian and distinguished man of letters. Although the young Benjamin Disraeli (as his name was normalised) was baptised into the Church of England in 1817 he did not attend university. In 1821 he embarked rather half-heartedly on a career in law, and enrolled at Lincoln's Inn three years later. More importantly for his intellectual development, Disraeli was travelling widely on the Continent at this period. In 1825, he was involved with Murray's* disastrous attempt to establish the *Representative* as a rival to *The Times*. The year following he published (anonymously and to settle embarrassing debts) his first novel, *Vivian Grey* (1826–27). Brought out with considerable fanfare by Colburn*, this ultra-fashionable tale helped popularise the silver fork* genre of fiction and established the young man as a bestseller. It was followed by *The Young Duke* (1831), *Contarini Fleming* (1832) and *Alroy* (1835). Extravagantly romantic in tone, these 'psychological studies' celebrate youth and the growth of the sensitive soul. Disraeli claimed that they contained 'the secret history of my feelings'. *Henrietta Temple* (1837) is a florid, heavily over-written story of young love between Ferdinand Armine, heir to an ancient Catholic family fallen on hard times and the heroine of the title. *Venetia** (1837) fictionalises the later career of Byron, Disraeli's literary idol. These works display the author as a main exponent with Bulwer-Lytton* of 'idealism', an aesthetic of the 1830s which aimed at the exaltation rather than the imitation of nature in fiction. As the other novelist put it: 'Art is that process by which we give to natural materials the highest excellence they are capable of receiving.' (Disraeli and Edward Bulwer were friends up to the point of Disraeli's marriage, when a separation occurred.) By this stage of his career Disraeli had made three unsuccessful attempts to enter Parliament. In 1837 he was finally elected as Tory member for Maidstone and the main line of his subsequent career was party-political. In 1839, he married the wealthy widow of a former political colleague, Wyndham Lewis. Around the same period Disraeli became preoccupied with the Chartist movement, and in the early 1840s he put himself at the head of a reform group within the Tory Party which was at odds with the leader, Peel. Partly to promote this Young England* lobby, he published a trilogy of powerful political novels, *Coningsby** (1844), *Sybil** (1845) and *Tancred** (1847). In them, he outlined his creed: an amalgam of neo-feudalist nostalgia, a disdain for the bourgeois ('Dutch') revolution of 1688, high Anglicanism and 'one nation' utopianism. Young England disdained utilitarianism, admired Bolingbroke, Puseyism and the Newmanite Tracts and opposed Peel's pragmatism. Their bible was Kenelm Digby's *The Broad Stone Of Honour, Or The True Sense And Practice Of Chivalry* (1822). Young England was as its epithet implies an intellectually juvenile creed. But *Sybil* also contains the most graphic depictions of working-class wretchedness to be found anywhere in the Victorian novel. *Tancred* asserts Disraeli's favourite religious proposition, that Christianity is the 'completion' of Judaism. All three of the novels express the optimistic belief that 'the Youth of the Nation are the trustees of Posterity'. In Parliament, Disraeli opposed the new Poor Law, and supported the Factory Reform Acts. The Young England movement effectively broke up in 1845, when Disraeli voted against an increased grant to the Catholic Seminary at Maynooth (a symbol of the 'Old Faith'). In 1846, he broke with Peel over the Corn Law issue. In 1848, Disraeli purchased Hughenden Manor and was elected MP for Buckinghamshire, a seat he held until 1876. In the 1850s and 1860s, he achieved a succession of high political offices culminating in the premiership in 1868. Resignation in the same year allowed time to write the political *Bildungsroman**, *Lothair** (1870). Like his last work, *Endymion**

(1880) it contains a narcissistic self-portrait of the author-politician as a young man. For this last work Disraeli was given the record sum of £10,000 by Longman*. His wife died in 1872. Disraeli was again Prime Minister from 1874 to 1880, and was created Earl of Beaconsfield in 1876. It is under this title that much of his fiction was subsequently reissued. BL 11. *DNB*. RM. *NCBEL*. Wol. Sad.

DIX, John ('John Ross', 1800?–65). Dix was born at Bristol evidently of humble parentage. For a while he trained as a surgeon. A volume of early poems appeared in 1829. In 1837, he published a life of Chatterton, which stirred up controversy and accusations of forgery. Around 1846, Dix emigrated to America where he probably lived until his death. In America he was moderately successful as a miscellaneous author (sometimes apparently under the name 'John Ross'). Dix wrote, among other books, a nautical novel, *Jack Ariel, Or Life On Board An Indiaman* (1847). Although the *Athenaeum** reviewer suggested its first voyage should be to the waste-paper basket, the work was popular. In America, among much else, he published a much reprinted temperance tale, *The Worth Of The Worthless* (1854). BL 2. RLF.

DIXIE, Lady [Florence Caroline] (née Douglas, 1857–1905). Poet, novelist, explorer and champion of women's rights. She was born in London, the youngest daughter of the seventh Marquis of Queensberry. Her sister, 'George Douglas*' (i.e. Lady Gertrude Georgina Douglas) was also a novelist. Precocious, Florence Douglas wrote accomplished girlhood verse under the pseudonym 'Darling' and published a dramatic tragedy, *Abel Avenged*, at the age of twenty. In 1875, she married Sir Alexander Beaumont Dixie. As Lady Dixie, she explored 'the unknown wastes of Patagonia' from 1878 to 1879 (see *Across Patagonia*, 1880) and was war correspondent for the *Morning Post*, during the Boer War of 1880–81. Her writing, as the *Academy** noted, displayed 'the brightness of a schoolgirl'. Among many other causes, she agitated for the rights of Zulus and women. Her first published novel was *Redeemed In Blood* (1889). An absurd melodrama of high life centred on the marital trials of Lord and Lady Wrathness, the novel has some vivid Patagonian scenes. Dixie's other fiction includes *Aniwee, Or The Warrior Queen* (1890), a tale of the Patagonian Arancanian Indians. Her best-known work in the twentieth century is *Gloriana, Or The Revolution Of 1900* (1890). In this bizarre futuristic fable Gloria of Ravensdale disguises herself as a boy, Hector D'Estrange, attends Eton and Oxford, and eventually gets herself into Parliament. The narrative ends with a visionary panorama of a regenerated London as seen from a balloon in 1999. In 1902 Dixie published a drama in verse on the persecution of women, *Isola, Or The Disinherited*. Although she was a good shot, a horsewoman and a strong swimmer she loathed blood sports and published a tract against them, *The Horrors Of Sport* (1905). Not a lover of the male sex, apparently, she claimed that 'horses and dogs were her best friends'. BL 6. *WW*.

DIXON, Ella Nora Hepworth ('Margaret Wynman', 1855–1932). Born in London, she was the daughter of William Hepworth Dixon*, editor of the *Athenaeum**. Ella Dixon was educated in London and Heidelberg, studied painting in Paris and followed in her father's professional footsteps by editing *The Englishwoman* until 1895. She never married, and travelled widely, even for a woman of her class in the 1890s. A journalist by profession, Dixon wrote short stories, collected as *One Doubtful Hour And Other Sidelights On The Feminine Temperament* (1904). Her only novel is *The Story Of A Modern Woman** (1894). Painfully autobiographical, it has as its heroine Mary Erle, the orphaned daughter of a renowned professor, who tries to live an independent life. Failing as an artist, she scrapes a living as a journalist, living in poor lodgings. Mary eventually loses her lover, Vincent, and is left at the end of the narrative independent but wretchedly solitary. Dixon also wrote *My Flirtations* (1892, by 'Margaret Wynman'), a 'lively and catty' series of sexual sketches, supposedly written by a coquette. Toward the end of her life she became increasingly militant for the cause of women's rights. BL 2. *WW*. Wol.

DIXON, William Hepworth (1821–79). Dixon was born in Manchester of an old puritan family enriched by trade. He came down to London in 1846, ostensibly to study for the law and was called to the Bar in 1854, but never practised. Meanwhile, he had embarked on a literary and journalistic career, under the patronage of Douglas Jerrold*. Clearly talented, Dixon became a young editor of the leading literary review in the country, the *Athenaeum**, in 1853. He held the post until 1869, when he resigned to become a JP in Middlesex and Westminster. A noted traveller (he helped found the Palestine Exploration Fund), Dixon suffered a series of misfortunes in the 1870s. In 1874, his home was wrecked by an industrial explosion. He was disabled by a fall from his horse in 1878. Two of his children died, and he had various financial reverses. In this unfortunate period of his life Dixon wrote a novel *Diana, Lady Lyle* (1877), presumably for money. The flimsy plot centres on the heroine's secretly being the daughter of a freed slave. The subsequent complications are a pretext for travelogue as the action shifts from England to Virginia, Niagara, France, Egypt, the South Seas and India. Another novel, *Ruby Grey* (1878), is restricted in setting to London and Paris. A tale of legal villainy, it has an exotic Romanian boyar as its villain. Dixon's brief career in fiction was cut short by his premature death. BL 2. *DNB*. RLF.

Doctor Birch And His Young Friends, W. M. Thackeray, 1849, 1 vol, Chapman and Hall. Thackeray's third Christmas* book. It offers, in panoramic sketch form, a humorous and lavishly illustrated introduction to the staff and pupils of 'Archbishop Wigsby's College of Rodwell Regis' where Dr Birch (a flogger) is head and Thackeray's ubiquitous *alter ego*, Michael Angelo Titmarsh, an assistant master.

Doctor Jekyll And Mr Hyde, R. L. Stevenson, 1886, 1 vol, Longman. (The full title is prefixed by *The Strange Case Of*.) This classic novel of horrific possession is alleged to have come to the author in a nightmare, in 1885. The central narrative is given in the posthumous confession of Dr Henry Jekyll, a successful London physician. In his youth Jekyll had lived a double life. Later as a scientist, he experiments with dual personality, devising a drug which will release his other, depraved self, Edward Hyde. Hyde finally commits murder, and increasingly dominates the appalled Jekyll who locks himself in his laboratory and kills himself to escape his double. The novella is told from the oblique perspective of Jekyll's friend Dr Hastie Lanyon, his canny lawyer, Utterson, who initially suspects that Hyde is blackmailing his client and Utterson's cousin, Enfield.

Doctor Phillips, A Maida Vale Idyll, Frank Danby (i.e. Julia Frankau), 1887, 1 vol, Vizetelly. An anti-semitic bestseller. The narrative opens at an evening party of middle-class Jews in Maida Vale. Their vulgarity and clannishness are savagely depicted. To this function Dr Phillips, a society (or 'ladies') doctor, brings his Gentile mistress, Mary Cameron, and their daughter Nita. Phillips's fat German Jewish wife Clothilde suspects nothing. Phillips subsequently goes on a medical expedition to Egypt in which he damages his health; and his fortune is squandered in speculation. His character 'retrogrades'. He murders his wife with an overdose of opium so as to inherit her money but to his despair discovers that Mary has meanwhile married an aristocrat of her own faith, Charlie Doveton. Their child Nita dies. His fellow Jews suspect Phillips to be a murderer and ostracise him. Accepting himself as the outcast, Phillips sets to and becomes the leading surgeon in England: 'he is scarcely known as an Israelite; he scarcely acknowledges the title'. The novel is remarkable for the viciousness of its satire on the English Jewish bourgeoisie and the subtle depiction of its 'complex' hero. It created a furore. Rather perversely, the *Athenaeum** read the novel as 'a deliberate insult to the medical profession'.

Doctor Thorne, Anthony Trollope, 1858, 3 vols, Chapman and Hall. The most sensational* of the Barsetshire* novels set mainly in the village of Greshambury. There were, originally, two Thorne brothers: Thomas, who became a doctor ('a modest country medical practitioner') and Henry, a scapegrace law student who in his youth seduced the sister of Roger Scatcherd, a stonemason. In his righteous rage, Scatcherd assaulted Henry Thorne, killing him, and was subsequently imprisoned a token six months for manslaughter. After the scandal, a former lover took the dishonoured girl away to America. The bastard child, Mary, was left in the care of her uncle, Doctor Thomas Thorne, who brought her up as his own adopted daughter. Not even her uncle, now Sir Roger Scatcherd, a railway construction millionaire whose one close friend is the doctor, knows the secret of Mary's birth. Nor does she. The main part of the narrative has to do with the complications of Mary Thorne's love life. She is wooed by Frank Gresham, an eligible squire related to the aristocratic and snobbish De Courcys. The match is frustrated by his mother, Lady Arabella and Frank's ambitious sister Augusta. There are other complications. Greshambury Park, the property to which Frank is heir apparent, is mortgaged to Sir Roger. He and his degenerate son Louis Philippe Scatcherd (who also loves Mary), are both drinking themselves to death. This happily occurs, so as to make Mary the heiress who can save the Gresham fortunes. All obstacles being removed, she and Frank finally marry. The novel is particularly effective for the depiction of the bluff Doctor Thorne, and the crises of conscience he suffers. The level-headed heiress Martha Dunstable also figures entertainingly. Frank's family persuade him to propose to this lady, who good-naturedly declines, so surviving to marry Dr Thorne himself in the later *Framley Parsonage* (1860).

Dr Wortle's School, Anthony Trollope, 1881, 2 vols, Chapman and Hall. (Serialised in *Blackwood's Magazine**, May–December 1880.) A late and short story, with a fashionable bigamy* theme. Henry Peacocke and his American wife Ella are employed at Dr Wortle's school, an exclusive establishment which prepares pupils for Eton. Peacocke is a classical scholar of great ability, and a clergyman. But there is some mystery about his marriage in America. It emerges that he and his 'wife' are, in fact, living in sin since she has a first husband who deserted her in America. Wortle doggedly stands by the Peacockes under moral pressure from the local bishop and indignant parents. Finally, an expedition to America by Peacocke reveals that the first husband is now dead, and the couple can legitimise their union. The portrait of the admirably obstinate doctor is one of Trollope's best.

A Dog Of Flanders, Ouida (i.e. Marie Louise de la Ramée), 1872, 1 vol, Chapman and Hall. (Originally published in *Lippincott's Magazine*.) A sentimental animal fable and study in Flemish genre subject-matter. Nello lives with his ancient guardian, Jehan Daas, on the outskirts of Antwerp. Daas is a peasant who is assisted by a Flemish dog, Patrasche, who draws his milk cart to market. Patrasche is well used by his masters (unusual enough in Belgium, as Ouida notes) and adores them. Nello grows up with artistic yearnings he can never fulfil. And his love for the miller's daughter Alois is forbidden because of his poverty. Finally he freezes to death outside Antwerp Cathedral (whose Rubens paintings are his inspiration) with the loyal dog Patrasche in his arms. Ouida makes the story a text for her lifelong campaign for kindness to animals.

Dombey And Son, Charles Dickens, 1848, 1 vol, Bradbury and Evans. (Serialised in monthly instalments, October 1846–April 1848, with illustrations by Phiz*.) The novel opens with the frigid and self-righteous Mr Dombey being presented with a son who will eventually take over his commercial firm. His mother dies in childbirth and the christening is ominously cold and cheerless. Little Paul Dombey is a strange and unnaturally perceptive child. He is sent to Dr Blimber's school but sickens and also dies. Dombey is devastated, but continues to neglect his loving daughter Florence and Walter Gay, who loves her, is sent off to the West Indies. Dombey goes to Leamington, where he meets the proud and beautiful widow Edith Granger. They marry. The match is disastrous. Edith allows herself to be involved with her husband's villainous manager, James Carker, and elopes with him to France. Dombey hunts down the guilty pair, and Carker is finally destroyed by an onrushing train. (The railways permeate the novel as an ambiguous symbol of industrial progress.) Dombey's firm fails, and he is at last reconciled with Florence, a chastened father. Walter returns, having been thought lost at sea, and the novel ends in muted happiness. The narrative is rich in incidental studies of characters like the self-preening Major Joey Bagstock, the incompetent but warm-hearted maker of nautical instruments Solomon Gills, and Paul's nurse Polly 'Richards', who marries the train driver Toodle. The novel marks Dickens's growing interest in using his art for purposes of social criticism in the late 1840s and introduces a distinctly darker tinge to his fiction.

Domestic Fiction. Although scarcely a 'school', the domestic novel exists as a well-defined anti-type, which gave the sensation* novelists of the

1860s a sense of their identity. It was with this in mind that Henry James contrasted Braddon's* *Lady Audley's Secret** (1862) with 'the novel of domestic tranquillity'. Less politely, Charles Reade* pointed out in a footnote to *Love Me Little, Love Me Long* (1859) that 'domestic is Latin for tame'. It was, however, tameness that Anthony Trollope* aimed at in his bestselling *Framley Parsonage** (1861): 'the story was thoroughly English. There was a little fox-hunting. There was no heroism and no villainy.' As Trollope indicates, the principal founder of the domestic novel was Thackeray* with *Vanity Fair, A Novel Without A Hero** (1847). Bulwer-Lytton's* *The Caxtons, A Family Picture** (1849) was also influential in making the domestic novel fashionable. Charlotte Brontë's* declaration in the preface to *Shirley** (1849) that she intends a a novel as undramatic 'as Monday morning' indicates a domestic purpose. So too do the opening paragraphs of *Tom Brown's Schooldays** (1857) with their aggressive celebration of the unspectacular 'Browns' of the world. But it is George Eliot* who brought domestic fiction to its highest pitch in her story of provincial life, *Middlemarch** (1872). The mid-Victorian opposition of domestic and sensational fiction can plausibly be linked with the running debate on gothicism* and realism which goes back at least to the beginning of the century.

Doreen, The Story Of A Singer, Edna Lyall (i.e. A. E. Bayly), 1894, 1 vol, Longman. (The novel was first published in America, where it was presumably targeted at the large Irish readership of the Eastern seaboard.) An unusually powerful novel dealing with the Fenian agitations that rocked late-Victorian England. The story opens in the 1870s with the rich English Hereford family spending a summer in Southern Ireland. They meet a young Irish girl, Doreen O'Ryan and her mother. Doreen possesses a magnificent voice, is thoroughly politicised and has a father who has been imprisoned for Nationalist activities. Young Max Hereford and Doreen enter into a pact of silence when his friend and tutor, John Desmond, kills a land agent (Fenians are suspected of the crime). The narrative jumps forward fifteen years. Doreen and her parents return from America; but the father, weakened by his years in jail, dies before he can take up his English newspaper appointment. Mrs O'Ryan soon follows. With Max's help, Doreen embarks on what is to be a successful singing career. His own career in Parliament is destroyed by a vengeful French servant, whom he earlier dismissed. Doreen and Max become engaged, but break up when she refuses to give up singing for the Irish cause. In a complicated climax, Max narrowly escapes conviction for associating with terrorists; Doreen is imprisoned and loses her singing voice in jail; Desmond confesses all on his deathbed. The novel ends with Max (now a Liberal MP enlightened on the question of Home Rule) and Doreen married. They have a son, Dermot, who has inherited Doreen's musical talent. Gladstone's speeches on Ireland figure centrally in the last pages and the novel is dedicated to him 'in gratitude and reverence'.

Dorothy Forster, Walter Besant, 1884, 3 vols, Chatto. The most charming of Besant's historical* romances and the author's own favourite work. The subject is the Jacobite uprising of 1715, as it affected the Forsters of Bamborough Castle, in Northumberland. Thomas Forster raises a force for the Pretender, and is joined by the luckless Earl of Derwentwater (fated to be beheaded after the rebellion). The novel, which is based on fact, is narrated from the historical sidelines by Thomas's sister. She is loved by Derwentwater, but rejects him on grounds of religious conscience, he being a Catholic. She lives on, a spinster attended by her faithful suitor and tutor Antony Hillyard whose sage opinions Dorothy dutifully repeats throughout her narrative. He appends an obituary after her early death in 1739.

DOUDNEY, [Miss] Sarah (1843–1926). Born in Portsmouth and educated privately, Doudney began contributing to the magazines early in life. Her first successful novel was *Archie's Old Desk*, put out under the imprint of the Sunday School Union in 1872. She was clearly pious (many of her subsequent works were published by the RTS*) and lived mainly in London. Her main line of fiction was high-minded romances for young girls and much of her income must have come from Christmas* tales, in which she was a specialist. Her plots are typically thin and concentrate mainly on feminine psychology and routine moral dilemmas. Her novels for older readers include: *A Woman's Glory* (1883); *The Missing Rubies* (1886); *Lady Dye's Reparation* (1899). A lifelong spinster, she gave as her recreations to *Who's Who* 'walking, antiquarianism'. BL 55. *WW*. Wol.

DOUGALL, L[ily] (1858–1923). Born in Montreal, Canada she had her school education there and in New York. As an older girl, she lived with an aunt in Edinburgh and attended university lectures in the city. In the 1870s, she moved to London. Dougall's fiction is mostly devoted to propagating the theories of the Christian-mystical sect she helped found. But she wrote four novels with Canadian backgrounds. *What Necessity Knows* (1893) which depicts the prejudices of English immigrants is reckoned the best of this group, although *The Zeit-Geist* (1895), set in Prince Edward's Island, was well received. *The Madonna Of A Day* (1896) has a new woman* heroine who falls off a train and undergoes various adventures in the lumberjack camps of the Canadian North-west. Dougall also wrote a heavily researched novel about Mormonism, *The Mormon Prophet* (1898). BL 11. *WW*. Wol.

DOUGLAS, George (i.e. Lady Gertrude Georgina Douglas, 1842–93). A daughter of the seventh Marquis of Queensberry (1818–58) and an older sister of Lady Florence Dixie*, she wrote under her male pseudonym Scottish regional fiction aimed at the 1870s library market, mainly published by Tinsley*. The tone of her novels is robust (after the style of G. A. Lawrence*) and they feature hoydenish heroines. Most reviewers took her to be a male writer. Douglas's titles include: *Brown As A Berry* (1874); *The Red House By The River* (1876); *Linked Lives* (1876); *Mar's White Witch* (1877). None of them had any great success, though reviewers generally found Douglas a 'rather above average' writer. In 1882 she was entrusted by her clergyman brother, the Rev. A. E. Douglas, with looking after his London school while he was temporarily abroad. Lady Gertrude chose the best-looking schoolboy, Thomas Stock, and married him. He was seventeen, she forty. After their marriage, the couple kept a baker's shop for a while in Kensington. It did not pay, and the marriage broke up. The young husband went to South Africa to be a policeman. She died of consumption in a convent hospital, evidently having converted to Catholicism. She published a last, bitter novel: *A Wasted Life And Marr'd* (1892). BL 8. Boase. Wol.

Douglas Jerrold's Shilling Magazine (1845–48). Jerrold* conducted this fiction-carrying monthly from January 1845 to June 1848. It was printed at the *Punch** office, by Bradbury and Evans. The price was low for the mid-1840s, and maximum circulation of the magazine reached around 9,000 per month. The contributors were partly drawn from the *Punch* stable: Angus B. Reach*, Mark Lemon*, Henry Mayhew*, Henry Fothergill Chorley*. The editor, Jerrold, opened the magazine's first issues with his own novel, *St Giles And St James*, illustrated by John Leech*. Otherwise (apart from a serial by R. H. Horne*) it carried little fiction. The tone of the journal reflected the editor's radical sympathies and is specifically addressed to the 'masses of England'. *BLM.*

The Dove In The Eagle's Nest, Charlotte M. Yonge, 1866, 2 vols, Macmillan. (Serialised in *Macmillan's Magazine**, May–December 1865.) A tale for children, set in the mid-fifteenth century. The heroine Christina Sorel, a maiden of Ulm, is carried off by a baron to Schloss Adlerstein to nurse his sick daughter. Christina civilises his pagan household and is secretly married to the young Baron Eberhard. He is supposed to have been murdered and Christina subsequently devotes her life to bringing up their twin sons alone. At the end of the story, Eberhard returns to see his wife's good work.

DOWIE, Ménie Muriel (later Mrs Henry Norman, 1867–1945). A prominent exponent of the new woman* novel, fashionable in the 1890s. Dowie was born in Liverpool, a grandchild on her mother's side of Robert Chambers, the author of *Vestiges Of Creation* (1844). Dowie was educated in Germany and France. In 1891, she married Sir Henry Norman a journalist, an MP and, like her, a tireless traveller. (In later life he was well known for his campaign to preserve the Niagara Falls from urban intrusion.) Using her foreign experience, Dowie produced a lively first book, *A Girl In The Karpathians* (1891). The heroine-narrator is a young Scot who travels through the Balkans, Russia and middle Europe, smoking, drinking and dressed like a man. The work was popular and, as the author reported, of the 400 reviews it received, not one was bad. Dowie also wrote some militantly pro-feminist non-fiction books such as *Women Adventurers* (1893) which features chapters on such things as 'The Woman In Battle'. Dowie made considerable stir with the militantly feminist novel *Gallia** (1895), a work in which, as the *Saturday Review** thought, the author 'goes further in sheer audacity of the treatment of the sexual relations and sexual feelings of men and women than any woman before'. Gallia is a new woman, brought up without feminine indoctrination ('Gallia never had a doll'). Oxford educated, she chooses the future father of her child on ultra-rationalistic eugenic criteria, ignoring any considerations of bourgeois love. *Some Whims Of Fate* (1896) contains shorter pieces collected from the *Yellow Book**. *The Crook Of The Bough* (1898) is a satire on conventional femininity. It has as its hero a modernised Turk, trapped between Western and traditional oriental ideas about the place of woman. (The 'crook of the bough' is where the monkey rested, before he took up the responsibility of being a man.) *Love And His Masks* (1901) depicts British high society reacting to the Boer War. In 1903 Dowie (having divorced Norman) married Major E. A. Fitzgerald. This second husband (b. 1871) was younger than her, a Guards officer and a world-famous mountaineer. In later life, farming in Britain was one of Dowie's occupations and she gave up writing almost entirely. BL 5. *WW*.

DOWLING, Richard ('Marcus Fall', 1846–98). Richard Dowling was born at Clonmel, Co. Tipperary, and educated at Limerick. A cousin of the better known Edmund Downey*, he worked for some years in a shipping office in Waterford. Dowling subsequently moved to Dublin in 1870, where he was a journalist on the *Nation*, and from there he moved on to London in 1874. Five years later he began a career writing popular Irish* regional* novels, such as: *The Mystery Of Killard* (1879), a story of Co. Clare fishermen in the 1820s; *Sweet Inisfail* (1882), a romance set in the author's native Clonmel; *The Skeleton Key* (1886), a 'shilling shocker'; *Old Corcoran's Money* (1897). The last of these is a rather bleak tale of crime and punishment in the small town of 'Ballymore'. Dowling's vision of rural Ireland is generally less jolly than his cousin's. Dowling habitually wrote under the pseudonym Marcus Fall and contributed to most of the leading magazines of the period. BL 26. Boase. Wol. RLF.

DOWNEY, Edmund ('F. M. Allen', 1856–1937). Downey was born, grew up and eventually died in Waterford, Ireland, the son of a Catholic ship-broker. He was educated at the Catholic University School, and St John's College Waterford. A keen observer of the life of the port, he used what he saw extensively in his later fiction. In 1878, Downey moved to London where he worked with the publishers Tinsley* Bros. In 1884, he formed his own publishing house, Ward and Downey. The firm specialised in three-volume fiction for the library market. Downey retired in 1890, only to start up as Downey and Co. in 1894. Subsequently he returned to Waterford, where he was proprietor from 1906 of the *Waterford News*. His fiction (the comic part of it composed under the pen name 'F. M. Allen') was largely loose-knit 'yarns' with a strong regional* flavour. Although an ostentatiously Irish* author, he was popular with English readers. Downey's titles include the collections of tales: *Anchor Watch Yarns* (1884) and *In One Town* (1886), the town being Waterford. *The Merchant Of Killogue* (1894) was his first full-length novel, set in Munster with a political sub-plot. It was followed by *Ballybeg Junction* (1894); *Pinches Of Salt* (1895); *Mr Boyton* (1899). Downey also wrote on Irish life and put together an interesting account of his career as a publisher entitled *Twenty Years Ago* (1905). BL 8. *WW*. Wol.

DOWSON, Ernest [Christopher] (1867–1900). Remembered principally as a decadent* poet, Dowson also had aspirations to be a novelist. He was born near London, the eldest son of a well-off dry-dock owner in Limehouse. Young Dowson did not go to school, but was educated at home by his bookish father. In 1886, he went to Oxford. At the university he dabbled in Catholicism, and left without a degree. Dowson began publishing short stories as early as 1888. His first, 'Souvenirs Of An Egotist' (a tale of love, music and Paris) appeared in *Temple Bar**. On leaving Oxford, Dowson worked in his father's dock business for six years. At the same time, he collaborated with a university friend, Arthur Moore, on a novel, *Doctor Ludovicus*, which no publisher would take. The same fate met the writers' second novel. Their third effort, *A Comedy Of Masks* (1893), was accepted by Heinemann*. A study of artistic and bohemian life in London, the novel is a classic expression of the mood of the 1890s and in the character of Rainham offers a self portrait of Dowson. The family business meanwhile had failed and in 1894 Dowson's father died, probably by his own hand. Dowson spent 1894–99 in France. He befriended Oscar Wilde* after his disgrace and finally made a name for himself as a poet. Moore and Dowson published another novel, *Adrian Rome*, the story of a young artist's love life, in 1899. He also translated Balzac and Zola and a collection of his short stories, *Dilemmas*, was published by Elkin Mathews in 1895. *Verses* appeared in 1896. In 1897, his lover Adelaide Foltinowicz finally discarded him after a six-year-long affair. Dowson's last months were consumed in absinthism, failing health and chronic poverty. He died at the home of a novelist friend, Robert Sherard*. BL 3. *DNB*. RM. *NCBEL*. Wol.

DOYLE,[Sir] Arthur Conan (1859–1930). The creator of Sherlock Holmes. Doyle was born in Edinburgh, one of seven children of a municipal civil servant. Doyle's parents were Irish and Catholic. His uncle was Richard Doyle*, the illustrator. Doyle was educated at the Catholic public school Stonyhurst. At sixteen he spent a year in Austria, then he enrolled at Edinburgh University to study medicine. Doyle wrote from an early age and his first story was published in *Chambers's Journal** in 1879. In 1880, he spent seven months in the Arctic as ship's doctor on a whaler. The following year he graduated with a respectable degree and made another trip to Africa. By this period of his life, Doyle and his family were feeling the economic effects of his father's growing alcoholism, and his start in the medical profession was humble. After an unsuccessful experiment in partnership, he set up in medical practice at Southsea, near Portsmouth, in July 1882. His income reached £300 a year by 1885, enabling him to marry. All this while Doyle had kept up his writing and in 1886 became interested in the detective* story as a genre. The outcome was the successful Sherlock Holmes novella, *A Study In Scarlet** (1887). This mystery of double murder in Utah and London caught the public taste and Doyle followed it up with another Holmes adventure, *The Sign Of Four** (1890). Doyle put something of himself into Sherlock Holmes, but the sleuth was mainly inspired by a sharp-eyed teacher at Edinburgh, Joseph Bell. Early in 1891, Doyle submitted two stories to Greenhough Smith of the *Strand** magazine. The editor reportedly realised 'that here was the greatest short story writer since Edgar Allan Poe'. These Sherlock Holmes stories were devised to correct 'the great defect' in current detective fiction, lack of logic. They were illustrated by Sidney Paget*, who supplied the detective with his famous deerstalker and aquiline profile. But Doyle's heart was never in detective fiction. Holmes, he complained, 'takes my mind from better things'. Nevertheless the stories were phenomenally popular in Britain and America and overshadowed everything else Doyle was to write. In fact, his output was extremely diverse. *The Mystery Of Cloomber* (1888) is a sensational* melodrama with a trio of Indian assassins stalking their prey in an English castle. (The plot is obviously lifted from Wilkie Collins's* *The Moonstone**.) More ambitious was *Micah Clarke** (1889), a story of the 1685 Rebellion and its defeat at Sedgemoor, told autobiographically by one of Monmouth's humble followers. *The Firm Of Girdlestone* (1890) is set in the nineteenth century and is interesting for its evocation (in Chapter 4) of Doyle's years at Edinburgh University. Less effective is the main plot in which two rascally London merchants plan to murder their ward and are foiled by her gallant lover. *The White Company** (1891), another historical* romance, was the author's own favourite work. The action is set in the Hundred Years War with France, and follows the exploits of a company of English bowmen. Like all of the author's period fiction it maintains a rattling pace. But Doyle was doomed to be the creator of Sherlock Holmes, however he chafed under it. In 1893, he killed the detective, only to bring him back to life in 1901 and again in 1903. Much as he came to hate him, Holmes made Doyle rich. With the aid of the agent A. P. Watt, the novelist was earning as much as £1,600 a year from his writing in 1891 and by the end of the century was one of the richest of British men of letters. Literary fame brought him friendship with such writers as J. M. Barrie* and Jerome K. Jerome*. It was Jerome who originally commissioned the realistic (and occasionally supernatural) stories of medical life which were collected as *Round The Red Lamp* (1894), a red lamp being 'the usual sign of the general practitioner in England'. *The Refugees* (1893) is a Franco-Canadian romance set in the period of Louis XIV. *The Parasite* (1894) is a story of mesmeric villainy which reveals Doyle's growing fascination with the paranormal. (He was converted to spiritualism in the first World War, and in 1926 went on to write a full-length *History Of Spiritualism.*) *The Stark Munro Letters* (1895) is an epistolary account of 'the evolution of a young medico' (i.e. the author). *Rodney Stone* (1896) reflects Doyle's enthusiasm for pugilism. Set in the early nineteenth century, it introduces Brummel and other historical notables. The work earned the author £5,000. *Uncle Bernac* (1897) is a Napoleonic tale dealing with the projected invasion of England in 1804. It cost the author pains to write and was relatively unsuccessful. Doyle was a hearty man of letters, loving cricket, shooting and motoring. He was a convinced imperialist. During the Boer War he offered his medical services to the armed forces and propagandised for the English cause. He was knighted in 1902. Doyle was also active as a patriotic front line reporter in the First World War. (See his *Visit To Three Fronts*, 1916.) All his adult life, Doyle was extraordinarily diligent as a writer to the press and attached himself to innumerable causes. Some, such as his defence of wrongly convicted criminals, were noble. Other causes (notably his crusade for spiritualism and his belief in fairies) brought him into some ridicule. Among his notable post-Victorian novels are: *The Hound Of The Baskervilles* (1902); *The Adventures Of Gerard* (1903); *Sir Nigel* (1906); *The Poison Belt* (1913). In later life the author hyphenated his name as Conan-Doyle. BL 31. *DNB*. RM. *NCBEL*. Wol. Sad.

DOYLE, Richard (1824–83). Illustrator and artist. Doyle was born in London, the son of a Catholic artist and caricaturist, John Doyle. He was educated at home by his father, and displayed an early talent for drawing. In 1843 Doyle became associated with *Punch** and designed its famous cover. But he broke with the journal following its anti-Catholic campaign of 1850. He subsequently worked for *Cornhill** during his friend Thackeray's* editorship. Doyle illustrated a number of works of fiction; most memorably Ruskin's* *King Of The Golden River** (1851) and Thackeray's

The Newcomes* (1853–55). His style (particularly in his crowd scenes) is fluid and inventively detailed. Doyle's work represents a high point of the comic illustrative tradition pioneered by Cruikshank* in the 1830s. It was superseded in the 1860s by the more naturalistic illustrations of artists like Millais* and Du Maurier*. *DNB*. Hou.

Dracula, Bram Stoker, 1897, 1 vol, Constable. Bram Stoker claimed that inspiration for *Dracula* came to him in a nightmare. A more plausible source is J. S. Le Fanu's* story of vampirism *Carmilla** (1872). Stoker, however, had the idea of making his vampire a historical figure, Vlad the Impaler, a ruler who had tyrannised over Wallachia in the fifteenth century. Stoker borrowed for his tale Wilkie Collins's* high-impact, multi-narrative style. *Dracula* unfolds through various diaries (including, topically, a 'phonograph' diary), letters, press cuttings and journals. The story is simple crime and chase. The solicitor Jonathan Harker is sent to Transylvania, on the ostensible business of Dracula's house purchase in England. The young lawyer is thoroughly vampirised, but escapes. The Count, meanwhile, has had himself transported by coffin to Whitby devouring the ship's crew and driving the captain mad on the way. Arrived, the ghoul deposits fifty hideaway coffins around London, and renders the Harkers' friend, Lucy Westenra, one of the undead. The vampirologist Dr Van Helsing and his companion Dr Seward track Dracula back to his castle in Transylvania. They finally trap the monster at sunset and decapitate him. The theatrical potential of Stoker's story was subsequently exploited by the dramatist Hamilton Deane and by many twentieth-century film makers.

A Dream Of John Ball, William Morris, 1888, 1 vol, Reeves. (The story was first published in Morris's socialist journal, *Commonweal*, 1886–87.) A political fable, associated with the Trafalgar Square 'riots' of 1887. The narrative opens with Morris in the 'land of nod', subconsciously worried about his lecturing commitments. He wakes up (as he imagines) 'on a strip of wayside waste by an oak copse just outside a country village'. It is medieval Kent at the time of the Peasants' Revolt of 1381. A transmuted Morris finds himself talking Middle-English and as the Oxford educated 'Man from Essex' is befriended by Will Green. The centrepiece of the story is the priest John Ball's speech on 'fellowship' (communism) which is followed by Jack Straw's mobilising the Kent yeomen to march on London. The hero consoles the doomed Ball with the prophecy that 'thy death will bring about that which thy life has striven for'. At the end of the story, Morris returns to the 'Great Wen' and the dawn cacophany of hooters calling workmen to their labours. A strong undertone of pessimism runs through the work.

DRUMMOND, Hamilton (1857–1935). An Irish author, about whom little is known other than that he was the son of a Dublin JP, and himself later became a JP in the same city. In his forties, Drummond began publishing a string of historical* romances catering for the market that Stevenson* had created. Drummond specialised in French and Spanish settings for his tales which enjoyed some success. His titles include: *Gobelin Grange* (1896), a collection of supernatural stories; *For The Religion* (1898); *A Man Of His Age* (1900); *A King's Pawn* (1900). BL 25. *WW*. Wol.

DRURY, Major W[illiam] P[rice] (1861–1949). Drury was born in Essex, the son and grandson of senior naval officers. On leaving school, he went to Plymouth College and was commissioned in the Royal Marines. As a young officer, Drury saw active service in Crete in 1898, and was eventually promoted to a staff post at the Admiralty. During this phase of his life (when he was in his forties) Drury wrote plays and fiction. A selection of Kiplingesque* short stories first printed in service magazines were gathered as *Bearers Of The Burden* (1899). *The Petrified Eye* (1899) contains horror stories, some of which have lasted well. In 1926, Drury published his interesting *Memoirs Of A Marine*. He married a daughter of the novelist Annie Thomas (i.e. Mrs Pender Cudlip*), but there seem to have been no children. Drury wrote a spate of works on seafaring in the twentieth century and rejoined the Royal Navy when hostilities broke out in 1914. BL 9. *WW*.

The Dublin University Magazine (1833–77). Founded by a disgruntled caucus of Tories at Trinity College, Dublin after the Reform Bill, the journal was modelled on the co-political *Blackwood's** and *Fraser's** magazines. Like them it was monthly, and featured fiction among its politically flavoured miscellany. Initially the journal was published by William Curry*, and after 1846 by James McGlashan*. In 1856, Hurst and Blackett* bought an interest in the paper (which led to a greater emphasis on popular fiction). In its early years the *Dublin University Magazine* carried stories by William Carleton*. Its devotion to fiction was enhanced, however, with the appointment of Charles Lever* as editor in 1842. Although he only held the post three years, Lever made the journal the vehicle for his finest Irish* tales and under his management circulation rose to a respectable 4,000. Another major novelist, J. Sheridan Le Fanu*, was associated with the magazine from 1861–69 as editor and proprietor. It was the serial outlet for some of his best fiction (e.g. *Uncle Silas**). Other notable contributions of the 1860s came from Mortimer Collins* and, pre-eminently, Rhoda Broughton*. The level of fiction dropped off in the last decade. The magazine never liberated itself from its original Fraserian format, declined to illustrate itself (which put it at a sales disadvantage to *Bentley's Miscellany** and the *Cornhill**) and its Irishness was less to the public taste after the 1840s. But it was a pioneer in the serialisation of long fiction. *WI. BLM*.

DUCLAUX, Mme [Agnes Mary Frances] (née Robinson, 1857–1944). By her own description, Duclaux was a 'poetess'. She was born in Leamington, the daughter of a Fellow of the Society of Antiquaries, and educated on the Continent and at University College, London. Her older sister, Frances Mabel Robinson* also wrote novels in later life. Agnes Robinson's first marriage was to James Darmesteter, a French writer who died in 1894. In 1901, she married another Frenchman, Emile Duclaux, a professor at the Pasteur Institute in Paris. Duclaux began her writing career with a novel, *Arden* (1883), which went through at least three editions. She also published translations from the Greek and literary criticism. Her collected poems appeared in 1902. BL 1. *WW*.

DUDENEY, Mrs Henry E. [Alice] (née Whiffin, 1866–1945). Born in Brighton, Alice Whiffin went to school in West Sussex, a region that figures strongly as a setting in her later fiction. In 1884, she married Henry

Dudeney (1857–1930), the famous deviser of newspaper puzzles. In her personal life Dudeney seems to have been very domestic. (In *Who's Who* she lists her recreations as 'gardening and collecting old oak furniture'.) She began to publish novels some years after marriage. Her plots are morbidly preoccupied with the drama of illegitimate pregnancy and other fashionable 'sex problems' of the 1890s. *Folly Corner* (1899) has as its heroine a London girl who takes up residence in an ancestral Sussex farm with subsequent bigamous complications. *The Maternity Of Harriott Wicken* (1899) is a story of murder, which ends wretchedly with the death of a mother and child from measles. *Men Of Marlowe's* (1900) is a set of bohemian tales set in Gray's Inn, London ('Marlowe's'). *The Third Floor* (1901) follows the misfortunes of a young girl, alone in London and sexually victimised. Dudeney continued writing well into the twentieth century. BL 48. *WW*. Wol.

DUFF, Henrietta Anne (1842–79). A daughter of Vice-Admiral Norwich Duff of Huntley, she was a lifelong invalid and died of heart disease at Brighton aged thirty-seven. During her short writing career she published *Virginia, A Roman Sketch* (1877). Immediately after her death, *Honor Carmichael, My Imperialist Neighbour* and her 'Fragments of Verse' were published in 1880. BL 3. Boase. Wol.

W. and J. Dugdale. Publishers of pornography and seditious material. William Dugdale (1800–68) was born at Stockport. In 1819, he was implicated in the Cato Street conspiracy and during his life was repeatedly imprisoned, dying in a house of correction. He ran his business mainly at 23 Russell Court, Drury Lane where he was, as Ashbee puts it: 'one of the most prolific publishers of filthy books'. He catered for the well-heeled middle- and upper-class client. (WD)Boase.

The Duke's Children, Anthony Trollope, 1880, 3 vols, Chapman and Hall. (Serialised in *All The Year Round**, October 1879–July 1880.) The final novel in the Palliser* series. The story opens painfully with Glencora, Duchess of Omnium, dying of a cold. Left alone, her husband Plantagenet has various parental trials. Lord Silverbridge, his heir, has been sent down from Oxford, and shows a dangerous weakness for gambling. His younger brother, Palliser, is similarly sent down from Cambridge. Mary, his daughter, has formed an unsuitable alliance (as Plantagenet thinks) with one of Silverbridge's Oxford friends, Frank Tregear. Tregear belongs to the Cornish gentry, is handsome and capable but is insufficiently grand a match for Mary in her father's view. His conscience is troubled on the matter, however, since it emerges that his dead wife approved of the affair. Silverbridge becomes entangled with a shifty racing associate, Major Tifto. Tifto lames the horse they jointly own, which is favourite to win the St Leger and Silverbridge loses £70,000 in bets. This brings matters between him and his father to a head. The young man finally assumes his aristocratic responsibilities, marries a vivacious American heiress, Isabel Boncassen (about whom the Duke has some initial British prejudice) and enters Parliament. Frank Tregear also enters Parliament, and wins the Duke's consent to marriage with Mary. The Duke himself returns to office as President of the Council. The novel's portrait of Palliser in proud old age is among the best things that Trollope achieved in fiction.

DU MAURIER, George [Louis Palmella Busson] (1834–96). With Thackeray*, the most accomplished artist-novelist of the century. Du Maurier's grandfather was a French glass-blower named Busson who fled the Revolution, and in England added the aristocratic 'Du Maurier' to his name. The novelist's father (1797–1856) was an inventor. His mother was English, a daughter of Mary-Anne Clarke, a notorious mistress of the Duke of York. The family circumstances were impoverished, although the fiction was resolutely maintained that the Du Mauriers had aristocratic origins. The young George was born in Paris and was brought up in a bilingual household that moved erratically between England and the Continent during his childhood. As critics have noted, duality was to be an obsession in his later novels. Du Maurier started his university study at the Sorbonne, and continued it desultorily at the University of London, in 1851. After embarking on an abortive career in chemistry he returned to Paris after his father's death in 1856, to study art and live for a year in the Latin Quarter. This experience provided the inspiration for his best-known novel, *Trilby** (1894). Among Du Maurier's artist friends in Paris at this time was the American James Whistler. In 1857, for unknown reasons, Du Maurier moved to Antwerp to study at the Academy. His ambitions received a setback, in 1857, when he suddenly lost the sight of his left eye. (The shocking experience was later used in *The Martian**, 1897.) This was the end of Du Maurier's ambition to be a painter. In 1860, he moved to London, and took up residence with Whistler, in Newman Street. In the same year, Du Maurier's long association with *Punch** started. Eventually, he was to become one of the magazine's best known cartoonists and a major contributor to the 'Things One Would Have Left Unsaid' series. Du Maurier also illustrated serials in fiction-carrying magazines like *Once A Week** and *Cornhill**. Retrospectively he supplied Smith, Elder* with fine illustrations to de luxe reissues of the work of Mrs Gaskell* and Thackeray. Du Maurier's work in this line is florid and theatrical in composition. But he stands out in a period generally marked by a decline in the illustration of popular fiction. In 1863, he was confident enough of his prospects to marry. For the next fifteen years he was principally occupied with *Punch*. He settled down with his now large family in Hampstead and set himself up as an opponent of bohemianism and aestheticism. In 1880 Du Maurier was passed over for the editorship of *Punch* and he began to take on more outside work and lecturing. At the same period he became friendly with Henry James, whose *Washington Square* (1881) he illustrated. Artistic work was increasingly straining Du Maurier's eyesight and he was again pinched for money. It was James who urged Du Maurier to try his hand at a novel. The result was *Peter Ibbetson** (1892). This first novel (which the author himself illustrated) was moderately successful. It was followed by *Trilby* (1894), a novel which was popular to the point of mania with the British and American reading public. As well as having hats (and even a town) named after it, Trilby (especially in its dramatic adaptation by Beerbohm Tree in 1895) created the stereotype of bohemian artistic life which persists today. The work enraged James Whistler, however, who was satirically portrayed as Joe Sibley in the narrative. Libel suits were threatened, and Du Maurier withdrew the character from later issues of the novel. Before his death in 1896 Du Maurier wrote and himself illustrated another work of fiction, *The Martian* (1897). All three of his late novels recall his early

French experience nostalgically, and introduce the occult elements which were fashionable at the end of the nineteenth century. Du Maurier, whose health had never been good, died prematurely of heart failure at sixty-two. BL 3. *DNB*. RM. *NCBEL*. Wol. Sad.

DUNN, [Mrs] Gertrude ('G. Colmore', née Renton, 1860?–1926). Born in England, Gertrude Renton was educated at Frankfurt am Main, and worked before her marriage as a governess in London and Paris. Her first marriage, which ended in divorce, was to a barrister, Henry A. Colmore Dunn. In 1901 she married Harold Baillie Weaver, another barrister. She wrote under a confusing array of names and pseudonyms: G[ertrude] Colmore, Gertrude Renton Weaver, Mrs Gertrude Dunn. Her fiction includes: *Concerning Oliver Knox* (1888); *A Conspiracy Of Silence* (1889); *A Living Epitaph* (1890); *The Strange Story Of Hester Wynne* (1899); *The Marble Face* (1900). BL 15. *WW*.

DURAND, [the Rt Hon. Sir] Henry Mortimer ('John Roy', 1850–1924). The son of an army general, Durand had his school education at Tonbridge public school. He afterwards read for the Bar and was called to it in 1872. Durand entered the Bengal Civil Service in 1873. His subsequent career as a diplomatist was distinguished, and he rose to be Consul-General at Madrid in 1900 and British ambassador at Washington in 1903. Drawing on first-hand experience of the Afghan War of 1879, Durand wrote *Helen Treveryan, Or The Ruling Race* (1891) whose story follows the adventures of a young English officer in the campaign. The work contains some trenchant criticism of the English colonial mentality. BL 1. *DNB*.

DURRANT, Valentine (1850?–92). The son of a baker at Brighton, Durrant came to London where he lived in great poverty in Fulham. In the early 1870s, he was writing for boys' magazines. About the same period he received a grant from the Royal Literary Fund*. His main effort in fiction were the 'Cheveley novels' which Blackwoods* brought out, 1877–79. These were an attempt to revive the practice of monthly part serialisation which had been pioneered by Dickens*. The first of the series was *A Modern Minister* (1877). It was followed by *Saul Weir* (1879) and *Souls And Cities* (1885). The enterprise was not successful and reviews were unrelievedly savage. Durrant died destitute, and after a long illness at Bournemouth. BL 3. Boase. Wol. RLF.

E

Eason and Son. 'The Irish W. H. Smith*'. Charles Eason (1823–99) began to work for Smith's at Victoria Station, Manchester. In 1857, he was transferred to the firm's Dublin branch. He managed the division profitably until 1886. At this point, it became politically embarrassing for W. H. Smith II (who had just been appointed Chief Secretary for Ireland) to operate an Irish network and it was sold to Eason. By the end of the century, Eason's controlled most of the bookstall and wholesale newspaper trade in Ireland, and continued to do so in the twentieth century. (CE) Boase.

EASTLAKE, Lady [Elizabeth] (née Rigby, 1809–93). Elizabeth Rigby was born in Norwich the fifth child of a doctor, who died in 1821. In 1827 Rigby went to Heidelberg and spent two years there mastering the German language. In the 1830s and 1840s she wrote for the magazines, usually on European topics. From 1842, she lived in Edinburgh with her mother and wrote the contributions to the *Quarterly Review* for which she is best remembered (notably the libellous attack on *Jane Eyre** in 1848, which accused Charlotte Brontë* of being Thackeray's* mistress). In 1838 and 1844, Rigby visited Russia (where she had a sister married to an Estonian baron) and out of the experience created some works of fiction: *The Jewess* (first published as a slim volume in 1843); *The Disponent* (i.e. bailiff) and *The Wolves*. These were collected as *Livonian Tales* (1846). The stories have interesting local colour, but are extremely awkward stylistically. In 1849, Rigby married the well-known painter, Sir Charles Lock Eastlake. She was forty, he fifty-six. The couple settled in Fitzroy Square, London, and moved in the highest society after he became director of the National Gallery in 1855. After his death in 1865 she was awarded a Civil List pension of £60. BL 2. *DNB. NCBEL.*

East Lynne, Mrs Henry Wood, 1861, 3 vols, Bentley. (Serialised in the *New Monthly Magazine**, January 1860–August 1861.) The most famous melodramatic novel of the century. The heroine, Lady Isabel Vane (vain by nature), is left bankrupt and friendless on her father, Lord Mount Severn's, death. She marries a high-minded lawyer, Mr Archibald Carlyle, who buys her former home, East Lynne. Isabel's married life is made uncomfortable by her priggish sister-in-law Cornelia and, eavesdropping, she misconstrues her husband's relationship with another woman. Disastrously, she is tempted to elope ('a blind leap in a moment of passion') with the caddish Frank Levison, a former lover. Carlyle divorces her. She bears Frank's child, is deserted and is thought killed in a French train crash. Disfigured, white haired and disguised by green spectacles she returns as Madame Vine to East Lynne as governess to her own children. Carlyle has meanwhile remarried his former sweetheart, Barbara Hare. Isabel has her child William die in her arms, without knowing her. After revealing herself to Carlyle she is forgiven and herself dies. Levison, after unsuccessfully contesting an election with Carlyle, is revealed to be a murderer and condemned to death. The novel embodies Wood's stern conviction that for a married woman, adultery is 'far worse than death'. By 1895, Bentley had sold 400,000 copies of the work. (It is, incidentally, in the popular stage version, not the novel, that the luckless heroine is made to scream at the deathbed of her child, 'dead! dead! and never called me mother'.)

EDEN, Charles Henry (1839–1900). A younger son of a magistrate in Madras, India, Eden was educated at the English public school Marlborough. In adult life, he travelled widely in South Africa, Australia and Canada. Eden went on to write a large number of books based on his experiences and residence abroad. They include novels aimed principally at the juvenile reader, such as *Ralph Somerville, Or A Midshipman's Adventures*

In The Pacific Ocean (1876) and *Afloat With Nelson* (1897). *Found Though Lost* (1881) and *George Donnington* (1885) are aimed at the older reader. The last of these has a wildly adventurous plot that transports the hero to Siberia. After a lifetime's travel, Eden died in London. BL 14. *WW*. Wol.

EDEN, the Hon. [Eleanor] Lena (1826–79). Niece to Emily Eden*, whose letters she edited. The first-born child of the third Baron Auckland and Bishop of Bath and Wells, Eleanor Eden wrote mainly children's books using the diminutive form of her Christian name, 'Lena'. Her output also includes some adult fiction, mostly set in idyllic rural England. *False And True* (1858) is a village comedy as is *Dumbleton Common* (1867), Eden's most popular work. Its narrator, 'Little Miss Patty', chronicles local intrigues in a small hamlet five miles outside London. The work is clearly inspired by Elizabeth Gaskell's* *Cranford**. Eden never married. She evidently passed most of her life in the country, dying in Wiltshire. BL 5. Boase. Sad.

EDEN, the Hon. Emily (1797–1869). She was born in Westminster, the seventh daughter of William Eden, first Baron Auckland and a career diplomat. In early womanhood, Emily Eden and her sister Fanny travelled with their brother George (Lord Auckland) to India, and kept house for him during his term of residence there as Governor-General, 1835–42. On her return to England, Eden published lively epistolary accounts of travel and society in India. She continued as social hostess for her brother until he died in 1849. She also wrote two very successful novels: *The Semi-Detached House* ('Edited by Lady Theresa Lewis', 1859) and *The Semi-Attached Couple** (1860). The first has as its sprightly heroine Lady Blanche Chester, whose husband is obliged to leave her in England while he is posted abroad. She is pregnant, and must share a semi-detached residence in 'Dulham' with a robust middle-class family, the Hopkinsons. The comic complications are heightened with the arrival of the *nouveau riche* Jewish Baron Sampson and his wife who eventually come to commercial grief. The novel is an accomplished study in the social contrasts of aristocratic style, bourgeois respectability and crass vulgarity. The narrative is propelled by lively dialogue, for which Eden had a fine ear. *The Semi-Attached Couple* was first written in 1829. It narrates the marital difficulties of Helen Beaufort and Lord Teviot, who, despite all the advantages of youth, beauty, wit and fortune find they cannot always get on well together. Both works are marked by a comic touch that critics frequently compare to Jane Austen's (Emily Eden's favourite author). There was no compulsion on Eden to write. Her condition of life was comfortable, and she did not need the pin-money her works brought. Eden never married, and in the later years of her life lived at Eden Lodge, Kensington, where she entertained all the celebrities of the day at her forenoon receptions. BL 2. *DNB*. RM. *NCBEL*. Wol. Sad

EDWARD[E]S, Mrs Annie (née Edwards, 1830?–96). Little is known of her life, or of her husband, L. E. Edwards. She may have been a cousin of Matilda Betham-Edwards*, and may have had the same East Anglian gentry background. But the settings of her fiction make it clear that at some stage of her life she spent considerable time in the Channel Islands, and on the Continent. Edwards's first novel, *The Morals Of May Fair*, an overwritten story of fashionable adultery, appeared anonymously in 1858.

The heroine, Marguerite, dies causing huge remorse and anguish in the guilty hero, Earnscliffe. *Creeds* (1859) is a quite different story of the conflict between profane love and Catholicism. In his memoirs, the publisher William Tinsley* recalled Edwards as a 'clever writer' who could change her style of fiction at will. Her early work is sensational* and reminiscent of Rhoda Broughton*. Like the other novelist, it often had a somewhat risqué quality, and was occasionally banned by the librarian Mudie*. Much of her fiction was first serialised in *Temple Bar*. From the 1870s, Mrs Edwardes (she added the final 'e' to her surname in 1870) wrote new-womanish* novels, with lively young heroines who conform to the bohemian, hoydenish stereotypes of the genre. *Archie Lovell* (1866) was her first success; set in France, it recounts the adventures of a tomboy ('Archie') who scandalises the little community of 'Morteville'. 'What grace, what playfulness, what naughtiness', one reviewer sarcastically observed of the heroine. But readers liked bohemian heroines like the one in *Jet* (1878), who were fast and even on occasion smoked cigarettes and they put Edwardes in the well-paid £500-a-work bracket of authors. Edwardes's other fiction includes: *Steven Lawrence, Yeoman* (1867), the story of two cousins' ruthless rivalry in love for the hero; *Susan Fielding* (1869); *Ought We To Visit Her?* (1871), the heroine, Jane Theobald, having been a ballet dancer before marriage; *A Ballroom Repentance* (1882), which chronicles a young girl's adventures on the continent; *A Girton Girl* (1886) is one of her more interesting novels, dealing as it does with the dilemmas of the woman newly admitted into Cambridge University. In fact, the heroine Marjorie Bartrand does not get to college giving up her academic ambitions to become a good wife ('I need no other life, no other wisdom'), but as in *A Blue Stocking* (1877), Edwardes deals quite interestingly with the issue of female education. She died at Clifton, where her son, a doctor, was in practice. BL 20. Boase. Wol. Sad.

EDWARDS, Amelia [Ann] B[lanford] (1831–92). Novelist, journalist and Egyptologist. Edwards was born in London, the only child of a banker. The family background was East Anglian gentry. Confusingly for bibliographers, she was related to Matilda Betham-Edwards* and possibly to Annie Edward(e)s*. As a young girl Amelia was educated at home by her mother and displayed extraordinary precocity in writing, drawing and music. Her first poem was published when she was seven, and her first story when she was twelve. When her family's financial difficulties obliged Edwards to earn a living, she chose authorship, having had an early piece accepted by *Chambers's Journal*. She went on to write other stories for the journals and made a small name for herself as a producer of ghost* tales for the Christmas numbers of magazines. Her early short fiction was collected as *Miss Carew* (1865). In the late 1850s there were some openings for women in journalism, and Edwards found work on the staff of the *Saturday Review* and the *Morning Post*. She wrote eight novels, from 1855 onward. Fiction came easily to her, although each novel took her as she claimed two years' work. Her early novel *The Ladder Of Life* (1857), 'A Heart History', was criticised by reviewers as spasmodic and overwritten. But popular success came with *Barbara's History* (1864). It has a young English heroine who goes to college in Germany. The subsequent love complications introduce the bigamy* that was fashionable in the early 1860s. *Half A Million Of*

Money (1866) has a young hero, Saxon, who is brought up in the wilds of Switzerland, who subsequently inherits a fortune in England but is so innocent of civilisation that he does not know what a banknote is. R. L. Wolff especially admires Edwards's novel *Debenham's Vow* (1870) which has a musician hero who is swept up in the naval battles of the American Civil War. *In The Days Of My Youth* (1873) is about growing up in France. Reviewers particularly liked Edwards's women characters. 'It is a joy to be among them', the *Athenaeum** wrote. Edwards's promising career as a novelist was interrupted by the most influential event of her life, a trip to the middle East in 1873. Thereafter, she became a passionate enthusiast for everything to do with ancient Egypt, and helped found the Egypt Exploration Fund in 1882. Although this work preoccupied her, she wrote some good late fiction, notably *Lord Brackenbury* (1880), a story of English country life. Edwards never married. After 1864 she lived with a female friend at Westbury-on-Trym. A public figure of some standing, she visited America in 1889–90, although by then her health was very poor and a broken arm she sustained in Columbus, Ohio, may have advanced her death in 1892. In the same year she received a Civil List pension of £75, for her services to literature and archaeology. Politically, Edwards supported suffrage for women. By legacy she helped found the first English chair of Egyptology at University College, London. BL 13. *DNB*. Wol. Sad.

EDWARDS, Mrs H[arry] B[ennett] (née Cox, 1844–1936). She was born in London, where her father was a lawyer and where she was educated largely at home. Together with her two brothers, she became proprietor of her father's the *Field* and *Queen* magazines. From these and other enterprises, she drew as she claimed an income 'of some £20,000 a year', upon which she lived as a 'country gentlewoman' with her husband, Captain Harry Bennett-Edwards (m. 1866). Cox began writing at the age of twelve, and had some early stories published in the *Queen*. In her early thirties she wrote her first three-volume novel, *A Tantalus Cup* (1878) and turned out two other novels in the same twelve months. (According to *Who's Who*, the first of these was written when she was twenty, 1864). They were all marked by a gorgeous style of writing. Edwards's later fiction includes the romantic melodrama *In Sheep's Clothing* (1880) which has as its heroine a woman who marries a man she does not love, who turns out to be a murderer. He goes to Australia, but returns to make her miserable in later life. *Pharisees* (1884) was reckoned her best novel. The hero is a young squire who returns from Australia after ten years with an actress wife called Star. She provokes pharisaical responses from the local English gentry and even her husband reverts to type and is ashamed of her. BL 6. *WW*.

EDWARDS, H[enry] Sutherland (1828–1906). Edwards was born in Hendon, the son of an independently wealthy father. He was educated at Brompton Grammar School, and in France. In the later 1840s he became involved with the world of London journalism, writing and doing occasional illustrations for *Punch**. In 1856 Edwards was in Russia, as a correspondent for the *Illustrated Times**. There he met his future wife, Margaret Watson, the daughter of a Scottish engineer. In 1869, Edwards was appointed first editor of the newly founded *Graphic* and a year later, he covered the Franco-Prussian War for *The Times*. During the course of a busy literary career

Edwards produced a wealth of books, plays and opera libretti. He also wrote fiction including a mystery novel set in the eighteenth century, *The Missing Man* (1885) and the social comedy *What Is A Girl To Do?* (1885), a work narrated by the perplexed maiden of the title. Meanwhile he (or probably his wife) turned out a string of better than usual novels for the libraries. *The Three Louisas* (1866) is an 'art' novel, dealing with the world of music. *The Governor's Daughter* (1868) is set in the Polish uprising of a few years before. *Dutiful Daughters* (1890) is a reworking of *King Lear*, in modern English society. *The Secret Of The Princess, A Tale Of Country, Camp, Court And Cloister Life In Russia* (1891) draws on Mrs Edwards's childhood experiences of Russia in the 1850s. *The Dramatist's Dilemma* (1891) was a collaborative work, written with Florence Marryat*. Edwards's publishers (mainly Tinsley*) presented these novels as by 'H. Sutherland-Edwards', leading reviewers to believe the husband was the author. This confusion is perpetuated in the BL Catalogue, which credits all but one of the Edwards's eight novels to him. BL 8. *DNB*. Wol. RLF.

EDWARDS, M[ary] E[llen] ('M.E.E.', 1839–1910). Illustrator. Edwards was born near London. Little more is known of her life, except that she worked as M. E. Edwards until 1869, when she became Mrs Freer. Her first marriage evidently soon ended and from 1872 she signed herself Mrs Staples in her work. Edwards was a prolific if undistinguished illustrator in the 1860s naturalistic school. Novelists and editors evidently liked her designs. She worked regularly for *Good Words*, *Argosy*, *Cassell's Magazine* and the *Girl's Own Paper*. Her best-known illustrations are those in 1867 for Trollope's* *The Claverings* and for M. E. Braddon's* *Birds Of Prey* (1868). According to Forrest Reid in *Illustrators Of The 1860s*, 'Edwards would occupy a higher position among our illustrators had she not repeated herself so monotonously.' Hou.

Edwin Drood, Charles Dickens, 1870, 1 vol, Chapman and Hall. (Full title, *The Mystery Of Edwin Drood*, six out of a planned twelve instalments being issued, April–September 1870, illustrated by Luke Fildes*.) Dickens's last, tantalisingly incomplete novel. Two widowers, now deceased, have betrothed their children Edwin Drood and Rosa Bud to each other. Rosa is brought up in Cloisterham (i.e. Rochester). Edwin's guardian is John Jasper, a precentor at Cloisterham cathedral (which dominates the action) and a secret opium smoker. Rosa's is the amiable London lawyer Mr Hiram Grewgious. Jasper gives Rosa lessons in music and makes advances which she disgustedly rejects. She and Edwin, despite their parents' wishes, do not love each other. Two other orphans arrive at Cloisterham, Neville and Helena Landless. Neville and Edwin quarrel over Rosa, and Edwin mysteriously disappears on a stormy Christmas Eve. Jasper reacts strangely. Neville is arrested for possible murder of Edwin, but in the absence of any corpse is released without trial. It is supposed that Edwin has been drowned. The novel breaks off with Jasper's continued persecution of Rosa in London. How Dickens intended the work to continue is itself mysterious. The best guess is that Jasper murdered Edwin on Christmas Eve and buried him in the cathedral crypt.

EGAN, Pierce ('the younger', 1814–80). The son of a famous namesake father who wrote *Life In London* (1821) and was for some years the sports editor of *Bell's* popular newspapers. Egan the younger was born in London, and educated at the art school of the Royal Academy. He began professional life as an artist, illustrating his father's work. He later turned to writing low-grade serials, beginning with *Quintin Matsys, The Blacksmith Of Antwerp* (1839). A year later he produced a very popular 1d. serialisation, *Robin Hood And Little John*, which initiated what has been called 'a whole Robin Hood industry in popular fiction'. After he had established himself Egan mainly wrote for the *Weekly Times* and the *London Journal**. So popular was he in the second of these that when they tried to drop him in 1859 sales plummeted and the proprietors were obliged to bring Egan back on his own terms. Of the fifty or so romances he produced, only a handful were deposited in the British Museum. His speciality was historical* fiction, some of which he illustrated himself. Representative titles are: *Wat Tyler* (1841); *Adam Bell* (1841); *Paul Jones, The Pirate* (1842); *Fair Rosamund* (1844); *The Thirteenth, Or The Fatal Number* (1849); *Clifton Grey, A Tale Of The Crimea* (1854). Little is known of Egan's life other than that he married, had several children, enjoyed a fair income from his literary work and held radical political views. *Eve, Or The Angel Of Innocence* (1867) was his most popular novel. BL 8. *DNB*. Wol. Sad. RLF.

EGERTON, George (i.e. Mary Chavelita Bright, née Dunne, 1859–1945). Author of *Keynotes** (1893), the most influential of the so-called new woman* fictions. Egerton's life is complicated by the official accounts she put out in her lifetime. She was born in Melbourne, Australia. Her father was Irish and an army officer, her mother Welsh. As a child, she witnessed something of the New Zealand wars against the Maoris. The young Egerton had hopes of being an artist, 'but family affairs prevented the course of study'. Like Iota*, she instead trained as a nurse. In 1888, Egerton eloped with a married man Henry Higginson (called in the official account 'H. H. W. Melville'). The couple lived in Norway where Egerton became imbued with the Ibsenism which is prominent in her later work. Higginson was, apparently, a drunken brute and Egerton left him after a year (the official version has him die in 1889). She moved to England (although she seems to have spent considerable periods in Ireland) and in 1891 married what one commentator calls 'an idle destitute Canadian', Egerton Clairmonte. Officially, he was a respectable minor novelist. In 1901, they divorced. (The official version has Egerton widowed again.) Meanwhile, as Mrs Clairmonte, Egerton achieved a huge success with *Keynotes*, and apparently became the mistress of its publisher, John Lane* (among many other literary notables). It was followed by similar collections of modish short stories and sketches of the *femme incomprise*: *Discords* (1894); *Symphonies* (1897); *Fantasies* (1898). *The Wheel Of God* (1898) is a full-length autobiographical work, interesting for its depiction of the formation of a young Irish girl's character as she travels to New York, supporting herself as a journalist. *Flies In Amber* (1905) collects various short stories, including 'The Marriage Of Mary Ascension', a sharp portrayal of middle-class Irish life. For all its feminist toughness, Egerton's writing has great delicacy. More than her sister new woman novelists, she was influenced by the aesthetics of decadence*, and by the European novel (particularly Knut Hamsun, to whom *Keynotes* is dedicated). In 1901 she made a third marriage to the author's agent Reginald

Golding Bright, and herself became a leading dramatic agent for such writers as G. B. Shaw* and Somerset Maugham*. BL 7. *WW.* Wol.

The Egoist, George Meredith, 1879, 3 vols, C. Kegan Paul. (Serialised in the *Glasgow Weekly Herald*, June 1879–January 1880.) The egoist is Sir Willoughby Patterne of Patterne Hall. Willoughby is brought up in a setting of wealth and female adoration. On coming into his inheritance, he announces his engagement to Constantia Durham. But she sees through him and elopes shortly before the marriage with Harry Oxford, a captain in the hussars. Willoughby tours the world for three years. On his return he brings with him two relatives, the dashing Vernon Whitford and Crossjay Patterne (the humble son of an army man). Willoughby selfishly continues to ignore Laetitia Dale, a shy but intelligent woman who has always loved him. Instead, he courts Clara Middleton, the daughter of a wine-loving clergyman and scholar. Willoughby's courtship of Clara and her increasing reluctance form the main plot of the novel. To protect himself from another humiliation in the eyes of his county neighbours Willoughby secretly proposes to Laetitia, while still formally engaged to Clara. Laetitia rejects him. The exposure of Willoughby's treachery brings about the break Clara wants and she marries Vernon. Willoughby again offers himself to Laetitia and she finally accepts him in a disillusioned spirit of mere 'egoism'. The narrative embodies the aesthetic theory of Meredith's essay 'On The Idea Of Comedy And Of The Uses Of The Comic Spirit' (1877).

ELIOT, George (née Mary Anne Evans, 1819–80). Mary Anne Evans was the daughter of a land agent, Robert Evans, in the service of the Newdigate family, of Arbury Hall, in Warwickshire. (Caleb Garth in *Middlemarch** is an admitted portrait.) Mary Anne's mother was Evans's second wife, and like him of respectable working-class background though of slightly higher station. In her childhood, which was happy and rural, Mary Anne was particularly attached to her brother Isaac, three years older than her. (The relationship is evoked by that of the young Tullivers in *The Mill On The Floss**.) Mary Anne was educated at school locally, and read widely on her own account. (Scott, whom she first read in 1827, was a strong early influence). From the age of thirteen to sixteen she attended a girls' school in Coventry. The following year (1836) her mother died and Mary Anne took over much of the running of her father's house. At this period she was particularly drawn to theology, in which she read assiduously. She was also steeping herself at the period in the Romantic poets, notably Wordsworth. In the early 1840s her intellectual development was powerfully influenced by association with Charles and Cara Bray*. Charles indoctrinated Mary Ann (as she called herself after 1837) with his idiosyncratic blend of Christianity and free-thought. This provoked an early crisis in 1842, when Mary Ann for a while refused to attend church with her father. Bray also introduced her into provincial journalism. In 1844, Charles Hennell (whom she had met through the Brays) asked Mary Ann to translate D. F. Strauss's *Das Leben Jesu* into English. The translation (1,500 pages of German, for which she received £20) came out in 1846. In 1848, she met Emerson, a meeting which had a profound effect on her. In 1849, Robert Evans died, leaving his daughter a small inheritance of around £90 a year. After her father's death she travelled abroad for some months. Marian (as she yet again renamed herself) was sufficiently independent financially to take what was virtually unpaid work as assistant editor on John Chapman's *Westminster Review*. For this journal she wrote learned but lively articles. And through association with Chapman (with whom she was romantically involved) she entered the literary world of London. In 1852, there was an unhappy love affair with Herbert Spencer, who seems to have been deterred by Marian's superficial lack of physical beauty. In the same year, she became involved with George Henry Lewes*, journalist and philosopher. Lewes, a free-thinker, had amiably surrendered his wife to his journalist colleague, Thornton Hunt. In 1855, Marian and Lewes set up home together. Having condoned his wife's adultery, Lewes could not divorce. Nevertheless, Marian called herself Mrs Lewes and resolutely referred to Lewes as her 'husband'. She continued to write for the *Westminster*, and between them the couple earned less than £1,000 in their early years together. In 1854, Marian worked on her translation of Spinoza's *Ethics*, a work whose influence is felt in her later fiction. Lewes meanwhile was finishing his life of Goethe, and the couple visited Germany in 1854. In London, they suffered some ostracism and moral condemnation for their defiantly unorthodox 'marriage'. In 1856, Marian began writing fiction, with the story *Amos Barton*, later published in *Scenes Of Clerical Life** (1858). Lewes negotiated for the publication of the 'Scenes' with John Blackwood* who was initially kept in ignorance of the identity and sex of their pseudonymous author 'George Eliot'. The 'Scenes' which drew closely on Marian's memories of her early life in Warwickshire, were published first in *Blackwood's Magazine**. They were well received, and Marian was encouraged to write a full-length novel, *Adam Bede** (1859). Set in the rural Midlands at the time of the Methodist revival, the novel was sensationally popular with library readers. It was no longer possible to keep her authorship a secret (more so as an impostor Joseph Liggins was making obstreperous claims to be George Eliot). In 1859, Marian took over the role of mother to Lewes's three sons. In 1860, Blackwood published *The Mill On The Floss*, the most autobiographical of Eliot's novels. Despite some objection to the near seduction of Maggie Tulliver by Stephen Guest in the third volume, the work confirmed Eliot's standing as a novelist of the first rank. But the Leweses were still not socially accepted by their respectable contemporaries. Over the period 1859–61, she produced the shorter works of fiction: *The Lifted Veil** (1859; a tale of clairvoyance told autobiographically, an unusual form for Eliot) and *Silas Marner**, the finest of her studies of humble rural life. Eliot's next major project was a story of fifteenth-century Florence, *Romola**. For once, the novelist deserted Blackwood and for an unprecedented offer of £10,000 (later somewhat reduced) allowed the new work to be published in George Smith's *Cornhill Magazine**. Despite the fortune it earned her, Eliot's historical novel was judged her least successful. In 1863, however, the Leweses were sufficiently well off to buy a new and more luxurious house, the Priory in St John's Wood. In 1866, during the political ferment over the second Reform Bill (on which she had rather conservative views), Eliot produced the social problem* novel, *Felix Holt, The Radical**. Lewes ably handled the now famous author's social and literary relationships, and a salon was established at the Priory on Sunday afternoons. In 1869, Eliot began writing her novel of English life, which eventually appeared as *Middlemarch**. The novel was first published by Blackwood in eight serial parts over 1871–72. In 1876, Blackwood published Eliot's last novel, *Daniel Deronda**, on the same serial pattern as its predecessor. Despite its preoccupation with Judaism, the work was immensely successful and in 1876 the Leweses purchased a large country house, the Heights at Witley, near Haslemere. But Lewes, whose health was chronically poor, died in November 1878. An inconsolable Eliot devoted the remainder of her intellectual energies to editing his *Problems Of Life And Mind*. In 1879 John Blackwood died and the next year Marian married John Walter Cross (1840–1924). Cross was twenty years Marian's junior, and had been a serviceable friend for many years. A few months later, on 22 December 1880, Marian died of a kidney disorder. She left a little under £43,000. Cross's *Life Of George Eliot* (1885) is a notable example of the Victorian whitewash biography, excluding as it does everything questionable in the author's life. BL 10. *DNB. NCBEL.* Wol. Sad.

Ellen Middleton, Lady Georgiana Fullerton, 1844, 3 vols, Moxon. The author's most interesting and popular novel, written at a religious crisis of her life. The fifteen-year-old heroine slaps an eight-year-old cousin and causes the child to fall to her death down some stairs. The accident makes Ellen an heiress. But she has been observed, by whom she does not know. Her subsequent life is haunted by blackmail and the pangs of conscience. Finally she confesses her crime and dies absolved. The novel was warmly reviewed by Gladstone, who approved its 'eloquence' and 'pathos'.

ELLESMERE, the Earl of [Francis Charles Granville Egerton] ('Charles Granville', 1847–1914). The Ellesmere family pioneered the Lancashire canal system. Charles Granville (as he called himself authorially) was born in London and educated at Eton and Cambridge from where he graduated BA in 1867, having succeeded his father to the earldom in 1862. Heir to some 13,000 acres of Lancashire countryside, he was an enthusiastic sportsman. In 1868, he married a daughter of the second Marquis of Normanby (the first being the well-known silver fork* novelist) by whom he had nine children. Over the course of his life, Granville published a number of works of fiction and is probably the highest-ranking novelist in the century. *Sir Hector's Watch* (1887), 'an amateur detective* novel', was found to be a 'tame and disappointing mystery', although some reviewers liked its aristocratic charm of manner. *A Broken Stirrup Leather* (1888) is a straightforward sporting* novel narrated by 'Sir Charles Egremont', who may be a self-portrait. *A Sapphire Ring* (1895) is a thriller featuring nihilists and Russian terrorists. Like all Granville's fiction it is defective in construction. *John Carruthers* (1900) has a man-about-town hero who unexpectedly inherits £75,000. The author listed his recreations as 'cricket, racing, shooting', and he was a Conservative in his politics. Granville's novels were published by Murray*, presumably as a favour since the publisher normally avoided fiction. BL 7. *WW*. Wol.

ELLIS, Mrs Edith Mary Oldham (née Lees, 1861–1916). Edith Lees was born in Cheshire. Her mother died shortly after, and Edith is reported to have hated her father, an idle man of private means. At twelve, Edith was put into a convent school but on her wanting to convert to Catholicism her father removed her to London. For a while, as a young woman, Lees ran a school in Sydenham. But when Havelock Ellis (1859–1939) met her in 1890, she was a thoroughly emancipated new woman*. He was on the rebound from his affair with Olive Schreiner*, and the couple married in 1891. Her career was thereafter overshadowed by his. Before her marriage she was one of the moving spirits in the Fabian Society. She gave up political activity but wrote the interesting novel *Seaweed, A Cornish Idyll* (1898; republished in 1907 as *Kit's Woman*) whose plot anticipates Lawrence's *Lady Chatterley's Lover*. A Cornish miner is crippled, and encourages his wife to have a child by another man, which she does, to everyone's satisfaction. The connection with Havelock Ellis's advanced ideas on sexual mores is clear enough (both were strongly influenced by the pioneer sexologist, James Hinton). The Ellis marriage seems to have been tempestuous. Before marrying, Edith was a lesbian. Within the marriage, the couple lived largely separate lives and she died prematurely of diabetes after a series of shattering nervous breakdowns. BL 1. *DNB*.

ELLIS, Mrs William [Sarah] (née Stickney, 1812–72). Didactic writer. Sarah Stickney was born a Quaker, but became a Congregationalist on her marriage in 1837 to William Ellis. Ellis (a widower) was a missionary, and the couple devoted their lives to practical evangelism. Both were active in the cause of temperance and women's education in the furtherance of which Ellis started a school for ladies, Rawdon House, in the 1840s. She also wrote a wealth of improving literature, including fiction, much of which is addressed correctively to the young or the socially inferior. Her best-known novel is *Home, Or The Iron Rule* (1836) which inspired a genre of 'home novels'. Among her other titles, *Northern Roses, A Yorkshire Story* (1868) is less sermonising than most. Ellis gained wide fame with her manual: *The Women of England, Their Social Duties And Domestic Habits* (1839). (A work which infuriated freer-thinking women, like Geraldine Jewsbury*.) She died of the same chill as her husband, caught on a train journey. BL 11. *DNB. NCBEL*. Wol. Sad.

ELTON, Sir Arthur Hallam (1818–83). Elton, a baronet (after 1853), was born at Clevedon, a brother of Jane Brookfield*. In young manhood he was a lieutenant in the army for a year, 1840–41, before selling out. In later life he was MP for Bath (1857–59), and a well known Victorian public figure. He wrote anonymously the novel *Below The Surface* (1857). An ambitious work, it purports to expose 'the secret workings of modern English society' and ranges from the saloons of the aristocratic to the lunatic asylums and workhouses of England. Selfishness is seen as the *primum mobile* of British life. Reviewers quickly identified Elton's hand in the work which drew mixed reviews. He wrote another novel, *Herbert Chauncey* (1860) which attracted less attention. A story of business fraud it is, like Lever's* *Davenport Dunn* (1859), based on the career of the swindler John Sadleir (1814–56), presented by Elton as 'a man more sinned against than sinning'. BL 2. Boase. Wol. Sad.

Endymion, Benjamin Disraeli, 1880, 3 vols, Longman. The last and most self-indulgent of Disraeli's novels. The action is set in the years 1827–50 (corresponding with the author's own début in politics). It contains a number of political portraits from life, and gives Disraeli's romanticised view of the administrations of Peel and Melbourne in the 1830s. Endymion and Myra are twins, the children of a passed-over Whig politician, William Pitt Ferrars. His failures oblige Endymion to leave Eton and take a clerkship in the Treasury. Myra goes as companion to Adriana Neuchatel a rich banker's daughter. Ferrars kills himself. Both twins rise meteorically in the world. Myra makes a first marriage with Lord Roehampton, the Foreign Secretary, and a second with a monarch, King Florestan. Endymion marries the influential Lady Mountfort and eventually becomes Prime Minister, boosted by his insatiably power-hungry sister. The novel's weakness is its vapid hero. An incidental point of interest is Disraeli's venomous depiction of Thackeray* as the ultra-snobbish St Barbe.

Erewhon, Samuel Butler, 1872, 1 vol, Trübner. Butler's dystopian satire draws initially on his own experience rearing sheep in New Zealand. The hero Higgs (as he is later called), assisted by a native, Chowbok, makes a perilous journey over a mountain range. This brings him to a country called Erewhon (i.e. 'nowhere'). The main body of the work is a satiric anatomy of the topsy-turvy world of the Erewhonians. They punish sickness, but cure crime. Higgs for instance is taken up by a patron, Nosnibor (i.e. Robinson), who is 'recovering' from embezzling a widow and children out of their money. The Erewhonian young people attend universities of Unreason, where nothing useful is taught. And Erewhon has proscribed machinery, on the superstitious grounds that if allowed to develop it will take over society. The state religion is a worship of the goddess Ydgrun (i.e. 'Mrs Grundy'). Higgs falls in love with an Erewhonian woman, Arowhena Nosnibor, and escapes with her by air balloon. Butler wrote a sequel, *Erewhon Revisited* (1901), in which a widowed Higgs returns in 1890 to discover that following his disappearance he has become the centre of a religious 'Sunchild' cult.

Eric, Or Little By Little, Dean [Frederic W.] Farrar, 1858, 1 vol, Black. The most reprinted of improving stories for Victorian and Edwardian boys, *Eric* went through twenty-four editions in thirty-one years. The novel chronicles the sad decline of little Eric Williams. The rot sets in at his school on the Isle of Roslyn where he is a boarder. Provoked by the school tyrant Barker and misled by the corrupt Brigson, Eric gradually slips away from the influence of his saintly school fellow, Edwin Russell, and takes to smoking, cribbing his lessons, swearing and drinking. (Discreetly, masturbation and homosexuality are also hinted at.) Edwin dies in a cliffside accident, as does Eric's little brother, Vernon. Eric, drunk from brandy tippling at the Jolly Herring, attacks a schoolmaster and becomes involved with low-life characters. He is suspected of theft, and runs away to sea where he is ill-treated and bitterly feels his loss of respectability. He returns to find that although his name is cleared, his mother has died of shame. Eric himself dies of remorse, joining 'those he loved, in the land where there is no more curse'. Together with Thomas Hughes's* *Tom Brown's Schooldays**, Farrar's depiction of Roslyn school had a formative influence on subsequent boys' literature. Although religious to excess, Farrar was also an experienced teacher and the novel offers sensible counsel on such things as bullying. Quotations from Wordsworth stress the book's Romantic conception of childhood.

Ernest Maltravers, E. G. E. L. Bulwer-Lytton, 1837, 3 vols, Saunders and Otley. The novel and its sequel, *Alice, Or The Mysteries* (1838, 3 vols, Saunders and Otley) compose a *Bildungsroman** or 'an experiment in typical fiction' as Bulwer called it. The narrative is set in the early years of the century. Ernest, a rich young student steeped in Kantian philosophy, loses himself on the moors. He takes shelter in the hovel of a criminal, Luke Darvil. Darvil's beautiful daughter Alice warns Ernest that his life is in danger. In gratitude, he helps her escape, and sets her up in a secluded cottage. Masked under the alias Butler, Maltravers then undertakes to educate the young woman. Instead, he seduces her. Alice is then abducted to Ireland by her father before Ernest knows she is pregnant. Over the subsequent years, the hero has various adventures and romances. His life is complicated by the enmity of Lumley Ferrers with whom he tours the Continent. In Italy, he falls in love with Valerie de Ventadour and meets the frenzied homicidal poet Cesarini, who eventually drowns himself in the Seine. Returned to England, Ernest enters Parliament and falls in love again with an heiress, Lady Florence Lascelles. He also becomes involved with Evelyn Cameron, whom he discovers may be his daughter. (She is not, it emerges.) Eventually after eighteen years, he is reunited with Alice (now ennobled as Lady Vargrave), a marriage symbolising the end of the philosophical quest which has been the hero's life.

ERRYM, Malcolm J. (i.e. James Malcolm Rymer, 1804–82?). Rymer was probably born in the Scottish highlands, of middle-class parents. In the 1830s he was resident in London, as a civil engineer. In this capacity he first met the publisher Edward Lloyd* at a Mechanics' Institute in London. Rymer subsequently turned to popular fiction and under his anagrammatic pseudonym 'Errym' produced sensationally popular penny serials for working-class readers. They include: *Ada The Betrayed* (1842); *The Black Monk* (1844); *The White Slave* (1844); *Varney The Vampire** (1847). For a while in the 1840s he was editor of *Lloyd's Penny Weekly Register* and must have turned out more low-grade serial fiction than will ever be traced. There is also an apparently irreducible confusion over what he and Thomas Peckett Prest* respectively wrote. In his prime, Rymer is said to have written up to ten novels simultaneously, using a battery of pseudonyms (he was particularly fond of teasing names such as 'Errym' and 'Malcolm J. Merry'). At some point in his career he visited the USA, where he was a popular writer. Rymer was productive up to the 1860s. *The Doge's Daughter* (1864) seems to have been his last work. He retired early and left an £8,000 estate on his death. BL 10. (Only a small small fraction of Rymer's multitudinous books and serials were deposited in the copyright collection.)

ESLER, E[rminda] Rentoul (née Rentoul, 1860?–1924). Born in Donegal, the daughter of a clergyman doctor, she was educated in France and Germany. In 1879, she graduated from the Royal University of Ireland, and in 1883 married a doctor, Robert Esler. The couple thereafter lived in London. Esler's fiction specialised in depictions of 'idyllic' village life and includes: *Almost A Pauper* (1888); *The Way Of Transgressors* (1890); and *The Way They Loved At Grimpat* (1894). These works are set in rural England. *A Maid Of The Manse* (1895) has an Irish setting as does Esler's best-received novel, *The Wardlaws* (1896), which covers a family's fifty years of genteel decay. BL 8. *WW*. Wol.

Esther Waters, George Moore, 1894, 1 vol, Walter Scott. Moore's most successful novel. The working-class heroine is forced out of home at the age of seventeen by a drunken stepfather, and goes into service at Woodview, a racing stables on the Sussex Downs. There, she is seduced by a fellow servant, William Latch, who abandons her to run away with a daughter of the house. Esther, now pregnant, is obliged to leave by her not otherwise unsympathetic mistress, Mrs Barfield. Moore vividly portrays Esther's subsequent grim experiences at the lying-in hospital and with the baby-farmer who offers to do away with her young son Jackie for a fiver. Esther is on the point of conversion by the Plymouth Brethren when Latch reappears, willing to make amends. He marries her and they set up a public house in Soho. But his activities as a bookmaker lead once more to ruin and he dies, leaving Esther destitute. At the end of the novel the worn-out heroine returns to find refuge at Woodview (now decayed) with her old employer Mrs Barfield. The novel is a conscious attempt by Moore to emulate Zola and Turgenev. Because of the frankness of its sexual episodes, circulating libraries refused to stock it. Walter Scott was an obscure publisher active in the 1890s and based in Newcastle upon Tyne.

The Eternal City, Hall Caine, 1901, 1 vol, Heinemann. Caine's most ambitious novel. The story opens in London. A little Italian boy, pressed into beggary by 'white slavers', is freezing to death in a snowstorm. He is rescued by a compatriot, a doctor Roselli (who is not a doctor, but a refugee politician, Prince Volonna). The boy, David, is adopted by his saviour and brought up with Volonna's daughter Roma. The novel jumps twenty years to Rome, currently in political ferment. Roma is the mistress of the Prime Minister, Baron Bonelli. David Rossi is now a Tolstoyan socialist, preaching a revolution based on the Lord's Prayer. The main plot of the novel is intricate and improbable. Roma and Rossi marry, but she is blackmailed by Bonelli into denouncing him. Bonelli is then assassinated by Roma, as it is thought (in fact she is innocent). Rossi is discovered to be the son of the Pope, and brings about a peaceable republic. Roma dies of a mysterious ailment. In an epilogue, the novel travels into the future and foresees a utopian 1950. C. Arthur Pearson commissioned *The Eternal City* for his *Ladies' Magazine* and later sued Caine on the grounds that the work was too immoral to publish.

The Eustace Diamonds, Anthony Trollope, 1872, 3 vols, Chapman and Hall. (Serialised in the *Fortnightly Review**, July 1871–February 1873.) The third of Trollope's *Palliser** novels, although the narrative is only loosely connected with the sequence's principals. Lizzie Greystock is an orphan who with the help of her aunt Lady Linlithgow contrives to trap the vicious Sir Florian Eustace into marriage. Within a year, she is a widow. The main part of the plot concerns the Eustace diamonds, which may or may not belong to her, given the ambiguity of law on the subject of heirlooms and 'paraphernalia'. Lizzie, who is quite unscrupulous, is determined to keep them. In a hotel in Carlisle thieves break into her bedroom and steal the metal safe in which she normally keeps her jewels. But, without letting the world know, she has secreted them under her pillow. Largely shunned by decent society, Lizzie surrounds herself with a raffish set of hangers-on. Her life is further complicated when the diamonds are really stolen from her house in London. They end up adorning the breast of a Russian princess on the Continent, and Lizzie is entirely disgraced by the criminal trial of the (London) thieves. During her widowhood she attempts to trap a number of eligible gentlemen into marriage. Lord Fawn is saved by his own timidity. Lizzie's cousin, the young MP Frank Greystock, is almost induced to jilt his governess fiancée Lucy Morris, but at the last moment pulls back. Finally, Lizzie is herself captured by the odious Joseph Emilius, a clergyman of middle-European Jewish background. As we learn in *Phineas Redux**, the union is mutually displeasing and does not last. *The Eustace Diamonds* was popular with readers, and shows Trollope adopting some of the detective* story tricks of Wilkie Collins's* *The Moonstone**.

Evan Harrington, George Meredith, 1861, 3 vols, Bradbury and Evans. (Serialised in *Once A Week**, February–October 1860 with illustrations by Charles Keene*, and the subtitle 'He Would Be A Gentleman'.) Meredith's anatomy of gentlemanliness. The hero is the son of a socially ambitious Lymport tailor, Melchisedec Harrington ('the Great Mel'). The novel charts Evan's rise in life. His three sisters have already risen by marriage; Harriet to a brewer; Caroline to an army officer; Louisa to a Portuguese nobleman. All the children keep their father's trade a secret. Evan himself escapes 'tailordom' by taking a minor diplomatic position in Lisbon where he falls in love with the envoy's niece, Rose Jocelyn. Most of the novel follows the working out of these emotional complications in England. Despite the secret of his shameful origins becoming public knowledge, Evan wins Rose's heart. But the match is broken by the meddling of Evan's sister, and the machinations of a rival suitor for Rose, Ferdinand Laxley. In defiance, Evan sets up as a tailor in London. All is made well when Rose's invalid cousin, Juliana, dies and leaves Evan (whom she loves) a fortune and property expected by the Jocelyns. Evan renounces this bequest in favour of the family and the marriage can go ahead. Meredith's grandfather was a Portsmouth tailor, and the novel has an autobiographical element.

EVANS, the Rev. Albert Eubule ('Roy Tellet', 1839–96). Evans was educated at Oxford, graduating BA in 1864. He was ordained shortly after, and pursued a clerical career in Slough and later in Derby. As 'Roy Tellet' he produced a number of popular novels. *The Outcasts* (1888) has a religious theme. *Prince Maskiloff* (1889) is a romance of modern Oxford. *Pastor And Prelate* (1892) is set in a Yorkshire town, and tells the sensational* story of a clergyman falsely accused of crime. *A Draught Of Lethe* (1891) is an out-and-out thriller, set in Germany. In his own name Evans produced a string of uplifting tract novels for the Christian Knowledge Society, including: *Elma's Trial* (1886); *The Stepmother's Will* (1888). 'Tellet', who published with most of the principal houses, was apparently a favourite writer with circulating library patrons. (Roy Tellet) BL 4. (A. E. Evans) BL 10. Boase. Wol.

Evelyn Innes, George Moore, 1898, 1 vol, T. Fisher Unwin. The heroine is a singer of Wagnerian opera. She is brought up in Dulwich by a father who has himself rejected a public career in music for the Church. Grown-up, Evelyn is followed through the conflicting pulls of love, art and religion. Born a Catholic, she succumbs to a charming but agnostic man of the world, Sir Owen Asher. Asher induces her to accompany him to the Continent, where she becomes his mistress. Evelyn subsequently falls under the spell of a mystic poet, Ulick Dean, in whose Celtic opera *Grania* she offers to sing. Finally a Roman Catholic priest, Monsignor Mostyn, induces her to renounce her immoral life and enter a sisterhood to spend her remaining years in penance. The narrative breaks off with Evelyn unsure of how her future course will be determined. The heroine is supposed to be a malicious portrait of John Oliver Hobbes* (i.e. Mrs Craigie) and Evelyn's second lover is partly based on the poet W. B. Yeats. Moore's original draft of *Evelyn Innes* was some 300,000 words long and he published the second half in the form of a sequel, *Sister Teresa* (1901). It chronicles the spiritual ordeals of the former Evelyn, under the discipline of conventual life. Peace only comes when she loses her magnificent voice. The conclusion finds her the replica of her father, a teacher of music who has subordinated all ambition to religious duty. Moore was himself a lapsed Catholic, and the religious tone of the works is ambiguous. Neither was popular.

EVERETT-GREEN, E[velyn] ('Cecil Adair', 1856–1932). Her father was G. P. Everett-Green, the artist, and her mother Mary (née Everett-Wood) was an author of historical books. Evelyn went to school in London, and to Bedford College. She then studied music for two years, and worked for a while as a nurse in a London hospital. Later, in 1883, Everett-Green moved to the country, where she wrote some novels for adults, and a vast amount of 'blameless fiction' for young people, much of it published under the auspices of the RTS*. Her full-length adult fiction includes: *The Last Of The Dacres* (1886); *A Clerk Of Oxford* (1898), a historical* tale of the Barons' wars; *Monica* (1900). The last of these recounts the story of Lady Monica Trevlyn who is hoodwinked into thinking her husband does not love her. Reviewers found its complications very feeble. *Olivia's Experiment* (1901) has the more interesting plot of an orphaned heroine unexpectedly finding herself the possessor of a foundling child. In the twentieth century, Everett-Green lived largely abroad and wrote among other things romances for adults under the pseudonym 'Cecil Adair'. BL 254. *WW. NCBEL*. Wol. Sad.

Eve's Ransom, George Gissing, 1895, 1 vol, Lawrence and Bullen. (Serialised in the *Illustrated London News**, January–March 1895.) The hero Maurice Hilliard is a Black Country drudge, who unexpectedly receives a windfall of £436 as conscience money from a former partner of his bankrupted father. He leaves his job in Dudley and goes on a spree to Paris, persuading the attractive Eve Madeley, a book-keeper with whom he is obsessed, to leave London and join him there (chaperoned). When they return to England, she agrees to marry him when he is able to support her in middle-class respectability. Hilliard sets out on the road to improvement by apprenticing himself as an architect. He is helped by a well-off friend, the industrialist Robert Narramore. Narramore also proposes to Eve, ignorant of Hilliard's interest in her. When he finds out, Hilliard sacrifices his claim and Eve marries Narramore so attaining the comfort she requires. Hilliard goes on eventually to succeed in architecture, a 'free man'. The novel is one of Gissing's more sardonic efforts.

EWING, Mrs Juliana Horatia (née Gatty, 1841–85). A leading Victorian author of children's* books. Born in Ecclesfield, Yorkshire, she was the daughter of a clergyman father (the Rev. Alfred Gatty) and an author mother, Margaret Gatty*, who also wrote for children (notably the long-running *Parables From Nature*, 1855–71). As a girl, Juliana was her mother's favourite child, showing precocious skill in drawing and music. She also entertained her seven siblings with improvised stories. (An activity cosily recalled in *Melchior's Dream.*) By all accounts, the Gatty household was unusually happy. Juliana published her first story ('A Bit Of Green', the touching story of a slum child's affection for a green plant) in the *Monthly Packet** in 1861 and brought out her first miscellaneous volume of fiction, *Melchior's Dream*, the following year. The collection takes its allegorical title from the mythical boy who refuses to share a bed with his brother and sits up all night by the fire. He is visited by personifications of Time and Death, a salutary experience which brings him back to a proper love for his siblings. Juliana and her sister Horatia Katherine edited *Aunt Judy's Magazine** (founded in 1866), after the death of their mother in 1873. The magazine was called after Juliana's family nickname. (Horatia was to keep the journal going until it wound up in 1885.) In 1867, she married Major Alexander 'Rex' Ewing (1830–95) of the Army pay corps and travelled with him round the world. A posting in Canada (1867–69) furnished settings for many of her later narratives. Her most admired story for children is *Jackanapes** (1883). Its theme of self-sacrifice by a gallant young fellow is handled with less cloying sentimentality than usual. Her other much reprinted fiction includes *Lob Lie By The Fire* (1873), the story of a gypsy child found by a pair of old spinsters under a bush. They adopt him, he runs away to join the army, returns and secretly makes amends until he feels morally fit to announce himself to his guardians. The Ewings lived much of their later married life at Aldershot. In 1879, Ewing collapsed while travelling to Malta with her husband, now a senior officer. She spent the remainder of her life quietly in Devonshire and at Bath, dying prematurely of cancer of the spine. BL 19. *DNB. RM. NCBEL.* Wol.

An Eye For An Eye, Anthony Trollope, 1879, 2 vols, Chapman and Hall. (Serialised in the *Whitehall Review*, August 1878–February 1879.) A novella of violent passion, set in Ireland. An aristocratic English cavalry officer, Fred Neville, is stationed in Co. Clare where he seduces a local girl, Kate O'Hara. Fred inherits an earldom in England and intends to desert Kate, who is pregnant. Her mother pushes him over the cliffs. She is consigned to a lunatic asylum and Kate goes to live with her reprobate father in France. The novel is more passionate than most of Trollope's tales, possibly the outcome of its wild Irish setting.

F

Fabiola, Or The Church Of The Catacombs, Nicholas Wiseman, 1854, 1 vol, Burns and Lambert. The first title in Cardinal Nicholas Wiseman's 'Catholic Popular Library', designed to counter-attack Charles Kingsley's* *Hypatia** (1853) on its own classical historical ground. It opens: 'It is on an afternoon in September of the year 302, that we invite our reader to accompany us through the streets of Rome.' Fabiola is a patrician maiden who is introduced to Christianity by Syra, one of her slave girls from Antioch. It is a period of tribulation for the Church, which is in hiding, and the martyrdom of the emperor's favourite, Sebastian, and Fabiola's cousin, Agnes (both saints' deaths are described in gruesome detail), persuade the heroine to embrace the new faith. She improbably survives the subsequent persecution and lives to see the final victory of Christianity in 312 AD. Wiseman's novel, which is heavily detailed and pedantic, was popular and much reprinted.

FAITHFULL, Emily (1836–95). Feminist and publisher. Faithfull was born at Headley Rectory, Surrey, the youngest daughter of a clergyman. She went to school in Kensington, but retained a strong feeling for the English countryside throughout her life. At the age of twenty-one, she was presented at Court. A couple of years later, she broke with her background to associate herself in 1859 with the Langham Place group of feminist militants. She interested herself particularly in the employment of women and in 1860 founded her Victoria Press, entirely staffed by females. The venture was successful and in 1862 she was appointed 'Printer and Publisher in Ordinary to her Majesty' (a purely honorary title). In 1863, Faithfull founded the *Victoria Magazine* which ran until 1880. Although the journal carried some fiction (by male as well as female writers) its main function was as a political organ for the women's movement. Faithfull remained single all her life, but was unpleasantly involved in the highly publicised divorce case in 1864 between Henry (later Admiral) and Helen Codrington. In 1868, Faithfull wrote, printed and published a novel, *Change Upon Change, A Love Story* (1868). The jilted and jilting heroine, Tiny Harewood, was found feeble by reviewers although the work generally was regarded as an interesting oddity. After leading a man on, for inscrutable reasons, the heroine crushes him by a letter of dismissal, the novel ending: 'The iron had entered Wilfred's soul as only the hand of Tiny could have driven it.' In 1872–73, Faithfull lectured in America and her novel was published there as *A Reed Shaken With The Wind* (1873). She was given a Civil List pension in 1889 and died six years later in Manchester. BL 1. Boase. Sad.

FALKNER, J[ohn] Meade (1858–1932). The eldest son of a clergyman, Falkner was born in Wiltshire and educated at Marlborough School and Oxford, graduating with a degree in history in 1882. In adult life he was passionately interested in ecclesiastical and county history. He supported himself, however, by tutoring the sons of Sir Andrew Noble, one of the directors of the armaments firm Armstrong and Co. When his teaching was no longer required, Falkner himself went to work for the company, and eventually rose to be chairman of the board, 'a position in which', his biographer notes, 'he can hardly be called a success'. In addition to historical scholarship and various county guidebooks for John Murray*, Falkner wrote three very successful works of fiction. *The Lost Stradivarius* (1895) is a 'psychic romance' centred on a violin, unearthed in Oxford, which gradually takes possession of an undergraduate. *Moonfleet* (1898) is a Stevensonian* romance, set in eighteenth-century Hampshire and Dorset. Its plot concerns a lost diamond and various smuggling adventures ensue. *The Nebuly Coat* (1903) is another tale of mystery, set in a quiet cathedral town and involving a quantity of the church history in which the author was expert. BL 3. *DNB*. RM. *NCBEL*. Wol.

Fantasy. Fantasy as a staple fictional commodity, for either juvenile or adult readers, first emerges in the Victorian period, although its origins can be traced back to the Romantic poets (notably Coleridge). In 1823, the Grimm brothers' tales were first translated by a London lawyer, Edgar Taylor, and published in England. They were immensely successful and were widely reprinted, often with illustrations by George Cruikshank*. In 1839–41, E. W. Lane's translation of *The Arabian Nights* was published and in the mid-1840s numerous volumes of Hans Christian Andersen's tales. In 1847 Andersen visited England and stayed with Dickens* (whose fantastic *Christmas Carol** had been published in 1843). These works, together with the general revival of interest in Gothic, inspired a stream of experiments in fantasy by major and minor British authors. They include: F. E. Paget's* *The Hope Of The Katzekopfs* (1844); Ruskin's* *The King Of The Golden River** (1851); George MacDonald's* *Phantastes** (1858); Thackeray's* *The Rose And The Ring** (1855); Kingsley's* *The Water-Babies** (1863); Lewis Carroll's* *Alice's Adventures In Wonderland** (1865). A number of late Victorian writers such as Jean Ingelow*, William Morris*, Arthur Machen*, F. Anstey*, Oscar Wilde* and Andrew Lang* came to specialise in fantasy as a genre which had evolved into full sophistication by the 1880s. Richard Burton's authoritative translation of *The Arabian Nights* also appeared in this decade, in 1885-88. Fantasy also feeds into the early development of science fiction*, as practised by H. G. Wells*.

Far From The Madding Crowd, Thomas Hardy, 1874, 2 vols, Smith, Elder. (Serialised in *Cornhill**, January–December 1874, illustrated by H. Allingham*.) The Wessex* novel with which Hardy broke through into general popularity. The story opens with a description of Gabriel Oak, a sheep farmer who is in love with the beautiful but capricious Bathsheba Everdene, just now visiting her aunt at a nearby farm. Oak's hopes of proposing are dashed when a badly trained dog drives his flock of ewes over a cliff. Bathsheba, now the owner of a fine property, is subsequently courted by the dashing Sergeant Troy. With a hypnotising display of swordmanship he dazzles and wins her. Meanwhile his other deserted love, Fanny Robin, dies with her child in the workhouse. As a husband, Troy has abused Bathsheba. Finally, he disappears and is thought drowned. Another former suitor enters

Bathsheba's life, the rich gentleman farmer William Boldwood. She promises to marry him in six years. But as the house is being prepared for Christmas festivity, Troy returns to reclaim his wife. Boldwood takes a shotgun from the wall, and murders his rival. At his trial he is found mad, and imprisoned for life with the criminally insane. Bathsheba finally and quietly marries the faithful Oak who has been managing her farm all the while. The narrative was the most complex and melodramatic Hardy had hitherto attempted.

Fardorougha The Miser, Or The Convicts Of Lisnamona, William Carleton, 1839, 1 vol, Curry. (Serialised in the *Dublin University Magazine**, irregularly, February 1837–February 1838.) Carleton's most powerful novel. The story starts with the birth of a child, Connor, after thirteen years of marriage, between Fardorougha, a peasant farmer, and his wife Honor O'Donovan. The father's temperamental miserliness is complicated and exacerbated by his love for his son. He takes on as a servant in his household Bartle Flanagan, the son of a man he previously ruined. Bartle, a secret Ribbonman, plots O'Donovan's downfall. He burns the barn of Bodagh Buie (whose daughter Una has been refused Connor in marriage, because of Fardorougha's meanness). Connor is condemned to hang, but the sentence is commuted on account of his gentle nature. Suffering tempers Fardorougha, who sells up his farm and with his wife follows Connor to transportation in New South Wales. Bartle is eventually caught and confesses. The O'Donovans are brought back by public subscription to their home. The novel is notable for its close depiction of Irish subsistence farming life and for its sympathetic analysis of avarice, encouraged in Ireland as it was by the ever-present likelihood of ruin and starvation.

FARGUS, Frederick John ('Hugh Conway', 1847–85). Born in Bristol, he was the son of an auctioneer. As a boy, his ambition was to go to sea. (Fargus took his *nom de plume* from the name of his school frigate, the *Conway*.) This desire was frustrated by his father, who directed him instead towards a sensible career in accountancy. From the age of seventeen, Fargus wrote songs for the stage and short tales, with some local success. In 1868, his father died and he took over the family auctioneering business, carrying it on until two years before his own death. He married in 1871. His first published volume was a collection of poems in 1879. It was followed two years later by a collection of tales. Fargus's writing was encouraged by the leading Bristol publisher, Arrowsmith* and in 1881 the more prestigious *Blackwood's Magazine** accepted his story, 'The Secret Of The Stradivarius'. And world-wide fame came in 1884 with his first full-length fiction, *Called Back**. Published by Arrowsmith at 1s. this sensational story of murder, amnesia, Siberian exile, political assassination and detection made a tremendous hit. It was translated all over Europe, a dramatised version ran for a year and the novel sold over 350,000 copies in four years. The triumph was quite unexpected; the first agreement for the novel specified £150 payment for 10,000 copies. Before his premature death from tuberculosis (aggravated by typhoid) in Monte Carlo, Fargus published another nine volumes of fiction, including *A Cardinal Sin* (1886), or 'The Red Hill Mystery', and *Living Or Dead* (1886). The second of these evidently contains a recollection of the author's childhood in Bristol. *Somebody's Story* (1886) is a gimmicky short story, published in facsimile hand-writing, followed by an orthodox printed transcription of the 'confession'. Fargus's late work, *A Family Affair* (1885), also appeared posthumously. The study of two bachelor brothers, the Talberts of Oakbury, it was well received, and suggests that given a longer life he might have developed into a writer of consequence. BL 10. *DNB. NCBEL.* Wol. Sad.

FARJEON, Benjamin [Leopold] (1838–1903; some accounts give his date of birth as 1833). Farjeon's father, Jacob, was a London merchant and an orthodox Jew newly come to Europe from North Africa. Young Farjeon was brought up in some poverty, 'almost without education' in Whitechapel. At thirteen, after reading Bulwer-Lytton's* *The Caxtons*, he determined on authorship as his career, allegedly declaring: 'I should be content to die if I had written such a book.' He began working life as a printer's devil at fourteen on the *Nonconformist* newspaper. He broke with his family at the age of seventeen, and went off to make his fortune in the Australian goldfields, travelling steerage to Melbourne. On the eighty-day voyage he completed his first sizeable piece of writing. He later moved on to New Zealand at the age of twenty-three, where he supported himself by journalism, working on the *Otago Daily Times* with Julius Vogel*. About the same period, Farjeon began to write fiction. From the first, the dominating influence on his writing was Dickens*, whose disciple he proclaimed himself. In 1866, his story of a Melbourne street arab, *Grif*, enjoyed considerable success. (The work was not however published in Britain until 1870.) The young vagrant hero is closely modelled on Jo in Dickens's *Bleak House* (1852), even down to the catch-phrase: 'He wos wery good to me, he wos.' A couple of years later, in 1868, Farjeon returned to England, encouraged by a letter from his idol, offering to accept 'any original communication' in *All The Year Round*. Over the following ten years, he turned out a stream of novels, mostly with the publisher Tinsley*. They show the strong influence of Dickens, Walter Besant* and Wilkie Collins*. *Blade O' Grass* (1871), a Christmas* story, has a hackneyed plot, in which twin sisters are adopted, one by a respectable and one by a slum family, with predictable consequences. Rather better is the cockney* novel, set in Soho, *London's Heart* (1873). Other Farjeon titles include: *Joshua Marvel* (1871), a picaresque nautical* tale with elopement and shipwreck at its centre; *The Duchess of Rosemary Lane* (1876); *Great Porter Square, A Mystery* (1885), a detective* story with the inevitable London setting; *Toilers Of Babylon* (1888); *For The Defence* (1891); *The Last Tenant* (1893), a Pooteresque comedy of middle-class London life with genteel house-hunting as its main business; *Aaron The Jew* (1894). The last is a powerful indictment of anti-semitism in the 1870s. The hero, Aaron Cohen, is a devout Jew whose daughter, Ruth, is in fact a secretly adopted Gentile. *Aaron The Jew* is one of four novels Farjeon wrote on the topic of race. The others include: *Solomon Isaacs* (1877) and *Pride Of Race* (1901). The second of these is the saga of the rise and fall of Moses Mendoza and his Anglicized son Raphael. Farjeon also wrote successful plays and was actively connected with the theatre. In 1877 he married Margaret, the daughter of the American actor, Joseph Jefferson. She was a Protestant. Farjeon did not himself convert to Christianity, but neither did he impose Judaism on his children. In later life he gave popular readings of his short pieces (like *Blade O' Grass*) in

America, following the touring example of his mentor Dickens. He died comfortably off in Hampstead. His daughter, the well-known children's author Eleanor Farjeon (1881–1965), evoked her father's household vividly and his personality fondly in *A Nursery In The Nineties* (1935). Especially poignant is her description of his waning grip on public popularity at the turn of the century. BL 51. *DNB*. RM. *NCBEL*. Wol. Sad.

FARRAR, [Dean] Frederic W[illiam] (1831–1903). Novelist, historian and theologian. Farrar was born in Bombay, where his father was a church missionary. At the age of three, he was sent back to England and the care of maiden aunts in Aylesbury. The young Farrar was sent as a boarder to King William's College in the Isle of Man, the original of his fictional 'Roslyn School'. He rose to be head boy. After attending university in London and Trinity College, Cambridge (where he took a first-class degree in classics and maths in 1854 and won the Chancellor's medal for poetry), he was ordained priest in 1857. Farrar had meanwhile embarked on his teaching career at Harrow School where he was a house-master from 1855 to 1871, and at Marlborough College where he was headmaster from 1871 to 1876 and where he wrote his *Life Of Christ*. He subsequently had a successful career as a churchman, eventually becoming Chaplain to Queen Victoria and to the House of Commons and earning promotion in 1895 to Dean of Canterbury. In the last of these posts he was energetic in raising funds for the repair of the Cathedral. He married in 1860, fathering five sons and five daughters. Farrar actively involved himself in theological controversy, on the question of damnation (about which his views were liberal). He also wrote a famous novel of Victorian school life, *Eric, Or Little By Little** (1858), which shows both his religious faith and his schoolmasterly sagacity. His other fiction (mainly aimed at juveniles) includes: *St Winifred's, Or The World Of School* (1862); *Julian Home* (1859), a moralistic novel of college life at 'St Werner's' college, 'Camford'; *Darkness And Dawn, Or Scenes In The Days Of Nero* (1891), a story of martyrdom with climactic scenes of St Paul's defiance of the pagan emperor; *Gathering Clouds, A Tale Of The Days Of Saint Chrysostom* (1895). The last two are specifically aimed to chronicle the struggles of early Christianity and are written in the style of C. Kingsley's* *Hypatia**. Farrar was a member of the Royal Society, to which he was proposed by Charles Darwin. As an educationalist, he opposed excessive corporal punishment and advocated expansion of the school curriculum beyond its traditional classicism. Although a lesser figure than Dr Arnold of Rugby and Thomas Hughes*, he was an architect of the extraordinarily durable English public school ethos. He died after a long, paralysing illness. BL 6. *DNB*. *NCBEL*. Wol. Sad.

FARRER, Henrietta Louisa [Lear] (1824–96). The youngest daughter of James Farrer, a master in Chancery, she began publishing pious volumes for juveniles early in life. They include: *Baby's Baptism* (1848); *Carry And Milly* (1848); *The Little Traveller* (1849). In 1859, she married the Rev. Sidney Lear, a clergyman five years younger than her. When he died prematurely in 1867, Farrer settled herself in a house in Salisbury Cathedral Close and went on to become one of the more prolific Victorian writers for children with more than fifty works, including some fiction, to her credit. BL 6. Boase. Wol.

Felix Holt, The Radical, George Eliot, 1866, 3 vols, Blackwood. Eliot's social problem* novel. Set in the period of the first Reform Bill of 1832, it clearly alludes to the second bill, of 1866–67. The hero is a young man of the people. The son of a quack apothecary he has himself taken up the trade of watch repairing, although his intellectual qualities could have made a middle-class life available to him. Felix maintains that working-class advance is less dependent on legislation than moral regeneration. He is contrasted with the aristocratic 'radical' Harold Transome. Transome, a dilettante, has returned to England from luxurious life abroad to fight the coming election. The heroine of the novel is Esther Lyon, the supposed daughter of an energetic nonconformist minister. Both Esther and Harold discover an unexpected parentage. Esther is the adopted daughter of a Frenchwoman whom the Reverend Lyon once passionately loved. And to his horror, Harold finds he is the illegitimate son of Matthew Jermyn, a lawyer whom he has always instinctively hated. (The recognition scene, as both men look into a mirror, is a powerful moment in the narrative.) The action climaxes with a riot which Felix is helpless to control. He is tried, and only saved from transportation by Esther's testimony. The narrative has an extraordinarily complicated legal subplot, to do with the ownership of the Transome estate which Esther eventually inherits, then renounces to throw in her lot with a pardoned Felix. Critics agree in finding the best thing in the novel the depiction of Mrs Transome, a woman of indomitable will worn out by the guilty secret in her past.

FENN, George Manville (1831–1909). Henty's* closest rival, as a spinner of manly yarns for juvenile readers. Fenn was born in Pimlico, London, the eldest of three sons and reportedly received little early education. As he later wrote: 'At the age of thirteen, I was thrown entirely on my own resources. My father met with troubles and I had to fight my own way.' As a young man, he attended Battersea Training College for Teachers (1851–54) where he was influenced by the educationalist, Samuel Clark. In the late 1850s, Fenn taught in Lincolnshire where in 1855 he married. (There were to be eight children, six of them daughters.) In 1862, he bought a small press, and started his own poetry magazine. Eventually, he drifted out of teaching into the more congenial world of London journalism and by the mid-1860s was living by his pen. Fenn was a talented reporter. His pieces on working-class life, published in the *Star* by Justin McCarthy* and republished as 'Readings By Starlight', are among the best of their kind. In 1864, Dickens* acccepted the story *In Jeopardy* for *All The Year Round**, and Fenn embarked on a career in fiction. *Hollowdell Grange*, his first tale for boys, was published in 1867. Thereafter, his production was torrential. Around 170 books (largely fiction and natural history, for juvenile readers) were turned out in the next forty years. He also published over a thousand articles for the popular press. In 1870, Fenn took over the editorship of *Cassell's Magazine*. And in 1873, he purchased *Once A Week** from James Rice*, and carried the journal on (as a loss-making venture) until 1879, by which time it was wholly unprofitable. Fenn was a lover of the English countryside, gardening and books. From 1889, he lived in some comfort at Syon Lodge, Isleworth, earning a handsome living from his writing. He died shortly after finishing his disciple's life of Henty, in 1909. In addition to his juvenile fiction, Fenn produced some multi-volume novels for adults, such as: *The Sapphire Cross* (1871); *The New Mistress* (1883); *The Master Of The Ceremonies* (1886), a period melodrama, set in the fashionable seaside resort of 'Saltinville' in the Regency period; *The White Virgin* (1894), a story of mining. He wrote adventure stories for boys set everywhere and at many different historical periods. But his best works are reckoned to be those drawing on his knowledge of coastal Devon and Cornwall (e.g. *Cormorant Crag*, 1895, 'A Tale Of Smuggling Days'). BL 164. *DNB. NCBEL.* Wol.

The Fifth Form At St Dominic's, Talbot Baines Reed, 1887, 1 vol, RTS. (First serialised in the *Boy's Own Paper**, 1881–82, illustrated by Gordon Browne.) The most famous of late-Victorian public school stories (although its author, a former day-boy at the City of London School, had no first-hand experience of the institution which he immortalised). The fifth form at St Dominic's is dominated by Horace Wraysford and Oliver Greenfield, who conduct ceaseless warfare against their foes in the sixth, particularly the cad Loman (closely related in type to Thomas Hughes's* magnificent rotter, Flashman, in *Tom Brown's Schooldays**). The heroes of the fifth also patronise the 'tadpoles and guinea pigs of the fourth' a class below them. The main episode, in a very diffuse plot, concerns Oliver's being suspected of stealing the £50 Nightingale scholarship examination paper from the head's study. In fact, the culprit is Loman, who needs the prize to pay off Cripps, the dubious landlord at the Cockchafer Inn. The story is strong on slang, school types and such rituals as prize days and football matches.

FILDES, [Sir Samuel] Luke (1844–1927). Illustrator. Fildes was born at Liverpool and later studied at the Royal Academy Schools in London. He fell in with the new 1860s style of magazine illustration and began his career working for *Cornhill**, *Once A Week** and the *Graphic*. Dickens* liked his naturalistic designs and contracted Fildes for the unfinished *Edwin Drood** (1870). He also did the famous posthumous study of the great novelist's 'empty chair'. Among other novels, Fildes illustrated serial versions or reprints of Charles Reade's* *Peg Woffington** and *Griffith Gaunt**; Wilkie Collins's* *The Law And The Lady*. But after 1872, he turned his efforts more to painting. He was elected to the Royal Academy in 1887 and knighted in 1906. *DNB.* Hou.

FINDLATER, Jane Helen (1866–1946) and Mary (b. 1865). Born in rural Lochearnhead, the Findlater sisters were daughters of a Kirk minister and educated at home in their birthplace and later at Prestonpans. They never married, and in later life set up home together at Rye in Sussex. Under their separate names and jointly they wrote Scottish tales set mainly in and around Edinburgh where they had been brought up. Their early writing was carried out in conditions of some hardship, Jane actually writing her first novel on paper discarded by a neighbourhood grocer. Mary produced as her independent work *Over The Hills* (1897), a portrait of spinster life in 'Ubster'; *Betty Musgrave* (1899) and *A Narrow Way* (1901). The last is a relatively ambitious chronicle of a young girl's struggle to escape the Presbyterian repression of her aunt's household, stimulated as she is by love and Rossetti's sonnets. Jane put out as her sole work the more atmospheric *The Green Graves Of Balgowrie* (1896) and *A Daughter Of Strife* (1897), an eighteenth-century tale. Of the sisters, Jane was the more ambitious literary stylist. Together, they published *Tales That Are Told* (1901). The Findlater sisters continued writing their mild stories well into the twentieth century by which time their brief vogue had faded. (JHF) BL 10. (MF) BL 7. (JHF and MF) BL 5.

FISHER, Admiral William (1780–1852). Fisher was born in Norfolk, and entered the navy at fifteen. He served during the Napoleonic Wars, and from 1816 to 1817 saw some particularly exciting action against slavers and pirates off the Guinea coast. He was made rear admiral in 1847. During his retirement, he wrote two novels: *The Petrel, Or Love On The Ocean* (1850) and *Ralph Rutherford* (1851). The first of these, a nautical* picaresque tale of a midshipman's adventures, enjoyed some success, but more for the credentials of its gallant author than its minimal literary worth. BL 2. *DNB*. Wol.

FITZGERALD, Percy H[etherington] ('Gilbert Dyce', 1834–1925). Born in Co. Louth, Ireland, Fitzgerald was educated at the Catholic school, Stonyhurst, and at Trinity College, Dublin. He subsequently qualified as an Irish barrister, and in time rose to the rank of Crown Prosecutor. His literary output consists mainly of works of history, with a specialism in the Hanoverian era. He was a friend of John Forster who first introduced him to Dickens* and encouraged him to write in 1856. Fitzgerald had further encouragement from Richard Bentley* and he remained faithful as an author to that publishing house throughout his career. Fitzgerald contributed usefully to early Dickens scholarship and his two-volume *Memoirs Of An Author* (1895) offers the closest record of the sub-Dickensian bohemian coterie of authors: Edmund Yates*, G. A. Sala*, Wilkie Collins*, etc. In the 1860s and 1870s, Fitzgerald wrote a number of light novels usually with flirts, fops and lovers prominent in them. His first novel (serialised in the *Dublin University Magazine**) was *Mildrington The Barrister* (1863) and his best selling work was *Bella Donna, Or The Cross Before The Name* (1864). Fitzgerald capitalised on its popularity with two sequels: *Jenny Bell* (1866) and *Seventy-Five Brooke Street* (1867). Fitzgerald's pen was very fluent, and it was his practice to run two serials simultaneously ('the Briarean system', as he called it). Half a dozen of his novels were serialised in *All The Year Round**. His fiction includes: *Fairy Alice* (1865); *The Second Mrs Tillotson* (1866); *The Dear Girl* (1868); *Beauty Talbot* (1870); *The Middle Aged Lover* (1873); *The Parvenu Family* (1876). The last, subtitled 'Phoebe, Girl And Wife' is a typical Fitzgerald romance chronicling Phoebe Dawson as she progresses from finishing school in the first volume to troubled marriage into the parvenu Pringle family in the second volume and resolution of all problems in the third. *Fatal Zero* (1886), written in the form of a Homburg diary, is a powerful study of gambling mania. At the end of his life, Fitzgerald had some 200 published volumes to his name, but he effectively gave up writing fiction after the late 1870s in favour of works of popular eighteenth-century history. In *Recreations Of A Literary Man, Or Does Writing Pay?* (1882), Fitzgerald reckoned that his fiction brought him close on £3,000. BL 21. *WW. NCBEL*. Wol. Sad.

The Fixed Period, Anthony Trollope, 1882, 2 vols, Blackwoods. (Serialised in *Blackwood's Magazine*, October 1881–March 1882.) The oddest item in all Trollope's fiction. *The Fixed Period* is set in the future republic of Britannula, an island off Australia. The president has decreed that all citizens reaching the age of sixty-seven are to enter a 'college'. There, they will be prepared for death at age sixty-eight. (Trollope was sixty-seven when he wrote the story and died five months before his sixty-eighth birthday.) The first candidate for this euthanasia, Gabriel Crasweller, loses his enthusiasm for the 'fixed period' scheme as his own term approaches. Rescue is provided by the British navy, which returns Britannula to the rational rule of the Empire. Critics have sneered at the poverty of science fiction* imagination in this work. But the story is a nice reworking of Trollope's *The Warden* (1855) where the elderly inhabitants of Hiram's Hospital are prepared for death in more traditional fashion.

FLETCHER, Alfred H. (1859–1902?). Fletcher was born and brought up in Chelmsford, and as a young man worked on various local Essex newspapers. He succeeded in journalism, and eventually became managing editor of the *Yorkshire Herald* in 1899. Out of his experience in the North he wrote a number of short stories and novels, including: *Lost In The Mine, A Tale Of The Great Coal Strike* (1896) and *Clevelands Of The Peak, A Derbyshire Romance* (1897). BL 2. *WW*.

FLETCHER, J[oseph] S[mith] (1863–1935). Fletcher was born and raised in Halifax, Yorkshire, a clergyman's son. He was educated privately and worked as a journalist in London in the early 1880s, returning as leader writer for the Leeds *Mercury* in the 1890s. Fletcher wrote extensively on rural life, especially that of his native Yorkshire. (In various papers, he wrote a syndicated column as 'A Son Of The Soil'.) As a senior provincial newsman he was special correspondent for the *Yorkshire Post* at the King's coronation in 1902. Among his many books are several novels in the style of Jefferies*: *The Wonderful Wapentake* (1894); *Where Highways Cross* (1895); *Life In Arcadia* (1896); *From The Broad Acres* (1899). All of these are prominently set in Yorkshire and a number of them present a grim picture of the region. Fletcher also wrote simple thrillers such as *Morrison's Machine* (1900), the story of a stolen invention, and a large number of adventure yarns for boys. According to Michael Sadleir, of all Fletcher's voluminous work, the early historical* novel *When Charles I Was King* (1892) has lasted best. Narrated by 'William Dale, Yorkshireman' the romance contains local as well as national history of the Civil War period. BL 39. *WW*. Wol. Sad. RLF.

FORBES, the Hon. Mrs Walter [Eveline Louisa Michell] (née Farwell, 1866–1924). Little is known of her life. Eveline Farwell was born in Tettenhall, the granddaughter of an admiral, after whom ('Michell') she was named, and was educated at home. In 1888 she married Walter Forbes, a captain in the Gordon Highlanders and the son of a baron, and the couple subsequently lived in the West End of London. Her fiction includes: *Fingers And Fortune* (1886); *Her Last Run* (1888); *Blight* (1897). In the last, Blight is the nickname of a *femme fatale* who cuts a swathe through English aristocratic society. Her fiction is adorned by profuse quotation and high-flown language. Reviewers found Forbes's addiction to the upper classes absurd. BL 10. *WW*.

The Forest Lovers, Maurice Hewlett, 1898, 1 vol, Macmillan. An extremely popular and sophisticated medieval romance of the 1890s. The young knight Prosper le Gai leaves the household of his elder brother, Baron Malise, on an undefined quest which brings him to Morgraunt Forest. There he rescues Isoult la Desirous from the clutches of a lecherous monk, Dom Galors, who has terrified the girl with the information that her mother was a witch. A long feud ensues, during which Prosper and Isoult marry and only afterwards fall in love. Galors (now a knight in armour) abducts the girl and in a final combat Prosper slays him, tying his severed head to his saddle bow ('the times were grim times'). Isoult is revealed to be the highborn Lady Pietosa and the lovers live happily ever after. The tone of the work verges on the fey.

FORTESCUE, the Hon. John William (1859–1933). The fifth son of an earl, Fortescue was born in Madeira. He was brought up in Barnstaple, and educated at Harrow and Trinity College, Cambridge. On leaving university, he tried law but in 1880 left it for the study of military history. As a military historian his output was large and distinguished. For a nine-year-old nephew, however, Fortescue wrote a charming animal tale set on Exmoor, *The Story Of A Red Deer* (1897). The work became very popular and has been much reprinted. Fortescue wrote another tale for children, *The Drummer's Coat* (1899), illustrated by H. M. Brock*. BL 2. *DNB*.

The Fortnightly Review (1865–1954). The *Fortnightly* was devised by Frederic Chapman (of the publishing firm, Chapman and Hall*), Anthony Trollope* and George Henry Lewes* (its editor, 1865–66) as an English equivalent of the *Revue Des Deux Mondes*. It was Liberal in politics, and pitched at a higher intellectual level than other English journals of its class. At Trollope's insistence, its reviews were signed, a departure from usual Victorian practice. The first issues (May 1865–January 1866) serialised Trollope's *The Belton Estate*, and altogether three of his novels (including *The Eustace Diamonds*) appeared in its pages. It also serialised Meredith's* *Diana Of The Crossways** and four other of his major novels. Soon after publication, the journal ran into financial difficulties. Paradoxically, it became a monthly after November 1866 around which time Trollope ceased to be a leading spirit. And in 1867, John Morley took over the editorship which he held until 1882 and under his management, the journal established itself as a progressive organ for the Victorian intelligentsia. It had a late lease of life under the vigorous proprietorship and editorship of Frank Harris*, 1886–94, who recruited most of the leaders of late Victorian literature to the paper. *WI. BLM*.

FOTHERGILL, Miss Jessie (1851–91). Jessie Fothergill was born in Manchester, the eldest child of a cotton merchant who died when she was fifteen leaving his dependants 'much reduced in circumstances'. Her family background was northern Quaker and she was educated at boarding school in Harrogate. Fothergill never married, living most of her adult life quietly twenty miles from where she was born, at Littleborough. From this vantage point she closely observed the life led by cotton workers and carefully transcribed it into her later fiction. In 1874, Fothergill visited Germany and on her return she published a novel of Lancashire life, *Healey, A*

Romance (1875). Her German experience (together with her lifelong love of music) is also reflected in her second novel, *The First Violin* (1877). Its English heroine, May Wedderburn, escapes marriage by travelling to Germany where, after various mishaps, her destiny becomes intertwined with that of a leading violinist, Eugen Courvoisier, in whose background there is a mystery to do with accusations of forgery. May resourcefully puts all right. The novel (which was first serialised in *Temple Bar**) enjoyed considerable popularity and was later successfully dramatised. Her price as an author gradually rose to a very respectable £600 a novel. Most of her life she was a semi-invalid with a lung disorder and in later life she travelled extensively to avoid the British winter. Fothergill moved to Rome in 1890, and died in Berne. *Aldyth* (1876) is the story of a girl who refuses to emigrate with her lover, in order to look after her sisters, one of whom then treacherously steals him from her. The disappointed heroine thereafter 'lived for all, and in so living fulfilled her mission upon earth'. Her other fiction includes: *Probation* (1879), a tale of the disastrously sudden 1863 cotton famine caused by the American war; *Kith And Kin* (1881), whose hero is the disinherited grandson of a wealthy squire, and has to earn his living as a clerk; *Borderland* (1886), a country town chronicle set around the river 'Tees'; *The Lasses Of Leverhouse* (1888), a Lancashire tale first published in the local *Bolton Journal.* Reviewers credited Fothergill with telling a straightforward narrative well, and with creating consistently interesting minor characters. She had an authentic feel for northern dialect. Much of her fiction was published anonymously, in keeping with her reticent personality. She had a sister, Caroline Fothergill, who also wrote novels of much the same unambitious kind. BL 13. *DNB.* Wol. Sad.

FOTHERGILL, John M[ilner] (1841–88). Fothergill was born in Westmorland and studied medicine at the University of Edinburgh, at Vienna and at Berlin. After a short period practising in Leeds in the early 1870s, he moved to London, where he made an international reputation for himself as a heart specialist. For reasons which are mysterious, Fothergill wrote and published in 1884 a three-volume novel, *Gaythorne Hall,* dealing with English political agitation between the first Reform Act and the Chartist movement of the 1840s. Reviewers were respectful but rather baffled by the work. BL 1. *DNB.* Wol.

Foul Play, Charles Reade and Dion Boucicault, 1868, 3 vols, Bradbury and Evans. (Serialised in *Once A Week**, January–June 1868.) A novel with a purpose, written against the current scandal of scuttling. (This was the period in which the MP, Samuel Plimsoll, introduced his reforms in shipping regulation.) The hero, Robert Penfold, is originally encountered as tutor to Arthur Wardlaw, the villain. Penfold is falsely accused of forgery and transported. On his release, he books a passage aboard a ship owned by the Wardlaws. The owners intend to scuttle it in the Pacific, for the marine insurance. Ironically, a passenger on board is Arthur's ailing fiancée, Helen. After the shipwreck, Robert finds himself alone on a desert island with Helen. He masquerades as a missionary, the Rev. Mr Hazel, and performs prodigies of chivalrous service. As George Orwell observed: 'he is hero, saint, scholar, gentleman, athlete, pugilist, navigator, physiologist, botanist, blacksmith and carpenter all rolled into one. It is only a month or two before this wonderful clergyman has the desert island running like a West End hotel.' Robert makes his fortune from the island's natural resources, Helen recovers her health, Arthur goes mad. Reade (without Boucicault) adapted *Foul Play* for the stage in 1876, as *The Scuttled Ship*.

The Fourth Generation, Walter Besant, 1900, 1 vol, Chatto. (A very short version of the novel was first published in the Rationalist magazine, the *Humanitarian*, as 'To The Third And Fourth Generation', in 1893). Besant's most ambitious novel, a wide-ranging investigation of the theme of genetic consequence clearly inspired by Ibsen. The narrative opens with a striking depiction of an old man walking solitary in an overgrown garden in Buckinghamshire. He is Algernon Campaigne. For seventy years, since the mysterious murder of his best friend Langley Holme in 1826, the old man has uttered not a word. The main subsequent action follows the career of the old man's great-grandson, Leonard Campaigne, a rising young lawyer and politician. Leonard initially has no idea of any stain on his family's history. But a disreputable trickster, Uncle Fred, returns from Australia to embarrass him. Another uncle, Christopher, supposed to be a successful barrister is disclosed to be a composer of other men's after-dinner speeches. A cousin, Sam, emerges from the slums of Commercial Road, divulging horrible secrets of various relatives' crimes and madness. Finally, the old man is confronted. Leonard's fiancée Constance (a great-granddaughter of Langley Holme) stirs his memory so that he confesses to the murder and dies. His enormous wealth is left to Constance as reparation. Apart from its too providential ending, the novel is one of the best of the thirty or so that Besant wrote and was the author's own favourite.

FOWLER, Ellen Thorneycroft (1860–1929). An elder daughter of Viscount Wolverhampton (also the town where she was born), Fowler was brought up in a Methodist household while remaining herself Anglican. She was educated and lived in the parental home until she was forty-three, spending three months each year in London. Her first major publication was a volume of *Songs And Sonnets* in 1888. She was, apparently, encouraged to write fiction by a family friend, Sir William Robertson Nicoll. In 1898, Fowler made a name for herself as a novelist with the bestselling *Concerning Isabel Carnaby*. The plot, which has evident autobiographical origins, concerns the contrast between Methodist domesticity and high London society. The heroine, Isabel, recently returned from India, falls in love with her nonconformist tutor, Paul Seaton, provoking the usual moral dilemmas. He nobly takes responsibility for a sneering novel she has written. All turns out well in the last chapter with the couple married and he a Liberal MP. The tone of Fowler's fiction was agreeeably light and witty and reviewers acclaimed her as a 'brilliant' observer of society. She followed up with *A Double Thread* (1899) in which a soldier, Captain Jack Le Mesurier, has a love affair with two sisters, the rich Elfrida and the poor Ethel Harland. By a supremely artificial stroke of theatre, they turn out to be one and the same woman. The work was very successfully dramatised. *The Farringdons* (1900) is the saga of a Methodist, ironworks-owning family in the Black Country. Fowler's underlying piety is reflected in *How To Make An Angel* (1901), a temperance tract. In 1903, Fowler married A. L. Felkin, an inspector of schools. The couple produced a jointly written love story, *Kate*

Of Kate Hall (1904). Fowler continued writing fiction of mild marital and pre-marital complication up to *Signs And Wonders* (1926). BL 13. *DNB*. Wol.

Framley Parsonage, Anthony Trollope, 1861, 3 vols, Smith, Elder. (Serialised in *Cornhill**, January 1860–April 1861, with illustrations by John Everett Millais*.) Trollope's first serial novel with which he broke through into mass popularity. The setting is Barsetshire. The Rev. Mark Robarts of Framley Parsonage and Ludovic, Lord Lufton of Framley Court, have been friends since early childhood. Lady Lufton (Ludovic's mother) firmly believes that 'her' clergymen should be married, and has virtually arranged Mark's union with Fanny Monsell. Mark whose life seems to be one long run of good luck finds himself taken up by Nathaniel Sowerby, MP, who flatters the young clergyman. Sowerby, in fact, is a dangerous man. He has run into debt gambling and has designs on Martha Dunstable, heiress to a patent medicine fortune. He persuades Mark to countersign a promissory note, with the assurance that he will soon have the Dunstable wealth. But when Miss Dunstable marries instead Dr Thorne, the bill (together with another one Mark has signed) falls into the hands of moneylenders and the bailiffs prepare to take over Framley Parsonage. Meanwhile another crisis has developed. Lord Lufton has fallen in love with Mark's sister, Lucy. The match is fiercely opposed by Lady Lufton, who thinks Lucy too 'insignificant' for her son. Eventually she is won round by the girl's extraordinary sweetness. Lord Lufton steps in to rescue Mark from his creditors and all ends happily.

FRANCILLON, R[obert] E[dward] (1841–1919). Francillon was born in Gloucestershire, the son of a county court judge and (like a surprising number of Victorian novelists) of Huguenot family origins. He was himself called to the Bar in 1864 (after taking a first in law at Cambridge), but moved across to journalism, joining the staff of the *Globe*, where he worked from 1872 to 1894. Francillon went on to write quite extensively as a serial novelist for the journals. His fiction is composed of light adventure with love sub-plots designed to appeal to the not very serious magazine reader. Typical titles are *Olympia* (1874); *King Or Knave* (1889), the story of a trickster whose schemes to create a new Port of London fail; *A Real Queen* (1884); *Romances Of The Law* (1889), short stories; *Jack Doyle's Daughter* (1894). The last concerns the misadventures of a heroine and heiress with six possible fathers. Reviewers found the work pleasant but incoherent in the extreme. Francillon published an autobiography, *Mid-Victorian Memories*, in 1914. BL 15. *WW*. Wol. RLF.

Frank Fairlegh, Or Scenes From The Life Of A Private Pupil, Frank E. Smedley, 1850, 1 vol, A. Hall, Virtue. (Serialised in monthly parts, January 1849–March 1850, illustrated by George Cruikshank*. Early chapters of the story were first published in *Sharpe's London Magazine**.) A *Bildungsroman** similar to Dickens's* *David Copperfield** (1850) and Thackerary's* *Pendennis** (1851). The story is told autobiographically and is set in the 1830s. Frank is first discovered, fifteen years old, in the coach taking him to Dr Mildman's establishment at Helmstone where he is to be a private pupil. Once arrived, he meets George Lawless, a practical joker who is to be a lifelong friend. Frank is subjected to such rites of passage as having his trousers stolen on his first day. At Mildman's, he also meets the manly Harry Oaklands and the cad Richard Cumberland. His father dies, and he leaves Mildman's. But he is reunited with his friends and foes at Cambridge, where once again Frank enjoys high jinks and has thrilling adventures. Oaklands is almost killed in a duel, which he fights for the honour of a working-class girl abducted by Cumberland and his accomplice Wilford. Frank dutifully attends to his studies and comes out fourth wrangler. The last chapters recount his wooing of Clara Saville (Cumberland is his rival and is initially favoured by Clara's guardian). Oaklands meanwhile pays court to Fanny Fairlegh who is also loved by the comical, but adoring Lawless. Wilford and Cumberland attempt to kidnap Clara, and are foiled. Wilford dies, and Cumberland flees to America where he eventually drinks himself into destitution. The novel ends with the expected marriages. The work is rich in the horseriding scenes that Smedley (himself a cripple) loved.

FRANKAU, Julia ('Frank Danby', née Davis, 1864–1916; the *DNB* gives her date of birth as 1864, and other accounts as 1859). The daughter of a Jewish (but religiously lapsed) artist, Hyman Davis, she was educated at home by Mme Paul Lafargue, the eldest daughter of Karl Marx. Her brother, James Davis ('Owen Hall*') was also a writer and composer. In 1883, Julia married a wholesale cigar merchant, Arthur Frankau (d. 1904). Frankau began writing for the *Saturday Review** and as 'Frank Danby' produced a novel, *Dr Phillips, A Maida Vale Idyll**, in 1887. The work (which was allegedly partly written by George Moore*) provoked notoriety for its savage denigration of Jewish life as philistine, dull, money-grubbing and devoted to 'the Deity of Gain'. Nevertheless, the novel went through five editions in ten years. Frankau followed this bestseller with *A Babe In Bohemia* (1889). A grim tale of seduction, it tells the story of a venereally diseased epileptic girl, Lucilla Lewisham, who finally goes to the bad and cuts her own throat with an open razor, in a seizure. 'The blood was bad', the narrator concludes: 'and drains into the soil. But who will clean the soil?'. *A Babe In Bohemia* is one of the hardest-hitting books of its time. The chronically cautious *Athenaeum** disgustedly called it 'a further excursion into the drains and dustbins of humanity'. The book, inevitably, was banned by Mudie*. Frankau subsequently gave up fiction to study engraving. In 1902 she very successfully returned to the novel with *Pigs In Clover*, another anti-semitic novel dealing with the vulgar comedies (as Frankau maliciously saw them) of Anglo-Jewish life. Her last satire on Judaism, *The Sphinx's Lawyer*, was published in 1906. Frankau's eldest son, Gilbert (1884–1952) was also a bestselling novelist. BL 13. (GF) *DNB*. Wol.

FRASER, Mrs Augusta Zelia ('Alice Spinner', née Webb, 1868?–1925). Born in Scotland, Augusta Webb was educated at home, and spent some time abroad before her marriage in 1889. Her husband, Affleck Fraser, was a diplomat and in 1892 she accompanied him to Jamaica to take up a government appointment. At a friend's suggestion in 1894, she published as 'Alice Spinner' some stories inspired by the West Indies: *A Study In Colour* (1891); *Lucilla* (1895); *A Reluctant Evangelist* (1896). They are sharply observed and were well received by English readers. BL 3. *WW*. Wol.

FRASER, Mrs Hugh [Mary] (née Crawford, 1815–1922). The daughter of Thomas Crawford the sculptor, and a sister of the American novelist F. Marion Crawford, she was educated largely in Italy. Mary Crawford married Hugh Fraser, HM Minister to Japan, and accompanied him on his various tours of duty. She became a Catholic in 1884, a widow in 1894 and a novelist in 1895 with *The Brown Ambassador*. This was followed by: *Palladia* (1896); *A Chapter Of Accidents* (1897); *The Looms Of Time* (1898); *The Splendid Porsenna* (1899); *The Customs Of The Country* (1899). The last is the most interesting of her fiction, a collection of tales and sketches, highly appreciative of the 'new' Japan. BL 9. *WW*.

FRASER, James Baillie (1783–1856). Fraser was born in Invernesshire. In his early life, he voyaged to India and the West Indies and far-flung travel was to be the main feature of his career thereafter. A trip to the Himalayas in 1815 resulted in a popular book. Fraser later specialised in books on Persia, and the East. He brought out various novels, drawing on his experience abroad: *The Kuzzilbash* (1828); *Alli Neemroo, The Buchtiaree Adventurer* (1842), a tale of Louristan; *The Dark Falcon, A Tale Of The Attruck* (1844), a Persian romance; *The Khan's Tale* (1850). His fiction is undistinguished, and indicates the decline of the Eastern tale from the level to which James Morier* had brought it in the 1820s and 1830s. BL 6. *DNB. NCBEL*. Wol.

Fraser's Magazine (1830–82). Founded as a London equivalent of *Blackwood's Edinburgh Magazine** the journal had the same monthly format, miscellaneous contents and Tory political flavouring. The first editor was a former *Blackwood's* contributor, William Maginn*. Articles were anonymous and often collectively written. (Contributors made great play with a pseudonymous editor, 'Oliver Yorke'.) The magazine took its title from its reticent publisher, James Fraser. But its character was entirely the creation of Maginn who remained in the editorial chair until 1836, recruiting a distinguished band of 'Fraserians' who included: Thackeray*, Carlyle, James Hogg and T. C. Croker. In its early years, the magazine took a keen critical interest in contemporary fiction and led by Thackeray conducted a savage assault against the Newgate* novel and its main practitioner Bulwer-Lytton*. In the late 1830s, it carried the serialised versions of Thackeray's early fictions: *Catherine**, *The Yellowplush Correspondence* and *A Shabby Genteel Story** (1840). In the 1840s, under the editorship of G. W. Nickisson, it became more sober and largely steered clear of fiction. But under John W. Parker* (1847–60) it serialised C. Kingsley's* *Yeast** and *Hypatia**. Longmans* acquired the magazine in 1865. *WI. BLM*.

FRAZER, R[obert] W[atson] (1854–1921). Frazer was born in Dublin, and educated at the university there. He subsequently entered the Indian Civil Service, and became a noted scholar on the country, its history and languages. In addition to his specialist works, he wrote (as 'R. W. Frazer, LL.B., I.C.S., Retd.') a collection of sketches and stories of ancient and modern India, published as *Silent Gods And Sun Steeped Lands* (1895). BL 1. *WW*.

FRERE, M[ary Eliza Isabella] (1845–1911). Born in Gloucestershire, she was the eldest child of Sir Bartle Frere (1815-84), and privately educated at school in Wimbledon. In 1863, when she was eighteen, Frere went out to Bombay, where her father was now governor. From this experience, she produced twenty-four tales, gathered as *Old Deccan Days* (1868). This collection sold well, and demonstrates genuine feeling for the sub-continent. But the remainder of Frere's literary output comprises only some drama and poetry of the most minor kind. In 1877 she accompanied her father to South Africa. They returned to England and her remaining years were spent in travel and, latterly, biblical study. Frere never married. BL 1. *DNB*. Wol.

FRISWELL, [James] Hain (1825–78). Friswell was born at Newport in Shropshire, the youngest son of a prosperous London lawyer whose clients 'were mostly titled people'. A delicate child, James was devoted to his mother. The original intention that he should study for the law evidently came to nothing. In 1842, he was articled to learn engraving and five years later he married and settled in Pentonville. By now he was determined on a literary career. In the 1850s, he duly became a contributor to the *Puppet Show*, a magazine conducted by Angus Reach* and Albert Smith*. His early London experiences are reflected in the novel *Diamonds And Spades* (1857). In 1856, Friswell's father died, leaving nothing but a vexatious lawsuit for his son. By the mid-1850s, Friswell was writing extensively for the magazines, contributing to such fashionable organs as Yates's* *Train* and the *Welcome Guest* (he finished the American novelist G. W. Curtis's *Trumps* for that journal in 1859). Meanwhile (1856–63) Friswell was also employed as an engraver to a Bond Street jewellers. Notably philanthropic, Friswell devoted much of his energy to the extension of working-class literacy and education. His literary output was miscellaneous and largely forgettable. An authority on heraldry, he wrote some good essays, and a few brisk novels which include: *Sham, A Novel Written In Earnest* (1861); *Daughter Of Eve* (1863); *A Splendid Fortune* (1865). The last is a social comedy set in 'Bilscombe Regis' in the 1840s. *Our Square Circle* (1880), a panoramic survey of the characters living in a London square, was completed by his daughter. As a reviewer put it, Friswell's fiction is generally marked by 'good intentions and weak effects'. Facetiousness was his dominant narrative tone. In 1869, he ruptured a blood vessel and his remaining years were spent as an invalid. Never the less, in 1870, in a volume called *Modern Men Of Letters Honestly Criticised*, Friswell savagely libelled G. A. Sala*, and was fined £500. His daughter, Laura Hain, wrote some stories and a memoir of her father. BL 5. *DNB*. *NCBEL*. Wol. Sad. RLF.

FRITH, Walter (1857?–1941). The third son of the artist William Powell Frith, he was educated at Harrow School and studied law at Trinity Hall, Cambridge. He was called to the Bar in 1880 and seems to have practised law successfully. Relatively late in life (1898) he married a clergyman's widow, Maud Law. A well-regarded man of letters, Frith was a member of the exclusive Athenaeum Club. His literary output is mainly numerous melodramatic plays, and he was for many years the drama critic of *Pall Mall*. He also wrote the novels: *In Search Of Quiet* (1895), a 'Country Journal'; *The Sack Of Monte Carlo* (1897); *The Tutor's Love Story* (1904), 'an adventure of today'. Reviewers found Frith's fiction quiet and in its way rather charming. BL 3. *WW*.

Froggy's Little Brother, Brenda (i.e. Mrs G. Castle Smith), 1875, 1 vol, RTS. Together with Hesba Stretton's* *Jessica's First Prayer**, the best known of the 'street arab' stories for children. Froggy and little Benny are orphaned and destitute. The story follows the older boy's brave struggles to look after his doomed sibling, Benny, who eventually dies. Froggy is rewarded for his virtue with a berth in a comfortable orphanage where he acquires a new 'brother'. 'How many a beautiful lesson can we learn from the poor', the author concludes.

FROST, Thomas (1801–86?). One of the most popular of writers of working-class* fiction, little is known of Frost's life (even his dates are uncertain, some accounts giving 1821–79). He was evidently born in Croydon, where he later worked as a printer. He retired from this line of work in the mid-1840s, devoting himself to the Chartist cause, then at its height. Frost took a prominent part in the great Chartist demonstration of 1848 and was a delegate to the 1852 Reform Conference. At various periods in his later life he was editor of the *Sheffield Evening Post*, the *Barnsley Times* and the *Barnsley Independent* which indicates that he moved to the north of England. As a novelist, Frost made his name with *Sixteen String Jack* (1845); *Emma Mayfield, Or The Rector's Daughter* (1847); *Paul The Poacher* (1850), a tale of life in the West Country; *Obi, Or Three-Fingered Jack* (1851); *Alice Leighton, Or The Murders At The Druids' Stones* (1857). Edward Lloyd*, the publisher, thought some of Frost's material was too strong sexually, and for a time the author was employed by the pornographer, William Dugdale*. Among his more powerful works is *The Black Mask* (1850). In later life, a regenerate Frost wrote for the RTS*. BL 8.

FROUDE, J[ames] A[nthony] ('Zeta', 1818–94). Historian and biographer. Froude was born at Dartington, Devon, the youngest son of the Archdeacon of Totnes. His fifteen-years-older brother, Richard Hurrell Froude, went on to make a name as a High-Church clergyman. After graduating from Oriel College, Oxford, Froude was offered a fellowship at Exeter, and took deacon's orders in 1844. He had been influenced by Newman*, and collaborated with him on the *Lives Of The English Saints*. Froude's Life of St Neot came out in 1844. In 1845, Newman left the Church of England for Rome. Shortly afterwards, Froude dramatically lost his faith. This crisis is recorded in his two works of fiction: *Shadows Of The Clouds* (by 'Zeta', 1847) and *The Nemesis Of Faith** (1849). Both recall Froude's early life at Westminster School and university. Both were considered in their different ways scandalous. *Shadows Of The Clouds* (which features seduction) was bought up from the bookshops by Froude's ashamed father, and destroyed. A copy of *The Nemesis Of Faith* (being the story of a young man who takes religious orders only to fall into disbelief and adulterous passion) was publicly burned at Exeter College by the Rev. William Sewell*. Froude having taken orders was commonly regarded as an apostate of the worst kind. He resigned his fellowship and took to writing for the London magazines, and in 1849 met Carlyle, a momentous event in his life. In the same year he married Charlotte Maria Grenfell (a sister of Mrs Charles Kingsley*), who died in 1860. Froude was editor of *Fraser's Magazine**, 1860–74 and in 1884 completed his biography of Carlyle. This work has always been controversial. His *History Of England* was completed in twelve volumes in 1869. In 1892, Froude was appointed to the Regius Chair of Modern History at Oxford. BL 2. *DNB*. RM. *NCBEL*. Wol. Sad.

FULLERTON, Lady Georgiana [Charlotte] (née Leveson-Gower, 1812–85). Lady Fullerton was born at Tixall Hall, in Staffordshire, into the English nobility. She was brought up largely in Paris, where her father, Lord Granville Leveson-Gower, was ambassador, 1824–41. Her grandfather was the Duke of Devonshire. In 1833, she married a young Irish Guards officer attached to the embassy, Alexander George Fullerton. The couple continued to live in the British Residence in Paris until 1841. He was received into the Catholic Church in 1843; she followed in 1846, 'after an interval of devout Puseyism'. Her first novel, *Ellen Middleton** (1844) was approved by Lord Brougham* and warmly commended by Gladstone in the *English Review*. The narrative, which ends with the pathetic death of the heroine, is a study of piety in the upper classes. Her next, and better novel, *Grantley Manor** (1847) is a well-devised plea for the toleration of Catholicism, using all the melodramatic devices of romantic fiction. In 1854, she was shattered by the death of her only son, and devoted the rest of her life (which she spent in deep mourning) to philanthropic works and religious devotion. A highly cultivated woman, Fullerton wrote two of her novels in French and translated works of her French friends. Her fiction includes: *Lady-Bird* (1852); *Too Strange Not To Be True* (1864), a historical* tale based on the murder of Charlotte Sophia of Brunswick and accompanied by a pedantic appendix on sources; *Mrs Gerald's Niece* (1869). The last is a story of a couple's conversion and is, as the *Saturday Review** tartly put it, 'a novel for persons about to turn Roman Catholics'. Written for the publisher Richard Bentley* (her earlier work was put out by Edward Moxon), the work was better devised to appeal to the secular library reader. Fullerton was closely involved in the founding of the Catholic journal the *Month* in July 1864, and her story *Constance Sherwood* (1865), 'an autobiography of the sixteenth century', was serialised in its pages. The story deals with the sufferings of Catholics in the reign of Elizabeth I in the style of Anne Manning's* pseudo-documentary historical* reconstructions. Fullerton was an intimate friend of Mrs Augustus Craven*. BL 9. *DNB*. *NCBEL*. Wol. Sad.

FURNISS, Harry (1854–1925). Illustrator. The youngest son of an English civil engineer, Furniss was born in Wexford, Ireland, and educated at the Wesleyan School in Dublin. In 1873 he came to England. His first commissions were from Florence Marryat*, then editor of the magazine, *London Society*. In 1876 he joined the staff of the *Illustrated London News**, and in 1880 did his first work for *Punch**, becoming a member of that journal's staff four years later. In 1889 he illustrated his friend Lewis Carroll's* *Sylvie And Bruno*. In 1894 Furniss launched a humorous weekly of his own, *Lika Joko*, which lasted only a year. Among the Victorian fiction that he illustrated was Walter Besant's* *All In A Garden Fair* (1883) and John Davidson's* *Perfervid* (1890). In the early twentieth century, Furniss was a pioneer of British cinematography. *DNB*. Hou.

G

GALLETTI DI CADILHAC, Countess (née the Hon. Margaret Isabella Collier, 1846–1928). The daughter of Baron Monkswell (1817–66), a judge with a passion for landscape painting, she married an Italian count and active politician in 1873. Galletti's fiction reflects her experience as a married woman in Italy. It includes: *The Camorristi And Other Tales* (1882); *Prince Peerless* (1886), a 'Fairy-Folk Story Book', illustrated by the Hon. John Collier; *Babel* (1887); *Rachel And Maurice* (1892); *Annals Of An Italian Village* (1896). Galletti's husband died in 1912, and she returned to spend her later life in Devon, England. BL 5. *WW*.

Gallia, Ménie Muriel Dowie, 1895, 1 vol, Methuen. A full-blooded new woman*, pro-eugenics novel. Essentially, the narrative is a portrait gallery of modern types. At the outset, Mark Gurdon, a staid young civil servant, is dispatched to look into the affairs of his former college-friend Robbie Leighton, who has left England to study art in the Latin Quarter of Paris. In Paris, Mark becomes involved with a bohemian model, Cara Lemuel, whom he later looks after in London and who is supposed there to be his mistress. The other centre of the narrative is Gallia Hamesthwaite, Robbie's cousin. Oxford-educated, Gallia is a woman of 'immediate honesty'. She loves, and is loved by, 'Dark' Essex. But he has a weak heart and with dandyish nobility does not press his suit on Gallia. Finally, she agrees to marry Mark whom she does not love, but whom she feels she can learn to love. Before the wedding, he confesses that he has previously loved Dark's sister, Margaret Essex. The novel is primarily concerned to present a modern psychology of eugenics.

GALLON, Tom (1866–1914). Born in London, Gallon started working life as a clerk in the City, then became an usher in a private school. For a while he was secretary to a mayor in a provincial town. He fell ill in middle life, and went on a long tramp through England as a prelude to a career in authorship which began in 1895 with journalistic commissions for 'stray guineas'. Gallon went on to write sub-Dickensian* fiction of sentiment and low-life in London, typically written in an elliptical, rather graceless style. His works (mainly short stories) include: *A Prince Of Mischance* (1897); *Dicky Monteith* (1898); *The Kingdom Of Hate* (1899), a Zendaish romance set in 'Labyrinthia'; *Comethup* (1899), the story of a young orphan named after the verse in *Ecclesiastes*. *A Rogue In Love* (1900) is a typical Gallon low life romp, about the exploits of a lovable cockney* inmate of Wormwood Scrubs. Gallon (who never married) also wrote successful plays after 1900. BL 34. *WW*.

GARVICE, Charles (1850?–1920). Little is known of Garvice's life. His writing career began with a volume of poems, *Eve*, in 1873. His first three-decker, *Maurice Durant*, followed two years later. In later life, Garvice also wrote moderately successful plays. But he mainly supported himself by free-lance journalism for various English and American papers. His fiction includes (to take just one year's output): *Her Heart's Desire* (1900), *Nance* (1900), *The Outcast Of The Family* (1900), *A Coronet Of Shame* (1900). Among the public positions Garvice held during the course of his life were those of county councillor in Northam, Devon; President of the Farmers and Landowners Association and President of the Institute of Lecturers. In his later years, he lived in Henley on Thames. DL 57. *WW*.

GASKELL, Elizabeth Cleghorn (née Stevenson, 1810–65). Mrs Gaskell, as she was to be universally known, was born in Chelsea, London, of Unitarian parents. After quitting the ministry and unsuccessfully trying farming, her father had taken up the comfortable official position of Keeper of Records to the Treasury. Elizabeth's mother came from Cheshire thus setting up from birth the cultural clash of North and South which was to preoccupy the future novelist. Mrs Stevenson died when her daughter was just over a year old, and the very young Elizabeth was effectively adopted by her aunt Lumb, in Knutsford, Cheshire (the original of Cranford*). Elizabeth grew up in the small country town with its outlying farms, whose life she was later to chronicle. She was brought up a Unitarian and well educated at school locally and at Stratford upon Avon leaving at the age of seventeen with a good knowledge of modern and classical languages. In 1828, her brother John Stevenson, a lieutenant in the merchant marine, disappeared at sea. His loss affected her strongly, and the brother thought dead who returns to life appears as a motif frequently in her subsequent fiction. Around the same period, her father remarried a woman whom Elizabeth did not much like (a situation which is recalled as the central event of *Wives And Daughters**). She nevertheless remained with her father until his death in 1829, after which she returned to Knutsford. In 1832, she married the Rev. William Gaskell, a Unitarian assistant minister at the Cross Street Chapel in Manchester. The union was to be very happy. Elizabeth now settled in Manchester, sixteen miles from Knutsford but, as the most advanced industrial city in the world, different in every way from what she had been brought up with. The first dozen years of her marriage were occupied in family and parochial business. But she found time to write the odd piece of prose and verse. In 1837, for instance, she embarked on a descriptive poem, in the style of Crabbe, called *Sketches Among The Poor*. Her first serious venture in authorship came, however, after the death of her only son Willie from scarlet fever in 1845. Partly to console herself, she wrote a story of industrial life and strife in Manchester originally called 'John Barton', later changed to *Mary Barton** (1848). Mrs Gaskell had some difficulty in finding a publisher for this tale of 1840s strife, strike and assassination. But eventually Chapman and Hall* took it, paying her £100. The novel, which was published anonymously in two volumes, enjoyed a huge success. Carlyle (prominently quoted on the novel's title page) admired it, and only the mill owners (represented by the articulate W. R. Greg) objected. Her identity soon became known, and she was overnight a literary celebrity. On the strength of *Mary Barton*, Dickens* invited Gaskell to contribute to his new venture, *Household Words** and she produced *Lizzie Leigh* for the paper's first issue. Gaskell was thereafter a regular contributor for

Dickens, publishing *Cranford* (1851–53), a small town idyll in *Household Words*. *A Dark Night's Work** (1863), a more sensational* work to do with the grim consequences of manslaughter, came out in Dickens's *All The Year Round**. Gaskell's second full-length novel, *Ruth** (1853), again attacked the middle-class conscience by dealing with a social problem*, this time bastardy. The story of a repentant fallen woman and her relationship with a dissenting minister, *Ruth* provoked some controversy, but in general confirmed Gaskell's status as a major novelist and social commentator. *North And South** (1855; first serialised in *Household Words*) marks a new level of maturity in her art. The story of the socially complicated love affair of a well-bred Home Counties girl and a northern mill owner reflected many of the tensions of the author's own life, and her double cultural inheritance. And following hard on the Preston cotton strike (that Dickens for his part was dealing with in *Hard Times**), the novel was unusually topical. In the same year that *North And South* was published, Gaskell's friend Charlotte Brontë* died. Brontë's father and husband asked her to undertake a biography, so as to forestall the wilder rumours circulating about the sisters' lives. *The Life Of Charlotte Brontë* appeared in 1857. George Smith gave Gaskell £800 for the work, which is reckoned among the best of Victorian literary biographies. It none the less aggrieved a number of living acquaintances of the Brontës, and there were legal consequences and a forced retraction in *The Times*. By now, Gaskell was earning enough to live comfortably and travel extensively. In Rome, in 1857, she met the American scholar Charles Eliot Norton, with whom she formed a lasting friendship. Meanwhile her fiction output continued at a fast pace. In 1858 she published the slightly disappointing *My Lady Ludlow*, a study of amiable aristocratic prejudice, in *Household Words*. This work became the centrepiece of a two-volume set of miscellaneous fiction entitled *Round The Sofa* (1859), the various stories being linked by a framework device in which each is supposed to have been told by friends to distract the sufferings of an Edinburgh doctor's crippled sister. (Gaskell had herself spent a winter in Edinburgh when she was twenty.) Her next major novel, *Sylvia's Lovers**, was begun in 1859 with extensive research into eighteenth-century Whitby in which the narrative is set. But domestic preoccupations distracted her from this historical* tale of love, smuggling and pressgangs. The work finally came out in 1863, under the imprint of Smith, Elder*, who paid £1,000 for the copyright, her highest reward to date. *Cousin Phillis** (1864), a gentler idyllic piece, is thought by many critics to be Gaskell's masterpiece. It was followed by *Wives And Daughters*, which was being serialised in *Cornhill** at the time of the author's death. An 'everyday story', this last novel recapitulates in the experiences of its heroine Molly Gibson much of the author's own early years. Mrs Gaskell died of a heart attack while visiting the house she had just bought at Holybourne with the £1,600 proceeds of *Wives And Daughters*, surrounded by three of her daughters. She was buried at Knutsford. BL 15. *DNB*. RM. *NCBEL*. Wol. Sad.

GASPEY, Thomas (1788–1871). Thomas Gaspey was born in Hoxton, north-east London, the son of a Royal Navy lieutenant, At an early age he took up work as a political journalist on the *Morning Post*, working on the paper for sixteen years in all. In 1828, Gaspey bought a share in the

Sunday Times and did much to raise the paper to a leading position among British weekly journals. He also wrote drama reviews, and undertook a wide range of miscellaneous journalism and was a leading member of the Royal Literary Fund*. Throughout his working life, he published occasional novels of which the first was *The Mystery* (1820). All Gaspey's subsequent fiction was published in the pre-Victorian period, with the exception of *The Self Condemned* (1836; still in print as a new novel when Victoria came to the throne) and *Many Coloured Life* (1842), subtitled 'Tales Of Woe And Touches Of Mirth'. For the last twenty years of his life, Gaspey lived in quiet retirement at Shooter's Hill in Kent. BL 9. *DNB. NCBEL*. Wol. Sad. RLF.

GATTY, Mrs Alfred [Margaret] (née Scott, 1809–73). Born at Burnham in Essex, she was the youngest daughter of Lord Nelson's former chaplain on the *Victory*, the Rev. Alexander Scott. Her mother died when she was two, and the little girl was raised by her bookish father. At a young age, she showed a remarkable talent for drawing, calligraphy and literature. In 1839, Margaret Scott married the Rev. Alfred Gatty, a vicar at Ecclesfield, Yorkshire, where she was to spend the rest of her life. Both Gattys were authors. He began writing verse as an undergraduate at Oxford and produced a number of works of theology and literary criticism over the years. Margaret Gatty's first book (co-written with her husband) was a memoir of her father, in 1842. Gatty's first fiction, in the style of Hans Christian Andersen, *The Fairy Godmothers*, was published in 1851, when she was in her early forties. In 1858, she brought out one of the most successful mid-Victorian volumes of fiction for children, *Aunt Judy's Tales*. 'Aunt Judy' was in fact the nickname for Gatty's daughter, Juliana [Ewing*], later to be a famous children's author in her own right. A sequel, *Aunt Judy's Letters*, appeared in 1862. In May 1866, Gatty founded *Aunt Judy's Magazine** which she edited until 1873 at which point it was taken over by her daughters, Mrs Ewing* and Horatia K. F. Gatty. Her most substantial work is the five-volume collection of improving tales, *Parables From Nature* (1855–71), a series which was much reprinted and illustrated by Holman Hunt, and John Tenniel* among others. She died at Ecclesfield, having been paralysed for some years. BL 7. *DNB*. RM. *NCBEL*. Wol.

The Gentleman's Magazine (1731–1907). The longest running of all British literary magazines, the *Gentleman's Magazine* was founded in the eighteenth century by Edward Cave as a social 'intelligencer'. As such it carried obituaries, news items, antiquarian notes and poems. In 1868, however, the magazine was transformed into a middlebrow Victorian magazine, publishing undistinguished serial fiction by such authors as: Joseph Hatton*, R. E. Francillon*, Helen Mathers*, G. Whyte-Melville* (his *Satanella*, which ran through the journal's pages in 1872, was a cut above the usual fiction fare for this period). In 1877 Chatto and Windus* acquired the magazine, and added illustrations. But the experiment in illustrated fiction stopped in 1880. Among the more interesting works which appeared at this period was Eliza Lynn Linton's* *Under Which Lord?** (1879). Chronically unsure of its character, the journal never prospered and long fiction dropped from its pages in the mid-1880s. *BLM*.

George Geith Of Fen Court, F. G. Trafford (i.e. Mrs J. H. Riddell), 1864, 3 vols, Tinsley. Mrs Riddell's first hit with the English reading public. The novel combines a fashionable and rather hackneyed bigamy* plot with the author's unusual familiarity with the ins and outs of London 'City' (or commercial) life. The action opens in 1847. George Geith is first encountered an austere accountant in Fen Court, a *cul de sac* in the City. It emerges that there are secrets in his past. In his youth, at university, George injudiciously married a woman beneath him socially. Having taken holy orders, he fled his living to escape her blackmail. Learning that this wife is now dead, Geith allows himself to fall in love with Beryl Molozane, the daughter of a Hertfordshire squire whose affairs he is putting in order. Misfortune crowds on the Molozanes. The father is bankrupted and is forced to sell his estate. His talented literary daughter, Louisa, dies and he soon follows. George marries Beryl Molozane, but they too are doomed. He is ruined by a bank failure and then his wife returns, not dead after all. In a trial for bigamy, it is proved that she forged her own death certificate, and George is acquitted. But he cannot divorce; he and Beryl must separate. She pines and dies. A devastated Geith carries on to make himself a power in the City again, for the ultimate benefit of his (illegitimate) son Walter. A complicated sub-plot involves George's being kept out of his inheritance by his cousin Sir Mark Geith, who is in fact his father's bastard by a housekeeper. Riddell's novel is extraordinarily gloomy in tone and in the relentless catalogue of its stoic hero's sufferings. But readers of 1864 clearly loved it, and 'F. G. Trafford's' high-handed narrative manner.

George St George Julian, The Prince Of Swindlers, Henry Cockton, 1841, 1 vol, Grattan and Gilbert. (Illustrated by T. Onwhyn*.) Cockton observes in his preface to this work: 'it is computed that in London alone, there have never, since the panic of 1825, been less than five thousand men living by unequivocal swindling'. *George St George Julian* is a novel in the early Dickensian* social problem* pattern, which aims to expose a current scandal. Cockton's hero, George, becomes involved with speculative banking and specious emigration schemes, earning the nickname 'Prince of Bankers'. Guilty only by rash association with the real swindler, Tynte, he is tried for embezzlement and sentenced to fourteen years' transportation. (The trial is well handled by Cockton.) At the eleventh hour, George is rescued, restored to his wife, Julia, and awarded by providence a handsome inheritance. Tynte dies violently.

GERARD, Dorothea [Mme Longard de Longgarde] ('E. D. Gerard', 1855–1915). Born in Lanarkshire, into a well-off, Catholic family, Dorothea Gerard was educated at home, with governesses. She was later sent to a convent school in Austria. In 1886, she married an army officer, Julius Longard de Longgarde, later a field marshal in the Austrian forces. With him she lived in Galicia, the setting for much of her subsequent fiction. The last years of her life seem to have been spent in strict seclusion. In collaboration with her sister Emily Gerard* (whose career exactly parallels her own) she wrote *Reata* (1880). Subtitled 'What's In A Name?' the novel features an exotic half-German, half-Mexican heroine. It opens, typically: 'The shock of discovering that her heart was not broken, that her life was not blighted and that she did not love Otto was a severe one to Reata.' The affairs of

Reata and Otto nevertheless occupy the ensuing three volumes of narrative. The Gerard sisters also jointly wrote: *Beggar My Neighbour* (1882), a story set in Poland in the 1850s; *The Waters Of Hercules* (1883), a story set on the borders of Hungary and Romania; *A Sensitive Plant* (1887), the portrait of a morbidly shy woman, Janet, in her native Scotland and in Venice. Independently, Dorothea Gerard wrote voluminous romantic fiction. It includes: *Orthodox* (1888), the story (told by an anti-semitic comrade) of a Polish Jewess who falls in love with an Austrian officer; *Recha* (1889), in which again the heroine is a Polish Jewess, who this time loves an unworthy Austrian officer; *A Queen Of Curds And Cream* (1892); *Lot Thirteen* (1894); *The Rich Miss Riddell* (1894); *An Arranged Marriage* (1894); *The Wrong Man* (1895); *Angela's Lover* (1896); *A Spotless Reputation* (1897); *Miss Providence* (1897); *A Forgotten Sin* (1898); *The Impediment* (1898); *Things That Have Happened* (1899), a collection of stories. *One Year* (1899), a gloomy story of love and suicide set among the Polish inhabitants of east Galicia, is Gerard's most powerful work, and is representative of both her strengths and her repetitive themes as a novelist. The story is told autobiographically by a narrator-heroine transplanted, as was the author, from Britain to Poland. (DG and EG) BL 4. (DG) BL 43. *WW*. Wol.

GERARD, Emily Jane [Madame de Laszowski] ('E. D. Gerard', 1849–1905). Sister of the above, Emily Gerard was born in Scotland and educated at home until she was fifteen. At this age she was consigned to a convent at Riedenburg in the Tirol, ostensibly to master European languages. There, like her sister, she married an Austrian officer, Chevalier Miecislas de Laszowski, later a general in the imperial armed forces. For a while Emily Gerard reviewed German literature for the London *Times*. She began to write fiction in 1879, in collaboration with her sister under the joint pen name 'E. D. Gerard'. Their first effort was entitled *Reata* (1880) and was successful enough to warrant a number of jointly written successors. Emily's independent productions (mainly short stories) draw heavily on European settings and themes and reviewers often accused her of being unduly influenced by German writers. Her works include: *The Land Beyond The Forest* (1888); *Bis* (1890); *A Secret Mission* (1891); *The Voice Of A Flower* (1893); *A Foreigner* (1896); *An Electric Shock* (1897); *The Tragedy Of A Nose* (1898). The last is a sprightly story of two Austrian officers who cut off off each others' noses in a duel. They are subsequently replaced on the wrong faces. Gerard lived most of her life in Vienna, although she evidently kept strong personal links with England and the house of Blackwood* with whom she published most of her fiction. (DG and EG) BL 4. (EG) BL 9. *WW*. Wol.

Ghost Stories. The nineteenth century is the period in which the ghost story came into its own as a 'particular sort of short story', as M. R. James* called it. The ghost story can claim ancestry in various traditional forms: tales of terror and the supernatural, gothic* fiction, the folk-tale. As with much else in Victorian fiction, it was Dickens* who gave the genre its decisive character with *A Christmas Carol** (1843) and *The Haunted Man* (1848). Dickens's journals *Household Words** and *All The Year Round** came to specialise in ghost stories, particularly in their bumper Christmas numbers.

Writers associated with Dickens, such as Wilkie Collins* and Bulwer-Lytton* produced classics in the form. (See the latter's *The Haunted And The Haunters**, 1859.) Another pioneer, J. S. Le Fanu*, began publishing his distinctive ghost stories in the *Dublin University Magazine** in the early 1840s. His masterpiece of psychological suspense, *Uncle Silas**, appeared in 1864. *In A Glass Darkly* (1872) reprints both his tale of vampirism *Carmilla** (a work which inspired Bram Stoker's* later *Dracula**) and the study in horrific possession, *Green Tea**. Women authors with an interest in spiritualism also contributed powerfully to the development of the Victorian ghost story; see, for instance, Mrs E. Riddell's* *Weird Tales* (1882) and Mrs M. Oliphant's* *A Beleaguered City** (1880) and *Two Stories Of The Seen And Unseen** (1885). The artistic high point of the ghost story was attained in the late 1880s and 1890s, when it merged with decadence* and aestheticism to produce such works as: Stevenson's* *Dr Jekyll And Mr Hyde** (1886); Vernon Lee's* *A Phantom Lover* (1886); Wilde's* *The Picture Of Dorian Gray** (1891); Arthur Machen's* *The Great God Pan** (1894); Henry James's *The Turn Of The Screw* (1896).

GIBBON, Charles (1843–90). Gibbon was born to working-class parents on the Isle of Man, but moved early in life to Glasgow where he first worked as an office clerk. At the age of seventeen, he was working as a journalist. One of his reviews in 1860 attracted favourable attention from the actor Charles Kean, then on provincial tour. Gibbon subsequently migrated to London around 1861–62, where he soon became well known as a writer and clubman. The last years of Gibbon's life were spent in poor health and poverty in East Anglia. He died at Yarmouth. Gibbon brought out his first three-volume novel, *Dangerous Connexions*, in 1864. The work (a jaunty sensation* novel after the style of Braddon*) was well received, and he followed up with *The Dead Heart* (1865) 'A Tale Of The Bastille'. *Robin Gray* (1869) is the story of a young Scottish girl, Jeanie Lindsay, who falls in love with a fisherman who is wrongly thought lost at sea. She marries a farmer she does not love, with predictable melodramatic consequences. Gibbon is at his best with Scottish regional settings, as in the romantic *The Braes Of Yarrow* (1881). *The Golden Shaft* (1882) is the story of a crossed love affair between a provost's daughter and a young Scottish industrialist. Other Scottish-flavoured works are: *By Mead And Stream* (1884) and *A Princess Of Jutedom* (1886), 'Jutedom' being Dundee. Gibbon also wrote a life of George Combe, the Scottish phrenologist in 1873 and edited the six-volume *Casquet Of Literature* (1873–74). Michael Sadleir, who gives a comprehensive list of Gibbon's works, describes him as a 'sentimental counterpart of the sensational Farjeon*.' BL 29. *DNB*. Wol. Sad. RLF.

GIBERNE, Agnes [De] (1845–1939). Agnes Giberne was born in India, where her father was an army officer. Educated at home, she attributed her subsequent literary sensibility to her mother and her scientific curiosity to her father. Giberne began to publish children's stories anonymously at the age of seventeen. (Some of them she illustrated herself.) By 1880, she had established herself as a writer also on scientific topics for the young. In 1895 Giberne wrote a life of the outstanding Victorian author of children's books, Charlotte M. Tucker* ('ALOE'). Giberne herself never married and lived her adult life quietly at Eastbourne. In addition to tales for the very young, she wrote some fiction aimed at the adolescent girl, and mainly published by the RTS*. It includes: *The Curate's Home* (1869); *Miss Devereux, Spinster* (1891), 'a study of development' which ends with 'banns, frocks and veils'; *The Girl At The Dower House* (1896), a glum story of crossed love. BL 11 (a grossly small number, most of her volumes having come out as undeposited tracts). *WW*. RLF.

GILBERT, [Sir] John (1817–97). Illustrator. Called 'the most prolific black and white artist of his time', Gilbert was born in Blackheath, the son of an estate agent. He initially took up work himself in an estate agent's office in the City of London in 1833. In the early 1840s, he began working for *Punch** but he is most closely associated with the *London Journal**, for whom he became the star illustrator of serial fiction in 1845. At the same period, he was working for the recently founded *Illustrated London News** and his style had a formative influence on the new 'pictorial journalism'. Gilbert's workmanlike designs were imitated by most illustrators of historical* fiction during the century, and he himself illustrated some of the early fiction of W. H. Ainsworth*. Gilbert was knighted in 1872 and elected to the Royal Academy in 1876. In later life he was famous as a painter of historical subjects. *DNB*. Hou.

GILBERT, Lady Rosa ('Ruth Murray', née Mulholland, 1841–1921). Born in Belfast, she was the second daughter of a doctor, and educated privately at home. In 1891, Rosa Mulholland married Mr (later Sir) John Thomas Gilbert, the Irish historian and secretary of the Public Record Office of Ireland, 1867–75. Twelve years older than her, he died in 1898 leaving her a young widow. She resided thereafter in Dublin. Dickens* encouraged her early attempts at fiction and published her short stories in *All The Year Round**. Writing as 'Ruth Murray', she put out the full-length *Dunmara* in 1864, the story of a young Irish girl brought up in Spain who comes to England to make her way as an artist. In her own name, she subsequently put out a large quantity of novels with a strong Irish regional flavour. They include: *Marcella Grace* (1886); *A Fair Emigrant* (1889); *Hetty Gray* (1899); *Onora* (1900); *Cynthia's Bonnet Shop* (1900). Gilbert's later work was largely directed to the young girl reader. All her stories stoutly celebrate female independence. BL 49. *WW*. Wol.

GILBERT, William (1804–90). Gilbert was born at Bishopstoke, the younger son of a colonial broker and merchant. He attended school in Clapham and in 1818 enrolled as a midshipman in the East India Company. He quit the service under something of a cloud in 1821, having clashed with his superiors on issues of rights and liberty, never much respected at sea. Gilbert then went to Italy, where he mastered the country's language and steeped himself in its literature. He himself began to write poetry. On his return to England around 1825, he studied medicine at Guy's Hospital, and returned to sea for a while as a navy surgeon. He then drifted into journalism, and was eventually relieved from the need to earn his living by an inheritance when his father died. Late in life, Gilbert published (anonymously) his first book *Dives And Lazarus* (1858), a well-received study of London slum life. At this point of his career, Gilbert was evidently encouraged by the publisher Alexander Strahan*. He followed with other novels, including: *Margaret Meadows* (1859), a 'Tale For The Pharisees'; *Shirley Hall Asylum* (1863), a powerful study of monomania (the narrator is a lawyer gone mad trying to solve the problem of perpetual motion); *De Profundis* (1864), 'a tale of the social deposits'; *The Washerwoman's Foundling* (1867); *King George's Middy* (1869); *Clara Levesque* (1872); *Legion* (1882), a powerful semi-documentary study of alcoholism or 'the modern demoniac'. In the 1860s, Gilbert was a regular contributor to *Good Words**. Staunchly Liberal in his political views, he died at Salisbury. Much of his personality is revealed in his autobiographical novel, *Memoirs Of A Cynic* (1880). He was the father of the famous librettist, W. S. Gilbert. BL 13. *DNB. NCBEL.* Wol. Sad.

GILCHRIST, R[obert] Murray (1868–1917). Gilchrist was born in the north of England at Sheffield, and was educated at the city's grammar school. For a while he worked for the *National Observer* under the famous Victorian editor, W. E. Henley. Gilchrist's later fiction is almost entirely devoted to his native Peaks region in Derbyshire, and the 'Milton Folk' who lived there. It includes *A Peakland Faggot* (1897); *Willowbrake* (1898); *Nicholas And Mary* (1899); *The Courtesy Dame* (1900); *Natives Of Milton* (1902). His stories are rich in folklore and descriptions of characteristically local things such as well-dressing. Gilchrist, who never married, gave as his main recreation 'long moorland walks'. In an obituary, Eden Phillpotts* likened his art to that of Turgenev. BL 37. *WW.* Wol.

GILLIES, R[obert] P[earse] (1788–1858). Gillies was born at Arbroath in Scotland, and inherited his father's considerable estate there in 1808. His background was bookish. He studied at Edinburgh University (where his literary bent was evident) and was admitted as an advocate (i.e. Scottish lawyer) in 1813. Gillies lost most of his inherited fortune in speculation, and gave up law for the life of an Edinburgh man of letters in 1815. He was one of the early contributors to *Blackwood's Magazine**, was a friend of Scott's and corresponded with Wordsworth. Gillies was particularly interested in Germany, and spent a *Lehrjahr* there, meeting Goethe and Tieck. He later founded the *Foreign Quarterly Review* in 1827, and moved at the same period to London which was increasingly overtaking Edinburgh as the centre of the magazine world. Gillies' subsequent career was one long financial embarrassment and in 1840 he fled with his wife and children to Boulogne to escape creditors. On his return to England in 1847, he was thrown (not for the first time) into debtors' prison, not regaining his freedom until 1849. He wrote a variety of miscellaneous works, including (late in life, and presumably for money) the fiction: *Thurlston Tales* (1835) and *Palmario, Or The Merchant Of Venice* (1839). He died at Kensington. BL 2. *DNB.* Wol. RLF.

Ginx's Baby, John Edward Jenkins, 1870, 1 vol, Strahan. Jenkins's first published novel, and his most sensationally popular. Ginx is a £1-a-week navvy who deposits his thirteenth child on the Catholic 'Sisters of Misery'. The baby is rescued from Papist error by the 'Protestant Detectoral Society' who (after spending over £1,000 in the affair) dump the baby on the parish. The parish returns him to his lawful parents. Ginx next abandons his baby in the doorway of the Reform ('Radical') Club. The unwanted thing grows up criminal, finally drowning himself off Vauxhall Bridge, the solution originally intended by his father at the unlucky child's birth. The work went through thirty-seven editions between 1870 and 1877. It is written in a jagged, satirical manner derived from the 'Moving On!' chapter in Dickens's* *Bleak House*.

The Girl's Own Paper (1880–1965). Sister publication to the immensely popular *Boy's Own Paper**, also published by the RTS*. Starting a year later than its companion, *GOP* featured the so-called 'girl's story' which had been pioneered by L. T. Meade* and Evelyn Everett-Green*. *GOP* shared the same format as *BOP*, making some conventional concessions to the milder and more domestic nature of the Victorian girl.

GISSING, Algernon (1860–1937). Gissing was born at Wakefield, the third son of Thomas Waller Gissing, a retail chemist, and brother of the better known novelist George Gissing*. Algernon was educated at a private school near Manchester, and on leaving trained as a solicitor. From 1887, he lived in the country, in Gloucestershire, and wrote fiction. His first novel, *Joy Cometh In The Morning*, came out in 1888. 'An agreeable and tolerably written tale of country life' (as one modern critic calls it), it sold 392 copies and earned all of £16 in royalties for its author. Algernon's fiction generally is more rural and idyllic in tone and subject-matter than George Gissing's. He also experimented with Meredithean* complexity as in *A Masquerader* (1892). His other works include: *Both Of This Parish* (1889); *A Village Hampden* (1890); *A Moorland Idyll* (1891); *Between Two Opinions* (1893); *The Sport Of Stars* (1895); *The Scholar Of Bygate* (1897), a Scottish story. *A Secret Of The North Sea* (1899) is one of his best novels, with a Northumberland coast setting and some closely observed melodrama of village life. Gissing, who evidently catered for a loyal library readership, suffered badly with the decline of the three-decker in 1894. His income in the early twentieth century slipped below the £100 per annum level, on which even the most frugal middle-class family could barely exist. As one of his sponsors to the Royal Literary Fund* put it: 'the wonder is that with his children to keep and his wife an almost helpless invalid, he was still able to produce his volume a year'. Gissing survived in penury virtually into the modern period, a casualty of the New Grub Street* his more talented brother chronicled. BL 28. *WW*. Wol. RLF.

GISSING, George [Robert] (1857–1903). Gissing was born at Wakefield, Yorkshire. His father was a pharmaceutical chemist with strong liberal opinions, and during George's childhood, the family lived over the shop. Gissing attended local Wakefield schools until he was thirteen, when his father died. He then went to Owens College, Manchester, where he gained a sound education in the classics and in modern languages. Gissing was a prize pupil and worked to the point of nervous breakdown. He seemed set for Oxford or Cambridge. But in 1876, when he was eighteen, he fell in love with a local seventeen-year-old prostitute, Nell Harrison. To keep her off the streets, Gissing embarked on a series of thefts of clothing and money from the college. He was found out, disgraced and sentenced to a month's hard labour. This episode had a profound effect on the young man's subsequent career, and doubtless inspired the pessimistic and frequently morbid themes found in his later fiction. On his release, Gissing fled in shame to America in September 1876. He spent a year there, restlessly working as a teacher, journalist and photographer's assistant. By this period his political opinions had become strongly radical. On his return to England he was reunited with Nell Harrison, whom he married in 1879. The marriage was disastrous. She was alcoholic and had no sympathy with his intellectual aspirations. The couple separated in 1883. Meanwhile, Gissing was supporting himself in a hand-to-mouth way by taking pupils. In 1880, he published at his own expense *Workers In The Dawn**, a grim study of slum life. The novel attracted little general attention but brought Gissing to the notice of the literary world. Frederic Harrison, the positivist thinker, was particularly useful to Gissing at this formative stage of his career and helped the young writer to some journalistic commissions. And at the same period, Gissing came strongly under the influence of another new friend, the German socialist Eduard Bertz. In 1884, he produced another novel of working-class life, *The Unclassed**, which was published by Chapman and Hall*. Gissing's circumstances improved (particularly after his separation from Nell) and he moved into a comfortable flat near Regent's Park in London. In his subsequent novels, he turned an ironic gaze on to the English middle classes. *Isabel Clarendon* (1886); *Demos** (1886); *A Life's Morning* (1888) all enjoyed some success of critical esteem and sales. *Thyrza** (1887) returned to slum life, with the depiction of an idealised working-class girl and her somewhat more interesting lover, Gilbert Grail. *The Nether World* (1889), written during the terrible trade depression of the mid-1880s, offers Gissing's harshest depiction of the life of the English lower classes. Gissing was himself now relatively comfortably off, and in 1888 he went to the Continent for five months. An Italian setting is introduced into *The Emancipated* (1890), a work which is lighter and more deftly ironic than Gissing's previous efforts. *New Grub Street** (1891) is generally regarded as his masterpiece. A bitter survey of the contemporary literary life and its rewards, the novel's indictment holds for the twentieth-century world of letters as much as for the age in which Gissing wrote. In 1891, Gissing married again, choosing another girl of the working classes, Edith Underwood. As before, the marriage was a catastrophic failure. Its wretchedness is reflected in the excessively gloomy *Born In Exile** (1892). In the same year, Gissing turned out a one-volume novel with a political theme, *Denzil Quarrier*. The hero, whose career is ruined by sexual delinquency, would seem to have some autobiographical origins. *The Odd Women** (1893) is interesting for its engaged attitude towards the question of women's rights. *In The Year Of Jubilee** (1894) is the last of Gissing's three-deckers. Its subject, that of a woman's surrender of her freedom for marriage, is again politically topical. The novel also vividly depicts the celebrations of the fiftieth anniversary of Victoria's reign, and expresses the author's pessimistic evaluation of mass culture. *The Whirlpool* (1897) is another major work, dealing with the socially and psychologically disintegrating effect of life in London. Edith Gissing's behaviour had meanwhile become increasingly unstable, and had made normal home life impossible. In 1897, Gissing deserted her. In 1897, he visited Italy again, and began to write his major critical work, *Charles Dickens, A Study* (1898). The trip also inspired the travel book, *By The Ionian Sea* (1901). Gissing moved to Dorking, in Surrey, having put his children into care. For the last five years of his life, he lived happily with a Frenchwoman, Gabrielle Fleury. Fleury, who was intellectual (she translated *New Grub Street* into French), supplied the companionship lacking in Gissing's previous unhappy relationships with women. Since (as guilty party) Gissing could not divorce Edith, the union was irregular. In 1903, Gissing produced his most popular work, the essayistic *Private Papers Of Henry Ryecroft*. By this time, the author was living in France and was crippled by emphysema of which he died in 1903. Two novels were published posthumously. *Will Warburton* is complete. *Veranilda*, a story of sixth-century Rome, is incomplete. Gissing's fiction is notable for its agnosticism, realism and ironic pessimism. BL 26. *DNB*. RM. *NCBEL*. Wol. Sad.

GLANVILLE, Ernest (1856-1925). Glanville was born in Wyneburg, South Africa, of Devonshire parents. He was educated at Graham's Town. His father was a journalist, and as a boy Ernest helped him set up the first printing press at Kimberley. Later, Glanville Sr rose to be a leading South African politician. As a young man, Ernest Glanville dug for diamonds in the Kimberley fields, and was a war correspondent for *The Times* and other London papers during the Zulu War of 1879. He afterwards settled down as a journalist in Cape Town. During the 1890s, he was based mainly in England. For the English public Glanville wrote a quantity of fiction with South African settings, including: *Among The Cape Kaffirs* (1887); *The Fossicker* (1891), a Mashonaland romance; *Kloof Yarns* (1896). *The Lost Heiress* (1891) is a story of 'Love, Battle And Adventure'. *Max Thornton* (1901) is a lively tale of the Boer War, which made Glanville a very popular writer on the home front. It was particularly valued for its revelations of the Boers' guerrilla 'dodges'. He returned to South Africa around 1908. BL 21. RM. Wol.

GLASCOCK, Captain [William Nugent] (1787?-1847). Glascock is the least interesting representative of the nautical* school of nineteenth-century fiction. He entered the Royal Navy in 1800 and served with distinction in the Napoleonic Wars. From 1818 until his death he had various commands and distinguished himself in duty off the Portuguese coast in the early 1830s. In 1847, he was appointed one of the Poor Relief Act's inspectors in Ireland, to superintend aid to victims of the famine there. During his slack periods of half pay, Glascock would write novels, or, to borrow one of his titles, *Tales Of A Tar* (1836). They are mostly feeble, although evidently the vogue for Marryat's* fiction (and Richard Bentley's* advertising) was sufficient to sell them. His most successful novel was probably *Land Sharks And Sea Gulls* (1838) illustrated by George Cruikshank*. He also wrote an officers' manual in 1836, which was widely reprinted. Glascock died in Ireland, carrying out his official duties during the Famine. BL 3. *DNB*. RM. *NCBEL*. Wol. Sad. RLF.

GLEIG, G[eorge] R[obert] (1796-1888). Military historian and novelist. Gleig was born in Stirling, Scotland, the son of an episcopalian clergyman, later Bishop of Brechin. After attending grammar school locally he went to Balliol College, Oxford, leaving prematurely in 1811 to take up a commission in the army. (Some accounts have him entering Glasgow University at the age of thirteen, before embarking on a military career at an only slightly less surprising early age). Gleig served in the Peninsular War as a lieutenant. He later saw action and was wounded in the subsequent hostilities with America. After Waterloo, Gleig, like most officers, went on half pay and returned to Oxford in 1816. He completed his studies and was ordained in 1820 and was for a while an impecunious curate. In 1826, he sold up his half-pay pension and wrote his first work of fiction *The Subaltern*. Its success led to a string of similar racy military novels, all with a pronounced autobiographical element. Most were published by Blackwood's*, a house with whom Gleig formed a close alliance and with whose Conservatism he was in political sympathy. *The Hussar* (1837) is presented as the autobiography of Norbert Landsheit, beginning with his birth in Germany in 1777 and ending with his admission to the Chelsea Hospital for superannuated soldiers in 1819. Gleig's later fiction includes: *The Light Dragoon* (1844). As a historian, Gleig's most popular work was *The Story Of The Battle Of Waterloo* (1847), a source which was used extensively by Thackeray* for his novel *Vanity Fair**. The major components in Gleig's diverse career were neatly combined in 1844, when he was appointed Chaplain-General of the Forces, a post he held for thirty years. BL 10. *DNB*. *NCBEL*. Wol.

GLYN, Elinor (née Sutherland, 1864–1943). Although famous as a best-selling author of twentieth-century women's romance, Glyn made a Victorian début and the core of her authorial personality was formed in the period. Elinor Sutherland was born in Jersey, the daughter of a civil engineer who had unsuccessfully laid claim to the title of Lord Duffus. He died shortly after his daughter's birth. Her mother returned to her native Canada, and remarried in 1871. The Sutherland children disliked their aged and strict Scottish stepfather David Kennedy. Elinor was educated at home by governesses and grew up an imaginative child (her favourite book was Charles Kingsley's* *The Heroes*). She was from childhood temperamentally independent. Pretty, with red hair and green eyes, she successfully entered English high society, and was thought to have made a fine catch with her husband, Clayton Glyn, a wealthy landowner whom she married in 1892. But the marriage was not a success (partly because she could only provide two daughters, and no son). Glyn's first book, *The Visits Of Elizabeth* (1900) which was immediately popular, takes the form of letters written by the heroine to her mother, describing dazzling visits to English and French country houses such as Heaviland Manor and the Chateau de Croixmare. Its success led to a sequel (*Elizabeth Visits America*, 1909) and to other novels of contemporary high society, culminating in the tremendously successful *Three Weeks* (1907). The story of a Balkan queen and her English lover, this work was sexually explicit for its time. Glyn's career subsequently took her to Hollywood, and authorial stardom. Her best-remembered novel is probably *It* (1926). In 1936, she published an autobiography, aptly entitled *Romantic Adventure*. BL 31. *DNB*. RM. *NCBEL*.

God And The Man, Robert Buchanan, 1881, 3 vols, Chatto. Buchanan's most popular and melodramatic novel, set at the turn of the century. The action starts from an inveterate feud between Squire Orchardson and Robert Christianson of Fen Farm. When the latter dies, the enmity is carried on by the next generation, young Richard Orchardson and Christian Christianson, rivals in love for the daughter of a Methodist preacher, Priscilla Sefton. All three find themselves on board a ship bound for America. Disguised as a common seaman, Christian attacks Richard (who earlier seduced his sister) and is put in irons. Richard maliciously sets fire to the vessel and by an unlikely series of events, the rivals find themselves abandoned in the snowy wastes of Labrador. Here, reduced to animal existence, they are finally reconciled. Richard dies. Christian, his hate purged, returns to marry Priscilla. The novel was successfully dramatised.

God's Fool, Maarten Maartens, 1892, 3 vols, Bentley. (Serialised in *Temple Bar*, January–December, 1892). The most strikingly original of Maartens's 'Koopstad Chronicles', the series of realistic tales of middle-class Dutch life, set just outside Amsterdam. Hendrik Lossell, a rich tea merchant and town councillor, makes two marriages. The son of the first, Elias, is blinded, deafened and brain-damaged at the age of nine when a flowerpot drops on his head. By his grandfather's will, it is Elias, the 'fool', who is left heir, rather than his younger twin half-brothers, Hendrik and Hubert (who mischievously pushed the flower pot). Aided by a villainous lawyer, Alers, Hendrik contrives to cheat the amiable idiot of his heritage, persuading him (by touch language) that he is giving money to the poor, 'like Christ'. Hubert stabs his brother to death. Elias nobly sacrifices himself to the authorities. The highly unusual conception of the hero is strikingly done but the novel provoked charges of blasphemy which Maartens publicly rejected, noting tartly that the satirist kicks the world like a football, 'but always towards the goal'.

The Gods, Some Mortals And Lord Wickenham, John Oliver Hobbes (i.e. Pearl Mary-Teresa Craigie), 1895, 1 vol, Henry. (First serialised in the *Pall Mall Budget*, 1895.) The scheming anti-heroine, Anne Delaware, entices an aristocratic young doctor, Simon Warre, away from Allegra, the young Italian beauty he originally loves and whose father wants the match for money reasons. At his wedding to her, Simon discovers the facts about Anne's sexual past when her brutal lover, Algernon Dane, suffers an accident riding. It emerges that she gave herself to him 'for money'. Simon refuses to consummate the marriage or to divorce Anne (despite flagrant infidelity). He eventually goes off to the tropics to work himself to death. Allegra survives to marry the amiable Lord Wickenham. The novel is depressive and 'sensitively' written (i.e. almost impossible to read), in the style fashionable in the 1890s. It has been suggested that the marriage-trap theme may have inspired the central episode in Hardy's* *Jude The Obscure** (the two novelists were friends).

GODWIN, Mrs Catherine Grace (née Garnett, 1798–1845). The daughter of a Glasgow doctor, Catherine Garnett's mother died delivering her and she was entirely orphaned four years later with the death of her father. Brought up by family friends in Westmorland (at this time the poetic centre of Britain) she married a senior employee of the East India Company, Thomas Godwin, in 1824. As Catherine Godwin she went on to publish verses that were well thought of by Wordsworth in the 1830s. She died prematurely after a long affliction of spinal disease. Although the *DNB* asserts that she wrote little after the death of her sister in 1832, she has to her credit a number of excessively well-meant stories for children such as: *Alicia Grey, Or To Be Useful Is To Be Happy* (1837); *Basil Harlow* (1836); *Cousin Kate, Or The Punishment Of Pride* (1836); *Josephine, Or Early Trials* (1837); *Louisa Seymour, Or Hasty Impressions* (1837); *Scheming* (1838). BL 7. *DNB*.

The Golden Butterfly, Walter Besant and James Rice, 1876, 3 vols, Tinsley. (Serialised in the *World*, 1876.) After *Ready Money Mortiboy**, the most successful of Rice and Besant's fourteen collaborations. This novel's main interest is in its central character, Gilead P. Beck, probably the first American millionaire to be portrayed in English fiction. The grandiose and vulgar Beck has 'struck oil' ('ile', as he calls it) and throws his 'greenbacks' about in a futile attempt to buy English society. He plans a national art collection, theatre and newspaper. The funniest scene has Gilead duped at the Langham Hotel by what he takes to be a company of the leading literary men in England (Carlyle, Tennyson, Ruskin*, Sala*). Beck's oil runs out, and he ends the novel without a 'red cent'. The golden butterfly of the title is his lucky charm, a lump of quartz 'quaintly marked' with the exact shape of a butterfly. A romantic plot is attached to Beck's three-months' misadventures through his connection with Jack Dunquerque, an English youth who saved him from a grisly bear in the Wild West, before his fame and fortune. And Besant makes Beck's grandiose patronage of the English arts the occasion for running satire on the country's incurable philistinism: 'Successful authors make a few hundreds a year; successful grocers make a few thousands; and people say – How well is Literature rewarded!'.

The Golden Lion Of Granpere, Anthony Trollope, 1872, 1 vol, Tinsley. (First serialised in *Good Words**, January–August, 1872.) The title refers to the name of the single hotel in Granpere, a village in the Vosges Mountains in France. The plot is unsensational. The owner of the Golden Lion, Michel Voss, has been twice married. The son of his first marriage, George, is in love with the niece of his present wife, Marie Bromar. Voss peremptorily forbids the match. George goes away, to start up his own inn at Colmar. He does not write and Marie is induced to accept the marriage proposal of Adrian Urmand, a linen buyer from Basle, who frequently uses the Golden Lion when travelling. George hears of the proposed marriage, and returns to claim Marie. His father, overjoyed by the reunion, offers no more resistance. The novel was originally conceived as one of a series which Trollope hoped to bring out anonymously, but the experiment did not work.

Good Words (1860–1906). The most popular fiction-carrying monthly (after 1861) magazine of the nineteenth century, before Newnes's* *Strand** appeared in 1891. *Good Words* was devised by the Scottish publisher and magazine proprietor, Alexander Strahan* whose bright idea it was to find a way of recruiting the large evangelical readership of magazines for something lighter than theology and church news. As a pilot, he had launched the weekly *Christian Guest, A Family Magazine For Leisure Hours And Sundays* in 1859. The motto for *Good Words* was: 'Good Words are Worth Much and Cost Little'. It was the only journal of its kind to receive an endorsement from the Society for Purity in Literature, in 1861. At around seventy pages, with illustrations, costing 6d., the magazine was good value. Much of its success is attributable to the editor Strahan appointed, the Rev. Norman

Macleod*, a hero of the Established Church of Scotland. In addition to editing and writing on theological matters, Macleod contributed many of the journal's most popular pious stories, notably: *The Old Lieutenant And His Son* (1861), the story of an evangelical sailor who spreads lavish amounts of Christian good wherever he goes. Under Macleod, the tone of the journal was consistently instructive, with a preference for articles of travel and geographical interest. Among other more secular novelists who contributed to the journal were Dinah Mulock (Craik*), Anthony Trollope* (although *Rachel Ray*￼ in 1863 led to a painful breach, arising from its alleged anti-evangelical satire), 'Sarah Tytler' (i.e. Henrietta Keddie*), Charles Kingsley*, George MacDonald*, Thomas Hardy* (*The Trumpet Major*), and Mrs Henry Wood*. The journal started off with a circulation of 30,000 and rose to five times that figure by 1864. But it never quite shook off the dark suspicions of strict Christians that it was the insidious enemy of Sabbatarianism. A notable feature of the paper was its use of distinguished illustrators, including W. Q. Orchardson*, Arthur Hughes* and J. E. Millais*. Despite its bounding circulation, *Good Words* was not an unqualified commercial success, largely due to the incompetent business management of its proprietor Strahan. There were a series of financial crises in the late 1860s, culminating in near bankruptcy of the publisher's whole enterprise in 1872. Strahan was forced to retire from business, although *Good Words* continued to come out under his firm's name. The journal gradually fell back from the first rank it had occupied in the 1860s, but it survived until the twentieth century when after various take-overs it became an unrecognisable tabloid. In the 1860s a stable of journals sprang up around *Good Words*, including: *The Sunday Magazine* (founded in 1864) and *Good Words For The Young* (founded in 1868, edited in the 1870s by George MacDonald), *Good Cheer* (the journal's special Christmas issues) and *Argosy*￼ (founded in 1865). BLM.

The Gordian Knot, Shirley Brooks, 1860, 1 vol, Bentley. (Subtitled 'A Story Of Good And Evil' the novel was serialised in twelve irregular monthly parts, December 1857–December 1859, with illustrations by John Tenniel*.) Brooks's most interesting novel. A young lawyer, Philip Arundel, falls in love with an apparently parentless young beauty, Margaret Spencer, at a fête on the bank of the Thames. (There is a fine Tenniel illustration, showing her with bow and arrow.) Margaret has been brought up in the country town of St Oscar's by relatives, her Anglo-Indian parents having separated. Despite this blot, and despite rivalry from a doctor cousin, Alban Cheriton, Margaret and Philip marry. After marriage, rifts emerge. He falls back into dissolute clubman ways. A former mistress, Maria, emerges. Disreputable elements of Margaret's family past also resurface. And as family physician, Alban cunningly plays on the couple's problems. Alban finally goes mad, and the Arundels are reconciled 'in the Sacrament of Death' over the body of the dying Maria whose last words are: 'Perhaps, if I go to Heaven, we may both love him there.' The novel has lively theatrical and opera scenes.

GORDON, the Rev. Charles W[illiam] ('Ralph Connor', 1860–1937). Born in Glengarry, Ontario, Gordon was one of six sons of a Scottish Free Church minister. After graduating from the University of Toronto with a BA in 1883, Gordon spent a year studying theology in Edinburgh. He was ordained in 1890, and undertook missionary work among lumbermen and miners in the Rocky Mountains. In 1894, he settled down in a ministry at Winnipeg, where he was to remain until 1936. He married in 1899, fathering a large family (six daughters and one son). As an author, Gordon began (as 'Ralph Connor') writing sketches and fictional stories for the Presbyterian *Westminster* magazine. This led to his first book, *Black Rock, A Tale Of The Selkirks* (1898). The work was a bestseller, and was followed by the even more successful *The Sky Pilot* (1899) and *The Man From Glengarry* (1901). These stories all feature the civilising effects of ministers of religion (i.e. 'sky pilots') in the Canadian wilderness. Despite his age, Gordon served as a chaplain to the Canadian forces in the First World War. His later novels were comparatively unsuccessful. BL 27. *WW*. RM.

GORDON, Samuel (1871–1927). Gordon was born in Buk, Prussia, and came to England with his family at the age of thirteen. He was educated in London and at Cambridge University, where he read classics. Gordon subsequently gained some fame in Britain as 'an authority on all things Russo-Jewish'. His fiction, which deals mainly with Jewish themes and stands out against the perils of assimilation, includes: *In Years Of Transition* (1897); *A Handful Of Exotics* (1897); *A Tale Of Two Rings* (1898); *Daughters Of Shem* (1898); *Lesser Destinies* (1899); *Sons Of The Covenant* (1900). This last is Gordon's outstanding novel, an unflinching examination of the place of Jews in London's East and West Ends through the intertwined careers of two brothers. As the *Athenaeum** condescendingly noted: 'the work has more interest for the Hebrew community in England than for the reading public at large'. It was sponsored by the Philadelphia-based 'Jewish Publication Society of America', who also commissioned the early work of Israel Zangwill*. A recent critic of Gordon argues that his endorsement of Jewish separateness (in works such as *The Queen's Quandary*, 1903) encouraged legislation to curb immigration in the early twentieth century. BL 12. *WW*.

GORE, Mrs C[atherine Grace] F[rances] (née Moody, 1799–1861). The undisputed leader of the silver fork* school of fashionable fiction and one of the most prolific novelists of the century. Gore's fiction (which has never been fully annotated bibliographically) amounts to at least seventy full length works between 1824 and 1862 if one includes translations and 'edited' novels. Anonymity was essential to her enterprise, lest she be seen to be drugging the market. Thus, in the same week of 1841, *Greville* and *Cecil** were published, in keen rivalry with each other. (In the same year, there appeared a sprightly sequel *Cecil, A Peer*.) Mrs Gore was born Catherine Moody into a family of respectable background. Her father, C. Moody, was a wine merchant in East Retford, Nottinghamshire. At an early age she showed literary ability and was nicknamed 'the Poetess'. In 1823, she married Captain Charles Arthur Gore, of the Life Guards. Although he left the service in the same year, Catherine evidently saw at first hand some of the fashionable life she describes in her fiction. As the *Athenaeum** put it in 1837: 'Mrs Gore writes for the world, and she is herself a woman of the world'. R. H. Horne*, in his portrait of Gore in *The New Spirit Of The Age*, astutely notes that 'she excels in the portraiture of the upper section of the middle class, just at that point of contact with the aristocracy'. She herself, in the preface to *Pin Money* (1831), claimed that she was transferring 'the familiar narrative of Miss Austen to a higher sphere of society'. Gore's writing career apparently began with *Theresa Marchmont, Or The Maid Of Honour* (1824). She was puffed extravagantly by Colburn*, and for him had her first hit with *Women As They Are, Or The Manners Of The Day* (1830). George IV, no less, pronounced it 'the best bred and most amusing novel published in my remembrance'. In the 1830s, in the post-Reform ferment, Gore embarked on a series of novels illustrative of the hazards and volatility of English society of which the finest is *The Hamiltons* (1834), a depiction of the social consequences of the Reform Bill. In 1832, for reasons which are not clear (but which may involve debt or scandal) Gore moved to France, and thereafter lived a life of seclusion. Domestically, her life was full. She had ten children. Although her fiction is all of it consistently lively and entertaining, by general agreement her finest work is to be found in *Mrs Armytage, Or Female Domination** (1836), *Cecil, Or The Adventures Of A Coxcomb* (1841) and *The Banker's Wife, Or Court And City* (1843). Although she never managed to break out of the constricting frames set up by the social and historical* fiction of the 1830s, Gore's is a considerable literary talent. She is, it should be emphasised, much more versatile than Thackeray's* good-natured burlesque, *Lords And Liveries* ('by the author of *Dukes And Déjeuners, Hearts And Diamonds, Marchionesses And Milliners*, etc.') would suggest. She has, at her best, as easy a manner as Thackeray himself. Her fashionable novels are set in, and sharply reflect, the present day. She writes a vigorous, slangy prose, with sharp epigrams embedded in it. In novels like *Men Of Capital* (1846); *Mammon, Or The Hardships Of An Heiress* (1855) and the early *Stokeshill Place, Or The Man Of Business* (1837) Gore handles the theme of money and social mobility very ably. As a sociologist of English society she is impressive (see, for example, her *Sketches Of English Character*, 1846). Her later fiction, in key with the times, is more moral and domestic*. At the end of her life, Gore was blind, though still writing. Of her ten children, only two survived her. After a heroically long writing career, she inherited a substantial property in 1850. But she was impoverished five years later when her former guardian, Sir John Dean Paul (1802–68), defrauded her of £20,000. (He was subsequently sentenced to four years' imprisonment for this and other crimes against clients.) Gore died, prematurely, at the age of sixty-one. BL 53. *DNB*. RM. *NCBEL*. Wol. Sad.

GOSSE, [Sir] Edmund [William] (1849–1928). The son of a fundamentalist zoologist who quixotically tried to align faith and science, Gosse gives a wonderful account of his early family life in *Father And Son* (1907). In adult life, Gosse worked in the British Museum Library from 1865 to 1875 and in the twentieth century made an internationally famous name for himself as critic, man of letters, scholar and biographer. He also composed poetry, and wrote one novel, *The Secret Of Narcisse* (1892). A melancholy tale, it is set in Bar le Duc in the sixteenth century and has as its hero an artist falsely accused of witchcraft by a scorned lover. Gosse's fellow writers (such as Hardy*) admired the work but it made no hit with the reading public. BL 1. *DNB*. RM. *NCBEL*. Wol.

Gothic Fiction. Gothic fiction flowered in the eighteenth and early nineteenth century, notably with the romances of M. G. Lewis (1775–1818),

Charles Maturin (1782–1824) and Ann Radcliffe (1764–1823). The mainstream of Victorian fiction took a quite different direction towards domestic* realism. A persistent gothic strain is found in historical* fiction, however, (particularly that of Ainsworth*, see his *Auriol**) and in Walter Scott influenced work, such as that of the Brontës (particularly Emily). Gothic horror survived in the fiction for the millions produced in the 1840s by the so-called Salisbury Square publishers (i.e. those who set up business around Fleet Street) such as Edward Lloyd* and G. W. M. Reynolds* and hack writers such as Pierce Egan Jr*, Thomas Peckett Prest* and James Malcolm Rymer (or Errym*). The latter's *Ada The Betrayed* (1842) and *Varney The Vampire** (1847) may be considered late, if coarse, classics of nineteenth-century gothic. And the genre can be seen to resurface strongly in the decadent* novels of the 1880s and 1890s by such writers as Arthur Machen* and R. L. Stevenson*, who was strongly impressed by 'penny dreadfuls*' in his boyhood. But in general, gothic, with all its conventional furniture of ghastly castles, mysterious apparitions, sex and sadism, and Italianate mystery remains a minor byway of Victorian fiction.

GOULD, Nat[haniel] (1857–1919). Gould was born in Manchester, the son of a tea merchant and educated at nearby Southport. His father died during Nat's schoolhood and after a brief try at the family business, which did not suit him, he went into farming. This also was unsuccessful, although it served to develop his lifelong interest in horses. Gould next moved into provincial journalism, and in 1877 gained a post on the *Newark Advertiser*. In 1884, he emigrated to Australia, where he worked on various newspapers, largely as a racing correspondent. He also began writing short stories, and in 1891 turned out a long serial, *The Double Event* (called *With The Tide* in Australia). This 'tale of the Melbourne Cup' which mixed racing scenes with a detective* plot was a hit and Gould followed it with other lively yarns of the turf. In 1886, he married and in 1895 returned to England after eleven years' absence. He was now a well-known novelist and on his return he made an agreement with Routledge* to furnish them with five works of fiction a year. By 1919, working at this extraordinary rate, Gould had over 150 books to his name. All his narratives centre around horse-racing. His output for 1899 is typical: *Racecourse And Battlefield*; *The Old Mare's Foal*; *The Dark Horse*; *The Pace That Kills*. BL 172. *WW*. Wol.

GRAHAM, R[obert] B[ontine] Cunninghame (1852–1936). Graham was born in London. His father, William Cunninghame Graham Bontine of Gartmore in Perthshire was a former major in the Scots Greys, a laird and a fierce Whig. His mother was half-Spanish and had been born in South America. The surname Graham was adopted from his great-grandfather. The family could claim indirect descent from the Stewarts and Andrew Lang* nicknamed Graham 'the uncrowned king of the Scots'. In later life he was also called 'El Hidalgo' (the nobleman). Graham received a miscellaneous school education, which included two years at Harrow. Incurably romantic, at the age of seventeen he went to South America. This was the formative experience of his life and altogether he was to spend around sixteen years in the sub-continent. He rode with the gauchos mastering the lasso and bolas, travelled north to befriend Buffalo Bill Cody and assumed the airs of a Spanish don for the remainder of his life, although his political views were (at their most extreme) revolutionary. In 1878, Graham married a Chilean grandee's daughter. In 1883, his father William Graham died, following an accident riding. The estate was found to be heavily in debt. Nevertheless, Cunninghame Graham spent the following ten years in a vain attempt to save Gartmore, in the role of gentleman farmer. In 1886, he was elected Liberal MP for North Lanarkshire and in Parliament was a firm supporter of Parnell, making a name for himself as an orator. Subsequently he became an ardent socialist and was briefly imprisoned for taking part in the 1887 'Bloody Sunday' Trafalgar Square riot. Graham wrote various books throughout the course of his remarkable life. He began, in the Victorian era, with a travel work: *Mogreb-el-Acksa* (1898). His Victorian fiction is found gathered in collections of sketches, travel writing, essays and stories: *The Ipané* (1899); *Thirteen Stories* (1900); *Success* (1902). These volumes are consciously nostalgic and retrospective in tone, Graham writing as a man 'who has not only seen but lived with ghosts'. A flamboyant adventurer, Graham, together with W. H. Hudson* (with whom he was personally friendly after 1894) created a powerful mystique in the Anglo-Saxon reading public around the idea of South America. During the First World War, Cunninghame Graham served his country by buying horses for the government in South America. His later years were largely devoted to equine pursuits and causes. BL 12. *DNB*. RM. *NCBEL*.

GRAHAME, Kenneth (1859–1932). Grahame was born in Edinburgh, the son of a lawyer who traced his descent from Robert the Bruce. (As, coincidentally, did Grahame's mother.) Grahame went to school in Oxfordshire, and in 1879 began his working life in the Bank of England. Around 1886, he started writing essays and sketches for the reviews. He published a collection entitled *Pagan Papers* in 1893. During the magazine's short existence Grahame wrote for the *Yellow Book**. In 1895, he published *The Golden Age*, a collection of sketches and tales which delicately recapture childhood experience. A sequel, *Dream Days*, came out in 1898. In the same year, Grahame became secretary of the Bank of England. He held the post until 1908, when ill-health forced him to retire. His most famous book, the animal fable *The Wind In The Willows*, was published in 1908. BL 3. *DNB*. RM. *NCBEL*.

GRAND, Sarah [Frances Elizabeth McFall] (née Clarke, 1854–1943). The most interesting of the novelists who engaged their fiction with the political issues of the new woman*. Grand was born in Northern Ireland, into a middle-class background. Both her parents were English by birth, her father being a Royal Navy lieutenant. She gives a sharp picture of her childhood and its shabby gentility in the Castletownrock chapters of *The Beth Book**. In 1861, on the death of her father, the family returned to England. She attended two boarding schools, unhappily, and emerged much less well educated than her two brothers. In 1870, at the age of sixteen, she was married to an army surgeon, Lieutenant-Colonel David McFall. Her husband was twenty-three years older than her, an army surgeon and a widower with children. His tyrannous character is portrayed in Dan Maclure in *The Beth Book*. The marriage was not a happy one, although the couple travelled widely to Hong Kong and the Far East. In England they lived in Norwich and subsequently in Warrington. (He eventually died in 1898, many years after their separation.) Grand began writing the preachy *Ideala* in 1880, although the work was not published until eight years later. The small profits from the novel enabled her to leave her husband and take her young son to London where she supported herself writing. Grand's reputation was made with the scandalous *The Heavenly Twins** (1893). Blackwood's* were nervous about taking the work, since syphilis figures centrally in the plot. George Meredith*, as publisher's reader, turned the work down for Chapman and Hall*, because he found it too clogged with 'ideas'. When it was eventually published the novel sold 20,000 copies and was reprinted six times in the first year. Four of Grand's polemical novels, *Ideala* (1888); *A Domestic Experiment* (1891); *The Heavenly Twins* (1893) and *The Beth Book* (1897) are influential feminist works to this day. The last, particularly, is revealingly autobiographical. *Ideala*'s heroine, 'by suffering made strong', defies convention by living flagrantly in sin. In a fighting preface answering accusations of hideous immorality, Grand asserted: 'Doctors spiritual must face the horrors of the dissecting room.' *A Domestic Experiment* is a story of justified adultery which scandalised reviewers. A cult figure in the 1890s, Heinemann* were careful to preface volumes of her fiction with striking portraits of the beautiful author. Grand lived a long life, but wrote (or published) relatively little. (Although one of her novels, *The Winged Victory*, came out as late as 1916.) After her husband's death she lived in Tunbridge Wells where she was president of the local branch of the National Union of Suffrage Societies. In 1920 she moved to Bath and was subsequently mayoress of the city on six occasions. In *Who's Who* she put down as her principal recreation 'sociology'. BL 11. *WW*. RM. *NCBEL*. Wol. Sad.

Grania, the Hon. Emily Lawless, 1892, 2 vols, Smith, Elder. Subtitled 'The Story Of An Island', Lawless's highly sentimental story is set on the Aran isles off the Galway coast. Grania is a young girl brought up among the island's fisherfolk. Her dark complexion and passion witness to Spanish blood, inherited from her mother. When she is eighteen, her father dies and Grania is left in charge of her family. An impetuous woman, she drowns when her betrothed, Murdough Blake, does not come to her aid as she tries to cross the foggy channel to fetch a priest for her dying sister Honor. Swinburne called *Grania* 'one of the most exquisite and perfect works of genius in the language'. The *Athenaeum** thought that 'Grania, heroic in her failings as in her strength, and Honor, the pale saint, are beautiful types of Irish womanhood'. In fact, the novel is little more than a vehicle for Lawless's densely regional* depiction of a distinctive local way of life and an unusual community that she knew at first hand. A map of the island was appended to Smith, Elder's first edition.

GRANT, James (1822–87). Military novelist and Scottish Nationalist. Grant was born in Edinburgh, into an old Scottish family with inherited Jacobite sentiments. His father was an army captain in the Gordon Highlanders, who had served in the Peninsular War. After his mother's death in 1833, Grant and his two brothers were taken to Newfoundland. The family spent six years in North America, at which point Captain Grant resigned his commission. James Grant was by patronage himself gazetted as an ensign in the 62nd Foot, in 1840. But in 1843, he too resigned his commission, and entered the office of an Edinburgh architect. Grant began his long authorial career with a sub-Dickensian* series *Sketches In London* (1838; the work was illustrated by Phiz*). He also wrote extensively for Colburn's* *United Service Magazine*. In 1846–47 he published his four-volume *The Romance Of War, Or The Highlanders In Spain*, the narrative of the 92nd Highlanders' contribution from the Peninsular campaign to Waterloo. This work which drew heavily on his father's army experience was popular and set the pattern for Grant's later books which typically rang the changes on Scottish, Jacobite and military themes. Two of his most characteristic novels are *The Scottish Cavalier* (1850), set in the late seventeenth century; and *The Cameronians* (1881), a work written to coincide with the disbandment of the famous regiment in current army reforms (about which the author evidently had his doubts). Grant was an active spokesman for his country and in 1852 founded the National Association for the Vindication of Scottish Rights. He was also an enthusiastic supporter of the local Volunteer movement, designed to equip civilians as part-time soldiers. As a military expert, he was occasionally consulted by the War Office. An opportunist, Grant was always ready to write a novel on whatever war was going on (see, for instance, his novel about the current Sudan hostilities, *Playing With Fire*, 1887). He died destitute, having embraced the Catholic faith in 1875. His work is reckoned somewhat superior to that of his fellow military novelists, Gleig* and Maxwell*. BL 60. *DNB*. RM. *NCBEL*. Wol. Sad. RLF.

Grantley Manor, Lady Georgiana Fullerton, 1847, 3 vols, Moxon. One of the author's more interesting works, fuelled, like *Ellen Middleton**, by her pro-Catholic sentiments. Ginevra, a young English girl, meets and marries Edmund Neville in Italy. She is Catholic, the daughter of Colonel Leslie and a beautiful Italian mother. Edmund's father is a strict Anglo-Irish Protestant with all the religious prejudices of his class, so the marriage is kept secret. The pair meet, apparently casually, in society. Women fall in love with Edmund, men woo Ginevra. There is a domestic theatricals episode, with ironies reminiscent of those in Jane Austen's *Mansfield Park*. The obstructive father dies, leaving a will declaring that his wealth will not go to Edmund (who has run up huge debts) should he marry a Catholic. All problems are providentially solved in the third volume after Ginevra has almost died. It turns out that the will was only a test, to see whether the couple really were married. As the *Athenaeum** reviewer noted: 'the tension is somewhat too remorselessly protracted'. The narrative is replete with Fullerton's lush descriptions and silver-forkery*. The novel was, however, very popular in its day and was boosted by the so-called 'Catholic Aggression' following Newman's* defection to Rome.

GRATTAN, Thomas Colley (1792–1864). Irish* novelist and travel writer. Grattan was born in Dublin, the son of a solicitor who retired early to country life. He went to school in Athy, and after a false start himself in law in Dublin he joined the Louth militia and served in northern England. Failing to get a commission when the wars with France ended, Grattan left intending to fight in the South American wars of independence. On the voyage to Venezuela he met, fell in love with and married Eliza O'Donnel. They settled in France, and Grattan took to writing for his living. He contributed extensively to the English magazines, and translated French poetry. He was also, for a time, a correspondent for *The Times*. Always hard-up, he undertook a series of minor government commissions. In 1839, he was appointed British consul at Massachusetts and helped settle the boundary quarrel between America and Canada. In 1846, Grattan returned to England and spent his last years in London, churning out volumes of commentary on Anglo-American affairs and a number of inferior novels. They include: *The Cagot's Hut And The Conscript's Bride* (1852); *The Forfeit Hand* (1857); *The Curse Of The Black Lady* (1857). BL 8. DNB. RM. *NCBEL*. Wol. Sad.

GRAVES, Clo[tilde Inez Mary] ('Richard Dehan', 1863–1932). Graves was born at Buttevant, Co. Cork, the daughter of an Irish army officer. As a young woman she studied at the Royal Female School of Art, Bloomsbury, and later settled in Hampstead. From 1887, she enjoyed some reputation as the author of light plays and pantomimes. 'Clo' Graves was also a journalist, and wrote novels with up-to-date feminist themes in an exalted style. *Dragon's Teeth* (1891) has a villain heroine who preys on men. *Maids In A Market Garden* (1894) tells the story of a band of women who set up their own smallholding. *A Well Meaning Woman* (1896) comically portrays the misadventures of the busybody Lady Baintree's matchmaking. Of the last, the *Athenaeum** wrote: 'it is delightful to meet a book so full of high spirits'. As 'Richard Dehan' Graves wrote the successful *The Dop Doctor* (1910), a story of South Africa. BL 10. *WW*. Wol. RLF.

GRAY, Rev. E[dward Dundas] McQueen (1854–1932). Gray was born a doctor's son in Lanarkshire, and after attending school at Uppingham studied at a number of British and European universities including Heidelberg and London, where he was an 'octuple honoursman'. Ordained a priest of the Protestant Episcopal Church and a Ph.D. he worked as a teacher of classics and modern languages, travelling widely in adult life. In 1898, he settled in New Mexico, and became President of the State University. He wrote, in addition to professional and scholarly works, the novels: *Ronald Graeme* (1884); *Time's Revenges* (1885); *My Stewardship* (1892); *The Stepsisters* (1892). *Elsa* (1891) is a melodrama set in Venice and Munich and typically encrusted with redundant literary allusion. Gray's light romances did not meet with critical favour and were described by one reviewer as 'pleasant, long-winded and unconvincing'. BL 5. *WW*.

GRAY, Maxwell (i.e. Mary Gleed Tuttiett, 1847–1923). Gray was born at Newport on the Isle of Wight, the only daughter of a surgeon. In adult life she interested herself keenly in womens' rights which often protrude, melodramatised, in her fiction. She never married apparently and wrote under a male pseudonym. Her best-known and successfully dramatised novel was *The Silence Of Dean Maitland** (1886) in which a young curate seduces a girl, commits manslaughter, allows a friend to go to prison for the crime, goes on to lead a useful life, but finally dies of remorse when the betrayed friend is released and forgives him. Gray's other novels include: *The Reproach Of Annesley* (1886); *In The Heart Of The Storm* (1891), a story of the siege of Lucknow during the Indian Mutiny; *An Innocent Impostor* (1892); *The Last Sentence* (1893), whose hero is a judge agonisingly obliged to sentence his own daughter, Cicely, to death for child murder; *A Costly Freak* (1893); *Sweethearts And Friends* (1897); *The House Of Hidden Treasure* (1898). The 'stimulating psychology' of these books was generally admired. Tuttiett lived most of her life and died at Ealing, in London. BL 27. *WW*. Wol. Sad.

Great Expectations, Charles Dickens, 1861, 3 vols, Chapman and Hall. (Serialised in *All The Year Round**, December 1860–August 1861.) The author's finest exercise in autobiographical narration. The story's hero Pip (Philip Pirrip) is an orphan, brought up by his sister and her husband Joe Gargery. Joe is a simple-minded blacksmith who treats his young brother-in-law kindly. But Mrs Joe is a tyrant. Visiting his family's graves, Pip is seized by a convict, escaped from the hulks in the mouth of the Thames. Terrified, yet pitying the man, he brings him a supply of food and a file to break his manacles. Later, when the convict is recaptured he does not betray Pip. The young man's eventual apprenticeship in the forge is preceded by a summons to visit the imperious Miss Havisham in Satis House. Abandoned at the altar, she has kept the interior exactly as it was on the day she was jilted. At her house, Pip is humiliated and tormented by Miss Havisham's young ward, the beautiful but heartless Estella. Some time later, Pip is visited by an inscrutable lawyer, Jaggers, who informs him that he has expectations. He is to go to London and become a gentleman. Pip and the Gargerys naturally assume Miss Havisham to be his benefactor. In London, Pip sets up in lodgings in Barnard's Inn and becomes involved with Herbert Pocket. In the metropolis, Pip feels himself above his old friends and Biddy, the country girl who loves him. It is his vain hope to marry Estella, who has become a pitiless breaker of men's hearts. Meanwhile, Mrs Joe has been attacked and beaten into imbecility. Dolge Orlick, a journeyman blacksmith employed by Gargery is suspected. (Later, he will make an attempt on Pip's life as well.) On reaching his majority, Pip is visited by his mysterious patron who to his dismay turns out to be the convict whom he assisted years before: Abel Magwitch, alias Provis. Having prospered in Australia, it has been his intention to make a gentleman of his own, both in gratitude and as a 'revenge' on society. Having come back from transportation without leave, Magwitch risks hanging. Pip, suffering keen mortification, gives his degraded patron refuge. He goes to Miss Havisham to protest at her cruelly misleading him. There he learns that Estella is to marry Bentley Drummle, an odious 'gentleman' who had been his fellow-pupil in London and who has discovered his low social origins. Miss Havisham has encouraged Estella to avenge her own suffering on the male sex. Later, during another visit by Pip in which she finally implores his forgiveness, the old woman dies in a fire which destroys Satis House. It emerges that Magwitch is Estella's father and that his great enemy, Compeyson, is the man who jilted Miss Havisham. Compeyson contrives to have Magwitch arrested before Pip and Herbert can smuggle him out of the country. In a desperate fight in the Thames, Compeyson is drowned and Magwitch is mortally wounded. He dies before sentence is executed on him. Before he dies, Pip expresses a Christian forgiveness for Magwitch. He later falls dangerously ill himself, and is nursed back to health by Joe. Now a widower, Joe marries Biddy, whom Pip earlier spurned. Penniless, Pip sets to in business with Herbert and by dint of hard work abroad pays his creditors and rises in the world. Eleven years later, Pip returns to visit Joe and Biddy. Returning to the ruin of Satis House, he is reunited with Estella who has also been drawn there. The narrative suggests they will at last marry (Drummle having died). Dickens suppressed a rather bleaker ending in which Pip meets a remarried Estella in Piccadilly and after a brief exchange, they part. Dickens originally intended the serial for monthly parts but inserted it into *All The Year Round* to stem the loss of readership provoked by Lever's* feeble *A Day's Ride*.

The Great God Pan And The Inmost Light, Arthur Machen, 1894, 1 vol, John Lane. (Volume V of Lane's *Keynotes** series). *The Great God Pan* is an occultist extravaganza with decadent* overtones. The tale begins with a brain surgeon, Dr Raymond, performing an experiment in 'transcendental medicine' on a simple country girl as a result of which she has a vision of Pan, and is reduced to total idiocy. Later a daughter is born to her, whom Raymond farms out. From various fragmentary accounts, we learn that the child is called Helen Vaughan and that sinister events are associated with her. The scene shifts to London where Villiers, an Oxford man, meets his former friend Charles Herbert in Soho in rags. It emerges that his wife is driving him to his death. The wife is Helen Vaughan. When Herbert does indeed die, Villiers exorcises the Pan in Helen, by means of a hempen rope with which she hangs herself. Before she dissolves into gelatinous nothing she undergoes bestial and sexually explicit metamorphoses. *The Inmost Light* is another tale of occult scientific experiment and diabolism in London.

Green Tea, J. Sheridan Le Fanu, 1872, 3 vols, Bentley. (The story originally appeared with others in the three-decker *In A Glass Darkly*.) Le Fanu's most anthologised tale of spiritual possession. *Green Tea* is told as one of the cases investigated by the 'metaphysical investigator' Dr Hesselius. The narrative is made up of an exchange of letters between Hesselius and his colleague Professor Van Loo, edited by an unnamed medical secretary. The subject is the Rev. Mr Jennings, a rich unmarried clergyman with a living in Warwickshire. Jennings is prey to strange visitations. Hesselius discovers that these take the form of a hallucinatory monkey, of obscene appearance. A mental hypersensitivity induced by green tea is diagnosed, but Jennings cuts his throat before Hesselius can treat him. The story is as notable for the subtlety of its telling as for the gothic* horror of the haunting.

GREENAWAY, Kate [Catherine] (1846–1901). Illustrator. Greenaway was born in Hoxton, London, the daughter of John Greenaway, an engraver who had worked for the *Illustrated London News** and *Punch**. The young Greenaway studied art herself at the Slade school of the University of London. By 1868 she was exhibiting her paintings and had her work accepted by the Royal Academy in 1877. In 1889 she was elected a member of the Institute of Painters in Water Colours. She remains best known for her charming depictions of young children. In 1879, her collection for the young reader, *Under The Window*, was a great hit. She illustrated stories for *Cassell's Magazine** and did the pictures for Lady Colin Campbell's* story *Topo* (1878) and Yonge's* reprinted *The Heir Of Redclyffe** in 1879. Her distinctive images of innocent, chubby childhood had a durable influence on book covers and greeting cards in the twentieth century. Hou.

GREENWOOD, Frederick (1830–1909). One of the most famous literary journalists and editors of the late Victorian period, Greenwood touched the careers of many novelists including George Meredith* and, most notably, J. M. Barrie*. He was born in London, the eldest of eleven children of a coachbuilder and was educated at private school in Kensington, rather more extensively than his class origins might suggest. As a boy of fifteen he was apprenticed to a publisher and printer where he soon distinguished himself. A qualified tradesman at the age of sixteen, he married at twenty a Quaker girl, Katherine Darby. The couple had five children. Greenwood quickly rose to the responsible position of publisher's reader and by the early 1850s he was writing extensively for the papers and magazines. At this early period of his life, Greenwood also had ambitions to be a writer of fiction. In 1853, he published the Christmas tale *The Loves Of An Apothecary* and in 1859 *The Path Of Roses*. With his brother James (1832–1929, also a minor novelist and story teller at this period) he wrote the three-decker *Under A Cloud* (1860). Greenwood's strongest effort in fiction is *Margaret Denzil's History** (1864; 'annotated by her husband'). A sensitive editor, he constructed intelligent completions of Mrs Gaskell's* *Wives And Daughters** and Thackeray's* *Denis Duval**, both of which had their serialisations in *Cornhill** broken off by death. Greenwood was editor of the *Queen*, on the journal's foundation in 1861. From 1864 to 1868, he edited *Cornhill* and became a close business adviser to its publisher, George Smith. From 1865 to 1880, Greenwood edited the congenially Liberal *Pall Mall Gazette*, and it was during this stint that he established himself as one of the greatest of Victorian editors. From 1880, he edited the newly set up *St James's Gazette*. James Greenwood wrote loose picaresque stories of the day such as *Humphrey Dyot* (1867) and *Dick Temple* (1877). He also wrote street arab stories such as the popular *The True History Of A Little Ragamuffin* (1866). (FG) BL 3. (JG) BL 28. (FG and JG) BL 1. *DNB. NCBEL.* Wol. Sad.

GREENWOOD, Thomas (1851–1908). Principally remembered as an advocate of free public libraries, Greenwood was born at Woodley in Cheshire where he was educated at the local village school. As a youth, he benefited from the facilities of the newly opened Manchester public library. Subsequently Greenwood took up work as a clerk and himself worked in libraries for a while. Eventually, he set up his own publishing firm, Scott, Greenwood and Co., specialising in technical and trade journals. In later life, he was a passionate propagandist for public libraries, and by his personal efforts persuaded a number of local authorities to set them up. A book lover, he wrote voluminously, including *Grace Montrose, An Unfashionable Novel* (1886). BL 1. *DNB.*

GREG, Percy (1836–89). Born in Bury, Lancashire, he was the son of William Rathbone Greg (1809–81), the essayist and economist who led the reactionary attack on Mrs Gaskell's* *Mary Barton** in the late 1840s. Percy Greg was educated locally and went into journalism, contributing to the *Manchester Guardian* and *Saturday Review**. His opinions changed wildly during the course of his life. In youth an atheist, he later became a spiritualist. Pro-American at one stage, in 1887 he wrote a hysterically antagonistic history of the country. His most interesting work of non-fiction is the satirical dialogue, *The Devil's Advocate* (1879) which is lively, if wrong-headed. Greg wrote a number of idiosyncratic novels. *Errant* (1880) is 'a life story of latter day chivalry' in which the extravagant hero, Lionel Darcy, Marquis of Ultramar, fights for the Southern cause in the American Civil War. *Across The Zodiac* (1880) is a work of science fiction*, depicting life on Mars in 1830. 'A very odd and curious book', the *Athenaeum** called it. *Sanguelac* (1883) is another story of the American Civil War, with a strong bias for the cause of the defeated South. It finishes with a paean of praise for the activities of the Ku Klux Klan. Greg's other works include *Ivy, Cousin And Bride* (1881) and *The Verge Of Night* (1885). BL 6. *DNB.* Wol.

GRESLEY, the Rev. W[illiam] (1801–76). Gresley was born in Kenilworth in Warwickshire, the eldest son of a landowner. His mother was related to the Grote banking family, and the Gresleys' circumstances were very comfortable. William attended Westminster School, and went on to Oxford. An eye injury prevented him following a planned career in law, and he took orders in 1825. Gresley was appointed to a curacy in Lichfield, an area to which he was to be attached for the rest of his life. Excessively High Church, he was an early and enthusiastic follower of Newman*. In 1839, together with a fellow disciple, Edward Churton, Gresley began 'The Englishman's Library'. The aim of the series was frankly propagandistic. Gresley contributed six works of fiction to his library. They include *Charles Lever* (1841), a work warning the unwary against dissent and *Church Clavering* (1843), a narrative which argues for Church control of education. (The first edition of the novel was prettily embellished with pictorial vignettes by its publisher, James Burns*.) Outside this venture, Gresley also wrote such novels as *Bernard Leslie, Or A Tale Of The Last Ten Years* (1842), the story of a parochial clergyman, and a number of historical novelettes for the 'Juvenile Englishman's Library', in the late 1840s. Gresley's writing is heavy handed, and interesting only for the light it throws on so-called 'Condition of England' fiction in the period. He made a good marriage to an heiress in 1828. In 1840, he was appointed a prebendary at Lichfield Cathedral and moved to a comfortable living at Brighton in 1850. Over the subsequent years he published a vast number of theological works. BL 8. *DNB. NCBEL.* Wol.

GREY, Mrs Colonel [Elizabeth Caroline] (née Duncan, 1798–1869). The niece of 'Miss Duncan', a well-known actress of the late eighteenth century, she kept a school for girls in London. On the side, she wrote silver fork* novels, and through her husband (a reporter on the *Morning Chronicle*) she became associated with Edward Lloyd*, the 'Salisbury Square' publisher of fiction for the millions. In the early 1840s she won Lloyd's 100 guineas prize for a gothic* thriller with *Ordeal By Touch* (1847). She went on to write such penny dreadfuls* as *The Iron Mask* (1846–47). *Sybil Lennard* (1846) is the story of a Swiss orphan who becomes a governess in England. The work (which was published by Newby*) has some resemblance to the fiction of the Brontës*. Grey also wrote more sober society novels, well into the 1860s, such as: *Passages In The Life Of A Fast Young Lady* (1862); and *Good Society* (1863). At some point in her early career she married Colonel Grey, about whom virtually nothing is known. BL 26. Boase. Wol.

GRIBBLE, Francis Henry (1862–1946). Gribble was born in Barnstaple. He attended a private school in the area and went on to complete his education at Exeter College, Oxford, where he gained a first in classics in 1884. For a while thereafter he taught at Warwick Grammar School. In 1887, he came to London to write for the newspapers specialising in European (particularly Swiss) affairs. He was the first editor of *Phil May's Annual*, and wrote numerous short stories and full-length novels. His fiction includes: *The Red Spell* (1895), a bloody tale of the Paris Commune; *The Things That Matter* (1896); *The Lower Life* (1896); *Only An Angel* (1897); *Sunlight And Limelight* (1898). The last is a story of 'the stage life and the real life', offering a convincing depiction of the repertory theatre world in the English provinces. BL 12. *WW*.

GRIER, Sydney C[arlyon] (i.e. Hilda Caroline Gregg, 1868–1933). Grier was born in Gloucestershire and educated privately. After gaining a BA from London University, she tutored pupils for a while. From 1881, she wrote for her living. Her first short story was accepted by the *Bristol Times* in 1886. At some point she evidently travelled extensively in the East. Her subsequent full-length fiction is marked by its partiality for exotic situations. *In Furthest Ind* (1894), is the 'autobiography' of an East India Company man (Edward Carlyon, presumably an ancestor), in the late seventeenth century. *His Excellency's English Governess* (1896) has an English heroine (Miss Cecil Anstruther, BA, London University) recruited to teach a young potentate in Baghdad. *An Uncrowned King* (1896) and its sequel *A Crowned Queen* (1898) are Balkan romances 'of high politics'. *Peace With Honour* (1897) has as its heroine a female doctor, working in darkest Ethiopia. *Like Another Helen* (1899) is an epistolary novel, dealing with the Black Hole of Calcutta outrage. The narrative is elaborately researched. Grier never married, apparently, and coolly gave as her principal recreation in *Who's Who*, 'reading.' BL 30. *WW*.

Griffith Gaunt, Or Jealousy, Charles Reade, 1866, 3 vols, Chapman and Hall. (First serialised in *Argosy**, December 1865–November 1866, illustrated by William Small.) The work which Reade labelled 'my masterpiece' but which raised a storm of protest for its sexual frankness. The action is set in eighteenth-century Cumberland. The heroine, Kate, is rich, high-spirited and Catholic. She has two lovers: George Neville and Griffith Gaunt. She also has to decide whether to marry or take the veil. She chooses Griffith over his more eligible rival. After marriage, Griffith becomes a straightforward English squire. Sexual attraction develops meanwhile between Kate and her spiritual adviser, Father Leonard. Griffith's jealousy is worked up by a vicious servant, Caroline Ryder. Griffith falls ill, and is nursed back to health by Mercy Vint, an innkeeper's daughter, whom he marries bigamously under the assumed identity of his half-brother, Thomas Leicester. Griffith is later supposed murdered by Kate (who does in fact stab him), but the corpse proves to be that of the real Thomas Leicester. Mercy goes on to marry Neville, and the Gaunts are reconciled. Their reunion is confirmed by a remarkable blood transfusion and some very explicitly described sexual intercourse. The novel was widely attacked by critics whom Reade energetically counter-attacked as 'prurient prudes'. In a bitingly condescending judgement, Mrs Oliphant* called *Griffith Gaunt* 'the most powerful of Reade's lesser productions'.

GRIFFITHS, Major A[rthur George Frederick] (1838–1908). Griffiths was born in Poona, India, the son of a senior army officer. Having gone to boarding school in the Isle of Man, Griffiths in his turn entered the army as an ensign in 1855, and went on to serve in the Crimea. He subsequently had a long and successful military career, finishing in 1870 as a brigade major at Gibraltar. On leaving the army Griffiths went into the prison service, and held a series of deputy governorships, including that at Wormwood Scrubs, 1874–81. Thereafter, he was an inspector of prisons until 1896. By this stage in his career Griffiths enjoyed the status of the country's leading expert on penology, and in 1896 he represented Britain at the international conference on criminal anthropology in Geneva. He wrote extensively on the subject and popularised it with a series of sensational* tales of convict life and the criminal underworld such as: *Secrets Of The Prison House* (1893); *A Prison Princess* (1893); *Mysteries Of Police And Crime* (1898); *The Brand Of The Broad Arrow* (1886), the story of a jailbreak from the high-security facility at Portland. These were immensely successful. Griffiths also wrote detective* stories in the style of Gaboriau, such as: *Fast And Loose* (1885); *Number 99* (1885); *The Rome Express* (1896), his most popular work; *In Tight Places* (1900). Least successful of his novels are the military tales which draw on his youthful adventures in the Crimean War, such as *The Queen's Shilling* (1873) and *The Thin Red Line* (1900). The last of these introduces major historical figures (such as Raglan) and has some quite interesting business about the establishment of military espionage as a respectable department of the British army. Griffiths died in the south of France. BL 32. *DNB*. Wol.

GROOME, Francis Hindes (1851–1902). Groome's major claim to fame is as a Romany scholar. Born in Suffolk, the son of an archdeacon, he attended school at Weymouth and locally in Ipswich. Having gone up to Oxford he left without taking his degree in 1871 to travel with gypsies all over Europe. Groome subsequently married an English gypsy, Esmeralda Locke, from whom he soon separated. After 1876, Groome's life suddenly and inexplicably became more conventional. He moved to Edinburgh, and devoted himself to hardworking literary pursuits. He was a sub-editor on *Chambers's Encyclopaedia*, and wrote for various magazines always retaining a scholarly interest in Romany matters. Like Borrow* (to whom he may have been related, and whose *Lavengro** he edited) Groome turned his bohemian wandering life into fiction. His novel of gypsy life, *Kriegspiel* (1896), is unusual and interesting as are the more miscellaneous *Gypsy Folk Tales* (1899), drawn as they are from many lands. Their appeal was the greater at a period when as one reviewer put it, 'thanks largely to railways, the true gypsies are dying out'. BL 2. *DNB*. *NCBEL*.

GROSSMITH, George (1847–1912) and **GROSSMITH**, Walter Weedon (1854–1919). The Grossmiths were born in London, sons of a *Times* court reporter. George joined his father in Bow Street on leaving school, but soon showed himself a talented singer and entertainer. In 1864, he began to give paid performances. From 1870, he was a professional entertainer, specialising in patter songs and humorous recitative. He went on to make a name for himself as a performer in Gilbert and Sullivan operettas, 1877–89. He died at Folkestone. His published works include the volumes of reminiscences *A Society Clown* (1888) and *Piano And I* (1910). Weedon studied art at the Royal Academy and Slade schools. He established himself rather earlier as a comedian and artist. As the *DNB* notes, 'his successful career was mainly occupied in acting "dudes" and small, underbred, unhappy men, in which he excelled'. Weedon was also an illustrator and wrote the novel *A Woman With A History* (1896). The Grossmiths jointly produced *The Diary Of A Nobody** (1892) which was first published as an immensely popular serial in *Punch**. The diary is kept by Charles Pooter, a charming and pathetic nonentity. The pathos of the *petit bourgeois* clown has never been better caught and looks forward to H. G. Wells's* Mr Polly and the film creations of Charlie Chaplin. BL 1. *DNB*. RM. *NCBEL*. Wol.

GRUNDY, Sydney (1848–1914). Grundy was born in Manchester, the son of a mayor of the city. He was educated at Owens College, Manchester, and was called to the Bar in 1869. He practised law in Manchester until 1876. Grundy subsequently made a name for himself as a dramatic author. His only novel is the three-decker with a London theatrical setting published early in his career by Tinsley* in 1876, *Days Of His Vanity*. The *Athenaeum** noted: 'ten years hence Mr Grundy will be sorry to think he ever wrote this novel'. Grundy subsequently had a number of stage hits with such plays as *The New Woman* (1894). His play, *Sowing The Wind* (1893) was based on his earlier novel, which was reissued by Chatto* for the occasion with an apologetic preface. BL 1. *WW*. Wol. Sad.

Guy Deverell, J. S. Le Fanu, 1865, 3 vols, Bentley. (Serialised in the *Dublin University Magazine**, January–July 1865.) A gothic* melodrama whose action is dominated by the brooding presence of Marlowe Hall and its mysterious 'green room'. The hall's owner is Sir Jekyl Marlowe MP, who earlier in life killed Guy Deverell in a duel. The victim now has a grown-up son, also called Guy Deverell. Sir Jekyl's comfortable middle age is disturbed by a sinister, indeterminately foreign intruder, M. Varbarriere, who is, in fact, Herbert Strangways, whose sister was married to the original Guy. Sir Jekyl is finally driven to deathbed contrition. The estate goes to his brother, the Rev. Dives Marlowe, frustrating Varbarriere's schemes. But Guy marries Sir Jekyl's daughter, Beatrix. The narrative creates an atmosphere of gathering mystery by the artful withholding of information and by centring on the dull but anguished sensibility of the villain, Sir Jekyl.

Guy Fawkes, W. H. Ainsworth, 1841, 3 vols, Bentley. (Serialised in *Bentley's Miscellany**, January 1840–November 1841, with illustrations by George Cruikshank*.) The story opens vividly with the public execution of Catholic priests at Manchester in 1605. From the first, Fawkes's fanatic revenge for this persecution is doomed. A prophetess, Bess Orton, not only predicts his failure on her deathbed but is resuscitated from her tomb by Dr Dee to repeat the warning. Fawkes nevertheless perseveres. Human interest (entirely fictional) arises from his involvement with the aristocratic, but Catholic, Radcliffe family. The beautiful Viviana is loved by Fawkes, his fellow conspirator Robert Catesby and the young Manchester merchant Humphrey Chetham. It is Fawkes whom she finally marries (secretly).

The novel follows Fawkes's attempt to blow up Parliament, step by step: landing the powder, burrowing the mine, laying the train. (Cruikshank's night scenes are excellent.) Captured, Fawkes is hideously tortured. Viviana dies. Chetham survives, never marries and becomes famous to posterity as the founder of the Manchester hospital which bears his name.

Guy Livingstone, G. A. Lawrence, 1857, 1 vol, J. W. Parker. (Subtitled 'Or Thorough'.) Regarded as the *ne plus ultra* of the muscular* School of fiction, *Guy Lawrence* was the hit of 1857. Like Tom Brown, Guy is an idealised product of the Rugby–Oxford system of education. He is first encountered a fifteen-year-old cock of the school and the scourge of all bullies. After college, and a brief spell in the crack Household Brigade, he devotes himself to the life of an English squire. Livingstone is a descendant of Norman, or 'thoroughbred' aristocracy. He also embodies the 'new generation' of manhood. Physically massive (he rides at fourteen stone and pulverises professional boxers), very dark haired but pale of skin, 'vast proportioned but lean in the flanks like a wolf-hound', he is the 'berserker', or Charles Kingsley's* saga hero, reborn to lord it in evening dress over contemporary society. The novel's plot is thin. A womaniser ('immoral, but never cruel'), Livingstone is discovered in a conservatory, kissing the coquette Flora Bellasys, by Constance Brandon, to whom he is engaged. The match is broken off. Livingstone throws himself into an orgy of dissipation at Paris. Constance, her constant heart broken, sickens and dies. There is a pathetic deathbed reconciliation between the lovers. After a few more listless demonstrations of his potency, Livingstone is mortally injured on the hunting field. The novel ends with his protracted death, which like that in *The Heir Of Redclyffe**, is very uplifting. The novel is narrated by Guy's adoring, consumptive friend, Frank Hammond.

H

HAGGARD, Lt.-Col. Andrew [Charles Parker] (1854–1923). Two years the elder brother of Rider Haggard*, he was born in the family home at Bradenham Hall, Norfolk. Educated at Westminster School, he joined the King's Own Borderers in 1873 serving with the regiment in India and Aden. Haggard saw action in Egypt at the battle of Ginness in 1885, and having won a DSO rose to the rank of lieutenant-colonel. The fiction which he largely wrote in his retirement reflects his far-flung military postings and adventures. It includes: *Dodo And I* (1889); *Leslie's Fate* (1889); *Ada Triscott* (1890), a story of love, war and esoteric Buddhism; *Tempest Torn* (1894), the melodramatic tale of a soldier who loves two women at once, it also has a heroine who wins the VC disguised as a drummer boy. Haggard wrote his personal reminiscences of military service in the East as *Under Crescent And Star* (1896). He also dabbled in poetry, married in 1906 and spent much of his later life in the wilds of Canada hunting, shooting, fishing and exploring. BL 14. *WW*. Wol.

HAGGARD, Major Edward Arthur ('Arthur Amyand', 1860–1925). A brother of Rider Haggard's, he was born at Bradenham Hall, the youngest son of William Meybohm Haggard. Edward was educated at Shrewsbury School and Pembroke College, Cambridge. He joined the King's Shropshire Light Infantry in 1884, and served in the East. Like his brother Andrew, he saw active service in Egypt. In 1889 he transferred to the Service Corps and in 1892 he retired with the rank of major, rather early in his career, having married in 1887. In his retirement, he was active in military matters, organising veterans' associations and militia units. Generally, however, his time seems to have been occupied with hunting, shooting, fishing and a little writing. His fiction, which is military in its preoccupations, was written under the pen name Arthur Amyand. It includes: *Only A Drummer Boy* (1894); *With Rank And File* (1895); *Comrades In Arms* (1895); *The Kiss Of Isis* (1900). The last is a story of the supernatural, set in Egypt. More than his brothers, Edward Haggard wrote short stories for male readership magazines. BL 5. *WW*.

HAGGARD, [Sir] H[enry] Rider (1856–1925). Haggard was born at West Bradenham Hall, Norfolk, the sixth son of William Meybohm Haggard, a barrister. His mother was an heiress, enriched with East India Company money, and the family lived the life of prosperous rural gentry. Henry was educated at Ipswich Grammar School and privately. At the age of nineteen he went to South Africa as secretary to Sir Henry Bulwer. There he was attached to the government of Natal, during stirring times in the colony. From 1877 to 1879 he was Master of the High Court of the Transvaal. On his return to England in 1879, he married a Norfolk heiress, Mariana Margitson. The couple spent some time (1880–81) in South Africa. But Haggard was so disgusted with British concessions to the Boers that in 1881 he left Africa 'for good'. There were one son (who died young) and three daughters to the marriage. Haggard trained for the Bar (1880–84) and although he qualified in 1885, decided that the work did not suit him. Two pursuits preoccupied the remainder of his life: farming the land and writing romance*. He became an authority on English agriculture, producing *A Farmer's Year Book* in 1899 and a two-volume survey of *Rural England* in 1902. His political aspirations were disappointed when he failed to win East Norfolk for the Unionists in 1895. But his career as an author enjoyed meteoric success. *King Solomon's Mines** (1885) was an immediate bestseller as were the similarly exotic *She** (1887) and *Allan Quatermain** (1887). *Jess* (1887) and *Swallow* (1889), a tale of the Great Trek, draw on Haggard's knowledge of Africa (which he revisited at the time of the Boer uprising), as do *Nada The Lily** (1892) and the various episodes of the Quatermain saga, of which the last, *Allan And The Ice Gods*, came out in 1927. Haggard also experimented with other settings for his violent and gripping romance in *Cleopatra** (1889), *Montezuma's Daughter* (1893) and *Heart Of The World** (1896). In the twentieth century, Haggard undertook various government commissions, and was knighted for public service in 1912. He was awarded the KBE in 1919, in recognition of his war work. A stalwart member of the Society of Authors*, Haggard published a posthumous autobiography, *The Days Of My Life*, in 1926. Haggard continued writing his vivid romances up to his death, elaborating the long-running sagas of Quatermain and She. His fiction marks the resurgence of popular escapist romance (mainly for male readers) in the late nineteenth century. BL 60. *DNB*. RM. *NCBEL*. Wol. Sad.

The Half Sisters, Geraldine Jewsbury, 1848, 2 vols, Chapman and Hall. In the author's view, her best novel, written against the attitude embodied in Mrs Ellis's* series of manuals advocating female submissiveness. The heroine is Bianca, a passionate actress who has risen from the sordid circus world. The bastard of Philip Helmsby and a beautiful Italian mother whom he has deserted, she loves the unworthy Conrad Percy. Bianca's legitimate half-sister, Alice, a docile and conventional girl, marries William Bryant, a successful ironmaster. Ignorant of their relationship, the half-sisters become friends and Conrad (whom Bianca has been forced to discard) falls in love with Alice. On the brink of eloping, she dies of convulsions. Bianca survives to marry a lord. Some reviewers professed to find the novel immoral. Like the author's *Zoe** it was strongly influenced by George Sand and to some extent by Madame de Stael's *Corinne*.

HALIBURTON, Thomas Chandler (1796–1865). Immortal as the creator of 'Sam Slick', Haliburton was born at Windsor, Nova Scotia, the son of a Canadian judge of New England origins. He himself had a successful career in the law and as a politician, rising eventually to the supreme court of Nova Scotia. In 1829, he wrote a history of the province and in 1837, there appeared the first series of *The Clockmaker, Or The Sayings And Doings Of Samuel Slick Of Slickville*. This protracted comic dialogue, centred on the pithy wisdom of a Yankee pedlar, was an instant bestseller on both sides of the Atlantic. For all its dialect comedy (which anticipates that of Twain, and may have influenced Dickens*) the Slick character expresses Haliburton's ambivalence about Americans and their imperial confidence. A second series appeared in 1838, and a third in 1840. *The Attaché, Or Sam Slick In England* appeared in 1843, and it too spawned a second series the next year. There followed *The Old Judge, Or Life In A Colony* (1849); *Sam Slick's Wise Saws* (1853) and its sequel *Nature And Human Nature* (1855). In 1856, Haliburton retired from his post in Nova Scotia and came to England. Three years later he was elected a Tory MP, and held the Launceston seat until just before his death. As an English politician, he specialised in the country's frequently vexed relations with North America. BL 9. *DNB*. RM.

HALL, Owen (i.e. James Davis, 1849?–1907). Davis studied law at University College, London, but evidently left early to become articled. He worked as a solicitor in London from 1874 to 1886. He then abandoned the legal profession for literature. A regular contributor to magazines, Davis edited the *Bat*, 1885–87. He was also dramatic critic for the *Sporting Times*. (Horseracing was a passion with him, and in later life he was himself an owner.) Hall wrote successful plays in the 1890s such as *A Gaiety Girl*; *An Artist's Model* and *The Geisha*. His main work of fiction is *The Track Of A Storm* (1896), the story of a highwayman, Charles Fortescue, who is falsely convicted and transported to Australia in the 1830s. Reviewers found the story gripping but badly put together. His other fiction comprises *Jetsam* (1897), a mystery story, and *Hernando* (1902). Davis stood unsuccessfully as Conservative candidate at Dundalk in 1880. BL 3. *WW*.

HALL, Mrs S[amuel] C[arter] [Anna Maria] (née Fielding 1800–81). Anna Fielding was born in Dublin, and brought up in Ireland. Her father died early, and she and her mother went to London in 1815. In late girlhood, Anna Fielding wrote the kind of Irish* sketches which went down well with the English reading public in the early nineteenth century. In 1824, she met Samuel Carter Hall (1800–89), a journalist, literary patron, editor (notably of Colburn's* *New Monthly Magazine*) and later founder of the *Art Union Journal* (a publication which made high quality pictures available cheaply to the general population). Genuinely and practically philanthropic, she was instrumental in setting up the Hospital for Consumption at Brompton and the London Home for Decayed Gentlewomen. Under her married name, Mrs S. C. Hall was herself an active woman of letters. Her *Sketches Of Irish Character* (1829–31) were popular. Her first novel, *The Buccaneer*, a historical* novel of the seventeenth century, appeared in 1832. Her later fiction includes: *Uncle Horace* (1837); *Marian, Or A Young Maid's Fortunes* (1840); *The White Boy* (1845), a story of Ireland in 1822; *A Woman's Story* (1857), written by a self-proclaimed 'Nobody'; *Can Wrong Be Right?* (1862). The last, judged Hall's best novel, is the story of a rural schoolmaster's daughter who has to protect her virtue against the assaults of the local lord. They marry, and the narrative follows several years of their wretched life together. Like most of Hall's fiction, the tone of the work is excessively moralistic and glories in the self-sacrifice of the heroine. Hall wrote travel books, edited *Sharpe's London Magazine** in the 1840s and *St James's Magazine** in the 1860s, wrote successful plays and ran something of a salon in London. Despite the persistent Hibernian flavour in her writing, she was never popular in Ireland. BL 52. *DNB*. RM. *NCBEL*. Wol. Sad.

HAMERTON, Philip Gilbert ('A. Segrave', 1834–94). Hamerton was born near Oldham, Lancashire, the only son of a lawyer. His mother died at his birth and he was brought up by aunts. He was educated at Burnley and Doncaster grammar schools. His father, who had utterly neglected him, died in 1844. On leaving school, Hamerton was for a short while an officer in the Lancashire militia during the Crimean crisis. From 1855 to 1858 he studied painting in London and Paris, wrote poems and married a French wife. The Hamertons lived from 1858–61 on a lonely islet in Argyllshire. They returned to France in 1861. Hamerton was art critic of the *Saturday Review**, and founded the *Portfolio* magazine in 1869. He also wrote extensively on art, particularly etching. On the side, and particularly after a severe nervous breakdown in 1868, he wrote some fiction which includes: *Wenderholme, A Story Of Lancashire And Yorkshire* (1869); *Harry Blount* (1875); *Marmorne* (1878). The last of these (written under the pseudonym Adolphus Segrave) has effective Franco-Prussian War settings, and tells the story of three brothers, all Catholic. *Wenderholme* remained the best known of Hamerton's novels and he brought out an abridged version of it in 1890, reduced from its original three volumes. A powerful saga of the Ogdens, a nonconformist manufacturing and farming family, the narrative has a strong temperance tendency. Set in the 1850s, it also recalls Hamerton's militia service during the national emergency of the Crimean period. Hamerton also wrote extensively about French life and art and left an autobiography, completed by his widow in 1897 after his sudden death from heart disease.

Although small in amount, Hamerton's fiction suggests strong talents left undeveloped. BL 3. *DNB*. *NCBEL*. Wol.

HAMILTON, Lord Ernest [William] (1858–1939). The sixth son of the first Duke of Abercorn, he was educated at Harrow and Sandhurst. He subsequently entered the army, and rose to the rank of captain in the 11th Hussars. On resigning his commission, he was Conservative MP for North Tyrone, 1885–92, and married in 1891. He wrote on Irish affairs, and his fiction includes: *The Outlaws Of The Marches* (1897), set in sixteenth-century Liddesdale; *The Mawkin Of The Flow* (1898), a romantic tale set in the Scottish borders, the Mawkin being a mysterious spectral maiden; *The Perils Of Josephine* (1899), the story of a heroine who must unwillingly accept the Catholic suitor selected by her father; *Mary Hamilton* (1901). The heroine of the last tale is one of Mary Queen of Scots' attendants, Anne Cunninghame. Hamilton's brisk historical* romances capitalised on the new one-volume 6s. form of fiction in the 1890s. BL 7. *WW*. Wol.

HAMILTON, Lillias (d. 1925). An MD, Hamilton was in private practice in Calcutta, 1890–93. She was subsequently the physician in charge of the Dufferin Hospital, Calcutta, 1893–94. Thereafter, in the course of what must have been a highly unusual medical career, she served as court physician to the Amir of Afghanistan, 1894–97. Out of this experience came a sombre story of the Hazara War, *A Vizier's Daughter* (1900). The narrative is set in Kabul, and has as its heroine a rebel princess, Gul Begum, who is eventually destroyed. This work also contains a portrait of the potentate whom Hamilton served. The *Athenaeum** reviewer recommended the work as essential reading for all British administrators in India. From 1908 to 1924 Hamilton was Warden of Studley Horticultural College for Women. In 1907 Hamilton published *A Nurse's Bequest*, a study of the working woman's life in the 1880s. BL 1. *WW*.

HAMLEY, [Lt.-Gen. Sir] Edward Bruce (1824–93). Edward Hamley was born at Bodmin, Cornwall, the fourth son of an admiral. The Hamleys were a family which seems to have specialised in high-ranking army officers who wrote novels. Edward's older brother, William George Hamley (1815–93), was also born at Bodmin and educated at the local grammar school. William went into the Royal Engineers in 1833 as a second lieutenant and by 1866 had made colonel. He retired in 1872, to take up minor governmental posts in the West Indies. As a civilian he wrote the novels *Guilty Or Not Guilty?* (1878); *The House Of Lys* (1879) and a military novel dealing with the post-Waterloo period, *Traseaden Hall* (1882). Edward Hamley was trained at the military academy at Woolwich and entered the Royal Artillery in 1843. He began publishing articles in *Fraser's** and *Blackwood's** magazines around 1850. His first novel (written when he was still a captain), *Lady Lee's Widowhood*, was published in 1850 and reissued four years later, with illustrations by the author. A facetious tale, it chronicles the trials of an eligible young widow whose remarriage with the soldier she loves is frustrated by the terms of her dead husband's will. Hamley served with distinction in the Crimean War, and was promoted to lieutenant-colonel in 1855. On his return to England, he entered literary circles and was friendly with, among others, Bulwer-Lytton* and Thackeray*. In 1858, he edited a first series of *Tales From Blackwood* which contained some of his own short fiction. In 1859, he was appointed professor of military history at Sandhurst. His military theoretical writing was influential and he held the important post of commandant of the army Staff College, 1870–77. Hamley was promoted general in 1877. In 1882, he returned to active service in Egypt; but the episode formed a disappointing conclusion to an otherwise distinguished and varied career. He was made a KCMG in 1880 and a KCB in 1882. He was twice elected a Conservative MP in the 1880s. Percy Fitzgerald* gives a vivid picture in *Memoirs Of An Author* of Hamley as 'a unique specimen of the *literary* soldier who haunted the Athenaeum club and not the club of the services opposite'. (EBH) BL 2. (WGH) BL 3. *DNB.* Wol. Sad.

The Hand Of Ethelberta, Thomas Hardy, 1876, 2 vols, Smith, Elder. (Subtitled 'A Comedy In Chapters', the novel was serialised in *Cornhill**, July 1875–May 1876, illustrated by George Du Maurier*.) Hardy's fifth published novel, and one of his slighter efforts. Ethelberta, a butler's daughter, finds herself at twenty-one the widowed daughter-in-law of Lady Petherwin who sends the young woman abroad to finish her education. The women fall out over a volume of poems Ethelberta writes and on Lady Petherwin's death the heroine is forced to fend for herself. Initially she earns her way by public readings of her work, with some success. From three eligible suitors she chooses the ancient Lord Mountclere, overriding the protests of her family. The marriage turns out well, despite ill auguries.

Handley Cross, Robert S. Surtees, 1843, 3 vols, Colburn. (Serialised in the *New Sporting Magazine*, 1840–41. Reissued in enlarged serial form by Bradbury and Evans* in seventeen irregular monthly parts, March 1853–October 1854, with illustrations by J. Leech*.) The middle part of Surtees's Jorrocks* trilogy. The story begins with the death of Michael Hardey, a gentleman of the old school and master of the Sheepwash Vale Farmers' Hunt. Meanwhile, the previously sleepy Handley Cross has been undergoing great changes. The wholesale gentrification of the little spa town is masterminded by Captain Miserrimus Doleful, whose committee decides to appoint Jorrocks as the master of the newly formed and more ambitious hunt club for the next season. John Jorrocks turns out be a vulgar, comic, twenty-stone, cockney enriched by greengrocery. His wife and eligible niece Belinda accompany him to his new post at Diana Lodge. The main body of the narrative deals with Jorrocks's hilarious season's misadventures on and off the hunting field together with the sublimely maladroit huntsman, James Pigg. There is also a lawsuit between him and Doleful over a dubious piece of horse trading. And for a while Jorrocks is incarcerated in Hoxton lunatic asylum on account of his hunting mania. Belinda eventually marries her Handley Cross beau, Charley Stobbs. The story is more connected than its predecessor *Jorrocks's Jaunts And Jollities* (1838) and funnier than its successor, *Hillingdon Hall** (1845). Leech's illustrations (particularly that of Jorrocks's entering Handley Cross in triumph) are masterly.

Handy Andy, Samuel Lover, 1842, 1 vol, Lover and Groombridge. (Illustrated by Lover, the work was serialised in *Bentley's Miscellany**, January 1837–May 1839 and in monthly parts over 1842.) Andy Rooney, an idiotic

Irish manservant, bungles himself and his master into innumerable comic scrapes. The structure of the novel is episodic to the point of total disintegration. It is, however, redeemed by Lover's pretty songs and competent engravings. There is also some attempt to give a picture of 'real Ireland' (although Andy himself is no national advertisement). The story loosely follows the activities of two squires, one good one bad. There is some satire of the Englishman in Ireland, in the character of the lisping, foppish Furlong. But in general, the narrative is a farrago of duels, hunting, comic feuding and jesting. There is some attempt to gather things at the end, when it is disclosed that Andy is actually aristocratic. He assumes the title Lord Scatterbrain, and is the victim of an assassination attempt. The work, with its Irish* 'Wellerism', was popular and much reprinted. 'Handy Andy' has become a catchphrase for clumsiness and a figure in popular mythology.

HANNAY, James (1827–73). Hannay was born in Dumfries, Scotland, the son of a businessman there. His father, David Hannay (1794–1864), was also the author of an unsuccessful novel, *Ned Allen, Or The Past Age* (1849), and a man of wide intellectual interests. Hannay joined the Royal Navy at the age of thirteen, and saw active service. He made strenuous efforts at this early period to educate himself. At eighteen, now a midshipman, he was court-martialled for insubordination and riotous conduct. He was dishonourably discharged and although the sentence was later reversed, he remained embittered by the experience. Thereafter, Hannay supported himself by writing; mainly for the newspapers, his first post being on the *Morning Chronicle*. In 1857, he stood unsuccessfully as a Conservative at Dumfries. He edited the *Edinburgh Evening Courant* from 1860 to 1864. In 1848, Hannay had made the acquaintance of Carlyle and Thackeray*, both of whom had a profound influence on him. He continued rigorously to improve his mind in middle age, learning Greek in his thirties. He wrote what is probably the best full-length Victorian appreciation of Thackeray's fiction, and helped edit the other writer's lectures on the eighteenth-century humorists. Hannay was appointed British consul at Barcelona in 1868, and died there. He wrote some quite impressive fiction early in his career, all of it drawing on his navy experiences and derived in style from Marryat*. *Biscuits And Grog* (1848) is a collection of nautical* sketches. *Singleton Fontenoy, RN* (1850) is his best work, containing the author's autobiographical recollections from the 1840s. *Sketches In Ultramarine* (1853) reprints his shorter naval fiction. *Eustace Conyers* (1855) is a rather flat narrative of an *ingénu*'s progress in life. BL 7. *DNB. RM. NCBEL.* Wol. RLF.

Hard Cash, Charles Reade, 1863, 3 vols, Sampson Low. (Serialised as *Very Hard Cash* in *All The Year Round**, March–December 1863.) A sequel to *Love Me Little, Love Me Long* (1859), and by general agreement the best of Reade's propaganda novels. The cash of the title refers to Captain David Dodd's £14,000. This life's earnings is resolutely preserved through all shipwrecks and pirate attacks. But when he returns to England, Dodd entrusts his precious cash to his old rival in love, the banker Richard Hardie. Hardie is a villain. He embezzles Dodd's money, driving the sailor mad. Hardie's son Alfred meanwhile has fallen in love with Dodd's daughter Julia. When he threatens to expose his father, the banker has Alfred confined to a private lunatic asylum. Julia thinks she is deserted. As a patient, Alfred

is tortured horribly, even more than the other inmates when he repulses the
sexual advances of his gaoler, Mrs Archbold (a physically magnificent figure
of a woman). Alfred spends what was to have been his wedding night, strait-
jacketed in a cell. Dodd Sr and Hardie Jr make their escape from the asylum
during a fire. Dodd, still mad, joins the navy as a common seaman and is
(apparently) killed saving a comrade. His body is saved for embalming, and
a mosquito bite reveals, at the last minute, that he is not dead after all
but in suspended animation. He recovers his senses. Hardie's other victim,
Alfred, has reunited himself with Julia, defended himself from criminals
employed by his father, taken a first-class degree at Oxford and cleared
himself in court. He and Julia marry and retire to their 'happy little villa'.
Dodd recovers his cash and he and his wife Lucy are blessed with another
infant. Hardie goes senile and mad, and ends his days in a lunatic asylum.
The novel (especially its gruesome madhouse scenes) displeased *All The
Year Round*'s readers, and circulation dropped.

Hard Times, Charles Dickens, 1854, 1 vol, Bradbury and Evans. (Serialised
in *Household Words**, April–August 1854.) Dickens's major social problem*
novel. Because of its conception for publication in the weekly columns
of *Household Words*, the narrative is some three-quarters shorter than
Dickens's usual novels in numbers. Dickens confided that originally he had
intended taking a year's rest after *Bleak House**, but 'the idea [of *Hard
Times*] laid hold of me by the throat in a very violent manner'. One main
inspiration was the Preston strike. Over 20,000 cotton workers were out
for over six months, with the slogan 'ten per cent and no surrender'. The
strike ran from October 1853 to April 1854, when it ran out of funds. *Hard
Times* is set in 'Coketown' (i.e. Preston). It opens in the model school of
Mr Gradgrind, a utilitarian. Gradgrind's educational philosophy is devoted
to the extinction of imagination in favour of 'facts'. The opening chapters
introduce the reader to Gradgrind's two repressed children, Tom and Louisa,
Sissy Jupe, whose father, a circus performer, has deserted her, and Bitzer,
the school's automaton-like prize pupil. Years pass. Louisa takes on Sissy
as her maid. Tom goes into the business owned by Bounderby, a supposedly
self-made and vulgar business man. Bitzer is employed as a clerk in the
same establishment, and is very friendly with Bounderby's housekeeper,
Mrs Sparsit. To Sparsit's disgust, Bounderby marries Louisa, a match
which is promoted by Gradgrind despite a dangerous difference in age and
temperament. Louisa is betrayed into indiscretion and near adultery with
Jem Harthouse, a cynical young London gentleman visiting Coketown as a
political aspirant. Tom embezzles funds from Bounderby's firm. The prying
Mrs Sparsit abetted by Bitzer gleefully observes Louisa's involvement with
Harthouse but in announcing to Bounderby this and other discoveries fails to
ingratiate herself to him. Finally, Gradgrind has it demonstrated to him that
his educational system is a terrible failure. Tom is smuggled away by Sleary's
travelling circus (from which Sissy originally came), despite a last minute
attempt by Bitzer to apprehend him. Bounderby is unmasked as a fraud,
the mother whom he claimed had deserted him as a child being discovered a
respectable and solicitous parent. A sub-plot to these main events concerns
the textile worker, Stephen Blackpool. Blackpool cannot free himself from
a marriage with a drunken wife. He promises the good woman whom he

loves, Rachael, that he will not join the union and is 'sent to Coventry'. He leaves Coketown, suspected of having stolen Bounderby's money (Tom Gradgrind being in fact the culprit). Crossing the moors, Blackpool falls into an old mineshaft, is rescued, but dies piously soon after. *Hard Times* has been taken as Dickens's most powerful plea for the necessity of imagination and the inadequacy of mere reason as the guide to human conduct. The strike scenes in the novel (especially the depiction of the outside agitator, Slackbridge) have been most objected to, Bernard Shaw calling Dickens's treatment of the episode 'pure middle-class ignorance'. In fact, Dickens gave a much more sober and friendly picture of the Preston strikers and their organisers in an essay, 'On Strike', published in *Household Words*, in February 1854. *Hard Times* is dedicated to Carlyle.

HARDY, Elizabeth (1786–1854). Elizabeth Hardy was born in Dublin, a zealous Protestant. She was ruined by bank failure and dishonest lawyers and in 1830 turned to authorship. In 1848, while writing what she intended should be her masterpiece (a novel based on the life of Owen Glendower), she ran into debt and was imprisoned in 1852, dying two years later in the Queen's Bench Prison. Her published fiction includes: *Michael Cassidy, Or The Cottage Gardener* (1845); *Owen Glendower* (1849); *The Confessor, A Jesuit Tale Of The Times* (1854). All were published anonymously. BL 3. Boase. RLF.

HARDY, Lady [Mary Anne] Duffus ('Addlestone Hill', née MacDowell, 1824–91). Mary MacDowell was born in London, shortly after the death of her father. In 1850 she married (as his second wife), Thomas Duffus Hardy. Hardy had been born in the West Indies, and was a Civil Servant. From 1861 until his death in 1878 he was Deputy Keeper of Records, in which capacity he was knighted in 1873. Mary Hardy wrote around a dozen novels, including: *Savile House* (1853), published under the pseudonym 'Addlestone Hill'; *The Two Catherines* (1862); *Paul Wynter's Sacrifice* (1869), a Cornish saga, following the connected fortunes of two families; *Lizzie* (1875); *Madge* (1877); *A Dangerous Experiment* (1888). The last is a luridly melodramatic study of ill-assorted marriage and arsenic poisoning damaged, as reviewers thought, by the lack of any sympathetic character. None of her novels was more than ordinarily successful although she studiously introduced passionate crime into all her plots. She died in Maida Vale, leaving one daughter, Iza Duffus Hardy (1852?–1922), who was also a novelist. Iza Hardy lived a very private life, and little is known of her. It seems from the content of her books that she visited the southern USA with her mother in the early 1880s. (See *Love In Idleness*, 1887, the story of a winter in Florida.) Evidently she never married. Her fiction includes: *Only A Love Story* (1877); *A Broken Faith* (1878); *Love Honour And Obey* (1881), the story of Zeb and Silas from courtship to tragedy, when death does them finally unite; *A Woman's Loyalty* (1893). The last has a typical plot, in which the heroine Clemaine learning that her lover has poisoned his former wife faces the dilemma of obeying heart or conscience. (MAH) BL 15. *DNB*. Wol. (IDH) BL 28. *WW*. Wol.

HARDY, Robina Forrester (d. 1891). Hardy was born in Edinburgh, where as an adult she worked among the poor in the Grassmarket slums of the city, apparently in connection with the nearby Greyfriars church. She published a volume of verse, *Whin Bloom* in 1879. More successful were her stories of Edinburgh life such as *Jock Halliday, A Grassmarket Hero* (1883); *Archie* (1885) and *Fickle Fortune* (1886). Her stories are moralistic, but have some charm. She collaborated on a volume with Annie S. Swan*, shortly before her death. She never married, apparently, and lived in a flat by the slums where she worked. BL 19. Boase.

HARDY, Thomas (1840–1928). The greatest regional* novelist of the nineteenth century. The Hardys were an old Dorchester family. Thomas was born in the village of Higher Bockhampton in Dorset where his father was a builder. His mother came from a family of small landowners and had worked as a servant before marriage. The new-born Hardy was first thought dead by the midwife, a gloomy omen which it pleased the author to recall in later life. From his father he inherited a love of music. His mother on her part encouraged his literary taste, giving him Johnson's *Rasselas* and Dryden's *Virgil* to read at the age of ten. The young Hardy was exposed to the life of rural England before the incursions of railways and Victorian industrialism reached Dorset. After attending the village school, Hardy graduated to the British School at Dorchester, three miles distant, in 1849. Here he received what was in the circumstances a remarkably good education, including a grounding in classics. In 1856, he was entered as a pupil in the office of Dorchester architect John Hicks. Hicks was a congenial employer, specialising in church restoration, a subject which resurfaces in such later novels as *The Laodicean* (1881). At this early period of his life Hardy made the acquaintance of the Dorset poet William Barnes and of Horace Moule. Moule, sophisticated, upper-class and Cambridge educated, encouraged Hardy's literary inclinations and later, as a man of letters, promoted his friend's authorial career. Hardy gave various impressions of Moule in his fiction, notably as Angel Clare in *Tess Of The D'Urbervilles*. A dipsomaniac, Moule evidently inspired something of Michael Henchard in *The Mayor Of Casterbridge*. From 1862 to 1867, Hardy was employed as an assistant architect in London. He worked in the West End and lived in lodgings. All the while, he was reading furiously and writing poetry, little of which survives. Chronically shy, he had few close friends at this or any other period of his life. But a fellow worker had stimulated his interest in Christianity, and he toyed for a while with the idea of attending theological college. In the summer of 1867 his health failed, and he returned to Dorchester to work for Hicks again while he recovered. Here he became sexually involved with a cousin, Tryphena Sparks. The affair was probably over in 1870 when she left for teachers' training college in London. Now an atheist (albeit reluctant) and a pessimist, Hardy completed his first long work of fiction, *The Poor Man And The Lady*, in 1868. The manuscript was submitted to publishers, duly rejected and subsequently was either cannibalised into later works or lost. But Alexander Macmillan took the trouble to correspond at length with the aspiring author and George Meredith* (on behalf of Chapman and Hall*) actually gave him an interview. Meredith recommended imitation of Wilkie Collins* and Hardy went on to produce the extravagantly sensational* *Desperate Remedies*, which William Tinsley* published in 1871. The work made no money and little critical impression. But Tinsley was confident enough of Hardy's ability to take the shorter *Under The Greenwood Tree** (1872) and *A Pair Of Blue Eyes** (1873) as a serial for his house magazine. Hardy was still employed by Hicks's successor, G. R. Crickmay and on an architectural commission to restore a church at St Juliot in Cornwall in 1870 he met Emma Lavinia Gifford. They married in 1874. Meanwhile his career as a writer was looking up. In late 1872, Leslie Stephen wrote as editor of *Cornhill** to request a serial. Hardy supplied *Far From The Madding Crowd** (1874). This powerful anti-pastoral was the author's most ambitious work hitherto and gained him fame. But it attracted complaints from *Cornhill* readers at the sexual explicitness of the Fanny Robin episode. And when the story was a third written, Horace Moule cut his throat in his rooms at Cambridge. The event cast a shadow over later portions of Hardy's narrative and probably over his whole later life. The Hardys' early marriage was happy, although the couple had no permanent home. In 1876, he produced *The Hand Of Ethelberta** and two years later the more sombre *The Return Of The Native**, a work which returned to the Wessex* with which Hardy was by now inextricably associated. He was at this period well known in London literary circles, if uncomfortable with them, and among the friends he made at this period of his life was Edmund Gosse*, the country's most influential literary critic. A lifelong obsession with the Napoleonic era found expression in Hardy's only historical* romance, the charming *The Trumpet Major** (1880). By this date, his price per work was well over the £1,000 mark. But his preference as a writer was always for his relatively undervalued poetry. By the end of the 1870s, strains had shown in the Hardys' marriage. Temperamentally, Emma's vitality was at odds with her husband's morbid reticence. *Two On A Tower** (1882) elaborates Hardy's post-Darwinian pessimism by reference to the 'stupendous background of the stellar universe'. Hardy was also at this time turning out short stories which like Dickens's* indulge his taste for the supernatural. By now, he had returned to Dorchester and in 1885 moved into his fine Victorian mansion, Max Gate, which he had himself designed. He celebrated Dorchester in his tragic novel, *The Mayor Of Casterbridge* (1886), his most powerful study of 'character' and 'destiny'. It was followed by the mellower *The Woodlanders** (1887), the author's own favourite work. The Hardys visited Italy in 1887. By the early 1890s, his fame was at its peak. But he chafed at the discipline of 'respectability' imposed on the novelist and consciously rebelled in *Tess Of The D'Urbervilles* (1891), whose plot revolves around rape, illegitimate birth and adultery against a background of rural spoliation. The work provoked a furious reaction. *The Well-Beloved** (1892) similarly shocked middlebrow readers. But *Jude The Obscure** (1895) topped both in its offensiveness to the English Mrs Grundy. Following *Jude*'s hostile reception, Hardy gave up fiction (a 'trade' he had never much respected) for good. At the same time, the Hardy marriage was irreparably broken down. There had been no children, and his barrenness disturbed Hardy intensely. He had what seems to have been an affair with Florence Henniker* in 1893. The remainder of Hardy's authorial energies were devoted to his first love, poetry. Initially, his grand Napoleonic verse epic, *The Dynasts* (1903–06), thereafter the lyrics on which his reputation as a poet mainly rests. In 1910, he received the Order of Merit. In 1912, Emma died and two years later he married Florence Dugdale. She was thirty-five to his seventy-three. Florence served as Hardy's secretary-cum-biographer. On his death, his ashes were buried in Westminster Abbey and his heart in his first wife's grave. BL 16. *DNB*. RM. *NCBEL*. Wol. Sad.

HARKNESS, Margaret ('John Law', 1861–1921). The details of this author's life are tantalisingly obscure. Harkness was evidently an ardent socialist; a cousin of Beatrice Webb and a friend of Eleanor Marx and Olive Schreiner*. According to Wobb, Harkness was the child of clerical and conventional parents who tried to repress her extraordinarily active mind. She began her literary career with hack work in the British Museum. Engels admired her first novel *A City Girl** (1887) with its attack on the industrial vice of sweated labour and his comments on it are a classic instance of early Marxist literary criticism. As John Law, Harkness wrote seven novels in all, including *Out Of Work* (1888), an ironic juxtaposition of the Jubilee of 1887 with the Trafalgar Square riots of that same year; *In Darkest London* (1889); *A Manchester Shirtmaker* (1890). In the 1880s, she was working among workers and the poor in the East End of London (an episode reflected in *George Eastmont, Wanderer*, 1905). Some accounts suggest she was a member of the Salvation Army for a while. In the 1890s, Harkness seems to have become disillusioned with Socialism. BL 7.

HARLAND, Henry ('Sidney Luska', 1861–1905). Harland was born in St Petersburg, the only son of an American lawyer. He completed his education at Harvard Divinity School, having studied in Paris and Rome, where after graduation he subsequently returned. He soon lost his religious vocation and his career as a novelist (under the pseudonym Sidney Luska) began with *As It Was Written** (1885). A 'Jewish Musician's Story', it offered realistic melodrama, set in contemporary New York. This work was popular and inspired successors on the same lines such as *Mrs Peixada* (1886) and *The Yoke Of The Thorah* (1887). The second of these is often reckoned the best of Luska's fiction. Its hero is a young Jew who jilts a Gentile girl at the behest of a stern Rabbi uncle (Harland was not himself Jewish). *Grandison Mather* (1890) is more directly autobiographical and recalls the author's early experiences in the writing profession. After 1890, Harland formally abandoned 'sensation* literature'. He moved to London, with the intention of making himself a master of literary craft. An Anglophile, he regarded himself as a 'dormant baronet' of the United Kingdom, through his Harland connection. He is recorded as being 'handsome, with charming manners'. In his own name he published *Two Women Or One?* (1890), a study of double personality, and *Mea Culpa* (1891). Of the last, a psychological study of murder written as the confession of an emigré Russian, the *Athenaeum** noted wryly that it 'must have been easier to write than to read'. He also began to turn out quantities of highly wrought short stories in the approved 1890s style: *Mademoiselle Miss And Other Stories* (1893); *Grey Roses* (1895); *Comedies And Errors* (1898). Harland was literary editor of the *Yellow Book** during its short but influential lifetime, 1894–97. His most Jamesian and admired novel, *The Cardinal's Snuff-Box**, appeared in 1900. Harland suffered from tuberculosis in his later years and spent his winters in San Remo, where he died. His wife (née Aline Merriam) completed his last novel, *The Royal End* (1909). BL 17. *DNB*. Wol. Sad.

Harold, The Last Of The Saxon Kings, E. G. E. L. Bulwer-Lytton, 1848, 3 vols, Bentley. The novel partners the author's *The Last Of The Barons** and his most ambitious poetical work, *King Arthur* (1848–49), which he called 'the grand effort of my literary life'. Set in the closing years of Edward the Confessor's reign, Harold Godwinson is conceived in Carlylean terms as a liberal and a patriot, the embodiment of true national spirit. Bulwer-Lytton confessed to 'dryness' in this library-made novel, with its cast of 'ceorls, thegns, cnehts'. The opening words set the tone of the work: 'Merry was the month of May in the year of our Lord 1052'. The story climaxes with William's invasion, fourteen years later. Between these dates, Lytton embroiders a fanciful romantic plot. Edith, the ward of Hilda, an ancient Scandinavian prophetess, loves the future king Harold. But for state reasons, he discards her ('the loving Fylgia of his life') to marry Aldyth. After his death at Hastings, Edith tends his corpse and finds her name inscribed over his heart, and underneath the more patriotic slogan, 'England'. In the context of the turbulent 1840s, Bulwer-Lytton's celebration of ancient English democracy had a political overtone, as does the pro-Saxon tendency in Disraeli's* Young England* trilogy of the same period and the narrative ends with a prophecy of ultimate racial triumph: 'Eight centuries have rolled away, and where is the Norman now? Or where is not the Saxon?' *Harold* was the last of the author's historical* novels.

HARRADEN, Beatrice (1864–1936). Harraden was born in Hampstead, the daughter of a musical-instrument importer. She finished her education at Dresden, and at Bedford College, London where she studied classics and mathematics. She devoted her subsequent life to travel, and to unobtrusive activity on behalf of the women's movement. In later life she was one of the leaders of the Women's Social and Political Union and campaigned energetically on behalf of the suffragettes. Personally unassuming, physically small and pretty she was, on her entry into London society, a protégée of Eliza Lynn Linton* (who condescendingly termed her, 'my little BA'). Harraden wrote a short tale for children, *Things Will Take A Turn*, in 1891. Her first novel, *Ships That Pass In The Night** (1893), was outstandingly successful. The story is excessively gloomy, the hero and heroine being invalids who fall in love at an Alpine sanatorium for consumptives. Harraden followed this bestseller with a collection of stories, *In Varying Moods* (1894); *Hilda Strafford* (1897), a Southern Californian story; *Untold Tales Of The Past* (1897), tales for children; and *The Fowler* (1899). The last is titled after a vicious sexual predator, Theodore Bevan, who violates women's minds and bodies. Sadleir, who evidently disliked Harraden's fiction, indicates her favourite theme, that of the brief encounter between soon to be forever parted lovers. He notes: 'this obsession probably arose from the tragic experience of her life, for she fell deeply in love with a man who falsified his clients' accounts and whose body was found not long after in a crevasse on a Swiss glacier'. BL 15. *DNB. NCBEL.* Wol. Sad.

HARRIS, Emily Marion (1844?–1900). Born of Jewish parents in London, and evidently brought up in the faith, Harris worked for various charitable organisations during the course of her life. She never married and she wrote improving works of fiction for the younger reader, such as *Echoes* (1871). *Mercer's Gardens* (1876) is a panorama of London life. Her most interesting novel is her seventh, *Estelle* (1878). It chronicles the life of a Jewish family, the Hofers, who live in an English cathedral town. There are two daughters, Estelle and Lexie, who are raised in orthodox Judaism. The main action of the novel deals with the social tensions which Estelle undergoes in a prominently Gentile society, as she attempts to follow her artistic vocation. Eventually, she is driven to reject a Christian lover, determining on a life of spinsterhood. Her single life in London among the Russo-Polish immigrant community is described in a sequel, *Bonodictus* (1887). Harris's treatment of her complex social themes is low-keyed and often comic. She also wrote less ambitious historical* romances such as *The Lieutenant Of The Tower* (1881). Her last major effort was a multi-volume series of tales from the Bible, which suggests that at some point of her adult life she converted to Christianity. BL 12. Boase. Wol.

HARRIS, Frank [James Thomas] (1856–1931). One of the most notorious of Victorian adventurers and autobiographers, Harris was, with everything else, a considerable writer of fiction (indeed, it has been argued that he never wrote anything else). He was born the son of a Welsh seaman and ran away to the USA at the age of fourteen. Thereafter he drifted for a few years among a variety of jobs (including driving cattle). During this period, Harris educated himself, attending Kansas State University in 1872, and also gave evidence of his genius for journalism. He returned to London in 1883. Possessed of tremendous energy and self confidence, he had made himself editor of the *Fortnightly Review** by 1886. A year later, he married a wealthy Park Lane widow and embarked on a political career as a socialist. It failed, as did the marriage. In 1894, he eloped with Miss Helen O'Hara, whom he later married. Harris published his first book in 1894. *Elder Conklin And Other Stories* is interesting for its vivid recollection of his rough life in Kansas. The long title piece is the portrait of an iron-willed Christian patriarch who stands up against General Custer's attempt to give his farmland to Indians as part of a treaty. The story ends unhappily with the Elder's daughter running away from his domestic tyranny. Other stories, such as 'The Best Man In Garotte', are routine tales of gunslinging in the Wild West. Also 1894 Harris bought the *Saturday Review**, and went on to make it the most brilliant political and literary weekly in the country. He sold the paper in 1898. By the turn of the century, Harris was a ruined man. His attempt to run luxury hotels on the Riviera failed utterly, and the rest of his later life is a catalogue of disgrace (including a spell in prison). From 1922 to 1926 he published his scandalous, unreliable but fascinatingly readable *My Life*. His second volume of fiction is *Montes The Matador* (1900). Apart from the title story (an authentic tale of the corrida) the most admired piece in the collection is 'Sonia', the story of a young MP's infatuation for a Russian nihilist. BL 4. *DNB*. RM. *NCBEL*.

HARRIS, Richard ('Benedick Whipem', 1833–1906). Harris was born in Surrey. He trained as a lawyer and was called to the Bar in 1864 rising to the rank of QC in 1888. He began publishing poetry as early as 1853, and followed with an epic, *The Siege Of Candia* in 1860. Harris remained a productive amateur author throughout his life, using the pen name 'Benedick Whipem'. In addition to a number of works on law (some useful, some humorous) and some plays he wrote the novels: *New Nobility* (1867) and *Mayfair To Millbank* (1870). Sensational* in style, the works were pronounced 'dull and foolish' by reviewers. BL 2. *WW*.

HARRISON, Mary St Leger ('Lucas Malet', née Kingsley, 1852–1931). The younger daughter of Charles Kingsley*, she was born at the family home at Eversley in Hampshire. Mary Kingsley was gifted and studied art at the Slade School in London, under Edward Poynter. But she gave up her career in 1876, on her marriage to the Rev. William Harrison (d. 1897). With him, she set up home at Clovelly in north Devon. As a clergyman's wife (before the couple separated) she had leisure which she used for writing. Harrison used a resoundingly male-sounding pseudonym, Lucas Malet, so as to avoid association with her famous writing relatives and presumably to escape identification as the girl of the family. Malet's early fiction includes: *Mrs Lorimer* (1883) and *Colonel Enderby's Wife* (1885). The second of these made her name as a novelist. It is the pessimistic study of a failed marriage between a middle-aged man and a younger, heartless woman. Marriage breakdown, of one kind or another, was to be a staple theme of Malet's fiction. 'Clever' and 'painful' were two terms often applied to her work by reviewers. *Little Peter* (1887) is a 'Christmas Morality'. *A Counsel Of Perfection* (1888) has a middle-aged heroine who is cruelly exploited by both her father and lover. *The Wages Of Sin* (1891) is a work which somewhat resembles Hardy's* *Jude The Obscure*. It has a young painter hero, who becomes involved with a Cornish girl. She later returns with their child to destroy his relationship to a woman of his own class and breeding. The novel was much reprinted. *The Carissima** (1896) is a more melodramatic story of sexual destructiveness, with a Swiss setting. *The Gateless Barrier* (1900) is a spiritualist romance about a man who falls in love with a ghost which inhabits a satinwood escritoire. It was found absurd. ('A barrier would not be a barrier if it had a gate in it', sneered one reviewer.) Malet's most ambitious novel is *Sir Richard Calmady** (1901). The hero of the title is unpleasantly deformed, and his relationships with various women, some sexual, are closely described. There were no children to the Harrison marriage, and as a widow she was received into the Catholic Church in 1902. (She revised some of her fiction after conversion.) In 1906, she bought a home at her native Eversley. But she spent much of her later life on the Continent, and as late as the 1920s was a well-known literary hostess at Montreux. She numbered among her friends numerous men and women of letters, including Henry James, Romain Rolland and Robert Hichens*. BL 12. *DNB*. *NCBEL*. Wol. RLF.

Harry Richmond, George Meredith, 1871, 3 vols, Smith, Elder. (The full title is prefixed by 'The Adventures Of' and the novel was serialised in *Cornhill*, September 1870–November 1871, with illustrations by George Du Maurier*. In magazine form, the story was anonymous and was attributed by some readers to Charles Lever*.) Autobiographical in form (and also in content, although less so than the author's *Evan Harrington**, 1861) the novel opens in the 'Hampshire heath-country' with a vivid scene of a young boy, Harry, being reclaimed by his absentee father, Roy Richmond. The separation between father and son and 'the gradual changes of the growing Harry' are to be the narrative's subsequent main concern. For most of his life, the hero is 'a kind of shuttlecock', batted about by powerful adults.

His father was originally a music master who seduced and eloped with the squire's daughter he was hired to teach. The subsequent marriage proved disastrous and after his mother died, Harry, the only child, was packed off to be brought up by his maternal grandfather and an aunt at Riversley. After being abducted by his father at the age of five, Harry returns again to Riversley. Some years later, he runs away from school to London, hoping to find Roy. He and a friend are kidnapped by a well-meaning sea-captain and taken to Germany. Here, by accident, father and son are reunited. Yet again, the hero is returned to Riversley while Roy goes to Bath where he lays siege to an heiress. At the age of twenty-one, Harry is promised his grandfather's fortune of £20,000 a year, on condition that he marries Jane Ilchester. Instead, he goes off with his father to Ostend, where he pursues the Princess Ottilia, whom he met and fell in love with earlier in Germany. On his grandfather's death, Harry ends up with a disappointing £3,000 a year inheritance. Ottilia marries a German prince. Janet becomes engaged to a marquis. Eventually, however, Harry and Janet are reconciled and united. Roy dies in a fire at Riversley, the narrative ending with the laconic comment, 'He was never seen again'.

HARTLEY, Mrs May (née Laffan, 1850?–1890?). May Laffan was born in Dublin and married Walter Noel Hartley, a Fellow of the Royal Society, and professor of chemistry at King's College, London who was knighted in 1911. The couple either separated in later life or more likely she died young. (No new work is listed by her after 1890 and she is not mentioned in her husband's later *Who's Who* entries.) May Hartley's most successful novel was the early *Hogan MP* (1876); a story set in contemporary Dublin attacking the self-imposed shackles of the Catholic community. The hero is a venial Home Rule MP, manipulated by unscrupulous peers and financiers. According to the *Spectator* (which assumed the author to be a man), 'we have seldom read through a modern novel which left a worse taste behind it than this'. Hartley's other fiction includes: *The Hon. Miss Ferard* (1877), a comedy of Irish manners; *Flitters, Tatters And The Counsellor* (1879), a collection of four stories, the first two dealing with street arabs of the Dublin slums; *The Game Hen* (1880); *Christy Carew* (1880), a story written denouncing Catholic hostility to mixed marriage; *Ismay's Children* (1887), a tale of Fenian times. As reviewers noted, Hartley's later fiction tended to be little more than Irish sketch-books richly larded with pathos. She published her work anonymously. BL 9. (WNH) *WW*. Wol.

HARWOOD, Isabella Neil ('Ross Neil', 1838?–88). The daughter of Philip Harwood, an editor of the *Saturday Review** (1868–83), she produced a batch of successful novels between 1866 and 1870. They include: *Abbot's Cleve* (1864); *Carleton Grange* (1866); *Raymond's Heroine* (1867); *Kathleen* (1870). Harwood's romances were found by critics to be excessively wholesome. In the 1870s, under her male pseudonym, Ross Neil, she turned to drama, publishing a number of historical plays in blank verse. BL 5. *DNB*. Wol.

HARWOOD, John Berwick (1828–86?). His life is a mystery. Sadleir writes: 'according to the Bentley* *Catalogue* he was born in 1828, published a volume of poems with Pickering in 1849, married in 1850 and celebrated his honeymoon abroad in a book entitled (regrettably) *The Bridal And The Bridle*. His first novel appeared in 1854 [*Falconbeck Hall*] and his last in 1885 [*Sir Robert Shirley, Bart.*] He wrote at least nineteen novels.' Most of them deal with love and aristocracy. Harwood's most popular works with the contemporary reader were *Lady Flavia* (1865) and *Lord Lynn's Wife* (1864). The second is one of the many bigamy* novels that were the rage in the 1860s. A novel on modern Russia (*The Serf Sisters*, 1885) suggests that Harwood may have travelled widely. The author also wrote an industrial novel, *Paul Knox, Pitman* (1878). R. L. Wolff surmises that the obscure Harwood may in fact have been a woman. BL 15. Wol. Sad.

HATTON, Joseph (1841–1907). A versatile author and journalist, Hatton was born at Andover, Hampshire, the son of a writer and bookman. He began a career in law, but quickly turned to writing for his living. An energetic man with connections in the USA, Hatton became foreign correspondent of several international papers including (after his first visit to America in 1876) the *New York Times*. He was also editor of the *Gentleman's Magazine** from 1868 to 1874. He wrote travel books, plays and fiction which includes: *Bittersweets* (1865), a work which the *Athenaeum** pronounced 'unreadable'; *Christopher Kenrick* (1869), the disjointed autobiography of a modern journalist; *Clytie* (1874). This last work displays Hatton's florid melodrama at its crudest. The heroine, Clytie, is a musician's daughter loved by two students at 'Dunelm University'. To escape them she runs away to London, where she narrowly escapes being recruited into a brothel, and goes on the stage. Later she makes a fine marriage with a lord. Ten years on, Clytie is blackmailed about her early London career by one of her former student lovers. Her husband brings an action for libel, which forms the climax of the plot and which was, evidently based on an actual recent case. The other (and more gallant) student lover returns enriched from California and everything ends in a welter of blood. The *Athenaeum*, which loathed Hatton, called *Clytie* an 'utterly worthless book'. Despite such fulminations, Hatton was a popular author. *By Order Of The Czar* (1890) is a lively late romance. Hatton wrote mysteries towards the end of his career and had some success with his sombre London stories and studies, such as *Cruel London* (1878), which the author himself dramatised. His work for the stage includes a successful dramatisation of Hawthorne's *The Scarlet Letter*. Hatton's son Frank was killed in 1883, exploring in Borneo and the father published a novel on the affair aimed at the juvenile market, *Captured By Cannibals* (1888). BL 24. *DNB. NCBEL*. Wol.

The Haunted And The Haunters, Or The House And The Brain, E. G .E. L. Bulwer-Lytton, *Blackwood's Magazine*, August 1859. One of the earliest and finest Victorian ghost* stories. A gentleman scholar hears of a haunted house off Oxford Street in London. He persuades the owner (who has been unable to keep any tenant for more than a few hours) to let him spend a night there. His manservant is terrorised by a hideous spectre and runs away. His dog dies of a mysteriously broken neck. But the hero stands his ground and locates the source of the house's supernatural energy in a single room. By detective investigation he also discovers that the murder of a child took place in the house. He helps the owner dismantle the haunted room where a safe is found containing strange chemicals and apparatus. After their removal the house is exorcised.

HAWKER, Mary Elizabeth [Morwenna Pauline] ('Lanoe Falconer', 1848–1908). Born in Inverary, Aberdeenshire, she was the daughter of an army officer who had her educated at home and in France. When her father died in 1857 and her mother remarried in 1862 the family moved to the Continent. Following this, Hawker became proficient in French and German. In 1890, she contributed a work to Fisher Unwin's 'Pseudonym* Library', *Mademoiselle Ixe**, by 'Lanoe Falconer'. ('Lanoe' is an ingenious anagram of 'alone'; 'Falconer' a synonym of hawker.) The work was a great hit, selling a reported 40,000 copies. It tells the story of an governess who becomes involved with a Russian nihilist assassination attempt. In 1891, Falconer followed this success with the morbid psychic romance, *Cecilia De Noël*, and *The Hotel D'Angleterre*. She never married and evidently lived with her mother, whose death in 1901 hit her hard. Hawker was victim to failing health and consumption in her last years. BL 4. *DNB. NCBEL*. Wol.

HAWKINS, Sir Anthony Hope ('Anthony Hope', 1863–1933). Hawkins was born in Clapton, the younger son of a clergyman headmaster of a school for the sons of poor clergy. The writer Kenneth Grahame* was a cousin on his mother's side. Hawkins was educated at Marlborough School and Oxford, where he was a noted athlete and President of the Union. He capped a brilliant undergraduate career with a first-class degree. On graduation, he entered law as his chosen profession and was called to the Bar in 1887. As a young lawyer, Hawkins lived for seventeen years with his widowed father at St Bride's, near Fleet Street, not marrying until 1903. His energetic attempts to enter politics as a Liberal MP failed. But by 1893, he had published five moderately successful novels. The best of them are: *Father Stafford* (1891), a country-house comedy (Stafford is a high-living Anglican priest) and *A Change Of Air* (1893), a light tale in which a revolutionary poet falls in love with the daughter of a county squire. 'Brilliant' was a word often applied to Hope's early novels, although they were also accused of frothy insubstantiality. Hawkins had by this time also made a name for himself as a lawyer. The success of *The Prisoner Of Zenda** (1894) confirmed writing romances as his main occupation and he gave up his promising career in law the following year. This work was thrown off at the rate of two chapters a day, and enjoyed immense popularity in book, stage and eventually in a number of film versions. The story centres on Rudolf Rassendyll, who is the exact double of a Ruritanian monarch, and who becomes embroiled in middle European intrigue. 'Anthony Hope' as he called himself in print, followed up with *The Dolly Dialogues* (1894), a witty semi-dramatic reflection on high London society. Hope's other principal Victorian works include: *A Man Of Mark* (1890), which features revolution in an imaginary South American republic; *The God In The Car* (1894), which has a hero, 'Juggernaut', who aims to buy up vast estates in South Africa; *Simon Dale* (1898), a historical* romance, with Nell Gwyn at the centre of the action; and the inevitable Zenda sequel, *Rupert Of Hentzau* (1898). Hope was knighted in 1918 for public service during the war. He lived the last thirty years of his life on his farm at Walton-on-the-Hill, in Surrey. BL 34. *DNB*. RM. *NCBEL*. Wol.

Hawkstone, A Tale Of And For England, William Sewell, 1845, 2 vols, Murray. (Published anonymously.) A fanatic anti-Catholic novel addressed to 'a distracted and degraded England'. Sewell was an early friend of Newman's* and a fellow tractarian. But he was alienated by Tract 90 (1841). In reply, he produced this work, an extreme instance of Jesuit paranoia. The Catholic villain of the story ('the stranger') inflicts himself on the town of Hawkstone, committing various crimes against England. They include fanning rebellion among the industrial workers, the kidnapping of Anglican clergy and the assassination of English gentlemen's children. He is punished by being eaten alive by rats in the vaults of Hawkstone Priory (a symbol of the obsolete England he wants to resurrect). The narrative has some garishly hostile chapters set in Popish Italy, as seen through the eyes of the robust hero, Villiers. Sewell gained fame in 1849 as the senior representative of Oxford University who publicly burned Froude's* *Nemesis Of Faith**.

HAYES, Frederick William (1848–1918). Hayes was born and educated in Liverpool. He initially trained as an architect, but showed an early preference for water-colours, and landscape painting. (His favourite scenery was that of northern Wales.) Hayes exhibited at the Royal Academy in 1871. He was also actively involved in Fabianism and dabbled in psychical research. His novels (which he illustrated himself) include: *A Kent Squire* (1900), a historical* novel set in the same period as *Henry Esmond**; and its sequel *Gwynett of Thornhaugh* (1900), whose action moves to France. Critics found Hayes's work tediously long-winded. His other publications extend well into the twentieth century. BL 6. *WW*.

He Knew He Was Right, Anthony Trollope, 1869, 2 vols, Strahan. (Serialised in thirty-two weekly parts published by Virtue* and illustrated by Marcus Stone*, October 1868–May 1869.) Trollope's most powerful depiction of sexual jealousy. Louis and Emily Trevelyan are, as we first encounter them, the most fortunate of couples. He is rich, well educated and handsome. She, the daughter of a governor in a West Indian colony, is beautiful. They have a fine London house, and a healthy baby son. Trouble arises, however, when Emily receives the visits of one of her father's friends, Colonel Osborne. Despite the gentleman's advanced age, Trevelyan chooses to be suspicious. This leads to arguments, and eventually Emily is driven out of the house, to stay with a clergyman relative, the Rev. Outhouse, in the East End of London. Trevelyan, by now demented, sets a private detective on her and kidnaps his son. He then absconds to Siena, where he retreats to a desolate villa called Casalunga. There his condition deteriorates until his friends conspire to bring him back to England, where he dies, monomaniacally convinced of his rightness. On his deathbed, he induces his wife to 'confess' her infidelity, which she does to humour him. A number of sub-plots intersect with the main story of the Trevelyan marital tragedy. Emily's sister, Nora, is loved by Hugh Stanbury, a journalist. But she cannot accept him as he is wayward and penniless. But for love of him, she rejects the proposal of Charles Glascock, heir to a title and a fortune. Hugh and Nora eventually marry and in Italy Glascock falls in love with a vivacious young American, Carry Spalding. The novel is notable for its gallery of comic figures: Hugh's redoubtable Exeter aunt Stanbury; the private detective Bozzle; the American feminist Wallachia Petrie.

The Headless Horseman, A Strange Tale Of Texas, Captain Mayne Reid, 1866, 2 vols, Chapman and Hall and Bentley. (Serialised in 6d. monthly parts, March 1865–October 1866 with illustrations by L. Huard.) The first pulp Western in England. The tale revolves around the passionate love between Louise Poindexter, a beautiful Creole heiress, and Maurice Gerald, 'better known as Maurice the Mustanger', a wild Irishman. The mysterious headless horseman is a spectre, called up by the misdeeds of Cassius Calhoun, who killed and decapitated his own cousin (Louise's brother), under the misapprehension that his rival Maurice was the victim. The hero narrowly escapes lynching for the crime. Villain and hero finally have it out with 'shooting irons'. Victorious, Maurice takes possession of Louise and reveals himself to be Sir Maurice. In this story, Reid provides all the props of the Western genre, which descended direct to Hollywood. The Comanche attack, the saloon brawl, the mainstreet shoot-out, sunset on the mesquite, virtuosity with the lasso, bowie knife and six-gun are all found here. And Reid's descriptions of Texas, which he knew at first hand, have a crude vitality to them.

Heart Of The World, H. Rider Haggard, 1896, 1 vol, Longman. (Serialised in *Pearson's Weekly*, August 1894–January 1895.) A colourful adventure set in Mexico. The Heart of the World is a secret city, located in the interior. An Indian, Ignatio, has inherited various sacred relics and believes that if he finds the city he will be able to lead an uprising to free his people from their European conquerors. With an Englishman, James Strickland, who has saved his life in a mine, he travels far inland. After adventures they arrive at the Golden City of the Indian and become swept up in a power struggle for kingship. Strickland falls in love with the beautiful Maya, who is killed with their baby. The city is destroyed by flood and the two adventurers struggle back. But Strickland soon dies. Ignatio has smuggled back a girdle of emeralds, with which he sets up his own estate.

Heartsease, Or The Brother's Wife, Charlotte Mary Yonge, 1854, 2 vols, J. W. Parker. The follow-up to *The Heir Of Redclyffe**. The Martindales are a noble family. They, and his sister Theodora particularly, are shocked when Arthur Martindale (a Guards officer) marries the insignificant Violet who, true to her name, is shy and unassertive. But Violet's goodness works wonders, and Arthur is saved from the life of dissipation into which he was falling. (Yonge does not specify his vices.) Theodora loses her looks, and is eventually cured of her unchristian haughtiness. Charles Kingsley* called *Heartsease* 'the most delightful and wholesome novel I ever read'. But it did not appeal to general readers as much as its predecessor had.

The Heavenly Twins, Sarah Grand, 1893, 3 vols, Heinemann. (The work was first privately printed at the *Guardian* office, Warrington, 1892.) One of the most notorious of the new women* novels of the 1890s. Using three loosely connected exemplary case studies, Grand attacks conformity and the sexual double standard. The first heroine, Evadne Frayling, marries the elderly Colonel George Colquhoun, only to discover that he has a disreputable past. Her parents demand that she give in to convention: 'Evadne, remember', her mother tells her, 'a woman has it in her power to change even a reprobate into a worthy man.' Evadne nevertheless deserts her husband, giving him the slip at a railway station. Relenting, she returns and accompanies him on garrison duty to Malta, but only on condition that the marriage is not consummated. The strain of this unnatural celibacy leads to depression and attempted suicide. Evadne is treated (but not entirely cured) by the enlightened Dr Galbraith, whom she marries after Colquhoun's convenient death from heart disease. The second story concerns Edith Beale, a bishop's daughter. Misguided by her parents, Edith marries Sir Mosley Menteith (one of Colquhoun's fellow officers). He is a man rotten with venereal disease; Edith delivers a child like a 'speckled toad', and dies. The third tale gives the collection its enigmatic title. Angelica Hamilton-Wells is twin to the boy Diavolo. Her life is constrained, his is free to develop wherever his talent draws him. Angelica proposes to and marries Mr Kilroy. But she insists that she must be free within the marriage 'to do as I like'. Exploiting this freedom, she dresses in male clothes and cultivates a friendship with a singer. Rescuing her from drowning, he discovers to his surprise that she is a woman. He subsequently dies of pneumonia, and Angelica returns to her husband. The novel which the author had initially printed at her own expense was immensely successful. Heinemann claimed a sale of 40,000 within a few weeks. Its popularity was probably due to Grand's unusually frank description of syphilis.

Heinemann and Co. (1890–). Publisher. The founder, William Heinemann (1863–1920), was born in Surbiton, the son of a naturalised German. The young man joined Nicholas Trübner* in 1881 leaving that firm on its amalgamation with Kegan, Paul and Trench to start his independent publishing house in January 1890. The following month he put out Hall Caine's* *The Bondman**. The novel was a huge success and set Heinemann up for life. He subsequently brought out *The Manxman** (1894), as a 6s. new novel (sealing the fate of the obsolete three-decker). Heinemann also published in his 'popular 6s. series' such major writers of the 1890s as Sarah Grand*, R. L. Stevenson*, Flora Annie Steel*, Israel Zangwill*, R. S. Hichens* and Rudyard Kipling* and was the proprietor of the *New Review* (1895–97). An active member of the Publishers' Association after its formation in 1896, he was President from 1909 to 1911. As a publisher, he was cosmopolitan, speaking a number of languages and introducing the English reading public to such writers as Dostoevsky. In 1899, Heinemann married one of his novelists: Donna Magda Stuart Sindici (they divorced five years later). Heinemann left a fortune of £33,000 on his death. *DNB*.

The Heir Of Redclyffe, Charlotte Mary Yonge, 1853, 2 vols, Parker. There are two heirs in the novel. One is Guy Morville, Byronic and an orphan. Guy is driven by wild passions which he gradually learns to subdue to Christian duty. Transferred to the religiously high-toned Edmonstone household he forms a strong bond with Charles, his guardian's crippled son, and falls in love with Amy Edmonstone before going off to Oxford University. But Guy's reputation is blackguarded by Philip Morville, who is next in line to the Redclyffe fortune. Philip, an army officer, is conceited and jealous. He proposes to Amy's sister, Laura, without the means to support her. Worse than this, he tells old Edmonstone that Guy needs £1,000 to pay off gambling debts. (In fact, he wants the money to found a religious sisterhood and to pay off a delinquent uncle's debts of honour.) Banished to his crumbling mansion, Guy is taken back into favour after performing great feats of daring in a sea rescue. He and Amy marry. On honeymoon in Italy, they find Philip sick. Guy nurses his former enemy back to health, but catches the fever himself. He dies, in a famous deathbed chapter. His last moments are comforted by an Anglican priest, who hears his confession. Philip, chastened, survives to marry Laura Edmonstone and inherit the Redclyffe estate. The novel is a classic instance of Tractarian piety in fiction, and was a tremendous bestseller (although it was turned down by John Murray*, and only reluctantly accepted by Parker). John Keble scrutinised the manuscript, before publication. Some part of the book's massive profits were donated to Bishop Selwyn of New Zealand who used them to fund a missionary ship, the *Southern Cross*.

Helbeck Of Bannisdale, Mrs Humphry Ward, 1898, 1 vol, Smith, Elder. Alan Helbeck is a Catholic ascetic who lives in his run down country home in the 'Flent Valley' (Westmorland). His sister, Augustina, has rejected her family's faith and married a Cambridge free-thinker. When he dies, she returns to Bannisdale, with her young and sexually eligible stepdaughter, Laura Fountain. Laura is torn between the legacy of her sceptical father and her growing attraction towards Alan. The tensions of Catholicism (which Ward knew from her own family background) are carefully depicted. Alan is wholly admirable. His Jesuit advisers, such as Leadham, are portrayed less favourably. Laura's dilemma is sharpened by her involvement with her relatives, the farming and sturdily Protestant Masons and the Liberal Dr Friedland. Alan and Laura finally admit their love for each other and find temporary happiness. But she cannot accept the disciplines of his faith, and drowns herself. He becomes a Jesuit. The novel is notable for its treatment of the austere, doctrinaire hero.

Held In Bondage, Ouida (i.e. Marie Louise de la Ramée), 1863, 3 vols, Tinsley. (Serialised in the *New Monthly Magazine**, as 'Granville De Vigne, A Tale Of The Day', January 1861–June 1863.) A very early novel, written when the writer was strongly under the influence of the muscular* school. The hero Granville de Vigne is first encountered at public school. The heir to £20,000 pounds a year, Vigne is a superb sportsman and general swell. The novel is narrated by his hero-worshipping friend, Arthur Chevasney. After three fast years at Cambridge, Vigne lords it over London society, with his inseparable companion Vivian Sabretasche. Despite his mother's anxieties, he woos and wins the reigning beauty, 'the Trefusis'. As she signs the register after the wedding, Trefusis discloses herself to be Lucy Davis, a Welsh girl whom Vigne earlier seduced and abandoned. She has married Vigne only to destroy his happiness forever. The story jumps ten years. Vigne and Sabretasche are discovered as soldiers of the Queen fighting Indian bandits. They return to England, where Vigne falls in love with Alma Tresillian, an artist. On his part, Sabretasche wins the heart of Violet Molyneux. But just after their wedding, he discovers that a former wife, whom he thought dead, in fact lives. He too is in bondage. Vigne wrongly thinks that Alma has deserted him. He and Chevasney go to the Crimea, where both take part in the glorious Charge of the Light Brigade. Sabretasche is eventually liberated, when his hag of an Italian wife finally drinks herself to death. And Trefusis is revealed to be a bigamist, releasing Vigne who at last marries

Alma. The work is clearly written in the excitement of the divorce law reform of 1857. Ouida was not proud of the novel, and apologises in a later preface for its want of art.

HELPS, Sir Arthur (1813–75). Born at Streatham, Surrey, Helps was educated at Eton and Trinity College, Cambridge. He showed some early talent for writing but sensibly suppressed it to follow a career in politics and the Civil Service. His progress was rapid. Beginning as private secretary to the Chancellor of the Exchequer, he rose to be Clerk of the Privy Council in 1860 and a trusted adviser to Queen Victoria whose 'Highland Journal' he edited. Helps turned out a wealth of essays, biographies and works of history, none of which has lasted at all well. He also wrote fiction for a few years. In 1868, he brought out his most successful novel, *Realmah*, a political fable set in the prehistoric Lake District artfully interrupted by modern dialogue on the same vexing subjects by a group of sophisticated 'Friends in Council'. Less well received were *Casimir Maremma* (1870), the story of an Eastern nobleman who submerges himself in London's proletariat and *Ivan De Biron* (1874), a story of Russian court life in the 1750s. Critics generally rather liked Helps's engaging way of setting his novels up as a series of stories exchanged between 'Friends in Council'. BL 3. *DNB*. R.M. *NCBEL*. Wol. Sad.

HEMYNG, [Samuel] Bracebridge (1841–1901; there is considerable disagreement over this author's dates, which can also be found recorded as 1829–1904). Creator of Jack Harkaway*. Hemyng was born in India, a son of the Registrar of the Supreme Court of Calcutta. He was educated at Eton (see his *Eton School Days*, 1865) and was called to the Bar in 1862. Hemyng subsequently became an extremely popular and prolific author, writing low-grade serials for the *London Journal**. His early novels include: *The Curate Of Inveresk* (1860); *Gaspar Trenchard* (1864). Hemyng also did the 'London Prostitution' section in Henry Mayhew's* *London Labour And The London Poor* (1861). On 23 July 1871, in the magazine *Boys Of England*, Hemyng published 'Jack Harkaway's Schooldays'. The Harkaway character went on to make the fortune of the journal's publisher, E. J. Brett* and of Hemyng himself. He travelled to the USA in 1874 at the invitation of the publisher Frank Leslie, where he wrote for the *Police Gazette* and produced several Harkaway stories set in America. Hemyng eventually returned to England, where he died at Fulham writing Harkaway stories until Brett's death in 1895. Among Hemyng's later works is *The Stockbroker's Wife* (1885), 'sensational* tales of the stock exchange'. BL 18. Wol. RLF.

HENNIKER, the Hon. Mrs Arthur [Florence Ellen Hungerford] (née Milnes, 1855–1923). A daughter of the first Baron Houghton and a sister to the Marquis of Crewe. She married an army officer, Arthur Henniker-Major (d. 1912), a baronet's son, in 1882. As an author, Florence Henniker specialised in studies of wretched marriage. Her fiction includes: *Sir George* (1891), the story of an uncle who falls in love with the girl entrusted him by his nephew; *Bid Me Goodbye* (1892); *Foiled* (1892), a story of adultery, forgery and suicide; *In Scarlet And Grey* (1896), a *Keynotes** volume of stories concerning 'soldiers and others' including one, 'The Spectre Of The Real', written in collaboration with Thomas Hardy*; *Sowing The Sand*

(1898). Her fiction was sometimes labelled unwholesome, particularly with regard to its obsessive interest in old men's love for young girls. Henniker wrote plays in the twentieth century. She was President of the Society of Women Journalists in 1896. She and Thomas Hardy were closely associated in 1893, and Henniker is supposed to have been the original of Sue Bridehead in *Jude The Obscure**. BL 5. *WW*. Wol.

Henry Esmond, William Makepeace Thackeray, 1852, 3 vols, Smith, Elder. (The full title of the work is, *The History Of Henry Esmond, Esq., A Colonel In The Service Of Her Majesty Queen Anne, Written By Himself*). Thackeray's finest achievement in historical* fiction. The work is a third person autobiography with an occasional artful lapse into 'I narration'. Henry is the supposed bastard son of Thomas Esmond. In fact, Thomas married the Flemish girl who was Henry's mother and the boy is legitimate although he is not aware of the fact. Thomas Esmond inherits the estate of Castlewood and is made Viscount. Henry is appointed page to the absurd Lady Isabel Castlewood. At this stage of his life he first encounters the Jesuit Father Holt, a man who profoundly influences Harry's later life. The Castlewoods support the Jacobite uprising, and the Viscount is killed at the battle of the Boyne. The estates and title pass to the good-natured and apolitical Colonel Francis Esmond. Henry attaches himself with what is to be lifelong fidelity to his patron's beautiful young wife, Rachel. As a young man, Henry brings smallpox into the household; Rachel is infected and her looks are damaged. She and her husband are increasingly estranged (his boorishness is partly due to his knowledge that Harry is the true heir). Harry goes to Cambridge, and on his return finds the Viscount has fallen in with the villainous Lord Mohun. An aspersion is made against Rachel's honour, and Castlewood fights a duel with Mohun in which he is killed, but before dying he tells Harry the truth of his birth. Harry is imprisoned for a year for his part in the duel, and Rachel unkindly blames him for her husband's death. Once released, Harry serves as a soldier on the Vigo expedition. On his return, he is reunited with Rachel at Winchester cathedral, and forgiven by her. He meets her daughter, Beatrix, now full grown, and falls in love. Harry is swept up in the War of the Spanish succession, and is wounded at Blenheim. After the battle of Wynendael, Harry fights a duel with Mohun in which neither party is killed. Rachel learns of Harry's sacrifice for her family (particularly her son, the present Viscount Frank) and comes to love him even more. Harry, meanwhile, is entranced by the dazzling Beatrix, the toast of fashionable London. But her lover, the Duke of Hamilton, is killed in a duel with the fateful Mohun who also dies of his wounds. Largely to win Beatrix, Esmond engineers a plot to return the Young Pretender to the throne of England. This almost succeeds, but at the last minute fails when the young Prince delays in order to seduce Beatrix. Finally disillusioned, Harry marries the faithful Rachel and emigrates to Virginia, the scene of *Henry Esmond*'s sequel, *The Virginians** (1858–59).

HENTY, G[eorge] A[lfred] (1832–1902). 'The boys' Dumas'. Henty was born at Trumpington, near Cambridge, the son of a stockbroker and coal-mine owner. The young Henty was brought up near Canterbury and was educated at Westminster School. He attended Cambridge University, but left without a degree in 1853. A sickly child (but cured, as he claimed, by health salts) Henty was a robust young man and on the outbreak of the Crimean War he volunteered for service, and his famous 'active life' began. George and his brother (who was to die of cholera at Scutari) were accepted for the Hospital Commissariat. Later he became Purveyor of the armed forces. G. Manville Fenn*, Henty's disciple and biographer, notes apologetically that 'his place would more naturally have been in the fighting line'. Nevertheless Henty was evidently a born leader, and showed much pluck. After the hostilities, with the rank of captain, he remained on in Asia Minor, to observe other wars going on in the region. For the next ten years, his life was unsettled. In 1859 he went to Italy to organise field hospitals for that country's war against Austria. In 1858 he married the widow of a fellow officer and had four children in as many years before she died of consumption in 1865. After a brief interlude helping his father manage a colliery in the early 1860s, Henty turned to journalism with striking success. Together with Archibald Forbes and William Howard Russell*, he became a pre-eminent Victorian war correspondent. Henty covered the Austro-Italian War for the *Standard* (and was an eyewitness to the naval battle of Lissa, 1866); reported the Franco-Prussian War, the Ashanti Wars and in the mid-1870s, the Carlist insurrection in Spain and the Turco-Serbian War. Often, he risked his life and was almost killed in Abyssinia in 1867. Henty also wrote on politics (he was a Conservative) and wrote three-volume novels for the adult market, beginning with *A Search For A Secret* (1867). But neither this nor its two successors was popular. Indeed, the *Athenaeum** cruelly observed that Henty's characters were no more like human beings than monkeys. Henty's first story for boys, *Out On The Pampas*, was written in 1868. It found its mark and adventure stories streamed from his pen thereafter. 'His one great excess', Fenn wryly notes, 'was his indulgence in ink.' Henty signed a contract with the publisher Blackie to provide three books a year and eventually turned out over 100 works for the boys' market (and about a dozen relatively unsuccessful straight novels for adults). He routinely put down 6,000 words a day. His novels tended to be tales of military history, with a young boy protagonist latched on to some great event. 'With' is a significant preposition in the Hentyan title as in *With Clive In India* (1884) or *With Cortez In Mexico* (1891). Henty was proud of the factual authenticity of such romances: 'lads', he declared, 'may rely upon the information contained in my books to be trustworthy'. His books for boys dwelt exclusively on adventure and manly episode. 'Once', he recalled, 'I ventured to make a boy of twelve kiss a little girl of eleven, and I received a very indignant letter from a dissenting minister.' Famously, Henty extolled the dogma of imperialism for young minds, with stirringly entitled works like *A Dash To Khartoum*; *True To The Old Flag*; *Hold Fast For England*. He took over the *Union Jack** magazine from the ailing W. H. G. Kingston* in 1880 but could not make it pay. Nor did he succeed with the *Boy's Own Magazine*, of which he was proprietor, 1889–90. But he was a stalwart of the hugely popular *Boy's Own Paper** (which had a juvenile readership of 500,000). Henty prospered from his writing, remarried (unhappily) in 1890 and died on his yacht, *Egret*, in Weymouth Harbour, 1902. Meredith*, whom he met as a fellow-journalist in 1866, was a lifelong friend and admirer. BL 107. *DNB*. RM. *NCBEL*. Wol. Sad. RLF.

Her Two Millions, William Westall, 1887, 3 vols, Ward and Downey. The most memorable of Westall's voluminous works by virtue of its autobiographical element and first-hand descriptions of continental life. The contrived plot, which extends from the Garibaldian era down to 1871, turns on the hoary device of a missing heir. It opens dramatically with the heroine's father being shot dead at Lago Maggiore. Most interesting in the narrative is Westall's well-informed account of how an English-language Swiss newspaper is run. (The author was editor of the *Swiss Times*.) The narrative, which ranges internationally, also introduces episodes set among the Paris Commune of 1871.

Hereward The Wake, Charles Kingsley, 1866, 2 vols, Macmillan. (Serialised as *Hereward, The Last Of The English* in *Good Words**, January–December 1865.) Kingsley's last novel, and his most pugnacious advertisement for the 'berserker' spirit as England's regenerative force. Hereward (later called Wake, in recognition of his alertness) is first encountered a boisterous lad, the son of Earl Leofric and Lady Godiva. His God-fearing mother has him outlawed, which leads to various adventures, in the company of Martin Lightfoot. In the north of England, Hereward makes his mark by defeating a polar bear in single combat. Hereward then brawls his way through Cornwall and finds himself eventually at the Court of Baldwin of Flanders. There Hereward shows his prowess against the over-armoured knights and wins the love of Torfrida. They marry and she civilises her wild husband. It is 1066, the year of the Norman invasion. Three years later, Hereward and Martin return to their country and discover Norman brutalities against their people. Hereward musters a rebel army, and takes up his camp in the Fens. Gradually, Hereward's resistance is worn down by William's army and by the subtle wiles of Alftruda who succeeds in separating the hero from his wife. Finally, Hereward's foe, Ivo Taillebois, surprises him in his ancestral home. He is killed after valiant struggle, calling Torfrida's name. He is the last of the old English leaders and is followed by more civilised, peace-loving Englishmen. But, the novel argues, primitive energies and virtues must not be entirely forsaken by modern man, lest effete degeneracy sap the racial virtue.

HERMAN, Henry (1832–94). Herman was born in Alsace and educated at a military college there, after which he emigrated to America. He fought in the Civil War, on the Confederate side, and lost an eye in action at the battle of Bull Run. He returned to England, and in 1875 began writing plays (mainly comic), in which he enjoyed considerable success. His first hit was *Silver King* (1882), written in collaboration with H. A. Jones. Herman also wrote novels. In collaboration with D. C. Murray* over the period 1887–91, he co-authored (among other works of the same melodramatic kind): *A Dangerous Catspaw* (1889); *The Bishop's Bible* (1890), a pathetic story of what happens when a clergyman's bible is stolen; *He Fell Among Thieves* (1891); *Only A Shadow* (1891); *A Leading Lady* (1891), a story of the stage. Under his single authorship, Herman published *His Angel* (1891), a story which starts vividly with a lynching in New Mexico; *Eagle Joe* (1892), 'A Wild West Romance'. Reviewers found his novels hastily written but exciting. He was, however, sometimes accused of repeating his plots unduly. Herman amassed a valuable theatrical library, which fetched £16,000 at auction after his death. His talent, in drama and fiction, was in the devising of story-lines and plot situations which are often ingenious. BL 17. *DNB*. Wol.

HEWLETT, Joseph Thomas James (1800–47). Joseph Hewlett was born in London. After receiving his school education at Charterhouse he went on to Worcester College, Oxford. Having graduated BA in 1822, he duly took holy orders in 1826, and went on to become headmaster of Abingdon Grammar School. Hewlett failed as a schoolmaster, and retired to Berkshire, intending henceforth to support himself by his pen. His subsequent life was, as the *DNB* puts it, 'a prolonged struggle with poverty'. A friend of Theodore Hook*, and a Colburn* author, he attempted to save his financial position by writing popular comic novels. Few writers (with the possible exception of Hook), have succeeded under this kind of pressure. Hewlett published *Peter Priggins, The College Scout* in 1841. The work was illustrated by Phiz*, serialised Dickens*-style in monthly numbers and 'edited' by Hook. It did not catch the public. It was followed by the similarly facetious, Hook-edited *The Parish Clerk* (1841); *College Life* (1843); *Parsons And Widows* (1844); and the historical* work, *Dunster Castle* (1845). *Great Tom Of Oxford* (1846) may be seen as a precursor of Thackeray's* *Pendennis** (1849–51). Hewlett's financial distress was relieved by his friends, who in 1840 helped obtain for him a curacy in Essex, worth £175 a year. BL 6. *DNB*. RM. RLF.

HEWLETT, Maurice Henry (1861–1923). Hewlett was born in Weybridge, Surrey. His father was a senior Civil Servant at the Land Revenue Records Office, specialising in legal affairs. Distantly, the family was of Huguenot origin and one of Hewlett's uncles was J. T. Knowles, founder of the magazine *Nineteenth Century*. The young Hewlett was educated at Sevenoaks Grammar School. In 1878, after three years at the Isleworth experimental International College (which he left without a degree), he went into the family law business in Lincoln's Inn to learn his profession from the bottom. In 1888 he was sufficiently well off to marry the daughter of a clergyman, Hilda Herbert (later a pioneer aviator). He was called to the Bar in 1890 and in 1897 succeeded his father as Keeper of Land Revenue Records, a post which he held until 1900. The turning-point of Hewlett's career was in 1898 with the publication of his novel *The Forest Lovers**. This romantic fable of a knight, Prosper le Gai, and a peasant girl, Isoult la Desirous, whom he rescues, in an idealised medieval New Forest, was so successful as almost to embarrass its author. It was followed by *Little Novels Of Italy* (1899), five stories set in Renaissance times; *The Life And Death Of Richard Yea And Nay* (1900), a whimsically fictional chronicle of Richard the Lion Heart; *The New Canterbury Tales* (1901); and *The Queen's Quair* (1904). From 1904 to 1914, Hewlett wrote numerous novels (his favourite line was Regency romance). He regarded his literary genius as principally poetic, and particularly valued his epic of 'Hodge', *The Song Of The Plow* (1916). Hewlett was a talented essayist and in later life was a committed socialist. BL 32. *DNB*. RM. *NCBEL*.

HICHENS, Robert [Smythe] (1864–1950). The eldest son of a clergyman, Hichens was born in Speldhurst, Kent, and educated at Clifton College. His early ambition was to be a musician, and he studied for some years at the Royal College of Music. Later in life, he was music critic on the *World*, in succession to Shaw*. He also travelled widely, and was particularly drawn to Egypt where he first went for his health in the early 1890s. Hichens had shown early literary talents. His novel *The Coastguard's Secret* (1886) was written when he was only seventeen. He made his name as an author with *The Green Carnation* (1894); a topical satire on Wilde* ('Esmé Amarinth'), Lord Alfred Douglas ('Reggie Hastings') and ultra-aestheticism. The work made clear allusion to Wilde's homosexuality and was withdrawn in 1895, by which time it had laid the way for the author's public disgrace. There followed Hichens's first hit: *An Imaginative Man** (1895). A study of madness, it is set in Cairo, and its honeymooning hero, Harry Denison, after sexual adventures, finally dies by dashing his brains out against the Sphinx. The work is an interesting example of the decadent* style and the kind of superheated romanticism about the Orient that was to be the staple of the early-twentieth-century bestseller, culminating in Edith M. Hull's *The Sheik*. It was published by one of the new houses of the 1890s, Heinemann*. Hichens's other early fiction includes: *The Folly Of Eustace* (1896), stories, some supernatural; *Flames* (1897), 'a London fantasy', with resemblances to Stevenson's* *Dr Jekyll And Mr Hyde**; *The Londoners* (1898), 'an absurdity' satirising decadent London society; *The Slave* (1899), a fantasy, centring on a wondrous emerald; *Tongues Of Conscience* (1900), five rather gloomy stories strong on horror, among which 'How Love Came To Professor Guildea', a story of supernatural visitation, is claimed by some to be the best thing he did in fiction. Hichens had international bestselling success with his oriental romance, *The Garden Of Allah* (1904). But it is for his satire on the literary and depraved nineties that he remains most worth reading. He lived abroad, in Switzerland and on the Riviera for most of his later life, unmarried. His memoirs, *Yesterday*, were published in 1947. BL 61. *DNB*. RM. *NCBEL*. Wol.

Hidden Depths, Felicia Mary Frances Skene, 1866, 2 vols, Edmonston and Douglas. Skene was a high Anglican, who did philanthropic work in Oxford (here called 'Greyburgh') as well as writing novels to raise money for her favourite charities. The heroine of *Hidden Depths* is Ernestine. Well-born and earnestly true to her name, she sets out to save from prostitution a girl whose sister Ernestine's brother had earlier seduced and abandoned. She is helped by Thorold, a High-Church clergyman. The novel effectively attacks middle-class hypocrisy. Ernestine's suitor, for example, is unmasked as the first seducer of a dying prostitute, being comforted by the heroine. Some of the brothel scenes are horrific, and stand out as unusually realistic for the 1860s. Originally put out anonymously, the novel was later republished with the author's name attached. She asserted that the narrative was entirely based on eyewitnessed fact and subtitled her work 'Veritas Est Major Charitas', truth is the greater charity.

HILL, Headon (i.e. Francis Edward Grainger, 1857–1927). Grainger was born in Lowestoft, the eldest son of a clergyman, formerly a teacher at Eton. He himself was educated at Eton, before joining the army. On his discharge he married, became a journalist and began to write fiction around 1890. By 1918, he had over fifty pot-boiling novels to his credit. They include: *Clues From A Detective's Camera* (1893); *Cabinet Secrets* (1893); *Zambra The*

Detective (1894); *The Rajah's Second Wife* (1894); *By A Hair's Breadth* (1897); *The Plunder Ship* (1900). The last is typical, being the story of an expedition to recover a sunken galleon's treasure in the Indian Ocean with, as one reviewer put it, 'a crisis in every chapter and enough villainy to stock a Drury Lane melodrama'. The work starts with a memorably full description of riding the nineteenth-century London underground. *The Spies On The Wight* (1899) is an early novel of espionage in which the hero, Philip Monckton, 'a new journalist', defeats the schemes of a gang of German imperialists. BL 73. *WW*. Wol

Hillingdon Hall, R. S. Surtees, 1845, 3 vols, Colburn. (Serialised in the *New Sporting Magazine*, February–June 1844, with illustrations by 'Wildrake' and Henry Heath.) The final part of the Jorrocks* trilogy. In this instalment, the comic London grocer (now too old to hunt) becomes the owner of Hillingdon Hall on the death of its venerable occupant, Mr Westbury. Jorrocks's attempts to play the gentleman farmer are predictably hilarious. He becomes a magistrate and a local dignitary. The narrative climaxes with Jorrocks's opposing the Marquis of Bray in a local election. Topically, Jorrocks stands as the pro-Corn Law candidate (that is, a true friend to the English farmer and countryside). He wins by two votes.

Hill-Top Novels. A term devised by Grant Allen*, in the preface to *The British Barbarians* (1895). According to Allen, 'A Hill-Top novel is one which raises a protest in favour of purity'. Arising from his experience with the bestselling but controversial *The Woman Who Did** (in its eighteenth edition with John Lane* as the author wrote), Allen noted the intrusive, censorious influence of editors in magazines. And he declared: 'I will willingly forgo the serial value of my novels, and forfeit three-quarters of the amount I might otherwise earn, for the sake of uttering the truth that is in me, boldly and openly, to a perverse generation.' Henceforth, Allen declared, all his novels would carry the description 'Hill-Top' as a trade mark, guaranteeing their fearless 'purity'. In fact, Allen's description came to be associated with defiant new women* heroines of the Herminia Barton variety, who flew in the face of bourgeois morality. The original Hill-Top novel, *The British Barbarians*, is the fantasia of a twenty-fifth century alien ('Bertram Ingledew') who returns to the 1890s, only to find them hopelessly primitive and irrational. Most irrational are the marriage conventions, which he blithely proceeds to flout. At the end of the novel, he is shot by an aggrieved husband, Robert Monteith.

HIND, C[harles] Lewis (1862–1927). Hind was born in London where his father was a JP. He was educated privately and at Christ's Hospital. At one point, he evidently contemplated a career in medicine but became instead a professional journalist and all-purpose man of letters. Hind was sub-editor on the *Art Journal* (1887–92); editor of the *Pall Mall Budget* (1893–95) and editor of the *Academy** from 1896. Hind also wrote articles and stories for various magazines. His fiction comprises *The Enchanted Stone* (1898), an updating of *The Moonstone** (1868) and *Life's Little Things* (1901), a collection of London sketches. BL 2. *WW*. Wol.

HINKSON, H[enry] A[lbert] (1865–1919). Born in Dublin, Hinkson was educated at the High School, Trinity College (where he studied classics) and in Germany. For a while he taught at Clongowes Wood School. He married in 1893, enrolled to study law and was called to the English Bar in 1902. He remained thereafter some years in England. Hinkson was a Catholic convert, and this is reflected in his fiction which includes: *Golden Lads And Girls* (1895), a modern love story, set in Galway; *Up For The Green* (1898), one of the many romances written to commemorate the Irish rebellion of 1798; *When Love Is Kind* (1898). Reviewers found the last 'pretty', and generally declared Hinkson to be a skilled story-teller. In later life, he returned to Ireland where he was a magistrate in south Mayo. Hinkson married the novelist Katharine Tynan* and was the father of the well-known writer Pamela Hinkson (1900–82). BL 13. *WW*. Wol. RLF.

His Natural Life, Marcus Clarke, 1875, 3 vols, Bentley. (A long version of the novel was serialised in the *Australian Journal*, March 1870–June 1872. The Australian volume edition was published by George Robertson, 1874.) The greatest Australian novel of the nineteenth century. The narrative begins in London, in 1827, with a complicated inheritance, crime and transportation prelude. Richard Devine, heir to a rich shipbuilder, takes on a false personality and is falsely accused of the murder of his Dutch father-in-law. He is transported to Van Diemen's Land, and supposed in England to have died. Over the next twenty-five years, his destiny criss-crosses with that of his cousin, Maurice Frere, who does not know his true identity. As a prison commandant, Frere brutally abuses 'Rufus Dawes' (as Richard now calls himself) and poisons the mind of Dora Vickers (whom the convict chastely loves) against him. The main part of the novel is written after the manner of Charles Reade's* *Put Yourself In His Place** and graphically details the vileness of convict life in Hobart and, particularly, on Norfolk Island, off Sydney. Devine escapes with the help of a sympathetic gaol chaplain, the Rev. North. He rescues Frere's daughter from shipwreck and adopts her. Subsequently he strikes gold (the Eureka Stockade episode figures in one section of the sprawling narrative). Meanwhile, a fellow convict goes back to England and falsely assumes Richard's inheritance. (This is based on the Tichborne case, in which an Australian butcher passed himself off as an English baronet, thought lost at sea. The first trial concluded in 1872.) Frere is killed by his illegitimate son, whom he has tortured in prison. Richard is finally vindicated and returns to England and to his wife (a character entirely ignored by the narrative). The novel has great power in the prison scenes, and the descriptions of Australian landscape are effective (that of the blowhole near Eaglehawk Neck stands out). But the work was perceived as grossly too long in its original serial state. Clarke brought out a much-revised and shortened version for the Australian and English library reader in 1874. This has a much more melodramatic opening and a climax in which Rufus dies with Silvia (i.e. Dora) Frere at sea in a storm. There is considerable critical disagreement as to which version is the better.

Historical Fiction. The most numerous and least honoured of Victorian fictional genres. None of his later-nineteenth-century disciples was able to repeat Scott's feat in the *Waverley Novels* of consistently raising the historical romance to high art. Nevertheless every self-respecting novelist tried his hand at the form: Dickens* with *A Tale Of Two Cities**; Thackeray* with *Henry Esmond**; Trollope* with *La Vendée**; Gaskell* with *Sylvia's Lovers**; Reade* with *The Cloister And The Hearth**; Wilkie Collins* with *Antonina**; George Eliot* with *Romola**; Hardy* with *The Trumpet Major**. And a surprising number of Victorians would have claimed that Reade's, Thackeray's or Dickens's historical romances were the very greatest literary works of the age. On no matter relating to the Victorian novel has posterity more diverged from contemporary nineteenth-century thought. The least interesting Victorian historical romancers are those who conceived themselves Scott's direct descendants: G. P. R. James* and Harrison Ainsworth*. James wrote nothing which posterity has thought worth keeping in print. And Ainsworth's fiction only became memorable for that brief period when, as with *Jack Sheppard**, it was interfused with the Newgate* criminal novel. In the 1830s only Bulwer-Lytton* achieved anything worthwhile, even rising to the challenge of the notoriously difficult classical historical setting with *The Last Days Of Pompeii* (1834). But his historical romance, as his critics often complained, 'smelled of the lamp'. His last essay in the genre, *Harold** (1848), is his most successful and has been taken to indicate a 'new seriousness' in the genre. Nevertheless, the 1840s probably represent the nadir of nineteenth-century historical fiction; and at the end of the decade the young Anthony Trollope received the immortal advice from his publisher: 'Do not make it historical. Your historical novel is not worth a damn.' Thackeray contrived to raise the form's status in the early 1850s with his brilliant eighteenth-century reconstruction, *Henry Esmond*. Most effectively, he treated the historical novel as an aesthetic challenge in which narrative and memory have an intimate and complex interaction. And Thackeray, like Kingsley and Dickens, had imbibed Carlyle's thinking in *Past And Present* (1843), taking an altogether more intellectual line on the problem of historical fiction than the immediate imitators of Scott. Macaulay's *History Of England* (1848) was also influential on Thackeray. At the end of the decade, Dickens produced his great melodrama of the French Revolution. But the most energetic adaptations of the form were in reaction to the religious quarrels of the day. Charles Kingsley's* ultra-Anglican *Hypatia** matched on their own classical ground J. H. Newman's* Catholic parable of persecution, *Callista**, and Cardinal Wiseman's* *Fabiola**. The Crimean War also inspired the muscular novelists like the Kingsleys and G. A. Lawrence* to write patriotic romances set in the glorious national past. With less distinction, the military historical novel flourished with the nostalgic camp-fire yarns of James Grant* and W. H. Maxwell*. In the later decades of the period there were some startling experiments in historical fiction such as Pater's* *Marius The Epicurean* and Shorthouse's* *John Inglesant**. And in the 1880s, R. L. Stevenson* came near to equalling Scott's achievement with *Kidnapped** and *The Master Of Ballantrae**. But by this late period, the main impulse had shifted down-market via Rider Haggard* to the juvenile sector dominated by G. A. Henty*, W. H. G. Kingston* and their numerous followers. Increasingly historical romance (even Stevenson's) was beneath the notice of the adult reader.

The History Of Margaret Catchpole, Richard Cobbold, 1845, 3 vols, Colburn. (Unusually for a three-decker, the novel carried illustrations, by the author.) A historical* and authentically regional* tale of Suffolk smuggling at the turn of the nineteenth century. Margaret 'A Suffolk Girl', is a farm labourer's daughter who goes into service. She has two lovers: the dashing smuggler Will Laud and the solid countryman, John Barry. In the climax of the narrative, Margaret steals a horse to ride to London and marry Will. But she is caught; sentenced to death; then reprieved. She later escapes daringly from Ipswich gaol and in a bloody shoot-out (in which Laud is killed) she is recaptured. After ten years as a transported convict in Australia Margaret returns to Suffolk to marry John Barry and end life as a respectable matron. The novel is loosely based on fact and the actual Margaret Catchpole was helped by the novelist's mother, Elizabeth Cobbold. The narrative is amateurish and condescending in tone. But it captures common life in East Anglia well and was a bestseller.

The History Of St Giles And St James, Douglas Jerrold, 1851, 1 vol, Bradbury and Evans. (Serialised in *Douglas Jerrold's Shilling Magazine**, January 1845–May 1847, with illustrations by John Leech*.) The story was devised as the lead item for Jerrold's ambitious new magazine. It is an unusual novel. Extraordinarily savage politically, it sets out (in the words of the preface of 1851, for which the text was revised) to show the 'ignorant disregard of the social claims of the poor upon the rich, of the governed million upon the governing few'. Jerrold uses the hackneyed device of the doubled heroes (as had Ainsworth* in *Jack Sheppard**) to make his points. St Giles is a 'hero of the gutter'; St James (as the London associations of their names suggest) a young marquis. The novel opens in the 1820s with an atmospheric night storm scene, in which the baby St Giles is found at the breast of a dead woman of the streets. He is brought up in the slums of Seven Dials. As a young criminal, he robs St James of his hat outside Covent Garden, but escapes prosecution when the young nobleman generously declines to press charges. St Giles subsequently steals a pony worth £20 from the young lord and is condemned to death (this being the due penalty in what Jerrold bitterly calls 'the Good Old Times'). He is reprieved and transported to Botany Bay, but returns at the risk of being hanged. At the end of the novel, by a series of highly theatrical twists, St James is himself imprisoned for murder, together with St Giles who faces execution as an illegally returned convict. St James is acquitted and makes a speech in Parliament which wins the freedom of St Giles who goes on to become 'a decent shopkeeper and churchwarden'. In following St Giles's career as a condemned, reprieved, transported and returned convict, Jerrold nags at the reader with harsh tirades: 'we make them outcasts, wretches, and then punish, in their own wickedness, our own selfishness, our own neglect'. The story is solved with the discovery of St Giles's parentage, inheritance, marriage and providential justice.

HOBBES, John Oliver (i.e. Pearl Mary-Teresa Craigie, née Richards, 1867–1906). The most accomplished Catholic novelist of the late nineteenth century. Pearl Richards was born in Boston, America. Her family was enriched by patent medicines, notably Carter's Little Liver Pills. The Richardses moved to London in 1868, and it was there the young girl spent her formative years. Pearl Richards was brought up in the style approved of for upper-class English girls, attending boarding schools in Berkshire and at Paris. Her literary sensibility was extremely precocious, her first story being published when she was nine. Richards was presented at Court in

1886. At nineteen, she married an English banker, Reginald Walpole Craigie, whom she met in America. There was one child of the marriage, a son, born in 1890. In the same year, the couple parted. Her partisans claim he was drunken, unfaithful and infected her with venereal disease. Whatever else, he gave her the principal theme of her subsequent fiction, utterly wretched marriage. The couple were eventually divorced messily (on the grounds of his adultery) in 1895. In 1892, she converted to Catholicism. At about the same time, she resolved both to educate herself and to pursue a career in literature. In 1891, she published her first novel, *Some Emotions And A Moral**. The story of an ill-assorted and mutually unfaithful marriage, the work is written with a light, cynical touch. It was very successful. Since it first appeared in Fisher Unwin's 'Pseudonym Library*', the author was obliged to devise a pen-name: John Oliver Hobbes. She followed up her success with other modish studies of sex and Bohemian manners, dedicated to her view that 'if the gods have no sense of humour they must weep a great deal' and written in a diamond-hard manner. They include: *The Sinner's Comedy* (1892); *A Study In Temptations* (1893); *The Gods, Some Mortals And Lord Wickenham** (1895); *The Herb Moon* (1896). The last is the depressing story of the courtship between a young clerk, Robsart, and an older woman, Rose, whom he initially supposes to be a widow. In fact, she is married to a husband locked up in a lunatic asylum. After many years (and his winning a VC in the Indian Mutiny) they eventually marry. The odd title is a proverbial reference to long engagements. On the strength of such studies of sexual cross purpose, her striking presence and her independent wealth, Hobbes became a fashionable London woman of letters. She also tried less successfully for theatrical success in the early twentieth century. Her most enduring work has been the pair of connected novels, with a pronounced Catholic theme: *The School For Saints** (1897) and *Robert Orange* (1900). Hobbes's fiction is clearly influenced by Meredith* and, more venerably, by Disraeli* and Newman*. It is teasingly indirect and digressive in manner. George Moore*, with whom she was sexually and emotionally involved, represents her vindictively in a number of his novels. In later life, she was (like Mrs Humphry Ward*) a member of the Anti-Suffrage League and president of the Society of Women Journalists, 1895–96. She never enjoyed good health, and died very young. A John Oliver Hobbes scholarship was established in her memory at University College, London. BL 13. *DNB*. RM. *NCBEL*. Wol.

HOBHOUSE, [Mary] Violet (née McNeill, 1864–1901). Violet McNeill was the daughter of the Deputy Lieutenant of Co. Antrim. In 1887, she married the Rev. Walter Hobhouse, a bishop's son. Although a Unionist, Hobhouse studied Irish traditions, and was fluent in the Irish national language. In 1887, and after, she spoke against Home Rule from English platforms. Her fiction includes: *An Unknown Quantity* (1898), 'A Sad Story Of Modern Life' and *Warp And Weft* (1899), 'A Story Of The North Of Ireland', dealing with the linen weaving community, and its Presbyterian culture. Reviewers found Hobhouse's writing laboured but admired the documentary authenticity of her picture of Ulster. She also wrote poetry. BL 2. (WH) *WW*.

HOCKING, Joseph (1860–1937). Hocking was born at St Stephen, Brannel, in Cornwall, the youngest son of a tin-mine owner. He reportedly read all Scott's fiction by the time he was twelve, and had written his own first novel a year later. Despite these early literary prodigies, he was apprenticed to land surveying at the age of sixteen. He felt (as had his brother Silas Hocking*) a call to the Methodist ministry, however, and attended Owens College and the Crescent Range Theological College in Manchester, where he proved a prize pupil and was ordained in 1884. In 1887, he married and undertook an extensive tour of the Middle East. On his return, he was minister at Woodford Green, Essex, 1888–1910. Hocking published over fifty books, of which the first was the novel *Jabez Easterbrook* (1890). One reviewer summarised it thus: 'a sturdy young Wesleyan minister encounters a fascinating young lady of agnostic tendencies. They argue throughout the tedious length of the novel.' Much of his fiction (which a large number of readers in fact found highly entertaining) was serialised in the *British Weekly*. His most effective narratives are his Cornish romances, which draw on his childhood memory, for example: *Ishmael Pengelly, An Outcast* (1893); *The Mist On The Moors* (1896); *And Shall Trelawney Die?* (1897); *The Birthright* (1897). *The Madness Of David Baring* (1900) is one of Hocking's more interesting works, the story of a young man's struggle to establish a utopian community in Cornwall. Hocking's fiction generally has a tendency towards preachiness. His views of the literary world are reflected in *Fields Of Fair Renown* (1896). He died in Cornwall. BL 82. *DNB*.

HOCKING, Silas K[itto] (1850–1935). A brother of the above, he had parallel childhood experiences. Intended originally to follow his father into the mining business, he was ordained a Methodist minister in 1870, and took up his vocation in the industrial north-west of England, where he proved himself an unusually brilliant preacher, marrying in 1876. Hocking resigned the ministry in 1896, in order to devote himself to writing, Liberal politics and journalism. He also wrote fiction principally aimed at children. Even more than his brother Joseph, he has a tendency to the didactic in his novels. His first published work was *Alec Green* (1878). He had an immense success shortly after with *Her Benny* (1879), a tale of the Liverpool 'street arab'. When his saintly sister dies, Benny heroically resists becoming a thief and grows up instead to be worthy of marrying his master's daughter. Ill-advisedly, Hocking sold the copyright of this bestselling work for £20, outright. But it established his reputation, and Hocking became one of the most popular authors in England. In 1894, he became editor of the *Family Circle* and two years later helped establish the *Temple Magazine*, an organ devoted to entertaining Sunday reading in the style of *Good Words**. He revisits the scene of his Cornish childhood in *The Strange Adventures Of Israel Pendry* (1899). His other fiction includes: *God's Outcast* (1898), a study of guilt; *To Pay The Price* (1900), a moralistic fable of theft and painful redemption. Hocking's autobiographical *My Book Of Memory* was published in 1923. He died in London. BL 48. *DNB*. *NCBEL*. Wol.

HOCKLEY, W[illiam] B[rowne] (1792–1860). Hockley was born in Bury St Edmunds, the son of an army officer. He was educated locally and entered the Indian government service in 1813. He eventually rose to the rank of judge, but was accused of receiving bribes in 1821. Only partially cleared, he was dismissed in 1824, with a pension of £150 a year. He wrote a number of oriental tales, drawing on his Indian experience. *Pandurang Hari* (1826) was the first. The last, *The Memoirs Of A Brahmin, Or The Fatal Jewels* (1843) falls into the Victorian period. But by this date, the vogue for this highly coloured genre had long passed. Hockley died in London. BL 5. Boase. RM. *NCBEL*. Wol. Sad. RLF.

HOEY, Mrs Cashel [Frances Sarah] (née Johnston, 1830–1908). Frances Johnston was born in Dublin, one of the eight children of the registrar of Mount Jerome Cemetery. She was educated at home, largely teaching herself. She married (on her sixteenth birthday) Adam Stewart, by whom she had two children. Some years later (around 1853) she began to write for the Dublin papers and magazines. Her husband died in 1855. The young widow came to London, with an introduction from William Carleton* to Thackeray*. She began writing reviews, and was soon well known in literary circles. In 1865, she began a long association with *Chambers's Journal**, then edited by James Payn*. In 1858, she married the journalist John Cashel Hoey (1828–93). Politically he was associated with Young Ireland. She converted to his Catholicism, and over the course of her marriage wrote eleven novels, most of them fast paced melodramas with high-society settings and far-flung travels interspersed among the narratives. She particularly relished complicated love situations. Hoey's most popular works were: *A House Of Cards* (1868); *Falsely True* (1870); *The Question Of Cain* (1882), the story of a burglary syndicate whose action goes as far afield as India; *A Stern Chase* (1886). The 'chase' in the last takes the melodramatic action to Cuba which is vividly described but which Hoey had never seen, as her preface to the novel candidly admits. According to the *DNB*, drawing on the testimony of William Tinsley*, Hoey was 'largely responsible' for novels usually attributed to Edmund Yates*: *Land At Last* (1866); *Black Sheep!** (1867); *Forlorn Hope* (1867); *The Rock Ahead* (1868), a story of love and poison; *A Righted Wrong* (1870). She was allegedly, the sole author of this last work, a lurid drama of bigamy* and illegitimacy. Mrs Hoey helped Edmund Yates found the *World* in 1874. In 1892, she was awarded a Civil List pension of £50. Among other literary work, Hoey made translations from French and Italian. In 1871, she visited Paris and reported enthusiastically on the Commune. She died in Beccles, Suffolk. BL 11. *DNB*. Wol.

HOFLAND, Barbara [Hoole] (née Wreaks, 1770–1844). She was born in Sheffield, where her father, Robert Wreaks, was a manufacturer who died in his daughter's infancy, leaving her to be brought up by an aunt. In 1796, she married T. Bradshawe Hoole, a Sheffield merchant who died of consumption in 1798. Barbara Hoole was left a rich widow, but was later ruined by the failure of the business in which her money was invested. In 1805, she began writing to support herself and her young son. A volume of poems attracted charitable subscriptions (from friends, mainly) and with this nest egg she opened a school at Harrogate. The venture was unsuccessful. Hoole had better luck with her fiction, which was of a domestic uplifting kind (e.g. *The Clergyman's Widow*, 1812). In 1808, she married the artist, Thomas Hofland (1777–1843). Like her, the son of a rich northern manufacturer, he was gifted, but improvident and added to her financial burdens. When he fell ill, she was obliged to write harder than ever. But by now, she was an established and popular writer. Hofland was a friend of Miss Mitford*, but her fiction is generally considered much inferior. It consists mainly of children's tales and very tame works with an insistent Christian message. *Emily's Reward* (1844) is a typical later work. Hofland also wrote some Victorian three-deckers towards the end of her life, such as: *The Czarina* (1842); *The King's Son* (1843); *The Unloved One* (1844), 'a domestic story'; *Daniel Dennison* (1846), the story of a country apothecary in early-nineteenth-century Cumberland. According to the *DNB*, during the many trials of her life, she was a 'true-hearted, cheerful, and affectionate woman'. BL 61. *DNB. NCBEL.* Wol.

HOLDSWORTH, Annie E. (d. 1910?). Holdsworth was born in Jamaica, the daughter of a clergyman and educated in London and Scotland. She married Eugene Lee-Hamilton (1845–1907) in 1898. He was also a writer, principally of poetry and in 1898 published a translation of Dante's *Inferno*. Lee-Hamilton was also a half-brother of the novelist Vernon Lee* and an acquaintance of Henry James. Annie Holdsworth worked on W. T. Stead's *Review Of Reviews* in the 1890s, was an active feminist, and was co-editor with Lady Henry Somerset of *The Woman's Signal.* Her most discussed novel was *Joanna Traill, Spinster* (1894), the story of an old maid who changes her life at the age of thirty-five, told in a style reminiscent of Meredith*. The narrative ends gloomily with solitary death for the heroine. The so-called 'superfluous woman' was an issue of the day and according to the *Observer*, Holdsworth's 'picture is a beautiful one, which it would be well for many women to ponder on'. The work was published in Heinemann's* 'Pioneer Library', devoted to the discussion of new ideas and social themes. Her other fiction includes: *The Years That The Locust Hath Eaten* (1896), the story of a wife's wasted devotion to a selfish husband; *Spindles And Oars* (1887), kailyard* stories; *The Gods Arrive* (1897), a love story with Emersonian overtones. BL 15. *WW.* RLF.

HOLLAND, Clive (i.e. Charles James Hankinson, 1866–1959). Hankinson was born in Bournemouth, the son of a civil engineer and later mayor of the town. After attending Mill Hill School, he trained initially for the law. As Clive Holland, he began writing for boys' papers in 1887, and devoted himself entirely to journalism after 1893 writing for many of the leading papers and magazines. Hankinson also travelled widely and Eastern settings feature prominently in his work. His Victorian fiction includes: *The Golden Hawk* (1888); *Raymi* (1889); *My Japanese Wife* (1895); *Marcelle Of The Latin Quarter* (1900). The last is a tepid account of art student life in Paris. BL 14. *WW.* Wol.

HOOD, Tom [Thomas] (1835–74). The only surviving son of Thomas Hood (1799–1845), the humorist. Hood the younger was born at Wanstead, and spent his early years travelling with his parents on the Continent. He was educated at schools in London, and subsequently left Oxford University neither taking a degree nor taking holy orders (as had been expected). As a young man, Hood supported himself by writing, and journalism. From the mid-1850s until 1860 he lived in Cornwall, whose scenery he exploited in his first novel, a saga of the Tresellans of Tresellan entitled, *A Disputed Inheritance, A Cornish Tale* (1863). As the author candidly observed in a preface, if the work were to receive 'a not unkindly welcome,

I shall be encouraged to attempt a more ambitious story'. It was not welcomed. In 1860, through the friendship of Lady Molesworth, Hood was given a clerkship in the War Office. He left in 1865, to become editor of *Fun*, a magazine for which he wrote reams of verse, and which he also helped illustrate. Hood's forte is agreed to be amusing doggerel, in his father's vein. But he wrote several novels in the 1860s, including: *Vere Vereker's Vengeance, A Sensation In Several Paroxysms* (1864), an illustrated burlesque; *A Golden Heart* (1867); *The Lost Link* (1868), a tale of bigamy* and detection; *Money's Worth* (1870), a sensational* story with a writer hero; *Love And Valour* (1871), which has some Oxford scenes which may be autobiographical. Reviewers regularly accused Hood's fiction of carelessness and occasionally of downright plagiarism. BL 6. *DNB. NCBEL.* Wol. RLF.

HOOK, Theodore [Edward] (1788–1841). A famous wit, and the most renowned practical joker of the nineteenth century. Hook was born in London, the son of the composer and organist James Hook (1746–1827), and educated at Harrow School from 1804 to 1805 (when he was a contemporary of Byron's) and at Oxford University. From an early age, Hook was drawn to the theatre and was writing for it in his teens. In his twenties, he already enjoyed considerable success as a comic dramatist. Hook quickly made himself a favourite jester in Regency high society (Thackeray* was later to satirise him unkindly as Wagg, parasite of the Marquis of Steyne, i.e. the Marquis of Hertford). In 1811, he gave up writing plays and the next year, through the patronage of the Regent, he was made Accountant-General and Treasurer to the island of Mauritius, newly won from the French. Hook was entirely unsuited for responsibilities of this kind. In 1818, he was arrested on the charge of embezzling 62,000 dollars and imprisoned for two years. For the rest of his life he was technically bankrupt and always chronically in debt. (On his death Hook was supposed to have still owed the enormous sum of £30,000.) He was, however, infinitely resourceful and in 1820, he founded the scurrilous Tory paper, *John Bull.* In 1824, his novel *Sayings And Doings* originated the silver fork* fashion of novel, and Hook was for the rest of his life a star Colburn* author. Among his popular early novels of high life was *Maxwell* (1830), although his leadership in the genre was soon overtaken by Mrs Gore*. In 1836, Colburn appointed him as editor (annual salary £400) of the revamped *New Monthly Magazine** to match Bentley's* success with Dickens* and *Bentley's Miscellany**. In the six years of life that remained to him, Hook turned out a quantity of anecdotal comic fiction, under extreme duress of poverty and ill health. In the circumstances, much of it is surprisingly good. It includes: *Gilbert Gurney* (1836), a rag bag of miscellaneous essays, sketches and comic episodes pegged on to the progress of a hero born 'in the same year as Lord Byron [and Hook]', 1788; *Jack Brag** (1837); *Gurney Married* (1838); *Births, Deaths and Marriages* (1839); *Precept And Practice* (1840); *Peregrine Bunce* (1842). Hook was working on this last novel at the time of his death in August 1841, and it was finished by another hand. On his death aged fifty-three at Fulham, Hook's property was, yet again, seized for unpaid debt. His funeral was unattended by any of his rich patrons, friends or employers. His common-law wife of twenty years and his five children (four daughters) were left destitute although his works remained favourites throughout the Victorian period. BL 14. *DNB*. RM. *NCBEL*. Wol. Sad.

HOOTON, Charles (1813?–47). Hooton's background is obscure. He was evidently born in Yorkshire, and as a young man edited a newspaper in Leeds. He came to London around 1837 and was associated with *Bentley's Miscellany**. For that paper, he wrote his best-known work (illustrated by John Leech*); *Colin Clink* (1841). After some other desultory literary activities, Hooton left for Texas, where 'for nine months he led an almost savage life'. After some unsuccessful ventures in American journalism, Hooton returned to London, exhausted. He renewed his acquaintance with Ainsworth*, and wrote *Launcelot Widge** for *Ainsworth's Magazine**. He died, during this novel's serial publication in Nottingham, of an overdose of morphia in 1847. His sub-Dickensian* fiction, though quirky, has its powerfully atmospheric and comic moments. BL 4. *DNB*. Wol. Sad. RLF.

Hopes And Fears, Or Scenes From The Life Of A Spinster, C. M. Yonge, 1860, 2 vols, Parker. The novel has a complex plot. Honora, the heroine, loves Owen Sandbrook, a clergyman intent on converting the Red Indian. He lapses from his high ideals, takes a comfortable living, marries a rich wife and has two children. Honora, although she has marriage offers from her rich cousin, Humfrey, remains a spinster. Years later, having become trustee of her cousin's wealth, she and Owen (now a widower) are reconciled just before his death from overwork. Honora takes charge of his children, both of whom go to the bad, before repenting and returning to Christian courses. Honora is assisted by Phoebe, a virtuous girl who marries the long-lost heir of the rich cousin. Charlotte Yonge herself was thirty-seven and unmarried when she wrote this novel.

HOPKINS, [William] Tighe (1856–1919). Hopkins was born in Cheshire, the son of an Anglican clergyman, and educated at Oundle Grammar School. In 1881 he married Ellen Crump, the step-daughter of the novelist Mortimer Collins*. As his name suggests, Hopkins's background was Irish, and he edited a number of William Carleton's* works for the modern reader. He was also interested in penal reform, which is reflected in his best work of fiction, *The Silent Gate, A Voyage Into Prison* (1900). The narrative is made up of eleven prisoners' tales, narrated with cool good humour. Hopkins's other novels include: *'Twixt Love And Duty* (1886); *The Nugents Of Carriconna* (1890); *The Incomplete Adventurer* (1892); *Lady Bonnie's Experiment* (1895), social comedy at the expense of the new cult of primitivism; *Nell Haffenden* (1896), 'a strictly conventional story' and a double decker which must have been one of the last Victorian multi-volume novels. BL 10. *WW*. Wol. RLF.

HORNE, Richard [Henry] Hengist (1802–84). A versatile and highly eccentric author, Horne was born in London. He attended the military academy at Sandhurst, but failed to get the commission he applied for in the East India Company's service. He subsequently left England, and joined the Mexican navy to fight in war against Spain. In the following years, Horne travelled extensively in North America, undergoing various adventures. When he returned to England in the late 1820s, he made himself an all-purpose man of letters. In 1839, he entered into correspondence with Elizabeth Barrett (the letters were eventually published). And in 1841, he served on a commission investigating the conditions for female and child workers in industry. His information on the subject inspired Barrett's poem, 'Cry Of The Children' (1843). In 1844, Horne brought out his *A New Spirit Of The Age*, an updating of Hazlitt's famous cultural survey. A year earlier, there had appeared his *Orion*, an epic poem following the growth of the poetic mind. Famously, it was sold at a farthing, and earned Horne the sobriquet, 'The Farthing Poet'. Horne married in 1847, but left his wife in 1852 to travel to the Australian goldfields with William Howitt*. He remained in Australia until 1869, and was among other things a magistrate there. As an author of fiction, Horne wrote some fine children's stories in the 1840s: *Memoirs Of A London Doll* (1846); *The Good-Natured Bear* (1846); *King Penguin* (1848). His fiction for adults includes *The Dreamer And The Worker* (1851), 'a story of the present time'. The work ambitiously tries to show the ways in which art (specifically poetry) can cooperate with labour. Unfortunately, as reviewers sourly noted, Horne chooses at the end to enrich his hero and heroine with providentially unearned riches and solves all social problems with an 'Institute for Artizans'. The work was first published in Douglas Jerrold's* radical 1s. magazine before the better-known (and frankly better) social problem* novels of Mrs Gaskell* and Charles Kingsley*. Horne himself certainly rated as more important his epics and tragedies (such as his 'miracle play', *Judas Iscariot*, 1848). In 1874, he was awarded a Civil List pension. Horne was well-regarded by his contemporaries. Carlyle, for instance, declared that he had 'the fire of the stars in him'. BL 5. *DNB*. RM. *NCBEL*. Wol. RLF.

W. B. Horner and Son. Publishers of popular fiction in the late Victorian period. The firm was originally founded in Dublin, but moved to London. In the 1890s, it specialised in penny dreadfuls* of a less dreadful kind than E. J. Brett's*. In 1889, the firm's list was around 150 novels, selling at 1d. Up to 450,000 of the most popular items were printed. Horner's was taken over in the 1920s by the Amalgamated Press.

HORNUNG, E[rnest] W[illiam] (1866–1921). E. W. Hornung was born in Middlesborough, and educated at Uppingham School. He spent 1884–86 in Australia in order to mend his poor health. Australian settings were to prove useful to him in his later fiction. In 1893, he married A. Conan Doyle's* sister. By this time, he was firmly established as a journalist (associated principally with the *Strand** magazine) and as a novelist. Hornung's fiction includes: *A Bride From The Bush** (1890); *Under Two Skies* (1892); *Tiny Luttrell* (1893); *The Unbidden Guest* (1894); *My Lord Duke* (1897). *Peccavi* (1900), the story of an erring parson, is regarded as the most serious of Hornung's early novels. But his most famous work remains *The Amateur Cracksman* (1899), which features the elegant man-about-town criminal, Raffles*. Hornung served with the YMCA in the First World War in which, tragically, his only son, still a boy, was killed. He wrote up his war experiences movingly as *Notes Of A Camp Follower On The Western Front* (1919). BL 29. *WW*. RM. Wol.

HORT, Richard (1804–57). Not much is known of his life. Richard Hort entered the Life Guards in 1819, and rose to the rank of major with the brevet rank of lieutenant-colonel. Thereafter he was editor of the *Royal Military Magazine*. Hort's fiction is described by Michael Sadleir as a mere 'vehicle for bringing forward his admirable illustrator, Alfred Ashley'. Hort's novels include: *The Man Who Eloped With His Own Wife* (1850); *The Horse Guards* (1850); *The Embroidered Banner* (1850); *Penelope Wedgebone* (1850); *The Guards And The Line* (1851). Hort can also claim to have produced the longest title in the annals of Victorian fiction: *The White Charger That Cost Me Two Hundred Pounds; Lost Me Seventy Thousand Pounds; Drove Me From Society; And Eventually Deprived Me Of My Friends; And Finally Compelled Me To Quit The Service* (1850). Some bibliographical confusion has arisen over Hort's identity. *The Horse Guards* is an attack on Wellington's administration of the army, and was published anonymously. The British Museum credited the work later to another 'Colonel Hort', namely Sir John Josiah (1824–82). This error is followed by a number of subsequent bibliographers. BL 6. Boase. Wol. Sad.

HOTTEN, John Camden [William] (1832–73). Elsewhere entered as the founder of Chatto and Windus*, Hotten is also noteworthy as a pioneer in the publication of pornography. He was born in Clerkenwell, into a family with Cornish roots. His father was a master carpenter and undertaker. Well educated, Hotten revealed an early passion for books and at the age of eleven he had a 'respectable' library of 450 volumes. At the age of sixteen he went to the West Indies with his brother and after various adventures (including a cholera epidemic) found himself in the USA where he applied himself to journalism. In 1855 he returned to England, where he opened a small bookshop, married and settled down. Hotten thereafter figured on three important fronts in the British book trade. He became a publisher of respectable works. He introduced a number of American writers to the British public, such as Bret Harte and Mark Twain. And he cultivated what he called his 'flower garden' of libertine books. He published (clandestinely) R. Payne Knight's *Worshipping Priapus* among other classics of prohibited literature. His interest in flagellation (he published, for instance, a *History Of The Rod*) connects with his championing of the poet Swinburne. Hotten also himself wrote a comic opera in two acts, *Lady Bumtickler's Revels* (1872). *DNB*.

The House With The Green Shutters, George Douglas (i.e. George Douglas Brown), 1901, 1 vol, Macqueen. Brown's novel was designed to demolish kailyard* sentimentality about the beauties of rural Scottish existence. The setting is the village of Barbie, in the late nineteenth century. John Gourlay is a self-made man; a contractor with twelve wagons. He has a slatternly wife and daughter, and a weak son, John. Gourlay's enemy James Wilson returns rich after fifteen years abroad to continue a bitter rivalry. He sets up a store which stocks items previously hauled in by Gourlay. He also starts a competitive carting service. Young John goes to Edinburgh University where by fluke he wins an essay prize. Briefly, he has his father's approval but promptly forfeits it when he is expelled for drunkenness. Gourlay's business fails and he so torments his son that he strikes him dead with a poker. The Gourlay women convince the authorities that the death was accidental. But John, haunted by the memory of his father's eyes, poisons himself. His mother who is dying of cancer and his consumptive sister follow him, after reading the scriptural text on charity. The house with the green shutters is sold off.

Household Words (1850–59). A 2d. weekly, founded by Charles Dickens* in collaboration with Bradbury and Evans*, who had a quarter share in the venture. Dickens was assisted by W. H. Wills as sub-editor and the paper's circulation was a healthy 40,000 a week, rising to almost three times that for special Christmas issues. *Household Words* paid a guinea per two-column page printed. The contents were miscellaneous (although book reviews were excluded), featuring general interest articles, politics (Dickens agitated for such things as workers' education) and current affairs. Short fiction was also featured. Mrs Gaskell* contributed the sketches that came together in volume form as *Cranford*. Wilkie Collins* also supplied short fiction and his was one of the careers (together with G. A. Sala's*, Percy Fitzgerald's* and Harriet Parr's*) that was launched in the paper. Dickens published some longer pieces, such as Gaskell's *North And South** and his own *Hard Times**. He fell out with Bradbury and Evans over their refusal to print in *Punch** his explanation for parting from Mrs Dickens. Dickens subsequently bought the property of *Household Words* at auction in 1859 and promptly extinguished the paper to start in its place the ambitiously conceived and independent *All The Year Round**. BLM.

HOUSMAN, Laurence (1865–1959). Housman, a younger brother of the poet A. E. Housman, was born at Perry Hall, Bromsgrove, the son of a solicitor with eccentric Tory views. His mother died when he was six, and the young man became very attached to his stepmother. After attending Bromsgrove School he did not go to university, but instead at eighteen went to study art in London. In straitened circumstances, he lived with his sister Clemence Annie Housman. In 1893, he published a well-received selection of Blake's poetry and from 1895, he was art critic of the *Manchester Guardian*, a paper with which he retained close ties throughout his life. Housman published a number of volumes of poetry including *Green Arras* in 1896 and *Spikenard* in 1898. He also wrote essays, plays, tales, political satires (e.g. *John Of Jingalo*, 1912), fables and fiction. His novels were mainly published (stylishly) by John Lane* and include the whimsically oriental *Gods And Their Makers* (1897) and his notorious investigation of female psychology *An English Woman's Love Letters* (1900). This last work was extremely successful and earned its author £2,000. He also wrote stories for children. Housman was a pacifist in the first World War. In late life, he wrote an autobiography, *The Unexpected Years* (1937). His sister, Clemence (d. 1955), with whom he lived until her death, also wrote such allegorical fictions as: *The Were Wolf* (1896), first serialised in *Atalanta**; *The Unknown Sea* (1898). The second of these is her most ambitious work and rhapsodically chronicles the symbolical love affair between a self-martyrising 'Christian' and a heartless mermaid, Diadyomene. Neither Housman married. BL 9. *DNB*. RM. *NCBEL*.

HOWARD, Edward (1793?–1841). Howard's life is obscure. He served in the Royal Navy in the Napoleonic Wars and was a shipmate of Frederick Marryat's*. He left the service in 1810, being afflicted with deafness. In civilian life, Howard made some injudicious speculations, with money which may not have been his. After a series of small jobs (which included tutoring and painting on ivory), he drifted into the literary world and was Marryat's sub-editor on the *Metropolitan** in 1835. Howard made a hit with his lively nautical* novel *Rattlin The Reefer*, which ran in the magazine from 1834 to 1836 and which contains many recollections of the author's life afloat. The hero, Ralph Rattlin, is found abandoned in Reading in the 1790s, and brought up in working-class London. The narrative spends some time on Ralph's experiences at Mr Root's unpleasant academy, before he goes to sea as a junior midshipman on the frigate HMS *Eos*. He travels to the West Indies with his vessel, sees action and hideous floggings on board ship, and falls in love on furlough. Ralph eventually returns to England where, inevitably, his true identity is discovered to be that of Sir Ralph Rathelin. Howard's narrative (delivered autobiographically by Ralph) contrives to be both amusing and in places graphically horrible. Following up the success of *Rattlin The Reefer*, he brought out a string of inferior rollicking tales of the sea: *The Old Commodore* (1837); *Outward Bound* (1838) and *Jack Ashore* (1840). Their content is indicated by their salty titles. Howard took over editorship of the *Metropolitan* after Marryat sold it to Saunders and Otley*. In 1841, he took up an appointment under Thomas Hood at the *New Monthly Magazine** but 'following a good Christmas dinner', he died before setting to work. He did not live to see the decline in popularity of the nautical novel of which he was the second greatest practitioner. BL 4. *DNB. NCBEL.* Wol. Sad. RLF.

HOWARTH, Anna (1854?–1943). Howarth was born in London, the daughter of a clergyman. On her father's death she was shipped out to South Africa, partly for her health, partly because of financial difficulties at home. In 1894, she trained as a nurse and lived for some time in the countryside with the family of Selina Kirkman, who was to be her lifelong companion. Howarth drew on her first-hand acquaintance with South African locations for her first novel, *Jan, An Afrikander* (1897), a work which is unusual for its treatment of racial miscegenation. *Katrina, A Tale Of The Karoo* (1899) is a more domestic tale, which has a vivid depiction of South African drought. *Sword And Assegai* (1899) is a historical* tale, set during the 1820s settler wars. *Nora Lester* (1902) is a Boer War novel. (The war gave a topicality to all Howarth's novels, which were popular in England.) Reviewers found her style 'heavy'. Howarth also wrote poems, and lived most of her life in South Africa with Kirkman. But on her friend's death, she returned to England in 1935. BL 5.

HOWITT, Mary (née Botham, 1799–1888). Born at Coleford, Gloucestershire, her father was a prosperous business man, with an interest in mining. Mary Botham was brought up a Quaker although in later life she rebelled against the sect's disciplines. In 1821, she married William Howitt* (1792–1879), and embarked with him on a productive literary career. The couple settled first in Nottingham, then moved to Heidelberg in 1840. Howitt acquainted herself with the literature of Europe, and between 1842 and 1863 translated from the Scandinavian the fiction of Fredrika Bremer (whom she introduced to an English readership) and Hans Christian Andersen. She also published the three-volume novel *Wood Leighton* (1838) whose narrative chronicles a year of closely observed rural village life. Most of her writing is, however, ephemeral and was published in magazines and annuals. In 1847, Howitt and her husband started *Howitt's Journal*, a venture which failed. In later life, both Howitts were attracted by the cult of mesmerism and spiritualism. In 1870, they moved to Italy, William dying at Rome in 1879. His widow went to live with their daughter, Margaret Howitt, in the Tyrol. (Margaret was herself the author of children's fiction, such as *Birds Of A Feather, Or Two Schoolboys*, 1867.) Mary was received into the Catholic Church in 1882, a few years before her death. An interesting and intellectually powerful woman, Howitt began writing popular stories for children in the late 1830s. She also produced a later three-volume novel *The Cost Of Caergwyn* (1864), a story of inheritance and legal dispute set in a densely described rural Wales. Her *Collected Tales Of English Life* were published in 1881, prefaced by a nostalgic recollection of a 'slower England', since disappeared. BL 13. *DNB. NCBEL.* Wol.

HOWITT, William (1792–1879). Born in Derbyshire, Howitt's father was a farmer and a Quaker. The boy William showed himself unusually precocious, and largely educated himself. He was particularly gifted in foreign languages. Travel and travel books were to feature prominently in his later career although he retained a strong feeling for the English countryside throughout his life. (See his novel *Woodburn Grange*, 1867, the story of a rural community with some revealing Quaker scenes.) After marriage to Mary Howitt* in 1821, Howitt supported himself for a while as a druggist. From an early age he held radical political views, which are evident in his novel, *The Man Of The People* (1860), a story set in the stirring years preceding the first Reform Bill. He also published the more idyllic *The Hall And The Hamlet* (1848), a novel of community. Both he and his wife were progressive in their intellectual and artistic views. (They admired, for instance, the Pre-Raphaelites.) Temperamentally restless, Howitt went to Australia when he was sixty. The episode is reflected in his novels: *A Boy's Adventures In The Wilds Of Australia* (1854) and *Tallangetta, The Squatter's Home* (1857). In the 1860s, he became fascinated by spiritualism, and wrote widely on the topic. He died in Rome having been awarded a Civil List pension in 1865. Fiction is a small part of Howitt's large and commercially successful literary output. His major work was his five-volume *Popular History Of England* which he undertook for Cassell's*, 1856–62. BL 5. *DNB. NCBEL.* Wol.

HUBBACK, Mrs J[ohn] C[atherine Anne] (née Austen, 1820?–1880?). Proudly listed by her publisher as 'the niece of Miss Austen', she was the daughter of the admiral, Sir Francis Austen (1774–1865), a brother of Jane the novelist. She married the lawyer John Hubback (1811–85) in 1842. Her fiction rings the changes on her famous aunt's themes and includes: *The Younger Sister* (1850); *The Wife's Sister, Or The Forbidden Marriage* (1851); *Life And Its Lessons* (1851); *Malvern, Or The Three Marriages* (1855); *The Mistake Of A Life* (1863). The last ('a dreary tale', the *Athenaeum** called it) is the story of a young heiress who foolishly marries a treacherous Italian. Hubback was, reportedly, a popular author. BL 10. Boase. Sad.

HUDSON, W[illiam] H[enry] (1841–1922). Hudson was born on a small cattle ranch near Buenos Aires, in Argentina, the fourth child of American emigrant parents who had gone south for the sake of their lungs. He was brought up among ranchers, and had a random education at the hands of a series of tutors. At fifteen, an attack of typhus, complicated by rheumatic fever, ruined his health and rendered him a semi-invalid for life. He was told that he might drop dead at any moment (he was, in fact, to live to the age of eighty-one). Living where and as he did, the young man felt the blow strongly. Over the next few years, Hudson read obsessively (almost blinding himself in the process) and developed the gloomy Darwinistic views which accompanied the passionate love of nature he had cultivated in his childhood. He was particularly drawn to ornithology on which he was expert enough to dispute with Charles Darwin himself in 1870 on the habits of the pampas woodpecker. (Among Hudson's more specialist productions is a comprehensive survey of Argentinian bird life.) In the 1860s he travelled all over South America, and served with the Argentine National Guard. In 1868 his father died and in 1874 Hudson sailed to England, never to see his native Pampas again. In London, he lived a lonely and narrow existence. In 1876, he married Emily Wingrave, a woman eleven years his senior. The union was evidently friendly, but Hudson remained essentially the solitary man he had always been and there were no children. The couple ran a boarding house, which failed in 1884. Another suburban boarding house which the couple set up failed in 1886. Hudson's life was to be plagued by petty anxiety over money. In 1885, he published his first and bizarrely titled volume of fiction, *The Purple Land That England Lost**. It was wholly unsuccessful, the *Saturday Review** calling it a 'vulgar farrago of repulsive nonsense'. Undeterred, Hudson went on to publish the utopian, William Morris* style romance, *A Crystal Age** (1887). The work is hostile to urbanisation, and foresees a future extinction of the sex drive in man. Hudson enjoyed rather more success with his essayistic books, *The Naturalist In La Plata* (1892) and *Birds In A Village* (1893), a study of English ornithology which he followed with *Birds In London* (1898). He wrote one three-volume novel, *Fan* (1892) and his post-Victorian fiction includes the savage *El Ombú* (1902), set in 1808 and named after the distinctive Argentine tree, and his best-known work *Green Mansions* (1904), 'a romance of the tropical forest', which contains the remarkable creation of the bird-girl Rima. As a laureate of the English countryside, Hudson belongs with Jefferies*, Hardy* and Baring-Gould*. As a romancer of the South American plains, he belongs with Cunninghame Graham*. Hudson received a Civil List pension of £150 in 1901 (in recognition for his services to natural history), and published a history of his early childhood, *Far Away And Long Ago* in 1918, just before his death. BL 7. *DNB*. RM. *NCBEL*. Sad.

HUGHES, Arthur (1832–1915). Painter and illustrator. Hughes was born in London and educated initially at Archbishop Tenison's Grammar School. His artistic abilities were noticed early, and in 1846 he was taken on at the government school of design at Somerset House, progressing from there to the Royal Academy schools. He came strongly under the influence of the Pre-Raphaelites and gained a name for himself as a painter in the 1850s. *The Long Engagement* is probably his best-known painting. As an illustrator of fiction, Hughes supplied pictures for the 1869 edition of Thomas Hughes's (no relation) *Tom Brown's Schooldays** and for a number of George MacDonald's* fantasies; most effectively *At The Back Of The North Wind** (1871). *DNB*. Hou.

HUGHES, Thomas (1822–96). Hughes wrote little fiction in an otherwise hectically busy life. But *Tom Brown's Schooldays** has transcended its period popularity to become the archetypal boys'-school tale. Like his fictional Tom, Hughes was born into the landowning, professional middle classes. His father, John Hughes of Donnington Priory, was a farmer and a JP. Thomas was brought up in Berkshire, a county whose landscape haunts his fiction, and attended Rugby (like Brown again) under the revolutionary regime of Dr Arnold. As a schoolboy he was captain of the cricket and football teams. From there, he went at nineteen to Oriel College, Oxford in 1842 (playing cricket for the University) and after graduation proceeded to a career in law in 1845. He was admitted to the Bar three years later. At Lincoln's Inn, he fell under the charismatic influence of the chaplain, F. D. Maurice, the greatest preacher, Hughes thought, since St Paul. From 1848 (the climax of the Chartist movement), he associated himself with Maurice's militant Christian Socialism. He wrote pro-Chartist tracts (on the Charles Kingsley* model), lectured, and helped set up Working Men's Associations and the Working Men's College in Great Ormond Street. He married in 1847, and the responsibilities of family (there were nine children) led to a more bourgeois form of life as a professional lawyer in the 1850s. *Tom Brown's Schooldays* (1857) was written at a time when Hughes's own eight-year-old son Maurice was about to enter Rugby. Some manuscript chapters were shown to Macmillan*, who seized on the work. The book was a runaway succcess, was enthusiastically reviewed and went through five editions in seven months, earning Hughes over £1,200. More importantly, it established a new genre in fiction. And although published anonymously by 'an old boy', it quickly made Hughes a famous public figure. He did a sequel, *Tom Brown At Oxford*, to kick off Macmillan's new magazine in November 1859. It is much less vigorous a tale than its predecessor. Hughes wrote one other work of fiction, the Christmas story *The Scouring Of The White Horse** (1858). It features a London clerk who visits Berkshire and witnesses the local rite of cleaning the white horse inscribed in the chalk hills. The remainder of Hughes's life was largely occupied with the law. He was made a QC in 1869 and appointed a county court judge in 1882. He was a Radical MP for Lambeth from 1865. But he kept up his energetic practice of lay preaching on such subjects as 'The Manliness Of Christ' (1879). He also argued publicly for better relations with America, a country in which he took a particular interest and which he visited in 1870. He suffered serious financial reverses in 1880 through helping set up a cooperative settlement ('Rugby') in Tennessee and was obliged to live in reduced style thereafter. Hughes wrote a memoir of Daniel Macmillan (1882) and of his elder brother George (whom he had hero-worshipped) in 1873. Hughes died a widely known and loved public figure. BL 3. *DNB*. RM. *NCBEL*. Wol. Sad. RLF.

HUISH, Robert (1777–1850). Huish was born in Nottingham. In his teens, he attended university in Frankfurt, where he acquired an unusually close knowledge of German literature. He subsequently spent some time in Russia, apparently as a tutor. Most of his later life was passed in London and he died in Camberwell. In the 1820s he was frequently in prison for debt, leaving his wife and five children to fend for themselves. Huish had an unusually long run as a novelist: his early fiction appearing in the 1790s (e.g. *The Sorcerer*, 1795) and his last novel, *Our Grandpapa's Chest*, coming out in 1850. Huish's early efforts are conventionally gothic* and Germanic. A militant radical, he later wrote silver fork* works which (as did G. W. M. Reynolds's* notorious *Mysteries Of London*) expatiate salaciously on the delinquencies of the upper classes (e.g. *The Memoirs Of George IV, 1830*) Towards the end of his long career, Huish wrote penny dreadfuls* for Edward Lloyd*. BL 3. RLF.

HUME, Fergus[on] [Wright] (1859–1932). Born in England, Hume's family emigrated to New Zealand in his childhood. He was educated at school in Dunedin, and the University of Otago. Before turning to literature as his livelihood, he worked as a barrister's clerk and was himself called to the New Zealand Bar in 1885. He subsequently moved to Melbourne, where, in a famous literary anecdote, he asked a bookseller what kind of fiction was selling. On being told that the detective* stories of Gaboriau were in vogue, he wrote his immortal *The Mystery Of A Hansom Cab** (1886), for which he received only £50 for the outright sale of the copyright. The work made little stir in Australia. But when it was published in Britain, a year later, it was phenomenally successful and made Hume's name as a leader in the exciting new field of detective fiction. It also helped set up the speculative 'Hansom Cab Publishing Company'. Many claimed authorship of this story, and Hume himself claimed he received nothing from its English triumph. He came to England in 1888, which was thereafter his literary base. By 1900, he had written forty-six novels. His Victorian fiction includes: *Madame Midas* (1888), a 'shilling shocker' of Australian mining life, dedicated to 'Miss Alice Cornwall, the first Victorian Lady Miner'; *Monsieur Judas* (1890); *Island Of Fantasy* (1892); *The Dwarf's Chamber* (1896); *The Bishop's Secret* (1900). The last is the story of an ecclesiastic improbably blackmailed by gypsies. None of his subsequent fiction matches his first work, although Hume plugged away writing mysteries until the year of his death. In his *Who's Who* entry he aggressively labelled himself not 'novelist' but 'story teller'. BL 134. *WW*. RM. Wol.

HUNGERFORD, Mrs Margaret Wolfe ('The Duchess', née Hamilton, 1855–97). A popular Irish novelist, Margaret Hamilton was born in Co. Cork, where her father, Canon Fitzjohn Stannus Hamilton, was a clergyman at Ross Cathedral. She married twice; first to Edward Argles (d. 1878), a Dublin solicitor, in 1872; secondly in 1882 to Thomas Hungerford. Each marriage produced three children. A fertile writer, she produced around thirty novels before her premature death by typhoid. Of these the most successful was *Molly Bawn* (1878), 'a love tale', featuring a light-headed but irresistible Irish colleen. Hungerford affected the pen name 'The Duchess', after one of the titles of her novels. Her Irish* tales (for which there was an end of the century vogue) include: *Her Week's Amusement* (1885); *A Little Irish Girl* (1891); *Nor Wife Nor Maid* (1892); *The Red House Mystery* (1893); *The Hoyden* (1894). Hungerford's fiction is mainly insubstantial and frothy. As the *Academy** put it, 'Miss Hungerford's Irish girls have always been pleasant to meet upon the dusty highways of fiction'. An exception is

Lady Verner's Flight (1893), which deals with the sufferings of an abused wife. BL 48. *DNB*. Wol.

HUNT, Mrs Alfred [Margaret] ('Averil Beaumont', née Raine, 1831–1912). Born in Durham, she was the daughter of a lawyer with a scholarly interest in local history. In 1861 she married Alfred W. Hunt (1830–96), an artist specialising in Turneresque water-colour landscapes. Hunt was associated with the Pre-Raphaelites, which lends some interest to his wife's novel *Magdalen Wynyard, Or The Provocations Of A Pre-Raphaelite* (1872). Her other fiction, which is generally exuberantly comic and satirical, includes *Thornicroft's Model* (1873); *Under Seal Of Confession* (1874); *The Leaden Casket* (1880), a satirical survey of the London literary and artistic worlds through the career of a vivacious heroine Olive Brooke; *Mrs Juliet* (1892); *A Black Squire* (1894). Hunt wrote under her 'Beaumont' pseudonym until the mid-1870s. Her novel *The Governess* was finished by her daughter Violet Hunt* and published in 1912 with a preface by Ford Madox Hueffer. BL 12. (AWH) *DNB*. Wol. Sad.

HUNT, [Isobel] Violet (1866–1942). The daughter of Mrs Alfred Hunt*, she was born in Durham and grew up among the Rossetti circle. Her father, himself a water-colourist, intended her to be a painter, and she studied art until the age of twenty-eight. Thereafter, she was a well-known hostess and woman of letters. A consort of Ford Madox Ford (i.e. Hueffer, 1873–1939) she was for a while after 1911 known as 'Mrs Hueffer', unofficially, as the first Mrs Hueffer from whom he separated in 1909 was unwilling to divorce her husband. Hunt nevertheless defiantly entered 'married 1911' into her *Who's Who* entry without specifying her husband. Her previous lovers included the novelists Oswald Crawfurd*, Walter Pollock* and Somerset Maugham*. She took an active interest in women's suffrage activities, and founded the Women Writers' Suffrage League. She was the friend of Henry James and an early patron of D. H. Lawrence. Her own fiction includes: *The Maiden's Progress* (1894), 'A Novel In Dialogue', which follows the career of 'Moderna' a modish heroine of eighteen, first discovered in her bedroom in Queen's Gate, languishing on her bed in a white peignoir; *A Hard Woman* (1895), 'A Story In Scenes' with an anti-heroine called Lydia Munday; *The Way Of Marriage* (1896); *Unkist, Unkind!* (1897), an ultra-romantic tale, set at a country-house party in Northumberland; *The Human Interest* (1899), a story of modern sex problems with a novelist-heroine, Egida, who is a 'great Ibsenite'. *Affairs Of The Heart* (1900). Hunt's fiction generally is smart, cynical, and usually comic. BL 13. *WW*. Wol.

HUNTER, Peter Hay (1854–1909). Hunter was born in Edinburgh, the son of a paper merchant. He was educated at Edinburgh University, at Leipsic and the Sorbonne. He was subsequently ordained as a minister in the Church of Scotland, and took up his first post at Elie in 1883. He subsequently had a successful career, preaching several times before Queen Victoria. Hunter was made an honorary doctor of divinity in 1902. Two of his novels were written in collaboration with Walter Whyte: *My Ducats And My Daughter* (1884), a story of Scottish capitalism and electioneering; and *The Crime Of Christmas Day* (1885). Hunter's other fiction under his own name is more overtly religious and includes: *The Story Of Daniel* (1883); *Sons Of The*

Croft (1893); *James Inwick* (1894); *The Silver Bullet* (1894). Hunter was a keen observer of the Scottish scene, an enthusiastic mountaineer and a yachtsman. He died in Edinburgh. BL 6. *WW*. Wol.

HUNTER, Sir William Wilson (1840–1900). Hunter was born in Glasgow, the son of a prosperous manufacturer. He graduated from Glasgow University in 1860 and chose a career in the Indian Civil Service taking first place in its open examination. Hunter became a distinguished Indian administrator, and made himself a world authority on the sub-continent's history and languages. He was appointed by the government to conduct the statistical survey of the Indian Empire, a massive task which took him twelve years. In 1887, he retired from the service, and thereafter published a number of books from his home in Oxford. His output includes the interesting novel, *The Old Missionary* (1895), set in India in the early days of the century. It tells the story of an old sailor, 'Trafalgar Dawson', who settles down as a hard-working missionary in Northern Bengal. His experiences are the pretext for a close historical reconstruction of Indian life from 1820 to 1850. BL 1. *DNB*.

Hurst and Blackett (1852–1926). The publishing firm founded by Daniel Hurst (1802?–1870) and Henry Blackett (1826–71) in succession to Henry Colburn* at Great Marlborough Street. The partners took over Colburn's business in good running order and continued his policy of supplying the libraries with popular three-deckers by such writers as Mrs Marsh (Caldwell*) and Geraldine Jewsbury* (one of the firm's literary advisers). The house was absorbed by Hutchinson* in the 1920s, who revived a Hurst and Blackett list in the 1960s for romantic fiction, appropriately enough. (DH and HB) Boase.

Hutchinson (1887–). Publisher, founded by George (Sir George after 1912) Thompson Hutchinson (1857–1931), who began working life as an apprentice of Alexander Strahan*. An early bestseller published by the firm was Joseph Hatton's* *By Order Of The Czar* (1890) and thereafter popular middlebrow fiction remained Hutchinson's main line of goods. Hutchinson was one of the publishers who exploited the disappearance of the three-decker in 1894. (GTH) *WW*.

HUTCHINSON, Horatio [Horace] G[ordon] (1859–1932). The son of an army general, he was educated at Charterhouse (where his grandfather had earlier been a headmaster) and at Corpus Christi College, Oxford. Hutchinson took his BA in classics, but his heart was in golf. He was amateur national champion 1886–87 and wrote extensively on sport. He also wrote some successful works of Victorian prose fiction: *Peter Steele The Cricketer* (1900); *Little Lady Mary* (1900) and *Her Best Friend* (1900). BL 9. *WW*.

HYNE, C[harles] J[ohn] Cutcliffe [Wright] (1865–1944). Hyne was born in Bibury, Gloucestershire, the eldest son of a clergyman. He was educated at Bradford Grammar School, and at Clare College, Cambridge, where he studied science and rowed for the Varsity. Hyne married in 1897. Throughout his life he was an active sportsman and travelled extraordinarily widely. It was his boast that he covered 10,000 miles of new ground every year. His fiction (which reflects his far-flung wanderings in its settings) includes: *The New Eden* (1892); *The Recipe For Diamonds* (1894); *Honour Of Thieves*

(1895); *The Stronger Hand* (1896); *The Paradise Coal Boat* (1897); *The Adventures Of Captain Kettle* (1898); *The Further Adventures Of Captain Kettle* (1899); *The Lost Continent* (1900). Kettle, a lovable old sea dog in the merchant marine with a long-suffering wife in South Shields, is the author's best-known creation and was effectively portrayed in accompanying illustration by Stanley L. Wood. Hyne also invented the popular detective Mr Horrocks in *The Derelict* (1901). He concentrated on historical* romance, in his later career. BL 46. *WW*. *NCBEL*. Wol.

Hypatia, Or Old Foes With New Faces, Charles Kingsley, 1853, 2 vols, J. W. Parker. (Serialised in *Fraser's Magazine**, January 1852–April 1853.) The 'foes' of the title are proselytising Catholics. The story is set in fifth-century Alexandria. The initial narrative line begins with Philammon, a young monk at Laura, 300 miles above Alexandria. In a deserted Egyptian temple, he has a vision and is moved to persuade his superiors to let him go to the city. Canoeing down the Nile, he is picked up (after a misadventure with a hippopotamus) by a party of Goths searching for Asgard, city of the Norse gods. They are accompanied by the beautiful courtesan, Pelagia (later revealed to be the hero's sister). At Alexandria, a complicated cast of characters is introduced: Orestes, the cunning Roman Prefect; Cyril, the arrogant head of the Church; Hypatia, a Neoplatonist philosopher and teacher. Raphael Aben-Ezra is a cultivated Jew and one of Hypatia's pupils. Later for love of another woman, Victoria, he becomes a Christian. There follow complicated intrigues. Philammon, intending to denounce Hypatia, is entranced by her. The novel climaxes with a series of set-piece scenes, saturated with Kingsleyan eroticism and violence. At the spectacle of Alexandria, Pelagia performs a pagan dance on the back of a white elephant. The performance (bizarre even by Kingsley's standards) explodes into pandemonium. A coup, planned by Orestes and Hypatia, fails. In the lecture hall, where Hypatia aims to recant her paganism, she is stripped and torn limb from limb by Cyril's monks, under a gigantic image of Christ. The scene is one of the most sexually charged in all Kingsley's fiction. Philammon escapes with Pelagia to the desert. The novel concludes with a coda, twenty years on. Cyril's Church has sunk under its own corruption. Philammon is now abbot of his own monastery and Pelagia is a chaste recluse.

I

The Idler (1892–1911). An illustrated monthly, costing 6d. Until 1898, the magazine was published by Chatto and Windus*. Its first editors and shapers were Jerome K. Jerome* and Robert Barr*. The *Idler*'s contents, in accordance with its editors' style of writing, was miscellaneous, paragraphic and facetious. It carried occasional serials by the Americans Mark Twain and Bret Harte, and Barr went on to contribute light fictional sketches under his pseudonym 'Luke Sharp'. Conan Doyle* also contributed many of the short pieces later collected as *Round The Red Lamp* (1894). A number of novelists supplied non-fiction articles to Jerome's paper. By 1896, the *Idler* was featuring short stories by such writers as W. W. Jacobs*, Israel Zangwill*, H. G. Wells* and longer fiction by Anthony Hope (i.e Hawkins*). From 1893 to 1897 Jerome ran an illustrated 2d. weekly, *To-Day*, using *Idler* personnel. But an expensive libel suit in 1897 forced him to dispose of his interest in both journals. *To-Day* continued under the editorship of Barry Pain* until 1905. *The Idler* was taken over first by Barr, then by Arthur Lawrence. Among other fiction, *To-Day* serialised R. L. Stevenson's* *Ebb Tide* (1893–94). *BLM*.

The Illustrated London News (1842–). A weekly 6d. publication which pioneered new illustrative techniques and a distinctive 'pictorial journalism'. The paper was founded by Herbert Ingram (1811–60), formerly a compositor and Nottingham newsagent. Ingram was inspired by the attractiveness of the occasional woodcut illustration in the otherwise staid *Morning Chronicle*. First issues of the *ILN* were sixteen folio pages and triple-columned. Among the original contributors were Mark Lemon* and the Mayhew* brothers, stalwarts of *Punch**. Artists associated with the *ILN* in its first years of publication were John Gilbert*, John Leech*, J. Kenny Meadows* and Alfred Crowquill*. During its early career, the *ILN*'s stress was exclusively on current affairs. But in the early 1880s, spurred by its rival the *Graphic* (founded December 1869), it began to feature serial fiction by novelists such as R. L. Stevenson*, Walter Besant*, R. E. Francillon*, Rider Haggard* and Maarten Maartens*. Hall Caine's* *The Scapegoat** ran from July to October 1891, with the sexually explicit (i.e. bare-breasted) illustrations that evidently added to *ILN*'s appeal to the general reader. By 1901, the weekly novel instalment was routinely the leading item in the paper. The *ILN* developed a lighter and more homogenised pictorial style than the *Graphic* whose leading artists were the socially realistic Arthur Boyd Houghton (1836–75), Luke Fildes* and Hugo von Herkomer (1849–1914).

An Imaginative Man, R. S. Hichens, 1895, 1 vol, Heinemann. An early success by the author of the superselling *The Garden Of Allah* (1904). After three months of marriage, the clever, thirty-eight-year-old, idle and ironic Harry Denison discovers that his beautiful wife is, despite appearances, incorrigibly empty-headed. The couple travel to Egypt for a 'second honeymoon'. In Cairo, Harry becomes prey to strange fascinations. The Sphinx obsesses him and he goes out at night into the desert to contemplate the enigmatic monument. In their hotel, Mena House, he falls in with a vivacious widow, Mrs Aintree, whose son Guy is dying of consumption and dissipation. Harry accompanies him on a ghastly round of night visits to the 'inferno' of Cairo's brothels. Finally, Guy dies of exhaustion and Harry goes to the Sphinx and dashes his brains out 'against the mighty rock that has defied the perpetual intangible embrace of the gliding ages'. Hichens's tone perfectly catches the elegant nihilism fashionable in the 1890s.

In The Year Of Jubilee, George Gissing, 1894, 3 vols, Lawrence and Bullen. The novel is set in the fiftieth year of Victoria's reign, 1887 and Gissing's jaundiced view of the country's jubilation features centrally in the action. The main characters belong to neighbouring families in Camberwell: the Lords and the Frenches. The head of the Lord family deals in pianos, and has two children: Horace (a young wastrel) and Nancy (a flirt). There is a mystery about the absent Mrs Lord. The Frenches are principally three vulgar young women, possessed of a small inheritance from their builder father: Fanny, a sexual adventuress (she eventually runs away to Paris); Beatrice, hard-headed and selfish (she sets up a successful fashion shop) and Ada, a shrew married to the mild clerk Arthur Peachey (whom she eventually drives to flight). The opening narrative centres on Nancy. She rejects the overtures of the pompous autodidact Samuel Barmby Jr; encourages but finally rejects an advertising agent, Luckworth Crewe and finally allows herself to be seduced by a well-bred man about town, Lionel Tarrant. They marry secretly, only to discover on her father's death that neither she nor Horace will inherit if they marry within five years. Nancy and Lionel keep their marriage (and their eventual son) secret. He goes to the Bahamas to make his fortune, but fails. He travels on to America, and does not write; Nancy thinks herself deserted or widowed. Her secret leaks out, and she suffers malicious persecution. Meanwhile, Horace has become involved with the unscrupulous Fanny French. The relationship is broken up by a society hostess, Mrs Damerel, who takes a suspicious interest in Horace. (She is his mother, it later emerges.) Lionel eventually returns, and after some bitterness becomes a moderately successful writer. He and Nancy reveal their marriage, and finally find themselves able to live together. Horace, meanwhile, has contracted consumption. He marries the soiled Fanny, and dies abroad. The novel contains some biting satire on petty bourgeois society, and is principally remarkable for the sensitive depiction of Nancy's growing maturity under physical hardship. Gissing's odd views on marriage are reflected in the ultra-rational Tarrant union.

In The Roar Of The Sea, S. Baring-Gould, 1892, 3 vols, Methuen. One of Baring-Gould's Cornish romances. The story is set on the estuary of the Camel in the eighteenth century. It opens with the death of the Vicar of the church of St Enodoc (an establishment which symbolically needs to be excavated from the tidal sand that constantly engulfs it). The Rev. Trevisa leaves a pair of twins. Judith is beautiful and wilful; Jamie an idiot. They are put in the care of their aunt Dionysia, who is housekeeper to the villainous Cruel Coppinger, skipper of the *Black Prince* and one of the wreckers who lures ships to destruction on the Cornish coast. Despite her initial horror, Judith is attracted to Cruel, and saves him from the Revenue men. He comes to adore her. But at their marriage ceremony, she faints and is unconscious at the moment of union. She regards herself as thereafter only 'half married'. Judith refuses to consummate the marriage after Cruel uses the witless Jamie as 'Jack o' the Lantern' to entice a ship onto Doom bar. Their relationship deteriorates further when Jamie tries to poison Cruel, and he assumes Judith to be the culprit. The story ends with the self-destruction of Cruel in his lair, Othello Cottage. Judith marries the suitably virtuous Oliver Menaida, and the couple emigrate to happiness in Portugal. The work offers rich regional description of the kind Baring-Gould was famous for.

INGELOW, Jean (1820–97). Born at Boston, Lincolnshire, Ingelow was the eldest child of a banker, and educated at home (which seems to have been in Suffolk). Her mother was Scottish. In 1863, the family moved to London.

By this date Ingelow had shown ample evidence of literary talent. Her first published volume of poems came out in 1850. Subsequent collections of poetry (especially that in 1863) established her as a leading author of the day. Among her more famous lyrics are *When Swallows Build* and *Wedlock.* For many years she was an editor of the evangelically flavoured *Youth's Magazine.* Ingelow also wrote fiction. She was, as one critic put it, a good story-teller but a poor novelist. The semi-fictional *Studies For Stories From Girls' Lives* (1868) was illustrated by J. E. Millais*, among others. Her story for children, *Mopsa The Fairy* (1869), is both ingenious and charming. Of her novels for adults, foremost is *Off The Skelligs** (1872). Ostensibly a melodrama of tangled love and peril at sea the work contains autobiographical material. As do all her novels, it displays a quantity of larded-in verse and high-flown conversations about the meaning of things. Ingelow devised a sequel, *Fated To Be Free* (1875). *Sarah De Berenger* (1879) is a melodrama in the style of *East Lynne**. It tells the story of a mother married to a convict who conceals her shame by pretending to be her children's servant. *Don John* (1881) gloomily chronicles the misfortunes which follow on two children being exchanged at birth. Ingelow did well with her writing (which included many short stories) and was socially acquainted with the great writers of the period, who regarded her as an equal, a reputation she has since lost. She never married and died at Kensington. BL 11. *DNB. RM. NCBEL.* Wol.

The Invisible Man, H. G. Wells, 1897, 1 vol, Pearson. (Serialised in *Pearson's Weekly*, June–July 1897.) The story begins comically in rural Surrey. 'The stranger', muffled, bespectacled and morbidly reclusive, installs himself at the Coach and Horses inn, provoking the curiosity of all in Iping village. He is in fact a young student, Griffin. The unveiling of the stranger's secret over the next two months is initially hilarious. But when driven to flight things become gradually more ominous as he revenges himself on his tormentors. In the next phase of the story, he recruits a tramp (a type Wells always handled well) as his assistant. He breaks into the house of a former student friend, now Dr Kemp, and tells him his story. It emerges that he is a figure to be pitied, rather than feared (particularly effective are the invisible man's descriptions of his lonely alienation in London). Kemp betrays him, when the invisible man proposes setting up a reign of terror by selective murder. Alone and hunted and increasingly demented, he declares the 'Epoch of the Invisible Man'. But it is he who is hunted and beaten to death by the decent country folk he intended to rule. As it lies in the street, his albino corpse finally materialises. In one of the stupider reviews of the century, the *Athenaeum** declared the work to be 'uninteresting'.

IOTA, (i.e. Kathleen Mannington Caffyn, née Hunt, 1855?–1926). One of the most powerful if soft-centred, of the new woman* novelists. Kathleen Hunt was born at Tipperary in Ireland (she acknowledged her origins by retaining a preference for Irish heroines in her fiction). She was educated expensively by English and German governesses, but showed her independence by training as a nurse at St Thomas's Hospital, London. In 1879 she married Stephen Mannington Caffyn* (1851–96), a surgeon. The following year, the couple went to Australia where the husband held a number of medical posts, made some useful inventions, and wrote some fiction. His *Miss*

Milne And I (1889) was very popular, and inspired a successor, *A Poppy's Tears* (1890). Iota began publishing her work after her return to England in 1892 and had a sensational success with *A Yellow Aster** (1894), which traces the intertwining complications of love, marriage and free-thought in a fashionably modern setting. *Children Of Circumstances* (1894), has a hero who marries his cousin but subsequently falls in love with a social worker in London's East End. The three meet and discuss their triangular 'mistake' in adult fashion. The wife, Beatrice, nobly arranges for her rival to take over after her death. 'Love is all', the novel portentously concludes. Iota's later fiction includes: *A Comedy In Spasms** (1895), first published in Hutchinson's** aptly named 'Zeitgeist Library', and *A Quaker Grandmother* (1896), the first of which is another powerful new woman tract. *Poor Max** (1898), published shortly after Stephen Caffyn died, has a typical plot, in which a powerful woman dominates a weak, artistic husband. *Anne Mauleverer* (1899) is one of the wilder feminist novels of the period. The extravagantly emancipated heroine is half-Irish, a sculptress and an expert in horseflesh capable of advising the King of Italy on equine matters. At the beginning of the narrative she is found nursing the man she loves. He dies, she adopts his child and remains for the rest of her life defiantly celibate. Iota seems to have been a physical, hard-living woman. Affairs of the horse as well as the heart figure frequently in her fiction. In *Who's Who*, she listed her recreations as riding, hunting, watching polo matches, and gave her club as the Ladies' Army and Navy. BL 14. *WW*. Wol.

Irish Novels. The Irish novel, like the American (under Fenimore Cooper) came into vogue following the success of Scott, in 1814, with *Waverley*. But the Irish regional* novel had distinct differences from the Scottish. Dublin had a better established publishing industry and more sophisticated literary world than early-nineteenth-century Edinburgh. Thus Maria Edgeworth was producing her national tales as early as 1800, with *Castle Rackrent*. But the main differentiating factor was the more turbulent and wretched history of Ireland. Like Scotland, Ireland had imposed on it an Act of Union in 1800 (only two years after the uprising of 1798). The Young Ireland movement and the tithe wars of the 1830s were notably unsettling but were entirely overshadowed by the genocidal famine of 1846–48, from which the country has never fully recovered. And there was the insoluble religious conflict, inflamed by the gross unfairness of the disposition of Irish wealth and property under the terms of the Protestant Ascendancy. Not surprisingly, Irish fiction tends to have a sharper political consciousness than its Anglo-Saxon equivalent. Particularly in the late 1830s and 1840s, William Carleton* with works like *Fardorougha The Miser** (1839) and *The Black Prophet* (1847) brought the novel closer to actual social calamity than any other British writer. In a work largely devoted to buffoonery like *Handy Andy** (1842), Samuel Lover* will break out (in Chapter 38) 'Oh! Rulers of Ireland, why have you not sooner learned to lead that people by love, whom all your severity has been unable to *drive*?'. But at the same time, the Irish novel indulged a vein of Celtic romance and pathos more extreme than any found in England. This strain finds its origins in Sydney Owenson's *The Wild Irish Girl* (1806) and Charles Maturin's *The Wild Irish Boy* (1808). In the Victorian period Hibernian sentimentality permeates the popular fiction of Mrs S. C. Hall*, Emily Lawless*, May Hartley*, Annie Keary*, May Crommelin*. A third strain in Irish fiction is the social anthropological, exemplified in the work of John and Michael Banim*, and their *Tales By The O'Hara Family* (1826). Irish fiction reached its peak of popularity with the early serials of Charles Lever* in the *Dublin University Magazine*. But in 1846 Lever shifted his literary base to London, with the collapse of the Irish book market (and the main Dublin publisher, William Curry*) in the famine induced business recession of the period. It was Lever who largely created the Englishman's favourite Irishman; a happy-go-lucky picaresque fellow roistering his jolly way through life. Lever accepted, as a fact of publishing life, that although his subjects might be Irish, his readership would be overwhelmingly English and would expect their prejudices to be confirmed. Meanwhile, J. S. Le Fanu* who had remained in Dublin, moved away from Irish topics (as in the early *The Cock And Anchor*, 1845) to ghost* stories (in which Irish literature has always been rich). Lever largely ceased writing about Ireland directly in the second half of his career. Arguably the greatest Irish novelist of the 1860s and after is the archetypally English Anthony Trollope*, with works such as *Castle Richmond* (1860) and *An Eye For An Eye* (1879). By the last decades of the century it is noticeable that the most gifted Irish writers (Wilde*, Shaw*, Moore*) are generally, but not invariably, disinclined to write about their country. And in his study of the genre, Thomas Flanagan makes the point that for all its numerousness 'the history of the Irish Novel is one of continuous attempts to represent the Irish experience within conventions that were not innately congenial to it'.

Is He Popenjoy?, Anthony Trollope, 1878, 3 vols, Chapman and Hall. (Serialised in *All The Year Round*, October 1877–July 1878.) This late and rather dark novel by Trollope hinges on an inheritance plot. The Marquis of Brotherton, a depraved hedonist, has lived many years in Italy completely cut off from his respectable English family. He suddenly returns in the company of a mysteriously acquired Italian wife and 'heir', Lord Popenjoy. The dowager Countess, her three unmarried daughters and her younger son Lord George Germain (who previously presumed himself heir) are evicted from the family house at Manor Cross. George, meanwhile, has married Mary Lovelace, daughter of the pugnacious Dean of Brotherton. Mary is unworldly but in no sense spineless. The subsequent narrative follows two tracks. One is the legal counter-attack against the Marquis on the grounds of Popenjoy's probable illegitimacy. This plot concludes with the death of the young pretender, it never being clear whether he was born in wedlock or not. The other track is marital and romantic. The Germains' marriage is doubly threatened. Mary nearly becomes entrapped into adultery with the dashing and Byronic Jack de Baron. On his part, George Germain becomes dangerously involved with an old flame, Mrs Adelaide Houghton. Finally all comes well. The wicked marquis dies, George inherits, husband and wife are reconciled, a true Popenjoy is born to them. The novel has a number of incidental points of interest such as lively hunting scenes and Trollope's blisteringly prejudiced satire on the emergent women's movement and their absurd leaders, the German Baroness Banmann and the American Doctor Olivia Q. Fleabody.

The Island Of Dr Moreau, H. G. Wells, 1896, 1 vol, Heinemann. The most morbid of Wells's scientific romances. The story begins with a shipwreck in which the survivors are driven to the brink of cannibalism. The hero-narrator, Prendick, is rescued by a ship carrying a cargo of animals. On board he is succoured by the friendly but weak Montgomery. Cast adrift again by the drunken captain (who is enraged by Montgomery's animalic servant) Prendick finds himself on a Pacific island. There he discovers that Dr Moreau (earlier hounded out of England for torturing animals) has perfected techniques of vivisection by which he can accelerate evolution. Under his scalpel, brutes are raised to quasi-humanity. Pain and severe puritanical morality are used to keep the monsters in check. Rebellion and blood lust break out. Moreau is killed by a puma he was tormenting and Montgomery dies mumbling: 'the last of this silly universe. What a mess.' Prendick returns to England to live a hermit's life on the South Downs. Contemporary reviewers affected to find Wells's fable utterly revolting.

It Is Never Too Late To Mend, Charles Reade, 1856, 3 vols, Bentley. Reade's first major success in fiction, and his first social problem* novel. It drew largely on the author's melodrama *Gold*, which had a successful run at Drury Lane in 1853. The hero of the novel, George Fielding, an honest Berkshire farmer, is ruined by the moneylending villain, Meadows, who covets George's sweetheart, Susan Merton. George is forced to emigrate and seek his fortune in Australia. The parallel (prison-centred) plot revolves around the thief Tom Robinson. Before transportation, Robinson is tormented by the sadistic prison governor, Hawes. There are vivid descriptions of the 'silent system', solitary confinement and the horrors of the 'black hole'. Hawes is opposed by the saintly prison chaplain, Francis Eden. The British prison scenes are very powerful and culminate in the cell suicide of Edward Josephs, imprisoned for stealing food when starving. The last third of the novel moves to the gold diggings in Australia, showing Tom and George mending their fortunes down under. Henry James thought this entirely researched section superior to Henry Kingsley's* eyewitness account in *The Hillyars And The Burtons* (1865). Particularly successful are the characters of the morally precise Jew Isaac Levi, and the aborigine Jacky. Robinson's antecedent 'Autobiography Of A Thief' was later published in Reade's volume of short stories, *Cream* (1858).

J

Jabez Easterbrook, Joseph Hocking, 1890, 3 vols, Ward, Lock. A Yorkshire tale. Jabez arrives as the new minister for the Methodist church at Heathertown. He converts drunkards, outpunches bruisers and generally shines in his work. The agnostic and haughty daughter of a prominent local Methodist, Margaret Ashton, is drawn to Jabez but cannot conquer her intellectual scruples against his primitive Christianity. More seriously, Jabez falls foul of the more orthodox elders in his church and is faced with a credal inquisition. The doubts he expresses oblige his resignation. A bene-factor whose daughter he has saved from drowning at Windermere gives Jabez £1,000 and with it he starts his own independent church. Unusually, it has a library, a gymnasium and public baths attached. Margaret is fi-nally won over and together the Easterbrooks (now married) continue in their civilising mission to the industrial classes of northern England. The narrative is handled simply and vigorously by Hocking, himself a Methodist minister.

Jack Brag, Theodore Hook, 1837, 3 vols, Bentley. A snob's progress. Jack is the son of a London wax and tallow-chandler who thinks himself born for better things than trade. He rents a front door in Grosvenor Street and a non-existent place in the country. He attaches himself to Lord Tom Towzle and spurns the love of a woman of his own class, Anne Brown of Walworth. In his search for a rich wife, Jack answers an advertisement by a rich widow who turns out to be his own mother. Mrs Brag eventually marries one of her apprentices, Jim Salmon, who promptly squanders her fortune. Jack's attempts to raise himself all fail and eventually he changes his name and goes to Spain in an army commissary department as 'acting-assistant-deputy-deputy-assistant-commissary-general'. Salmon eventually dies after being thrown out of his gig (following an illicit lunch with a young actress) and a chastened Brag is reconciled to his mother and life in the tallow business. Like most of Hook's fiction, *Jack Brag* is a virtually plotless series of farcical misadventures.

Jack Harkaway. The famous juvenile hero, created by S. Bracebridge Hemyng*. Harkaway was launched in 1871 in a serial in Edwin Brett's* *Boys Of England*. He was immensely popular from the first, and was everywhere pirated by other publishers of boys' stories, including the American Frank Leslie (who later invited Hemyng to come and work in the USA). Jack is a scapegrace who runs away from school to experience myriad scrapes and adventures some coarse by the standards of the age.

Jack Hinton The Guardsman, Charles Lever, 1843, 1 vol, Curry. (Se-rialised in monthly parts, January–December 1842 with illustrations by Phiz*.) Like *The Confessions Of Harry Lorrequer*, this is the story of an ingenuous English officer in Ireland. Hinton arrives in the country in the turbulent second decade of the century. Like other Lever heroes he steeplechases, makes love, and duels. Hinton is accompanied by a faithful native servant, Corny Delany. In his passage through Irish society his path crosses those of the Dublin snobs, Mr and Mrs Paul Rooney, the Irish priest Tom Loftus and 'Tipperary Joe'. The last sections of the narrative trans-port the action to Spain, France and Italy. The novel has good dialogue and in the course of his jolly adventures Hinton learns something of the real Ireland.

Jack Sheppard, William Harrison Ainsworth, 1 vol, Bentley. (Serialised in *Bentley's Miscellany*, January 1839–February 1840 and issued in fifteen weekly numbers in 1840, all issues illustrated by George Cruikshank*.) The narrative is divided into three 'epochs': 1703, 1715, 1724. It opens with a fine set piece, the great November storm of 1703. The story then follows the careers of two mysteriously born boys (they eventually turn out to be cousins, connected with a noble Lancashire family). Jack Sheppard is a 'flash cove' and Thames Darrell a flawless hero. As apprentices to the London carpenter Wood, they are versions of Hogarth's idle and industrious young men. (Cruikshank's illustrations also allude directly to Hogarth's pictorial sequence.) Absurdly complicated, the plot is one of Ainsworth's favourites, that of the true heir (here Thames) kept out of his inheritance by a villainous relative and his accomplice (here Jonathan Wild). After various adventures, Thames is disclosed to be a marquis and marries Wood's daughter. Jack, meanwhile, has gone utterly to the bad as a thief and gaol breaker. The narrative climaxes with Jack's being carried from Newgate to Tyburn for riotous public execution. (Cruikshank's triptych of this episode is probably the best fiction illustration he did.) *Jack Sheppard* was at the centre of the Newgate* novel controversy, and the murderer Courvoisier in 1840 claimed that he was inspired to his crime by Ainsworth's hero. Nevertheless, *Jack Sheppard* was immensely successful, pushing *Bentley's Miscellany*'s sales even higher than had *Oliver Twist**. There were at least eight dramatic versions produced, and as many plagiarised versions for the semi-literate public.

Jackanapes, Mrs J. H. Ewing, 1883, 1 vol, SPCK. (Serialised in *Aunt Judy's Magazine**, 1879, with illustrations by R. Caldecott*.) One of the most famous of Victorian tales for and about children. Jackanapes is a wild child whose father was killed at Waterloo. But he is civilised by his upbringing with his maiden aunt. Grown up, the hero lays down his life on the battlefield (which war is not clear) for a friend. There is a pathetic last scene in his mourning home village. The story was supposedly inspired by the death of the French Prince Imperial during the Zulu Wars.

JACOBS, W[illiam] W[ymark] (1863–1943). Jacobs was born in Wapping, the eldest son of a wharf manager. The family was large and poorly off. The young Jacobs ran wild in the Thameside locality which is vividly portrayed in his later fiction. But he also spent some time in rural East Anglia, which inspired his other favourite locale, 'Claybury'. Doggedly self-improving, Jacobs attended Birkbeck College's night classes, where he met another future novelist of London life, Pett Ridge*. In 1879, he became a boy clerk in the Civil Service, working in the savings bank department. Jacobs remained at the work until 1899. He had, however, begun writing sketches in 1885 and his first success came in the early 1890s, when Jerome K. Jerome* accepted some of his pieces for the *Idler**. In 1895, Jacobs joined the staff of Newnes's* new magazine, the *Strand**. Here he began his fruitful collaboration with the illustrator, Will Owen, with whom he devised many of his later stories. For the *Strand*, Jacobs began producing his ironic yarns of sailors' lives, and introduced his best-known character, the night-watchman. Jacobs's early, and by far his best work, was collected as the volumes: *Many Cargoes* (1896); *The Skipper's Wooing* (1897); *Sea Urchins* (1898); *A Master Of Craft* (1900); *Light Freights* (1901). These works feature the author's famous trio of heroes, Sam Small, Peter Russet and Ginger Dick. From 1899, he was a full-time writer. By this date, he was financially secure and in 1900 he married Agnes Williams, the daughter of a bank accountant. Jacobs's subjects are described by Michael Sadleir: 'he wrote stories of three kinds: describing the misadventures of sailor-men ashore; celebrating the artful dodger of a slow-witted village; and tales of the macabre'. It is for the famous macabre tale of three horribly granted wishes, *The Monkey's Paw* (published in 1902) that Jacobs is best remembered today. BL 22. *DNB*. RM. *NCBEL*.

JAMES, Charles T[homas] C[lement] (1858–1905?). James was born in London, and educated privately. By his wife, Eliza, he was related to Thomas Hancock, the Quaker. Otherwise little is known of his life, other than that he was the lieutenant-colonel of the Royal West Kent Regiment in 1900. A novelist and dramatist, his fiction includes: *A Bird Of Paradise* (1889), the portrait of a heartless wife; *The New Faith* (1890), the story of a ruthless religious revivalist, stricken with paralysis at the moment of his triumph; *One Virtue* (1893); *A Worker In Iron* (1894). Reviewers rather liked James's extravagant melodramas, although his plots were found very hackneyed. BL 20. *WW*. Wol. RLF.

JAMES, G[eorge] P[ayne] R[ainsford] (1799?–1860). The doyen of hack historical* novelists, and author of more romances than anyone has ever managed to count. James was born in London, the son of a physician, previously a navy surgeon. His grandfather, also a medical man, was the inventor of James's powders, the famous patent medicine. The young James attended school in Putney, taught himself languages and elegant manners, met Byron and in his later youth travelled extensively on the Continent. He subsequently claimed to have seen active service in the Napoleonic wars, and according to one account was taken prisoner by the enemy. During this period James perfected his French and fought a duel. (The propensity to duel was one of James's later affectations.) He returned to England, with high social and political ambitions. When these failed, in 1827, he turned to literature. In 1829, James produced his first and best historical romance, *Richelieu*, under Colburn's* imprint. The work sold well and was praised by Scott whose *Quentin Durward* was clearly the pattern James worked from. James, who had married in 1828, was now set up to turn out historical romances with industrial speed and efficiency. For the next two decades (during which he lived for long periods in France) he produced up to three full-length works a year. His total output is enormous, and he thrived on the unexacting literary standards of the 1830s. His price rose to the £1,000-a-work mark, allowing him to reside in a succession of country houses and think seriously of a career in politics. The end of James's popularity as a writer was signalled (and possibly precipitated) by Thackeray's* devastating parody in *Punch** ('Barbazure', 1847). A similarly devastating review in the *Athenaeum** (1846) dismissed his work as 'sloppy'. James's fiction is rigidly formulaic and he was notorious for his 'two horsemen' openings. Nevertheless, he occasionally experimented with other than historical romance, as in *A Whim And Its Consequences* (1847) and varied his normal narrative manner as with the autobiographical *Henry Masterton, Or The Adventures Of A Young Cavalier* (1832), a popular work which is among James's most reprinted. He evidently fell on hard times in 1849 with the failure of a complete edition of his works and he was obliged to sell all his copyrights to the Irish reprinters, Simms M'Intyre, for railway* editions. Nevertheless the works he produced at this period, such as *Agincourt** (1844), *The Smuggler** (1845), *The Castle Of*

Ehrenstein* (1847), and *Henry Smeaton* (1851), are among his better efforts. Around 1850, he accepted the appointment of consul to Massachusetts. (An American novel of Indian fighting, *Ticonderoga*, 1854, inevitably ensued.) In New England, James was a literary celebrity and he lectured on 'Civilisation' to students at Yale. James moved to Norfolk, Virginia, two years later, and in 1856, was promoted to the consul-generalship of the Austrian ports in the Adriatic at a salary of £700 a year. After his removal from England, James wrote only a handful of novels. He was evidently a conscientious diplomat but he had entirely ruined his health by the mid-1850s and was drinking heavily enough to alarm his friends. He died at Venice of apoplexy. A Tory of the old school, whose political and public personality was formed in the 1820s, James also wrote popular history, and served as Historiographer Royal under William IV. BL 67. *DNB*. RM. *NCBEL*. Wol. Sad. RLF.

JAMES, M[ontague] R[hodes] (1862–1936). Montague James was born at Goodnestone in Kent, the fourth and youngest child of a clergyman, formerly a Cambridge don. In 1865, James's father moved to a living near Bury St Edmunds where he was to remain for the remainder of his life. At an early age, Montague was fascinated by church architecture and history. After Eton, he went to King's College, Cambridge where he took a double first in classics and archaeology. He remained at the university to become the most distinguished palaeographer of his generation. In 1905, he was elected Provost of King's College. He never married and his later life was loaded with academic honours and distinction. On the side, James wrote learned and donnishly clever ghost* stories, which typically were first read to friends at King's before being published. *Canon Alberic's Scrapbook* (first published in the *National Review*, 1894) tells the story of an Englishman, Denniston, who buys a book from a French sacristan which turns out to be guarded by a terrifying demonic attendant. In an interesting late essay ('Stories I Have Tried To Write') James noted: 'I have neither much interest nor much perseverance in the writing of stories.' This seems confirmed by his desultory literary output which although it continued until 1927 amounts to very little in bulk. BL 7. *DNB*. RM. *NCBEL*.

James II, William Harrison Ainsworth, 1848, 3 vols, Colburn. (Serialised in *Ainsworth's Magazine**, January–December 1847, advertised as merely 'edited' by Ainsworth.) Ainsworth may have farmed part of the composition of this work to one of his hacks. The story, subtitled 'Or The Revolution Of 1688', is feeble in the extreme. The main historical event chronicled is the abdication of King James, which Ainsworth writes up in the style of the last chapters of Scott's *Redgauntlet*. There is a sub-plot with perfunctory love interest. Ainsworth's absurd habit of dragging in historically famous characters is displayed at a dissenters' meeting where George Fox, John Bunyan and Richard Baxter are found casually in conversation. The anti-Catholic sentiment in the novel is topical.

JANE, Fred[erick] T[homas] (1870–1916). Jane was born at Honiton in Devon, the son of a vicar (a distant descendant of the Vicar of Bray). He was educated at Exeter School, and inherited the traditional West Country love of the sea. A career in the navy, however, was precluded by his delicate health. In 1890, Jane began training as an artist. His nautical passion found expression in 1898 with his illustrated catalogue of *The World's Fighting Ships*. (The series still runs.) He also invented the popular 'Naval War Game', and was naval correspondent for the *Daily Chronicle*. In 1906 he contested Portsmouth as the Naval Interests candidate (unsuccessfully). Jane wrote novels, of a Jules Verne kind such as: *Blake Of The Rattlesnake* (1895), 'a story of torpedo warfare'; *The Incubated Girl* (1896); *To Venus In Five Seconds* (1897); *The Violet Flame* (1899), a story of future destruction ('Armageddon') by a mad scientist, Mirzarbeau, using death rays, illustrated apocalyptically by Jane himself; *The Port Guard Ship* (1900), a story of the present day navy. BL 6. *WW*. Wol.

Jane Eyre, Currer Bell (i.e. Charlotte Brontë), 1847, 3 vols, Smith, Elder. The story begins in 1800 and is told autobiographically by 'a heroine as plain and small as myself'. Jane is encountered a young orphan, unhappily lodged with her sadistic relatives, the Reeds of Gateshead Hall. She suffers years of maltreatment, but after a particularly brutal imprisonment in the room where old Reed died, she collapses. On being nursed back to health Jane is sent to Lowood School, fifty miles away. There she is exposed to another set of evangelical tyrants, the Brocklehursts. At school, Jane is befriended by the long-suffering Helen Burns (Jane is passionate by nature), who dies. She is also taken under the wing of a friendly teacher, Miss Temple. After the school is ravaged by an epidemic of fever, the Brocklehursts are dismissed and Jane's life becomes easier. On growing up, she remains for a while at Lowood as a teacher, but her restless nature craves more adventure than school can supply. She applies for a position as governess, advertised by a Mrs Fairfax of Thornfield Hall. She discovers that her pupil is Adele Varens, a spoiled girl of unexplained French origins. There is no mistress of the house, and Jane learns that the master, Edward Rochester, is away on business. She first encounters the sinister Rochester as he rides back, falls from his horse, and requires her assistance to bring him home. He impresses her as a figure of Byronic energy, mystery and sexual power. Jane discovers that Adele is the offspring of one of his former mistresses, a French dancer. Jane also discovers that the house has a strange occupant whose maniac laughter she occasionally hears. She assumes it is Grace Poole, a servant known to drink. Rochester is now in residence and spites Jane (who is strongly drawn to him) by paying court to the haughty Blanche Ingram. In one surreal episode, Rochester appears before the assembled company disguised as a gypsy and reads Jane's fortune. A strange Mr Mason comes to Thornfield, but leaves mysteriously wounded the next morning. A servant arrives to tell Jane that her former guardian, Mrs Reed, is dying and must see her. She has a confession. She has told a rich relative, John Eyre, that Jane is dead, so keeping her out of an inheritance. Mrs Reed's own children have gone to the bad, and she dies wretched. Jane returns to Thornfield where Rochester at last proposes to her. But two nights before the wedding, Jane discovers her bridal veil torn in half. And at the church, the marriage service is interrupted by a mysterious stranger. On behalf of Mason, this stranger announces that Rochester is already married. He confesses that there is a wife, Bertha. He met her in the West Indies, and was tricked into marriage. She subsequently went mad and he now keeps her locked in the attic of his house. Jane sees the horrific Mrs Rochester and runs away from

Thornfield in moral terror. In the northern Midlands, she is taken in by a clergyman, St John Rivers, and his two sisters, Mary and Diana. These are her cousins, although Jane (who now calls herself Elliot) is unaware of the fact. She takes up work teaching in a girls' school. St John tells Jane that his relative John Eyre has recently died in Madeira. Her true identity is discovered and the heroine finds herself a rich heiress. St John Rivers, who in his cool way loves her, asks Jane to accompany him on his missionary work to India. She declines. In a vision, she hears Rochester calling to her. Trusting her heart, she returns to Thornfield where she finds that fire has destroyed the house, killed Bertha and blinded Rochester. She can now marry him, tamed as he is by physical handicap. Two years later, he partially recovers his sight.

JAY, Harriet (1857–1932). A sister-in-law, and later adopted daughter of the Scottish writer Robert Buchanan*. Jay was born in London, educated in Scotland and lived some years in Mayo, on the strength of which she wrote novels with an Irish* flavour. They include: *The Queen Of Connaught* (1875), the story of an Englishman, John Bermingham, who becomes involved with a west of Ireland community when he marries Kathleen O'Mara; *The Dark Colleen* (1876), the story of a French sailor, wrecked on the west coast of Ireland ('Eagle Island'), nursed back to health by an Irish maiden whom he marries and deserts; *Madge Dunraven* (1879); *The Priest's Blessing* (1881), an anti-Catholic tract written, as reviewers thought, 'in a very melancholy groove'; *Two Men And A Maid* (1881); *My Connaught Cousins* (1882); *Through The Stage Door* (1883), a theatrical novel; *A Marriage Of Convenience* (1885). Jay became an actress in 1881 and Buchanan dramatised some of her fiction. She seems to have collaborated with him as 'Charles Marlowe'. In *Who's Who*, Jay gives her date of birth as 1863 which would have had her publishing fiction at twelve. She also claims never to have married. BL 9. *WW*. Wol. RLF.

JEAFFRESON, John Cordy (1831–1901). Jeaffreson was born at Framlingham, Suffolk, the ninth child of a local surgeon (a pioneer of ovariotomy). His mother was the daughter of a prosperous local tradesman. Jeaffreson attended the grammar school at Woodbridge, after which he was apprenticed to his father's profession. He decided he did not like medicine and instead went to Oxford, where he was friendly with Henry Kingsley* and evidently moved in a fast undergraduate set. Jeaffreson graduated in 1852, and spent the next six years in London, tutoring and lecturing. He also began to write fiction early in life. *Crewe Rise* was published in 1854 and *Hinchbrook* was serialised in *Fraser's Magazine* a year later. This set him on the path to writing numerous three-deckers over the next thirty years, none of which has the slightest literary distinction. His most successful novels were the sensational* *Live It Down* (1863), a tale of crime and inheritance set in the 1830s, and *Not Dead Yet* (1864). The second of these is a wild story of illegitimacy and disputed inheritance in which the hero arrives back just too late to prevent his beloved's wedding. The author was so pleased with the idea of this novel that he wrote a preface ('Ladies and Gentlemen, Attention!') in which he drew attention to its originality. His other fiction includes: *A Woman In Spite Of Herself* (1872), a tale set in Canada; *The Rapiers Of Regent's Park* (1882); *Cutting For Partners* (1890). His writing in general is marked by a jaunty, smart tone and short, brisk sentences. In 1856, Jeaffreson abandoned teaching for journalism as his main profession. From 1858, he was a regular contributor to the *Athenaeum**. He also wrote his pioneering survey *Novels And Novelists* in 1858. In the late 1850s he made yet another change of vocation and was called to the Bar in 1859. But he never practised, although he thereafter moved in legal society. Through friendship with Sir Thomas Duffus Hardy (whose wife Mary* and daughter Iza were novelists) Jeaffreson was appointed to a post in the Public Record Office in 1874. He became a leading authority on historical archives and in his later years wrote popular (and critically despised) biographies of Shelley and Nelson. *A Young Squire Of The Seventeenth Century* (1878) is a reconstruction (apparently from manuscript sources) of the early life of one of the author's ancestors, Christopher Jeaffreson of Dullingham House, Cambridgeshire. BL 10. *DNB. NCBEL.* Wol.

JEFFERIES, [John] Richard (1848–87). The best-known naturalist-cum-novelist of the Victorian period, Jefferies was born near Swindon in Wiltshire where his father was a farmer in a small way, with forty acres. (James Luckett Jefferies is pictured as Iden in *Amaryllis At The Fair**.) He spent the first thirty years of his life in this area, whose Downs-dominated landscape was of overriding emotional importance to him. Jefferies was educated locally and at Sydenham in Kent. At sixteen, he demonstrated his independence, by running away to France with a friend. They intended eventually to make their way to Moscow. Jefferies subsequently moved to Swindon, and before he was twenty began to write descriptive and local historical articles for the Wiltshire newspapers. Even at this early date, his political views were strongly Conservative. He also tried his hand at novels and tragedies. In 1867, he suffered severe illness, and was never to be robust in health again. He married Jessie Baden, a farmer's daughter, in 1874, and published, partly at his own expense, his first novel, *The Scarlet Shawl*. A conventional and romantic work published by Tinsley*, it was followed by *Restless Human Hearts* (1875); *The World's End* (1877) and *Greene Ferne Farm* (1879). None of them did well, and for some time Jefferies could not find a publisher for his next work, the far more introspective and sensitive *The Dewy Morn* (eventually published in 1884), a work which combines fiction and country essay; the hybrid form that was to be Jefferies' unique contribution to Victorian literature. He had, however, contrived to make a name for himself as a writer of straight descriptive sketches of rural nature and some letters on rural distress to *The Times* in 1872 brought him to public notice. In 1876, he moved to London, and in 1878, his reprinted papers, *The Gamekeeper At Home*, caught the public taste as did *Wild Life In A Southern County* (1879), a work which is often reckoned to be Jefferies' best. The naturalist and novelist in Jefferies came together with his remarkable animal fable, *Wood Magic* (1881), a work which stresses the inherent intelligence of natural creations. This was followed by the childhood autobiographical novel, *Bevis** (1882) and the spiritual autobiography of adolescence, *The Story Of My Heart* (1883), a work which he claimed to have been meditating for seventeen years. *After London** (1885) is an extraordinary visionary work, which foresees the end of urban civilisation and the final victory of nature. It also articulates the complex feelings which the author had about the city. Jefferies also produced less portentous bucolic fiction, such as *Amaryllis At The Fair* (1887). In 1881, his health collapsed. Tuberculosis and a painful fistula (and numerous operations on it) made writing an agony. The remainder of his life was passed, as an invalid, in various resorts. Jefferies refused, however, financial aid from the Royal Literary Fund*. His last works were dictated to his wife, from his deathbed. He died of tuberculosis at Goring, by the sea, aged only thirty-eight. The Jefferies had three children. The death of the youngest, Oliver, from meningitis in 1886 intensified the author's temperamental melancholy. As a novelist, Jefferies is *sui generis*. And he was a heroic figure to his fellow authors. Walter Besant* wrote a generous eulogy, which describes his talents well. And the poet Edward Thomas wrote a book-length appreciation of Jefferies in 1908. Never popular with a large public, he has none the less always enjoyed a cultish following and was one of the first Victorian novelists to have a society formed to his memory. BL 12. *DNB*. RM. *NCBEL*. Wol. Sad. RLF.

JENKIN, H[enrietta] C[amilla] (née Jackson, 1807?–85). Henrietta Jackson was born in Kingston, Jamaica, where her father was a colonial administrator. Her mother was Scottish. In 1832, she married a midshipman (later Captain) Charles Jenkin RN. She began to write, reportedly under the pressure of poverty. Her early fiction includes: *Wedlock* (1841); *The Smiths* (1843); *The Maid's Husband* (1844); *Lost And Won, Or The Love Test* (1846). The Jenkins lived on the Continent, 1847–51. In Italy, she associated with Ruffini, and the Liberal faction of politicians. In 1858, she published *Violet Bank And Its Inmates* (the *DNB* wrongly assumes this to be her first novel). Her first notable success was with *Cousin Stella, Or Conflict* (1859), a love story drawing on her childhood experience, set in Jamaica just before the Act of Emancipation. She followed with *Who Breaks, Pays* (1861), a study of coquetry; *Skirmishing* (1862); *Once And Again* (1865), a novel set in Paris. Jenkin's favourite topic, as her titles indicate, is matrimony and its dilemmas. In 1868, her son Henry Charles Fleeming Jenkin (1833–85), was appointed to a professorship in engineering at Edinburgh University and she lived with him thereafter, becoming a well known personage in the city. According to R. L. Stevenson*, who wrote a memoir of her son, Jenkin wrote for no other motive than money. BL 12. *DNB*. Wol.

JENKINS, John Edward (1838–1910). Born in Bangalore, India, Jenkins was the son of a Wesleyan missionary. The family moved to Canada during the author's childhood and he was educated at school in Montreal, and later at McGill University. (See his lively melodrama with scenes of Canadian life, *Jobson's Enemies*, 1882.) Jenkins came to London, and was called to the Bar in 1864. As a lawyer, he worked energetically in the anti-slavery and aborigine protection cause, while remaining a staunch British imperialist. In 1870, he had a tremendous success with *Ginx's Baby**, one of the most efficacious social problem* novels of the century. The story satirically chronicles the sectarian tug of war over the religious education of an abandoned child. The novel had a liberalising effect on the religious clauses of the 1870 Education Act. Jenkins followed this success with a less effective sequel, *Little Hodge* (1872), dealing with rural distress. Jenkins represented Dundee as a radical MP, 1874–80. (A man of volatile opinions, he later tried to re-enter Parliament as a Conservative provoking a near riot among his former Dundee supporters.) In 1876, he produced *The Devil's Chain**, a full-blooded polemical tale against the infinitely far-reaching evils of alcohol. Like *Ginx's Baby*, it was reprinted in the hundreds of thousands. Jenkins's other fiction includes: *Lutchmee And Dilloo* (1877) 'A Story Of West Indian Life'; *The Captain's Cabin* (1877), a Christmas 'yarn' written 'without a purpose'; *A Week Of Passion* (1884), which starts with a vividly described explosion in central London; *A Secret Of Two Lives* (1886); *Pantalas* (1897), the original novel of the 'Elephant Man', who is shown visited in turn by a futile succession of late Victorian do-gooders: a Salvation Army general, a parson, a philanthropist, a politician, etc. Jenkins married in 1867, and had seven children. He was editor of the *Overland* and *Homeward Mail* from 1886. His writing career was cut short in later life by paralysis. BL 11. *DNB*. Wol. Sad.

JENNINGS, Hargrave (1817?–90). Little is known of Jennings's life. Around the age of fifteen, he began writing for Marryat's* *Metropolitan Magazine**, which suggests some nautical* connections. For many years, he was secretary to Colonel Mapleson, manager of the Italian Opera in London. In later life Jennings was intensely interested in the occult, esoteric Buddhism and Rosicrucianism, and is supposed to be the original of Ezra Jennings in Wilkie Collins's* *The Moonstone** (1868). Jennings's own fiction includes: *The Ship Of Glass* (1846); *Atcherley* (1846); *St George* (1853). The first is a Poe-like tale of the supernatural; the second (bound together with it) a historical* tale of the Rye House plot in the Restoration period. Reviewers deprecated Jennings's wild gothicism*, which was increasingly out of fashion in the realistic 1840s. Jennings's publisher was the dubious Newby*. BL 3. *DNB*. Wol. Sad.

JENNINGS, Louis John (1836–93). Jennings was born into an old Norfolk family. In his early twenties, he entered the employment of *The Times* and in 1863 was sent as special correspondent to India, where for some years he edited the *Times Of India*. Jennings was subsequently posted to America where he eventually settled and married in 1868. For a while he was editor of the *New York Times* and was notably courageous in opposing political corruption in his columns. Jennings returned to England in 1876, where he founded the *Week* and became a Tory MP for Stockport in 1885 (a fact he proudly proclaimed on the title pages of his novels). Among much else, Jennings wrote some novels, including two with American themes: *The Millionaire* (1883) and *The Philadelphian* (1891). In the second of these a Confederate Colonel (aided by a northern compatriot, Rufus Snapper) comes to Britain and solves a Fenian murder. BL 3. *DNB*. Wol. Sad.

JEPSON, Edgar [Alfred] (1864–1938). Jepson was born in London, went to school at Leamington and later graduated from Balliol College, Oxford. He subsequently took up work as a schoolmaster in Barbados, 1889–93, after which he worked as a crammer in London, 1893–97. His first published novel was *Sibyl Falcon* (1895). R. L. Wolff describes it as: 'juicy, sensational, sadistic, girl warrior, naked black villains, much stabbing, strangling, etc'. (In *Who's Who*, Jepson mildly listed his recreations as 'lawn-tennis, the opera, bridge.') His other fiction includes: *The Passion For Romance* (1896); *The Keepers Of The People* (1898). The second of these fantasises a Utopia, Varandaleel, somewhere in northern India, where women are sternly kept down. In his later years the misogynistic Jepson evidently considered England hopelessly 'hag-ridden'. With Captain D. Beames, Jepson wrote a story of frontier life in India, *On The Edge Of The Empire* (1899). BL 7. *WW*. Wol.

JEROME, Jerome K[lapka] (1859-1927). Jerome K. Jerome was born at Walsall, the son of a Staffordshire colliery proprietor and nonconformist preacher. (A vocation which seems to have left no mark on the son.) His mother was Welsh and it was with her money that Jerome's chronically unsuccessful father bought his coal-pits. The unusual middle name was adopted from the Hungarian nationalist G. Klapka, who stayed with the Jeromes while in English exile. Following business misfortune in 1860, the family moved to the East End of London, during Jerome's childhood. There his father scraped a living as a wholesale ironmonger. The boy went to Marylebone Grammar School from 1868, leaving at the statutory minimum age of fourteen to make his way in the world by himself (his father having died in 1871 and his mother in 1873). Jerome thereafter was successively: railway clerk, schoolteacher, actor, solicitor's clerk, and finally a journalist. Three of his plays were put on in 1888. In 1886, he brought out his charmingly casual collection of essays *The Idle Thoughts Of An Idle Fellow*. Three years later, there appeared his comic masterpiece, *Three Men In A Boat**, the hilarious story of a summer boating trip up the Thames. Literary success had meanwhile enabled Jerome to marry in 1888. In 1892, with Robert Barr* and George Brown Burgin*, Jerome founded the illustrated 6d. monthly, the *Idler**. It was highly successful, and he edited the magazine from 1892 to 1897, during which time it carried the work of many of the lively younger generation of writers such as W. W. Jacobs*, Anthony Hope (i.e. Hawkins*) and Eden Phillpotts*. Jerome meanwhile brought out several volumes of tales and sketches, of which the best is *Three Men On The Bummel* (1900; this time, the summer trip is to Oberammergau in Bavaria, for the passion play). Jerome's most ambitious effort in fiction is the long autobiographical novel, *Paul Kelver* (1902), which opens with the hero's East End origins. Eventually, Paul makes his way (as did Jerome) in the world of the theatre. In the twentieth century, Jerome wrote successful plays, and served as an ambulance driver in the first World War. He died on a motoring tour through England. Jerome's autobiographical *My Life And Times* (1926) contains interesting recollections of his powerful sense of childhood degradation and deprivation in London. BL 11. *DNB*. RM. *NCBEL*. Wol.

JERROLD, Douglas William (1803-57). A famous wit, successful playwright, magazine proprietor and very minor novelist, Jerrold flourished on the edge of the Victorian fiction scene. He was born into a theatrical family in London, and seems largely to have educated himself with whatever help he could get from his father's acting associates. That he should in manhood have been intellectual and scholarly is one of the heroic feats of Victorian self-improvement. Jerrold went to school in Sheerness until in 1813, aged ten, he was enrolled in the navy to serve in the last stages of the Napoleonic

Wars. As he put it: 'I began the world at an age when, as a general rule, boys have not laid down their primers; then the cockpit of a man of war was at thirteen exchanged for the struggle of London.' His years of London struggle saw him graduate from the trade of printing to the profession of journalism. Jerrold had developed a passionate hatred of tyranny in the navy (still ruled by flogging). In the 1820s, a period of excited reform agitation, he developed the political radicalism which he held throughout his life ('savage little Robespierre' is one nickname he attracted). Jerrold had begun writing plays as early as 1818 and in 1829 he had a stage success with *Black-Eyed Susan*, 'a nautical and domestic melodrama'. Jerrold married in 1824, and the next ten years were a period of professional consolidation, largely devoted to the theatre. In 1835 he was established as a journalist of note, contributing to *Blackwood's Magazine**. He was one of the founders of *Punch** in 1841 and from the first wrote sharp political squibs (as 'Q'). It was for *Punch* that Jerrold devised his greatest popular works, the apolitical *Story Of A Feather** (1843); *Mrs Caudle's Curtain Lectures** (1845); *The Life And Adventures Of Miss Robinson Crusoe* (1846). His initially formative influence on *Punch* was in 1847 replaced by Thackeray's* mellower brand of humour. The years 1846–47 represent the high point of Jerrold's career. In this period he founded *Douglas Jerrold's Shilling Magazine** and his weekly newspaper. Unfortunately neither prospered. Nor, apparently, did his monthly serial *A Man Made Of Money** (1848) appeal to the reading public. Jerrold was thereafter editor of *Lloyd's Weekly Newspaper* from 1852 until his death in 1857 at a salary of £1,000 a year. Under his editorship, the paper grew in strength and survived well into the twentieth century. Jerrold's best loved serials are situation comedies, which use techniques of fiction but have relatively little narrative progression. (Mrs Caudle's nagging, for instance, denies her husband the release of sleep every night.) His one novel proper, *The History Of St Giles And St James**, illustrated by Leech*, was designed as the lead serial for Jerrold's new monthly magazine in 1845. It is an unusual performance. Extraordinarily savage politically, it sets out (in the words of the preface of 1851) to show the 'ignorant disregard of the social claims of the poor upon the rich, of the governed millions on the governing few'. Jerrold was much loved by his fellow bohemian writers who relished his company and his famous caustic wit. After his death, Dickens* led the drive to raise a charitable subscription for the author's surviving family. BL 5. *DNB*. RM. *NCBEL*. Wol.

JERROLD [William] Blanchard (1826–84). The eldest son of Douglas Jerrold*, and his father's biographer. William Jerrold was born in London and educated at Brompton Grammar School. His original intention was to be an artist, but his eyes failed and he turned instead to his father's trade of bohemian journalism. On his father's death, he took over the editorship of *Lloyd's Weekly*. In spite of this duty, Jerrold contrived to spend at least half his subsequent life in Paris. He was closely associated with Gustave Doré and collaborated with him on his pictorial survey, *London* (1872). In a wide-ranging literary career, which generally parallels his famous father's, Jerrold produced a number of successful plays, a life of George Cruikshank*, books on gastronomy and a handful of novels often with London or Paris settings and bohemian themes, including: *Two Lives* (1862), a story of crime and politics set in 1830s France; *Up And Down In The World* (1863), an anecdotal survey of the roistering lives lived by young lawyers in chambers; *Passing The Time* (1865), the story of a young city gent, Arthur Newlands, whose love life goes wrong; *Black-Eyed Susan's Boys* (1876). BL 8. *DNB. NCBEL.* Wol. RLF.

Jessica's First Prayer, Hesba Stretton (i.e. Sarah Smith), 1867, 1 vol, RTS. (First published in *Sunday At Home*, 1866.) One of the most popular of tales for Victorian children which pioneered the popular 'street arab' genre of improving fiction. The heroine of the tale, Jessica, is the daughter of a drunken and failed actress. Jessica takes to the streets and the irrepressible goodness which shines through her rags converts the middle-class gentleman who adopts her. In the sequel, *Jessica's Mother* (1868), her guardian dies trying to save Jessica's degraded parent from drowning. The two narratives are notable for their unsentimental presentation of squalor and for their attack on 'respectable' Christianity which ignores the plight of children in the street outside its churches. (Child abuse was Stretton's great concern, in and out of fiction.)

Jessie Phillips, A Tale Of The Present Day, Mrs F. M. Trollope, 1843, 3 vols, Colburn. (Serialised in monthly parts, December 1842–November 1843, illustrated by John Leech*.) A novel with a purpose. The work attacks (as had *Oliver Twist**) the workings of the 1834 Poor Law Amendment Act, which was still in force as Trollope wrote. Jessie Phillips, a beauty and seamstress, is artfully seduced by the son of the Deepbrook squire, Frederic Dalton. Thanks to the bastardy clause in the Act, he cannot be made responsible for his illegitimate child and Jessie is forced into the horrific workhouse when her mother dies. Suspected of infanticide, she is befriended by a resourceful middle-class saviour, Martha Maxwell, who entraps the seducer Frederic, who also has designs on her. It is in fact he who has killed his own child. Frederic is denounced by his long-suffering sister Ellen and drowns himself in the aptly named deep brook. Jessie is pronounced not guilty, but dies before hearing the verdict. The work caused some stir, not just for its fierce propaganda but for Trollope's vagaries during the course of the serial publication. As she candidly admitted, evidence furnished to her about the 1834 Act changed her mind (half way through her story) on the iniquities of the new law.

JESSOP, George H. (1850?–1915). Jessop was born in Ireland, and went to the USA in 1873. Little else is known of his life other than that he wrote some successful plays and returned at some point to London, dying in Hampstead where it is reported he was received into the Catholic Church on his deathbed. His novels include: *Check And Counter Check* (1888); *Judge Lynch, A Tale Of The Californian Vineyards* (1889) and *Gerald Ffrench's Friends* (1889). The last is a collection of linked short stories, the hero being a young Irishman who emigrates (as did Jessop) to San Francisco in the early 1870s. BL 7.

JEWRY, Laura (d. 1899). The daughter of a navy officer, Laura Jewry married the Rev. Richard Valentine in 1853. He died a year later, presumably leaving his wife to fend for herself. As a novelist, Jewry specialised in florid historical* romance (mainly for the publishers F. Warne and T. C. Newby*) such as: *The Ransom* (1846), a tale of the thirteenth century; *Kirkholme Priory* (1847); *The Vassal* (1850). She also wrote improving books of travel, tales and history for young people, and was editor of the *Girl's Home Book* from 1877. BL 16. Wol.

JEWSBURY, Geraldine E[ndsor] (1812–80). The most accomplished all-round lady of letters of the nineteenth century. Jewsbury was born and raised in northern England, during the height of the industrial revolution. Her father was a Manchester cotton merchant and insurance agent. Her mother died prematurely and what to do with young Geraldine posed the family problems. Largely raised by her sister Maria Jane (later a woman of letters herself) she showed herself extremely clever, but did not want to teach or be a governess. Although she had love affairs during her life, she never married. After her father's death, in 1840, she kept house for her brother Frank until he married in 1853. But the most important relationship in her life was with the Carlyles, whom she first came to know in 1841 (it is for her letters to Jane Carlyle that Jewsbury is principally remembered today). She became a self-confessed Carlylean disciple. He, on his part, was evidently fond of 'the fair pilgrimess from the North', as he once called her, although he could not, on principle, always approve of her novels. In the late 1840s, Jewsbury wrote competent social commentary for *Douglas Jerrold's Shilling Magazine**. But gifted as she was in this line, Jewsbury was not a full-time journalist. In 1854, she moved to Chelsea, to be near the Carlyles at Cheyne Walk. Her first novel, *Zoe**, came out with Chapman and Hall* in 1845. In 1848, there appeared *The Half Sisters**, and in 1851, *Marian Withers*. John and Alice Withers are brought up in the workhouse at the turn of the century and put to work in the Lancashire cotton mills. He rises to become a successful businessman and model employer and has a daughter, Marian, who eventually marries the man, Mr Cunningham, who can save her father from financial ruin. (The work was first published in the *Manchester Examiner And Times* and makes an interesting companion to Mrs Gaskell's* better-known Manchester novels.) Though the industrial setting was topical, it is not the heart of the novel. Jewsbury's main concern was always the 'woman question': women's need for employment, the tyranny of the marriage market, the inadequacy of their educational chances. Jewsbury wrote a number of other novels, which sometimes offended orthodoxy. She did not, however, put her best into her fiction and it remains good second-rate quality. *Constance Herbert* (1855) is dedicated to Carlyle and is a story of confused love, broken engagements and noble renunciations. The heroine Constance nobly refuses to marry, lest she pass on her mother's insanity. *The Sorrows Of Gentility* (1856) is the story of Gertrude Morley, an innkeeper's daughter who overcomes the snobbish barriers that stand in her way. *Right Or Wrong* (1859) is set in historical France and has a hero who for twenty years lives a double life, spending six months of the year as a family man, the remaining six months as a celibate monk. It is more than a historical* novel, since once again the woman's peculiar role (included the half-deserted wife's) is not forgotten. Jewsbury's later fiction was published with Hurst and Blackett*, and conforms to that house's preference for romantic melodrama. Otherwise she was a sound and hard-headed reviewer in the pages of the *Athenaeum** and for fifteen years was a reader ('literary adviser') for Richard

Bentley*. (Commentators have found much of interest in her confidential reports on submitted manuscripts.) She wrote children's books, of which *The History Of An Adopted Child* (1852) is most interesting. In 1874, she was awarded a Civil List pension of £40 for her 'services to literature'. From 1866 she lived at Sevenoaks in Kent, and was less among the literary world, dying a lingering death from cancer. Jewsbury can claim to be the most successful disciple of George Sand and exponent of Sandism* in England of the Victorian period. BL 8. *DNB*. RM. *NCBEL*. Wol. Sad.

The Jilt, A Yarn, Charles Reade, 1877, 1 vol, Harper. (Serialised in *Belgravia**, March–June 1877, illustrated by J. Nash and part of a series generally entitled 'Good Stories Of Man And Other Animals'. The work was not published in book form in England until 1884.) The jilt of the title is Ellen Ap Rice, a Welsh beauty. She promises to marry a worthy sailor, Arthur Greaves. But while he is away on duty, she marries instead the wealthy yachtsman Edward Laxton. Laxton subsequently becomes deranged, and turns pirate. (Oddly, this same idea is used by Mortimer Collins*, in *The Vivian Romance*, 1870.) After melodramatic adventures at sea, Edward is captured, declared insane and dies. A chastened Ellen and loyal Arthur finally marry. The work is very short and brisk in the telling.

JOCELYN, Mrs Robert [Ada Maria] (née Jenyns, 1860–1931). Born in Aldershot, Ada Jenyns was the daughter of an army colonel. In 1892, she married R. J. O. Jocelyn, also a distinguished soldier and later the seventh Earl of Roden. Ouida* and Whyte-Melville* were Jocelyn's principal literary models. Her fiction which is by turns dashing, jokey (particularly her ghost* stories about 'spooks'), military and horsey includes: *A Distracting Guest* (1889), a story of apparitions, mesmerism, love and country houses; *The MFH's Daughter* (1889); *A Big Stake* (1892); *A Dangerous Brute* (1895), the brute being Hawthorne, a brown horse; *Juanita Carrington, A Sporting Novel* (1896); *Miss Rayburn's Diamonds* (1898). Jocelyn wrote plays and apparently gave up fiction around 1898. BL 20. *WW*. Wol.

John Halifax Gentleman, Dinah Mulock (Mrs Craik), 1856, 3 vols, Hurst and Blackett. The best-known Victorian fable of Smilesian self-improvement. The story is set in the early Industrial Revolution, 1790–1830. Mr Abel Fletcher, a Quaker manufacturer, has an invalid son, Phineas, who narrates the story. The Fletchers take on John Halifax, a fourteen-year-old orphan, to work for them. He starts at the bottom, in the tannery, hauling stinking animal hides. But he proves himself a willing worker, and befriends Phineas. As time goes on, John performs heroic services for his employers, saving their mill from bread rioters and otherwise proving himself invaluable. In their twenties, he and Phineas take a cottage together in the country. There they meet Ursula March, who is nursing her dying father. Although she is an heiress, John woos and wins her. After their marriage, they live together with their ever faithful friend, Phineas. The Halifaxes have a beloved blind daughter, who later dies, devastating her parents. John is now himself a master, and uses steam power to modernise his works. He prospers, goes into politics, and becomes a great man. But his grown-up children cause various tribulations. His son Guy goes to the bad, and is forced to emigrate to America. His daughter Maud falls in love with a worthless nobleman, Lord William Ravenel, and John forbids the match. After some years, Guy and Ravenel return, reformed characters, to console the old age of Halifax who dies serenely in his armchair, a prosperous paterfamilias and thorough gent. The insistent didacticism of the narrative is somewhat relieved by Mulock's briskly unsentimental mode of narration.

John Inglesant, J. H. Shorthouse, 1880, 1 vol, privately printed. A philosophical romance set in the seventeenth century. Shorthouse claimed to have found the germ of the story in an 'old book' chronicling a returned crusader who forgave the murderer of his brother. The Inglesant family are loyal Royalists, but also drawn to Rome. In 1622, twins are born: Eustace (the older by some minutes) and John. Their mother dies in birth. Eustace is brought up the more worldly of the pair by his father at Court. John is bookish, delicate in health and is brought up at Westacre Priory, where he becomes steeped in Platonism and mysticism. He also comes under the influence of the Jesuit, Father St Clare, whose aim it is to return England to the true Catholic faith. Clare has John placed as a Queen's page. He advises against conversion, thinking that the young man will be a better instrument if still nominally Anglican. The main characters are now swept up in the Civil War. On a secret mission John is taken prisoner by the Roundheads, and is sentenced to execution. But Clare contrives his release. The King meanwhile (in 1649) is beheaded. On his way to France, Eustace (who brought his brother's order of release) is murdered by an Italian enemy, Malvolti, and John swears revenge. But first he undertakes a long journey to Rome. On route in France, he is tempted by the asceticism of Hugh de Cressy. In Rome he is drawn to the quietism of Miguel de Molinos. But he decides to serve the Church and is sent on a mission by the Jesuits to Umbria, where he falls in love and marries Lauretta Capece. During a terrible outbreak of plague in Naples, John at last finds his brother's murderer, now a blind, penitent friar. He forswears revenge, laying his sword on the altar of a nearby chapel. But on his return, he finds that his wife and child have died of the epidemic. In Rome, he falls foul of the Inquisition, and eventually returns to England where he lives out what remains of his life in quiet contemplation and is last seen an English gentleman at Worcester Cathedral. Shorthouse commissioned a first printing of 100 elaborately-bound copies of his work, expecting no sale for such a strange production. But the novel became a bestseller when transferred to Macmillans* in 1881. Their two-volume edition sold 10,000 copies in its first year. The work dramatises vividly the spiritual tensions of the late-Victorian period and was a strong influence on Mrs Ward's* *Robert Elsmere**.

John Manesty, The Liverpool Merchant, William Maginn, 1844, 2 vols, Mortimer. (Serialised in *Ainsworth's Magazine**, intermittently from July 1843 to February 1844, with poorly executed illustrations by George Cruikshank*.) Maginn ended his short and debauched life in 1842. To relieve the financial distress of his family, this 'inedited work' was generously published by Ainsworth* in his magazine. Only the opening sections and the idea are Maginn's, the work being completed by Charles Ollier*, one of Ainsworth's hack employees. The novel starts brilliantly. Describing the hero and Liverpool in the 1760s, it maliciously indicates how the wealth of the city is built on slavery, black and white. As it continues by other hands, the narrative is grotesque. The sober-sided abolitionist merchant Manesty is finally revealed to be none other than Dick Hoskins, pirate captain of the *Bloody Juno*. This equation between pious businessman and murderous freebooter would probably have inspired Maginn's wit (had he completed the work) rather than Ainsworthian theatricality.

John Marchmont's Legacy, M. E. Braddon, 1863, 3 vols, Tinsley. (Serialised in *Temple Bar**, December 1862–January 1864.) The most intricate of Braddon's sensation* novels. The rich John Marchmont, knowing he will die, marries the beautiful Olivia Arundel. His motive is to provide a protector for his young daughter Mary. But Olivia loves her cousin, Captain Edward Arundel. On his part, Edward loves and (despite some difficulties) marries Mary secretly. After the wedding, he is injured in a rail crash and lies comatose for three months. When he recovers, Olivia and an ill-intentioned cousin, Paul Marchmont, tell him that his wife has drowned herself. In fact, they have secreted her in a boat-house with her new-born baby. As Edward is about to marry Belinda Lawford, Olivia (in a fit of jealousy and spite) interrupts the service to reveal all. The Arundels are reunited and Paul Marchmont burns himself to death in Marchmont Towers. After a year, Mary dies, and Edward (having served out a short widowerhood fighting in India) at last marries Belinda. As with all Braddon's fiction, the absurd plot is handled with verve.

JOHNSTON, Grace L[eslie] Keith ('Leslie Keith', 1843?–1929). Born in Edinburgh, she was the fifth daughter of the distinguished geographer and cartographer, Alexander Keith Johnston ('the elder', 1804–71). Keith was her grandmother's maiden name, and she used the sexually ambiguous 'Leslie' to create her mystifying pseudonym. Keith was educated at Edinburgh and in Germany. Her first published novel was *A Simple Maiden* (1878). She followed it with such works as: *Surrender* (1881); *A Hurricane In Petticoats* (1887); *A Lost Illusion* (1891), a story of love complicated by quakerism; *The Indian Uncle* (1896); *My Bonnie Lady* (1897); *Wayfarers All* (1899). The *Athenaeum** dryly commended the last as 'a not unfavourable specimen of the religious novelette'. Johnston did not apparently marry and ceased publishing novels around 1907. BL 41. (AKJ) DNB. Wol.

JOHNSTON, Henry (1842–1919). Johnston was born in Ireland, of Scottish parents. He came to Glasgow in his youth, and worked there as an accountant, writing for magazines in his spare time. In later life he published some moderately successful and quietly humorous stories of Scottish small-town life, including: *The Dawsons Of Glenara* (1877), his first and best-known work; *Martha Spreull* (1884); *The Chronicles Of Glenbuckie* (1889); *Kilmallie* (1891), like its predecessor, a tale of Scottish village life in the 1830s; *Dr Congalton's Legacy* (1896). The last is the story of the complications which ensue when a Scottish doctor's will leaves his property equally among three incompatible heirs. Johnston was much admired by Mrs Oliphant*. BL 5. Wol.

JOHNSTON, William (1829–1902). Johnston was born at Downpatrick, Ireland and graduated MA from Trinity College, Dublin. He was called to the Irish Bar in 1872. Johnston resided in later life at Ballykilbeg, and was one of the most strenuous Northern Irish opponents of Home Rule. A

Unionist and Orangeman, Johnston was Grandmaster of the Grand Black Chapter of Ireland and was, from 1865 to 1878, MP for Belfast. From 1878 to 1885 he was Inspector of Irish Fisheries. His novels reflect his fierce politics. They include the polemical *Nightshade* (1857) and *Freshfield* (1861), both of which have melodramatic scenes of political skulduggery, assassination and Catholic unscrupulousness. *Under Which King?* (1872) recounts the events of 1688–91 with the inevitable Williamite glee at the outcome of the Battle of the Boyne. BL 3. *WW*.

JONES, Ernest Charles (1819–68). Chartist poet and novelist. Jones was born of Welsh parents in Berlin. Jones's father was a major in the hussars on the staff of the Duke of Cumberland and the boy was educated in Germany. Intellectually he was precocious, publishing his first poems at the age of ten. A year later he showed his mettle by attempting to run away and fight with the Polish insurgents. In 1838, his family returned to England. At this period, Jones evidently conformed to the rules of the station in which he was born and was presented at Court by the Duke of Beaufort in 1841, and married a high-born wife in 1844. In the same year, he published a romantic novel, *The Wood Spirit*. It made little impact. Jones mainly supported himself by journalism in the 1840s. He also enrolled in law and was called to the Bar in 1844 but did not go into practice. Jones was radicalised by the events of the turbulent 1840s. In 1846, he joined the Chartists, and espoused the tough doctrine of Feargus O'Connor's physical (as opposed to moral) force faction. A fiery orator and journalist, he eventually became editor of the movement's organ, the *Northern Star*. At Manchester in 1848 he was convicted of making seditious speeches and sentenced to two years' imprisonment. In prison, he later claimed to have written the poem *The Revolt Of Hindostan* with his own blood. He was a rebellious inmate, and refused to pick oakum for which he was further punished. On release, by now a working-class hero, Jones threw himself into political activities (with some law practice and much writing) until his death. He died, at Manchester, at a moment when for the first time after several attempts, he looked likely to occupy a seat as a radical candidate. Jones's fiction largely conforms with his political activities. *De Brassier, A Democratic Romance* appeared in 1852. Subtitled 'The History Of A Democratic Movement, Compiled From The Journal Of A Demagogue, The Confessions Of A Democrat And The Minutes Of A Spy', the work chronicles the career of a nobleman who carves his way to the leadership of a popular movement only to betray the cause finally. In 1854 Jones published the colourfully historical* tale *The Maid Of Warsaw, Or The Tyrant Czar*. It was followed in 1855 by a violently political novel, *The Lass And The Lady* (published in parts and 'completed by Thomas Frost*'). *Women's Wrongs* (1855) is a collection of five tales about women from varied backgrounds, with franker sexual reference than is common in middle-class fiction of the period. This fiction is devoted to the view that, as Jones puts it: 'it is folly to say we can't help it, we are creatures of circumstances, we are are what society makes us. We *can* help it, we can *create circumstances*, we can *make* society.' Jones also wrote a number of poems, some with a political tendency. He is remembered principally as the author of powerful verses, such as 'The Song Of The Poor'; 'The Song Of The Day-Labourers'; 'The Song Of The Factory-Slave'. BL 5. *DNB*. RLF.

JONES, Hannah Maria (1801–54; some accounts give Jones's dates as 1796–1859). The 'Queen' of cheap fiction and one of the two women to succeed in the 'penny dreadful*' field, the other being Miss Emma Robinson*. A prolific author of sub-Radcliffian romances, Jones had some success in the 1820s and 1830s with her popular gypsy novels, such as: *The Gypsy Girl* (1834) and *The Gypsy Mother, Or The Miseries Of Enforced Marriage* (1835). Before the 1840s, her works ('Illustrated By Beautiful Steel Engravings') sold in the tens of thousands in 1d. and 6d. serial parts. And with the semi-literate public, she remained a voluminously reprinted novelist long after her death. Montague Summers comments: 'her popularity was enormous, and continued so that until the end of the century many of her romances were appearing in cheapest guise with crudest woodcuts, generally without date or printer's name.' For all her popularity, she was the least proud of authors and claimed that no one could have a lower opinion of her works than did she herself. And despite her sales, Jones survived in a state of constant penury and what little is known of her life comes from her repeated applications to the Royal Literary Fund* with the waning of her popularity in the late 1830s. Her first novel was, apparently, *Gretna Green* (1820). Throughout her career she worked for extremely small amounts and even in the 1850s was receiving under 1s. a page. Her work was ruthlessly plagiarised by other hacks. Her husband, John Jones, was an out-of-work compositor and normally depended on rather than supported his wife. In later life, she lived with another hack author, John Lowndes, and although they were not married called herself Mrs Lowndes. Her end was wretched and in its obituary notice of her *The Times* noted that: 'Her remains await, in all probability, a pauper's funeral.' Her Victorian fiction includes: *The Ruined Cottage, Or The Farmer's Maid* (1846); *The Shipwrecked Stranger* (1848), a sequel; *Katherine Beresford, Or The Shade And Sunshine Of A Woman's Life* (1850). *The Gypsy Chief* (1841) was her best-known work in the last years of her life. BL 18. RLF.

Jorrocks. R. S. Surtees's* cockney* greengrocer and tea-dealer (of St Botolph's Lane, in the City), who has a love of the hunting field. Rich, twenty-stone, in his fifties when first encountered, Jorrocks's catchphrase ejaculation is 'My vig'. He was first introduced in the pages of the *New Sporting Magazine* (1831–36), in July 1831. He figures centrally in the trilogy: *Jorrocks's Jaunts And Jollities* (1838); *Handley Cross, Or The Spa Hunt** (1843); *Hillingdon Hall, Or The Cockney Squire** (1845). In various reissued forms, the Jorrocks saga was memorably illustrated by Phiz* and John Leech*.

Joseph's Coat, David Christie Murray, 1881, 3 vols, Chatto. (Serialised in *Belgravia**, November 1880–December 1881, illustrated by Fred Barnard*.) Murray's novel was very popular with Victorian readers. A prologue sets it in the Black Country in the 1850s. Joseph Bushell has risen by trade to great wealth, his wife being a noted female preacher. After a camp meeting at which his mother has preached, young Joseph Bushell, the well-educated but over-indulged heir, falls out with his best friend Sydney Cheston, argues with his parents, and strikes an evangelical friend of the family when he warns the young man against the sins of the flesh. Aided by his uncle George (a villain who wants to inherit the Bushell fortune) young Joseph runs away to California and is not heard of again. His sweetheart, Dinah Banks, is left pregnant. She and Joseph have in fact married, although since she does not have her 'lines' (i.e. certificate) Dinah assumes that the union has no validity. Her son, George, is brought up as her nephew. Twenty-three years later, George is secretary to old George Bushell. Headstrong like his father before him, the young man forges a cheque for £300. In the ensuing investigation, all comes to light. The rightful heir, Joseph, returns from abroad; old George repents and young George is rehabilitated through hard work. The novel ends with the formal remarriage of Joseph and Dinah. Murray's novel has a number of points of interest: the closely observed Midlands setting, the intricately sensational* plot, the broad-minded attitude to criminal lapses in the young.

Joshua Davidson, Christian And Communist, Eliza Lynn Linton, 1872, 1 vol, Strahan. (Full title, *The True History Of*, etc.) Linton's most popular work, which went through three editions in its first three months of publication. The novel daringly recasts the life of Christ (Jesus, son of David) in a modern setting. Joshua is born in 1835, the son of a Cornish carpenter. As a child in his native village of Trevalga, he falls foul of the pharisaical clergy (particularly the Reverend Grand), whom he accuses of betraying the Gospel. As a young man, Joshua goes to London, where he works at his trade and tries to live the literal Word of Christ. He befriends and reforms two sinners: Mary, a prostitute and Joe, a drunken burglar. Joshua graduates from his scriptural fundamentalism to civilised Anglicanism. But every denomination denounces him as 'infidel, unsound, irregular'. He eventually persuades himself that a Victorian Christ would be a socialist politician, or 'class organiser', and joins the newly founded Working Men's Association. In this phase of his career he goes to the recently declared Paris Commune. On his return, Joshua is kicked to death by a crowd of enraged Christians (led by his relentless adversary, Grand) for his proclaimed belief in the creed of communism. Joshua's story is told, gospel-fashion, by an unnamed apostle who has known him from birth. The narrative ends with Linton's familiar conundrum: 'Is practical Christianity impossible?'. The novel, like Ward's* *Robert Elsmere*, represents a Victorian attempt to reconcile the conflicting claims of secular politics and religion. By the sixth edition in 1874, Linton had acknowledged her previously withheld authorship. Up to that point, the volume appeared with no name at all on the title page.

Jude The Obscure, Thomas Hardy, 1895, 1 vol, Osgood, McIlvaine. (Serialised and bowdlerised in *Harper's New Monthly Magazine*, December 1894–November 1895. In this form the novel's title was first *The Simpletons*, then *Hearts Insurgent*.) Hardy's last published full-length novel which provoked a storm of criticism for its 'anti-marriage' doctrines. The narrative opens at Marygreen village, where the schoolteacher Richard Phillotson is about to leave, to enlarge his prospects at the university city of Christminster (i.e. Oxford). Phillotson's instruction and his aspirations have had a strong effect on young Jude Fawley. Jude is an orphan (there is a mysterious tragedy in his past), looked after by his aunt Drusilla, a baker. The youth embarks on the path of educational self-improvement. He apprentices to a stone mason, whilst assiduously applying himself to study at night. His plans are demolished, however, by a lusty country girl, Arabella Donn. She first attracts Jude's notice by throwing a pig's pizzle at him and she then traps him into marriage, by feigning pregnancy. The marriage is wretched. Jude attempts suicide (to which he is genetically prone), and begins to drink heavily. Then suddenly Arabella deserts him and he is a free man, but not free to marry. Jude subsequently goes to Christminster where he meets his beautiful but high-strung cousin, Sue Bridehead, who works in an ecclesiastical warehouse. He also rediscovers Phillotson whose grand dreams have come to nothing; he is still a schoolmaster. Sue is induced to become his assistant. Jude, meanwhile, succumbs to drink and loses his position. He returns to Marygreen where the minister persuades him to apply for ordination by licence (i.e. without the normal university degree). Sue, on her part, is now at teachers' training college in Melchester. Jude and she pass an innocent night together, which nevertheless leads to her expulsion. And her free-thinking erodes the foundation of Jude's faith in Christianity. Sue marries Phillotson and Jude rediscovers Arabella, now a barmaid in Christminster. Jude gives up his vocation. And at the funeral of his aunt Drusilla, he and Sue decide they cannot live without each other. They go together to Aldbrickham, where they hope to be unknown. Phillotson and Arabella concede divorce, but Sue cannot bring herself to marry and the lovers live in sin. Arabella sends to Jude a child, Little Father Time, who is a living embodiment of the age's spiritual and physical enfeeblement. For several years Sue and Jude contrive to live in a kind of peace. But Jude is hounded out of his work, and the family go to Christminster yet again (in Remembrance Week) where Sue is insulted by a prudish boarding-house keeper. Time is profoundly affected, and hangs his two little siblings and himself, because 'we are too many'. Sue miscarries. After this holocaust, which she sees as divine judgement, she returns to Phillotson. Jude falls again into the clutches of Arabella, who remarries him. On a last visit to Sue in the rain he catches cold. His drink-weakened constitution gives out and he dies, the cheers from celebrating students ringing distantly in his ears. As Virginia Woolf observed, *Jude* is the one unequivocally pessimistic work in Hardy's fictional corpus. After publishing it, he seems to have given up fiction as a bad job.

The Jungle Books, Rudyard Kipling, 1894–95, 2 vols, Macmillan. (The stories were earlier published separately in a variety of magazines. The first book issue was illustrated by Kipling's father, John L. Kipling, P. Frenzeny and W. H. Drake.) The books comprise fifteen animal fables, accompanied by verse and written in a pleasantly stilted idiom. The narrative opens with the toddler Mowgli straying from his Indian village into the jungle. He is stalked by the lame tiger, Shere Khan, but escapes to be brought up as a man cub by father and mother wolf. He learns the law of the jungle in the ordered society of the Seeonee Pack, under the democratic leadership of Akela. Mowgli's other teachers, as he grows to wolfhood, are Baloo the bear and Bagheera the black panther. The main body of the subsequent jungle books is composed of discrete tales, of which the best known is probably that of Rikki Tikki Tavi, the mongoose who gallantly protects a white family's bungalow against cobras. The second book begins with 'How Fear Came To The Jungle' and ends with Mowgli's conquest of the fearsome *dhole*, red hunting dogs. At the end of his adventures in the jungle, Mowgli accepts his own manhood and returns to human society 'seeking new trails'. The stories embody a potent anthropomorphic mythology and a romanticised view of the colonist's power to absorb the essence of the wilderness while preserving his racial superiority. The rituals of Akela's idealised wolf pack were taken over by Baden Powell's scout 'cubs'.

K

The Kailyard. Scottish dialect for 'the cabbage patch', the term applies to a popular but largely reviled school of late-nineteenth-century fiction. It was first used by J. H. Millar in the *New Review*, 1895, with reference to the recent bestselling works of J. M. Barrie*, Ian Maclaren (i.e. John Watson*) and S. R. Crockett*. (See the epigraph to Maclaren's *Beside The Bonnie Brier Bush*: 'There grows a bonnie brier bush in our kailyard'.) The distinguishing kailyard feature was taken to be a syrupy sentimentalism about Scottish (usually lowland) rural life and a pawky humorous tone of narrative interspersed with heavy pathos. Representative kailyard works are: Barrie's *Auld Licht Idylls* and (notoriously) Crockett's *The Stickit Minister*. George Douglas Brown's* extravagantly grim *The House With The Green Shutters*￼ was written to contradict the kailyard's rosy view of life in a Scottish village.

KAVANAGH, [Miss] Julia (1824–77). Born at Thurles in Ireland, she was the only child of Morgan Peter Kavanagh*, philologist and novelist. In an extraordinary literary quarrel Julia was obliged in 1857 to disown any connection with a novel (*The Hobbies*) which her father wrote, and tried to pass off as partly hers. In her childhood, the Kavanagh family lived largely in Paris and Normandy. French settings, and foreign (usually French) heroines recur in Julia's subsequent fiction, such as: *Madeleine, A Tale Of Auvergne* (1848), a story of 'heroic charity and living faith founded on fact'; *Nathalie* (1850); *Beatrice* (1865); *Silvia* (1870); *Bessie* (1872). Kavanagh's plots also tend to contain resourceful, independent women (sometimes orphans) at their centre, such as: *Adèle* (1858), which opens ominously with 'The funeral was over' and *Dora* (1868). The Kavanagh family returned to London in 1844, evidently separating from the father. Thereafter Julia supported herself and her invalid mother by her writing. Her first book for children (*The Three Paths*) came out in 1847. Her subsequent fiction was aimed at younger women readers and was fashionably domestic* in style while remaining wholly 'ladylike' in tone. Her last work, *Forget-Me-Nots* (1878), is a series of linked tales. Kavanagh was a popular and consistent writer, who evidently built up a loyal reading public with her many novels which she published with Bentley*, Colburn* and Hurst and Blackett*. After her mother's death, she lived in Nice, a devout Catholic, where she died unmarried. Her last words, in French, were: 'Oh Mama! how silly I am to have fallen'. With her mother Bridget (who was evidently a lifelong companion) she published a volume of fairy stories in 1876. BL 21. *DNB*. RM. *NCBEL*. Wol. RLF.

KAVANAGH, Morgan Peter (1800–74). The father of Julia (see above), Kavanagh began his authorial career as a poet. He wrote what the *DNB* calls a 'ridiculous work' on linguistics, *The Discovery Of The Science Of Languages* (1844), which locates the origin of speech in prehistoric physical mime. His domestic life was evidently unsettled and unhappy. He wrote two novels: *Aristobulus, The Last Of The Maccabees* (1855), 'A Tale Of Jerusalem', and *The Hobbies* (1857). This second work, which the *Athenaeum** labelled 'an insult to the public', involved him in public controversy with his better-known daughter when he, or his unscrupulous publisher Newby*, indicated on the title page that she had 'edited' the narrative. Kavanagh also wrote entirely unregarded epic poetry. BL 2. *DNB*.

KAYE, Sir John William ('Sullivan Earle', 1814–76). Kaye was born in Acton, the son of a successful lawyer. He was educated at Eton, and the Royal Military College, Addiscombe. In 1832, he went to India, as a cadet in the Bengal Artillery. He resigned the army in 1841, but remained in India to found the *Calcutta Review* in 1844. A year later he returned to England. In 1856, Kaye accepted a post in the administrative branch of the East India Company and later took over John Stuart Mill's secretaryship at the India Office. Kaye was a voluminous writer, especially on military history. (See his *History Of The War In Afghanistan*, 1851; and his *History Of The Sepoy War*, 1876.) He also wrote fiction anonymously, usually in small privately printed runs and under the pseudonym Sullivan Earle. It includes: *Jerningham* (1836); *The Story Of Basil Bouverie* (1842); *Peregrine Pultuney* (1844); *Long Engagements, A Tale Of The Afghan Rebellion* (1845). Kaye's novels draw extensively on his Indian experience. BL 6. *DNB*. Wol.

KAY–SHUTTLEWORTH, Sir James Phillips (1804–77). Born and educated in Rochdale, Kay-Shuttleworth first went to work in a bank. Finding the occupation uncongenial, he enrolled at Edinburgh University in 1824, to study medicine. He had a brilliant career as a student, and on qualifying settled in Manchester as a physician. Kay-Shuttleworth became deeply involved with the Lancashire working people in his care, and he agitated effectively for sanitary reforms in the city. He also performed heroic feats of medical aid during the cholera epidemic of 1832. In 1835, he was appointed an Assistant Poor Law Commissioner. From 1841 onwards, Kay-Shuttleworth devoted himself to the introduction of a national system of education, a campaign which bore late fruit in 1870. He was created a baronet in 1849. A man of cultivated literary tastes, it was at his house that Charlotte Brontë* met her sister novelist and her eventual biographer, Elizabeth Gaskell*. Kay-Shuttleworth published anonymously two novels, both rich in local colour and topography, rendered with scrupulous 'fidelity'. They are: *Scarsdale, Or Life On The Lancashire And Yorkshire Border Thirty Years Ago* (1860) and *Ribblesdale, Or Lancashire Sixty Years Ago* (1874), a story of feuds between ancient gentry and commercially enriched newcomers. Reviewers found Kay-Shuttleworth's stories laudably 'Ainsworthian*'. BL 2. *DNB*. Wol.

KEARY, Annie [Anna Maria] (1825–79). The daughter of an Irish clergyman and former soldier, Annie Keary was born near Wetherby, Yorkshire (some accounts say Bath), and educated largely at home. She gives a portrait of the small town where she was brought up in her later novel *Oldbury* (1869). Keary was a precocious story-teller, and from a young age used her talent to entertain the younger members of her family. As a young woman she took charge of her brother's motherless children. On his remarriage and their removal, coupled with the breaking of her own engagement, she evidently suffered a severe breakdown. In 1858 she travelled to Egypt where she experienced a religious crisis. Much of her later fiction was written in a condition of semi-invalidism, in the south of France. Keary published a popular children's book *Mia And Charles* in 1856 and followed it a year later with the popular *Sidney Grey*, a tale of school life. In the 1860s, she put out a series of popular domestic novels such as *Janet's Home* (1863) which some critics found lugubrious and over-pious in tone. The *Saturday Review**, for instance, declared her fiction to be 'not brilliant but it possesses qualities that are more valuable than brilliance'. Her best work, *Castle Daly* (1875), subtitled 'The Story Of An Irish Home Thirty Years Ago', is set during the Irish famine, is sympathetic to Home Rule, and re-creates an Ireland for which, reportedly, she had no real affection and no first-hand knowledge. Nonetheless, the work had gone through twelve editions by 1900. *A Doubting Heart* (1879), Keary's last novel, was completed by Mrs MacQuoid*. A typical homely story of the love affairs of two girl cousins, it features some descriptions of the Riviera where the author spent her last months. A Macmillan* author, Annie Keary made plentiful use of epigraphs and dialogue. She never married. Her sister, Eliza Keary, also wrote verses and some stories for children and in 1882 a memoir of Annie. BL 15. *DNB*. *NCBEL*. Wol.

KEARY, Charles Francis (d. 1917). Keary was educated at Marlborough school, and at Trinity College, Cambridge, before taking up literature as a career. For some years he seems also to have been employed by the British Museum. As an author, he specialised in numismatics and Scandinavian history. His fiction, which is strongly influenced by French Naturalism and the drama of Ibsen, includes: *A Mariage De Convenance* (1890), a modern epistolary novel; *The Two Lancrofts* (1893), a story of Oxford college life; *Herbert Vanlennert* (1895), a *Bildungsroman**; *The Journalist* (1898). The last evidently contains autobiographical material describing the life of a young man of letters, Richard Vaux, who becomes an Ibsenite. Reviewers claimed to discern barely concealed literary identities in the novel's dramatis personae. BL 8. *WW*.

KEATING, Joseph (1871–1934). Keating was born in South Wales, of Irish Catholic parents. His father was a miner and Keating himself went into the work at the age of twelve (for 6s.9d. a week) but hated it. As he wryly put it, he later gave up 'work' and turned to writing for his living. Keating subsequently published fiction drawing on his early Welsh experience. His most powerful early work in this vein is the melodramatic *Son Of Judith, A Tale Of The Welsh Mining Valleys* (1901). Its central character is a son brought up by his mother to avenge his father's murder; the work has a terrific climax evidently inspired by Zola's *Germinal*. BL 13. *WW*.

KEDDIE, Henrietta ('Sarah Tytler', 1827–1914). Henrietta Keddie was born in Cupar, Fife, the daughter of a lawyer. Early in her life, she moved to Elie on the Scottish coast, where the family had coal mining interests. Keddie was educated at home, largely by an elder sister. At sixteen she went to Edinburgh, where she was helped by the well-known man of letters, Dr John Brown, and early in life placed her work in *Blackwood's Magazine**. From 1848 to 1870 she and her sister ran a school for girls at Cupar. She never married. Her first book was published in 1854 and by the late 1860s, Keddie was writing regularly under her pseudonym Sarah Tytler. In 1870, she came to London, to support herself solely by literature. In addition to numerous educational works, she eventually wrote over 100 works of fiction, largely aimed at the girl reader. Her many works include: *Nut Brown Maids* (1860); *Citoyenne Jacqueline* (1865), a revolutionary tale from a woman's point of view; *St Mungo's City* (1885), a portrait of Glasgow; *French Janet* (1889); *The Witch Wife* (1897), a story of witch burning in the seventeenth century; *A Loyal Little Maid* (1899). Her most revealing work is probably *Logie Town* (1887) in which she describes the Fife that she knew as a child. BL 101. *WW. NCBEL.* Wol. RLF.

KEELING, Elsa D'Esterre (née Esterre, 1860–1935). Elsa Esterre was born and went to school in Dublin, finishing her education in Germany. Evidently an able linguist, she worked for a while as a translator for the British Foreign Office. She was thereafter a schoolmistress at Oxford and London (1884–90), rising eventually to the rank of principal of the Chelsea School of Elocution. Her fiction includes: *Three Sisters, A Highly Original Family* (1884); *Bib And Tucker* (1884), 'being the revelations of a babe in arms'; *A Professor's Wooing* (1886). In later life she suppressed reference to her novels and her marriage. BL 7. *WW.*

KEENE, Charles [Samuel], (1823–91). Illustrator. Born at Hornsey, outer London, Keene was the son of a lawyer. He was brought up in his mother's home town of Ipswich and after school returned to London to work in law. He soon gave this up in order to apprentice himself to a wood-engraver. In 1847, he became associated with the newly founded *Illustrated London News**, and shortly after with *Punch**, an association he retained until his death. With the establishment of Bradbury and Evans's* *Once A Week* in 1859, Keene became one of the principal illustrators of the fiction that ran in its pages (for instance, Charles Reade's* *A Good Fight*, Mrs Henry Wood's* *Verner's Pride* and George Meredith's* *Evan Harrington**, the designs for the last of which the art critic Forrest Reid considered the most beautiful the artist ever executed). He also illustrated George Eliot's* *Brother Jacob** for *Cornhill**. Keene was immensely influential, and his highly naturalistic (but comically tinged) designs are largely credited with bringing about the revolution in book illustration that occurred in the 1860s. Keene never married, was a bohemian in life-style and died in London, which had always provided his most congenial subject-matter.

KEIGHTLEY, [Sir] S[amuel] R[obert] (1859–1940). Keightley was born in Belfast, the son of a JP, and educated at Queen's College, Belfast. (In later life he was elected to the University Senate.) He was called to the Irish Bar in 1883, married in 1892 and was knighted in 1912. Politically active, he contested Antrim as an Independent Unionist in 1903. At the turn of the century Keightley wrote poetry and a number of Dumas-inspired historical* romances with Irish* settings. They include: *The Crimson Sign* (1895), a story of the siege of Derry; *The Cavaliers* (1896); *The Silver Cross* (1898); *Heronford* (1899); *The Return Of The Prodigal* (1900); *A Man Of Millions* (1901), a contemporary thriller. BL 9. *WW*. Wol.

KELLY, William Patrick (1848–1916). Kelly was born in Co. Kilkenny, Ireland and was educated at Clongowes Wood College. After training at the Royal Military Academy, Woolwich he was commissioned into the Royal Artillery in which he served until 1878. He lived at Harrogate thereafter and wrote a quantity of historical* adventure stories. His best work is *Schoolboys Three* (1895), recalling life at a Catholic school in the early 1860s which evidently contains autobiographical material. Reviewers found the story's tone 'healthy'. BL 12.

The Kellys And The O'Kellys, Or Landlords And Tenants, Anthony Trollope, 1848, 3 vols, Colburn. Trollope's second published novel. Like the first, it had a topical Irish* theme (given the current famine) and according to its author failed utterly with the English reading public. The story has two intertwining plot lines. The first concerns Frank O'Kelly's (Lord Ballindine's) quest for the hand of the heiress Fanny Wyndham. He is frustrated in his suit by her guardian, the Earl of Cashel, who wants Fanny for his own wastrel son, Lord Kilcullen. The other plot line concerns the progeny of Simeon Lynch, who has made a dishonest fortune managing Frank's family estate. Lynch's son, Barry, drunkenly tries to murder his sister Anty so as to inherit her half of the money. Taking refuge with an innkeeper (Mrs Kelly), Anty eventually finds a husband, Martin Kelly, to protect her. Frank finally overcomes all obstacles and marries Fanny. Barry and Lord Kilcullen, villains both, are driven abroad. Frank is the first of Trollope's many horsey, reckless heroes.

KEMBLE, Adelaide [Sartoris] (1814?–79). Born in Covent Garden, London, she was a daughter of Charles Kemble and a member of the famous theatrical family. Herself a talented singer, she performed professionally from 1835 on the stage and in opera in London and European capital cities. Kemble's debut was in Venice and her first appearance at Covent Garden was in 1841. Thereafter she travelled widely (including one tour with Liszt). In 1844 she married Edward John Sartoris and her professional career effectively ended. To relieve the inactivity of her marriage, she wrote and published quite extensively. Her fiction includes the lively *roman-à-clef* first serialised in *Cornhill**, *A Week In A French Country House* (1867), and *Medusa And Other Tales* (1868). BL 3. *DNB*. Wol. Sad.

KENEALY, Arabella (1864–1938). Kenealy was born in Sussex, the daughter of a lawyer. She graduated from the London School of Medicine for Women, and practised as a doctor in London and Watford (1888–94) until ill health forced her retirement. She also wrote a number of novels with contemporary settings which mainly deal with modern sex problems in a melodramatic but not unhumorous way. Her most successful work was *Dr Janet Of Harley Street* (1893), Dr Janet being the wise friend and helper of the young love-crossed heroine, Phyllis Eve. Phyllis is promised in marriage

to the aged and debauched Marquis of Richeville. Rather than submit to
sexual violation, she runs away, still *virgo intacta*, two hours after the wedding ceremony. After various adventures, she is adopted by the fifty-year-old
Dr Janet and herself trains as a doctor. A theatrical climax ensues in which
Richeville attempts to enforce his conjugal rights before blowing his head
off during a tremendous fit of delirium tremens. 'I thank God that he did
it', concludes an unremorseful Dr Phyllis. The lesbian relationship between
the older and younger woman is (by Victorian standards) frankly depicted.
Kenealy's other fiction includes: *Molly And Her Man Of War* (1894); *Some
Men Are Such Gentlemen* (1894); *The Hon. Mrs Spoor* (1895), the story
of a woman with a dreadful secret in her past which reviewers were im-
plored not to divulge; *Woman And The Shadow* (1898); *A Semi-Detached
Marriage* (1898), a gloomy story of illicit sexual relationships and bigamy;
Charming Renée (1900), the heroine being 'a beautiful problem'. Kenealy
wrote some fierce tracts on vivisection and in late life became preoccupied
with occultism, particularly the role played in human evolution by the gy-
roscopic rotation of the earth. BL 25. *WW*. Wol.

Kenelm Chillingly, E. G. E. L. Bulwer-Lytton, 1873, 3 vols, Blackwood.
A novel of intellectual quixoticism. Kenelm is the only child, born late in
married life, to Sir Peter and Lady Chillingly of Exmundham. He grows up
solemn, precocious and sceptical. After graduation from Cambridge, he sets
out on a long questing tour of the world, incognito and with only a few
pounds in his pocket. The main section of the narrative concerns his wanderings and his occasional resurfacing in respectable society. Among other
adventures, he thrashes a lecherous blacksmith, Tom Bowles (who promptly
reforms), and wins the heart of Squire Leopold Travers's daughter, Cecilia.
Cecilia tells Kenelm the tragic story of Alfred Fletwode, an aristocrat who
killed himself on being discovered in forgery (intended to repair his ruined
family fortunes). By coincidence, Kenelm falls in love with a descendant
of this criminal, Lily Mordaunt. She, however, is promised in marriage to
her guardian, Walter Melville, and eventually dies of a broken heart. The
novel ends with Kenelm and his father contemplating Parliament with the
prospect of a political career and marriage to the ever faithful Cecilia. The
novel is remarkable for the character of its intellectually rootless hero, the
finest type of the Bulwerian 'student'.

KENNARD, Mrs [Mary] Edward (née Laing, 1850–1914). The daughter
of Samuel Laing, MP for Orkney, himself an author who wrote books
of popular history, folklore and a novel, *A Sporting Quixote, Or The
Life And Adventures Of The Hon. Augustus Fitzmuddle* (1886). Mary
Laing was educated by governesses, and at finishing school in Germany. In
1870 she married Edward Kennard (b. 1842), a Northamptonshire country
gentleman, keen fisherman and JP. By her own account, Mary Kennard
'took to writing when her two sons went to school; began with sporting*
tales to amuse them, entitled *Twilight Tales* [1886]; then wrote *The Right
Sort* [1883], which was well received; and shortly published *Straight As A
Die* [1885]; since then wrote steadily till eyesight grew bad; had a bad fall
out hunting with a concussion to the brain which forced her to reduce her
hours'. Kennard wrote some thirty books. Her fiction, which revolves almost
exclusively around hunting and equestrian sport in the shires, includes:

Killed In The Open (1886); *The Girl In The Brown Habit* (1887), her best-known work, a sporting novel told by Miles Mannington, the girl being Nell Fitzgerald; *A Hunting Girl* (1894); *Fooled By A Woman* (1895), whose heroine enterprisingly murders her mother-in-law; *Morals Of The Midlands* (1899), a rattling tale of Leicestershire hunting and Norwegian fishing; *Tony Larkin, Englishman* (1900), a story which intersperses English hunting scenes with the hero's colonial exile in Africa. This unusual woman listed her main hobby as automobilism: 'driving a 40 hp. Napier car, a De Dion volturette, and a 15 hp. Darracq and riding a motor tricycle, being one of the few ladies in England at present [1900] to do so'. It would seem that her ubiquitous sporty heroines (as in *Wedded To Sport*, 1892) are projections of the author herself. Reviewers liked her slapdash, highly ungrammatical style of writing in which they discerned 'lots of go' and a 'thoroughly healthy tone'. BL 23. *WW*. Wol.

KENNEDY, Bart (1861–1930). Kennedy was born in Leeds, of Irish parents. As an author, he is one of the early advocates of 'tramping', as the source of literary inspiration. He describes his own life somewhat romantically in *Who's Who*: 'picked up education in knocking about the world. Reared in Manchester; was a half-timer at the age of six in a cotton mill; worked up to the age of twenty in mills and machine shops in Manchester; went to sea before the mast; been a labourer and a tramp in the USA; lived or fought with the Indians; goldmined up in the Klondike before the gold rush; became an opera singer and an actor; drifted into writing.' He also drifted into marriage in 1897. His fiction (much of it short) includes: *Darab's Wine Cup* (1897); *The Wandering Romanoff* (1898); *A Man Adrift* (1899), an autobiographical work, subtitled 'Leaves From A Nomad's Portfolio'; *A Sailor Tramp* (1902), another geographically far-flung tale which evidently contains a large measure of autobiography. BL 11. *WW*. RLF.

KENYON, Edith C. (d. 1925). Kenyon was born at Doncaster, where her father practised as a doctor. She was educated at home and as an adult woman lived with her brother (another doctor) in Bradford until 1898, when she moved to London. She began her authorial career translating works from German, graduating into writing original stories for the young, and thence to fully fledged adult fiction. Kenyon wrote fluently, often for the RTS* and had some thirty-five books to her credit by 1907. Her novels include: *The Squire Of Lonsdale* (1896) and *The Hand Of His Brother* (1897). BL 48. *WW*.

KEON, Miles Gerald (1821–75). Keon was born at Co. Leitrim, Ireland, in a family castle ('Keon's Folly') on the banks of the Shannon. His father was descended from an old Irish family, and a barrister. He died in 1824 and his wife followed a year later, leaving the young boy to be brought up by his maternal grandmother. Keon attended the Jesuit college at Stonyhurst, and for a while served as a soldier of fortune in North Africa. He was subsequently a student of law at Gray's Inn, married in 1846 and drifted, by the familiar route, into writing for his living. He worked for the *Morning Post*, 1847–59, mainly as a correspondent sympathetic to the Conservative cause. Keon had influential friends (including Bulwer-Lytton*) and he was made colonial secretary to Bermuda in 1859, a post he held until his death. His novels include: *Dion And The Sibyls* (1866), 'a romance of the first century', and *Harding The Money Spinner* (1879) which was first serialised in the *London Journal** in 1852. His novels were popular. BL 2. *DNB*. Wol. Sad. RLF.

KERNAHAN, [John] Coulson (1858–1943). Coulson Kernahan was born in Ilfracombe, and was educated largely at home by his father, a scientist and biblical scholar admired by the Bishop of London, whose endorsement his publications carried. The young man began his career as an author writing for such heavy journals as *Nineteenth Century* and the *Fortnightly**. He also served for many years as literary adviser to the publisher, Ward, Lock and Tyler*. His own fiction includes: *A Dead Man's Diary* (1890); *A Book Of Strange Sins* (1893); *God And The Ant* (1895), a religious parable; *Captain Shannon* (1897), a story of Fenian outrages in the 1890s. *The Child, The Wise Man And The Devil* (1896) was immensely successful, and is estimated to have sold upward of a quarter of a million copies. It takes as its premiss the discovery of Christ's body, and the subsequent disproof of his divinity. BL 5. *WW*.

KERNAHAN, Mrs Coulson [Mary Jean Hickling Bettany] (née Gwynne, 1857–1941). Jeannie Gwynne was born in Taunton, the daughter of a mathematics teacher and was related to the historian W. H. Prescott. She was educated by her father and later at University College, London. Her first marriage was to Professor G. T. Bettany of Caius College, Cambridge, by whom she had three children. She subsequently married the novelist, Coulson Kernahan*, by whom she had her fourth child, a daughter. Mrs Kernahan herself began writing novels such as: *Trewinnot Of Guy's* (1898), a medical story; *The House Of Rimmon* (1899), a story of industrial life set in the Black Country; *Frank Redland, Recruit* (1899); *The Avenging Of Ruthanna* (1900), the story of a wronged heroine. This last work ends on a melodramatic note: 'Cecil saw his wife in Forsyth's arms. He was showering kisses on her upturned face. Ruthanna was avenged'. She went on to write a quantity of romance in the twentieth century. Much of her Victorian fiction was serialised in *Temple Bar** and the *Argosy**. BL 40. *WW*.

KETTLE, R[osa] M[ackenzie] [Mary Rosa Stuart] (d. 1895). Born at Overseale, in Leicestershire (or Ashby de la Zouch, according to another account), she assumed her mother's maiden name 'Mackenzie' as part of her *nom de plume*. From 1863 to 1883, she lived near Poole, in Dorset and the region colours her subsequent numerous novels of action and romance. Her first anonymous effort seems to have been *Max Wentworth* (1839). Kettle's other fiction includes: *The Earl's Cedars* (1860); *The Mistress Of Langdale Hall* (1872); *Over The Furze* (1874), a chronicle of the heathland of Dorset; *The Wreckers* (1876). The last is set in Yorkshire, and has an industrial theme. The *Athenaeum** found it decent but 'dull'. In general, her work tends to be excessively melodramatic and romantic. Kettle was in the habit of using her own verse extensively for epigraphs in her fiction. BL 29. Boase. Wol.

Keynotes, George Egerton (i.e. Mary Chavelita Melville Bright), 1893, 1 vol, John Lane and Elkin Mathews. Egerton's first collection of stories. It

was immensely successful for her, for the publishing house of John Lane*
and for the new woman* school of fiction. Stressing the musical theme,
Egerton followed up with *Discords* (1894), *Symphonies* (1897) and *Fantasies*
(1898). Each of the collections is composed of sketches, or studies of the
modern *femme incomprise* as she undergoes various crises: alcoholism, sex
problems, suicidal anomie. The whole tendency of Egerton's work is away
from narrative, offering instead snapshots of the woman at a significant
'psychological moment' in her life. *In toto*, the volumes offer half answers
to the 'riddle of the *ewig weibliche*'. The original volume had a frontispiece
designed by Beardsley* and a dedication to Knut Hamsun, who is made
to appear in one of *Keynotes*'s stories (several of which have fashionable
Scandinavian settings). The work was seen as instrumental in establishing
a feminist literary voice. As the *Queen* noted: 'not since *The Story Of
An African Farm** was written has any woman delivered herself of so
forcible a book'. The elegantly slim single-volume format of *Keynotes*
contributed to making the work a bestseller and Lane devised a series
modelled on it featuring the cream of the new generation of writers. Among
the subsequent thirty-three *Keynotes* titles were stories by Henry Harland*,
Fiona Macleod*, George Egerton*, Grant Allen*, M. P. Shiel*, Ella D'Arcy*
and Arthur Machen*.

KICKHAM, Charles J[oseph] (1828–82). Kickham was born at Mullina-
hone, Tipperary, where his father was a shopkeeper. He was injured and
handicapped for life by an accident with gunpowder in his youth. An early
enthusiast for the Irish Nationalist cause, Kickham contributed verse and
tales to the *Shamrock*. In the 1840s, he involved himself with the Young Ireland movement. From 1860, he was more dangerously associated with the
Fenians and in 1865, he was arrested and sentenced to fourteen years' penal
servitude for sedition. Although he was freed after four years on compassionate grounds, his health (particularly his sight) was irreparably damaged.
Kickham published a number of novels, including *Rory Of The Hill*, as early
as 1857. His best-known work of fiction was *Sally Cavanagh* (1869), set in
the 1840s in Tipperary. The heroine has to fend off the lecherous attentions
of a landlord while her husband is in America. He returns to find their children dead and Sally a madwoman living in a graveyard. *Knocknagow* (1879)
was also frequently reprinted. An elegiac chronicle of life in a depopulated
Tipperary village, it has been called 'one of the greatest, if not the greatest
of all Irish* novels'. Others find it overlong and over-sentimental. Kickham
also wrote *For The Old Land* (1886), an idyllic story of peasant life in the
1870s. He is a prime example of the closer connection of politics and fiction
in Victorian Ireland than in Victorian England. BL 4.

Kidnapped, R. L. Stevenson, 1886, 1 vol, Cassell. (Serialised in *Young
Folks*, May–July 1886.) Stevenson's most popular romance, set in 1751 in
the aftermath of the Scottish rebellion. David Balfour comes from the Forest
of Ettrick, where his father was a schoolmaster, to stay with his uncle,
Ebenezer of Shaws. Ebenezer is a miser, and covets David's inheritance.
After trying to kill his nephew by luring him on to a broken stairway he
conspires with Captain Hoseason to have David kidnapped on the brig
Covenant. The vessel runs down a rowing boat that carries Alan Breck
Stewart, a Jacobite escaping to France. Alan and David join forces, and are

forced to defend themselves in the ship's round-house against Hoseason's murderous crew. The *Covenant* runs aground off Mull, and the heroes escape on shore. There they make their way south to Edinburgh, to reclaim David's fortune. On the way, they witness the Appin murder in which the 'Red Fox', a King's Factor, is shot and killed. Alan and his Jacobite kinsman, James Stewart of the Glens, are suspected. David and Alan undergo other adventures and perils, and narrowly escape capture by the English soldiery. Eventually, they reach Edinburgh and restore David's rights. Alan escapes to France. The novel works well as an adventure tale, and also as a study in conflicting personality; Alan being romantic and Jacobite, David canny and realistic in his politics. Stevenson devised a sequel, *Catriona* (1893, serialised in *Atalanta**, December 1892–September 1893, as *David Balfour*), which narrates David's 'further adventures' as a 'landed laird', Balfour of Shaws. David falls in love with Catriona Drummond, the daughter of a highland rebel (James More Drummond, a rogue) whom he meets in 'the old black city' of Edinburgh. The hero is at the time engaged on an unsuccessful attempt to bring about the release of James Stewart who is condemned to hang for 'political reasons' rather than any crime. Catriona's father gives false evidence which damns Stewart and otherwise obstructs David's marriage with the long-suffering heroine. The match is finally brought about by the vigorous intervention of Alan Breck. *Catriona* is a ramshackle narrative, but as Stevenson ruefully notes in his dedication, 'it is the fate of sequels to disappoint'. The Appin murder is historical, and the Scottish locations closely observed, as always with Stevenson. There are also some Dutch locations towards the end of the story, following the *émigré* communities of the Scottish Jacobites after 1745.

Kim, Rudyard Kipling, 1901, 1 vol, Macmillan. (Serialised in *McClure's* and *Cassell's* magazines, December 1900–November 1901, with illustrations by H. R. Millar, E. C. Weeks and the author's father, J. L. Kipling.) The hero is Kimball O'Hara, the son of a drunken Irish sergeant in the Mavericks, stationed in India. On his father's death, Kim is left in the care of a native guardian, and in six years grows up so sunburned, and so much a denizen of the bazaar that he passes for Indian. Among his associates is Mahbub Ali, a horse dealer and British secret agent. Kim attaches himself to a Tibetan lama, dedicated to finding a sacred river. Kim accompanies him in his quest and also carries a secret message from Mahbub Ali to the English in Umballa warning of a rising in the North. On the journey, they come across the Mavericks. Kim's amulet is recognised by the Rev. Arthur Bennett and the boy is unwillingly made a sahib again. Assisted by money from the lama, he goes off to St Xavier's boarding school (although he keeps his links with the bazaar). After some initial difficulties, Kim finds he likes school. Having become 'civilised' and mastered the little games of school he is recruited by Mahbub Ali into the 'great game' of espionage. The novel ends excitingly with international intrigue in the Himalayas, and with the lama's at last discovering his sought-for river. The novel allegorises the early events of Kipling's own first six years, spent in Lahore, although genetically Kim is a variant on the popular 'street arab' hero of Victorian fiction.

KIMMINS, Mrs G[race] T[hyrza] ('Sister Grace of the Bermondsey Settlement', née Hannam, 1870–1954). Grace Hannam was born in Lewes, the daughter of a cloth merchant. In 1897, she married Charles W. Kimmins, a local government official, who was later appointed Chief Inspector of Education for London. After her marriage, Kimmins became passionately concerned about the welfare of handicapped children and worked with slum families. In 1894, she formed the Guild of the Brave Poor Things, and set up a settlement at Bermondsey, where she was known as Sister Grace. She continued working in charitable causes throughout her life and was made a Dame of the British Empire in 1950. In 1899, Kimmins published the successful novel with a purpose, *Polly Of Parker's Rents* (1899), illustrated by F. Mabell Pearse. The little heroine is a street arab, who has to fight against the influence of a thieving family and a slum background. BL 1. *WW*.

KING, Alice (1839–94). Born in Cutcombe, Somerset, Alice King was the daughter of a clergyman. Blind from the age of seven, she was educated by her mother, and sufficiently overcame her handicap to learn seven languages by ear and to conduct Bible classes for up to eighty children. King subsequently contributed pieces to the *Argosy** and the *Quiver**, and was the author of eleven novels in all. They include: *Forest Keep* (1861); *Queen Of Herself* (1870); *Hearts Or Coronets* (1876); *A Strange Tangle* (1887). The last is a story of murder and detection set in a Hampshire village. It shows King keeping resolutely up with fashions in fiction. BL 11. Boase. Wol.

KING, Richard Ashe ('Basil', 1839–1932). King was born at Ennis in Co. Clare and educated at Trinity College, Dublin. Ordained into the Church of England in 1862 he was posted to Yorkshire where he was for a while a curate in Bradford. In the early 1880s he gave up his living and came to London, where he contributed to the *Cornhill** and *Pall Mall*. He otherwise supported himself as a lecturer and a private tutor. His fiction, which frequently has Irish* themes and which he wrote as 'Basil', includes: *Love The Debt* (1882); *The Wearing Of The Green* (1884); *A Drawn Game* (1884). *Bell Barry* (1891) is his best-known work. The story of shipboard romance, it features a gallery of racy Irish types. King returned to Ireland for long periods in his later life but died in London where he had been for some years President of the Irish Literary Society. BL 7. *WW*. Wol. RLF.

The King Of The Golden River, John Ruskin, 1850, 1 vol, Smith, Elder. Subtitled 'Or The Black Brothers, A Legend Of Stiria' this fable was written in 1841 for the girl whom Ruskin was later to marry, Effie Gray (then twelve). The story is set in Treasure Valley, a fertile area watered by rivers which gleam gold in the sun. The main characters are three brothers. Schwartz and Hans (nicknamed the 'black brothers') are cruel. Little twelve-year-old Gluck is good and kind. While he is turning the roast, Gluck is visited by a strange little man, with a bugle-like nose. He treats the queer visitor well, but on their return the black brothers try to turn him out of the house. The visitor swears revenge. That night the roof of the brothers' house is torn off (although Gluck is untouched) and a visiting card found from 'South West Wind, Esq.' Thereafter, the valley is windless, rainless and infertile. The black brothers turn to goldsmithing, and much to his dismay melt down Gluck's personal drinking mug. In the furnace, the metal forms into a dwarf, who tells the brothers how to turn the valley's river into gold.

They must drop holy water into the stream. The elder brothers' attempt to do this fails, and they are transmuted to black stone. Gluck passes the test, and the river turns not to literal gold but to new irrigation for Treasure Valley. Ruskin's fantasy* (which effectively rewrites the Cinderella theme) was illustrated by Richard Doyle*.

King Solomon's Mines, H. Rider Haggard, 1885, 1 vol, Cassell. The most successful adventure story of the century. It is narrated by Haggard's recurrent hero, Allan Quatermain* of Natal, big-game hunter and guide to the interior of the dark continent. Quatermain is approached by Sir Henry Curtis and Captain John Good who are looking for Curtis's younger brother, now called George Neville. Neville quarrelled and left his family some years before. Allan has heard rumours of someone by that name associated with King Solomon's diamond mines in the interior. He has a map, taken from a dying Portuguese, which may guide them there. After an arduous trek across the desert and the Breasts of Sheba mountains, the three adventurers discover King Solomon's Road, a magnificent architectural feat remaining from an earlier civilisation. They are captured by the Kukuanas, a people tyrannised by a cruel King, Twala, and his sorcerers. Their servant, Umbopa, eventually discloses himself to be Ignosi, the true King, and the central section of the narrative deals with his successful resumption of his throne. In a great battle, Twala is killed by Sir Harry. Ignosi, to reward his helpers, orders the sinister old witch Gagool to take them to the treasure cave of King Solomon's mine. There, she traps them. But they escape via a secret tunnel. On their return to civilisation they discover George Neville, lying wounded in a native village and finally reach safety, with a handful of the diamonds to enrich themselves.

The King With Two Faces, M. E. Coleridge, 1897, 1 vol, Arnold. An unusual and much-reprinted historical* novel. Set in Sweden in the late eighteenth century, the narrative opens with an exciting scene in which the loyal hero, Count Adolf Ribbing, is about to be murdered by four revolutionary assassins (called merely A, B, C and D). He escapes by showing them a prophecy that says he will one day kill their enemy, King Gustav III. Released, Adolf becomes one of the King's most faithful followers. He and his comrade Axel Fersen save the besieged city of Gothenburg from the Danes by blowing up its main bridge. In the turbulent period of the French Revolution, Adolf is imprisoned in France and later returns to Sweden where a complicated series of events leads to the frustration of his desire to marry his cousin Tala. Adolf later becomes a conspirator against the King. But on his deathbed, the mercurial monarch forgives him his treachery. The end of the novel finds the hero a world-weary exile, having lost everything but mindful 'that he was only twenty-three'. The title refers to Gustav's having two strikingly different left and right profiles. Coleridge's quirky, oblique mode of narration grows on the reader.

KINGSLEY, Charles (1819–75). Leader of the Christian Socialist and muscular* schools of fiction. Kingsley was born at Holne Vicarage in Devonshire, the son of a well-off and well-educated clergyman. Charles spent his early childhood at Clovelly, whose landscape made an enduring impression on him. He was an unusually precocious child, allegedly writing sermons at the age of four. In 1831 he witnessed the Bristol riots while attending Clifton School, an experience which he records as influential. In 1836, the Kingsleys moved to London where Charles's father took up a living at Chelsea. Two years later, Kingsley entered Magdalene College, Cambridge. It was a period of extreme religious upheaval and as an undergraduate he suffered conventional 'doubts'. Otherwise he was a hearty and successful student, winning a first-class degree in classics in 1842. In the same year he was ordained as a curate at Eversley in Hampshire where he was to remain for most of the rest of his life. In 1844 he married Fanny Grenfell, to whom he had been attached for five years. And in 1844 he was also presented to the living at Eversley, by petition of the parishioners. Over the next few years, Kingsley was preoccupied with parochial work and by his growing family. (Four children were born between 1845 and 1858.) In 1848, he published his first major work, the blank-verse drama *The Saint's Tragedy*. The work brought him into contact with the Christian Socialist F. D. Maurice, the most influential intellectual relationship of his career. And in 1848, he became a colleague of Maurice's by accepting the professorship of English literature at Queen's College, London. This period (1848) was the highpoint of Chartist agitation in England, and Kingsley entered on an actively political phase of his development, which lasted until 1852. He wrote various pamphlets under the pseudonym 'Parson Lot' and in 1848 began publishing a social problem* novel in the pages of *Fraser's Magazine** entitled *Yeast**. The story proved controversial and Kingsley suffered a severe breakdown, resigned his academic appointment and retired to Ilfracombe to recuperate. During this period he was associated with J. A. Froude*, whose recently published *The Nemesis Of Faith** was causing a sensation. Over the winter 1849–50, Kingsley completed *Alton Locke**, the story of a radical working-class poet. Urged by Carlyle, Chapman and Hall* accepted the work. At this date, Kingsley was regarded as a politically dangerous figure and in 1851, after a particularly trenchant sermon, the Bishop of London forbade him from preaching in the capital. Thereafter, Kingsley's activism effectively ceased. His next novel, *Hypatia** (1853), was safely historical*. Maurice had meanwhile been ousted from King's College, London and Fanny Kingsley suffered a physical breakdown following a miscarriage. Spending the winter 1853–54 in Torquay, Kingsley became fascinated by marine biology and published *Glaucus, Or The Wonders Of The Shore* in 1855. The Crimean War inspired his bloodthirsty romance of Drake's age, *Westward Ho!** (1855). *Two Years Ago** (1857) recalls the stirring events of 1854 in fictional form. By now Kingsley was an establishment figure. In 1859 he was appointed one of the Queen's chaplains and in 1860 was made professor of modern history at Cambridge. (His domestic base remained Eversley, however.) He earned a genuine reputation as a historian. In 1864, Kingsley lost much public respect by his religious controversy with J. H. Newman* in which the Catholic came off best and which inspired the *Apologia Pro Vita Sua*. At this period, Kingsley produced what has remained his most popular book, the fantasy *The Water-Babies** (1863). By now his health was poor and much of his life was taken up in convalescence and recuperative travel. But he continued to work for his favourite social causes (such as sanitation, public education) and his last novel, the extravagantly heroic *Hereward The Wake**, appeared in 1865. In 1869, with his daughter Rose, he made a trip to the West Indies, having resigned his Cambridge chair earlier in the year. *At Last, A Christmas In The West Indies* was duly published in 1871. In 1873, Kingsley was appointed a canon at Westminster and in the following year he undertook a tour of North America. During the trip, his health finally gave way. He died of pneumonia at Eversley in early 1875. BL 10. *DNB*. RM. *NCBEL*. Wol. Sad.

KINGSLEY, Henry (1830–76). The black sheep of the distinguished and otherwise highly respectable family of whom the most famous author was Henry's elder brother, Charles. A niece, 'Lucas Malet' (i.e. Mary St Leger Harrison*), also wrote novels. Born in the village of Barnack in Northamptonshire, where his father was vicar, Kingsley was brought up and educated at London. He seems not to have had instilled in him the passionate love of the countryside so evident in Charles. From King's College, London, he proceeded to Worcester College, Oxford. At university he was notably hearty and lived a fast college life. He inevitably ran into debt and left without a degree, a grave disappointment to his family. In 1853, Henry Kingsley left for the Australian goldfields with some fellow students. He remained there enduring considerable hardship and danger for five years. He did not, however, make his fortune. His Australian experiences are commemorated in his first published novel, *The Recollections Of Geoffrey Hamlyn** (1859) whose hero migrates from Devon to the sheep pastures of New South Wales, in constant conflict with his villainous foe George Hawker. On returning to England and having atoned by hard work, Kingsley was reconciled with his family. Charles prevailed on his friend and publisher, Macmillan*, to take *Geoffrey Hamlyn* which was duly a terrific hit with the reading public. In 1864, Henry married a cousin and the couple went to live at Wargrave near Henley. By the early 1860s Kingsley was supporting himself comfortably by writing. *Ravenshoe** (1862) was another success. It follows its hero to the Crimea, where he rides in the Charge of the Light Brigade. There is much confusion in the plot to do with changelings and frustrated inheritance. Already Kingsley's preference for cluttered, incoherent designs was pronounced and it was to become a vice in his later stories. *Austin Elliot* (1863) is a somewhat thinner work, which follows the consequences of a duel on a family's fortunes between 1789 and 1845. As usual with Kingsley, the geographical locations of the narrative are diverse, starting at Christ Church, Oxford, and ending after wide-ranging excursions in Argyllshire, Scotland. *The Hillyars And The Burtons* (1865) is the story of two families, one high- the other low-born. *Silcote Of Silcotes* (1867) is another tangled chronicle of a country family as is *Stretton* (1869). *Leighton Court* (1866) has fox-hunting, gambling, crimes of passion and a 'dead but not dead' marriage plot, all set in the 1850s. *Mademoiselle Mathilde* (1868) is a historical* novel, dealing with the French Revolution. Kingsley continued to be improvident, and was dogged by bad luck (notably his wife's chronic ill health). Nor was his manner of life steady enough for any solid literary achievement. In 1869, he went to Edinburgh to edit a Free Church newspaper. The venture was a failure. He had more luck in 1870 when he travelled to the Franco-Prussian war, to write dispatches for the *Daily Review*. Kingsley witnessed the battle of Sedan, and wrote some genuinely distinguished war correspondence. He also turned out a Hentyesque* story on the war, *Valentin, A French Boy's Story Of Sedan* (1872). But as a novelist, Kingsley no longer pleased the public. The 1870s found him desperate, and reduced to scrounging from his famous brother Charles. In extremity, he produced some very poor novels such as *The Harveys* (1872), *Oakshott Castle* (1873) and the unreadable *The Grange Garden* (1876). In 1873, a windfall legacy had supplied Kingsley with enough money to make his remaining months of life comfortable. He developed cancer of the tongue, and retired to Cuckfield, Sussex, to die A number of legends have clustered round Henry, whose life evidently had its share of dissipations. He may well have been homosexual and was almost certainly alcoholic. His life and work trace the pathological edge of the muscular* school, where its cult of virility merges into narcissistic depravity. At its best, his fiction has a picaresque jollity, and devil-may-care verve. BL 20. *DNB*. RM. *NCBEL*. Wol. Sad. RLF.

KINGSTON, W[illiam] H[enry] G[iles] (1814–80). One of the two or three greatest authors for boys in Victorian literature. Kingston was born in London, the son of a prosperous merchant and the grandson of a judge, Sir Giles Rooke. His father's business was based in Portugal and the author as a boy spent some years in Oporto. He left for England around his tenth birthday to continue his education in London. Some of the formative years of his boyhood were spent at the house of his Rooke relatives (a nautical family) by the Solent. Kingston's first desire at the age of nineteen was to enter the navy, but he was now considered too old for that career. Instead he joined his father in business at Oporto. His commitment to this line of work was enforced by the death of his father in 1844. In the 1840s, Kingston became increasingly interested in emigration and wrote *The Emigrant Voyager's Manual* in 1850. His first bestselling book for boys, the popular *Peter The Whaler**, came out the next year. In 1853, Kingston married and spent several months travelling the world on his honeymoon, writing the episode up as *Western Wanderings* (1855). From the mid-1850s onward, Kingston produced well over 100 books of adventurous tales for young readers, many with a nautical* flavour. They include: *Salt Water* (1857); *The Cruise Of The Frolic* (1860); *The Fire Ships* (1861); *Ben Burton* (1871); *The Three Midshipmen* (1873); *The Three Lieutenants* (1874); *The Three Admirals* (1877); *The Two Supercargoes* (1877). Kingston also wrote up tales of actual heroism and adventure (including a life of Captain Cook, 1871) and popular educational books for young people such as: *The Boy's Own Book Of Boats* (1860). And he was one of the translators and popularisers of Jules Verne for English readers. As an editor and proprietor, Kingston conducted *Kingston's Magazine For Boys* (1859–63) and was a founder contributor to the *Boy's Own Paper** in 1879. Some months before his death, he helped launch *Union Jack**, a magazine subsequently taken over by G. A. Henty*. Knowing that he was dying, Kingston as his last literary act wrote a gallant open letter to his readers which ended: 'Dear Boys, I ask you to give your hearts to Christ, and earnestly pray that all of you may meet me in heaven.' BL 167. *DNB*. *NCBEL*. Wol. RLF.

KIPLING, [Joseph] Rudyard (1865–1936). The laureate of Empire and the white man's burden. Kipling's family had Yorkshire origins. His father, John Lockwood Kipling, was an artist and pottery designer. He became engaged to the author's mother (whom he met in a factory) alongside the Rudyard reservoir, at Stoke-on-Trent. In 1865, the Kiplings left for India, where John took up a position as principal at the new art school in Bombay. Rudyard was born there, and grew up steeped in Indian life until his sixth year when (as was usual with the children of Anglo-Indians) he was shipped back to England with his sister. He was boarded at Southsea with an unpleasant family. In 1878, he was sent to the United Services College in Devon, a new minor public school, as a preparation for an army career. The experience inspired the unusually realistic story sequence, *Stalky And Co.* (1899), a work which studiously debunks the mythology of the public school cult. Kipling began writing seriously while at school, and when he left his father obtained him a post on the *Lahore Civil And Military Gazette* in 1882. He soon began publishing verse and short stories. *Plain Tales From The Hills* appeared in 1888, as did the story of Indian adventure, *Soldiers Three*. The children's work, *Wee Willie Winkie*, came out in 1889. In the same year, Kipling returned to England. The ambitious novel, *The Light That Failed** appeared in 1891. The story of a blinded war artist, it is an ambitious experiment in an end-of-century decadent* style of fiction that in the event did not suit Kipling. In 1892, he married the American Carrie Balestier. Their honeymoon trip round the world was cut short when the bank holding Kipling's savings failed. The couple returned to Vermont, where Kipling wrote the *Jungle Books** (1894–95). They were immensely successful. *Captains Courageous** (1897) is his most American novel and *Kim** (1901) his most Indian. In 1896, the Kiplings returned to England. Three years later, their daughter Josephine died, an event which prostrated her parents. In 1902, Kipling moved to Sussex. In the twentieth century, he became a great man of letters, though always better known for his verse than his fiction. BL 20. *DNB*. RM. *NCBEL*. Wol.

KIRBY, William (1817–1906). Kirby was born at Kingston upon Hull, and emigrated to the USA with his family in 1832. A lingering sentiment of Britishness led him in 1839 to move to Canada, where he settled in the border town of Niagara and where he was employed as a journalist and a customs officer, 1871–95. Kirby also wrote poems and pamphlets, most with a strong imperialist theme. His major work, however, is the historical* romance, *The Golden Dog* (1877, revised 1896). The product of years of historical research, this novel attacks the French neglect of Canada and its justified seizure by the British in 1759–60. Apart from its political bias, the work has vivid scenes of pioneer days. BL 2. Boase.

KNOWLES, J[ames] Sheridan (1784–1862). Knowles was born in Cork, the son of the lexicographer James Knowles (a first cousin of the dramatist Richard Brinsley Sheridan). Knowles was brought to London at the age of nine, and later studied medicine in Scotland. He made a name for himself writing romantic plays for the London stage, of which the best known (e.g. *The Hunchback*) were produced in the 1830s and he was panegyrised by Bulwer-Lytton*. In the early 1840s, he underwent a religious conversion, and became a baptist. He acquired a reputation as a preacher, and relatively late in life turned out two novels: *George Lovell* (1846), the story of the adventures of a jeweller's son, and *Fortescue* (1847), a fashionable novel dedicated to his 'highly respected relative', Caroline Norton*. They are much inferior to his plays and were found too 'earnest' in their tone by reviewers. BL 2. *DNB. NCBEL.* RM. Wol. RLF.

KNOX, Captain Charles [H.] (d. 1855). Knox joined the army in 1826 as an ensign. He made captain in 1836 and retired on half pay in 1838. In his retirement he served as a lieutenant-colonel in the Royal Glamorgan Militia, and wrote books on a number of topics including a history of the polka, and a quantity of military history. His fiction includes the fashionable novels: *Hardness* (1841); *Softness* (1841); *Harry Mowbray* (1843). Of the first two, the *Athenaeum** jested: 'are *Fatness* and *Leanness* to follow?' BL 5. Boase. Wol.

L

La Vendée, Anthony Trollope, 1850, 3 vols, Colburn. Having failed with two Irish* novels, Trollope tried historical* romance for his third. Famously, he proved the wisdom of the publisher who warned him, 'Your historical novel is not worth a damn!'. For this work, Trollope received only the £20 which Colburn* injudiciously advanced him. The subject, though historical, was topical, given the recent French Revolution of 1848. The narrative follows the fortunes of the Larochejaquelin family, in the Vendéan counter revolution of 1793. A number of historical figures, such as Robespierre (who brutally represses the revolt), are introduced. And there is the obligatory romantic complication between young Henri Larochejaquelin and his cousin Marie de Lescure. It ends tragically with Henri's death, as Commander in Chief of the Vendéan forces. *La Vendée* is the least reprinted and probably the least read work in Trollope's corpus. It is also his only historical novel.

The Ladies Lindores, Margaret Oliphant, 1883, 3 vols, Blackwood. (Serialised in *Blackwood's Magazine*, May 1882–May 1883.) This novel, with its sequel *Lady Car* (1889), is one of the more interesting and darker of Oliphant's later works. The Lindores family receive an unexpected inheritance and peerage which change the hitherto middle-class life they have led. Lady Car[oline], the daughter, is persuaded by her dictatorial father to marry a rich brute, Pat Torrance. The central part of the narrative depicts her six years of wretched marriage. Torrance eventually falls over a cliff riding and Edith Lindores' lover, the young laird John Erskine, is suspected of murder. Finally the culprit is revealed to be Car's brother, Lord Rintoul. A year after being widowed (and in defiance of her father) the heroine marries her early lover, Edward Beaufort. In the subsequent *Lady Car* her story is continued. Happiness still eludes her. Edward loses his literary ambition and shamelessly sponges off his rich wife. The son of the first marriage grows up the image of his odious father and Lady Car dies a wretched woman. Oliphant evidently poured many of the disappointments of her own life into this work.

Lady Anna, Anthony Trollope, 1874, 2 vols, Chapman and Hall. (Serialised in the *Fortnightly Review**, April 1873–April 1874.) Trollope gives a succinct synopsis in his *Autobiography*: 'A young girl, who is really a lady of high rank and great wealth, though in her youth she enjoyed none of the privileges of wealth and rank, marries a tailor who had been good to her, and whom she had loved when she was poor and neglected.' The core of the narrative is Lady Anna's long quarrel with her mother over keeping her pledge to the aforesaid journeyman tailor, Daniel Thwaite. After an unsuccessful attempt on his life by the Countess, Daniel and Lady Anna emigrate to a new life in Australia.

Lady Audley's Secret, Mary E. Braddon, 1862, 3 vols, Tinsley. (Serialised partially in *Robin Goodfellow**, July–September 1861; wholly serialised in the *Sixpenny Magazine*, January–December 1862 and rerun in the *London Journal**, March–August 1863.) The most sensationally successful of all sensation* novels. The heroine is originally a beautiful governess, when she catches the eye of rich old Sir Michael Audley of Audley Court in Essex. He marries and ennobles her. But there is a secret in Lucy Graham's past. Earlier in life, she had married George Talboys, a dragoon. He absconded to the Australian goldfields. Three years later, and a reformed character, George arrives back with £20,000 to reclaim his wife ('Helen') and baby. He is told they are dead, but does not believe it. He tracks her down as the bigamous Lady Audley. She lures him to a deserted spot, and pushes him down a well. She thinks she has murdered him but he survives with only a wounded arm. For obscure reasons George secretly takes himself off to America. His friend, Sir Michael's barrister nephew Robert, turns sleuth to discover the truth about his suspicious aunt. Handwriting connects her with the Helen Maldon who had married Talboys. Increasingly desperate, she tries to burn down the inn where Robert is staying. He survives to denounce her. Lady Audley finally goes (or pretends to go) mad, and dies in Belgium. 'Audley Court is shut up – a curtain hangs before the pre-Raphaelite portrait.' The work has one of the accidental bigamy* plots fashionable in the early 1860s.

Lady Pokingham, Or They All Do It, Anon, 1880. (Serialised in the *Pearl*, 1879–80.) A classic of Victorian pornographic fiction. The heroine, Beatrice Pokingham, experiences the usual sexual initiation at her school, after which with a friend, Alice Marchmont, she goes to live with a Roman Catholic in London. There she joins the 'Paphian Circle', devoted to flagellation and orgy. Beatrice marries the aged rake, Lord Crim-Con (a pederast by preference). He dies mid-orgy, and as a widow she embarks on a strenuous career of debauchery. Sick with galloping consumption, she is ordered to Madeira for her health and seduces the doctor on her deathbed. Four more volumes of Pokingham adventures were extracted from the pages of the *Pearl*.

LANDON, Laetitia Elizabeth ('L. E. L.', 1802–38). The most celebrated poetess of the 1820s and 1830s. Laetitia Landon was born in Chelsea, into an upper-class family ruined by the South Sea Bubble. Her father worked as an army agent, in Pall Mall. She was educated at home, and at school in Chelsea. Precocious, she published her first poem in 1820 and was quickly noticed by William Jerdan, of the *Literary Gazette*, who managed her early career. For the next twenty years, L. E. L. enjoyed an almost

Byronic degree of fame with the English public. Like Byron, too, her private life was popularly imagined to be scandalous. Among others, she had a notorious liaison with William Maginn*, the dissolute editor of *Fraser's Magazine*. She earned large sums with her poetry, but never secured financial independence. In 1838, she contracted an injudicious marriage to George Maclean, the governor of Cape Coast Castle, a man rumoured to have a living wife in Africa. Three months after the marriage, L. E. L. was found dead at the castle, a vial of prussic acid by her side. The circumstances of her death were universally considered suspicious. By virtue of her last publications, L. E. L. is a Victorian novelist, by date, if not in spirit. A year before her death, the author published her finest novel, the historical* *Ethel Churchill* (1837). Set in the early Hanoverian era, it is a sentimental story of love in high places, showing off the author's elegant turn of phrase. Historical characters are introduced. *Lady Anne Granard* was published posthumously, in 1842. BL 4. *DNB*. RM. *NCBEL*. Wol. Sad.

John Lane (1887–). Publisher. John Lane (1854–1925) was born in West Putford, Devon, to yeoman-class parents. After leaving school, he went to work as a clerk in the Railway Clearing House, in 1869. By 1887, he had resolved to make himself a publisher and set up in premises in Vigo Street, Piccadilly, with Elkin Mathews, an antiquarian bookseller from Exeter. The partners named their firm Bodley Head, after the Devon hero, Sir Thomas Bodley. The Bodley Head made an immediate name for itself as a producer of fine books. It also attracted a nucleus of the most advanced writers of the 1890s; among them, John Davidson*, Richard Le Gallienne*, Ernest Dowson* and Oscar Wilde*. The house gained fame with its magazine the *Yellow Book**, published from April 1894 to 1897 and its *Keynotes** series of one-volume novels and short stories, featuring such literary fashionables as George Egerton*, Ella D'Arcy*, Henry Harland* and Arthur Machen*. After Wilde's disgrace in 1895, the tone of Bodley Head's literary offerings became more cautious. But the firm survived this crisis and many others to survive to the present day. (JL) *DNB*.

LANG, Andrew ('A. Huge Longway', 1844–1912). Noted folklorist and versatile man of letters. Lang was born into an old Border family at Selkirk where his father was the sheriff-clerk. In his early childhood, he was steeped in Scottish balladry and folk culture, and the rest of his career may be seen as growing out of this formative experience. At ten, Lang was sent to the Edinburgh Academy and progressed from there to the University of St Andrews, an institution for which he retained a lifelong fondness. He finished his education at Oxford, where he eventually became a don and fellow of Merton in 1868. On vacation in France (where he had gone to improve his weak lungs) he met and formed a friendship with Robert Louis Stevenson* in 1874. Lang was, thereafter, to be an advocate for the simple historical* romance against the modernist and realist fiction of Henry James and Thomas Hardy*, which he detested. In 1875, he married and left his comfortable berth at Oxford for a career in London journalism and letters. He wrote leaders for the *Daily News*, reviewed widely and translated Homer. Lang's publications are vast in number. His most distinguished contributions are in the field of folklore and anthropology. As well as collecting, he wrote fairy stories such as: *The Princess Nobody* (1884) and *The Gold Of Fairmilee*

(1888). He also wrote some interesting novels for the juvenile and adult reader. *Much Darker Days* (1884), written under the pseudonym 'A. Huge Longway', is a sensational* Christmas* book. *The Mark Of Cain* (1886) is a contemporary 'shilling shocker' of crime and detection, published by Arrowsmith* and *In The Wrong Paradise* (1886) is a series of romantic tales dedicated to H. Rider Haggard*. *A Monk Of Fife* (1895) is told by a Scottish former archer, Norman Leslie, now a Benedictine monk at Dunfermline, who tried to rescue Joan of Arc from her martyrdom in the French Wars. The work is anti-imperialist in tone and ends with a 'curse on the cruel English and the coward French'. It is presented as a chronicle (translated from the original French) and the first edition was illustrated with medieval-looking capitals and drawings by Selwyn Image. With Rider Haggard, Lang wrote the popular *The World's Desire** (1890), the imagined story of Odysseus's last voyage, to ancient Egypt. And with A. E. W. Mason*, Lang wrote a lively story of the Jacobite plotting against George I, *Parson Kelly* (1900). With Paul Sylvester, Lang put out a collection of tales from the French entitled *The Dead Leman* (1889). BL 6. *DNB*. RM. *NCBEL*.

LANG, John ('The Mofussilite', 1817?–64). The first Australian author to publish works of fiction. Lang was born at Paramatta in New South Wales. He went to college in Sydney, finishing his studies in Cambridge, England, in 1838. He subsequently qualified as a barrister, and returned to Sydney in 1841. A year later, Lang left for India where he practised law and journalism, eventually dying there. Lang wrote stories and essays for *Household Words** in the 1850s. His full-length fiction includes: *Too Clever By Half* (1853), his most popular work, obscurely pseudonymised as 'by the Mofussilite' (i.e. Bengali for 'provincial', or 'yokel'); *Too Much Alike* (1854); *The Forger's Wife* (1855), an 'Australian Tale'. The work of Lang's which lasted best is probably *The Wetherbys* (1853). Subtitled 'A Few Chapters Of Indian Experience', it contains an interesting description of the country in the 1840s, before the Mutiny. A dramatist, Lang collaborated with Tom Taylor on a number of plays. BL 10. Boase. Wol.

LANGBRIDGE, [Rev.] Frederick (1849–1922). Langbridge was born in Birmingham, apparently into a family of Irish origin. He went to school in the city and later graduated from Merton College, Oxford. A scholar of distinction, Langbridge was awarded a D Litt. by Trinity College, Dublin, in 1907. After graduation, he was ordained around 1878, when he also married and took up a post as Rector at St John's, Limerick. A writing clergyman, Langbridge published a number of volumes of verse, beginning with *Gaslight And Stars* (1880). He also wrote the novels: *Rider's Leap* (1887), an adventure story with scenes set in the Zulu War; *Miss Honoria* (1893), a sentimental and pathetic Irish* story of a gentlewoman who survives disappointment in love to become Lady Bountiful to a village; *The Dreams Of Dania* (1897), which chronicles the romantic upsets of what the *Athenaeum** called 'an exceedingly foolish young woman'. Langbridge specialised in such sweet young women betrayed by cads. He also turned out tract fiction for the RTS*. His daughter, Rosamond (b. 1880), wrote a number of novels in the twentieth century. BL 10. *WW*.

The Last Chronicle Of Barset, Anthony Trollope, 1867, 2 vols, Smith, Elder. (Serialised in 6d. weekly parts, December 1866–July 1867, with illustrations by George H. Thomas*.) Trollope's magnificent conclusion to his Barsetshire* saga, and his finest study of agonised conscience. The author's first intention was to give the work the sensational* title, 'The Story Of A Cheque For Twenty Pounds And Of The Mischief Which It Did'. Although cumbersome, this discarded title sums up the main story-line fairly enough. Josiah Crawley, the cross-grained perpetual curate of Hogglestock, is suspected of having stolen a cheque. So confused is Crawley, that he cannot clearly remember how he came into possession of the money order, and he is arraigned before Barchester Assizes on suspicion of having stolen it from the pocket-book of Lord Lufton's agent, Mr Soames. The Bishop's wife, Mrs Proudie, leads the persecution of Crawley and her husband is induced to set up an ecclesiastical commission to inquire into the matter. Mrs Proudie is finally put in her place, however, and suddenly dies of an unsuspected heart complaint. (In a famous anecdote, Trollope claims he did it because he heard a couple of fellow clubmen complaining about what a bore the woman had become.) Crawley, who has been supported by his noble wife Mary and his eldest daughter Grace, is finally exonerated. Obstacles preventing Grace's marriage to the eligible Major Henry Grantly are overcome. Part of the novel's action moves to London where more is given of the later life of Lily Dale, her false lover Adolphus Crosbie and her true lover Johnny Eames. (See *The Small House At Allington**, 1864.)

The Last Of The Barons, E. G. E. L. Bulwer-Lytton, 1843, 3 vols, Saunders and Otley. The story is set in the years 1467–71, but clearly reflects on the politically troubled 1840s in which the author was living. The action begins, Scott-fashion, with an archery contest. This brings together (as victors) two foster brothers, Nicholas Alwyn and Marmaduke Nevile. They have taken different paths in life. Alwyn has seen his future in trade, and is a goldsmith. Marmaduke, a kinsman of the kingmaking Earl of Warwick, seeks preferment at Court. Marmaduke saves a young girl from a mob who is revealed to be Sibyll Warner, the daughter of an eccentric alchemist and inventor, thought by the ignorant masses to be a wizard. Sibyll nurses Marmaduke back to health, after a band of Lancastrian brigands have set on him. Recovered he attaches himself to Warwick. The main political plot of the novel concerns the power struggle between Warwick and Edward IV. The lecherous King attempts to ravish the Earl's daughter, Anne, and war breaks out. Warwick subsequently appoints Henry VI to the throne but the House of York restores Edward. All the main characters are caught up in the affairs of state. Sibyll and her father die. Marmaduke is imprisoned. Alwyn thrives under the new regime. The ending of the novel is enigmatic, reflecting Bulwer-Lytton's own political uncertainties at the period. Historically, the most interesting feature is the novel's sympathetic portrait of Richard of Gloucester, Shakespeare's villain.

LATEY, John (1842–1902). Latey was born in London, where his father, John Lash Latey, was from 1858 to 1890 editor of the *Illustrated London News**. The family had roots in Devon and was strongly Radical in its politics. Young John Latey was educated at Barnstaple and the Working Men's College in London. In 1861, he began a successful career in journalism. He himself became assistant editor on the *ILN* and later editor in chief of the *Sketch* and the *Penny Illustrated Paper*. He also collaborated with Captain

Mayne Reid* on the *Boy's Illustrated News*. In later life he founded the Press Club. Latey translated Dumas and himself wrote a number of historical* romances and stories of London life, including: *Love Clouds* (1884), 'a story of love and revenge'; and *The River Of Life* (1886), 'A London Story'. Latey was, as he records, 'a steadfast advocate of all manly exercises calculated to promote a sound mind in a sound body'. BL 2. *DNB*.

Launcelot Widge, Charles Hooton, 1849, 3 vols, Newby. (Serialised in *Ainsworth's Magazine**, January–December 1847). The luckless Hooton's last novel. Like other works published in *Ainsworth's Magazine* it may have been tidied up by some hired hack. The work opens conventionally. The villain, Mrs Thornton, spirits away the new-born child of her sister, so she may inherit the family estate. The child is disposed of in the Adelphi vaults, under the Strand. (Hooton is strong on London scenes.) But by providence and the aid of a mysterious astrologer, Saul le Blanc, he survives to become an artist. Later he recovers his title and estate. The main interest centres on the hero, a vain would-be artist who has pretensions to paint in the grand manner. His career and mishaps in the lower bohemian world of Bloomsbury have some documentary interest.

Lavengro, George Borrow, 1851, 3 vols, Murray. Subtitled 'The Scholar, The Gypsy, The Priest', *Lavengro* is the thinly veiled and somewhat romanticised autobiography of a man whose life is stranger than fiction. The hero's father is an army officer during the Napoleonic Wars period, and the family follows him to garrisons all over the British Isles. At the age of six, the hero reads *Robinson Crusoe* and develops a strong sense of himself as outsider. At the same period, he meets a band of gypsies, and because of his skill with snakes (one of which he has in his pocket) is named 'Sapengro'. He swears brotherhood with a gypsy boy, Jasper Petulengro. Later in Ireland, he meets Jasper again who is now a 'Romany Kral', or king. The hero, on account of his mastery of the Rom language, is renamed 'Lavengro'. But he falls foul of an old witch, Herne. In the civilised world, Lavengro goes into a solicitor's office, but his facility with words and language draws him into the realm of letters. He is exploited by publishers (who want him to turn out gothic* pot-boilers). Eventually, Lavengro becomes a tinker. On the road, Herne tries to poison him. Recovered, he takes up with a Welsh preacher, Peter Williams. From Petulengro, he learns that Herne has finally hanged herself. The two heroes are obliged to fight, for honour's sake (Herne being Jasper's kinswoman) and a little blood is harmlessly drawn. More seriously, Lavengro defeats a gypsy champion, the Flaming Tinman. The end of the novel finds him united with the beautiful Isopel Berners. The story is extraordinarily rich in incident and furnished a sequel, *The Romany Rye**.

LAWLESS, the Hon. Emily (1845–1913). Lawless was born in Co. Kildare, a daughter of the third Baron Cloncurry. The family was of wealthy Anglo-Irish extraction. But it was famously tragic: Emily's father and two of her sisters committed suicide. Privately educated, Emily Lawless grew up gifted and somewhat eccentric. She never married, and spent most of her life at her family home in Ireland, in whose history she was steeped. In *Who's Who* she listed her recreations as 'dredging, mothing, gardening, geologising'. Her novels are updated versions of the Banim* brothers' studies of 'Irish

Peasantry' and occasional historical* romance. Her first novel was the atypical and socially panoramic *A Chelsea Householder* (1882). Its successor *Hurrish* (1886), dedicated to Mrs Oliphant*, was more successful. It is a story of the 1870s in the 'wildest west' of Co. Clare. In the context of Home Rule agitation of the 1880s, it was topical although Lawless's loyalist views were controversial. *Major Lawrence, F.L.S.* (1887), the story of an English officer returned from India and *Plain Frances Mowbray* (1889), a novel set in Venice, are simpler studies of character which unkind reviewers found dull. *With Essex In Ireland* (1890) is an oddity. Originally passed off as a genuine historical document, it is the account by a private secretary, Henry Harvey (edited by John Oliver Maddox, MA), of Essex's 1599 expedition. The work is in the documentary style of the 'spurious antique' novel, popularised by Anne Manning*. *Grania* (1892), 'The Story Of An [Aran] Island' was Lawless's most successful novel. It was read and enthused over by Gladstone and brought her to the notice of leading English critics and literati (such as Mrs Humphry Ward*, who became a close friend). Among Lawless's subsequent novels are: *Maelcho* (1894), a story of the bloody Desmond rebellion of 1579, centred on a 'noble savage'; *Traits And Confidences* (1898); *The Race Of Castlebar* (1913) a light-hearted work about a threatened French invasion in the late eighteenth century, on which the author collaborated with Shan F. Bullock*. Lawless died, leaving the other writer to write the last chapter by himself. She also wrote poetry, and a biography of Maria Edgeworth. Lawless spent her last years in Surrey, in poor mental and physical health. BL 10. *WW. NCBEL.* Wol.

LAWRENCE, G[eorge] A[lfred] (1827–76). The leading exponent of the muscular* novel. Lawrence was born at Braxted, Essex, the son of a clergyman. From 1831, his father's living was at Sandhurst in Kent. George, the eldest son of the family, was sent to Rugby in 1841, then under the revolutionary regime of Dr Arnold. He was profoundly affected by the new public school ethos as was the other (more pious) novelist, Thomas Hughes*. *Guy Livingstone* opens with a rather more violent picture of Rugby life than Tom Brown* experiences. (The novels appeared in the same year, 1857, and Lawrence may have intended to contradict Thomas Hughes's namby-pambyism.) Lawrence went to Oxford, where he led a fast and hearty undergraduate existence. He graduated in 1850, entered law and was called to the Bar in 1852. Thereafter, he drifted into writing for which he had a natural and untutored aptitude. The runaway success of *Guy Livingstone* in 1857 led to a career of full-time fiction writing. (His subsequent novels all appeared as 'by the author of *Guy Livingstone*'.) None of his later works was as popular, although all earned handsomely for their author. *Barren Honour* (1862) is another study of magnificently chivalrous self-destruction demonstrated in the person of Sir Alan Wyverne, another 'thoroughbred all through'. He dies in a luridly described shipwreck, holding the picture of the woman he loves to his lips, to the end an image of masculine power 'if a very imperfect Christian'. *Maurice Dering* (1864) replays the theme, with the difference that Maurice is not a squire (like Alan) but a soldier (like Guy). Lawrence's early work, up to 1862, was put out by Parker* and *Fraser's Magazine*, the favoured publishing combination of the muscular novelists. His middle-period work was taken over by the semi-respectable

Tinsley*. Finally, after 1869, Lawrence was a Chapman and Hall* author (Fred Chapman, who took over in the mid-1860s, had a fondness for manly fiction). An officer in the militia, Lawrence affected the title 'Major' in social life and a military brusqueness in his literary manner. In the American Civil War, he quixotically offered his services to the South. Deported, he wrote the interesting volume of reportage, *Border And Bastille* (1863). An improvident author, Lawrence would use his normal £1,000-per-novel payment from Tinsley to stake gambling jaunts on the Continent. His nine novels after *Guy Livingstone* show no progress in art. His first, and best-known work, stands as the most brutal of the muscular novels and earned the tribute of a hilarious Bret Harte parody, *Guy Heavystone*. Lawrence's *Sword And Gown* (1859), a tale of bigamy* and the Crimea (climaxing inevitably on the Charge of the Light Brigade), remains enjoyable, as does *Brakespeare* (1868), the story of a 'free lance' in the Hundred Years War, with a good chapter on the Battle of Poitiers. *Breaking A Butterfly* (1869), contains more pathos than the author's previous work. *Hagarene* (1874), the highly coloured portrait of an unscrupulous adventuress, shows the old Lawrence trying to learn new tricks, without much success. The *Athenaeum** review was devastating, and declared: 'that an author who has so little idea of how to write a novel should have made a name of whatever sort speaks ill for the discernment of his contemporaries'. Lawrence died in Edinburgh, impoverished and ruined in health. BL 10. *DNB*. RM. *NCBEL*. Wol.

LAWSON, Henry [Hertzberg] (1867–1922). Lawson was the son of a Norwegian seaman, Peter Larsen, who left his ship to dig for gold in Australia. He married Louisa Albury in 1866, and Henry Lawson was born in a tent at the Grenfell goldfield. A lifelong victim of deafness, he attended the local Catholic school, leaving at thirteen. Lawson provides vivid descriptions of his early childhood in *A Fragment Of Autobiography* (written in 1904 and published intermittently after 1908). His home life, he recalls, was 'miserably unhappy'. He read as a boy Dickens*, Marryat* and Bracebridge Hemyng's* 'Jack Harkaway*' stories. His father died prematurely of heart disease in 1888. The dominant intellectual influence in his life was not the Catholic Church, but his energetic and politically radical mother, Louisa, a woman reported to have had 'a strong prejudice against men in general'. Lawson's adult life was extraordinarily restless. He had any number of menial and manual jobs in Australia and New Zealand. In 1887, he published his popular poem *The Song Of The Republic* (at this period he seems to have been working as a housepainter). He wrote other successful ballads, for which there was a larger Australian than British market. He married in 1896 and in 1900 came to England with his wife and two children to boost his literary career. But the country did not suit him. London bohemianism led him to dissipation. The fact that he was pro-Boer and Radical in his politics did not endear him to his English hosts and he returned to Australia in 1902, claiming to have 'grown old in three years'. His marriage subsequently broke up and the remainder of his life was pathetically drunken and unproductive. In fiction, Lawson's reputation rests on some powerfully realistic short stories of bush-ranging life, collected as: *While The Billy Boils* (1896); *The Country I Come From* (1901); *On The Track* (1901). Three volumes of his short stories, were published in 1964. BL 13. *WW*. RM.

LEE, Edgar (1851–1908). Born in Pembrokeshire, Lee was educated at the Pembroke Grammar School and later at the London Institute. He subsequently took up a career in journalism, and became moderately famous as 'Rambler' in the *Sunday Times*, 1876–77. Lee was acting editor of *St Stephen's Review* (1883–90) and coeditor, with Florence Marryat*, of *Once A Week** (1884–87; this must be different from Bradbury and Evans's* journal, which ceased publication in 1880). In the 1890s, Lee was editor of the *Court Circular*. His fiction (mainly 'shilling shockers' for Arrowsmith*) includes *Pharaoh's Daughter* (1887), 'A Story Of The Ages'; *Maria And I* (1890). BL 5. *WW*. Wol.

LEE, Vernon (i.e. Violet Paget, 1856–1935). Paget was born in France, near Boulogne. Her father had been involved in the Warsaw insurrection of 1848, and was forced to flee Poland. The son of a French nobleman, De Fragnier, he took his wife's maiden name, Paget, as his own. He became tutor to Eugene Lee-Hamilton (1845–1907, later a morbid, and chronically invalid poet) and subsequently married the boy's invalid mother in 1855. Violet, the child of this marriage, was strongly influenced by her half-brother Eugene, and assumed his name in her pseudonym. Precociously brilliant, 'Vernon Lee', as she called herself, brought out her *Studies Of The Eighteenth Century In Italy* in 1880, aged twenty-four. Normally resident on the Continent, she made her first visit to England in 1881 (J. S. Sargent did a striking portrait of her in this year). In addition to criticism, Lee wrote well-received travel books and in later life became obsessed with what she called 'psychological aesthetics'. (Lee is credited with having invented the English term, 'empathy'.) In 1920, she brought out a volume on pacifism entitled *Satan The Waster*. Her fiction includes: *Ottilia, An Eighteenth-Century Idyl* (1883), set in Germany during the *Sturm und Drang* period; *A Phantom Lover* (1886), a 'shilling shocker'; *Miss Brown** (1884), a witty satire on aestheticism; *Hauntings* (1890), a collection of four 'Fantastic Stories'. *Vanitas* (1892) comprises three so-called 'Polite Stories' with cosmopolitan settings. Lee's forte was the psychological analysis of evil, and fantasy. Eugene Lee-Hamilton, in addition to some pessimistic and hypersensitive poetry, wrote the novels: *The Lord Of the Dark Red Star* (1903) and *The Romance Of The Fountain* (1905). He married the novelist Annie E. Holdsworth* in 1898. (VL) BL 12. (ELH) BL 2. *DNB*. RM. *NCBEL*. Wol.

LEECH, John (1817–64). Illustrator and artist. Of Irish background, Leech was born in London where his father kept a coffee-house at Ludgate Hill. He was educated at the nearby Charterhouse School, where he was a friend of the somewhat older Thackeray*, who took a paternal interest in the young artist's career. (Leech was famous for his lovable personality.) For a while he studied medicine at St Bartholomew's, where he met the other failed doctors (and later collaborators on *Punch**) Albert Smith*, Percival Leigh and Gilbert à'Beckett. By 1840, Leech was drawing full time for the magazines and after 1841 he was the country's favourite cartoonist in *Punch*. Leech illustrated a number of novels in *Bentley's Miscellany**, beginning with Theodore Hook's* *Jack Brag** (1837). Leech also illustrated some of the best known of Dickens's* Christmas* stories. But his most effective illustrations, displaying his unrivalled mastery of horsey subjects, were of

R. S. Surtees's* sporting* novels. Unlike many illustrators, Leech earned as much as the best-paid novelists for his work and died rich, if prematurely. *DNB*. Hou.

LE FANU, J[oseph Thomas] Sheridan (1814–73). Le Fanu was born in Dublin, into an old Huguenot family. On his father's side, he was distantly related to the famous playwright, Richard Brinsley Sheridan. A slow child, Le Fanu was two before he could speak. As a young boy he was educated at the Royal Hibernian Military School, where his father was chaplain. When Le Fanu was twelve, his father was appointed Dean of Emly and the family moved to Abington, Co. Limerick. There he was educated at home until he entered Trinity College, Dublin in 1832. At university, Le Fanu made a name for himself as a public debater. In 1839 he was called to the Irish Bar, but never practised. Instead he went into journalism. In 1838 he began contributing to the *Dublin University Magazine**, a journal with which he was to have lifelong links (he was its proprietor, 1861–70). Le Fanu's politics, Irish Tory and Protestant, were reflected in the magazine's personality. In the 1840s, he went on to own and run various Irish newspapers which occupied most of his creative energies for a decade. In 1843 Le Fanu married Susanna Bennett, the daughter of a barrister. There were four children to the marriage, which lasted fourteen years, and the Le Fanus, in their house in Merrion Square, were prominent in Dublin life. Busy as he was, Le Fanu found time to write fiction and began his experiments with the ghost* story, in which he was to excel. In 1851 Susanna fell ill and died seven years later at the age of thirty-four. Her husband was devastated. Thereafter, he lived the life of a recluse, earning the Dublin nickname of 'the Invisible Prince'. Up to this point, Le Fanu had written relatively little full-length fiction. *The Cock And Anchor* (1845) is a 'Tale Of Old Dublin', and full of the gloomily gothic* violence the author relished. *The Fortunes Of Colonel Torlogh O'Brien* (1847) is an Irish* historical* novel (illustrated by Phiz*), set at the turn of the seventeenth century climaxing at the 'last battle of the Irish against the English'. Le Fanu's *Ghost Stories And Tales Of Mystery* were collected in volume form in 1851. But his major fiction begins with *The House By The Churchyard* (1863), an intricate story of murder, ghastly visions (notably 'a white fattish hand') and detection set in eighteenth-century Ireland. It was followed by *Wylder's Hand* (1864), a murder mystery set in England with an aristocratic cast of actors. *Uncle Silas** (1864) is Le Fanu's best-known novel, a story of a villainous old man's schemes to steal his ward's fortune. *Guy Deverell** (1865) was Le Fanu's most gory novel to date. All these 1860s works feature such gothic trappings as guilty secrets, inheritance and atmospheric mystery finally dissolved by bloodily violent action. *All In The Dark** (1866) introduces Le Fanu's other specialism, the occult. His subsequent novels (which became more sensational* with the years) include: *The Tenants Of Malory* (1867); *A Lost Name* (1868); *Haunted Lives* (1868); *The Wyvern Mystery* (1869); *Checkmate* (1871); *In A Glass Darkly* (1872), which contains the widely-anthologised vampire story, 'Carmilla*' and the story of hallucinatory possession, 'Green Tea*'; *Willing To Die* (1873). Le Fanu passed his last five years in virtually complete isolation, dying in Dublin at a relatively young age from bronchitis. BL 21. *DNB*. RM. *NCBEL*. Wol. Sad.

LE GALLIENNE, Richard [Thomas] (1866–1947). Richard Gallienne was born in Liverpool, where his father was manager of the Birkenhead brewery. He was educated at Liverpool College. A chronic sufferer from asthma, he inherited a bookish disposition from his mother, and began writing poetry at a young age. For his first appearance in print, with *My Ladies' Sonnets* in 1887, he added the prefix 'Le' to his name. In 1888 he moved down to London, where a year later he became involved with the publishers Elkin Mathews and John Lane*. As an adviser, and contributor to the *Yellow Book**, Le Gallienne was a literary force in the 1890s. In addition to verse, essays and reviews, he wrote some novels. *The Quest Of The Golden Girl* (1896), the whimsical account of a young (thirty-year-old) man's walking tour in search of an ideal bride, was unexpectedly popular. *The Romance Of Zion Chapel* (1898) is a gloomier story of bereaved love, set in provincial 'Coalchester', described as 'a very ignorant, meanly grim little provincial town' dominated by a gasometer. It was written in Le Gallienne's exaggeratedly arch style, which irritated middlebrow reviewers intensely. *Young Lives* (1899) is Le Gallienne's most moving novel. It records his upbringing and his brief but happy marriage with a former Liverpool waitress, Mildred Lee ('Angel' in the novel), who died in 1894. Le Gallienne's second marriage (with a Danish woman of his own class and intellectual abilities) dissolved in 1901, and he went to live in the USA. The break up of the 1890s movement with the Oscar Wilde* scandal made London inhospitable. Thereafter, Le Gallienne lived the life of a cosmopolitan man of letters, dying in Mentone. BL 7. *DNB*. RM. *NCBEL*.

LEHMANN, Rudolph Chambers (1856–1929). Lehmann was born near Sheffield of a German father and a Scottish mother. He was educated at Highgate School and at Trinity College, Cambridge where he was President of the Union in 1876. Lehmann subsequently went into law and was called to the Bar in 1880. A staunch Liberal, he made several attempts to enter Parliament. From 1890 to 1917 he was a journalist for *Punch**, one of his first commissions being to update Thackeray's* 'Prize Novels' burlesques. His fiction, which is all in the comic paper vein, includes: *Harry Fludyer At Cambridge* (1890); *In Cambridge Courts* (1891), sketches of university life; *The Billsbury Election* (1892). These books were mainly reprinted pieces that had already appeared in *Punch* and *Granta*. Lehmann married an American, Alice Davis, in 1898 and was appointed editor of the *Daily News* in 1901. His study, *Charles Dickens As Editor* (1912), is a valuable work of literary criticism. BL 3. *WW*. Wol.

LEIGHTON, Marie [Mrs Robert Flora Barbara] (née Connor, 1869–1941). Marie Connor was born in Clifton, the daughter of a captain in the Royal Irish Fusiliers. She was educated mainly in Calais, France, and began publishing her fiction at the unusually young age of fifteen, with the three-decker *Beauty's Queen* (1884). An extraordinary mishmash of romantic and religious passion, it provoked most reviewers to sarcastic drollery; but women readers liked it. Connor followed rapidly with a string of similar romances: *A Morganatic Marriage* (1885); *Sweet Magdalen* (1887), described as 'only a love story'; *Husband And Wife* (1888); *The Triumph Of Manhood* (1889). In 1889, still just twenty, she married the author and journalist Robert Leighton*. The couple had two children. In the

1890s, as Mrs Robert Leighton, she wrote around thirty serials for various Harmsworth journals, the firm for which her husband worked. Together the Leightons put out *Convict 99* (1898), a powerful anti-prison tract which became their best-known work. It has a highly sensational* plot in which the hero, Laurence Gray, is framed by a rival in love on false charges of embezzlement and murder. Sent to Grimley Prison as Convict 99 on a life sentence, Laurence suffers various indignities before escaping and proving his innocence. The force of the book lies in its graphic and credible depictions of life in jail (particularly the part played by corporal punishment, or the 'cat'). The authors dedicated the novel to Alfred C. Harmsworth, proprietor of the *Daily Mail*, in recognition of his 'earnest enthusiasm on behalf of those ground down beyond redemption under the iron rigour of a merciless convict system'. *In The Shadow Of Guilt* (1901) is another crime story. After 1896, the Leightons were primarily committed to writing fiction for the *Daily Mail*. Leighton's last published novel was *In The Plotter's Web* (1937), but effectively she had given up all serious writing by the early 1920s. (MCL) BL 79. (MCL and RL) BL 3. *WW*. Wol.

LEIGHTON, Robert (1858–1934). Leighton was born at Ayr, the son of a Scottish poet of the same name. He was educated at Liverpool. At the age of fourteen he took up work in local journalism and moved to London in 1879 where he became editor of *Young Folks*, 1884–85. He was subsequently employed by the booming Harmsworth publishing combine and from 1896 to 1899 he was literary editor of the *Daily Mail*. With his wife Marie Connor Leighton* he co-authored a number of serial novels for the Harmsworth journal, *Answers*. On his own account Leighton wrote a string of historical* romances and adventure stories for juveniles, including: *The Pilots Of Pomona* (1892), a story of Orkney in the 1840s and his best-known work; *The Thirsty Sword* (1893); *In The Grip Of The Algerine* (1893); *Olaf The Glorious* (1895); *Under The Foeman's Flag* (1896), a story of the Spanish Armada; *The Golden Galleon* (1897). In later life, Leighton became intensely interested in dogs, and wrote a number of books on the subject. (RL) BL 33. (RL and MCL) BL 3. *WW*.

Leisure Hour (1852–1905). An illustrated penny-weekly paper, published in quarto format and featuring fiction with woodcut illustrations. Subtitled 'A Family Journal Of Instruction And Recreation', *Leisure Hour* featured moralistic, self-improving serial novels, most of them anonymous. Some better-known contributors who occasionally published fiction in its pages were Mrs Oliphant*, Frances Browne* and (in the 1890s) Leslie Keith (i.e. Grace Keith Johnston*). The journal was endorsed by the Society for Purity in Literature, in the early 1860s.

LEMON, Mark (1809–70). The first and most influential editor of *Punch**. Lemon was born in London, the eldest son of a Lincolnshire hop merchant. His father died in 1817, and the young Mark was brought up by his grandfather at Hendon. He made an unsuccessful try at the brewing business after leaving school but this did not last long in the face of the attractions of a literary life. Lemon's first play was performed in 1835 and thereafter drama was always his first love. He had a strong sense of what the public wanted and over the years turned out a vast number of plays, burlesques and farces. He was also a keen amateur actor like his fellow bohemians Charles Dickens* and Douglas Jerrold*. But even less than Jerrold, his plays have not lasted and Lemon's durable reputation is as an editor. At various times he conducted the *Field*, the *Illustrated London News** and the *London Journal**. Most significantly, he was a founder and the convivial first editor of *Punch*, in 1841. He occupied the magazine's editorial chair for twenty-nine years (his salary rising from £80 to £1,500 per annum) and although he was not the most famous contributor, Lemon can take most credit for forming the distinctive *Punch* brand of humour. In the leisure and diminished energy of his later years, Lemon began a career as a novelist, aged fifty-four, and wrote a number of artificially plotted sensational* stories. They include: *Wait For The End* (1863), a story of the rivalry of two half-brothers, Gerard and Gilbert Norwold, with forgery and robbery as its main plot; *Loved At Last* (1864), the story of two heroines who come to a combined happy romantic destiny; *Falkner Lyle* (1866), subtitled 'The Story Of Two Wives' and a man's wrong choice between them, usually considered his best novel; *Leyton Hall* (1867), a collection of tales, the first one of which is historical* and set in the seventeenth century; *Golden Fetters* (1868), a tale of legal shenanigans, with a London setting. *The Taffeta Petticoat* was left unfinished at his death. Critics were respectful, but unimpressed by Lemon's fiction which is digressive and very amateur-looking. His main motive in writing was to leave a few extra pounds for his family. He had married in 1839, and had ten children. BL 7. *DNB. NCBEL.* Wol. RLF.

LENNOX, Lord William [Pitt] (1799–1881). Born at Winestead Abbey in Yorkshire, Lennox was the fourth son of the fourth Duke of Richmond. His godfather was William Pitt and one of his cousins was Charles James Fox. While still a thirteen-year-old boy at Westminster School, he was gazetted to a cornetcy. He then joined Wellington's staff as an *aide-de-campe*, remaining in the post until three years after Waterloo. He missed the battle itself, though in Brussels his mother threw the ball for him which is commemorated in *Vanity Fair** and *Charles O'Malley**. Disraeli* lampooned him as 'Lord Prima Donna' in *Vivian Grey*. Lennox sold his commission in 1829, and served as a Whig MP from 1832 to 1834. He was, however, more interested in sport (particularly racing) and literature than in public service. Lennox went on to write extensively for the journals and was the author of fashionable novels, which hit the taste of the day but are very feeble. In his later years, he was a broken-down figure willing to hire himself out for lectures on the theme of 'Celebrities I have known'. None the less his volumes of reminiscences, published in the late 1870s, are lively. His fiction includes: *Compton Audley* (1841); *The Tuft Hunter* (1843); *Percy Hamilton* (1851); *Philip Courtenay* (1855); *The Adventures Of A Man of Family* (1864). BL 13. *DNB.* Wol. Sad.

LE QUEUX, William [Tufnell] (1864–1927). Le Queux was born in London. His father was a French draper's assistant and his mother English. He was educated on the Continent and for a while studied art in Paris. As a young man, Le Queux undertook a foot tour of Europe after which he supported himself writing for the French newspapers. Eventually he returned to London in the late 1880s, where he edited *Gossip* and *Piccadilly*. Le Queux joined the staff of the *Globe* as a parliamentary reporter in 1891. Two years later he gave up journalism to concentrate on fiction and travelling. In his later life, Le Queux undertook various minor diplomatic functions and was generally resident in Italy. In *Who's Who* he listed his main recreation as 'revolver practice'. He also claimed to be a consultant to the British government on account of his 'intimate knowledge of the secret services of foreign powers'. He was also fascinated by radio, and made himself an expert in its use. In later life, his political views (as reflected in his many novels) were anti-semitic and pro-Fascist. Le Queux wrote a large quantity of fiction much of it serialised in newspapers where his gloomy prophecies of European war had most impact. *A Secret Service* (1896), 'being the strange tales of a Nihilist', is a book which, Le Queux claimed, had attracted the interest of the Russian secret service, and their active cells in London. His best-known works are chauvinist anti-German invasion fantasies such as *The Great War In England In 1897* (1892) and *The Invasion Of 1910* (1906), a work sponsored by Harmsworth's *Daily Mail* which was phenomenally popular. Pseudo-documentary in style it charted the German advance over those parts of England where the newspaper's readership was particularly strong. But Le Queux also wrote works of espionage such as *England's Peril* (1898); tales of the occult such as *Stolen Souls* (1895); low-life London stories such as *A Madonna Of The Music Halls* (1897) and detective* stories such as *Guilty Bonds* (1890). BL 132. WW. Wol.

LEVER, Charles [James] (1806–72). The best-known Irish* novelist of the century. Lever was born in Dublin, the son of a building contractor from Lancashire. The family enjoyed the privileges of Anglo-Irish life, and Charles went to Trinity College, Dublin at the age of sixteen, graduating BA five years later. As a schoolboy and undergraduate he was renowned for jests and irrepressible wit. He also took to writing and his first publication seems to have been an essay on opium taking, published in 1826. His twenties were active. In 1827 he went to Canada where he travelled to the frontier and passed some time with Indians. In 1828 he made a tour through Germany, studying at Göttingen and visiting Goethe at Weimar. He returned to Dublin where he studied medicine desultorily. He failed the examination of the Royal College of Surgeons but gained a bachelor of medicine degree in 1831. (He never took the MD.) In 1832, Lever helped out heroically in the Co. Clare cholera epidemic. But at his first post at Portstewart he fell out with his superiors. In 1832 he married his childhood sweetheart Kate (by whom he was to have four children) and his father's death the following year set him up with a small legacy. In 1836, W. H. Maxwell* persuaded him to take up writing again. Lever soon began contributing to the *Dublin University Magazine** and in 1839 his story of military ups and downs in the 1790s, *The Confessions Of Harry Lorrequer**, made a terrific hit. Curry* republished it in Dickensian* monthly parts, with illustrations by Phiz* and the work was even more popular in book form. *Lorrequer* began as a single anecdote, and its *ad hoc* continuation shows in the virtually narrativeless sequence of events which take the military hero from Cork all over Europe. *Charles O'Malley** (1841) repeated the formula and was even more popular (largely with the English reading public; the Irish frequently suspected Lever of perpetrating objectionable national caricatures). Lever followed with similar good-humoured Irish picaresques under the general title 'Our Mess': *Jack Hinton** (1842) deals more seriously with the clash of English and Irish attitudes; *Tom Burke Of Ours** (1844) is probably the best novel of the Napoleonic Wars hitherto written in England. *Arthur O'Leary** (1844) records much of the author's own travellings as a young man 'In Many Lands'. Lever himself claimed to 'detest' this work. Meanwhile, his personal life had undergone transformations. During the course of *Lorrequer*'s serial run he took up a post as physician to the British community in Brussels. In 1842, increasingly famous as a novelist, he gave up medicine and returned to Ireland to edit the *Dublin University Magazine*. Prosperous for the first time in his life he set himself up in a mansion at Templeogue, where he lived the life of a country gentleman. Courageously, Lever softened his journal's habitual anti-Nationalist attitudes and attempted to conciliate between the fierce factions of Irish cultural life. But the task was exhausting and thankless. He suffered the first attacks of the gout that was later to cripple him. And in 1845 political factionalism forced him to leave Dublin for the Continent where he was to remain based until his death. *The O'Donoghue* (1845) is 'A Tale Of Ireland Fifty Years Ago'. The tone of the work is more favourable to the English than his earlier fiction, and in fact Lever was moving his literary base to the mainland. *St Patrick's Eve* (1845) was written as a Christmas* Book for Chapman and Hall*. It is the grimmest story Lever had hitherto published, a gloomy picture of small farmers starving to death in 1832. Lever was now experiencing financial difficulties, and (as he was to do for the rest of his life) writing too much too fast. *The Knight Of Gwynne* (1847), although an unsuccessful rival in serial form to *Dombey** and *Vanity Fair**, is an ambitious work. Set at the turn of the century, it creates in the quixotic Knight a nobly pathetic figure. With the 1845 famine, the vogue for Irish comedy of the kind Lever had invented was much less saleable. *Roland Cashel* (1850) varies his pattern with an Irish hero who hails from Colombia. *The Daltons* (1852) is the longest narrative Lever had hitherto attempted. It deals critically with the question of absentee landlordism, and has lively scenes set in Austria and Florence. Lever by now knew these places well, having himself settled in Italy after 1847. *Maurice Tiernay** (1851) opens with the French revolutionary terror, and thereafter follows the fortunes of a young Irish Jacobite. *The Dodd Family Abroad* (1854) is a charmingly humorous study of British gaucheness in foreign places with a confessed self portrait of the author as the amiably downtrodden Kenny Dodd. Lever was now varying his style from work to work. *The Fortunes Of Glencore* (1857) deals with the psychology of unhappy marriage, *Davenport Dunn** (1859) with vast financial crime. Lever, however, failed to regain the first rank of writers with the British public, and was forced to overproduce. His son Charley was giving him increasing domestic anxiety. After service in the Crimea, the young man left the army and went to the bad, eventually dying of dissipation at the age of twenty-six. In 1858, Lever was appointed to a consular position in Spezia, Italy, which he held until 1867. The work was boring, and he spent most of his time in Florence, where his wife was increasingly invalid (as was he himself). During this period he continued to turn out a ceaseless stream of fiction, now usually serialised first in journals like *Cornhill** and *Blackwood's**. But increasingly he was forced to come to terms with his diminishing authorial value. When Dickens serialised Lever's quixotic *A Day's Ride* (1863) in *All The Year Round** the work caused the journal's sales to plummet. Dickens himself was obliged to weigh in with *Great Expectations** to restore circulation. Lever's later titles include: *One Of Them* (1861), a story using the author's diplomatic experience in Florence; *Barrington** (1863), a comedy of middle-class life set in Co. Kilkenny; *The Bramleighs Of Bishop's Folly* (1868), a family saga; *Paul Gosslett's Confessions In Love, Law And The Civil Service* (1868). His last work, the gloomy *Lord Kilgobbin** (1872), a 'Tale Of Ireland In Our Own Time' written, as the dedication to the author's recently dead wife declares, 'in breaking health and broken spirits', has found some modern admirers as evidence of an emerging 'dark' Lever. In general, the author has been undervalued by English readers as a lightweight comedian and by the Irish as a traducer of the national image. In 1867, the Conservative government charitably appointed Lever to a consulship at Trieste and he died there shortly after. BL 33. *DNB*. RM. *NCBEL*. Wol. Sad.

LEVY, Amy (1861–89). Levy was born at Clapham into a cultured and orthodox Jewish family who actively encouraged her literary talents. She was educated at Brighton, and at Newnham College, Cambridge, where she was the first Jewish girl to matriculate. At university in 1881 Levy's first volume of poems was published. Entitled *Xantippe* (after Socrates' fabled shrew of a wife) the work indicated her feminist sentiments. The details of Levy's subsequent life are tantalisingly mysterious. She may have taught, or even have worked in a factory from idealistic motives. She was a close friend of Olive Schreiner* and of Clementina Black*. Her novel *Reuben Sachs* (1888) is the story of a sexually unscrupulous politician. Its depiction of Jewish life in London as grossly materialistic caused a furore, and was widely taken as a race libel, as had been Julia Frankau's* similarly anti-semitic *Dr Phillips** (1887). Levy's subsequent novel, *Miss Meredith* (1889) was less tendentious. It is the story in autobiographical form of an English governess, Elsie Meredith, who falls in love with the son of the Italian household where she is employed. Its lightness of tone suggests that it may have been written some time before actual publication. Levy also wrote the shorter fiction *The Romance Of A Shop* (1888), in which four Lorimer sisters set up their own photography business in Baker Street. A prey to melancholy, Levy committed suicide by suffocating herself with charcoal fumes shortly after correcting her fifth and last volume of poems for the press. BL 3. *DNB*.

LEWES, G[eorge] H[enry] (1817–78). George Eliot's* consort. Lewes was born in London into a theatrical family and went to school haphazardly in Britain, the Channel Islands and France. His formal education finished when he was sixteen and he went to work as a clerk in a notary's office. A tireless self-educator, Lewes subsequently enrolled himself as a student of medicine, but gave up the profession because of his sensitivity to others' suffering. But he retained a lifelong interest in physiology, and the physiological basis of existence was an article of faith in his subsequent philosophy in which the other main components were the ethics of Spinoza and the 'sociology' of Auguste Comte. From 1838 to 1840 Lewes was in Germany, and made himself an authority on German literature and culture, publishing a well-received life of Goethe in 1855. In 1841, he married Agnes Jervis, whose tutor he probably was. At this period, Lewes was supporting himself more or less by journalism, and attempting to write for the stage for which he had a passion. But his attempts to make a career as either a dramatist or an actor failed. He did, however, succeed as an intellectual journalist, writing for the serious magazines on a range of aesthetic, philosophical and scientific topics. Now a confirmed free-thinker, he did not object to the unusual liaison that his wife formed with Thornton Hunt (son of Leigh Hunt). In 1850, Hunt and Lewes became joint editors of a radical weekly, the *Leader*, to which Lewes contributed some of his best literary criticism. Lewes eventually separated from his wife, amicably and rationally, on learning that the paternity of her fourth son was not his, but Hunt's. In 1852, Herbert Spencer introduced him to Mary Ann Evans, the young bluestocking whom he was to help form into George Eliot. Divorce being impossible (Lewes having condoned his wife's misconduct) the two lived together, publicly proclaiming their unconsecrated 'marriage' after 1854. Lewes was protective of Eliot's genius and their union also helped foster his own lesser talent. Encouraged by her, he went on to write his monumental *Problems Of Life And Mind*, of which the last volume was published posthumously in 1879 (at tremendous intellectual and emotional cost to Eliot). In the 1860s Lewes was (albeit briefly) editor of *Cornhill** and the *Fortnightly** and he continued to write voluminously for the magazines. He no longer had to. By the mid-1860s, his and George Eliot's financial situation was extremely comfortable. In 1863, the couple bought the Priory, St John's Wood, where they entertained extensively, despite the social taint that attached to their household. Lewes's health was never strong, and he predeceased Eliot. Lewes's novels are: *Ranthorpe** (1847) and *Rose, Blanche and Violet* (1848). They are laboured performances, although the first has some interesting scenes of literary apprenticeship and is an early instance of the *Bildungsroman** genre of fiction which became fashionable in the 1850s. The second, with its multiple heroines, is very awkwardly put together. BL 2. *DNB*. RM. *NCBEL*. Wol. Sad.

The Lifted Veil, George Eliot, *Blackwood's Magazine*, July 1859. Unusually for Eliot, this is a short story of the occult set in the 1830s. The hero and narrator, Latimer, develops clairvoyant powers after falling ill in Geneva. But this faculty produces nothing but misery for its morbid possessor. He has visions of a destructive woman, whom he finally meets in the person of his brother Alfred's betrothed, Bertha Grant. At first, he cannot read her thoughts. Alfred dies in a hunting accident, and Latimer marries Bertha. Now he can see into her mind, and he discovers that she intends to poison him. They separate, and the story ends with Latimer awaiting his death, which he knows will occur from angina pectoris on 20 September 1850. The work found little favour with Eliot's literary advisers or her readers. It was written in the 1850s, but not published in volume form in Britain until 1878.

The Light That Failed, Rudyard Kipling, 1891, 1 vol, Macmillan. (First published in the USA in 1890 and in *Lippincott's Magazine*, January 1891, with a 'happy' ending.) A grim tale of 1890s bohemian life. Dick Heldar and Maisie are first encountered as middle-class orphans, boarded out with the uncongenial Mrs Jennett at Fort Keeling. (The episode draws on Kipling's own unhappy childhood experiences.) Both are strong-willed, and they forge what is to be a lifelong 'bond'. Grown up, Dick becomes a war artist, following the bloody imperial campaign in the Sudan. He devises a brutally unsentimental aesthetic philosophy. On his return to London, after some hardship, he becomes a successful artist lodging with his fellow special correspondent, Torpenhow. Together the young men live a carefree life, which is interrupted when Dick meets Maisie again. She too is now an artist, but studying in the grand style which Dick finds pompous and empty. They renew their relationship, but at her insistence it goes no further than professional connection. An old wound, received in battle, causes Dick gradually to lose his sight. To win Maisie, he creates a masterpiece, an ambitious painting of 'Melancolia'. But unknown to him, it is ruined by the jealous model who sat for it. Unconscious that it is now a mess of paint, Dick offers his canvas to Maisie, who leaves his life for ever. On discovering what has happened, Dick laboriously makes his way to the Egyptian desert where he is mercifully shot by an enemy sniper, dying in the faithful Torpenhow's arms.

LILLY, William Samuel (1840–1919). Lilly was born in Dorsetshire, the son of a landed and Catholic West Country family. He was educated at Cambridge University, graduating in the law tripos in 1861. He subsequently took the Indian Civil Service examination. On passing, he began a promising career, rising in 1869 to an under-secretaryship. But his health failed, and in 1870 he returned to England where he was belatedly called to the Bar in 1873. Lilly maintained a keen interest in questions of philosophy and theology and wrote extensively on them. He married in 1878 and was towards the end of his life a London JP. He wrote an interesting, 'society novel' describing the career of a fashionable hero, Sir Philip Savile, published by John Lane* as *A Year Of Life* (1900). The work stirred up some polite interest among the reviewers and went into a speedy second edition. BL 1. *WW*. RLF.

Linda Tressel, Anthony Trollope, 1868, 2 vols, Blackwood. (Serialised in *Blackwood's Magazine**, October 1867–May 1868.) Trollope's story is set in Nuremberg. The heroine, Linda, loves a young political extremist, Ludovic Valcarm. She is an orphan, and her alarmed but well-meaning aunt, Madame Staubach, tries to marry her ward to an old Civil Servant, Peter Steinmarc. Instead Linda elopes with Ludovic, but he is arrested at Augsburg station. Linda, who has discovered meanwhile that she does not really love Ludovic, is returned to Nuremberg. But Steinmarc now declines to take her back. She dies. This short depressive novel, like *Nina Balatka** (1867), was first published anonymously; but the experiment was not successful in terms of sales and Trollope did not persist with it.

LINSKILL, Mary ('Stephen Yorke', 1840–91). Mary Linskill was born in Whitby, Yorkshire, the daughter of a worker in jet, who died leaving his family in financial distress. She was apprenticed to a milliner, and later turned to literature and art to support her family, living with her mother all her life, mainly at a little cottage near Newholme. In *Good Words** and under her 'Yorke' pseudonym, she published *Tales Of the North Riding* (1871). She went on to specialise in sentimental love stories with strong regional* (particularly north Yorkshire) settings and hearty heroines. Much of her fiction came out under the imprint of the SPCK*. Her titles include:

Cleveden (1876); *Between The Heather And The Northern Sea* (1884); *In Exchange For A Soul* (1887); *Hagar* (1887), 'A North Yorkshire Pastoral'. BL 12. *DNB*. Wol. RLF.

LINTON, E[liza] Lynn (née Lynn, 1822–98). Eliza Lynn was born in the Lake District (an area for which she retained a lifelong fondness) at Keswick, the twelfth child of a clergyman of staunch Conservative opinions. Linton's maternal grandfather was Dr Goodenough, Bishop of Carlisle. Her mother died five months after Eliza's birth and her father was generally indifferent to his many offspring, leaving his youngest child with a perpetual sense of emotional deprivation and loneliness. She was, however, surrounded by books and taught herself comprehensively. In her early girlhood, she underwent what was evidently a severe religious crisis, which finds a later record in her fiction. In 1845 Eliza Lynn enterprisingly took her future into her own hands and went off to London, to live by her writing. There she worked on the *Morning Chronicle* for three years and published three unsuccessful novels. *Azeth The Egyptian* (1847) was accepted by Newby* for a fee (payable by the author) of £50. The work's historical background was boned up from reading in the British Museum. *Amymone* (1848) is a 'Romance Of The Days Of Pericles'. It earned the young author £100 from Bentley* and with a further £30 from her father allowed her another year's subsistence in London. *Realities* (1851) avoided the absurdities of historical* fiction but its plot remains desperately artificial. In 1851, Lynn quarrelled with her employer at the *Morning Chronicle*, John Douglas Cook, and for three years from 1853 she worked as a foreign correspondent in Paris. By this time she had become acquainted with most of the senior men and women of English letters. She became a hero-worshipping friend of Walter Landor (whom she called her 'beloved father') and knew G. H. Lewes*, John Forster, Thornton Hunt and Charles Dickens* to whom in 1856 she sold Gad's Hill (a property inherited together with £1,500 from her father). In 1858, Lynn married William James Linton, the noted engraver and artist. He was ten years her senior, politically radical and a widower with seven children. He quickly ran through her little fortune. The marriage failed and the couple soon separated (though she never divorced and kept on good terms with her husband, who eventually drifted to the USA, and with her stepchildren, especially the daughters). In the 1860s, Lynn Linton (as she was known) started a new phase of her career in which fiction was to play a larger part. From 1866, she worked on the *Saturday Review** and wrote an extraordinarily powerful sequence of anti-feminist articles, collected as *The Girl Of The Period* (1869). Hitherto, she had been something of a proponent of women's rights. She became a novelist of the first rank with the success of *Joshua Davidson** (1872), a work which sardonically recasts the gospel in a modern setting. The free-thinker Charles Bradlaugh bought 1,000 copies to distribute for his cause, and the novel sold best of all Linton's works during her lifetime. Her other major achievement, *The Autobiography Of Christopher Kirkland** (1885), remains one of the best depictions of the writer's spiritual growth to be found in Victorian fiction. She called it 'the book of my whole career'. Lynn Linton's other fiction has considerable interest. *Grasp Your Nettle* (1865) is a story of genteel life in the country, concentrating as usual on 'the trials in a woman's existence'. Sharper in its

observations than Mrs Gaskell's* *Cranford**, its plot involves bigamy* and
the return of a wife supposed dead. *Lizzie Lorton Of Greyrigg* (1866) is set
in a Cumberland parish in the early nineteenth century whose congregation
a young Ritualist priest vainly tries to civilise. It all leads to a tragic
ending, in which the heroine drowns herself. (Self-destruction is common
with Linton's leading ladies.) *Sowing The Wind* (1867) is a powerful story
of a disastrous marriage with a journalistic subplot. *The Atonement Of
Leam Dundas* (1877) has a passionate half-Spanish heroine who poisons her
stepmother and atones by dying on the Cumberland fells. Like much of
Linton's fiction, it was attacked as immoral. In *Under Which Lord?** (1879)
a wife is torn between the conflicting demands of an agnostic husband and a
persuasive priest. Among Lynn Linton's late fiction, *Dulcie Everton* (1896)
is a simpler domestic* tale of marital delinquency and redemption. And
the author's very last novels are remarkable for their vituperative attack
on the so-called 'girl of the period', whom she loathed. *The One Too Many*
(1894) satirises the cult of the Girton girl, whom Lynn Linton portrays as
a smoking, drinking harlot. The novel is dedicated to 'the sweet girls still
left among us'. *In Haste And At Leisure* (1895) attacks women's societies in
the form of the 'Excelsior Club' where ladies are taught misconduct under
the guise of discussing current affairs. In later life, the author is reported
to have declared: 'All the reforms we have striven for have been granted.
Nothing further is now required.' Lynn Linton died of pneumonia, leaving a
lively memoir, published posthumously as *My Literary Life* (1899). BL 26.
DNB. RM. *NCBEL*. Wol. Sad.

LITTLE, James Stanley (1856–1940). Little was born in Herne Hill, south
London, and educated at King's College, London. He visited the Cape and
Natal in the early 1880s and the experience shaped the rest of his life. On his
return to England he wrote dozens of books on South Africa and lectured
extensively on the country from a pro-imperialist standpoint. From 1886 to
1895 he was the moving spirit on the South Africa Committee. (Little was an
enthusiastic committee man, and also helped Walter Besant* organise the
Society of Authors*.) In 1895, he married a French viscountess. Little wrote
the novels: *My Royal Father* (1886), a story for women; *Doubt* (1888); *Whose
Wife Shall She Be?* (1888). The last is the story of a painter's complicated
love life. The work has some army chapters and was dedicated to the
author's friend, Rider Haggard*. All Little's novels were found slapdash
by the reviewers. BL 5. *WW*.

Little Dorrit, Charles Dickens, 1857, 1 vol, Bradbury and Evans. (Serialised in monthly parts, December 1855–June 1857, illustrated by Phiz*.)
One of the three great works of Dickens's last period, and a novel which
examines the early experience of imprisonment for debt in the Marshalsea
Prison which his luckless father, John Dickens, underwent in 1824. The novel
is extraordinarily rich and diverse, but the main narrative line follows Arthur
Clennam. Middle-aged and spiritually exhausted, Clennam returns to London from his family business affairs in the East. His mother is a crippled,
housebound religious zealot. In her household, he meets Amy ('Little') Dorrit who earns a little money by domestic needlework. A saintly young girl,
her father William Dorrit is the father of Marshalsea, the longest serving
debtor in the prison, a weak but morbidly proud man. His financial troubles

have arisen from involvement with the 'Circumlocution Office' (i.e. the Civil Service, the object of Dickens's satire partly for their chronic bureaucratic bungling during the Crimean War). Clennam befriends the Dorrits who are released from their bondage by an unexpected inheritance. The Dorrits (except for Amy and her uncle Frederick) become arrogant *nouveaux riches.* Arthur, who has not returned Amy's love, is himself ruined and finds himself in the Marshalsea. Amy nurses him through a dangerous illness, and the couple are eventually united. Arthur is revealed not, after all, to be the son of the stony Mrs Clennam. Moreover, she has suppressed the codicil to a will which would have enriched the Dorrits. The novel has a rich cast of secondary characters: Merdle the financier who cuts his throat after his speculative bubble bursts; the down-to-earth inventor Daniel Doyce who is baffled by the Circumlocution Office and its bureaucracy; the Barnacle clan who nepotistically infest the Circumlocution Office; the villain Rigaud, alias Blandois and Lagnier. The setting is also more cosmopolitan than any of Dickens's previous novels, ranging all over Europe.

Little Lord Fauntleroy, Frances Hodgson Burnett, 1886, 1 vol, Warne. (Serialised in *St Nicholas**, November 1885–October 1886, illustrated by Reginald B. Birch.) The first international bestseller of children's* fiction (though arguably always more popular with their parents). Seven-year-old Cedric Errol is first encountered in New York City living with his mother, whom he calls 'Dearest'. He wears velvet suits, ruffs and has cascading golden curls but is nevertheless a regular kid. His particular friends are the local bootblack and Hobbs the store-keeper. Cedric and his mother unexpectedly learn that he is heir to an earl, and an English lord. They return to England to the castle of Cedric's crusty grandfather, the Earl of Dorincourt ('the Wicked'). It emerges that this old tyrant banished his son (Cedric's father) for marrying an American, a people he hates. Even now, he refuses to see Dearest. By sheer good nature, Cedric wins him over and makes him, against all his habits, a good old man. A rival to the title appears, but Cedric's New York friends expose him as a fake. Hobbs comes over to set up a shop in England. The novel was widely popularised by its stage and later film versions. Fauntleroy suits remained fashionable for many years after.

Little Meg's Children, Hesba Stretton (i.e. Sarah Smith), 1868, 1 vol, RTS. Stretton's follow-up to her popular *Jessica's First Prayer** (1867). Like the previous work it is a 'waif romance'. Meg Fleming is the eldest daughter in a slum family forced by her mother's death and her sailor father's absence to fend for her siblings by charing. The heroine is entrusted by her dying mother with forty sovereigns which she virtuously keeps intact until her father's return. Meg's good conduct is contrasted with her neighbour Kitty, who has become a drunken prostitute. The father finally returns and the family goes off to Canada to a new, happy life.

The Little Minister, J. M. Barrie, 1891, 3 vols, Cassell. (Serialised in *Good Words**, January–December 1891.) One of the author's 'Thrums' (i.e. Kirriemuir) stories. The narrative is told by Dominie Ogilvy. Gavin Dishart is the twenty-one-year-old little minister of the title, renowned for the power of his preaching in his small 'Auld Licht' parish. His mother,

Margaret Dishart, now a widow, has a complicated married history. Her first husband, Adam, disappeared three months after his marriage to her and was presumed drowned. She subsequently married Gavin ('Dominie') Ogilvy, little Gavin's father. But after six years, Adam returned to claim his wife and 'his' child. Now she watches with neurotic closeness over her son and unknown to her, Ogilvy watches over her. Gavin becomes acquainted with Babbie, a gypsy girl ('the Egyptian'), during a riot of weavers in Thrums. He becomes sexually entangled with her, to the alarm of his parishioners, and during a fierce drought he deserts a prayer service for rain in order to marry Babbie by gypsy ceremony in the forest. While he is doing so, a flash of lightning reveals him to his rival in love, Lord Rintoul, and to his congregation who have come to look for their minister. Babbie is kidnapped. Gavin saves Rintoul from drowning and the Little Minister is accepted back by his flock, now married to his Egyptian, who is eventually revealed to have a respectable family background.

LLOYD, Edward (1815–90). Publisher of popular fiction. Lloyd was born in Thornton Heath, Surrey, the son of a farmer. As a very young boy, he went into bookselling, setting up a shop in Shoreditch while still in his teens. His first publication seems to have been the 1d. serial, *Lives Of The Most Notorious Highwaymen* (1836) which ran for sixty weekly numbers. Lloyd followed with *The Calendar Of Horrors* (1836). By the end of the 1830s he was an established publisher of cheap fiction at a period when the industry was booming with the expansion of London. He founded a number of 'People's' newspapers, including in 1842 *Lloyd's Illustrated London Newspaper* which as *Lloyd's Weekly London Newspaper* was edited by Douglas Jerrold (after 1852) and achieved sales of 90,000, rising to half a million by the end of the century. Lloyd was one of the pioneers of the American Hoe rotary press, and set up his own paper factory in Kent to supply his vast output of printed matter, supplied with raw materials from 100,000 acres of esparto grass which the publisher leased in Algeria. In the 1840s particularly he produced hundreds of eight-paged, double-columned, crude woodcut-illustrated, 1d. serials, employing such famous stars of the form as T. P. Prest* and Malcolm Errym*. According to Thomas Frost*, Lloyd's normal 'honorarium' was '10s. per weekly instalment of the story'. His premises (after 1843) in London's Salisbury Square were adopted as a label for the genre of working-class* fiction. *DNB.*

LOCKE, William J[ohn] (1863–1930). Locke was born in Barbados, and went to school in Trinidad. He attended St John's College, Cambridge, graduating with a degree in mathematics in 1884. Locke subsequently trained as an architect and was from 1897 to 1907 secretary to the RIBA. In his later life he lived on the Continent (largely in the Riviera), edited English translations of French authors and wrote novels, including: *At The Gate Of Samaria* (1895); *The Demagogue And Lady Phayre* (1896), a story of political life and moral temptation; *A Study In Shadows* (1896), a novel of *pension* life in Geneva; *Derelicts* (1897). In the last, the gentleman hero, having served a sentence for fraud, attempts to rehabilitate himself in a pharisaical society which (with the exception of a redeemingly noble woman) resists all his efforts. *Idols* (1898) is an ambitious study in modern sex problems. BL 32. *WW.*

The London Journal (1845–1912). A popular weekly specialising in working-class* fiction, heavily illustrated. It was started by George Stiff, an engraver, with George Vickers as its first publisher and G. W. M. Reynolds* as its first editor. In the late 1840s, circulation rose to the half-million mark. Reynolds quarrelled with Stiff and soon left to start his rival *Miscellany* in 1846. Under the editorship of J. W. Ross, the *London Journal* continued to thrive, and John Gilbert's* woodcuts contributed to its distinctive appearance. J. F. Smith's* serial *Minnigrey* brought circulation to a peak in 1850 and Pierce Egan Jr* was one of the journal's later editors. The success of Vickers's publication inspired many rivals. Its crude romantic, gothic* or historical* fictions were largely disregarded by the middle-class readership although in the 1860s it serialised several stories by M. E. Braddon*.

London Society (1862–98). An illustrated monthly magazine, devoted to 'light and amusing literature for hours of relaxation'. An inferior imitator of Smith's *Cornhill*, the journal was published independently and contained articles of miscellaneous interest and some substandard fiction (initially anonymous). In 1874, it serialised Mrs J. H. Riddell's* *Above Suspicion* and in the same period Florence Marryat's* *Open Sesame*, she evidently being the journal's editor at the time. Among the illustrators featured in *London Society* were: M. E. Edwards*, R. Caldecott*, Harry Furniss*, F. A. Fraser and George Cruikshank Jr. The journal's Christmas numbers were lavish and featured stories by such writers as Le Fanu*, Shirley Brooks*, G. A. Sala* and Edmund Yates*.

Longman (1724–). The oldest-established of British commercial publishers. The firm was founded by Thomas Longman (1699–1755) at the Sign of the Ship and Black Swan, Paternoster Row. Successive Longmans directed the firm for 200 years. The house acquired a dominant stature in the eighteenth and nineteenth centuries with a mixed list of books in which fiction was present but not prominent. Longman were the publishing force behind the founding of the *Edinburgh Review* in 1802. They also published many of the major Romantic poets (Wordsworth, Coleridge, Southey). In 1856, they made a publicity splash by giving Macaulay a £20,000 cheque for his *History*. At the same time they were helping Anthony Trollope* get started in his career, publishing *Barchester Towers* (£100). In 1880, they again made a sensation by giving Disraeli* £10,000 for his novel *Endymion*, representing the highest single payment in the Victorian period. The firm took a more purposive interest in fiction with the setting up of *Longman's Magazine* in November 1882. The magazine kicked off with James Payn's* *Thicker Than Water* and in its first year published various of Mrs Oliphant's* *Stories Of The Seen And Unseen*, and other stories by Thomas Hardy*, F. Anstey* , Dinah Craik* and R. L. Stevenson*. In its early years, the magazine showed the strong influence of the firm's current literary adviser, Andrew Lang* (although the editor for the magazine's twenty-three years of life was C. J. Longman). A monthly costing 6d. (and unillustrated) the journal made fiction its main item. Kipling*, Rider Haggard*, and Walter Besant* were authors who published over the years in *Longman's Magazine*, which embodied Lang's belief that romance*, not realism or modernism, represented the strength of English fiction. Longman reprinted its magazine fiction writers in one-volume book form in the 1880s and 1890s, thus contributing to the downfall of the three-decker in 1894. The magazine, which was drab in appearance, lost ground to the new illustrated papers such as Newnes's* *Strand**. By 1900, it was a much less impressive publication, featuring such minor novelists as Arthur W. Marchmont* and L. B. Walford*. It ceased publication in 1905. *BLM. WI.*

Lord Kilgobbin, Charles Lever, 1872, 3 vols, Smith, Elder. (Serialised in *Cornhill**, October 1870–March 1872.) Lever's last novel, described as 'A Tale Of Ireland In Our Time'. Set in the 1860s, the work portrays a seedy Ireland, infested with Fenianism. Matthew Kearney, styled Lord Kilgobbin, is a ruined landowner, the last of a Catholic family ennobled by James II. He lives in a decayed castle by the Bog of Allen with his daughter Kate. As is normal in Lever, the plot is less interesting than the gallery of characters introduced. Joe Attlee is the usual rollicking hero, a bohemian Trinity College student. Daniel Donogan, the Nationalist, is less stereotyped as is also the dashing heroine, Nina Kostalergi. Half-Irish, the daughter of a Greek prince and a niece of Matthew's, she uses her sexual charm to work her political will. The gloomy tone of the work has attracted some interest among modern critics of Lever.

Lord Ormont And His Aminta, George Meredith, 1894, 3 vols, Chapman and Hall. (Serialised in the *Pall Mall Magazine**, December 1893–July 1894, illustrated by J. Gülich.) Lord Ormont, a cavalry general, inspires the hero worship of two young people: Matthew ('Matey') Weyburn and Aminta ('Browny') Farrell. An early love affair between them while they are still at school is firmly put down. Lord Ormont falls out with his superiors and resigns the service in anger. He marries the still adoring Aminta in Madrid, but insists that the match be kept secret. When they return to England, she is supposed to be his mistress. Matey re-enters her life as Ormont's secretary and the old passion revives. Ormont fails to win his disaffected wife with gifts of jewels and she and Matey elope to Switzerland. Some years later, Lord Ormont visits the school they have set up in Berne and the trio are reconciled. When he dies soon thereafter, the young couple at last marry. As usual with Meredith, the complexities of unhappy marriage are examined with super-subtlety.

LORIMER, Norma [Octavia] (1864–1948). Lorimer was born in Scotland. But her father was a Manxman, and she was educated at the Castletown High School, spending fifteen formative girlhood years on the Isle of Man. In later life she travelled widely in Europe, the USA and the Orient. She never married, apparently, and lived her later life mainly in Italy. Lorimer's Manx background is drawn on for *Mirry Ann* (1900). In *A Sweet Disorder* (1896) the heroine, Molly Collister, is an independent girl who takes up writing novels. *Josiah's Wife* (1898) features a wife, Camela, who takes a year's Italian holiday from marriage to an American Baptist husband. Lorimer was a regular contributor to the *Girl's Own Paper**. BL 18. *WW.*

Lorna Doone, A Romance Of Exmoor, R. D. Blackmore, 1869, 3 vols, Sampson Low. The most popular regional* historical* novel of the century. Set in Exmoor at the end of the seventeenth century the story is told by John Ridd, of the parish of Oare in Somerset. Ridd's farmer father is killed by the lawless Doone bandits while his son is still at school, setting up what is to be a lifelong feud. John grows up immensely strong, and falls in love with Lorna, supposedly the daughter of the Doone who killed his father. He and Lorna have a secret relationship, but a crisis arises when she is promised in marriage to Carver Doone, the lawless leader of the clan. With the blessing of old Sir Ensor (and the gift of a diamond necklace) John carries Lorna off to the safety of his farm. Through his connection with a highwayman relative, Tom Faggus, John becomes involved in the rebellion against King James, is taken prisoner and narrowly escapes execution. But in return for gallantry, John is eventually knighted. He returns to Somerset, where the Doones have finally been put down. But at his wedding to Lorna, Carver returns to shoot the bride. An epic chase and fight ensues between Carver and John in which the hero is victorious and the villain is swallowed in the Exmoor bog. Lorna survives her wound. In addition to its exciting action, *Lorna Doone* is remarkable for its close observation of West Country life and scenery.

Loss And Gain, The Story Of A Convert, John Henry Newman, 1848, 1 vol, Burns. Together with Thackeray's* *Pendennis**, one of the earliest English novels of university life. Biographically, *Loss And Gain* also chronicles the interval of doubt and uncertainty which preceded Newman's entry into the Catholic Church in 1845. The hero is Charles Reding. The son of an Anglican clergyman, Reding goes up to 'St Saviour's College', Oxford. With his friend William Sheffield, he embarks on a strenuous examination of the articles of faith which the University requires of him. He rejects the worldly attitudes of his tutor Vincent and the stupid Anglican prejudices of his college masters who see 'subtile Jesuits' everywhere. After his father's death, spies (wrongly) inform the authorities that Reding is a secret Catholic. He is examined and rusticated. Eventually, Reding takes his finals, gaining a second-class degree, but does not graduate. Instead, after being proselytised by a variety of religious fanatics and repudiated by his mother he goes over to Rome. His initiation is helped by a former classmate, Willis, now Father Aloysius. The novel ends with the exaltation of Charles's conversion.

The Lost Brooch, Harriet Mozley, 1842, 2 vols, Burns. A tale for older girls by Cardinal Newman's* novel-writing sister. The plot centres on a maid, falsely accused of theft. Eventually she is acquitted, her virtue proved and tested. The interest of the work is less in the process of detection than the complex personal relationships described, an unusual feature in the normally stereotyped genre of juvenile moral fiction.

Lost Sir Massingberd, James Payn, 1864, 2 vols, Sampson Low. Marmaduke Heath lives in Fairburn Hall, the ward of a dissolute uncle, Sir Massingberd, who covets his nephew's fortune. Marmaduke befriends the narrator, Peter Meredith, and while the two young men are out riding, Marmaduke has a fall from his horse, engineered by Sir Massingberd. A gypsy, whose son the wicked nobleman has had transported and whose sister he has seduced, curses him to death by inches. Marmaduke recovers from his fall and discovers that his uncle's gypsy paramour, Sinnamenta, still lives, a maniac. Sir Massingberd goes missing, and suspicion falls on the gypsies. It emerges that he has been trapped in an old oak, searching for poachers, dying horribly caught in the depths of the tree's rotten trunk. The now ennobled Marmaduke survives to marry Lucy Gerard, the daughter of an old friend. Payn's novel was extraordinarily popular and is narrated with characteristic breeziness. It contributed something to the development of the English detective* novel.

Lothair, Benjamin Disraeli, 1870, 3 vols, Longman. Disraeli's least political novel, written in one of the intervals in which he was out of power. The hero is an orphan, left the ward of a stern Scottish peer, Lord Culloden, and the wily Catholic, Cardinal Grandison. Brought up in strict seclusion in Scotland, Lothair is obliged by the terms of his father's will to attend Christ Church, Oxford. There he makes friends with Bertram, the son of a duke, and is invited to the country house Brentham, where he falls in love with the beautiful Lady Corisande. His ingenuous proposal to marry her is gently refused. The early chapters, dealing with the inexperienced hero's introduction into society, are the most amusing and effective section of the narrative. Its later course is connected with the power struggle for his allegiance and massive wealth. He becomes involved in the Garibaldian uprising of the 1860s, and takes part in the popular resistance to the Papal forces. On her deathbed, the patriotic Theodora makes Lothair promise never to convert to Rome. Lothair is wounded at the battle of Mentana and comes again under the influence of his Cardinal guardian. Finally, he returns to England and Corisande. The story ends idyllically at Brentham, where Corisande receives some magnificent pearls, 'the offering of Theodora to Lothair's bride'.

Lovel The Widower, W. M. Thackeray, 1861, 1 vol, Smith, Elder. (Serialised in *Cornhill**, January–June 1860, with illustrations by the author.) The somewhat unsatisfying story with which Thackeray opened his new magazine. The hero-narrator, Frederick Lovel, is a middle-aged widower, sadly henpecked by his mother and mother-in-law, Lady Baker. Consternation is caused in the Lovel household by Miss Prior, a pretty young governess. Lovel is one of those attracted by her, but to the infinite disgust of Lady Baker it emerges that Miss Prior once danced on the stage to support her family. But Lovel revokes her dismissal, marries her, and is gratified by the departure of Lady Baker from his house for good. The story is told interestingly from Lovel's restricted and amiably stuffy point of view.

LOVER, Samuel (1797–1868). Lover was born in Dublin, in the Protestant middle class. His father was a stockbroker and as eldest son Samuel could look forward to a comfortable career in business. But he showed an early inclination towards music and art and after a false start in commerce he took up painting as his vocation at the age of seventeen and did moderately well as a miniaturist. Lover's first success, however, was as a song writer, in the style of Thomas Moore. In 1828, he was elected to the Royal Hibernian Academy. And four years later, he published his first book, a collection of Irish* tales and legends. In 1833, Lover helped found the *Dublin University Magazine**. In addition to its political (anti-Nationalist) programme the journal was the inspiration for later fiction-carrying magazines in England. In 1835, Lover moved to London. He exhibited pictures at the Royal Academy, and did some work for the theatre. In 1837, there appeared his first novel (inspired by one of his own ballads) *Rory O'More*, a 'National Tale', containing a sympathetic presentation of the Irish peasantry during the 1798 rebellion. It was dramatised, and later became a starring vehicle for Tyrone Power at the Adelphi Theatre. In the same year, Lover (together with Dickens* and Richard Bentley*) helped found *Bentley's Miscellany*. His contribution to the design of this journal, particularly its intermixture of text and illustration, has been undervalued. Lover's best-known work, *Handy Andy** (1842), an 'Irish Tale', appeared in *Bentley's*, illustrated by himself. Lever's third novel, *L.S.D. Or Treasure Trove*, appeared in 1844. A historical* tale set in the period of the Young Pretender's uprising it features the obligatory Irish hero. In 1847, Lover's first wife died (he remarried in 1852). At this period Lover's sight was failing and handicapped his work with both pen and pencil. Versatile as ever, he devised a public entertainment, 'Irish Evenings', which he took, as a one-man show, to America, with great success, in 1846. The *DNB*, too harshly, labels Lover 'a second-rate Lever* and a third-rate Moore'. In fact, his career is of great interest. His ambidexterity with pen and pencil (and his facility with verse and song) anticipates Thackeray* (and he was probably a better illustrator than the other novelist). His public readings and performances were surely remembered, and later exploited by Dickens*. Some of his songs (such as *The Low Backed Car*) have survived into twentieth-century repertoire. And he is regarded of significance as an early figure in the growth of Irish national consciousness. Throughout his later life, Lover moved between the English and Irish capitals, dying in Jersey. BL 5. *DNB*. RM. *NCBEL*. Wol. Sad.

Sampson Low (1819–1914). Publisher. Sampson Low (1797–1886) was the son of a namesake father who was a London printer and publisher. The junior Sampson Low was apprenticed to Longman's*. In 1819, he started up his own business, together with a reading room at Lamb's Conduit Street. In 1837, he assumed a leading role in the British booktrade as the delegated publisher of the *Publisher's Circular*, a journal centred on an authoritative fortnightly list of new publications. In 1867, the journal became his sole property. Low had a number of premises, mainly around Fleet Street. He retired in 1875, and the death of his heir resulted in the firm being taken over by one of his partners, the energetic Edward Marston (1825–1914), in 1881. Sampson Low specialised in the publication of American authors, and in the marketing of British authors in America. Among many other bestselling novels, the house was responsible for works by R. D. Blackmore* (including *Lorna Doone**, 1869), by Wilkie Collins* and by William Black*. (SL) *DNB*.

LOWRY, H[enry] D[awson] (1869–1906). Dawson was born in Truro, the eldest son of a bank clerk. His father moved to Somerset and Lowry was educated at school in Taunton and at Oxford, where he graduated with a degree in chemistry in 1891. Lowry gave up a career in science for literature in 1893 and wrote for the *National Observer*, the *Morning Post*, and the *Pall Mall Gazette*. In 1897, he became editor of the *Ludgate Magazine*. He died, unmarried, at Herne Hill, London. Lowry wrote successful stories of Cornish life such as *Wreckers And Methodists* (1893). His other fiction, all of which is strong on regional* colour, includes: *Women's Tragedies* (1895), a set of stories of Cornish life, including the allegorical sequence 'The Former Age';

A Man Of Moods (1896), a love story set in the Scilly Isles; *Make Believe* (1896); *The Happy Exile* (1897), a collection of sketches and studies. BL 5. *WW*. Wol.

Lucretia, Or The Children Of The Night, E. G. E. L. Bulwer-Lytton, 1846, 3 vols, Saunders and Otley. *Lucretia* is based on the career of Thomas Wainewright (1794–1852), convicted forger and unprosecuted poisoner of his sister-in-law for insurance gain. As well as being a criminal, Wainewright was an artist and a literary man. Such characters were of interest to Bulwer-Lytton. The novel has an extravagantly complicated plot. Part the first opens with the strongest scene in the narrative. An architect of the Terror takes his son to see his own mother guillotined. These spectators are revealed as Olivier Dalibard and Gabriel Varney, the two villains of the action. Dalibard has learned the poison recipes of the Borgias. His son Varney is an artist. From the Parisian opening, the action moves to London at the turn of the century. The Dalibards are installed at Laughton, the country seat of the aristocratic St John family. At this point, interest shifts to Sir Miles St John's niece, Lucretia Clavering. Naturally vicious, Lucretia is utterly corrupted by Dalibard. In a complicated episode (involving four suitors) Lucretia is disgraced and cut out of Sir Miles's will. She marries Dalibard. Part the second moves to the early 1830s. In the interim, Lucretia has murdered Dalibard, remarried and poisoned her second husband. The child of the second marriage is mislaid and lost. We discover Lucretia now crippled, but still dangerous. With Varney, she conspires to poison her niece Helen. In an absurdly theatrical climax, Lucretia is exposed by the illiterate crossing sweeper Beck. Lucretia kills him with a poisoned ring. He turns out to be her lost son. She goes mad. Varney is transported for forgery. *Lucretia* provoked a storm against the Newgate* novel, *The Times* calling it 'a disgrace to the writer, a shame to us all'. Lytton revised the work in 1853 (allowing Helen to live).

LUCY, [Sir] Henry W[illiam] (1843–1924). Lucy was born at Crosby the son of an engineer, and went to school in Liverpool. He was apprenticed to a Liverpool hide merchant but by 1864 had moved to the more congenial occupation of journalism, in Shrewsbury. In 1869, he spent a year at the Sorbonne in Paris, studying the French language and literature. He returned to England, and joined the staff of the *Pall Mall Gazette* in 1870. He subsequently held a senior editorial position on the *Daily News* and created the character 'Toby MP' for *Punch** (the column ran from 1881 to 1916). Lucy also did a popular series of regular parliamentary sketches, 'From Behind The Speaker's Chair', for the *Strand**. He himself made several unsuccessful attempts to win a parliamentary seat. He was knighted in 1909. Lucy's fiction includes: *Gideon Fleyce* (1882), a political novel about a young man's thwarted parliamentary career and *The Miller's Niece* (1892). BL 2. *DNB*. Wol.

LUMLEY, Benjamin ('Hermes', born Levy, 1811–75). Born in London, he was the son of a Canadian Jewish merchant, Louis Levy. Changing his name, Lumley trained as a lawyer but soon took up profitable employment as a theatrical (specifically opera) manager. He took over Her Majesty's Theatre in the 1840s and over the next eighteen years was responsible for the first performance in England of a number of major Italian works. He also managed the Italian Opera House in Paris for a period. In late life, Lumley published two works of mystical science fiction*: *Sirenia, Or Recollections Of A Past Experience* (1862), an astral love story dealing with the transmigration of souls; and *Another World* (1873), by 'Hermes', a utopian vision of civilisation on a neighbouring planet. The second of these went into three editions in its first year of publication. BL 2. *DNB*, Wol.

LYNAM, Colonel William [Francis] (1845?-94). Lynam was born in Galway. He gained his military rank in the 5th Royal Lancashire Militia, which he joined in 1867 and in which he served until 1881. He lived at Dundrum, 1863-87, then at Clontarf until his death. For many years, Lynam was proprietor and editor of *Shamrock*, a weekly paper. For this journal, he invented the tremendously successful 'Mick McQuaid' series. This devious schemer's adventures, begun in 1867, were continued by other hands until well after their original author's death. The McQuaid tales were reprinted in volume, and 1d.-part form. Lynam actually became tired of his famous character, and tried to replace him. (The most successful substitution was 'Dan Donovan'.) But any cessation caused an immediate loss of circulation of *Shamrock* and as with Sherlock Holmes, resurrection was forced on an unwilling author. BL 1. Boase.

LYNCH, Hannah (1862-1904). Lynch was born in Dublin. As a young girl she joined the 'Ladies' Land League' and when *United Ireland* was suppressed, published the paper from Paris. In later life, she lived for various periods in Spain, Greece and France. For many years she was the Paris contributor of the *Academy**. A Catholic, in the 1880s Lynch was associated with Miss Anna Parnell and various militantly Nationalist Irish associations. Her fiction is the vehicle for her political convictions. It includes: *Through Troubled Waters* (1885); *The Prince Of The Glades* (1891), a story of Fenianism; *Daughters Of Men* (1892), a wild melodrama set in Greece; *Jinny Blake* (1897), the portrait of an idealistic new woman's* girlhood ; *An Odd Experiment* (1897), the story of a woman who morally reclaims her husband's mistress by setting up a domestic threesome ('a very curious experiment', the *Athenaeum** thought); *Rosni Harvey* (1892), another melodrama set in Greece. Lynch's *Autobiography Of A Child* (1899) is a literary curiosity. Originally published in *Blackwood's Magazine** it purports to be the actual life story of an abused Dublin girl, for whom Lynch was merely the amanuensis. BL 10. *WW*. RLF.

LYNCH, Theodora Elizabeth (née Foulks, 1812-85). Elizabeth Foulks was born in Sussex, the daughter of a Jamaica sugar planter. In 1835, in the West Indies, she married Henry Lynch, a lawyer who died in 1845 of yellow fever. The widow returned to England, and devoted herself to fiction, much of it set in the Caribbean and directed at juvenile readers. Her works include: *The Cotton Tree* (1847), 'Or Emily, The Little West Indian'; *The Family Sepulchre* (1848), 'A Tale Of Jamaica'; *Maude Effingham* (1849); *The Red Brick House* (1855). Lynch's tales became markedly more pious with advancing age. BL 13. *DNB*.

LYSAGHT, Sidney Royse (1860?-1941). Lysaght was born in Co. Cork, and eventually became a rich ironmaster in Bristol. In his younger years a poet, dramatist and occasional novelist, his first publications were *A Modern Ideal* (1886), a dramatic poem, and *One Of The Grenvilles* (1899), the story of a family with aristocratic and mercantile branches. His most interesting novel is *The Marplot* (1893). It is the story of a young Irishman, Dick Malory, who marries a music hall artiste. When her immoral past emerges he is disillusioned, emigrates to America to become a cowboy. Subsequent twists of plot involve desert war in Khartoum and Irish* episodes before all comes straight. Reviewers complained at the ramshackle nature of Lysaght's narratives. BL 2. *WW*.

LYTTON, Edward [George Earle Lytton] Bulwer- (1803–73). How to term this author is an initial problem. Before 1843, he is properly 'Bulwer', thereafter 'Bulwer Lytton' (optionally hyphenated). On the paternal side, Bulwer's family had been ennobled since the Conquest. His mother's family (the Lyttons) were distinguished scholars. How to blend the aristocrat's with the 'student's' role was a lifelong aspiration for Bulwer. After one of the unhappy marriages that ran in the family, Bulwer's father died in 1807. Edward, the youngest of three sons, was brought up by his mother, a smotheringly possessive woman. (Harriet Martineau* was later to make the cruelly precise jibe that Bulwer dressed a woman's spirit in man's clothing.) He was thought too delicate for Eton. Like Scott's Edward Waverley, young Edward Bulwer was left alone with books rather than boys for company, and carefully over-educated at home. He duly emerged a prodigy of learning and precocious authorship. At sixteen, he had his first and as he claimed his only perfect love affair. The name of his idealised first love is unknown, and the young people were separated by command of her father. Supposedly she died soon thereafter. In 1820, there appeared Bulwer's first book, *Ismael, An Oriental Tale*. At Cambridge, his preferred literary form was verse and he won the Chancellor's medal for poetry in 1825. As a young 'pseudo Byron', Bulwer had a scandalous affair with Lady Caroline Lamb. After a continental tour, the young fashionable, as he now was, married the Irish coquette Rosina Wheeler after a tumultuous courtship, in 1827. It was a disastrous relationship. Rosina was clever (later she devoted her intelligence to writing novels of vengeance against her luckless husband) but hopelessly spoiled. Bulwer had married wholly against his mother's wishes and she cut off his allowance. This had two consequences for his subsequent writing career. First, he was forced write for money (effectively this meant writing fiction). Secondly, feeling himself an outcast, he developed his keen interest in the outsiders, recluses and criminal exiles who populate his fiction. *Falkland*, a gloomy two-volume affair, was brought out in 1827. The public did not take to it, nor did Bulwer himself think much of the novel. But the opportunistic Colburn* sniffed bestsellerdom in *Pelham* (1828) and launched it with a powerful advertising campaign. Bulwer's anatomy of dandyism was the book of the year. Success is reflected in Bulwer's price, which soared to £1,000. He also earned £20 a sheet for contributions to Colburn's fashionable *New Monthly Magazine*. Between 1827 and 1834, he produced eight full-length novels, a sociology of Britain (*England And The English*, 1833) and a torrent of journalism and poetry. He was a Liberal MP who in 1832 reformed himself out of a seat. He returned to Parliament the same year, and continued to represent Lincoln until 1841. Bulwer edited the *New Monthly* from 1831 to 1832, and while his marriage held together, he and Rosina lived a furiously fashionable social life, at Hertford Street in Mayfair, despite the inconvenient arrival of two children. But his health broke down and on a recuperative visit to Italy in 1834 so too did the marriage. After much squalid quarrelling, the separation was formalised in 1836. Bulwer's fiction in this early phase is versatile but uneven. *The Disowned* (1828) is too long (four volumes) and a poor successor to *Pelham*, *Devereux* (1829) is a stilted historical* novel set in Queen Anne's reign. *Paul Clifford* (1830) is more interesting. This story of a gentleman highwayman owes something to Gay. As a novel with a purpose, written against the 'universal medicine' of capital punishment, it is also somewhat Godwinian. The inclusion of low-life 'flash', or slang, made up the recipe for what was to become known as Newgate* fiction. Legend has it that *Paul Clifford* cleared the largest impression ever of a novel on its first day of publication. The work established Bulwer as the undisputed successor to Scott. It also made him a mark for the satirists on *Fraser's Magazine**. Their campaign against Bulwer, as conducted by Maginn* and later Thackeray*, is the most virulent in Victorian literary history. *Eugene Aram* (1832), the novelisation of a notorious scholar-murderer's career, 'took all Europe by storm'. But the implication in the narrative that Bulwer condoned Aram's murderous theft (on grounds of his superior 'genius') gave his opponents, notably Maginn, the cast-iron moral justification that they needed for further persecution. Bulwer, 'the corrupter of youth', was to be mercilessly baited over the next fifteen years. And to add to his miseries, Rosina chose to humiliate him publicly, with novels like the extravagantly libellous *Cheveley** (1839). Nevertheless, his position as England's leading novelist was, by the turn of the decade, secure. Bulwer was the first nineteenth-century novelist to project himself as an intellectual, interested in ideas, and how fiction can be their vehicle. Professionally, he was very astute, and understood clearly the way in which an ambitious writer needed to take possession of his career, and not become the slave of ruthless publishers. But for all its achievement and stimulating variety, there are flaws in Bulwer's early work, which tended to augment over the subsequent years. Increasingly, he fancied himself as a 'philosopher' and drags his narrative through 'mazes of metaphysical investigation' to what he takes to be 'the arcana of the universe'. His obsession with Idealism is especially tedious. Another fault is that of wilful amateurism. He never entirely rid himself of the pose that novels were an 'idle' pursuit, something thrown off by a brilliant mind in low gear. It was as a historical novelist that Bulwer scored most heavily with his early readers. In Italy in 1834 he may have lost a wife, but he came back with the ideas for two bestsellers, *The Last Days of Pompeii* (1834) and *Rienzi* (1835). *Rienzi* is the more interesting (if less spectacular) of the two. Set in mid-fourteenth-century Rome, the novel plays off republicanism (embodied in the Roman tribune, Rienzi) against autocratic monarchy and aristocratic hegemony. *Rienzi*'s moral is, as Bulwer puts it, 'to be great and free, a People must trust not to individuals but themselves'. As an MP, Bulwer resigned his seat in 1841, and did not return to Parliament until 1852, by which time he was a land-owning Tory with Disraelian views (having inherited the family Knebworth estate in 1843). From 1858 to 1859, he was Secretary of State for the Colonies after which his political career effectively came to an end. Bulwer-Lytton's literary production diversified greatly in the ten years after *Rienzi*. There were highly successful plays such as: *The Duchess De La Valliére* (1836); *Richelieu* (1839); *Money* (1840). He also wrote well-received poems such as the controversial *The New Timon* (1846), a work which presumed to attack Tennyson. But fiction remained his main line of work. *Night And Morning* (1841) centres on an ill-assorted marriage. With his next novel, *Zanoni** (1842), Bulwer embarked on his career of writing 'mystical novels'. Other notable occult fictions of Bulwer-Lytton's are *A Strange Story** (1862), the ghost* story, *The Haunted And The Haunters** (1859) and the pioneering science fiction* tale, *The Coming Race** (1871). In 1843, he had analysed English nationalism with *The Last Of The Barons**. Popular as it was at the time, and long after, Bulwer-Lytton's historical fiction now seems turgid. *Harold** (1848) conceives the last Saxon King as a liberal patriot. Bulwer-Lytton underwent a severe physical breakdown in 1844. When he returned to fiction writing, it was with two extremely different works, conceived, as he claimed, simultaneously. These were the Newgate novel *Lucretia** (1846) and the domestic* novel *The Caxtons** (1849). The 'arsenical' Lucretia subjected Bulwer-Lytton once more to the abuse whipped up by his earlier murderer-hero Eugene Aram. After this final exercise in crime fiction, he devoted himself to the domestic* mode, and followed the well-received *Caxtons* with a sequel, *My Novel** (1853). Bulwer-Lytton had been returned to Parliament in 1852, and was now very much a public man, a Conservative and more serene in his private life. He continued writing, but evidently the effort of full-length fiction was less attractive to him. His remaining long novels are relatively few in number: *What Will He Do With It?* (1859); *Kenelm Chillingly** (1873); *The Parisians** (1873). The last is unfinished, although still substantial. Supposedly narrated by the hero of *The Coming Race*, it is set in Paris just before the Commune. This novel displays, to the end, all Bulwer-Lytton's plot artifices: lost relatives, lost fortunes, complicated narrative surprises. It is not easy to sum up Bulwer-Lytton's achievement. He was over-valued in his own day, and has been under-valued by posterity. He can plausibly claim to be the father of the English detective* novel, science fiction, the fantasy* novel, the thriller, and the domestic realistic novel. BL 25. *DNB*. RM. *NCBEL*. Wol. Sad.

M

MAARTENS, Maarten (i.e. Joost Marius Willem Van der Poorten Schwartz, 1858–1915). Schwartz was born in Amsterdam, the son of a doctor. His father, a German Jew by birth, was converted to Christianity, and worked for the Scottish Presbyterian Church's campaign to propagate the Gospel among Jews (a vocation that on at least one occasion brought him close to being lynched). His mother was a well-born Dutch lady. The boy was educated in England from his sixth to his twelfth year when his father suddenly died and he returned to Amsterdam. His education was completed in Bonn where the family moved in 1873 and at the law faculty of the

University of Utrecht, where he earned a doctorate and was considered a brilliant student. In 1883, Schwartz married a cousin and settled down in Zonheuvel Castle, near Doorn. But her chronic invalidism and his own poor health led to the couple spending much of their married life on the Riviera and in Switzerland. In 1885, he began publishing verse (in English) which was well received. Three years later, Schwartz took the pen name of 'Maarten Maartens' and began writing (in English) various trial novels, initially published at his own expense. Oddly, his début was with a detective* story, *The Black Box Murder* (1889). This led to the first of his 'Koopstad' sequence, *The Sin Of Joost Avelingh** (1890), the story of a nephew who marries so as to disoblige his rich uncle. These 'Dutch Tales Told In English' were in the genre tradition, primarily for a British readership. Others in the series are: *An Old Maid's Love* (1891); *God's Fool** (1892), whose hero is saintly and imbecilic; *A Question Of Taste* (1892), a biting study of Dutch bourgeois mores; *The Greater Glory* (1894), 'a story of high life'; *My Lady Nobody* (1895), which has a complex legal sub-plot around the heroine, Ursula. These last two works create a fictional world of near Balzacian scale and represent Maartens's finest achievement. His other fiction includes *Her Memory* (1898), a psychological study of marital bereavement which evidently draws on the author's feelings for his own wife. The widowed English hero, Anthony Stollard, is finally brought back from his fruitless grief to a useful social existence. Maartens was one of the most popular writers of the Victorian era and in 1907 he made a triumphant trip to the USA. He was mortified by the outbreak of war in 1914, and died a year later. His invalid wife (to whose health much of his life had been devoted) survived Maartens by ten years. Much of his fiction embodied a hatred of established religion and he is unusual among Dutch writers of his age in having taken his principal inspiration from English rather than French fiction. It was a matter of regret to him that he was always unpopular as an author in Holland where he was generally taken to offer travesties of the national character. BL 17. *WW*. Wol. Sad.

MABERLY, Mrs [the Hon. Catherine 'Kate' Charlotte] (née Prittie, 1805–75). Kate Prittie was born in Corville, Tipperary, and in 1830 married William Leader Maberly (1798–1885), an army officer and later an MP. Maberly was appointed permanent secretary to the Post Office in 1846 and figures as an obstructive administrator in Anthony Trollope's* *Autobiography*. On her part, Mrs Maberly wrote a number of frothy three-volume silver fork* and historical* romances: *Emily Or The Countess Of Rosendale* (1840); *Leontine, Or The Court Of Louis XV* (1846); *Fashion* (1848); *The Lady And The Priest* (1851); *Display* (1855); *Leonora* (1856). The last is 'the history of a bold, bad, beautiful woman who having lost her character plunges into crime to preserve her reputation'. The *Athenaeum** found it 'slipshod and vulgar'. Remembering her origins Maberly also published a volume on Ireland's suffering in the year of the great famine, 1847. BL 8. *DNB*. Wol.

MacCABE, William Bernard (1801–91). MacCabe was born in Dublin of Catholic parents. He began working life as a journalist in 1823 and in the early 1830s moved to London where he wrote for the *Morning Chronicle*. A man of scholarly interests (especially in Anglo-Saxon history) he travelled widely. In the 1850s he left Britain to live in Brittany and follow various antiquarian pursuits. MacCabe wrote historical* romances, such as *Bertha* (1851), a romance of the dark ages, and *Adelaide, Queen Of Italy* (1856). In 1861, he published the more interesting *Agnes Arnold*, an Irish* novel dealing with the rebellion of 1798. He died in Dublin, aged ninety. BL 2. *DNB*. Wol.

McCARTHY, Justin (1830–1912). Irish politician and writer. McCarthy was born near Cork, a Catholic, and the second son of a clerk to the Cork city magistrates. Justin was first intended for the legal profession but family hardship forced him out to work at the age of seventeen. His first employment was with the *Cork Examiner*, for whom he later wrote articles on the Irish Famine. McCarthy for a while allied himself with the radical Young Ireland movement and in 1853 he emigrated to Liverpool. There he worked on the *Northern Daily Times* and in 1855 married. (His wife was to die prematurely in 1879.) In 1859 he moved on to London, to work for the *Morning Star*, and in 1864 became editor of the paper. In the 1860s, McCarthy associated with leading Liberal politicians and political theorists such as John Stuart Mill. He visited the USA in 1868, returning in 1871 on the grounds that he could best serve the Nationalist cause in Britain. On his return, he worked for the *Daily News*. Around the same period he began to write fiction. His first novel, *Paul Massie*, appeared anonymously in 1866 under Tinsley's* imprint, and was moderately successful. It was followed by *The Waterdale Neighbours* (1867). As early as 1868, McCarthy had prospered sufficiently to resign much of his newspaper work. In 1879, he was invited by Parnell to stand for Parliament as a Nationalist, and was elected. He defected from Parnell after the other politician's public disgrace in the O'Shea divorce scandal of 1890. From 1890 to 1896 McCarthy was chairman of the Nationalist Party. In 1897, his health collapsed. Almost blind, he retired from Parliament in 1900 to spend his remaining years quietly at Westgate on Sea. In 1903, Balfour awarded him a Civil List pension. McCarthy's fiction represents only a particle of a full life's activity. But *Dear Lady Disdain* (1875), the story of an uncompromisingly scornful heroine, Lady Marie Challoner, and the similarly conceived *Miss Misanthrope* (1878) stand out as superior works. Both suffer as narratives from not much happening in the plot apart from scene-setting, world travel and conventional love-making. In general, McCarthy's main skill is in the creation of vivacious young heroines. Critics also agreed in finding his English clear and concise. *Mononia* (1901) is a retrospective and autobiographical 'Love Story Of Forty-Eight' which the *Athenaeum** called 'an amiable narrative of youthful patriotism'. As usual, the young heroine, Munster-born Mononia, found favour. *Lady Judith* (1870) is a melodrama set in London in the year of the Great Exhibition, 1851. *A Fair Saxon* (1873) is generally thought his best Irish* novel. It chronicles the love of an English girl for a radical Irish MP, Maurice Tyrone, and has a Fenian sub-plot. McCarthy wrote three novels with Mrs Campbell Praed* (e.g. *The Right Honourable**, 1886, a story of parliamentary ambition wrecked by passion; *The Ladies' Gallery*, 1888). These collaborative works which combine political settings with romance enjoyed considerable popularity. BL 11. (JM and CP) BL 3. *DNB*. *NCBEL*. Wol.

McCARTHY, Justin [Huntly] (1860–1936). Only son of the above. Justin McCarthy was educated at University College, London. In later life he travelled widely, cultivated an interest in oriental literature and was elected to Parliament in 1884 as a Nationalist MP. His career as a published author began in 1881. McCarthy was a moderately successful dramatist and historian, as well as a novelist. His fiction includes: *Lily Lass* (1889), a novel chronicling the Young Ireland movement with a striking opening set in the American Civil War; *A London Legend* (1895), a novel which reviewers found reminiscent of his father's *Dear Lady Disdain* (1875); *The Royal Christopher* (1896). The last of these is clearly derived from Stevenson's* *Treasure Island*. McCarthy's first wife, Marie Cecilia (b. 1876), whom he married in 1894, was a music hall artiste (stage name 'Cissie Loftus') who composed songs and wrote tales for young people. BL 20. *WW*. Wol.

The Macdermots Of Ballycloran, Anthony Trollope, 1847, 3 vols, Newby. Trollope's first published novel. It was begun in September 1843, after the move to Ireland on Post Office work which he saw as marking a great reform in his life. Trollope married in 1844 (another reform) and completed his novel by June 1845. Through the agency of his mother, the work was taken by Newby*, a notoriously unreliable publisher. *The Macdermots* exploited current interest in Ireland, ravaged by the 1847 famine. Its narrative chronicles the tragic demise of a landowning family. Larry Macdermot lives in a dilapidated mansion in Co. Leitrim, whose mortgage (enforced by his enemy, the vulgar builder Joe Flannelly) he cannot keep up. Enmity between the Macdermot and Flannelly families is sharpened by Larry's having declined to marry Joe's daughter, Sally. Macdermot's daughter, Feemy, is herself seduced by the locally hated English police officer, Captain Myles Ussher. Ussher, who enforces the excise laws against poteen distilling, is murdered by Feemy's brother, Thady. He is hanged, his father Larry goes mad, Feemy dies bearing Ussher's bastard and the Ballycloran house is finally vacated of Macdermots. As Trollope records, the work was an abysmal failure with the reading public.

MacDONALD, George (1824–1905). Scottish clergyman, editor and wide-ranging writer, MacDonald's fame today rests mainly on his fantasies*. (Ironically, many Victorians thought these his weakest writing.) MacDonald was born at Huntly, West Aberdeenshire, where his father was a farmer. Young George was brought up in the country, where he imbibed a quantity of folklore and raw Calvinism. He subsequently won a bursary to Aberdeen University. Two years into his courses, in 1842, MacDonald's studies were interrupted, either because of lack of funds or because of rustication. During the enforced leisure of the summer of 1842, the young man read widely in German Romantic literature and formed much of his later literary personality. After graduation (with a degree in science) MacDonald moved to London in 1845 where he worked as a tutor and apparently discovered a religious vocation. In 1848 he entered an independent theological college, and went on to become a Congregational minister at Arundel, in 1850. His ministry there was not happy. His lungs began to reveal a hereditary disposition to tuberculosis. His flock found his sermons doctrinally lax and he left for Manchester in 1853 with the intention of supporting himself by literary work. Here he made the acquaintance of the poet Henry Septimus

Sutton and Alexander John Scott, principal of Owens College. MacDonald had meanwhile married in 1851. He published his long-conceived dramatic poem, *Within And Without* in 1855, and three years later, his allegorical ('Faerie') romance in prose, *Phantastes**. MacDonald's subsequent writing career followed separate tracks. He wrote 'weird' visionary visions of imagined worlds such as *The Portent* (1864). In a quite different vein he wrote vernacular tales, set in a solidly described and actual Scotland such as: *Alec Forbes Of Howglen** (1865); *Annals Of A Quiet Neighbourhood* (1867); *The Seaboard Parish* (1868); *Robert Falconer** (1868); *Malcolm* (1875). MacDonald also wrote historical* tales such as *St George And St Michael* (1876), a tale of the English Civil War. Some of MacDonald's fiction is overtly didactic, such as *Paul Faber* (1879), in which the hero is a doctor finally won round to faith in God, or *Sir Gibbie** (1879), the affecting story of a city street arab. MacDonald also has sensation* stories (e.g. *Donal Grant*, 1883) and light-textured Scottish romances (e.g. *Heather And Snow*, 1893) to his credit. All in all, MacDonald should be ranked a more versatile writer than his conventional reputation as a fantasist suggests. And some of his novels such as *David Elginbrod* (1863) and *Adela Cathcart* (1864) mix his realistic and fantastic modes to powerful effect. But not all readers liked the heterogeneity of his fiction, and he was accused of offering the public 'ragbags' on occasion. Despite his resignation from the ministry, he continued to preach in a lay capacity. After various travels (including a stay in Algiers in 1856, for his health) MacDonald settled in London in 1860. Here he was friendly with F. D. Maurice, Carlyle, Ruskin* and the Brownings. He was closely allied with the publisher Alexander Strahan*, and in 1870 took over the editorship of Strahan's *Good Words For The Young*, in which his affecting allegory *At The Back Of The North Wind** (1871) was serialised. MacDonald was by now a celebrity and lectured widely. In 1872, he toured America, meeting among others, Emerson. In 1877 he was awarded a Civil List pension of £100. From 1881, his health rapidly declined, and he spent a large part of each year in Italy for the sake of his lungs. In 1902 he settled at Haslemere, in a house erected for him by his son Greville. MacDonald's imaginative stories for children are among the finest of the century and his own children carried on some of their father's literary creativity. Ronald MacDonald (b. 1860) wrote the historical novel *The Sword Of The King* (1900), a tale of England under James II. Greville MacDonald (1856–1944, in later life a distinguished medical man) wrote fantasies in the Edwardian period. BL 37. *DNB*. RM. *NCBEL*. Wol. Sad.

MACDONALD, James Middleton (1857–1916). Macdonald was born in Melbourne, Australia, of Scottish parentage. His father was a minister, and he was educated at the Scottish College, Melbourne, and Exeter College, Oxford. On graduation (with a second-class degree in theology) Macdonald was ordained, and held a succession of chaplaincies which took him all over the Empire, the Americas and the East. He married the editress of *The Ladies' Field* in 1884, and the couple settled in Nowgong, India. Among other books with exotic settings, Macdonald wrote *Thunderbolt, A Bushranging Tale* (1894) and *The Baba Log* (1896). The last is a story about Indian children for English children and contains overt imperial propaganda (about how to 'lick the Boers', for instance). BL 2. *WW*.

MACFALL, Captain [Chambers] Haldane [Cooke] (1860–1928). Macfall, the eldest son of an army officer, was himself educated at Sandhurst military academy. He was subsequently commissioned and in 1885 joined the West India Regiment in Jamaica. Macfall's stepmother was the novelist, Sarah Grand*, who spelled her married name 'McFall'. He does not mention her in his *Who's Who* entry. On his retirement from the service in 1890 (with the rank of lieutenant) Macfall turned to writing for his livelihood. Jamaica forms the background for his lively picaresque novel, *The Wooings Of Jezebel Pettyfer* (1897). Subtitled 'Being The Personal History Of Jehu Sennacherib Dyle, Commonly Called Masheen Dyle', the work is unusual in having a West Indian Negro hero and a densely documented depiction of black life. The bulk of his fiction and publications in art history and military theory fall into the twentieth century. Of Victorian interest is his novel, *The Masterfolk* (1903), a chronicle of 1890s Bohemian life in London and Paris, dedicated to George Meredith*. Macfall was also a talented artist and designed numerous book covers. BL 3. *WW*. Wol.

MACFARLANE, Charles (1796?–1858). Historian and historical* novelist. Macfarlane was born in Scotland, and in his younger years travelled widely in Europe and the Near East, spending the years from 1816 to 1827 in Italy and from 1827 to 1829 in Turkey. Apparently at this stage of his life he was wealthy. In 1829, Macfarlane settled in London. There he was associated with the popular educator Charles Knight, and produced a stream of popular histories, historical biography and travel books. His workmanlike historical novels include: *The Armenians, A Tale Of Constantinople* (1830); *The Camp Of Refuge* (1844), a much reprinted story of Hereward the Wake and Ely in the eleventh century; *A Legend Of Reading Abbey* (1845); *The Dutch In The Medway* (1845). These last two were gathered up as 'Old English Novelettes' (1846–47). As a man of letters, Macfarlane's status is a notch above that of hack. Like Thackeray's* Colonel Newcome, he ended as a poor brother of the Charterhouse in 1857, where he died a year later. BL 4. *DNB*. Wol. RLF.

James McGlashan (1846–55). Dublin publisher. McGlashan (1800?–58) was probably born in Edinburgh and began working life there as an assistant in Blackwood's* publishing house. From 1830 to 1846, he worked with William Curry* in Dublin, becoming a partner in the firm in 1837. From its start in 1833 he took a keen interest in the house's *Dublin University Magazine**. When Curry died in 1846, McGlashan took over as sole owner, in conditions of considerable financial difficulty precipitated by the Famine. McGlashan remained the principal Dublin publisher until his retirement in 1855 to Edinburgh, where he died insane, three years later. Boase.

MACHEN, Arthur (i.e. Arthur Llewellyn Jones, 1863–1947). Welsh novelist, fabulist and translator. For the purposes of literary periodisation, Machen is awkwardly suspended between the nineteenth and twentieth centuries. But although critical recognition came late, his literary personality was clearly formed in the Victorian 1890s. He was born in Caerleon-on-Usk, and (particularly in his later career) took his Celtic heritage seriously. His father was a clergyman, and young Machen tried unsuccessfully in 1880 to enter the Royal College of Surgeons. One reason he failed was that his head was evidently too full of poetry to contain medical facts. He published (at his own expense) a first volume, *Eleusinia* ('The Mysteries') in 1881. This was followed in 1884 by another vanity publication, the Burtonesque *Anatomy Of Tobacco*. In the same year, Machen picked up various writing and translating commissions. In 1887 he married and his father died, leaving him an inheritance that ensured financial independence for the next fifteen years. In 1888, he brought out a collection of fantastic and occult pieces, *Thesaurus Incantatus*. At the same time, he was translating Casanova's *Memoirs* (they appeared in print in 1894). On the edge of English letters in one of its more interesting phases (before Wilde's* downfall), Machen was acquainted with many of the leaders of literary fashion. In 1890, there appeared his *Fantastic Tales* and in the same year he wrote his first novel proper, the mythic-erotic *Great God Pan**. This was eventually published in John Lane's* prestigious *Keynotes** series in 1894. It was, Machen later claimed, the quintessence of 'yellowbookery'. In 1895, his second novel, *The Three Impostors**, appeared also under Lane's imprint. The reception of this work was tainted by the Wilde scandal. From 1895 to 1897, Machen worked on his masterpiece, *The Hill Of Dreams*. This 'Robinson Crusoe Of The Soul' follows its author hero, Lucian Taylor, through literary London, Rome and to an imagined and drug-induced infernal region. It ends with his death. The work was eventually published by Grant Richards in 1907. In the late 1890s, Machen became more involved with Celtic mythology and in 1900 he joined the Hermetic Order of the Golden Dawn. He subsequently had a long and productive career as a twentieth-century author, and belatedly gained a deserved measure of literary fame, though not, surprisingly, an entry in the *DNB*. BL 13. *WW*. RM. *NCBEL*. Wol. RLF.

MACHRAY, Robert (1857–1946). Machray's family emigrated from Aberdeenshire to Canada during his early childhood. Brought up in the new country, he returned to Cambridge University and after graduating BA was ordained in 1883. Machray subsequently taught English at the University of Manitoba, marrying in 1886. Thereafter, he took up a ministry in Rupert's Land, where his uncle (also Robert Machray, 1831–1904) was Anglican Archbishop. But illness forced him into semi-retirement after 1889. In this period Machray began to write fiction. His novels include: *Grace O'Malley* (1898), a pro-Celtic Irish historical romance; and *The Vision Splendid* (1899), a romance of the modern stage, co-written with Florence Bright; *Sir Hector* (1901), the story of a Scots gentleman. Machray was war editor of the *Daily Mail*, 1904–05, by which date he had evidently returned to Britain. He wrote some detective* thrillers towards the end of his career. BL 15. *WW*.

McILROY, Archibald (1860–1915). McIlroy was born at Ballyclare, Co. Antrim, of Irish Protestant stock. He began working life as a bank clerk. Thereafter he moved into the insurance business and was active in local Irish politics. The last three years of his life were spent in Canada before going down with the *Lusitania* as a neutral casualty of the first World War. His fiction, all strongly Irish*-regional in flavour and mild in content, includes: *The Auld Meetin' Hoose Green* (1898), a story of Antrim peasantry in the mid-century which one sarcastic reviewer called 'a crop of Ulster kail' (in reference to the kailyard*, or 'cabbage patch' school); *When Lint Was In*

The Bell (1898); *By Lone Craig-Linnie Burn* (1900), a story of the Scots-Irish in Ulster; *A Banker's Love Story* (1901). BL 5.

McILWRAITH, Jean Newton ('Jean Forsyth', 1859–1938). The daughter of a leading ornithologist who emigrated from Scotland in 1853, McIlwraith was born in Canada and educated at the Ladies College, Hamilton, Ontario. She began her career writing short stories for magazines, and worked as a publisher's reader in New York, 1902–19. Her main achievemont is a historical* novel, dealing with the afteimath ot 1745 among the Scottish omigi ant community in Canada, *The Curious Career Of Roderick Campbell* (1901). She also collaborated with fellow Canadian William McLennan* to write *The Span O' Life, A Tale Of Louisbourg And Quebec* (1899). McIlwraith apparently never married, occasionally wrote as 'Jean Forsyth' and died in Ontario. BL 3. *WW.*

MACKAY, Charles (1814–89). Mackay was born in Perth, Scotland. His father was a former army officer, a disabled veteran of Walcheren. His mother dying during his childhood, Mackay was brought up in a foster home at Newhaven, and picked up a miscellaneous education in Scotland, London and Belgium. Having mastered several languages, he decided against the army and became instead a successful journalist in the 1840s. Mackay went on to found various papers, earned a doctorate from Glasgow University in 1846 and from 1852 to 1859 was editor of the *Illustrated London News*. In 1860, he established the *London Review* and a year later (with John Maxwell*) *Robin Goodfellow*. Neither did well. Nor did he succeed in the early 1860s as a journalist in America. Mackay's greatest success was in writing songs. (His most famous lyric is 'The Good Time Coming'.) He published a number of books, including the novels: *Longbeard, Lord Of London, A Romance* (1841), the story of a mill-owner MP; *The Gouty Philosopher* (1862), 'Or The Opinions, Whims And Eccentricities Of John Wagstaffe'; *Luck And What Came Of It* (1881), a political 'Tale Of Our Times'; *The Twin Soul* (1887), 'A Psychological And Realistic Romance'. Mackay married twice. By his first wife (whom he married at eighteen) he had three sons and a daughter. When the first Mrs Mackay died in 1859, he married Mary Elizabeth Mills, by whom he had earlier (in 1855) fathered a daughter, Mary (i.e. 'Marie Corelli*'). Mackay passed on to his eccentric daughter many of his curious interests in topics such as Celtic philology. He suffered a collapse of health in 1883 and spent the last seven years of his life semi-paralysed. BL 3. *DNB. NCBEL.* Wol. Sad. RLF.

MACKIE, John (1862–1939). Mackie was born in Stirlingshire, and educated at school there. After studying agriculture at college, he emigrated to Australia in 1882, and 'became in turn explorer, pioneer, gold-digger'. Mackie claimed to be the first man to settle in the far northern territories by the Van Alphen river. He subsequently moved on to Canada, where for a while he served in the Mounties. Mackie later travelled widely over North America. He also fought for the British forces in South Africa, and was decorated for gallantry. His fiction, largely devoted to sagas of colonial adventure, includes: *The Devil's Playground* (1894), 'A Tale Of The Wild North West'; *Sinners Twain* (1895), a romance of the 'Great Lone Land'; *They That Sit In Darkness* (1897) 'A Story Of The Australian Never-Never'; *Tales Of The Trenches* (1901). BL 8. *WW.*

McLENNAN, William (1856–1904). McLennan was born in Montreal, and educated at McGill University where he read law. He subsequently practised as a notary in Montreal, and devoted much of his energy to the promotion of a Canadian cultural consciousness. His fiction includes the historical* romance, *Spanish John* (1898), a narrative based on the life of the Scots-Canadian soldier of fortune, John MacDonell (1728–1810). McLennan also wrote *In Old France And New* (1899) and in collaboration with Jean McIlwraith* *The Span O' Life* (1899), an eighteenth-century tale of Louisbourg and Quebec. BL 2. *WW*.

MACLEOD, Fiona. Her creator William Sharp* gave this figment of his authorial imagination a well-worked-out identity and even a separate entry from his own in *Who's Who* (1900). Allegedly born in the Hebrides, resident in Iona and unmarried, Fiona Macleod 'wrote' sixteen mythic novels or collections of tales, including: *Pharais, A Romance Of The Isles* (1894); *The Mountain Lovers* (1895); *The Sin Eater And Other Tales* (1895), the title piece being the story of a man who takes on himself a corpse's sins, so as to give it release; *The Washer Of The Ford* (1896); *Green Fire* (1896); *The Divine Adventure* (1900). In this last, the most exalted of Macleod's works, the soul, the will and the body go on a joint pilgrimage to the 'hills of dream'. In its totality, Macleod's fiction exalts mystic Celtic consciousness (as did George Meredith*, the 'Prince of Celtdom') and the Gaelic tongue at a period when the culture was vanishing. Her recreations are solemnly listed as: 'sailing, hill-walks, listening'. Her work was published by the firm of P. Geddes, of which Sharp was an adviser. After the novelist's death, to compound the sexual complications, Macleod's collected works were edited by Sharp's widow. BL 16. *WW*. Wol. *NCBEL*.

MACLEOD, Norman (1812–72). Scottish ecclesiastic, editor and writer for children. Macleod was born at Campbeltown, Argyllshire; his father (also Norman Macleod) was a minister, a moderator of the Church of Scotland and eventually (after 1841) Chaplain in Ordinary to the Queen. The young Norman went to Edinburgh University where he came under the personal influence of Thomas Chalmers at the period of the Disruption. Theologically, Macleod was moderate at a time when extreme opinions were common. He was ordained into the Church of Scotland in 1838. His first ministry was in Ayrshire where he was much loved by his parishioners as he was at Dalkeith, where he went in 1843. In 1851 Macleod moved to Glasgow and began to interest himself in evangelical journalism. In 1857 he was appointed Chaplain to the Queen (with whom he was a favourite) and a year later was awarded his doctorate of divinity by the University of Glasgow. Also in 1858, Alexander Strahan* approached him to edit what eventually (in 1860) became *Good Words**. The magazine was phenomenally successful, and soon claimed sales of 160,000. Macleod extended the journal's range beyond the narrowly evangelical, inviting authors such as Trollope* to contribute. (Although he was obliged to reject *Rachel Ray**, which he had commissioned, allegedly because it contained a scene of dancing.) Macleod was passionate about missionary work and in 1864, he himself travelled on church business to Egypt, and in 1867 made a voyage to India. On this trip, Macleod's health gave way, and he never fully recovered although in 1869 he was appointed Moderator of the Church of Scotland. In his fifties, Macleod wrote fiction of an improving kind (mainly for *Good Words*). It includes: *The Gold Thread* (1861), a moralistic fairy tale; *The Old Lieutenant And His Son* (1862) 'life-sketches' woven around the character of a half-pay navy man in a Scottish seaport; *Wee Davie* (1864), 12,000 copies of this uplifting story of an exemplary young Christian being sold in a week; *The Starling* (1867), 'A Scotch Story, By One Of Her Majesty's Chaplains' with poaching and redemption as its main subject; *Reminiscences Of A Highland Parish* (1867). BL 4. *DNB. NCBEL.* Wol.

Macleod Of Dare, William Black, 1878, 3 vols, Macmillan. (The novel was first serialised in *Good Words*,* and illustrated by a dozen artists, including the author's 'good friends' W. Q. Orchardson* and J. E. Millais*.) Like all Black's fiction, this novel deals with the clash of national cultures, and was inspired by his own sense of being an alien Scot in London. Keith Macleod is a Scottish baronet, and the last of his line, his five brothers having died in battle. Dare is his ancestral home in the Highlands. He comes to London, and falls desperately in love with a stunning actress, Gertrude White. She is attracted (no more) to him. On his return to Castle Dare, Macleod's faithful retainer, Hamish, his cousin Janet and his mother detect a profound change in him. After a gift of otter skins is well received, he goes to London again and declares his love to Gertrude. She is reluctant to surrender her career and a visit to Castle Dare does nothing to reassure her. Macleod finally sails down on his boat *Umpire* and abducts her. Off the coast of Mull, the yacht is sunk in a wild storm. The novel is rich in the land- and sea-scapes in which Black excelled.

MACLISE, Daniel (1806–70). Illustrator and artist. Maclise was born at Cork, the son of a former Scottish soldier, evidently a shoemaker at the time of his son's birth. The young Maclise was educated in Cork and began working life in a bank. In 1825, a sketch drew him to the attention of Sir Walter Scott. And two years later he moved to London. In 1829 he exhibited at the Royal Academy and over the next forty years established himself as a major historical and portrait painter. He also influenced the styles of later Victorian fiction illustrators with his contributions to *Fraser's Magazine* * (1830–36). Maclise himself illustrated some of Dickens's* Christmas* stories to good effect. *DNB.* Hou.

MacMAHON, Ella (d. 1956). A daughter of the Chaplain to the Lord Lieutenant of Ireland, Ella MacMahon was born in Dublin and educated at home. She evidently never married and apparently converted to Catholicism at some later point in her life. MacMahon was also keenly interested in local Dublin history and wrote extensively on the topic. She worked as a Civil Servant in which she was evidently extremely competent and during the first World War held senior posts in the newly formed government intelligence department. Late in life, she was awarded a Civil List pension. MacMahon's fiction, all of it lush romance, includes: *A New Note* (1894); *A Modern Man* (1895); *A Pitiful Passion* (1896); *The Touchstone Of Life* (1897); *Fortune's Yellow* (1900). The title of the last refers to a rose which recalls to the heroine her lover of twenty years earlier whom she gave up to marry for money. MacMahon continued writing novels until the late 1920s. BL 23. *WW.* Wol.

MacMANUS, Seumas [James] (1870–1960). MacManus was born in Donegal, the son of a peasant farmer. As he put it in later life: 'I am one of the mountain people. By the time I was seven I could tell a hundred of the old tales.' MacManus was for some years a National School teacher. From this humble work, he moved to journalism. Having first visited the USA in 1898, he made a number of lecture tours there in later life. His folkloric stories were immensely popular with American audiences and he was awarded an honorary doctorate by Notre Dame University in 1917. His fiction exploits the comic and idyllic stereotypes of Irish peasant life and includes: *The Leadin' Road To Donegal* (1896); *'Twas In Dhroll Donegal* (1896); *The Bend Of The Road* (1897); *The Humours Of Donegal* (1898). He died in New York City. English reviewers found MacManus's fiction too Irish* for reading comfort. BL 21. *WW*. Wol.

Macmillan (1843–). Publishers. Alexander (1818–96) and Daniel Macmillan (1813–57) were by birth Scots, sons of an Ayrshire farmer who died in 1823. Daniel came to England to work in the book trade in 1833, Alexander (who had been keeping a small school) followed six years later. In February 1843, they set up a bookshop in Aldersgate Street in the City of London, from which they published (non-fiction) books in a very small way. A year later, the brothers moved their business to Cambridge. And it was at the university town that they evolved what was to be their principal characteristics as publishers: intellectual earnestness, evangelical mission, a keen desire to prosper. The firm's early lists were strongly academic and theological in tone. In 1850, they incorporated themselves as Macmillan and Co. The first novel the firm put out was Charles Kingsley's* Christian Socialist and extravagantly muscular* *Westward Ho!** (1855). This bestseller was followed by another, Thomas Hughes's* *Tom Brown's School Days** (1857). In 1857, Daniel died and a year later the firm moved to its new enlarged premises in Henrietta Street, Covent Garden, which it was to occupy for a century. In 1859, *Macmillan's Magazine** was successfully launched. The publication of Kingsley's *The Water-Babies** (1863) and Lewis Carroll's* *Alice's Adventures In Wonderland** (1865) led to a productive specialisation in children's* books (both for leisure reading and after 1870 for school education). In 1869, the house opened what was to be a highly profitable New York branch. Macmillan's (under the management of John Morley) published early work by Mrs Humphry Ward*, J. H. Shorthouse* and Henry James. In the 1880s and 1890s, the firm became the regular publisher of Hardy* and Kipling*. The Macmillan dynasty kept a firmer hold on the family firm than almost any other Victorian publisher, with the possible exception of Blackwood*. And even in fiction, Macmillan's contrived always to retain two features of their early character: high-mindedness and intimate friendly relations with authors. In the 1890s, under Frederick Macmillan (1851–1936, Daniel's son), the firm was a pioneer in setting up the Net Book Agreement (1899) and the Publishers' Association (1895), innovations essential to the stability of the British book trade in the twentieth century. (AM and DM) *DNB*.

Macmillan's Magazine (1859–1907). The Macmillan brothers, Daniel and Alexander, had the idea to start a house magazine as early as 1855. In fact, it was not until the end of the decade (after Daniel's death, and the setting up of a London branch of the publishing house) that the magazine got off the ground. *Macmillan's*, when it first appeared in November 1859, pipped *Cornhill** by a couple of months as the first 1s. monthly magazine. Under its first editor, David Masson, *Macmillan's* was a more earnest organ than George Smith's venture and unillustrated. But it prominently featured serial fiction, kicking off with Hughes's* *Tom Brown At Oxford*. Works by the Kingsley* brothers succeeded (including *The Water-Babies**). In general, *Macmillan's* tended to concentrate more on closely associated house-authors than *Cornhill*. Subsequent editors after Masson departed in 1868 adopted a conservative line (notably Mowbray Morris, editor from 1885 until the journal's decease in 1907). Throughout its career, however, *Macmillan's Magazine* upheld its proprietors' evangelical, intellectual, Arnoldian–Liberal cast of thought, while at the same time offering a wider array of fiction than any comparable journal. Among the authors who provided major novels for *Macmillan's* were Frances Hodgson Burnett*, Annie Keary*, Thomas Hardy*, Mrs Oliphant*, William Black*, R. D. Blackmore*, Charlotte M. Yonge*, William Clark Russell* and Henry James. *BLM*. WI.

MACNAUGHTAN, S[arah] (d. 1916). The fourth daughter of a JP, Macnaughtan was widely travelled (spending part of her childhood in Canada) and was evidently a student of music and painting. Little is known of her life although she evidently had substantial private means, and served with the Red Cross in the Boer War. Macnaughtan's fiction includes the much reprinted *Selah Harrison* (1898), the story of a Scottish prodigal who reforms, does good works in the East End of London, devoting his life to missionary work on Taro Island, where he finally dies. 'A most gloomy book', the *Athenaeum** called it. Macnaughtan also wrote *The Fortune Of Christina McNab* (1901), the story of a young daughter of the Kirk who unexpectedly inherits £18,000 p.a., and sundry post-Victorian novels along the same romantic lines. Her last book, *Some Elderly People And Their Young Friends* (1915) was dedicated to her publisher, Reginald Smith, of Smith, Elder*. She died at her home in Park Lane, London. BL 12. *WW*.

MacQUOID, Katharine S[arah] (née Thomas, 1824–1917). Kate Thomas was born in Kentish Town, suburban London, and was educated largely in her parents' home. In her youth she seems to have used her mother's name, Gadsden. An early visit to France evidently made a deep impression on her. In 1851, she married the artist Thomas Robert MacQuoid. (Later, he was to illustrate her books of travel. He died in 1912.) Mrs MacQuoid began her writing career with a short story in the pages of John Maxwell's* *Welcome Guest* in 1859. At this period of her life she seems to have been encouraged by G. H. Lewes*, who sagaciously advised her to capitalise on her 'early impressions' of France. Her first works include: *Piccalilli* (1862); and *A Bad Beginning* (1862). The second of these chronicles a fashionably loose 'French marriage' and was the prelude to a huge output of popular fiction aimed at the woman reader of which *Patty* (1870), was probably the most popular item. In her middle years as a writer, MacQuoid was helped by John Morley of *Macmillan's Magazine** and as a devout sideline also produced tract fiction for the SPCK*. Among MacQuoid's many later novels are: *Wild As A Hawk* (1868); *Too Soon* (1873), 'The Study Of A Girl's Heart', like most of her works; *Beside The River* (1881), the river being the Meuse; *Her Sailor Love* (1883); *At the Red Glove** (1885); *Joan*

Wentworth (1886), which follows its heroine between France and England; *An Old Chateau* (1891); *Maisie Derrick* (1892); *Appledore Farm* (1894); *His Last Card* (1895). The last is the study of a virtuous heroine entrapped by a heartless gambling villain. MacQuoid lived mainly in London, and also wrote travel books, some with her son, Gilbert Samuel MacQuoid. She was a perennially popular writer in the American market and her last work of fiction seems to have been *Molly Montague's Love Story* (1911). BL 65. *WW*. Wol. Sad. RLF.

Macrone (1835–37). Publisher. Probably a Manxman by origin, John Macrone (1809–37) came to London in the early 1830s, and with some small capital behind him, entered into partnership with James Cochrane in 1833. Two years later, Macrone set up independently in St James's Street. His short career thereafter was brilliant. In 1836, he reissued Ainsworth's* *Rookwood**, illustrated by George Cruikshank*. He went on to publish Ainsworth's *Crichton** (1837). Over 1836–37, Ainsworth went on to partner Dickens* with Cruikshank on the highly successful *Sketches By Boz*. Macrone contracted for further work from his star novelists, but a chronic shortage of cash led to his having to sell his Dickens property to Chapman and Hall* and his Ainsworth property to Bentley*. He was one of the first publishers to recognise the talent of the young Thackeray*. Macrone died bankrupt and prematurely from influenza. His business was taken over by Hugh Cunningham.

Mademoiselle Ixe, Lanoe Falconer (i.e. Mary Elizabeth Hawker), 1890, 1 vol, Fisher Unwin. (First published as Volume I in T. Fisher Unwin's 'Pseudonym*' Library. The series was eccentrically pocket-sized and the rule was that authors must write under a *nom de plume*.) A story of Russian nihilism. Mademoiselle Ixe is governess to an English family where she wins the affection of the daughter of the house, Evelyn Merrington. The Merringtons give a ball, at which a Russian count is to attend. Ixe uses Evelyn to approach the Count during the function, and shoots him. Evelyn and her lover subsequently help the would-be assassin to escape, and during their flight Ixe explains that it is love of country which has motivated her. She is, in fact, an aristocrat herself in disguise. The Count recovers. Three years later, when she marries, Evelyn receives a cryptic letter of congratulation from a Russian prison, signed 'X'.

MAGINN, William (1793–1842). Maginn packed an astonishing amount of literary activity into his short, debauched life. He was born in Cork, the son of a schoolmaster. Unusually precocious, he went to Trinity College, Dublin, in 1811 and took a degree in classics. For a while Maginn helped his father teach, then in 1819 took his doctorate in law. About this period, he began to contribute to *Blackwood's Magazine** and the *Literary Gazette*. In 1821, he went to Edinburgh and became a leading Blackwood's* author, generally writing under the pseudonym Morgan O'Doherty. In 1823, he moved on to London. There he began a connection with L. E. L. (i.e. Laetitia Landon*) which continued (at least as an item of popular gossip) until her mysterious death in 1838. Maginn was already a byword for dissipation. In 1827, he produced a satirical novel, *Whitehall, Or The Days Of George IV*. A year later, he broke with *Blackwood's* and founded a rival,

*Fraser's Magazine**, in 1830. In 1836, one of his fiercer reviews (of the novel *Berkeley Castle*) led to a duel with its bullying author, the Hon. Grantley Berkeley*. As the 1830s progressed, Maginn became increasingly drunken and desperate. In 1837, destitution drove him to debtors' prison. Thackeray* (a Maginn protégé) gives an affectionate, but none too flattering portrait of the imprisoned Maginn as 'Captain Shandon', in *Pendennis**. Maginn began to write another novel around the time of his death, *John Manesty, The Liverpool Merchant** (1844). It was completed haphazardly by Charles Ollier*. BL 3. *DNB*. RM. *NCBEL*. Wol. Sad. RLF.

The Maid Of Sker, Richard D. Blackmore, 1872, 3 vols, Blackwood. (Serialised in *Blackwood's Magazine**, August 1871–July 1872.) The narrative begins in 1872. In the Bristol Channel, 'Fisherman Davy' Llewellyn finds a young girl in a drifting boat. Her condition recalls the ballad heroine, the Maid of Sker. Having recently lost his wife and his sailor son, Davy adopts the foundling. By various physical signs, Bardie (as she is called), is eventually found to be of aristocratic family. In the interim, Davy voyages to Devon where he falls foul of the villainous Parson Chowne and has a number of random adventures. The interest of the work largely centres on the narrator Davy's quaintness and roguery. Among the novel's notable set-pieces are the burying of the local ship-wrecker Black Evans's five sons in a sandstorm and some lively action at sea in the Napoleonic Wars.

MAITLAND, A[gnes] C[atherine] (1849–1906). Agnes Maitland was born in London, the daughter of a merchant. The family moved when she was five to Liverpool. Maitland had her early education at home and later studied domestic science at college in Liverpool. In her subsequent career, she became an educationalist and was for fifteen years examiner to the National Union of Schools of Domestic Economy and an inspector of schools in north-east England. In 1889, she took up the post of principal of Somerville College, Oxford. Maitland, who never married, wrote on miscellaneous educational topics, cookery and hygiene. Her fiction which was aimed principally at the young reader includes: *Elsie* (1875), a 'Lowland Sketch' about a miller's daughter; *Madge Hilton* (1884); *Rhoda* (1886); *Nelly O'Neill* (1889). BL 3. *WW*.

MAITLAND, Edward ('Herbert Ainslie, BA', 1824–97). Maitland was born in Ipswich, the son of an evangelically inclined clergyman. The family was solidly upper class, and boasted a number of distinguished military, professional and churchmen. The young Maitland was educated at Brighton, and brought up in an atmosphere of strict religious orthodoxy. He graduated from Cambridge in 1847. The 'doubts' that were epidemic in this decade prevented him from immediately entering the Church. To clear his mind, he travelled to America, where he became a forty-niner. From the Californian minefields, he travelled to Australia. There he married (his wife dying soon after) and became a commissioner of crown lands. Maitland returned to England in 1857 where he supported himself by literary work. In addition to journalism and reviewing, he produced novels mostly with a pronounced mystical element. The autobiographical and essayistic *The Pilgrim And The Shrine* (1867) and *The Higher Law* (1869) were found strikingly original and well received. The first, subtitled 'Passages From

The Life And Correspondence Of Herbert Ainslie, BA', is ostentatiously a novel of ideas, using letters, conversations and poetic interludes to chart the hero's journey towards religious conviction. *The Higher Law* is a mystical study of marriage. Through the prophetic novel set in a mystically conceived African Utopia, *By And By, An Historical Romance Of The Future* (1873), Maitland formed an acquaintance with Anna Kingsford (1846–88), the wife of a Shropshire vicar. A highly unusual Anglican vicar's lady, she was a journalist and since 1870 (but not for long) a Catholic. Kingsford congealed the spiritual tendencies of Maitland's mind into something like fanaticism. Together in 1874, they went to Paris and turned out a stream of writing directed against materialism, meat-eating and vivisection. (Kingsford qualified as an MD in this period.) Maitland claimed to have visions, and to be himself the reincarnation of St John the Evangelist (whose experiences he could accurately recall). After a brief flirtation with theosophy and Blavatsky in 1883, the couple founded their own hermetic society. In 1888, Kingsford died (inevitably, Maitland claimed to be in touch with her beyond the grave). Maitland thereafter returned to England, and in 1891, 'in response to astral intimations', founded the Esoteric Christian Union. He died at Tonbridge. BL 3. *DNB*. Wol.

Major Gahagan, W. M. Thackeray, 1841, 1 vol, Cunningham. (Full title, *Some Passages In The Life Of Major Gahagan*. Serialised in the *New Monthly Magazine**, February 1838–February 1839.) An early burlesque which takes the form of a boastful autobiography by Major Goliah O'Grady Gahagan, commander of a battalion of Irregular Horse, Ahmednuggar. There are four comic targets: Irish braggadocio; the tall stories of the Indian service; the current vogue for oriental adventure stories; and heroism. (One perceives early stirrings of *Vanity Fair**, Thackeray's 'Novel Without A Hero'.) The funniest episode in the story has the intrepid hero destroy 134 elephants with a single cannon-ball.

The Making Of A Marchioness, Frances Hodgson Burnett, 1901, 1 vol, Smith, Elder. (Serialised in *Cornhill**, June–July 1901.) Burnett's heroine is Emily Fox-Seton, a well-born but poor (£20 p.a.) youngish (thirty-four) lady who supports herself. She is invited by a rich friend, Lady Maria Bayne ('the cleverest, sharpest-tongued, smartest old woman in London'), to attend a house party at Mallowe, in the country. The aim of the party is to find a mate for an eligible marquis. Emily modestly does all she can to promote his match with the beautiful Lady Agatha Slade. But unaccountably, the Marquis of Walderhurst chooses the good and simple Emily herself with the peremptory explanation 'You are the woman I want'. A late Victorian version of the Cinderella fable.

MALLOCK, W[illiam] H[urrell] (1849–1923). Mallock was born near Crediton, Devonshire, the eldest son of a clergyman. His family was long established in the county, and Mallock was through his mother related to J. A. Froude*. His early education was by private tutor. In 1869, Mallock went to Balliol College, Oxford, where he won the 1871 Newdigate Prize for poetry. Otherwise, he did not have a brilliant undergraduate career. As he put it in *Who's Who*, he 'never adopted any profession though at one time [he] intended for diplomacy'. Instead, Mallock published *The New Republic**, his most famous work, in 1877. It takes the form of a Platonic–Peacockian debate. ('Culture, Faith And Philosophy In An English Country House' is the work's subtitle.) The central conversations feature various Victorian sages (Carlyle, Arnold, Ruskin*, Pater*, etc.) under thin disguise. This witty essay in philosophical fiction was followed by *The New Paul And Virginia, Or Positivism On An Island* (1878), the hero and heroine being shipwrecked returning from Australia. The butts in the idea-laden work are T. H. Huxley, Frederic Harrison and the Comteans. Mallock subsequently wrote various scholarly, satirical and philosophical works, and a quantity of fiction. *A Romance Of the Nineteenth Century* (1881), is a story set on the Riviera (like other of his narratives), and the work's heroine, Cynthia Walters, irritated reviewers by her 'indecency'. *The Individualist* (1899) is a satire deriding the view that the lower classes can be fed culture from above, the main target being Mrs Norham, 'an ornament of intellectual Bloomsbury' who has the dubious distinction of having written 'a novel with a purpose'. One of Mallock's more popular novels was the wittily reactionary *The Old Order Changes* (1886) which has a heroine, Consuelo Burton, whose mind becomes troubled by 'writings of modern agitators' and who conducts long dialogues with a 'highly connected and highly intellectual priest, Father Stanley'. Mallock's wit troubled his contemporaries. As the *Athenaeum** complained: 'No writer of fiction succeeds better than Mr Mallock in leaving a nasty taste on the palate and a nasty smell in the nose of his readers.' A self-conscious stylist and purveyor of ideas, Mallock declared the purpose of his writing to be 'the exposure of the fallacies of Radicalism and Socialism'. His other fiction includes: *A Human Document* (1892); *The Heart Of Life* (1895); *The Veil Of The Temple* (1904). Mallock's work sold surprisingly well, 8,000 copies of *A Human Document* being cleared in three years. He never married, and was converted to Catholicism on his deathbed. An autobiography, *Memoirs Of Life And Literature*, was published in 1920. BL 9. *DNB*. RM. *NCBEL*. Wol. Sad.

Man And Wife, Wilkie Collins, 1870, 3 vols, F. S. Ellis. (Serialised in *Cassell's Magazine*, January–September 1870.) Collins's novel with a purpose, written against the iniquities of the English and Scottish marriage laws. After a complicated prologue the novel's action opens at the Scottish estate of Windygates, home of the Lundie family. Anne Silvester, a governess, has been seduced and made pregnant by a young aristocrat, Geoffrey Delamayn, a brute who cares for nothing but athletics. Anne cajoles Delamayn into spending the night with her at a nearby inn so as to make her his common-law wife. But on hearing that his father Lord Holchester is dying, Delamayn prevails on Arnold Brinkworth to go in his place. Arnold does so, and is falsely identified by the innkeeper as Anne's 'husband'. Lord Holchester recovers and insists that his wayward son marry an heiress, Mrs Glenarm. To do so, he disowns Anne, who bears a stillborn baby. Meanwhile, Arnold has married Anne's pupil and friend, Blanche Lundie. This match is declared bigamous, when the affair at the Scottish inn becomes public knowledge. By virtue of an injudicious note Delamayn wrote, he in his turn is eventually forced to take the now unwilling Anne as his wife. He proceeds to lock her up in a secluded London mansion, under the custody of a homicidal housekeeper, Hester Dethridge. Delamayn dies of a stroke, while trying to smother Anne. She is reunited with her friends and marries Sir Patrick Lundie, who has been her ally throughout. The plot is among Collins's less convincing but was successfully dramatised by the author.

A Man Made Of Money, Douglas Jerrold, 1848, 1 vol, Bradbury and Evans. (Serialised in six monthly parts with illustrations by John Leech*, October 1848–January 1849.) The shrewish wife of the man of the title, Solomon Jericho, nags him (like Jerrold's famous Mrs Caudle*) until he utters the unlucky Midas-wish, 'I wish to Heaven I was made of money!' His body subsequently turns into a fund of banknotes, on which he can draw. But each withdrawal shrinks him physically. At first Solomon rises in the world but finally becomes a misanthropic miser, despising the human race that would consume him. He dies after accidentally throwing one of his banknotes in the fire. The story is one of Jerrold's most effective satires on capitalism. He evidently borrowed the idea for his novel from Balzac's *La Peau De Chagrin* (1831).

The Manchester Man, Mrs G. Linnaeus Banks, 1876, 3 vols, Hurst and Blackett. (Serialised in *Cassell's Family Magazine* January–November 1874.) Despite a hackneyed foundling-hero plot, the novel contains an exact chronicle of Manchester during its critical years of growth from the Napoleonic Wars to the period of the first Reform Bill. It begins with a baby being found floating on the waters during the great Lancashire flood of August 1799. The waif is saved by a cotton spinner, Simon Clegg, and called Jabez. Jabez Clegg grows up a fine lad and forms at the Blue Coats school what is to be a lifelong enmity with the well-born Laurence Aspinall. On leaving school, he goes to work for a small-ware manufacturer, Mr Ashton. His steadiness earns him promotion. Meanwhile, Manchester suffers the corn-law riots of 1816 and the Peterloo massacre of 1819, where Jabez is wounded (although he refuses to testify against the militia man who slashed him). By now, Jabez can presume to hope for the hand of his master's daughter, Augusta Ashton. But the wily Laurence elopes with her (despite having already a local mistress). Jabez nobly makes a charitable marriage with a rich invalid, Ellen Chadwick, who loves him. She soon dies, leaving her wealth to the hero. By the 1830s, Jabez has risen to be Ashton's partner, having helped him weather the terrible bank crashes of 1826. Aspinall dies, after years of abusing his wife and 'better late than never', Jabez, now the rich 'Manchester Man', marries his first love.

MANN, Mary E. (i.e. Mrs Fairman Mann, née Rackham, 1848–1929). Mary Rackham was born at Norwich, a merchant's daughter. She married and had four children, but gave no details about her husband in her *Who's Who* entry. Mann evidently lived in Norfolk all her life, mainly on the Suffolk border at Thetford, and wrote about rural life in East Anglia. Her fiction includes: *The Parish Of Hilby* (1883), 'A Simple Story Of A Quiet Place'; *Susannah* (1895), the story of a well-bred young lady who disguises herself to go into service as a 'maid of all work' at 11s. a week; *Mrs Peter Howard* (1886); *Confessions Of A Coward And A Coquette* 1886, 'As Told By Herself'; *Moonlight* (1898), the love story of an older man for a young woman. In *The Patten Experiment* (1899), one of her livelier efforts, a wealthy family tries to live on the wages of an ordinary labourer. Reviewers appreciated the ingenuity of Mann's plots. BL 34. *WW*. Wol.

MANNERS, Mrs Catherine (later Lady Stepney, née Pollok, 1785–1845). The daughter of a Wiltshire clergyman, Catherine Pollok's first marriage was to Russell Manners. As Mrs Manners, she published the gothic*-historical* novels *Castle Nuovier* in 1806, and *The Lords Of Erith* in 1809. Widowed, she married Sir Thomas Stepney (d. 1825) in 1813. In later life, she lived in fashionable style as the again-widowed Lady Stepney, in Cavendish Square. Stepney was a frequent contributor to the annuals, and wrote a quartet of silver fork* novels: *The New Road To Ruin* (1833); *The Heir Presumptive* (1835); *The Courtier's Daughter* (1838); and *The Three Peers* (1841). BL 6. *DNB*.

MANNING, [Miss] Anne (1807–79). Anne Manning was born in London, the daughter of a Lloyd's insurance broker with a legal family background. She was brought up in Chelsea (which seems to have stimulated her youthful historical imagination) and educated at home by her mother, an accomplished woman, distantly connected with Charles Lamb. An artistically inclined child (who won a medal from the Royal Academy for a copy she made of a Murillo painting) Anne passed on her education to her younger siblings. This led to her first book, *A Sister's Gift* (1826), 'Conversations On Sacred Subjects'. Initially published at her own expense, the work eventually yielded £60 for its young author. Manning's adult life was singularly uneventful. From the 1850s, she lived as a spinster daughter at Reigate Hill for over twenty years. When her mother died, she moved to Tunbridge Wells, where she again lived (and eventually died) quietly. As a novelist, Manning specialised in spuriously authentic historical* 'diaries'. Her first notable success was with *The Maiden And Married Life Of Mary Powell* (1849), Mary Powell being the later Mrs John Milton. The work was first published in *Sharpe's London Magazine** and was an immediate hit. Its popularity led to a sequel, *Deborah's Diary* (1858). These works were written in a pastiche seventeenth-century style and printed with the old-fashioned typography and page layout for which there was a vogue at the period. (The most famous example being Thackeray's* *Henry Esmond**.) Of Manning's other fifty or so books, *Cherry And Violet, A Tale Of The Great Plague* (1853; also a diary, written by 'Cherry') stands out. Michael Sadleir observes a dualism in her fiction: 'through a bibliography predominantly historical, ran a vein of quiet comedy of village and small town contemporary life'. Into this second category falls her first published novel, *Village Belles* (1838) and her most successsful, *The Ladies Of Bever Hollow* (1858), a study of small-town life in the Midlands. In the first category would fall *The Good Old Times* (1857) and *A Noble Purpose Nobly Won* (1862). Manning was scrupulously anonymous as an author, always listing herself as 'the author of *Mary Powell*'. Some records give Manning the married name Mrs Anne Rathbone, although details of any husband are missing. BL 43. *DNB*. RM. *NCBEL*. Wol. Sad.

The Manxman, Hall Caine, 1894, 1 vol, Heinemann. Hall Caine's most powerful and characteristically regional* novel. The work has a genetic theme typical of the 1890s. The Christian family have furnished Deemsters (judges) for the Isle of Man for six generations. But the two sons of 'Iron' Christian have gone to the bad. One, Thomas, although trained as a lawyer in England, disobeys his father by marrying below his class. His wife takes to drink, and Thomas dies disappointed, leaving a son, Philip. Iron's other son Peter also dies, leaving a bastard, Pete Quilliam. Philip and Pete grow up friends. And when Pete goes off to make his fortune in South Africa, he entrusts his sweetheart, Kate Cregeen, to his cousin's care. Kate is repelled by Pete's semi-literate letters home, and is gradually attracted to the more genteel Philip. One obstacle to their love seems removed when Pete is reported dead. But Philip is warned by his Aunt Nan not to repeat his father's mistake and marry a peasant. He seduces Kate. Unexpectedly Pete returns (now a captain) to claim his bride. They marry, and a daughter Kate (in fact Philip's child) is born. Philip, meanwhile, has embarked on a promising career in law, and eventually fulfils the family destiny by becoming Deemster. Unable to bear her guilt, Kate runs away to England. She eventually returns to the Isle of Man, is arrested for street-walking and tried before Philip. He publicly confesses his guilt, and the ostracised couple leave the island together. The novel is marked by Caine's love of sexually charged melodrama and his close attention to the picturesque details of Manx life and lore.

Marcella, Mrs Humphry Ward, 1894, 3 vols, Smith, Elder. Marcella Boyce, the beautiful heroine, is first discovered in London where she is an art student and an associate of the Venturists (i.e. Fabians). Her life is transformed when her father inherits the family estate, Mellor Park. But he is not happy in his inheritance; earlier disgrace he brought on the family results in the Boyces still being ostracised by local society. Marcella, however, soon catches the eye of Aldous Raeburn, the Conservative son of Lord Maxwell. Despite their political differences, Aldous and Marcella become engaged. But they are driven apart when one of Maxwell's keepers is killed by a crippled poacher (hunting to feed his starving family). The poacher, Jim Hurd, is sentenced to hang and Marcella does all in her power to save him, in vain. After this crisis, Marcella works as a nurse in the East End of London. She becomes involved with a debonair Liberal, Harry Wharton, while Aldous makes a name for himself in the Government. Wharton is a newspaper proprietor whose paper, the *Clarion*, is supporting the striking steel workers. But he sells out to the owners, and when the fact leaks out a disillusioned Marcella is gradually reconciled to Aldous. They eventually marry, and inherit the Maxwell title and property. The principal characters are reintroduced in a sequel, *Sir George Tressady*** (1896). *Marcella* focuses many of its author's ambivalences about philanthropy (while writing it, she was setting up a benevolent institution in Bloomsbury, University Hall).

MARCHMONT, Arthur W[illiams] (1852–1923). Marchmont was born in Southgate, Middlesex, the son of a clergyman. He was educated first privately, then at Pembroke College, Oxford. On graduating he moved into journalism, rising to be editor of the *Lancashire Daily Post*. In 1888, Marchmont entered Lincoln's Inn with a view to a career in law. About the same time, he began writing fiction. His novels, which are largely Zendaish romances for Longman*, include: *Isa* (1888); *By Right Of Sword* (1897); *The Greatest Gift* (1899), a work which opens with the sea-captain hero unexpectedly finding himself heir to £10,000 a year; *In The Name Of A Woman* (1900); *For Love Or Crown* (1901), the crown in question being that of 'Saxe Lippe', a central European Grand Duchy. Marchmont's last novel seems to have been *By Right Of Sex* (1923), the 'By Right' prefix being his hallmark. BL 3. *WW.*

Margaret Denzil's History, Frederick Greenwood, 1864, 2 vols, Smith, Elder. (Subtitled 'Annotated By Her Husband', the story was serialised in *Cornhill*, November 1863–October 1864.) A sensational* bigamy* novel, typical of the 1860s and notable principally for its ingenious mode of narration. The history is told by an extraordinarily innocent heroine, with worldly-wise interpolations and editings by her 'husband', John Denzil. Margaret is a child of mysterious origins, brought up by a family of cottagers (the Forsters) in the New Forest. Margaret is clearly not their daughter and she is eventually sent to school in France, then to Mrs Lamont's finishing establishment in Brighton. At this point, Margaret's life becomes very complicated. The wandering Lamont son Arthur returns from service abroad and falls in love with her. Arthur has a guilty secret, having killed, as he thinks, the seducer of his sister Charlotte. After a conversation with Charlotte, he suddenly leaves to fight in the Russian wars. What she has told him is that Margaret is the daughter of her seducer, Wilmot, who was supposed to have killed his wife. Margaret knows nothing of this. For many years she has been financially supported by John Denzil, a sailor who married well. John's 'torment' of a wife refuses to adopt Margaret, and he has over the years fallen in love with the girl. His wife supposedly drowns herself. John gratefully proposes to Margaret, is accepted and they settle down as man and wife at Twickenham, where they have a son, Ishmael. Finally, Margaret discovers the secret of her birth and the fact that her mother actually died accidentally. It also transpires that Lamont did not, as he thought, kill Wilmot and the two men are reconciled before both dying on the battlefield in Russia. As a final stroke of theatre, it emerges that Denzil's wife has in fact staged her death, in order to torture her husband. At the end of the novel the heroine is living alone, a wife but no wife, with her fatherless child. John Denzil returns sadly to sea.

Margaret Maitland, Margaret Oliphant, 1849, 3 vols, Colburn. (Full title, *Passages In The Life Of Mrs Margaret Maitland Of Sunnyside.*) Oliphant's first book and her first success. (Colburn* gave the young Scottish authoress £150, and the work went into several editions.) The story is told by the heroine herself. A god-fearing lowland Scot spinster ('a quiet woman of discreet years and small riches') and a daughter of the Manse, she becomes the guardian of a young relative, Grace Maitland. Grace's romance with Mistress Maitland's minister-nephew, Claud, provides the dramatic element to the plot. The main interest, however, is in the shrewd but devout personality of the narrator and the exactly rendered regional setting ('the parish of Pasturelands'). Oliphant wrote a 'conclusion', *Lilliesleaf*, in 1855, with a livelier action, involving a heroine's attempt to clear her brother's name. *Margaret Maitland* is a precursor of the kailyard* school and introduces in passing the town of 'Thrums' that J. M. Barrie* later picked up for his lowland idylls.

Margaret Percival, Elizabeth Missing Sewell, 1847, 2 vols, Longman. (The first edition was advertised as having been 'edited' by the author's brother, William Sewell*.) *Margaret Percival* was written at the request and with the aid of the author's brother, William, to warn against the dangerous inroads Catholicism was making into the Anglican establishment. The story is set in the small town of Staunton. Margaret, the older daughter, is put in charge of the education of her six younger brothers and sisters. She is conspired against by the Countess Novera, a twenty-six-year-old Italian widow, and her private confessor, Father Andrea. Subtle and intellectual, he succeeds in unsettling the young girl's faith and she comes to the brink of religious perversion. Margaret is rescued by her uncle, Mr Sutherland, a High Anglican clergyman who has 'come to peace with his God'. He offers no intellectual argument but commands simple, unquestioning obedience to the Church of her fathers, 'Crush doubts!'. Margaret gives up the friendship of Beatrice Novera. Her father, Dr Percival, dies of exhaustion, and the daughter and her mother go to live in a cottage near Mr Sutherland, having found their haven in the local Anglican church (where Margaret's brother now officiates). The novel is on the same lines as William Sewell's *Hawkstone** (1845) though less fierce in its anti-Catholicism.

Maria Monk, 'Maria Monk', 1836, 1 vol, Harper. The most widely circulated of scurrilous anti-Catholic fictions in the early Victorian period. Although the text varies from printing to printing, it invariably concentrates on 'The Hidden Secrets Of A Nun's Life In A Convent Exposed'. The work takes the form of an authentic confession by Maria Monk, dated January 1836, and purports to expose the cruelties and sexual delinquencies practised at the Congregational, Grey and (particularly) Black nunneries, in Montreal, Canada. Maria takes the veil and with her friend Jane Ray penetrates to the inner mysteries of the notorious *Hôtel-Dieu*. Among other allegations, Monk professes to reveal that the nuns exist principally as concubines for insatiably lecherous priests. After routine trials and tribulations, Maria is supposed to escape to New York, from which haven she writes her account. The narrative was actually the work of an impostor arrived in New York from Montreal, very pregnant. She was assisted in her composition by the Rev. George Bourne (1780–1845), a Presbyterian from England with fanatic anti-Catholic views. Monk was soon discredited (although her 'disclosures' continued to circulate) and died in a New York prison in 1848, where she had been sent on a charge of theft.

Marion Fay, Anthony Trollope, 1882, 3 vols, Chapman and Hall. (Serialised in the *Graphic*, December 1881–June 1882.) The narrative hinges on one of the inheritance plots which fascinated Trollope in his later period. The Marchioness of Kingsbury has three sons, but chafes under the thought that her husband's title will go to the child of his first marriage, Lord Hampstead, an aristocrat with perversely radical views on society. She plots with the Kingsbury domestic chaplain, the Rev. Thomas Greenwood, to do away with Hampstead. Marion is the beautiful daughter of an old Quaker clerk, Zachary Fay. Hampstead loves Marion, but she refuses to marry him, knowing that she will soon die of consumption. Hampstead's friend George Roden (a post office clerk) loves Lady Frances Trafford, one of the Kingsbury daughters. The match is fiercely opposed by the family. Opposition melts when Roden inherits an Italian dukedom. He declines the title, but the change in his fortunes (and promotion) allow the marriage to take place.

Mark Rutherford's Deliverance, Mark Rutherford (i.e. William Hale White), 1885, 1 vol, Trübner. The sequel to *The Autobiography Of Mark Rutherford**, bringing the hero's life to its premature conclusion, or 'deliverance'. Like its predecessor, this volume is supposedly edited from the subject's journal by his friend, Reuben Shapcott. The narrative initially finds Mark alone in London. He works as a parliamentary correspondent and lives around Goodge Street, in the centre of the city. He has gradually accepted that 'there is nothing in him'. He is a person of no consequence. But he retains some sense of his early evangelical zeal, although he can no longer worship with the 'Independents'. With a friend, McKay, he opens a small mission in Drury Lane. Few attend, or are converted to Rutherford's doctrine of 'living Christ'. In the most unromantic circumstances, Mark is reunited with Ellen, a girl who rebuffed him earlier in his provincial young manhood. She is now a widow, and he marries her. After a trip to Bexhill, she catches typhus and Mark discovers the true worth of his stepdaughter Marie (whom he previously disparaged). Ellen recovers, but Mark soon after dies unexpectedly of a weak heart. The firm where he has worked as a copying clerk sends back his few belongings wrapped in brown paper, with his last week's salary and no letter. The novel, like its predecessor, is remarkable for its articulate humility and passivity in the face of dreary circumstance. At the age of seventy-eight White provided for his son some notes entitled *The Early Life Of Mark Rutherford* (1913). These fill in some of the blanks left in 'Rutherford's' autobiography. The town where he was brought up is revealed to be Bedford. The bookseller with whom Rutherford worked in London after his expulsion from the ministry is identified as John Chapman and 'Theresa' as the young George Eliot*.

MARRIOTT, Charles (1869–1957). Marriott was born in Bristol, where his father was a brewer. He was educated privately by clergymen, and at art school in South Kensington. Marriott subsequently took a strong interest in photography, and qualified as a dispensing chemist. He worked from 1889 to 1901 at a lunatic asylum as photographer and druggist. After this miscellaneous preparation, he became a popular novelist and art critic. Marriott's novels typically alternate adventure with psychological romance. His one Victorian novel, by chronological reckoning, is *The Column* (1901), published by John Lane*. The work is set in Cornwall, where the heroine Daphne's father erects a Doric column, of towering symbolic significance. The narrative ends with Daphne drowning herself, overwhelmed by what the monument represents. Reviewers of the period reckoned *The Column* a major work of English literature. Marriott seems to have given up writing fiction just before the first World War. BL 21. *WW*. Wol.

MARRYAT, Florence (1838–99). The youngest and eleventh child of Frederick Marryat*, she was born in Brighton, largely educated at home and, as she later claimed, 'by myself'. In 1854, at the age of sixteen in Penang, she married a soldier, T. Ross Church, and thereafter lived with him in India. The couple had eight children. He rose in the service but they divorced in 1879. (Later, the wife misreported herself a widow.) In 1879 she married Captain Francis Lean. Marryat had returned to England as early as 1860 and wrote her first novel (as 'Miss Marryat'), *Love's Conflict* (1865) 'to distract her mind in the intervals of nursing her children with scarlet fever'. It is the story of a young wife bound to a despicable older husband with the bitter epigraph, 'He jests at scars who never felt a wound'. Thereafter Marryat turned out some ninety works of fiction. They were largely sensation* novels and superheated domestic romances. Typical samples are: *Too Good For Him* (1865), the story of a dissipated husband and a saintly wife; *Petronel* (1870) the story of a love affair between a middle-aged doctor and his young ward partly set in Belgium; *Her Lord And Master* (1871), a story with two heroines, one a wife one a nun; *On Circumstantial Evidence* (1889), a divorce melodrama; *A Fatal Silence* (1891); *A Passing Madness* (1897); *A Rational Marriage* (1899). In her early career, Marryat's sexual themes affronted reviewers who would occasionally pointedly refer to her (in defiance of her title pages) as 'Mrs Ross Church'. Michael Sadleir notes that 'during the first part of her writing life, Florence Marryat was bracketed with Annie Thomas [i.e. Cudlip*] as a purveyor of dangerously inflammatory fiction, unsuitable for reading by young ladies, but much to their taste'. A Catholic, Marryat was fascinated by spiritualism which she frequently introduces into her novels. As a spiritualist she wrote the popular book *There Is No Death* (1891). She was also an accomplished singer and playwright. Over the period 1872 to 1876 she edited the magazine *London Society* and worked with George Grossmith* on various entertainments. With her own theatrical company she toured in the late 1880s, featuring among her repertoire plays by herself (some taken from her novels) and by one of her eight children, Frank Marryat. (See *My Sister The Actress*, 1881.) Marryat supposedly gives a portrait of herself and her novel-writing sister Augusta in *Fighting The Air* (1875). There were also other Marryat daughters who wrote novels, Emilia Norris* and Blanche Marryat (author of *Briars And Thorns*, 1867). BL 81. Boase. Wol. Sad.

MARRYAT, Frederick (1792–1848). Marryat demonstrates how, almost accidentally, men of accomplishment in the early nineteenth century might stumble on a triumphant career of novel-writing. Like Scott, Marryat wrote 'impromptu novels to buy farms with' and invariably professed himself a bluff amateur in the finer points of his craft. Like Scott again, Marryat's life was remarkably full. It was as a naval man primarily that he presented himself to the fiction-reading world, and it is as 'Captain' that the novelist is usually titled. Marryat's naval career was, in fact, genuinely distinguished, and recommended him to a British public far enough removed in time to bask in Trafalgar's remembered glories and the 'Great' war against the French. Marryat's life in fact reads like one of his own nautical novels. He was born in the City of Westminster, where his father had once been an MP. The Marryats had property in the West Indies, and Frederick's father was a chairman of Lloyd's. In his youth, Marryat is supposed to have run away to sea three times. (The Royal Navy had a front-line role for cabin boys and powder monkeys; one reason that the sea always excites young readers.) In September 1806, young Marryat joined the *Imperieuse*, a 'crack' frigate under the command of Lord Cochrane, and saw active service against the French, his name appearing frequently in dispatches. He passed his lieutenant's examination in 1812 and after some illness was again in action off the coast of America in 1814. The end of the war a year after found him a commander at the precocious age of twenty-three. He was not, however, given command of a vessel until 1820 and his immediate postwar years were frustrating. In 1820, he took over a ten-gun brig, the *Beaver*. But this and subsequent service at sea continued to be boring and unfulfilling. Things looked up in 1824, however, when he again saw active service in the Burmese campaign. Between 1815 and 1829, he wrote his manual on the code of signals (1817), a pamphlet on naval impressment, and in 1810 married Catherine Shairp, a daughter of Sir Stephen Shairp. In 1828, following a dispute with the Admiralty (Marryat was notoriously hot-headed) he resigned the service (as a post-captain with a CB) having off-handedly, even by his standards, written two novels: *Frank Mildmay* (1829) and *The King's Own* (1830). His first hope was for a political career. But his attempt to enter Parliament as a Liberal MP in 1833 failed. And he quickly ran through the fortune his father had left him. From 1830 until his death, Marryat was a man of letters, and an exceedingly busy one. He travelled on the Continent (1835–36) and in America (1837), farmed in Norfolk, lived an increasingly full social and empty family life. All were expensive occupations, especially the separation from his wife, which cost him £500 annually after 1839. (There were eleven children.) And everything had to paid for out of his inkwell. Marryat's production was accordingly rapid; sometimes, as in 1834, frantic. *Frank Mildmay*, his début work, is the most indiscreet and autobiographical of his novels, being the story of an engaging naval scapegrace made good. *The King's Own* deals graphically in its early sections with the Nore mutiny and its ruthless suppression. These early novels and their successor, *Newton Forster* (1832), employ supremely theatrical and artificial narrative devices, such as the 'lost heir' plot (always Marryat's stand-by). But they also show Marryat's allegiance to *Don Quixote* and Le Sage's *Gil Blas* (as translated by Smollett). *Peter Simple** (1834) is Marryat's most sustained work. *Jacob Faithful* (1834) continues his obsession with foundling heroes. This story of a roguish Thames lighterman is, however, more London-proletarian than anything else Marryat wrote and its slang, ballads and low-life scenes align it with Ainsworth's* bestseller *Rookwood** (also 1834). *Japhet In Search Of A Father* (1836) is also land-based, and again has a foundling hero who devotes himself to finding a father whom he feels must be a great man. Having worked out the nautical* vein, Marryat's subsequent fiction thrashes around, never finding another entirely satisfactory formula, but never, apparently, alienating a loyal public. *Snarleyyow* (1837) is a strange exercise, nautical but centred on a dog whom the ship's crew think to be a fiend. *The Phantom Ship* (1839) is warmed-over Flying Dutchman, but it reveals the increasingly dark tone of Marryat's fiction. *Poor Jack* (1840) tells the story of a Thameside waif or mudlark. The novel was issued none too successfully in monthly numbers, illustrated by Clarkson Stanfield*. *Percival Keene* (1842) is yet another *Roderick Random*-derived picaresque autobiography. Marryat's enduring works from his last phase are *The Children Of The New Forest** (1847) and *Masterman Ready** (1842) with which he decisively turned the British nautical novel towards a juvenile readership. This trend is confirmed in *The Settlers In Canada* (1844), specifically subtitled 'Written For Young People'. In 1841 his health collapsed and he retired from his fine town-house in London's Manchester

Square to his Norfolk estate, Langham. Here he was cared for by his four surviving daughters, three of whom were to go on to be novelists in their own right. Florence Marryat* also wrote his biography. Marryat's eldest son, Frederick, drowned at sea in 1848, which precipitated the father's own death from apoplexy a few months after. *The Little Savage* was finished by another hand (presumably Frank Marryat's); it is yet another variation on the Crusoe theme. *Valerie, An Autobiography* (1849) is incomplete and Marryat's only experiment in using a female narrator. Marryat was one of the consistently best-paid novelists of the nineteenth century. Colburn* enticed him into the novel-writing profession with £400 for *Frank Mildmay*. Saunders and Otley* gave £1,200 for *Mr Midshipman Easy* (1836). Among magazines, Marryat was most closely associated with the *Metropolitan**. Marryat became editor and proprietor in 1832, an interest which he sold to Saunders and Otley for just over £1,000 in 1836. (He promptly transferred his services to Colburn's rival and nearly identical *New Monthly Magazine**.) Marryat initiated that ambidextrous practice by which a novelist might run his own fiction through a magazine (preferably his own) then lease it to the publishers for volume publication. Among his non-fiction productions are *A Diary In America* (1839) and *Olla Podrida* (1840). Everyone knew that Marryat was a slapdash writer. He made no secret of it himself. But though the critics might give him a 'confounded licking', contemporary readers and their descendants loved his easy-going novels. He is among the most reprinted of Victorian novelists. Marryat was also popular with his fellow authors. Dickens* liked him (and *Oliver Twist** may owe something to Marryat's many waif heroes). Thackeray*, throughout his life, remembered his 'dearly beloved' Marryat affectionately. BL 25. *DNB*. RM. *NCBEL*. Wol. Sad.

MARSHALL, Emma (née Martin, 1830–99). Emma Martin was born in Cromer, the daughter of a prosperous Norwich banker and a Quaker mother. Emma was named after an elder sister who had just died of consumption. Her early life was spent quietly in Cromer and Norwich, and as a young girl she conceived an enthusiasm for the poetry of Longfellow which in 1851 led to a lifelong correspondence with the American poet. In 1849 she went with her mother to live at Clifton near Bristol. In 1852, the two ladies were baptised into the Anglican Church. Emma subsequently married Hugh Marshall, a banker, in 1854. Two years later the couple moved to Wells where they remained until 1869 and seven children later. From 1869, the Marshalls were at Exeter, and from 1874 at Gloucester. Financial hardship struck in 1878 with the collapse of the West of England Bank, and the wife (now with nine children) became the main breadwinner. Her first published story had been *Happy Days At Fernbank* (1861), a work directly inspired by Charlotte M. Yonge*. She subsequently wrote 200 stories. Among all this prodigious output her most popular novel was *Life's Aftermath* (1876) which recreates the Quaker ethos of her childhood. Marshall specialised in historical* tales which introduced historically actual personages such as *Penshurst Castle* (1894) which has Sir Philip Sidney as its protagonist. Her other fiction includes: *In Colston's Days* (1883), a story of Bristol in the Great Rebellion; *Alma* (1888), the portrait of a quiet music mistress; *Bristol Diamonds* (1888); *Winchester Meads* (1890), a romance which features Bishop Ken; *In The Service Of Rachel, Lady Russell* (1892); *The Young Queen Of Hearts* (1898), a story of Elizabeth I; *The Parson's Daughter* (1899). Marshall's readership was juvenile in the main and she wrote extensively for the SPCK* and the religious publisher Nisbet*. Her later life was spent largely in Bristol, where many of her historical tales are set. Marshall's fiction was much admired by the critics Alfred Ainger and J. A. Symonds. BL 142. Boase. Sad.

The Martian, George Du Maurier, 1897, 1 vol, Harper's. (The work was first serialised in *Harper's Monthly Magazine*, from the month of the author's death, October 1896, until July 1897. The text was illustrated by Du Maurier himself and marketed in Britain by the American firm.) Du Maurier's last novel. The first half of the narrative is set in a Parisian boarding school, the Pension Brossard, in the late 1840s and early 1850s. The narrator is a British pupil, Robert Maurice, the son of a wine merchant. Maurice attaches himself to a new boy, Barty Josselin. The son of an aristocrat (killed in a duel) and a beautiful actress, Barty is dashing and brilliant. The school sections draw heavily on Du Maurier's own early experience at the Pension Froussard and the two main characters combine aspects of his own experience. On returning to London, the grown-up Maurice studies chemistry at London University (as did Du Maurier in 1851). Barty joins the Brigade of Guards. But his life is darkened (literally) when he begins to lose his sight, as did Du Maurier, at the age of twenty-five. Thinking the affliction irreversible, he is about to poison himself when he has a visitation from a Martian maid. This 'Martia', as she calls herself, informs Barty (through a secret shorthand) that his eyes will not deteriorate further and that henceforward she will be his inspiration. He marries a former love, the Jewess Leah Gibson, and writes (to Martia's dictation) a stream of fabulously successful visionary books (e.g. *The Fourth Dimension*). Leah and Barty have a number of children, including a daughter who is the incarnation of Martia. She falls from a tree, injures her spine, and dies. Barty joins her in death. The novel is told by a bereaved Maurice.

MARTIN, Violet Florence ('Martin Ross', 1862–1915). Violet Martin was born at Ross House, Galway, the eleventh and youngest daughter of the Deputy Lieutenant of the county. The family (Protestant in religion since the nineteenth century) had been established since the sixteenth century in Northern Ireland and had several members distinguished in literature and law. The Martin estate had suffered badly in the 1845 famine in which, unlike most of their class, the Martins were conscientious landlords. Violet's father shut up the family home, took up journalism in London to recover the Martin fortunes, and succeeded sufficiently to retire and die at Ross House in 1872. After her father's death, Martin lived in Dublin (although for most of her later life, a large part of her literary income was subsequently eaten up by the insatiable expense of keeping up the family property at Ross, which Violet's mother opened again in 1888). In Dublin, where the Martins lived in a series of rented houses, Violet was was educated at home by governesses who came three evenings a week, and later at Alexandra College. As a young lady, her diaries already reveal a sharp eye on middle-class life. (Much of her girlhood is recalled in the early chapters of *The Real Charlotte**, 1894.) On leaving college, she lived mainly in Ireland, making frequent trips abroad in the company of her cousin, intimate companion and collaborator in fiction, Miss Edith Oenone Somerville*. Somerville had been brought up in the country at Drishane. The cousins first met at Castletownshend in 1886. Both ladies rode enthusiastically to hounds. Martin had very poor eyesight, however, and was seriously injured riding in 1898, never fully recovering. This pastime is reflected in their best-loved work, *Some Experiences Of An Irish RM* * (1899; 'RM' stands for 'Resident Magistrate'). Their other fiction includes: *An Irish Cousin* (1889); *Naboth's Vineyard* (1891); *The Silver Fox* (1897). The alliance was supposed to have continued after 1915, by 'psychic' communication. In 1932, Ross was awarded a posthumous honorary doctorate of letters by Trinity College, Dublin. Martin never married but evidently had a long love affair with the minor poet, Warham St Leger. The sardonic fiction of Ross and Somerville offers a comprehensive satire on the Protestant Ascendancy and its foibles. Of the two, Martin seems to have had the warmer sense of humour and to have been the more intellectual and literary. She was also an ardent feminist and keen churchgoer. (EOS and MR) BL 16. *DNB*. R.M. Wol. Sad.

MARTIN, William ('Peter Parley', 1801–67). Martin was born in Woodbridge, Suffolk, the illegitimate son of a garrison laundress. His father may have been Sir Benjamin Bloomfield, a soldier stationed at Woodbridge during the Napoleonic Wars. Apart from dame's school, Martin was largely self educated. Nevertheless, he succeeded sufficiently to teach at a school in Uxbridge, a post he held until 1836. He also edited the *Educational Magazine* in the 1830s. Martin's success as an author came with *Peter Parley's Annual* (1840). He was, in fact, only one of the Parleys, and not the original. The editorial persona was the invention (in 1838) of the American Samuel Griswold Goodrich. Essentially the formula served to string together various tales and homilies for the young. The Parley books were incredibly successful in the 1840s. Of the half dozen piratical English practitioners, Martin and George Mogridge are reckoned best. Martin married three times, and spent his last years in dissipation. BL 4. Boase. RLF.

Martin Chuzzlewit, Charles Dickens, 1844, 1 vol, Chapman and Hall. (Full title prefixed with *Life And Adventures Of*. Serialised in monthly numbers, January 1843–July 1844, with illustrations by Phiz*.) The novel begins at Salisbury, in the domestic establishment of a hypocritical architect, Mr Pecksniff. Pecksniff routinely passes off the work of his articled pupils as his own. The action opens with the angry departure of one such student, John Westlock, and the arrival of another, Martin Chuzzlewit. There is considerable mystery attaching to Chuzzlewit's background. His grandfather (also Martin) is sick (possibly dying), attended by an orphaned young woman, Mary Graham, whom the young Martin loves. This love affair has vexed the grandfather who requests Pecksniff to dismiss the young man, which he does. The meek and good-natured Tom Pinch remains to be exploited by Pecksniff and his daughters, Charity and Mercy. Martin's villainous uncle Jonas proposes to the latter (having made love to the former), and after his father dies in suspicious circumstances becomes director of the fraudulent Anglo-Bengalee Disinterested Loan and Life Insurance Company. Martin emigrates to America, accompanied by a noble-hearted servant, Mark Tapley. The trip across the Atlantic (which Dickens himself had recently undertaken) is vividly described. In New York, he discovers snobbery and ludicrous pretension. He is swindled into buying land in the new southern township of Eden, which turns out to be nothing more than a poisonous swamp. Martin falls ill of fever, and is nursed back to health by the faithful Mark. The experience serves to cure Martin of his egoism and selfishness. They return to England and are reunited with Tom Pinch, now a librarian employed by a mysterious benefactor (in fact old Martin) Jonas murders Montague Tigg, who is blackmailing him. On being arrested, Jonas poisons himself. The two Martin Chuzzlewits are eventually reconciled, and the younger marries Mary Graham. Westlock marries Pinch's sister, Ruth. Mark Tapley marries the proprietress of the Blue Dragon inn. Pecksniff is denounced, falls on hard times, and finishes life a broken-down beggar, attended by his daughter Charity.

Martin Hewitt, Investigator. The general title for detective* stories by Arthur Morrison*, mainly published in the *Strand** and *Windsor* magazines, 1894–96. The most successful rival to Conan Doyle's* Sherlock Holmes, Morrison's sleuth is distinctly different. A 'private investigator', he has an office and charges fees. He is genial and plump, unlike the saturnine, cadaverous, amateur Holmes. Hewitt's cases are recounted by a confidant, Brett, a journalist who is much less obtrusive than Dr Watson.

MARTINEAU, Harriet (1802–76). A versatile woman of letters, philosopher and economist, Martineau was in one of her many parts a didactic novelist. She was born in Norwich, the sixth of eight children of a textile manufacturer of Huguenot extraction. One of her younger brothers was the later theologian, James Martineau. The family was Unitarian (a doctrine which favoured female education) and their circumstances (during Harriet's childhood at least) prosperous. Harriet was precocious, and read Milton at the age of seven. At the age of twelve there appeared the deafness that was to blight her life. By 1816 her hearing was largely gone, and with it most of her marriage chances. (Her fiancé, John Hugh Worthington, went mad and died shortly after the couple's becoming engaged in 1826. In her later autobiography, Martineau stoically records the tragedy as a lucky escape.) In 1829, the family was utterly ruined and thereafter Martineau lived by her pen. She claimed to find the loss of gentility liberating. Her material needs were simple, and as a political economist (from the age of fourteen), she invested her substantial earnings wisely. Ideologically, Martineau moved from religiosity to rationalism (though famously, she was to dabble with the mystical cult of mesmerism in her later years, claiming a miraculous cure from it in 1845). In 1832 she moved to London and her first major success in writing came with the *Illustrations Of Political Economy* which were serialised in monthly parts, 1832–35. Up to 10,000 copies of these exemplary fables were sold monthly. Within crude fictional narratives, the *Illustrations* introduced many of the themes of the later social problem* novel. Martineau found herself famous, and (within a couple of months) £600 richer. Other series of *Illustrations* were less successful. And her subsequent *Forest And Game Law Tales* (1845), based on research supplied by a parliamentary committee, were overshadowed by the Corn Law repeal, and flopped. Martineau's major full-length fiction is *Deerbrook** (1839), a work which Carlyle pronounced 'very ligneous, very trivial didactic, in fact very absurd for the most part'.

Edward Moxon (better known as a publisher of poetry) first brought the novel out and Martineau later sold the copyright to Smith, Elder* for £50 in 1853. This study of provincial life was not popular with early Victorian readers, but has its modern admirers. Martineau had one of the most powerful minds and wide-ranging interests of any writer of the period and fiction is a small part of her claim to notice. In 1834 she travelled to America (not an easy trip at this date) and wrote her impressions up in *Society In America* (1837). She was, unsurprisingly, strongly in favour of Abolition. In 1846, she travelled to Egypt. She is probably best remembered for her candid autobiography (published posthumously in 1877), her forthright views on the woman question and for her popularisation (and translation in 1853) of the inventor of sociology, Auguste Comte. Martineau's fiction includes (in addition to the titles mentioned above): *Five Years Of Youth* (1831); *The Playfellow* (1841), children's stories, variously reprinted; *The Hour And The Man* (1841), a romance on the career of the Haitian revolutionary, Toussaint L'Ouverture; *Dawn Island* (1845); *The Billow And The Rock* (1846). In her later life she lived in the Lake District where she had built her own house. She was by her own order buried without any religious ceremony. BL 13. *DNB*. RM. *NCBEL*. Wol. Sad.

Mary Barton, A Tale Of Manchester Life, Mrs Gaskell, 1848, 2 vols, Chapman and Hall. Gaskell's first published novel, and the most directly influential of the social problem* genre. The novel opens with an idyllic picture of John Barton's family enjoying well-earned leisure from the working week in the textile mills. Gaskell is careful to emphasise the dignity of working-class home life. There are, however, some ominous rifts in Barton's happiness. His sister-in-law Esther has been seduced and abandoned, and John has no sympathy for the castaway's plight. And his daughter Mary (apprenticed to a dressmaker) is flighty and likely to take after her aunt. Barton is subsequently put out of work by one of the trade depressions that ravaged industry around 1839. A union man, he goes to London to deliver the great Chartist petition to Parliament, but no good comes of that. His wife and baby have died of starvation and fever; cholera kills his fellow strikers. Meanwhile, Mary has rejected the addresses of an honest (and clever) worker of her own class, Jem Wilson, in favour of the flatteries of a young mill-owner's son, Harry Carson. Carson's father is the most obdurate of the employers. The union decide on the desperate remedy of assassination: Harry Carson is the chosen victim, John Barton the chosen assassin. After the murder, suspicion falls on Jem Wilson. Mary is put in a terrible dilemma, since she increasingly apprehends her father's guilt. Finally, by resourcefully tracking down an alibi for Jem (in the shape of the sailor Will Wilson, about to leave from Liverpool), she saves her lover. John Barton and old Carson are reconciled, before Barton (weakened by remorse and opium) dies. Jem and Mary emigrate to Canada. Gaskell originally intended to make John Barton and his crime, rather than Mary and her love, the story's centre of interest. The novel is informed by Gaskell's first-hand observation and a passionate desire to be fair to all parties.

MASON, A[rthur] E[dward] W[oodley] (1865–1948). Mason was born at Camberwell, London, the son of a chartered accountant. After receiving his school education locally at Dulwich College he went to Trinity College, Oxford to read classics. At university he was a noted speaker in the Union and active in the dramatic society. On graduating, Mason tried the stage, but never amounted to much as an actor. Encouraged by Arthur Quiller Couch* and Oscar Wilde*, Mason brought out his modern romance of murder set in the Lake District, *A Romance Of Wastdale*, in 1895. This was followed by: *The Courtship Of Morrice Buckler* (1896), a story of an English gentleman during the years 1685 87; *Lawrence Clavering* (1897), a stolid romance set in the period of the 1715 Rebellion, narrated autobiographically; *The Watchers* (1899), a romance set in the eighteenth century. Around this period, Mason deserted costume historical* fiction for modern adventure. He had his first triumph in this genre with *The Four Feathers* (1902), one of the finest of imperialist–heroism stories chronicling the cowardice and redemption of highly strung Harry Feversham in the colonial Sudan Wars. Following this breakthrough, Mason established himself as a bestselling author who richly capitalised on English patriotism in the twentieth century. Personally adventurous, he travelled widely, climbed mountains and yachted all over the world. He was elected to Parliament in 1906 and did useful intelligence work abroad for his country in the first World War. During his long writing career, Mason wrote successful plays, detective* fiction (inventing the sleuth 'Inspector Hanaud') and had a massive sales success with the novel *Fire Over England* (1936). BL 31. *DNB*. RM. *NCBEL*. Wol.

The Massarenes, Ouida, 1897, 1 vol, Sampson Low. Ouida's most successful satire on high English society. The story opens at Homburg, where the vivacious but corrupt Lady Kenilworth ('Mouse') sets herself to plunder the new rich Massarene family. William Massarene is an American robber baron, originally from Ulster. His wife, Margaret, is a former milkmaid. His daughter, Kathleen, has been brought up in New York, and is a bluestocking. Mouse contrives to sell a family property, Vale Royal, to the gullible Massarenes. And it is her intention to marry her brother Ronald Hurstmanceaux to Kathleen. But her own husband, Lord Kenilworth ('Cocky'), dies of drink shortly after inheriting his father's dukedom. He takes pains to keep his wife out of the family money, but cannot prevent the title descending to his 'son' Jack, whom he knows to be the offspring of an adultery between Mouse and Harry Brancepeth. Soon after being widowed, Mouse is sexually blackmailed by William Massarene, who has recovered some family jewels for her. But he is murdered by an American cripple, whom he earlier cheated out of his land. Kathleen inherits everything, and gives it back to the American poor from whom it was extorted. Hurstmanceaux is so impressed that he marries her, to Mouse's chagrin. Mouse finally contrives to marry a German prince, but her reputation is forever tainted. The work is smart, in Ouida's usual fashion, but also an effectively bitter picture of modern degeneration. Reviewers were unfairly sarcastic about the old woman's novel.

The Master, Israel Zangwill, 1895, 1 vol, Heinemann. A fashionable (for the 1890s) study of the conflict of art and society. The hero, Matthew Stang, is brought up in poverty in Nova Scotia, his father having died at sea. As a young man, Matthew goes to Halifax (Canada) where he works in a furniture store to earn money for his trip to London. In London he supports himself as a taxidermist and fails as an artist, his Impressionist paintings being rejected by the Royal Academy. He returns disappointed to Nova Scotia to work as a hack artist and marries an uncongenial woman, Rosina. Matthew's second attempt at fame is more cynical. His sentimental study 'Motherhood' wins popular acclaim in England. Now a celebrity, he has an affair with the sophisticated Eleanor Wyndwood. But finally he renounces her and what she represents for Rosina and his children. By returning to domestic servitude, Matthew discovers that he can at last produce great works of art. The novel avoids Zangwill's usual Jewish themes and critics found it excessively wordy and tendentious, 'a monumental waste of energy'.

Master Humphrey's Clock (1840–41). The weekly 3d. magazine which Dickens* and Chapman and Hall* optimistically hoped would serve as the flexible framework for his fiction and other writing in small units. After *The Old Curiosity Shop** and *Barnaby Rudge** came out in this format, Dickens (in December 1841) returned to his more congenial monthly number form of issue. Master Humphrey, the supposed narrator, or master of narrative ceremonies, is a crippled old man, addressing the reader alongside his old clock. The device is cumbersome.

The Master Of Ballantrae, Robert Louis Stevenson, 1889, 1 vol, Cassell. (Serialised in *Scribner's Magazine*, November 1888–October 1889.) Stevenson's most intense psychological study of fraternal rivalry, written during his exile in the South Seas. The story is set in Scotland, in the aftermath of the 1745 uprising. Lord Durrisdeer has two sons; the elder, James, is Master of Ballantrae, and has a 'diabolic' character. The younger, Henry, is a duller, more virtuous fellow. On Prince Charles's landing, the family hedge their bets by having James join the Pretender, while Henry remains loyal to the English Crown. After Culloden, James is thought dead. In fact, he survives to blackmail his brother, who has assumed the role of family heir. In Paris, James disgraces himself and returns incognito to the house of Durrisdeer. There he alienates the love of Henry's wife and child, and a duel is fought between the brothers. James is thought dead (again), but survives. His father dies of shock, and Henry suffers a brain fever, which permanently unhinges him. James subsequently drifts to America, where he continues to disgrace the family name, by setting up as a tailor with an Indian servant picked up on his travels. Henry follows him, and there ensues a desperate chase in the North American wilderness. James tries to escape by having himself buried alive by his Indian servant. But the ruse misfires, and he is resuscitated only momentarily. The shock is too much for Henry, who himself dies. The brothers are buried together. The narrative is told episodically, in pseudo-documentary style by the family's faithful steward, Ephraim Mackellar.

Masterman Ready, Or The Wreck Of The Pacific, Captain Marryat, 1841, 3 vols, Longman. Marryat's retort in fiction to *The Swiss Family Robinson*. The Seagrave family, returning to New South Wales on board the *Pacific*, are shipwrecked on a desert island. The crew have made off in the lifeboat, leaving the passengers to their fate. The Seagraves (father, invalid mother, four childen) have with them a faithful black servant Juno, and an omnicompetent old sailor, Masterman Ready, a veteran of fifty years at sea. The most interesting portions of the subsequent narrative are Ready's autobiographical reminiscences of his earlier life. Least interesting are the merry pranks of young Tommy Seagrave. With the assistance of Ready, the family survive their ordeal without having to surrender the middle-class amenities of life and all the while learning lessons on natural history and discovering evidence of the Almighty's benevolence on every side. They are, however, besieged by savages and Ready is wounded on a mission to get water for the family. Just as all seems lost, rescue comes in the form of a British schooner. Ready dies and is buried on the island.

MATHER, J[ames] Marshall (1851–1916). Mather was born in Darlington, and educated at Lincoln. His first intention was to be an architect. But his father was minister of a nonconformist church, and Mather eventually followed him into the Ministry. He subsequently took up pastoral work in Manchester where the remainder of his life was to be spent. Mather's published work includes a treatise on Ruskin*, and a series of very popular sketches and stories reflective of Lancashire life. These were collected as *Lancashire Idylls* (1895). The volume is made up of eight stories, in a Lancashire kailyard* style. Mather's other fiction includes: *By Roaring Loom* (1888); *The Sign Of the Wooden Shoon* (1898). Mather's fiction was consciously thickened with Lancashire dialect and it pleased him to pose as the literary heir of Mrs Gaskell*. BL 3. *WW.*

MATHERS, Helen (i.e. Ellen Buckingham Mathews, 1853–1920). Ellen Mathews was born in Somerset, into a well-off family. At an early age, apparently, she was afflicted with deafness. In 1876, she married Henry Albert Reeves (d. 1914), a distinguished surgeon, and set up house with him in Grosvenor Street, London. His *Who's Who* entry pointedly avoids all reference to his wife, and the couple may well have separated. Otherwise her subsequent life seems to have been uneventful. In her *Who's Who* (1901) entry she gave as her recreations: 'needlework and cycling'. With her first novel, *Comin' Thro' The Rye** (1875), the bubblingly autobiographical story of a heroine's graduation from tomboy to womanhood, Helen Mathers (as she called herself in print) had a huge hit. The work (which clearly owes much to Rhoda Broughton's* more intelligent romance) went on to sell 35,000 copies over the next twenty years for her publisher, Bentley*. Thereafter, she turned out a book a year for the next three decades and was much reprinted in the early twentieth century. Her work strikes modern readers as soft-centred romance. But *Comin' Thro' The Rye* was found, by contemporaries, to be fairly frank in its sexual reference. Her fiction (with its typical titular allusion to popular song) includes: *Cherry Ripe!* (1878), 'a disgusting book', according to the *Athenaeum**; *As He Comes Up The Stair* (1878), a short love idyll set in Devon; *My Lady Greensleeves* (1879); *Sam's Sweetheart* (1883). In addition to stories of the heart, Mathers tried her hand successfully at sensational* melodrama, as in *Murder Or Manslaughter?* (1885). Like Trollope*, she used contemporary settings for her fiction but also affected a highflown style which irritated reviewers, who often devoted much of their space to correcting her solecisms. By the end of the century with works like *Cinders* (1901), Mathers's once scandalously fast and slangy heroines were regarded as very tame. This last work has, however, some interesting topicality in its depictions of the effects of the

Boer War on the bright young (but very belligerent) maidens left behind. BL 31. *WW. NCBEL.* Wol. Sad.

MATHEW, Frank (1865–1924). Mathew was born in Bombay, the son of a civil engineer and a grand nephew of Father Mathew, the apostle of temperance (young Mathew later did a life of his famous relative, published in 1890). Mathew was sent to London in his childhood and studied at London University, graduating in 1888. He eventually took up work as a barrister and married in 1899. Mathew wrote fiction, often with romantic Irish* themes and rambling narratives that reviewers found charming. His novels include: *At The Rising Of The Moon* (1893), twenty tales set in the west of Ireland; *The Wood Of The Brambles* (1896), a story of the rebellion of 1798; *A Child In the Temple* (1897); *The Spanish Wine* (1898); *A Defender Of The Faith* (1899); *The Royal Sisters* (1901), i.e. Elizabeth and Mary. BL 8. *WW.*

MATURIN, Edward (1812–81). Maturin was born in Dublin, the son of the better-known novelist (and clergyman) Charles Robert Maturin (1782–1824). After graduating from Trinity College, Dublin he qualified as a barrister. Thereafter Maturin emigrated to the USA. For a while he taught classics at the College of South Carolina and at New York, where he died. Maturin published two novels with Nationalist Irish* themes: *The Irish Chieftain* (1848) and *Bianca* (1852), 'A Tale Of Erin And Italy'. He also published the more exotic romance, *Montezuma, The Last Of The Aztecs* (1845). BL 3. Boase.

MAUGHAM, W[illiam] Somerset (1874–1965). A major twentieth-century literary figure, Maugham, by virtue of literary precocity, made a Victorian début. He was born in Paris, where his father was solicitor to the British Embassy. Both parents died before he was ten, and the boy was brought up by a clergyman uncle in Kent. He attended the King's School, Canterbury, and was clearly headed for university and eventually some respectable profession. Instead, he went to Heidelberg and in 1892 enrolled at St Thomas's Hospital, London. Although he qualified, Maugham never practised. His first published novel, *Liza Of Lambeth* (1897), recounts a year in the life of a doomed factory girl, neglected by a drunken mother and seduced by a married neighbour. It is a starkly Zolaesque exercise and was well enough received to allow him to give up medicine. It was followed by: *The Making Of A Saint* (1898); *Orientations* (1899), five short stories; *The Hero* (1901). The last is the bitter tale of James Parsons VC, who returns from the wars to keep an engagement to his former love with disastrous consequences. Maugham's pedigree is normally assumed to be in French realism, and his major achievements fall in the post-Victorian period. Never the less, in the 1890s reviewers noted a clear literary debt to Thackeray*. BL 43. *DNB.* RM. *NCBEL.* Wol.

Maurice Tiernay, Charles Lever, 1852, 1 vol, Hodgson. (Serialised in the *Dublin University Magazine*, April 1850–December 1851.) The hero is a young Irish boy, brought up in Paris during the Terror. His father, an officer in the *Garde du Corps*, is guillotined and young Maurice is only saved by the personal intervention of Robespierre. (One of the many historical notables dragged into the narrative.) After living by his wits in the Paris streets, Maurice becomes a camp follower, then a hussar. Service takes him to Germany and (in the most interesting episode in the novel) to his native Ireland, where he organises the Free Irish Army to resist the British. Under the command of Masséna, Maurice eventually rises to the rank of colonel, and catches the eye of Napoleon, whose favour allows him to marry an aristocratic bride. He ends 'one of the richest and the very happiest among the Soldiers of Fortune'. The novel is interesting for its shrewd analysis of French revolutionary politics. It does not seem to have been a popular work.

MAXWELL, [Sir] Herbert [Eustace] (1845–1937). Maxwell was born in Edinburgh, the son of a baronet and had his education at Eton and Oxford. Failing to get a degree, he entered the Scots Fusilier Guards. On leaving the service, he settled on his father's estate, in Wigtownshire, and lived the life of a country gentleman. On his father's death, in 1877, he became the seventh Baronet Monreith and a Conservative MP. Maxwell was also a dilettante author. His most substantial work is a life of Wellington (1899). He wrote (as 'Sir Herbert Maxwell, Bart. MP') a number of novels, including: *The Art Of Love* (1889), a story contrasting rural Scotland and London clubland; *A Duke Of Britain* (1895), a romance of the fourth century about whose artless anachronisms the reviewers made merry; *The Chevalier Of The Splendid Crest* (1901), a Scottish historical* romance, set during the reign of Edward I. BL 4. *DNB*. Wol.

John Maxwell (1860–95). Publisher. John Maxwell (1824–95) is best-known as the husband of Mary Elizabeth Braddon*. An Irishman, he came to London in the late 1830s to arrange for the publication of Gerald Griffin's works. He began his independent business career as a newspaper agent in the City of London, 1851–57. From 1857 to 1860 he was a contractor for advertisements. Around 1860, he set up his publishing house with Robert Maxwell at 4 Shoe Lane. The firm survived (with some ups and downs) until 1887. Maxwell was an inveterate founder of magazines. In 1858, he started *Town Talk*, a weekly which lasted a year and a half. He launched the 1d. weekly *Welcome Guest* (1858–61) and lost, as he reckoned, £2,000 on the venture in two years. The price was raised to 2d. and the venture converted into *Robin Goodfellow**. *The Halfpenny Journal*, an eight-page, three-column weekly, was more successful, running from 1861–65. In December 1860, he established *Temple Bar**, as a monthly rival to *Cornhill** but could not hold on to the journal. In April 1861, Maxwell founded yet another monthly, *St James's Magazine**, and in 1866 (most successfully) *Belgravia**. Expansion led Maxwell into severe financial difficulties in the early 1860s. In 1862, his firm was put into receivership, with the copyright and stock valued at £23,500. He executed a deed of assignment of all his estate and effects in December of the same year. Maxwell was helped out of his crisis by the earnings of Elizabeth Braddon, with whom he was living. He could not at the time marry Braddon, since his first wife (whom he had married in 1848 and by whom he had five surviving children) was alive in a lunatic asylum. When she died in 1874, his relationship with Braddon was regularised. Maxwell was the main publisher of the sub-Dickensian* bohemian authors and a specialist in cheap reprint fiction. Boase.

MAXWELL, W[illiam] H[amilton] (1792–1850). In his day, a well-known military novelist and rival of Charles Lever*. Maxwell was born at Newry,

Co. Down, the son of a prosperous merchant. He attended Trinity College, Dublin 'in a somewhat desultory manner' and was widely supposed to have seen service in the Peninsular War with the Black Watch (a recent commentator, Royal Gettmann, disputes this) and at Waterloo, where he served as a captain of infantry. With the peace, and chronically short of cash, Maxwell toyed with the idea of going off to fight as a mercenary in South America. Instead he returned to Newry, married an heiress, took orders, and as Rector of Ballagh, Connemara, took up the undemanding vocation of sporting clergyman. In 1825, he produced the novel *O'Hara, Or 1798* (the story of a Protestant landowner, who becomes involved with Nationalists). His most popular works of fiction were the semi-autobiographical and eye-witness accounts collected as *Stories Of Waterloo* (1829) and *The Bivouac, Or Stories Of The Peninsular War* (1834). In the 1830s, Maxwell was a popular Bentley's* author, producing such works as *The Dark Lady Of Doona* (1834), a gothic* tale set in seventeenth-century Ireland; *The Adventures Of Captain Blake* (1838); *Captain O'Sullivan* (1846), 'Or Adventures Civil, Military And Matrimonial Of A Gentleman On Half-Pay'. But the vogue for military (and nautical*) 'adventures' by bluff soldier types was worn out by the 1840s. The comic Irish* mode (as Lever discovered) was also old hat. Maxwell suffered other misfortunes. His wife died, and her money was squandered. He was deprived of his living in 1844 for non-residence. His last years, plagued by failing sight and utter destitution, were wretched. He died at Musselburgh, near Edinburgh. BL 14. *DNB*. RM. *NCBEL*. Wol. Sad. RLF.

MAYHEW, Augustus ['Gus' Septimus] (1826–75). Mayhew was born in London, one of the seventeen children of an attorney, Joshua Mayhew (a 'respectable man' as another son, Henry*, called him in an ironic poem of 1848). Augustus had seven brothers, among the more famous of whom are Henry and Horace (1816–72). Early home life seems to have been materially comfortable, but unhappy. The Mayhews had a strong bent towards writing. But whereas his brothers specialised in comic journalism, Augustus was more inclined to fiction. His best-known work (written in collaboration with his brother Henry) was *The Greatest Plague Of Life, Or The Adventures Of A Lady In Search Of A Good Servant* (1847; issued in monthly numbers and memorably illustrated by Cruikshank*). The serial was popular and the brothers Mayhew followed up with *Whom To Marry, And How To Get Married* (1848). Augustus, like his brother Henry (author of *London Labour And The London Poor*) was strong in metropolitan settings. They feature prominently in *Kitty Lamere, Or A Dark Page In London Life* (1855); *Paved With Gold, Or The Romance And The Reality Of The London Streets* (1857), a work written to show the horrors of slum life, especially for working-class children, and embellished with brilliant Phiz* illustrations; *The Finest Girl In Bloomsbury* (1861); *Faces For Fortunes* (1865). It is not always easy to work out which brother wrote which parts of such works as *Whom To Marry* (1848) or *The Image Of His Father* (1848); *Living For Appearances* (1855). Augustus Mayhew also wrote drama, some of it in collaboration with Henry Sutherland Edwards*. He lived in London, and died prematurely of an operation for hernia. (ASM) BL 6. (ASM and HM) BL 6. *DNB*. RM. *NCBEL*. Wol. RLF.

MAYHEW, Henry (1812–87). A brother of the above, Henry Mayhew was born in London and educated at Westminster School. In 1827, indignant at a flogging, he ran away from home. He was subsequently sent to sea for a year and returned to become articled to his attorney father, a man whom the Mayhew sons evidently regarded as a tyrant. Law did not suit him, and three years later he drifted into journalism and theatrical work, supported the while by a £1-a-week allowance from his father. His first farce, *The Wandering Minstrel*, appeared in 1834 and in the later 1830s, he was the lessee of the Queen's Theatre in London. In the 1830s Mayhew worked on various precursors of *Punch**, notably *Figaro In London*, and for a short period in 1841–42 was himself an editor of Bradbury and Evans's* new paper. Mayhew married Jane, a daughter of Douglas Jerrold*, in 1844. The marriage seems to have been uneasy and the Mayhews went bankrupt in 1846, having run up debts of £2,000 on an annual income of £400 (comfortable enough by Victorian standards). As a result Henry was cut out of his father's will. To recover his fortune, he embarked on a series of novels with his brother, Augustus. They collaborated on *The Greatest Plague Of Life* (1847), and Henry singly wrote *1851, Or The Adventures Of Mr And Mrs Sandboys* (1851), a story of the Great Exhibition (memorably illustrated by George Cruikshank*). Henry Mayhew's major work, however, was the journalistic *London Labour And The London Poor*. First produced as articles (or 'letters') for John Douglas Cook in the *Morning Chronicle* in 1849, the series was carried on intermittently in various forms and places over the next fifteen years making up one of the classic texts of early urban sociology. Mayhew wrote a number of children's and travel books. He was associated with liberal causes and interested himself in working-class welfare. His last twenty years are obscure. Having fallen out with the *Punch* set early on, he figures less prominently than he should in official histories of the magazine. As Raymond Williams observes: 'Mayhew remains a puzzling character, and some final clue seems missing'. BL 1. (HM and ASM) BL 7. *DNB*. RM. *NCBEL*. Wol. RLF.

MAYO, Isabella ('Edward Garrett', née Fyvie, 1843–1914). Isabella Fyvie was born in London, the youngest child of Scottish parents and educated privately at a girls' school near Covent Garden. In her informative *Recollections Of Fifty Years* (1910), Fyvie recalls as her earliest memory being turned away from the British Museum, aged four. By this age, 'I could read easily', she reports. Another early memory was that of her sister Elizabeth dying, aged eighteen, Isabella then being only six. By the age of eight, she was familiar with Blair's *Belles Lettres* and was addicted to Jean Ingelow's* tales, as they were then appearing in the *Youth's Magazine*. At thirteen, Isabella actually submitted a tale to the journal, which was kindly rejected with a long helpful letter from Ingelow. Fyvie's father was a prosperous West End baker whose business failed. All four of his sons died, and in despair he followed in 1851, leaving a large debt of £800. Aged seventeen, Isabella was thrown into 'the battle of life', shouldering (without any legal obligation), her father's financial responsibilities. Throughout the 1860s she made a living copying legal documents and addressing envelopes at the rate of 1,500 a day for 3s. She also acted as amanuensis to an unidentified 'literary woman' ('Miss Y') at 6d. an hour, and succeeded eventually in paying off the family debts. Around the middle of the decade, Fyvie became acquainted with various literary patrons: Isa Craig*, Mrs S. C. Hall* and Edwin Arnold*. (She was also active at this period in the 'Office for the Employment of Women' at Langham Place.) Through her friends' good offices, she began to publish poems and stories under the pseudonym Edward Garrett, and had encouragement from the congenially evangelical publisher Alexander Strahan* who in 1867 commissioned her serial *The Occupations Of A Retired Life* for £300. So ended her 'life and death fight for bread and indepependence'. In 1870, she married a solicitor, John R. Mayo (d. 1877). A pious woman (although she was not as strict as Strahan would have liked), she lived most of her writing career in Aberdeen. Towards the end of her life she was one of the pioneering translators of Tolstoy into English. Her novels (which reviewers generally found beneath their notice) include: *The Crust And The Cake* (1869), a story of respectable poverty in London; *Seen And Heard* (1871), nostalgic sketches and portraits; *Premiums Paid To Experience* (1872); *The House By The Works* (1879); *A Black Diamond* (1893); *Rab Bethune's Double* (1894); *A Daughter Of The Klephts* (1897), a story of the Greek war of liberation; *Chrystal Joyce* (1899). BL 28 (6 as 'I. Fyvie', 28 as 'Edward Garrett'). *WW.* Wol.

The Mayor Of Casterbridge, Thomas Hardy, 1886, 2 vols, Smith, Elder. (Serialised in the *Graphic*, January–May 1886, illustrated by Robert Barnes.) Hardy's reworking of *Oedipus Rex*. Michael Henchard, a journeyman labourer, arrives at the village of Weydon-Priors. At a fair he gets himself drunk on laced furmity (a milk drink), and sells his wife Susan for five guineas to a sailor. On sobering up, he takes a solemn vow not to touch liquor for twenty-one years. Eighteen years later, he has prospered as a corn factor and is Mayor of Casterbridge. At this point, his wife and a daughter Elizabeth-Jane return from Canada. Susan's marriage to the sailor Richard Newson is illegal; and he is thought dead at sea. Henchard devises an elaborate plan to court and 'remarry' Susan, which he does. Meanwhile, he has taken on as manager a clever young Scot, Donald Farfrae. But the men fall out, and Farfrae sets up as Henchard's rival. On Susan's death, Henchard discovers that Elizabeth-Jane is not, after all, his daughter, but Richard Newson's, and his manner towards her hardens. A woman from Jersey, Lucetta Le Sueur, with whom Henchard previously had an affair, inherits property nearby Casterbridge and takes Elizabeth-Jane into her household, so that Henchard can decently call on her. But she secretly marries Farfrae. Henchard's business affairs are increasingly desperate. And the old furmity seller returns, to expose the original wife sale, completing his public disgrace. Through the treachery of a former employee called Jopp, Henchard's sexual indiscretions become common knowledge, and the dregs of Casterbridge mount a mocking parade ('skimmity ride') with effigies of the adulterous pair, the humiliation of which kills Lucetta. Henchard is now a drunkard, his twenty-one years being up. Newson returns, and Henchard tells him that both Susan and Elizabeth-Jane are dead. But the sailor persists in his search and is reconciled to his daughter. Farfrae (now Mayor of Casterbridge) eventually marries Elizabeth-Jane, and Henchard ends as he began, a penniless, vagrant, journeyman labourer. He dies in solitude in a hovel on Egdon Heath. The novel contains Hardy's blackest description of his native Dorchester (i.e. Casterbridge) and in Henchard his most powerful study of will and 'character'.

MEADE, L[illie] T[oulmin Elizabeth Thomasina Smith] (1854–1915). The author of some 250 books, and for six years (1887–93) editor of *Atalanta**, a periodical for girls, Meade was the most industrious of Victorian authors. She was born in Cork, the daughter of the Rector of Nohoval, and wrote her first book at the age of seventeen. As a young woman, she came to London. There she worked in the British Museum, and studied life in the East End of the City. (She turned this observation to use in social-realistic works like *Good Luck*, 1896, and *Princess Of The Gutter*, 1895), although she conscientiously noted in the work's preface that: 'the language of East London cannot, for obvious reasons, be altogether reproduced in these pages.' Meade's publications begin to stream out in the 1870s. As a writer for the juvenile market, she practised most of the fashionable modes: rewards*, street arab tales, allegories, fantasies*, fictional tracts, adventure stories, sensation* novels, ghost* stories. Works like *The Medicine Lady* (1892) deal with such things as medical advances in the treatment of tuberculosis and the role of women in hospitals. The most interesting category in Meade's fiction is that group of tales relating to her native Ireland, which she wrote towards the end of her life. Her most influential work was *A World Of Girls* (1886), an enormously succcessful book which pioneered a whole genre of school stories. As a writer for older readers, Meade was similarly versatile. This can be illustrated by briefly summarising the output of just one year, 1898: in *Mary Gifford* a woman doctor establishes a practice in the East End. In *The Cleverest Woman In England* a wife devotes herself so entirely to propagating the cause of the new woman* that she ruins her marriage and dies of smallpox. *Girls Of St Wode's* is a story of the new university-trained Girton and Newnham girls. In *A Handful Of Silver* the heroine Audrey refuses to marry the man she loves, because she is encumbered with her father's debts. In *On The Brink Of A Chasm* a nurse Clara uses hypnotism to rescue a young baronet from a villain. *The Rebellion Of Lil Carrington* traces a hoyden's career left as she is at fifteen in the care of a harsh aunt. In *The Siren**, the heroine is a socialist and nihilist ordered by her Russian masters to assassinate her own father. Through this decade, Meade was churning out such fiction at the rate of half a dozen titles a year. She married Toulmin Smith in 1879, and had three children. BL 251. *WW*. *NCBEL*. Wol.

MEADOWS, [Joseph] Kenny (1790–1874). Illustrator. Meadows was born in Cardigan, Wales, the son of a retired naval officer. Nothing is known of his early life but by the 1830s he was active in London as an artist. One of his greatest successes was a series in monthly numbers, *The Heads Of The People* (1838–40), to which Douglas Jerrold* and Thackeray* contributed. He also illustrated some of the serial fiction of Henry Cockton*. In later life, Meadows worked extensively on children's* books, illustrated Shakespeare (memorably) and was employed by the *Illustrated London News**. He received a Civil List pension in 1864. *DNB*. Hou.

MEANY, Stephen Joseph (1825–88). Meany was born in Ennis, Co. Clare. For a while he worked as a constable but was dismissed from this work.

He subsequently turned to journalism. A friend of Daniel O'Connell's, he was imprisoned in 1848 for his association with the Nationalist movement. Meany thereafter left Dublin for Liverpool, where he founded the first English-Catholic newspaper outside London, the *Lancashire Free Press*. By 1862, he was bankrupt. Later details of his life are scarce, but in 1882 he was imprisoned for theft, and spent some time in America. On his return to England in 1886, he was arrested on charges of Fenianism, and sentenced to fifteen years in prison. He did not serve this time, dying shortly after in New York. Meany's one exercise in fiction is of a piece with his life. *The Terry Alt* (1841) is a 'Tale Of 1831', and chronicles agrarian agitation in Munster. BL 0. Boase.

Mehalah, S. Baring-Gould, 1880, 3 vols, Smith, Elder. Baring-Gould's most reprinted work of fiction, set in the early nineteenth century in the parish where the author was vicar, 1871–81. The heroine, Mehalah (or 'Glory') Sharland, lives with her mother on a leased farm in the coastal salt-marshes by Mersea, Essex. Their property, called 'the Ray', is bought for £800 by Elijah Rebow, a violent man, whose desire is to marry the wilful Mehalah. She however loves a local fisherman, George De Witt, who helps her when Rebow distrains on the Ray for debt. De Witt mysteriously disappears, the Ray is burned down by an unknown arsonist (in fact Rebow), Mrs Sharland is chronically ill. Under these afflictions, Mehalah is finally induced to marry Elijah. But immediately after the wedding he tells her that it was he who abducted her lover George, keeping him in the cellar at Red Hall, until he finally went mad. In her anger, Mehalah dashes vitriol in her new husband's eyes, blinding him. Subsequently remorseful, she thereafter makes herself his slave. Finally, George returns to the scene. It emerges that Elijah did not kidnap him. He was taken off by a pressgang to fight the French. Finding Mehalah married, George himself marries an old sweetheart, Phoebe Musset. During the service, Elijah takes the semi-conscious Mehalah out in a boat and scuttles it, drowning them both. The novel contains vivid descriptions of Essex locations, although the conception of the black-haired, passionate heroine is standard Baring-Gould.

MELDRUM, D[avid] Storrar (1856–1940). Meldrum was born in Kirk-caldy, and educated at Edinburgh High School. After false starts in business and journalism he became a literary adviser to Blackwood's* publishing house. In their service, Meldrum edited John Galt's works. He also wrote novels set in his native Fife, in the early nineteenth century. They include: *The Story Of Margrédel* (1894), a tale of family intrigue; *Gray Mantle And Gold Fringe* (1896), short stories; *The Conquest Of Charlotte* (1902), 'A Fifeshire Romance'. BL 3. *WW*. Wol.

Men's Wives, George Fitz-Boodle (i.e. W. M. Thackeray), 1843. The collective title of a trio of short stories centred on the theme of marriage, published in *Fraser's Magazine**, March–November 1843. *Dennis Haggarty's Wife* is a savage, anti-Irish, misogynistic tale. *Mr & Mrs Frank Berry* is the study of a henpecked husband. *The Ravenswing* is a rather more amusing comedy of sexual manners. These three early pieces show Thackeray at his most bitter.

MEREDITH, George (1828–1909). The least read major novelist of the Victorian period. Meredith was born at Portsmouth where his grandfather, Melchizedek Meredith, ran the town's principal tailor's and naval outfitter's establishment. The business was subsequently taken over by George's less enterprising father, Augustus Armstrong Meredith (1797–1876). The Merediths' trade background was later to figure importantly in the novelist's most accessible work, *Evan Harrington** (1861). George was the only child of his parents' marriage (in 1823) and his mother died when he was five years old. The family tailoring business had declined with peace after Waterloo, and Augustus Meredith emigrated to South Africa, only to return in 1860 after which he was to be a constant drain on his son's finances. Meredith went to schools in Portsmouth up to his fourteenth year. He then (in 1842) spent a formative two years in Germany. In 1844, he returned to England to be articled to a solicitor. A year later (and very hard up for money) Meredith began to write. His early efforts were mainly in poetry and higher journalism. In 1849, he married Thomas Peacock's widowed daughter, Mary Ellen Nicolls. The couple lived a semi-bohemian life at Weybridge and Meredith clearly came under the stylistic influence of his novel-writing and eccentric father-in-law. The marriage, however, was to prove ill-assorted and ultimately wretched. (The pain is reflected in Meredith's powerful sonnet sequence, *Modern Love*, 1862.) Having borne a son (Arthur) Meredith's wife ran off in 1858 and died, deserted by her lover Henry Wallis, three years later. Meredith's first volume of poems appeared in 1851. They were generally regarded as modern and difficult. His first published work of fiction was the grotesque *The Shaving Of Shagpat* (1855), 'An Arabian Entertainment'. It was followed by the similarly whimsical *Farina* (1857), 'A Legend Of The Rhine'. More substantial was *The Ordeal Of Richard Feverel** (1859). This novel deals with the issues of education and sex, and has a maturity unusual in Victorian fiction. Inevitably it was banned by the librarian Mudie*. Following *Feverel*'s poor sales, Meredith worked for a while in provincial journalism, devoting himself to his son. *Evan Harrington* (1860) was more popular with the reading public, possibly because it was serialised in *Once A Week**. In 1862, Meredith took on the position of literary adviser to Chapman and Hall*, a post which he was to hold for most of the rest of his life. In the role of 'reader', he helped the early careers of George Gissing*, Olive Schreiner* and Thomas Hardy* and exercised considerable influence on what Victorians read. Meredith was, by the 1860s, a respected man of letters but regarded as somewhat strange by his contemporaries. *Sandra Belloni** appeared in 1864. In the same year, Meredith was elected to membership of the Garrick Club and remarried. His wife was Marie Vulliamy, whose family was of Swiss Huguenot extraction. A son, William Maxse, was born in 1865, named after Meredith's close friend (and original of Beauchamp), Frederick Augustus Maxse (1833–1900). In 1867, the Merediths moved to Flint Cottage, Box Hill, near Dorking. In 1866, Meredith had been sent by the *Morning Post* to Italy to cover the country's struggle for independence. The experience enriches *Vittoria** (1866). After 1867, he became closely involved (together with John Morley) in the running of Chapman and Hall's *Fortnightly Review**. Several of his novels were serialised in the journal. But *Harry Richmond** (1871), one of his more popular works, was first published in *Cornhill**. Meredith's idiosyncratic theory of comedy was given practical expression in *Beauchamp's Career** (1875) and *The Egoist** (1879). His essay on 'The Idea Of Comedy' was delivered in 1877, and somewhat bemused his contemporaries. *The Tragic Comedians* (1880), based on the career of Ferdinand Lassalle, represents the purest crystalisation of Meredith's theories of fiction. It was followed by three novels with feminist concerns: *Diana Of The Crossways** (1885); *One Of Our Conquerors** (1891); *The Amazing Marriage** (1895). From 1885, Meredith was increasingly disabled by a spinal complaint and was for the last sixteen years of his life virtually paraplegic although to the end 'conspicuously handsome'. On Tennyson's death, he was elected President of the Society of Authors* in 1892. In 1905 he received the Order of Merit and his last years were passed in the unchallenged glory of being the nation's Grand Old Man of letters. BL 20. *DNB*. RM. *NCBEL*. Wol. Sad.

MERIVALE, Herman Charles (1839–1906). Merivale was born in London, the son of a senior Civil Servant at the India Office. He was educated at Harrow School and at Balliol College, Oxford (where Swinburne was his contemporary). Merivale showed an early interest in drama and the stage, but prudently prepared himself for a legal career. He was successful as a lawyer and held a number of official and semi-official appointments. (From 1870–80, for instance, he was editor of the *Annual Register*.) He meanwhile kept up his literary and artistic contacts; Anthony Trollope* and J. E. Millais*, for instance, were his sponsors for membership of the Garrick Club in 1864. In 1874, when his father died, Merivale left law, and gave himself over entirely to literary pursuits. He had his first stage success in 1875, with an adaptation of Dickens's* *A Tale Of Two Cities** (melodramatically retitled 'All For Her'). Merivale went on to produce a succession of plays, burlesques and farces. He also wrote a well received novel, *Faucit Of Balliol* (1882). The work was later dramatised by the author as 'The Cynic'. The plot contains a disputed inheritance and attempted seduction and offers in its first volume a lively evocation of Merivale's life at college, clearly displaying the influence of Thackeray*, a writer whom Merivale admired intensely. Merivale married in 1878, but had no children. His mental condition was always precarious and in 1879 he published *My Experiences In A Lunatic Asylum*, 'By A Sane Patient'. In 1891, his health again broke down, while he was writing the authorised life of Thackeray. He voyaged to Australia to recover, and was shipwrecked on route. On his return, he discovered that he had been financially ruined by the embezzlements of a dishonest lawyer. He published his memoir, *Bar, Stage And Platform* in 1902. Merivale's last years were miserable. In 1900, he was relieved by the award of a Civil List pension, and he converted to Catholicism shortly before his death. BL 2. *DNB*. RLF.

MERRICK, Leonard (born Miller, 1864–1939). Miller was born in Belsize Park, London, of Jewish parentage. He was educated at Brighton, and at Heidelberg, where his father's financial problems interrupted his study of law. As young man, Miller subsequently travelled to South Africa, where he worked for a while in the diamond fields. He eventually returned to England, where he went on the stage changing his name by deed poll to 'Merrick'. Failing in his theatrical career he turned to fiction and play-writing, in which he had better fortune. Merrick's novels are somewhat plotless, but lively.

They include: *Mr Bazalgette's Agent* (1888), a detective story; *Violet Moses* (1891), the study of a Jewish financier and his troubled young wife; *The Man Who Was Good* (1892); *The Worldlings* (1900), an ingenious investigation of the psychology of crime; *Conrad In Quest Of His Youth* (1903). The last, subtitled 'An Extravagance Of Temperament', is judged his most successful work. The hero, aged thirty-seven, having passed most of his life in the colonies comes into an inheritance and returns to Europe and the scenes of his early romance. BL 17. *WW. NCBEL.* Wol. Sad. RLF.

Mervyn Clitheroe, William Harrison Ainsworth, 1858, 1 vol, Routledge. (Chapman and Hall* began issuing the novel in monthly numbers illustrated by Phiz*, from December 1851. The public did not take to the serial, and publication was suspended in March 1852. In December 1857, Routledge* undertook to complete the work, in twelve numbers, following up with a one-volume edition). Ainsworth's ill-fated rival to *Pendennis** and *David Copperfield**. The early numbers are autobiographical in form. They evidently recall Ainsworth's schooldays at Manchester (here 'Cottonborough') Free Grammar School. The middle and later parts of the story are done in the novelist's floridly romantic manner. They involve Mervyn's struggle for the inheritance which has been filched from him by his family rival Malpas Sale, aided by an assorted band of villains and gypsies. After convoluted intrigues and adventures, Mervyn finally gains his estate and wins the hand of his early sweetheart, Apphia Brideoake. The early chapters retain a freshness which suggests that had his public been more tolerant, Ainsworth could have broken the historical* romance mould which confined him.

Methuen (1889–). Publishers. The firm was founded by Algernon Methuen Marshall Stedman (1856–1924), a classical scholar and writer of school textbooks. Stedman began publishing from a single room in Bloomsbury, his first book being Edna Lyall's (i.e. Bayly's*) somewhat controversial novel, *Derrick Vaughan* (1889), a work which went on to be a bestseller. The proprietor changed his professional name to Methuen in 1899. Early novelists published by the house were Marie Corelli*, E. F. Benson*, Anthony Hope (i.e. Hawkins*), Stanley Weyman* and Rudyard Kipling*. Methuen's was one of the new publishers which flourished on the ruins of the three-decker system after 1894. The firm retained a mixed list, however, in which educational books enjoyed a principal place with fiction. (AM) *WW.*

The Metropolitan Magazine (1831–50). The *Metropolitan* pioneered the serialisation of fiction in England, particularly under its second editor and proprietor (1832–36), Frederick Marryat*. The journal was founded as a highbrow miscellany in 1831 (on the lines of Colburn's* *New Monthly Magazine**), under the editorship of Thomas Campbell. But he was soon succeeded by the more dynamic Marryat. Two of Marryat's novels were serialised and three others excerpted in the magazine. Marryat was assisted as sub-editor by the similarly nautical* Edward Howard*, whose *Rattlin The Reefer* (1836) first appeared in the magazine's pages. The journal was eclipsed by *Bentley's Miscellany** after 1837. For most of its existence (1832–47) the *Metropolitan* was published by Saunders and Otley*. *BLM.*

Micah Clarke, Arthur Conan Doyle, 1889, 1 vol, Longman. (The work was serialised in 1894 in *Longman's School Magazine*, preparatory to its long career as an approved school textbook.) A historical* romance, set at the period of the Monmouth Rebellion, 1685. The hero Micah is a young Puritan, brought up at Havant near Portsmouth, the son of one of Cromwell's most loyal soldiers, 'Ironside Joe'. Micah and his friend Reuben Lockarby (an innkeeper's son) are recruited by a soldier of fortune, Decimus Saxon, to fight for the rebel army. After various adventures, they join 'King' Monmouth at Taunton. Micah quickly ingratiates himself with the Pretender, and is dispatched to Bristol, to recruit the Duke of Beaufort. Beaufort is secretly sympathetic, and Micah's message persuades Monmouth to march to Bristol to unite with his powerful new ally. But the rebels are forced to make a stand at Sedgemoor, where they are defeated by the King's forces (as a prophecy foretold). Micah is captured, sentenced by the hanging judge, Jeffreys, but ransomed by Saxon. He goes off to fight as a mercenary abroad. The novel is notable for Doyle's skill in handling rattling action and an engaging troupe of simply conceived characters. The narrative is presented autobiographically as Micah's statement to his three grandchildren, Joseph, Gervas and Reuben 'during the hard winter of 1734'.

Michael Armstrong, The Factory Boy, Mrs Frances Trollope, 1839, 3 vols, Colburn. (Serialised in twelve monthly numbers March 1839–February 1840, with illustrations by A. Hervieu, R. W. Buss* and T. Onwhyn*.) With the exactly contemporary *Helen Fleetwood* (by C. E. Tonna*) the pioneer 'industrial novel' of the early 1840s. Mrs Trollope (with introductory letters from Lord Shaftesbury) undertook first-hand research in the textile towns of the North to prepare for *Michael Armstrong*. The theme (following *Oliver Twist**) concentrates on child abuse in modern England. Michael, a little factory boy, is adopted by the brutal mill owner, Sir Matthew Dowling, to mollify one of his refined lady companions. Later, when Dowling wearies of philanthropy, Michael is disposed of as an apprentice. Surviving this, the typhus, and work in the factory he is eventually rescued (together with his crippled brother and the little girl he loves) by the vigorous heroine, Mary Brotherton. Like the black slaves in Mrs Trollope's earlier *Jonathan Jefferson Whitlaw* (1836) these genteel waifs are given haven on the Continent. The work shocked, particularly with its depictions (and graphic illustrations) of the industrial town Ashleigh, and the Deep Valley factory, where a starved Michael scrambles with pigs for the offal in their troughs. Politically, the novel is a tract in favour of the Ten Hours Bill; a measure whose virtues are ceaselessly propagated in the narrative by the Rev. George Bell.

Middlemarch, George Eliot, 1872, 4 vols, Blackwood. (Serialised in eight bi-monthly and latterly monthly parts or 'books', December 1871–December 1872.) George Eliot's study of provincial life, set in the English Midlands around the end of the 1820s. The opening section centres on the growth to maturity of Dorothea Brooke. Together with her sister Celia, Dorothea is left orphaned and in the care of her uncle, Mr Brooke of Tipton Grange. Dorothea is courted by Sir James Chettam, but has no interest in marriage. Sir James makes do with Celia. Dorothea is eventually attracted to Edward Casaubon, a scholarly clergyman at the nearby parish of Lowick. In her 'theoretic' desire to sacrifice herself, Dorothea overlooks the sterility of Casaubon's mind and becomes his wife. The light-headed Mr Brooke does nothing to prevent this disastrous mismatch. Dorothea realises her mistake during the honeymoon in Rome. And her awakening sensibility is stimulated by conversations with a distant cousin of her husband's, Will Ladislaw. Meanwhile, in Middlemarch, a young physician, Dr Lydgate, has similarly come to grief. A scientist who believes that one day he will extend the boundaries of knowledge, Lydgate is trapped into stultifying marriage by the selfish Rosamond Vincy. Lydgate has also been compromised by Rosamond's uncle, Nicholas Bulstrode, founder of the new fever hospital. A third strand of the plot concerns Rosamond's brother Fred. A scapegrace, Fred hopes that a bequest from the miserly Featherstone will enable him to pay his debts and marry the virtuous (but strong-minded) Mary Garth. Fred's eventually making himself worthy of Mary (without any legacy) is one of the more optimistic sections of *Middlemarch*'s narrative. Meanwhile, Edward Casaubon develops heart disease, and becomes increasingly jealous of Dorothea's affection for Will who has returned to Middlemarch, to assist Mr Brooke get into the newly reformed Parliament (which, comically, he fails to do). When Casaubon dies, a codicil to his will disinherits Dorothea if she marries Ladislaw. And after her husband's death, Dorothea discovers that his great work, 'The Key To All Mythologies', is worthless. The novel's plot becomes increasingly complex and close-knit towards its conclusion. Lydgate is driven into bankruptcy by his wife's extravagances, and is mortified by her vulgarity. Bulstrode is blackmailed by a sporting man, Raffles, who knows that Bulstrode's fortune really belongs (by inheritance) to Ladislaw, via his mother who married a Polish exile. Bulstrode eventually lets Raffles die, by feeding him brandy during a bout of delirium tremens. When the fact emerges, the doctor in charge, Lydgate, is also publicly disgraced. Dorothea relieves the Lydgates' immediate financial wants, and finally marries Ladislaw. The couple leave for London, where he subsequently enters Parliament and Dorothea (who once aspired to be a modern St Theresa) consoles herself with inconspicuous goodness. The Lydgates go off to a watering place, where he lives the life of a successful, but unfulfilled society doctor. Before conceiving her eventual massive design, Eliot intended a simpler story about Dorothea.

MILES, Henry Downes (1806–89). Montague Summers writes of Miles: 'He was a very prolific writer and journalist. He shows himself to have been a scholar and a man of wide reading in English literature.' Only a few biographical details can be gleaned. Henry Miles inhabited the sporting, theatrical, journalistic Bohemia of London. He was sub-editor of the *Constitution* in 1833, a paper which was set up in opposition to *The Times*, and failed. Miles subsequently served as ring reporter for the sporting newspaper, *Bell's Life*. (He went on to publish a three-volume history of boxing, in 1881.) In 1873 he was editor of the *Licensed Victuallers' Year Book*. He also translated Sue's *Mysteries Of Paris* (1846). Miles's own fiction belongs to the Newgate* genre, and clearly owes much to Ainsworth*. It includes: *Dick Turpin* (1839); *Will Watch, The Bold Smuggler* (1840?); *Claude Du Val* (1849). Miles also wrote a life of the clown Joseph Grimaldi (1838) and died at Wood Green, London. BL 3. Boase. RLF.

The Mill On The Floss, George Eliot, 1860, 3 vols, Blackwood. The most autobiographical of Eliot's novels. Maggie and Tom are the children of

Edward Tulliver, the owner of Dorlcote Mill on the river Floss. Maggie is wild, passionate and dark-haired. She contrasts with the neat, well-mannered blondness of her cousin, Lucy Deane. Tom is less intelligent than his sister, but firm and moralistic. Maggie never the less worships him. Tom is sent to a private tutor's together with Philip Wakem, the son of a lawyer for whom the miller Mr Tulliver has conceived a particular hatred. Philip is hunchbacked, but very clever. He and Maggie find a natural affinity. Mr Tulliver is finally ruined at law, by Wakem. Dorlcote Mill is lost, and in his fury the miller has a seizure and is partially paralysed. He recovers sufficiently to make Tom swear vengeance against the Wakems. The Tullivers scrimp to pay off their debts, and Maggie enters womanhood in an increasingly bitter and impoverished home atmosphere. She consoles herself by reading the works of early English divines, and by dint of ruthless self-suppression achieves some serenity. When Tom discovers that she has been seeing Philip, he cruelly forbids the relationship. When finally enough has been earned to pay off the family debts, old Tulliver horsewhips Wakem publicly, and thereafter dies of the excitement. Maggie goes off to be a teacher while Tom devotes himself to making enough money to repossess the Mill. Two years later, Maggie returns. She and her cousin Lucy's betrothed, Stephen Guest, fall in love. On a river trip, Stephen and Maggie are swept away, and are thought to have eloped. On their return, Tom feels disgraced at his moment of triumph, having at last recovered the Mill. At the end of the novel, brother and sister are swept away on a great flood, and drowned in the Floss. Their last act is an embrace of reconciliation as the torrent sweeps down on them.

MILLAIS, [Sir] J[ohn] E[verett] (1829–96). Famous as a Victorian painter and President of the Royal Academy, Millais was also among the finest illustrators of mid-Victorian fiction. Millais was born in Southampton. His family (which was well off) had lived for some generations in Jersey and returned there shortly after his birth. The young Millais was prodigiously gifted and precocious. He entered the Royal Academy Schools in 1840 and later in the decade came under the influence of the Pre-Raphaelites. In 1855 he married Effie Ruskin, John Ruskin's* wife, her earlier marriage having been annulled on grounds of non-consummation. In 1863 he was elected RA, was made a baronet in 1885 and president of the Royal Academy in 1896, just before his death. Millais' major illustrations of novels were executed for Trollope's* *Framley Parsonage** (1861); *Orley Farm** (1862); *The Small House At Allington** (1862) and *Phineas Finn** (1869). They represent the most notable alliance of the woodcut style of the 1860s with the realistic novel of the period. *DNB*. Hou.

MILLER, Mrs Lydia Falconer ('Harriet Myrtle', née Fraser, 1811?–76). Lydia Fraser was born in Inverness, the daughter of an unsuccessful tradesman, and educated at Edinburgh. Later she lived with her mother in Cromarty and took pupils at home, 1833–36. In 1831, she became acquainted with Hugh Miller (1802–56), the geologist, and after a long engagement the couple were married in 1837. After marriage, she helped Miller edit the church paper, the *Witness*, and supported his activity during the Disruption which was currently transforming the Church of Scotland. In 1847, Hugh Miller published his refutation of Chambers's *Vestiges Of Creation*, entitled *Footprints Of The Creator*, a work defending the Genesis account. Lydia Miller fell severely ill in 1855, and was thereafter in chronically poor health. As 'Harriet Myrtle' (a pseudonym she shared with Miss Mary Gillies) Miller wrote numerous stories for the young: e.g. *Little Amy's Birthday* (1846); *The Little Sister* (1852); *Aunt Maddy's Diamonds* (1864). She also wrote a novel for adults, on the subject of the Disruption, entitled *Passages In The Life Of An English Heiress* (1847). In 1857, Miller received a Civil List pension of £70. A widow for sixteen years, she died in the manse of her son-in-law. Hugh Miller, who predeceased her by twenty years, also wrote some fiction recalling his early Scottish origins: *Scenes And Legends Of The North Of Scotland* (1835); *My Schools And Schoolmasters* (1854). (LFM) BL 21. (HM) BL 3. *DNB*.

MILLER, Thomas ('the basket-maker', 1807–74). One of the very few Victorian novelists of proletarian origins, Thomas Miller was born in Gainsborough, the son of a wharfinger. His father disappeared in 1810 during political agitations in London and Miller was brought up in great poverty and deprivation. At a very early age he was apprenticed to a basket-maker, and became acquainted with Thomas Cooper*, the Chartist. Like Cooper, Miller wrote poetry, and in 1835 moved to London. As the poetic basket-maker, he gained the patronage of the Countess of Blessington*. In 1836 he published *A Day In The Woods*, 'a connected series of tales and poems'. This won him some success, and with the help of Samuel Rogers, Miller set up as a bookseller in Newgate Street in 1841. In addition to poetry, he wrote tales for the popular *London Journal** and historical* romances for children. His fiction includes: *Royston Gower, Or The Days Of King John* (1838); *Fair Rosamond* (1839); *Gideon Giles The Roper* (1840); *Lady Jane Grey* (1840); *The Mysteries Of London* (fifth volume, 1849); *The Village Queen* (1852); *Langley On The Lea* (1860); *Jack Of All Trades* (1867). By far his most interesting novel is the autobiographical *Godfrey Malvern, Or The Life Of An Author* (1842). The hero is a poor schoolteacher who comes to the London literary world. Here he has various adventures, sexual and authorial, before returning to his wife and family in the country. Miller's later years were impoverished. Disraeli* awarded him £100 from the Royal Bounty Fund in 1874, but he died utterly destitute. BL 15. *DNB. NCBEL*. Wol. RLF.

MILLIKEN, E[dwin] J[ames] (1839?–97). Inventor of the archetypal cockney* character, 'Arry. Born in Ireland, Milliken began his working life as an engineer. He came to London where he was first employed as a journalist on *Figaro* in 1874. Four years later, he joined the staff of *Punch**. For this journal he wrote *The 'Arry Papers* (1874–97). Other of Milliken's comic productions include: *The Modern Ars Amandi* (1883); *Fitzdotterel* (1885); *Untiled, Or The Modern Asmodeus* (1890). Etymologists credit Milliken with furnishing the most exact phonetic reproduction of spoken cockney cant words and city dialect. BL 3. Boase. RLF.

MILLINGEN, John Gideon (1782–1862). Millingen was born at Westminster, London, the son of a Dutch merchant. At the age of eight, he was taken by his father to Paris, where he lived through the most exciting period of the Revolution (in which his brother James was imprisoned). He later studied medicine in Paris, and took up work as a British army surgeon in 1802. Millingen subsequently served in the Peninsular War, and at Waterloo. During a later posting in the West Indies his health collapsed, and he retired on half pay in 1823. As a civilian, he was physician to various lunatic asylums. As an author Millingen wrote popular medical books and works (mainly farces) for the stage. His fiction (which has attractive autobiographical elements) includes: *The Adventures Of An Irish Gentleman* (1830); *Stories Of Torres Vedras* (1839); *Jack Hornet, Or The March Of Intellect* (1845). BL 3. *DNB*. RLF.

MILLS, George (1808–81). Mills was born at Glasgow, the son of the Lord Provost, and educated at Glasgow University. After graduation in 1827 he went into his father's shipping company, and eventually became an extremely successful shipbuilder himself. An energetic man, Mills also practised as a stockbroker (particularly in the trade depression of the 1840s) and went into newspaper proprietorship in 1857 with the *Glasgow Advertiser*. On the side he wrote some fiction with a vernacular Scottish flavour: *Craigclutha, A Tale Of Old Glasgow* (1857); *I Remember* (1857); *The Beggar's Benison* (1866). The last was thought by the *Athenaeum** reviewer to be the most distasteful novel he had ever read, recounting as it did the ruthless rise to power by a Clydesdale 'getter on'. As with everything that Mills turned his hand to, his fiction made him money. BL 3. *DNB*.

MILLS, John ('D'Horsay', d. 1885?). Very little is known of Mills other than that he lived in Essex, and wrote rollicking hunting books, which include: *The Old English Gentleman* (1841); *The Stage Coach Or The Road Of Life* (1843); *D'Horsay* (1844), a lampoon on the Count d'Orsay, consort to the Countess Blessington*; *The Old Hall* (1847); *A Capful Of Moonshine* (1849); *Our County* (1850); *The Belle Of the Village* (1852); *The Wheel Of Life* (1855); *The Life Of A Foxhound* (1861), a work narrated autobiographically by a dog; *On The Spur Of The Moment* (1884). Michael Sadleir (in *XIX Century Fiction*) grotesquely confuses him with the Calvinist minister of the same name (1812–73) written up in the *DNB*. BL 16. Boase. *NCBEL*. Wol. Sad. RLF.

MINTO, William (1845–93). A Scot, Minto was born in the village of Auchintoul in Aberdeenshire, of humble parentage. He won a bursary to Aberdeen University, where he covered himself in glory, winning more prizes than any other student of the century. After graduation, in 1865, he spent a year at Merton College, Oxford before returning to teach English and logic at his Alma Mater. He left a notable mark on his academic subject (his *Manual Of English Prose Literature* appeared in 1872). In 1873, however, he changed course and travelled to London to support himself by journalism. A Liberal in politics, he wrote leaders for the *Daily News* and the *Pall Mall Gazette*, and was editor of the *Examiner* from 1874–78. He returned to Aberdeen as professor of English in 1880, marrying at the same date. During the tenure of this chair, he wrote three novels: *The Crack Of Doom* (1886), the story of what happens when an earth-threatening comet is predicted by an eccentric professor; *The Mediation Of Ralph Hardelot* (1888), a historical* romance set in the period of Wat Tyler; and *Was She*

Good Or Bad? (1889), a slighter comedy of modern manners. Minto's career reflects the Scottish intellectual's easy mobility between the academy and higher journalism. His novels are not his major claim to fame, but they are of a piece with his all-round achievement. BL 3. *DNB. NCBEL.* Wol.

Miriam's Schooling, Mark Rutherford (i.e. William Hale White), 1890, 1 vol, Kegan Paul. Like White's other works, this novella is supposedly 'edited by his friend, Reuben Shapcott'. The story is set in 'Cowfold' (White's native Bedford), in the early century. Miriam is the daughter of an Italian watchmaker, Giacomo Tacchi. A girl of powerful, if untutored, character she dominates her brother Andrew. He goes to London to work as a clerk, and Miriam accompanies him to keep house. In London, Andrew falls in with bad company and is dismissed for drunkenness. Miriam nurses him to recovery, and they return to Cowfold. There she marries an oafish basket-maker, Didymus Farrow. By various acts of mutual friendliness, the couple gradually school themselves into an affectionate relationship. The novel is one of the author's many celebrations of the moral virtue of humility.

The Miser's Daughter, William Harrison Ainsworth, 1842, 3 vols, Cunningham and Mortimer. (Serialised in *Ainsworth's Magazine**, January–October 1842, illustrated by George Cruikshank*.) The novel with which Ainsworth launched his magazine. The work's principal distinction is that it provided a platform for Cruikshank's finest illustration to fiction. The narrative is set in 1744, and offers a wealth of topographic detail. The plot is complex, and ill knit. Randulph Crew, a young paragon, has honourably sacrificed his father's estate in Knutsford to creditors. He comes to London. There he delivers a mysterious packet to the miser Scarve, and falls in love with Scarve's daughter, Hilda. The match is opposed both by the father (who intends his daughter for the rake Philip Frewin) and by Randulph's own guardian, his uncle Abel, for reasons which are initially obscure. Randulph is subsequently introduced into fashionable circles. There, among other adventures, he fights a duel with Beau Villiers, to protect Hilda's honour. A complicated sub-plot has Randulph blackmailed to join the Jacobites, which he honourably refuses to do. Philip attacks Randulph with his myrmidons, and is fatally wounded. To protect his treasure (of which Philip was the heir) the miser buries it in his cellar. But, having dug the hole, it becomes his grave as, over-exerted, he dies. (This is the occasion of one of Cruikshank's most powerful nocturnal illustrations.) A complicated set of denouements reveals that the hero's uncle Abel was earlier Scarve's rival for the love of Hilda's mother, and that there was a contract between Randulph's father and Scarve for the marriage of their children. Enriched by the miser's money, the hero and heroine marry and 'all the rest of their life was a honeymoon'.

Miss Bretherton, Mrs Humphry Ward, 1884, 1 vol, Macmillan. Ward's first published novel, inspired by a visit to the theatre with Henry James to see the acclaimed American actress, Mary Anderson. The novelists found her beautiful, but technically amateurish. Ward's heroine, Isabel Bretherton, is an actress (from the colonies) who wins the heart of a fastidious Oxford man of letters, Eustace Kendal. Despite his love for her, Eustace is obliged to tell Isabel that she lacks true dramatic art. Isabel retreats to the Continent where with the help of Eustace's sister, Marie, she learns her craft from European masters. On her return to London, Isabel triumphs in the lead of a new play written for her by Eustace's American friend, Edward Wallace. Marie, dying, effects a reconciliation between the lovers. The novel is a slight effort and gives no hint of its successor, *Robert Elsmere** (1888).

Miss Brown, Vernon Lee (i.e. Violet Paget), 1884, 3 vols, Blackwood. A satire on aestheticism. Miss Anne Brown is a beautiful girl, working as nursemaid to an artist's family in Italy. She is taken up by another bored artist, the Pre-Raphaelite poet and painter, Walter Hamlin, who settles money on her to allow her to be educated in Germany. Afterwards she may or may not become his wife; it is her 'soul' he is principally interested in. In the event he fails to make her his ideal aesthetic woman. She is radicalised by her Scottish cousin Richard Brown and becomes instead a socialist. But when Hamlin is finally a broken man, Miss Brown relents and in a spirit of self-sacrifice marries him. The last rather ghastly image in the novel is Hamlin's face by gaslight: 'radiant with the triumph of satisfied vanity'. The story's extended satire on the contemporary art world went down well with middlebrow reviewers but the second volume sags badly. Much against his wishes, Paget dedicated this first novel to Henry James.

Miss Mackenzie, Anthony Trollope, 1865, 2 vols, Chapman and Hall. One of Trollope's experiments in anti-romanticism. Margaret Mackenzie is a thirty-five-year-old spinster, who has spent her youth keeping house for and finally nursing her brother Walter. When he dies, she is left his heir. Out of duty, she lends some of her new fortune to her disappointed brother, Tom. His oilcloth business has gone to the bad, and Samuel Rubb, the son of his dishonest partner, lays siege to Miss Mackenzie hoping to secure the rest of her money. She escapes, but at Littlebath (i.e. Bath) she is wooed by the greasy Rev. Jeremiah Maguire, who wants her money to set up his church. She is also proposed to by a decent man, her cousin John Ball. A widower, Ball is connected to the aristocratic branch of the heroine's family. The plot comes to a crisis with the death from cancer of Tom Mackenzie. His widow (a woman who has always looked down on Margaret as an old maid) is left destitute. Miss Mackenzie nobly shares her money with her sister-in-law. But she discovers that after all, the fortune was not her brother's to leave. All the while it has belonged to John Ball. He resumes his suit, and she finally accepts him. The novel is principally attractive for its tender portrait of the plucky but unworldly heroine.

Miss Marjoribanks, Margaret Oliphant, 1866, 3 vols, Blackwood. (Serialised in *Blackwood's Magazine**, February 1865–May 1866.) The most sharply comic of the Carlingford* chronicles. Lucilla Marjoribanks (pronounced 'Marchbanks') is a Victorian Emma: domineering, self-willed, constantly defeated in her ambitious attempts to lead Carlingford society. Losing her mother when she is fifteen, Lucilla's first campaign is to console and take charge of her father, the doctor of Carlingford, described as 'too busy a man to waste his feelings on a mere sentiment'. Lucilla subsequently embarks on her mission to bring about 'a revolution in the tastes and ideas of Carlingford'. The plot covers ten years, and climaxes with an election in the town. The victor, Mr Ashburton MP, proposes to the heroine. But she marries instead a faithful cousin, Tom Marjoribanks, who has been labouring in India to make himself worthy of her love. The narrator concludes: 'there is something consoling in our own mind in the thought that Lucilla can now suffer no change of name.' *Miss Marjoribanks* is thought by some to be Oliphant's masterwork. It was, however, less popular with Victorian readers than earlier tales in the Carlingford series.

Mr Scarborough's Family, Anthony Trollope, 1883, 3 vols, Chatto and Windus. (Serialised in *All The Year Round**, May 1882–June 1883.) Trollope's forty-fifth novel; he died during its serial run. The work, appropriately, is a patriarchal meditation on wills, death and unworthy heirs. Mr John Scarborough has been enriched by clay workings on his estate at Tretton. But his two sons are, in their different ways, unworthy of his fortune. Mountjoy, a captain in the Guards, is a ne'er-do-well. His younger barrister brother, Augustus, is cold and calculating. Mr Scarborough has taken the precaution of marrying his wife twice on the Continent. The second 'marriage' postdates Mountjoy's birth, thus rendering him illegitimate if divulged. When Mountjoy runs hopelessly into debt, Mr Scarborough (about to undergo an operation which will probably be fatal), has him legally declared a bastard. Mountjoy disappears and is even thought murdered, for a while. But Augustus proves so keen to see his father buried, that Scarborough relents (having meanwhile paid all Mountjoy's debts on the cheap) and reinstates his firstborn before finally dying. Mountjoy immediately takes himself off to Monte Carlo, presumably to squander the inheritance. There is a subplot, concerned with Mr Scarborough's niece, Florence. She is competed for between the Scarborough sons, and another expectant heir, Harry Annesley. After Harry too has lost and regained his inheritance, Florence marries him. The novel has a complex legal plot, and is (for Trollope) notably humourless.

Mr Sponge's Sporting Tour, Robert Smith Surtees, 1853, 1 vol, Bradbury and Evans. (Serialised in monthly numbers, January–December 1852, with illustrations by John Leech*. An earlier version of the novel was published in Ainsworth's* *New Monthly Magazine**, January 1849–April 1851 as 'Soapey Sponge's Sporting Tour'.) The narrative covers a season in the life of a hunting man about town and country. Soapey Sponge is first encountered as a rather seedy racing man in London. He pulls off a coup in the horse-trading way by buying two mounts, which set him up for a season's hunting at Laverick Wells, where his cockney* manners initially go down very badly. Never the less, an attempt by the Master of the Hunt, Waffles, to show Sponge up in the field misfires. And Sponge gets his revenge by selling Waffles one of his horses, the unridable Hercules. Sponge later (by devious means) gets invitations to hunt with Lord Scamperdale (who mistakenly thinks him rich) and Mr Puffington (who mistakenly thinks Sponge an influential sports writer). After numerous knockabout adventures, Sponge ends his season's sport by marrying an actress, Lucy Glitters, and setting up a betting shop in London. The serial was successful and inspired a series of rollicking hunting tales from Leech and Surtees, including a sequel *Mr Facey Romford's Hounds* (1865) in which Soapey Sponge is seen absconding to Australia, leaving Lucy behind to fend for herself.

Mrs Armytage, Or Female Domination, Mrs C. G. F. Gore, 1836, 3 vols, Colburn. (Gore's novel was very successful when it first came out. It was reissued in 1848, with a typical Colburn promotion stunt, the novel being alleged to have been found, bloodstained, on the bed of 'the unfortunate Duchesse de Presslin on the night of her assassination'.) Arthur, a lifeguardsman with only £450 per annum settled on him, has married so as to disoblige his wealthy, domineering mother, Mrs Armytage, mistress of Holywell Park and £17,000 a year. He further offends by beating her candidate in the county election. An imperfect reconciliation between mother and son is brought about by the saintly Sophy Armytage. Arthur eventually turns up a codicil to his father's will: the inheritance is his, not his mother's. He does nothing until she falsely accuses her daughter-in-law of infidelity. In a melodramatic third-volume climax, the browbeaten Sophy dies of a broken heart and proud Mrs Armytage (now nothing more than a 'jointured dowager') flounces off to the Continent. But she has an incurable cancer. Just before her death, all parties forgive each other and the mother is brought back to Holywell to die in peace. Despite her protestation that 'I believe a woman of first-rate faculties would constitute only a third-rate man', Gore invests her stubborn heroine with a queer admirableness. The action is set in the present day.

Mrs Caudle's Curtain Lectures, Douglas Jerrold, 1845, 1 vol, Bradbury and Evans. (Serialised in *Punch**, January–December 1845, illustrated by John Leech*.) Jerrold's most popular comic serial. Job Caudle is a good-natured toyman and doll merchant. Every night in bed, he is nagged unmercifully by his shrew of a wife and prevented from going to sleep. As the narrator notes, 'Minerva's bird, the very wisest thing in feathers, is silent all the day. So was Mrs Caudle. Like the owl, she hooted only at night.' The text (supposedly edited after Job's death) is made up of Mrs Caudle's nightly monologues to her suffering and feebly protesting partner on such themes as: 'Mr Caudle Has Remained Downstairs Till Past One, With A Friend.'

Mrs Keith's Crime, Mrs W. K. Clifford, 1885, 1 vol, Fisher, Unwin. A powerful tale of euthanasia. Mrs 'Maggie' Keith is left a widow with two children when her artist husband Arthur is drowned at the seaside. She ekes out a living painting portraits but her little son Jack dies of consumption and her six-year-old daughter also shows ominous signs of sickness. With a loan from a good-natured friend, Frederick Cohen, she goes to live in Malaga, Spain. There she falls in love with her doctor, George Murray. She also contrives to matchmake for two young lovers at her hotel. But Mrs Keith's daughter Molly gets worse, her lover leaves and she herself develops terminal symptoms of heart disease. Lest her little girl be left to die motherless, she hastens her death with chloroform. The novel, which is narrated autobiographically as a 'record' tails off with Mrs Keith's dying thoughts. The early sections of the story draw on the author's own experiences, widowed as she was at the age of twenty-six with two small children. *Mrs Keith's Crime* was hugely popular and was successfully dramatised.

Mrs Perkins's Ball, M. A. Titmarsh (i.e. W. M. Thackeray), 1847, 1 vol, Chapman and Hall. (Illustrations by the author.) Thackeray's 1846 Christmas* Book. Michael Angelo Titmarsh, mild-mannered tutor in the flute, French and drawing, is invited to the Christmas ball of his employers, the Perkinses of Pocklington Square. Somewhat against his will, he is prevailed on to take along his wild Irish friend The Mulligan (of Ballymulligan). The liberally illustrated book is made up of vignettes and snapshots (e.g. Miss Bunion, the poetess author of *Heartstrings*, *The Deadly Nightshade*, *Passion Flowers*, etc.) The proceedings end with Mulligan's getting drunk, offering to fight his host and being ejected.

MITFORD, Algernon Bertram [Freeman] (1837–1916). Mitford was born into the outer fringe of the English aristocracy, and was educated at Eton and Christ Church, Oxford. In 1858, he took up a career in the diplomatic service and was posted to Japan in 1868, an experience which marked him profoundly. He left the Foreign Office in 1873. In 1886 he assumed the name Freeman. From 1892 to 1895, he was a Conservative MP. Mitford wrote fiction, using his knowledge of the East. It includes: *Tales Of Old Japan* (1871), a work illustrated by Japanese artists; *The Bamboo Garden* (1896); *The Attaché at Peking* (1900). His novels were evidently popular. BL 3. WW.

MITFORD, Bertram (d. 1914). Apparently a relative of the above author. Bertram Mitford was born at Mitford Castle, Northumberland, and spent much of his adult life in world travel. A fellow of the Royal Geographical Society, he lived after 1873 mostly in South Africa, and produced numerous adventure novels many with that country as background. They include: *The Fire Trumpet, A Romance Of The Cape Frontier* (1889); *The Gun Runner* (1894), a tale of Zululand; *A Veldt Official* (1895); *Fordham's Feud* (1897), an adventure story set in the Swiss Alps. *The Sign Of The Spider* (1897) has a huge man-eating spider as its blood-curdling subject. *Aletta* (1900) is a pro-British 'Tale Of The Boer Invasion'. BL 31. WW. Wol. Sad. RLF.

MITFORD, Mary Russell (1787–1855). Mary Mitford was born at Alresford, Hampshire, the only child of an incorrigibly spendthrift doctor father and an heiress mother. Mitford's father soon ran through his wife's fortune. Mary was precociously clever, could read before she was three and at the age of ten won a lottery worth £20,000. She was educated at private school in London, and in 1802 settled with her parents. By 1810, she had published some well-received poems. Her first serious writing attempts were in tragedy, in which she was encouraged by the poet Coleridge. Ten years later, however, when her father had reduced the family to penury, Mary was obliged to write for money. In 1819, she began the sketches 'of rural character and scenery' subsequently collected as *Our Village*, for the *Lady's Magazine*. In terms of literary genre, Mitford thus laid the foundations of the domestic* novel, or 'novel of community', centred on English parochial life and doings. In 1823, Macready produced her tragedy *Julian*. Mitford occupied the first rank of popular writers in the pre-Victorian period, but her father's depredations continued to keep her relatively poor. In 1835, she brought out *Belford Regis, Or Sketches Of A Country Town* (i.e. Reading). By this stage, her invention as a writer was clearly flagging. In 1837, Mitford was granted a Civil List pension of £100, and in 1842 her father finally died. In 1852, she brought out her *Recollections Of A Literary Life*, and in

1854, her last effort in fiction, *Atherton, And Other Tales*. In her last years she was crippled with rheumatism, but still enjoyed some fame as a woman of letters and conversationalist. BL 7. *DNB*. RM. *NCBEL*. Wol

Modern Chivalry, Or A New Orlando Furioso, William Harrison Ainsworth and Mrs C. G. F. Gore, 1843, 2 vols, Mortimer. (Serialised in *Ainsworth's Magazine**, July–December 1843.) Although usually attributed to Ainsworth (who at different times claimed to have 'edited' and to have written it), the sprightly prose of this work argues for Mrs Gore as the principal author. It is a loosely strung, but sharply observed study of egoism and social uselessness. The hero, Howardson of Greyoke (later Lord Buckhurst) lives a fashionable life, his one desire being to escape the 'alligator', boredom. His career is followed from his social début in London to his death in Paris where 'even the headstone, erected by contract, has sunk into the soil, so as to render illegible his right honourable name'. Although largely disregarded and slight, this work is better than most of what either Ainsworth or Gore published as their major fiction.

MOLESWORTH, Mrs Mary Louisa ('Ennis Graham', née Stewart, 1839–1921). Mary Stewart was born in Rotterdam into a Scottish merchant's family. In 1841, the Stewarts moved to Manchester. (For a version of the novelist's childhood memories, see *The Carved Lions*, 1895.) Mary was educated at home, and in Switzerland. As a child, she wrote stories for her amusement. In 1861, she married Major Richard Molesworth, late of the Royal Dragoons, and a viscount's nephew. The couple had four children and travelled extensively. Mary Molesworth began writing novels very young, 'as an amusement'. Her first published work was *Lover And Husband*, in 1869. All her fiction up to 1874 was written under the pseudonym 'Ennis Graham' and was mainly directed at adults. It includes *Not Without Thorns* (1873) and *Cicely* (1874). In 1876, Molesworth discovered her vocation as a children's* writer, and brought out in that year her best-known work, *Carrots*. The hero, Carrots, is, as J. S. Bratton puts it, 'a child who precipitates family chaos by finding and keeping a half-sovereign, thinking it a special sort of sixpence. He is rescued from the threat of a whipping, all is explained, and his elder brother, who has failed to be compassionate towards him, is the more severely reprimanded.' This work was followed by other very popular tales: *The Cuckoo Clock* (1877); *The Tapestry Room* (1879). *Miss Bouverie* (1880). Her fiction includes fantasies* like *Christmas Tree Land* (1895); stories of growing up like *The Third Miss Quentin* (1889); and ghost* stories like *Uncanny Tales* (1896). Molesworth's husband died in 1900 and she continued writing up to the 1920s. BL 120. *WW*. RM. *NCBEL*. Wol.

MOLLOY, J[oseph] Fitzgerald (1858–1908). Molloy was born in New Ross, Co. Wexford, Ireland. He was originally intended for the Catholic Church, but was drawn to music and (particularly) literary pursuits. In 1878, he emigrated to London, accompanied by letters to his compatriots Mr and Mrs S. C. Hall*, who became his patrons. Equally helpful to him was Sir Charles Gavan Duffy, who engaged him as private secretary and secured a place for him in the office of the agent-general for New Zealand. Molloy wrote biography, and history (mainly to do with the Hanoverian reigns).

He also wrote a number of novels, most of which were serialised in the London and Liverpool papers. They include: *Merely Players* (1881), a story of crossed love in high places; *It Is No Wonder* (1881), 'A Story Of Bohemian Life'; *What Hast Thou Done?* (1883); *That Villain Romeo* (1886); *A Modern Magician* (1887), a Corelli*-style story of the occult; *An Excellent Knave* (1893); *His Wife's Soul* (1893), a contemporary melodrama of crime, death and distraught spouses; *A Justified Sinner* (1897), a highly coloured story of deceit in love with the kind of tremendous emotional climax that was the author's speciality. BL 15. *DNB*. Wol.

MONKHOUSE, William Cosmo (1840–1901). Monkhouse was born in London, the son of a solicitor. He attended St Paul's School, leaving in 1856 to enter the Board of Trade. He served the whole of his working life in the Civil Service, travelling world-wide and rising eventually to the rank of assistant secretary to the Finance Department. He married in 1865, but seems to have divorced soon after. Distinguished principally as an art critic, Monkhouse wrote for such journals as the *Academy** and the *Saturday Review**. He also wrote nature poetry, and one three-volume novel, *A Question of Honour* (1868). BL 1. *DNB*.

MONKSWELL, [Sir] Robert Collier (1845–1909). Collier was born in London and educated at Eton and Trinity College, Cambridge, where he took a first-class degree in law. He inherited the title of second Baron Monkswell in 1885. A Liberal, he was a servant of the London County Council for many years and Under-Secretary for War in 1895. He wrote extensively on the law, and produced one novel, *Kate Grenville* (1896), the story of a lawyer's daughter who nobly sacrifices her birthright. BL 1. *WW*.

MONTGOMERY, Florence (1843–1934). An admiral's daughter, Florence Montgomery began her career in fiction telling stories to her four younger sisters. She was eventually persuaded to publish her writing by the veteran novelist, Whyte-Melville*. Her work is largely composed of moral tales for children, with adolescent girls as both subject-matter and readers. In a preface of 1872 she confessed her inclination even in adult fiction 'to side, as it were, with the children against the parents'. She never married. Montgomery's fiction includes: *A Very Simple Story* (1866); *Misunderstood* (1869), her most popular tale; *Thrown Together* (1872); *Thwarted* (1873); *Seaforth* (1878), the story of a country house; *Herbert Manners* (1880); *Transformed* (1886); *Colonel Norton* (1895), the story of a 'thoughtless, frivolous girl' eventually brought to maturity; *Prejudged* (1900). The last is intended for older readers and has love in a French *pension* as its subject. BL 20. *WW. NCBEL*. Wol. Sad.

The Monthly Packet (1851–99). A magazine, published by the evangelical firm of Mozley as an aid to the more liberal kind of Sunday-School teacher. The journal's full title was: 'The Monthly Packet Of Evening Reading For Younger Members Of The English Church'. For most of its existence, the *Packet* was edited by C. M. Yonge*, assisted latterly by Christabel Coleridge* (after 1890). It featured a diet of general interest articles and improving fiction.

MONTRESOR, Miss F. F. (1843–1923). An admiral's daughter, she was born in Kent. She never married, apparently. Her fiction includes: *Into The*

Highways And Hedges (1895), the story of marriage between a clever, well-bred girl, and a strict evangelical preacher; *The One Who Looked On* (1895), the story of an aunt who quizzically regards the family dramas around her; *Worthwhile* (1896), a collection of tales; *False Coin Or True?* (1896), the story of an orphan who becomes the medium of a French mesmerist; *At The Cross Roads* (1897), a melodramatic romance with a modern heroine and a convict lover; *The Alien* (1901), the story of a villainous mother who conspires to embezzle for her child another child's inheritance. Montresor evidently wrote one-volume romance to the taste of late-Victorian library subscribers and employed a portentous style with numerous moralistic asides. She had a knack, however, for eye-catching titles such as: *The Celestial Surgeon* (1904) or *The Burning Torch* (1907). Not even the British Library Catalogue knows what her initials stand for. BL 13. *WW*. Wol.

MOODIE, Mrs Susannah (née Strickland, 1803–85). The younger sister of Agnes Strickland* (author of *The Lives Of The Queens Of England*, 1840–48), she was born in the family home at Reydon Hall, Suffolk. Like her sisters, Susannah was precocious and published a first novel, *Spartacus, A Roman Story*, in 1822, when she was only nineteen. In 1831, she went on to publish an innocuous volume of verse, and married Lieutenant John Wedderburn Dunbar Moodie (1797–1869), the traveller and adventurer. The newly-married couple voyaged to Canada in 1832 where for a while they farmed. Moodie later served in the Niagara militia, and eventually became a sheriff in Ontario. In 1852, the family fell on hard times. To earn money, Mrs Moodie began publishing books, the most interesting of which recall her pioneer experiences. The first of these, *Roughing It In The Bush* (1852), is generally regarded as her best. It was followed by *Life In The Clearings Versus The Bush* (1853); *Mark Hurdlestone* (1853), the story of a 'gold worshipper' or miser, written 'during the long cold, winter nights of 1838–39'; *Flora Lindsay* (1854); *Matrimonial Speculations* (1854); *The World Before Them* (1868). Mysteriously, Moodie stopped writing fiction on her husband's death in 1869, and it is suggested he may have been the author of the works which bear her name. BL 16. *DNB*. RM. RLF.

The Moonstone, Wilkie Collins, 1868, 3 vols, Tinsley. (Serialised in *All The Year Round**, January–August, 1868.) According to T. S. Eliot 'the first, longest and best of English detective* novels'. The plot begins with the storming of Seringapatam in 1799 when an English adventurer, John Herncastle, steals a sacred Indian diamond called the Moonstone. The action moves to the 1840s. Despite the menace of three Hindu thugs, Herncastle has held on to the stone (and his life) by threatening to have it cut up, in the event of his death. The Moonstone is left to his niece, Rachel Verinder. Her cousin, Franklin Blake, delivers it in person and the young people fall in love. But after a party, the gem is found to be stolen. Sergeant Cuff of Scotland Yard is called in. Rosanna Spearman, Rachel's maid, is suspected and commits suicide by throwing herself into quicksands. She leaves a letter which turns up evidence seeming to incriminate Franklin. Rachel meanwhile has become engaged to a young charity worker, Godfrey Ablewhite. But the match is broken off, after he seems all too interested in her fortune. An experiment with laudanum reveals that Franklin did indeed take the Moonstone, while drugged. It was thereafter stolen by Ablewhite. Ablewhite (disguised as a sailor) attempts to make off with the gem but is finally murdered by the patiently waiting Hindu assassins. The Moonstone is last heard of restored to the forehead of the idol from which it was originally stolen.

MOORE, Frank [Francis] Frankfort (1855–1931). Moore was born in Limerick, Ireland and educated at the Royal Academical Institute, Belfast. He began to write at the age of sixteen, had his first volume of verse published in 1872 and spent sixteen years on the staff of the *Belfast Newsletter*. As a journalist he travelled widely, and from 1876 to 1892 worked for several London newspapers. Moore wrote plays with some success, married twice and turned out many novels. His early fiction mainly took the sea or fragrant young maidens as its subject. He had his first major success late on, however, with *I Forbid The Banns* (1893) and *The Jessamy Bride* (1897). The second of these is an eighteenth-century historical* romance which introduces as characters on the first page: Dr Johnson, Oliver Goldsmith, Edmund Burke, David Garrick, James Boswell and Sir Joshua Reynolds. Moore's earlier novels include: *Sojourners Together* (1875); *The Mate Of The Jessica* (1879), a story of the South Pacific; *The Mutiny On The Albatross* (1885), an SPCK* volume; *The Great Orion* (1886); *Under Hatches* (1888); *From The Bush To The Breakers* (1893), an Australian tale; *One Fair Daughter* (1894); *Nell Gwyn* (1900); *According To Plato* (1901). Moore wrote some interesting Irish novels, late in his life (e.g. *The Ulsterman*, 1914). BL 64. *WW*. Wol.

MOORE, George [Augustus] (1852–1933). The leading naturalist novelist of the late Victorian period. Moore was born at Moore Hall in Co. Mayo, the eldest son of a wealthy Liberal MP and stable-owner (a background later used in *Esther Waters**, 1894). Young George was educated at home and at the Catholic public school Oscott, near Birmingham. As a child he was chronically ill, missing many months of education. At the age of eleven, he had his first significant literary experience, reading *Lady Audley's Secret**, after which he methodically steeped himself in Miss Braddon's* fiction. His father died (of 'political frustration', allegedly) when Moore was eighteen, by which time he had already committed himself to a bohemian life in Paris. Never the less he now owned over 12,000 acres of Irish property and an income for life. In Paris, Moore absorbed the new aesthetic doctrines of Impressionism and Naturalism (although in personal habits he remained austerely abstemious). A vivid recollection of this period of his life is given in *Confessions Of A Young Man* (1888). Failing as an artist, Moore returned to Mayo (where the estate's financial affairs were in disorder) in 1879, making London his literary base. His first novel, *A Modern Lover* (1883), the story of a young artist in London, was a frank homage to 'Zola and his odious school', as the *Spectator* put it. The hero, Lewis Seymour, callously betrays the three women who sacrifice their virtue to him. *A Mummer's Wife** (1885) entered new areas of sexual frankness for the Victorian novel, and established Moore as a rebel against the kind of decency represented by Mudie's* 'select' circulating library. About the same time, Moore discovered the prose of Walter Pater* and a new aestheticism enters his writing. There followed *A Drama In Muslin* (1886), the carefully interlaced life stories of five convent-educated Irish girls and *A Mere Accident* (1887), a work which shows the influence of Huysmans. In 1889, Moore was deeply affected by his aged publisher Henry Vizetelly's* being sent to prison for publishing Zola's novels. And his own novel, *Mike Fletcher* (1889) was not a success, although its depiction of a thirty-year-old poet's dissolute life and suicide in bohemian London still reads well. Various experiments in drama failed. But Moore re-established himself as one of the leading British authors of the 1890s with his masterpiece, *Esther Waters* (1894), among much else the most English of his novels. Around the mid-1890s, he began to cultivate his skills as a short story writer. *Evelyn Innes** (1898) and its sequel *Sister Teresa* (1901) are musical novels, which sensitively explore the artistic and religious pathology of creativity. At the turn of the century, partly moved by disgust at the Boer War, Moore became disillusioned with England and made his residence in Ireland. In 1905, he was appointed High Sheriff of Mayo. Moore continued to build a reputation as a leading modern writer in the early twentieth century, with works such as *Memoirs Of My Dead Life* (1906) and the *Hail And Farewell* (1911–14) trilogy. At this period, he also made a determined effort to reconnect himself with his Irish roots. His later works are excessively stylised and he rewrote or extensively revised many of his earlier novels. Moore's sexual involvement with John Oliver Hobbes* (i.e. Mrs Craigie) reverberates through the fiction of both writers. He first met her in 1893, at a period when she was involved in a divorce suit. Their affair was troubled, and he gives a version of it in the 'Mildred Lawson' section of *Celibates* (1895). Moore spent the last twenty-three years of his life in London, where he was regarded as a Grand Old Man of Literature. Of his later works, *The Brook Kerith* (1916), a novelisation of the Gospels, caused considerable stir. BL 19. *DNB*. RM. *NCBEL*. Wol. Sad.

MORIER, James [Justinian] (1780–1849). Morier was born in Smyrna, the son of Isaac Morier, the Consul General of the Levant Company, at Constantinople. The family origins were Huguenot. James was educated at Harrow School, and later entered the diplomatic service which took him on a mission to the Persian Court in 1809. He revisited the country and the Orient generally over the next few years. Morier left the Foreign Office in 1817, having already published some well-received travel books and the remainder of his life was devoted to literary pursuits. He had a great success with his first Oriental Tale, *Hajji Baba* (1824), the book which is usually reckoned his best. It was followed by other novels in the new and fashionable genre of which Morier was the undisputed master: *Zohrab The Hostage* (1832); *Ayesha* (1834); *Abel Allnutt* (1837); *The Mirza* (1841); *Misselmah, A Persian Tale* (1847); *Martin Toutrond, Or The Frenchman In London* (1849). The last work was translated from his own French text by the author. A brother, David Richard Morier (1784–1877) was also a noted Eastern traveller and wrote the novel *Photo The Suliote, A Tale Of Modern Greece* (1857). BL 7. *DNB*. RM. *NCBEL*. Wol. Sad.

MORRAH, Herbert Arthur (d. 1939). Morrah was born in Winchester, the son of an army colonel. He was educated at Highgate School, London, and St John's College, Oxford where he was President of the Union, 1894. He began his literary career with the volume of verse *In College Groves* (1894). He also produced the novels, *A Serious Comedy* (1896); *The Faithful City* (1897); *The Optimist* (1898). BL 3. *WW*. RLF.

MORRIS, William (1834–96). Morris was born in Walthamstow, the eldest son of a bill-broker in the City. In 1840, the family moved to Woodford Hall near Epping Forest. The young William went to Marlborough in 1848, and entered Exeter College, Oxford in 1853, where he formed an influential friendship with the painter Edward Burne-Jones. At this period, Morris came under the influence of Carlyle, Ruskin* and Charles Kingsley*, forming the aesthetic-political theories that were to dominate his later life. He was particularly fascinated by fellowships and communes and in 1854 formed 'The Brotherhood' with like-minded social idealists. In the 1850s, Morris's extraordinary energies expressed themselves in architecture, poetry and journalism. He helped found *The Oxford And Cambridge Magazine* in 1856, studied as a painter 1857–62 and in 1859 married Jane Burden. In the 1860s, among much else, he produced the bulk of his major poetry (much of it in the saga tradition) and in the 1870s he promoted the arts and crafts movement from Kelmscott Manor, Oxfordshire. During the active political phase of his career, inspired by his reading Marx in 1883, Morris produced a quantity of visionary fiction. It falls into two large categories. Most effective with his, and subsequent reading publics, were the political utopias and near science fiction* works, such as *A Dream Of John Ball** (1888) and *News From Nowhere** (1890). The second category contains dreamy prose romances* such as: *The House Of The Wolfings* (1889); *The Roots Of The Mountains* (1889); *The Story Of The Glittering Plain* (1891); *The Wood Beyond The World* (1895); *The Well At The World's End* (1896); *The Water Of The Wondrous Isles* (1898); *The Sundering Flood* (1898). The source of these works is to be found in the political optimisms and idealisms which sustained Morris's socialist vision of the 'Earthly Paradise'. They typically feature love quests and ordeals in mythic landscapes. In 1890, Morris withdrew from the Socialist League and founded the Kelmscott Press which published some fifty-three beautifully made books, 1891–98. BL 9. *DNB. RM. NCBEL.*

MORRISON, Arthur (1863–1945). Morrison was born at Poplar in east London. A morbidly secret man, little is known of his early life. His father was a steam fitter and it is likely that Morrison's early home life was impoverished. In 1887, he took up work in the People's Palace in Stepney. (The institution was founded by Walter Besant* and grew out of his novel, *All Sorts And Conditions Of Men**.) The palace fell into financial difficulties around 1890, leading Morrison to become a freelance journalist. (His first commissions were to write on cycling topics.) He subsequently joined the *National Observer* under W. E. Henley and on its collapse worked for *Macmillan's Magazine** and *Tit Bits*. Morrison's naturalistic sketches of East End life were published as the volume *Tales Of Mean Streets* in 1894. It was successful, and at the invitation of a missionary in the slums, the Rev. A. Osborne Jay, Morrison went on to research and write his best-known novel of London squalor, *A Child Of The Jago* (1896)*. *To London Town* (1899) is rather less pessimistic than its two East End predecessors with which it was intended to form a trilogy. *Cunning Murrell* (1900) is a historical* novel of witch-finding in Essex in the mid-nineteenth century with close topographical descriptions. The work is based on the historical fact that 'a man was swum for a witch in Essex ten years after the date of this tale [i.e.

1854]'. Morrison was an early contributor to Newnes's* *Strand Magazine*. For this journal in the early 1890s he devised a popular sub-Sherlock Holmes detective, 'Martin Hewitt*, Investigator'. *The Dorrington Deed Box* (1897) reprints a collection of the author's other detective* stories. In 1902 he wrote another fine novel of slum life, *The Hole In The Wall*. Thereafter he largely gave up as a writer of serious fiction. But between 1902 and 1910, he made himself an expert on Japanese art, producing an authoritative study, *The Painters Of Japan*, in 1911. As a novelist, Morrison was remarkable for the authenticity of his observations (at one point, he worked in a matchbox factory, to gather local colour), and the sensitivity of his ear to cockney* dialect. He married in 1892, and had one son, who died of injuries sustained in the first World War. In later life, Morrison was an FRSL. BL 16. *WW*. RM. *NCBEL*. Wol.

MOTT, Edward Spencer ('Nathaniel Gubbins', 1844–1910). Mott was born near Lichfield, where his father was a JP, and Deputy Lieutenant of the county. He was educated at Eton, and at the Royal Military College, Sandhurst. In 1862 he was commissioned into the army and served for five years in India and Burma, leaving in 1867 to become a 'strolling actor'. In 1877, Mott joined the staff of the *Sporting Times*. He wrote pantomime, burlesque, and light fiction (some of it with a sporting* background). His novels include: *Pink Papers* (1899); *The Flowing Bowl* (1899); *The Great Game* (1900); *Bits Of Turf* (1901); *Dead Certainties* (1902). BL 6. *WW*.

MOZLEY, [Mrs] Harriet Elizabeth, (née Newman, 1803–52). The sister of Cardinal Newman*, she married another influential Tractarian, Thomas Mozley (1806–93), in 1836. The couple lived at Cholderton, where he was rector, 1836–47. (There was one daughter to the marriage, Grace.) Thomas Mozley wrote extensively for the London newspapers on ecclesiastical topics. On her part, Harriet Mozley wrote children's stories. Young children were aimed at in *The Fairy Bower* (1841); older children with *The Lost Brooch* (1842). Mozley's fiction was important in liberating children's writers from ultra-evangelical didacticism. She died in London, prematurely, and her husband remarried in 1861. BL 4. *DNB*. *NCBEL*. Wol.

MUDDOCK, J[oyce] E[merson] Preston ('Dick Donovan', 1843–1934). Muddock was born in Southampton, the son of a shipping manager. He was educated partly in India and began his working life at a gun foundry, near Calcutta. Muddock was in the sub-continent during the Mutiny of 1857, an experience which he recalls in one of his more enduring novels, published in 1896, *The Great White Hand* (i.e. 'colonial rule'). He subsequently travelled widely through the East, writing for papers and magazines. For five years, he was Swiss correspondent of the *Daily News*. In addition to his journalism, Muddock wrote about two dozen volumes of crime detection* fiction as 'Dick Donovan' (a name which he took from an eighteenth-century Bow Street runner). The creation was immensely successful. His other novels (many with international themes and settings) include: *A Wingless Angel* (1875); *As The Shadows Fall* (1876); *Stormlight* (1888), 'A Story Of Love And Nihilism In Switzerland And Russia'; *The Dead Man's Secret* (1889), the secret being a map to the 'Valley Of Gold'; *The Man From Manchester* (1890), stories from the logbook of a thief-catcher; *For God And The Czar*

(1892), a very popular work which was much reprinted around 1917; *The Star Of Fortune* (1894), a tale of the Indian Mutiny; *The Chronicles Of Michael Danevitch* (1897), a tale of the Russian Secret Service. Muddock published an autobiography, *Pages From An Adventurous Life* in 1907. BL 51. *WW*. Wol.

MUDFORD William (1782–1848). Mudford was born in London At the age of eighteen, he was appointed assistant secretary to the Duke of Kent and seemed set for a political career. But he lost all his money speculating in the 1820s, and thereafter supported himself independently as a man of letters with strong Conservative opinions. In this capacity he contributed to *Blackwood's Magazine**, and himself edited the Tory journal *John Bull* after Theodore Hook's* death. Mudford hob-nobbed with senior politicians and among much else wrote novels from his twentieth year onwards. *Stephen Dugard* (1840) falls into the Victorian period, as does *Arthur Wilson*, a novel published posthumously in 1872. Mudford's well-known tale of terror, *The Iron Shroud*, first published in *Blackwood's*, came out as a book in 1840. BL 5. *DNB*. *NCBEL*. Wol. RLF.

Mudie's Circulating Library (1842–1937). The 'Leviathan' of lending libraries, Mudie's played a central part in the institutionalisation of the three-volume novel, and the imposition of censorious middle-class values on the creative writer in the mid-Victorian period. Charles Edward Mudie was born in 1818 in London, of Scottish parents. His father was a newsagent, and the young Mudie went into the same line of business. Around 1842, he began lending books from his shop in Southampton Row. Thereafter his expansion was extraordinarily rapid. His main selling point was the one-guinea, one-year, one-volume subscription. For this purpose, the 31s.6d. three-decker (which could cater to three customers at the same time) was ideal. Mudie's was (as his advertisements insisted) a 'Select' library, and from the first he exercised a strict control on the content of the books he loaned. In 1852, Mudie moved to large new premises in New Oxford Street, by the British Museum. In 1860, his establishment was further expanded by the addition of a large central hall for deposits and withdrawals of books. By 1861, he was claiming to purchase some 180,000 volumes a year and his orders had a palpable effect on the British publishing industry. Branch outlets were opened in Birmingham and Manchester. (London deliveries were by van, country deliveries by train. Books were also shipped abroad in tin boxes.) Mudie successfully vanquished competition in the 1860s from the Library Company Ltd, which soon went bankrupt. Mudie himself formed his business into a limited liability company in 1864. By the late 1860s, there were no sizeable competitors, apart from W. H. Smith*, whose reliance on the railway system made him a complementary rather than a rival operator. Mudie encountered major problems in sustaining his dominating position after the 1880s. Writers increasingly chafed against his interference with the content of their books, George Moore* going so far as to write a polemic, *Literature At Nurse, Or Circulating Morals* (1885). The intended successor, Charles Henry Mudie, died in 1879: a blow from which his father never recovered. Around 1884, his younger son, Arthur, took over. At this period, the three-volume novel was under strong attack from new publishers like

Chatto and Windus*. Smith and Mudie finally combined to kill the three-decker in 1894, by jointly agreeing not to purchase multi-volume fiction at more than 4s a volume. This led the way to the emergence of the new novel at 6s; a price which remained constant for fifty years. Mudie's declined with the disappearance of the three-decker, but maintained a large share of the London circulating library carriage trade, at least until the 1930s.

MULHOLLAND, Rosa [Lady Gilbert] ('Ruth Murray', 1841–1921). The younger of two writing sisters born into an old Belfast family, prosperous from textile manufacture. Her father was a doctor, and a Catholic. Rosa (the better-known sister) married Mr (later Sir) John T. Gilbert (d. 1898) in 1891. As a young writer, she was encouraged by Dickens*, who published her early work in *All The Year Round**. Her subsequent novels are intensely Catholic, but her stories for young readers are less tendentious. Her full-length fiction includes: *Dunmara* (1864), written as 'Ruth Murray'; *Hester's History* (1869); *Eldergowan* (1874); *Four Little Mischiefs* (1884), the story of Kitty, Jock, Bunko and Ba, who are sent into the country to recover from mumps; *Marcella Grace* (1886), 'An Irish* Novel'; *A Fair Emigrant* (1889), her most popular work, the emigration being between Ireland and America; *Nanno* (1899), 'A Daughter Of The State'; *Onora* (1901); *Cynthia's Bonnet Shop* (1900). [Ellen] Clara Mulholland, Rosa's sister, was educated at convents in England and Belgium. She married to become Lady Russell of Killowen. Her fiction was mainly aimed at the young reader, with a relatively restrained improving tendency. It includes: *The Little Bogtrotters* (1878); *Linda's Misfortunes* (1885); *Little Snowdrop* (1889); *Kathleen Mavourneen* (1890). (RM) BL 52. (CM) BL 12. *WW*. Wol.

A Mummer's Wife, George Moore, 1885, 1 vol, Vizetelly. An early and notorious exercise in the French Naturalist style, which led Mudie* to ban Moore's novels from his library. The story begins in Hanley, a manufacturing town in the Potteries where Kate Ede runs a small haberdashers with her puritanically nonconformist mother-in-law. Kate's husband, Ralph, is a chronic asthmatic and the novel begins with a harrowing description of one of his attacks. Kate's narrow horizons are widened by the arrival of Dick Lennox, an actor, who lodges above the shop while his company plays in Hanley. Lennox seduces Kate (who has romantic dreams of a richer life than Hanley offers) and persuades her to elope with him. On the road with Morton and Cox's company, she reveals acting talent and as Kate D'Arcy makes a reputation. Now divorced and pregnant, she marries Lennox. But she has taken to drink, and through drunken neglect her baby dies. Lennox separates from her. In London, she by chance meets her former husband Ralph who has remarried an assistant in the shop, Hender. Kate finally dies alone, of a protracted bout of delirium tremens. The novel is relentlessly Zolaesque and detached in its description of Kate's futile career.

MUNRO, Neil ('Hugh Foulis', 1864–1930). Neil Munro was born in the Highlands of Scotland, at Inveraray. He worked in Glasgow, and lived much of his life at Helensburgh, Dumbartonshire, where he died. As 'Neil Munro', he wrote Highland romances. As 'Hugh Foulis' (and after 1904) he wrote droll stories of life in the west of Scotland. His Victorian output is exclusively in the first authorial character. His Neil Munro fiction includes:

The Lost Pibroch, And Other Sheiling Stories (1896); *John Splendid* (1898), a historical* work, set in the Highlands in 1645, being the 'tale of a poor gentleman and the Little Wars of Lorn'; *Gilian The Dreamer* (1899), a story of village life, in the early years of the nineteenth century; *Doom Castle* (1901), a tale of the western Highlands, in 1745. It is as a humorist that Munro is chiefly remembered. (NM) BL 14. *WW*.

MURPHY, James (1830–1921). Murphy was born at Glynn, Co. Carlow in Ireland. He began working life as a teacher, and rose to be a school principal, a local government educationalist and also a professor of mathematics at the Irish Catholic University, Dublin. Murphy wrote a number of popular novels with Irish* historical* themes, tinged with Nationalist sentiment. They include: *The Haunted Church* (1889); *The Shan Van Vocht* (1889), 'A Story Of United Irishmen'. The most powerful of Murphy's novels, *Convict No. 25* (1886), deals with the clearances in Meath in the early nineteenth century. BL 9.

MURRAY, [Sir] Charles Augustus (1806–95). Murray was educated at Eton and at Oriel College, Oxford (where he successfully resisted the charismatic influence of Newman*). A classical scholar, with a cultivated literary sensibility and rich by birth, Murray studied law and moved in the best London circles. In the 1830s, he also travelled widely. Famously, he went to America in 1835, and joined a tribe of Pawnees for three months, experiencing many adventures. (See his *Travels In North America*, 1839.) In America he fell in love with Elise Wadsworth. The match was forbidden by her father, and in 1844, Murray communicated with his beloved by means of a novel, *The Prairie Bird*. The work, a story of Red Indian life and warfare, set in Ohio, was very popular. On his return from America, Murray went into the Queen's household and in 1844 he entered the diplomatic service. Out of his subsequent experience in Egypt, he wrote his other main work of fiction, *Hassan, Or The Child Of The Pyramid* (1857), set in Egypt and Libya in the 1820s. After years of residing at Old Windsor, Murray died in Paris. BL 2. *DNB. NCBEL*. Wol. Sad.

MURRAY, David Christie (1847–1907). Born in West Bromwich, Staffordshire, before the town was industrialised, Murray went to work in his father's printing office at the age of twelve. This evidently was as the result of 'a serious fall in the family business'. By his own account, his early reading was derived from his father's stock of popular magazines. Some accounts talk obscurely of a 'domestic trial' which placed the young man 'in difficult circumstances'. (Perhaps, like some of his heroes, he fathered an illegitimate child.) At eighteen, Murray was sent to London to complete his training as a printer. This did not suit him and he enlisted in the army which suited him even less. After a year he was discharged and gravitated into journalism. Initially he worked on various Birmingham papers under the editor George Dawson (who was a major influence on him). Some of Murray's assignments were memorable. He covered the Russo-Turkish War, 1877–78, for the *Scotsman* and *The Times*. In 1878 he undertook a tramp's tour of England, for the magazine *Mayfair*. From 1881 to 1886 he was based mainly in France and Belgium, although still writing for an English periodical readership. From 1889, Murray (who had been widowed early in life) lived in Nice, although he continued to travel widely and as far afield as Australia. After 1898, he campaigned energetically for the release of Dreyfus. In this he was originally encouraged by Edmund Yates*. Murray wrote some thirty novels, about one a year from 1879 onwards, many of them set in his native Staffordshire. Six of his works were written in collaboration with the novelist and dramatist, Henry Herman*. They include *Paul Jones's Alias* (1890) and *He Fell Among Thieves* (1891), a society novel. His most popular titles under his own name are *Joseph's Coat** (1881), the ingenious story of a young man who embezzles his own property, and *Val Strange* (1882), one of the author's many exploitations of the inheritance plot. Murray's other forte was colliery settings, as in *Coals Of Fire* (1882). His other fiction includes: *By The Gate Of The Sea* (1883) and *Rainbow Gold* (1885). *A Rising Star* (1894) is a novel about struggling authorship. Murray wrote detective* stories in the early twentieth century and two books about authorship: *A Novelist's Notebook* (1887) and *The Making Of A Novelist* (1893). His *Recollections* (1908) are revealing. (HH and DCM) BL 6. (DCM) BL 29. *WW*. Wol. RLF.

MURRAY, [Eustace Clare] Grenville ('Trois-Etoiles', 1819–81). An illegitimate son of Richard Grenville, second Duke of Buckingham and Chandos, Murray entered the diplomatic service and was sent as an attaché to Vienna in 1851. He was at the same time a journalist, writing for the *Morning Chronicle* and Dickens's* *Household Words** (for whom he was 'the Roving Englishman'). He was thereafter vice-consul at Mitylene (1852) and Consul-General at Odessa (1855–68). In later life, Murray styled himself Count Rethel. An occasionally scurrilous journalist, he was publicly horsewhipped outside the Conservative Club by Lord Carrington in 1869, for a satirical article in the *Queen's Messenger*. For a while, he was a partner of Edmund Yates's* on the *World*. On the side, Murray wrote a number of novels, including: *Walter Evelyn* (1853); *The Member For Paris* (1871); *The Boudoir Cabal* (1875). His most interesting work is *Young Brown, Or The Law Of Inheritance* (1874), a savage satire on his own aristocratic background. The work was first serialised in *Cornhill**. Murray wrote much of his fiction under the pseudonym 'Trois-Etoiles'. BL 6. *DNB*. Wol.

John Murray (1768–). Publisher. The first John Murray (1745–93) started the firm in 1768. He was succeeded by John Murray II (1778–1843) and John Murray III (1808–92). In the early nineteenth century, the house was a dominant literary force, publishing Byron and founding the *Quarterly Review* (the Tory counterpart of the *Edinburgh Review*) in 1809. But although they were early publishers of Jane Austen, Murray's showed a marked distaste for publishing fiction in the Victorian period. Instead, they concentrated on travel literature, biography and political works. As a negative force, the house of Murray confirmed a pervasive belief throughout the nineteenth century that the novel was beneath serious book-people's notice. (JM) *DNB*.

MURRAY, John Fisher (1811–65). Murray was born in Protestant Belfast, the son of an eminent doctor credited with the discovery of liquid magnesia. He graduated from Trinity College, Dublin in 1830. He subsequently studied medicine and gained some reputation as a *Blackwood's Magazine** contributor, and as a poet. Murray was a supporter of Young Ireland. He wrote one novel (first serialised in *Blackwood's**), *The Viceroy* (1841). The work satirises Dublin Castle, and the Protestant Ascendancy while even-handedly lampooning Irish Catholics. BL 1. *DNB.*

The Muscular School. A loose term (probably invented by the *Saturday Review**) to describe the coterie of novelists centred on Charles Kingsley* in the late 1840s and early 1850s. A number of ideological and literary influences helped form the school. Carlylean hero worship is the main ingredient. There was also the growing fascination with race purity and the saga and berserker spirit. In muscular novels, this appears as the cult of the 'manly' hero. The Crimean War inspired the most vigorous of the muscular novels: *Westward Ho!**, *Tom Brown's Schooldays**, *Guy Livingstone**, *Ravenshoe**. Muscularity also manifests itself as a mystical celebration of English national struggle in works such as *Hereward The Wake** and G. A. Lawrence's* *Brakespeare.* The muscular novelists were notably 'earnest' and engaged themselves with social problems*. Kingsley's sympathy with Chartism (culminating in the great petition of 1848) inspired *Alton Locke** and *Yeast**. The influence of Christian Socialism (via F. D. Maurice) was also formative on Kingsley and Thomas Hughes*. More than Kingsley, Hughes devoted himself to the regeneration of the nation's youth. The least amiable aspect of the school is its obsession with violence. As Hughes puts it: 'from the cradle to the grave, fighting, rightly understood, is the business, the real, highest, honestest business of every son of man'. In the works of G. A. Lawrence, the hero accordingly degenerates into the condition of a thug in evening dress. In the late 1850s and early 1860s, the sturdy, muscular hero attracted novelists not centrally in the school. Adam Bede* (first discovered in a workshop fight) is kin to Kingsley's Amyas Leigh. Thackeray's* Philip Firmin is also cast in the muscular mould. Two publishing houses were principally associated with muscular fiction: J. W. Parker* (and their journal, *Fraser's Magazine**) and Macmillan* (and their journal, *Macmillan's Magazine**).

Myddleton Pomfret, William Harrison Ainsworth, 1868, 3 vols, Chapman and Hall. (Serialised in *Bentley's Miscellany**, July 1867–March 1868.) In the late 1860s, Ainsworth attempted unsuccessfully to revive his flagging popularity with three novels of contemporary life: *Old Court* (1867), *Myddleton Pomfret* (1868) and *Hilary St Ives* (1870). They appealed to the public of the day even less than his standard historical fare. This work borrows the fashionable bigamy* and 'dead yet not dead' devices, popularised by the sensation* novelists Charles Reade* and Mary Elizabeth Braddon*. It opens with an 'ill-omened marriage'. Julian Curzon, one of the 'handsomest men about town', marries a penniless girl, Sophy Leycester. Subsequently, he is financially ruined and declared bankrupt. Julian fakes his death by drowning in a lake, while his wife watches. Presumed dead, he goes off to India to make a new life. Four years later, his debts of £6,000 are mysteriously settled by 'Myddleton Pomfret', a merchant claiming to be Julian's intimate friend. Myddleton, of course, is Julian. His wife (widow as she thinks) remarries a treacherous friend, Captain Musgrave, who in fact knows that Julian still lives. The scene is set for routine complications when Myddleton-Julian returns. Sophy dies in a paroxysm of shame. A duel ensues, in which Julian slays Musgrave ('Sophy is avenged'). The hero dies soon after, on a return voyage to India. The narrative is written in the choppy style of the sensationalists and was clearly designed to prop up the slumping sales of *Bentley*'s, which in fact came to its end later in the year.

My Novel, E. G. E. L. Bulwer-Lytton, 1853, 4 vols, Blackwoods. (Subtitled 'Or Varieties In English Life'.) One of Lytton's sprawlingly panoramic studies of provincial life, predominantly comic in tone. The narrative is conducted by Pisistratus, hero of the earlier novel, *The Caxtons**, with frequent interruptions by other family members. The opening setting is the village of Hazeldean and there is some mild comedy on the subject of the squire William Hazeldean's intention of restoring the local stocks. Among others involved in this affair are a local Italian refugee, Dr Riccabocca (who voluntarily shackles himself, as a scientific experiment). The subsequent plot lines centre on the squire and his smoother half-brother, Audley Egerton. There are two spirited election episodes in the narrative and a wily Jewish financier who schemes in the background. But the main strand of the plot follows the career of a young peasant of genius, Leonard Fairfield. Leonard is educated by the perceptive Riccabocca, and after apprenticeship in London is discovered to be the legitimate son of Audley Egerton. By the end of the action he is a famous poet and has been reconciled with his dying politician father. A villain, Randal Leslie (a false friend of Hazeldean's son Frank) schemes to abduct Riccabocca's daughter, Violante, and is foiled. His political ambitions collapse with Egerton's death and he ends the novel a drunken usher in a village school. The Italian is revealed to be the wealthy Duke of Serrano, in the novel's unconvincing denouement.

The Mysterious Mr Sabin, E. Phillips Oppenheim, 1898, 1 vol, Ward and Lock. The thriller which launched Oppenheim's career of xenophobic espionage fantasy. The Mr Sabin of the title is a ruthless criminal mastermind, determined to restore the monarchy of France and put his niece Hélène on the throne. To this end he has stolen plans of various American inventions and secrets of English coastal defence. These will allow Germany to invade. A sinister handsome man of cosmopolitan origins who walks with the aid of a jewelled stick, Sabin is opposed by a young Englishman, Lord Wolfenden. Wolfenden's father, Admiral Deringham, is generally thought to be mad. But in fact he has drawn up accurate details of Britain's defence installations which Sabin must have. By various ruses, Sabin steals the papers. But before he can hand them over to the German ambassador he is visited by a leader of a Russian secret society of which he was earlier a member. On orders, Sabin destroys Deringham's documents, and world peace is preserved. Wolfenden and Hélène marry. The novel sustains a rattling pace and features the café society that Oppenheim loved.

The Mystery Of A Hansom Cab, Fergus Hume, 1886, 1 vol, Hansom Cab Co. The most sensationally popular crime and detection novel of the century. It begins with a classic enigma. A dead body is found in a Melbourne cab; there are no evident clues as to the murderer. Spurred by the promise of reward, a local private detective, Gorby, discovers that the corpse is Oliver Whyte, a young man recently arrived from England. He deduces that Whyte was chloroformed to death by Brian Fitzgerald, he and Whyte being rivals for the hand of Madge Frettlby, a millionairess. Fitzgerald is tried but acquitted by resourceful work by another detective, Kilsip. In an unexpected climax, the murderer is revealed to be Madge's father. Whyte had discovered his former attachment to a Melbourne prostitute and was blackmailing him. Frettlby dies before justice can take its course. Hume consciously modelled his novel on Gaboriau's detective* fiction and initially hoped for success with a stage adaptation. After publishing the work himself in Australia, he sold the English rights for £50 only to see the work printed by the hundred thousand over the next few years by the impudently named Hansom Cab Publishing Company.

N

Nada The Lily, H. Rider Haggard, 1892, 1 vol, Longman. (Serialised in the *Illustrated London News**, January–May 1892, illustrated by R. Caton Woodville. First book-form edition illustrated by Charles Kerr.) The most gripping of Haggard's Zulu sagas. In winter, a white man takes refuge in the kraal of an old witch doctor. He reveals himself to be Mopo, the assassin of Chaka, the Zulu 'Napoleon', who died in 1828. Mopo tells the white man the strange saga of his life. As a child, among the Langeni tribe, he gave the outcast Chaka, then a boy, a gourd of water. Later, himself cast out with his sister Baleka, Mopo found refuge with Chaka, now leader of the insurgent Zulus. Baleka became one of Chaka's concubines and Mopo saved her child from the death Chaka decreed for all his offspring, passing the baby off as his own son. Umslopogaas thus grew up as the brother of Mopo's light-skinned child, Nada. Fearful for his family's safety, although he was now Chaka's chief wizard, Mopo went through the motions of divorcing his wife Macropha, sending her to safety in Swaziland with Nada. Umslopogaas was meanwhile carried off by a lioness. The narrative subsequently divides. One strand follows Umslopogaas's growing up. Rescued from the lion's den by Galazi, King of the Wolves (in fact a relative of Chaka's), he wins by combat the great axe, Groanmaker, and forms his own tribe, the People of the Axe. He also declares his love for Nada. Chaka interrogates Mopo while forcing him to roast his left hand in the hut fire, finds him true, and rewards him still further. But to revenge his slaughtered sister, Mopo plots with Dingaan, to assassinate Chaka. At his death, the great warrior foresees the defeat of his Zulu people by the white invader. Dingaan tracherously attacks the People of the Axe, and Nada dies immured in a cave, her hand held by a wounded Umslopogaas outside, too weak to free her. He survives to become Allan Quatermain's faithful ally in *King Solomon's Mines**. Having told his story, the old witch doctor dies.

The Nautical Novel. Nautical fiction flourished in the 1830s, much of it centred round the person of the 'Sea Fielding', Captain Frederick Marryat*. A whole list of lesser writing captains can be mustered: Barker*, Glascock*, Howard*, Chamier*. There were historical reasons for the boom in nautical stories. British naval power was decisive in the Napoleonic

War, of which the leading novelists were bemedalled veterans. These ex-naval men were also associated with the sailing boat which, like the stage-coach, was sentimentally regarded in the age of steam. Service at sea required an officer to be literate (keeping a log-book), involved travel, supplying leisure while withholding drink and the company of women. The vast number of officers retired on half pay after 1815 swelled the always sizeable ranks of would-be authors. Retired and serving naval men also constituted a large reading public in their own right in the 1830s, catered for by journals such as Henry Colburn's* *Naval And Military Gazette*. The literary progenitor of the nautical novel was Smollett's *Roderick Random* (1748). Also influential was J. Fenimore Cooper's *The Pilot* (1823), a work written specifically with the landlubberly inaccuracies of Sir Walter Scott's novel *The Pirate* (1822) in mind. (Authenticity was a main claim of the nautical novel. Marryat, for instance, wrote *Masterman Ready* * because he was disgusted at the seamanship displayed in *The Swiss Family Robinson*, 1813.) Nautical expertise did not extend to technical aspects of narration. Notoriously the form was associated with senile garrulity, and typically disintegrates into loosely connected 'tales', 'sketches' and adventures. Representative examples are Glascock's *Tales Of A Tar* (1830); the 'Old Sailor' of M. H. Barker's *Tough Yarns* (1838); William J. Neale's* *Will Watch* (1834). Marryat was the undisputed star of the genre and his *Metropolitan Magazine* * was its main vehicle. Apart from Marryat's novels, the best work produced in the style was Edward Howard's *Rattlin The Reefer* (1836). By 1836, the nautical novel was played out. The *Athenaeum* * in that year noted that the reading public was tired of 'salt water babble'. By 1840, Richard Bentley*, the leading purveyor of the genre, had given it up as unprofitable. One of the last examples of its heyday was James Hannay's* *Singleton Fontenoy* (1856). The tale of nautical adventure enjoyed a new lease of life, however, in the juvenile fiction of G. A. Henty*, R. M. Ballantyne* and W. H. G. Kingston*. For adults, nautical fiction fostered the late Victorian talents of F. Frankfort Moore*, W. Clark Russell* and Joseph Conrad.

NEALE, Erskine ('C. F. Haldenby', 1804–83). The son of an army physician, Dr Adam Neale, and brother of William Johnson Neale*, he was educated at Westminster School and Cambridge, graduating in 1828. Neale subsequently took orders, and settled down as a rector in Kirton, Suffolk. Among the interests of a quiet clerical life, Neale became an expert on handwriting. He wrote voluminously, and has two religious novels to his credit: *The Bishop's Daughter* (1842) and *Self Sacrifice* (1844). His most popular book was the semi-autobiographical miscellany, *The Experiences Of A Gaol Chaplain* (1847). Neale seems to have submitted this work to the original publisher (Bentley*) under an alias, Charles Francis Haldenby. BL 2. *DNB*. Wol. RLF.

NEALE, John Mason (1818–66). Neale was born in London. His father was a clergyman of scholarly disposition and the family atmosphere narrowly evangelical. Neale's father died in 1823, and his early years were unsettled, although financially secure. Precociously clever, he won a scholarship to Trinity College, Cambridge, where he was judged the best classical scholar of his year. He graduated from the university in 1840 and with others of his generation Neale was swept up in the High Church movement of the period. In 1842, he was ordained a priest and appointed to a small living at Crawley, Sussex. Almost immediately, his health collapsed and in 1843 he travelled to Madeira to convalesce. During the enforced leisure of the following three years he took up writing. In 1846, Neale was appointed Warden of Sackville College, East Greenstead, a charitable institution founded in the seventeenth century. Here, in line with his Puseyite sentiments, he founded a nursing sisterhood. Neale was formidably erudite, especially on historical and theological subjects. In 1843, he published a devotional novel, *Agnes De Tracey, A Tale Of The Times Of St Thomas Of Canterbury*. He also wrote shorter stories for the magazines. But Neale is best remembered as the author of the novel, *Theodora Phranza* (1857), a historical* work dealing with the fall of Christian Constantinople. Together with *John Inglesant** and *Hypatia**, it is one of the few successful religious-historical novels of the century. The work is written in a rigid style and with much prurient revelling in the dissipation of Constantinople in the 1450s. Among Neale's novels for the young and other minor fiction are: *Herbert Tresham* (1842); *A Mirror Of Faith* (1845), collected tales and legends of the Church of England; *Ayton Priory, Or The Restored Monastery* (1843); *The Unseen World* (1847); *Duchenier, A Tale Of The Revolt In La Vendée* (1847). BL 20. *DNB. NCBEL*. Wol.

NEALE, W[illiam] Johnson [Nelson] (1812–93). A younger brother of Erskine Neale*, W. Johnson Neale entered the navy at the age of twelve and saw active service at Navarino in 1827. In 1833, he came ashore to begin what was to be a moderately successful career in law. In 1846 he enterprisingly married a granddaughter (and co-heiress) of the Viscountess Nelson and in 1859 he was appointed city recorder at Walsall, a post which he held until his death. Like other veterans of the navy Neale produced a string of sub-Marryat* nautical* yarns, based on his adolescent experiences. The first (and probably most popular) was *Cavendish, Or The Patrician At Sea* (1831), a work published when the author was only eighteen years old. His subsequent works include: *The Port Admiral* (1833); *Will Watch* (1834); *Gentleman Jack* (1837); *The Flying Dutchman* (1839); *The Naval Surgeon* (1841); *The Captain's Wife* (1842). Neale continued writing until the late 1840s, turning out *The Scapegrace At Sea* (1847) long after the vogue for nautical novels had passed. His most enjoyable tale is *Paul Periwinkle, Or The Press Gang* (1841), serialised in monthly numbers, and illustrated by Phiz*. Neale had a memorable public row with his mentor, Marryat, in 1834 over *The Port Admiral*. A duel was offered and declined by Marryat on the insulting grounds of Neale's social inferiority. The two men went on publicly to disgrace themselves by scuffling on Guy Fawkes' night in Trafalgar Square. He died at Cheltenham. BL 13. *DNB. NCBEL*. Wol. Sad.

NEEDELL, Mrs John H[odder] [Mary Anna] (née Lupton, 1830–1908?). Mary Lupton was born at Vanbrugh Castle, Blackheath, south London and married J. H. Needell, of Dorset. She describes the duality in her subsequent career, in *Who's Who* (1907): 'From the earliest age, I was a student and writer up to the period of marriage; during a long married life of engrossing claims my literary production was suspended, to be resumed in 1881'. Little else is known about her. Lupton's fiction includes: *Ada Gresham* (1853);

Catherine Irving (1855); *Julian Karslake's Secret* (1881); *Lucia, Hugh And Another* (1884), three character sketches opening with a characteristically imperative 'Come and look at this scene'; *The Story Of Philip Methuen* (1886), the portrait of a modern ascetic and his problems in love, this work was the author's most popular although some reviewers complained at its 'heaviness'. *Unequally Yoked* (1891), is the tragedy of a clergyman who marries beneath him; 'a very inferior and somewhat unpleasing tale', the *Athenaeum** called it. Among her later novels are: *Passing The Love Of Women* (1893); *The Honour Of Vivien Bruce* (1899). Mrs Needell published little if anything after 1902. BL 10. *WW.* Wol.

Nelson and Sons (1835–). One of the leading publishers of cheap reading matter in the nineteenth and twentieth centuries. Thomas Nelson (1780–1861) was born in Throsk, near Stirling, Scotland. He learned his publishing in London and returned to Edinburgh to set up his own business in the 1830s. In 1835 he admitted his son William (1816–87) into partnership and in 1840 his more dynamic younger son Thomas (1822–92). From the older Thomas Nelson, the firm inherited a preference for improving (theological and educational) books. Thomas the younger introduced new printing technology, and the firm was employing around 500 men by 1850. After the 1870 Education Act, Nelson's became the largest supplier of school-books in the Empire. Among its other innovations, the firm was instrumental in the 1880s in standardising the 6d. uniform reprint of popular fiction. (TN) *DNB.*

The Nemesis Of Faith, J. A. Froude, 1849, 1 vol, John Chapman. The most notorious religious novel of the century. The story is told in confessional autobiographical form. Markham Sutherland, a young Oxford undergraduate, prepares for ordination in the Anglican Church, but is agonised by doubts which are expressed in a series of letters to a friend, Arthur, in the early 1840s. He cannot believe in the savage God of the Old Testament. At his family's urging and after six months' inward struggle, he takes orders, but resolves only to give ethical, not religious instruction. He is denounced by his co-religionists and obliged to give up his living. At this point of the narrative, Markham's epistolary record becomes the 'Confessions Of A Sceptic', comprising straight theological disquisition. The last section of *The Nemesis Of Faith* is the disjointed tale of the secular complications of the hero's life. He goes to Italy where he falls in love with Mrs Helen Leonard. Markham subsequently blames himself when Helen's daughter dies of a fever, seeing it as God's punishment for his adulterous desires ('the sin which he had wished to commit'). He is saved from suicide by an English Roman Catholic priest (based on J. H. Newman*) and dies shortly after in a monastery, still unsettled in his religious faith. The novel was publicly burned at Oxford by William Sewell*. In a pugnacious preface to the second edition, Froude insisted that the story was not autobiographical. Most readers disbelieve him.

The New Antigone, [Father] William Barry, 1887, 3 vols, Macmillan. An interesting pro-Catholic novel of ideas. The central strand of the narrative follows the career of Colonel Edgar Valence; atheist, socialist and terrorist. Valence's daughter Hippolyta is the New Antigone of the title. Brought up a dedicated free-thinker, she enters into an open sexual liaison with Rupert Glanville, an artist. Gradually she discovers the need for (Catholic) religion in her life and in the world. She leaves Rupert who joins the nihilist anarchists in an attempt to find her. Hippolyta atones for her political enlightenment by becoming a nun. Rupert falls in love with an earl's daughter, Lady May Davenant. There is a terrific climax in Spain, bringing together all the principals (including a secret son of Colonel Valence, Ivor, who dies a convert to Catholicism, having just saved a suicidal Lady May from drowning). The novel ends with Rupert and May happily married, his genius 'chastened and glorified'. Hippolyta is now a missionary in the far east. Colonel Valence is last seen on the brink of going over to Rome. The revolutionary secret society reappears in a number of other novels of the period: William Black's* *Sunrise* (1880); Henry James's *The Princess Casamassima* (1886); W. H. Mallock's* *The Old Order Changes* (1886). Like these other works, *The New Antigone* makes play with brilliant conversation and extended country house episodes. The work was published anonymously and the *Athenaeum** guessed, obtusely, that the author was 'a learned young lady'. It was extremely popular, being reprinted three times in its first year of publication and running into seven editions by 1906.

New Grub Street, George Gissing, 1891, 3 vols, Smith, Elder. Gissing's biting satire on the Victorian literary profession. The narrative covers a range of authorial types. At the centre is the novelist, Edwin Reardon. Reardon, the author of two delicate fictions, is destroyed by the drudgeries of Mudie's* library system, and by grinding poverty. As an artist he cannot sustain his art in the face of commercial dictates. His wife Amy brings him no dowry; their love withers under the pressure of trying to keep up a genteel habitation in Regent's Park. When the failure of his books forces Edwin to return to clerking, Amy protests at the loss of caste, and the marriage is doomed. Even after Amy inherits a fortune, the indelible memory of Edwin's shabbiness prevents any genuine reconciliation. The Reardons' child dies, and an exhausted Edwin soon follows after. His career is contrasted with that of the cynical opportunist, Jasper Milvain. Good-natured, but unredeemably venal, Jasper has an eye for the main chance. He makes a name for himself in smart journalism, and it is he who eventually marries Amy and reaps the benefit of her £10,000. To win this prize, Jasper is obliged to jilt a fellow writer, Marian Yule. Marian slaves for her editor father, who runs a small circulation highbrow magazine. Although she too inherits money, her prospects are blighted by her father's impending blindness, and the financial collapse of the firm which is to provide her legacy. The prudent Jasper decides that she is not, after all, the best partner for an aspiring young writer like himself. Marian is left to drudge in libraries for the rest of her life. Harold Biffen, a dedicated (but uncommercial) realist novelist also figures in the action. He falls in love with Amy, and finally kills himself. Jasper ends the novel happy, benevolent and successful.

The New Monthly Magazine (1814–84). The pioneer of monthly miscellany magazines. The journal was founded by Colburn* as a Tory counterpart to the *Monthly Magazine*. It attracted the talents of many of the leading authors of the 1820s and 1830s. (Bulwer [-Lytton*] was editor, 1831–33.) Although the magazine featured short stories, and minor fiction items, serial novels were not a principal ingredient until 1837. At this date, provoked by the launch of *Bentley's Miscellany**, Colburn recruited Theodore Hook* as editor, and renamed the journal *The New Monthly Magazine And Humorist*. In the next few years, it carried novels by Hook (*The Gurney Papers*, 1837), Mrs Trollope* and Marryat* (*The Phantom Ship*, 1837), among others. But it made no impact on the success of Bentley's rival organ which at half a crown cost 1s. less. Thomas Hood succeeded to the editorship on Hook's death in 1841. In 1845, Colburn sold the property to Ainsworth*, then at the height of his popularity. Ainsworth remained proprietor and editor until 1870, using the magazine as a vehicle for his, and other novels. After 1837 the *New Monthly* was decidedly a second-rank publication. It was unillustrated and never managed to outgrow its randomly miscellaneous format. *WI. BLM.*

The New Republic, W. H. Mallock, 1877, 2 vols, Chatto and Windus. (Serialised in *Belgravia**, June–December 1876. Subtitled 'Culture, Faith, And Philosophy In An English Country House'.) The most successful conversation novel of the period. The setting is Mr Otho Laurence's cool seaside villa, 'towards the close of last July, when the London season was fast dying of the dust'. While setting out place cards for 'a select party of friends' invited to a weekend party, it occurs to Laurence (a Tory, opposed 'quietly' to 'Christianity and Fundamentalism') to list as well the topics for discussion. He proposes: 'the Aim of Life'; 'Society'; 'Art and Literature'; 'Love and Money'; 'Riches and Civilisation'; 'the Present'; 'the Future'. The company comprises the great sages of the day, under thin disguise. 'Luke' is Matthew Arnold; 'Rose' Walter Pater*; 'Herbert' Ruskin* (the main speaker); 'Storks' T. H. Huxley. Mallock's epigrammatic satire on liberalism, radicalism and cant plays freely over the ensuing talk and talkers. It ends inconclusively with the half-hearted verdict that things are best as they are.

New Woman Fiction. Many novels of the 1890s reflected and contributed to the debate over the so-called 'new woman'. The concept arose from end-of-the-century controversies over 'rational' dress, contraception and venereal disease, occupations and votes for women. Fiction touching on these topics ruffled feathers. Mrs Oliphant*, for instance, was inspired to write her famous polemic against the 'anti-marriage league' of new women novelists in 1896. Although many of its practitioners were women (even new women) men also participated in the genre. The two most widely-read new women novelists were, in fact, Grant Allen* with his notorious *The Woman Who Did** (1895) and Thomas Hardy*. Another male writer, Henrik Ibsen, whose *The Doll's House* and *Hedda Gabler* appeared on the London stage in the early 1890s, was extremely influential. In her study of the genre, Gail Cunningham divides the new woman novel into two principal sub-categories: (1) the purity school (sometimes also called 'Hill-Top* Novels' after Grant Allen's subtitle to *The British Barbarians*, 1895); (2) the neurotic school. Leading exponents of the purity line of new woman fiction are Sarah Grand*, Iota* and Allen. The neurotic style is represented by George Egerton*, Emma Frances Brooke*, Mona Caird* and Ménie Muriel Dowie*. The novel solely and militantly concerned with the new woman burned itself out in a few years. But interest in the type enriches female characterisation in mainstream fiction of the late Victorian period. Hardy's last three novels are a case in point (Sue Bridehead in *Jude The Obscure** is a fine example of the 'neurotic' species). Meredith* (e.g. *One Of Our Conquerors**, 1891) and Gissing* (e.g. *The Odd Women**, 1893) also contributed to the debate.

NEWBOLT, [Sir] Henry [John] (1862–1938). Newbolt was born at Bilston, Staffordshire, the son of a clergyman. He was educated at Clifton and later at Corpus Christi College, Oxford, where he gained a first-class degree in classics. In 1887 Newbolt was called to the Bar and successfully practised law for twelve years. He retained strong literary inclinations, however, and eventually embarked on a second career in authorship. Newbolt's first book, *Taken From The Enemy* (1892) is a romance, set in 1821, fantasising an attempt to rescue Napoleon from St Helena. *Mordred*, a tragedy in blank verse (not, as it turned out, Newbolt's forte) came out in 1895. His popularity was boosted sky-high by 1s. volumes of his poems, published in 1896 (notably, the nautical ballad, 'Drake's Drum'). Newbolt's later volumes of poetry, *Admirals All* (1897) and *The Island Race* (1898) both flaunted hearty imperialistic sentiments and made their author the most popular poet in England after Kipling*. In 1899, he gave up law. Newbolt subsequently had a distinguished career in letters and public service, being knighted in 1915. In later life he published other prose romances, including: *The Old Country* (1906), a part medieval, part modern story which reviewers took to be his début in fiction and another feudal romance, *The New June* (1909). BL 6. *DNB*. RM. *NCBEL*.

Newby and Co. (1843–74). Publisher. Thomas Cautley Newby (d. 1882) was, without doubt, the most notorious publisher of fiction in the Victorian period. Newby started up business on his own account in 1843, at 72 Mortimer Street. His publishing style was based on that of Henry Colburn* and his main line of goods three-deckers for the newly emerging metropolitan libraries. In 1847 he brought out the first novels of Emily Brontë*, Anne Brontë* and Anthony Trollope*. He seems to have acted dishonestly with all three authors (advertising Anthony's *Macdermots Of Ballycloran** as by his more famous mother, Mrs Frances Trollope*). Famously, Newby took money from eager young writers. Eliza Lynn Linton* recalls having to pay £50: 'Mr Newby's standing price for first books by young authors'. Newby subsequently capitalised on the mysterious identity of the author of *Adam Bede**, much to George Eliot's* disgust. He dishonestly presented a book by Julia Kavanagh's* father as by her in 1857. And as Mrs Riddell's* first publisher, he is lampooned in her *A Struggle For Fame** (1883). Newby moved his headquarters to 30 Welbeck Street in 1849 and retired in 1874 after a long career in cheap commercial roguery. Boase.

The Newcomes, W. M. Thackeray, 1855, 2 vols, Bradbury and Evans. (Serialised in monthly parts, October 1853–August 1855, with illustrations by Richard Doyle*. Subtitled 'Memoirs Of A Most Respectable Family. Edited By Arthur Pendennis Esq.') Thackeray's largest, and most sentimental panorama of mid-Victorian middle-class life. The hero is Clive Newcome, a younger contemporary of Arthur Pendennis at Grey Friars (i.e. Charterhouse) School. Clive's father is a serving Indian officer, Colonel Thomas Newcome; his mother (respected but unloved by her husband) is dead. Clive grows up a lively, spirited lad who wants to be an artist. He falls in love with his cousin Ethel, the daughter of a rich banker, Sir Brian Newcome. Ethel's devious brother, Barnes Newcome, becomes Clive's sworn enemy. And Ethel's grandmother, the Countess of Kew, intends that the girl shall make a great match. (The novel attacks the marriage of convenience at great length.) Much of the central part of the narrative is set on the Continent where Ethel plays with suitors such as her cousin Lord Kew and the fabulously wealthy Marquis of Farintosh. Clive, meanwhile, has qualified himself as an artist, together with his more brilliant but physically deformed working-class friend, 'J. J.' Ridley. The colonel has returned from India, to live with his son in London's West End. But father and son (although they love each other dearly) find it difficult to get on. Disastrously, the colonel allows himself to be entangled in a fraudulent Anglo-Indian bank scheme. He and many friends he has recruited are ruined. Clive has only moderate success as an artist. And having despaired of winning Ethel, he allows himself to drift into marriage with Rosey Mackenzie, the niece of one of his father's comrades. Rosey is docile enough, but her widowed mother 'the Campaigner' is a frightful bully. She makes the ruined colonel's life wretched, and he finally takes refuge as a pensioner at Grey Friars. He dies, in one of the most famous scenes in Victorian fiction, murmuring 'adsum' as the evening attendance bell rings. Around his bed are gathered his son, grandson and the French woman whom he has always secretly loved. Rosey dies, and Thackeray leaves the reader to imagine that Ethel and Clive are subsequently united, 'in fable land'.

The Newgate Novel. The controversy about so-called Newgate fiction raged most violently over the period 1830–47. Novelists centrally associated with the genre were Bulwer[-Lytton*], Ainsworth* and Dickens*. (Repudiation of Newgate fiction was also formative in Thackeray's* development as a satirical novelist.) Very simply, Newgate novels dealt with criminals recorded in the *Newgate Calendar*. Simply, again, to write fiction about criminals was misapprehended as condoning (or even advocating) criminal behaviour. Prohibition of criminal complexity as a fit subject for the writer marked a damaging setback to the novel of ideas pioneered by William Godwin, some years before. Thus for a large part of the era (unlike France where Victor Hugo and Eugéne Sue were less hampered) the depiction of social deviance was left to the downmarket penny dreadfuls*. The Newgate novel controversy also became confused with the abolition of wholesale capital punishment in 1837 (the year of *Oliver Twist*). The first bolts of Newgate reaction discharged on Bulwer's *Paul Clifford* (1830), *Eugene Aram* (1832) and Ainsworth's *Rookwood* (1834). All three were sensationally popular. They also provoked the English intelligentsia in a number of ways. Under William Maginn*, the radical Tory *Fraser's Magazine* became a ruthless opponent of Newgate fiction, and particularly venomous towards Bulwer. When Maginn retired in 1836, Thackeray wielded the *Fraser* lash even more effectively than his mentor. A second phase of the Newgate controversy began with the foundation of *Bentley's Miscellany* in 1837. The two sensationally popular early serials in the magazine were *Oliver Twist* and Ainsworth's *Jack Sheppard* (both graphically illustrated by George Cruikshank*). Dickens's novel did not have a Newgate original in its dramatis personae. But Fagin was identifiably Ikey Solomon, the notorious fence. *Oliver Twist* is also typical of Newgate novels in its insistence that social conditions cause crime. (Or, as Bulwer put it in *Paul Clifford*, 'Circumstances make Guilt'.) Dickens was shielded by his eminence (even in 1837), and a greater moral fury fell on *Jack Sheppard*. Anger was sustained by the revelation that the youth Courvoisier had been motivated to murder his master by 'the perusal of that detestable book'. In *Fraser's*, Thackeray published his masterpiece of corrective satire, the 'cathartic' *Catherine** (1840). This novella chronicles the most loathsome Newgate tale Thackeray's research into the *Calendar* could turn up. The next, and final phase of the Newgate controversy covers 1841–47. The principals are Thackeray and Bulwer-Lytton (as he was called after 1843). The main text involved was Bulwer-Lytton's 'arsenical' *Lucretia** (1846). The story is based (as the author admitted) on the career of the poisoner Thomas Griffiths Wainewright (1794–1852). Although Bulwer-Lytton was careful not openly to sympathise with his murderer hero (as he had injudiciously done earlier in *Eugene Aram*), the work was bitterly attacked. *The Times* called it 'a bad book of a bad school'. Thackeray wrote the brilliant parody, 'George De Barnwell' in *Punch**. Bulwer-Lytton wrote no crime novels thereafter. Generally, respectable English novelists had been warned off murder as a subject, and did not return to it until the rise of the sensation* novel in the 1860s and the detective* novel in the 1880s.

NEWMAN, Cardinal [John Henry] (1801–90). The most influential Anglican (and later Catholic) churchman of the Victorian period. A banker's son, Newman was born in London and educated at Ealing. In 1817, he went to Trinity College, Oxford and was elected a fellow of Oriel College in 1822. In 1824, he took Anglican orders and went to work in a curacy in Oxford. In 1832, he travelled to southern Europe with Hurrell Froude (brother of James Froude*). Newman saw Rome, composed the famous hymn 'Lead, Kindly Light' and fell dangerously ill. On his return he began a campaign (the 'Oxford movement', irreverently called 'Newmania') to regenerate the Anglican Church. In 1833, the 'Tracts For The Times' began to appear. Newman's position through the decade became increasingly that of an Anglo-Catholic. And in 1845, he went over to the Church of Rome. As Rome's principal apologist, Newman went on to play a dominant part in the controversy on 'Papal Aggression' in the early 1850s. In 1851, he was made Rector of the Catholic University in Dublin. (His influential lectures on 'The Idea Of A University' were delivered over the following years.) In 1864, Newman published his *Apologia Pro Vita Sua*, as part of a public quarrel on the issue of Catholics and 'truth' with the fiercely chauvinistic Charles Kingsley*. He was appointed a cardinal in 1879. A small but integral part of Newman's immense achievement was in fiction. His *Callista, A Sketch Of The Third Century** (1856), is one of the more successful of Victorian classical historical* novels, a melodrama of faith, persecution and martyrdom in Roman Proconsular Africa. *Loss And Gain** (1848) is a *Bildungsroman** which can bear comparison with Thackeray's* *Pendennis** which it may in fact have influenced. BL 2. *DNB*. RM. *NCBEL*. Wol. Sad.

Newnes (1881–). Publisher. [Sir] George Newnes (1851–1910) was one of the principal architects of twentieth-century journalism. Newnes was born at Matlock, the youngest of six children of a Congregational minister. On leaving school at sixteen, he went into business. He soon conceived the idea of a new kind of weekly miscellany, made up of small items of gossip, news and anecdote. The result in October 1881 was *Tit-Bits*, which was an immediate and sensational success. Within three years, Newnes was a tycoon, and in 1885 he entered Parliament as a Liberal. In 1891, with W. T. Stead, he founded the *Strand Magazine**, a periodical which had a dominant influence on the shape of late-nineteenth- and twentieth-century fiction. In 1897 Newnes founded *Country Life*. Newnes's innovations were developed by his early associates, Cyril Pearson and Alfred Harmsworth.

NEWNHAM-DAVIS, Lt.-Col. N[athaniel] (1854–1917). Born in London, he was educated at Harrow School. Newnham-Davis was subsequently commissioned into the Buffs regiment in 1873, and fought in the Zulu Wars with conspicuous gallantry. Later military service took him all over the Empire. At the end of his career he was engaged with the intelligence service in India. Newnham-Davis retired from the army in 1894 and joined the staff of the *Sporting Times*. For many years he remained the paper's assistant-editor. He was also editor of *The Man Of The World*, 1894–1900 and wrote some moderately successful musical comedy. Newnham-Davis's fiction comprises three volumes mainly of short stories: *Three Men And A God* (1896); *Jadoo* (1898), an Anglo-Indian novel, Jadoo being Hindustani for 'magic'; *Baby Wilkinson's VC* (1899), a collection of colonial military stories. Reviewers found the 'sensual' aspects of his Indian stories disturbing. BL 3. *WW*.

News From Nowhere, William Morris, 1891, 1 vol, Reeves. (Serialised in the *Commonweal*, January–October 1890.) Morris's final vision of the future socialist utopia (inspired by the American Edward Bellamy's immensely popular *Looking Backward*, 1888). The narrative opens with a 'brisk' discussion at the Socialist League about the 'Morrow of the Revolution'. The narrator goes home on the new underground railway, falls exhausted into bed and awakes from a long sleep to find himself in the twentieth century, at Hammersmith. He bathes in the Thames (proverbially filthy in the Victorian age but now teeming with salmon) and after sight-seeing around a transformed London, spends the day in what used to be the British Museum, discussing politics, economics and education. The next day, the narrator travels up the Thames via Runnymede, the *fons et origo* of English democracy. He is in the company of two young people, Dick and Clara. At Oxford, he takes part in haymaking. The narrator ('William Guest') subsequently becomes romantically involved with the beautiful, but remote woman of the future, Ellen (Morris's familiar unattainable feminine ideal). Guest returns to 'dingy' Hammersmith in the 1890s, with a sense that what he has experienced is 'a vision, not a dream'. Generally, the narrative fleshes out Morris's ideas of social salvation by the revival of medieval arts and crafts. Shortly after publishing the work, he left the Socialist League.

Nicholas Nickleby, Charles Dickens, 1839, 1 vol, Chapman and Hall. (Serialised in monthly parts, April 1838–October 1839, with illustrations by Phiz*.) Dickens's second novel in monthly, 1s. numbers. The Nicklebys are left destitute by the death of Mr Nickleby. Nicholas, a spirited and noble young man, applies to his uncle, Ralph Nickleby, for help. Pretending to assist (although in fact his motives are vicious) Ralph arranges for Nicholas to take up work in a Yorkshire school, Dotheboys Hall. The headmaster, Wackford Squeers, is revealed to be a money-grubbing sadist. Nicholas rejects the overtures of his repellent daughter, and befriends Smike, a pupil brain-damaged by Squeers's brutality. Nicholas is provoked into thrashing Squeers in front of the school, and escapes with Smike. He supports himself for a while with the theatrical company of Vincent Crummles, and subsequently takes up employment with the amiable Cheeryble brothers. His sister, Kate, has been apprenticed to a dressmaker, Madame Mantalini. Ralph Nickleby (who makes the most of Nicholas's degradation) encourages a sensual nobleman, Sir Mulberry Hawk, in his campaign to seduce Kate. Mrs Nickleby is entirely ineffectual; but Nicholas physically fights off the lecherous peer and sets up his womenfolk in a respectable home. He meanwhile falls in love with Madeline Bray. The villainous Ralph has his own plans to marry Madeline off to a disgusting old moneylender, Gride. Smike dies, and is revealed to be Ralph's son. Nicholas is aided by his uncle's clerk, Newman Noggs and together they foil Ralph, who hangs himself. Nicholas marries Madeline and Kate marries one of the Cheerybles' nephews. Like its predecessor, *Pickwick**, the novel is episodic and indomitably optimistic in tone.

NICHOLSON, Edward Williams Byron (1849–1912). Nicholson was born at St Helier, Jersey, the son of a navy officer. He was educated at Tonbridge School, and at Trinity College, Oxford. An outstanding scholar, at the age of only thirty-three he was appointed librarian of the Bodleian Library, in 1882. Among Nicholson's many interests were Celtic antiquity, philology and folklore. He was also a fierce opponent of vivisection, and held radical political views. Among his diverse publications is a volume of fiction: *The Man With Two Souls And Other Stories* (1898). The volume comprises four tales, one of mesmerism, another centred on an epic mile footrace. Reviewers were generally unkind. BL 1. *DNB.*

NICHOLSON, Joseph Shield (1850–1927). Nicholson was born in Banbury, the son of an Independent minister in the town. He read philosophy at King's College, London, and mathematics at Edinburgh and Cambridge universities. Before he was even thirty years old Nicholson was recognised as one of the leading economists in the country and in 1880 he was appointed to a professorship in political economy at Edinburgh University where he distinguished himself as a teacher. Over the years 1891–1901 Nicholson brought out his great work, *The Principles Of Political Economy.* (His theories were sternly anti-Marxist and anti-socialist.) Among his varied accomplishments, Nicholson wrote three allegorical romances: *A Dreamer Of Dreams* (1889); *Thoth* (1888), an Athenian romance in which a heroine, Daphne, is kidnapped and carried off to a modern technological utopia founded by the Egyptian Thoth I; *Toxar* (1890). The last also has a Hellenic setting and is largely composed of philosophical dialogues. Nicholson received a number of honorary degrees and among much else conducted the chess column in *The Times.* BL 3. *DNB.*

NICHOLSON, Renton (1809–61). Nicholson was born probably illegitimate in Hackney, London. At the age of twelve he was apprenticed to a local pawnbroker, and worked in the trade until 1830, when he set himself up as a jeweller in Regent Street. He soon went bankrupt, however, and thereafter spent long periods in debtors' prisons. For some time, he supported himself as a billiard- and card-sharp. In 1837, Nicholson's literary career formally began, when he was employed by a London printer, Joseph Last, to edit the journal of 'flash life', the *Town*. The paper ran until May 1840, when he took up the management of the Garrick's Head and Town Hotel in Covent Garden. Here he founded 'The Judge and Jury Society', over whose mock trials he would preside as 'The Lord Chief Baron Nicholson'. Nicholson who was famous for his repartee later took over 'The Coal Hole' in the Strand in 1844. Among his miscellaneous publications is the fiction: *Cockney Adventures* (1838) and *Dombey And Daughter* (1850), a work serialised in 1847 while *Dombey And Son** was still coming out. Both shamelessly exploit Dickens's* popularity and were first issued in 1d.-weekly parts. Nicholson died at the Gordon tavern, in Covent Garden. BL 2. *DNB*. Wol. Sad.

Nina Balatka, Anthony Trollope, 1867, 2 vols, Blackwood. (Serialised anonymously in *Blackwood's Magazine**, July 1866–January 1867.) A short tale, set in Prague. Nina is a Christian maiden who loves a Jew, Anton Trendellsohn. His family disapprove of the match, and set a trap by which it will seem that she has been dishonest. The ruse works, and a distraught Nina attempts suicide in the Moldau, but is saved. A servant confesses, all is made well and the marriage goes ahead. Trollope was interested both in Bohemia as a location and in the complexities of mixed marriage. In collaboration with John Blackwood, Trollope deliberately had the tale appear anonymously, but the results of the experiment were discouraging.

NISBET, Hume (1849–1921?). Nisbet was born in Stirling, Scotland. He left at the age of sixteen, to spend seven years wandering around Australia. On his return to his native country, he worked as an art master at Watt College, Edinburgh, a post he resigned in 1885. For a while Nisbet travelled for the publisher Cassells* in Australia, after which he turned to full-time novel writing. By 1900, Nisbet had written some forty 'tales of adventure'. They draw heavily on his colonial experience and include: *Bail Up* (1890), his best-known work, a romance of bush-ranging in Queensland, the title being the command given by thieves to their victims; *A Bush Girl's Romance* (1894); *The Great Secret, A Tale of Tomorrow* (1895); *In Sheep's Clothing* (1900). An artist, Nisbet also illustrated some of his books. BL 46. *WW*. Wol.

Nisbet and Co. (1809–). Evangelical publisher. The founder, James Nisbet (1785–1854) was the son of a farmer at Kelso in Scotland. An inspired educationalist, Nisbet founded the Sunday School Union in 1803. In 1809, he set up his bookselling and publishing business in London. Nisbet published and distributed tracts and by the 1830s had his own circulating library. Together with the SPCK* and the RTS*, Nisbet circulated much of the improving fiction of the early Victorian period. In the 1860s, his list featured more secular fiction, including the tales of R. M. Ballantyne*. Boase.

No Name, Wilkie Collins, 1862, 3 vols, Sampson Low. (Serialised in *All The Year Round**, March 1862–January 1863.) The novel starts sedately enough in Combe-Raven, Somersetshire. The Vanstones are a happy, comfortably off family; husband, wife, two daughters and a faithful governess. But it emerges that the parents are not legally married, and although they eventually legitimise their union, they neglect to correct their will. Consequently the document is invalid and the father's fortune goes to an ill-natured brother, and after his death to the brother's cretin son, Noel Vanstone. Norah, the older Vanstone sister, becomes a governess. Magdalen, the younger, becomes a stage artiste, with the assistance of an amiable rogue, 'Captain' Horatio Wragge. The main concern of the subsequent narrative is Magdalen's resourceful campaign to recover her father's fortune, aided by Wragge. A master of disguise, she bewitches Noel Vanstone, and as 'Miss Bygrave' succeeds in luring away his villainous housekeeper, Mrs Lecount, long enough to marry the heir. But on her return, Lecount persuades Noel into changing his will. She also penetrates Magdalen's disguise. On her husband's death, Magdalen can inherit nothing without revealing her deceptions. But by further ingenious detective work she confounds Lecount by discovering another will which returns her father's money to its rightful owners. Norah marries a rich cousin, George Bartram, who inevitably turns out to be the Vanstone heir. Magdalen marries a naval captain; Wragge is enriched by having invested in a proprietary medicine. The novel is principally attractive for its resourceful and near-criminal heroine.

A Noble Life, Dinah Mulock Craik, 1866, 2 vols, Hurst and Blackett. An unusual study of heroic Victorian invalidism, set in Scotland, 'many years ago'. The Earl of Cairnforth is a sweet-natured congenital cripple, obliged to pass his life in a wheelchair. The scene in which his pregnant mother is traumatised by seeing her husband drown in a loch opens the novel. She gives birth and herself dies soon after. Once he has come into his estate, the Earl makes a will benefiting Helen Cardross, the saintly daughter of a local minister. As a prospective heiress, she is married by a Byronic fortune-hunter, Captain Ernest Bruce, who mistreats her terribly. Bruce dies of dissipation in an Edinburgh garret, and the benevolent Earl adopts Helen's son, Alexander, as his heir before himself dying aged only forty-three, just as his morally exemplary successor comes of age. The main focus of the work is on the long-suffering, Christian sweetness of Cairnforth. The *Athenaeum** found the work 'too depressing'.

NOEL, [Lady] Augusta [Mary] (née Keppel, 1838–1902. Some accounts give the date of birth as 1825). Born Lady Augusta Keppel, second daughter of the Earl of Albemarle, she married Ernest Noel (JP and Deputy Lieutenant of Sussex) in 1873. Her fiction includes: *Owen Gwynne's Great Work* (1875), the grim story of a middle-aged scholar's fatuous devotion to his research in fifteenth-century history, his notes eventually being lost in a shipwreck; *From Generation To Generation* (1879); *Hithersea Mere* (1887). The last is the mild story of a clergyman with a not too shocking secret in his past. Noel lived her later life in Norfolk. BL 6. *WW. NCBEL*. Wol. Sad.

NORRIS, Emilia (née Marryat, 1835–75). Third daughter of Frederick Marryat*. She was born at Brighton, and in 1862 married Henry Edward Norris at Winchester. Like her sisters Augusta and Florence Marryat*, she wrote fiction from an early age, including: *Temper* (1854); *The Early Start In Life* (1867), the story of a boy who goes to the bad in Australia and eventually reforms; *Theodora* (1869); *Paul Howard's Captivity* (1875). Most of Norris's fiction was designed for the juvenile reader. She died at Charmouth. There seems to have been a daughter, Cecil Marryat Norris, who also wrote fiction in the 1880s. BL 18. Boase. Wol.

NORRIS, W[illiam] E[dward] (1847–1925). The son of Sir William Norris, Chief Justice of Ceylon, Norris was born in London and educated at Eton. He was called to the Bar in 1874, but never in fact practised law. He instead wrote a vast quantity of fiction, mostly light romantic in nature. His work was popular and enabled Norris to sustain the style of life into which he had been born. He resided at Torquay, beside the ocean which was the main setting for his romances. Many of his works were first serialised in magazines and reviewers often compared his easy-going style to Thackeray's*. His fiction includes: *Heaps Of Money* (1877); *Mademoiselle De Mersac* (1880), a story partly set in Algiers; *Matrimony* (1881); *No New Thing* (1883), the hero, like Norris, is Anglo-Indian; *Adrian Vidal* (1885), the hero, like Norris again, is a young novelist; *Chris* (1888), the story of a young heiress, and her lovers; *Major And Minor* (1888), an unhappy story of love, politics and money; *The Rogue* (1889); *Billy Bellew* (1895); *The Dancer In Yellow* (1896), a pathetic, saccharine romance; *Clarissa Furiosa* (1897), a novel of high life; *The Widower* (1898); *The Fight For The Crown* (1898), the comedy of a Conservative husband, burdened with a Liberal wife; *The Widower* (1898); *Giles Ingilby* (1899). The last is the story of a noble young writer who makes a name for himself but declines to press his attentions on Cynthia, the woman he loves, when he discovers himself illegitimate. He goes off instead to fight in South Africa. All ends well, as it invariably does in this author's fiction. R. L. Wolff thinks very highly of Norris, calling him 'an almost forgotten novelist who had a real power to depict fashionable people and their often serious predicaments'. Late Victorians found his fiction refreshingly 'wholesome' and well-bred. He was personally friendly with Henry James who privately despised Norris's artless novels. BL 74. *WW*. Wol.

NORTH, William (1824–54). North's fiction (or near fiction) comprises: *Anti-Coningsby* (1844), a satire on Disraeli*; *Anti-Punch* (1847); *The Impostor* (1845); *The Slave Of The Lamp* (1855). In connection with this last posthumous work, Sadleir offers some sparse biographical details: 'William North left England for America in 1852, full of idealist expectation for the liberty he expected to find there. Two years later, he committed suicide in New York. The MS of this autobiographical novel, found in his room, was published within a year of his death.' BL 4. Sad.

North And South, Mrs [Elizabeth] Gaskell, 2 vols, Chapman and Hall, 1855. (Serialised in *Household Words**, September 1854–January 1855). Gaskell's follow up to *Mary Barton**, and consciously fairer to the mill-owners. Margaret Hale is transplanted from comfortable life in the home counties to 'Milton-Northern' (i.e. Manchester) in 'Darkshire' when her clergyman father's doubts force him to surrender his church living in Hampshire. In Milton, Margaret comes into contact with the industrial world. She befriends a free-thinking worker, Nicholas Higgins, and his invalid, mill-girl daughter, Bessie. Sexually, Margaret is attracted to John

Thornton, a stiff-necked master. A number of impediments come between Thornton and Margaret: his proud mother; a labour dispute in which he leads the owners in their obdurate lock-out policy; a case of mistaken identity in which Margaret's disgraced brother Frederick is supposed to be her secret lover. Margaret courageously proves her love, however, by protecting Thornton from an angry mob of workers. At the end of the novel Margaret returns to London and the rural area of Helstone where she was brought up, but having experienced the more vital life of the North she finds the South unsatisfying. She inherits a fortune, and is able to rescue a now bankrupt Thornton. The couple marry and return to Milton where he becomes a model employer, searching always to discover a relationship with his workers beyond that of 'cash nexus'. The novel is notably conciliatory in tone.

NORTON, [the Hon.] Mrs Caroline [Elizabeth Sarah] (later Lady Stirling-Maxwell, née Sheridan, 1808–77). Caroline Sheridan was born into a distinguished and literary family. Her grandfather was Richard Brinsley Sheridan, the dramatist, her mother was herself a novelist. Her father died when Caroline was ten. The King gave the widow and her seven children apartments at Hampton Court. The young Caroline was intellectually precocious, literary and beautiful. Her first major work (a drama) was written when she was thirteen. At the age of sixteen, she was sent to a boarding school. While there she met and in 1827 married the Hon. George Chapple Norton, a barrister, eight years her senior, later an MP and a man of small means and violent temper. The marriage was wretched. Caroline Norton was obliged to support the family largely by her writing. She had a notable success with the poem *The Sorrows Of Rosalie* (1829), and she was publicised as a female Byron. In 1831, Norton took over as editor of *La Belle Assemblée*, a Court magazine. Her first novel, *The Wife And Woman's Reward*, appeared in 1835. At this period her marriage was breaking up messily. In 1836, her husband brought an unsuccessful, but luridly sensational, action against Lord Melbourne, accusing the famously womanising politician of alienating his wife's affections. (The episode may have inspired Dickens's* *Bardell* v *Pickwick*.) The couple separated, and Caroline rejoined her mother at Hampton Court. Her poetry at this period took on a more sombre aspect. She wrote two long 'social problem*' poetic sequences, *A Voice From The Factories* (1836) and *The Child Of The Islands* (1845). Her private life was meanwhile preoccupied by her struggle for the custody of her children. In 1851, she produced (for Colburn*) the autobiographical novel, *Stuart Of Dunleath*. As the *Athenaeum** noted: 'a tale of trial accumulated upon one poor woman's head more melancholy than this novel is not within our recollection'. Subtitled 'A Story Of Modern Times', the novel carries a florid dedication to the Queen of the Netherlands. The heroine Eleanor is grossly abused by her 'brute of quality' husband, Sir Stephen Penrhyn. Norton's own husband continued to persecute her, even attempting to acquire her literary copyrights as his property. Unsurprisingly, Norton was an enthusiastic proponent of divorce-law reform, a campaign which was finally successful with the Divorce Bill of 1857. In 1863, she brought out the novel, *Lost And Saved*, another saga of domestic misery. Her last work of fiction was *Old Sir Douglas* (1868), first serialised in *Macmillan's Magazine**. It is the story of a noble old gentleman, a suffering wife and a 'vile and treacherous sister-in-law'. Norton's husband finally died in 1875, and she remarried an old friend, Sir William Stirling-Maxwell. Norton's marital experiences are supposed to have inspired Meredith's* magnificent heroine in *Diana Of The Crossways* (1885). BL 4. *DNB. NCBEL.* Wol. Sad.

NORWAY, Arthur Hamilton (1859–1938). Norway was born in Cornwall. He was educated at the Liverpool Institute and entered the postal branch of the Civil Service as a clerk in 1883, rising to the senior post of assistant secretary in 1907. He retired in 1920, having been made a CB in 1918, for war service. In later life he published extensively on local and Post Office history and wrote a romance, *Parson Peter* (1900), a 'Tale Of The Dart' with a Devonshire setting and featuring smuggling episodes and R. D. Blackmore*-style regional* colour. The work was published by Murray*, presumably on the strength of its topographical interest. Although he lived most of his adult life in London, Norway evidently retained a fondness for the West Country where he had been born and brought up. BL 1. *WW*.

O

Oakfield, Or Fellowship In the East, W[illiam] D[elafield] Arnold, 1853, 2 vols, Longman. A militantly moral novel by one of Dr Arnold of Rugby's younger children. Edward Oakfield leaves Oxford without sufficient vocation to enter the Church. Instead, he enrols as an officer in the military forces of the East India Company (an institution which strongly resented Arnold's novel). In Hajepoor, Edward is revolted by the 'ribaldry' of his fellow officers and boycotts the mess. His example converts the young Arthur Vernon, who dies piously after a river accident. Edward goes up country to Allahabad, where he becomes friendly with a sagacious magistrate, Mr Middleton. He refuses to be provoked into a duel by the local mess bully, Stafford, who speaks coarsely to Middleton's daughter Fanny. Oakfield is provoked, however, into horsewhipping Stafford's insolent emissary and is court-martialled but exonerated. The most lively section of the novel ensues, namely Edward's fighting in the Sikh Wars of 1846. Later, he becomes a magistrate, administering justice to the natives of whom he has a higher opinion than most Englishmen. He dies after six years' exhausting work raising the moral tone of the colony. His friend Wykham returns to England to marry Edward's sister, Margaret.

O'BRIEN Charlotte G[race] (1845–1909). The daughter of William Smith O'Brien (1803–64), the Young Ireland leader who was sentenced to be hanged, drawn and quartered for insurrection in 1848. O'Brien was later reprieved (much against his will) and transported to Tasmania for high treason. He returned to Europe in 1854 with a pardon and from 1854 to 1856 he and his daughter lived in Brussels. Otherwise, Charlotte O'Brien passed most of her life in Co. Limerick, where she had been born and where her uncle was a baronet. She was active in Nationalist politics and the Gaelic

League, becoming a Catholic in 1887 (in later life she was also afflicted with deafness). She had some effect in improving the sailing conditions for young Irish women emigrating to the USA. As an author, O'Brien wrote lyrics and fiction, all with strong Nationalist themes; e.g. *Dominick's Trials* (1870); *Light And Shade* (1878). The second of these is a story of the Fenian uprising of 1867. It contains a strong protest against the conditions in Mountjoy Prison for interned Irishmen held under the suspended Habeas Corpus act, and ends with the hero and heroine emigrating to America 'carrying with them hatred of English law and passionate love for Ireland'. BL 13. (WSO) *DNB*.

O'BRIEN, Richard Baptist ('Father Baptist', 1809–85). O'Brien was born at Carrick on Suir, Tipperary. He subsequently entered the priesthood, rising (in 1859) to the position of Dean of Limerick, a post he held until his death. Alongside his clerical career he wrote poems for the *Nation*, under the name of 'Father Baptist'. His novels, which tend to be Irish history lessons, include: *Ailey Moore* (1856), subtitled meaningfully 'A Tale Of The Times, Showing How The Evictions, Murder And Such-like Pastimes Are Managed And Justice Administered In Ireland'; *Jack Hazlitt, AM* (1875) 'A Hibernian-American Story'; *The D'Altons Of Crag* (1882), another tale of Irish suffering, 1848–49. BL 3. Boase.

O'BRIEN, William (1852–1928). O'Brien was born at Mallow, Co. Cork, the son of a solicitor's clerk. His parents were Roman Catholics but he was educated at a Protestant school. O'Brien took up employment as a journalist, and in 1875 joined the staff of the *Freeman's Journal*. Parnell made him editor of the militant *United Ireland* in 1881. The journal was eventually suppressed and O'Brien jailed. In all, he was prosecuted nine times and spent two years in prison. While a prisoner, O'Brien was elected to Parliament as a Nationalist MP in 1883. Also in prison (where he regarded himself as a political prisoner, and refused to wear uniform) he wrote the novel *When We Were Boys* (1890), a tale of Ireland in Fenian times with some high society London episodes. It ends with the hero, Ken Rohan, sentenced to life imprisonment and the uplifting message, 'Courage, this is not the end!'. Thematically, the work records the progress of republican American ideas in modern Ireland. O'Brien's other fiction includes *A Queen Of Men* (1897), the chronicle of Grace O'Malley, a heroine of ancient Ireland. Reviewers found O'Brien's fiction excessively theatrical, containing as one critic wittily put it, 'plenty of mustard, little beef'. His wife Sophie (née Raffalovich) wrote the novel, *Rosette, A Tale Of Dublin And Paris* (1907), which ends with the heroine taking the veil (a repugnant kind of 'happy ending', the *Athenaeum** thought). BL 2. *WW*. Wol.

The Odd Women, George Gissing, 1893, 3 vols, Lawrence and Bullen. A biting study of the dilemma of the 'superfluous' Victorian female of whom there were half-a-million in contemporary England. The odd women of the title are six sisters. They have been brought up genteel and well educated but their doctor father dies in a riding accident without leaving enough money to keep up their position at the seaside resort where they live. Nor do they have unusual gifts or beauty. The story jumps fifteen years to 1887 and south London. Three Madden sisters have died prematurely (one of consumption, one of suicide, one in a boating accident). Three survive more or less wretchedly. Virginia, a lady's companion, takes to drink. Alice, the eldest, takes up governessing; but cannot make a living at it. The youngest daughter, Monica, just twenty-one and working in a draper's shop in Lambeth, has better chances. For a while she attends an establishment set up to train women as clerks, run by Rhoda Nunn and Mary Barfoot. But instead of honest work, she chooses marriage with the well-to-do, but stodgy Edmund Widdowson. The match is disastrous, and the husband's neurotic jealousy drives him to set detectives on his wife. Monica eventually dies in childbirth. Alongside the powerfully graphic narrative of the Maddens' miseries is a sub-plot centred on the relationship of Everard Barfoot (a rich young man of leisure) and Rhoda. After much modish discussion of the ethics of marriage, the couple break up unhappily. Pensioned by a remorseful Widdowson, Alice and Virginia (once rehabilitated) look forward to a better future caring for Monica's child.

Off The Skelligs, Jean Ingelow, 1872, 4 vols, King. The Skelligs are rocky islands, off the south-west of Ireland. Ingelow's heroine, Dorothea Graham, tells her own story. Her mother and father emigrate to Australia, leaving Dorothea and her brother Tom to be brought up by a rich, yacht-owning uncle. Off the Skelligs, they pick up a boatload of survivors from a fire at sea. Dorothea nurses Giles Brandon back to health, and accompanies him (after an interlude in Chartres) to his English home. There Dorothea is wooed by Giles's impulsive young stepbrother, Valentine. Eventually, she surrenders and prepares to go with him to New Zealand (largely for the sake of his weak lungs). But at the last minute, he jilts her. She forgives him, and eventually marries the steadier Giles. Tom, meanwhile, marries a barmaid. The work is over-written, with much inserted poetry, in Ingelow's habitual narrative manner.

O'FLANAGAN, James Roderick (1814–1900). O'Flanagan was born at Fermoy barracks, Ireland, the son of an army officer. He was called to the Irish Bar in 1836. By 1846, he had risen to the position of Crown Prosecutor in Cork. In 1872 he retired from his legal career with failing sight. O'Flanagan wrote authoritative treatises on the law and a variety of miscellaneous works of biography and local history. He also turned out some novels with a strong Irish* flavour and featuring the sporting* scenes which were his speciality. O'Flanagan's fiction includes: *Gentle Blood, Or The Secret Marriage* (1861), a melodrama based on the sensational Yelverton divorce case in which bigamy* figured centrally; *The Life And Adventures Of Bryan O'Regan* (1866); *Captain O'Shaughnessy's Sporting Career* (1873). He died where he had been born, at Fermoy. BL 2. Boase.

The Ogilvies, Dinah Mulock Craik, 1849, 3 vols, Chapman and Hall. Mulock's first novel, dedicated to her dead mother. It opens in the genteel setting of Summerwood Park, and the narrative examines the complexities of marriage choice, through the courtships of three female cousins. Isabella Worsley is a calculating husband-hunter. Eleanor Ogilvie is an orphan, whose match with Philip Wychnor is soundly based on mutual knowledge and respect (if contrary to the wishes of his aunt and guardian). Philip goes on to become a famous author. More problematic are Katharine

Ogilvie's love affairs. As a sixteen-year-old, 'pretty-faced, pretty-spoken, pretty-mannered' and an heiress, she is infatuated with the handsome man of letters and politician, Paul Lynedon. But on discovering that he does not return her passion (and in fact loves Eleanor, who rejects him), she marries a rough and ready cousin, Hugh. During her marriage, Katharine grows in beauty and social accomplishment. Lynedon is now attracted, and when Hugh conveniently dies 'in the midst of his careless sports' the lovers promptly marry. But under the strain of guilt, Katharine herself succumbs at twenty to a fatal heart-failure. 'Oftentimes', the narrator concludes, 'living is harder than dying'.

O'GRADY, Standish [James] ('Luke Netterville', 1846–1928). O'Grady was born at Castletown Bere, Ireland, a son of a Protestant clergyman and small landowner. He was educated at Tipperary Grammar School, at Trinity College, Dublin (where he was a brilliant student), and was subsequently called to the Irish Bar in 1872. From law, which he never seriously practised, O'Grady drifted into full-time journalism and novel writing. His books, both fiction and non-fiction, have a pronounced national flavour. O'Grady's novels include: *Red Hugh's Captivity* (1889); *Finn And His Companions* (1892), tales of the Irish heroic age; *The Bog Of Stars* (1893), stories of Ireland in the age of Elizabeth; *Lost On Du Corrig* (1894), an adventure tale for boys; *The Chain Of Gold* (1895), a tale of adventure on the north west coast of Ireland; *Ulrick The Ready* (1896), a story of the Elizabethan age in Cork; *In The Wake Of King James* (1896); *The Flight Of The Eagle* (1897). The last is yet another of the author's stories of Elizabethan Ireland. O'Grady's narratives of Ireland's heroic age had a strong influence on the literary revival of the 1890s and the growth of Nationalist consciousness in the early twentieth century. He also wrote science fiction* under pseudonym (e.g. *The Queen Of The World*, by 'Luke Netterville', 1900). BL 13. *WW*. RLF.

The Old Curiosity Shop, Charles Dickens, 1841, 1 vol, Chapman and Hall. (Serialised in *Master Humphrey's Clock*, April 1840–February 1841 with illustrations by George Cattermole* and Phiz*.) The work was originally intended for Dickens's new weekly periodical, and Master Humphrey in fact intrudes as the narrator in the early chapters. The loose-knit narrative revolves around the saintly heroine, Little Nell (Trent), who lives in the quaint Old Curiosity Shop run by her grandfather. He is well-meaning, but feckless and has been impoverished by Nell's spendthrift older brother, Fred. To keep the shop going, he injudiciously borrows money from a villainous dwarf, Daniel Quilp, who has sexual designs on Nell. When Quilp discovers that the old man has gambled away his money and is not (as thought) a rich miser, he seizes the shop. Nell and her grandfather are forced to wander through England, as beggars. They undergo various adventures, while being tracked down by a relative returned from abroad. He finds them, but Nell dies (in a famously sentimental scene) and is shortly followed by her grandfather. Quilp, who has been unmasked for the villain he is, drowns in a Thames flood. Kit Nubbles, the young lad whom he falsely incriminated, is saved. Among a host of lively minor characters are the amiable ne'er-do-well, Dick Swiveller, and 'the Marchioness' whom he eventually marries.

An Old Man's Love, Anthony Trollope, 1884, 2 vols, Blackwood. Trollope's last complete novel. Written in the year of his death (1882) it was published posthumously. The 'old man' (fifty years old) is William Whittlestaff. He becomes the guardian of Mary Lawrie, the daughter of a dead friend, and falls in love with her. But Mary has another lover, John Gordon. Gordon, forbidden to woo Mary while he is penniless, emigrates to the South African diamond fields to make his fortune. Mary hears no word from him for three years. She explains that she still loves John, but accepts Whittlestaff. The next day Gordon returns rich, to claim his bride. Chivalrously, but with considerable pain, the old man withdraws his suit, leaving the way clear for his young rival. Trollope handles the dilemma of his hero's conscience, torn between selfish desire and unselfish duty, with great delicacy.

Old Saint Paul's, A Tale Of The Plague And The Fire, William Harrison Ainsworth, 1841, 3 vols, Cunningham and Mortimer. (Serialised in the *Sunday Times*, January–December 1841, and in monthly parts over the same period, with illustrations by John Franklin. The novel was serialised for a third time in *Ainsworth's Magazine**, 1846.) One of Ainsworth's most vigorous and popular romances, derived from Defoe's *Journal Of The Plague Year* and Hugo's *Notre Dame* (1831). The novel's main strand chronicles the fortunes of grocer Bloundel's family during the eventful months April–December 1665. Amabel Bloundel is loved by the the worthy apprentice Leonard Holt, but is seduced by Maurice Wyvil, alias the Earl of Rochester (like other of Ainsworth's early works, *Old Saint Paul's* has a strongly populist theme). Rochester arranges a fake marriage and Amabel, her honour ruined, succumbs to the plague. Leonard becomes involved with Mike Macascree, a blind piper, and his daughter Nizza. In reality, she is Lady Isabella Argentine. Leonard performs heroically during the Great Fire of London which Ainsworth portrays as being started by the apocalyptic mad prophet, Solomon Eagle. The young hero devises a system of firebreaks and saves the King's life for which he is ennobled, and finally marries Nizza. There are some effective characters at the level of sub-plot, notably the corpse-robbers Judith Malmayns (a murderous nurse) and Chowles the coffin maker. This grisly couple are finally trapped in the vaults of the cathedral and swallowed in molten lead with their loot.

OLIPHANT, Laurence (1829–88). Born in Cape Town, the only child of Sir Anthony Oliphant, a colonial law-officer, the young Laurence Oliphant was brought up in an evangelical household which even abroad retained its Scottish character. His father was twenty years older than his wife and the domestic atmosphere during Laurence's childhood was strained. Shortly after his birth Lady Oliphant lapsed into chronic invalidism. He went to school briefly in England, but in 1841 followed his father to his new appointment as Chief Justice in Ceylon. Thereafter, Oliphant's education was very interrupted, although there was always plentiful stimulus for his unusual mind. After travel in Europe during the revolutionary era (1846–48) he served as his father's private secretary, having decided against Cambridge as too dull. He was eventually called to the colonial Bar in 1849. It was an unsettled period and Ceylon was a wild outpost of the Empire. Over the following two years, Oliphant appeared in twenty-three cases of murder. In

1851, he returned to England to pursue his legal career. He had the usual letters of introduction to the leaders of good evangelical society. His first travel book (*A Journey To Khatmandu*) came out in 1852. In the same year Oliphant travelled to Russia with his friend Oswald Smith and his ensuing book on the country was boosted by the Crimean War. It also earned him £400 and cemented what was to be a lifelong association with the house of Blackwood*. Using family connections, Oliphant attached himself to Lord Elgin (1811–03) and followed the diplomat on various asssignments around the world (notably to China and the USA, about which he wrote more travel books). In this way Oliphant observed at first hand all the significant wars and rebellions of the period. His own life was endangered at the Edo uprising in Japan in 1861. He also served as a secret agent in Europe for the Foreign Secretary, Lord John Russell, in 1862. In 1865 he resigned the diplomatic service and entered Parliament as a member for Stirling. His most popular novel, *Piccadilly, A Fragment Of Contemporary Biography* appeared as a book in 1870 with illustrations by Richard Doyle*. (The work had been serialised in *Blackwood's Magazine** five years earlier.) The hero, Frank Vanecourt (a self-portrait), is heir to the Duke of Dunderhead. He takes rooms in the West End of London to watch the world go by. And, after foiling the various attempts of society mothers to entrap him, he escapes to America, the novel being finished 'on his last night in England'. The work is remarkable for its lively, embittered portrait of English high society. It was initially published anonymously and provoked speculation as to who its brilliant author could be. Oliphant did little of note in Parliament, and judging by *Piccadilly*, was evidently disillusioned by English public life. In 1867, he seems to have gone somewhat mad. He resigned his seat in 1868 and subjected himself to the authority of an American prophet, Thomas Lake Harris, the leader of a utopian community (The Brotherhood of the New Life) at Brocton in New York state. Oliphant rendered himself Harris's slave, giving the community all his property, and persuading his mother to join the cult. In 1870, still a devotee, he was *The Times* correspondent covering the Franco-Prussian war. In 1872, he married an heiress, Alice le Strange, and induced his wife to become part of the austere and tyrannical Brocton community. (The couple were, for instance, forbidden to sleep together.) At Harris's instruction, Oliphant undertook various commercial activities for the enrichment of the Brotherhood (whose headquarters had meanwhile moved to Santa Rosa, California). Oliphant was finally disillusioned in Harris with whom he quarrelled over money in 1881 (his mother, however, remained faithful). And Harris tried to use his hold over Alice to have Oliphant declared insane. Meanwhile, another enthusiasm had seized him. From 1879, Oliphant was a tireless advocate of Zionism, and actively supported schemes to populate Palestine with the Jewish exodus from Russia. He spent long periods in the East, and at Haifa, among a community of Jewish immigrants, where he wrote the novel *Altiora Peto** (1883). Essentially a picture of modern society, the work expounds the ideas Oliphant had been developing over the previous few years. In 1886, Oliphant publicly denounced Harris. The following year his wife died of a fever and in 1888 he married Rosamond Dale Owen, an American granddaughter of Robert Owen, the social reformer. *Massollam, A Problem Of The Period* was published in 1886. The main character is a portrait of Harris and the plot concerns the struggles of his daughter to escape his domination. The novel, which opens with a vivid picture of the House of Commons, is the author's most autobiographical. The action ends, centred on the eastern sage Massollam, in Palestine. In 1887, Oliphant collected various of his stories as *Fashionable Philosophy*. In 1887 there also appeared his *Episodes In A Life Of Adventure*. Five months later he died at Twickenham. Dark rumours subsequently circulated about Oliphant's sexual delinquency and his idiosyncratic 'Symphneuma' creed. Harris continued publicly to abuse his errant convert as 'the greatest apostate since Judas Iscariot' until his own death in 1906. Oliphant stands out from the history of his age as a notable Victorian eccentric. *Piccadilly* suggests a real talent for fiction, left uncultivated among all the other activities of a furiously busy life. A fictional portrait of Oliphant is given in Haskett Smith's novel *For God And Humanity, A Romance Of Mount Carmel* (1891). BL 3. *DNB*. RM. *NCBEL*. Wol. Sad.

OLIPHANT, Mrs [Margaret Oliphant] (née Wilson, 1828–97). One of the most prolific Victorian novelists, and like Trollope* (whom she in fact outwrote two-to-one), an author who contrived to combine mass production with a high degree of artistry. Margaret Wilson was born near Edinburgh, at Wallyford, and although she lived most of her adult life in London always retained a pronounced Scottishness in her manner and personality. Francis Wilson, her father, was an ineffectual figure, apparently employed in the custom and excise service and his work involved frequent household moves. In atmosphere the Wilson family was firmly bourgeois, and the major influence on her childhood character was her energetic and resourceful mother. Margaret Wilson, whose subsequent life was dogged by domestic tragedy, was to need these qualities in full measure herself. Her parents were Presbyterian and strongly affected by the Disruption of 1843, but Margaret, when she had discretion in the matter, chose to be Anglican. Her career in writing began when her brother Willie filched her novel, *Margaret Maitland*, and sent it off to the publisher Henry Colburn*. Colburn, whose eye for new talent was always sharp, published the tale in 1849. The work duly went into three editions, was praised by Charlotte Brontë*, and the novelist was launched at the age of twenty-one. Over 100 books were to follow. For Colburn, she did a couple of other historical* romances. But the most important professional relationship of her career was formed in 1853, when with *Katie Stewart* (a domestic*-historical romance of the 1745 uprising) she became a 'Blackwood's* author'. In the early 1850s, she came to London. And in 1852 (against her mother's wish, evidently) she married her cousin, Francis William Oliphant, and settled in Harrington Square. He was an artist specialising in stained glass who worked with Pugin on the remodelling of the Houses of Parliament. (Although she wrote his biography, Mrs Oliphant disclaimed any family connection with the gifted and eccentric namesake writer, Laurence Oliphant*.) She went on to write a stream of novels including: *The Athelings* (1857), the story of three children each with a distinctively different talent; *Orphans* (1858); *The Laird Of Norlaw* (1858). Mrs Oliphant was happier at this stage of her life than she was ever to be again; there were children, she was earning around £400 for every novel she turned out, and she was a minor celebrity in London literary life.

There were already vexations, however. Her husband Frank was talented but a poor provider. Margaret, moreover, was obliged to support her charming, alcoholic brother, William. (Before drink destroyed him, William Wilson wrote an interesting novel, *Matthew Paxton*, 1854, based on his experience as a clergyman in a small Northumberland community.) In 1859, Oliphant's world collapsed. Her husband contracted consumption, and died within a few months, after a nightmarish journey to Italy. The young widow had two surviving children, was pregnant, and was virtually penniless. Her suffering at this period is recalled in two later novels: *Agnes* and *A Son Of The Soil**, both published in 1866. *Agnes*, for instance, tells the story of the daughter of a blacksmith who marries the heir to a baronet but is left a penniless widow with three young children to care for. In 1860, to make things worse, Oliphant's fiction (of which there was an over-supply on the market) no longer seemed to appeal to the reading public. Resourcefully, having returned to England to live with her brother Frank, she pulled herself up with what was to be her most enduring achievement in fiction, the seven-volume 'Chronicles of Carlingford*'. The series got off to a successful start with *Salem Chapel** (1863) and was promptly followed by *The Rector And The Doctor's Family* (1863) and *The Perpetual Curate** (1864). For this last, a delighted John Blackwood gave the author £1,500, her highest payment ever. The seven-part sequence was clearly influenced by Trollope's *Barsetshire** novels, which ran from 1855 to 1867. But Oliphant's Carlingford dramas were less ambitious in their social scope, and more theological in their content with a nagging preoccupation with religious vocation. (For Trollope, clergymen tended to be Civil Servants in dog-collars.) Together with Trollope and Eliot*, Oliphant was, at the end of the 1860s, a leader of the domestic genre of fiction. But financial crisis and domestic tragedy continued to dog her. In 1864 her daughter died. At about the same time, she took charge of three of her widowed brother Frank's four children. Her own boys went to Eton. Both were to be a source of infinite vexation to their mother, and both predeceased her with pulmonary ailments. As the *DNB* notes, 'after 1866, the rest of her life might have been described as slavery to the pen, if writing had not been a real enjoyment to her.' In addition to novels, Oliphant wrote biography (including the standard life of Edward Irving, leader of the 'Catholic Apostolic Church'); an excellent history of Blackwood's publishing house; literary history, and powerful reviews. Like all Blackwood's authors, she cultivated a strong line in short stories. (A collection of her work was made by J. M. Barrie*, who regarded her as a master of the form.) In the 1870s, she began to turn out a successful series of travel books. Her autobiographical 'fragment' is fascinating, if tantalisingly incomplete. She pleased the leading critics of the day, and was Queen Victoria's favourite novelist. Among her many titles are: *John* (1870); *May* (1873); *The Greatest Heiress In England* (1880); *Hester* (1883); *Joyce* (1888); *Kirsteen* (1890); *Janet* (1891). The works of Oliphant's which have survived best are the 'Carlingford Chronicles', and her various 'Stories Of The Seen And Unseen'. Indomitably modest, she regarded herself as 'rather a failure'. BL 95. *DNB*. RM. *NCBEL*. Wol. Sad.

Oliver Twist, Boz (i.e. Charles Dickens), 1838, 3 vols, Bentley. (Serialised in *Bentley's Miscellany**, February 1837–April 1839, with illustrations by

George Cruikshank*. The story was reissued in monthly parts by Bradbury and Evans, December 1845–September 1846.) The story opens dramatically. A woman comes to a workhouse and dies giving birth to a child. Nothing is known of her background, and the boy is brought up as Oliver Twist, a foundling. Having reached boyhood, Oliver is farmed out as an apprentice to an undertaker. After various afflictions (notably from his bullying fellow apprentice, the odious Noah Claypole) Oliver runs away to London. There he falls in with the Artful Dodger, a young street criminal, who takes him to the den of a Jewish fence, Fagin. There, Oliver is trained in the arts of pickpocketing. An unsuccessful attempt to lift the handkerchief of the amiable Mr Brownlow leads to Oliver's being rescued for a while. But he is abducted again by Nancy, a member of Fagin's gang, while doing an errand for Brownlow. It transpires that a mysterious stranger, Monks, wants Oliver to be thoroughly criminalised. Under Fagin's direction, Bill Sikes takes Oliver off to help with a burglary. Oliver is shot, and nursed back to health by Mrs Maylie and her ward, Rose. Nancy repents, and warns Rose and Brownlow that there is a mystery about Oliver's origins and that Monks and Fagin are conspiring against the boy. Claypole (now in Fagin's service) overhears the conversation, and Sikes brutally murders Nancy. He then takes flight, but cannot escape either conscience or a vigilant London populace who finally hunt him down to the Rookery (a notorious slum) where he accidentally but appropriately hangs himself. Fagin is arrested, and judicially hanged. In a complex denouement, Monks is revealed to be the half-brother of Oliver, and Rose his aunt. He is adopted by Mr Brownlow, and at last joins the middle class he spiritually belongs to. Monks emigrates, and eventually dies in prison. *Oliver Twist* specifically attacks the New Poor Law of 1834, and in a wider sense Benthamism as a social philosophy. Bumble, the vastly self-important beadle who has conspired with Monks, himself becomes an inmate of his own workhouse. Oliver asking for more gruel has become probably the single best-known scene in Victorian fiction.

OLLIER, Charles (1788–1859). Ollier was descended from a French Protestant family which fled to England in the 1685 persecution. Brought up in London he began his working life in Coutts's Bank but subsequently (around 1816) entered the publishing business with his brother James. (Keats was one of the Olliers' authors. They also published Shelley, Lamb and Peacock.) For many years, Charles Ollier was literary adviser to Richard Bentley*. He also wrote some negligible novels. They include: *Altham And His Wife* (1818); *Inesilla, Or The Tempter* (1824); *Ferrers* (1842). The last is a historical* novel about Earl Ferrers, executed in 1760. In the 1840s, he was evidently employed by Ainsworth* as a hack on his various magazine enterprises. And it was Ollier who was assigned by Ainsworth to finish off Maginn's* incomplete romance, *John Manesty*, which he did execrably. BL 5. *DNB*. Sad. RLF.

OLLIVANT, Alfred (1874–1927). Ollivant was born at Nuthurst, Sussex, the son of a senior army officer. He was educated at Rugby School, and at the Royal Military Academy, Woolwich (where he won his class prize for riding). The young Ollivant was subsequently commissioned into the Royal Artillery (his father's corps), in 1893. Badly injured in a fall from a horse, he resigned the army in 1895, and took up writing. He married in 1914 into an aristocratic family. The Sussex Downs form the usual background to his fiction. Ollivant wrote well into the twentieth century, always with a strong line in animal narratives. His main work of Victorian fiction is *Owd Bob, The Grey Dog Of Kenmuir** (1898) which with Ouida's* *A Dog Of Flanders** (1872) is one of the few Victorian novels to have a canine hero. BL 15. *WW.*

O'MEARA, Kathleen ('Grace Ramsay,' 1839–88). O'Meara was born in Dublin, and was taken to Paris by her parents as a young child. The family had strong French connections, O'Meara's grandfather (Barry Edward, 1786–1836) having been Napoleon's personal physician on St Helena. It seems unlikely that Kathleen O'Meara ever saw Ireland again, although it features prominently and nostalgically in her subsequent fiction, written under the pen-name Grace Ramsay. O'Meara also wrote biographies, and was for many years Paris correspondent of the Catholic journal, the *Tablet.* Her novels include: *A Woman's Trials* (1867), the story of a heroine who is sent to boarding school in Paris and becomes a Catholic, thus provoking her father into disowning her; *Iza's Story* (1869); *A Salon In The Last Days Of The Empire* (1873); *The Battle Of Connemara* (1878); *Are You My Wife?* (1878); *The Old House In Picardy* (1887); *Narka The Nihilist* (1888), a Russian assassination story. She died in Paris. BL 6. *DNB.* Wol.

On The Face Of The Waters, Flora Annie Steel, 1896, 1 vol, Heinemann. The most famous novel of the Indian Mutiny, by a writer who knew the country and its history at first hand. The narrative opens strikingly. The fleshily handsome Major Erlton buys his mistress, Alice Gissing, a cockatoo at a public auction. Ominously (although he does not know it) the bird has been taught to cry the Islamic call to arms. And, equally ominously, Erlton's wife, Kate, passes on the way to a church service. Erlton goes off to ride in a race whose result he has had fixed. The bulk of the novel follows Kate's experiences in Delhi during the uprising. She is chastely beloved by an English undercover agent, first called Greyman, later identified as Jim Douglas (who has a native mistress). Passing for a native, Douglas rescues Kate when Alice Gissing and the other Europeans in the city are massacred. Erlton, who had planned to marry Alice, is killed at the storming of Delhi by the English forces (under John Nicholson, whom Steel idolised). He is recommended for a posthumous VC. Kate, meanwhile, has been preserved in native disguise, with Douglas's former concubine Tara. An epilogue reveals that the couple marry, and enjoy a comfortable afterlife in Scotland as landed gentry. The novel is notable for the sharpness of its depictions (particularly of colonial morals).

Once A Week (1859–80). In 1858, Bradbury and Evans* broke with Dickens* (over their refusal to carry an advertisement explaining his separation from Mrs Dickens). *Household Words** was wound up in consequence and Dickens founded the weekly *All The Year Round** in 1859, a journal he decided would be independent of any publisher. In opposition Bradbury and Evans set up *Once A Week* under the editorship of Samuel Lucas. The paper departed from its predecessor in a number of ways. At 6d. it was more expensive. More significantly, it was illustrated. For their illustrators Bradbury and Evans drew on the extensive stable of artists associated with their other weekly magazine, *Punch**: notably John Leech*, John Tenniel*, George Du Maurier*. *Punch* writers (Mark Lemon*, Shirley Brooks*, Tom Taylor) also featured prominently in the magazine's pages. Serial fiction was a main attraction, and the early issues of *Once A Week* carried Reade's* *A Good Fight* and Meredith's* *Evan Harrington**. In its first year, *Once A Week* probably sold around a million copies. But it was expensive to produce, probably underpriced, and went into a decline after Lucas died in 1865. At some point thereafter *Once A Week* was acquired by James Rice* who owned and edited it until 1873 when G. Manville Fenn* bought it. By this stage it was a shadow of its former self. Historically the magazine's main achievement was to provide an outlet for the innovative group of illustrators of the 1860s. *BLM.*

One Of Our Conquerors, George Meredith, 1891, 3 vols, Chapman and Hall. (Serialised, in different form, in the *Fortnightly Review**, October 1890–May 1891.) A striking study of marital misery. Victor Radnor marries a wealthy widow, only to discover that he really loves her young companion, Natalia. Natalia and Victor subsequently set up home together, and have a daughter, Nesta Victoria. Victor is prosperous and successful, but as she grows up Nesta comes to realise that she is unrespectable. The facts of her birth complicate her relationship with an eligible suitor, the Hon. Dudley Sowerby. Things are made even more difficult when it emerges that her friend Mrs Marsett is also living in sin. The novel ends tragically. Overcome by shame, Natalia dies; Victor's wife outlives her (thus removing any possibility of legitimising Nesta). Nesta eventually marries Captain Dartrey Fenellan, who loves her for herself.

ONWHYN, Thomas ('Peter Palette', 1811–86). Illustrator and artist. Onwhyn was born in London, the son of a bookseller in the Strand. He furnished some of the plates for the popular plagiarisms of Dickens's* *Pickwick Papers** and *Nicholas Nickleby** in the late 1830s. He subsequently illustrated Henry Cockton's* *Valentine Vox** (1840) and half-a-dozen other novels by the same author. Stylistically, Onwhyn was influenced by George Cruikshank* and Phiz*, and specialised in etching and engraving on steel. According to the *DNB* he was 'an indifferent draughtsman but showed real humour in his designs'. He contributed to *Punch**, 1847–48 and at the end of his life switched largely to guide-book work. *DNB.* Hou.

OPPENHEIM, E[dward] P[hillips] (1866–1946). Oppenheim was born in London, the son of a leather merchant, who later moved to Leicester. The son attended the local grammar school and in 1882 dutifully went to work in the family leather business (which was failing). He published his first novel, *Expiation* (1887), 'A Novel Of England And Canada', at his own expense. Its success led to a contract to write no less than six serials for the *Sheffield Weekly Telegraph*. On the strength of his success, he married Elsie Hopkins (an American) in 1891. Oppenheim subsequently made his name with *The Mysterious Mr Sabin** (1898). This work inaugurated his successful formula of thrilling intrigue and espionage in high and cosmopolitan places. His early fiction includes: *The Man And His Kingdom* (1899), a Zendaish romance, set in a South American dictatorship; *The World's Great Snare* (1900), a tale of adventure and love in the American mining camps; *A Millionaire*

Of Yesterday (1900), set in colonial Africa; *The Survivor* (1901), the story of a brilliant young poet's encounter with a bewitching siren. All these works were written in the author's characteristically terse, telegraphic style. Oppenheim went on to become a bestselling author of the twentieth century, and a fixture on the pre-war French Riviera. His last published novel was *Burglars Must Die* (1945). Oppenheim was also a skilled illustrator of his own work. BL 171. *DNB*. RM.

ORCHARDSON, [Sir] W[illiam] Q[uiller] (1832–1910). Painter and illustrator. Orchardson was born in London, the only son of a tailor. His mother was Austrian. In 1845, he went to art school in Edinburgh and three years later was exhibiting at the Scottish Royal Academy. He returned to London in 1862 and went on to become a famous painter in the high Victorian manner. He also illustrated some fiction, notably that of his friend William Black*. Orchardson was knighted in 1907. *DNB*. Hou.

The Ordeal Of Richard Feverel, George Meredith, 1859, 3 vols, Chapman and Hall. The novel with which Meredith made his name. The hero's mother deserts her husband and Richard Feverel is brought up by his father Sir Austin on scientific educational principles. The 'system' (which has kept Richard secluded at home) is tested to breaking point when the boy falls in love with Lucy Desborough, the niece of a neighbouring farmer. Sir Austin opposes the match, and the young couple marry secretly. In London, Richard and Lucy are exposed to various trials. He is seduced by a courtesan; she attracts the attention of Lord Mountfalcon. The couple separate (a frequent event in Meredith's stories) and Lucy, unknown to her husband, bears a child. Sir Austin is finally brought round to approval of his daughter-in-law. But Richard is badly wounded in a duel with Mountfalcon. Lucy goes mad and dies while her husband lies paralysed, a triumph of his father's 'system'. The novel was held to be dangerously frank in its sexual passages and was boycotted by Mudie*, fatally damaging its early sales and blighting Meredith's reputation.

O'RELL, Max (i.e. Leon Paul Blouet, 1848–1903). O'Rell was born in Brittany, and educated at Paris. As a young man he fought with the French cavalry in the Franco-Prussian War, and was severely wounded. He came to England in 1872, initially as a foreign correspondent. From 1876 to 1884, O'Rell was a teacher at St Paul's School in London. He also lectured and travelled extensively in the English-speaking world, and had a great hit with *John Bull And His Island* (1883). His fiction includes: *Drat The Boys* (1886) and *Woman And Artist* (1900). The last is the study of strained marriage in English bourgeois life. It was initially published in France, and subsequently translated for the English public by the author's wife. BL 4. *WW*.

Orley Farm, Anthony Trollope, 1862, 2 vols, Chapman and Hall. (Serialised in twenty monthly parts, March 1861–October 1862, with illustrations by J. E. Millais*.) Trollope's first novel in 1s. numbers. He thought the plot the best he ever created, and Millais's designs the best he had ever seen. When Sir Joseph Mason dies, he leaves as his hopeful heirs a young widow (with a baby son, Lucius) and a grown-up son and three daughters from an earlier marriage. Among a generally equitable disposition of the dead man's wealth, a codicil to his will leaves Orley Farm to his new-born son,

Lucius. The older son Joseph (irascible by nature) had always understood the farm would be his and disputes the codicil. A trial acquits Lady Mason of forgery. Years later, Lucius has grown up to be the efficient manager of his farm. But he excites the enmity of a local lawyer, Samuel Dockwrath. Dockwrath is married to one of the original witnesses to Sir Joseph's will, and he rakes up enough evidence to warrant another trial for perjury. Lady Mason is gallantly protected by Sir Peregrine Orme, an old gentleman who loves her. And in court, she is defended by the unprepossessing but legally brilliant Mr Chaffanbrass. One of his juniors, Felix Graham, provides much of the love interest in the novel with his courtship of Madeline Staveley. In the second trial, Lady Mason is again acquitted. But in the process Lucius discovers that she has indeed forged the codicil, and returns Orley Farm to the incorrigibly surly Joseph Mason. Sir Peregrine does not withdraw his offer of marriage, but Lady Mason releases him. Lucius takes his mother out of the country, and himself emigrates to Australia.

Osgood, McIlvaine (1891–1898?). Publishers. The firm was started by James Ripley Osgood (1836–92), an American who came to London in 1886 as Harper's English agent. Following the passing of the International Copyright Bill in 1891, he went into partnership with another American employee of Harper's, Clarence McIlvaine. The firm set up in Albemarle Street and published fiction by Hardy* (notably *Tess Of The D'Urbervilles**, after Macmillans* turned it down), Henry James and Vernon Lee*. Much of the vision left the business, however, with the premature death of Osgood in 1892.

O'SHEA, John Augustus ('The Irish Bohemian', 1839–1905). The son of a journalist, O'Shea was born at Nenagh, and educated at the Catholic University, recently established under Newman* in Dublin. He moved to London in 1859, eventually joining the staff of the *Standard* where he worked for twenty-five years and for whom he reported the war in France in 1870. Much of his professional life was subsequently spent in Paris. O'Shea was active in Irish politics and his fiction includes *Military Mosaics* (1888) and a tale of France during the Second Empire, *Mated From The Morgue* (1889). His sister, J. J. O'Shea, wrote the novel *Dark Rosaleen* (1884). O'Shea was paralysed towards the end of his life, and died in London. BL 3. *DNB*. Wol. RLF.

O'SULLIVAN, Mortimer (1791?–1859). O'Sullivan was born at Clonmel, Co. Tipperary. His father was a Catholic schoolmaster, but the son converted to Protestantism and took his degree at Trinity College, Dublin. He subsequently took up work as a schoolteacher, and eventually went into the Protestant Church. O'Sullivan particularly interested himself in the political problem of religious factionalism in Ireland. He lived most of his life in or around Dublin, wrote a number of books and some fiction, notably *The Nevilles Of Garretstown* (1860), 'A Tale Of 1760'. BL 1. *DNB*. Wol.

OUIDA, (i.e. Marie Louise de la Ramée, 1839–1908). Ouida's French-sounding *nom de plume* derives from a childhood corruption of her christian name. She was born, humbly enough, Louise Ramé at Bury St Edmunds, Suffolk, where her Guernsey-born father, Louis Ramé, was a teacher of French. Her mother (née Sutton) was English. Monsieur Ramé gave his quick-witted, artistic and precocious daughter an unusually good education for a country girl of her background. (In the 1860s he moved back to Paris, and disappeared during the upheaval of the 1871 Commune.) In 1859, while staying at Hammersmith, Louise Ramé was introduced to Harrison Ainsworth*, and sent the veteran author a short story, 'Dashwood's Drag, Or The Derby And What Came Of It' for *Bentley's Miscellany**. (Despite its name, Ainsworth was currently the proprietor-editor of the journal, which he had taken over in 1854.) By the end of 1860, Ainsworth had taken a score of similarly 'fast' stories of fashionable (and typically military) life from the young authoress. He also accepted her first novel, *Granville De Vigne* (1863), for the *New Monthly Magazine**, which he also edited. The novel was subsequently published in volume form by Tinsley* as *Held In Bondage**. As 'Ouida', Ramée had bestselling success with: *Strathmore** (1865); *Chandos** (1866); *Under Two Flags** (1867), her best-known, most reprinted and most imitated work; and *Idalia* (1867), a work which had been written when she was only sixteen. *Tricotrin* (1869) is the 'story of a waif', Viva, who is adopted by a French vagabond musician. The narrative is set in France and dedicated to the American people of the North and South, 'whose friendship honours me'. After her triumphant début in the early 1860s, Ouida lived largely in Italy, now styling herself socially 'de la Ramée'. She remained a fascinating and glamorous figure in the mind of her English readers, and sensational rumours attached to her. There were also absurdly high claims made for her romantic fiction. Bulwer-Lytton*, for instance, hailed *Folle Farine* (1871), Ouida's highest-flown and most allegorical investigation into the plight of the orphan, as a major work of literature. Even Henry James claimed to admire her 'artistry'. In 1874, Ouida settled with her mother at a villa in Florence. Here, for a few years, she lived very well. She was an idealist, of sorts. She loved dogs, and campaigned against vivisection. She wrote sympathetically about the Italian peasantry (in, for example, *A Village Commune*, 1881), and intelligently about international politics. (She supported the Boers' struggle in South Africa, for instance.) And social satires such as *Moths* (1880) proved her to be sharp-eyed about European high society. In 1897, Ouida published another and better novel attacking the English aristocracy, *The Massarenes**. But by the 1890s, she had outlived her vogue. Nor had she looked after her copyrights (her novels were still selling well in cheap reprint form, but earning the author nothing). Ouida's last eighteen years were passed in increasing penury, and she died in virtual destitution, aided by a Civil List pension in 1906. She remained indomitably proud, however, and strongly resented Marie Corelli's* vulgar attempt to publicise her plight in the London papers. She died at Viareggio of pneumonia. Ouida is commemorated by a monument in Bury St Edmunds, a town she herself seems not to have remembered once in her cosmopolitan, high-flown fiction. She wrote forty-four novels and collections of stories, of which some of the more memorable are: *Puck* (1870), the monologue of a garrulous and unusually philosophical dog; *A Dog Of Flanders** (1872), the story of a working-class canine; *Two Little Wooden Shoes* (1874); *Wanda* (1883), a story of Russian princes and Austro-Hungarian countesses. *Under Two Flags* continued to sell massively in the twentieth century and inspired a successful (if unfaithful) Hollywood adaptation. BL 44. *DNB*. RM. *NCBEL*. Wol. Sad. RLF.

Our Friend The Charlatan, George Gissing, 1901, 1 vol, Chapman and Hall. Gissing's malicious portrait of a Victorian gigolo. The hero is Dyce Lashmar, a well-trained Oxford man of refined sensibility who lives on women. Initially a private tutor to a rich widow, he ingratiates himself with a patroness, Lady Ogram. With her support he puts himself up for Parliament. He has no views of his own, but cleverly plagiarises fashionable political philosophy. Things go badly for Lashmar. Lady Ogram is infuriated when he makes love to her grandniece, May Tomalin, and insists that he marry the less attractive Constance Bride. When Lady Ogram dies and Constance inherits, Dyce indeed proposes, but is turned down. He also loses the election. Finally, Lashmar marries the widow he originally tutored, only to discover that her fortune has been embezzled by criminals sharper than he. The novel ends with the couple uneasily reconciled to each other. The tone of this late novel is extremely elusive.

Our Mutual Friend, Charles Dickens, 1865, 2 vols, Chapman and Hall. (Serialised in monthly parts, May 1864–November 1865, with illustrations by Marcus Stone*.) Dickens's last complete novel, and his most complex plot. The story opens on the river Thames, with boatmen fishing out the night's corpses. This watery setting and the business of bodies being pulled from death casts a symbolic mood over the whole narrative. John Harmon, 'our mutual friend', has been brought back to England by the death of his father, a dust contractor. (The mountains of rubbish accumulated in Victorian London also figure symbolically in the action. There has been considerable critical controversy over whether Dickens's use of the term 'dust' is in fact a euphemism for 'excrement'.) It was old Harmon's mysterious intention that before inheriting his son should marry a girl he has never met, Bella Wilfer. John confides to a sailor on board that he means to conceal his identity on landing and thus decide whether to marry Bella. The sailor subsequently tries to kill Harmon, but himself dies. His waterlogged body is subsequently mistaken for Harmon's, who can thus keep the fact of his survival secret. He takes on the identity of John Rokesmith, and works as secretary for Boffin, old Harmon's employee, who has now inherited the highly lucrative dustheaps. Boffin has adopted Bella, who becomes unbearably haughty in the enjoyment of new riches. She rejects Rokesmith's proposal. Boffin meanwhile is being blackmailed by Silas Wegg, a one-legged stall keeper whom he originally employed to read to him, being himself illiterate. Boffin finally discovers the true identity of Rokesmith, and helps him win the heart of a by now chastened Bella. A Thameside story with largely proletarian characters runs alongside this main plot. Lizzie Hexam, who helps her father fish for bodies in the river, is loved by a self-improved teacher, Bradley Headstone, who has befriended her brother. For all his virtue, and for all her gratitude, Headstone is physically repulsive to Lizzie who is drawn instead to the idle, but handsome, young lawyer, Eugene Wrayburn. Madly jealous, Headstone attacks his rival Wrayburn by night, and almost kills him. On his recovery (having been nursed by Lizzie) Eugene is transformed into a man worth her love. Headstone, meanwhile, is blackmailed by Rogue Riderhood, a Thames sailor who knows of his assault on Eugene. The two men are drowned struggling together. Among the novel's extensive cast of characters are little Jenny Wren (i.e. Fanny

Cleaver) a doll's dress maker, the saintly Jew, Riah, and Betty Higden, an old woman terrified of the 'charitable' workhouse.

Our Street, W. M. Thackeray, 1848, 1 vol, Chapman and Hall. Thackeray's second Christmas* Book. Liberally illustrated by the author, it offers a comic panorama of the various respectable (and would-be respectable) inhabitants of Pocklington Gardens. The work is supposedly written by Thackeray's amiable authorial persona, Michael Angelo Titmarsh. It is in the 'social physiology' genre which Thackeray made particularly his in the 1840s. It is also one of the relatively few books that he wrote for Dickens's* principal publisher, Chapman and Hall.

Owd Bob, The Grey Dog Of Kenmuir, Alfred Ollivant, 1898, 1 vol, Methuen. The most successful Victorian novel with a dog as its hero. The story is set in Cumberland, where 'Owd Bob' is a sheepdog, 'a grey dog of Kenmuir'. A dalesman, the narrator tells us, 'would as soon think to sell his child as part with a grey dog'. Bob's owner, James Moore, feuds with a fellow farmer, the Scot Adam McAdam, and Bob is pitted against the other man's villainous dog, 'Red Wull', as champion courser. Moore wins the shepherd's trophy in a vividly described hillside competition. After various adventures and much mystery, Red Wull is discovered to be a secret sheep killer. He is torn to pieces by a pack of more law-abiding tykes and McAdam dies soon after, being buried alongside his beast, 'one just within, the other just without the consecrated pale'. The work pioneered a whole genre of anthropomorphic dog tales but is principally memorable for its exact description of dales' dialect and mores. Unlike most canine novels, *Owd Bob* does not unduly sentimentalise its subject.

OXENHAM, John (born William Arthur Dunkerley, 1860–1941). Oxenham was born and educated at Old Trafford, in Manchester. At some point in his life he seems to have changed his name, whether for authorial or other reasons is not clear. On leaving the local university, he went into the business world, but could not apparently settle down. He travelled to France and the USA, and for a while tried orange growing and sheep farming in the west and south of that country. With Robert Barr* (another writer with American connections) Oxenham was instrumental in introducing the weekly *Detroit Free Press* to England and subsequently went on to help Barr and Jerome K. Jerome* found the *Idler** magazine. He eventually returned to England where he 'took to writing as alleviative and alternative to business, found it much more enjoyable than business, so dropped business and stuck to writing'. In fact, he was to become a prolific and moderately popular Edwardian author, turning out light romance in large quantity. Oxenham's Victorian fiction (by chronological reckoning) includes: *God's Prisoner* (1898), 'The Story Of A Crime, A Punishment, A Redemption', with some American scenes; *Rising Fortunes* (1899), the story of 'two Scotch Whittingtons' who come to London to make their fortunes; *A Princess Of Vascovy* (1900), set in a Ruritanian kingdom. His best-known work was to be *Flies In Amber* (1913). Oxenham died at Worthing in Sussex. He had six children, one of whom, Elsie Jeanette Oxenham, became a well-known writer for children in the twentieth century. BL 42. *WW*.

P

PAE, David (1828–84). Pae was born in Amulree, Perthshire, the son of a miller. From 1848, he worked for Thomas Grant, the Edinburgh bookselling and publishing firm. On the side, Pae wrote stories for the *Edinburgh Penny Post*, and the *North Briton*. For some years, Pae was editor of the *Dundee People's Journal*, for which he wrote twenty-seven serialised works of fiction. They include: *Jessie Melville, Or The Double Sacrifice* (1856), the story of a heroine with two lovers that the *Athenaeum** called 'a tissue of foolishness unredeemed by any qualms of common sense'; *The Merchant's Daughter* (1857); *Hard Times* (1868), like Dickens's* novel of the same name, a tale of the Lancashire cotton famine. According to his son (also named David Pae), he was 'the founder of the system of serial publication in newspapers', later exploited by the Tillotson* syndicate. Pae's most reprinted work was the apocalyptic treatise, *The Coming Struggle Between The Nations Of The Earth* (1853), and he was clearly among everything else a religious zealot. BL 7. Boase.

PAGET, Frances E[dward] (1806–82). The eldest son of the famous soldier, General Sir Edward Paget (1775–1849), he was educated at Westminster School and Christ Church, Oxford. Paget stayed at university from 1825 to 1836, and was swept up by religious enthusiasm for the Oxford Movement, inspired by Newman*. In 1835, he was appointed Rector of Elford, near Lichfield. Paget thereafter remained at Elford all his life, and superintended the restoration of his beloved parish church in 1848. (Restoration was also to be the main theme of his fiction.) Paget was for many years chaplain to the Bishop of Bath and Wells and was an invalid for much of his later life. His novels are frankly designed to promote his brand of high Anglicanism. They include: *Caleb Kniveton, The Incendiary* (1833); *Tales Of The Village* (1841); *Milford Malvoisin* (1842); *St Antholin's* (1842), a novel with a purpose written against the evils of modern church architecture; *The Hope Of The Katzekopfs* (1844), a fairy-tale; *Tales Of The Village Children* (1843–44); *The Warden Of Berkingholt* (1843). Paget had less of a thumping touch in his fiction than other novelists with a Tractarian tendency. His *Lucretia* (1868) is a witty send-up of the sensation* school and his last novel, *Homeward Bound* (1875) created a small stir. BL 7. *DNB. NCBEL.* Wol.

PAGET, Sidney E[dward] (1860–1908). Illustrator. Paget was born in London, the fourth son of a vestry clerk. He entered the Royal Academy School in 1881, where he was to be a prize-winning student. Although his early vocation was for painting, it was as an illustrator that Paget made his name. He is particularly remembered for his definitive portraiture of Conan Doyle's* Sherlock Holmes in the *Strand** magazine, 1892–94. He also illustrated Arthur Morrison's* Martin Hewitt* detective* stories. Paget's brothers Henry Marriott (1856–1936) and Walter (1863–1935) were also illustrators of fiction. *DNB*. Hou.

PAIN, Barry [Eric Odell] (1864–1928). Pain was born at Cambridge, the son of a linen draper. He attended the local university (Corpus Christi College), graduating in 1886 with a third-class degree in classics. More usefully, Pain made a name for himself while a student as a brilliant contributor to *Granta*. His work for the undergraduate paper was subsequently collected and published as *In A Canadian Canoe* (1891). This volume was followed up by other comic miscellanies: *Stories And Interludes* (1892); *Playthings And Parodies* (1893); *The Octave Of Claudius* (1897); *Wilmay* (1898). In 1890, Pain settled in London as a full-time writer and journalist. He succeeded the congenially humorous Jerome K. Jerome* as editor of *To-Day* in 1897. In 1900, he published *Eliza*, the first of a series of books supposedly written by a suburban clerk. (The *Eliza* books continued until 1913.) In the first years of the twentieth century Pain firmly established himself as the leading comic writer in England, writing among much else multitudinous facetious novelettes (i.e. *Proofs Before Pulping*, 1909, published in Mills and Boon's 'Laughter Library'). BL 57. *DNB*. RM.

A Pair Of Blue Eyes, Thomas Hardy, 1873, 3 vols, Tinsley. (Serialised in *Tinsley's Magazine**, September 1872–July 1873.) Hardy's first major success in fiction. A Wessex* tale, the setting is Endelstow in north Cornwall. A young architect, Stephen Fitzmaurice Smith, is commissioned to restore a church tower. (Hardy had strong objections to this kind of refurbishing.) Stephen has been helped in his career by Henry Knight, a well-bred and influential literary man. There is no hotel and the young architect lodges with a local vicar, the Rev. Swancourt. Stephen subsequently falls in love with Elfride Swancourt, the blue-eyed daughter of the Vicar. Stephen, whose father was a mason, has no hope of winning the Swancourts' favour. He and Elfride elope, but at the last minute her nerve fails. Stephen emigrates to India, to make his fortune. Elfride is subsequently wooed by Knight. (In an odd little subplot, he unknowingly reviews harshly a novel she has published.) In a dramatic scene, Elfride saves Knight's life on a cliffside by making a rope out of her petticoats. But Knight discovers her previous affair with Stephen. Disgusted, he breaks off the engagement. Stephen returns, and both men go down to Cornwall on the same train, only to find that Elfride's corpse has accompanied them in the baggage van.

PALGRAVE, Francis Turner ('Henry J. Thurstan', 1824–97). A son of Sir Francis Palgrave (1788–1861), a historian and converted Jew, F. T. Palgrave attended Charterhouse and Balliol College Oxford. Having taken a first-class degree in classics he became a private secretary to Gladstone (then Secretary of State for War and the Colonies). This led to a distinguished career as a Civil Servant and educationist. Palgrave's main claim to literary fame is as the anthologising editor of *The Golden Treasury Of Songs And Lyrics* (1861) and as the professor of poetry at Oxford (1885–95). Among much else, Palgrave wrote some incidental and idiosyncratic works of fiction under the pseudonym Henry J. Thurstan, including: *Preciosa* (1852), a journal novel which was more prosy than precious, the *Athenaeum** thought; *The Passionate Pilgrim* (1858), a series of poetic discourses, subtitled 'Eros And

Anteros' and carrying a heavily learned appendix on sources and allusions; *The Five Days' Entertainments At Wentworth Grange* (1868). BL 3. *DNB*. RM. *NCBEL*. Wol.

The Pall Mall Magazine (1893–1914). Founded with the American wealth of William Waldorf Astor and published by Routledge*, the *Pall Mall* was a monthly magazine, incorporating the popular fictional and pictorial styles of the 1890s. The magazine's policy was to steer a respectable middle course between the morbid excesses of the 1890s aesthetes and the crassness of the English philistine. Its first editors were Lord Frederick Hamilton and Sir Douglas Straight. The magazine carried articles of general and political interest, together with high-quality serial novels by, among others: Meredith*, Hardy*, Stevenson*, Hall Caine*, Kipling*, Doyle*, Zangwill*. The *Pall Mall* could not, however, compete with Newnes's* dynamic *Strand Magazine*, and by 1900 had become boringly middlebrow in tone. In 1914, it merged with *Nash's*. BLM.

The Palliser Novels. The collective title for Anthony Trollope's* linked sequence of political (or as he preferred to call them, 'parliamentary') novels. The recurrent (but not always central) character is Plantagenet Palliser, later Duke of Omnium and sometime Prime Minister of England. The Palliser novels comprise: *Can You Forgive Her?** (1865); *Phineas Finn** (1869); *The Eustace Diamonds** (1873); *Phineas Redux** (1874); *The Prime Minister** (1876); *The Duke's Children** (1880).

PANTON, Mrs J[ane] E[llen] (née Frith, 1848–1923). Born in London, she was a daughter of the famous Victorian painter, William Powell Frith. Jane Frith married James Panton in 1869. As Mrs J. E. Panton (and mother of five children) she was a journalist on household topics (1882–1900) and also wrote much fiction, most interestingly a group of late 1890s semi-fictional books with domestic themes and suburban settings: *Homes Of Taste* (1890); *Within Four Walls* (1893); *Suburban Residences* (1896); *Simple Homes* (1898); *A Dream House* (1898). Panton's fiction proper includes: *One Year In His Life* (1881); *Jane Caldecott* (1882), 'A Story Of Cross Purpose'; *The Curate's Wife* (1886); *Dear Life* (1886); *A Tangled Chain* (1887). The last is the story of a young woman whose life is warped by her tyrannous father. The narrative opens with his death, which may or may not be from natural causes. *Bypaths And Crossroads* (1889) is a collection of sketches. Panton also wrote books of sensible advice for young Victorian wives and was a Fellow of the Zoological Society. BL 12. *WW*. Wol.

PARDOE, Julia (1806–62). Born in Beverley, Yorkshire, the daughter of an army officer (a veteran of Waterloo) Julia Pardoe distinguished herself as a child author, having a volume of her poems published at fourteen. Suspected consumption led to her travelling extensively abroad during her adolescence, an unusual experience for a girl of the time and one which was to be her main qualification as a popular writer. In 1835, she travelled to Turkey with her father and familiarised herself sufficiently to write a standard guide to the country, *The City Of The Sultan* (1837). Pardoe never married, underwent a physical crisis brought on by overwork in 1842 and lived much of her life with her parents. She was an industrious writer, producing a creditable amount of competent travel books, history and fiction. Her first novel was *Lord Morcar Of Hereward* (4 vols, 1829). Her most successful effort in fiction was *Confessions Of A Pretty Woman* (1846), written for Colburn* (whose silver fork* style of novel suited her). Other works by Pardoe which fall into the Victorian period are: *The Jealous Wife* (1847); *The Rival Beauties* (1848); *Flies In Amber* (1850); *Reginald Lyle* (1854); *Lady Arabella* (1856); *The Poor Relation* (1858); *The Rich Relation* (1862). Pardoe became a figure of fun in her later years, and Elizabeth Barrett Browning mocked the ageing author's vanity about her youthful looks. She was given a Civil List pension of £100 two years before her death. BL 13. *DNB*. Wol. RLF.

The Parisians, E. G. E. L. Bulwer-Lytton, 1873, 4 vols, Blackwood. (Serialised in *Blackwood's Magazine**, October 1872–January 1874.) Bulwer-Lytton's last novel, left unrevised on his death in 1873. The work is also the author's most mature statement in fiction of his political sentiments. The setting is Napoleon III's Second Empire; the action moving from 1869 to the Franco-Prussian War of 1870. The main plot centres on Graham Vane, a young Englishman, who has been charged by a rich uncle, Richard King, to find a lost daughter, so as to pass on King's fortune. The search leads Graham to France where a second line of plot follows the career of a French nobleman, Alain de Rochebriant, struggling to sustain himself in the face of crippling debts. The novel is made into a vehicle for Bulwer-Lytton's scepticism about French political romanticism as propagated by writers like Victor Hugo.

PARKER, E[lizabeth] M[ary] (b. 1849?). Supposedly the only servant maid in the Victorian period to have written and published a novel for the circulating libraries. The one-volume *The Rose Of Avondale* (1872) was noticed by Arthur J. Munby, the eccentric man of letters, in the window of the Charing Cross bookseller, R. J. Bush. The publisher made a selling point of the fact that the author of the book was a servant girl. On inquiry, Munby discovered that Parker was in service at St James's Place. Munby (who had a sexual fetish for servant girls) found Parker 'as nice and modest a woman of twenty three or so as you need wish to see; just like any other servant in manner, only very quiet'. Parker, he discovered, was born in Buckinghamshire, where her father kept an inn. Nothing more is known of her. (See *Munby, Man Of Two Worlds*, ed. D. Hudson, 1972.) In reviewing the work, the *Athenaeum** could observe no 'signs of genius' but thought the tone commendably 'refined'. BL 1. Wol.

PARKER, Eric [Frederick Moore Searle] (1870–1955). Parker was born in East Barnet, the eldest son of a solicitor and educated at Eton and Merton College, Oxford where he took a second-class degree in classics. After some schoolmastering he took up work as a journalist at the age of thirty, writing for the *St James's Gazette* and the *Spectator*. Over the years he came to specialise in pieces for sporting periodicals, notably the *Gamekeeper* and the *Field*. Within the Victorian period, he also put out a novel *The Sinner And The Problem* (1901), a domestic story tinged with kailyard* sentimentality which follows the tribulations of two schoolboys. The work was popular and was twice reprinted in its first three months of publication. In the twentieth century Parker wrote numerous books on cricket, wildlife, gardening and his

English public school. He published another novel of childhood experience in 1912, *The Promise Of Arden*. BL 2. *WW.*

PARKER, Sir [Horatio] Gilbert [George] (1862–1932). Parker was born in Ontario, Canada, where his father had been a militia officer. He went into schoolteaching at the age of seventeen, intending eventually to take holy orders. But instead he went to Australia in 1885 and joined the staff of the *Sydney Herald*. Parker travelled on to England in 1889. His first published volume of fiction, *Pierre And His People* (1892), contains epic tales of the Canadian North-west. Critics have found it excessively sentimental and inaccurate as to local detail, but the work was successful. Parker followed it with *Mrs Falchion* (1893), a study of cold female egotism, and a series of Canadian epic tales, including: *The Trail Of The Sword* (1894); *When Valmond Came To Pontiac* (1895), a melodrama of French Canada featuring a (fictional) son of Napoleon; *An Adventurer Of The North* (1895), which continues the saga of Pierre and his people; *The Seats Of The Mighty* (1896). The *Athenaeum** summed up Parker's achievement as a national chronicler as 'meritorious rather than engrossing'. *The Battle Of The Strong* (1898) deals with the Channel island of Jersey during the period of the French Revolution. The *DNB*, in a hostile assessment of Parker, describes his prose style as turgid and his imperialist prejudices as obnoxious. Parker was a Conservative MP for Gravesend (1900–18) and was knighted for his services to England in 1902 and created a baronet in 1915. BL 38. *DNB.* RM. Wol.

J. W. Parker (1832–63). Publishers. The firm was founded by John William Parker (1792–1870). At fourteen, Parker was apprenticed to the printer Clowes. Clowes had close professional connections with Cambridge University Press, which Parker inherited when he went into business himself in 1832 in the Strand. Initially, Parker specialised in religious items, and was an agent for the Christian Knowledge Society. In 1836, he was appointed printer to Cambridge University and maintained the relationship until 1854. From 1847, J. W. Parker were proprietors of *Fraser's Magazine** and in this capacity they acquired rights to the fiction of leading members of the muscular* school of novelists, notably Charles Kingsley*, whose early work they published. In 1863 the firm was acquired by Longman*. (JWP)*DNB.*

PARKER, Joseph (1830–1902). Parker was born in Hexham, the only son of a stonemason and Congregationalist deacon. He was a bright child and rose above his station in life (his father originally intended he too should be a stonemason) to become a schoolteacher and eventually a minister. As a Congregational preacher, Parker had no equal. In 1858, he took over the Cavendish Chapel in Manchester. He moved from this post to a central London ministry in 1869. Parker went on to become influential in Congregational Church politics, and as an ambassador for his denomination made frequent visits to the USA. He wrote a variety of works, including the novels: *Springdale Abbey* (1868), 'Extracts From The Diaries And Letters Of An English Preacher'; *Weaver Stephen* (1886); *Tyne Chylde* (1889), an autobiographical story; *Paterson's Parish* (1898). BL 24. *DNB.*

PARR, Harriet ('Holme Lee', 1828–1900). Parr was born in York where her father was a traveller in silks, satins and other fine textile products. In 1854, she published her first novel, *Maud Talbot*, a story of mill life, with forgery, murder and social problems* to beguile the reader. The novel was well reviewed. Her second, *Gilbert Massinger* (1855), a regional* story of fatal family pride, was sent to Charles Dickens*, who thought well of it. A third work, *Thorney Hall* (1855), followed promptly. From 1854 to 1882, Parr turned out some thirty novels under the pen name Holme Lee. They include: *Against Wind And Tide* (1859); *Annis Warleigh's Fortunes* (1863); *Her Title Of Honour* (1871); *Straight Forward* (1878); *A Poor Squire* (1882). Lee was a favourite novelist of Mudie*, the circulating library owner, to whose sense of decency her fiction strictly conformed with its depictions of shy maidens and their decent love problems. Her most ambitious work was the life of Joan of Arc which came out in 1866 under her own name. Parr died at Shanklin on the Isle of Wight, where she had been living for some years, never having married. BL 21. *DNB. NCBEL.* Wol. RLF.

PARR, Mrs [Louisa] ('Mrs Olinthus Lobb', née Taylor, 1848?–1903). The only child of a naval officer, she spent her early years in Plymouth. In 1868, she published a story, 'How It All Happened', in the evangelical magazine *Good Words** under the pseudonym 'Mrs Olinthus Lobb'. The work was well received, and gave her a flying start as an author. In 1869, she married a doctor and London historian, George Parr, and settled in Kensington. In 1870, she brought out *Dorothy Fox*, a novel of Quaker life, which was successful, particularly in America. In 1880, she published what is generally thought her best novel, *Adam And Eve*, a story of Cornish smuggling life, Adam being the smuggler and Eve his London cousin. Parr often returned in her fiction to the nautical* scenes and themes associated with her childhood. She wrote nine novels in all, including: *The Prescotts* (1874); *The Gosau Smithy* (1875); *Robin* (1882); *Loyalty George* (1888), a story of fishing life around Plymouth; *Dumps* (1891); *The Squire* (1892); *Can This Be Love?* (1893), the story of the trials of a young woman with a snobbish lover and vulgar relatives. Parr wrote a short life of her fellow novelist Dinah Mulock Craik* in 1897. BL 9. *DNB.* Wol.

PASTON, George (i.e. Miss E[mily] M[orse] Symonds, d. 1936). Very little is known of her life. She was a cousin of John Addington Symonds, and apparently never married. Under her invariable male pseudonym, Miss Symonds wrote plays, popular eighteenth-century history and novels which frequently portray new woman* heroines and dilemmas. In *A Modern Amazon* (1894), Regina Haughton, a high-spirited beauty marries Humphrey Kenyon MD on the understanding that the union will remain unconsummated. Her other fiction includes: *A Bread And Butter Miss* (1894), the story of an ingenuous seventeen-year-old, suddenly immersed in sophisticated society; *A Study In Prejudice* (1895); *A Fair Deceiver* (1897), the story of a girl who steals her sister's fiancé; *A Writer Of Books* (1898), the writer being a separated wife. BL 7. *WW.* Wol.

PATER, Walter [Horatio] (1839–94). Walter Pater was born in Shadwell, the son of a doctor who died when his son was five years old. Mrs Pater moved with her four children to Enfield, on the northern outskirts of London. In 1853, they moved again to Kent and Walter entered the King's School. A year later his mother died, and the surviving family was taken charge of by an aunt. As a schoolboy, Pater was miserable. Physically misshapen, he took no pleasure in sports. But he was clever and in 1858 won a scholarship to Oxford, the city that was to be his home until he died. At the university he read classics and on his own account absorbed much contemporary German philosophy. In 1862, he took a second-class degree and two years later was elected to a fellowship at Brasenose College. His desire to be a candidate for ordination in the Church of England was apparently blocked by the authorities. Throughout the 1860s, Pater evolved his aesthetic theories. These were sharpened by his first visit to Italy in 1865. *Studies In The History Of The Renaissance* (1873) with its famous injunction to Oxford's young men to burn with a 'hard gemlike flame' enjoyed a success of scandal and esteem. Pater's next major work was the philosophical romance, *Marius The Epicurean* (1885). Pater intended this work to be the first part of a trilogy. The unfinished *Gaston De Latour* (partly published in *Macmillan's Magazine**, 1888) comprised a sequel set in sixteenth-century France. What the last part of the trilogy was to be is not clear. The aim of the 'triplet' (as Pater called it) was to reconcile the problems of religious belief, secular philosophy and the claims of the beautiful. In the larger sense, this was the endeavour of Pater's whole life. After 1885, he spent a greater amount of his time at his sisters' house in London (while retaining his Oxford post). He was a dominant influence on the emergence of aestheticism in the 1890s, although his personal attitude to frankly deviant figures like Wilde* was ambivalent. Pater himself never married, and may have been homosexual. He remained, however, a cautiously establishment and time-serving figure inspiring as well as the decadents* of the 1890s such pillars of Victorian society as Mrs Humphry Ward*. In 1893, Pater's *Plato And Platonism* was published. He died the following year of a weakened heart. BL 2. *DNB*. RM. *NCBEL*.

PATERSON, Arthur [Henry] (1862–1928). Paterson was born in Bowdon, Cheshire, the son of a doctor. He was educated at University College School, London, after which he set off to wander the world. He was subsequently a sheep rancher in New Mexico, 1877–79, and a farmer in west Kansas, 1879–80. Paterson returned to Liverpool, to work in business, 1881–84. The novels which he wrote in later life divide into cowboy and historical romances. They include: *The Better Man* (1890); *A Partner From The West* (1892); *A Man Of His Word* (1894); *A Son Of The Plains* (1895). The last follows the adventurous career of Nat, brought up by the Comanches after being caught on the Santa Fe trail. Paterson was very interested in social work and wrote a novel about it, *John Glynn* (1907). BL 17. *WW*. Wol.

PATERSON, William Romaine ('Benjamin Swift', 1871–1935?). Paterson was born in Glasgow, the son of a doctor. He was educated at Lausanne and at Glasgow University, where he took a first-class degree in philosophy. After graduation, Paterson toured Europe, with the aim of acquiring foreign languages. On his return, he based himself in Edinburgh and took up writing for a living. Paterson's fiction, as Benjamin Swift, includes: *Nancy Noon* (1896); *The Tormentor* (1897); *The Destroyer* (1898), dedicated humbly to Maeterlinck on the strength of its 'Northern Chapters', set in Russia; *Siren City* (1899); *Dartnell* (1899), a story of adultery in high places; *Nude Souls* (1900). The last is a fashionably 1890s hotchpotch of sexual victimisation, diabolism and German metaphysics with an Aleister Crowley-style first chapter warning the unwary reader 'against the true nature of the book'. In his own name, Paterson wrote books on theology and philosophy, such as: *Problems Of Destiny* (1935), apparently his last publication. BL 15. *WW*.

PATMORE, P[eter] G[eorge] (1786–1855). Father of the noted Victorian poet, Coventry, Patmore was born in London, himself the son of a jeweller. He was the friend of leading men of letters of the early century, and edited the *New Monthly Magazine** from 1841 to 1853. His best-known book is the mildly indiscreet memoir, *My Friends And Acquaintances* (1854). Patmore wrote a couple of fashionable novels, *Chatsworth, Or The Romance Of A Week* (1844) and *Marriage In Mayfair* (1854). The works introduced literary notables in fictional disguise. He died at Hampstead. BL 2. *DNB*. *NCBEL*. Wol.

Paul Ferroll, Mrs Archer Clive, 1855, 1 vol, Saunders and Otley. A highly unusual Victorian novel. The hero is conventionally heroic; rich, handsome, masterful, cultured and a benevolent lord of the manor. The opening section of the novel portrays Ferroll as the squire of Mainwarey going about his daily business. His wife is found murdered in her bed, the assailant unknown. Some years after, enriched by his first wife's death, Ferroll remarries and has a daughter, Janet. Gradually, over the next eighteen years, from evidence accumulated by Janet's lover, Hugh Bartlett, it emerges that Paul murdered his first wife. A harridan, she tricked him into marrying her. So he killed her. To save an old servant from prosecution, he confesses his crime publicly. Extraordinarily, the novelist does not seem to criticise Paul for this divorce Victorian-style. She is as tolerant of his putting down a workers' riot by summary execution of the ringleaders. Was Clive advocating murder as one of the rights of man, the *Athenaeum** wondered? At the end of the novel, Ferroll is condemned to death and his wife dies of shock. Janet and Hugh conspire to spring the hero from prison on the eve of execution and he escapes into exile, attended by his ever-devoted daughter. The novel's last words are his question 'Can you still love me, Janet?' and her passionate reply: 'Love you? Oh, yes – my father!'. In a fourth edition, Clive added a rather more moralistic conclusion. A sequel, *Why Paul Ferroll Killed His Wife* (1860), extenuates still further and is correspondingly weaker.

PAYN, James (1830–98). Payn was born in Cheltenham. His father was clerk to the Thames Commissioners and passed on to his son (before dying early) a love of the countryside. As a family, the Payns were friendly with Miss Mitford* and Harriet Martineau*. Payn went to school at Eton, where he was unhappy and is recorded as having been a poor classics scholar. His health was too delicate for the army, and it was decided that he should enter the Church. He was accordingly put under a tutor in Devonshire to study for his university entrance. While undergoing this year's tuition, Payn sent an article to *Household Words**, and received an encouraging reply (and publication) from Dickens* himself. At Cambridge, Payn did brilliantly; he was President of the Union, published two volumes of verse, and took a first-class degree. He was, as Mary Mitford put it, 'splendidly handsome'. On graduation, Payn determined on a literary career. He contributed regularly to *Household Words* and to *Chambers's Edinburgh Journal**. From 1857 to 1861, he was co-editor in Edinburgh of the second of these journals, together with the veteran hack Leitch Ritchie*, who soon retired. But from 1861 until the end of his life, London was to be Payn's literary base and he came to exercise formidable power as a literary broker and patron. As a commentator on the metropolitan scene, he wrote a regular column for the *Illustrated London News**. In 1874, having fallen out with William Chambers, Payn resigned his editorship and became a reader for the publishing house of Smith, Elder*. From 1883 to 1896, he was editor of the *Cornhill Magazine**. Payn published his first novel, *The Foster Brothers* in 1859. (The narrative is loosely based on his college experiences.) His first major success in fiction was with *Lost Sir Massingberd** (1864). As a serial in *Chambers's Edinburgh Journal*, it is supposed to have raised circulation by 20,000. The story of a wicked baronet who disappears, the novel is an early example of the detective* genre. According to Payn himself, *By Proxy** (1878) was his bestselling work and is one of the few novels of the period to use China as a location. Payn contracted what was (by some accounts) a happy marriage with Louisa Edlin in 1854 and settled in the Lake District. But in 1861, he moved his family to Maida Vale. In London he was evidently a much-liked figure in the club world and played his rubber of whist every day. Around 1880 he seems to have separated from his family, living at his office. His other fiction includes: *Married Beneath Him* (1865); *Blundel Parva* (1868), the story of a ruined man who fakes his disappearance; *Bentinck's Tutor* (1868), a sensation* novel, in which a young heir disappears; *Not Wooed But Won* (1871); *Fallen Fortunes* (1876); *Less Black Than We're Painted* (1878), a novel about theatre people; *The Canon's Ward* (1884); *The Talk Of The Town* (1885), based on the Shakespeare forgeries of the eighteenth century; *The Heir Of The Ages* (1886), the story of a governess who writes a novel and becomes the toast of literary London; *The Disappearance Of George Driffell* (1896), a mystery, dedicated to Conan Doyle*. In general, Payn's fiction is marked by a love of sensational plot and excessively melodramatic complication. In later life he was crippled by gout, and he died at Maida Vale. BL 61. *DNB*. RM. *NCBEL*. Wol. Sad.

PEACOCK, Captain Ferdinand Mansel (1861–1908). Peacock was born in Wiltshire, the son of a clergyman. He was educated at Marlborough School and at Sandhurst Military Academy. Peacock was subsequently commissioned into the Somerset Light Infantry in 1882, and served in India from 1883 onwards. Peacock was wounded in the Burma Campaign, 1885–87, and decorated for gallantry. He later saw action in South Africa, 1899–1900, winning the Queen's Medal and five clasps. Having married in 1899 he retired with the rank of major in 1904 and lived his remaining years in Ulster. Alongside an eventful military career, Peacock wrote military novels, including: *A Change Of Weapons* (1895); *A Soldier And A Maid* (1890), 'a romance of the late war in Burma'; *A Curled Darling* (1896). BL 9.

PEARCE, J[oseph] H[enry] (1856–1909?). Pearce wrote novels set in rural Cornwall. They tend towards Hardyan* melancholy rather than idyll, concentrating on 'the seamy side of peasant life'. His titles include: *Esther Pentreath* (1891), a romance of tin mining in the early nineteenth century; *Inconsequent Lives* (1891), tales of Cornish fisherfolk; *Drolls From Shadowland* (1893); *Jaco Treloar* (1893), a melodrama of love and jealousy involving a peasant husband and his wife's curate lover, a 'squalid little tragedy' as the *Athenaeum** called it; *Eli's Daughter* (1896); *Ezekiel's Sin* (1898), the story of a fisherman who steals gold from a corpse with tragic consequences. BL 9. Wol.

PEARD, Frances Mary (1835–1923). The daughter of a naval captain, Peard was born at Exminster, Devon. In later life she lived at Torquay, never apparently marrying. Her family boasted a number of distinguished soldiers and sailors in its history and this tradition evidently had its effect on the young woman who often introduces war into the background of her later fiction. Peard wrote books for both adults and juveniles, specialising in French settings. Her novels include: *The Rose Garden* (1872); *The White Month* (1880), a romance set in Brittany, during the Franco-German war; *Jeannette* (1883), a story of the Huguenots; *His Cousin Betty* (1888), a Devonshire love story; *Catherine* (1893), a love story, set during the Napoleonic Wars; *An Interloper* (1894), a love story set in France; *Donna Teresa* (1899), a story of innocent matchmaking set in Rome and Sicily. The *Athenaeum** noted: 'Miss Peard is one of the few modern authors who can, without being dull, write for the young girl and for those readers who shrink from too violent an appeal to the imagination.' BL 40. *WW*. Wol.

PEARSE, the Rev. Mark Guy (1842–1930). Pearse was born at Camborne, Cornwall, the son of an evangelist of the same name. He went to school locally and later attended the Wesleyan College at Sheffield. He entered the Methodist ministry in 1863. Thereafter he lived and worked in Leeds, Brixton and Ipswich. From 1890 to 1900, he was minister at the West London Mission. Alongside his religious duties Pearse wrote improving fiction, much of it in tract form, for the juvenile reader. It includes: *Daniel Quorm, And His Religious Notions* (1875–80); *Mister Horn And His Friends* (1872); *Good Will* (1878), a collection of Christmas* stories; *Simon Jaspar* (1883); *Cornish Stories* (1884); *Rob Rat, A Story Of Barge Life* (1888); *The Story Of A Roman Soldier* (1899). BL 24. *WW*.

Pearson's Magazine (1896–1939). One of the *Strand** inspired periodicals of the 1890s. *Pearson's* was named after its publisher, Pearson (principally a newspaper and magazine firm), and was edited by C. Arthur Pearson. Heavily illustrated, the magazine was directed at a middle to lower-class 'home readership'. Among the miscellaneous contents were short stories and serial novels by, among others: Max Pemberton*, Rafael Sabatini, and Rudyard Kipling* (whose school story *Stalky And Co*. ran in the magazine). *BLM*.

Peg Woffington, Charles Reade, 1853, 1 vol, Bentley. Reade's first published novel. It was adapted from his stage hit *Masks And Faces* (1852) and dedicated to his 'coadjutor' on that work, Tom Taylor. The 'dramatic story' centres on the (historically actual) eighteenth-century actress of the title. Witty, immoral and beautiful, Peg catches the heart of a Shropshire gentleman, Ernest Vane. She becomes his mistress; at which point Vane's virtuous wife, Mabel, comes to town. In a famous scene, Peg masquerades within a portrait frame, overhears Mabel's pious prayers and the rivals confront each other. Mabel urges Peg to give up her husband. Moved by the other's goodness, Peg does so, proving herself 'something more than a picture or an actress'. In a coda to the main narrative, we follow Peg through various successes on and off the boards to an eventual moral conversion before she dies, prematurely. The novel which introduces a cast of actual historical personages (such as Colley Cibber) was popular. But so slender was Reade's payment that he took his publisher Bentley to court.

PEMBERTON, [Sir] Max (1863–1950). Pemberton was born in Birmingham, where his father, Thomas Joshua Pemberton, had a brass foundry business. Max was educated at Merchant Taylors' School, and at Caius College, Cambridge. He graduated and married in 1884 a daughter of the Tussaud family. His first novel, *The Diary Of A Scoundrel*, was published in 1891. Pemberton was editor of the boys' paper *Chums**, 1892–93, and of *Cassell's Magazine*, 1896–1906. He was later a director of Northcliffe Newspapers Ltd. As a novelist, Pemberton specialised in Jules Verne-like stories of imaginative adventure which sold vastly well. His novels include: *The Iron Pirate* (1893), a saga of ironclad buccaneers; *Jewel Mysteries I Have Known* (1894), stories 'from a dealer's notebook'; *The Impregnable City* (1895), a fantasy about a fortified citadel in the Pacific which repulses both the French and Russian fleets; *The Little Huguenot* (1895); *A Puritan's Wife* (1896); *A Gentleman's Gentleman* (1896); *Christine Of The Hill* (1897); *Queen Of The Jesters* (1897); *The Phantom Army* (1898), the story of a band of European outlaws; *The Garden Of Swords* (1899), a tale of the Franco-Prussian War; *Signors Of The Night* (1899), a story of early eighteenth-century Venice. Pemberton wrote plays, was one of the first automobile owners in Britain, founded the London School of Journalism in 1920 and was knighted in 1928. BL 62. *WW*. Wol.

PEMBERTON, T[homas] Edgar (1849–1905). Brother of the above, he went to school in Birmingham, and at the age of nineteen entered the family brass foundry firm, marrying soon after in 1873. He remained working at Pemberton's until 1900, living all his life at Birmingham where he was dramatic critic for the *Daily Post*. He himself wrote plays and was an acquaintance of the American author Bret Harte about whom he wrote a life and several books. Pemberton wrote some well-regarded non-fiction (e.g., a book on Dickens's* London, 1875). His novels include: *Charles Lysaght* (1873); *Under Pressure* (1874); *A Very Old Question* (1877), a melodrama of London business life; *Born To Blush Unseen* (1879). BL 4. *WW*. Wol.

Pendennis, W. M. Thackeray, 1850, 2 vols, Bradbury and Evans. (Serialised in monthly parts November 1848–December 1850, with illustrations by the author. Full title, *The History Of Pendennis. His Fortunes and Misfortunes. His Friends, And His Greatest Enemy*.) Thackeray's autobiographical masterpiece. Arthur Pendennis (Pen) is the son of a snobbish Devonshire apothecary who has prospered in his business. Pen, as the only child, is spoiled, particularly by his indulgent mother Helen. When Pen is sixteen, John Pendennis dies and the hero returns as master to the family home Fairoaks where he falls in love with the tawdry star of a visiting dramatic company, Emily Costigan ('Miss Fotheringay'). She is older than Pen, Irish and in every way unsuitable. As is her habit, Helen Pendennis appeals for help to her worldly brother-in-law, Major Pendennis. The major ingeniously frustrates the rash engagement Arthur has made. The next episode takes Pen to Oxbridge, where he lives the life of a fashionable undergraduate. He duly fails his finals and runs horribly into debt. The Pendennises are saved by the assistance of Laura Bell, an orphan whom Helen has adopted. Pen spends some idle months at Fairoaks, during which time he has a flirtation with Blanche Amory, a young lady attached (in no very clear way) to the neighbouring household of Sir Francis Clavering. At his mother's prompting, he proposes to Laura. But she will not have the immature young man, although she secretly loves him. Pen eventually gains a respectable degree and enrols as a lawyer in London. He shares chambers with George Warrington (a distant descendant of Henry Esmond*). Warrington is the epitome of manliness, but has a secret in his past which prevents him from ever being more than a bohemian journalist. (His secret is eventually revealed to be a wretched marriage.) Pen drifts into journalism, and writes for the newly founded *Pall Mall Gazette* (whose imprisoned editor, Captain Shandon, is based on Thackeray's early mentor, William Maginn*). He goes on to write a bestselling novel, *Walter Lorraine.* In London high society, he renews his relationship with Blanche. An inveterate coquette, she also captivates the heart of Pen's ingenuous but wealthy friend, Harry Foker. More dangerously, Pen becomes sexually attracted to Fanny Bolton, the daughter of his housekeeper. Pendennis falls dangerously ill (as did Thackeray during the course of the novel). He is nursed by Fanny, who is brutally repulsed by a righteous Mrs Pendennis when she arrives in London. On his recovery, the Pendennises and Warrington go on the Continent to aid his recovery. On their travels, Pen discovers that Helen has held back from him letters from Fanny. Mother and son are hopelessly estranged and only reconciled by Warrington who confides details of his own disastrous marriage to justify Helen's conduct. She dies, at peace with her son. On his return to England Pen comes more and more under the influence of his worldly uncle who has parliamentary ambitions for his nephew. Major Pendennis perceives that Blanche Amory has some hold over the Claverings and urges Pen to marry the girl. Pen, now thoroughly cynical, proposes. In a complicated unravelling, it emerges that the Clavering fortune depends on what may be a bigamous marriage. But finally Pen marries the virtuous and infinitely patient Laura. The early rural chapters of the novel and Pen's experiences as a tyro man of letters are as fine as anything Thackeray wrote in fiction.

Penny Dreadfuls. The term penny dreadful (or 'bloods') came into general use in the 1840s. The term was originally applied to the gothic* tales, in eight-page, double-column instalments, luridly illustrated with woodcuts, for the working-class reader, mass produced by publishers like Edward Lloyd*. The most famous were probably *Varney The Vampire** (1845–47), *The String Of Pearls* (1846), the tale of Sweeney Todd, and the various adventures of Springheeled Jack. But in addition to these original works there were also crude plagiarisms of middle-class favourites like Dickens*, Ainsworth* and G. P. R. James*. The best known practitioners in the style were Thomas Frost*, T. P. Prest*, Percy B. St John*, John Malcolm Rymer ('Errym*'), G. W. M. Reynolds*, Pierce Egan Jr* and James Lindridge (1820–91). In the last quarter of the century, however, penny dreadfuls came to refer more exclusively to tales for the young reader, many more of whom were literate after the 1870 Education Act. As the popular educator Charles Knight put it: 'the penny magazine produced a revolution in popular art throughout the world.' This later generation of 'dreadfuls' was less dreadful and stressed adventure rather than gore. Frequently they featured a boy who ran away to find his fortunes abroad, or in a life of glamorised crime. This fiction had a long pedigree, going back to chronicles and registers of 'dreadful' crime and horrors. A natural link was forged in the penny dreadfuls to folk heroes and demons like Robin Hood, Dick Turpin and Sawney Beane, the Scottish cannibal. Publishers specialising in penny dreadfuls for Victorian boys were Charles Perry Brown of the Aldine Publishing Company*; Samuel Dacre Clark ('Guy Raynor'); Charles Fox of the Hogarth House Publishing Company; John W. Allingham ('Ralph Rollington' and publisher of the *Boy's World*); Edwin J. Brett* (publisher of *Our Boys' Paper*); George Vickers, the London newsagent who was also associated with the founding of the *Illustrated London News** in 1842. In the late 1880s, the depraved quality of juvenile reading matter sparked off a middle-class moral panic. Protest was articulated most forcefully by Edward Salmon, in various articles in the *Fortnightly Review** and *Nineteenth Century*. *Punch** joined the crusade to purify boys' adventure literature. Numerous cases were cited of children seduced into crime by unwholesome fiction. The campaign lent strong support to the *Boy's Own Paper**, founded in 1879 by the RTS*.

A Perilous Secret, Charles Reade, 1885, 2 vols, Bentley. (Serialised in *Temple Bar**, September 1884–May 1885.) Published in the year of Reade's death, the novel is the work of an exhausted mind. To the end, Reade retained his love of excessively theatrical plot. The central character is an inventor, William Hope. Hope's little daughter, Grace, is made to substitute for a dead heiress, whose fortune would otherwise leave the family with her death. In subsequent twists of plot, villains are confounded, matches made, providential rewards and punishments contrived. The strongest scene (possibly borrowed from Zola's *Germinal*) has Hope and his daughter trapped in a flooding mine with one of the villains of the piece. Hope is the last in Reade's long line of supremely resourceful and inventive heroes.

Perlycross, R. D. Blackmore, 1894, 3 vols, Sampson Low. (Serialised in *Macmillan's Magazine**, June 1893–July 1894.) Blackmore's most satisfying re-creation of village life. The novel (written at the end of the author's life) recalls his earliest experiences when his father took up the post of curate at Culmstock in Devon, in 1835. (Blackmore portrays his father in the story as the widowed Parson Penniloe.) The action is minor. After the death of Sir Thomas Waldron the village blacksmith, Joe Crang, claims to have seen a grave-robbing. A superficial examination of the grave excites the whole village into a hysterical search for the supposed resurrection men. Among others, suspicion falls on Dr Fox. He wants to marry the new squire's sister, and sets his own ruse to discover the villain. The novel climaxes (very effectively) at Perlycross Fair, with a general brawl and a terrific storm. The missing corpse is discovered, and all is made well.

The Perpetual Curate, Margaret Oliphant, 1864, 3 vols, Blackwood. The fourth of the 'Chronicles Of Carlingford*' and Oliphant's most explicit treatment of the Oxford Movement in fiction. The curate hero is Frank Wentworth, a personable young man inclined, however, towards Rome.

He officiates in the chapel of St Roque. But he has also helped found a sisterhood (a High Anglican practice) and preaches to Carlingford's poor in another chapel in the slums. Frank's Romanism terrifies the evangelical womenfolk of his family. There are other vexations. Frank's half-brother Gerald (who has a wife and five children) is determined to resign his comfortable living and become a Catholic priest. The novel has a happy ending. Gerald converts, but as a layman, Frank inherits the rectorship at Carlingford. Mrs Oliphant had her highest payment ever from John Blackwood for this work, £1,500.

PERRIN, A[lice] (née Robinson, 1867–1934). The daughter of an Indian army general (and the sister of a baronet, Sir Charles Robinson), Alice Robinson was educated in England. In 1886, she married Charles Perrin, an engineer in the Indian Public Works Department. The couple thereafter lived in India for many years and the sub-continent forms the normal setting of her novels. They include: *Into Temptation* (1894), her first novel, the story of a girl in India who marries an older man and takes a young lover; *Late In Life* (1896), an Anglo-Indian story of two sisters; *East Of Suez*, (1901); *The Spell Of The Jungle* (1902). The Perrins evidently returned to England around 1900. In later life, and presumably widowed, she lived in Switzerland. BL 23. *WW*. Wol.

Peter Ibbetson, George Du Maurier, 1891, 2 vols, Osgood, McIlvaine. (Serialised in *Harper's Monthly*, June–December 1891, with illustrations by the author.) Du Maurier's remarkable first novel, published 'in the afternoon of his existence' aged fifty-five. The story is the prison confession of Gogo Pasquier, later called Peter Ibbetson. The early sections of the narrative cover Pasquier's idyllic childhood in Passy. The son of an English mother and a French father, Pasquier is orphaned and taken in charge by a relative, Colonel Ibbetson. He has the boy (now renamed) brought up an English gentleman. Peter qualifies as an architect and while carrying out a commission for an aristocratic client falls in love with the Duchess of Towers. (She turns out to be a childhood sweetheart from Passy days, now grown up.) The Duchess introduces Peter to the practice of 'dreaming true' by which the past may be revisited in their dreams. Peter, meanwhile, falls out with his guardian and during a violent argument kills him. He is condemned to die, but the sentence is later reduced to life imprisonment. Confined to a cell in an asylum for the criminally insane, Ibbetson and the Duchess live a wonderfully full night-life, travelling back as far as the world of their own grandparents. After twenty-five years, the Duchess dies. But she returns in a vision to Peter, promising an even richer life after death. The novel was a bestseller.

Peter Simple, Captain Marryat, 1834, 3 vols, Saunders and Otley. (Serialised in the *Metropolitan Magazine**, June 1832–December 1833.) The best of Marryat's nautical* tales for adults. *Peter Simple* is written in autobiographical form and the hero is as ingenuous as the title implies. But unlike most of Marryat's heroes he is neither an orphan nor a foundling. Peter is sent from a respectable background to sea as 'the fool of the family' and fit for nothing better. While a greenhorn midshipman he has a number of comic scrapes, all of which revolve around his simplicity (e.g. 'As I had never heard of a gun having breeches before, I was very curious'). By chapter twelve, Marryat gets his hero to sea. The novel's subsequent action is set in the 'Great' (i.e. Napoleonic) war in the blockade years after Trafalgar and before Waterloo. Simple and his Irish comrade O'Brien (based on a real-life figure) are captured and imprisoned in France. They escape, Simple disguised as a girl. On their return to England, the patronage of Simple's aristocratic grandfather secures them berths on a crack frigate. Thereafter their careers run parallel. We follow, in all, fifteen years of the sailors' service, as they climb the ranks. In the second volume, Simple matures into a brave and knowledgeable seaman. The last volume is packed with episode. Simple is conspired against by a malicious captain and villainous uncle. He survives an undeserved court martial, foils his family rival (who at one point has Simple confined in Bedlam) and concludes the novel happily married and Viscount Privilege. Notable characters in the narrative include the snobbish boatswain, Mr Chucks.

Peter The Whaler, W. H. G. Kingston, 1851, 1 vol, Grant and Griffith. Kingston's first and prototypical adventure story for Victorian boys. The hero, Peter Lefroy, is a scapegrace son of a vicar in the south of Ireland, sent to sea for poaching. Peter's first voyage on the *Black Swan* exposes him to the worst of life at sea. A brutal captain falsely accuses him of mutiny and binds the young boy to the vessel's bowsprit. Meanwhile, the ship's cargo of coal catches on fire, and the hero is saved from death by a friendly old sailor, Silas Flint. After various adventures, Peter eventually reaches New Orleans. In America he becomes involved with pirates, joins the US navy, is shipwrecked on an iceberg (the most gripping episode in the narrative) and after his rescue joins a whaler, the *Shetland*. Over the course of his eventful adolescence, Peter learns the lessons of manly Christian conduct. At the end of the novel, the hero is shipwrecked yet again, this time on his home Irish shore to be welcomed as a returned prodigal. The novel is told autobiographically, with great energy. Kingston followed it with *Mark Seaworth* (1852) and innumerable other tales of far-flung adventure and moral improvement in exotic places.

Phantastes, George MacDonald, 1858, 1 vol, Smith, Elder. 'A Faerie Romance'. The narrator, 'Anodos', is just twenty-one and his father has given him the keys to an old secretary (or writing desk). As he sits in the study, the young man sees emerging from the piece of furniture a small and perfectly formed lady, apparently Greek. She informs him that he has fairy blood in his viens and leads him into Fairy Land. There follows a long, highly symbolic progress. The hero first finds himself in a forest, in which the trees are all animated (the ash is particularly malevolent, the beech good-hearted). For part of his passage through Fairy Land, the hero is accompanied by a mysterious shadow. And he precipitates a crisis by seizing his ideal 'White Lady' (transmuted, temporarily, into a statue). Later, he is dubbed a knight, and is killed in battle with a strange monster. His body is cherished by his lady and another knight. At this point, he is returned to reality and his earthly body. MacDonald's fantasy evidently allegorises the transition from boy's to the man's more hazardous world.

Philip, W. M. Thackeray, 1862, 3 vols, Smith, Elder. (Serialised in *Cornhill Magazine**, January 1861–August 1862, with illustrations by the author and Frederick Walker*. The full title is: *The Adventures Of Philip On His Way Through The World, Showing Who Robbed Him, Who Helped Him, And Who Passed Him By.*) Thackeray's last complete novel, containing much autobiographical recollection of his apprenticeship as a writer. Arthur Pendennis* figures as a narrator, with his moralistic wife Laura intruding as a choric figure. The prelude to the action is the unfinished story, *A Shabby Genteel Story* (1840). In that narrative, a young working-class girl was seduced by means of a fake marriage. The seducer was Philip's father, George Firmin, now a prosperous doctor. Philip's dead mother has left her son a fortune. While ill at school, Philip is nursed by the 'Little Sister', Mrs Brandon, who is revealed to be the woman Dr Firmin earlier betrayed. But for love of Philip (her own child having died) she takes no legal action. It is intended that Philip shall marry a cousin, Agnes Twysden. But Agnes's family break the match off so as to marry her to a rich mulatto, Captain Woolcomb. Meanwhile, Philip's fortunes have sunk. The trustee of his inheritance, General Baynes, has allowed Dr Firmin to speculate the money away. And Philip's father is meanwhile blackmailed by the clergyman who originally performed the marriage ceremony with the Little Sister. Firmin absconds to America, although he continues to vex his son with demands for money. Philip is obliged to make his own way in the world and enters journalism. On a visit to France, he falls in love with General Baynes's daughter, Charlotte. After some difficulty (largely caused by the shrewish Mrs Baynes) the couple become engaged. But the match offends Philip's rich relative, Lord Ringwood, who cuts the young man out of his will. Philip has a hard time as a man of letters. His mother-in-law is intolerable; his father continues to involve him in various fraudulent schemes; he falls out with the publisher who employs him, Mr Mugford. And the paper he launches goes broke. All is put right, however, when another will is found in an old postchaise, making Philip Ringwood's heir after all. As a heroic type, Philip conforms more to the muscular*, physical, hot-tempered ideal of the mid-1850s than do his more dandyish predecessors Pendennis* and melancholy Henry Esmond*. Although it has some fine passages of digressive commentary, the novel is generally thought Thackeray's weakest.

PHILIPS, F[rancis] C[harles] (1849–1921). Philips was born in Brighton, the younger son of a clergyman. He was educated at Brighton College and Sandhurst Military Academy. He subsequently entered the Queen's Own Regiment in 1868 and served in the army for three years. Philips resigned his commission to read law, being called to the Bar in 1884. He switched to literature as his profession, supporting himself by writing plays, journalism, and (increasingly) novels. His most famous work was *As In A Looking Glass* (1885). This was in fact his first work of fiction (daringly dedicated to Sarah Bernhardt who starred in its dramatic adaptation) and it climaxes with the heroine being poisoned with chloral. As Sadleir notes: 'it scandalised the critics to a degree which nowadays seems unreasonable'. Philips followed up with: *A Lucky Young Woman* (1886); *Jack And Three Jills* (1886); *The Dean And His Daughter* (1887); *The Worst Woman In London* (1895); *A Devil In Nun's Veiling* (1895); *A Question Of Colour* (1895), one of the few Victorian novels to deal frankly with love and race; *An Undeserving Woman* (1896). His novels are principally memorable for their full-blooded melodrama, and their invariable introduction of passionate murder. Lurid death scenes were one of Philips's specialities. BL 28. *WW*. Wol. Sad. RLF.

PHILLIPS, the Rev. Forbes Alexander ('Athol Forbes', 1866–1917). The son of a Civil Servant, Phillips was born and educated in the north-west of England. After attending Durham University, he was ordained an Anglican minister in 1889, and appointed to various parishes in East Anglia. He eventually settled as Vicar of Gorleston, near Yarmouth (about which he later wrote a book of local history). His fiction written under pseudonym is mainly churchy in tone and includes: *Cassock And Comedy* (1898) and *A Son Of Rimmon* (1899). Unusually for a clergyman, Phillips also wrote plays for London performance (e.g. *The Last Toast*, 1906). BL 3. *WW*.

PHILLIPS, Samuel (1814–54). Phillips was born in London, the son of a Jewish dealer in lamps and chandeliers in St James's Street. As a child, he was noted for his skill in recitation, and he appeared on the Covent Garden stage at the age of fourteen. He had his education at the universities of Göttingen and Cambridge (intending to enter the Church of England) but was forced to give up his studies when his father was ruined and died. For a while, Phillips attempted to carry on the family business. This failing, he supported himself and his new wife after 1841 by what he could earn writing. The early 1840s were difficult for Phillips. His wife died in 1843 (he remarried in 1845) and he himself was discovered to be consumptive. Almost destitute, he wrote a Jewish story *Caleb Stukely* (1842–43), for *Blackwood's Magazine**. The work marked a turn in his fortunes. In 1845, through the intervention of Lord Stanley, Phillips was appointed a leader writer on the *Morning Herald*. In the same year, he became a staff literary reviewer for *The Times*. As a reviewer Phillips was severe. (His notice is credited with 'killing' Thackeray's *Henry Esmond**, on its first appearance in 1852.) Phillips subsequently purchased the Tory paper, *John Bull*, but did not prosper with it. In 1853, just before his sudden death, he was made literary director of the Crystal Palace and wrote the standard guide to the institution. Phillips's main claim to posterity's interest is as a reviewer. But *Caleb Stukely* is an unusual novel. Written autobiographically, it is set in the eighteenth century and has a hero who goes to Cambridge and becomes involved with a Jewish moneylender, Solomon Levy, and his son Ikey. When Caleb's businessman father subsequently dies, the young man is cut adrift and becomes the 'travelling secretary of a Christian Instruction Society'. Various picaresque adventures ensue in which the hero comes into further contact with the Levys and with the villain of the piece, James Temple. The arch 'I narration' and the ingenuous hero both look forward to the *Bildungsroman** of the 1840s and early 1850s, such as *Pendennis** or *David Copperfield**. BL 1. *DNB*. *NCBEL*. Wol. Sad. RLF.

PHILLIPS, Watts (1825–74). Phillips's family background was Irish. He showed an early facility in acting and in drawing, and was for while a pupil of George Cruikshank's* (supposedly the only pupil the notoriously difficult artist ever had). In the 1840s, he studied art in Paris. Phillips's training was interrupted by the 1848 Revolution, and he moved to Brussels. Around 1853 he moved to London. There he wrote successful plays (e.g. *Dead Heart*, 1859) and did caricatures. In 1862, he published the novel *The Honour Of The*

Family in the magazine *Town Talk*. (The work, a story of country life in the seventeenth century, was reissued as *Amos Clark* and later dramatised.) A sequel, *Canary Bird*, was published in 1862. Phillips went on to write a quantity of pot-boiling serials for such papers as the *Family Herald*. Most seem not to have achieved the dignity of reprinting in book form. Just before his death Phillips's last novel, *Who Will Save Her?* (1874), came out. BL 3. *DNB*.

PHILLIPPS WOLLEY, [Sir] Clive (born Phillipps, 1854–1918). Clive Phillipps was educated at Rossall, and as a young man served as vice-consul at Kertch, 1873–76. He later read law, and was called to the Bar in 1884. Having practised law for a decade, Phillipps took up work as a colonial administrator in west British Columbia in 1896. Some time before this, he added 'Wolley' to his name, on succeeding to a large inheritance. On the side he wrote a number of works on hunting, big game shooting, exploring and other outdoor activities, as well as accounts of Canada. His novels include: *Savage Svanetia* (1883); *Snap* (1890), 'A Legend Of The Lone Mountain'; *One Of The Broken Brigade* (1897); *The Chicamon Store* (1900), a story of adventures in Alaska and the Yukon. Phillipps-Wolley was created a knight in 1914. BL 7. *WW*.

PHILLPOTTS, Eden (1862–1960). Phillpotts was born in India, the eldest son of an army officer and political agent who died while his son was still a small child. The Phillpotts family returned to England and settled at Dawlish. Eden Phillpotts was brought up by his widowed mother and developed a lifelong love of Devon. In later life, even after he had achieved international fame, the county was his home (first at Torquay, then near Exeter). After leaving school, Phillpotts worked for ten years as a clerk in the Sun fire-insurance firm in the West End of London. His mother hoped he would enter the Church. For his part he had some ambitions to be an actor but a brief experiment on the stage proved that he would not succeed in this line. Phillpotts had more success writing plays and short stories. (One of his early literary comrades was Arnold Bennett.) Phillpotts wrote *The End Of A Life* (1890) and followed this work with *Folly And Fresh Airs* (1892); *A Tiger's Cub* (1892); *In Sugarcane Land* (1893); *Some Everyday Folk* (1894), a tale set in a small village, on the edge of Dartmoor. As an avowed disciple of Hardy* he wrote the regional idyll *Down Dartmoor Way* (1895); *A Deal With The Devil* (1895); and *My Laughing Philosopher* (1896). *The Lying Prophets* (1897), considered his first major work, introduces as its dramatis personae the artists' colony at St Ives. In 1898, Phillpotts began his ambitious 'Dartmoor Cycle' with *Children Of The Mist*. (This novel was dedicated with 'heartfelt admiration' to Blackmore*, who with Hardy was a main influence on Phillpotts.) The action is set in the little town of Chagford and follows the career of a peasant, Will Blanchard, who in his past had enlisted as a soldier and deserted. Afterwards he marries Phoebe Lyddon, and takes up a farm. The couple experience various hardships (including the death of a son) but at the Queen's Jubilee of 1887 Will is finally pardoned. The cycle continued with *Sons Of The Morning* (1900) and nineteen successive works followed until 1923. The tone of the saga grew more richly descriptive as it progressed. Phillpotts was a fluent writer who turned out as many as four books a year. One of his last works of fiction was *The Fall Of The House Of Heron* (1948), an apocalyptic vision of his beloved Devon under assault by atomic weapons. In addition to his rural fiction, Phillpotts wrote workmanlike detective* stories. He lived most of his long life at Torquay, then at Broad Clyst, near Exeter. BL 186. *DNB*. RM. *NCBEL*. Wol. Sad.

PHILPOT, Joseph Henry ('Philip Lafargue', 1850–1939). Philpot was born in Stamford, the son of a clergyman (and distantly of Huguenot extraction). He was educated at King's College, London, and at Vienna, where he studied medicine, eventually taking up a post as obstetrician at King's College Hospital. He edited the *Medical Times* (1883–85) and earned an MBE for service in the first World War. As Philip Lafargue, Philpot wrote some fiction, including: *The New Judgement Of Paris* (1888); *The Salt Of The Earth* (1898); *Stephen Brent* (1898); *The Forsaken Way* (1899). BL 4. *WW*.

Phineas Finn, The Irish Member, Anthony Trollope, 1869, 2 vols, Virtue. (Serialised in *St Paul's Magazine**, October 1867–May 1869, with illustrations by J. E. Millais*.) The second of the Palliser* series, and the first of Trollope's 'parliamentary' novels (written at a period when he had political ambitions of his own). Phineas is a young, handsome, ambitious Irish lawyer. With luck and his father's help, he gets a seat in Parliament. His attempt to further his political career by marrying Lady Laura Standish fails, however. She helps the young man, but accepts as her husband the Glasgow millionaire, Robert Kennedy. Phineas recovers, and turns his attentions to the rich heiress, Violet Effingham. There are two objections to this match. First Phineas's wild friend, Lord Chiltern (Laura's brother), claims Violet as his own. Secondly, Phineas has an Irish sweetheart, Mary Flood Jones. Eventually, Phineas fights a duel with Chiltern in which he is slightly wounded. But his political patron is Lord Brentford, Chiltern's father, who withdraws his favour. Laura, meanwhile, has found Kennedy to be a tyrant. Her aspiration to be a powerful Whig hostess is frustrated by his calvinistic notions of a wife's duty. Ironically, Phineas saves Kennedy's life from garrotters. Despite reverses in his love life, the young man's fortunes flourish and he attaches himself with some success to the radical Mr Monk. Phineas's career as an outsider conquering English society is paralleled by that of Madame Max Goesler. A rich widow of uncertain racial origin, Madam Max induces the aged Duke of Omnium to propose to her. But finally she rejects him and offers herself to Phineas instead. Phineas has had to resign office in Gresham's Liberal ministry, because of his views on Irish tenant right. Without office he has no income and will have to give up Parliament. Nevertheless, he declines Madame Max's offer (they in fact marry in the sequel) and returns to Ireland. There he marries the faithful Mary and secures a position as a Poor Law Commissioner. Chiltern is finally accepted by Violet, and Laura is forced to run away from England to escape Kennedy.

Phineas Redux, Anthony Trollope, 1873, 2 vols, Chapman and Hall. (Serialised in the *Graphic*, July 1873–January 1874, illustrated by Frank Holl.) A direct sequel to *Phineas Finn** (1869) and the darkest of all Trollope's parliamentary works. The novel opens with the death of Phineas's young Irish wife, Mary. This releases the hero for a new political career.

He is invited by the Liberals to stand for Tankerville which, in a dirty election, he wins. His former love, Laura, is still living in Dresden, having taken flight from her husband Robert Kennedy. Phineas visits her, and finds her beauty sadly faded. Kennedy has become increasingly demented by jealousy, and attempts to shoot Phineas. He is removed to his vast estate at Loughlinter in Scotland, where he goes completely mad and dies. Phineas's new career in Parliament goes badly, and he falls particularly foul of another rising politician, Mr Bonteen. After a row in their club, Bonteen is found murdered. Phineas is arrested, although it is clear (to the reader at least) that the murderer was actually the Rev. Joseph Emilius (last encountered as Lizzie's second husband in *The Eustace Diamonds**). But Emilius (who is also a bigamist) has an alibi. By resourceful efforts on the part of Madame Max Goesler (involving detective work in Bohemia), Phineas is finally acquitted. But meanwhile, his faith in British justice has been forever shaken. He marries the fabulously wealthy Madame Max (to the disappointment of Laura) and retires from Parliament. In later Palliser* novels, Phineas returns as a senior politician; but he never achieves the supremely high rank promised in the early stages of his brilliant career.

PHIZ, (i.e. Hablôt Knight Browne, 1815–82). Illustrator. Browne was born in Kennington, educated in Suffolk and apprenticed in London, where he learned to engrave. After the unfortunate artist Robert Seymour killed himself in 1836 and R. Buss* proved inadequate to the task, Phiz (or 'Nemo' as he sometimes called himself) was recruited to supply the steel engravings for *The Pickwick Papers** (1837). This led to a long relationship with Dickens* through the 1840s. But although he is closely identified with Dickens's fiction, Phiz's payment for illustrating it seems to have been around £30 a month. Phiz went on to work for many of the leading novelists of the period: for Ainsworth* he illustrated *Old St Paul's** (1841), for Lever* most of his important early novels, for Frank Smedley* *Lewis Arundel* (1852), and for Trollope* *Can You Forgive Her?** (1865). But by the mid-1850s, Browne's scratchy caricature style of engraving was increasingly outmoded and fuller-textured naturalistic woodcuts were preferred. He had ambitions as a painter which were never realised. He suffered a paralytic stroke in 1867, and his later work is inferior. According to J. R. Harvey, 'He produced his best work very early in his career [for Dickens] and having done so he did not go on, as many artists do, to produce an impressive second-best for his remaining years; he went into a steady decline.' Phiz's younger son, Gordon Frederick Browne (1858–1932) was also an illustrator of talent (especially of children's fiction), and worked for R. L. Stevenson*, F. Anstey*, Grant Allen*, G. A. Henty* and Mrs Ewing*. *DNB*. Hou.

Phoebe Junior, A Last Chronicle Of Carlingford, Margaret Oliphant, 1876, 3 vols, Hurst and Blackett. Following Trollope's example with Barchester, Mrs Oliphant was inspired to devise a final part to her 'Chronicles Of Carlingford*'. The young hero, Reginald May, is publicly attacked for accepting a church sinecure. His father, the curate of St Roque's, forges the signature to a promissory note (recalling the plot of Trollope's *Last Chronicle Of Barset**, 1867). But the main interest centres on the heroine of the title. Phoebe comes from London to visit her country grandparents, the Tozers, in Carlingford. Like Oliphant's previous heroine, Miss Marjoribanks*,

Phoebe is a lively and enterprising young woman. Despite her dissenter and tradesman connections, she sets out to conquer Carlingford society. She succeeds in capturing the heart of Reginald May, but declines his offer in favour of the rough-diamond son of a contractor millionaire. The novel is the best constructed of all the 'Chronicles'.

PICKERING, Ellen (d. 1843). Ellen Pickering passed her early life at Bath. Her family owned property in the West Indies, but losses (following on the abolition of slavery) led to relative impoverishment and the family's removal to rural Hampshire. She began writing in 1825. According to the *DNB*, Pickering 'acquired some popularity, and earned, it is said, £100 a year'. Little is known of her life. The most successful of her books was *Nan Darrell* (1839), whose heroine is a crazed gypsy. Pickering died prematurely at Bath, of scarlet fever. Her last novel, *The Grandfather* (1844), was completed by Elizabeth Youatt, and published posthumously. Her other romances include: *The Marriage Of The Favourite* (1826); *The Heiress* (1833); *Agnes Serle* (1835); *The Merchant's Daughter* (1836); *The Squire* (1837); *The Fright* (1839); *The Prince And The Pedlar* (1839); *The Quiet Husband* (1840); *Who Shall Be Heir?* (1840); *The Secret Foe?* (1841); *The Expectant* (1842); *Sir Michael Paulet* (1842); *Friend Or Foe* (1843); *The Grumbler* (1843); *Kate Walsingham* (1848). BL 16. *DNB*. Wol.

The Pickwick Papers, Charles Dickens, 1837, 1 vol, Chapman and Hall. (Serialised in monthly numbers, April 1836–November 1837, with illustrations by R. Seymour, R. W. Buss* and Phiz*. Full title, *The Posthumous Papers Of The Pickwick Club*.) The most important single novel of the Victorian era. The project began without any clear prevision of its eventual outcome as a loose narrative strung around Robert Seymour's sporting plates. After Seymour's suicide, Dickens took firm charge of the project with (eventually) Phiz as his very subordinate assistant. The novel opens with a meeting of the Pickwick Club, under its president Samuel Pickwick. An expedition is mounted to Rochester by Pickwick, Mr Tracy Tupman, Mr Nathaniel Winkle and Mr Augustus Snodgrass. On route, they fall in with an incurable rogue, Alfred Jingle. Through a confusion of clothes and identities at a ball, Jingle involves Winkle in a duel with the bloodthirsty Dr Slammer. Slaughter is only narrowly averted. But blood is spilled when the Pickwickians visit Manor Farm in Suffolk and Winkle injudiciously tries his hand rook shooting. He accidentally wings Tupman. Jingle, meanwhile, has eloped with the elderly daughter of the house, Miss Rachael Wardle. Pickwick pursues Jingle to London and buys him off with £120. At the White Hart inn (where the transaction takes place) Pickwick meets with a sharp young bootblack, Sam Weller, whom he takes on as his personal servant. Pickwick's next adventure involves Mrs Bardell, his widowed housekeeper. She misunderstands her employer to be offering her marriage. In the breach of promise suit which follows, Pickwick is out-manoeuvred by the legal team of Dodgson and Fogg. When he refuses to pay the fine determined by the court he is thrown into debtors' Prison, where he he is later joined by Mrs Bardell. Pickwick rescues her from imprisonment and is released himself. Mr Winkle meanwhile has married to his father's displeasure Arabella Allen, a medical student's sister, whom the Pickwickians met at Bath. There are other romantic problems for Pickwick to solve. Snodgrass has fallen in love with Emily Wardle (Rachael's younger sister). All is finally put straight. Pickwick dissolves his club and retires to Dulwich with Sam Weller. The novel is the most zestfully comic that Dickens wrote.

The Picture Of Dorian Gray, Oscar Wilde, 1891, 1 vol, Ward and Lock. (Serialised in *Lippincott's Magazine*, July 1890). Wilde's famous parable of 1890s decadence*. The artist Basil Hallward creates a magnificent portrait of a golden youth, Dorian Gray, an embodiment of 'youth's passionate purity'. Dorian is later corrupted by one of Hallward's friends, Lord Henry Wotton. Following Wotton's lessons he breaks the heart of an actress, Sibyl Vane, who kills herself. Meanwhile Dorian remains unnaturally young while his portrait (hidden in an attic) secretly ages and turns ugly with sin. Hallward sees the picture and Dorian murders him. Finally Dorian destroys the now hideous portrait with a knife, and in so doing kills himself. The novel contains some of Wilde's finest epigrams.

The Pillars Of The House, Or Under Wode Under Rode, Charlotte Mary Yonge, 1873, 4 vols, Macmillan. With *The Daisy Chain** (1856), the most popular of Yonge's family chronicles. Edward Underwood, a parson, loses his family inheritance through a loophole in his uncle's will. He takes a curacy in the industrial North, and dies of consumption at the age of thirty-nine. On the day of his death, twins are born, bringing his surviving children to thirteen. Underwood's wife collapses into invalidism, and dies three years later. The family's income is subsequently provided by Felix, who gives up a career in holy orders to become an apprentice to the local printer. Domestic leadership falls on Wilmet, who contrives to run the house on £5 a week. As in *The Daisy Chain*, sub-narratives form around the Underwood children. Not all make good. Wilmet's twin, Alda, enters into a disastrous marriage to a baronet; Edgar, the black sheep, is deservedly scalped by Indians. Felix builds up a publishing business which is later taken over by his efficient brother, Lance. And the family is finally returned to their rightful inheritance and landed respectability. The work has been called 'the quintessence of Charlottery'.

POLLOCK, Walter Herries (1850–1926). The second son of Sir Frederick Pollock, Bt, he was educated at Eton and Trinity College, Cambridge. Pollock was subsequently called to the Bar, but instead turned to journalism. He eventually (in 1883) rose to be editor of the *Saturday Review**, holding the post until ill health forced his early retirement in 1894. Under his watch, the magazine, once famous for its sprightliness, became a dependable and rather dull pillar of the Conservative Party. Pollock had a passion for fencing, belonged to the Athenaeum, wrote French well, and was organiser of the Rabelais Club, which in the 1880s boasted R. L. Stevenson*, Henry James and Thomas Hardy* as members. Pollock wrote short fiction, collected in volume form as: *A Nine Men's Morrice* (1889); *Edged Tools* (1891); *King Zub* (1892). *The Picture's Story* (1883) is a full-length novel. BL 4. *WW*. Wol.

PONSONBY, Lady Emily [Charlotte Mary] (1817–77). The third daughter of the Earl of Bessborough (1781–1847, a Home Secretary under Canning), she never married, and after her father's death published (anonymously) a large number of romances for the library patron. They include:

The Discipline Of Life (1848); *Pride And Irresolution* (1850); *Clare Abbey* (1851); *Mary Gray* (1852); *Edward Willoughby* (1854); *The Young Lord* (1856); *The Two Brothers* (1858); *A Mother's Trial* (1859); *Nora* (1870); *Oliver Beaumont* (1873). A Catherine Ponsonby, who seems to be no relative, wrote five novels around the same period, including the regional tales: *The Border Wardens* (1844); *The Desborough Family* (1845). BL 14. *DNB.* Wol. (CP) RLF.

Poor Max, Iota, 1898, 1 vol, Hutchinson. As sarcastic reviewers noted, Iota (i.e. Mrs Mannington Caffyn) was more interested in poor Judith, Jewish Max Morland's Irish wife. The couple marry after a whirlwind courtship at Ballybruff in Ireland. Judith is subsequently reduced to financial insecurity by her artistic husband's impulsive generosity and becomes involved with another man. Max sickens and dies of diphtheria, his wife nursing him to the end. A steely Judith is last seen looking after her own interests by deserting her faithful lover to marry a rich debauchee, 'who has every vice Max hadn't'. The novel, which is told with Iota's usual wispy obliquity, represents a variation by the novelist on her usual heroine-centred new woman* formula.

POWER, Marguerite A[gnes] ('Honoria', 1815?–67). The daughter of an army colonel, she was also a niece of the Countess of Blessington*, with whom she lived in Paris after the break-up of Gore House in 1849. From 1851 to 1857, Power edited the *Keepsake*. In 1860, she wrote a long narrative poem, *Virginia's Hand*, which was dedicated to John Forster (Dickens's* friend) and earned the author some praise. Power's fiction includes: *Evelyn Forester* (1856), 'A Woman's Story'; *The Foresters* (1858); *Too Late* (1858); *The Letters Of A Betrothed* (1858), by 'Honoria'; *Nelly Carew* (1859), the story of the daughter of an Irish landlord who is forced into marriage with a wastrel; *Sweethearts And Wives* (1861). BL 6. *DNB.* Wol. RLF.

PRAED, Mrs Campbell [Rosa Caroline] (née Murray-Prior, 1851–1935). Rosa Murray-Prior was born at Bromelton in Queensland, Australia, the eldest daughter of the state's postmaster-general. At the time of her birth, her father was a sheep farmer. Subsequently she followed him to Brisbane, moving in the political society around Government House. In later life she claimed that her early experiences in the bush (at a period of sporadic warfare between squatters and aborigines) and her fascination with debates in the Australian House of Legislators had been formative influences. In 1868 her mother died, throwing the management of her father's house on to her. He was by now a Cabinet minister. She was by now writing novelettes for her own pleasure and rejected several proposals of marriage. In 1872, she married Campbell Mackworth Praed (d. 1901). Praed was an Englishman whose family had banking and brewing interests in the Midlands. The couple returned to England in 1876 to live at Earls Court in London. By now they had two sons and a handicapped daughter. Praed was an unfaithful husband and the marriage went sour. Despite this, they maintained a respectable appearance of harmony until his death. Her sexual energies were directed into writing. Fred Chapman (of Chapman and Hall*), advised by George Meredith*, encouraged her two first efforts *An Australian Heroine* (1880), written under her maiden name, and *Policy And Passion*

(1881), another story of growing up in Australia which lays the pattern for most of Praed's subsequent fiction. Honoria Longleat is the daughter of the Premier of Leichardt's Land (i.e. Queensland). Thomas Longleat is eventually impeached and commits suicide when it is revealed that he has a criminal past in England. After being betrayed by an English aristocrat, Barrington, Honoria marries a decent Australian politician, Dyson Maddox. In a preface, the author expressed her hope that the work 'would in some slight degree aid in bridging over the gulf which divides the Old World from the Young' Altogether, Praed was to publish some twenty novels and a book of sketches in the decade 1880–90. Her political romance *Nadine, The Study Of A Woman* (1882), has a heroine who is half-Russian, based on Gladstone's friend, Olga Novikoff. This work brought her to the notice of the Irish MP Justin McCarthy*, then fifty-five. McCarthy was Parnell's chief lieutenant in Parliament and an architect of Home Rule legislation. Through him, Praed met Parnell just before his disgrace in the O'Shea divorce case. McCarthy subsequently invited her to collaborate with him on a series of novels of English political life which proved popular. The association led to: *The Right Honourable** (1886), a picture of political infighting in the 1860s and *The Ladies' Gallery* (1888). The second of these was more consciously topical. It features an Australian, Rick Ransom, who becomes a millionaire from mining. In England, Ransom takes up Radical politics and the action of the novel climaxes tragically at the Trafalgar Square riots of 1887. Praed and McCarthy together wrote novels better than either achieved singly. Their next effort was *The Rebel Rose* (1888), a tale of contemporary Jacobitism. Praed seems to have had a protracted love affair with Edward de Fonblanque in the 1880s and early 1890s, a period when her marriage was clearly finished in all but name. In 1890, McCarthy's health failed, precluding further collaboration. On her own account, Praed wrote, among other novels: *Zéro* (1884), a tale of love and gambling in Monte Carlo; *Affinities* (1885), a satire on theosophy and Madame Blavatsky; *Outlaw And Lawmaker* (1893); *Christina Chard* (1894); *Mrs Tregaskiss* (1895), 'A Novel Of Anglo-Australian Life'; *Nùlma* (1897); *As A Watch In The Night* (1900). She became mystical in later life and was active in promoting spiritualism. Her interest in occultism and reincarnation is reflected in: *The Brother Of The Shadow* (1886); *The Soul Of Countess Adrian* (1891); *The Insane Root* (1902). In 1899, Praed met and set up house with the mystic Nancy Harward who was the dominant influence on her later life. *Nyria* (1904) expounds the doctrine of esoteric Buddhism. Although she never shook off the character of an Australian novelist, Praed spent most of her later life in London, where she finally died. (RCP) BL 45. (RCP and JM) BL 5. *WW*. RM. Wol.

PRESCOTT, E. Livingston [Edith Katherine] (née Spicer-Jay, 1830?–1901). The daughter of a barrister, Samuel Jay, she was educated privately. Her family had strong army connections and Edith Jay subsequently worked as the Honourable Lady Superintendent of the London Soldiers' Home, until herself incapacitated by ill health. Her fiction, which is of the sternly improving variety, military in subject and mainly for juvenile readers includes: *A Mask And A Martyr* (1896); *Scarlet And Steel* (1897); *The Rip's Redemption* (1899); *Helot And Hero* (1899); *Illusion* (1899), 'A Romance Of Modern Egypt'. BL 17. *WW*. Wol.

PREST, Thomas Peckett (1810?–79). Prest was a relative of the Right Reverend Edward Prest, Archdeacon of Durham Cathedral in the 1860s, which suggests a respectable family background. Little else is known of the writer's origins. He began his authorial career adapting farces and melodramas from the French and showed himself a talented musician and song writer. But Prest's main line of work was the production of low grade gothic* thrillers for the Salisbury Square publisher, Edward Lloyd*, highlighting torture, murder, sex and sadism. Prest, who led a dissipated, debt-ridden life, evidently died of lung disease in the late 1870s, a pauper in a cheap boarding house. His publications are numerous, and sometimes hard to identify. He wrote Dickens* plagiarisms in the 1830s, under the deliberately confusing pseudonym 'Bos'. His most famous work (often attributed to Rymer, or Malcolm Errym*, as he called himself) is *A String Of Pearls* (1846). First serialised in the *Penny Sunday Times*, this thriller about cannibalism and dubious meat pies was adapted into the perennially popular stage melodrama *Sweeney Todd, The Demon Barber Of Fleet Street*. A selection of Prest's fiction (much of it serialised in 1d. numbers) would include: *Angelina* (1841); *Gallant Tom* (1841); *The Death Grasp, Or A Father's Curse* (1842); *The Maniac Father* (1842); *Martha Willis* (1844); *The Gypsy Boy* (1847); *The Blighted Heart* (1849); *Jack Junk, Or The Tar For All Weathers* (1851); *Richard Parker, Or The Mutiny At The Nore* (1851); *The Miller And His Men* (1852); *Vice And Its Victim* (1854). BL 26. Wol.

PREVOST, Francis (i.e. Henry Francis Prevost Battersby, 1862–1949). Battersby, the son of a major-general and a baronet's daughter, was educated at Westminster School, and the Royal Military Academies of Woolwich and Sandhurst from where he graduated with distinction. He was subsequently commissioned as a lieutenant into the Royal Irish Rifles, but left the armed forces to enter journalism. In this capacity he was wounded reporting the Boer War for the *Morning Post*. He rejoined the colours to fight in the first World War, in which he was several times wounded and gassed. A versatile man of letters, Prevost (as he called himself in print) translated Tolstoy, wrote poetry and reported sporting events, particularly hockey, for the press. His fiction (mainly short) includes: *Rust Of Gold* (1895); *False Dawn* (1897), a psychological study of forbidden love, with an ambitious politician as hero; *In The Web Of War* (1900). BL 4. WW.

PRICHARD, Hesketh Vernon ('E. and H. Heron', 1876–1922). The posthumous son of an army officer, Prichard was born in Jhansi, India, his twenty-five-year-old father having died six weeks before in a typhoid epidemic. He was educated at Fettes School, Scotland, to which he won a Foundation scholarship in 1887. He later read law but never practised, and travelled extensively in remote parts of the world, shooting big game as he went. He was subsequently elected a Fellow of the Royal Geographical Society, and led an important expedition to Patagonia on which he published several books at the turn of the century. He also travelled to, and wrote about, Haiti. A noted athlete, Prichard played cricket as a fast bowler for the Gentlemen of Hampshire, 1903–05, and is recorded as 'a golden haired, gray eyed giant of six feet four inches'. Prichard's well-known 'Don Q' stories (about a Spanish Robin Hood) began to appear in the *Badminton Magazine* in January 1898 and the character became a cult figure of near

Sherlock Holmes stature. In collaboration with his mother, Kate O'Brien Prichard (a general's daughter), and under the joint pseudonym 'E. and H. Heron', Prichard wrote novels which include: *Tammer's Duel* (1898); *A Modern Mercenary* (1898), the adventures of a diplomat in Germany; *Karadac, Count Of Gersay* (1900), a historical* novel set on the Channel Islands. On his own Prichard wrote a large number of stories in the first decade of the twentieth century and in 1913 published *November Joe, A Detective Story Of The Woods*. Prichard married an earl's daughter, Lady Elizabeth Grimston, in 1908. In 1910, he led the conservationist fight to protect grey seals from being annually culled for their pelts. Although over age he won a DSO and MC in the first World War and died of delayed effects of his military service at the young age of forty-five. In 1924, Eric Parker wrote a memoir, graphically entitled: *Hesketh Prichard, DSO, MC, Hunter, Explorer, Naturalist, Cricketer, Author, Soldier*. E. W. Hornung* was a friend and quite probably modelled his hero Raffles* on the *preux chevalier*, Prichard. (EH and HH) BL 10. (HP) BL 1. *WW*.

The Prime Minister, Anthony Trollope, 1876, 4 vols, Chapman and Hall. (Serialised in eight 5s. monthly parts, unillustrated, November 1875– June 1876.) The fifth of the Palliser* novels, and the one which most closely focuses on Plantagenet Palliser himself, now Duke of Omnium. A deadlock between the old political opponents, Gresham (i.e. Gladstone) and Daubeny (i.e. Disraeli), leads to Omnium's becoming Prime Minister, in a coalition cabinet. His 'faineant' policies serve to steady the country. But he hates himself for the inefficacy of his three-year ministry. A related sub-plot deals with the marriage of a handsome adventurer, Lopez, to Edith Wharton against the wishes of her rich lawyer father, and in preference to a decent young suitor, Arthur Fletcher. Lopez plays on the inherent vulgarity of Glencora, Duchess of Omnium, at Gatherum Castle. She backs him as candidate for the local borough of Silverbridge. But Omnium is too scrupulous to give Lopez any endorsement, and he is forced to retire by Fletcher. Enraged, he demands financial compensation for his election expenses from the Duchess. The Duke pays Lopez off; the affair gets into the papers (via the disreputable journalist Quintus Slide, who earlier tormented Phineas Finn*). Omnium is not brought down, but is horribly mortified by the scandal, and the moral laxity it reveals in his wife. Lopez goes from bad to worse in partnership with a stockbroker, Sextus Parker. He extorts money from Emily's father, speculates in guano and Kauri gum and finally kills himself under a train at Clapham ('Tenway') Junction (a scene of great power). The novel, which was published in an unusual form of serial issue, did not please Trollope's contemporaries.

Prince Otto, Robert Louis Stevenson, 1885, 1 vol, Chatto. (Serialised in *Longman's Magazine*, April–October 1885.) Stevenson's most stylish romance. The hero is the irresponsible ruler of a German statelet, Grünewald. Out hunting, Otto rides incognito into neighbouring Gerolstein where he hears some home truths about himself from the farmer with whom he stays the night. His ruler's conscience is further awakened by the confiscated manuscript of an English traveller, Sir John Crabtree. This details Otto's total abdication of responsibility to the alien Baron von Gondremark and the prince's schemingly adulterous wife, Seraphina. Learning that these conspirators intend to take the Principality to war, Otto with the aid of Countess von Rosen (who loves him), attempts to seize control. But it is too late; revolution breaks out. Seraphina tries to kill Gondremark when she discovers that he has been merely using her. A republic is declared and the Prince and Princess, now reconciled, escape to live happily in the woods. A historical postscript traces the subsequent fortunes of little Grünewald. All that is recorded of the hero and heroine is an obscure volume of verse, *Poésies Par Frédéric et Amélie*. Stevenson's story is told with great incidental charm.

A Princess Of Thule, William Black, 1873, 3 vols, Macmillan. (Serialised in *Macmillan's Magazine*, March–December 1873). Two Englishmen, Edward Ingram, (a Civil Servant) and the fifteen-year younger Frank Lavender, an artist, spend a month on the Isle of Lewis (off western Scotland) fishing and hunting. Frank falls in love with a local girl, Sheila Mackenzie, 'The Princess of Thule', only daughter of the so-called 'King of Borva'. He marries her, and they come down to live in London. In the city, Sheila is increasingly unhappy. Lavender neglects her for another woman, the American Mrs Lorraine, despite the remonstrances of Ingram and a rich aunt. Finally, she flees back to her father. As atonement, Lavender returns to the Hebrides where he works at making himself a painter. Eventually, in this natural setting, he and Sheila (now a mother) are reconciled. Ingram marries Mrs Lorraine. The work was popular for its highly romanticised picture of Highland and island life and its vivid description in the opening chapter of Lewis.

PRINSEP, Val[entine] C[ameron] (1838–1901). Prinsep was born in Calcutta, where his father was a member of the Council of India (a number of other Prinseps held high office in the sub-continent). From his youth onwards, he was an intimate friend of the painter, G. F. Watts. Prinsep himself studied art under Gleyre in Paris. His painting style was strongly influenced by that of Lord Leighton, and his work was first exhibited at the Royal Academy in 1862. He published a 'Tale Of One Hundred Years Ago', the novel *Virginie* (1890). BL 1. *DNB*. Wol.

PRIOR, James (i.e. James Prior Kirk, 1850–1922). Kirk was born at Nottingham, where his father was a tradesman, born and brought up in the country. The young boy was forbidden novels, but Borrow's* *The Bible In Spain* was permitted him, due to a misapprehension about its contents. Kirk was, in fact, strongly influenced by George Borrow, and he was inspired to write regional* novels in the spare time from his work in a solicitor's office. Most were set in his native Nottinghamshire. They include: *Ripple And Flood* (1897), a story of the Trent; *Forest Folk* (1901); *Hyssop* (1904). Prior was a notorious hermit in his later years. BL 6.

The Prisoner Of Zenda, Anthony Hope, 1894, 1 vol, Arrowsmith. Rudolf Rassendyll, an Englishman visiting Ruritania, is swept up in a romantic intrigue on the eve of the coronation of King Rudolf (whom he uncannily resembles). The villainous half-brother of the King, Duke Michael, and his henchmen imprison the monarch at a hunting lodge at Zenda, hoping to precipitate a crisis. But Rassendyll successfully impersonates Rudolf at the coronation. And with the help of the loyal Fritz von Tarlenheim and

Colonel Sapt, Rudolf heroically rescues the real King. In the process Duke Michael is killed. Rassendyll, meanwhile, has fallen in love with the King's intended bride, the Princess Flavia. But she refuses to return with him to England, and does her duty as Queen of Ruritania. The hero thereafter lives a rather meaningless and celibate life at home, nagged by his sister Lady Rose Burlesdon. Hope's novel was immensely popular, especially in dramatic and film versions and inspired a whole genre of 'Ruritanian romance'.

The Professor, Charlotte Brontë, 1857, 2 vols, Smith, Elder. Brontë's first realistic novel, a conscious departure from the extended fantasies she, her brother and sisters wrote in their childhood. The hero William Crimsworth, not liking business, emigrates to Brussels, where he becomes a boarding-school teacher ('a professor'). The proprietress of another girls' school, Zoraide Reuter, attempts to entrap him sexually. But he resists her in favour of a Protestant pupil, Frances Henri, a demure young Anglo-Swiss. Crimsworth finds a better teaching position and marries Frances. The novel, like *Villette** (1853), draws heavily on the author's own two years in Brussels in 1842–44. The work was completed in 1846 and submitted to Smith, Elder who suggested a longer novel, which became *Jane Eyre** (1847).

PROWSE, Richard Orton (1862–1949). Prowse was born at Woodbridge in Suffolk, the son of a clergyman. He went to school at Cheltenham, and to university at Balliol College, Oxford. His fiction includes: *The Poison Of Asps* (1892), a tale of love and tragedy set in a small country town; *A Fatal Reservation* (1895); *Voysey* (1901), a sordidly realistic study of adultery. BL 7. *WW*.

PRYCE, Richard (1864–1942). Pryce was born in Boulogne, the son of an English army officer. His mother herself was the daughter of a general, and related to the English aristocracy. Pryce went to school in Leamington. Michael Sadleir writes: 'In this country, despite laudatory reviews, he never had the success he deserved. Neglect at the hands of the British public shook what little self-assurance he possessed and drove him inwards on his unpretentious self.' In addition to much fiction (most of it adventure stories) Pryce wrote plays. His novels include: *An Evil Spirit* (1887), a story of morphine addiction; *The Ugly Story Of Miss Wetherby* (1889); *Just Impediment* (1890); *The Quiet Mrs Fleming* (1890); *Miss Maxwell's Affections* (1891); *Time And The Woman* (1892); *Winifred Mount* (1894); *The Burden Of A Woman* (1895); *Elementary Jane* (1897); *Jezebel* (1900). Pryce lived most of his life in London's West End, never married and effectively ceased writing before the first World War. BL 21. *WW*. RM. Wol. Sad.

Pseudonym Library (1890–96). A series of one-volume tales, published by T. Fisher Unwin, in imitation of John Lane's* *Keynotes** series. As with the other series, 'Pseudonym' titles were self-consciously modish works of the 1890s. Women authors predominated. Over its six years the series put out fifty-four works, beginning with Lanoe Falconer's (i.e. Mary Hawker's*) *Mademoiselle Ixe**. Other authors who published in the series were Ouida* and John Oliver Hobbes* who devised her unusual pen-name for it. The volumes were physically eccentric, being diary-sized and oddly rectangular (shaped, apparently, to fit in a lady's reticule). Unwin partnered the series, which was successful, with an 'Autonym' list of new novels in which writers proclaimed their actual names.

PUDDICOMBE, Mrs Anne Adalisa ('Allen Raine', née Evans 1836–1908). Anne Evans was born in Wales at Newcastle Emlyn, the daughter of a solicitor. She was educated privately (at Cheltenham) and as a young woman met such leading writers as Dickens* and George Eliot*. From 1856 onwards she lived in Wales, steeping herself in its culture. In 1872 she married and went to live in the English Home Counties, her husband, Beynon Puddicombe, working for a London bank. She began writing fiction very late in life, apparently as the expression of an enduring love for her native Wales. At the National Eisteddfod in 1894, Puddicombe submitted a prize-winning story. In 1896, after some difficulty, she found a publisher for the novel *A Welsh Singer* by 'Allen Raine'. (The pseudonym was supposedly suggested to her in a dream.) This simple Welsh love story was followed by other similar works, all written at high speed: *Torn Sails* (1898); *By Berwen Bank* (1899); *Garthowen* (1900), the story of a Welsh homestead. Anne Puddicombe suffered bad health all her life. After her husband's mental breakdown in 1900 the couple retired to Wales where he died six years later. BL 12. *WW*.

PUGH, Edwin William (1874–1930). Born in London, the son of an advertising agent, Pugh was educated at a London board school and employed in a City office for eight years. During this period, he became a connoisseur of cockney* low life in the metropolis. In 1895, Heinemann* published a collection of his short stories, *A Street In Suburbia*, and Pugh followed with the well-received *A Man Of Straw* in 1897. Pugh's early writing was successful enough to induce him to become a full-time writer. His subsequent novels include *King Circumstance* (1898); *Tony Drum, A Cockney Boy* (1898); *Mother-Sister* (1900), the story of a prize-fighter's daughter who valiantly takes care of her family. With Godfrey Burchett, Pugh wrote *The Heritage* (1901), a grim study of alcoholism. By the turn of the century, Pugh's brief vogue (and the cockney novel's) had passed. The last thirty years of his life were dogged by chronic destitution. An avowed disciple of Dickens*, Pugh wrote several books on the earlier novelist celebrating him as 'the apostle of the people'. BL 28. *WW*. RLF.

PULLEN, the Rev. Henry William (1836–1903). Pullen was born at Little Gidding, Huntingdonshire, the son of a clergyman. He attended Marlborough School, and Clare College, Cambridge. After graduation in 1859, he was ordained. Thereafter Pullen taught for a while, and gained a reputation for himself as a skilled priest-pamphleteer. He used fiction for strictly polemical purposes, as in his most famous publication, *The Fight At Dame Europa's School* (1870). Subtitled 'Shewing How The German Boy Thrashed The French Boy, And How The English Boy Looked On', this satirical fable about the Franco-Prussian War sold by the hundred thousand. Pullen also wrote stories of school life. His fiction includes: *Tom Pippin's Wedding* (1871); *The Ground Ash* (1874); *Pueris Reverentia* (1892). The last is a sprightly attack on the British educational system. BL 3. *DNB*. Wol. RLF.

Punch (1841–). The most famous of Victorian comic newspapers. The first weekly issue of *Punch* appeared in July 1841, under the obscure imprint of Landells and Last. More significant to the magazine's future, the original coterie of contributors under the editorship of Mark Lemon* was already in place. Lemon was to remain editor until 1870 and must take credit for the formula of cartoons and short comic items which made an immediate appeal to the English middle classes. Bradbury and Evans* bought the paper in 1842 and (as Bradbury and Agnew) continue to own it to this day. Although fiction (at least long narrative fiction) did not feature in *Punch*, a number of fiction writers were among prominent early contributors: Henry Mayhew*, Douglas Jerrold*, Shirley Brooks* and, pre-eminently, W. M. Thackeray* whose easygoing irony was honed to perfection in early papers for the journal in the 1840s (notably in the *Snobs Of England** series, 1847). *Punch* also provided Bradbury and Evans with illustrators for fiction (some of which was featured in the house's other main magazine, *Once A Week**), such as: John Leech*, Richard Doyle*, George Du Maurier*. After 1846 (when Jerrold left) the tone of the journal became mellower. By 1874, when Tom Taylor took over the editorship (succeeded by Francis Burnand in 1880), *Punch* was a national institution. *BLM.*

The Purple Land, W. H. Hudson, 1885, 2 vols, Sampson Low. (In the first edition, the title continued: 'That England Lost'.) A picaresque story (loosely based on *Gil Blas*) set (unusually) in revolutionary South America. The English hero-narrator, Richard Lamb, marries a South American girl, Paquita, and runs away with her to Montevideo. There he leaves her with a relative, to find work in the interior. This section only takes a few prefatory pages. The main part of the narrative follows his adventures outward and his even more adventurous return journey. Finding no work as an *agregado* at the Estancia de la Virgen de los Desamparados (i.e. Vagabonds' Rest), Lamb picks up with a mysterious comrade, Marcos Marco, who is later revealed to be General Santa Coloma. Having rescued the general from jail and reunited him with his daughter, Lamb fights at the battle of San Paulo. But Coloma is defeated, and the hero barely escapes with his life from the victorious Colorados. On his way back to Montevideo he saves a rich heiress, Demetria Peralta, who falls in love with him. But he gallantly declines to take advantage of her. The narrative ends with Lamb and Paquita on route to Buenos Aires. As usual, Hudson's natural descriptions of the 'Bandu Oriental' are vivid. The American edition had an introduction by Theodore Roosevelt, approving the novel's appreciation of 'the wild picturesqueness of the old-time South American life'.

Put Yourself In His Place, Charles Reade, 1870, 3 vols, Smith, Elder. (Serialised in *Cornhill**, March 1869–July 1870, with illustrations by Robert Barnes.) The novel opens with a tag from Horace: 'I will frame a work of fiction upon notorious fact'. The notorious fact which inspired Reade was the persecution of non-members by the Sheffield trades unions in 1867. The novel is mainly set in 'Hillsborough', an 'infernal city' disfigured by industrialism. A prelude traces the hero's ancestry. He has been disowned after his mother disgraced herself by 'going into trade', marrying beneath the landowning class into which she was born. Henry Little intends to make his way in the world as an artisan. He falls foul of the Edge Tool

Forgers' Union. When he refuses to join, they put gunpowder in his forge. Reduced to a 'human cinder', Little none the less survives and prospers. He also falls in love with Grace Carden. Her father bars him from the house, unless he takes out £5,000 insurance on his life, which he does. But despite this Grace is finally forbidden to marry beneath herself. Henry meanwhile captures the heart of the magnificently Amazonian servant, Jael Dence, who saves him from yet another ETFU assassination attempt (by bow and arrow). His noble birth eventually revealed, Henry receives a bequest from the Philanthropic Society, and sets up as a manufacturer in his own right. On receiving yet more death threats, he determines to leave for America, to sell patents and raise capital. The villain of the novel, Coventry, who covets Grace, simulates Henry's death and suppresses his letters home. Henry returns to find Grace now married to this enemy. In a terrific final number (drawing on Samuel Harrison's *History Of The Great Flood At Sheffield*, 1864), the dam bursts over Hillsborough. Henry, performing prodigies of heroism, saves Grace and Coventry is providentially crippled ('below the waist, an inert mass'). The marriage is revealed to be invalid (the officiating clergyman being an impostor). Henry finally wins Grace and Jael marries a high-born lover. Reade appended an absurd essay, 'What Is To Be Done', showing how industrial peace can be achieved.

Q

QUIGLEY, the Rev. H[ugh] ('A Missionary Priest,' 1818–83). Quigley was born in Co. Clare, Ireland. He studied theology at Rome, and was eventually ordained as a priest there. Quigley subsequently took up work in the American higher education system, but resigned to live and minister among the Chippewa Indians and the Californian miners. He died in Troy, New York. His novels include: *The Cross And The Shamrock* (1853), 'An Irish-American Tale'; *The Prophet Of The Ruined Abbey* (1863), a romance set in the late eighteenth century; *Profit And Loss, Or the Life Of A Genteel Irish American* (1873). BL 1.

QUILLINAN, Edward (1791–1851). Quillinan was born in Oporto, Portugal, the son of an Irish wine merchant. He was educated in England and brought up in the Catholic faith. Quillinan later returned to Portugal to work in his father's counting house. But the family was forced out of the country by the French invasion of 1807. He subsequently joined the army, serving in the cavalry. Possessed of literary ambition, Quillinan began publishing poetry around 1814, which brought him into connection with Wordsworth. He was also associated with *Blackwood's Magazine**. Quillinan translated books from the Portuguese (including the epic *Lusiad*) and wrote a novel, *The Conspirators* (1841) which contains recollections of his military service in the Iberian peninsula. BL 2. *DNB*.

The Quiver (1861–1926). The *Quiver* was started by Cassell's* as a weekly paper, 'Designed For The Defence Of Biblical Truth, And The Advancement

Of Religion In the Homes Of The People', under the editorship of John
Cassell. But despite its religiosity, the paper from the first made serial
fiction its main attraction. And it was the vehicle by which Mrs Henry
Wood* made her name (among other novels, her *Mrs Halliburton's Troubles*
was published in *The Quiver* in 1862). After 1864, the religious tone of the
paper was loosened and even more so with the death of the straitlaced John
Cassell a year later. Few novelists of note, other than Wood, published in
the magazine's pages. The *Quiver*'s lavish Christmas numbers carried such
titles as: the *Mark* (1868); *Golden Arrows* (1869); the *Silver Bow* (1870);
the *Silver Shaft* (1871). *BLM*.

R

Rab And His Friends, Dr John Brown, 1855, 1 vol, Hamilton. The
earliest and probably finest canine story of the Victorian period. Rab is an
Edinburgh mastiff; old, grey and 'big as a little highland bull'. His friends
are his master, James Noble, a Howgate carrier and James's wife Ailie. Rab
displays indomitable loyalty as he guards the couple after she undergoes
an operation for cancer of the breast (graphically described), of which she
eventually dies. Rab is subsequently beaten to death by the carrier who takes
over James's business. Brown, a well-known Edinburgh doctor, evokes the
1830s city of his studenthood and its types while unsentimentally fleshing
out the character of Rab. The story, which was much reprinted, is pamphlet
length.

Rachel Ray, Anthony Trollope, 1863, 2 vols, Chapman and Hall. Like its
predecessor, *The Struggles Of Brown, Jones And Robinson** (1862), this
gently toned novel deals with the clash of old and new business methods.
Bungall and Tappitt's brewery at Baslehurst, Devon, has produced filthy
beer for generations. When the Bungall partner dies, Thomas Tappitt
expects to buy out the distant heir with £1,000. But Luke Rowan has other
ideas. He intends to introduce modern scientific techniques of brewing. He
also has a mind of his own where marriage is concerned. He declines to fall
in love with the Tappitts' eldest daughter Augusta, and chooses instead the
poor but pretty Rachel Ray. His suit is opposed by Rachel's strict widowed
sister, Dorothea Prime (nine years older), who sternly thinks 'cheerfulness a
sin'; by Rachel's morbidly devout widowed mother (for whom every young
man is a 'wicked wild beast') and by the odious evangelical clergyman, Mr
Prong ('not a gentleman', Trollope observes, meaningfully). Luke eventually
overcomes all opposition and ends in sole possession of the brewery and
of Rachel. The novel was originally commissioned by Trollope's friend Dr
Norman Macleod*, for *Good Words**. But Macleod was appalled by *Rachel
Ray*'s satire on evangelicalism, and refused to serialise the work, paying an
unmollified Trollope half the agreed fee by way of compensation.

RACKHAM, Arthur (1867–1939). Artist and illustrator. Rackham was
born in Lewisham, London. He studied at the Lambeth Art School, where

he was influenced stylistically by his fellow student Charles Ricketts (1866–1931), later an illustrator of Oscar Wilde's* work. Rackham went to work for the *Westminster Budget* in 1892, and illustrated some fiction, including Anthony Hawkins's* *The Dolly Dialogues* (1894). In the early twentieth century he evolved the distinctively mystical, allegorical manner which has been a dominant influence in modern book (particularly children's* book) illustration. *DNB*. Hou.

RAE, W[illiam] Fraser (1835–1905). Rae was born and went to school in Edinburgh. After studying at Heidelberg, he read law at Lincoln's Inn and was called to the Bar in 1861. He drifted into journalism and for a while served as the North American correspondent for the *Daily News*. In later life Rae's health was poor, and he spent considerable time in Austrian resorts. He wrote for *The Times* and produced books of travel, history and a number of three-volume novels, including: *Miss Bayle's Romance* (1887), the comic portrait of an American lady, Alma J. Bayle, who outfaces English high society in London and on the Riviera; *A Modern Brigand* (1888), a story of Sicilian banditry; *Maygrove* (1890), 'A Family History'; *An American Duchess* (1890), 'A Pendant To *Miss Bayle's Romance*', with the heroine now the 'Duchess of Windsor'. The last is rather more satirical than its predecessor, featuring such comic Yankee types as 'the lightning sculptress of the West', who carves millionaires' likenesses while they wait. In his later years Rae reviewed extensively for the *Athenaeum** and was a well-known London clubman. BL 3. *DNB*. Wol. RLF.

Raffles. The creation of E. W. Hornung*, Raffles was an ingenious variation on the detective* genre, pioneered by Conan Doyle* in the *Strand** magazine with Sherlock Holmes. A gentleman thief, or 'cracksman', A. J. Raffles is public-school educated, handsome (with a 'strong, unscrupulous mouth') and a superb athlete who plays cricket for the Gentlemen of England against the Players as 'the very finest slow bowler of his decade'. Off the field, Raffles teams up with a slower-footed accomplice, Bunny, a former school-fellow, down on his luck. Together they pull off daring jewel robberies and other capers. Hornung's stories were collected as: *The Amateur Cracksman* (1899) and *Raffles, The Further Adventures Of The Amateur Cracksman* (1901). In the last episode, 'The Knees Of The Gods', the genteel criminal is seen giving his life for Queen and country in the war against the Boers.

The Raiders, S. R. Crockett, 1894, 1 vol, Unwin. One of Crockett's most successful romances. The raiders are the tattered and outlawed remnants of the clans, living in Galloway in the late eighteenth century after the great 'killing' of 1745. The hero, Patrick Heron, the impoverished 'laird of Rathan', grows up in the smuggling community alongside the Solway Firth (wonderfully described by Crockett). Patrick falls in love with the bewitching 'May Mischief' (i.e. May Maxwell) of Craigdarrock. She is abducted to be the wife of the bandit Hector Faa, on one of his raiding forays from his stronghold in the northern hills. Accompanied by his mysterious friend 'Silver Sand' (in fact John Faa, king of the clan), Patrick rescues May from the 'murder hole' where she is held captive and the action climaxes with a great battle and a great hurricane. The work's similarity to Blackmore's* *Lorna Doone** is frequently noted.

Railway Fiction. The great Victorian railway expansion (or 'mania') took place in the late 1830s and early 1840s, creating a distinct new market for portable, entertaining books. In logistical terms, this market was more organised than other Victorian book markets by the licensing of W. H. Smith* as monopoly bookseller at the metropolitan stations, after 1848. Smith served as the outlet for a new range of reprints substantially cheaper than the previous 'Standard*' novels. Firms such as Simms McIntyre (Belfast based) with their 'Parlour Novelist' series (1846) embarked on a price war, which by the late 1840s had reduced the price of the reprint novel to 1s. George Routledge's* firm systematically exploited this new price and single format in 1848 with his all conquering 'Railway Library', which eventually amassed a thousand or so titles. The railway boom created a new lease of life for the authors who were favourites with the travelling public, who tended to be broader in their tastes than circulating library subscribers. Bulwer-Lytton*, a main favourite, had an unprecedented £20,000 from Routledge in 1854 for the lease of all his thirty-five copyrights. As W. H. Smith testified, by the mid-1850s Bulwer-Lytton was the most popular of all British novelists with the travelling public. Chapman and Hall* were encouraged in 1847 by the emergence of the new railway readership to embark on their 'popular' edition of Charles Dickens*, at a penny-halfpenny a part, the first of many cheap reprints of the author's works. Chapman and Hall were also (with W. H. Smith) pioneers in the creation of the new 1860s line of 'yellowback*' reprints, portable one-volume reissues of novels embellished by glossy, illustrated covers (of which the artist Edmund Evans was the principal designer). These led on to what were called 'Shilling Shockers' and the growth of rack-marketed fictional genres (the detective* novel, science fiction* etc.) in the 1880s and 1890s, with publishers like Arrowsmith* and the Hansom Cab Publishing Company (named after Fergus Hume's* bestseller) leading the way.

Ralph The Heir, Anthony Trollope, 1871, 3 vols, Hurst and Blackett. (Serialised as a supplement to *St Paul's Magazine,** January 1870–July 1871, with illustrations by F[rancis] A[rthur] Fraser.) The main line of the novel's plot follows Gregory Newton's attempts to pass on his property to his bastard son, Ralph. There is, confusingly enough, another (legitimate) nephew and heir, also called Ralph Newton. Gregory's schemes come to nothing when he dies hunting and Ralph the heir inherits Newton Priory. His namesake inherits £40,000 and is thus able to make a good marriage with his sweetheart Mary Bonner. Ralph the heir is one of Trollope's weak young heroes and proposes to no less than four young ladies during the year in the late 1860s that the narrative covers. The main interest of the novel lies in the sub-plots. Particularly powerful is the account of the gloomy lawyer Sir Thomas Underwood's attempts to enter Parliament as the member for Percycross. His failure recalls Trollope's own wretched experiences as a candidate at the 'dirty' Beverley election in 1868. Another subplot centres on the radical bootmaker, Ontario ('Onty') Moggs, legitimate Ralph's rival for the hand of wealthy Polly Neefit, the breeches maker's daughter. Trollope thought this 'one of the worst novels I have written'.

Ranthorpe, G. H. Lewes, 1847, 1 vol, Chapman and Hall. A novel about the growth of the author's soul. Percy Ranthorpe is first discovered a lawyer's clerk, with poetic ambitions. He quarrels with his businessman father and is thrown out of home. He also deserts the girl he has been brought up with, Isola Churchill, who loves him. On the strength of his first volume of verse, *Dreams Of Youth*, Percy is lionised. He almost marries a flirt, Florence Wilmington, but is warned off by his friend Wynton. Ranthorpe's second volume fails and his tragedy is hooted off the London stage. He is saved from suicide by an old man whom he meets in the London streets, and who introduces Percy to the great example of Goethe. The hero resolves to educate himself for authorship, and spends two years in Germany, at the end of which he returns, marries Isola and becomes a successful man of letters. The interest of the novel is principally in its early scenes of bohemian London around the teaching hospitals.

RATHBONE, Hannah Mary (née Reynolds, 1798–1878). Reynolds was born into a family of Quakers near Wellington in Shropshire. Her grandfather Richard Reynolds (1735–1816), having made a fortune in industry, became a famous philanthropist. At nineteen, Hannah married her half-cousin Richard Rathbone, by whom she went on to have six children, despite chronically delicate health. An accomplished artist, she specialised in calligraphy and illuminated manuscripts. Her publications are slight but stylistically influential. In 1840, she brought out a small volume of verse. More effectively, in 1844 she published the first part of her *Diary Of Lady Willoughby*. (Its full title was *So Much Of The Diary Of Lady Willoughby As Relates To Her Domestic History And To The Eventful Period Of The Reign Of Charles I.*) The work created a stir. There was considerable controversy as to its authorship and its supposed authenticity as a historical document covering 1635–48. The publisher, Longman*, brought out ('imprinted') the book with a period typeface, and it was presented superficially as a bona fide diary. The controversy was finally settled by a preface to the third edition indicating that the work was merely 'personated'. A sequel to the *Diary* ('Some Further Portions'), bringing the record to 1663, was published in 1847, and the joint work reissued in 1848. Rathbone's pseudo-historical narrative clearly inspired later 'diary' historical* novels such as Anne Manning's* *The Maiden And Married Life Of Mary Powell* (1850) and Thackeray's* *Henry Esmond** (1852) both of which Smith, Elder* brought out in facsimile old-fashioned type as 'spurious antiques'. Hannah Rathbone died in Liverpool. BL 2. *DNB*.

Ravenshoe, Henry Kingsley, 1862, 3 vols, Macmillan. (The novel was first serialised in *Macmillan's Magazine**, January 1861–July 1862.) The hero Charles is heir to the wealthy Ravenshoe family, of Stonington, Ireland. Following his mother, he is Protestant, the Ravenshoes (and his brother Cuthbert) being generally Catholic. On the death of his father (Densil Ravenshoe), Father Mackworth, the family's Jesuit confessor, reveals that Charles is not in fact the heir. He was changed at birth with the son of Densil's illegitimate half-brother, James Horton. The worthy but dull Cuthbert inherits the Ravenshoe estate. To multiply his woes Lord Welter, Charles's cousin and oldest friend, elopes with Adelaide the woman he loves, having seduced Charles's sister Ellen. The hero goes off to fight with the Hussars in the Crimea (the Charge of the Light Brigade figures vividly). He returns to England, desperate. He is saved at death's door by an old friend,

John Marston. And all is made well in a final denouement involving the death by drowning of Cuthbert and the discovery of Charles's legitimacy (a fact suppressed by the cunning Mackworth). The novel is notable for its gusto, and for a plot which Kingsley himself thought too 'intricate' to summarise. The early narrative has some lively Oxford University scenes.

RAYMOND, Walter ('Tom Cobbleigh', 1852–1930). Raymond was born in Yeovil, and remained a Somerset ('Ciderland') man all his life. For many years he ran a glove-making business, which he gave up in 1895 to write novels and books about the countryside. Little else is known about him, other than the fact that he lived in Taunton, married in 1878, had eight children (five daughters) and wrote a string of successful regional* 'idylls' which contemporary critics applauded for their 'simplicity and wholesomeness'. They include: *Misterton's Mistake* (1888); *Love And Quiet Life* (1894), 'Somerset Idylls', snapshots of 'Sutton Town' in the 1830s; *In The Smoke Of War* (1895), a romance set in the Civil War; *Tryphena In Love* (1895). The last features a rustic hero who after being crippled cultivates a love of literature. BL 13. *WW*. Wol.

REACH, Angus Bethune (1821–56). Reach was born in Inverness, Scotland, the son of a solicitor. After study at Edinburgh University, he was drawn into journalism and miscellaneous writing. In 1842, he moved to London, to work for the *Morning Chronicle*, then a paper with a strong line in vivid social reportage. For the *Chronicle* Reach was a parliamentary and trial correspondent and also wrote a powerful series of reports on industrial conditions in the north of England. He subsequently joined the *Punch** coterie in 1849 and collaborated at various times with Shirley Brooks* and Albert Smith*. (With Smith he brought out the bestselling comic serial *A Man In The Moon*, 1847–49.) Reach also hit the public taste of the late 1840s with a series of 'social zoologies', notably *The Natural History Of Bores* (1847) which was quickly followed by similar histories of 'Humbugs' and 'Tufthunters'. Among much other writing, Reach produced two rollicking novels: *Clement Lorimer, Or The Book With The Iron Clasps* (published in monthly parts, 1848–49, with illustrations by George Cruikshank*) and *Leonard Lindsay, Or The Story Of A Buccaneer* (1850). Reviewers applauded these works' 'meritoriously direct manner of narration'. Reach was famous for punishing stints of hard work and in 1854 he contracted softening of the brain. For the last painful months of his short life he was supported by friends like Shirley Brooks who did his writing for him. Thackeray*, Dickens* and Edmund Yates*, affected by the spectacle of Reach's death, staged various benefit readings and performances to relieve the wants of his surviving family. BL 4. *DNB*. *NCBEL*. Wol. Sad. RLF.

READ, Charles Anderson (1841–78). Read was born near Sligo, Ireland, the son of a ruined landowner turned schoolmaster. Having failed in business himself, Read came to London in 1863. In London, he went into business with James Henderson, the publisher, and contributed stories to Henderson's *Young Folks*. Read also wrote for the *Dublin University Magazine**. His major achievement was the preparation of *The Cabinet Of Irish Literature* (1876–78). Read wrote the novels *Savourneen Dheelish* (1867) and *Aileen Aroon* (1867), both of which enjoyed some popularity as 'People's Pocket Story Books'. BL 2. *DNB*.

READE, Charles (1814–80). Dramatist, novelist, controversialist and ec-centric. Reade was born, in the landed professional classes, at Ipsden Ox-fordshire, an estate which the Reade family had owned since the sixteenth century. Charles was the youngest of eleven children, and his mother (who died in 1863) had a profound influence on him. Evangelical and intellec-tual, she was a friend of Bishop Samuel Wilberforce. Charles was educated privately. He duly won a scholarship to Magdalen College, Oxford, and grad-uated in 1835 with a third-class degree in Greats. Later in 1835 Reade was made a probationary fellow of his college (he was to retain his rooms at Magdalen until his death). And in the same year, as regulations permitted, he enrolled at Lincoln's Inn to study law. Reade was called to the Bar in 1843; but never practised (although he was highly litigious by nature). In order to hold his Oxford fellowship, he was required to be, at least publicly, celibate. Reade consequently never married, nor did he smoke or drink. For a while, it was uncertain what he would do with his superabundant energies. (One of his projects was to sell violins.) For a number of years, he was a clubman largely resident in London, but spending quite large amounts of time in Oxford and Paris. He supported himself during this aimless period on his college stipend and various subsidies from his mother. (It has been suggested that her domination shows in his later fiction as an obsession with strong, sometimes sadistic, female types.) In 1849, Reade embarked on his literary career by adapting French drama for the English stage. With his fourth work for the theatre, *Masks And Faces* (1852), he achieved his first considerable success. (His collaborator on the play was Tom Taylor, another part-time barrister.) *Masks And Faces* yielded £150 profit for the two au-thors. In 1853 Reade, now at the advanced age of thirty-eight, produced his first novel, *Peg Woffington**, an adaptation of *Masks And Faces*. His motive for turning to prose fiction was impatience. Drama was not bringing him the fame he craved. *Peg Woffington* found its mark with the reading public and *Christie Johnstone** followed in 1853. It has been surmised that the work (which is set in Newhaven, near Edinburgh) records an affair of Reade's with a local woman, by whom he had a child. About this period, in 1853, Reade began collecting material on prison life. His play *Gold* (set in the Australian diggings) was also produced in 1853. In 1856, he published the novel with a purpose *It Is Never Too Late To Mend**, which resourcefully combined the prison research and goldfield melodrama to great effect. The work sold massively (2,700 copies of the cheap edition were cleared in two days) and laid the pattern for one main variety of sensation* fiction; namely the muck-raking novel directed towards the elimination of some crying social abuse. In 1854, Reade unsuccessfully tried his hand at theatre management. Also about this period, he formed a close connection with an actress, Mrs Laura Seymour. The relationship was probably platonic. Nevertheless, the couple set up house in 1869 (she she died in 1879, after a two decades long relationship). Reade was one of the first British novelists successfully to es-tablish a professional base in America, where he was (with the assistance of Ticknor and Fields), a bestselling author, despite the besetting problem of international copyright. In fact, of all Victorian novelists Reade took the keenest interest in the legal protection of intellectual property and in 1860 he wrote a book on the rights of authors entitled *The Eighth Command-ment* ('Thou shalt not steal. Except from authors'). In 1861 he successfully defended *It Is Never Too Late To Mend* against dramatic pirates. But paradoxically, Reade had a cavalier attitude towards what belonged to others. He fell out with Anthony Trollope* when, in 1872, he 'borrowed' the plot of *Ralph The Heir** (1871) for the play *Shilly Shally*. And from Mrs Burnett* (later famous as the author of *Little Lord Fauntleroy**) he similarly filched *That Lass O' Lowrie's** (1877) for his play *Joan* (1878). According to an infuriated Trollope, Reade simply did not know the meaning of the term 'literary honesty'. In 1861, there appeared Reade's massive historical fiction, *The Cloister And The Hearth**. (The work was first serialised in *Once A Week** as *A Good Fight*.) In 1863, he serialised *Hard Cash** in Dickens's* weekly paper *All The Year Round**. (It earned the high price of £3,000; and to Dickens's irritation proved both interminably long and unpopular with the journal's readers.) This 'Matter Of Fact Romance', directed at the abuses practised in private lunatic asylums, represented the perfection of Reade's 'Great System'. His idiosyncratic mode of composition involved the amassing of vast amounts of clippings, research and notebook materials. During the last twenty years of his life, Reade brought out half a dozen three-deckers, many stories, and much journalism. He was always one of the better-paid novelists. For *Put Yourself In His Place** (serialised in *Cornhill**, 1869–70) George Smith paid a total of £4,000. But this money and more was eaten up by the unsuccessful dramatic adaptation Reade made, *Free Labour* (1870), a play which ran to a Wagnerian length of four and a half hours. For all his popularity, Reade was never a comfortable, nor an entirely safe author. Mudie* refused to stock *Cream* in 1859. *Griffith Gaunt, Or Jealousy** caused another storm in 1866 for its frank treatment of sexual infidelity. Reade might protest that he was not offering a 'boatful of pap' for children; none the less, English publishers were chary of offending the family reader. George Smith, for instance, was afraid to take *A Terrible Temptation** (1871). But Reade had some late successes with the Tichborne case inspired novel *A Wandering Heir* in 1872 and the dramatic adaptation of Zola's *L'Assommoir*, *Drink*, in 1879. This last is supposed to have earned Reade £20,000. As a novelist, his achievement is hard to assess. He wrote, as he liked to say, 'solid fiction'. Many readers have found it solid to the point of indigestibility; lumpy with statistics, newspaper reports and bluebook extracts. Nor is his fiction with a purpose always directed at worthwhile targets, and frequently seems more the product of hobby-horsical irritability rather than genuine social conscience. Modern readers may well find the most interesting feature of Reade's dramatic technique to be his violently expressive typography. For effect, he will use gigantic or minuscule print; insert illustrations mid-text; or break into simulated newsprint, or legal gothic format. BL 26. *DNB*. RM. *NCBEL*. Wol. Sad.

READE, John Edmund (1800–70). Reade was born at Broadwell, Gloucestershire, into a well-to-do family, his paternal grandfather being a baronet. Reade's first collection of poems was published in 1825, and revealed his notorious authorial propensity for plagiarism. (The main victim of his literary plundering was Byron; although he also plagiarised Scott and Wordsworth.) Reade lived his adult life mainly at Bath, travelling frequently to Italy and southern Europe. Among much inferior poetry, he wrote three novels, all stilted melodramas: *The Light Of Other Days* (1858); *Wait And Hope*

(1859), a Bulwer-Lyttonian* farrago featuring smugglers, a pure heroine called Pearl and a wicked baronet; *Saturday Sterne* (1862). The odd title of the last is taken from the name of the heroine. BL 3. *DNB*. Wol.

READE, William Winwood ('Francesco Abati', 1838–75). A nephew of Charles Reade*, he was born at Ipsden House, Oxfordshire, and educated at Winchester and Oxford (which he left without a degree). Reade had a vocation for scientific investigation and in 1861, in a spirit of zoological curiosity, he travelled to the Gabon. His project was to discover whether or not gorillas were (as popular imagination maintained) ferocious beasts. He ascertained they were not. Aware of the dilettante nature of his intellectual pursuits, Reade made a serious attempt to master medical science in 1866, but seems not to have stayed the course. He subsequently made various explorations into Africa; notably in 1869, to search for the source of the Niger. On a third expedition in 1873 he reported the Ashanti Wars for *The Times*. He returned from this assignment (in which he himself fought) ruined in health. Reade was strongly affected by his famous novelist uncle, and himself wrote fiction. In 1859, he brought out *Charlotte And Myra, A Puzzle In Six Bits*. The narrative features a short-sighted hero who confuses the woman he loves with her identical twin and lands up with a breach-of-promise suit. The work was savagely assailed by the reviewers for its sexual innuendo. It was followed by: *Liberty Hall, Oxon.* (1860); *See Saw* (1865), by 'Francesco Abati', a Catholic narrator interrupted by Anglican Reade; *The Outcast* (1875), an epistolary novel dealing with questions of faith and doubt. Reade's fiction was, as the *Athenaeum** sternly put it, 'whimsical, fantastic, unwholesome' and 'such as no English gentleman should write'. He also produced several powerful polemics against religion, of which the most famous is *The Martyrdom Of Man* (1872). His abilities in fiction were never fully developed. BL 3. *DNB*. Sad.

Ready Money Mortiboy, Walter Besant and James Rice, 1872, 3 vols, Tinsley. (Serialised in *Once A Week**, 1871–72.) The first of nine collaborations by the authors and their most successful. Old Mortiboy is a skinflint who has amassed a fortune and built up his bank in Market Basing by extortion. He drives his only son Dick out of the country after a trifling forgery. Years later, Dick returns and persuades his father that he is now rich. Dick in fact intends to rob the bank, and while doing so is surprised by Old Mortiboy, who promptly suffers a paralytic seizure. Dick, now having charge of his father's ill-gotten wealth, turns philanthropist. But he is murdered by his accomplice to the original robbery and dies simultaneously with his paralysed parent. The idea for the story was Rice's and the telling of it Besant's contribution. Tinsley printed a meagre first edition of only 600 copies and everyone seems to have been surprised when the novel caught the public taste. The authors promptly converted their work into a stage hit.

The Real Charlotte, E. O. Somerville and Martin Ross, 1894, 3 vols, Ward and Downey. Generally considered the authors' finest work of fiction, set in the Ireland of the late-nineteenth-century Anglo-Irish Ascendancy. The Charlotte Mullen of the title is squat, 'startlingly plain', forty-years-old and ruthless. The daughter of the agent for the Dysart estates, she loves her father's (married) successor, Roderick Lambert, who uses her. Charlotte takes charge of her young and pretty cousin from Dublin, Francie Fitzpatrick, intending she shall marry the eligible landowner Christopher Dysart. Instead, Francie falls in love with a military man, Lieutenant Gerald Hawkins, and when they quarrel marries the now widowed Roderick Lambert on the rebound. All Charlotte's schemes, bullying, ruses and crime (including murder, by neglecting to administer medicine to Lambert's first wife, Lucy) succeed, except that she fails to get what she really wants. The novel has a complicated climax. A vindictive Charlotte betrays Lambert's embezzling to Dysart. It all ends with a powerful scene in the potato loft in which, with Lambert at her mercy, Charlotte loses control of her temper and angrily admits that it is she who has ruined him. At just this moment, the announcement arrives that Francie (who has been contemplating elopement with Hawkins) has been killed. The novel is a remarkable portrait of majestically powerful, malignant will.

Rebecca And Rowena, Mr M. A. Titmarsh (i.e. W. M. Thackeray), 1850, 1 vol, Chapman and Hall. (Serialised in shorter form in *Fraser's Magazine**, August–September 1846.) 'A Romance Upon [Scott's] Romance'. Having won Rowena, Ivanhoe finds that marriage palls. She is a shrewish wife, and to find relief he goes off to war again with the lion-hearted King Richard. He is thought killed at Chalus, and Rowena promptly marries Athelstane. Ivanhoe returns, and rescues Rowena. But she dies, making him promise never to marry a Jewess. Luckily he discovers that Rebecca has converted to Christianity. Chapman and Hall published this wittiest of burlesques as a Christmas* Book, illustrated by R. Doyle*.

The Recollections Of Geoffrey Hamlyn, Henry Kingsley, 1859, 3 vols, Macmillan. The narrator is a neighbour to the principal characters and himself plays little part in the action. The story begins in the 1820s in the Devonshire village of Drumston. The Vicar's daughter Mary Thornton is courted by a young rascal, George Hawker, a farmer's bastard son and half-gypsy. Hawker has already forged documents to rob his father (a hanging offence) and persuades Mary to elope with him, causing the Vicar to have a paralytic seizure. In Brighton he gambles away her fortune of £5,000 in the Funds and is transported for coining. Mary and virtually the whole of the village emigrate to Australia, where Hamlyn has been for some years sheep farming. George Hawker is now a bushranger and in a bloody battle he kills his own sixteen-year-old son. He is hanged, Mary remarries a cousin, Tom Troubridge. The story, with its extraordinary wholesale removal of a community across the world, is told with Kingsley's usual brio.

Red As A Rose Is She, Rhoda Broughton, 1870, 3 vols, Bentley. (Serialised in *Temple Bar*, May 1869–March 1870.) A self-consciously lyrical Welsh story. The heroine, Esther ('Essie') Craven, a farmer's daughter, consents after much domestic bullying to a marriage with Lieutenant Robert Brandon, a stolid military man whom she likes but does not love. Essie then falls genuinely in love with another man, the aristocratic St John Gerard, who (unconscious of Brandon's prior claim) proposes to her. Brandon releases her, but she undergoes various other trials before finally achieving married happiness with St John, Brandon meanwhile conveniently dying abroad. The story is prattled off in Rhoda Broughton's habitually vivacious fashion.

Red Pottage, Mary Cholmondeley, 1899, 1 vol, Edward Arnold. The narrative follows the careers of two friends, Rachel West and Hester Gresley. Rachel inherits money after years of impoverishment in the depths of which she scrapes a living as a free-lance typist. In society she catches the attention of a young man, Hugh Scarlett. Scarlett has had an affair with Violet Newhaven and as part of a suicide pact (on the grounds of honour) with her husband, Lord Newhaven, must kill himself within five months. During this period he and Rachel fall in love. On the due date, Hugh cannot keep his word; but Newhaven himself falls under a train. Violet knows of the pact, but does not know which of the men drew the fatal short straw. Rachel discovers the truth and forgives Hugh for his cowardice, but it is too late and he kills himself in an icy lake. For her part Hester is artistic and has written a novel, *An Idyll Of East London*. The death of an aunt, Lady Gresley, forces her to live with an unsympathetic clergyman brother, James. One evening he comes on the manuscript of Hester's latest work, for which she has been promised £1,000. It reminds him of the work of the detestable atheist George Eliot* and he burns it. Hester's situation recalls Cholmondeley's own years of servitude with her clergyman father. At the end of the novel, her writer heroine is liberated, travelling the world with Rachel. The novel contains a strong charge of protest against the exploitation of women in Victorian society, and became a bestseller in Britain and America. It is written in a smart, elliptic style verging on flippancy which amused contemporary readers.

REDDING, Cyrus (1785–1870). Redding was born at Penryn, in the West Country, the son of a Baptist minister. His father seems mainly to have educated him. In 1806, the young Redding came to London where he threw himself energetically into the world of letters and politics. Known principally as a newspaperman, a supporter of the Whig Party, an editor (principally of the *New Monthly Magazine**, 1821–30) and the author of *A History Of Shipwrecks* (1833), Redding also wrote novels late in life, as his journalistic energies waned. They are: *Velasco, Memoirs Of A Page* (1846); *Keeping Up Appearances, A Novel Of English Life* (1860); *A Wife And Not A Wife* (1867). Redding's fiction found no favour with the reviewers, who thought it stiff, overwrought with 'an intention prepense in every observation'. BL 4. *DNB*. Wol.

REDE, [William] Leman (1802–47). Rede's main claim to a place in literary history is as a writer for the London stage. He was born in Hamburg, and had his greatest success in the theatre with *The Rake's Progress* (1833). After 1841, he turned to writing for the journals. For a short while, he floated a rival to *Punch** called, inevitably, *Judy*. In 1846, Rede published serially in the *Sunday Times* a novel, *The Royal Rake*, based on the early career of George IV. (The work, 'a satirical romance', was published in book form in 1842). While running *The Man In Possession* through the same newspaper, he died suddenly of an apoplexy. The serialisation of fiction in a newspaper had a huge effect on contemporary publishing practice (even though the *Sunday Times* at this period cost 7d.) It directly inspired the founding of such fiction-carrying weeklies as *Reynolds's Miscellany* in 1846. His brother, Leman Tertius Rede (1799–1832) also wrote for the stage and died similarly young. BL 2. *DNB*. Sad. RLF.

REED, Talbot Baines (1852–93). The most influential writer of stories for Victorian boys. Reed was born in Hackney, London. His father, Sir Charles Reed (1819–81), had been an industrialist but during his son's childhood he was primarily an MP and a local government administrator with a special interest in education. Talbot Reed was educated at the City of London School and in 1868 he joined a type-founding firm owned by his father. Throughout his life, Talbot Reed took a scholarly interest in typography and helped found the influential Bibliographical Society in 1892. Always closely connected with the RTS* he was an original contributor to the *Boy's Own Paper** ('My First [Rugby] Football Match, By An Old Boy' was its opening story). Reed wrote numerous stories for juveniles, celebrating the public school cult of manliness. They include: *The Adventures Of A Three Guinea Watch* (1880), the 'autobiography' of a fashionable timepiece and Reed's first serial in *BOP*; *The Fifth Form At St Dominic's** (1882); *My Friend Smith* (1882); *The Willoughby Captains* (1887); *Roger Ingleton, Minor* (1891), the stirring story of a young hero's efforts to find his lost brother; *The Master Of The Shell* (1894), the author's most enduring work of school fiction, originally published by the RTS. The story follows the experiences of Mark Railsford, new housemaster of the Shell at Grandcourt. An all-round sportsman, Reed died at the age of forty-two from tuberculosis. His novels are relatively few in number for a juvenile market author, but were much reprinted and remained favourites up until the second World War. BL 17. *DNB*. *NCBEL*. Wol.

The Regional Novel. On the eve of the Victorian period a writer in the *Athenaeum** (28 May 1836) noted that regionalism as a theme for fiction was exhausted: 'Ireland with its White Boys, its racy wit and its squalid misery is exhausted; Scotland, too, for all the use of a romancer, is worn out.' After Charles Lever's* brief bestseller popularity (1839–47) it is true that Ireland was never consistently popular with the English reader. Nor, despite the appeal of writers like Mrs Oliphant*, was Scotland ever to regain the popularity it had enjoyed in the fiction of Scott and John Galt. Dickens* and Thackeray* were overwhelmingly novelists of London life and following their example the bulk of Victorian fiction is set in the capital. George Eliot's* fiction of provincial life, the Brontës'* novels of Yorkshire and Mrs Gaskell's* stories of industrial Lancashire are exceptions. All this is in cue with demographic trends. The 1851 census showed that for the first time more people were living in urban than rural situations. London grew at 20 per cent every decade over the period 1841-81, from 2 million to almost 5 million population. Industrial conurbations like Manchester also grew proportionately. In the 1870s a vogue for regional fiction that was essentially nostalgic in tone emerged with the Wessex* fiction of Hardy*, the southern counties stories of R. D. Blackmore* and R. L. Stevenson's* Edinburgh tales.

REID, Captain [Thomas] Mayne (1818–83). One of the most popular story-tellers for Victorian boys, Reid's life was itself an adventure. The son of a

Northern Irish Presbyterian minister and intended for the same career, he ran away to the USA as a youth to seek his fortune in 1840. He found adventure in plenty (which he was later to record in his tales). By his own account, he was variously a 'nigger driver', a store keeper, teacher, actor and literary hack. Reid settled in Pittsburgh in 1842, moving to Philadelphia in 1843 (where he met Edgar Allan Poe). In early 1846, he moved on to New York as a newspaperman. With the declaration of war against Mexico he joined the US army in December 1846, fought bravely, was promoted to captain and was seriously wounded at the storming of Chapultepec. He returned to Europe in 1849, intending to throw himself into the revolutionary fray. But discovering that the upheaval was largely over, determined instead on a career in authorship. His first work *The Rifle Rangers* (1850) was aimed primarily at adults and recounts his Mexican adventures, 1846-47. The narrative carries footnotes explaining such unfamiliar things to English readers as the Bowie knife, or 'Arkansas toothpick'. But with *The Desert Home, Or The English Family Robinson* (1851) he began his profitable vein of juvenile romance. In the mid-1860s, Reid had a massive success with *The Headless Horseman** (1866), a 'Strange Tale Of Texas'. Posters advertising this prototypical Wild West story were plastered over every railway station in Britain. But Reid squandered his subsequent wealth on a celebratory 'hacienda' in Gerrard's Cross, and his later years were an unsuccessful struggle for stage, magazine or fiction success. He spent the years from 1867 to 1870 in the USA again, but his health was no longer up to the labour of magazine work in that country. His remaining years were passed quietly in England. Mayne Reid's stories are remarkable for their lack of preachiness (the besetting fault of Victorian juvenile fiction). His obsession was the hunt; as in: *The Scalp Hunters* (1851); *The Hunter's Feast* (1855); *The Tiger Hunter* (1862); *The Boy Hunters* (1853); even surreally: *The Giraffe Hunters* (1867) and *The Plant Hunters* (1858). The last is the ingenious chronicle of how the typical English garden originally came by all its horticultural exotics. BL 124. *DNB*. RM. *NCBEL*. Wol. Sad.

REID, [Sir] Thomas Wemyss (1842–1905). Reid was born at Newcastle upon Tyne, the second son of a Congregational minister. At fourteen, he was put to work as a clerk. Intellectually precocious, he began writing for the newspapers while still in his mid-teens. By 1861, he was chief reporter on the *Newcastle Journal* and in 1862 his report on the Hartley Colliery disaster won him considerable fame. In 1864, he became editor of the *Preston Guardian* and from 1866 until his death he was 'writing editor' on the *Leeds Mercury*. With his roving reporter's commission, Reid travelled widely abroad and knew most of the leading authors of the day. He moved to London in 1890, to become manager of Cassell's* publishing firm. A Liberal in his politics, he was knighted by Lord Rosebery in 1894. Reid was President of the Institute of Journalists, 1898–99. At various points during his busy life, he wrote biography and fiction. Of special interest are his books on Charlotte Brontë* (1877) and on William Black* (1902). He died in South Kensington. Reid's most successful novels were: *Gladys Fane, A Story Of Two Lives* (1884) and *Mauleverer's Millions* (1886). The first, dedicated to William Black, is set in London and Monte Carlo, and features violent love, duels, and aristocratic intrigue. The hero, Rex Mansfield, cannot marry

Gladys, as he has an insane wife still living. Freed from marital bondage, he nobly dies after saving the heroine from burning in a *tableau vivant* of the martyrdom of Joan of Arc. *Gladys Fane* was extremely popular and was in its eighth edition by the early 1890s. The other novel is a quieter 'Yorkshire romance'. BL 2. *DNB*. RM. *NCBEL*.

The Religious Novel. Characterised as an age of 'Faith and Doubt', the Victorian period saw an unparalleled flowering of religious fiction. Impelled by the Tractarian (or 'Oxford') movement, many of these novels dealt directly with the issue of Catholic conversion. Leading figures in the religious debate employed fiction to proselytise. Newman*, for instance, published the self-justifying *Loss And Gain** (1848) shortly after going over to Rome. His *Callista** (1856) is uncompromisingly propagandistic as is his co-religionist Cardinal Wiseman's* *Fabiola** (1854). As uncompromising from the Anglican standpoint are William Sewell's* *Hawkstone** (1845) and Charles Kingsley's* *Hypatia** (1853). The Catholic theme continues less dogmatically with the fiction of John Oliver Hobbes* and Mrs Humphry Ward* (notably her *Helbeck Of Bannisdale**). And religiosity of an untendentious kind suffuses the Anglican fiction of Charlotte Yonge*, J. H. Shorthouse* and Walter Pater* (the last being tinged with intellectual agnosticism). Probably the finest novels of religious doubt are James Froude's* *Nemesis Of Faith** (1849) and Ward's *Robert Elsmere** (1888). And even free-thinkers or agnostics like George Eliot*, Eliza Lynn Linton* and Samuel Butler* were steeped in the faith which they questioned, qualified or frankly rejected. All varieties of religious belief are reflected in the Victorian novel: Anglican (clergymen and clergymen's daughters make up the largest band of authors); Unitarians (like Mrs Gaskell*); dissenters (like William Hale White*); Jews (like Grace Aguilar* and Israel Zangwill*); Calvinists (like George MacDonald* and Norman Macleod*). Mrs Oliphant* with her 'Chronicles of Carlingford*' and Anthony Trollope* with his 'Barchester* novels' anatomised the social and ecclesiastical dimensions of Victorian religion.

RTS (Religious Tract Society). This proselytising organisation was one of the largest producers of uplifting fiction over the first half of the nineteenth century. The society was founded in 1799 by a group of evangelicals led by the Congregationalist minister, George Burder (1752–1833). RTS tracts were devised to circulate through the distribution channels by which the poor customarily got their chapbooks, ballads and 1d. serials (e.g. street pedlars) and at giveaway price or free. By 1818, cumulative printing figures of up to 30 million tracts were claimed and by 1861, the annual output was a million pieces of printed material annually. Despite a puritan mistrust of fiction, the RTS began a line of imaginative works specifically for children in 1814. This initiative was further pursued in the 1820s, and a wholesale attempt to christianise fairy stories embarked on. And to the same end the society in 1824 began *The Children's Friend*, a 1d. monthly magazine which ran until 1860. It was patronised by the Princess of Wales and one of its early editors was the Rev. William Carus Wilson, whom Charlotte Brontë* was later to portray as the sadistic Mr Brocklehurst in *Jane Eyre** (1848). In its early years, the frank RTS aim was to convert and save souls. (Hence the popularity of deathbed stories for children.) By the 1840s, the tendency was more on using fiction as a guide to right conduct. At this later period favourite authors began to emerge, G. E. Sargent (1808?–83) being one of the first. And with the founding of their periodical *Sunday At Home* (1854) the RTS began to put out novels proper, as opposed to tracts clumsily sweetened with fiction. The best fiction, *qua* fiction, produced by the RTS in its early phase are the tales of Hesba Stretton* (i.e. Sarah Smith), author of the much reprinted *Jessica's First Prayer* (1867). Even more than most publishers of books for children, the RTS gave minimal payment to their authors. (Stretton, for instance, got under £50 each for her copyrights.) In the 1860s and after, the RTS made a conscious attempt to brighten their image with the juvenile reader, and to secularise (at least superficially) their product. They devised the immensely successful *Boy's Own Paper* in 1879 and published boys' adventure writers like W. H. G. Kingston*, R. M. Ballantyne*, G. A. Henty*, Gordon Stables* and Talbot Baines Reed*. (GB) *DNB*.

The Return Of The Native, Thomas Hardy, 1878, 3 vols, Smith, Elder. (Serialised in *Belgravia**, January–December 1878, with illustrations by Arthur Hopkins.) Hardy's most melodramatic novel, set in the 1840s and overshadowed by the lowering presence of Egdon Heath. The heroine, Eustacia Vye, is a passionate woman ('the raw material of a divinity') who has been jilted by Damon Wildeve, publican of the ironically named Quiet Woman inn (formerly an engineer). Wildeve has married the gentle Thomasin ('Tamsin') Yeobright, who is loved in turn by the vagrant reddleman, Diggory Venn, who supplies local farmers with ochre for marking sheep. Thomasin's cousin, Clym, is the native who returns. Finding his work as a gem merchant in Paris (and the whole of modern civilisation) meaningless he comes back to live with his mother at Blooms-End, Egdon Heath, intending to start a farm. He wants 'to do something worthy before I die'. Clym falls in love with and marries Eustacia. She hopes to persuade him to take up his former work. But in a complicated narrative sequence, Clym's mother dies as a direct result of Eustacia's haughtiness; he loses his sight and ends up a humble furzecutter or 'cropper' on the heath. Eustacia returns to Damon, but in a tremendous suicidal climax both are drowned in Shadwater Weir. Clym subsequently becomes a wandering preacher and 'lecturer on morally unimpeachable subjects'. In a happy ending (forced on Hardy by his magazine editor), Diggory Venn marries the widowed Thomasin. In the author's original design, Venn would have retained 'his isolated and weird conception to the last'. In his 1895 preface, Hardy draws the analogy between his novel and Shakespeare's *King Lear*, 'that traditionary King of Wessex', also associated with heaths.

The Revolt Of Man, Walter Besant, 1882, 1 vol, Blackwood. A literary curiosity. This tale of the future prophesies a gynocratic England. Women dominate the House of Commons, men are excluded. The male, by a complete role reversal, has become an ornamental appendage. Christianity is overthrown and replaced by a secular faith centred on the supreme woman. Society has become a gentle well-ordered place. In a loose plot, the oppressed males rise up led by Edward the Earl of Chester. They march on London and rout a force of guardswomen. The male is restored to superiority. The fable ends with some happy marriages. Following a notice in the *Saturday*

Review* Besant's tale became a bestseller. Its appeal was boosted by current fascination with the new woman*.

The Revolution In Tanner's Lane, Mark Rutherford (i.e. William Hale White), 1887, 1 vol, Trübner. Rutherford's finest novel, which takes the form of an anatomy of the mingled origins of nineteenth-century political radicalism and religious nonconformity. The action begins in London in 1814. After a scuffle in Piccadilly (where he refuses to remove his hat for the triumphant Louis XVIII), Zachariah Coleman is befriended by a fellow republican, 'Major' Maitland. Coleman is a printer and by faith an 'Independent'. He has recently married but sadly discovers that he does not love his wife. Maitland introduces Zachariah to a radical debating club whose secretary, a spy, is assassinated. Maitland and Coleman flee north to Manchester, where they continue as militant radicals. In 1817, during a political demonstration (as 'blanketeers') Maitland is cut down by a militiaman. Another of Zachariah's comrades is hanged and (now a widower) he marries the executed man's wife, Pauline. Zachariah himself subsequently spends two years in prison after which the action jumps forward twenty years to 'Cowfold' (i.e. Bedford) in the 1840s. The last section of the narrative chronicles a power struggle in the Tanner's Lane church of which Zachariah and his daughter are now members. White's novel examines with great convincingness the reasons why there should have been a revolution in Tanner's Lane in 1844, but no revolution in England in 1821.

Reward Books. Sometimes simply called 'Rewards'. They were books, stories or tracts given out at Sunday School, with a consciously improving purpose. Throughout the nineteenth century they were produced in mass by the RTS* and the SPCK*. Some established evangelical novelists (notably Charlotte Yonge*) wrote Rewards.

REYNOLDS, G[eorge] W[illiam] M[acArthur] (1814–79). Reynolds was born at Sandwich in Kent, the son of a senior naval officer, Sir George Reynolds. His well-born background gives no indication of his later republicanism. George Reynolds was entered at the Royal Military College at Sandhurst in 1828, but left after two years, 'a military career', we are told, 'being little to his taste'. Having been left £12,000, Reynolds travelled widely on the Continent in the 1830s, and was swept up by the revolutionary politics and the popular literature of France. (Notably, the criminal bestsellers of Vidocq, Eugène Sue and Victor Hugo.) He may have briefly become a French citizen. Reynolds's first published novel was *The Youthful Impostor* (1835). But he was principally concerned at this period with the proprietorship of French and English newspapers in which he gained much valuable experience and evidently lost most of his fortune. In 1836 Reynolds was bankrupt, and returned to England. In 1839, he had some success with the plagiaristic *Pickwick Abroad, Or The Tour In France*, a work reckoned to be the best of its derivative kind. Reviewers generally applauded this 'continuation' of Dickens's* narrative, in which Samuel Pickwick is called out of his retirement at Dulwich for a jaunt overseas. Reynolds's other bestseller of the period was the melodramatic novel about the heroic oarswoman, *Grace Darling* (1839). Around 1844, he married his wife, the author Susannah Frances Reynolds. In 1845, he became editor of the new *London Journal**.

At the same time, he began to publish his most famous serial, *Mysteries Of London* (various series ran until 1855, co-authored with Thomas Miller* and Edward Laman Blanchard). Based loosely on Eugène Sue's colourful *Mysteries Of Paris* (1842–43), the work was phenomenally successful with the lower class of English reader, and may have sold as many as a million copies in ten years. Reynolds's narrative is notable for its politically republican content, which may have alarmed the authorities. In 1846, there also appeared the first issue of the 1d. weekly *Reynolds's Miscellany*, a magazine which was made the vehicle of Reynolds's radical sympathies. Among the paper's most popular contributors after Reynolds himself was Edwin F. Roberts (1802–54). In 1848, however, he was again bankrupt. During the 1840s, Reynolds expressed strong sympathy with European revolutionary parties and himself became a leader of the Chartists in 1848, allying himself with the physical-force wing of the movement. Hatred of the landed aristocracy was always the main element in his political thinking. Following the collapse of organised labour in England, Reynolds founded *Reynolds's Weekly Newspaper* with a former clerk, John Dicks, in 1850. The paper, which initially cost 4d., lasted until 1967 and was his most enduring monument. By 1855 the *Miscellany* had a circulation of 300,000. Reynolds wrote (or put his name to) a mass of popular fiction, much of it issued in 1d. serial form. His novels include: *Faust* (1847); *The Coral Island* (1848); *The Pixy* (1848); *Pope Joan* (1851); *Mysteries Of The Court Of London* (1849–56); *Agnes* (1852); *The Soldier's Wife* (1853); *Rosa Lambert* (1854); *The Loves Of The Harem* (1855); *Ellen Percy* (1856). Reynolds translated from the French (and bowdlerised) several of the licentious novels of Paul de Kock (1809–91). His wife Susannah Frances Reynolds wrote *Gretna Green* (1848) and the Chartist melodrama (dedicated to 'the Industrious Classes of the United Kingdom'), *Wealth And Poverty* (1848). BL 43. *DNB*. RM. *NCBEL*. Wol. Sad. RLF.

REYNOLDS, H[enry] R[obert] (1825–96). Reynolds was born at Ramsey in Hampshire, the son of a Congregationalist minister and educated at Coward College. In 1846 he was himself ordained a Congregationalist pastor and two years later was elected (on the strength of his mathematical research) a fellow of University College, London. For the next ten years, Reynolds held various ministries around England. At the end of the 1850s his health collapsed. From 1860 to 1894, he occupied the less taxing position of President of Cheshunt College. He also took up writing during this quieter phase of his career. From 1866 to 1874, he coedited the *British Quarterly Review* and in the last three decades of his life was active as an evangelical writer. With his eminent physician brother, Sir John Russell Reynolds (1828–96), Reynolds wrote and published anonymously an 'ultra-Protestant' novel dealing with the religious controversies of the 1850s: *Yes And No, Or Glimpses Of The Great Conflict* (1860). The narrative takes the form of a Bulwer-Lyttonian* quest narrative, with much travel abroad and spiritual adventure for the hero. BL 1. *DNB*. Wol. Sad.

Rhoda Fleming, George Meredith, 1865, 3 vols, Tinsley. The novel's action begins in Kent. Rhoda and Dahlia Fleming are daughters of a farmer. Dahlia is seduced by an idle young man of higher class, Edward Blancove. Robert Eccles, a former soldier who loves Rhoda, sets out to rescue Dahlia. But the wily Blancove contrives to arrange a marriage between her and a hired ruffian, Sedgett. Eccles nevertheless preserves her purity by carrying Dahlia off immediately after the ceremony, and manages to establish that Sedgett was previously married. Blancove repents, but too late to prevent Dahlia from poisoning herself. She is however saved. Rhoda finally marries Robert. The novel earned the author a measly (as he thought) £400.

RHYS, Grace (née Little, 1856–1929). Born in Roscommon, Ireland, Grace Little in 1891 married Ernest [Percival] Rhys (1859–1946), the Anglo-Welsh poet best remembered as the founder of Dent's* *Everyman's Library*. The Rhyses lived in Hampstead, where they set up something of a literary salon. She was, as the *DNB* puts it, 'a lady of great charm and culture who published among other works two or three delicate volumes of belles lettres'. She also turned out some delicate novels with Irish* settings, such as *Mary Dominic* (1898), in which the heroine is a seventeen-year-old Irish girl of humble origins seduced by a rich lover and cast out by her parents. *The Wooing Of Sheila* (1901), a rural love story set in Ireland, seems to have been her only other effort in full-length fiction in the Victorian period. On his part, Ernest Rhys produced some Fiona Macleod* derived fantasies around the same end-of-century period, such as *The Fiddler Of Carne* (1896), a fable of art, using the character of an eighteenth-century vagrant musician, and *The Whistling Maid* (1900), a Welsh romance. (GR) BL 4. (ER) BL 2. *WW*. RM. RLF.

RICE, James (1843–82). A historian of English racing and magazine editor, Rice is best remembered as Walter Besant's* collaborator on his first dozen novels. Born in Northampton, Rice was Cambridge educated (though he seems not to have taken a degree). He subsequently read for the Bar and qualified in 1871. But he did not apparently practise. In London Rice was drawn into journalism and in 1868 took over the property and editorship of *Once A Week**, a post he held for four years before he sold the magazine to G. Manville Fenn* in 1873. A feature of Rice's journal was its reliance on a running serial novel. Rice discovered that he could not himself provide the needed commodity and he invited the young Besant to co-author with him. In 1872, they produced the hit *Ready Money Mortiboy** (the idea, or motif as Besant would say, was Rice's) and even more profitably adapted their story for the London stage. Encouraged by their success, the duo team-wrote a novel a year until Rice's premature death from cancer. Their most profitable title was *The Golden Butterfly** (1876), a comedy built around a vulgar, oil-rich American millionaire. Another good earner for them was *The Chaplain Of The Fleet** (1881), a story of the famous gaol in the reign of George III. Had Rice not died, it is likely that the partnership in fiction would have continued. Besant's subsequent eighteen novels without Rice lack a certain raciness and comic touch. (Although in his *Autobiography*, Besant regretted that their partnership had 'ever gone beyond *The Golden Butterfly*'.) Rice's history of the British turf appeared in 1879. (WB and JR) BL 14. *DNB*. RM. *NCBEL*. Wol.

Richard Cable, S. Baring-Gould, 1888, 3 vols, Smith, Elder. One of Baring-Gould's more unusual romances. The hero, Cable, is a lightship man off the Essex coast. A widower of ten months, 'half-way between thirty and forty', he has seven children. During a vividly described storm he rescues a young runaway girl, Josephine Cornellis, who subsequently falls in love with him and they marry. But ashore, Cable's crudeness appals his more civilised wife who discovers herself now an heiress. He declines to bathe every day, mispronounces words and gets himself fuddled at the Anchor inn, scandalising his in-laws. They part, and Cable, feeling himself 'a fish out of water', sails off to Cornwall. Josephine decides to lower her station in life and becomes a maidservant at the great house of Miss Otterbourne in Bath. In Cornwall, Richard has meanwhile established himself as a cattle-dealer. The couple eventually make up and go through another marriage ceremony to celebrate their strengthened union.

RICHARDS, [Lt.-Col.] Alfred Bate (1820–76). Richards is mainly known as a dramatist and as the moving force behind the Volunteer militia movement of 1859. He was born in Worcestershire, the son of an MP for Knaresborough (1832–37). Young Richards was educated at various boarding schools, including Westminster. After gaining his degree at Oxford, he read law at Lincoln's Inn, and was called to the Bar in 1845, but soon turned to literature. He went on to publish various well-received poems and tragedies, and was (briefly) the first editor of the *Daily Telegraph* in 1855. In 1859, he raised the third City of London rifle corps, remaining its commanding officer until 1869. Richards wrote one novel late in life, *So Very Human, A Tale Of The Present Day* (1871). It comprises a bitter satire on the morality of English society and commerce, prophetic of Trollope's* similarly jaundiced *The Way We Live Now** (1875). Its initial publication was held up a year for fear of libel action. BL 1. *DNB*. Wol.

RICHARDS, James Brinsley (1846–92). A son of Eustace Clare Grenville Murray* (himself the illegitimate son of the Duke of Buckingham and Chandos). At birth he was christened Reginald Temple S. C. Grenville Nugent Grenville-Murray, a name he later decided to change to something simpler and more proletarian. Richards was educated at Eton (about which he wrote a book in 1883). As a young man he lived for some time in France. He later worked as a journalist, reporting for *The Times* in Vienna from 1885 and in Berlin from 1892. Richards in this last phase of his life published anonymously a couple of novels of high life in Europe (which he evidently knew at first hand): *The Duke's Marriage* (1885) and *Prince Roderick* (1889). He died prematurely of a stroke in Berlin. BL 3. *DNB*. Wol.

RICHARDSON, Sir Benjamin [Ward] (1828–96). Richardson was born in Leicestershire and educated privately. After being apprenticed to a local surgeon he studied medicine first at Glasgow University, subsequently taking his MD from St Andrew's in 1854. (He was later to receive an honorary doctorate from the university in 1877.) From the early 1850s, Richardson practised medicine at Barnes in London and in 1856 was appointed physician to the Royal Infirmary for Diseases of the Chest. A man of superabundant energy, Richardson founded the *Journal Of Public Health And Sanitary Review* in 1855. Richardson went on to do important research on heart disease and introduced many effective drugs into medical use. He was also a believer in exercise (especially cycling), temperance and moderation as preventive medical techniques. Richardson had a distinguished and rewarded medical career and was knighted in 1893. He wrote prolifically, including a Bellamy-inspired romance, which ran to three tendentious volumes, *The Son Of A Star, A Romance Of The Second Century* (1888). The work's setting moves from Ancient Britain to Biblical Judea. He was a personal friend of Douglas Jerrold*, W. M. Thackeray* and George Cruikshank*. BL 1. *DNB*. Wol.

RICHARDSON, John (1797–1863). British only by military adoption, John Richardson was born of Scottish parents, near Niagara, in Canada and later served with the Canadian militia in the war of 1812. In 1815, he came to England where he married, and evidently spent some time in Paris. He subsequently published the ultra-fashionable novel *Ecarté, Or The Salons Of Paris* with Colburn* in 1829 and *Wacousta* in 1832. The second of these, which is set in Canada, is usually reckoned the author's most interesting work of fiction. In 1835, Richardson joined the British auxiliary legion, to fight in Spain on behalf of Queen Regent Christina against the Carlists. He saw active service, but fell out with his commander, Sir George De Lacy Evans, sparking off a feud that was to poison the rest of his life. His grievance led eventually to a House of Commons inquiry. With Hook*, he intended to libel Evans (and other of his enemies) in the latter's novel, *Jack Brag* (1837), but the scheme came to nothing. In 1838, Richardson was appointed *Times* correspondent in Canada, but was dismissed for biased reporting (his opinions were more fiercely Tory than the paper could stomach). In the late 1840s, he moved down to America. A veteran, but now destitute, writer he wrote a number of extremely feeble novels clearly to raise money. They include: *The Monk Knight, A Tale Of The Crusades* (1850); *Matilda Montgomerie* (1851), a romance of the American Revolution; *Wan-Nan-Gee* (1852), subtitled, 'Or The Massacre At Chicago'. Richardson died in the USA. BL 7. *DNB*. RM. Wol.

RICKETT, Sir Joseph [Compton] ('Maurice Baxter', 1847–1919). Born in London, Rickett was an industrialist (until 1902), lay preacher and politician. A Liberal MP for Scarborough from 1895, he achieved Cabinet office in 1916. On the side, he wrote voluminously. His major efforts were popular philosophy, but he also wrote poetry and fiction, under the pseudonym 'Maurice Baxter'. His major novel is *James Strathgeld* (1873). The hero (who tells his story partly autobiographically) is a monster of immorality who sacrifices all scruple to succeed in business. Rickett married in 1868, had eight children, was knighted in 1907, and went on to retitle himself by royal licence, Sir Joseph Compton-Rickett. BL 1. *WW*.

RIDDELL, Mrs J[oseph] H[adley] [Charlotte Elizabeth Lawson] ('F. G. Trafford', née Cowan, 1832–1906). Remembered as 'the novelist of the City' (i.e. of London), Mrs Riddell was a prolific and from 1864 to the mid-1870s, a popular author. She was born Charlotte Cowan, in Carrickfergus, Ireland, where her father was High Sheriff of the county. In general, she subsequently avoided Irish* settings in her later fiction, although some picture of her background is given in *Berna Boyle* (1882). Arrived in London in 1855, Cowan embarked on supporting herself and her sick mother by her pen. Without friends or literary patron she had the usual difficulty in placing her manuscripts, and first saw print with the notorious Newby*, whose female manageress had faith in the young novelist. The novel, *Zuriel's Grandchild* (1855), sank without trace. But this early story served to bring her to the notice of Smith, Elder*, who put out *The Moors And The Fens* in 1857, under the authorial pseudonym, 'F. G. Trafford'. The novel (which has a writer heroine who unhappily marries a baronet) enjoyed modest success and earned the author a niggardly £20. Riddell recalls her difficult apprentice years in one of her finest novels *A Struggle For Fame** (1883). In 1857, she married J. H. Riddell. Her husband, an engineer, provided her with the insider's financial background to the subsequent 'City novels' for which she is best known; e.g. *City And Suburb* (1861); *Mitre Court* (1885); *The Head Of The Firm* (1892). The last is the story of self-sacrificing Thomas Desborne who slaves for the firm of which his worthless nephew is the head. Riddell's observation of London is very sharp. And her career took off in 1863, when she moved to the Tinsley* brothers, then the most vigorous of purveyors of fashionable novels to the circulating libraries. Famously vulgar, William Tinsley exclaimed when she walked into his office: 'Here's "Too Much Alone". I have been wanting to find her.' From the Tinsleys, she had an agreement for £800 which produced *George Geith Of Fen Court** (1864), her eighth novel, the story of a clergyman who runs away from a disastrous marriage to become a successful accountant in the City. Hugely popular, *George Geith* was made into a successful play and became Riddell's hall-mark work, rivalling the Tinsleys' other bestseller of the period, *Lady Audley's Secret** (1862). In the late 1860s, Riddell was at the peak of her career. In 1867, she became editor and part proprietor of the *St James's Magazine** (founded by Mrs S. C. Hall* in 1861). Her mid-career fiction includes *Life's Assizes* (1871), a Scottish story; *Above Suspicion* (1876), a sensation* novel and short magazine stories such as 'The Prince Of Wales's Garden Party' (1882). For some years Riddell wielded literary power and patronage. But her popularity waned with the arrival of new favourites and in 1880 Joseph Riddell died, leaving ruinous debts. Scott-like, his widow undertook to pay these off with her pen. After 1887, she moved to Bentley* (from whom she had up to £400 per novel); from this point on she published wherever she could at ever lower payment. Her last novel, *Poor Fellow*, appeared in 1902, four years before her death. The mass of Riddell's fiction falls into three categories: (1) tales of commerce and City life; (2) tales of the supernatural; (3) tales of everyday life, typically suffused with sadness. Her ghost* stories (especially the influential *Weird Stories*, 1882) are highly regarded. Most of her supernatural fiction deals with haunted houses. BL 56. *DNB*. RM. *NCBEL*. Wol. Sad. RLF.

RIDGE, W[illiam] Pett (i.e. Warwick Simpson, 1860–1930). Ridge was born at Chartham, near Canterbury in Kent where he was also educated. He lived in the country for his first twenty years, before moving to London. Ridge worked for some years in the clerical grade of the Civil Service and studied by night at London University's Birkbeck College. He did not start seriously to write fiction until 1890 thereafter becoming one of the principal authors in the cockney* school, although his touch is lighter and more facetious than that of Arthur Morrison*, Israel Zangwill* or Edwin Pugh*. His novels include: *A Clever Wife* (1895); *An Important Man* (1896); *Mord Eml'y* (1898), the Walworth Road romance of a charwoman's daughter, Maud Emily; *A Son Of The State* (1899), the story of a young street arab from Hoxton; *A Breaker of Laws* (1900), the lawbreaker being a safebreaker, Alfred Bateson, who marries, reforms and relapses; *London Only* (1901), sketches of London life and character, subtitled 'A Set Of Common Occurrences'. Little is known of Ridge's life. In *Who's Who* he enigmatically gives his recreations as 'roaming east of Aldgate and south'. BL 63. *WW*. RM. Wol.

The Right Honourable, Justin McCarthy [MP] and Mrs Campbell Praed, 1886, 3 vols, Chatto and Windus. Subtitled 'A Romance Of Society And Politics', the novel presents itself as a *roman à clef*, tracing in piquant detail the careers of the two authors. The action opens with a prelude in Australia. An ambitious young politician, the Premier of South Britain, Sandham Morse, is about to leave for grander prospects in England. At his farewell, he converses with the daughter of a fellow politician, Kooràli Middlemist, nicknamed 'the Little Queen'. Ten years pass and the couple meet again in London. Morse is now a leading Radical politician, married to Lady Betty. Kooràli has married a selfish and small-minded Australian politician, Crichton Kenway. The Kenways are now in England on his business as Agent-General for South Britain. Kenway discovers that Morse has had dealings with an extreme socialist group and sets about blackmailing him in expectation that he will soon have political power. But Morse declines to form a ministry, disagreeing with the country's belligerent war policy. Meanwhile, he and Kooràli have fallen in love, retaining however their essential 'whiteness' of soul. Meanly suspecting adultery, Crichton drives Kooràli out of his house. Morse offers to elope with her, which would mean death to his political career. To spare him this sacrifice, Kooràli honourably returns by herself to Australia. The novel hints broadly at a passionate relationship between its authors.

Rita, Charles Aïdé, 1858, 2 vols, Bentley. 'An Autobiography.' The heroine is brought up in the English colony in Paris. Her father, Colonel Percival (formerly of the Guards), is a wastrel and Rita's education is neglected until her rich aunt Lady Dacre takes it in hand. The girl subsequently flowers into an eligible young lady in Parisian society, although she is haunted by a sense of some mystery in her past. Rita makes her début under the auspices of Lady Greybrook. Around the same time her mother dies of smallpox, warning Rita to beware of her father, who wants to force her into marriage with the Marquis D'Ofort. Rita is also pursued by a wild lover, Lord Rowdon. But finally, after various adventures, she marries the decent Hubert Rochfort. The novel is principally interesting for its depiction of British emigrant life in Paris, which the author knew at first hand.

RITCHIE, Lady Richmond [Anne Isabella] (née Thackeray, 1837–1919). Thackeray's* eldest child. She was born in London and after her mother went mad in 1844 lived her early childhood mainly in France with her paternal grandparents. In 1847, Thackeray set up home in Young Street, London, with his two daughters and thereafter Anne enjoyed the stimulating domestic life of a famous novelist's daughter, meeting socially most of the leading men and women of Victorian letters and travelling widely. In her teens and after Anny (as the family called her) also had the privilege of acting as her father's amanuensis. Just before his death in 1863, the Thackerays (less the mother, who was totally incapable and in care) moved to a fine new Queen Anne house at Palace Green in Kensington, designed by the novelist himself. On his death, the Thackeray girls were left short of money, although they were relieved by income from the editions of their father's work put in hand by George Smith (of Smith, Elder*) and by the sale of their father's mansion. (It is now the Israeli London embassy.) In 1867 the younger sister, Harriet Marian ('Minny'), married the well-known man of letters, Leslie Stephen, but not long after went mad and died in 1875. In 1877 Anne married a very young cousin, Richmond Thackeray Ritchie (1854–1912), seventeen years her junior. The union seems nevertheless to have been happy. From her young womanhood Anne Ritchie wrote voluminous biography and memoirs, her first publication being a sketch, 'Little Scholars', published in *Cornhill**, May 1860. She also turned out domestic* fiction (as 'Miss Thackeray') including: *The Story Of Elizabeth** (1863), a work recalling the author's early years in Paris which she probably began writing when she was seventeen. *The Village On The Cliff* (1867) is a mild governess melodrama set in the little seaside town of 'Petitport' (i.e. Arromanches, which the author had visited in 1864). Other successful works were: *Old Kensington* (1873), a loose-knit panorama of the London locations the Thackerays knew best; *Miss Angel* (1875) a novelised account of the life of the female artist, Angelica Kauffmann (1741–1807); *Mrs Dymond* (1885), a family melodrama set in the Lake District and Paris during the Franco-Prussian war. Richmond Ritchie had a successful career in the Civil Service and diplomacy. The couple had two children and he was created KCB in 1907 for service in the India Office. BL 6. *DNB*. RM. *NCBEL*. Wol. Sad.

RITCHIE, Leitch (1800?–65). Ritchie was born (by the best accounts) at Greenock in Scotland. Around 1817 he left his apprenticed position in a Glasgow banking office to come down to London, where he made his first attempts in literature. But failure obliged him to return to Glasgow and commerce. In 1818, when his firm went bankrupt, he tried London literary life again. Ritchie wrote miscellaneously for many journals in the 1820s and 1830s, producing a quantity of travel books and novels, of which *Tales And Confessions* (1829) and *The Game Of Speculation* (1830) were fairly successful. He edited Smith, Elder's* 'Library Of Romance' (1833–35) and various insignificant periodicals. Ritchie spent the later years of his life in Scotland, conducting *Chambers's Journal**, handing the post over to James Payn* in 1858. He was destitute at the end of his career and was awarded a Civil List pension of £100 in 1862 which allowed him to retire to London where he died. Ritchie's fiction is feeble, even more so in his last years. It includes: *The Magician* (1836); *Wearyfoot Common* (1855). BL 3. *DNB*. *NCBEL*. Wol.

Robbery Under Arms, Rolf Boldrewood (i.e. T. A. Browne), 1888, 3 vols, Remington. (Serialised in the *Sydney Mail*, 1883.) The most popular of Australian bush-ranging romances. The story takes the form of a confession written before execution by Dick Marston, in the death cell at Sydney gaol. The narrator reminisces randomly about the wild exploits of his outlaw family under the leadership of Captain Starlight. At the eleventh hour Dick is reprieved and marries the girl who has stuck by him.

Robert Elsmere, Mrs Humphry Ward, 1888, 3 vols, Smith, Elder. Probably the best-selling 'quality' novel of the century. Robert Elsmere is an excessively earnest young Oxford graduate. A robust younger son of an old-established Sussex family, he nevertheless has a strand of feminine weakness in his makeup. Following a good university career ('he was neither dull enough, nor great enough for a striking Oxford success'), he takes up a Church post in the gift of a relative. Meanwhile, visiting at Long Whindale in Westmorland (lovingly described by Ward), he meets and falls in love with Catherine Leyburn, a widow's daughter. Catherine has inherited from her unorthodox father an unusual intellectualism, together with her physical attractions. The two marry and return to Robert's parish. But his religious duties are complicated by doubts sown in his mind by the earnestly philosophical Edward Langham (Robert's Oxford tutor), Professor Grey (based on T. H. Green, the novel's dedicatee) and Squire Roger Wendover (based on Mark Pattison, a man who sacrifices everything to intellect). These worthy sceptics test Robert's faith by exposing it to various forms of rational doubt. To Catherine's distress, he gives up his appointment and goes to the East End of London, where he sets up a commune called the New Brotherhood of Christ. It is massively successful, but Robert finally dies of tubercular disease, exhausted by his missionary efforts among the poor. Catherine is left a widow, worshipping at the Anglican Church and keeping her husband's community going as well. ('The New Brotherhood still exists and grows.') The novel and its discussion of the 'great problem' of religion in the modern world provoked a long review article from Gladstone, '*Robert Elsmere* And The Battle Of Belief' (*Nineteenth Century*, May 1888) which helped the novel to its phenomenal sales success.

Robert Falconer, George MacDonald, 1868, 3 vols, Hurst and Blackett. (Serialised in the *Argosy**, 1867.) The hero is raised in Scotland by his grandmother. Robert's mother died in his infancy and his father, thought by the Calvinist standards of the place to be depraved, has decamped. Robert is brought up strictly to distrust pleasure and art (his grandmother, for instance, burns a violin which he has secretly taught himself to play). As a child, Robert befriends a waif, 'Shargar' Moray, and cares for him. Shargar duly becomes his slave for life. At university in Aberdeen his religious doubts are shared by a poetic friend, Eric Ericson. Eric intends to marry the orphan daughter of an English clergyman, Mary St John, (whom Robert also loves) but dies before he can do so. The hero, now qualified as a doctor, inherits money from a friend of his father, Dr Anderson. Robert subsequently goes to London to work charitably among the poor (assisted by Mary). He finally meets his father, whom he nurses back to health and well-being. Father and son take ship to India and (presumably) drown when the vessel sinks in the middle of the ocean.

ROBERTS, Morley (1857–1942). Roberts was born in London, the son of an income tax inspector. He was educated at Bedford Grammar School, and later at Owens College, Manchester, where he was a contemporary and became a lifelong friend of George Gissing's*. (After Gissing's death, Roberts wrote his biography in novel form as *The Private Life Of Henry Maitland*, 1912.) In 1876, Roberts went to Australia, to work on the railroads. He travelled, picking up employment here and there in New South

Wales, on cattle ranches and sheep stations. From Australia, Roberts drifted on to California and South Africa, working at ports, sawmills and wherever he could. This wandering equipped him to become a successful novelist of empire. (*A Son Of Empire**, 1899, was actually his most successful work; it is the story of a daring secret agent, 'Black Blundell'.) Roberts's novel-writing career began with *The Western Avernus* (1887). His subsequent fiction includes: *In Low Relief* (1890), a tale of London bohemian life; *The Earth Mother* (1890), a story of artistic life; *Maurice Quain* (1897), a realistic novel of London life which starts vividly with Maurice rowing down the Thames and dragging the suicidal heroine to land by her long hair; *The Mate Of The Vancouver* (1892), a nautical* tale; *The Reputation Of George Saxon* (1892), short stories. Roberts also wrote a fictionalised biography of Cecil Rhodes in *The Colossus* (1899) and a novel of the Boer War, *Taken By Assault* (1901). Somewhat to the impecunious Gissing's chagrin, Roberts was one of the best-paid novelists and short story writers of the 1890s. BL 53. *WW*. Wol. RLF.

ROBERTSON, T[homas] W[illiam] (1829–71). Robertson was the son of an actor and himself first appeared on the London stage in 1848. He soon after started his own company, married an actress and with her as leading lady toured the British Isles. Around the end of the 1850s, after the death of a daughter, he retired from management and acting, devoting himself thereafter to writing. He had a hit with his play *David Garrick* in 1864, and adapted it as a novel the following year. Robertson is best remembered for his melodramas *Society* (1865) and *Caste* (1867) which are still occasionally revived for the modern stage. He wrote two other works of prose fiction. BL 3. *DNB*. RM. *NCBEL*. Wol.

Robin Goodfellow (1861). The short-lived 1d. a week successor to John Maxwell's* *The Welcome Guest* (1858–61). Its editor was Charles Mackay* and the venture lasted only three months (July–September 1861). The paper's only claim to fame is that it serialised the early chapters of Mary Elizabeth Braddon's* *Lady Audley's Secret**. Maxwell had better luck with the further downmarket *Halfpenny Journal* which he launched at the same time and which ran until 1865.

ROBINS, Arthur (1836–1900). A son of the famously witty auctioneer, George Henry Robins (1778–1847), he was born in London and educated at Magdalen Hall, Oxford, graduating in 1866. Ordained a priest in 1867 Robins subsequently took up the post of domestic chaplain first to Lord Boston then to Lord Rossmore and a number of other dignitaries, including the Prince of Wales, 1881–1900. He was also for a while chaplain to the Household Brigade, earning the affectionate nickname 'the Soldier's Bishop'. Robins wrote novels, including: *Miriam May, A Romance Of Real Life* (1860); *Crispin Ken* (1861), the portrait of a power-crazed evangelical; *Black Moss* (1864), 'A Tale By A Tarn'. The last was described by the *Athenaeum** as 'absurd and unwholesome'. The story features a ruthless undertaker who allows the community drinking water to be polluted by effluent from his corpses. BL 3. Boase.

ROBINS, Elizabeth [Parkes] ('C. E. Raimond', 1863–1952). Actress, novel-ist, suffragette. Born in Louisville, Kentucky, she married George Parkes early in life. She came to London as a widow in 1889, where she soon made a starring name for herself in productions of Ibsen's plays. She also founded the Women Writers' Suffrage League and wrote a propaganda play, *Votes For Women*, produced in 1907. In addition to plays Robins wrote some fiction. Her most interesting novel is *George Mandeville's Husband* (1894), a satire on 'pseudo intellectual novelists', and particularly George Eliot*, whose moral rectitude she evidently detested. The novel was published in Heinemann's* influential 'Pioneer' series. As 'C. E. Raimond', Parkes also wrote *The New Moon* (1894) and *Below The Salt* (1896), a collection of short stories largely from the English servant's standpoint, 'generally unkind and ugly in its view of human nature', as the *Athenaeum** noted. BL 15. *WW*.

ROBINSON, Emma (1814–90). Robinson was born in London, the daughter of an Oxford Street bookseller. Few details of her life are known. Her father (d. 1856) apparently disapproved of her writing (her novels were accordingly published anonymously) and publicised them as *not* by her. His behaviour was regarded as eccentric in literary circles. She never married, and went mad in later life. Robinson's novels largely comprise florid Ainsworthian* historical* romances and include: *Whitehall* (1845), set in the Court of Charles I; *Caesar Borgia* (1846), a work considered immoral by the standards of the day; *The Maid Of Orleans* (1849); *Owen Tudor* (1849). Out of the run of Robinson's normal style is *The Gold Worshippers* (1851), 'a future historical novel'. In the late 1850s, Robinson turned to more domestic themes with: *Mauleverer's Divorce, A Story Of Woman's Wrongs* (1858); *Which Wins, Love Or Money?* (1862). Robinson wrote plays, received a small Civil List pension in 1862, stopped publishing around 1868 and died in the London County Lunatic Asylum at Norwood. BL 16. Boase. *NCBEL*. Wol. Sad. RLF.

ROBINSON, Frances Mabel ('W. S. Gregg', 1855?–1911?). Frances Robinson was born in Leamington, the daughter of G. T. Robinson, a Fellow of the Society of Antiquaries. She was educated partly abroad in Brussels and Italy, later taking her degree at the University of London. She herself became a secretary of Bedford College (London University's principal college for women). Robinson translated many works from the French and wrote a number of novels, mostly with feminist themes and often with Irish* settings. They include: *Mr Butler's Ward* (1885); *Disenchantment* (1886); *The Plan Of Campaign* (1887); *A Woman Of The World* (1890), a grim study of loveless marriage; *Chimera* (1895). She apparently never married. Her sister Agnes Mary (1857–1944) shared her upbringing and education. She married Professor James Darmesteter and later Emile Duclaux, director of the Pasteur Institute in Paris. Agnes wrote principally poetry and in 1883 a pioneering study of Emily Brontë*. In 1883, she also published a successful novel, *Arden.* It is the story of an English girl who is brought up in France then returned to the uncongenially robust Warwickshire bosom of her family. The work has clear echoes of William Black's* bestselling *A Daughter Of Heth** (1871). (FMR) BL 6. (AMR) BL 1. *WW*.

ROBINSON, F[rederick] W[illiam] ('A Prison Matron', 1830–1901). He was born at Spitalfields in London, the son of a property owner and brought up in the nearby Brixton and Kennington district of the capital.

At school, Robinson was a classmate of Henry Irving's. As a young man, he worked for a while as his father's secretary. Subsequently Robinson was drama critic of the *Daily News* for five years. From journalism he moved to novel writing in the early 1850s. He had some success with *The House Of Elmore* (1854), and followed up with some fifty other three-volume works, often with religious themes. (It was one of Robinson's mannerisms to introduce the word 'Church' into his titles.) They include: *Grandmother's Money* (1860); *High Church* (1860); *No Church* (1861), the story of Bessie Calverton, a self-improving heroine born while her mother is serving time in prison; *Church And Chapel* (1863); *Carry's Confessions* (1865); *Beyond The Church* (1866); *Christie's Faith* (1867). Robinson also wrote novels of London low-life, such as: *Owen, A Waif* (1862); *Mattie, A Stray* (1864). Under the pseudonym 'a Prison Matron', he also produced three influential semi-fictional studies of prison conditions which inspired reform. Robinson lived all his life in Brixton, and associated with leading men of Victorian letters such as Swinburne, Theodore Watts-Dunton* and Rossetti. In 1890, he produced no less than four novels: *A Very Strange Family*, *A Woman Of The World*, *The Keeper Of The Keys*, *Her Love And His Life*. But he ceased writing fiction with the demise of the three-decker in 1894. BL 48. *DNB*. Wol. RLF.

RODWELL, G[eorge] Herbert [Buonaparte] (1800–52). Best known as a musician, Rodwell studied under Vincent Novello, and himself became a professor at the Royal Academy of Music in 1828. In later life he developed theatrical interests and was proprietor (in succession to his brother James) of the Adelphi in London from 1825. G. H. Rodwell composed songs, libretti, wrote much drama and a little comic fiction, including: *The Memoirs Of An Umbrella* (1845), lavishly illustrated by Phiz*; *Woman's Love* (1846), 'A Romance Of Smiles And Tears', again heavily illustrated by Crowquill*; *Old London Bridge* (1848), a romance of the sixteenth century. Rodwell lived all his life in London. BL 4. *DNB*. Wol.

ROLFE, Frederick William [Serafino Austin Lewis Mary] ('Baron Corvo', 1860–1913). Rolfe was born in Cheapside, the eldest of five sons of a piano manufacturer. The family was nonconformist, but Rolfe was converted to the most ardent Catholicism at the age of twenty-six. His unsuccessful attempt to join the priesthood led to lifelong bitterness against Rome. (See his magnificently paranoid *Hadrian The Seventh*, 1904.) Rolfe quarrelled with all his friends and patrons, and suffered financial hardship verging on outright destitution throughout his short life. He supported himself with a series of teaching posts. Rolfe had a number of pieces published in the *Yellow Book**, later collected as *Stories Toto Told Me* (1898). His other Victorian fiction comprises *In His Own Image* (1901). Rolfe spent the last years of his life in Venice, sponging off acquaintances and boasting the absurd title, 'Baron Corvo'. BL 9. RM. *NCBEL*. RLF.

Romance. Like its conventional opposite 'realism', romance is a much used but virtually meaningless term for most of the nineteenth century. Ainsworth*, for instance, used the term 'a romance' in the subtitles of his works up to the 1870s as a simple synonym for 'novel'. In his later career he used the more neutral 'a tale' or nothing. Reade* routinely called his sensation* novels 'matter of fact romances' and Wells* labelled his science fiction* 'scientific romances' without apparently conceiving the term as loaded in a literary sense. But as the definition of realism became more precise in the period 1880–1900 with the influence of French theory, so romance was used more programmatically. Rider Haggard*, George MacDonald*, R. L. Stevenson* and William Morris* indulged escapist flights of imagination as a conscious reaction to the dominant realism of writers like Moore* and Gissing*. But in general, it makes more sense to see romance as a latent tendency in Victorian fiction rather than a clear-cut genre.

The Romance Of Lust, William Simpson Potter (ed.), 1873–76, 4 vols, Privately Printed. A classic of Victorian pornography. Charles, the massively phallic hero, is initiated into sex by a married woman at the age of fifteen. He seduces his two sisters and is himself seduced by two governesses. He leaves school for the home of an uncle who sodomises him. He seduces his aunt. The setting of Charles's subsequent adventures moves from Paris to London. (The third volume features a surreal episode at King's College, London.) As the bibliographer H. S. Ashbee notes, '*The Romance Of Lust*, though no masterpiece of composition, is far better written than most English works of its class.' The work was in fact written by several anonymous authors and put into assembled form by Potter.

A Romance Of Two Worlds, Marie Corelli, 1886, 2 vols, Bentley. (Corelli's first title for the work was 'Lifted Up'.) The narrator-heroine while recuperating from a nervous breakdown in the south of France is given an elixir by an artist called Raffaello Cellini. In a subsequent vision she encounters a man (or something greater than a man) called Heliobas. Heliobas is a Chaldean and instructed by Cellini the heroine travels to Paris to meet his reincarnation in the original flesh. There he is the prophet of a new 'Electric Creed'. Heliobas promptly dispatches the narrator on an intergalactic voyage, accompanied by the angel Azùl. This reveals to her various universal truths about space, time and Christianity. On her return (and after a tragic sub-plot concerning Heliobas's sister Zara and her lover Prince Ivan Petroffsky) the narrator again takes up her artistic life, refreshed. 'The electrician', Heliobas, disappears in the East, whence he came. Corelli's romance (her first published novel) is a conscious vehicle for her absurd and fanatic anti-materialism which she expounds polemically in a preface and afterword for the work as reissued by Methuen in 1896.

The Romany Rye, George Borrow, 1857, 2 vols, Murray. The uninterrupted sequel to *Lavengro**. The scholar-gypsy hero is now a traveller on the high roads of England, together with his love, the Romany beauty Isopel Berners ('Belle'). Like its predecessor, the story is essentially plotless. The main event is Lavengro's proposal of marriage to Belle. She promises to consider his offer, but then suddenly leaves on her own for America. He never sees her again. Lavengro has various chance encounters with the Man in Black (a Catholic priest), his old friend Jasper Petulengro, the horse dealer Jack Dale, and, finally, a recruiting sergeant who vainly tries to persuade him to go off and fight in India. The main interest of the book is in its discursive conversations and autobiographical ruminations on life.

ROMER, Isabella Frances (1800?–52). The youngest daughter of a general Isabella Romer married another soldier, Major Hamerton of the 7th Fusiliers, in 1818. The couple separated in 1827 and thereafter she reverted to her maiden name. Romer subsequently became a fanatic believer in mesmerism, and animal magnetism writing a novel on the subject, *Sturmer, A Tale Of Mesmerism*, in 1841. She also wrote travel books, and tales and sketches collected as *The Bird Of Passage* (1849). BL 2. *DNB*. Sad.

Romola, George Eliot, 1863, 3 vols, Smith Elder. (Serialised in *Cornhill Magazine**, July 1862–August 1863, with illustrations by Frederic Leighton.) George Eliot's single historical* novel, set in fifteenth-century Florence. The large background to the action is the spiritual revivalism of Savonarola and the political struggles of the Medicis. Charles VIII and Machiavelli figure on the edge of the plot. Eliot's heroine, Romola, is the daughter and amanuensis of a blind scholar, Bardo. She is wooed by a handsome young Greek, Tito Melema, who has enriched himself with some mysteriously acquired jewels. Tito is brilliant but, as it emerges, amoral. He has betrayed his adoptive father, Baldassare Calvo, setting in motion the processes of consequence and revenge that will eventually destroy him. But for the early section of the narrative, Tito thinks Baldassare safely a slave of the Turk and involves himself in political and private intrigues, with purely selfish motives. In disguise, he goes through a mock marriage with a simple peasant girl, Tessa, whom he earlier rescued from a mob. He marries Romola in earnest, only to betray her and her father (who soon dies, leaving his daughter to carry on his work). Baldassare comes back as a captive of Charles VIII, and contrives to escape, finding refuge with Tito's other victim, Tessa, who now has two children. Baldassare denounces his betrayer publicly, but is merely taken as a raving madman and imprisoned. But Romola credits his story and becomes wholly disillusioned both in her husband and in her spiritual director, the fanatic Savonarola. She flees Florence. Tito also tries to escape, having been uncovered for what he is, and is strangled on the bank of the Arno by Baldassare. Finally, Romola discovers salvation in her own moral and spiritual resources and devotes her life to the care of Tessa and Tito's children. Although its historical apparatus is unwieldy, the novel is the austerest expression of Eliot's ideals of selfhood.

Rookwood, W. H. Ainsworth, 1834, 3 vols, Bentley. (The work was reprinted by Macrone* in 1836 in one volume, with illustrations by George Cruikshank*.) Ainsworth's first great success in fiction (particularly in the illustrated Macrone edition). It was inspired, the author claimed, by a visit to Chesterfield in 1831 when he resolved to 'attempt a story in the bygone style of Mrs Radcliffe'. Ainsworth's new twist was to anglicise her Italian settings and have 'an old English highwayman for the Italian marchese'. *Rookwood*'s plot is tangled. The legitimate and bastard scions of the cursed Rookwood family intrigue for inheritance and the hand of Eleanor Mowbray. The villain Luke is aided by a mad sexton, Peter Bradley, and the highwayman Dick Turpin. The honest Ranulph Rookwood and Eleanor are finally married. The Turpin sub-plot (with its 'flash', or thieves' slang) was particularly successful and boosted the Newgate* fashion in fiction.

ROS, Mrs Andrew [Amanda Anna Margaret] (i.e Ross, née McKittrick, 1860–1939). Leading candidate for the worst Victorian novelist ever published. Anna McKittrick was born in Co. Down, Ireland. She trained as a schoolteacher, and married Andrew Ross, stationmaster at Larne. Amanda Ros (as she called herself professionally) wrote preposterous poetry, collected as *Poems Of Puncture* (1936?) and *Fumes Of Formation* (1933). Her novels (like all her works published locally in Ireland at her own expense) include *Irene Iddesleigh* (1897); *Delina Delaney* (1898); *Donald Dudley* (1900?). A club of London men of letters (including Lord Beveridge, Desmond MacCarthy, E. V. Lucas and F. Anstey*) met specifically to exchange the most ludicrous quotations from her work that they could find. Another connoisseur of Ros was Aldous Huxley. The quality of her prose is conveyed by the opening lines of *Irene Iddesleigh*: 'Sympathise with me, indeed! Ah, No! Cast your sympathy on the chill waves of troubled waters; fling it on the oases of futurity; dash it against the rock of gossip; or better still, allow it to remain within the false and faithless bosom of buried scorn.' BL 3. Wol.

The Rose And The Ring, W. M. Thackeray, 1855, 1 vol, Smith, Elder. A fairy-tale which Thackeray devised for his daughters, while in Rome (a situation recalled in the 'Prelude' by Michael Angelo Titmarsh, the narrator). The magic rose which belongs to Prince Bulbo of Crim Tartary makes its possessor irresistibly likeable. The magic ring which Prince Giglio of Paflagonia possesses bestows the same power. Giglio and the Princess Rosalba are deposed by wicked usurpers, who wish to set up Bulbo and the unlovely Angelica in their place. The hero and heroine are restored to their rightful station by the Fairy Blackstick (whose peculiarity it is to give each of her clients a little bad luck, as a salutary gift). The burlesque text and caricaturish illustrations are beautifully interwoven by Thackeray who called the work a 'Fireside Pantomine'.

ROSS, Charles H[enry] ('Ally Sloper', 1842?–97). Inventor of the first comic strip character in English. Ross was born in London, and on leaving school worked as a second-class clerk at the Navy Office in Somerset House, 1860–69. In 1868, he went bankrupt, presumably as the result of injudicious speculations in magazine proprietorship. He edited the rival to *Punch**, *Judy*, from 1869 until the late 1880s. Ross created his pictorial characters 'Ally Sloper and his friend Ikey Moses' around the same period in the late 1860s. The creation of the big-headed Ally, as later portrayed by the artist W. G. Baxter (1856–88), became immensely popular, and eventually attained folkloric status. Ross also wrote some comic fiction, including: *The Eldest Miss Simpson* (1866); *The Pretty Widow* (1868); *A London Romance* (1869); *A Private Enquiry* (1870). Ross illustrated some of his own work, not very impressively, under his wife's name, Marie Duval. BL 8. Boase. Wol.

Routledge (1836–). Publisher. George Routledge (1812–88) began his career in the book trade apprenticed to a bookshop in Carlisle. In 1836 he set himself up in London as a bookseller and casual publisher with his brother-in-law W. H. Warne. In 1848, Routledge's 1s. reprint series, the 'Railway Library', was launched. It was to be immensely successful. In 1851 Frederick Warne joined the business and he and Routledge made a fortune a year later in 1852 with cheap pirated reprints of *Uncle Tom's*

Cabin. In 1853 the firm could consequently afford to pay Bulwer-Lytton* the unprecedented sum of £20,000 for reprint rights to all his works. In 1854 Routledge and Warne opened a branch in New York (being one of the first British publishers to do so). In 1865 Frederick Warne left the house, which thereafter retitled itself George Routledge and Sons. In the 1880s, Routledge were in the forefront of the new style of children's books (notably those of Kate Greenaway*). Routledge died prematurely in 1888 and his sons even more prematurely in 1899. In the early twentieth century the firm underwent a series of reorganisations and mergers which in 1912 led to it emerging as Routledge, Kegan Paul Trench, Trübner and Co., with a somewhat academic character and little interest in fiction. It survives as Routledge and Kegan Paul.

ROWCROFT, Charles (1800?–56). Rowcroft was born into the English upper classes. After education at Eton, he served as a stipendiary magistrate in Australia and was later British consul at Cincinnati from 1852 until 1856. He died on the return trip to England after his exequatur had been revoked by the American President. Rowcroft's fiction includes: *Tales Of The Colonies* (1843), designed to entertain and also serve as instruction for new English settlers in Australia; *The Man Without A Profession* (1844); *The Bushranger Of Van Diemen's Land* (1846); *Confessions Of An Etonian* (1852), the first volume containing an extended description of school life early in the century; *Fanny The Little Milliner* (1853). BL 8. Boase. RM. Wol. Sad. RLF.

The Royal Literary Fund (1788–). Britain's principal charitable institute for authors. The Fund was founded by David Williams, a dissenting minister and man of letters, at the end of the eighteenth century. Initially, Williams foresaw something more than a charity, and projected an idea half way between an academy and a literary college. But these ambitious schemes remained unfulfilled. The Fund received royal patronage in 1842, after which it has been known as the Royal Literary Fund (RLF). The RLF has always had some notable beneficiaries (Samuel Taylor Coleridge was among the first). But generally, the more famous writers have tended to be subscribers and officers. In the nineteenth century, they included Trollope*, Thackeray* and Meredith*. Dickens* had rather vexed relations with the RLF and together with Bulwer-Lytton* set up the rival Guild of Literature and Art, in 1850. This body intended to provide not just money assistance (as did the RLF) but accommodations and salaries (or pensions) for needy writers. The Guild was not a success. The RLF was and is.

RUNCIMAN, James (1852–91). Runciman was born in Northumberland, the son of a coastguardsman. He attended naval school for two years (1863–65) with a view to going to sea but subsequently embarked on a career of teaching in London. While working, he read for a degree in science at London University, which he was awarded in 1876. By the end of the 1870s he was a part-time journalist and editor. Gradually he became a full-time man of letters, with a strong line in nautical* tales and essays. Runciman's fictional sketches and stories include: *Skippers And Shellbacks* (1885), nautical tales, reprinted from the magazines; *Grace Balmaign's Sweetheart* (1885), a story of love in a coastal town; *The Chequers, Being The Natural History Of A*

Public House (1888), a collection of temperance tales of drink-ruined lives, 'Set Forth In A Loafer's Diary'. No loafer himself, Runciman is reported to have died from overwork. BL 3. *DNB*. Wol. RLF.

RUSKIN, John (1819–1900). The greatest art critic of the century. Ruskin was born in London, the son of a wealthy wine merchant and brought up in a smotheringly evangelical household. He showed early artistic talent, and went to Christ Church, Oxford in 1837 where he was a brilllant student, but frail in health and hyperocnsitive. The first volume of *Modern Painters* appeared in 1843, by 'A Graduate of Oxford'. In 1848 he married Euphemia Chalmers Gray, the daughter of a Scottish lawyer. The marriage was never consummated. She deserted Ruskin and married the artist J. E. Millais* in 1855. For his future bride, when she was twelve years old (in 1841), Ruskin wrote the fine fairy story-cum-aesthetic fable, *The King Of The Golden River**. The work was belatedly published in 1851 by Smith, Elder* and illustrated charmingly by Richard Doyle*. BL 1. *DNB*. RM. *NCBEL*. Wol.

RUSSELL, Countess [Mary Annette Von Arnim] ('Elizabeth', née Beauchamp, 1866–1941). Mary Beauchamp was born in Sydney, Australia, distantly related to the novelist Katherine Mansfield's father. At the age of four, she came to London with her family who were well off but shiftless. She married twice; first, in 1891, to Count Henning August von Arnim (d. 1910), a wealthy Prussian landowner and friend of Wagner. The von Arnim estate and the castle of Nassenheide provided the background for the first of her novels, *Elizabeth And Her German Garden* (1898). In diary form an Englishwoman records a year in her beloved garden which serves as a refuge from an uncongenial husband ('The Man of Wrath') and children, whom she refers to only distantly. Meanwhile, Elizabeth expatiates on the roses which she has successfully cultivated. The work anticipates many modernist fictions in its displaced, hypersensitive intensity. The Von Arnims' marriage was unhappy. In the twentieth century (as the Countess Russell, sister-in-law to the philosopher Bertrand Russell) she became a woman of letters, achieving considerable success with her novel *Princess Priscilla's Fortnight*, in 1905. Her second marriage was as unhappy as the first and led to messy legal disputes. BL 16. RM. *WW*.

RUSSELL, T[homas] O'Neill ('Reginald Tierney', 1829–1908). Russell was born in Co. Westmeath, Ireland, the son of a Quaker. From 1858 to the end of his life, he devoted himself passionately to the revival of the Irish national language. Russell also espoused the Fenian cause and spent almost thirty years as a semi-exile in America. He returned to Ireland in 1895, and threw himself into the Gaelic renaissance. Russell wrote, among much else, some fiction; notably the popular tale of the 1814 famine, *Dick Massey* (1860), 'Or The Battles Of A Boy'. BL 1.

RUSSELL, W[illiam] Clark ('Sydney Mostyn', 'Eliza Rhyl Davies', 1844–1911). One of the greatest of late-Victorian nautical* novelists. Russell was born in New York, the son of the vocalist and composer Henry Russell (among whose best-known works is 'Cheer Boys Cheer'). On his mother's side he was related to the poet Wordsworth and she is credited with motivating her son with literary ambitions. After education in British private schools, Russell joined the merchant marine in 1858. He served until 1866; an experience which undermined his health and stored his mind as a novelist. In 1866 he retired from the sea and after an unsuccessful spell in business took to writing for his living. For some time, he was a journalist for the *Newcastle Daily Chronicle*. After a false start in drama, he had great success with two extravagantly adventurous nautical novels: *John Holdsworth, Chief Mate* (1875) and *The Wreck Of The Grosvenor** (1877). These led to a stream of similarly salty bestselling romances. Their content is prominently signalled in such titles as: *The Death Ship* (1888); *The Emigrant Ship* (1893); *The Convict Ship* (1895). Russell also remained active as a journalist, and was a regular writer for the *Daily Telegraph* under the pen name 'Seafarer'. His writings helped bring about substantial improvements for sailors at sea. Swinburne called Russell 'the greatest master of the sea, living or dead and the most judicious'. Conrad also admired him. His fiction includes: *As Innocent As A Baby* (1874); *Captain Fanny* (1876); *Auld Lang Syne* (1878); *The Frozen Pirate* (1887); *Marooned* (1891); *Master Rockafellar's Voyage* (1891); *A Noble Haul* (1897). Russell suffered severely from rheumatism in his later years and died at Bath. BL 65. *DNB*. RM. *NCBEL*. Wol. Sad.

RUSSELL, William Howard (1820–1907). A pioneer British war correspondent, Russell covered for *The Times* the Crimean, the American Civil, the Franco-Prussian and Zulu Wars. His front-line reporting was notable for its impartiality. (His accounts of British atrocities after the Indian Mutiny, for instance, showed the new power of the press to curb military excesses.) In 1868, he tried the experiment of writing a novel, *The Adventures Of Dr Brady* (1868). Closely autobiographical, it is the story of an Irish military surgeon whose eventful duty takes him to the battlefields of the Crimea and the Indian Mutiny. Tinsley* paid handsomely (£1,300) for the work and expected great things for it, running it as the first item in his new *Tinsley's Magazine** in August 1867. But, unaccountably, the novel failed. Probably the reason was that too long is spent on the hero's youth (it is not until the third volume that the action arrives at the Crimea). Russell did not repeat his novel-writing experiment. BL 1. *DNB*. Wol.

Ruth, Mrs E. Gaskell, 1853, 3 vols, Chapman and Hall. The heroine is Ruth Hilton. The daughter of a bankrupted (but decent) farmer, she takes up work as a dressmaker's assistant. Having been made pregnant and abandoned by a 'gentleman', Henry Bellingham, Ruth is given refuge by a nonconformist minister, Thurstan Benson, who finds her about to drown herself. Benson (a hunchback) induces Ruth to pass herself off as a decent widow ('Mrs Denbigh') and in this character she gets employment as a governess with the evangelical Bradshaw family. Several years later, Bellingham returns as Mr Donne, a prospective parliamentary candidate. He does not immediately recognise the mother of his child, being short-sighted. He proposes marriage to her, and she refuses. Ruth is later cruelly persecuted by Mr Bradshaw who discovers the truth about her past. (Providence punishes Bradshaw, when his son is subsequently disclosed by Benson to be a forger.) Ruth and her son Leonard are cast out. In a final act of reconciliation, Ruth nurses Bellingham on his sick-bed, catches his typhus fever and dies. Gaskell consciously took an 'uncomfortable' subject for this novel, her least popular. The gentle and inherently pure character of Ruth and small provincial town settings are well handled. But the Donne–Bellingham episodes are highly theatrical, as is the ending in which a chastened Mr Bradshaw adopts Leonard.

S

SADLIER, Mrs James [Mary Anne] (née Madden, 1820–1903). Mary Madden was born at Cootehill. In 1844, she emigrated to Canada, remaining in that country for the rest of her long life, having married her New York publisher D. James Sadlier in 1846. As Mrs Sadlier she wrote historical* novels (often with a strong Catholic tendency) and moral romances set in New York which enjoyed some success. Her fiction includes: *The Fate Of Father Sheehy* (1845); *Willy Burke* (1850); *New Lights, Or Life In Galway* (1855); *Berry Conway, Or The Irish Girl In America* (1864); *The Confessions Of An Apostate* (1864), a work which was frequently reprinted; *Maureen Dhu* (1869), a 'Tale Of The Claddagh In Galway' written against the evils of emigration; *The Knout, A Tale Of Poland* (1884). Towards the end of the century a daughter, Anna T[heresa] Sadlier (b. 1854), wrote some novels even more Catholic in tendency than her mother's. BL 14.

ST AUBYN, Alan (i.e. Frances L. Marshall, née Bridges, d. 1920). Frances Bridges was born in Surrey, the daughter of a solicitor and dramatist, George Bramstone Bridges. She married Matthew Marshall of St. Aubyn's, near Tiverton in Devon and used his residence for her male pseudonym. (Reviewers seem not to have penetrated the disguise and often took her for a male writer.) Educated at Cambridge University, Marshall worked for a while as a journalist and took a keen interest in archaeology. Her main line of fiction was insubstantial Varsity tales with a sideline in West Country idylls. Her titles include: *A Fellow Of Trinity* (1890), a work dedicated effusively to Oliver Wendell Holmes who replied in kind 'from the newer Cambridge'; *The Junior Dean* (1891); *With Wind And Tide* (1892); *Broken Lights* (1893); *A Tragic Honeymoon* (1894); *In The Face Of The World* (1894); *The Tremlett Diamonds* (1895), a detective* story; *A Proctor's Wooing* (1897), another Cambridge story; *Mrs Dunbar's Secret* (1899); *May Silver* (1901). BL 33. WW. Wol.

The St James's Magazine (1861–82). Published by W. Kent and Co., the journal was set up as a rival to *Cornhill** in April 1861. Like its model, it was monthly, illustrated (rather scantily) and cost 1s. Its first editor was the Irish woman of letters, Mrs S. C. Hall* who declared her editorial programme as being 'to promote the Interests of Home, the Refinements of Life and the Amusement and Information of all Classes'. Despite this sweeping agenda, the magazine principally addressed middle-class matrons. *St James's* featured substandard fiction (especially after its first year) and its most notable contributors were Dinah Mulock Craik* and Mrs Hall herself whose best novel, *Can Wrong Be Right?* (abysmally illustrated by Phiz*) was serialised in 1861. Hall kept the editorship only a year. Among her successors was Mrs J. H. Riddell* (1867–68), who was also evidently a part-proprietor as well. After 1871 the magazine added 'United Empire Review' to its masthead.

ST JOHN, Percy B[olingbroke] (1821–89). One of three brothers, all bohemian writers: Bayle, Horace Stebbing Roscoe and Percy B. St John. Their father James Augustus St John (1801–75) was a London journalist of Welsh extraction who himself wrote some fiction including *Margaret Ravenscroft* (1835); *Sir Cosmo Digby* (1843), a tale of the Monmouthshire riots; *Weighed In The Balance* (1864). Percy lived longest of the brothers. Having accompanied his father on travels to the USA and Spain he began working life as a journalist in Paris, reporting for the British papers. Later he evidently spent a longish period in America and was for many years a contributor to *Cassell's Illustrated Family Newspaper*. St John was also after 1846 editor of the *Mirror Of Literature* magazine. In 1861 he joined the *London Herald*. He wrote mainly adventure novels which include: *The Fireside* (1847), a domestic* tale; *Jessie The Mormon's Daughter* (1848), a work hostile to polygamy or 'the harem system'; *The Miser's Will* (1848); *The Eagle's Nest, A Romance Of Upper Texas* (1849); *The Snow Ship* (1867), an adventure tale set among Canadian immigrants; *The Blue Dwarf* (1869), one of the many Dick Turpin stories directed mainly at the lower-class reader. St John translated many of Gustave Aimard's Indian tales into English in the late 1870s. Bayle St John (1822–59), another journalist and traveller, wrote the novels: *The Eccentric Lover* (1845); *The Fortunes of Francis Croft* (1852). (JAS) BL 4. (BS) BL 2. (PBS) BL 24. *DNB. NCBEL.* Wol. RLF.

St Nicholas (1873–1940). An Anglo-American illustrated monthly magazine 'For Young Folks', published by Scribner's and after 1881 by the Century Company of New York, and by F. Warne and Co. in England up to 1885, thereafter by T. Fisher Unwin. The first editor was Mary M. Dodge. Henty*, Kipling*, Stevenson* and Burnett* published fiction in the magazine.

St Paul's Magazine (1867–74). *St Paul's* was set up by the publisher James Virtue* as a rival to *Cornhill**, whose monthly issue, format and 1s. cover price it exactly followed. Virtue designed the magazine around Anthony Trollope*, and for a while actually hoped to use the title *Anthony Trollope's Magazine*. Trollope in 1867 had political ambitions, and the magazine was carefully devised as a vehicle for his brand of independent Liberalism. He also ran through its pages his finest parliamentary novel, *Phineas Finn** (1869), illustrated by J. E. Millais*. Among his other major fiction, *Ralph The Heir** (1871) also first appeared in *St Paul's*. Other novelists whose work featured in the magazine were George MacDonald* and Margaret Oliphant*. But the venture never achieved the 25,000 circulation hoped for, and Virtue withdrew (under some financial distress). Alexander Strahan* took the magazine over, finally dispensing with Trollope's editorial services in 1870. In 1874 the unlucky enterprise was wound up altogether. *WI. BLM.*

SALA, George Augustus (1828–95). Sala was born in London, the youngest of four surviving children. His father, Augustus James Sala (1790–1829) was an Italian teacher of dancing and deportment. His mother Henrietta, originally the daughter of a prosperous estate owner in Demerara, had been an actress and opera singer of no great distinction, apparently. Marriage interrupted Madame Sala's career. But on her husband's premature death (nine months after George's birth) she supported her family by teaching singing and by occasional concerts. She too died early, in 1860. Physically frail, unusually precocious and multilingual (he wrote a French tragedy before he was ten, and a 12,000 word novel, *Gerald Moreland*, at fourteen) Sala was brought up in a bohemian household in Brighton and later educated partly in France. He showed an early talent for drawing and in 1844 was articled to Carl Schiller's studio in Charlotte Street. Sala was never to be anything more than a mediocre draughtsman, but (through his mother) he had connections with Dickens's* set of bohemian authors and in 1848 was appointed an illustrator for Albert Smith's* popular serial publication, *The Man In The Moon*, an assignment which brought him to the acquaintance of Angus B. Reach*, Shirley Brooks* and Phiz*. (On the debit side, the connection with *The Man In The Moon*, led to Sala's being blackballed from *Punch**, a journal with which Smith was at continual war.) The young man was by this date beginning to write for publication himself and by the early 1850s, he was one of the bohemian band of regular (and self-confessedly idle) contributors to Dickens's *Household Words**. (His first contribution to that journal, 'The Key Of The Street', provoked a mild sensation on its being printed in September 1851.) By the early 1850s, Sala had entirely given up art for journalism and Dickens sent him to the Crimea to cover the war for his paper. In 1856, with his fellow bohemian Edmund Yates*, he founded a successful journal of his own, the *Train*, which ran (for a bohemian publication) a healthy five years. One of the first such journals to cost a mere 1s., the *Train* quickly established itself as the *fast* magazine of the period. Sala intended to serialise a novel ('Fripanelli's Daughter') in the *Train*, but could not get round to writing it. Having quarrelled obscurely with Dickens, Sala went on to publish his first novel in Vizetelly's* *Illustrated Times* (*The Baddington Peerage*, 1858, 'A Story Of The Best And Worst Society'). A cynical panorama of high and low English life, the novel clearly reveals the author's besetting narrative sin, that of uncontrolled digression or 'maundering', as he put it. He himself called it 'the worst novel ever written', which is too harsh. In 1858, he also took on the editorship of the *Welcome Guest*, a new 1d.-a-week magazine founded by Vizetelly. (It was subsequently taken over by John Maxwell* in 1859.) It was for this journal that Sala wrote his best-known work, *Twice Round The Clock* (1864), a vivid account of twenty-four hours in a London street. Sala went on to establish the popular monthly magazine *Temple Bar** (another Maxwell venture) in 1860, editing it until 1866. Fiction was a main feature of the journal and Sala contributed a serial novel, *The Seven Sons Of Mammon** (1862). It was astonishingly successful, the *Spectator* going so far as to call it 'a work of broad and unquestionable genius'. To *Temple Bar* he also contributed his finest work of fiction, the eighteenth-century romance, *The Strange Adventures Of Captain Dangerous* (1863). (Its subtitle is explanatory enough: 'Who Was A Soldier, A Sailor, A Merchant, A Spy, A Slave Among The Moors, A Bashaw In The Service Of The Grand Turk, And Died At Last In His Own House At Hanover Square'.) Sala's short stories were collected as *The Ship Chandler* (1862).

For Dickens's *All The Year Round** he wrote *Quite Alone* (1864), although the work (which has some admirable Parisian scenes and a brilliant opening chapter, 'seule au monde', set in Hyde Park) had to be finished by Andrew Halliday and accusations of authorial unreliability were to plague Sala for the rest of his career. The author added an awkward preface, pleading the difficulties of serialising a novel while also working as the *Telegraph* correspondent in the United States and Mexico. In the early 1860s, Sala was one of the most highly regarded men of letters in the country and he moved with his family (having married in 1859) to a large country house, Upton Court. But by 1862, he had overreached himself, was nearly bankrupted and returned to London which was always more congenial. As he himself candidly admitted, Sala had no literary genius, but he was an unusually competent newspaperman. Since 1857, he had been contracted by J. L. Levy to write two articles daily for the *Telegraph*. This strenuous assignment (which he kept going for twenty-five years) made Sala the so-called 'king of journalists'. (He estimated his income from newspaper work at £2,000 a year; nevertheless he was always in chronic financial difficulties.) A connoisseur in his later years, Sala collected china and fine books. But over-writing (and probably dissipation) exhausted him as it did most of the free-living bohemians. For younger and more idealistic authors he came in his later years to epitomise the journalistic hack. Sala successfully sued James Hain Friswell* for libelling him in 1867 as 'often drunk, always in debt, sometimes in prison and totally disreputable'. In fact, Sala was a pioneer modern roving reporter and after 1863 covered a multitude of overseas stories for the *Telegraph*. He visited Garibaldi's troops, went to the American Civil War and was actually arrested as a suspected Prussian spy in wartime Paris in 1870. Sala made a final journalistic expedition in 1884, travelling and lecturing in America and Australia. Immediately on his return, in late 1885, his wife died. And for the last ten years of his life, which he passed mainly at Brighton, Sala was generally ill and increasingly poor. He married his secretary in 1890, launched an abortive weekly, *Sala's Journal*, in 1893. Before folding it carried the opening instalments of a new novel with a Faustian theme, *Margaret Forster*; the work eventually appeared in its entirety as a volume in 1897. Sala published his entertaining *Life And Adventures* in 1895, the year of his death. In the same year, he received a Civil List pension of £100. BL 5. *DNB*. RM. *NCBEL*. Wol. Sad. RLF.

Salem Chapel, Mrs Oliphant, 1863, 2 vols, Blackwood. (Serialised in *Blackwood's Magazine**, February 1862–January 1863.) The first novel-length work in the 'Chronicles of Carlingford*' series. The central strand of the narrative concerns Arthur Vincent, minister of the nonconformist chapel of the title and 'the only dissenting place of worship in Carlingford'. Vincent is intelligent, a gifted preacher but uneasy in the town's dissenting milieu. (His character is modelled on that of Edward Irving, on whom Oliphant had just written a biography.) He eventually loses his sense of mission and falls hopelessly in love with Lady Western, 'the highest luminary in all the society of Carlingford'. His flock turn against him and only a passionate speech by the Deacon, Tozer (one of Oliphant's finest creations), prevents them from expelling Vincent. But it is too late. He leaves his ministry and takes to higher journalism, founding the 'Philosophical Review' as the vehicle for his new beliefs. On to this study of failed vocation Oliphant attached an elaborately sensational* plot. One of Vincent's parishioners, Mrs Hilyard, ostensibly a needlewoman, has a secret past. She is being terrorised by a villainous husband. She asks Vincent to give her abused daughter sanctuary with his widowed mother and sister Susan. Susan meanwhile is being courted by a mysterious Mr Herbert Fordham, who turns out to be Mrs Hilyard's husband (real name, Colonel Mildmay). She shoots him. Susan is arrested for the crime, but cleared when Mildmay refuses to testify.

Sandism. The French influence on Victorian fiction was funnelled through a small group of innovative writers whose work circulated freely in England: Eugène Sue, Victor Hugo, Emile Zola and George Sand. Although she has survived least well into the twentieth century Sand (i.e. Amandine Lucile Aurore Dupin, Baronne Dudevant, 1804–76) was the most influential of this group. Between 1831 and her death, Sand turned out an average of two books a year. Her early novels of the 1830s are fictions of passion, permeated with the high romanticism of Byron and Rousseau. Their effect is plausibly traced in a Victorian novel like *Wuthering Heights** (1847), or in the early romances of Disraeli* and Bulwer-Lytton*. Sand's next novel-writing phase in the 1840s takes on social and political themes. (Connections with George Eliot* are easily drawn.) And in her third phase, with her *romans rustiques*, Sand popularised nostalgic regionalism as a theme for modern fiction. (Her tales of her native Berry countryside fall in naturally beside Hardy's* Wessex* stories.) Sand was widely read by thoughtful Victorians. As Patricia Thomson notes: 'What is very clear is that Sand's impact on the Victorian reading public and, more importantly, on Victorian writers, was enormous and that, although fully recognised at the time, it has now been almost completely forgotten.'

Sandra Belloni, George Meredith, 1864, 3 vols Chapman and Hall. (First published as *Emilia In England*, it was given the above title in 1886.) An art novel set in the early 1840s. Emilia Sandra Belloni, the daughter of an Italian musician, is adopted by the Pole family. In time she falls in love with the morally indecisive Wilfrid Pole. Pole senior is a speculator and financially entangled with a Mr Pericles, a man obsessed with managing the careers of singers. He attempts to recruit Emilia, but she resists. To save the family fortunes the young Poles are obliged to make rich marriages. Wilfrid duly courts Lady Charlotte Chillingworth. When Emilia discovers his infidelity, she is distraught and loses her voice. She is helped through her tribulation by Merthyr Powys, a romantic who later goes off to fight for Italy against the Austrians. To save the Poles Emilia finally consents to go to Milan for three years on condition that Pericles settles their debts. She also writes to Merthyr to tell him she will marry him when her contract expires. The novel's sequel is found in *Vittoria** (1866).

The Saturday Review (1855–1938). A weekly review of 'Politics, Literature, Science And Art' the paper was set up as a Conservative organ by A. J. Beresford-Hope under the editorship (1855–68) of John Douglas Cook. A prime vehicle for Victorian higher journalism, the paper's (anonymous) reviews of fiction were frequently severe. Dickens* was selected as a particular target by Fitzjames Stephen (1829–94) although Trollope* and Thackeray* were also given a hard time by the *Saturday*. The journal took over from the *Athenaeum** as the age's main former of advanced literary opinion. In the late 1860s the novelist Eliza Lynn Linton* became one of the main writers for the review and used it as the vehicle for her violently antagonistic opinions of the depraved 'Girl of the Period'. *BLM.*

SAUNDERS, John (1810–95). Saunders was born in Barnstaple, Devon, the son of a local bookseller and small publisher. He was educated at Exeter Grammar School and for some years thereafter lived with his sister Mary (b. 1813) in Lincoln. At some point in his early life he obviously came to know the industrial North well. In 1840 Saunders moved to London where he worked as a researcher and ghost-writer for Charles Knight, the popular educator. Saunders also founded the illustrated *People's Journal*, in 1846. As an original author he wrote verse and tragedy, his poetic drama *Love's Martyrdom* being put on at the Haymarket in 1855. Despite advertised commendation by W. S. Landor and Dickens*, the piece was not a hit. Towards the end of his life, Saunders fell on hard times and received assistance from the Royal Bounty. (R. D. Blackmore's* attempt to secure a Civil List pension for him failed.) Saunders also wrote a number of novels all moralistic, and some with industrial settings, including: *Abel Drake's Wife* (1862), 'The Story Of An Inventor', a lachrymose effort set in Lancashire with a child's death as its climax; *Martin Pole* (1863), co-written with Katherine Saunders; *Guy Waterman* (1864); *Hirell* (1869), 'Or Love Born Of Strife', a novel which was praised by Gladstone; *Israel Mort, Overman* (1876), 'A Story Of The Mine'. This last work is set in Wales and chronicles a hero who rises from pit-boy to pit manager (or 'overman'). The book is dedicated to former Home Secretary Lord Aberdare, with thanks for his legislation, 'the miner's Magna Charta'. Saunders's last novel seems to have been *Miss Vandeleur* (1884). Saunders had twelve children. His eldest daughter Katherine (1841–94) also wrote. In 1876 she married the Rev. Richard Cooper and in the 1870s and 1880s published numerous works of fiction (mainly for the RTS*), including: *Margaret And Elizabeth* (1873); *The High Mills* (1875); *Jasper Deane, Wood-Carver Of St Paul's* (1877); *Nearly In Port* (1886). As the titles indicate, Katherine Saunders specialised in nautical* settings. (JS) BL 18. (KS) BL 17. *DNB.* Wol. RLF.

Saunders and Otley (1824–71). Simon Saunders (1783–1861) and Edward John Otley (1798–1857) bought Henry Colburn's* Conduit Street Library in 1824, and set up business on the same lines as their predecessor. That is, they supplied mainly three-volume novels for circulating library consumption. In the 1830s, they established themselves as a leading London publisher with Bulwer-Lytton* and Marryat* starring on their list. They also published the successful *Metropolitan Magazine** in this decade, a journal in which all the leaders of the nautical* fiction vogue appeared. But Saunders and Otley ceased to recruit interesting new names after the 1830s. By the 1840s it was a second-rank publisher although the firm continued in business at Brook Street (after 1861) until 1871. (SS and EJO) Boase.

SAVAGE, Marmion W. (1803–72). Savage was born in Dublin, a Protestant clergyman's son. After graduating from Trinity College in 1824, he went to work for the Irish government as the clerk to council at Dublin Castle. During this period of his life, Savage also wrote for the *Dublin University Magazine**. His first published novel was the Peacockian *The Falcon Family, Or Young Ireland* (1845). Topically, it satirised the physical-force wing of the Young Ireland movement and was criticised as 'a malignant libel on the people of Ireland'. This did not prevent the work from being reprinted (with a witty preface by the author) in 1854. In 1847, Savage produced what is reckoned his best work, *The Bachelor Of The Albany*. 'An airy nothing', as the author called it, the story loosely chronicles the commercial doings of 'Spread, Narrowsmith and Co.' as they affect Mr Baker, 'the bachelor of the Albany' (i.e. the fashionable West End apartments). There is some incidental satire on the Oxford Movement. His other novels include: *My Uncle The Curate* (1849); *Reuben Medlicott, Or The Coming Man* (1852); *Clover Cottage* (1856), a novella successfully dramatised by Tom Taylor as *Nine Points Of The Law*; *The Woman Of Business* (1870). The last is the story of a feud over an estate between two sisters-in-law, one worthy, one vulgar. Savage's fiction is generally light and self-consciously entertaining. Critics sometimes complained about its 'slangy' tone. In 1856, he moved to London to succeed John Forster as editor of the *Examiner*. He resigned in 1859. Popular in English society, Savage married twice; first to a niece of Lady Morgan's (author of *The Wild Irish Girl*, 1806). He died at Torquay after prolonged illness, leaving no issue. No one apparently knows what the 'W.' stands for in Savage's name. BL 7. *DNB. NCBEL.* Wol. Sad.

SAVILE, the Hon. Charles Stuart (1816–70). The fourth son of the Earl of Mexborough, Savile was born at Mothley Park, near Leeds and educated at Eton and Cambridge. He subsequently joined the Foreign Office, and served for some years as a British attaché in Berlin. He was dismissed from this post in 1843 and thereafter concentrated on writing. His fiction includes: *Karah Kaplan, Or The Koordish Chief* (1842); *Night And Day* (1860); *Beating To Windward* (1866). He died at Geneva. His brother John Savile (1818–96), whose early diplomatic career runs parallel, was a noted connoisseur and later became Baron Savile of Rufford. BL 6. Boase. Wol.

The Savoy (January–December 1896). A short-lived effusion of the decadent* 1890s, this 'Illustrated Quarterly' (after July a monthly) was devised by the eccentric publisher Leonard Smithers*, and edited by the symbolist poet Arthur Symons. The cover design (which caused some censorship problems) was drawn by Aubrey Beardsley* who also published an expurgated version of his bawdy Wagnerian novel *Under The Hill* in its pages. The magazine carried modish short stories by Symons, W. B. Yeats, Hubert Crackanthorpe* and Ernest Dowson*. In criticism, it published Havelock Ellis's influential essay on Hardy's* *Jude**. The magazine was killed partly by poor sales, by a boycott by W. H. Smith's* and the savage backlash caused by Wilde's* conviction for sodomy in 1895. *BLM.*

Savrola, Winston Spencer Churchill, 1900, 1 vol, Longman. (Serialised in *Macmillan's Magazine**, May–December 1899). A Ruritanian romance, written by the future Prime Minister of England. The action opens on the day of a great parade in the capital of 'Laurania'. An old republic, the country has been a dictatorship under the presidency of Antonio Molara since the civil war of five years previous (1883). Savrola, a brilliant philosophical soldier in his thirties, has formed a revolutionary party to restore Laurania's 'ancient liberties'. An affair develops between Savrola and the President's wife, Lucile. She learns of the planned uprising but does not betray her lover to her husband. Savrola and Lucile are surprised by Molara at the very moment that the revolution breaks out (aided by British gunboats off the coast). Molara appears on the palace steps to surrender, but is shot by the socialist leader, Kreutze. A post-revolutionary coup by extremists forces Savrola and Lucile into exile, but an epilogue discloses that the hero later returns 'after the tumult had subsided and the hearts of the people turned again to the illustrious exile who had won them freedom'. The narrative is highly theatrical but Churchill handles crowd scenes excellently.

SAXBY, Jessie Margaret (née Edmonston, 1842–1940). Born in Halligarth in the Shetland Isles she was the ninth child of a doctor. By her own account she had 'no education save that acquired by much reading and a close study of nature and the society of literary and scientific parents. Early literary ambition suppressed for the sake of five young sons left fatherless.' Jessie Edmonston later married Henry L. Saxby also of Shetland and an authority on birds of the region. Mrs Saxby took a keen interest in Scottish affairs, declared herself a 'Radical-Imperialist' in politics, and was active in the causes of temperance and women's emigration. She wrote extensively in later life and had considerable success with a series of Shetland adventures for boys. They include: *Ben Hansen* (1884), a story of George Watson's College, the Edinburgh school; *The Lads Of Lunda* (1887); *Oil On Troubled Waters* (1888); *Wrecked On The Shetlands* (1890); *Tom And His Crows* (1894). BL 24. *WW*. RLF.

The Scapegoat, Hall Caine, 1891, 2 vols, Heinemann. (Serialised in the *Illustrated London News**, July–October 1891.) A novel with a purpose written to expose anti-semitic persecution. An English traveller in the 1860s stops at the Moroccan town of Tetuan. Among the Sultan Abderrahman's entourage he catches sight of a European-looking girl. She is, it emerges, a 'gift' to the Sultan from the local Chieftain. The main section of the narrative recapitulates the girl's story. She is Naomi, daughter of the Jew Israel Ben Oliel. For many years, Israel was the Kaid Ben Aboo's tax-gatherer and the most loathed person in Tetuan. Naomi was born deaf, dumb and blind; but in appearance recalls her less swarthy Anglo-Jewish ancestors. During the course of the ensuing story, she miraculously recovers her senses. And Israel descends to beggary, conceiving himself in the process to be the sacrificial scapegoat of his race. The story ends on a note of high melodrama. The English hero rescues Naomi from imminent violation by the Sultan ('a heartless sensualist with a black face') and makes her his own. Tetuan is stormed by a European expeditionary force and Ben Aboo is stoned to death by his enraged subjects. The whole aim of the novel is to convey Caine's revulsion for the native state of Morocco, 'a disgrace to the century'.

Scenes Of Clerical Life, George Eliot, 1858, 2 vols, Blackwood. (Serialised in *Blackwood's Magazine**, January–October 1857.) Eliot's first published fiction, comprising three short stories. 'The Sad Fortunes Of The Rev. Amos

Barton' is the study of an awkward and physically repellent curate who wins the sympathy of his Shepperton parishioners after the death (from exhaustion) of his wife Milly. The story is the grimmest embodiment of Eliot's theory that inner worth bears no relationship to outward appearance. 'Mr Gilfil's Love Story' deals with Barton's predecessor at Shepperton. Gilfil falls in love with Tina Sarti, the daughter of an Italian singer adopted by his (Gilfil's) patron, Sir Christopher Cheverel. But Tina has her heart broken by Cheverel's heir, Captain Anthony Wybrow. She finally marries Gilfil but dies soon after, leaving him forever bereft. 'Janet's Repentance' takes a wider social theme. The consumptive, but fiercely evangelical Rev. Edgar Tryan comes to the market town of Milby. His attempts at spiritual regeneration are resisted by a drunken lawyer, Robert Dempster. Dempster's brutality drives his wife Janet to drink. She is helped to recovery by Tryan and after his death, and her husband's (from delirium tremens), she devotes herself to a life of self-sacrificing service. Eliot's is the first intelligent treatment of alcoholism in English fiction.

The School For Saints, John Oliver Hobbes (i.e. Pearl Mary-Teresa Craigie), 1897, 1 vol, Unwin. Hobbes's most ambitious and over-written Catholic novel. (She had converted in 1892.) The narrative chronicles the career of Robert de Hausée Orange and is mainly set in the 1860s. In Brittany as a poetic and idealistic youth, he falls in love with Henriette Duboc, a Parisian actress (based on Sarah Bernhardt). He walks to Paris to throw himself at her feet but is repelled when he discovers that she has a child by her morganatic marriage with the Archduke of 'Alberia'. In her turn, Henrietta's child Brigit becomes the object of Orange's love when at sixteen she leaves her convent. Brigit, however, is forced into marriage with an old reprobate. Orange meanwhile has been taken up by an English family and is now by upbringing a young aristocrat with literary and political ambitions. He converts to Catholicism, despite Disraeli's* warning that it will damage his political prospects. Brigit (just seventeen and still virginal) is abandoned by her husband in the midst of the Spanish Carlist War and is rescued by Robert. Her disgraced husband, Parflete, is said to have killed himself and they marry under special licence at the Alberian Embassy. In the sequel, *Robert Orange* (1900), it emerges that the husband still lives and that the honeymoon was interrupted before sexual consummation. (A good half of Hobbes's narrative is devoted to this anticlimax.) The lovers separate and Robert eventually joins the priesthood, prostrates himself with overwork and dies a monsignor. Brigit becomes an actress; before he dies, Robert sees her on the stage and finds her 'the woman of his imagination', namely the ideal he first glimpsed in her mother all those years before. The novel ends with Disraeli's obituary for the tragically unfulfilled political career of the hero.

SCHREINER, Olive [Emilie Albertina] ('Ralph Iron', 1855–1920). Olive Schreiner was born in Wittebergen, Basutoland, the sixth of ten surviving children of a Methodist missionary of German origin. Her father, Gottlob, had come to the Cape in 1837 under the auspices of the London Missionary Society. Her mother, Rebecca (née Lyndall), was English and of respectable working-class origins. Schreiner was brought up, as her biographers put it, 'in a context of parental, certainly maternal severity and the brooding presence of a wrathful God'. A precocious girl who wanted above all else 'to be clever, to be wise', Schreiner educated herself and later claimed to have become a free-thinker at the age of twelve, when her little sister Ellie died. (Nevertheless, however secular, her thinking was to remain steeped in the fundamentalism of her father's stern faith.) Schreiner's childhood was unhappy and unsettled, Gottlob being forced to move his family to Cradock in the Cape Province following bankruptcy in 1869. In 1872, a broken engagement (and probable seduction) wounded her emotionally and coincided with a weakness of the chest that was to afflict her for the remainder of her life. In 1873, Schreiner left her parents' home to live with a sister in Fraserburg. She had medical friends and evidently considered becoming a nurse. But her health was not up to this vocation, and instead in 1874 she became a governess. Over the next seven years, working for a succession of families, she contrived painfully to save the £60 needed for her passage to England. Having become a free-thinker, she was alienated from her own family (more so when, after her father's death in 1876, her mother converted to Catholicism). While a governess, Schreiner began to write fiction, initially the autobiographical *Undine* (the author came to think ill of this first effort, and it was not published until well after her death in 1929). And in 1879, she began serious composition on *The Story Of An African Farm** (1883) whose heroine Lyndall's experiences are also clearly autobiographical. Finding no publisher by post, in 1881 Schreiner personally carried the manuscript to England. It was rejected by Macmillan*. But at Chapman and Hall* George Meredith* helped her revise the manuscript which was published in 1883 as by the masculine writer 'Ralph Iron'. Despite this, it was the unconventional heroine who attracted most attention. In the two years' interval between arriving in England and fame, Schreiner once again considered a career nursing. But the success of her novel (which went through three editions in its first year) established her as a professional author. *The Story Of An African Farm* exactly anticipated many of the concerns of new woman* fiction and provoked a storm of critical debate and brought her into contact with Eleanor Marx, who was to be a close friend (and, it has been alleged, lover). As a literary celebrity, Schreiner also made the acquaintance of Havelock Ellis in 1884. The couple had an intimate if strained relationship in which Ellis took it on himself effectively to psychoanalyse Schreiner. His free sexual doctrine was wholly incompatible with Schreiner's ineradicable puritanism, but he introduced her to the new ideas transforming English intellectual life, including Fabianism. At this period, she received an offer of marriage from her doctor Bryan (later Sir Bryan) Donkin and entered into a long correspondence with Karl Pearson, the brilliant mathematician (and later eugenicist) at University College, London. Their relationship (like others in Schreiner's life) seems to have broken down just at that point where it might have become sexually physical. Despite the intellectual stimulus, she was always unhappy and chronically ill in England. Nor did she capitalise on her success as a novelist. What promised to be a major work, *From Man To Man* (the story of two sisters brought up on an up-country farm and their different fortunes in life), was never completed. Begun as early as 1873, the novel was intended to engage with the problem of civilised prostitution. It, like *Undine*, was published only posthumously, in 1927. Other than her first great novel, the only literary publication to emerge from the London years was the collection of ethereal allegories, *Dreams* (1890). In 1889 Schreiner returned to South Africa. It was a period of extraordinary political ferment in the country, much of it stirred up by Cecil Rhodes. After an initial infatuation (which may have been based on a close personal relationship), Schreiner was violently disillusioned with Rhodes by 1892. This antipathy was heightened by the 1896 Jameson Raid, designed to take over the Transvaal republic for Britain. In the excited aftermath of this event (which led to Rhodes's downfall as Prime Minister and prepared for the Boer War four years later), Schreiner wrote *Trooper Peter Halket Of Mashonaland* (1897), a polemical allegory. The hero of the title is an English soldier engaged in 'pacifying' Rhodesia for the British South Africa Charter Company. Christ appears to Peter in a vision, and upbraids him for the atrocities committed by his comrades. The work was read as a political pamphlet and had some impact on an English reading public already apprehensive of war in the Cape. In 1894 Schreiner had married a politician and ostrich farmer, Samuel Cron Cronwright, a man eight years younger than her. The couple went to live in Kimberley where a daughter was born in 1895, dying almost immediately after. The experience despite its almost overwhelming pain for Schreiner helped formulate some of the ideas which were later to appear in her major feminist study, *Women And Labour* (1911). Cronwright devoted much of his energy to promoting Olive's literary and political career. During the 1890s and in the early twentieth century she was influential in the struggle for women's rights. But by the date of her return to England in 1913 she was exhausted and lonely. Her marriage had all but fallen apart. Cronwright remained farming in South Africa until 1920, when he joined her in London. But a month later, in August, she left for South Africa by herself, dying there in her sleep in December. BL 4. *DNB*. RM. *NCBEL*. Wol.

Science Fiction. In reviewing Bulwer-Lytton's* *A Strange Story** (1862) *The Times* called it a 'fairy tale of science'. And H. G. Wells* termed his end-of-the-century tales 'scientific romances'. But the term science fiction (and the self-conscious genre) is a twentieth-century invention. Nevertheless, the genre's roots are found in the earlier century. Even before the Victorian period, there existed the gothic* story (such as Mary Shelley's *Frankenstein*, 1818), the Utopia and the tale of the future. Before 1871, writing in these styles was marked by general ineptitude. Some exceptions stand out, for instance: R. F. Williams's *Eureka, A Prophecy Of The Future* (1837), a fable of Britain's conquest by Germany; H. Lang's *The Air Battle* (1859), a vision of a future Britain protected by 'Black Saharans'; H. N. O'Neill's *2,000 Years Hence* (1868), a prophecy of the terrible future consequences of the second Reform Bill. Such tales tended to be written by amateurs, and they were often short in length. Between 1871 and the end of the century, however, science fiction became more respectable and more purposive as a genre. In 1871 two masterpieces were published: Chesney's* *The Battle Of Dorking** and Bulwer-Lytton's *The Coming Race**. A year later, Samuel Butler* produced *Erewhon**, the finest satirical Utopia since Swift. And throughout the 1870s there had been the pervasive influence of Jules Verne's romances, widely translated for British magazines. On these three foundations British science fiction was erected. Later in the century, name authors frequently tried their hand at occasional scientific romances: Walter Besant*, for instance, with *The Revolt Of Man** (1882), or Anthony Trollope* with *The Fixed Period** (1882). And in 1889 there appeared in America Edward Bellamy's immensely influential utopian vision, *Looking Backward*. It was answered in 1890 by William Morris's* *News From Nowhere**. From the 1890s onwards, H. G. Wells poured out his scientific romances, beginning with *The Time Machine** (1895). Wells's *The Invisible Man** (1897) and more particularly *The Island Of Dr Moreau** (1896) re-established a link with the gothic tale of terror, also exploited by R. L. Stevenson*, Oscar Wilde* and Arthur Machen*. In 1898, Wells pioneered the alien invasion scenario with *The War Of The Worlds**. In 1898 M. P. Shiel* brought out his paranoid racial fantasy, *The Yellow Danger*, and followed it in 1901 with the cataclysmic *The Purple Cloud*. In the first, the human race is destroyed by Armageddon, in the second by 'natural' poison gas. By the turn of the century, the main tracks of British science fiction were firmly laid.

SCOTT, Lady [Harriet Anne] (née Shank, 1819–94). Harriet Shank was born in Bombay of Scottish parents. In 1844 she married Sir James Sibbald David Scott (1814–85), baronet and director of the East India Company. The couple had seven children and she wrote eight novels, the first four anonymously. They include: *The MP's Wife And The Lady Geraldine* (1838); *The Henpecked Husband* (1847); *The Only Child* (1852); *The Skeleton In The Cupboard* (1860); *The Dream Of A Life* (1862). Lady Scott, who also wrote a number of works of popular theology, died in London. BL 7. *DNB*. Wol. Sad (as 'Lady Lydia Scott').

SCOTT, Hugh Stowell ('Henry Seton Merriman', 1862–1903). With A. E. W. Mason*, Stanley Weyman* and Anthony Hope (i.e. Hawkins*), one of the masters of late Victorian romance*. Scott was born at Elswick, near Newcastle upon Tyne, where his father was a prosperous shipowner. His mother, who seems to have had a profound influence on him, was the daughter of the marine painter, James Wilson Carmichael. In 1873 he went away to public school in Scotland (Loretto) although he seems mainly to have been taught by private tutors. At eighteen, he went to work in his father's firm. In 1885 he joined Lloyd's underwriting office in London and seemed set for a successful career in business. But Scott had already developed a passionate love of travel (having voyaged to India in one of his father's ships in 1877–78). He chafed at office work and sent a first novel to Bentley*. *Young Mistley* (1888) duly appeared (anonymously) in two volumes. The work is immature, but indicates the author's future penchant for theatrical intrigue and rapidly shifting settings. In his next book, *The Phantom Future* (1888), a study of bohemian, artistic and student life, Scott took on his 'Merriman' pseudonym. His principal motive was to keep his writing a secret from his family although it is likely that he intended to emulate his namesake Walter Scott, 'the great Unknown'. As well as being secretive Scott was a severe critic of his own work. *Suspense* (1890, a sensation* novel which climaxes at the battle of Plevna) and *Prisoners And Captives* (1891) he considered unworthy and tried (unsuccessfully) to suppress the works in later life. But these two stories, with their exciting depictions of European war and Russian Nihilistic conspiracy, set the pattern for most of Merriman's subsequent romance. In 1889 he married.

The marriage seems to have been happy, although there were no children. Merriman's career took off in 1892, when the *Cornhill Magazine** (then edited by James Payn*) serialised *The Slave Of The Lamp*. The somewhat Ouidaesque* story of an intrepid newspaper reporter, Christian Vellacott, who is swept up in the underground of European politics, the novel reveals Merriman's growing mastery of fast-paced narrative. Buoyed up by the success of this novel and his next (*From One Generation To Another*, 1892, a psychological study of revenge) Scott was able to devote himself to writing full time and to the travelling which he loved. In 1894, there appeared his West African story of ivory and slave-trading, *With Edged Tools*, which went down well with the English reading public and with the critics. (The work can plausibly stand comparison with *The Heart Of Darkness*, by Conrad, also published in 1894, although its graphic violence and crude pro-imperialism have not worn well.) In 1895 he was confident enough of his achievements to identify himself to his family as a successful novelist, now earning £800 a year. (His father, who seems to have dominated the novelist psychologically, had meanwhile died.) *The Grey Lady* (1895) is a tale of seafaring life which shows a growing interest in character. It begins strikingly with a train 'tearing through the plains of Taunton'. In a first-class carriage are two boys, one of whom has just been accepted and one rejected for the Royal Navy. The subsequent narrative follows their linked careers. Like Stanley J. Weyman (with whom he liked to travel), Scott carefully studied the methods and emulated the success of Dumas. Like Weyman, he valued simple, fast, uncluttered narrative. He was particularly scrupulous about researching the background to his romances, steeping himself in the foreign locales in which his fiction was set. Probably his best work is the Russian story *The Sowers** (1896) which analyses with some skill the roots of nihilism. Merriman's later Victorian fiction includes: *Flotsam* (1896), a story of Delhi during the Mutiny; *In Kedar's Tents* (1897), a romance which contrasts English Chartist and Spanish Carlist fanaticism; *Roden's Corner* (1898), an attack on Anglo-Dutch corporate commerce; *The Isle Of Unrest* (1900), a tale of Corsican vendetta; *The Velvet Glove* (1901); *Barlasch Of The Guard* (1902), a historical* romance set in 1812 Danzig, a hotbed of intrigue and espionage during Napoleon's unsuccessful invasion of Russia. The last has survived as Merriman's most popular novel with later readers. The Dumas-like *The Last Hope*, a romance set in eighteenth-century France, was published posthumously in 1904. In some of his fiction, Scott collaborated with his sister-in-law, Miss E[velyn] Beatrice Hall ('S. G. Tallentyre', d. 1956) who was also a minor novelist in her own right. As Merriman he wrote eighteen novels in all. Reginald Pound notes: 'He was a disciple of Flaubert and the French clarity of thought pervades his writing, though precision of language does not. Strength of plot and careful character drawing override his lack of stylistic distinction. The dignified tone of his work was pleasing to many readers.' It has been suggested that like other writers, Scott may have been employed by the British secret services during his far-flung travels, ostensibly to gather material for his novels. By the turn of the century Merriman was a rich man, and he built himself a country house in rural Suffolk, near Woodbridge. He died prematurely, of appendicitis, aged forty-one. BL 18. *DNB*. RM. *NCBEL*. Wol. Sad.

The Scouring Of The White Horse, Thomas Hughes, 1858, 1 vol, Macmillan. (Illustrated by R. Doyle*.) Set, like the early chapters of *Tom Brown's Schooldays**, in the Vale of the White Horse. The hero, Richard, is a London clerk. A friend, Joe Hurst, invites him to spend his summer holiday in Berkshire. There Richard takes part in the ritual of cleaning the chalk outline of the White Horse, inscribed on the local hillside. In so doing, the young cockney gradually acquires a sense of England's heritage and his place in it. In addition to this education, he falls in love with Joe's sister Lucy. The novel ends with his return to London. During the train journey he dozes and has a vision of ideal England.

Scribner's Magazine (1887–1936). The premier American monthly magazine, published by Scribner's in America and co-published in Britain by Frederick Warne until 1892, thereafter by Sampson Low*. The magazine serialised a number of major English novels, including J. M. Barrie's* *Sentimental Tommy* (1896) and *Tommy And Grizel* (1900).

The Semi-Attached Couple, the Hon. Emily Eden, 1860, 2 vols, Bentley. Eden wrote this novel thirty years earlier, clearly under the influence of Jane Austen. Popular in its belated arrival ('a strange Chronicle of the Olden Time', the author modestly called it), the work has since achieved the status of a minor classic. Social comedy in mode, much of the narrative is refracted through incidental letters and onlookers' conversation. Helen, the eighteen-year-old and beautiful daughter of Lord and Lady Eskdale, makes a handsome marriage with Lord Teviot (somewhat to the chagrin of the Eskdales' neighbours, the Douglas family). But marriage is shown to have its problems. The morbidly self-conscious Teviot suspects his wife of insufficiently loving him. His suspicion boils over when rather than accompany him on a diplomatic mission to Lisbon she stays to look after a sick sister. The couple are reconciled by his serious illness following his return from Portugal. They are further brought together by the attempt of a bastard half-brother to assume the Teviot title. The dialogue and sharp epigrammatical style are delightful and the narrative contains a spirited election episode.

The Sensation Novel. Sensation fiction is a distinct but essentially minor sub-genre of the British novel that flourished in the 1860s. A pioneering authority, W. C. Phillips, entitled his book on the subject, *Dickens, Reade and Collins: Sensation Novelists* (1919) conceiving the style as a narrowly Dickensian* 'school'. For most critical purposes, it more loosely describes a cluster of bestsellers, such as *The Woman In White**, *Hard Cash**, *Lady Audley's Secret** and their clichéd imitations. Recent critics have explored the genre for what it reveals about dissident (i.e. criminal) womanhood in the Victorian period. However it is categorised, sensation fiction lived up to its name in the 1860s, alarming such authorities as the Archbishop of York, who preached a sermon against it as 'one of the abominations of the age'. One initial difficulty in defining the form is the ambiguity of the term 'sensation'. It can be taken psychologically, to describe the assault which fiction like Reade's* or Braddon's* makes on the nerves of the reader. Or, it can indicate that sensation fiction typically addresses itself to some journalistic sensation of the day: such as the forcible incarceration of the sane in lunatic asylums (e.g. *Hard Cash*) or bigamy* (*Lady Audley's Secret*, for instance, clearly derives its contemporary piquancy from the Yelverton divorce scandal which rocked England in 1861). The father of sensation fiction was Dickens. His habit of fixing on a particular abuse, his interest in topical crime, the disruptive immediacy of his style and devices were clearly influential. There was also an unusual (for Victorian literature) degree of fraternalism between him and Collins, and between Collins and Reade. Above all, Dickens was a serial novelist. As Mrs Oliphant* (who heartily disliked sensationalism) observed, it was the 'violent stimulation of serial publication' that inspired the most striking features of the genre. Its reliance, for instance, on 'curtain lines' or dramatic 'make 'em laugh, make 'em cry, make 'em wait' instalment endings. Other features of the sensation novel may be construed as refinements or exaggerations of Dickensian narrative technique. Sensation novels were up to the minute in their topicality, and were termed 'newspaper novels'. This writing to the historical moment quality can be traced back to *Oliver Twist**. The other great masters of the form can also be credited as innovators. Reade was a virtuoso of 'dramatic fiction', pacey, dialogue-centred, full of 'dead yet not dead' gimmickry, and false denouements. He wrote, as he put it, fiction 'with biceps'. The reading public after the 1860s has tended to find Reade's fiction sadly overstrained in its efforts at grandeur. But for all its forced tone and eccentricity, Reade's achievements with *Hard Cash*, *Put Yourself In His Place**, *Foul Play** and *It Is Never Too Late To Mend** are characteristic products of sensationalism. Collins's* contribution was the 'novel with a secret', the narrative built round a tantalising enigma. Collins also perfected the technique of multiple narration, assembling his stories from various journals, testimonies, diaries, newspaper reports. Swinburne was right to observe that Collins's early work such as *The Woman In White* and *The Moonstone**, which prefigure the detective* novel, are his finest. His later fiction with a reforming 'mission' is increasingly weak. On their part, Mrs Henry Wood* and Miss Braddon contrived to graft onto narrative fiction the energies and the range of effects associated with Victorian stage melodrama (in whose repertoire, Wood's *East Lynne** was a leading item). Viewed in terms of literary rather than social history, these novelists' main achievement was to subvert narrative conventions rendering fiction both more exciting and more suspenseful. Their influence was considerable. Dickens himself learned from Collins, and the enigmas around which *Great Expectations** and *Our Mutual Friend** are constructed owe something to the intricate plot work of *The Woman In White*. (As does the more supernaturally inclined *Uncle Silas** of J. S. Le Fanu*, 1864). Even Trollope*, arch-exponent of the domestic* school of fiction, borrowed from *The Moonstone* to create his *The Eustace Diamonds**. Hardy* certainly modelled his first published effort in fiction, *Desperate Remedies**, on the narrative tricks of Collins, Reade and Braddon*. So too, Ouida* was sensational in her début novel, *Strathmore**. Innumerable potboiling imitators followed the genre leaders, in writing crime fictions based on arson, bigamy, passionate crime and insanity.

Sequence Novels. Knitting novels together into large consanguineous sequences or patterns is less a Victorian English than a nineteenth-century French (Balzac, Hugo) and American (J. Fenimore Cooper) practice. The early Victorian most associated with the sequence novel is Thackeray* (who may have well been influenced by Balzac's *Comédie Humaine*). There are subtle connections between many of Thackeray's works, creating a sense of massive consanguinity. Warrington, in *Pendennis*, for instance, is the descendant of Henry Esmond* as (more closely) are the heroes of *The Virginians*. Trollope* took Thackeray's habit over (together with much else) in his 'Barsetshire* Chronicles' and, more particularly, the 'Palliser*' novels where Phineas Finn* and Plantagenet, Duke of Omnium connect the six massive works as carried-over heroes. Other notable sequence novelists of the period are Mrs Oliphant*, with her 'Chronicles of Carlingford*'; Rider Haggard*, with his Allan Quatermain* sagas; Conan Doyle*, with his Sherlock Holmes series; Maarten Maartens* with his 'Koopstad Chronicles'; E. F. Benson* with his 'Dodo' stories; J. M. Barrie* with his stories and sketches of 'Thrums' (i.e. Kirriemuir). Charlotte Yonge* wrote *The Trial* as a sequel to her popular *The Daisy Chain*, and connected both novels with her other bestseller *The Pillars Of The House*. In cases such as this, the larger design comes about merely by extension, when a writer wishes to follow up and exploit a success. In other cases, the writer requires a larger than one-novel scale to compose on. This was the case with Hardy's* Wessex* novels (in which the carried-over feature from work to work is region) or Philip Meadows Taylor's* ambitious chronicle of colonial India which began with *Tara* (1863).

SERGEANT, [Emily Frances] Adeline ('Adeline', 1851–1904). The author of some ninety novels, none of which has lasted, although at least a handful have some merit. (Her best works are probably the autobiographical *Esther Denison*, 1889, the story of an unsuccessful novelist, and *The Story Of A Penitent Soul*, 1892.) During her life, Sergeant's religious affiliation swung a complete 180 degrees from the Clapham Sect Methodism into which she was born through Anglicanism (to which she was converted in 1870, after her father's death) through Fabianism to Catholicism (which she embraced in 1899, shortly before her own death). Among this ideological merry-go-round it has been claimed that her most deeply felt work was written in the mid-1880s, a period during which she was temporarily agnostic. Sergeant was born at Ashbourne, Derbyshire, the second daughter of a Methodist clergyman and an authoress mother, Jane Sergeant (née Hall) who wrote under the pen name 'Adeline' (later incorporated by her daughter). Adeline Sr wrote popular improving stories for juveniles and adolescents such as *Amy's Christmas* (1861). She died in 1877. Emily was privately educated at Clapham and with her mother's aid broke into print at the precocious age of fifteen, with a volume of poems. She later attended Queen's College, London, where she gained first-class honours. She was writing fiction as early as 1879. But success came in 1882 when she won a £100 prize for a serial novel (*Jacobi's Wife*) awarded by the *People's Friend* of Dundee. The narrative opens dramatically with the sinking of a passenger ship at sea in 1870. Sergeant maintained her link with this journal, and became a popular and fertile provincial serial novelist. In 1884, she was an established author, and could afford to give up her position as a governess by which she had supported herself for ten years. From 1885 to 1887 she lived in Dundee. Shortly after she became a Fabian and was profoundly interested in the condition of the London poor and the fate of abandoned young girls in the capital. In *Esther Denison* she gives a remarkably powerful description of her own loneliness as a writer in London. In her writing prime, she turned out up to seven novels a year. According to her biographer, she averaged only around £100 a novel, but none the less managed to make a comfortable living. Her fiction includes *Deveril's Diamond* (1889), which has South African settings; *An East London Mystery* (1892); *A Broken Idol* (1893); *The Claim Of Anthony Lockhart* (1897), an inheritance story; *Blake Of Oriel* (1899), the story of an Oxford man who, despite an impressive exterior, is a villain. In 1892, she contributed to a novel by twenty-four hands, *The Fate Of Fenella.* (Her best-known collaborators on this venture were Conan Doyle* and Bram Stoker*.) Sergeant was an accomplished and professional woman of letters who acted for many years as Bentley's* literary adviser on submitted fiction manuscripts. Among her novels with religious themes are, *No Saint* (1886), which reflects her agnostic phase; *The Story Of A Penitent Soul* (1892), written in the form of an unhappy clergyman's journal; *The Common Lot* (1899), whose heroine sacrifices herself to look after selfish relatives. BL 70. *DNB.* Wol.

SERGEANT, Lewis (1841–1902). Sergeant (cousin of Adeline Sergeant*) was born in Barrow on Humber, Lincolnshire, the son of a schoolmaster. After leaving Cambridge University in 1865 with a degree in mathematics he taught for a while and wrote some school textbooks. He then took to journalism for, among other papers, the *Athenaeum*. Sergeant had a passion for modern Greece and wrote extensively about its history and politics. He wrote one novel under his own name, the facetious and autobiographically narrated love story, *The Caprice Of Julia* (1898), and others pseudonymously. BL 1. *DNB.* RLF.

The Seven Sons Of Mammon, G. A. Sala, 1862, 3 vols, Tinsley. (Serialised in *Temple Bar**, January–December 1861.) Sala's most effective novel, a biting satire on British commerce set in the early 1850s. Sir Jasper Goldthorpe, the father of seven sons, is 'the richest man on 'Change'. His origins are Quaker and he began business life as a small shopkeeper in the provinces. At the beginning of his career, Goldthorpe founded his fortune on the betrayal of a friend, Hugh Desborough. Desborough has subsequently returned from transportation as an omnipotent City moneylender. As 'Sims', he allies himself with a beautiful forger, Florence Armytage, who has documents proving Goldthorpe to be an embezzler. Armytage blackmails Sir Jasper and maliciously discloses his crime to his son Hugh. Hugh contrives to fake his death in Belgium, and returns to society under an alias. The novel (whose action is very intricate) ends with Goldthorpe bankrupted, Florence Armytage dying in a French prison and Hugh restored to respectability and the woman he loves, enriched by a suddenly benevolent Desborough. The novel is memorable for Sala's sprightly tirades on modern capitalism and it is clear that in writing it he had a recollection of Dickens's* *Our Mutual Friend*. The work is dedicated to Edmund Yates*, in memory of 'a very long and close friendship [and] a rational alliance'.

SEWELL, Anna (1820–78). The author of *Black Beauty** (1878), Sewell was born in Yarmouth, into a strict Quaker home. Her mother, Mary Sewell

(1797–1884), also wrote tales for the very young. (Her best-known work was the ultra sentimental *Mother's Last Words*, 1860.) Her father was a bank manager, later a commercial traveller for a Nottinghamshire lace firm. In a series of disasters, the Sewell family was impoverished and her childhood was disturbed. Most tragically, Anna was lamed, walking back from school at the age of fourteen. The ankle was evidently set badly, and she was to be severely disabled and in poor health for the remainder of her curtailed life. For any movement more than a few steps she was dependent on her pony and trap. During her last years, in which she was an invalid in her mother's care in Norfolk, she determined to write a book to improve the treatment of Victorian horses. *Black Beauty* ('The Autobiography Of A Horse, Translated From The Original Equine') was finished in 1877, and sold by Mrs Sewell to her publisher, Jarrold, who gave £20 for the copyright. By the time of the author's death a year later it had sold 100,000 copies. The most famous of Victorian animal stories, *Black Beauty* takes the form of a horse's reminiscences, as it comes down in the equine world to the condition of mere drudge. The work specifically attacks the use of the bearing rein, and was generally a boost to the newly formed RSPCA. BL 1. *DNB*. RM. *NCBEL*. Wol.

SEWELL, Elizabeth Missing (1815–1906). Like most women writers for children, Sewell was born into a religiously strict family, one of twelve offspring. Her father was a prominent solicitor and land agent. Elizabeth was brought up quietly at home on the Isle of Wight and at boarding school in Bath. Her brothers, all older than her, went on to win prominent positions for themselves in law, politics and the universities. So retiring was Elizabeth that she was unable even to tell her father that she had written and published her first book. Her closest brother William Sewell* (the author of *Hawkstone**, 1845) was an early Tractarian enthusiast, who reacted violently against Newman* after his conversion to Catholicism in 1845. Elizabeth remained a staunch High Church Anglican propagandist all her writing life. The autobiographical (and heavily evangelical) account she gives of her childhood stresses the cultivation of guilt feelings, and their sublimation into conscience. Her father died in 1842, heavily in debt and Mrs Sewell followed five years later. Elizabeth and the other children nobly undertook to pay their family's creditors. And Elizabeth additionally took over the support of the younger family, thus compromising her chances of marriage. In the 1840s, her life became easier when she gained fame with her novels (five of which proclaimed themselves to be 'edited' by William). In later life she was able to indulge her love of travel. *Amy Herbert* (1844) is a typical Sewell effort, with its study of social manners, adolescent feminine psychology and religious duty. The preface notes that 'the little tale was written by a lady for the use of a young member of her own family'. The girl growing up closely attached 'to the mother who to her was all in all' was to be Sewell's staple subject. A constant theme in her work is the value and rewardingness of the spinster's life. As an author, Sewell particularly disliked love stories and generally kept romance out or in the background of her narratives. She admitted that *The Experience Of Life* (1853), her most popular work, was also the actual record of her girlhood. (Appropriately, the story is narrated in the first person by the tough-minded and unmarried heroine, Sally.)

But in this novel, as in *Ursula, A Tale Of Country Life* (1858) the subtle chronicle of the growth of female consciousness is vitiated by a penchant for romantic and melodramatic climaxes and above all for pietistic conclusions. Sewell's most urgent religious novel, *Margaret Percival** (1847), was written at the instigation of her brother William and was intended to put down Catholic tendencies after Newman's defection. But so sweet-natured was Elizabeth that she felt obliged to present Catholics 'in an amiable light in order to avoid any appearance of prejudice or harsh judgement'. A similarly temperate vein of religious special pleading is evident in the multi-volume *Laneton Parsonage* (1846–48). *Katharine Ashton* (1858) is the somewhat bleak picture of a religious woman's life, dedicated to 'usefulness'. Sewell specialised in 'I' narration and had great success with such journal novels as *After Life* (1868). She enjoyed great popularity and esteem in England and America mainly among young female readers, although in the 1840s and 1850s large literary claims were made for her. Her proper position is probably in second place to Charlotte Yonge* (to whose *Monthly Packet** she was a contributor). In 1866 Sewell set up a small school with her sister Ellen in furtherance of her enlightened views on girls' education. BL 13. *DNB. NCBEL*. Wol. Sad. RLF.

SEWELL, the Rev. William (1804–74). An elder brother of Elizabeth Missing Sewell* and one of a talented family, he was born at Newport on the Isle of Wight. William Sewell attended Winchester College and Oxford from which he graduated with a first-class degree in classics in 1827. He entered the Church in 1830 and came under the spell of Newman* whom he knew personally. Sewell pursued an academic career at Oxford and it was he who was supposed publicly to have burned J. A. Froude's* *Nemesis Of Faith** in 1849. By the founding of various schools and colleges Sewell ran himself heavily into debt and his fellowship at Exeter College was sequestrated in 1862. He was forced to escape his creditors by moving to Germany. With the financial help of friends, he was able to return to England four years before his death. He never married. Sewell wrote fiction including the rabidly anti-Catholic *Hawkstone, A Tale Of And For England** (1845). He also 'edited' five of his sister's novels. As a preface to *Amy Herbert* (1844) sternly noted: 'books intended for the young should, as much as possible, be superintended by some clergyman who may be responsible for their principles.' BL 1. *DNB. NCBEL*. Wol.

A Shabby Genteel Story, W. M. Thackeray, *Fraser's Magazine*, June–October 1840. (The first book form version of the tale was published by Appleton, New York, 1852.) The early prelude to *Philip** (1862). Caroline Gann lives with her parents and her half-sisters at a boarding house in Margate. She has two suitors, the would-be poet, Andrea Fitch, and George Brandon. Brandon is a young fashionable gone underground from his creditors. He easily wins Caroline's heart and provokes a duel with the absurd Fitch to humiliate his rival. Fitch duly marries the bustling and wealthy widow Mrs Carrickfergus. Brandon's degenerate accomplices Lord Cinqbars and Thomas Tufthunt persuade him to go through a mock marriage ceremony which thoroughly dupes the innocent Caroline. Thackeray broke off his mournful little tale under the domestic crisis of his own wife's madness, which was confirmed at Margate in 1840. He picked up the strands of his shabby genteel story (from the point of the pregnant Caroline's inevitable desertion) twenty years later.

SHAND, Alexander Innes (1832–1907). Shand was born at Fettercairn in Kincardineshire. His father owned property in Demerara, and was ruined by the abolition of slavery in the West Indies in the first decade of the century. Young Shand was educated in Aberdeen, graduating from the city university in 1852. He subsequently went into law at his now widowed mother's request (turning down an offer of a commission in the Bengal Cavalry to do so). She died in 1855, upon which the young man undertook a long course of foreign travel and desultory writing. In 1865 he was admitted to the Scottish Bar, and settled down as a lawyer and married man in Edinburgh. But for his wife's health he moved shortly after to London, where his legal training was useless. Shand threw himself once more into magazine work. He did some early writing for *The Times* and for *Blackwood's Magazine**, and eventually joined the staff of the *Saturday Review**, whose sharp Conservative views were congenial to him. In London, he was a prominent man of letters, and a friend of Laurence Oliphant*, George Meredith* and George Smith (of Smith, Elder*). He was also an enthusiastic sportsman and wrote expertly on culinary matters. (See his *Cookery Of The Pheasant*, 1895.) Shand's novels include: *Against Time* (1870); *Shooting The Rapids* (1872), a story of Garibaldi's uprising; *Fortune's Wheel* (1886); *Kilcarra* (1891), an Irish* tale; *The Lady Grange* (1897). Shand's fiction is very strong on club scenes (see the opening of *Shooting The Rapids*, set in the 'Travellers') and reveals a close observation of the London business world. Trollope* maliciously portrayed Shand as Mr Ferdinand Alf in *The Way We Live Now** (1875). BL 4. *DNB*. Wol.

SHARP, William ('Fiona Macleod', 1855–1905). William Sharp was born in Paisley, Scotland, where his father was a merchant and he the oldest of eight children. Partly brought up in the Highlands, he succumbed as a child to Celtic romanticism, on one occasion running away to spend a whole summer with Scottish gypsies. Sharp was unhappy as a student at Glasgow University, and even more unhappy in 1874, when at his father's 'urgent request' he was put to work as a lawyer's clerk. (Sharp recollects the tension between his poetic self and his bourgeois parent with the Ruthven father and son relationship in his later novel, *Silence Farm*, 1899.) His family subsequently sent him to Australia in 1876 (shortly after his father died), there being some fear that he might have consumption. He did not take to the country, and came back to London to work once more in a bank in 1878. Sharp had poetic gifts (recognised early on by D. G. Rossetti) and began his authorial career by publishing a volume of sub-Shelleyan verse in the early 1880s. Critics were impressed particularly with his ambitious poem 'Motherhood', which examines maternal woman in civilised, primitive and savage settings. Over the next few years, Sharp was engaged with a series of commissioned biographies on romantic poets for Eric Robertson's 'Great Writers' series. He also threw himself into the profession of belletristic higher journalism, which at this period offered lucrative opportunities for his fluent pen. And he was helped make his way in the literary world by his strikingly impressive physical appearance, crowned by a full head of golden hair. Sharp made a number of visits to Italy in the 1880s. Two more volumes of poetry followed in 1884 and 1888. In 1890 he removed his literary base from London, spending much of his later life in worldwide travel. And notoriously, Sharp invented an alter ego, 'Fiona Macleod*' in 1894. Allegedly a cousin, this entirely fictional Celtic bard seems to have taken Sharp over. He insisted she was a real person and may even have convinced himself of the fact. Psychically, Macleod's 'land of the heart's desire' seems to have unlocked his creativity, particularly in the period 1894–96. (Sharp, incidentally, had married a cousin in 1884, but the union was probably companionate.) More importantly, as recent critics have pointed out, the Macleod device allowed the author to give play to his racial theory of inspiration, which expressed itself as an obsession with Celtic and Zionist themes. As William Sharp he wrote a number of novels, none of which has worn well. *The Sport Of Chance* (1888) is a sensation* novel, first serialised in the *People's Friend* which recalls scenes from Sharp's Scottish childhood and his 1876 visit to Australia. *The Children Of Tomorrow** (1889) is an art novel, chronicling the sexual and aesthetic relationship between a robust English sculptor and a fine-nerved Jewish poetess. In collaboration with the American author Blanche Willis Howard, he wrote the epistolary novel of marital entanglements, *A Fellowe And His Wife* (1892). It has been conjectured that the novel accompanied a crisis in Sharp's own married life. The author's shadowy double, Fiona Macleod, emerged in the early 1890s. Although her temperament was more suited to verse and folklore, she also wrote fiction. Her efforts in this field are represented by *Pharais, A Romance Of The Isles* (1894), 'Pharais' being the Gaelic for 'Paradise'; *The Mountain Lover* (1895); *The Sin Eater* (1895); *Green Fire* (1896). All are suffused with a heavy Celtic nostalgia and hypersensitivity. In his own person, Sharp wrote a number of thinly melodramatic late novels, including: *Wives In Exile* (1896), 'A Comedy In Romance'; and the autobiographical *Silence Farm* (1899). Fiona Macleod is plausibly considered to be a more vital, and creative artist than her prim creator. Maintaining the dual personality brought Sharp to the brink of nervous breakdown in 1897–98. He caught cold in Italy, dying suddenly at the young age of fifty. (WS) BL 5. (FM) BL 5. *DNB*. RM. *NCBEL*. Wol.

Sharpe's London Magazine (1845–70). *Sharpe's* was begun by the publisher T. B. Sharpe as a three-halfpenny weekly in November 1845. A miscellany, it aimed at the family reader. In 1848, Sharpe transferred ownership to Arthur Hall and the magazine became a 1s. monthly. From 1847 to 1849 its editor was Frank Smedley*, the novelist, who serialised much of his early fiction in the magazine's short instalments, including his best work, *Frank Fairlegh** (1849), for which he managed to get the services of the best illustrator of the day, G. Cruikshank*. Smedley was succeeded by another novelist, Mrs S. C. Hall*, in 1852. But her editorial tenure lasted less than a year. The magazine (although illustrated) was unable in the 1860s to compete with Dickens's* dynamic weekly *All The Year Round** or the new breed of quality monthlies inspired by *Cornhill**. BLM.

SHAW, [Miss] Flora L[ouisa] (later Lady Lugard, 1851–1929). The daughter of a British general, Flora Shaw was born in Dublin and privately educated. In the early 1880s she rebelled violently against her family. Helped by George Meredith*, she was taken on by W. T. Stead of the *Pall Mall*

Gazette and moved with him to *The Times*, where she rose to the senior position of head of the colonial department of the paper. As a journalist she undertook special commissions all over the Empire. In 1902, she married Sir Frederick Lugard, the colonial administrator. In the first World War, as Lady Lugard, she worked for the relief of refugees. Her first novel, *Castle Blair* (1878) was very successful and as 'A Story Of Youthful Days' consciously recalls her Irish childhood. As Ruskin* enthused: 'the book is good and lovely and true having the best description of a noble child (Winnie) that I ever read and nearly the best description of the next best thing, a noble dog'. Other lively romances followed: *Hector* (1883), 'A Story For Young People'; *A Sea Change* (1885); *Colonel Cheswick's Campaign* (1886), a tale of the domestic repercussions of the war in Egypt. BL 4. *WW. NCBEL.* Wol.

SHAW, George Bernard (1856–1950). The greatest playwright in English of the twentieth century. Shaw was born in Dublin, the youngest child and only son of a failed merchant, George Carr Shaw. Baptised a Protestant, his upbringing was religionless and loveless (his father, a secret drunkard, was seventeen years older than his wife). Shaw left school at fifteen, and worked in a land agent's office for 18s. a month. All the while, he was reading furiously. (He claimed to have read the whole of Dickens* at the age of twelve.) In 1876, he came to London (where his mother was now working as a singer) and for the next few years supported himself on a small inheritance, writing music criticism. On the side, he helped found the Fabian Society in 1884 and wrote five unsuccessful novels between 1878 and 1883. *Immaturity*, written in 1879, contains his early impressions of London boarding house life. It was rejected by George Meredith* for Chapman and Hall*, among others, and did not see print for fifty years. *The Irrational Knot* was written in 1880 and published eventually by Annie Besant in the magazine *Our Corner* (1885–87). The knot in the title is marriage. *Love Among The Artists* was written in 1881. A study of musical genius, it was also published in Besant's magazine (1887–88). *Cashel Byron's Profession** was written in 1882 and again rejected by Meredith. But eventually this lively romance of pugilism saw print in the socialist journal *To-Day* (1885–86) and was the first of Shaw's novels to be published in volume form, in 1886. *An Unsocial Socialist*, the last written, was the first of Shaw's novels to be printed (*To-Day*, 1884). But, as the author ruefully noted: 'the title of this novel finished me with the publishers' and it effectively ended his career as a Victorian novelist. Shaw's vocation was clearly not in fiction and it was not until the first performance of his Ibsenesque play *Widowers' Houses* in 1892 that his destiny as the nation's greatest modern dramatist was revealed. BL 5. *DNB.* RM. *NCBEL.*

She, H. Rider Haggard, 1887, 1 vol, Longman. (Serialised in the *Graphic* October 1886–January 1887, illustrated by E. K. Johnson.) The most popular of Haggard's African romances. At Cambridge, a dying student entrusts his young son, Leo Vincey, to the care of Ludwig Holly. On his twenty-fifth birthday, Leo opens a steel box left him by his father. From it he learns that he is descended from an ancient Egyptian priest Kallikrates and the Egyptian Princess for whom he broke his vows of celibacy. Leo is instructed to go to Africa and kill the wicked (and immortal) Queen who later murdered Kallikrates. Holly and Leo travel to central Africa. They encounter shipwreck, crocodile-infested rivers and a tribe of cannibals, the Amahaggers. Leo takes a native wife, Ustane. Through a tunnelled mountain they are finally conducted to the chambers of a heavily veiled queen, Ayesha or 'She'. She is possessed of magical powers, and recognises in Leo her ancient lover Kallikrates. She kills Ustane with a glance and takes the now bewitched Leo to the ancient city of Kôr. There at the heart of a cave she shows the white men the pillar of life, a flame which ensures immortality. She enters it first, to show there is nothing to fear. But perversely the flame returns her to her true age, 2,000. She dies a shrivelled monkey. After many more adventures the heroes return to England, Leo prematurely aged. Haggard wrote a sequel, *Ayesha* (1905). *She* was successfully dramatised in 1888 and there have been four film versions in the twentieth century.

Sheba, Rita (i.e. Mrs Desmond Humphreys), 1889, 3 vols, F. V. White. An autobiographical novel whose main interest lies in its first volume, which reconstructs the strange thirteen-year-old consciousness of Sheba Ormatroyd. Sheba is brought up in the Bush outside Sydney, and virtually educates herself from books left around her house. When her father, a clerk, dies, Mrs Ormatroyd goes to the city where she marries a rich merchant, Levison. (The marriage is the occasion for some vicious anti-semitism on Rita's part.) Resisting her mother's attempt to force her at sixteen into marriage with a French libertine, Sheba comes under the influence of a German philosopher, Franz Muller. She writes a novel, and falls in love with an opera singer, Paul Meredith. When it emerges that Paul has a disreputable wife in his past, Sheba never the less succumbs to 'the golden apples of temptation' and yields to him sexually. Paul goes to England, where he is the heir to an earldom. Meanwhile, his wife returns and brutally insults Sheba who collapses and has a miscarriage. At the end of the novel, narrowly rescued from suicide by drowning, the heroine has resolved to allow the world to think her dead. The work is subtitled, 'A Study Of Girlhood'.

SHEEHAN, [Canon] P[atrick] A[ugustine] (1852–1913). Sheehan was born at Mallow, Co. Cork. After attending Maynooth College, he was ordained a Catholic priest in 1875. Following a brief period of missionary work in England he passed the remainder of his career in Ireland, becoming Canon of Cloyne in 1903. Sheehan wrote poetry and some very popular fiction, including *Geoffrey Austin, Student* (1895), a story of school life; and its sequel, *The Triumph Of Failure* (1899). The novel was applauded by Irish critics as a major religious* novel yet at the same time, 'Irish* and heroic' and 'a trumpet call to our people'. His other fiction includes *My New Curate* (1899) and *Luke Delmege* (1901). Like many Irish writers, Sheehan was popular in the USA and the last novel was first serialised in the *American Ecclesiastical Review*. Set in New York, the narrative follows the tribulations of a priest who dies with a message for all mankind on his lips. Sheehan's short stories were collected and published in 1908. BL 6. *WW*.

SHEPPARD, Elizabeth Sara ('Beatrice Reynolds', 'E. Berger', 1830–62). Elizabeth Sheppard was born at Blackheath, London. Her father was an Anglican clergyman, unworldly but very scholarly. On her mother's side, Sheppard claimed Jewish descent, a fact which she invested with great romantic significance. Sheppard's father died, making no provision for his family and her mother opened a school at which Elizabeth taught, when she was old enough. She showed unusually precocious musical and linguistic gifts. At the age of ten, she wrote a drama, *Boadicea*. At eleven 'she was an excellent Latin scholar, wrote French fluently, and read Goethe and Schiller in the original'. At fourteen, she began to study Hebrew. At the age of sixteen, she began a novel, *Charles Auchester**. The work was dedicated to Disraeli*, whom she idolised. Not averse to idolatry, he read the manuscript enthusiastically and forwarded it to Hurst and Blackett* (successors to Disraeli's own publisher, Colburn*). It duly appeared in three volumes in 1853. A sensitive but painfully immature work, it fictionalises the life of Mendelssohn in the person of the Chevalier Seraphael. Other novels of Sheppard's are: *Counterparts, Or The Cross Of Love* (1854), dedicated to 'Mrs Disraeli', this is a 'romance of temperaments' with poets, painters and scientists in the dramatis personae; *My First Season* (1855), 'by Beatrice Reynolds'; *The Double Coronet* (1856); *Rumour* (1858); *Almost A Heroine* (1859). As 'E. Berger' (i.e. French for 'shepherd') she published two volumes of tales and fables. Sheppard died prematurely, in Brixton. Her fiction is often over-written and emotionally confused. BL 7. *DNB. NCBEL*. Wol. Sad.

SHERARD, Robert H[arborough] (1861–1943). Sherard was born in London, the son of a clergyman and a great-grandson of the poet Wordsworth. He was educated at school in Guernsey, and at the universities of Oxford and Bonn. Using his knowledge of German-speaking Europe, Sherard in the 1880s became a foreign correspondent for various English, American and Australian newspapers. In 1894 he married a daughter of the Baron de Stern. By this time, he had earned a reputation as a wild man, a dueller and an out-and-out bohemian. He was a loyal friend of Oscar Wilde* (about whom he published a sympathetic book in 1905) and of Ernest Dowson* who died in Sherard's cottage in 1900. In 1882, Sherard published a volume of poems, *Whispers*. He also turned out (among much else) novels including: *A Bartered Honour* (1884); *The American Marquis* (1888); *Rogues* (1889), a murder story; *Agatha's Quest* (1890); *Jacob Niemand* (1895), a brisk inheritance drama set in the Lake District; *The Iron Cross* (1897). Late in life Sherard made a second marriage having given up publishing fiction around 1904. BL 11. *WW*. Wol. RLF.

SHERER, J[ohn] W[alter] (1823–1911). Sherer was born at Nottingham, the son of a senior Bengal Civil Servant and was related on his mother's side to the Bishop of Madras. After going to school at Rugby, Sherer himself went to India in 1846, where he worked in various government posts. He was decorated for gallantry during the Mutiny in 1857, and served as a magistrate during the restoration of civil order that followed. Sherer married twice; on both occasions to eligible daughters of well-placed Anglo-Indian families. He eventually rose himself to the Indian bench, before retiring in 1877 to Bath, England. Sherer wrote numerous works on India and tales, mainly comic in tone, including: *Who Is Mary?* (1879); *The Conjuror's Daughter* (1880); *Myrtle And Nightshade* (1880), a tale of the Indian Mutiny; *Helen The Novelist* (1888), dedicated to F. W. Robinson*; *A Princess of Islam* (1897). BL 7. *WW*. Wol. RLF.

SHIEL, M[atthew] P[hipps] ('Gordon Holmes', 1865–1947). Shiel was born in Montserrat in the West Indies, where his father was a Methodist minister of Irish extraction. The ninth child, he was preceded by eight sisters. Young Shiel studied medicine at St Bart's, London, but did not qualify. He drifted into schoolteaching in Derbyshire and after 1895 supported himself mainly by writing. He published novels, short stories and some poetry. As a novelist, Shiel specialised in slick science fiction* and detective* novels (a group of the latter were produced in the early twentieth century under the pseudonym 'Gordon Holmes'). *Prince Zaleski* (1895), Shiel's first published work, appeared in John Lane's* *Keynotes* series. It takes the form of three mysteries (two murder, one theft) solved by the exotic hero. The novel was successful and was followed by *The Rajah's Sapphire* (1896), the story of a gem which haunts its owners. *The Yellow Danger* (1898) is a fantasy of Chinese domination of the globe. Improbably, the oriental potentate Yen How becomes infatuated with Ada Seward, a Fulham nursemaid, and starts a world war to get her. His hordes are foiled by Shiel's Anglo-Saxon hero, John Hardy, in a sea battle which claims the lives of 20 million. Some 150 million more of the earth's population die in a subsequent cholera epidemic. Shiel's other fiction includes: *Contraband Of War* (1899), a novel of intrigue on the seas during the Spanish-American War; *Cold Steel* (1899), a swashbuckling tale, set in the age of Henry VIII; *The Man Stealers* (1900), another historical* romance fantasising a French plot to kidnap Wellington in return for the imprisonment of Napoleon on Elba; *The Lord Of The Sea* (1901), Shiel's first science fiction work proper, with a hero who finds a meteorite full of diamonds and proceeds to rule the world. Shiel's *The Purple Cloud* (1901) is the work which posterity has come most to admire. The hero, Adam Jeffson ('the second parent of the world'), goes to the North Pole and so misses the poisoning of the rest of humanity by a cloud of cyanogen gas. He spends seventeen years in solitary, pyromaniac splendour before finding a mate sheltering in a cellar in Constantinople. The paranoid egoism of the hero is powerfully done and the much reprinted work earned Shiel the status of an apocalyptic prophet, a role he played with gusto over the following years. Shiel worked for the Government in the first World War, became increasingly preoccupied with racist fantasies of the 'Overman' and seems to have died a religious maniac. His last work, *Jesus*, was apparently finished but remains unpublished. His last published novel, *The Young Men Are Coming!* (1937), is a wild romance about a hero, Dr Warwick, who returns from outer space with an elixir of youth. Shiel's early work was rediscovered by science fiction enthusiasts in the 1930s. BL 30. RM. *NCBEL*. Wol. RLF.

The Ship Of Stars, Q (i.e. A. T. Quiller Couch), 1899, 1 vol, Cassell. Q's story about growing up in Cornwall in the 1860s. Theophilus ('Taffy') Raymond is the only son of a clergyman who accepts the offer of a living in remote Nanniabuloe. He falls out with his intemperate patron, Squire Moyle, while young Taffy falls in love with the squire's granddaughter, Honoria. Taffy grows up (experiencing some criminal shipwrecking episodes in the process) and for a while is apprenticed to a blacksmith. With his parents' sacrifices and Honoria's assistance (she now being married to a nobleman's son, George Vyell), Taffy goes to Oxford University. But Honoria wrongly suspects him of having made a local girl, Lizzie Pezzack, pregnant. George is in fact the culprit, and he dies saving his bastard child from drowning. The novel ends with Taffy and Honoria apparently separated. The work is memorable as the record of a Cornish childhood, the 'Ship of Stars' being a fantastic vessel imagined by the young hero and heroine in their daydreams.

Ships That Pass In The Night, Beatrice Harraden, 1893, 1 vol, Lawrence and Bullen. A weepy melodrama, set in a Swiss *Kurhaus*, or sanatorium, at Petershof. Bernardine Holme, an exhausted schoolteacher, is drawn to a fellow convalescent, Robert Allitsen, nicknamed 'the disagreeable man' on account of his surliness. They fall in love. Cured, Bernardine returns to England to work in her uncle's second-hand bookshop. Robert declares his love in a tender letter which he promptly tears to pieces. When his mother dies and he is suddenly rich, he appears at the bookshop in person and after a harrowing love scene, Bernardine is run over by a waggon. Robert returns to the sanatorium to spend the remainder (presumably short) of his life. *Ships That Pass In The Night* was a bestseller, and the title became a catchphrase for a certain kind of love affair.

Shirley, Charlotte Brontë, 1849, 3 vols, Smith, Elder. (The publishers originally proposed serialisation; but Brontë felt the lack of sufficient 'animal spirits'.) The conventional grouping of this work with the social problem* or 'Condition of England' novels of the 1840s is somewhat objectionable, since the action is set in 1811-12, and *Shirley* could as well be termed a regional*-historical* tale. The plot principally concerns Robert Gerard Moore (half-English, half-Belgian), a Yorkshire mill owner, determined to modernise his machinery in the face of Luddite protest, agitation, riot and, eventually, attempted assassination. His first love is Caroline Helstone, niece and ward of the local Rector. Her passive temperament is contrasted with the fire of Shirley Keeldar, an heiress and proud-spirited girl. Robert proposes to her, largely for financial motives, and is scornfully repulsed. The last page of the novel has the double marriage of Shirley to Robert's brother (formerly her tutor, and her true love) and Robert to his faithful and forgiving Caroline. The restrictive Orders in Council (1812) which have crippled Moore's export trade are lifted with Napoleon's defeat, and the 'social problems' (which Brontë depicts with historical accuracy) are dissolved in a wash of happy ending. *Shirley* has a number of points of interest. Brontë analyses, more than elsewhere in her fiction, the Yorkshire character and, particularly, the violent independence of her sister Emily (portrayed, it is generally accepted, in the heroine of the title). The work is marred by a melodramatic and morbid last volume, with Caroline recovering her lost mother, almost losing her life through illness, a riot, homicide and near death by violence for Robert. (Branwell died just as Brontë was embarking on this last third of her novel.) The tone of the work is sober: 'unromantic as Monday morning', the author claimed. *Shirley* is the only novel in which Brontë sacrificed first- for third-person narration.

SHORTER, Dora Sigerson (née Sigerson, 1866–1918). Born in Dublin, she was a daughter of the Irish surgeon and man of letters, George Sigerson (1836–1925). Well known as a poet (under the name Dora Sigerson), she married in 1896 the English critic and journalist C. K. Shorter (1857–1926), who had first been attracted to her by a photograph in the London papers. (She was a strikingly beautiful woman.) As Mrs Shorter, she wrote some gloomy stories, collected as *The Father Confessor* (1900). Her mother, Hester Sigerson, wrote the similarly gloomy novel: *A Ruined Race, Or The Last Macmanus Of Dramroosh* (1890). BL 2. RM. *WW*.

SHORTHOUSE, J[oseph] H[enry] (1834–1903). Shorthouse was born in Birmingham, the eldest of three sons of a manufacturer in chemicals (principally of sulphuric acid). His mother was the daughter of a glass manufacturer. Both parents were Quakers. Shorthouse's early education was disturbed by a paralysing nervous stammer which emerged in his fourth year. This handicap was to frustrate all attempts at a normal school education. In 1842, he was further disabled by a crippling attack of typhus. In his convalescence at Moseley (where his grandmother lived) the young Shorthouse read widely. At sixteen, he went into his father's business. He had, however, strong literary inclinations. He was an active member of a Friends' Essay Society and it was at its meetings that he first cultivated his literary sensibility, overcame his speaking disabilities and met his wife Sarah Scott (the daughter of a Birmingham accountant) whom he married in 1857. In his young manhood, Shorthouse was strongly influenced by Ruskin* and the Pre-Raphaelites. He also developed what was to be a lifelong obsession with seventeenth-century Anglicanism, which he romanticised powerfully. In 1861, he resigned the Society of Friends and was baptised into the Church of England, Sarah following soon after. His health continued to plague him. In 1858 he sustained a fall from his horse which concussed him. An attack of epilepsy followed in 1862 which was severe enough to render him a semi-invalid for the remainder of his life. In 1864 he began a nine-year stint as People's Warden at St John's Ladywood, in Birmingham, a High Anglican church. Three years later, in 1867, Shorthouse began writing *John Inglesant**. It was completed in 1876 and Shorthouse submitted it to various publishers. But the vogue for the historical* novel was over, the author was a nobody and the manuscript was everywhere rejected. In 1880, he circulated it in a private, vellum-bound edition of 100 copies printed by Cornish Brothers, Birmingham. The physical form of the book was based on the seventeenth-century volumes of theology of which Shorthouse was a discriminating collector. The following year Mrs Humphry Ward* forwarded a copy to Alexander Macmillan, who offered to publish the novel for a mass readership. It finally emerged in 1881. For an author who had never even been to Italy, *John Inglesant* is a remarkable performance ('the work', as he said, 'into which I put my life') and once published by Macmillan*, the novel enjoyed huge success. Gladstone, Huxley and Cardinal Manning were among Shorthouse's eminent admirers. He became a regular contributor to fashionable magazines (notably *Macmillan's**). He was lionised, and a cult formed around the book. He was taken up by literary London society, where his mannered, eighteenth-century appearance and love of colourful clothes made a striking impression. Shorthouse felt that *John Inglesant* was his great effort, and made no attempt to follow it with any fiction of a similarly ambitious scale. But he elaborated his eccentric line of Platonic mysticism and Anglican polemic in later minor works. *The Little Schoolmaster Mark* (1885) is 'A Spiritual Romance' set in eighteenth-century Germany. It follows the career of a tailor's son, Mark, whose destruction in the Court of a local prince allegorises the conflict of world and soul. *Sir Percival* (1886), subtitled 'A Story Of The Past And Of The Present', is in fact a tale of the present in which the Quixotic hero tilts against an array of modern 'ideas'. Failing in love, and still racked with doubt, Percival goes as a soldier to Africa where he dies gallantly attempting to rescue an English bishop from the natives. *The Countess Eve* (1888) is set in eighteenth-century Burgundy. A collection of shorter pieces was published in 1888 as *A Teacher Of The Violin And Other Tales*. His last work, *Blanche Lady Falaise* (1891), is a story of the present day and has a tragic heroine whose first love goes wrong. She subsequently marries a man she does not love, and who finally dies struck by lightning in the Austrian Alps. Like all of the author's fiction, the novel scrupulously notates protracted torments of conscience. Shorthouse died at Edgbaston, the Birmingham suburb where he had passed most of his life, having entirely given up business, due to bad health, in 1901. BL 6. *DNB*. RM. *NCBEL*. Wol. Sad.

The Sign Of Four, A. Conan Doyle, 1890, 1 vol, Spencer Blackett. (The story was first published in *Lippincott's Magazine*, February 1890.) The archetypal Sherlock Holmes story. The opening chapter, 'The Science Of Deduction', introduces the 'unofficial detective' Holmes describing his methods to the faithful Dr Watson. A young governess, Mary Morstan, soon presents Holmes with a teasing problem. Her father disappeared on his way back from service in India ten years before, and recently she has been receiving annually a mysterious gift of a priceless pearl. Holmes proceeds to unravel the matter. It emerges that Mary's father and a Major Sholto were prison officers in the Andaman islands. They cheated four of their prisoners out of a hidden treasure and in England Sholto accidentally killed his accomplice Morstan. As reparation after his own death he has his son send the yearly pearl. One of the cheated prisoners, wooden-legged Jonathan Small (assisted by his ruthless Indian servant Tonga), revenges himself on the Sholtos and is eventually captured after a Thames chase in which the treasure of Agra is scattered on the river bed. Watson marries Mary Morstan. Among other classic incidents, *The Sign Of Four* enunciates Holmes's essential dictum: 'when you have eliminated the impossible, whatever remains, *however improbable*, must be the truth.'

Silas Marner, George Eliot, 1861, 1 vol, Blackwood. Eliot's finest pastoral tale. Marner is a linen weaver in the village of Raveloe at the turn of the nineteenth century. In his early life he belonged to a strict sect from which he was expelled on a false charge of theft. In later life he has become a narrow-minded miser. Silas's store of gold is stolen from its hiding place under his cottage floor by Dunstan Cass, the depraved son of the local squire. Shortly after Silas's shattering loss a small baby, with strikingly golden hair, crawls into his house. Her mother has died in the snow outside. Silas adopts the child, called Eppie, who restores meaning to his life as she grows up a noble young woman. In later life, Eppie is revealed to be the daughter of another of the squire's sons, Godfrey Cass. But she refuses to leave Silas. The gold is eventually discovered on the corpse of Dunstan, in a drained quarry nearby. The story is notable for the sharpness of its rural detail, its tactful symbolism and its variation between high melodrama and the broad comedy of scenes in the Rainbow Inn.

The Silence Of Dean Maitland, Maxwell Gray (i.e. Mary G. Tuttiett), 1886, 3 vols, Kegan Paul, Trench. Gray's most popular and improbable melodrama. Cyril Maitland, a young clergyman, kills the father of Alma Lee, a village girl he has seduced. He allows a medical friend, Henry Everard (the lover of his twin sister Lilian), to stand trial for the crime. Everard is sentenced to twenty years' imprisonment in Australia during which time Cyril rises in the Church on the strength of his preaching, his ascetic devotion and his book, *Secret Penitent*. But his wife and children die, except for a daughter and a blind son. Everard returns having served his sentence and discovers the truth. He forgives the now shattered Cyril, Dean Maitland. On the day that he is to preach the sermon that will earn him a bishopric, Cyril confesses his sin publicly from his pulpit and dies, exhausted by the strain of his long silence. Henry and Lilian finally marry. The work was later adapted as a hit play.

Silver Fork Fiction. Also called 'the fashionable novel', the style was dominant from the mid-1820s until the mid-1840s. The master-mind behind silver forkery was the publisher Henry Colburn*. In 1825–26, at a time when the book trade was prostrated by a recession, Colburn embarked on a saturation campaign of publishing short-life bestsellers, exploiting post-Regency fascination with high life. His first hits were with Theodore Hook's* *Sayings And Doings* (1824); Disraeli's* *Vivian Grey* (1826); T. H. Lister's *Granby* (1826) and Robert Plumer Ward's* *Tremaine* (1825). Each of these works purported to be by an insider, privy to the intimate secrets of the aristocracy and willing to divulge all to a middle-class reading public. Colburn is estimated to have put his imprint on three-quarters of the 500 or so silver fork novels subsequently published. He was happiest when he could recruit actual aristocrats such as the Marquis of Normanby (i.e. C. H. Phipps), Lady Bury* and the Countess of Blessington* to perform. Colburn's biggest success, and probably the biggest long-term bestseller of the century, was Bulwer's (later Lord Bulwer-Lytton's*) *Pelham* (1828). This portrait of a modish 'gentleman' profoundly affected contemporary sensibility and fashion. (It led directly, for example, to the universal Victorian style of dark suiting for men.) The queen of silver fork fiction was Mrs Gore whose cascade of clever society-novels portrayed, as she put it, 'manners as they are'. Effectively, what fiction such as *Cecil** (1841) portray are manners as they were; specifically as they were in the dissolute days of George IV. Historically, the silver fork novel marks a transition between fiction of *ton* and the domestic*, bourgeois realism of the true Victorian novel. It was from a middle-class, 'common sense' standpoint that Thackeray* delivered his devastating critique of silver forkery in his burlesque: *Dukes And Déjeuners, Hearts And Diamonds, Marchionesses And Milliners*, etc. (1847). According to Michael Sadleir, the only silver fork novelist of any literary consequence is Mrs Gore*. This is probably harsh. (Hook's pioneering works are certainly worth consideration.) And, arguably, silver forkery was not extinguished by mid-century realism so much as driven underground only to resurface in the 1890s cult of Wildean dandyism.

SIME, William (1851–95). Sime was born at Wick, in northernmost Scotland. He died in Calcutta. Nothing else is known of his life, other than that he wrote some politically radical fiction. It includes: *King Capital* (1883), 'A

Tale Of Provincial Ambition' set in the Scottish industrial town of 'Lumside'; *The Red Route, Or Saving A Nation* (1884), a story of conspiracy, rebellion and repression in Ireland; *Boulderstone* (1885), 'Or New Men And Old Populations', a novel of riot and rebellion in modern Scotland; *Cradle And Spade* (1886), an imaginative story of gold mania in Scotland. In 1884 Sime published *Haco The Dreamer, A Tale Of Scottish University Life*, which implies that he may himself have been university-educated. BL 6. Boase.

Simpkin and Marshall (1814–1955). The major wholesaler of English books in the nineteenth and twentieth centuries, Simpkin and Marshall were also publishers. The firm was founded in the late 1800s by Benjamin Crosby, the son of a Yorkshire grazier. Crosby was one of the earliest booksellers to travel through the country, and he built up a trade supplying country booksellers. He was assisted by two assistants, William Simpkin (1772–1854) and Richard Marshall (1788–1863), who took over when Crosby was paralysed in 1814. (He died a year later.) The firm expanded through the century and in 1859 moved into specially constructed premises. By this period, Simpkin and Marshall were the country's largest book wholesaler and by the end of the century they enjoyed virtual monopoly status.

A Simpleton, Charles Reade, 1873, 3 vols, Chapman and Hall. (Serialised in *London Society*, August 1872–September 1873.) The simpleton is Rosa Lusignan, the 'dark but dazzlingly beautiful' heroine, who lives in a Kent villa near Gravesend with her businessman father. After he saves her from death by strangulation in her corsetry ('that diabolical machine'), she marries Dr Christopher Staines, who as the hero of the piece, deserves a stronger woman to help him in 'the battle of life'. Rosa is a bad household manager, and Christopher is forced to eke out his income by driving a London cab every night, disguised by a false moustache. When this is insufficient, he goes to sea as private physician to the touring Lord Tadcaster. He is later supposed drowned, but in fact is saved and taken to Cape Town by Captain Dodd (of *Hard Cash**). He decides to continue the pretence of his death, so as to let Rosa enjoy the £6,000 life insurance she has received. In South Africa, he becomes involved with diamond mining and lion hunting (the liveliest episode of the novel) and the Falcons. Phoebe Falcon is a strong, good wife whose brother Christopher has saved with an improvised tracheotomy; Reginald Falcon is a weak, immoral husband. Reginald (on the pretext of taking gems for sale) returns to London and offers to marry Rosa, for her money. She owes him what she conceives to be an overwhelming debt of gratitude, after he stage-manages the rescue of her son. He also shows her forged letters from a supposedly dying Staines recommending her to Falcon's care. As Rosa contemplates release by suicide, Christopher returns. The insurance money is given back and the couple are prosperously reunited. Falcon goes to prison, but is forgiven by the admirable Phoebe. In the preface Reade defends himself vigorously, if unconvincingly, against the charge of plagiarism persistently made against his writing.

SIMPSON, John Palgrave (1807–87). Simpson was born in Norwich, where his father was Town Clerk, and was a descendant on both sides of old

Norfolk families. He was educated at home by private tutor, and at Corpus Christi College, Cambridge. On graduation in 1829, Simpson declined to take orders and instead travelled widely on the Continent. While at Munich, in 1842, he became a Roman Catholic, and (as a mark of honour from the Pope) a Knight of St Gregory. In 1844, his father was ruined by bank failure, and Simpson was obliged to support himself by writing. *Second Love*, a three-volume collection of tales, appeared in 1846. It was followed by the Hungarian romance, *Gisella* (1847). Simpson wrote travel books, and reported on the 1848 French Revolution for *The Times*. He also wrote for *Blackwood's Magazine**. In 1849, he produced a historical* novel, *The Lily Of Paris*. In 1850, Simpson settled in London, and devoted himself, with some success, to writing for the stage. (He specialised in adaptations of Dickens's* and other popular authors' novels.) His own fourth novel, *For Ever And Never*, appeared in 1884. Simpson remained a confirmed bachelor. BL 4. *DNB*.

SIMS, George R[obert] (1847–1922). Born in London, Sims was educated at Hanwell College and at the University of Bonn. From 1874, he was a journalist and after 1877 wrote a regular column as 'Dagonet' for the *Referee*. His most notable work of journalism was a study of poverty for the London *Daily News* in the Henry Mayhew* style. (See his book, *How The Poor Live*, 1883.) Sims also wrote plays, of which the best-known is *The Lights Of London*. Sims wrote urban ballads, some children's* books and a large quantity of fiction, much of it with a realistic London setting in the naturalistic style of Arthur Morrison*. It includes: *Zeph, And Other Stories* (1880); *The Theatre Of Life* (1881); *Stories In Black And White* (1885); *Mary Jane Married* (1888); *Tales Of Today* (1889); *Dramas Of Life* (1890); *The Ten Commandments* (1896); *As It Was In The Beginning* (1896). The last two examine biblical themes in a modern environment. Not much is known about Sims. *Who's Who* records that he married late in life in 1901 and that his recreations were 'bulldogs, badminton, motoring'. BL 57. *WW*. Wol. Sad.

The Sin Of Joost Avelingh, Maarten Maartens, 1889, 2 vols, Remington. One of Maartens's Dutch regional 'Koopstad Chronicles'. An orphan, Joost is dominated by his uncle, Baron van Trotsem, who forces him to study medicine against his will and forbids him to marry Agatha van Hessel, whom he loves. The uncle dies of a heart attack, just as Joost is driving him to the lawyer who will enact a will disinheriting the nephew. Fortuitously enriched, Joost at last marries Agatha. But ten years later, a rival heir persuades a servant to testify that Joost murdered his uncle. The hero is eventually acquitted of the charge, but confesses publicly to the 'sin' of having *wanted* to kill the Baron and of having failed to stop the carriage while he died. He gives his fortune away and resigns his public offices, living henceforward as a humble lawyer's clerk. Townsmen thereafter treat him 'either with anger or with contempt'. But, 'his heart is at rest'. The narrative contains Maartens's usual quirky psychological twists.

SINCLAIR, Catherine (1800–64). The fourth daughter of the politician, Sir John Sinclair (1756–1835), she was born at Edinburgh and served as her father's secretary from the age of fourteen to thirty-five, when he died. A tyrannical father to his six ungainly daughters, Sir John insisted on their being inoculated for smallpox, which ruined their complexions and their marriage chances. Catherine Sinclair began to write on her own account after her father's death. (She added to *Modern Accomplishments*, 1836, a preface indicating that the work had been corrected by a 'venerated parent, now no more'.) She lived all her life in Edinburgh, and was noted for her public lectures and her philanthropy. Sinclair began in authorship writing children's* books (initially for her young nephew, the Hon G. F. Boyle, a son of the Earl of Glasgow). Her fiction for adults is represented by: *Modern Flirtations, Or A Month At Harrowgate* (1841); *Jane Bouverie, Or Prosperity And Adversity* (1846); *Sir Edgar Graham, Or Railway Speculators* (1849); *Cross Purposes* (1855), an anti-Catholic polemic. Sinclair's more pious tales for juveniles, collected as *Holiday House* (1839), have lasted well. Sinclair was indefatigably energetic in the setting up of kitchens for the poor and drinking fountains for wayfarers in her native Edinburgh. She died at her brother's vicarage in Kensington. An affectionate portrait of the author is given by her niece, Lucy Walford*, in *Recollections Of A Scottish Novelist* (1910). BL 26. *DNB. NCBEL.* Wol.

SINCLAIR, May [Mary Amelia St Clair] (1863–1946). May (an adaptation of 'Mary') Sinclair was born at Rock Ferry, Cheshire, the daughter of a Thomas Sinclair, a Scot and a prosperous Liverpool shipowner. May was the sixth child, and the first girl. When she was seven, her father's business failed, with the inevitable family upheaval. Her parents separated and she lived thereafter in genteel poverty with her mother. (This phase of her life is recalled in a later novel, *Mary Olivier*, 1919.) Sinclair read precociously in politics and philosophy from an early age. She briefly attended Cheltenham Ladies College (1881–82), but seems largely to have educated herself. During the 1880s her father and four of her brothers died, leaving May with the responsibility of caring for her mother. She began her authorial career writing verse, the first volume of which was published in 1892. In 1886 she entered into correspondence with Dorothea Beale, who introduced her to the idealist philosophy of T. H. Green which was to be overpoweringly influential on her. (As it was on her near contemporary, Mrs Humphry Ward*, who dedicated *Robert Elsmere** to Green.) As late as the 1920s she was publishing treatises defending Green's increasingly unfashionable doctrines. (See *The New Idealism*, 1922.) Sinclair's first story was published in 1895 and was succeeded by a novel which brought her some success, *Audrey Craven* (1896), a work which has been seen to pioneer modernist narrative techniques. It has a heroine who consciously assumes a whole range of fashionable intellectual poses in order to trap a series of men. *Mr And Mrs Nevill Tyson* (1898) is the story of a marriage that goes tragically wrong, the husband eventually dying for his country in the Sudan. *The Cosmopolitan* (1901) chronicles the doomed love of a spinster for a painter. Her most popular novel was the ultra-idealistic *The Divine Fire* (1904). So successful was this art novel (depicting the growth of a modern poet's mind and a corrupt world of modern letters) that on the strength of it the author made a literary tour of the USA. There she was received by such grandees as Theodore Roosevelt, an admirer. Sinclair never married and is recorded by contemporaries as having been prim, shy and spinsterish.

Yet she was an active suffragette in the period before the first World War and became the acquaintance of modernist writers like Ezra Pound and socialists like H. G. Wells*. Remarkably adaptive to new ideas, after 1914 she consciously introduced psychoanalysis as a theme into her fiction. Although in her forties, she drove an ambulance at the front in the Great War, and wrote an account of the experience as *A Journal Of Impressions In Belgium* (1915). Her novels in the 1920s and 1930s are generally found to be weakened by her excessively psychoanalytic preoccupations. BL 30. *WW* (which gives her date of birth as 1870). RM. Wol.

Singleheart And Doubleface, A Matter Of Fact Romance, Charles Reade, 1884, 1 vol, Chatto. (Serialised in *Life*, June–September 1882.) Reade's penultimate published novel, and probably his weakest. The Singleheart of the title is Sarah. She marries the doublefaced James Mansell. Thoroughly reprobate, Mansell flees to America. He later returns, and persuades his wife and daughter to come back with him to New York. Once there, he steals Sarah's £400, and takes up again with an American woman he has bigamously married. By wild coincidence, Sarah fortuitously finds lodgings in her husband's other wife's establishment, recovers her money, and escapes to England. Mansell's death and happy marriage for the singlehearted (and once more single) heroine are implausibly arranged by the author. The book is interesting in showing how obstinately from his first novel (*Peg Woffington**, 1852) to his latest, Reade retained his morbid obsession with bigamy*.

Sir George Tressady, Mrs Humphry Ward, 1896, 1 vol, Smith, Elder. (Serialised in the *Century Magazine*, November 1895–October 1896.) Ward's sequel to *Marcella** (1894), and inferior. The novel is more political and large parts of it focus on Lord Maxwell's campaign (aided by his wife Marcella) to pass a new Factory Bill into law. Sir George Tressady, a newly elected MP and a mine-owner, is of the opposite party. George injudiciously marries a pretty but shallow girl, Letty Sewell. The marriage is not easy and rendered even less so by George's vain and gullible mother. In London, he comes under the influence of Marcella, and has a demonstration of her pluck at an East End rally, where she is mobbed. Inspired by her, he turns coat and supports the government's Factory Bill. Letty, meanwhile, has nurtured small-minded jealousies about Marcella and has foolishly flirted with a bounder, Cathedine. Marcella nobly corrects Letty's misapprehension and persuades her to remain faithful to George. The climax of the novel is a disaster in the Tressady mining village. George dies leading a rescue attempt, fortified in his last minutes of life by a pure vision of Marcella as an angel beckoning him into the light.

Sir Gibbie, George MacDonald, 1879, 3 vols, Hurst and Blackett. (Serialised from September in the weekly *Glasgow Mail*.) A fable of natural goodness. Gibbie is a dumb street arab, first encountered grubbing in the gutters of a Scottish city. (His peculiar gift is for finding things.) Motherless, Gibbie's father is a hopeless drunkard, George Galbraith, who has come down in the world and now works as a cobbler. But in Mistress Croale's drinking shop, he is known as 'Sir George'. Gibbie adores and cares for his father. When drink finally kills him, the young orphan goes on a quest 'up

Daurside', to find his heritage. At Glashgar he invisibly helps at the farm of Janet Grant and is assumed to be a brownie. Discovered, Gibbie is cared for, given an education and taught to communicate. A series of accidents reveal him to be the heir to a fortune and indeed Sir Gilbert. The end of the narrative finds Gibbie a university graduate, prosperous and newly-married to his adored Ginevra. The strongest sections of the excessively sentimental story are those describing Gibbie as a plucky 'town sparrow', the ragged incarnation of untutored Christian goodness.

Sir Harry Hotspur Of Humblethwaite, Anthony Trollope, 1870, 1 vol, Hurst and Blackett. (Serialised in *Macmillan's Magazine**, May–December 1870.) Trollope's most poignant novella. Sir Harry Hotspur of Humblethwaite Hall in Cumberland has no male heir, his son having died. He makes arrangements for his estate to go to his daughter Emily. Sir Harry's nearest male heir, George Hotspur, is an adventurer. He deliberately sets out to woo his cousin Emily and wins her heart. But her father knows George to be worthless and forbids the match. George marries an actress, and shortly dies. Emily also dies of a broken heart.

Sir Richard Calmady, Lucas Malet (i.e. Mary St Leger Harrison), 1901, 1 vol, Methuen. One of Malet's grotesque psychological studies, embellished with her usual elusive smartness of narrative manner. In the 1840s, young Sir Richard, heir to the great Brockhurst estate, has an accident steeplechasing which leads to the amputation of both his legs. He dies, and a few months later his heir, the new Sir Richard, is born similarly legless with feet attached to his knees, 'thus dwarfing the child by a fourth of his height'. He is brought up by a fond mother, Katherine, goes to Oxford and enters society. But Richard is cruelly jilted by his fiancée, Lady Constance Quayle. He seeks solace in dissipation, falls ill and thanks to the love of his mother is nursed back to health. He subsequently sets up a house for cripples and finally marries happily Honoria St Quentin, who has always loved him. The novel contains some frank sexual description and its central idea was distasteful enough to turn some contemporary reviewers' stomachs.

The Siren, L. T. Meade (i.e. Elizabeth Thomasina Smith), 1898, 1 vol, White. The most interesting of the seven novels which the author turned out in 1898. The heroine is Vera: half-Russian, and a Socialist-Nihilist. Her father, an English colonel, discovers her existence after she has come of age. A complicated earlier sub-plot relates how Colonel Nugent twenty years before fell in love with a beautiful Russian aristocrat, widowed as she wrongly thought. In fact the Countess Chrisanto's husband lived, a fanatic Nihilist. She was exiled to Siberia and died in the mines leaving Vera to the ruthless Count Chrisanto. Vera comes to London, where she is a stunning social success. But Count Chrisanto has a double mission in mind for her. She will assassinate the Czar (with a cunningly poisoned bouquet of flowers) and also her father, Colonel Nugent, whom Chrisanto still implacably hates and whose estate he intends to appropriate for the terrorist cause. Vera confesses all to the Colonel, and kills herself with the deadly bouquet intended for the Czar. Meade was capable of turning such fiction out by the yard.

The Sisters, Or England And France, Henry Cockton, 1844, 1 vol, Nodes. (Serialised in the *Illustrated News*, 1843, illustrated by J. Kenny Meadows* and Alfred Crowquill*.) An unassuming 'romance of real life' whose principal function, like all Cockton's fiction (with the possible exception of *Valentine Vox*,* 1840) is to serve as vehicle for illustrators more talented in their field than the author in his. Set in the Regency, the heroines are high-born eligible ladies. Caroline (who represents sense) marries the ancient Sir Arthur Cleveland for money. Lucrece (sensibility) marries a poor army officer for love. Caroline is shamefully indulged, and conducts an affair with the caddish Vincent Darnley. Charles, Lucrece's husband, is captured at Verdun and she intercedes with Napoleon (in a scene reminiscent of *The Heart Of Midlothian*) for his release. On Sir Arthur's death, Caroline is disinherited and Vincent deserts her. After their various trials, both sisters are finally rendered happy wives. The novel testifies to the persistent influence of Jane Austen in Victorian fiction.

SKELTON, [Sir] John ('Shirley', 1831–97). Skelton was born in Edinburgh, the son of a lawyer. He went to school at Peterhead and to university in Edinburgh after which he qualified as a lawyer in 1854. But law did not suit him and he began to contribute to the magazines under the pseudonym 'Shirley' (taken from the title of Charlotte Brontë's* novel). As an essayist, Skelton gained a considerable reputation. In 1868, Disraeli* gave him a public position in the new public health board for Scotland and he continued to work for the improvement of Scottish health until the end of his life. From 1869 onwards, he was a prominent *Blackwood's** author, writing regularly for the magazine. Skelton wrote some minor and incidental fiction, including the political romance, *Thalatta! Or The Great Commoner* (1862). The main character is based on Disraeli, and the work was published at the instigation of J. A. Froude*, currently editor of *Fraser's**. Skelton wrote one other work of fiction, *The Crookit Meg* (1880), a picture of everyday life at Peterhead. He was made a KCB in 1897, the year of his death. BL 2. *DNB. NCBEL.* Wol.

SKENE, [Miss] Felicia M[ary] F[rances] (1821–99). A noted Victorian philanthropist, the novels Skene wrote (with the exception of *Hidden Depths**, 1866) were principally designed to raise money for her favourite charity. She was born at Aix-en-Provence the daughter of well-connected Scottish parents. Her father, James Skene (1775–1864), was a lawyer and a passionate admirer of Sir Walter Scott (on whose knee the young Felicia is supposed to have sat telling the great man fairy stories). Felicia Skene was educated at Paris, and in 1838 went with her family to Athens. Residence there inspired the young author's first book of travels. The Skenes returned to England in 1845 during the excitement of Newman's* defection to Rome and she came strongly under the influence of Anglo-Catholic clergymen. The family eventually settled at Oxford where the ferment was strongest. Skene's first novel, *Use And Abuse* (1849) is a bizarre fusion of gothic* fantasy and Tractarian propaganda which opens: 'Nature, visible and glorious, is the priestess of the Incomprehensible Unseen'. The work goes on to follow, very loosely, the careers of two rivals, Raymond and Arabyn. In 1854, Skene helped in Oxford with the cholera epidemic (an event which inspired Charles Kingsley's* *Two Years Ago**, 1857). And shortly after, she went on to train nurses for

Florence Nightingale in the Crimea. Skene's experience in Oxford's slums inspired her most powerful work, *Hidden Depths*. This novel courageously exposes the prostitution rife in the city (called 'Greyburgh' in the narrative). Skene's other (much less interesting) novels include: *More Than Conqueror* (1878); *A Strange Inheritance* (1886), the story of a family returning to Scotland from Australia; *The Lesters* (1887). Skene serialised evangelical novels in the mid-1870s in the *Quiver** which seem not to have been reissued in volume form. She edited the *Churchman's Companion*, 1862–80, never married and died in Oxford. BL 5. *DNB*. Wol.

SKETCHLEY, Arthur ('Mrs Brown', i.e. George Rose, 1817–82). Rose was born in London and began working life as a clerk at the Custom House. But discovering a vocation for the Church he enrolled at Oxford University in 1841. After graduation, he was ordained in 1848. Subsequently he travelled widely with his parents in Italy, eventually taking up a curacy in Camberwell, south London. Falling under the influence of the Oxford movement, he converted to Catholicism in 1855. For the next few years he supported himself as a private tutor to sons of the nobility, notably those of the Duke of Norfolk, the richest Catholic nobleman in the realm. Around 1863, Sketchley, as Rose called himself, embarked on what was to be a very successful literary career. His plays were performed on the London stage in the 1860s and in 1866 he invented his famous comic persona, 'Mrs Brown'. Until his death in 1882, Rose produced a stream of works in which the illiterate Mrs Brown pronounced on events of the day. Her monologues were immensely popular, and Rose made tours all over the world delivering them. He also wrote the straightforward novels, *A Match In The Dark* (1878) and *A Marriage Of Conscience* (1879). Rose himself never married, grew enormously fat, and died of heart failure. BL 2. *DNB*. Wol.

The Small House At Allington, Anthony Trollope, 1864, 2 vols, Smith, Elder. (The work was first published in *Cornhill*, September 1862–April 1864 with illustrations by J. E. Millais*.) One of Trollope's many studies of jilted love. The heroine, Lily Dale, lives with her sister 'Bell' and widowed mother in the 'Small House', attached to the estate of their relative, Squire Christopher Dale. Bell ideally should fall in love with the squire's heir, Captain Bernard Dale, but instead accepts Dr James Crofts, a young doctor in the neighbouring town of Guestwick. Lily loves even more unwisely. She is wooed by Adolphus Crosbie, a rising Government clerk. The couple are engaged. But Crosbie leaves his newly betrothed to visit Courcy Castle, in Barsetshire. There he is entrapped by Lady Alexandrina de Courcy. Although Alexandrina is hard, shallow and not young, she has aristocratic connections. Crosbie is seduced, and proposes. He sends Lily a letter, jilting her. Lily has a humble lover, Johnny Eames. Like Charley Tudor in *The Three Clerks**, Eames is a shiftless but essentially worthy young 'hobbledehoy'. He has already got the squire's good opinion by gallantry in the face of a charging bull. Encountering Crosbie on the London train, he gives the blackguard a black eye. Johnny's own love life is vexed, and runs a kind of parallel to Crosbie's. He has been almost entrapped by Amelia, the wily (and somewhat antique) daughter of his landlady, Mrs Roper. But he honourably extricates himself, and Amelia scoops up the other boarder, Joseph Cradell. The Crosbie–de Courcy marriage is a disaster from the honeymoon journey onwards. And thereafter, Adolphus's Civil Service career is also blighted, while Johnny's goes from strength to strength. But, to the frustration of the novel's readers, neither here nor in the sequel, *The Last Chronicle Of Barset**, does Johnny persuade Lily to marry him. Both remain single. Trollope regarded the creation of the gentle martyr Lily Dale somewhat ambivalently, thinking her the weakest thing in an otherwise 'good' novel.

SMART, [Henry] Hawley (1833–93). Smart was born in Dover, the son of an army major. The family had a long tradition in Kent and on his mother's side Smart was related to the famous sportsman and patron of the turf, Sir Joseph Henry Hawley (1813–75). Smart joined the army in 1849. He saw active service (and the fall of Sebastopol) in the Crimean War where he served as a captain of infantry, returning to England in 1856. The next year he sailed for India, and served during the Mutiny. From 1858, he served in Canada. In 1864, Smart sold out of the army and after some losses horse-racing supported himself as a novelist, taking the congenially easygoing Charles Lever* and Whyte-Melville* as his models. His fiction invariably revolves, increasingly nostalgically, around the 1850s era. His first novel was *Breezie Langton, A Story Of Fifty-Two To Fifty-Five* (1869). Typically, the story begins with a ghost in an English country house and ends with battles in the Crimea. Given the nature of Smart's fiction, Breezie Langton could be the name of a horse, a country house, or a guards officer. In fact, it is the name of the young heroine. Thereafter, Smart regularly produced two novels a year, usually with an emphasis on racing, hunting and military episodes. They include: *Pay Or Play* (1878); *The Great Tontine* (1881); *From Post To Finish* (1884), dedicated to George Meredith*, who apparently suggested the work; *The Outsider* (1886); *Saddle And Sabre* (1888); *Thrice Past The Post* (1891); *The Plunger* (1891); *Beatrice And Benedick, A Romance Of The Crimea* (1891). *Hard Lines* (1883) is a typical Smart effort, following the career of Captain Cis Calvert from a garrison posting with the '–th Lancers' in provincial York to service with the 'Royal Dunbars' in India to the 'real thing' in the Crimea where the hero is wounded at Sebastopol. Cis survives to marry his sweetheart Annie in York Minster. Smart himself made a late-life marriage in 1883 and died in Devon. The *Saturday Review** memorialised him as 'unequalled as a recorder of sporting life, manners and matters'. BL 50. *DNB. NCBEL.* Wol. Sad. RLF.

SMEATON, [William Henry] Oliphant (1856–1914). Smeaton was born in Aberdeen, the youngest son of a clergyman and university professor. He was educated at Edinburgh University and intended for the Church, 'but owing to difficulties over subscribing to the Confession of Faith, relinquished the intention'. He went instead to New Zealand in 1878. For some years he taught school. Then in 1883 he moved to Australia where he worked as a journalist. In 1893 he returned to Britain, where (based in Edinburgh) he exploited the current fashionability of things Scottish with the 'Famous Scots Series' of publications. He also (as Oliphant Smeaton) published some Kingsleyesque* novels including: *By Adverse Winds* (1895); *Our Laddie* (1897); *A Mystery Of The Pacific* (1899). BL 4. *WW.*

SMEDLEY, Frank [Francis Edward] (1818–64). Smedley was born at Great Marlow, Buckinghamshire, the only son of the former High Bailiff

of Westminster. Congenitally malformed feet rendered him a virtual cripple and prevented him from attending Westminster School where the male
Smedleys traditionally went. He was educated by tutor at Brighton then
privately near Cambridge by a clergyman uncle, where his observations of
Newmarket racing and university life were stored for his later fiction. Condemned to a sedentary existence, Smedley specialised in fiction that is hearty
and active, with a strong line in boisterous college escapades and adventurous equestrian exploits. His first success in fiction was with the serial story
Scenes From The Life Of A Private Pupil which he contributed to *Sharpe's
London Magazine** in 1846–48. This autobiographical narrative was eventually expanded into his best novel, *Frank Fairlegh** (1850). The second edition
of this work was handsomely illustrated by George Cruikshank*. Smedley
followed up the success of his first novel with *Lewis Arundel, Or The Rail-
road Of Life* (1852, published in monthly numbers and illustrated by Phiz*).
This picaresque work shows most clearly Smedley's predilection for the early
Dickens* of *Nicholas Nickleby**, whose narrative it closely resembles. For a
short period at this stage of his life, Smedley became editor of *Sharpe's*
magazine. He serialised the least impressive of his novels, *The Fortunes Of
The Colville Family* (1853), in its pages. In 1854, he was appointed editor
of the short-lived *George Cruikshank's Magazine* which failed after three
numbers. In 1855, he brought out *Harry Coverdale's Courtship* in monthly
numbers, again illustrated by Phiz. After 1854, Smedley collaborated with
Edmund Yates* (who was to become a firm friend) and wrote for Yates's
magazine the *Train*. But after 1856 Smedley's health deteriorated badly, and
his literary energies failed in the last few years of his short life. His health
was further damaged by an accident in his pony trap in 1856. In the preface
to *Harry Coverdale's Courtship* he records the crippling nervous headaches
which impaired the completion of the tale. He never married and died of
apoplexy at his Regent's Park house in London. (Smedley's last years were
made easier by an inherited fortune and his summer home at Beech Wood
near Great Marlow.) Menella Bute Smedley (1819?–80) was Frank's cousin
(although she is often wrongly listed as his sister). The daughter of the
Rev. Edward Smedley (Frank Smedley's Cambridge tutor), she never married. For many years, she acted as her cousin's housekeeper and amanuensis.
Menella Smedley wrote poetry and had some success with her patriotic lays
from English history. She also wrote a number of didactic stories, including:
The Maiden Aunt (1849); *Nina* (1861); *Twice Lost* (1863), the story of a
woman, almost forty, who goes into service as a lady's companion; *A Mere
Story* (1865). Her fiction lacks her brother's brio. (FS) BL 5. (MBS) BL 4.
(FS) *DNB*. (MBS) Boase. RM. *NCBEL*. Wol. Sad.

SMITH, Albert [Richard] (1816–60). Smith was born in Chertsey, Surrey,
the son of a not very successful surgeon. He attended the Merchant Taylors'
School (1826–31) and himself qualified as a surgeon and apothecary in
1838 (as did others of the early *Punch** set, which numbered several failed
doctors). After a couple of years in practice with his father in Chertsey,
he followed his natural bent and began to write. In 1841, he settled in
Soho, London and deserted medicine and dentistry altogether. A fluent and
inexhaustible writer with a good sense of humour, Smith had no difficulty
getting work with *Bentley's Miscellany**, and the newly formed *Punch*. He

also wrote plays in the early 1840s. In 1844, he produced the monthly serial, *The Adventures Of Mr Ledbury*, following it in 1845 with *The Adventures Of The Scattergood Family* and in 1847 with *The Struggles And Adventures Of Christopher Tadpole* (illustrated like *Ledbury* by John Leech*). All three works show the strong influence of Dickens's* writing with comic picaresque narratives. Typically, that of *Ledbury* flits from Paris, to London, to Ascot, to Germany, to Milan, to Switzerland, to Belgium, ending where it began in Paris. In the mid-1840s, Smith wrote a torrent of plays, pantomimes, burlesques and popular songs. He fell out violently with *Punch* and launched various burlesque attacks against his old Bouverie Street comrades. On their part, Thackeray* and Douglas Jerrold* vilified Smith as a loud-mouthed vulgarian. He was also drama critic for the new *Illustrated London News*. With A. B. Reach*, he was coeditor of a popular 6d. monthly entitled *The Man In The Moon* (1847–49). Also on this publication Smith recruited the artists Phiz*, Kenny Meadows*, H. G. Hine and the young G. A. Sala*. In 1847, he began to publish (under David Bogue's* imprint) a 1s. series of social 'physiologies'. (See his *Natural History Of The Gent*, 1847.) In 1848–49, he produced his best novel in numbers, *The Pottleton Legacy*, illustrated by Phiz*. In 1849, Smith travelled to Constantinople. Inspired by what he saw, in the 1850s he devised a series of public 'entertainments'. (His brother Arthur, 1825–61, acted as manager, and was later to serve Dickens in the same role.) These parlour dramatisations of his voyages were an immense hit at the Egyptian Hall in London. An ascent of Mont Blanc in 1851 and a visit to China in 1858 added to his repertoire. Smith wrote in addition to the novels mentioned: *The Wassail Bowl* (1843); *The Marchioness Of Brinvilliers* (1846), a romance of 'Old Paris'; *Wild Oats And Dead Leaves* (1860). He died of bronchitis, aged only forty-five, having married an actress eleven months previously. BL 6. *DNB. NCBEL*. Wol. Sad.

SMITH, Alexander (1830–67). Smith was born in Kilmarnock, Scotland, the son of a lace pattern designer who subsequently moved to Paisley, near Glasgow. Alexander attended school in Glasgow and was subsequently apprenticed to his father's trade in which he evidently showed no aptitude whatsoever. He drifted instead into literature and journalism. Endowed with a natural poetic gift he wrote verse and by 1851 had gained a local reputation. Smith's first volume of verse was published in 1853 to considerable praise. His poem 'Life Drama' was particularly admired and the volume earned its author £100. Buoyed up by success, Smith travelled to London to live as an author. But his fame was short-lived. His impressionistic or 'spasmodic' style was mercilessly burlesqued by Aytoun* in his mock tragedy *Firmilian* (1854). His second and third volumes of poetry fell flat and to add to his bitterness, there were accusations of his plagiarising Tennyson. Smith turned to prose with a collection of essays and sketches, *Dreamthorp* (1863), for which he remains best known. Finally, he published two novels in 1866: *Alfred Hagart's Household*, a story set in 'Greysley, a second-rate Scotch town' in the 1830s and serialised in *Good Words*; *Miss Oona McQuarrie*, a sequel. These largely autobiographical works were reviewed lukewarmly a year before the author's death from typhoid fever but evidently had he lived, he intended to write more fiction. Since 1854 he had supported himself and his family (having married in 1857) as Secretary and later Registrar of

Edinburgh University on a meagre salary of £150 a year. BL 2. *DNB*. RM. *NCBEL*. RLF.

SMITH, Alice ('Corisande', née Jerrold, 1849–72). A daughter of the man of letters William Blanchard Jerrold* (1826–84) she wrote serial fiction under the pseudonym Corisande. Her novels include *Love Without Wings* (1877) and *A Woman Of Mind* (1879), both of which were published in book form after her death in France. She was the wife of Adolphe Smith, about whom nothing is known. BL 2. Boase.

SMITH, Horace [Horatio] (1779–1849). Smith was born in London, the son of a solicitor. His older brother was James Smith (1775–1839), author and humorist. The young Horace went into stockbroking, and had made a sufficient fortune to retire by 1820. In his leisure he was the friend of Leigh Hunt, and of the poet Shelley. In 1812 the reopening of the burned-down Drury Lane Theatre inspired a prize-poem competition. James and Horace devised the brilliant set of parodies, *Rejected Addresses*. Horace, although less incisively witty than his brother, went on to write more. He produced among much else a number of novels, the first of which (*The Runaway*) was published in 1800. His best work of fiction is probably the pre-Victorian *Brambletye House* (1826), a historical* novel set during the Civil War. During Victoria's reign Smith published: *Jane Lomax* (1838); *The Moneyed Man* (1841); *Adam Brown, The Merchant* (1843); *Love And Mesmerism* (1845), tales. BL 21. *DNB*. RM. *NCBEL*. Wol. Sad.

SMITH, J[ohn] F[rederick] (1803–90). The son of a Norwich theatre manager, Smith began his literary career writing drama. He later lived for some years in Rome, where he came under the influence of the Jesuits (and was later suspected of belonging to the order). In the early 1830s, he was in London, writing voluminously for Edward Lloyd*. By 1849 he had joined the staff of the *London Journal*, in which his gothic* romances were enormously popular. *Minnigrey* (1851–52), illustrated by John Gilbert*, is supposed to have raised the circulation of the journal to half a million copies. In 1855, Smith transferred his writing services to *Cassell's Illustrated Family Paper*. Ten years later, in 1865, he returned to the *London Journal*. Smith, despite a considerable reputation as a bohemian, lived in a quiet way in a Bloomsbury lodging house, sealed off from social contact by deafness. In later life (some accounts say as late as 1880), he moved to America, where he continued to enjoy success with his low-grade romances. He died in New York. Smith's mid-Victorian novels include: *The Prelate* (1840); *The Plague Of London* (1849); *Stanfield Hall* (1850), a historical* novel first serialised very successfully in the *London Journal*; *Amy Lawrence, The Free Mason's Daughter* (1851); *Woman And Her Master* (1854); *The City Banker* (1856); *Milly Mogue* (1859); *Warp And Weft* (1863); *Sir Bernard Gaston* (1867). According to Louis James: 'Smith used to increase the tension of his [serialised] stories until the work-girls of the northern towns, one of his biggest class of readers, bought a copy each instead of waiting to borrow one, and the circulation would soar.' BL 24. Wol.

SMITH, William Henry (1808–72). Smith was born in Hammersmith, the son of a prosperous barrister (d. 1823). He was educated at the boarding school of Radley and at the University of Glasgow. Smith subsequently went into law himself, although he apparently had little love for the profession. In later life, he was on friendly terms with leading intellectuals of the day such as J. S. Mill, F. D. Maurice and John Sterling. Having inherited his father's wealth, he retired into a life of seclusion in the Lake District. He wrote tragedy (his *Athelwold* was produced by Macready in 1843), dabbled in philosophy and contributed to the occasional magazine, notably (after 1839) *Blackwood's**, with whose Conservative opinions he was evidently in sympathy, Smith wrote two mature works of fiction, loosely classified: *Thorndale, Or The Conflict Of Opinions* (1857) and *Gravenhurst, Or Thoughts On Good And Evil* (1861). Both take the form of philosophical dialogues. Smith is also credited with an early novel, *Ernesto* (1835). BL 3. *DNB*.

W. H. Smith and Sons (1792–). The leading British wholesaler and retailer of printed materials in the nineteenth and twentieth centuries. The Smith dynasty began in 1792 when Henry Walton Smith set up as newsvendors in Grosvenor Street, London. He was succeeded by his son, W. H. Smith I (1792–1865). By 1817, the business was also a booksellers and in 1820 Smith's moved to the Strand, where a large reading room was opened. Meanwhile, London and Fleet Street (centre of the capital's newspaper industry) were expanding as never before. In the 1820s, Smith's began to provide papers to the provinces, using the horse-drawn mails, under the slogan 'First with the News'. Under W. H. Smith I the firm eventually gained a virtual monopoly in the delivery of London periodicals to the country. W. H. Smith II (1825–91, nicknamed 'Old Morality') originally hoped for a career in the Church. But he was induced to follow the family business. And it was under him that the firm gained its dominating position as a railway newsvendor and bookshop chain. Between 1840 and 1870, nearly 15,000 miles of rail track were laid, effectively linking the country in a communications network for the first time. The first Smith's bookstall was opened at Euston Station, in 1848. Smith's were given the concession (for which they paid rent) on the understanding that they would clean up the quality of reading material for travellers. This they did and do. By the 1860s, the firm had bookstalls on all the main lines and in all the main stations of the realm. Smith's not only sold fiction from their outlets (notably Routledge's* 'Railway Library' 1s. reprints), they began from the 1860s onwards to take an interest in its production. They were instrumental (in partnership with Chapman and Hall*) in devising the yellowback* 2s. reprint of popular novels in the 1850s; handily sized, these volumes were embellished by pictorial covers and are the forerunners of the twentieth-century paperback. Lever*, Ainsworth*, Ouida*, Bulwer-Lytton* and Miss Braddon* were all yellowback favourites. Smith's expanded vastly in the second half of the century. From just thirty-five station bookstalls in 1851 they had 1,242 by 1902 and their workforce had risen from around 350 to over 8,000. Diversification came with expansion. In 1860, Smith's set up a circulating library to rival Mudie's* domination. Subscription costs were in line with Mudie's and like the other 'leviathan', Smith's exercised a firm moral control over the fiction they purveyed. A supply of volumes was held at every bookstall. For obvious reasons, Smith's system tended to favour the one-volume over the multi-volume novel Mudie specialised in.

This gave Smith's the edge over Mudie in the matter of distribution. On the other hand Mudie had the advantage of a central metropolitan location, and could handle vast numbers of the very newest novel with greater speed than the railway library. In 1870, Smith's library had a turnover of almost £34,000 annually which had doubled by the end of the century. Despite the competition between them, Smith's united with Mudie to boycott the three-volume novel in 1894, and survived the drastic upheaval that followed better than their rivals. After the firm's activities shifted to high street outlets in the early twentieth century, Smith's libraries continued in a flourishing condition until they were finally killed by the public libraries in 1961.

Smith, Elder and Co. (1816–1917). One of the top Victorian publishing houses. George Smith (a Scot) came down to London in the early years of the century and took up work first with the publisher Rivington and subsequently with Murray's* (a firm with which the Smiths always retained a close association). In 1816, Smith set up his own publishing house in Fenchurch Street in partnership with Alexander Elder. Shortly after, the new business moved to premises at 65 Cornhill (an address made famous by the later magazine). By the 1830s, the business had added new partners, and diversified profitably into East India agency and various other side lines. Smith, Elder had some publishing successes (notably with the illustrated annual gift books issued as *Friendship's Offering*, 1828–43). But it was still a minor publisher and it was only under George Smith the younger (1824–1901) that the firm achieved leviathan status. George Smith was born into money and educated in London. As a schoolboy, he was quick-witted but too indisciplined to win prizes or go to university. Throughout life, he regarded himself as a sadly ill-educated man. Young George was apprenticed to the family firm in 1837, aged thirteen. His father gave him the most menial tasks, with the aim of teaching him his profession from the ground up. Smith quickly established a reputation for himself as the 'boy publisher'. At the same time Smith, Elder was receiving windfall profits from its East India trade, £1,500 of which was given to young Smith as speculative capital. In 1843, as the new head of the firm's publishing operations he consciously began on a programme of expansion. Authority was thrust on the young man. In 1844, George Smith the elder began to show symptoms of brain softening and died in 1846. Embezzlement forced the departure of the other senior partner, leaving affairs entirely to Smith at the age of twenty-three. As a publisher his touch was not immediately golden. His attempt in 1844 to promote G. P. R. James* as a bestselling author failed expensively. But in 1847, he had the wisdom to accept the manuscript of *Jane Eyre**, submitted by 'Currer Bell'. (Smith was aided in this and other critical decisions by his literary adviser, W. S. Williams.) Brontë's* novel was fabulously successful, and laid the ground for a lifelong association. Between 1846 and 1856, Smith, Elder's volume of trade boomed from £48,000 annually to £176,000. Smith could afford to outbid his publishing competitors. Accordingly in 1852, he poached Thackeray's* *Henry Esmond** from Bradbury and Evans*. The novelist returned to Smith's service (at a massive salary) in 1860 to edit *Cornhill**. This magazine drew all the main novelists and writers of the day into Smith's orbit and he became not just the publisher but the friend of such Victorian literary notables as Ruskin*, Browning, Matthew Arnold and

Leslie Stephen. Smith now felt free to use his publishing power to express his Liberal political views and in 1865, together with Frederick Greenwood*, he founded the influential evening paper, the *Pall Mall Gazette*. In 1868, Smith divested the India agency side of his operations, to concentrate on publishing. (At the same period, he was making a fortune from owning the franchise to the popular mineral water, 'Apollinaris'.) In 1882, Smith inaugurated work on the *Dictionary Of National Biography* (a publication which he eventually donated to the English nation). In 1888, he took a risk by publishing Mrs Humphry Ward's* first superseller, *Robert Elsmere* (mainly as a favour to her uncle, Matthew Arnold) and with its success remained her partner for the rest of his life. In later life, Smith's firm published many of the major novelists of the last Victorian decades, notably George Gissing*. After his death, the business declined and was taken over by John Murray in 1917. (GS) *DNB*.

Smithers (1891–1900). Publisher. Leonard Smithers (1861–1909) was born in Sheffield of French parents and worked in that city as a solicitor. Around 1891, having inherited some money, he came to London and set up with H. S. Nichols as a bookseller and publisher. By 1895, he was the only publisher who would publish the work of Oscar Wilde*, was himself an 1890s dandy with depraved sexual tastes, and started (with Arthur Symons) the *Savoy* in 1895. The short-lived magazine became a vehicle for the leading literary lights of the English decadence* movement. Smithers was famous as a purveyor of pornography and is supposed to have displayed in his Bond Street window the sign 'Smut is cheap today'. He went bankrupt in 1900 and died nine years later from drink and drugs.

The Smuggler, G. P. R. James, 1845, 3 vols, Smith, Elder. One of James's less mediocre efforts. The scene is set off the Kent coast, in the 1750s. The 'gentleman smuggler' of the title is Mr Richard Radford of Radford Hall who becomes entangled (via his son, also Richard) with a less reputable smuggling clan and battles with the excise. Radford attempts to force the heroine Edith to marry young Richard, by threatening to send her father Sir Robert to the gallows with some forged evidence. A last-minute rescue saves all, and Radford kills himself in his cell, so cheating the hangman. Topically, James makes his novel a polemic in favour of free trade, the great political issue of the mid-1840s.

SMYTHIES, Mrs Yorick [Harriette Maria] (née Gordon, 1813–83). Harriette Gordon was born in Margate, the daughter of Edward Lesmoin Gordon. In 1835, she published a long and ambitious poem, *The Bride Of Siena*. The experiment was not successful and in 1838 she published her first novel, *Fitzherbert*, a tale of lovers and fortune hunters. This was followed by *Cousin Geoffrey* (1840) and *The Married Man* (1841), both published by Bentley*. In 1842, she married the Rev. William Yorick Smythies. In the following eight years, the couple had four surviving children and she wrote half a dozen romances. At this period, Smythies had earned herself the title, 'Queen of the Domestic Novel'. Her literary career remained moderately successful through the 1850s, when she was a regular serialist for the magazines (notably the large circulation *London Journal**). She also wrote articles on female etiquette for the *Ladies' Treasury*. Meanwhile, William Smythies had ruined himself financially, and she eventually left him (in the late 1850s), moving to lodgings in London. Her remaining years were spent in a desperate attempt to keep herself solvent and support a consumptive daughter. (All but one of her children predeceased her.) She was aided in her last years by donations from the Royal Literary Fund*. Smythies' fiction includes: *The Matchmaker* (1842); *The Breach Of Promise* (1845); *Courtship And Wedlock* (1853); *A Lover's Quarrel* (1858); *Guilty Or Not Guilty* (1864); *A Faithful Woman* (1865); *Acquitted* (1870). Nigel Cross notes: 'the quality of her best fiction suggests that she could have written works of more than ephemeral interest if her career had not, out of necessity, slotted so firmly into a commercial rut.' BL 21. Boase. Wol. RLF.

The Snobs Of England, by 'One of Themselves' (i.e. W. M. Thackeray), 1848, 1 vol, Bradbury and Evans. (Serialised in *Punch**, February 1846–February 1847, with illustrations by the author.) Thackeray's greatest hit in *Punch*, and supposed to have increased circulation by 5,000 a week. The fifty-two comic papers loosely follow the adventures of Mr Snob (the 'snobographer') as he travels through English society. Some of the episodes (notably Snob's visit to his snobbish country friends the Pontos) take a narrative form. But principally the work is a social physiology, anatomising the vice of 'thinking meanly of mean things'. Thackeray's series introduced the word 'snob' into the English language in its modern form. Bradbury and Evans published the one-volume edition as *The Book Of Snobs*.

The Social Problem Novel. Otherwise known as 'The Condition of England Novel', 'fiction with a purpose', 'the industrial novel', *roman à thèse*, *Tendenzroman*. The notion that fiction might have a place to play in social reform originates in the example of William Godwin's (1756–1836) propagandistic fiction and more particularly in the influence of Thomas Carlyle (1795–1881). Following Carlyle's cue (notably in *Chartism*, 1839) a number of novelists of the late 1830s and early 1840s began to address the social problems of the industrial age. Harriet Martineau's* story 'A Manchester Strike' in her *Illustrations Of Political Economy* (1835) is arguably the first true example of the genre. It was followed by Dickens's* *Oliver Twist** (1837) and Mrs Trollope's* *Michael Armstrong, The Factory Boy** (1839). In the 1840s, a new political sophistication was introduced to the genre by Disraeli*, with his Young England* trilogy (*Coningsby**, 1844; *Sybil**, 1845; *Tancred**, 1847). Disraeli's new Tory utopianism was countered by Charles Kingsley's* Christian Socialism in *Yeast** (1851) and *Alton Locke** (1850). Yet another panacea was offered by Mrs Gaskell* in her apolitical plea for universal sympathy, *Mary Barton** (1848), and its successor (putting the mill-owners' side of things) *North And South** (1855). After the politically troubled 1840s and the collapse of Chartism as a force in 1848 much of the fire went out of the social problem novel, which modulated in one direction into the novel of ideas, in another into the novel of social conscience and in a third into sensationalism*. Direct descendants are George Eliot's* reform-inspired *Felix Holt, The Radical** (1866) and Charles Reade's* trade union inspired *Put Yourself In His Place** (1870). Still later (and influenced by the French Naturalists such as Zola) George Gissing* (e.g. *Demos**, 1886) and Mrs Humphry Ward* (e.g. *Sir George Tressady**, 1896) wrote what may be called third-generation social problem novels. An unworthily forgotten late example of the genre is William Westall's* *Birch Dene* (1889). Just how much actual good social problem novels did is questionable. Clearly works like *Hard Times** (1854) encouraged sympathy for the industrial classes (the 'submerged sixth', as they have been called), who had no authentic literature of their own. But they did so by denying the validity of such things as trade unions (which Dickens attacks in the person of the London demagogue Slackbridge). Raymond Williams has gone so far as to call the Victorian industrial novel as nothing more than a spasm of middle-class 'alarm', a mere hiccup in the general complacency of the period.

The Society Of Authors (1883–). The formation of a British society of authors is inextricably bound up with the struggle for copyright protection. The most effective precursor was the 'Society of British Authors' which survived for a few months in 1843, under the leadership of Carlyle and Bulwer-Lytton*. But the society failed, as Walter Besant* later observed, because it could not agree on the primacy of material interests (i.e. copyright) as the one common ground that authors had. Besant himself was instrumental in founding a successful society of authors in September 1883. The society had sixty-eight paying members in its first year and 870 by 1892. Under Besant's direction, the organisation concentrated exclusively on the protection of literary property, in opposition to 'rapacious' publishers and booksellers (who founded their professional associations in the 1890s). In early conceptions of the society's role, Besant thought it might go on to become a publishing cooperative, or a general agent for the writing profession. But neither of these optimistic aims materialised. By the 1890s, most of the major novelists were loyal members and future presidents included Meredith* and Hardy*. The Society's journal, the *Author**, was begun in May 1890. In 1896, the Society's committee elected a number of women to its council, including: Charlotte Yonge*, Mrs Eliza Lynn Linton* and Mrs Humphry Ward*. The Society was instrumental in bringing about international copyright agreement (notably with America in 1891). The Society of Authors has survived and grown in professional authority throughout the twentieth century.

Some Emotions And A Moral, John Oliver Hobbes (i.e. Pearl Mary-Teresa Craigie), 1891, 1 vol, T. Fisher Unwin. Hobbes's first, and very successful novel. It was published in Unwin's 'Pseudonym* Library', hence the pen-name which the author was to use all her writing life. The story is fashionably brittle and hopeless. Cynthia jilts the writer Provence, whom she loves, because he is an artist and ought not to marry. She marries instead the down-to-earth Edward, who dies of typhoid. On his part Provence marries his cousin Grace. Cynthia and Provence meet in London, but Cynthia again rejects him. Meanwhile, Grace has entrapped Provence's best friend, George, who shoots himself. The ill-assorted Provence and his wife are left, after this slaughter, hopelessly separate within their marriage. *Some Emotions* was the hit of the season.

Some Experiences Of An Irish RM, Edith Somerville and Martin Ross, 1899, 1 vol, Longman. (First issued as stories in the *Badminton Magazine*, illustrated by Somerville.) Somerville and Ross's most popular book. It is made up of twelve episodes, linked by the narrator, Major Sinclair Yeates, a Resident Magistrate at Skebawn in south-west Ireland. The opening story has Yeates newly arrived, looking for a house. He sets up at Shreelane, in a dilapidated mansion that is, apparently, haunted by the ghost of 'Great-Uncle McCarthy'. It turns out that there are a disreputable couple camping out in the attic, supporting themselves by trapping and selling Yeates's foxes. This has enraged the local Master of Foxhounds and Yeates's landlord, 'Flurry' McCarthy Knox. The roguish Knox emerges as a central figure in the following narratives: 'he belonged to a clan that cropped up in every grade of society in the county, from Sir Valentine Knox of Castle Knox down to the auctioneer Knox, who bore the attractive title of Larry the Liar'. Subsequent stories deal with horsetrading, hunting (which Yeates does not much like), snipe shooting (which he does), the hero's marriage to Philippa, a remarkable dog (Maria), local fairs and races. The tone is generally comic, with occasional pathos (as in 'The Waters Of Strife'). The series was popular enough to warrant two sequels: *Some Further Experiences Of An Irish RM* (1908) and *Mr Knox's Country* (1915).

SOMERS, Robert (1822–91). Somers was born in Newton Stewart in Scotland and worked for most of his life as an influential political journalist in Edinburgh and Glasgow. From 1849 to 1859, he was editor of the *North British Daily Mail* and for eleven years after that of the *Morning Journal.* He died in London. Among a number of books on social questions, banking and current affairs (on all of which he took a Conservative line) Somers wrote the historical* romance, *The Martyr Of Glencree* (1878), a tale introducing yet again the villain John Graham of Claverhouse, so hated by the Scots. The work was published anonymously and no reviewer seems to have recognised its authorship. BL 1. *DNB*. Wol.

SOMERVILLE, Edith [Anna] Oenone (1858–1949). Edith Somerville, the eldest of six children, was born on the island of Corfu where her colonel father was stationed. In 1859 the family returned to their eighteenth-century house Drishane in West Cork, Ireland. Somerville's ancestors had come to Ireland in 1690, and eight generations of the family had lived at Drishane. Edith was educated by governesses and briefly at Alexandra College, Dublin, in the manner of other children of the Protestant Ascendancy. Somerville subsequently (and rather against her parents' wishes) studied art in London, Düsseldorf and, from 1884, in Paris. By 1885, her work was being accepted by the *Graphic* and it was while working on a commission for that paper in 1886 that she met her second cousin, Violet Martin* ('Martin Ross') at Castletownshend. The two young ladies were immediately attracted to each other, Somerville declaring that the meeting 'proved the hinge of my life'. They were both great-granddaughters of Charles Kendal Bushe, who had been Lord Chief Justice of Ireland at the time of the Union, and both were passionately interested in their family genealogy. They started work on their first novel late in 1887. Neither of the partners married, and at a time when opportunities for the Anglo-Irish middle-class spinster were virtually nil, they found a fulfilling vocation in joint authorship. Together (Martin under the pen name 'Ross', Somerville as 'Geilles Herring' which she soon dropped) they produced *An Irish Cousin* (1889), a novel for which Ross supplied most of the text and Somerville the pictorial illustrations.

The Irish cousin of the title is Theo Sarsfield, who returns from Canada to her dead father's home at Darrus in Cork. The work has a more gothic* flavour than the later collaborations and was accepted by Richard Bentley* for £50. The partners rewrote the novel in 1903. *Naboth's Vineyard* (1891) offers a somewhat harsher view of Catholic Ireland and is flawed by an unconvincingly melodramatic plot. In 1894, they had advanced in skill and produced their finest novel, *The Real Charlotte**, the story of an unscrupulous woman who ruins an innocent young girl. Since 1890, the partners had undertaken a number of tours through Ireland, England and Europe, writing them up as articles for magazines. Their next novel, *The Silver Fox* (1897) is set in the west of Ireland, and features numerous hunting scenes in a narrative generally concerned with the culture clash between the English and Irish middle-classes. According to Somerville, the fact that it was first serialised in a weekly paper led to flaws in construction and an over-reliance on unconvincing plot surprises. Their most successful and reprinted collaboration was the satirical stories gathered as, *Some Experiences Of An Irish RM** (1899). The first edition of 3,000 copies (published by Longman*) sold out in a month. A sequel (*Further Experiences*) appeared in 1908 and a third instalment (*Mr Knox's Country*) in 1915. The later collaborations included *Dan Russel The Fox* (1911), the story of an English heiress, Katherine Rowan, who becomes a hunting enthusiast during a visit to Ireland. After her mother's death in 1895, Somerville had taken over the running of Drishane which like her partner's country house Ross ate up most of her literary income. Both women began to learn Irish, in response to growing Nationalism, and allied themselves with the women's suffragette movement. (Neither advocated militancy or violence, however.) In 1903, Edith added to her financial burdens by taking over a pack of hounds. While the partners were at their respective estates they communicated by a stream of lively letters in which they seem to have poured some of their best writing. Ross was injured hunting on her horse 'Dervish' in autumn 1898, and was thereafter more or less an invalid. In 1915, she died. But Edith Somerville maintained that she was still in contact with her cousin and continued to publish her work as by Somerville and Ross. Trinity College, Dublin, conferred an honorary doctorate of letters on Somerville in 1932, who was still publishing fiction in the 1940s. She farmed with her brother Cameron (d. 1942) and younger sister Hildegarde until 1946, although latterly her property was plagued by debts. Somerville was active in the fight for women's rights, a devout Christian, founded the Castlehaven Nursing Association and was for some years a Master of Foxhounds. A Loyalist, but moderate advocate of independence for Ireland, she criticised the Government's brutal suppression of the 1916 uprising. Her last book, *Maria And Some Other Dogs*, appeared in the year of her death, 1949. She was buried alongside Ross. BL (ES) BL 3. (ES and MR) BL 23. *DNB*. RM. *NCBEL*. Wol. Sad.

A Son Of Empire, Morley Roberts, 1899, 1 vol, Hutchinson. Roberts's most successful novel; a cross between the new woman* and Kiplingesque* imperial genres. Madge Gretton is a tomboy heroine, given to hero-worship of military men who distinguish themselves in colonial battle. In Switzerland she develops a crush on Dick ('Black') Blundell, on furlough from India.

Blundell is thirty-nine years old, a womaniser and a passed-over captain whose career has been held back by the General father of one of Madge's friends. Madge steals the General's cipher and forges a telegram to the Indian High Command, ordering Blundell to active service on the North West Frontier. There, in company with Madge's sapper brother, Billy, Blundell gallantly wins the DSO. But Madge's forgery is discovered. She defends her action to the Commander-in-Chief and Blundell is sent on another secret mission in the Egyptian desert. He is reported dead, but Madge does not despair and eventually he returns to marry her. The narrative concentrates on Madge's attractively 'unladylike' high spirits and recklessness. The glory of the British Empire is bruited throughout the story.

A Son Of The Soil, Mrs Margaret Oliphant, 1866, 2 vols, Macmillan. (Serialised in *Macmillan's Magazine**, November 1863–April 1865.) One of the more depressing and Calvinistic of Oliphant's narratives. Colin Campbell, born to poor Scottish parents, wins a scholarship to Balliol. He returns idealistically to take charge of his local kirk but discovers that the flock does not respond to his brilliance, nor to his enthusiasm. And the childhood sweetheart, Alice, whom he nobly marries, is also now beneath him in mind and spirit. He reconciles himself to a life of reduced fulfilments and hard, unrewarding work.

The Sorrows Of Satan, Marie Corelli, 1895, 1 vol, Methuen. Corelli's most extravagantly narcissistic romance. A struggling novelist, Geoffrey Tempest (hero and narrator), receives an unexpected bequest of £5 million together with an introduction to the fascinating Prince Lucio Rimanez (i.e. Satan). The narrative thereafter concerns the destiny of Geoffrey's soul. He marries a rich society beauty, Lady Sibyl Elton. But she has been corrupted by reading new woman* novels and offers her body to Lucio, whom she secretly adores. When she is found out, Sibyl poisons herself. Following many long exchanges, Geoffrey has begun to understand the nature of his princely friend, who actually wants to be hated by mankind so that God will take him back. After a climactic voyage in Lucio's yacht (*Flame*), Geoffrey renounces suicide and mysteriously his millions evaporate. Salvation is found in a brilliant young novelist, Mavis Clare. A glorified self-portrait of Corelli, Mavis writes wholesome Christian fiction, is unfairly abused by the corrupt ranks of reviewers (whose notices she has trained her dogs to tear up) and represents the hope of Western civilisation. Lucio is last seen walking in the Houses of Parliament, arm in arm with a Cabinet minister.

The Sowers, Henry Seton Merriman (i.e. Hugh Stowell Scott), 1896, 1 vol, Smith, Elder. (Serialised in *Cornhill**, January 1895–January 1896.) Merriman's most flamboyant and popular romance. The action flits across the capitals of Europe with its main setting in the steppes of Czarist Russia. Prince Paul Howard Alexis is an enlightened estate owner, half-English and an Etonian. He has formed an illicit Charity League with other landowners to alleviate the plight of the peasants and is in the habit of disguising himself as a doctor to tend to their wants. In Paris, he falls in love with and marries Etta Bamborough, a young English widow. Paul does not realise that it is she who has previously betrayed the existence of his Charity League to the authorities, bringing down Siberian exile on a neighbouring landowner,

Stepan Lanovitch (whose plain daughter Catrina loves Paul hopelessly). On Paul's Osterno estate, Etta is blackmailed by a former lover, Claude de Chauxville, who foments the peasants into storming their master's castle. When they discover that Paul is in fact their beloved 'Moscow doctor', they disperse. Etta and Claude are killed in the uprising and Paul goes into exile in England, still working clandestinely for the well-being of the Russian peasant, 'sowing' reform by peaceful means. He has found love again with Etta's cousin, Maggie Delafield. The novel's handling of intrigue and violent action is characteristically deft.

SPCK. The Society for Promoting Christian Knowledge was founded in 1698. One of the Society's initial aims was the setting up of charitable schools, and the supply of printed materials quickly became an accepted part of its operation. Fiction was admitted in 1814, in the form of Mrs Trimmer's improving tales. In 1832, a Committee of General Literature and Education was set up (partly in a spirit of rivalry with the less conservative RTS*). Up to the 1850s, the SPCK concentrated on tract fiction for the lower orders. But after the mid-century it increasingly published entertaining stories for children, with less heavy-handed didacticism. In the same spirit, the society set up a journal, *The Home Friend*, in 1852. Its style of fiction was further relaxed after 1870, although the SPCK always trailed behind the RTS (founder of the *Boy's Own Paper** in 1879). Such Victorian notables as Mrs Ewing*, W. H. G. Kingston* and Hesba Stretton* published with the SPCK at various times.

SPEIGHT, T[homas] W[ilkinson] (1830–1915). Speight was born in Liverpool, and was probably illegitimate. He was educated at a foundation school at Kendal in the Lake District and from 1847 to 1887 worked for the Midland Railway Company. His fiction is made up of sensation* novels, thrillers and the occasional historical* romance. It includes: *Brought To Light* (1867); *In The Dead Of Night* (1874); *Mysteries Of Heron Dyke* (1880), a 'Novel Of Incident', centred on a country house; *A Barren Title* (1886), a 'shilling shocker'; *Wife Or No Wife?* (1887); *The Grey Monk* (1895); *Juggling Fortune* (1900). Speight was an extremely derivative writer. His *Under Lock And Key* (1869) was so close in plot to Wilkie Collins's* *The Moonstone** (1868) that the author was obliged to make an unconvincing public disclaimer of plagiarism. Speight lived most of his later life in London and contributed widely to the popular magazines including *All The Year Round** and *Belgravia**. BL 36. *WW*. Wol. RLF.

SPENDER, Mrs John Kent [Lily] (née Lillian Headland, 1835–95). The daughter of a West End doctor and a Spanish mother, Lily Headland was brought up in London and educated at home and at Queen's College (later part of the London University system). In 1858 she married a doctor, John Kent Spender, of Bath, the author of treatises on the tonic properties of spa water. As Mrs Spender, she contributed to a number of magazines and after 1869 principally wrote novels. They include: *Brothers In Law* (1869); *Parted Lives* (1873); *Jocelyn's Mistake* (1875); *Mark Eylmer's Revenge* (1877), the story of a poet's hardship; *Both In The Wrong* (1878); *Mr Nobody* (1884); *The Recollections Of A Country Doctor* (1885), a work drawing on her earlier experiences with her father, Edward Headland; *Kept Secret* (1888);

A Modern Quixote (1894). Spender's novels have cosmopolitan settings and mainly conventional themes. She also worked on behalf of educational causes and did social work in Bath. She evidently lived a full life. *Godwyn's Ordeal* (1879) is dedicated: 'To my five elder girls and boys, to whom the first volume was read as it was written on the seashore during a happy summer holiday'. Of Spender's eight children two (J. A. Spender and Harold Spender) became noted journalists. The poet Stephen Spender is a grandson. BL 22. *DNB*. Wol.

The Splendid Spur, Q (i.e. A. T. Quiller Couch), 1889, 1 vol, Cassell. A historical* tale, in the form of 'Memoirs Of The Adventures Of Mr John Marvel, A Servant Of His Late Majesty, King Charles I, In The Years 1642–43, Written By Himself'. Jack Marvel is a student at Oxford. A friend, Anthony Killigrew, persuades him to take a letter from the King to General Hopton. Killigrew is subsequently murdered. On the way to the West to deliver the letter, Jack undergoes various adventures. He befriends Sir Deakin Killigrew (who dies of a cold) and his beautiful daughter, Delia. They are taken prisoner by the Roundheads and duly escape. In the West Country, Marvel is aided by a peasant girl, Joan O' the Tor, who finally gives up her life to save him from Parliamentary soldiers. Jack's enemy, and the principal architect of his troubles, dies falling over a cliff. Delia goes off to France, leaving her lover Jack to fight for his monarch, having found the 'Splendid Spur', namely honour. Q's novel is typical of the full-blown romance* which enjoyed a revival at the end of the century.

Sporting Novels. The ethos out of which the Victorian sporting novel emerged has two main sources. One is the cockney*, or low-life interest in the turf, epitomised in Pierce Egan's *Life In London And Sporting Guide*, which subsequently evolved into the sporting journal, *Bell's Life In London*. The other source is the growing spread of hunting as a fashionable pastime among the middle classes in the later Victorian period. R. S. Surtees's* *New Sporting Magazine*, founded in 1834, was an important populariser of the hunting vogue. And Surtees's comic character Jorrocks* was one of the inspirations for *Pickwick Papers**, originally conceived as a sporting novel (a mould it outgrew with the death of Robert Seymour.) Less well remembered than Surtees but important in his own day was 'Nimrod' (i.e. Charles James Apperley, 1779–1843) who published a novel, *The Life Of A Sportsman*, in 1842. Other notable mid-Victorian sporting novelists were Charles Clarke* and (famously) Anthony Trollope* ('the novelist who hunted the fox') and Whyte-Melville* (who actually died on the hunting field). In illustration, John Leech* did much to popularise the horsey novel. Later in the century, the style was vulgarised by writers such as Nat Gould*, whose fiction is a mere adjunct to the racing pages of the yellow press. The twentieth-century memoirs of Siegfried Sassoon's George Sherston represent a more respectable legacy of the Victorian sporting and hunting novel.

Springhaven, A Tale Of The Great War, R. D. Blackmore, 1887, 3 vols, Sampson Low. (Serialised in *Harper's Monthly Magazine*, April 1886– April 1887.) The great war of the title is that against the French, and the main focus of the novel is the reaction of a small Sussex fishing village to the King's call to arms in 1802, in the face of French invasion. The narrative introduces a crowded cast (including Nelson). The most interesting of the sub-plots concerns the struggle between the village headman, Captain Zebedee Tugwell, and his fisherman son Daniel. Daniel contracts radical opinions and is thrashed by his father, making him ripe for the intrigues of the Gallic villain, Caryl Carne. All eventually comes right. The novel, timed to coincide with Victoria's Jubilee, expresses Blackmore's distaste for modern liberal values and his desire for a return to the ways of old, pre-industrial England.

Spy Fiction. Spies feature randomly in early and mid-Victorian fiction (see, for instance, the villain Lütterloh in Thackeray's* *Denis Duval** or Dickens's* *A Tale Of Two Cities** with its government informers). But the emergence of spy novels as a distinct genre is a feature of the 1880s and 1890s. Victorian interest in a permanent peace-time secret intelligence service (established belatedly in 1909) was the outcome of nineteenth-century war and growing national tension. Wellington's intrepid agent, Lieutenant John Grant, probably inspired something of Lever's* Charles O'Malley* with his daring forays behind Napoleon's lines. The Crimean War, particularly in combination with William Howard Russell's* journalistic coverage, highlighted the need for an organised military espionage service. (This is the theme of A. G. F. Griffiths's* *The Thin Red Line*, 1886.) The Prussian invasion of France (reflected in Chesney's* *The Battle Of Dorking**) and apprehension of Russian terrorist societies (see Lanoe Falconer's *Mademoiselle Ixe**, 1890) were contributory factors in the emergence of spy fiction proper in the 1890s in the romances of William Le Queux* and E. Phillips Oppenheim*. The genre was boosted in the early twentieth century by Erskine Childers's *The Riddle Of The Sands* (1903) and John Buchan's* Richard Hannay stories. Around the period of the first World War, a number of novelists were actually recruited to the SIS, confirming the mutual obsessions of fiction and espionage in the twentieth century.

STABLES, [William] Gordon (1840–1910). There is some doubt about Stables's date of birth, which the *DNB* gives as 1840. Subsequent events in the author's life suggest this is too late. There seems, however, little question that Stables was born in Banffshire, Scotland, the son of a vintner. In 1854 he entered Aberdeen University, remaining in the Arts Faculty until 1857. (Whether he took a degree is not clear.) Declining the offer of a commission in the army, he enrolled to study medicine, and qualified MD and CM (i.e. Church Missionary) in 1862. While still a student he had made a voyage to the Antarctic on a whaler and in 1863 he joined the Royal Navy as a ship's surgeon. He served at sea until 1870, when ill health forced him to resign his commission and go on half pay. For two years after, he worked in the merchant service, cruising in the South Seas, round the Americas and in the Indian Ocean. In 1874, Stables finally came ashore, married, settled in Berkshire and devoted himself to writing boys' adventure tales as 'Gordon-Stables'. Over the following thirty years he produced an average of four books a year. His fiction includes *Wild Adventures In Wild Places* (1881); *The Hermit Hunter Of The Wilds* (1889); *Kidnapped By Cannibals* (1899); *On War's Red Tide* (1900), a topical tale of the Boer War. Stables had some unexpected facets to his character. He was an early pioneer of caravanning, an enthusiastic bird-watcher and lover of rural nature. He lived his later life as a figure of some literary eminence (with his wife and six children) at his house 'The Jungle', Twyford. BL 137. *DNB. NCBEL.* Wol.

STACPOOLE, Henry de Vere (1863–1951). Stacpoole was born near Dublin, the son of a clergyman schoolteacher. He attended Malvern College and later studied medicine in London. Qualifying in 1891, Stacpoole signed on as a ship's doctor and travelled all over the world, experience which he later used in his novels. In the 1890s he became friendly with John Oliver Hobbes* (who assisted his early career) and a number of the *Yellow Book* coterie. The 1890s mood is clearly reflected in his early novels such as: *The Intended* (1894); *Pierrot!* (1896); and the ghost* story *Death, The Knight And The Lady* (1897). In the twentieth century Stacpoole's skill as a story-teller developed and with *The Blue Lagoon* (1908) he created one of the biggest bestsellers of the modern era. The romantic story of a boy and girl growing up marooned on an idyllic desert island went through innumerable editions (under Newnes's* imprint) and three film versions. Stacpoole spent his later life in rural Essex and the Isle of Wight, enriched by his fiction. BL 47. *DNB.* Wol.

Standard Novels. The standard novel was devised by Colburn* and Bentley* (then in partnership) in 1831. Essentially, it was a one-volume 6s. reprint usually appearing after a two-year interval. The innovation set up the two tier system between new expensive and cheaper reprint fiction which still survives today (in the hardback/paperback arrangement). In the 1870s, the price of the standard novel was reduced to 3s.6d. and early reprinting of the one-volume reprint (by such publishers as Chatto*) eventually led to the collapse of the three-volume system in 1894. Bentley continued his 'Standard Novel' series until 1855, when it numbered 126 titles. He was, however, obliged to sell the property (i.e. stock, stereotype plates and copyrights) to stave off bankruptcy. The term thereafter fell into disuse.

STANFIELD, [William] Clarkson (1793–1867). Illustrator and painter. Stanfield was born in Sunderland, and entered the Merchant Marine in 1808. The young sailor was subsequently pressed into the Royal Navy in 1812, retiring after the wars in 1818. Thereafter, nautical* subjects were to be his speciality. For some time in the 1820s he supported himself as a theatrical scenery painter. In this capacity and as a friend of the great author he later assisted in Dickens's* amateur theatricals in the 1850s. Stanfield's paintings were very popular, and he was publicly commended by Ruskin*. Among the fiction Stanfield illustrated was Marryat's* Thameside romance, *Poor Jack* (1840) and Dickens's *Battle Of Life* (1846). *DNB.* Hou.

Stanley Thorn, Henry Cockton, 1841, 3 vols, Bentley. (Serialised in *Bentley's Miscellany*, January 1841–February 1842, illustrated by George Cruikshank*.) A Victorian rewriting of Fielding's *Amelia*. The hero is the son of a beer merchant, risen in the world. He is spoiled as a child, runs wild at Eton and elopes to Gretna Green to marry his saintly wife, Amelia. The second volume of the novel (its strongest section) depicts Stanley's gambling adventures (there is a lively Derby episode) and his successfully standing for Parliament, done in a Dickensian* Eatanswill style. Downfall comes in the third volume. Stanley is unseated and financially ruined by an electoral petition. The villainous Sir William Wormwood conspires against Amelia's (impregnable) virtue. After a redemptive spell in debtors' prison, the chastened hero is granted romance's statutory £1,000 per annum and connubial bliss. Among the novel's strengths is the Wellerish servant, Bob, and the similarly Dickensian man of the world, Captain Filcher. Cruikshank's caricaturist illustrations are an asset.

STANNARD, Mrs Arthur [Henrietta Eliza Vaughan] ('John Strange Winter', 'Violet Whyte', née Palmer, 1856–1911). Henrietta Palmer was born at York, the daughter of a rector who had earlier been an officer in the Royal Artillery. In 1874 under the pen-name Violet Whyte she began her career as a published novelist in the *Family Herald*. She remained associated with the journal for ten years, contributing numerous short and full-length fictions. There was a strong military tradition in her family, and in 1881 she began writing regimental tales and sketches under the masculine pseudonym John Strange Winter. These were so authentic as to lead readers to believe her a cavalry officer. John Ruskin* (with whom the novelist corresponded) asserted that Winter was 'the author to whom we owe the most finished and faithful rendering ever yet given of the character of the British soldier'. Palmer married a civil engineer, Arthur Stannard, in 1884, and the couple settled in London. In 1885, she produced her most popular work, *Bootles' Baby, A Story Of The Scarlet Lancers*. The tale was first printed in the *Graphic*. Within ten years, there were estimated to be 2 million copies in print. Stannard has over 100 entries in the British Library catalogue, most of which are 'Winter' military tales. In 1891, she started a journal, *Golden Gates* (the name was changed in 1892 to *Winter's Weekly*, under which title it lasted until 1895). A thorough professional, Stannard was the President of the Society of Women Journalists, 1901–03. She is reported to have been an excellent wife and mother, and interested herself in the plight of dumb animals. Her novels include: *Army Society* (1886); *Pluck* (1886); *Mignon's Husband* (1887); *A Soldier's Children* (1892); *That Mrs Smith* (1893); *Grip* (1896). The last was publicised as her fiftieth published work, and was taken to 'break new ground' in its story of a young Englishman in 1840s Paris who is sentenced to fifteen years' *travail forcé*. Another novel published in the same year, *The Strange Story Of My Life* (also called *The Colonel's Daughter*), is more in the usual mould, telling (in the first person) the story of an English girl born in an Indian garrison who ends up with two husbands when one, like Tennyson's Enoch Arden, returns from the dead. In 1896, the failing health of her husband and daughter led to the Stannards moving to Dieppe, which furnishes the background to many of the later romances which continued to stream from her pen. BL 104. *DNB*. Wol. RLF.

The Star Chamber, William Harrison Ainsworth, 1854, 2 vols, Routledge. (Serialised in *The Home Companion*, April–December, 1853.) Written at the period when Ainsworth's decline was fast setting in. The plot (like that of its predecessor, *The Lancashire Witches*, 1849), is set in the reign of James I. It chronicles the criminalities of Sir Giles Mompesson and Sir Francis Mitchell, who use the Star Chamber to enrich themselves. There is a standard Ainsworth love plot connected to the narrative of their political overthrow.

STEEL, Mrs Flora Annie (née Webster, 1847–1929). Flora Webster was born in Harrow, outer London, the sixth of eleven children of the sheriff-clerk of Forfarshire, Scotland. Her mother, Isabella Macallum, was the heiress of a Jamaica sugar planter. Married at eighteen, she was seventeen years younger than her husband who is recorded as having been a man of savage temper. The conception of Flora marked a reconciliation after a quarrel which had suspended sexual relations between the Websters for some years. Flora was brought up in London until her tenth year when the family moved to Forfar, their fortunes having been reduced to bankruptcy in 1850. Born a Presbyterian, she joined the Anglican Church when she was sixteen. Her education was finished in Brussels and on New Year's Day 1868 (a 'baby bride', like her mother before her) she married Henry William Steel, currently on leave from the Indian Civil Service. The couple settled in the Punjab. The expected pattern of Steel's married life was interrupted when in 1870 her first child was aborted, to save the mother's life. Although a daughter was born soon after, Steele's maternal interests were thereafter directed in large part to the native Indians. Very unusually, Flora Steel identified herself with these despised colonials. She refused to regard them as heathens, and devoted herself particularly to the well-being and education of native women, training herself as a lay medical practitioner. Now a *burra mem*, or senior lady in the Indian Civil Service, she founded a school for native girls at the large station of Kasur in 1884 and as an inspector worked for the improvement of education generally in the sub-continent. A pragmatist, she thought Euclid of less use to a young Indian than lessons in culinary hygiene, and amended curricula accordingly. At the end of her stay, she estimated that no less than 20,000 Indian girls had passed through her care. In 1889 her husband retired and the Steels returned to Britain. Once home, aged forty-two, she began writing full time, drawing on her colonial experience. Her great success was a long-meditated novel of the Mutiny, *On The Face Of The Waters** (1896) which narrates the siege of Delhi from the standpoint of an English major's wife, Kate Erlton. Her other fiction includes: *Wide Awake Stories* (1884), tales of the Punjab illustrated by her friend, John Lockwood Kipling, Rudyard Kipling's* father; *Miss Stuart's Legacy* (1893), her first Anglo-Indian novel and a tale of seduction; *The Potter's Thumb* (1894), the title refers to Indian fatalism and the plot introduces lively racing episodes and a Eurasian (or 'black and tan') heroine, Elflida; *Red Rowans* (1895), set partly in the west Highlands of her childhood; *In The Permanent Way* (1897); *Hosts Of The Lord* (1900), which takes the great religious rituals of India as its principal subject. Her last major effort in fiction was a series of romances on the Mogul Empire, and her last Indian story, *The Curse Of Eve*, a novel advocating birth control for women, came out in the year of her death. By this date, she earned the nickname of 'the female Rudyard Kipling' which must have irritated her, since she seems to have thought little of the other writer. Steel revisited India twice more in 1894 and 1897, renewing her acquaintance with the northern states. In the twentieth century she allied herself with the suffragettes and spoke against Mrs Humphry Ward* (of the Anti-Suffrage League) in 1913. On this, as on every other matter, her views seem to have been eminently sensible. Her autobiography *The Garden Of Fidelity* was published posthumously. Among other works, she also wrote *The Complete Indian Cook And Housekeeper* (1887), a manual intended to assist young English wives coming to the country. BL 24. *DNB*. Wol. Sad.

STEPHEN, Sir George ('Caveat Emptor', 1794–1879). The fourth son of a master in Chancery, Stephen was born in London. Originally intended as an army surgeon, with the declaration of peace in 1815 he went to Cambridge University. After two years' idling there, his father placed him in a solicitor's office. This led to a succesful career in government service and a knighthood in 1838. Stephen quarrelled with his employers at the Bank of England shortly after and resolved in 1842 to become a private lawyer. He was accordingly called to the Bar in 1849 and practised in Liverpool until 1855, when he emigrated to Australia. He was unhappy in that country and could find little work. His wife died in 1869 in Melbourne, as did he ten years later. Throughout his life Stephen wrote extensively. His novels (by 'Caveat Emptor') include: *The Adventures Of A Gentleman In Search Of A Horse* (1835) and *The Adventures Of An Attorney In Search Of A Practice* (1839). Both were very popular. His topically anti-Catholic *The Jesuit At Cambridge* appeared in 1847, under Colburn's* imprint. BL 3. *DNB*. Wol.

STEUART, John A[lexander] (1861–1932). Steuart was born in Perthshire and trained as a banker. After a brief period of employment in Scotland he travelled to Ireland, and from there went to the USA, eventually settling in the far West. In America Steuart turned to journalism, and in the late 1880s returned to England, where he edited the *Publishers' Circular*, 1896–1900. The journal was entirely modernised under his supervision, short as it was. His fiction includes: *A Millionaire's Daughters* (1888); *Self Exiled* (1889), a story of the high seas and east Africa; *In The Day Of Battle* (1894), an autobiographical novel which begins in Edinburgh and climaxes in the forbidden city of Mecca; *The Minister Of State* (1898); *The Eternal Quest* (1901), a Scottish army melodrama. Steuart wrote light fashionable fiction well into the twentieth century and a number of works on his countryman R. L. Stevenson*. BL 34. *WW*.

STEVENSON, Robert Louis [Lewis Balfour] (1850–94). Stevenson was born in Edinburgh, into a family well known on the father's side for producing engineers (especially engineers with an interest in the design of lighthouses). Stevenson's mother, Margaret (née Balfour), was the daughter of a Scottish clergyman and introduced her son to the Highland romance and mythology which was to feature in his later fiction. As a child, Stevenson was lonely and chronically ill. And at this early stage of his life, he formed a psychically dependent relationship with his nurse, Alison Cunningham ('Cummie'). Stevenson was expected to follow his father's profession and with this in view entered Edinburgh University in 1867. At eighteen, he changed his name 'Lewis' to 'Louis' and in 1871, he gave up engineering for law. At the same period, he was exhibiting bohemian tendencies as a rebellion against his background and paternal authority. By 1875, he had established a name for himself locally as an author, and had made a number of visits to the artists' colonies at Grez and Fontainebleau. In the same year (1875), Stevenson was called to the Bar, met his influential friend and patron W. E. Henley (in an Edinburgh infirmary, his pulmonary ailments already being firmly established), and embarked on a love affair which eventually led to marriage in 1880 with an American divorcée, Fanny Osbourne. Mrs Osbourne was older than Stevenson, an author in her own right and had artistic connections. She resented Henley's clubbable friendliness and contrived to break the men's intimacy in 1888. Stevenson revealed an insatiable appetite for travel early in life. Over the period 1876–78 he undertook long rambles through France and its waterways. The outcome was the early travel books: *An Inland Voyage* (1878); *Travels With A Donkey In The Cévennes* (1879). In 1879 (having just written the Edinburgh play *Deacon Brodie, Or The Double Life*, with Henley) he left for America. He spent a longish period on the West Coast, living for a while in San Francisco. In August 1880, he returned to England (with his wife). Over the next few years, Stevenson passed considerable time in Switzerland and the south of France (his lungs were already incurably damaged). In 1881 he published the essays *Virginibus Puerisque*. The following year (1882) saw *Familiar Studies Of Men And Books* and the collection of stories, *New Arabian Nights*. In 1883, Stevenson put out his American travel book, *The Silverado Squatters*, and his perennially popular story for children, *Treasure Island**. In 1884, the Stevensons left France for the English seaside town of Bournemouth. The following year, Stevenson published his still-reprinted anthology *A Child's Garden Of Verses* and the romance *Prince Otto**. Two of his finest works of fiction came out in 1886, *Dr Jekyll And Mr Hyde** and *Kidnapped**. In 1887, the novelist's father, Thomas Stevenson, died. Their relationship had always been uneasy (a fact very evident in the themes of Stevenson's fiction). In the same year, Stevenson sailed for America, settling in Saranac for a year. In 1888, he and Fanny left for the South Seas in their yacht *Casco*. Their first cruise brought them to Hawaii. Further cruises landed them in Samoa in 1890, where they settled. Meanwhile, Stevenson had published *The Wrong Box* (1889), a tontine story written in collaboration with Lloyd Osbourne, and his finest novel of Scottish revolutionary history, *The Master Of Ballantrae** (1889). Although mythology has depicted the Stevensons' life in Samoa as idyllic, it was in fact hard and at times positively wretched. Stevenson was drained by constant financial worries. Fanny suffered a severe nervous breakdown in 1892. Two years later, Stevenson died of a stroke probably brought on by stress. His later fiction includes: *The Black Arrow** (1888); *The Wrecker* (1892); *The Beach Of Falesá** (1893); *Catriona* (1893); *The Ebb-Tide* (1894); *The Weir Of Hermiston** (1896) and the unfinished *St Ives* (1897). BL 21. *DNB*. RM. *NCBEL*.

The Stickit Minister, S. R. Crockett, 1893, 1 vol, T. Fisher Unwin. Subtitled 'And Some Common Men', the volume comprises sharply observed character sketches most of which were originally published by Crockett in the *Christian Leader*. They reflect the everyday working-class life and culture of the author's native 'grey Galloway land'. The title piece, which has become Crockett's best-known single work, concerns the 'renunciation of Robert Fraser, formerly student in Divinity'. Robert, now an impecunious humble tenant farmer, is generally thought by his neighbours to be a failed ('stickit') minister. The truth is otherwise. A doctor diagnosed consumption and gave him only six years to live. Robert voluntarily gave up his university career for a worthless, medical student brother who has just dispossessed him of his land. Robert will now 'flit' (i.e. leave his house and die). The other twenty-five pieces are by turn pawkily comic, pathetic, or self-consciously 'canny'. They include a couple of early episodes in the life of the Edinburgh street arab Cleg Kelly*, later the subject of a full-length novel.

STODDART, Thomas Tod (1810–80). Stoddart was born in Edinburgh, the son of a naval officer. He attended Edinburgh University and early in life began to show the skill in angling for which he is best remembered. In 1833, he qualified as a Scottish barrister, but never practised. He lived at Kelso by the Tweed and Teviot rivers and wrote extensively and authoritatively on freshwater fishing, an activity which he did much to make a popular sport. Stoddart also wrote some amateur poetry, drama and a futuristic novel, *Abel Massinger, Or The Aeronaut* (1846). BL 1. *DNB. NCBEL.* Wol.

STOKER, Bram [Abraham] (1847–1912). Stoker was born into the Dublin middle classes. His father was a minor Civil Servant, twenty years older than his wife Charlotte. Bram (a contraction of Abraham, his father's name) was the third of seven children and suffered illness in infancy, being bedridden from his third to his seventh year. He attended Trinity College, Dublin, 1864–68. At university he took honours in science, was President of the Philosophy Society and the champion athlete. On graduating, he went into the Irish Civil Service, where he was to remain until 1878, being Inspector of Petty Sessions in Ireland, 1877–78. But Stoker also showed an early interest in the Dublin theatre and while carrying out his official duties undertook a quantity of drama reviewing and short story writing. (His first horror story, 'The Chain Of Destiny', appeared in the *Shamrock* in 1875.) Intellectually, his major affiliation was to the new vogue of Whitmanism. And a formative influence on his later fiction was the work of fellow Irishman Joseph Sheridan Le Fanu* (especially his vampiric novel, *Carmilla**, 1872). In 1876 he had begun a friendship with the actor Henry Irving which was to be the most important relationship of his professional life. In 1878, he married and resigned the Civil Service to become the business manager of Irving's newly acquired Lyceum Theatre, throwing himself into a hectic round of London, provincial and American performances. Altogether, Stoker was to serve Irving twenty-seven years, and he published his personal reminiscences of the actor in 1906, a year after he died on tour in Bradford. Edward Marston of Sampson Low* brought out Stoker's first collection of short stories and 'fairy tales' in 1881, *Under The Sunset.* Over the next ten years Stoker threw off numerous other short stories, most successfully in the horror genre. (The most anthologised of these is *The Squaw*, the ingenious tale of a persistent Red Indian spirit, reincarnated as a cat, who pursues a plainsman enemy, finally bringing about his hideous death in a Nuremberg torture chamber.) Stoker cultivated friendships with Conan Doyle*, Hall Caine* (to whom his best-known work, *Dracula**, is dedicated) and Oscar Wilde* (a former suitor of Florence Balcombe, who eventually became Stoker's wife). Stoker's first novel was *The Snake's Pass* (1890), a tale of adventure, mystery and lost treasure on the west coast of Ireland. *Dracula* was published in 1897. Its triumph as a book coincided ironically with the Lyceum's storage building burning down, and consequent theatrical problems which were to torment Stoker and Irving. Stoker's highly coloured vampire story went through six editions in a year and has never been out of print since its first publication. Although he tried his hand at other styles (e.g. the romantic *Miss Betty*, 1898), it was as a writer of horror that he appealed to the public. *The Jewel Of Seven Stars* (1903) is a tale of Egyptian reincarnation; *The Lady Of The Shroud* (1909) is warmed-over *Dracula; The Lair Of The White*

Worm (1911) is an allegorical tale of the supernatural. All were moderately successful. But nothing Stoker wrote surpassed or equalled *Dracula*. In 1902 the Lyceum closed and Irving made his last US tour in 1904, a year before his death. Stoker published six books in his last six years of life. BL 12. *WW*. RM. Wol. RLF.

The Stolen Bacillus, H[erbert] G[eorge] Wells, 1895, 1 vol, Methuen. (Most of the fifteen stories in the volume were first published in the *Pall Mall Budget*.) This volume collects up Wells's early science fiction*. It was followed by *The Plattner Story And Others* (1897) and *Thirty Strange Stories* (1897). Comprising a brilliant cyclopaedia of science fiction themes, these collections reflect the range of Wells's extraordinary literary imagination. They extend from the richly comic title story where an anarchist steals a test-tube of supposed cholera bacillus and swallows it intending to become a human plague bomb only to discover that it is the bacterium designed to turn monkeys mottled blue. At the other end of Wells's range is the sombrely symbolic 'The Lord Of The Dynamos'. In this story an African, Azuma-zi, tending three dynamos at Camberwell, conceives them to be deities and eventually sacrifices his overseer Holroyd to them.

STONE, Marcus (1840–1921). Illustrator and genre painter. Stone was born in London, the son of an artist, Frank Stone (1800–59), who illustrated some of the minor work of Charles Dickens*. Marcus studied under his father and began exhibiting at the Royal Academy as early as 1858. He worked in later life for *Cornhill** and the *Illustrated London News** and was elected to the RA in 1887. Stone, whose style was naturalistic, specialised in interiors and figures. He illustrated serial versions of Dickens's *Our Mutual Friend** and Trollope's* *He Knew He Was Right**. *WW*. Hou.

The Story Of A Feather, Douglas William Jerrold, 1843, 2 vols, Bradbury and Evans. (Serialised in *Punch**, 1843.) With *Mrs Caudle's Curtain Lectures**, the most long-lastingly popular of Jerrold's books. Adopting the 'Adventures Of A Guinea' device, it recounts the passage of an ostrich feather, passing from hand to hand through English society. Among the panorama of social types, Jerrold fixes on the plight of Patty Butler, a poor featherdresser. (In this aspect, the work has connections with the social problem* novels of the 1840s.) Dickens* admired the work greatly.

The Story Of A Modern Woman, Ella Hepworth Dixon, 1894, 1 vol, Heinemann. One of the finest new woman* novels, and evidently closely autobiographical. It opens with an extended description of a Victorian funeral. Professor Erle, a widower, dies leaving his two children, Mary and James, to fend for themselves. Jimmy goes to college and Mary (urged by her emancipated friend Alison Ives) applies herself to study at the Central London School of Art. She fails, but does better as an all-purpose magazine writer. Meanwhile, she is proposed to by an old friend of the family, Vincent Hemming. In the 'supreme moment' of embracing her, 'Mary Erle tasted for the first time, in all its intensity, the helplessness of women, the inborn feeling of subjection to a stronger will, inherited through generations of submissive feminine intelligences.' Vincent, an advanced thinker, spends a year abroad to research the world-wide subjection of woman. He returns to jilt Mary by marrying a vulgar industrial heiress. In making her way, the heroine uncovers many other examples of male hypocrisy and female victimisation. Eventually a defeated Vincent offers to elope with Mary, an offer she refuses from an enlightened sense of solidarity with her lover's wife. The story ends with the heroine at twilight, alone at Highgate cemetery, a glimmering London at her feet. Among many other fine things, Dixon offers a remarkable analysis of a Victorian childhood, in her second chapter.

The Story Of An African Farm, Ralph Iron (i.e. Olive Schreiner), 1883, 2 vols, Chapman and Hall. One of the earliest and best new woman* novels. The setting is a South African farm (vividly introduced by moonlight). An English settler marries a Boer woman, Tant' Sannie, just before he dies. His motive is to provide for his motherless daughter, Em (who will inherit the farm), and Em's orphan cousin Lyndall. Lyndall is brought up in narrow Calvinist strictness. For company she has only Em and Waldo, the mystical and spiritually tormented son of the German farm-overseer, old Otto. When Lyndall is twelve, an Irish adventurer, Bonaparte Blenkins, comes to the farm and ingratiates himself with the trusting Waldo. But treacherously, he conspires with Tant' Sannie to have Otto dismissed and himself installed as foreman. Otto dies, and for a short period Blenkins tyrannises Waldo who is discovered in possession of a volume of the heretic John Stuart Mill. But Blenkins overreaches himself and is discovered by a furious Tant' Sannie making love to a rival. His jaunty departure (assisted by his long-suffering victim Waldo) marks the end of the novel's first section. Lyndall meanwhile grows up and goes away to school; Em grows fat and stolid on the farm; Waldo has a strange encounter with a 'Stranger' who communicates the meaning of life in the form of an allegory. An Englishman, Gregory Rose, arrives at the farm and proposes to Em. She breaks the engagement when a transformed Lyndall returns after four years' absence. Lyndall talks at length about the condition of woman and sex in this section of the narrative. And she passively allows Gregory to offer her marriage. But, as he later discovers, this is probably a tactic to bring pressure on the man she really loves and to whom she returns. Lyndall leaves and Gregory pursues her and her lover all over the Free State. Eventually she is discovered deserted in a small country hotel. She has had a child who died immediately after birth and is herself clearly dying. Disguised as a female nurse, Rose tends Lyndall, achieving for the first time a spiritual intimacy, and when she dies he brings her body back to the farm. In a conclusion which is usually read as overpoweringly pessimistic, Em and Gregory finally plan marriage; Tant' Sannie marries, grows enormously fat and has a child. The dreamer Waldo, who has also been wandering, returns to the farm where he devotes himself to the memory of Lyndall and eventually himself probably dies (as elsewhere, the text is enigmatic on this point).

The Story Of Bessie Costrell, Mrs Humphry Ward, 1895, 1 vol, Smith, Elder. (Serialised in *Cornhill**, May–July 1895.) Ward's most successful short fiction, and a careful study of English peasant life. John Bolderfield retires from a life of farm labouring in Clinton Magna. And before going off to the nearby Frampton for a few months, he entrusts the box containing his £71 life's savings to his relative Isaac Costrell, who has a young wife, Bessie. Isaac is an austere Congregationalist but Bessie succumbs to temptation and steals John's money to spend on drink. The surviving amount is stolen by Isaac's wastrel son, Tim. John Bolderfield returns, Bessie is forced to confess by an unforgiving Isaac and throws herself down a well. Isaac devotes himself to looking after John, now ruined. The story is told with remarkable economy and lack of condescension to its humble personages.

The Story Of Elizabeth, Miss [Anne] Thackeray [Ritchie], 1863, 1 vol, Smith, Elder. (Serialised in *Cornhill**, September 1862–January 1863, illustrated by Fred Walker*.) Anne Thackeray's first published novel and 'the story of a foolish woman who through her own folly, learnt wisdom at last'. Elizabeth Gilmour, 'Elly' as she is called, is eighteen and spends a season in Paris with her widowed (but still eligibly young) mother. Mrs Gilmour marries the somewhat tyrannically Protestant Pasteur Tourneur, against Elly's wishes who has to eat cabbage soup and wishes herself dead. Elly subsequently falls in love with a family friend, Sir John Dampier, who is older and more mature than she is. This infatuation leads to embarrassments, since he persists in regarding her as a 'weak-minded little girl'. Finally, after various complications, John (who breaks an engagement) and Elizabeth (who rejects two other proposals) are brought together, she having been cured of her weak-mindedness. Thackeray hinges the action cleverly on a scene at the theatre in which, against his will, Dampier is obliged to declare Elly his fiancée, so as to protect her reputation. The story evokes Parisian society vividly and has a sprightliness of narrative which inspired the young Rhoda Broughton* to write fiction on the same bright young girl lines. Critics disliked the implication that Elizabeth's mother was a rival for John Dampier, a thought which, as the *Athenaeum** put it 'is, or ought to be, quite inadmissible for a novel'.

Strahan (1859–82). Publisher and magazine proprietor. Alexander Strahan (1834?–1914) was born in the early 1830s in Rosshire, the sixth of nine children of a sheriff's officer. In his childhood, he was profoundly influenced by the 'Disruption' in which the Church of Scotland broke away from the English Established Church. In later life theological publishing was one of his main interests. In 1853, on the death of his father, Strahan went to work in the Edinburgh book trade and by the end of the decade was in business for himself. Modelling himself on the Chambers brothers, he founded his first magazine in 1859. Imaginatively, Strahan recruited Norman Macleod*, the royal chaplain for Scotland, to edit *The Christian Guest*. Within a year, the magazine was retitled *Good Words**. It cost 6d., was sixty-four pages long, monthly and illustrated. Combining as it did strict sabbath observance with the provision of entertaining fiction, the enterprise was fabulously successful. By 1864 *Good Words*'s sales were running at 160,000 an issue. On the strength of this success, Strahan went on to found the *Sunday Magazine* in 1864, the *Argosy** in 1865 and the *Contemporary Review* in 1866. In so doing, he overextended himself and became heavily indebted to, among others, the printer J. S. Virtue*. By a complicated manoeuvre, James Virtue founded *St Paul's Magazine** in 1867, which Strahan inherited in 1869. Strahan's business crashed in 1872, and he was forced to 'retire'. But he salvaged enough literary property (incuding the *Contemporary*) to carry on through the 1870s. But in 1882, he again faced bankruptcy and this time succumbed entirely. The remaining thirty years of his life were spent in obscurity though not, apparently, in hardship. The achievement of *Good*

Words gives Strahan some claim to be considered the premier evangelical publisher of the century. Certainly he devised a formula for mixing strict religiosity and fiction that was unprecedentedly effective.

STRAIN, Mrs E[uphans] H. (née McNaughton, d. 1934). Little is known about her. Born in Auchinleck, Ayrshire, she at some point married John Strain, an engineer. The couple, who had three children, lived in Glasgow, travelling extensively. They were friendly with the Stevensons*, whom they visited in Samoa. Mrs Strain wrote for the *Scotsman* newspaper and produced some fiction, including: *A Man's Foes* (1895), a story of the siege of Derry, from the Protestant viewpoint which the *Daily Mail* called the best historical* novel since Doyle's* *Micah Clarke**; *School In Fairyland* (1896), an allegory; *Elmslie's Drag Net* (1900), collected stories; *Laura's Legacy* (1903), a contemporary melodrama. She wrote her novels under the sexless authorial name 'E. H. Strain'. BL 5. *WW*. Wol.

The Strand Magazine (1891–1950). The so-called 'Mirror of the Century'. The magazine was the brainchild of George Newnes*. Newnes had enriched himself in 1881 with the founding of the fabulously successful weekly miscellany, *Tit-Bits*. He determined to set up a more intellectually respectable monthly stable-mate, costing 6d. From the first, the *Strand* hit the mark in attracting the middle-class family reader. The formula, like that of *Tit-Bits*, was miscellaneous, but less proletarian in tone. The journal was strongly pro-imperialist and favoured fiction with adventure or juvenile comedy at its core. Early contributors included A. E. W. Mason*, E. Phillips Oppenheim*, P. G. Wodehouse. Newnes's dislike of long items militated against full-length serial fiction. As a brilliant compromise, *Strand's* first editor H. Greenhough Smith hit on the short story sequence* using a recurrent hero who, when he caught on, became a household name. The system worked particularly well with detective* fiction, a genre which the magazine virtually owned in the 1890s when it had the services of Conan Doyle* ('Sherlock Holmes'); Grant Allen* ('Miss Cayley'); and Arthur Morrison* ('Martin Hewitt*, Investigator'). It was the *Strand's* illustrator Sidney Paget* who in fact created Holmes's distinctive aquiline, deerstalker-hatted profile by which he is best known. At its peak, the *Strand* commanded a circulation of half a million copies a month. *BLM*.

A Strange Story, E. G. E. L. Bulwer-Lytton, 1862, 2 vols, Sampson Low. (Serialised in *All The Year Round**, August 1861–March 1862.) One of the finest Victorian stories of the supernatural. The novel was conceived by Bulwer-Lytton as a refutation of the 'Materialist' doctrine, which reduces everything to rational explanation. Dr Fenwick comes to a small English town early in the nineteenth century. He discovers his only professional rival to be Dr Lloyd, a mesmerist. Fenwick, by contrast, is a confirmed sceptic in scientific matters. At a séance he ridicules Lloyd, who in his rage has a paralytic seizure. On his deathbed Lloyd curses his young antagonist and prophesies a terrible nemesis, 'the gibbering phantoms are gathering round you'. Lloyd's vacant house is let to a visiting family and Fenwick while treating the daughter, Lilian Ashleigh, falls in love with her. Later, she confesses she was attracted to him by a vision of her father, instructing her to do so. A mysterious stranger, Margrave, arrives. He is a student of the occult, searching for a mysterious 'pythoness'. Another resident, Sir Philip Derval a former traveller in the East and a mesmerist, recognises Margrave. Sir Philip is later found stabbed to death. Among his remains is a manuscript of Haroun of Aleppo, a document which reveals all the inner secrets of nature. Margrave needs it, and it later emerges that he earlier stole the elixir of life from Haroun. Fenwick, meanwhile, is arrested for the murder of Sir Philip. He is later released, but only to find that Lilian has fallen under Margrave's spell. He sees in her his sought-for pythoness. The final action of the novel takes place in a visionary Australia. Margrave offers to free Lilian from his thrall, but only if Fenwick helps him create more of the elixir. In a surreal climax on a deserted plateau, the cauldron containing the precious fluid is knocked over by a herd of stampeding cattle. Margrave vainly attempts to drink the unready elixir, and dies.

Strathern, Or Life At Home And Abroad, A Story Of The Present Day, the Countess of Blessington, 1844, 4 vols, Colburn. (Serialised in the *Sunday Times*, 1844.) A fashionable novel, set in Rome. It centres on the glittering social life of the beauty and heiress, Louisa Sydney, and her intercourse with 'scions of the nobility', one of whom, Strathern, she eventually marries. As with other silver fork* novels, a prime selling feature was the malicious *roman à clef* aspect of the work. (Bulwer[-Lytton*], heir to Knebworth, appears as the simpering 'Webworth'.) Per copy sold, this was one of the highest-paid-for novels of the era. Blessington had £600, although Colburn allegedly cleared only 400 sets of the work.

Strathmore, Ouida, 1865, 3 vols, Chapman and Hall. One of Ouida's early, garish efforts. Strathmore is highborn and ambitious. He falls in love with 'the Vavasour', an unscrupulous reigning beauty, and supposed to be the wife of the Marquis of Vavasour and Vaux. Mischievously, the Vavasour incites Strathmore (now her paramour) to duel with his bosom friend, Erroll (who has spurned her). Strathmore kills Erroll; then, in his turn, spurns the Vavasour. He discovers that she is not the wife, but the mistress of the Marquis whose name she bears, and vengefully publicises the fact. In reparation he adopts, and later marries, Erroll's daughter. As the critic, W. C. Phillips, pungently puts it: 'And so Strathmore lives happily ever after in the affection of the young wife whose father he murdered for a harlot.'

STRAUSS, Gustave Louis Maurice ('The Old Bohemian', 1807?–87). Strauss was born at Trois Rivières, Canada, of mixed European origins and educated in Germany where he took a Ph.D. He also took a degree in medicine in France. He was exiled from Germany and France for revolutionary activity and in the 1840s took up residence in London. In England, he became known as a famous bohemian, helped found the Savage Club and was one of a group of German homeopathic practitioners of medicine, of whom the best known was Julius Althaus. He also worked variously as chemist, cook, journalist and author, but in none of these lines was he successful. In 1879, Strauss found a charitable berth at the Charterhouse as a Poor Brother (as did Colonel Newcome, in Thackeray's* novel, *The Newcomes**). In 1882, he brought out his rambling *Reminiscences Of An Old Bohemian*. Strauss published a novel with Tinsley* in 1865, *The Old Ledger*, which became a centre of controversy. The *Athenaeum** reviewer found the work 'vulgar, profane and indelicate', and the author brought an action for libel against the paper. The affair was settled, and then flared up again in April 1866, when the *Athenaeum* repeated its original charges. A court decision eventually came down in favour of the paper's right to freedom of critical opinion. Strauss never married. BL 2. *DNB*. Wol. RLF.

STRETTON, Hesba (i.e. Sarah [Sara] Smith, 1832–1911). The century's most successful evangelical writer of children's fiction, particularly on the strength of her early million-seller, *Jessica's First Prayer** (1867). Sarah Smith was brought up in a nonconformist household, only a few notches up from the working class (a fact which may account for the extremely unromantic and closely observed pictures she gives of the lives of the poor in her later fiction). Her father was a printer and publisher in a small way and the young Sarah seems to have picked up and read many of his books. Her mother, a strongly evangelical woman, died when her daughter was eight. Unmarried, Sarah Smith entered authorship via governessing as did many of her sister-novelists. She began writing short fiction for the magazines after her sister successfully (and reportedly without Sarah's knowledge) sent 'The Lucky Leg' to Dickens's* *Household Words** in 1859. This led to a warm and professionally useful relationship between the two authors. Sarah brought her first sizeable work out with the RTS* in 1864. Notoriously stingy paymasters, they gave her only £30 for the copyright of *Fern's Hollow*, a story set in the coal-mining west country. She took the name 'Hesba' from the combined initials of her five siblings, and Stretton from Shropshire where she was brought up. Her next effort in fiction was *Enoch Roden's Training* (1865), a work influenced, as the title suggests, by Tennyson's *Enoch Arden*. These were trial shots and it was with *Jessica's First Prayer* (1867) that Stretton made her name. As J. S. Bratton notes: 'it was the foundation of a school of writing, the Sunday school story of the street arab, the homeless waif.' Stretton had moved from Shropshire with her sister to Manchester in 1863, which may have inspired a new vein of urban realism in her writing. Whatever the reason, the book was a success almost on the scale of *Uncle Tom's Cabin*. And like the other work, its appeal was international. Tsar Alexander, for instance, made it compulsory reading in all Russian schools. *Jessica*'s success was followed by *Little Meg's Children** (1868) and *Alone In London* (1869). About this period, she broke with the RTS, and her fiction became less didactic in its manner. She even wrote three-deckers for older readers. (e.g. *The Doctor's Dilemma*, 1872). Her other fiction includes: *A Chequered Life* (1862); *Hester Morley's Promise* (1873); *Through A Needle's Eye* (1879). The Stretton sisters moved to London in 1870. In the late 1870s and 1880s, Stretton became increasingly concerned about child abuse, and helped set up the London Society for the Prevention of Cruelty to Children, with the assistance of Dickens's patron, the Baroness Burdett Coutts. She resigned in 1894 (as did Coutts) when the society expanded to become a national institution. In 1892, she collected £1,000 for the relief of Russian peasants. Her later fiction reflects her philanthropic concerns. Stretton did well out of authorship and despite the relatively low prices given for children's books, was comfortably off after 1870. But, as the *DNB* notes, 'she never went to a theatre, cared nothing for dress and owned no jewellery'. She moved to Richmond in 1890 and was a total invalid after 1907. BL 68. *DNB*. RM. *NCBEL*. Wol.

STRETTON, Mrs Julia Cecilia ('Julia De Winton', née Collinson 1812–76). The second daughter of a clergyman at Gateshead she married Walter Wilkins (MP for Radnorshire, 1835–40) in 1831. Stretton took on the name De Winton in 1839, a year before her husband died. In 1857 she remarried a former army lieutenant, William Stretton, who died in 1868. Stretton produced in later life a number of romances, including: *The Lonely Island* (1852); *Margaret And Her Bridesmaids* (1856); *The Valley Of A Hundred Fires* (1860), a factory novel; *Three Wives* (1868). BL 11. Boase. Wol.

STRICKLAND, Miss Agnes (1796–1874). Strickland was the second surviving daughter of a Suffolk gentleman, formerly in shipping. He educated his daughters at home (there were nine Strickland children), and particularly cultivated their interest in history. The Stricklands, especially the girls, were a famous writing family especially after 1818, when their father died leaving them unexpectedly badly off. Elizabeth (1794–1875) helped her sister Agnes with *The Lives Of The Queens Of England* (1840–48), the family's most famous production. Jane Margaret (1800–88) wrote *Rome* (1854); Samuel (1809–67) emigrated to Canada and wrote of his experiences there. Mrs Susanna Moodie* (1803–85) wrote a quantity of fiction. Under her married name, Catherine Parr Trail (1802–99) wrote popular books of botany. On her part, Agnes wrote the novels: *Alda, The British Captive* (1841); *How Will It End?* (1865), a seventeenth-century historical* novel; *Guthred, The Widow's Slave* (1875); *The Royal Brothers* (1875), a historical romance. She also produced several volumes of tales adapted from British history for the child reader. Agnes Strickland lived a very quiet life, never married and was granted a Civil List pension of £100 in 1870. BL 8. *DNB*. *NCBEL*. Wol.

A Struggle For Fame, Mrs J. H. Riddell, 1883, 3 vols, Bentley. A closely autobiographical account of Riddell's experiences as an author and one of the finest Victorian novels about writing Victorian novels. The story opens in October 1854 on a ferry from Ireland landing at Morecambe Bay. The vessel carries a budding authoress, Glenarva ('Glen') Westley, and her genteel improvident father. Also on board is a resourceful young Irishman, Bernard ('Barney') Kelly. Glen and Barney meet casually on the boat and on the train to Euston and the subsequent narrative deals with their different but occasionally intertwining careers in the world of English letters. Glen sets out to support herself and her useless parent by writing fiction. She receives useful advice from the friendly but harrassed middlebrow publisher, P. Vassett (based on George Smith of Smith, Elder*, and Richard Bentley*). But her first, unfashionably Irish* novel is published by the opportunistic Pedland (i.e. Newby*). Gradually, she learns her craft, tramping round the publishing offices of London, and eventually has a hit. Mistakenly, she lets herself be bought over by a fly-by-night new firm, Felton and Laplash (i.e. the Tinsley* brothers). They do not stand by her when her popularity wanes (partly due to a savage review by Barney). Her final recovery of some kind of security is hard-won. Meanwhile, Glen has a series of personal trials. Her father dies, her health fails and she marries a shiftless (but charming) businessman, Mordaunt Logan Lacere, whom she has in fact to support. He dies prematurely. The last scene in the novel shows Glen standing alone at sunset, having turned down an offer of marriage from her faithful childhood sweetheart, Ned Beattie. The other strand of the story follows Barney's more picaresque progress through literary Bohemia. Failing as a novelist, he eventually makes his way as an all-purpose man of letters and magazine proprietor. His career seems to owe something to that of Edmund Yates*. In its incidental scenes, *A Struggle For Fame* offers a series of sharp vignettes of actual Victorian writers and book-trade people.

The Struggles Of Brown, Jones And Robinson, Anthony Trollope, 1870, 1 vol, Smith, Elder. (Serialised in *Cornhill**, August 1861–March 1862.) In retrospect, Trollope regarded this as the least satisfactory work he ever contrived to publish. The outline was turned down by two publishers before George Smith took it, in order to bind the rising star of Trollope more firmly to his house. Brown is a retired butter merchant. His go-ahead son-in-law, Jones, persuades him to put his cash into a haberdashery emporium. Another partner, Robinson, intends to establish the new concern on advanced commercial lines, with the full support of modern advertising techniques. The project ends in bankruptcy, and Brown is left with nothing but his faithful daughter, Maryanne (who rejects the proposals of Robinson). Robinson, undaunted, sets out to try again. The theme is interesting and ahead of its time (as with other of Trollope's failures such as *The Fixed Period**). But the work remains very odd.

A Study In Scarlet, A. Conan Doyle, 1888, 1 vol, Ward, Lock. (First published in *Beeton's Christmas Annual*, 1887. The first book edition had six illustrations by Charles Doyle, the author's father.) The first of the Sherlock Holmes stories which sets the scene for the forty-year-long series. Dr John Watson is invalided home from the Afghan Wars on a small pension. He moves into bachelor rooms with the mysterious Sherlock Holmes at 221B Baker Street. After some time Watson (a solid but unimaginative fellow) discovers that Holmes is a criminal investigator, called to assist Scotland Yard when cases prove insoluble. One such case arises and officers Gregson and Lestrade solicit the amateur sleuth's aid. An American business man, Enoch J. Drebber, has been found murdered in a pool of blood. By careful examination of the clues, Holmes arrives at an exact physical description of the assailant. Shortly after, Drebber's secretary Stangerson is found stabbed to death. Holmes, by a ruse, lures a cabman to his apartment whom he handcuffs and identifies as the killer. The cabman reveals himself as Jefferson Hope. He committed his murders for revenge. The woman he loved was earlier forced into Mormon marriage with Drebber, and died a month later. Hope has a heart condition and himself dies before execution.

STURGIS, Julian Russell (1848–1904). Julian Sturgis was born in the USA, at Boston, Massachusetts. He came to England with his family at the age of seven months and was educated at Eton and Balliol College Oxford, graduating with a second-class degree in classics in 1872. In 1876 he was called to the Bar, and the following year became an English subject. Over the next two years, Sturgis travelled extensively around the world and embarked on his career as a novelist specialising in light comedies. His first work of fiction was the chatty *John-A-Dreams* (1878). Other novels followed: *My*

Friends And I (1884), three tales, offering three self-portraits of the author; *John Maidment* (1885), a political novel with Oxford and American settings and Liberal sentiments; *Thraldom* (1887); *The Comedy Of A Country House* (1889); *The Folly Of Pen Harrington* (1897), a work dedicated to Rhoda Broughton*, whose comedy it emulates; *Stephen Calinari* (1901). Russell was, throughout his life, possessed of private wealth and fond of outdoor sports. He married in 1883. His fiction owes much to George Meredith* who was a friend. BL 9. *WW*.

A Superfluous Woman, Emma Frances Brooke, 1894, 3 vols, Heinemann. One of the bestselling of the new woman* novels, going through four editions in as many months between January–April 1894. The title was a catchphrase in demographic discussions of the late nineteenth and early twentieth centuries. Jessamine Halliday is first encountered as a social ornament, enervated and delicate in character. She is saved by the enlightened East End physician, Dr Cornerstone, who recommends the 'pill of reality' and on whose advice she travels to the Highlands of Scotland. Here she falls in love with the manly crofter, Colin Macgillvray of Dalfaber, with whom she labours in the fields and witnesses the majestic death of a stag. There is misunderstanding, however, when she offers Colin the 'unconditional surrender' of her body (intending to bear his child out of wedlock, being unable actually to marry a peasant). His old-fashioned chivalry will not allow this, and Jessamine returns to London where she marries the degenerate Lord Heriot whom she loathes. Ten years pass. She bears two idiot children (receptacles of 'the crimes and debaucheries of generations') and dies mad in childbirth with a third, also an idiot. Cornerstone goes north to tell the still faithful Colin that, after all, Jessamine loved only him. The novel expresses in melodramatic form current 1890s preoccupations with racial degeneration.

SURTEES, Robert Smith (1805–64). The creator of Jorrocks* and the best-loved of Victorian hunting novelists. Surtees was born (a second son) into the squirearchy at Hamsterley Hall, near Newcastle upon Tyne, Co. Durham. There were eight other children. The property had been in the Surtees family since his grandfather's time. A delicate child, he was not sent away to public school but instead at thirteen went to the local Durham Grammar School for a year. On leaving school it was necessary that as a second son he should find a profession. He duly took up the practice of law, being articled to a Newcastle solicitor in 1822 and a London solicitor in 1825. In 1828 Surtees was admitted in Chancery. He does not seem to have taken his legal vocation at all seriously. But from his earliest years, Surtees hunted enthusiastically. In 1829 he seems to have started writing a sporting* novel (subsequently destroyed) and he published his first contribution, 'Breaking Ground', in the *Sporting Magazine* in February 1830 which led to full-time sporting journalism as 'Nim South'. In 1831, his life took a number of decisive turns. He published his first book, *The Horseman's Manual*. (This, incidentally, was the only one of his books that Surtees would allow to carry his name.) In the same year, his elder brother Anthony died of smallpox, and he found himself in line to inherit his father's house and estate. With the publisher Rudolph Ackermann and in association with the famous sporting journalist C. J. Apperley

('Nimrod') he started up the *New Sporting Magazine* of which he was to be editor until 1836. In this journal were published the 'jaunts and jollities' of Surtees's most famous creation, the cockney* grocer, huntsman and squire, Jorrocks. There followed a number of other sporting tales, all serialised in numbers or in magazines and papers and centred on the popular Jorrocks, notably: *Handley Cross** (1843, reissued with John Leech's* illustrations, 1854); *Hillingdon Hall** (1845). Surtees had a very fruitful relationship with Leech, who illustrated five of his novels so memorably that he too is firmly associated in the mind of posterity with equestrianism. *Mr Sponge's Sporting Tour** (first published 1849-51 in the *New Monthly Magazine**, reissued in 1853, illustrated by Leech) shows Surtees at his best. In 1838, after some unsuccessful attempts to enter Parliament (as a Conservative), Surtees took up residence at Hamsterley Hall, his father having died in 1838 and he having married in 1841. One of his first acts was to start a pack of hounds (though he could not keep it going more than two years, for lack of hunting company). He was appointed Deputy Lieutenant for Durham and a JP the following year. Surtees also became a major in the Durham militia (1844-46), a High Sheriff (1856) and a county dignitary. An heir, Anthony, was born in 1847. His estate contained coal-mines, and Surtees farmed his land profitably. (He was an opponent of the repeal of the Corn Laws, and introduces the subject polemically into his Jorrocks sequence.) The fact that (like the other principal hunting novelist, Whyte-Melville*) he did not have to write for his living gives his fiction an engagingly slapdash and amateurish quality. His other novels (typically serialised by Bradbury and Evans*, with illustrations by Leech) include: *Hawbuck Grange* (1847), first serialised in *Bell's Sporting Life*; *Young Tom Hall* (1853), serialised in the *New Monthly Magazine*, interrupted and never completed when the editor, W. H. Ainsworth*, divulged Surtees's authorship; *Ask Mama* (1858); *Plain Or Ringlets?* (1860); *Mr Facey Romford's Hounds* (1865). The last is the story of an engaging confidence trickster who sets himself up as a free-lance Master of Foxhounds. Surtees also wrote as non-fiction: *The Analysis Of The Hunting Field* (1846) and edited a new edition of Blaine's *Encyclopaedia Of Rural Sports* in 1856. He died at Mutton's Hotel in Brighton (a resort he loved) of a heart attack. BL 8. *DNB*. RM. NCBEL. Wol. Sad.

Susan Hopley, Or Circumstantial Evidence, Catherine Crowe, 1841, 3 vols, Saunders and Otley. A simply written romance, which achieved considerable popularity and was reprinted throughout the century. The heroine is supposed to be a menial but eventually discovers herself (after years of domestic drudgery) to be a colonel's daughter, respectable and not obliged after all to work for her living. Excitement is added to this pleasant fantasy by Susan's enterprise in tracking down the murderer of her brother and by a climactic court scene.

SWAN, Annie S. [Mrs Burnett-Smith] (1859-1943). Annie Swan was born at Gorebridge, Scotland, where her father was a farmer. She was educated at the Ladies' College, Edinburgh and began her literary career writing children's books and pieces for the magazine *The Woman At Home*. Although she is principally remembered for the 200-odd slushy woman's romances she wrote in the twentieth century, Swan's early fiction is regional and (some of it) socially realistic. It includes: *Ups And Downs* (1878); *Aldersyde* (1883),

'A Border Story Of Seventy Years Ago', set near Gullane in East Lothian where the author lived; *Carlowrie* (1884); *Gates Of Eden* (1886), a Scots idyll in the bracken; *Who Shall Serve?* (1891), the story of a strike in a Clydeside shipbuilding yard. By 1898, Swan had thirty-six tales published in book form. She married Dr James Burnett-Smith (d. 1927) but throughout her career used her maiden name for authorial purposes. BL 197. *WW*. Wol.

SWAN, N[athaniel] Walter (1843–84). Swan was born at Monaghan in Ireland, and educated at Glasgow University. In the early 1850s he emigrated to Australia where he spent some time mining in Victoria. From this occupation he moved to journalism. A short story, 'Luke Myver's Harvest' won a *Sydney Mail* competition, and Swan began a mildly successful career in fiction. His work is collected as *Tales Of Australian Life* (1875) and *A Couple Of Cups Ago* (1885). BL 1.

SWEETMAN, Walter (1830–1905). Sweetman was born in Dublin, into a long established family of merchants. A Roman Catholic, he was educated at Stonyhurst. He took his degree at London University and was eventually called to the Bar. He seems not to have practised, however, living instead the life of a country gentleman. Sweetman wrote principally on religion and philosophy. But he also produced the novels: *Through The Night* (1869), 'A Tale Of The Times'; *Libertas* (1891), 'Or Through Dreamland To Truth'; *Roland Ryan* (1896), 'An Irish* Sketch'. BL 3. *WW*. Wol.

Sybil, Or The Two Nations, Benjamin Disraeli, 1845, 3 vols, Colburn. The second part of the 'Young England*' trilogy and the finest novel of the three. The work is also regarded as possibly the finest of Victorian social problem* novels. The two nations of the title are the rich and poor in England, an idea which Disraeli introduces strikingly into the action. The novel opens brilliantly with overheard conversations in St James's, London's clubland, on the eve of the 1837 Derby. Charles Egremont, 'the younger brother of an English earl' (Lord Marney), determines to investigate for himself the lower social levels of England in the disguise of plain Mr Franklin. This brings him to such eye-opening places as the wretched manufacturing towns (whose savage 'truck system', which keeps the workers in a state of virtual slavery, is vividly described). At Marney Abbey (a ruin, in the environs of the distressed rural town of Marney) Egremont meets by chance a highly intelligent working-class radical, Walter Gerard, who instructs him on the two nations that Victoria rules over. Egremont is highly impressed by his new mentor and even more impressed by the sudden 'divine melody' he hears being sung by Gerard's daughter, Sybil, dressed as a nun (or 'Religious') among the broken-down walls of the abbey. A jealous rival for Sybil's love, the moral-force radical Stephen Morley, conceives a morbid jealousy of Egremont, and assaults him in a deep mist. But the hero survives the cowardly attack, although a rift develops between him and Sybil when she discovers his true identity. The action climaxes with a great Chartist riot set in the early 1840s. During the storming of Mowbray Castle, Walter Gerard and Stephen Morley (now an outright apostle of violence) are killed. Egremont rescues Sybil from the mob. The novel ends with the inevitable reconciliation of the lovers and a rousing address to the youth of England:

'We live in an age when to be young and to be indifferent can no longer be synonymous. We must prepare for the coming hour. The claims of the Future are represented by suffering millions; and the Youth of a Nation are the trustees of Posterity.' The strength of the novel is its range of social coverage: from the 'saloons of the mighty' to Lancashire mill towns (during the great 'stick-out' of 1842) to the rurally deprived Home Counties. As a recipe for the social problems* of the day, Disraeli's Young England programme of nostalgic neo-feudalism is unpersuasive, symbolised as it is by the 'true' aristocratic union of Egremont and Sybil (who turns out to have blue blood in her veins). The 'One Nation' concept has, however, become a commonplace of subsequent Conservative political idealism.

Sylvia's Lovers, Mrs E. Gaskell, 1863, 3 vols, Smith, Elder. (The second edition of the novel, published in the same year, had four very fine illustrations by George Du Maurier*.) Mrs Gaskell's only historical* novel, set in the Napoleonic Wars and inspired by a holiday the author spent at Whitby on the Yorkshire coast (called 'Monkshaven' in the novel), a town dependent on whale-fishing at the turn of the century. Sylvia Robson, a farmer's daughter, has, as the title implies, two lovers. One is her cousin, the prudent draper's shop assistant Philip Hepburn who has been brought up among the Quakers and is on the way to becoming a prosperous business man. Sylvia's other lover is the wild 'specksioneer' (harpooner), Charley Kinraid, to whom she plights her troth with the traditional half-a-sixpence. By chance, Philip sees Charley taken by a navy press gang, and his rival shouts to him to let Sylvia know what has happened to him. But for his own mean motives, Philip lets her think Charley has been drowned, thus clearing the way for his courtship. Sylvia's father, Daniel Robson, hates the press gangs, and is hanged at York for murdering one of their number. His wife goes mad. Alone in the world, Sylvia consents to marry Philip. A year later, Kinraid returns a lieutenant. Shamed, Philip runs away and joins the army. At the siege of Acre (1799), Charley and Philip meet again. Philip saves his rival's life, and is horribly disfigured in the fighting. He returns to Monkshaven where Sylvia and his child Bella do not at first recognise him. Eventually he and his wife are reunited (Kinraid meanwhile having married a Bristol heiress) and Philip dies forgiven. Sylvia herself dies prematurely before her daughter grows up.

SYNGE, W[illiam] W[ebb] Follett (1826–91). Synge, the son of a clergyman, was educated abroad. In 1846 he took up a career in diplomacy and was attached to the British Legation at Washington from 1851 to 1853 where he met and married his American wife. At this period of his life, Synge came to know many of the leading men of letters of the day, including Thackeray*. He was subsequently Commissioner for the Sandwich Islands in 1861 and served as a commissary judge and Consul-General in Cuba in 1865. Synge's health collapsed and he retired from the Foreign Office in 1868 with a pension of £600 a year. In his retirement he contributed to *Punch** and the *Saturday Review**. He also wrote some fiction, including: *Olivia Raleigh* (1875) and *Tom Singleton, Dragoon And Dramatist* (1879), which the author dramatised himself for the stage. Synge died at Eastbourne. BL 2. *DNB*. Wol.

T

TABLEY, Baron De [John Byrne Leicester Warren] ('William P. Lancaster', 1835–95). Born in Tabley House, Knutsford, Cheshire, Tabley was the son of the second Baron de Tabley. As John Warren he was brought up (largely by his mother) in Italy and Germany and later educated at Eton and Christ Church, Oxford, graduating in 1859. He was called to the Bar in 1860, but seems not to have practised nor ever to have intended to. He instead lived a leisurely life at his father's estate in Cheshire, where he was an officer in the militia and pursued a lifelong interest in numismatics. In 1871, he returned to London, where he was well known as a clubman. Warren published numerous volumes of verse under the pseudonyms George F. Preston and William P. Lancaster. Anonymously he published tragedies on classical Greek themes. One of his plays, *The Soldier's Fortune*, succeeded in not selling a single copy. Warren also produced a survey of the flora of Cheshire and four novels (as 'Lancaster'): *A Screw Loose* (1868); *Ropes Of Sand* (1869); *Hence These Tears* (1872); *Salvia Richmond* (1878). BL 4. *DNB. NCBEL*. Wol. Sad.

The Tale Of Chloe, George Meredith, 1894, 1 vol, Ward, Lock. (First published in the *New Quarterly Magazine*, July 1879.) A tragic novella written in Meredith's most arch style, elaborating on the ballad of 'Fair Chloe'. Chloe (i.e. Miss Catherine Martinsward), a young lady living in eighteenth-century Bath, sacrifices her fortune to save her lover, the reckless Sir Martin Caseldy, a 'beau', from prison. But he deserts her. Caseldy eventually returns, but only to seduce 'the Duchess of Dewlap'. Formerly a dairymaid raised in station by marriage to a duke old enough to be her grandfather, the Duchess has been left in Chloe's and Beau Beamish's care. The heroine hangs herself on the door through which the errant Caseldy and his Duchess plan to elope. The rope is a skein in which she has made knots for every one of her lover's infidelities. The story is subtitled 'An Episode In The History Of Beau Beamish', who figures chorically throughout and narrates the events fifteen years after.

A Tale Of Two Cities, Charles Dickens, 1859, 1 vol, Chapman and Hall. (Serialised without illustrations in *All The Year Round**, April–November 1859 and simultaneously in monthly numbers June–December 1859, illustrated by Phiz*.) Dickens's romance about the French Revolution, with which he launched his new weekly magazine. The action of the novel shifts between the two cities of London and Paris. In France, Dr Manette has been imprisoned for eighteen years in the Bastille. His offence was to uncover the moral delinquencies of the Marquis St Evrémonde. In prison he maintains a precarious sanity by cobbling shoes. At the beginning of the story Manette has been brought to London by his solicitor Mr Lorry, to recover his wits in the care of his daughter Lucie. Lucie is loved by Charles

Darnay, a Frenchman who, although he conceals the fact, is a nephew of the Marquis. At a trial for espionage, a remarkable (and legally convenient) physical resemblance is observed between Darnay and an idle but brilliant young barrister, Sidney Carton. Carton also secretly loves Lucie. Having married Lucie, Darnay returns to Paris during the Terror, and is arrested for treason on the instigation of two embittered citizens, the Defarges. Carton follows Darnay to Paris, and nobly substitutes himself for the condemned man, dying at the guillotine with the famous melodramatic valediction: 'It is a far, far better thing that I do, than I have ever done.' The novel drew heavily on Carlyle's *The French Revolution* (1837) and may also owe something to Bulwer[-Lytton's*] *Zanoni** (1842).

Tancred, Or The New Crusade, Benjamin Disraeli, 1847, 3 vols, Colburn. The third part of Disraeli's Young England* trilogy. The theme of the novel is extravagantly mystical, unlike its social problem* predecessors. Tancred (Lord Montacute) is the son and heir of the Duke and Duchess of Bellamont and at the beginning of the novel is about to come of age. Rather than take his place in Parliament, Tancred (a paragon of talent and beauty) travels to the Middle East, in order to communicate directly with God on the subject of Duty and Faith. (The consternation of his aristocratic parents is one of the comic highlights of the novel, which is Disraeli's most amusing.) Before leaving, Tancred has a long discussion with the omnicompetent Jew, Sidonia, who earlier figured in *Coningsby**. At Sinai, God (appearing as a 'mighty form') instructs Tancred to spread the 'doctrine of theocratic equality'. The hero subsequently becomes involved in sectarian struggles in the Lebanon where he is duped by the intriguer Fakredeen and finally falls in love with a young Jewess, Eva. The novel climaxes with the unexpected arrival of his parents in Jerusalem. The novel is written in Disraeli's most flowery style and is dedicated to the cult of youthful heroism and racial regeneration that made up the main plank of the Young England programme.

Tauchnitz (1837–1943). Publisher. The firm was founded by the Baron [Christian Bernhard] Tauchnitz, in Leipzig, Germany, in 1837. From the first, Tauchnitz established itself as the principal publisher of cheap, one-volume reprints of English novels (in English) for continental readers. Unusually, Tauchnitz entered into contract agreements (for a standard £50 fee) with British authors. He was for this reason much admired by the British writing profession. Dickens*, for instance, sent a son to learn German with Baron Tauchnitz. The firm prospered until utterly destroyed by an RAF raid on Leipzig in 1943. Only a surprisingly small number of Tauchnitz reprints seem to have seeped back into the British market, despite their cheapness and attractive format.

TAUTPHOEUS, Baroness Von [Jemima] (née Montgomery, 1807–93). Jemima Montgomery was born in Seaview, Co. Donegal, the daughter of a gentleman and the niece of a baronet. At the age of thirty-one she married the Baron von Tautphoeus (1805–85), chamberlain to the King of Bavaria, and it was there that she spent most of the rest of her life. Her fiction contains sensitive observations of continental (especially German) life and manners. Her first published novel, *The Initials* (1850), was published in three volumes by Richard Bentley*. The story follows the experiences of Mr Hamilton, a young Englishman in Germany. Through a confusion with the initials of names on letters, he becomes acquainted with a Bavarian, Baron Zedwitz, and his wife. This leads to romance, and at the end of the narrative the hero has settled down in Bavaria with his sweetheart Hildegarde on the grounds that: 'a poor man really can enjoy life in Germany; it is only a rich one who could do so in England.' The novel is charmingly inconsequential, although it ends ominously on the eve of the 1848 Revolution. *The Initials* pleased English readers and was followed by: *Cyrilla* (1853), a tale of crime in high German places founded on certain 'facts' which the author suppressed in the reprinted text of 1872; *Quits* (1857), a lighter-toned story with a Tyrolean setting; *At Odds** (1863), a Bavarian-set historical* novel. Within her range of subject-matter, Tautphoeus is an underrated writer who consciously set out to explain German ways to a British readership. She died in Munich. BL 4. *DNB. NCBEL.* Wol. Sad.

TAYLOR, Captain [Philip] Meadows (1808–76). Taylor was born in the city of Liverpool, where his father was a merchant. Business troubles led to Philip, as the eldest son, being sent at fifteen to India, to work in the house of a Bombay merchant with the prospect of an eventual partnership. Chafing at commercial service, Taylor took a commission in the Nizam's forces in Hyderabad in 1824. This region in the Deccan was to be his base for the next thirty-six years. Soon after, in 1824, he re-entered civilian life and undertook a strenuous programme of self-education in engineering, law and surveying, preparatory to a career in the Nizam's administration. A man of powerful intellectual and physical energy, Taylor interested himself particularly in the Thug assassins' cult, recently uncovered by Colonel Sleeman. His first novel (and still his most widely read) was the semi-documentary *The Confessions Of A Thug** (1839). The work, written during convalescence from a bout of malaria in 1837, was suggested by Bulwer-Lytton* and published while Taylor was on furlough in England. It was an instant success with the English public (Queen Victoria was an early and avid reader). At his publisher's suggestion, Taylor followed in some haste with *Tippoo Sultaun* (1840), a tale of the Mysore War climaxing with the battle of Seringapatam. He also married in 1840 and returned to India where until 1853 he acted as *The Times* correspondent to the sub-continent. As an administrator in Hyderabad in 1841, Taylor pacified Shorapore without recourse to force of arms. In the capacity of Regent (for an under-age ruler) Taylor demonstrated similar finesse as a governor. After 1853 he had various high administrative posts, all of which he seems to have performed with distinction. He served twenty years without furlough, during which all thought of writing fiction was shelved. In 1860, his health (and apparently his mind) failed and he returned to England. In his retirement, he conceived a series of novels, covering the whole cycle of colonial Indian history: *Tara, A Mahratta Tale* (1863) deals with the imposition of Mahratta rule in 1657; *Ralph Darnell* (1865), a much weaker novel, follows the conquests of Clive at Plassey in 1757 marking the rise of English power; *Seeta* (1872) deals with the Mutiny of 1857. Taylor's *History Of India* came out in 1870 and his last novel, *A Noble Queen* (1878), was published posthumously. A feeble effort, it is set in the early seventeenth century and chronicles the heroic resistance to the Mogul invasion and the siege of Ahmednugger. Like other English novelists of India (Annie Steel*, or E. M. Forster, for instance) he evidently had more sympathy for the Muhammadans than the Hindus. And in general, he was incapable of presenting any English character convincingly in his fiction. Taylor was made a Companion of the Star of India in 1869, went blind in 1875, and published his autobiography, *The Story Of My Life*, in 1877. For a man who has been called 'the last of the adventurers' it is an astonishingly pedestrian document. He died at Mentone in France on the return from a last trip to his beloved India. Reviewing Taylor's last novel the *Spectator* claimed that he had done more to educate the English public on 'the natives of India than all the formal histories that were ever written'. BL 6. *DNB*. RM. *NCBEL*. Wol. Sad.

Temple Bar (1860–1906). The most successful of *Cornhill*'s* rivals. Like the other magazine, *Temple Bar* was a 'London Journal', and 1s. monthly, but (as originally conceived) unillustrated. The journal was launched in December 1860 by John Maxwell* with the gifted bohemian author George Sala* as its editor. Sala was also a main contributor of fiction and wrote his *The Seven Sons Of Mammon** (1862) and *The Strange Adventures Of Captain Dangerous* (1862) for the periodical. Another popular feature in the magazine's early numbers was Miss Braddon's* *Aurora Floyd** (1863). In a preface to the first volume, Sala confided in the reader that the editor and proprietor had toyed with the idea of woodcut illustrations, but decided instead to go for an extra sixteen pages of text. As a result, for his 1s. the purchaser had a massive 144 pages. The contents were miscellaneous, with a strong emphasis on serialised fiction. But the initial circulation of 30,000 soon dropped and the chronically impecunious Maxwell sold the property of the magazine to Sala around 1862. Sala retained ownership until 1866, when the magazine (now edited by Edmund Yates*) passed to Richard Bentley* who retained Maxwell's original conception. Under the new editorship of Bentley's son George, *Temple Bar* enjoyed a long period of prosperous stability. (It was merged with the ailing *Bentley's Miscellany** in 1868.) Contributors under the Bentley regime were Wilkie Collins*, Maarten Maartens*, Charles Reade*, Henry Kingsley*, George Gissing*, R. L. Stevenson* and Anthony Trollope*. Following Braddon's successful début, the magazine accommodated a high quality of woman novelist contributor, featuring major works by Mrs Henry Wood*, Rhoda Broughton* and A. B. Edwards*. George Bentley died in 1895, and the house of Bentley went under in 1898. Macmillan* kept the now unfashionable magazine going for another few years. Unlike many of the rivals to *Cornhill*, *Temple Bar* contrived to create a distinct personality for itself as a bohemian-flavoured journal. *WI. BLM.*

Ten Thousand A Year, Samuel Warren, 1841, 3 vols, Blackwood. (Serialised in *Blackwood's Magazine**, October 1839–August 1841.) One of the most successful comic novels of the century. Thanks to the legal forgeries of Snap, Gammon and Quirk, a diminutive draper's assistant, Mr Tittlebat Titmouse, inherits a fortune and a Yorkshire estate that is not rightfully his. He gives up his £35-a-year post in the Oxford Street establishment of Dowlas, Tagrag, Bobbin and Co. to live in high and vulgar style. The proper heir, Charles Aubrey MP, and his sister Kate are driven out of their house. Gammon proceeds to blackmail Titmouse who is in fact a bastard. Now a gentleman (at least in outward appearance) Titmouse contracts a fashionable marriage with Lady Cecilia Dreddlington and buys a seat in Parliament. He is courted by his former master, Tagrag. Finally, he is unmasked, stripped of his ten thousand a year and ends his life in a lunatic asylum. Gammon kills himself, Quirk and Snap are imprisoned and the virtuous Aubreys resume their property. The funniest things in the novel are the names and the cleverest things the intricate legal machinations.

The Tenant Of Wildfell Hall, Acton Bell (i.e. Anne Brontë), 1848, 3 vols, Newby. An epistolary novel, told in a series of letters between Gilbert Markham and his brother-in-law Mr Halford. The tenant of the title is Mrs Graham, a mother accompanied by a young boy, Arthur. Mrs Graham is mysterious; an accomplished artist, she is strangely nervous and anxious for her child, whom she always keeps by her. It emerges that her real name is Helen Huntingdon. And she is not, as given out, a widow but is married to a drunkard, Arthur Huntingdon. Helen confesses all to Gilbert by giving him her journal. It records how she was cajoled into marriage by an aunt. But the marriage was doomed by Huntingdon's chronic drinking and infidelity. Imprisoned in her husband's house, she finally contrived to escape and took on a new identity at Wildfell Hall. In a melodramatic climax to the narrative, Huntingdon falls from his horse and is nursed on his deathbed by his abnormally dutiful wife. He finally secures a bottle of wine, and hastens his end. A year later, Helen marries Gilbert. The story is notable for its depiction of the degradations of alcoholic addiction, presumably observed at first hand in Anne's brother Branwell.

TENNIEL, [Sir] John (1820–1914). Illustrator and cartoonist. Tenniel was born in London, the youngest son of a dancing master, and educated at the Royal Academy Schools . His illustrations to *Aesop's Fables* in 1848 brought him to the notice of Mark Lemon*, editor of *Punch**. Tenniel subsequently replaced Richard Doyle* in 1851 when he left (over the paper's anti-Catholic line). Ten years later, Tenniel became principal cartoonist for *Punch*, with the departure of John Leech* (who died in 1864). Over the years, Tenniel supplied more than 2,000 cartoons to the paper, including such immortal designs as 'Dropping The Pilot' (1890). He also illustrated Lewis Carroll's* *Alice's Adventures In Wonderland** (1865) and its successor, *Through The Looking Glass** (1871). He did the impressive pictures for Shirley Brooks's* *The Gordian Knot** (1860) and worked for *Once A Week** in the early 1860s. Tenniel specialised in studies of animals, although his figure drawing is also fine. He was knighted in 1893. *DNB*. Hou.

A Terrible Temptation, Charles Reade, 1871, 3 vols, Chapman and Hall. (Serialised in *Cassell's Magazine**, April–September 1871, with illustrations by F. T. Merrill.) After the social problem* novel, *Put Yourself In His Place**, Reade turned to a domestic* plot, using his favourite stage devices of mysterious birth and fraudulent inheritance. The early narrative centres on the rivalry of two cousins, Sir Charles and Richard Bassett. The latter is a malcontent who conceives himself done out of his inheritance. Moreover, Sir Charles is a rival suitor to Arabella Bruce, the red-haired heiress whom both men woo. Charles is the preferred lover and eventually marries

Arabella. The plot thickens with the replacement of one of Richard's bastard babies for the legitimate Bassett heir, Bella initially proving barren (the blood mother is a resourceful servant, Mary Wells). Sir Charles (who is unaware of the transfer) after being provoked by Richard, falls into an epileptic fit, and is kidnapped and incarcerated in a lunatic asylum. (The social propaganda around which Reade built this novel was the abuse of lunacy certification.) There follows Reade's customary rescue. The false heir Reginald grows up a scapegrace and his parentage is finally revealed after he burgles Richard Bassett's house. The cousins are reconciled at last and Richard's daughter marries Charles's second (and true-born) son. *A Terrible Temptation* has a number of incidental points of interest. Reade incorporates, in the character of Mr Rolfe, the author-detective, a portrait of himself and of his 'factual' working methods. The character of Sir Charles's discarded mistress, Rhoda Somerset, provoked extreme critical hostility and *The Times* advised mothers to keep the first volume away from unmarried daughters.

Tess Of The D'Urbervilles, Thomas Hardy, 1891, 3 vols, Osgood, McIlvaine. (Serialised in watered-down form in the *Graphic*, July–December 1891.) A Wessex* novel, set more nearly in the present than others Hardy wrote. Subtitled 'A Pure Woman', it is the melancholy life story of a peasant girl who ends on the scaffold. Her troubles begin when her drunken father, Jack Durbeyfield, is informed that he has the noble blood of the d'Urbervilles in his veins. Tess herself inadvertently jeopardises the family's income when their horse is killed while she is driving. In her guilt, she appeals to the rich d'Urbervilles (who have in fact bought the family name), and is seduced (or possibly raped) by her so-called cousin, Alec. Tess bears a child which dies and which she is forced to bury without benefit of Christian service. As a 'maiden no more' she takes up work at Talbothays dairy in Froom Vale. Here Tess evolves 'from simple girl to complex woman'. She falls in love with an idealistic young gentleman, Angel Clare, a clergyman's son who fondly imagines that in Tess he has found rustic purity. They marry. But the union is doomed when Tess's letter of confession (delivered on the night before the ceremony) goes astray. When he discovers what he has married, Angel cannot repress his disgust, and the couple part. Her life becomes ever harder, and she is obliged to labour in the fields at Flintcomb Ash Farm. At this stage, Alec reappears. He has undergone a spurious spiritual rebirth and now masquerades as a preacher. Tess's father dies and with his death the family lose their right to the cottage they occupy. Tess takes charge, and removes the surviving Durbeyfields to Kingsbere. Alec renews his attentions to Tess and she surrenders, just at the point when Angel returns from Brazil to forgive her. Tess murders Alec, and she and Angel take flight from the law. She is finally arrested by the police, sleeping on the sacrificial stone at Stonehenge. She hangs, and Angel is last seen walking away with her little sister. Hardy's ironic last word notes that 'the President of the Immortals (in Aeschylean phrase) had ended his sport with Tess'.

THACKERAY, William Makepeace (1811–63). Thackeray was born in India where his father held office as a Collector (i.e. senior Civil Servant), before dying in 1816. Thackeray's mother remarried Major Henry Carmichael-Smyth, immortalised later as 'Colonel Newcome', and the son was returned to England as a little boy in 1817. He had the education of a gentleman at Charterhouse ('Slaughterhouse' and 'Grey Friars' in the fiction) and Trinity College, Cambridge ('St Boniface' in *Pendennis**), though he left the university without a degree in June 1830. After false starts in law in England, drawing and journalism in Paris, Thackeray began a ten-year-long stint as a free-lance writer in the mid-1830s. By 1836 he had largely squandered his patrimony by gambling and newspaper proprietorship and had married improvidently an Irish girl with no dowry, Isabella Shawe (a fictional recollection of this formative period is given in *Philip**). Having borne him three daughters, two of whom survived, Isabella developed incurable insanity. After 1840 man and wife were permanently parted, she being put in care and he returning to the club life of his bachelorhood. Professionally, Thackeray had meanwhile made a reputation for himself, notably in the various pseudonymous pieces he wrote for *Fraser's Magazine**. Between 1838 and 1841 he produced the savagely satirical *Yellowplush Correspondence* and *Catherine**, and the somewhat more sentimental *A Shabby Genteel Story** and *The Great Hoggarty Diamond*. In 1844 *Fraser's* brought out his most substantial fiction to date, *Barry Lyndon**. His contributions to *Fraser's* (which include a multitude of lesser pieces, many of which have probably not been identified) diminished in the early 1840s, after he formed his connection with *Punch**, the newly established comic weekly. With this journal Thackeray had his first unequivocal success with the reading public, *The Snobs Of England** (1846–47, republished in 1848 as *The Book Of Snobs*). It was *Punch's* publishers, Bradbury and Evans*, probably encouraged by the triumph of Thackeray's satirical anatomy of England, who brought out the author's first major novel, *Vanity Fair**. Thackeray apparently began to write this work in February 1845, intending it for Colburn's* *New Monthly Magazine**, a journal which had published, among other things, his burlesque *Major Gahagan** in 1838. On rejection the early chapters of 'The Novel Without A Hero' (i.e. *Vanity Fair*) were set aside until Bradbury and Evans made a firm offer in January 1846, engaging to bring the work out in the middle of that year. Again publication was postponed, probably to avoid a clash with Dickens's* *Dombey And Son**. *Vanity Fair's* first monthly number finally appeared in January 1847, in the thirty-two page, illustrated format which Dickens had revived successfully with *Pickwick Papers** in 1836 (Thackeray's wrappers were yellow, as against the duck egg green of Dickens). Unlike Dickens, Thackeray did his own illustrations for *Vanity Fair*, offering in addition to the two full plates per instalment, numerous deft woodcuts, work for which the years in *Punch* had been a perfect training. (Thackeray also illustrated two other of his full-length works, *Pendennis* and *The Virginians**.) It is not clear that Bradbury and Evans intended *Vanity Fair* to go the full Dickensian quota of twenty numbers. In fact the serial did not do well at first, though it picked up after the third number. Thereafter it enjoyed great success with the discriminating reader, establishing Thackeray as the second novelist in Britain after Dickens. It should be noted, however, that he was never a popular novelist in Dickens's class: *Vanity Fair* sold under 10,000 per number in its monthly issue; *Dombey And Son* over 20,000 at exactly the same period and at exactly the same price. *Vanity Fair* marks the turning-point in Thackeray's professional career. It has been observed by his official biographer, G. N. Ray, that it marks the turning point in the novelist's personal life as well. In 1847 he gave up his largely bohemian life and settled himself with his two daughters in Kensington. Hitherto Thackeray had been a 'penny a liner'. Now he was a 'serious' novelist, and by virtue of the fame which *Vanity Fair* brought, was returned to his proper sphere as a 'gentleman'. He embarked on a strenuous career in this morally enlarged personality. In 1848–50 *Pendennis* came out in twenty-four monthly numbers (Bradbury and Evans, who had given £60 a number for *Vanity Fair* gave £100 for the instalments of *Pendennis*: they again sold about 10,000). In 1852 Thackeray changed publishers and produced the historical* novel *Henry Esmond** in the traditional three volumes (Smith, Elder* gave £1,200 for an edition of 2,750). He returned to Bradbury and Evans and serialisation with *The Newcomes**, 1853–55 (twenty-four numbers, £200 per number; around 14,000 sold of the monthly issues). Bradbury and Evans also brought out the sequel to *Esmond*, *The Virginians*, 1857–59 (twenty-four numbers, £250 per number, 13,000 average sale). The publishers lost money on *The Virginians*, nor did the slackly strung tale of the American Revolution find favour with the critics. Thackeray's career in fact seemed stalled in 1859 when Smith, Elder and Co. reappeared. George Smith, always a huge admirer of Thackeray, offered him the editorship of the newly conceived *Cornhill Magazine**. Thackeray accepted this lucrative post (it was to bring him up to £600 in some months). The venture was a huge success. *Cornhill* was the first 'quality' Victorian magazine regularly to break the 100,000 sales threshold. As well as editing it and recruiting such protégés as Trollope*, Thackeray contributed *Philip* and *The Roundabout Papers*. After giving up the editorship in 1862, and despite some rancour, Thackeray retained a connection. His last, incomplete novel, *Denis Duval**, was published posthumously in the magazine. The years of fame, 1847–63, had been tranquil, if not entirely happy ones for the novelist. Notable events were the illness which nearly killed him in 1849, and which suspended the publication of *Pendennis*; the painful 'Brookfield affair' in which the novelist seems to have fallen in love with his best friend's wife Jane Octavia Brookfield* (the melancholy produced by this episode, which reached a crisis in 1851, permeates *Esmond*); the American lecture tours in 1852 with *The English Humourists Of The Eighteenth Century*, and in 1855 with *The Four Georges*; the unsuccessful attempt to enter Parliament as an 'Independent Liberal' in 1857; the 'Garrick Club affair' in 1858, when the published insults of Dickens's protégé, Edmund Yates*, precipitated a public row with the other novelist; the removal to 2 Palace Green, Kensington in 1862, the house being built to Thackeray's architectural directions in his beloved 'Queen Anne' style. It was shortly after moving to this new luxurious home that Thackeray died, prematurely. His daughter Anne [Ritchie*] was to go on to become a successful novelist in her own right. BL 9. *DNB*. RM. *NCBEL*. Wol. Sad.

That Lass O' Lowrie's, Frances Hodgson Burnett, 1877, 3 vols, Warne. Burnett's first successful novel, and her most characteristically English work. The story is set in the Lancashire mining town of Riggan. Joan Lowrie ('that lass') is a pit-girl, the daughter of a drunken and brutal miner. She catches the attention of an engineer newly arrived from London, Fergus Derrick, and of his friend, the Curate, Paul Grace. These two young men become suitors for the hand of the Rector's daughter, Anice Barholm. But Fergus is attracted also to the Junoesque Joan. The love affair is threatened when he dismisses her father, Dan Lowrie, for imperilling pit safety by opening his Davy lamp. Lowrie plans to throw acid in Fergus's face, but is himself killed. In a tremendous climax, Joan heroically rescues Fergus after a pit explosion. When he recovers, he offers himself to her. She refuses, until she feels good enough for 'th' man I love'. The author handles local setting and dialect well, and the work (to Burnett's rage presumably) was successfully but piratically dramatised the following year by Charles Reade* as *Joan*.

THOMAS, George H[ousman] (1824–68). Wood engraver and illustrator. Thomas was born in London, the son of a shipbroker. He trained as a wood engraver, and began his career as a book illustrator in Paris. In that city he worked for American expatriates, and he subsequently went to New York in 1846. But his attempts to launch magazines in that country failed, and he returned to England in 1848. Over the next twenty years, he illustrated a number of novels, including Wilkie Collins's* *Armadale** and Anthony Trollope's* *The Last Chronicle Of Barset**. His brother, William L. Thomas (1820–1900), was also trained as an illustrator and engraver. He accompanied George to America on his ill-fated expedition in 1846. William Thomas began to work on their return for the *Illustrated London News** and was inspired to found the rival *Graphic* in 1869. The paper (which carried a great deal of illustrated fiction) was extremely successful, and Thomas followed up with the *Daily Graphic* in 1890, the first illustrated daily newspaper in England. Hou.

THOMAS, W[illiam] Moy (1828–1910). Thomas was born in Hackney, London, the younger son of a solicitor. He was educated under the supervision of an uncle, J. H. Thomas (also a lawyer). William, after a dutiful start in the legal profession, decided instead on literature for his career. For a while he served as private secretary to Charles Dilke (editor of the *Athenaeum**) and in 1850 became acquainted through him with Charles Dickens*, who hired him as a regular contributor to *Household Words**. (The stories which Thomas contributed to the journal were later collected in volume form as *When The Snow Falls*, 1859.) This led on to a wide-ranging career in higher journalism. Thomas was the first editor of *Cassell's Magazine* in which his sensation* novel set around Canvey Island in Essex, *A Fight For Life* (1868), was serialised. Otherwise his output was miscellaneous and his most enduring work was an edition of Lady Wortley Montagu's correspondence in 1887. In his later journalistic career (cut short by chronic illness in 1901) he was mainly the drama critic for various London papers. Thomas was also a prominent figure in the struggle for authors' copyright. BL 2. *DNB*.

THOMPSON, Sir Henry ('Pen Oliver, F.R.C.S.', 1820–1904). Thompson was born in Framlingham, Suffolk, a shopkeeper's son. On his mother's side he was the grandson of the artist Samuel Medley. Thompson came to London as a young man in the early 1840s and embarked on a medical career in which he was to excel. Graduating from University College as a gold medallist in 1851, he was made a Fellow of the Royal College of Surgeons in 1853. As a surgeon at University College Hospital (specialising in operations on genito-urinary organs) he rose to the top of his profession and was appointed Queen Victoria's personal physician. A man of a superabundant intellectual energy, he was also an amateur astronomer, artist and man of letters. Thompson was a passionate advocate of cremation (illegal in England until 1855) and it was largely due to his efforts that the first public crematorium at Woking was established. A friend of both Anthony Trollope* and Edmund Yates*, he persuaded both to be founders of the Cremation Society of England in 1874. Under the pseudonym 'Pen Oliver' he published two novels: *Charley Kingston's Aunt* (1884), 'A Study Of Medical Life And Experience' in the 1830s; and *All But* (1886). The second of these, a chronicle of country life, was illustrated by the author. Thompson was knighted in 1867 and was famous among his contemporaries as a London dinner party host. (His speciality was the 'Octave', companies of eight guests meeting at eight o'clock.) BL 2. *DNB.* Wol.

THOMSON, Mrs Anthony Todd [Katharine] (née Byerley, 1797–1862). Katharine Byerley was the seventh daughter of an employee (and relative by marriage) of the Wedgwood pottery family. In 1820, she married an eminent physician, Anthony Todd Thomson. He encouraged her to take up historical writing, which she successfully did with a series of anecdotal biographies of eighteenth-century and other notables. In the late 1830s and early 1840s the Thomsons were prominent in literary society and were friendly with Thackeray* and Bulwer-Lytton*. On her husband's death in 1849, she lived abroad as a widow for some years. The death in 1860 of her son Henry (with whom she had collaborated on two history books) was a blow from which she never recovered. Thomson's fiction (which was published for the library reader by Colburn* and Bentley*) includes: *Constance* (1833); *Widows And Widowers* (1842); *Tracey, Or The Apparition* (1847); *Faults On Both Sides* (1858). BL 10. *DNB.* Wol.

THORBURN, S[eptimus] S[met] (1844–1924). Little is known about Thorburn. He was educated at Cheltenham and served in the Bengal Civil Service (1865–99), rising to the high position of financial commissioner for the Punjab. In India, Thorburn took a scholarly interest in the country's history and published a number of books on the country, including the novels: *David Leslie, A Story Of The Afghan Frontier* (1879); *His Majesty's Greatest Subject* (1897), a future fantasy story about the hero who 'saved the Empire' in the early twentieth century when it was threatened by revolutionary independence movements; *Transgression* (1899), a story of the contemporary North West frontier. BL 4. *WW.*

The Three Clerks, Anthony Trollope, 1857, 3 vols, Bentley. An early and interestingly autobiographical novel, written before the author had earned any great fame. Two of the three clerks are Henry Norman and Alaric Tudor who work in the Weights and Measures Office of the Civil Service. The third, Charley Tudor, works in the Internal Navigation office. This male trio is partnered by the three daughters of Henry's cousin, Mrs Woodward. Henry is defeated by Alaric for the love of the eldest Woodward sister, Gertrude. He turns for consolation to the second Woodward sister, Linda. An unexpected inheritance enables him to marry her. Charley is that favourite Trollopian type, a 'hobbledehoy'. He has almost ruined himself by dissipation and entanglement with a barmaid, Norah Geraghty. (This parallels the description Trollope gives in the *Autobiography* of his first ill-spent years in the Post Office.) Despite all the bad signs, however, Charley makes good and, having overcome all prejudice against him, marries the sweetest of Mrs Woodward's daughters, Kate (a character of whom Trollope was especially proud). Alaric is led by his overweening ambition ('Excelsior!' is his motto) to ruin. He is seduced by a dishonest MP, Undy Scott, into using his official position to make profitable investments. He gets in too deep, is tried at the Old Bailey where, despite the efforts of his lawyer, Mr Chaffanbrass (who reappears in Trollope's novels, notably in *Orley Farm**, 1862), he receives six months' imprisonment. Gertrude stands by him, and helped by Henry the chastened couple emigrate to New Zealand. *The Three Clerks*, despite its divided plot, is among the most zestful of Trollope's comic novels. It also expresses his views on how ineffectively worth is measured by the public examination system recently introduced into the English Civil Service.

The Three Impostors, Arthur Machen, 1895, 1 vol, John Lane. (Published as No. XIX of the *Keynotes** series.) According to the author, 'an imitation I regret to say, of Stevenson's* *Dynamiters*'. Like the other work and like Conan Doyle's* Sherlock Holmes series this is a collection of short tales and fragments, connected by the narrating person of Mr Dyson. Dyson is a connoisseur of that part of London Machen loved best: Fitzrovia, north Soho, Bloomsbury. Dyson dedicates himself to 'piercing the city's veils of apparent monotony and meaness'. *The Three Impostors* contains a number of exercises in the macabre, culminating in demonic possession with 'A Strange Occurrence In Clerkenwell'. The book came out in the year of Wilde's* trial, and as a prime instance of literary decadence* was overwhelmed by the moral backlash.

Three Men In A Boat, Jerome K. Jerome, 1889, 1 vol, Dent. (Subtitled, 'To Say Nothing Of The Dog'.) Three friends, George, Harris, the narrator ('J') and the dog Montmorency decide on an expedition up the Thames from Kingston. The novel catalogues a subsequent train of minor comic disaster, beginning with the famous debacle in Hampton Court Maze, to which Harris foolhardily thinks he has the key. The first night under canvas at Runnymede is a catastrophe, climaxing on a meal of tinned pineapples but no tin-opener. The quartet finally reach Oxford. But rain on the return trip leads them to chuck the whole thing in and return furtively to London by train, where they end their expedition at the Alhambra Theatre. Jerome's humorous novel-cum-comic papers is deftly handled. It has been perennially popular and was filmed in the 1950s.

Three-Volume Novel ('three-decker'). The dominant form in which full length new fiction was published from the mid-1820s until 1894: namely three octavo volumes usually costing 31s.6d. and unillustrated. The large expanse of the form led to oversize print, wide margins and relatively few lines on the page. Notoriously, the form encouraged narrative padding, especially a profusion of short-sentenced dialogue by which expanses of white paper could be used up with relatively few words. The binding of the three-decker became progressively more ornate through the century. (Bentley* and Tinsley* covers after the 1870s were particularly brilliant.) The three-decker was almost exclusively purchased by libraries, notably the large metropolitan firms of Mudie* and W. H. Smith's* whose orders could consequently make or break a new novel. This led to de facto censorship and writers such as George Moore* and Henry James complained eloquently about the neutered English reading public, as compared to the French. The multi-volume form disappeared abruptly in 1894 when Smith and Mudie agreed not to buy any work of fiction costing more than 4s. a volume. The three-decker was succeeded by the one-volume novel costing 6s., a form of issue that remained essentially in place until 1939.

Through The Looking Glass, And What Alice Found There, Lewis Carroll (i.e. C. L. Dodgson), 1871, 1 vol, Macmillan. (Illustrated by John Tenniel*.) A sequel to *Alice's Adventures In Wonderland* (1865). In this fantasy, Alice travels into a mirror world, where everything is reversed. Her subsequent progress is based on chess moves during which she meets such figures as Humpty Dumpty and the riddling twins Tweedledum and Tweedledee. The sequel is more artificial and has less narrative than its predecessor but contains (among much else) Carroll's best-known verses about the Walrus and the Carpenter.

THYNNE, Lady [Harriet Frances] (née Bagot, 1816–81). The eldest daughter of Richard Bagot (1782–1854), Bishop of Bath and Wells (1845–54). In 1837 she married the Rev. Charles Thynne, youngest child of the Marquis of Bath. A canon of Canterbury Cathedral from 1845, he entered the Catholic faith in 1852 and died in 1894. Lady Thynne's fashionable fiction includes: *Eleanor Morrison* (1860); *Charlcote Grange* (1861); *Off The Line* (1867); *Colonel Fortescue's Daughter* (1868); *Maud Leslie* (1877). BL 13. Boase. Wol.

Thyrza, George Gissing, 1887, 3 vols, Smith, Elder. Gissing's most idealistic novel. The hero, Walter Egremont, an Oxford-trained idealist, determines to give lectures on literature to the workers in his father's oilcloth factory in Lambeth. Meanwhile, he unsuccessfully proposes marriage to a woman of his own class, Annabel Newthorpe. A young hat-trimmer, Thyrza Trent, also attends Walter's lectures and is inspired by them. She is courted by a middle-aged, self-improving candle maker, Gilbert Grail, whom Walter has put in charge of his working men's library. Walter and Thyrza fall in love, and to protect her from seduction, he leaves the country for America. But instead of marrying Gilbert, Thyrza herself disappears. Unknown to her friends she has taken refuge with a friend of Walter's, Mrs Ormonde, and is training to become a concert singer, to be worthy of her love. But when Walter returns, she is betrayed by her patroness, and finally agrees to marry Gilbert, dying almost immediately of heart disease. Egremont finally marries Annabel Newthorpe. The narrative gives its most intense focus to the heroine's aspiring purity.

Tillotson's Fiction Bureau (1873–1935). An agency founded by William Tillotson in 1873 in Lancashire. Tillotson was the proprietor of a chain of successful north of England newspapers, notably the *Bolton Weekly Journal*. Tillotson negotiated with authors for the serial rights to their novels for instalment publication in his and other, mainly provincial, papers (to whom he would act as agent). His initiative was followed by other bodies such as the National Press Agency, but Tillotson's dominated the field until the twentieth century. For late-Victorian novelists, subsidiary newspaper rights became an important source of income, although generally *feuilleton* serialisation started later and was less important than in France, where it was a main literary outlet from the 1830s onwards. The first major English novel to appear in a newspaper seems to have been Ainsworth's* *Old Saint Paul's**, which ran in the *Sunday Times*, January–December 1841.

The Time Machine, H. G. Wells, 1895, 1 vol, Heinemann. (The story was substantially anticipated in a short fiction, *The Chronic Argonauts*, written by Wells for his college magazine, the *Science Schools Journal*, April–June 1888.) The most famous of time travel science fiction* stories. The Time Traveller (never named) outlines to some friends at dinner his theory that time is a 'fourth dimension' and announces that he intends to travel through it on a device which he shows them. A week later, the dinner guests return, as does a dishevelled Time Traveller. He explains that he has travelled to the year 802,701. There he discovered that mankind has divided into two species. One is a breed of gentle decadents, the Eloi, child-people who spend their time in games and undemanding artistic pursuit. The other, more sinister species, is the Morlocks who live underground with what remains of human technology. They emerge at night to prey on the Eloi. The traveller after various adventures recovers his machine from the Morlocks who have taken it into their underground warren. Before returning to his own time, he travels forward to witness the heat death of the solar system. The novel ends with his departure on a time journey from which he does not return. As critics have observed, the Eloi and the Morlocks are pessimistic projections of the fashionably decadent* intelligentsia and the brutal urban proletariat of the 1890s.

Tinsley Brothers (1858–78). Publishers. The more important of the brothers was William (1831–1902). The son of a Hertfordshire gamekeeper, William Tinsley was educated at a dame's school and came to London at the age of twenty. His younger brother Edward joined him in 1854, and the pair went to work in the London book trade. In 1858 the Tinsleys set up in business together in Catherine Street by the Strand. Their first novel (a genre in which they were to specialise) was G. A. Sala's* *The Seven Sons Of Mammon** (1862). The house initially profited from the competition which arose in the early 1860s with the setting up of various competitors to Mudie's* circulating library, notably Smith's* and the Library Company Limited. Launched in 1862, the Library Company failed in 1865. But while it was in existence, demand for bestselling three-volume novels virtually doubled. The Tinsley brothers had the good fortune to publish Braddon's* *Lady Audley's Secret** in 1862, and its phenomenal success enriched the firm with over £10,000 worth of orders. The more competent brother, Edward, died in 1866, still in his early thirties, leaving the firm in the hands of the affable but too easygoing William. Nevertheless, it was William who founded *Tinsley's Magazine** in 1867 under the noted bohemian, Edmund Yates*. And it was William Tinsley also who had the perception to accept Thomas Hardy's* first published novel, *Desperate Remedies** in 1871, and the charming *Under The Greenwood Tree** (1872). But *Tinsley's Magazine* consistently lost money, and almost went under in 1881, the firm itself having gone bankrupt in 1878, owing some £33,000. William published his garrulous *Random Recollections Of An Old Publisher* in 1900, two years before his death. Most of the more popular novelists of the 1860–80 period published with Tinsley, and his lavishly and colourfully bound three-deckers were a hall mark. William Tinsley had a daughter, Lily (sometimes listed as 'Laura'), who published romances with the family firm in the 1880s. They include: *Cousin Dick* (1885); *In The Ring* (1886); *A London Secret* (1886). (LT) BL 6. (WT) *DNB*. Wol.

Tinsley's Magazine (1867–1892). One of the more popular of the post-*Cornhill** monthly magazines. Like its model, it was illustrated and its contributions (for the first few years, at least) strictly anonymous. *Tinsley's* kicked off with the serial novel, *The Adventures Of Doctor Brady*, by William Howard Russell* and Edmund Yates's* *The Rock Ahead*. For its first two years, the magazine was also edited by Edmund Yates (who had earlier edited the similarly conceived *Temple Bar**). His opening preface declared that the paper would take an interest in things Irish. When Yates resigned, the proprietor, William Tinsley, conducted the journal in an entirely apolitical vein. Serial fiction was a main component in the journal and Mrs Henry Wood* and Mrs J. H. Riddell* supplied stories. But the only novel of literary note to appear in the magazine's pages was Thomas Hardy's* *A Pair Of Blue Eyes** (1872–73). The magazine survived Tinsley's bankruptcy for a few years. By the 1880s, only utter nonentities were serialising fiction in its pages. The magazine suspended publication from June 1887–January 1888, contriving to limp on another four years, still under the flagging editorship of William Tinsley. *BLM*.

TODD, [Dr] Margaret Georgia ('Graham Travers', 1859–1918). Margaret Todd was born in Scotland, her father apparently being a business man with Indian connections. She was educated at Edinburgh, Berlin, Brussels and Glasgow universities, going on to qualify herself at the Edinburgh School of Medicine for Women. She subsequently worked as a physician at the Edinburgh Hospital for Women and Children. As Graham Travers she wrote the novels: *Mona Maclean, Medical Student* (1892); *Fellow Travellers* (1896); *Windyhaugh* (1898). BL 4. *WW*. Wol.

Tom Brown's Schooldays, 'By An Old Boy' (i.e. Thomas Hughes), 1857, 1 vol, Macmillan. The most famous of all boys' school stories. Hughes intended the one-volume tale for juveniles (more particularly, his own son, about to go to Rugby). None the less, *Tom Brown's Schooldays* has always delighted adults, as well. The action goes back to the 1830s, and the reform in education brought about by Dr Arnold. The great headmaster is seldom on stage in the novel, but he looms over it 'like the god in a Greek play'. Tom, the squire's son, enjoys an idyllic childhood in the Vale of the White Horse. At the age of nine, he is dispatched to Rugby. There he is befriended by Harry 'Scud' East and tormented by Harry Flashman. (Hughes does not skirt the sadism rampant in boarding-school life.) The young heroes finally turn on Flashman and thrash him. Eventually, their enemy is expelled for drunkenness. On their part, Tom and his comrades are morally regenerated, but more by the example of their saintly school-fellow George Arthur than by the Olympian 'Doctor'. (Although it was Arnold who sagaciously put Tom in the same study as George, thinking correctly that the contact would christianise him.) The main events of the novel are football, cross-country running, fishing, feasting and various innocent scrapes. At the end of his last term, Tom captains his school cricket team against the MCC. We finish with a whiskered Brown, on vacation from Oxford, hearing of the Doctor's death in 1842, and returning to his beloved Rugby to pay his final respects at his mentor's graveside. The hero's name, Hughes observed, was 'a synonym for the middle classes of Great Britain'. Brown is thus a type. The most acceptable of 'muscular*' heroes, he represents a fusion of the Carlylean Hero, the new post-Crimean joy in physical force and imperial ambition. He is one of 'the great army of Browns who are scattered over the whole empire on which the sun never sets'. *Tom Brown At Oxford* (1861; serialised in *Macmillan's Magazine**, November 1859–July 1861) takes the hero through three years at 'St Ambrose's College', and disastrous near-seduction of the barmaid Patty (again he is saved by a friend, Hardy's, good counsel) to eventual blissful marriage. Hughes's novel has some interesting recollection of the impact of the Oxford movement on undergraduates of the 1840s. But as a narrative it is almost entirely lacking in structure and has never enjoyed the popularity of its predecessor.

Tom Burke Of Ours, Charles Lever, 1844, 2 vols, Curry. (Serialised in monthly parts, February 1843–September 1844, illustrated by Phiz*.) Tom Burke is first discovered a sixteen-year-old Irish orphan of good breeding and little means. Harassed by his father's attorney, Basset, he runs away, with only £100 of his patrimony. He picks up with a companion 'Darby the Blast' who accompanies him through all his later adventures. In Dublin Tom falls in with military friends and gains the nickname 'Burke of Ours'. A French officer Charles de Meudon (one of those who came over to help the Irish in the uprising of 1798) gives the hero an introduction to the French *Polytechnique* (military school) before dying. In Paris Tom becomes an officer of the Hussars and is dangerously involved with the Bourbonists. Charles's sister, Marie de Meudon, secures his release from prison and he goes off to serve gallantly at Austerlitz and Jena. But he is still under suspicion, so he retires to Ireland where he comes into a handsome inheritance. Civilian life soon palls, and Tom returns to serve Napoleon who personally promotes him to the rank of colonel and gives him the Cross of the Legion for bravery against the Austrians. But the imperial cause is lost, as the Emperor tells Burke, advising him to return to Britain. Tom does so, having married Marie (conveniently widowed). The novel is Lever's finest picaresque military tale and pleased its English readership.

TONNA, Mrs [Charlotte Elizabeth] ('Charlotte Elizabeth', née Browne 1790–1846). The daughter of a clergyman and minor canon at the cathedral in Norwich, Charlotte Browne married early in life an army officer, Captain Phelan. She followed him for two years' service in Nova Scotia after which the couple returned to his native Ireland. The Phelans separated around 1824, and she went to live with a brother, Captain John Browne, at Clifton. Here she made the acquaintance of the evangelical writer, Hannah More. She later moved to London and her husband having died in 1837, she married Lewis Hippolytus Tonna (1812–57) in 1841. He was a writer and controversialist on exclusively religious subjects. 'Charlotte Elizabeth', as she called herself, had begun writing tracts (often anti-Catholic) as early as the 1820s. She continued producing a stream of didactic fiction until her death of which *Conformity* (1841) and *Falsehood And Truth* (1841) are typical. Her most interesting work is the early social problem* story, *Helen Fleetwood* (1841), 'A Tale Of The Factories'. BL 36. *DNB*. Wol.

The Tower Of London, W. H. Ainsworth, 1840, 1 vol, Bentley. (Serialised in monthly parts, January–December 1840, illustrated by George Cruikshank*.) *The Tower Of London* covers the period of Lady Jane Grey's rise and fall, July 1553–February 1554. In the manner of Scott's *Kenilworth*, Ainsworth creates a love rivalry between Elizabeth and Mary for the unworthy Courtenay. A mysterious gothic* fringe is added to the historical chronicle with the villainous Simon Renard, counsellor to the Catholic Queen. Below this, is a fictional plot around the young lovers, Cuthbert and Cicely (high-born, if she but knew it). Cicely is coveted by Lawrence Nightgall, the evil Keeper of the Tower. He is privy to all manner of dungeon horrors. Comic relief is provided by the Stone-Kitchen trio of giant warders, Og, Gog, Magog, and their attendant dwarf. The happy ending is furnished by the union of the young people and the hideous death of Nightgall, who plunges from the tower (a climax which inspires one of Cruikshank's finest grotesque illustrations). For all its crudity of technique, *The Tower Of London* is topically effective. The preface concludes with a rousingly loyal address to Queen Victoria and this saga of two beautiful queens flattered the sentiment of the three-year-old Victorian reign. The nationalism of the work is blatant. *The Tower Of London* is the first successful English exploitation of London topography along the lines of Eugène Sue's *Mysteries Of Paris* and, pre-eminently, Victor Hugo's *Notre Dame De Paris*.

TRACY, Louis (1863–1928). Tracy was born in Liverpool and educated privately there and partly in France. From 1884 he worked for some time as a journalist in Darlington in the north of England before undertaking extensive travel in the East (notably in India, 1889–93, where he spent several years, and about which he later wrote a book) and in the USA. On his return, Tracy made a name for himself in London journalism as both a reporter and a proprietor, starting up the *Sun* in 1894. During the first World War he held various responsible staff positions and in 1917 was appointed to the British War Mission to the US. From the early 1890s, Tracy published extensively, including numerous volumes of mystery and adventure. His imperialistic Victorian novel of England against the whole world, *The Final War* (1896), enjoyed some success. BL 38. *WW*.

Treasure Island, Robert Louis Stevenson, 1883, 1 vol, Cassell. (Serialised as 'by Captain George North' in *Young Folks*, October 1881–January 1882.) A strong candidate for the finest boys' adventure story published in the Victorian period. The young hero, Jim Hawkins, helps run the Admiral Benbow inn with his mother and sick father. They have a mysterious sailor, Captain Bones, who lodges with them. After a visit by Blind Pew (who delivers the ominous black spot, the pirates' death sentence) Bones dies. Resourcefully, Jim discovers a map Bones was hiding. It records the island in the Spanish Main on which Captain Flint buried his pirate treasure. Together with Squire Trelawney and Dr Livesey, Jim sets off from Bristol in the *Hispaniola* to find the treasure. A one-legged ship's cook, Long John Silver, incites a mutiny among the crew. It breaks as the *Hispaniola* reaches Treasure Island. There ensues a series of treacheries and fights to the death on board and in Flint's old stockade. Jim discovers Ben Gunn who was marooned on the island, and contrives to take the *Hispaniola* from the mutineers single-handed (shooting the villainous coxswain, Israel Hands, in the process). When a truce is called, and Flint's chest dug up, it is found to be empty. Gunn has removed it. This final trick defeats the mutineers, although Silver escapes with a sackful of coins in the West Indies. The story is told through Jim's perceptive, but often naïve view of things.

Trilby, George du Maurier, 1894, 3 vols, Osgood, McIlvaine. (Serialised in *Harper's Monthly Magazine*, January–July 1894, illustrated by the author.) Du Maurier's sanitised version of the *vie de bohème* was possibly the bestselling single novel of the century. In the Latin Quarter of Paris, there live three British art students: Taffy, Sandy and Little Billee. While they are entertaining a sinister Jewish musician, Svengali, an artist's model comes in. She is Trilby O'Ferrall and is possessed of a magnificent voice. Unfortunately she is also tone deaf. Trilby takes up with the Britons. But when she models naked, Little Billee (who loves her) leaves Paris. She becomes a decent laundress, and she and Billee are reconciled. But his mother persuades her not to ruin her son's life by marrying him. Nobly, Trilby acquiesces. Five years pass and Billee becomes a famous artist. At a reunion in Paris the former art students discover that Trilby is now a famous singer. Svengali has contrived to overcome her tone deafness by hypnotism, of which he is a master. She is completely under his control. In a subsequent London concert, Svengali dies and Trilby reverts to her natural bellowing incompetence on stage. Her friends comfort her; but she has no memory of her singing career and slowly pines away. Just before dying, a large photograph of Svengali rouses her to magnificent song once more. A coda reveals that shortly after her death Little Billee dies too. The novel was phenomenally successful, inspiring, among other things, a vogue for the felt hat since universally called after the heroine.

TROLLOPE, Anthony (1815–82). He was born in London, the youngest son of Frances Milton Trollope* (later a distinguished novelist in her own right) and Thomas Anthony Trollope, a barrister given to fits of suicidal melancholy. In the year of his birth, the Trollopes moved to Harrow, where Thomas unsuccessfully tried his hand at farming. The farm (which was leased) proved the grave of the Trollopes' prosperity and the family's misfortunes translated into inadequate and disturbed schooling for the young Anthony. From 1823 to 1825 he was a day-boy at Harrow School; from 1825 to 1827 he was a pupil at a private school at Sunbury. From 1827 to 1830 he was at Winchester College (his father's school), but was forced to leave when his fees were not paid; and from 1831 to 1834 he was again a dayboy at Harrow. During this period he was 'always in disgrace' and exquisitely miserable, a misery which he records eloquently in his *Autobiography*. Meanwhile, the family fortunes went from bad to worse. In 1827 his mother made her ill-fated attempt to set up a bazaar in the

United States and three years later she returned penniless with the older members of the family who had accompanied her. Trollope's father was by now eccentric to the point of mania. His elder brothers Tom and Henry had managed to make some decent start in professional life, but Anthony's future seemed already blighted. The family finances were improved somewhat by the runaway success of Mrs Trollope's first book, *The Domestic Manners Of The Americans* (1832). Never the less, the Trollopes were obliged to flee from their creditors to Bruges in April 1834. There, Henry Trollope (1811–34) died of consumption in December. Less than a year later, Anthony's father died. Meanwhile, the young man tried his hand unsuccessfully as classical usher at a private school in Brussels and in November 1834 (by family influence), aged nineteen, procured a place as a junior clerk in the General Post Office in London at £90 a year. In 1840, after seven years' undistinguished service (commemorated in Charley Tudor's experiences in *The Three Clerks**, 1857), Trollope fell seriously ill. (Oddly, Trollope makes no mention of this illness, which seems to have been partly asthmatic, in his *Autobiography*.) Surviving, his character seems to have changed. He left 'twenty-six years of suffering, disgrace and inward remorse' behind him, and took a demanding post as a surveyor's clerk in the Central District of Ireland. Trollope did well in this outlying branch of the Post Office service and spent seventeen years in the country, going from strength to strength. He developed his lifelong love of hunting in Ireland. In September 1843 he began to write his first novel, *The Macdermots Of Ballycloran** (1847). In June 1844, he married Rose Heseltine, whom he had met two years earlier, shortly after his arrival in the country. The marriage was happy, and a first child, Henry Merivale Trollope, was born in 1846. *The Macdermots* was published somewhat ignominiously by Newby* in 1847 and earned its author nothing. Equally unsuccessful was a second Irish* novel, *The Kellys And The O'Kellys**, published by Colburn* in 1848. A French Revolution novel, *La Vendée** (1850), similarly failed, despite there having been a French Revolution in 1848 to stimulate sales. Nothing daunted, Trollope wrote a play in 1850, *The Noble Jilt*, which found no theatrical buyers. Despite the misery which Ireland (in the throes of the Famine) was undergoing, Trollope's years in the country were probably the happiest of his life. Meanwhile, his Post Office career was moving ahead satisfactorily. Over the period 1851–52 he was sent to the west of England and the Channel Islands on work for the extending of local delivery of letters. He travelled an average of forty miles a day, helping lay down a postal system which was to be the envy of the civilised world. (Among Trollope's many achievements as a Civil Servant was the introduction of the pillar-box into England.) At Salisbury in 1852, he conceived the idea of his first Barsetshire novel, *The Warden** (1855). Duly published by Longman*, this quiet story of ecclesiastical infighting enjoyed a greater success than anything Trollope had previously published. He was now based in England, and over the next ten years travelled extensively both to his mother and brother in Florence, and on Post Office business. Finding Longman uninterested in his Carlylean survey of latter-day England, *The New Zealander* (written in 1855, published eventually in 1972), Trollope returned to ecclesiastic fiction with *Barchester Towers** (1857). The novel marked up another increment of success, but Longman were unwilling to advance the £200 Trollope wanted for its successor, *The Three Clerks*, which Bentley* brought out in 1857. Bentley would not pay the price Trollope wanted for this novel's successor, *Doctor Thorne** (1858) which went to Chapman and Hall*, who were, in fact, to remain the novelist's preferred publisher during the rest of his career. Trollope actually wrote a large portion of *Doctor Thorne* during an official trip to Egypt; and once returned from this journey he immediately embarked on a voyage to the West Indies and the USA. He duly wrote *Tales Of All Countries* (1861). Trollope returned summer 1859, and later the same year he was commissioned by Thackeray* and George Smith to write the lead serial for the new *Cornhill Magazine**. Smith offered £1,000 (Trollope's largest reward by far). Initially, he hoped the magazine would take his work in progress, the Irish story *Castle Richmond** (1860). But Smith declined this tale of the Famine, which Chapman and Hall eventually put out. For *Cornhill*, Trollope devised another Barchester tale, *Framley Parsonage** (1861). The work was extremely well received. In the same year, Trollope took up the post of Surveyor of the Eastern District of England, and settled at Waltham Cross, Hertfordshire, an address from which he could conveniently hunt. Trollope's next novel, *Orley Farm** (1862), was published in monthly numbers, and with its fine illustrations by J. E. Millais* consolidated his reputation as the new Thackeray. In 1861–62, Trollope travelled to the USA and, like his mother before him, produced a pungent travel book, *North America* (1862). Visiting his brother in Florence in October 1860, Trollope had begun what was to be a lifelong (and almost certainly platonic) relationship with a young American girl, Kate Field (1839–96), who seems to have given him the inspiration for many of his later heroines. Field was a journalist, feminist and actress and evidently a dynamic contrast to the domestic Rose Trollope. *The Small House At Allington** (1864) continued the Barchester panorama, with its long-suffering heroine, Lily Dale. In 1864, however, Trollope embarked (probably without any long-term plans) on another fiction sequence with *Can You Forgive Her?**. This work introduced at full length Plantagenet Palliser, whose parliamentary fortunes were to feature in five subsequent works. Trollope was by now a dominant man of letters, and was elected to the Athenaeum Club in 1864. In 1865, he was one of the architects of the new journal, *The Fortnightly Review**. Although the publication failed commercially, it left a distinctive mark on the thinking of the age. Trollope was also involved less directly in the launch and early years of George Smith's Liberal paper, *The Pall Mall Gazette*, for which he wrote numerous public affairs articles. And in 1867, he launched his own magazine with James Virtue*, *St Paul's**. Fiction meanwhile cascaded from his pen, written in the everyday before-breakfast sessions which he describes in his *Autobiography*, and which have sometimes been used against him as indicating him to be a mere mass-producer of novels. *Rachel Ray** (1863), a picture of dissenting culture, ran into trouble with Norman Macleod*, who refused to serialise it in *Good Words**. *Miss Mackenzie** (1865) took the awkward subject of middle-aged spinsterhood. *The Claverings** (1867) concentrated on the kind of weak, hobbledehoy hero who fascinated Trollope. *The Belton Estate** (1866) kicked off the *Fortnightly Review*, but the novel has never found many admirers. Much more successful was *The Last Chronicle Of Barset** (1867), a powerful study of monomania that some critics have seen as ushering in a 'dark phase' in Trollope's authorial career. Trollope had for some time felt stalled in his Post Office activities. And as a wealthy man of letters with parliamentary ambitions, he resigned from the Post Office, effective October 1867. At the same period he wrote his most cheerful political novel, *Phineas Finn** (serialised in *St Paul's*, 1867–69). During the course of this novel's appearance, Trollope took the plunge and stood as a Liberal candidate at the Beverley election in November 1868. He was defeated in what was a very dirty contest of which he gives a vivid picture in *Ralph The Heir** (1871). At this stage in his career, Trollope's fortunes began to wane. *St Paul's* never did as well as expected, and Trollope was obliged to give up the editorship in 1870. He had probably produced too many novels too quickly, and he made a moderately successful attempt to cash in on the sensation* fiction vogue with *The Eustace Diamonds** (1872). *Phineas Redux** (1873) is a depressed sequel to Finn's fortunes which expresses considerable doubt about the efficacy of Britain's justice. Over the period 1871–72, the Trollopes undertook a round-the-world trip, principally to see their son Fred now a sheep farmer in New Zealand. (The trip resulted in one of his best travel books, *Australia And New Zealand*, 1873.) On his return, Trollope took up residence at Montague Square in London, and began his savage satire of contemporary English morals, *The Way We Live Now** (1875), a work which many commentators regard as his masterpiece. But it did not appeal to his contemporary readers, any more than did the next instalment in Palliser's career, *The Prime Minister** (1876). In 1875, he undertook yet another trip to Australia. It was now rather harder to place his fiction and *Is He Popenjoy?**, partly written on the trip, could not be published until 1878. At this period, Trollope began putting together his *Autobiography*, published posthumously in 1883. His later fiction (for which he received ever lower payment) includes: *The American Senator** (1877); *The Duke's Children** (1880), the final instalment of the Palliser series; *John Caldigate* (1879), a novel drawing on Trollope's Australian experiences; *Ayala's Angel** (1881); *Marion Fay** (1882); *Mr Scarborough's Family** (1883); *An Old Man's Love** (1884). Much of this fiction (including the incomplete *The Landleaguers*, 1883) appeared posthumously. Following a trip to Ireland in September 1882, Trollope suffered a stroke in early November and died in a London nursing home on 6 December. The publication of his frank *Autobiography* had been held back until after his death. Trollope's son, Henry Merivale Trollope (1846–1926) wrote a novel, *My Own Love Story* (1887). BL 47. *DNB*. RM. *NCBEL*. Wol. Sad.

TROLLOPE, Cecilia (1818–49). Sister of Anthony Trollope*. She was by all accounts a quiet young lady and it was her brother Anthony who introduced her to his close friend John (later Sir John) Tilley (1813–98), whom she subsequently married in 1839. Tilley was a colleague of Anthony's in the Post Office. She died of the family disease, consumption, having borne five children in ten years. She also had the family addiction for writing fiction and published the High Church novel *Chollerton, A Tale Of Our Own Times* (1846). BL 1. (FMT) *DNB*. Sad.

TROLLOPE, Mrs [Frances] (née Milton, 1779–1863). The author of thirty-five novels and mother of Anthony*, author of forty-seven, of Thomas Adol-

phus*, author of twenty, of Cecilia, author of one and mother-in-law of
Frances Eleanor* author of eleven. Frances Milton was the second daughter
of the Rev. William Milton, Vicar of Heckfield and was brought up in the
professional-mercantile milieu of Bristol. In 1809, she married Thomas Anthony Trollope (1774–1835), a rising thirty-six-year-old barrister, possessed
at marriage of a comfortable £700 a year. Mrs Trollope was a good mother
(as Anthony movingly testifies in his *Autobiography*); but she was also very
unlucky. Only two of her seven children (all born between 1810 and 1818)
survived her. And of the five grand-children she had by her daughter Cecilia (herself a premature victim of consumption in 1849) only one reached
adulthood. There were other trials. The farm which Thomas Trollope took
over in Harrow in 1813 proved a millstone to the family, and an intolerably
depressing psychological burden from which he personally never recovered.
There were other afflictions. In 1820 Trollope lost an expected legacy. He
exacerbated his plight by alienating legal clients. In 1827 there was a disastrous agricultural depression. In the same year Mrs Trollope (accompanied
by three of her children and partly to escape her husband's morbid temper)
went to western Tennessee where she joined a slave emancipation colony
at Nashoba. The following year she attempted to restore the family fortunes by setting up a bazaar in Cincinnati, designed to furnish this remote
corner of the New World with high European culture. The venture failed
disastrously. Now fifty-two, Mrs Trollope resolved both to revenge herself on
America and to earn money by writing a book. She returned to England in
1831 and in 1832, *Domestic Manners Of The Americans* came out. Spiteful
and topical (given the Reform Bill and British interest in republicanism) the
book was a hit and brought in about £600 for its author. In the same year
she went on to produce her first novel, with a similarly Yankee theme, *The
Refugee In America* (1832). At this period, Trollope broke with her first
publisher, Whittaker, and formed an alliance with the more enterprising
Richard Bentley*. This lasted until the early 1840s, when she transferred to
Bentley's great rival, Henry Colburn*. After Colburn's retirement in 1852,
she formed her final relationship with his successor in business, Hurst and
Blackett*. (Unlike her son Anthony, she was fairly loyal to her publishers.)
The 1830s were a rich period for fashionable authors, and Trollope had
£400 for the first edition (1,250 copies) of her first novel. Her pattern of
work, which was to remain constant during her lifetime, was to alternate
between racy travel books (e.g. *Paris And The Parisians*, 1836; *Vienna And
The Austrians*, 1838; *A Visit To Italy*, 1842) and even racier novels. In the
mid-1830s, despite her literary success, the Trollope family was devastated
by a series of disasters. Farming finally bankrupted Thomas, and the bailiffs
moved in to Julians (the home on which Anthony based *Orley Farm**). The
family was forced to decamp to Bruges in Belgium, where Thomas Trollope
died a broken man in 1835. Consumption was taking its toll of the children. Anthony, who at least was robust, was apparently drifting into listless
failure. Among all this, Mrs Trollope remained indomitably cheerful. She
rose at four in the morning to write her books while the family slept, and
composed her jaunty fiction beside the bed of her dying son Henry in 1834.
(Anthony, who could write his daily quota through sea-sickness, felt this
would have been too much even for him.) In 1835, there appeared *Tremor-
dyn Cliff*, the study of a dominant woman (a character type which was

to become Trollope's trademark in fiction). It was followed by her savage anti-slavery novel, *Jonathan Jefferson Whitlaw* (1836) and her witty anti-evangelical novel, *The Vicar of Wrexhill** (1837). These works, powerful and coarse by the standards of the time, were attacked by the critics. But Bentley gave Trollope £600 a novel (making great play in his advertisements with her now notorious name) and with the two works a year which she could turn out (aged sixty) she was never to be poor again. The 'Widow Barnaby*' trilogy (1830 43) represents her best comic–satiric effort. And in 1839, she took on Dickens* himself with a social problem* novel in numbers, *Michael Armstrong, The Factory Boy** (for which Colburn paid £1,000). This scathing attack on industrialism, together with her other monthly serial, *Jessie Phillips** (1843) attracted the now customary acccusations of unwomanly literary conduct. The critics were, of course, wrong. The period 1839–46 represents the high-point of Trollope's novel-writing career. In *One Fault* (1840) she gave a retrospective analysis of her own marriage and its undramatic wretchedness. At the same period, she published two sharp comedies of modern literary life: *Charles Chesterfield, Or The Adventures Of A Youth Of Genius* (1841) and *The Blue Belles Of England* (1842). After 1843, she settled permanently in Florence with her son and long-time companion, Thomas Adolphus. (She exploited her continental observations for the characteristically sarcastic picture of John Bull and family abroad, *The Robertses On Their Travels*, 1846.) *Father Eustace, A Tale Of The Jesuits* (1847) is a propaganda novel, written in the wake of Newman's* defection to Rome two years earlier and featuring a Romish priest given to spiritual and sexual seduction. Her subsequent fiction revolves largely around the same themes. Strong women and 'petticoat government' (as she entitled her 1850 novel) continued to fascinate her. And she provides a full gallery of woman in the conditions of spinster, wife and widowhood. Mrs Trollope continued to put out novels until her seventy-sixth year, her last being *Fashionable Life, Or Paris And London* (1856). She died at the age of eighty-four, her last words being 'Poor Cecilia'. For someone obliged to start writing in extremis when most people contemplate retirement, Mrs Trollope's was a remarkable career. BL 35. *DNB*. RM. *NCBEL*. Wol. Sad.

TROLLOPE, Frances Eleanor (née Ternan, 1834?–1913). T. A. Trollope's* second wife and an elder sister to Dickens's* shadowy mistress (after the late 1850s), Ellen Ternan. Their mother, also called Frances Eleanor Ternan (née Jarman, 1803?–73), was a well-known London actress as was Ellen. Anthony, who knew the Ternans well, introduced Frances to his brother after the death of his first wife, Theodosia, in 1865. For a while Ternan was a governess to T. A. Trollope's twelve-year-old daughter, Bice (i.e. Beatrice), before the couple married in 1866 in Paris. (Anthony was one of the witnesses.) Her novels are marked by pathos and a strain of feminine masochism. They include: *Aunt Margaret's Trouble* (1866), advertised on the title page as by 'A New Writer'; *Mabel's Progress* (1867), the story of a young woman making her way in a difficult world; *The Sacristan's Household*, (1869); *That Unfortunate Marriage* (1888); *Among Aliens* (1890), the story of a pretty young English governess working for a noble Italian family, this work probably contains some autobiographical material; *Madame Leroux* (1890), another work with a governess subplot. *A Charming Fellow* is a typical F. E. Trollope story, chronicling the rise and fall of Algernon Errington. Algie is well connected and charming, but a rogue. He drives his long-suffering wife to her death, but the world insists on excusing his faults on the ground that he is a 'charming fellow'. The work is narrated with an effectively brittle sarcasm against the hero. Frances Trollope was apparently interested in spiritualism at the end of her life, and it figures in *Black Spirits And White* (1877). After her husband's death, she evidently fell on hard times and was granted a Civil List pension in 1893 by Gladstone, of all British prime ministers the most friendly to novelists. BL 11. Boase. Wol. Sad.

TROLLOPE, T[homas] Adolphus (1810–92). The oldest son of the Trollope family, he was born in Bloomsbury, London, and educated at Harrow and Winchester. He was less affected by the family disturbances and poverty of the late 1820s than his brother Anthony*, and in 1829 entered Magdalen College, Oxford. (The straitened Trollope finances did not permit his younger brother to follow him.) For a while he was a master at King Edward's School, Birmingham, having graduated from Oxford in 1835. He also travelled with his mother, who by the late 1830s was a novelist of note and could support a small entourage. Thomas eventually decided on journalism as his profession and was one of the early contributors to Dickens's* *Household Words**. From 1843, he lived in Florence, again with his mother. In Italy, he developed a sympathy for the country's radical politics (while remaining more conservative in his views on English affairs). In 1873 he based himself in Rome to become the Italian correspondent of the London *Standard*. He was well-liked in the country, and from King Victor Emmanuel he received the Order of St Maurice and St Lazarus. In 1890, he returned to England, a country he had rarely seen since the 1830s. He soon after died at Clifton. Trollope married twice. His first wife, whom he married in 1848, was Theodosia Garrow (1825–65). An accomplished linguist, poet and a cultivated woman, she superintended over the so-called Villino Trollope which was visited by many of the literary and political notables of the day. She died in 1865. The following year, Trollope married Frances Eleanor Ternan [Trollope*] (1834?–1913) who had initially joined the family as a governess. An author in her own right, she wrote a biography of her mother-in-law, Frances Trollope*, and a number of popular novels. T. Adolphus Trollope himself wrote fiction equivalent in quantity but far inferior to that of his mother and brother. Much of it reflects his long residence in Italy. His novels include *Filippo Strozzi* (1860), a historical* romance which may plausibly have influenced George Eliot's* *Romola**. It was followed by: *La Beata* (1861); *Marietta* (1862); *Giulio Malatesta* (1863), set largely in 1820s Bologna; *Beppo The Conscript* (1864), set along the Adriatic; *Gemma* (1866), set in Siena; *Artingale Castle* (1867); *Leonora Casaloni* (1868), a Roman story; *The Garstangs, Of Garstang Grange* (1869), a sequel to the similarly English rural *Artingale Castle*; *A Siren* (1870), set in Ravenna; *Durnton Abbey* (1871); *The Stilwinches Of Combe Mavis* (1872); *Diamond Cut Diamond* (1875), a story of Tuscan life. Trollope was evidently fertile in the conception of plots for fiction. He is credited with giving Frances the idea for *Petticoat Government* (1850) and Anthony that for *Doctor Thorne** (1858). He wrote an autobiography, *What I Remember* (1887), which differs interestingly from his brother's account of the same family events and characters. BL 20. *DNB. NCBEL.* Wol. Sad.

Trübner (1851–1912). Publisher. Nicholas Trübner (1817–84) was born in Heidelberg, and having worked as a clerk with Longman* set up his own business in 1851. An oriental scholar he was himself an author of some note. As a publisher he specialised in American agency work. On commission, he also published some classics of Victorian fiction which regular publishers short-sightedly turned down: notably Charles Reade's* *The Cloister And The Hearth** (1861), Samuel Butler's* *Erewhon** (1872) and the early fiction of William Hale White* ('Mark Rutherford') and Mona Caird*, as well as fiction by such exotic writers as Turgenev and Tolstoy. After various mergers, the firm was eventually swallowed up in the early twentieth century by Routledge*. *DNB.*

The Trumpet Major And Robert His Brother, Thomas Hardy, 1880, 3 vols, Smith, Elder. (Serialised in *Good Words**, January–December 1880, with illustrations by John Collier.) A Wessex* novel set in the Napoleonic Wars, a period which fascinated Hardy. The trumpet major (i.e. regimental chief trumpeter) is John Loveday. The son of the local miller, John is a suitor for the hand of Anne Garland, whose mother is a tenant of Overcombe Mill near the port of Budmouth. John's sailor brother Bob also comes to love Anne as does the odious Festus Derriman, the local squire's nephew. Festus is bested and finally disinherited in favour of Anne. Robert wins glory at Trafalgar and finally has Anne's hand in marriage; Miller Loveday marries Mrs Garland and John goes off to die in the Peninsular War. The novel is Hardy's sole exercise in historical* fiction.

TUCKER, Charlotte Maria, ('ALOE', i.e. 'A Lady Of England', 1821–93). One of the most successful writers of fiction for Victorian children. Tucker was born at Barnet into the upper-professional classes, her father (a dominant influence, as with many women authors) being a senior Indian Civil Servant and financier. Charlotte was the sixth child and third daughter. She was educated largely at home. In 1822, the family moved to central London, where a number of the most famous men and women of the time visited (including, on one occasion, Wellington). In 1848, Charlotte underwent a conversion to strict evangelicalism. Her father died in 1851, and she never married, devoting herself to a life of useful spinsterdom. Tucker was active in helping the London poor before 1851, but did not publish any fiction until after her father's death. Her first work was the unabashedly didactic *Claremont Tales, Or Illustrations Of The Beatitudes* (1852). Their success encouraged her to express more of her philanthropy in print. Her subsequent work is versatile, within the standard modes of Victorian children's* books. She wrote homilies in prose (e.g. *Precepts In Practice*, 1858); Bible stories (e.g. *Rescued From Egypt*, 1871); allegories (e.g. *The Giant Killer, Or The Battle Which All Must Fight*, 1868); animal fables (e.g. the autobiographical *The Rambles Of A Rat*, 1854); adventure stories (e.g. *The Robbers' Cave*, 1862). In general, ALOE avoids the crude moralism of the reward* genre of children's story, in which good behaviour is encouraged by the promise of divine favour. And her fiction is, for the age, notably realistic. As J. S. Bratton notes: 'drunkenness, child abuse, starvation, rapacious landladies, fevers, harsh employers, swindling and jeering fellow-servants are regular features in many of her stories.' On the other hand, her stories often have a lighter didactic touch, as indicated by the final words of her amiable rambling rodent: 'Perhaps the human race would despise us less proudly if our characters and instincts were better known. Who can say that some truth may not be learned, some lesson of kindness gained, even from the history of the Rambles of a Rat'. The last years of Tucker's life were extraordinary. At the age of fifty-four she went to India as a missionary (having taught herself Hindustani) and spent the last eighteen years of her life as a Zenana visitor (i.e. calling on secluded Indian women). She was also an active educationalist, converting the natives to Christianity as she taught them. She eventually died at Amritsar, having been long weakened by illness in 1885. Some of her later work (e.g. the volume of stories, *Pomegranates From The Punjaub*, 1878) has an Indian setting and flavour of narration. BL 74. *DNB*.

TUPPER, Martin [Farquhar] (1810–89). Remembered primarily as the author of *Proverbial Philosophy*, Tupper was born in London, a West End doctor's son (distantly of Huguenot ancestry). Martin was a delicate child, reportedly as a result of his solicitous father over-bleeding him. He had his early education from a tutor and in 1821 went on to Charterhouse School where he was a contemporary of Thackeray* and John Leech*. In 1828 he entered Christ Church, Oxford. As an undergraduate, he wrote a torrent of verse and in 1830 he pipped Gladstone for the university theological essay prize. (Gladstone nevertheless remained a friend and patron for the remainder of Tupper's life.) Tupper took his degree in 1832. He began his working life in law and was called to the Bar in 1835, but he never practised and seems to have qualified only so that he could marry (which he did, the day after). The newlyweds had four children in as many years. Tupper's authorial fortunes rose meteorically with the publication of his sermonistic poems *Proverbial Philosophy* in 1838. The work was fabulously successful, and by 1880 was in its fiftieth edition. On the strength of his earnings, Tupper in 1840 set himself up in a spacious new mansion, Albury House, near Guildford in Surrey. At this period he was contributing to *Ainsworth's Magazine**, and he evidently decided to try his hand at fiction. He accordingly wrote some uplifting novels, starting with *The Crock Of Gold* (1844). It tells the story of a pious labourer, Roger Acton ('honest Roger'), who digs up a crock of gold, and subsequently takes to drink and goes to the bad. He is finally charged with murder and only providentially saved at the last minute. Despite its insufferably moralistic tone, the work was successful and went through five editions promptly. Tupper followed up with *The Twins* (1844) and *Heart* (1844). Tupper intended these three works respectively to illustrate the sins of covetousness, adultery and false witness. In 1845, his father died and he came into his inheritance. For a while he followed various amateur pursuits, and made some quite significant archaeological discoveries. In 1850, he was mortified not to get the laureateship which very properly went to Tennyson. Always popular in America, Tupper visited the country in 1851, and had a triumph reading his work to packed halls. (He was to make the trip again, less successfully, in 1876.) By the late 1850s, however, he was suffering from the anti-middlebrow movement led by such journals as the *Saturday Review**, for whom Tupper's poems represented all that was worst in Victorian literary culture. Hawthorne, who visited him at this period, declared him 'the vainest little man of little men'. Increasingly, Tupper was in financial difficulties. His uncle's patent galvanised iron company lost him a small fortune. And in the late 1860s his eldest son Martin (an army officer) ran up huge gambling debts. Tupper tried to raise a subscription for himself (on the dubious grounds of his 'services to literature') which was unsuccessful. But in 1873 he received a Civil List pension which somewhat relieved his financial crisis. He was also a beneficiary of the Royal Literary Fund*. In addition to the fiction mentioned, Tupper also wrote *Stephan Langton* (1858), a saga of Albury in the reign of King John. The work has always had a local sale in Guildford but critics of the time found it a very stiff and unconvincing historical* romance. BL 4. *DNB. NCBEL.* Wol. RLF.

Two Marriages, Dinah Mulock Craik, 1867, 2 vols, Hurst and Blackett. Two short novels, bundled together under a thematic title. In the first, 'John Browerbank's Wife', the rich heroine is forbidden by her father from marrying the poor man she loves. Married instead to a rich widower she pines and dies. The second story, 'Parson Garland's Daughter', is more moralistic. The low-born heroine, Charlotte Dean, follows the parson's son Keith Garland to Cambridge, where she forces him to make an honest woman of her. Keith's father, Parson Garland, sends his son off to Canada and takes Charlotte into his family. There he gradually overcomes his distaste for her vulgarity and educates her into a respectable daughter of the house. The stories do not rank among Mulock's best fiction.

Two On A Tower, Thomas Hardy, 1882, 3 vols, Sampson Low. (Serialised in *Atlantic Monthly*, January–December 1882.) A melodrama in which Hardy consciously juxtaposes the little love problems of humankind against the immensities of interstellar space. The hero is an astronomer of humble birth, Swithin St Cleeve. Swithin falls in love with a noblewoman, Lady Viviette Constantine, on whose estate is the column, or tower, where he keeps his telescope. Her brutal husband, Sir Blount, has decamped to Africa. She learns with relief that he is dead, and promptly marries Swithin secretly. The match is disastrous. Swithin discovers that by marrying before the age of twenty-five he forfeits a legacy from his uncle. And it emerges that at the time of their wedding, Lady Constantine's husband was still living in a sordid liaison with a native princess. Although he subsequently blew his head off, the lovers' marriage is legally null. She persuades Swithin to take a position in South Africa, and herself accepts the offer of Bishop Helmsdale of Melchester. The marriage is doomed when he discovers whose is the child she bears. The Bishop dies and Swithin returns to the tower to find Lady Constantine prematurely aged. Nevertheless, he offers to marry her honestly, and she collapses dead with the joy of his proposal. The novel has never been reckoned one of Hardy's best and its grand cosmic theme is left largely undeveloped.

Two Stories Of The Seen And Unseen, Margaret Oliphant, 1885, 1 vol, Blackwood. This volume contains two of Oliphant's best, and most anthologised supernatural tales. 'The Open Door' (first published in *Blackwood's*

Magazine*, January 1882), is a story of haunting and exorcism, set in Scotland. A young boy hears an eerie wailing in some ruins on his family grounds. Colonel Mortimer (the level-headed narrator) investigates. Together with the local minister, he makes contact with a guilty spirit, returned from the dead in search of his former family. The minister persuades it to go and seek among the dead, and leave the living in peace. 'Old Lady Mary' (first published in *Blackwood's Magazine* in January 1884) has a similar theme. Lady Mary, an autocratic lady, dies. Perversely, she has drawn up her own will and hidden it. As a result, the little goddaughter whom she intended to be her heir is dispossessed. Lady Mary returns, but can make no contact with the living. Eventually, the will is found by accident. Like all eavesdroppers, Lady Mary discovers truths about herself that she was unaware of in life but also learns she is forgiven by her goddaughter.

Two Years Ago, Charles Kingsley, 1857, 3 vols, Macmillan. Kingsley's most hobby-horsical novel. The principal purpose is the propagation of the author's (inherently sensible) views on sanitation. The setting is a Cornish village Aberalva, 'two years ago' (i.e. 1855), during a cholera epidemic. The crisis throws into heroic or ignoble relief the village doctor Tom Thurnall (very heroic), the Anglican Curate Frank Headley (heroic), the nonconformist schoolmistress Grace Harvey (heroic) and the decadent, apothecary's assistant turned poet, John Briggs (ignoble). After knocking all round the world, Thurnall was shipwrecked off Aberalva and saved (alone of his fellows) by Grace. But he refuses to be converted by her. In the rescue, Tom loses his money belt with £1,500 in it. All this is forgotten in the epidemic. Afterwards, Tom proposes to Grace, but is repulsed. He goes off to the Crimea. Discovering that her mother has taken the belt, Grace follows Tom to the battlefield, as a nurse. But she does not find him and returns to England. Finally (released from a Russian prison) Tom comes home and the lovers are at last united. The novel has never been among Kingsley's more popular.

TYNAN, Katharine [Hinkson] (1861–1931). Katharine Tynan was born near Dublin, Ireland, the fourth daughter of a cattle trader with strong Nationalist sympathies. As a child, her eyes were damaged by measles, leaving her partially sighted for life. Tynan's early family background was Catholic and strict, but she read novels secretly and wrote poetry. Her first poem was published in 1878 and her first Pre-Raphaelitish collection of verse came out in 1885 with the help of a £20 subsidy from her father, Andrew. In the 1890s she began writing prose and her first novel, *The Way Of A Maid*, was published in 1895. This opened the way for a career writing slushy romantic fiction, of which she turned out up to six volumes a year. Meanwhile she reserved her more serious literary energies for religious verse. In 1893 she married Henry Hinkson*, a barrister (later a resident magistrate), whom she converted to Catholicism. He too published novels. The Hinksons became friendly with all the leaders of the Irish Renaissance movement, including W. B. Yeats. Hinkson died in 1919, and his widow spent most of the remainder of her life in England, dying at Wimbledon. Her Victorian fiction includes: *The Handsome Brandons* (1899); *She Walks In Beauty* (1899). BL 94. *DNB*. RM. *NCBEL*. RLF.

U

The Unclassed, George Gissing, 1884, 3 vols, Chapman and Hall. A story of the London slums. As he often does, Gissing uses a large cast and an intricate multiplot structure. There are three heroines, initially encountered in a London school. Ida Starr is the daughter of a prostitute, who herself drifts into vice. Harriet Smales is vulgar and Maud (Ida's friend) is shabby genteel. These women's destinies intertwine with those of Osmond Waymark, an unsuccessful novelist of the lower classes, and Julian Casti, an even less successful writer. Casti is duped into marriage with Harriet. Ida falls in love with Waymark and tries to reform but Harriet maliciously contrives to have her sent to prison on a charge of theft. Osmond becomes engaged to Maud. In a melodramatic climax, Ida inherits a fortune from her slum landlord grandfather; Maud relinquishes her claim on Osmond who marries Ida; Casti deserts Harriet only to die of consumption. The novel is notable for its depiction of the clash between middle-class culture (here represented by the would-be author heroes) and squalid working-class circumstances.

Uncle John, G. J. Whyte-Melville, 1874, 3 vols, Chapman and Hall. (Serialised in *Temple Bar*, November 1873–August 1874.) A breezily attractive novel in Whyte-Melville's sub-Trollopian style. The narrative opens with a January country-house party at Plumpton Priors. The host, (Uncle) John Dennison, is a hunting man. Among his guests are a cricketing parson, Algernon Lexley, Uncle John's niece, Annie, a young Etonian, Perigord, a bored man of the world, Percy Mortimer, and Laura Blair, a woman with a past. There are some hunting scenes but the novel's main action concerns Lexley's proposal to Laura. She tells him that she is in fact the widow of a gambler killed by pirates. They nevertheless marry and Laura's first husband, Delancy, unexpectedly returns. The couple separate, but are later reunited. Delancy is killed trying to escape from prison (Algernon converts him to Christianity on his cell deathbed). The other, quieter strand of the novel follows the courtship of Annie. The end of the novel is darkened by the death (or 'run-in' as he calls it) of the amiable Uncle John.

Uncle Silas, Joseph Sheridan Le Fanu, 1864, 3 vols, Bentley. (Serialised in the *Dublin University Magazine**, July–December 1864 as 'Maud Ruthyn And Uncle Silas, A Tale Of Bartram-Haugh'.) Often considered the best ghost* story of the period. On the sudden death of her father Austin Ruthyn from a heart attack, Maud is left to the care of her Uncle Silas in Derbyshire, until she comes of age. Silas is suspected of having earlier murdered in his house a man to whom he owed gambling debts, but he has never been brought to justice. Sinister in appearance and a consummate villain, Silas plots first to marry Maud to his oafish son Dudley (who is, it emerges, already married). When this falls through, father and son conspire to murder their ward and so inherit her fortune. A French governess, Madame de la Rougierre, is brought in to help with the plan by which the victim is to be killed with a spiked hammer. The main focus of the story is on Maud's sense of impending doom as reflected through her ingenuous first-person narrative. The plot fails, the French governess is murdered in Maud's place, and the heroine escapes in the nick of time from Silas's house of horror. Silas kills himself with an overdose of laudanum. Maud goes on to live happily as Lady Ilbury, the 'wife of a noble-hearted husband'. The novel is suffused with the author's Swedenborgianism.

Under The Greenwood Tree, Thomas Hardy, 1872, 2 vols, Tinsley. (Subtitled, 'A Rural Painting Of The Dutch School'.) A short and early idyll which marks the beginning of Hardy's Wessex* cycle of novels. The action is set in Mellstock in the early nineteenth century. The social event which overshadows the plot is the replacement of the old church choir (or orchestra) by a modern cabinet organ. The hero, Dick Dewy, is a tranter, or jobbing carrier who falls in love with the clever new teacher and organist at the Mellstock Church School, Fancy Day. Her father, the keeper of Yalbury Wood, favours his suit. But Fancy has higher hopes. In the way of Hardy women, she betrays Dick by encouraging another offer of marriage from the local Vicar, Arthur Maybold. But this is withdrawn when he discovers her previous attachment, and Dick eventually marries his bride ignorant of her treachery. All ends with a festive country wedding. The novel is among the most charming and cheerful that Hardy wrote.

Under Two Flags, Ouida (i.e. Marie Louise de la Ramée), 1867, 3 vols, Chapman and Hall. Ouida's bestseller. The story is preposterous, but is carried through with the author's usual reckless verve. The Hon. Bertie Cecil of the Life Guards is a dashing man about town, a champion of the race course, a lover of beautiful women and a gambler. He fakes death and leaves London to protect the reputation of a lady and the honour of a younger brother. Enlisted as a chasseur d'Afrique as Louis Victor, Bertie performs prodigies of heroism against the Arab rebels in Algeria while incurring the implacable enmity of the sadistic Colonel Chateauroy. He is loved by Cigarette, a beautiful camp follower who has saved Bertie's life on the field of battle. But although he treats her courteously, Bertie gives his heart to the mysterious Princess Corona (who eventually turns out to be Bertie's best friend's sister). The hero's older brother, Lord Royallieu, dies and the title (rightfully Bertie's) goes to his unworthy young brother, Berkeley (who also turns up in Algeria). In a tremendous climax, Bertie strikes Chateauroy for insulting the Princess Corona and is sentenced to death by court martial. Cigarette informs a marshal of France of his true identity and so wins a reprieve. Galloping back, she arrives in the nick of time, hurling herself into the fusillade intended for Bertie. She dies a martyr to love and Bertie marries the Princess. In its cheap form (with Chatto*) the novel sold millions of copies and in the twentieth century was successfully filmed.

Under Which Lord?, E. Lynn Linton, 1879, 3 vols, Chatto. (Serialised in the *Gentleman's Magazine**, January–December 1879, illustrated by A. Hopkins.) Linton's powerful blast against Ritualism. The story opens with the marriage of a young army officer, Richard Spence, to an heiress, Hermione Fullerton, of Crossholme Abbey. He is a free-thinker, and she mentally passive; but nevertheless, the match is happy. In deference to her being the property owner, he takes his wife's name on marriage. The couple have a daughter, Virginia, who grows up to be a pleasant young woman of no particular views. Troubles begin for the Fullertons with the arrival of a new vicar, the Rev. Launcelot Lascelles. He is a fanatic Ritualist, dedicated to the recovery of the Abbey, and the whole community, to his brand of Anglicanism. Lascelles spiritually seduces Hermione, while his sister wins over Virginia. Richard stands helpless as his womenfolk and their property are alienated from him. His rationalist arguments are dismissed by them as 'atheism'. Virginia, although underage, is abducted to France, where she is enrolled as a nun (Lascelles's sister turning out to be a secret Catholic, unknown even to him). The Fullertons separate. She, however, is disillusioned in 'Superior' (as she calls Lascelles) when he finally marries for money. She is reunited with Richard, only to watch him die nobly and agnostically. It all ends, enigmatically, with the widowed Hermione wondering whether she has done the right thing: 'Had it been a holy sacrifice of the baser human affections to the nobler spiritual aspirations? or had it been the cruelty of superstition? the inhuman blindness of fanaticism?' The asperity of Linton's narrative tone indicates her opinion on the matter.

Ungava, R. M. Ballantyne, 1858, 1 vol, Nelson. Subtitled 'A Tale Of Esquimaux Land', *Ungava* recalls the physical details of the author's own early experiences with the Hudson's Bay Company. Frank Morton (six feet one inches tall, twenty-two-years-old, single) and George Stanley ('nearly six feet high', forty-years-old, married) set up a trading post (with fifteen volunteers) for their fur company in Canada's frozen north at Ungava, among the warring Eskimo and Indian natives. Various adventures ensue, such as the heroes being buried alive in a snowfall. The climax of the narrative is Frank's rescue, snow-blinded and wounded, from the elements and the wolves by ten-year-old Edith Stanley whom, seven years later, he marries. The story has revealing descriptions of Eskimo life and as Ballantyne claimed, 'most of its major incidents are facts'.

Union Jack (1880–83, 1894–1933). A weekly journal for boys, originated by W. H. G. Kingston* and subsequently taken over by G. A. Henty*. It collapsed in 1883 (under competition from the *Boy's Own Paper**) but the title was later revived by Alfred Harmsworth. In this second incarnation of *Union Jack*, the detective* Sexton Blake first made his appearance and Blake stories were thereafter published (by various hands and in various places) until the 1960s. The detective's first chronicler was Harry Blyth (1852–98) writing under the pseudonym 'Hal Meredith'.

UPWARD, Allen (1863–1926). Upward was born at Worcester, the son of a land-owner and JP. He was educated at Great Yarmouth Grammar School and at the Royal University of Ireland, where he won the O'Hagan gold medal for oratory. Upward subsequently read law at the Inns of Court, winning two first-class scholarships in the process. He was called to the Irish Bar in 1887 and the English Bar in 1889. Upward stood unsuccessfully for Parliament in 1895 and fought as a volunteer in the Greco-Turkish War in

1897. Although nearly sixty, he also volunteered for the first World War in 1914. Upward never married. He was the author of numerous romances including: *The Prince Of Balkistan*, (1895); *A Day's Tragedy* (1897), 'A Novel In Rhyme'; *The Secrets Of The Courts Of Europe* (1897); *The Wrongdoer* (1900). Upward was also the author of the 'International Spy' series in *Pearson's Magazine** (1895–1905) and wrote *The Secret History Of Today, Being Revelations Of A Diplomatic Spy* (1904). His novel *Athelstane Ford* (1899) opens with a typical flourish: 'It has not happened to many men, as I think, to have fallen into the hands of as cruel and bloodthirsty a monster as ever defiled God's earth, and to have escaped to tell the tale.' BL 34. *WW*. Wol.

V

Valentine Vox, The Ventriloquist, Henry Cockton, 1840, 1 vol, Lea. (Serialised in monthly numbers March 1839–October 1840, illustrated by T. Onwhyn*.) Cockton's first, most popular and much reprinted work. The loose Pickwickian narrative is hitched on to the adventures and capers of Valentine, a Suffolk boy who discovers at four that he has ventriloquial powers. Once grown up, he travels to London to make his way and to practice his 'art'. There is predictable hilarity when he throws his voice into the statue of Memnon in the British Museum ('How's your mother?'); into a murderer's skull at a phrenological lecture; into figures at a waxwork; into the orang-utan in Regent's Park Zoo. Cockton adeptly catches the actuality of life in London (such things, for instance, as what an omnibus ride from Piccadilly Circus to the Elephant and Castle in the 1830s was like). He was, apparently, strongly influenced by *Nicholas Nickleby**, and Dickens's* creation of Dotheboys Hall. Valentine's friend, Goodman is seized from the London streets and forcibly incarcerated in Dr Holdem's private lunatic asylum on the instigation of his wicked brother Walter. There he is goaded into madness, and dies shortly after being rescued. A remorseful Walter drowns himself in the Thames. In the happier part of the story, Valentine gets his Louise, together with a handsome inheritance, and restrains his ventriloquial extravagances in later life.

VANDAM, Albert D[resden] (1843–1903). Vandam was born in London, of Jewish extraction, his father being a senior Dutch Civil Servant in charge of Holland's state lottery. He was brought up in Paris and after the Franco-Prussian War settled in London, where he worked as a journalist. From 1882 to 1887 he was Paris correspondent for the *Globe*. His fiction includes *An Everyday Heroine* (1877), a work set in Holland and derived from the Dutch original of J. J. Cremer. Vandam also wrote criminal and detective* stories (some documentary) gathered in volume form as: *Masterpieces Of Crime* (1892); *A Coroner's Story* (1893); *The Mystery Of The Patrician Club* (1894). BL 4. *DNB*. Wol.

Vanity Fair, William Makepeace Thackeray, 1848, 1 vol, Bradbury and Evans. (Serialised in monthly numbers, January 1847–July 1848, with illustrations by the author.) Thackeray's masterpiece. The story begins in 1813 with two young girls of different character leaving Miss Pinkerton's private school in Chiswick. Amelia Sedley is a demure young lady, the virtuous daughter of a City of London merchant. Becky Sharp is the orphaned daughter of a bohemian artist, half-French and totally unscrupulous. Becky goes to spend a short holiday at the Sedley house in Russell Square, before taking up work as a governess. There she tries to entrap Amelia's fat nabob brother Jos into marriage. But the scheme is frustrated (in a notably comic episode at Vauxhall Gardens) by Amelia's lover, Captain George Osborne. Having taken up her position at Queen's Crawley, Becky employs her sexual charms to fascinate the boorish Sir Pitt Crawley who, when his feeble wife dies, proposes to his unscrupulous governess. But it is too late, Becky has already secretly married Sir Pitt's raffish dragoon son, Rawdon Crawley. Meanwhile, Amelia's affairs have gone awry. Following Mr Sedley's commercial failure, George's father forbids his son to marry her. Urged by his more honourable friend Captain Dobbin, George (who has few honourable instincts himself) does so. The newly married Osbornes and Crawleys spend their honeymoons together at Brighton, before embarking to Belgium to help the Iron Duke counter Napoleon's threat. In Brussels, Becky entraps George into a foolish offer of elopement. But Waterloo intervenes, and George dies at Quatre Bras. After the battle Amelia and Becky (now mothers) go their separate ways. Becky after some years on the Continent comes to London where, aided by the lecherous Lord Steyne, she conquers English society and is presented to George IV. But she is ruined when her husband (whom she has arranged to have arrested) surprises her in her private apartments with Steyne. They part, he to be governor of Coventry Island, where he dies of fever. Becky takes herself off to the Continent, where she lives a bohemian existence. Amelia has meanwhile suffered increasing poverty living with her parents at Fulham. And, with great suffering and heartsearching, she has entrusted the care of young George to his vulgar but rich grandfather, Mr Osborne. Meanwhile she is faithfully loved by Dobbin. Old Osborne finally dies, leaving Amelia prosperous. Dobbin returns from Indian service with Jos Sedley and they go on a continental tour with Amelia and George. In Pumpernickel (i.e. Weimar) they meet up with Becky. She finally entraps Jos, and with perverse good humour, induces Amelia to give up her worship of the deceased George ('that padded booby!') and accept Dobbin. In an ironic postscript, we learn that Becky poisons Jos and enriched by his life insurance reinstates herself as a respectable lady in Vanity Fair (i.e. middle-class England). Thackeray's novel is one of the century's finest feats of satiric narration in a style derived directly from Fielding and with a moral severity drawn from Bunyan.

Varney The Vampire, Or The Feast Of Blood, James Malcolm Rymer [Errym], 1847, 3 vols, Lloyd. (Serialised in 1d. numbers, 1845–47.) The most famous of the 1d. gothic* serials, together with T. P. Prest's* *String Of Pearls* (1846). Although J. W. Polidori's *The Vampyre* (1819) is the first novel on the fascinating theme in English, and Bram Stoker's* *Dracula** the most famous, Rymer's 868-page epic is both original and, in its crude way, a powerful fiction. It opens with a tremendous chapter: 'Midnight. The Hailstorm. The Dreadful Visitor. The VAMPYRE.' An amateurish, but sufficiently bloodcurdling, woodcut shows the fiend 'at his hideous repast'. The vampire (Sir Francis Varney, the new owner of Ratford Abbey by day) attacks Flora Bannerworth by night. She is protected by her brothers and by her lover Charles Holland (later imprisoned by Varney in a vile dungeon). The narrative becomes extremely digressive and inconsequential after the initial clash between the forces of family decency and obscene monstrosity. Rymer was evidently persuaded by the popularity of the work to extend it far beyond the elasticity of his imagination. Finally, Varney is consumed with remorse at the death of another victim, Clara Crofton. He confesses his gruesome history to a clergyman. He has been a vampire since the time of the English Civil War. 'I cannot help it, I am what I am', he declares, with a Byronic flourish. Varney finally destroys himself on Vesuvius: 'He took one tremendous leap, and disappeared into the burning mouth of the mountain.' The work has often been misattributed to Thomas Peckett Prest.

VELEY, Margaret (1843–87). Veley was born at Braintree, Essex, the daughter of a solicitor. She was educated locally and lived at home until 1880, when she moved to London. The deaths of her father and two sisters at this date seem to have had a profound effect on her. Veley's published career as an author began in 1870, with 'Milly's First Love', a story which she contributed to *Blackwood's Magazine**. She subsequently contributed serials to various top-flight magazines: *For Percival* (1878), first published in *Cornhill**, being the liveliest of her works. The dedication which describes the work as 'my first book' suggests that it may have been written some years before. A story of love, inheritance and wasted chances, it follows the career of Percival Thorne, who finishes the novel having lost self-respect, the woman he loves and the chance of a political career. *Mitchelhurst Place* (1884) was serialised in *Macmillan's Magazine**; *Mrs Austin* (1887) and *Damocles* (1882) in *Cornhill*. The last is another rueful story of loss in an otherwise comfortably middle-class station of life. It concludes with the typical Veley moral: 'People talk of life as a vale of tears till the expression is repulsively hackneyed. Rachel [the heroine] was astonished when she suddenly discovered the meaning of it.' Veley's later work tends to be depressed and world-weary in this way. Her shorter pieces were collected as *A Garden Of Memories* (1887). She never married and died young. BL 4. *DNB*. Wol.

Venetia, Benjamin Disraeli, 1837, 3 vols, Colburn. A fantasia on Byronic and Shelleyan themes. Marmion and Lady Annabel Herbert separate on account of his republican sympathies. He goes off to become a general in the American revolutionary army, and after the war lives in Italy. The Herberts' daughter Venetia grows up fascinated with her father, whom she knows by his portrait and by his vibrant poetry. Venetia's love affair with Lord Cadurcis is obstructed by her mother, who objects to the young man's radical politics. Venetia suffers a physical breakdown and goes to Italy with her mother to recuperate. There she effects a reconciliation between her parents. Moreover Cadurcis arrives and is also reconciled to Lady Annabel. The story ends tragically, however, when Mrmion and Cadurcis are drowned, after much high-flown conversation, in a squall in the bay of Spezzia. Venetia subsequently marries Cadurcis's cousin, Captain George.

VERNEY, Lady Frances [Parthenope] (née Nightingale) (1819–90). The oldest daughter of William Edward Nightingale (born 'Shore') of Lea Hurst in Derbyshire, a rich and cultivated lover of travel. She was also the nurse Florence Nightingale's (1820–1910) sister. Frances had her odd middle name from Naples, where she was born. In 1852 she published a volume of 'hints on mathematics' for governesses. In 1858 she married the Rt Hon. Sir Harry Verney MP, as his second wife. Frances Verney subsequently wrote the novels: *Stone Edge* (1868), a tale of the moor; *Lettice Lisle* (1870), a novel consciously intended to commemorate the rich dialect of the northern Midlands, in the spirit of Max Müller's linguistics; *Ferneyhurst Court* (1871); *Llanaly Reefs* (1873), a novel of wrecking on the Welsh coast. The author's short stories were collected as *The Grey Pool* (1891). Verney also wrote knowledgeably about the condition of peasant life on the Continent. BL 6. *DNB*. Wol.

The Vicar Of Bullhampton, Anthony Trollope, 1870, 1 vol, Bradbury and Evans. (Serialised in monthly parts, July 1869–May 1870, illustrated by H. Woods.) A deliberate attempt by Trollope to deal with the 'unpleasant' topic of prostitution. Carry Brattle is a 'castaway' around whom the plot revolves. Seduced and abandoned by her lover in London, she is a source of bitter shame to her father, Jacob Brattle, the miller of Bullhampton. The Brattles' miseries are multiplied when a son, Sam, is accused of murdering a local farmer. The Marquis of Trowbridge, the main landowner in the area, peremptorily demands that the Brattles' landlord, Squire Harry Gilmore, evict them. But Gilmore refuses, and is supported by the vicar of Bullhampton, Frank Fenwick and his wife Jane. Fenwick resourcefully detects the real murderers and reconciles Brattle to his luckless daughter. The Marquis has spitefully released some ground near the vicarage to Primitive Methodists. But when it emerges that the property is not his to give the nonconformists are obliged to pull down their unpleasant tabernacle. In a pathetic sub-plot Harry Gilmore loves and loses (gracefully) Mary Lowther to his rival, Walter Marrable. The novel outlines Trollope's ideals of traditional English manliness.

The Vicar Of Wrexhill, Mrs Frances Trollope, 1837, 3 vols, Bentley. (The novel was illustrated by Trollope's protégé, Auguste Hervieu.) A powerful novel, written during Mrs Trollope's early phase of social-critical fiction. The action is set in the early 1830s. Middle-aged Mrs Clara Mowbray is left a widow, with a fortune of £14,000-a-year when her husband dies suddenly of apoplexy. Weak-minded and unfit for anything but domestic responsibilities, she puts her trust in a newly arrived and slimily evangelical clergyman, the Rev. William Cartwright. He consoles the bereaved heiress, divides her from her children Charles (at Oxford), Fanny, Helen and Rosalind who are not provided for in their father's will. Cartwright proposes marriage before others can claim the prize. Mrs Mowbray accepts and discovers his true nature just before her death with her new-born baby. The reading of her will is the climax of the novel. Despite Cartwright's watching her day and night she has added a secret codicil, leaving everything to Charles. The villainous Vicar is disgraced and driven out of Wrexhill together with his evangelical henchman and cousin, Stephen Corbold. The work gave offence on three counts. First, it was an attack on the established Church. Secondly, it was startlingly frank in its description of Cartwright's seducing young girls and widows in his flock. (Mrs Trollope seems at times to be aspiring to write an Anglican version of *Maria Monk**.) Thirdly, the author of this distasteful material was not a man, nor anonymous, but a woman. Thackeray* (one of many hostile reviewers) sternly observed in *Fraser's Magazine** that Mrs Trollope 'had much better remained at home, pudding-making or stocking-mending'.

Villette, Charlotte Brontë, 1853, 3 vols, Smith, Elder. The author's most revealingly autobiographical novel. The story is told in the first person by Lucy Snowe. Left alone in the world, Lucy resourcefully makes her own way; first as a paid companion, then as a teacher in a Brussels ('Villette') boarding school, or *pensionnat*. There she has a strained relationship with the establishment's proprietress, Madame Beck. The school's doctor, John Bretton (who turns out to be the son of Lucy's godparent) is attracted to Lucy, but she discourages him. He turns to the flirtatious and spoiled Ginevra Fanshawe before finding a more suitable lover in his childhood sweetheart, Paulina. On her part, Lucy is fascinated by the dominating professor, Paul Emanuel. After a number of awkward and testing encounters (in one of which she breaks his spectacles) the couple admit their love for each other, despite the obstructions put in their way by Madame Beck. At the end of the novel, Paul is returning from the West Indies, and may have been drowned at sea. (Lucy will not tell the reader.) The heroine is left in charge of their school. The novel is an evocation of Brontë's own experiences in Brussels in the 1840s.

VINCENT, Sir Francis (1803–80). Vincent was born in London. In 1809 he became the tenth Baronet Vincent and was in adult life MP for the city of St Albans (1832–35). His first novel was a tale of the French Revolution, *Arundel* (1840). He went on to write: *Sir Hubert Marston* (1867); *On The Brink* (1868); *The Carylls* (1871); *The Fitful Fever Of A Life* (1872). Vincent was a Newby* author, and doubtless wrote out of vanity rather than for profit. No critic seems to have thought well of his fiction. BL 5. Boase. Wol.

The Virginians, William Makepeace Thackeray, 1859, 2 vols, Bradbury and Evans. (Serialised in monthly parts, November 1857–October 1859, with illustrations by the author.) Thackeray's American Revolution novel, continuing the dynastic history of the Henry Esmond* family. Rachel Esmond Warrington has twin sons, heirs to the Virginian estate of Castlewood. The elder, George, is bookish and a reincarnation of his gallant grandfather. Harry is boisterous and good-natured. George joins the forces of Braddock and is thought killed by the French in Canada. Now the sole heir, Harry goes to England. There he falls in with the degenerate main branch of the Castlewood family, and becomes a favourite of Baroness Bernstein (formerly Henry Esmond's love, Beatrix). Harry is rogued out of his money by Will Castlewood and is entrapped by the ageing Castlewood daughter Maria (the match is eventually frustrated by the Baroness Bernstein with some judicious misinformation about the other lady's false teeth). Harry is ruined and in debtors' prison when miraculously George reappears, not dead after all. He clears his brother's debts and settles down to live the struggling life of a man of letters in London. He marries Theo Lambert, a colonel's daughter.

(Sadly, Harry does not marry her sister Hetty, who loves him.) George unexpectedly becomes Sir George when a distant relative dies. Harry goes off to fight with Wolfe against the French. The novel's climax centres around the War of Independence. George fights for the crown, Harry with Washington (an old personal enemy of his brother's). Thereafter, the Warringtons live separate lives, united still in love for each other. By his own confession, Thackeray handled the American War action of the later narrative badly, postponing and underplaying it. But the novel is among the finest written of the author's career, showing off his urbane prose to perfection.

Virtue (1855–69). Publisher, printer and, for a short period in the 1860s, magazine proprietor. James [Sprent] Virtue (1829–92) was the son and business successor of George Virtue (1793–1868) who earlier in the century founded a firm specialising in the printing of illustrated works (notably the hugely successful *Art Journal*). James continued the Virtues' tradition of finely printed books, after taking over the family printing and publishing business in 1855. In 1867 with Trollope*, Virtue founded *St Paul's Magazine* and for two years (until the magazine was taken over by Strahan*) published the novelist's major works, paying him at the highest rate of his career. But after this brief experiment with fiction, Virtue returned to his safer, specialised line of illustrated book production. *DNB*.

Vittoria, George Meredith, 1866, 3 vols, Chapman and Hall. (Serialised in the *Fortnightly Review**, January–December 1866.) The sequel to *Sandra Belloni** (1864). Emilia is now in Milan, an opera singer and collaborator with the Italian resistance to the Austrian occupation. (But, as the narrator interjects, 'he who tells this tale is not a partisan'.) Her professional name is (symbolically) Vittoria, and she will signal the start of the War of Independence by breaking into an agreed song on stage at La Scala, during a performance of *Camilla*. Vittoria's relations with the Italian patriots are complicated by Wilfrid Pole (or 'Pierson'), now an officer with the Austrians, and by the machinations of the vengeful Anna von Lenkestein and Violetta d'Isorella. Her old friend Merthyr Powys reappears, but she marries neither of her British suitors, choosing instead an Italian count, Carlo Ammiani. The narrative concludes with 'Episodes Of Revolt And War'. Ammiani is killed in a confused duel and Merthyr delivers the 'burden of death' to Vittoria who 'lived through it as her Italy had lived through the hours which brought her face to face with her dearest in death'. She bears a son, Carlo Merthyr Ammiani.

Vizetelly (1842-89). Engraver and publisher. Henry [Richard] Vizetelly (1820–94) was born in London, the son and grandson of printers. (Italian ancestors had migrated from Italy at the end of the seventeenth century.) He was apprenticed as a wood engraver and assisted in the setting up of the *Illustrated London News** in 1842. In 1843 Vizetelly started his own rival, the *Pictorial Times*, recruiting as writers Douglas Jerrold*, Mark Lemon* and Thackeray*. In 1852 Vizetelly published a highly profitable pirated edition of *Uncle Tom's Cabin*. He also started the magazine the *Welcome Guest* in 1858. In the 1860s he returned to work for the *Illustrated London News* and from 1865 to 1872 was the paper's Paris correspondent. In the 1870s he returned to England. By this time he had a considerable reputation as a writer on continental literature and as a connoisseur of wines. In 1884, he published translations of Zola's *Nana* and *L'Assommoir* followed a year later by *Germinal* and *Pot-Bouille*. Other of the French novelist's works appeared until 1888 when *La Terre* provoked a legal action by the authorities. Vizetelly pleaded guilty to publishing obscene articles and was fined £100. In 1889, Vizetelly reissued his Zola titles, slightly expurgated by his son Ernest. Again he was tried and at the Old Bailey sentenced to three months' imprisonment. He was sixty-nine and in poor health. The firm collapsed. In 1893, Vizetelly published his autobiographical *Glances Back Through Seventy Years*. Vizetelly wrote a 'fictitious narrative' in 1849, purporting to be his observations of some 'Forty-niners' in California. Entitled *Four Months Among The Gold Finders Of Alta California* (1849, 'By James Tyrwhitt Brooks, MD'), the work was generally supposed to be authentic. Vizetelly's son, Ernest Alfred (1853–1922), was a precociously young journalist and wrote fiction with French and other European settings, including *The Scorpion, A Romance Of Spain* (1894) and *A Path Of Thorns* (1901). Ernest Vizetelly was decorated with the Legion of Honour for gallantry during the siege of Paris, 1870. (EV) BL 2. *DNB*. Wol. RLF.

VOGEL, [Sir] Julius (1835–99). Vogel was born in London of Jewish parents who died when he was sixteen. He was educated at University College School and the Royal School of Mines, after which he emigrated to Victoria in 1852 where for the next nine years he worked first as a goldminer then as a journalist. Vogel settled in Dunedin, New Zealand, in 1861, where he started the first daily newspaper in the country. His fellow editor was the novelist B. L. Farjeon*. Vogel subsequently went into politics and was the New Zealand Premier for two spells in the early 1870s (in the aftermath of the Maori Wars), service which culminated in a knighthood in 1875. The rights of women were among his special interests. Vogel spent the last eleven years of his life in England, where he was active in pro-imperialist lobbying. He died in London. Vogel wrote a number of miscellaneous books and pamphlets, including the immensely long and tedious work of science fiction*, *Anno Domini 2000, Or Woman's Destiny* (1889). BL 1. *DNB*. RM

The Voice Of The Charmer, L. T. Meade (i.e. Elizabeth Thomasina Smith), 1895, 3 vols, Chatto. At this period of her life, Meade was churning out six novels a year. This tells the melodramatic story of John Ward. Possessed of hypnotic power, he enslaves his wife, and forces her to collaborate in crime with him. She finally regains her will, and makes amends. They are both eventually killed in a flood. Meade was interested in hypnotism and wrote several novels on the subject in the 1890s. This work must have been one of the last three-deckers.

VOYNICH, Ethel [Lilian](née Boole, 1864–1947?). Youngest of five daughters of the mathematician, George Boole (1815–64), whose algebra is the basis of twentieth-century computer systems. Ethel Boole was brought up in Cork. She married the Polish Count Wilfrid Voynich (1865–1930) and through him was introduced to revolutionary European politics. This resulted in her first and most successful novel *The Gadfly* (1897), a story of revolution in Italy culminating in the uprising of 1848. The novel enjoyed a huge and durable success in the twentieth century, particularly in communist countries. In 1910, Voynich produced a sequel continuing the narrative of *The Gadfly* and called *An Interrupted Friendship*. By her own account, in 1911, she gave up writing to concentrate on music. But several decades later she produced a third instalment of the *The Gadfly* saga called *Put Off Thy Shoes* (1945) which takes the story back to the heroine's Cornish childhood. Voynich wrote other novels, of less weight, in her later life which she largely spent in America. BL 7. *WW. NCBEL.*

W

WALFORD, L[ucy] B[ethia](née Colquhoun, 1845–1915). Lucy Colquhoun was born at Portobello, near Edinburgh, the daughter of a sportsman, author of *The Moor And The Loch* and formerly an army officer. The family was well connected and Lucy was the granddaughter of a baronet, Sir James Colquhoun. Her childhood was, as she recalled, 'old-fashioned, peaceful, absolutely quiet'. At seven, she was reading 'avidly', and was strongly influenced by the works of Charlotte Yonge* virtually in her infancy. Her aunt was the Scottish novelist Catherine Sinclair*, author of *Holiday House*. She was educated at home by English and foreign governesses. The domestic atmosphere at the Walford house was sternly Presbyterian (the author later remembered 'terrible Sundays') but the family moved in good Edinburgh society. In 1868, Lucy Colquhoun read Jane Austen for the first time, an experience that was, she claimed, 'to exercise an abiding influence over all my own future efforts'. In 1869, she married Alfred Saunders Walford (d. 1907), of Cranbrook Hall, Ilford, Essex. After marriage, she began to write (at first secretly). As Lucy Walford, she contributed to *Blackwood's Magazine** and produced numerous sketches and stories, many with an Edinburgh setting. Her first novel, *Mr Smith, A Part Of His Life* (1874) had been years in the writing, and was successful when it first appeared. A domestic, jaunty tale marked by one-sentence paragraphs and elliptical comedy, the work had the approval of Queen Victoria herself ('I wish we had more literature of this kind'). Walford's other fiction includes: *Pauline* (1877), first serialised in *Blackwood's Magazine*; *The Baby's Grandmother* (1884); *Cousins* (1885); *The History Of A Week* (1886), the story of three young heroines in Galloway; *A Mere Child* (1888); *A Stiff-Necked Generation* (1889); *The Havoc Of A Smile* (1890); *The Mischief Of Monica* (1892); *Sir Patrick, The Puddock* (1899). In the 1890s, Walford extended her range beyond Blackwood's (which had been less congenial since the death of John Blackwood in 1879) and wrote for the London magazines (including Edmund Yates's* *World*) and was from 1889 to 1893 London correspondent for the New York *Critic*. She retained her irrepressible vivacity up to her last novel, *David And Jonathan On The Riviera* (1914). Walford wrote an autobiography rich in childhood memories, called *Recollections Of A Scottish Novelist* (1910). BL 42. *WW*. Wol.

WALKER, Fred[erick] (1840–75). Illustrator. The son of a jeweller, Walker was born in London and educated at the Royal Academy Schools. In 1855, he was apprenticed to an architect. Already a proficient artist on wood, he was recruited in 1860 by Thackeray* to illustrate his novel *Philip* for the new *Cornhill Magazine*. Walker went on to illustrate other serials in the magazine, including Anne Thackeray Ritchie's* *The Story Of Elizabeth*. He also worked in the 1860s for *Good Words*, the *Graphic* and *Once A Week*. Walker is probably best remembered in the twentieth century, however, for his rather sombre illustrations to late reissues of Dickens's* fiction. Towards the end of his short life he was concentrating on painting in water colours. His style is powerful and realistic, in the 1860s fashion. *DNB*. Hou.

WALMSLEY, Hugh Mulleneux (1826–79). Born in Liverpool, he was a son of Sir Joshua Walmsley (1794–1871), the politician who was mayor of Liverpool in 1838, knighted in 1840 and an MP from 1849 to 1857. The young Walmsley was a man of strong religious convictions, being for some years President of the National Sunday League. He also travelled widely (notably in Africa) and wrote stories of adventure by land and sea, including: *The Life Guardsman* (1871), an eighteenth-century historical* novel, set in France; *Branksome Dene, A Sea Tale* (1872), dedicated to the recently died publisher, Richard Bentley*. He published a dutiful life of his father, Sir Joshua, and had some success with *Wild Sports And Savage Life In Zululand* (1872). BL 5. (JW)*DNB*. Wol.

The War Of The Worlds, H. G. Wells, 1897, 1 vol, Heinemann. (Serialised in *Pearson's Magazine*, April–December 1897, illustrated by Warwick Goble.) Although its own source lies fairly clearly in Chesney's* invasion-phobia fable, *The Battle Of Dorking* (1871), the imitators of Wells's story in subsequent twentieth-century science fiction* are legion. As in *The Invisible Man*, the tale generates its powerful impact by imagining a gross violation of George Orwell's 'gentle' England. The Martians, driven by the inhospitability of their dying planet and assisted by superior technology, colonise earth. Their first cylinders land at Horsell Common and excite the normally torpid inhabitants of Chobham and Woking. (Among whom is the narrator, currently writing a paper on morality; a subject rendered meaningless by the interplanetary *Realpolitik* of the Martians.) Wells charts the panic and the break-up of civilisation in the Home Counties and the capital. After the inadequate resistance of human artillery and ironclads (in a dramatic Thames estuary scene) against the enemy's fighting machines, heat ray and black smoke, all is lost. In his desperate flight and his struggle to reach his wife at Leatherhead, the narrator has a series of adventures, 'grotesque gleams of a time no history will ever record'. In a ruined house at Halliford, he is trapped with a maniac curate. (Here it is that the Martians' diet of human blood is revealed; one of the few gothic* excesses in an otherwise soberly documentary narrative.) At Putney he meets an artilleryman whose plans for a rebel race of humans ('big, savage rats') are revealed as pipe-dreams. Finally, in the wasteland of 'dead London' mankind's salvation is found to be the smallest of earth's inhabitants, the disease germ: 'there are no bacteria on Mars'. The novel (published during one of Victoria's Jubilee years) is a striking illustration of national bad conscience on the matter of British imperialism. As the narrator muses: 'the Tasmanians, in spite of their human likeness, were entirely swept out of existence in a war of extermination waged by European immigrants, in the space of fifty years.'

WARBURTON, 'Eliot' [Bartholomew Elliott George] (1810–52). Warburton was born in Tullamore, Northern Ireland, where his father was a former Inspector General of the Irish Constabulary. After graduating from Cambridge University in 1833 he was admitted to the Irish Bar in 1837 but soon gave up the legal profession in order to write and to travel. His taste for exotic voyages was stimulated by a trip to the Middle East in 1843. While in Paris, he came under the influence of De Tocqueville and in 1844 he was persuaded by Charles Lever* (for whom as editor of the *Dublin University Magazine** he had written some articles) to produce his sociological travel book, *The Crescent And The Cross, Or Romance And Realities Of Eastern Travel*. Together with Kinglake's *Eothen* (also 1844) this account of life in the Orient was immensely popular and was skilfully marketed by Henry Colburn* (who regarded it as the best contemporary book he ever published). Warburton was killed, prematurely, in a ship's fire, on his way to the Isthmus of Darien. Towards the end of his short life he edited the travel book (by George Drought Warburton), *Hochelaga, Or England In The New World* (1846). He also wrote a pair of novels: *Reginald Hastings* (1849), a tale of Ireland in the seventeenth century; *Darien, Or The Merchant Prince* (1852). The last was Warburton's most popular work of fiction; it features some bloody scenes of torture and a scene of shipboard fire which uncannily predicts the author's own death. BL 2. *DNB. NCBEL*. Wol.

WARD, Mrs T[homas] Humphry [Mary Augusta] (née Arnold, 1851–1920). Mary Augusta Arnold was born in Hobart, Tasmania. Her father was a son and namesake of Dr Thomas Arnold of Rugby School, and Matthew Arnold was one of Mary's uncles. Thomas Arnold the younger had been infected with the dangerous enthusiasms of the Oxford movement, and went to Australasia out of muddled religious idealism. Farming did not suit him, and he became a school administrator. But this position was forfeit in 1854, when he formally entered the Catholic Church. The Arnolds returned to Britain in 1856. Thomas Arnold was given a teaching position with Newman* at the Catholic University in Dublin. The young Mary (one of eight children) spent much time at Fox How near Ambleside in the Lake District, whose surroundings left a lifelong impression on her. They reappear glowingly in much of the later fiction. The young girl's school education was disrupted and unsatisfactory (she gives her vivid recollections of the boarding schools she was sent to in the early chapters of *Marcella**, 1894). In 1865, very fortuitously from Mary's point of view, her father reconverted to Anglicanism. This permitted Arnold to accept the post teaching English at Oxford for which his training, intellect and family connections qualified him. And in 1867, the family was united at Oxford. Resourcefully, and with the assistance of Mark Pattison, Mary educated herself at the Bodleian (there was at this date no chance of her receiving a formal university education). By her own efforts she had made herself by the early 1870s one of the world's leading authorities on early Spanish history and literature. Arnold had also been writing fiction since childhood, and in 1869 her first story, 'A Westmoreland Story', was published in the *Churchman's Companion*. The next few years were eventful. In 1872, she married a young fellow of

Brasenose, Thomas Humphry Ward. The next nine years were spent in Oxford as a don's wife. She bore three children (the first in 1874) and was active as Secretary of the Oxford Association for the Education of Women in opening the university to women students. This led to the founding of Somerville College in 1879. In 1876, her father returned to Catholicism, a blow which finally shattered whatever relationship survived between him and his wife Julia. Mary, meanwhile, had swung round to a position bordering on Christian belief and agnostic rationalism. The 1870s were quiet years for her authorially; her major effort was reserved for the more than 200 entries she wrote for Dean Wace's *Dictionary Of Christian Biography*. And she wrote a not very successful children's story, *Milly And Olly* (1880). In 1881, she was strongly influenced by the Rev. J. Wordsworth's Bampton lecture and brought out a pamphlet entitled 'Unbelief And Sin'. In the same year, the material circumstances of her life changed when T. Humphry Ward took up a position as a leader writer and art critic on *The Times*. The family moved to Russell Square. London was stimulating to the still young Mary Ward, who had more money and more leisure than hitherto, enabling her to contribute fairly regularly to *Macmillan's Magazine**. She quickly gave up her ideas of writing a history of French literature and with the encouragement of Henry James published her first sizeable work of fiction, *Miss Bretherton**, in 1884. The work was slight, and although moderately well received, sold badly. She had difficulty finding a publisher for her next work, and even more trouble writing it. The work, when it finally appeared in print with Smith, Elder*, was *Robert Elsmere** (1888), probably the most popular novel of the century. A story of doubt, faith, privilege and poverty the novel crystallised a whole spectrum of Victorian ideological debate. Famously, even Gladstone was moved to pass judgement on the book, in *Nineteenth Century* in May 1888. Ward followed up with a novel set largely in the Lake District, *David Grieve** (1892). Although not as good a novel as its predecessor, the author had a huge sum (£7,000) for the American rights, that country having recently subscribed to international copyright law. In 1892, Ward was now wealthy enough to buy a large country house for herself, Stocks, near Tring. She was also able to establish a 'settlement' (or working people's centre) in Bloomsbury, called initially 'University Hall'. (It survives to the modern day as the Mary Ward Centre.) She paid a personal price for the terrible labour which it took her to write in the form of crippling physical disorders, and never enjoyed good health again for the rest of her life. In 1894 Ward published *Marcella*. This work was one of the last of the Victorian era's three-volume novels, and Ward was instrumental in helping abolish the obsolete form, aided by her friend and loyal publisher, George Smith. Her idyllic *The Story Of Bessie Costrell** was published in Smith's *Cornhill** in 1895. In 1896, Ward published Marcella's further adventures in the social problem* novel, *Sir George Tressady**. The following year, the Passmore Edwards Settlement, as University Hall was renamed, was opened, serving the local population of King's Cross and St Pancras. In 1898, Ward published her sensitive study of Catholicism, *Helbeck Of Bannisdale**, a work which recalls much of her family's sufferings in the wake of Thomas Arnold's religious conflicts. In 1899, Ward pioneered the setting up of nurseries for working women (another of her lasting bequests). By 1905, there were eight evening play-centres for children of working mothers in

London. At the same period, she was active against women's agitation for the vote, being a leader of the Anti-Suffrage League. Ward's later fiction rarely achieves the energy or imaginative power of *Robert Elsmere*. It includes *Eleanor* (1900); *Lady Rose's Daughter* (1903); *The Marriage Of William Ashe* (1905); *Fenwick's Career* (1906); *The Testing Of Diana Mallory* (1908); *The Case Of Richard Meynell* (1911), a sequel to *Robert Elsmere*; *The Mating Of Lydia* (1913); *Missing* (1917); *Harvest* (1920). Ward was active for her country during the first World War. She had always been immensely popular in North America. In 1908, she had visited Canada and the United States to lecture on education. Her propagandistic *England's Effort* (1916) was the outcome of first-hand experience visiting the trenches (which she did for a second time, in 1917). The book was written partly at the invitation of Theodore Roosevelt, to mobilise pro-war sentiment in the USA. It was followed by *Towards The Goal* (1917) for which Roosevelt wrote the foreword and *Fields Of Victory* (1919). In 1918, Ward published her incomplete but revealing *A Writer's Recollections*. In 1920, the year of her death, she became one of the first women magistrates in England and was awarded an honorary doctorate from Edinburgh University. BL 25. *DNB*. RM. *NCBEL*. Wol. Sad.

WARD, Robert Plumer (1765–1846). Robert Ward was born in Mayfair, London, the son of a merchant normally resident in Gibraltar. He was educated at Westminster School, and at Christ Church, Oxford. He read for the law, and was called to the Bar in 1790. Ward subsequently spent some time in France during the revolutionary period and on his return to England involved himself in politics. Helped by the patronage of Pitt he was elected to Parliament in 1802, and remained an MP until 1823. He made a first marriage in 1796; widowed, he remarried Mrs Plumer Lewin in 1828, adding part of her name to his. He eventually rose to be Sheriff of Hertfordshire and when his second wife died in 1831 made a third marriage with an heiress. He died at Chelsea Hospital, where his father-in-law was governor. Ward wrote three novels which (with the promotional assistance of Henry Colburn*) are pioneers of the silver fork* genre of fashionable fiction: *Tremaine, Or The Man Of Refinement* (1825); *De Vere, Or The Man Of Independence* (1827); *De Clifford, Or The Constant Man* (1841). The last, written at the age of seventy-six, is a novel published well out of its time. Plumer also wrote the social sketches *Illustrations Of Human Life* (1837); *Pictures Of The World At Home And Abroad* (1839) and edited the *roman-à-clef, Chatsworth, Or The Romance Of A Week* (1844). BL 4. *DNB*. RM. *NCBEL*. Wol. Sad.

Ward, Lock and Tyler (1854–). Publishers. The firm was founded in 1854 as a partnership between Ebenezer Ward and George Lock (d. 1891). The house absorbed the business of S. O. Beeton* in 1866 and that of Edward Moxon in 1870. The firm published the *Windsor Magazine* and the fiction of leading authors, including: Oscar Wilde* (notably his *Picture Of Dorian Gray*); Conan Doyle*; Arthur Morrison*; H. Rider Haggard*; Rudyard Kipling*.

The Warden, Anthony Trollope, 1855, 1 vol, Longman. This short work, the first of the Barchester series, marked a turn in Trollope's career. He wrote the story between July 1852 and autumn 1854, taking much longer over it than many of his vast later novels. The warden of the title is the Reverend Septimus Harding, precentor of Barchester Cathedral. Harding has charge of Hiram's Hospital, an almshouse founded in the Middle Ages to comfort a dozen old 'bedesmen'. This arrangement is upset by the suitor of Harding's daughter Eleanor, John Bold. Bold, a surgeon, is also a reformer. And he has friends among the London press who publicise the iniquity (as they see it) of Harding's sinecure. Battle is joined between the forces of conservatism (led by Harding's magnificently reactionary son-in-law, Archdeacon Grantly) and the forces of reform, led by Bold and the 'Thunderer' (i.e. *The Times*). Harding, a gentle, conscientious old man, is cruelly tormented by the thought that perhaps he is wrong to accept his warden's emolument. In the end, and to the disgust of the archdeacon, he retires. The result of all the wrangling is that the Hospital falls into dilapidation, and the bedesmen (who had wild ideas of becoming rich) are left uncomforted. Trollope used comedy to express his (conservative) opinion on the reform movement currently sweeping through the Anglican Church. *The Warden* was based on an actual recent case at Winchester Cathedral.

WARDEN, Florence [Alice] (i.e. Mrs George E. James, née Price, 1857–1929). Florence Price was born in Hanworth London, the daughter of a stockbroker. She was educated at Brighton and in France where she had the services of a finishing governess. From 1880 to 1885 she was on the stage (see her novel *From Stage To Peerage*, 1911) and she went on to marry George E. James in 1887. He was later dropped from her *Who's Who* entry, which presumably indicates separation. Warden's fiction comprises a huge quantity of romances for women readers and includes: *The House On The Marsh* (1882); *At The World's Mercy* (1884); *A Woman's Face* (1888); *The Witch Of The Hills* (1888); *A Passage Through Bohemia* (1893); *A Perfect Fool* (1895); *Kitty's Engagement* (1895); *The Inn By The Shore* (1897); *Joan The Curate* (1898), an eighteenth-century smuggling story; *A Lowly Lover* (1900). BL 158. *WW*. Wol. Sad. RLF.

WARREN, Samuel (1807–77). Warren was born near Wrexham, the elder son of a Methodist minister (earlier a French prisoner of war), and brought up in a strict religious atmosphere. Warren's father later took Anglican order and became a rector at Ancoats near Manchester. Young Warren studied medicine at Edinburgh, 1826–27. Even at this stage Warren's main interests seem to have been literary; he won a university prize for poetry in 1827 that brought him to the notice of the famous Blackwood's* writer, 'Christopher North' (i.e. John Wilson). On leaving university, Warren switched to law, working for six years in the courts. He was called to the Bar in 1837, and practised for the remainder of his working life, writing a number of legal works on the side. In 1851, Warren was made a QC and from 1852 to 1874 he was Recorder at the city of Hull. From 1856 to 1859 he served as a Conservative MP, resigning to become Master in Lunacy at a munificent £2,000 a year stipend. Warren, who modelled himself on Walter Scott, maintained strict anonymity in his lighter authorship, most of which appeared first in the pages of *Blackwood's Magazine**. *Passages From The Diary Of A Late Physician* (1833) caused some stir. Its successor, *Ten Thousand A Year** (1841) was immensely successful. *Now And Then*

(1847) was, by comparison, a disappointment. Warren, though he was proud of his literary productions, clearly wrote fiction as an interlude in a life predominantly devoted to the legal profession and posterity (perhaps unfairly) has viewed him as a one book author. BL 3. *DNB*. RM. *NCBEL*. Wol. Sad.

The Water-Babies, Charles Kingsley, 1863, 1 vol, Macmillan. (Subtitled 'A Fairy Tale For A Land Baby', the story was serialised in *Macmillan's Magazine**, August 1862–March 1863.) In *The Heroes* (1856) Kingsley adapted his moral teaching for the child reader. *The Water-Babies* similarly adapts his religious and (post-Darwinian) scientific thinking. The hero Tom is the epitome of Victorian abused childhood, a chimney sweep. Bullied by Grimes, his master, and ignorant as he is grimy, Tom blunders down the chimney of Harthover House into the bedroom of Ellie, the Squire's daughter. Suddenly ashamed of himself, he realises he is 'dirty' and runs away. Obsessed with the idea that he must be clean, he throws himself into a stream (an image which combines baptism with Kingsley's mission to reform English sanitation). Reborn in the water, Tom embarks on an adventure fantasia, involving among others, Ellie, Grimes (who is finally dispatched on the Sisyphean task of sweeping Mount Etna) and the mysterious Mother Carey. Kingsley is successful in mixing surreal episode (such as Tom's growing prickles when he steals sweets), Bunyanesque personification (e.g. Mrs Doasyouwouldbedoneby), scientific instruction and satire on various topical issues (e.g. the infidel materialist Professor Ptthmllnsprts). At the end of the tale Tom, who has undergone a literal sea-change, is united with Ellie. He goes on to become 'a great man of science'. The fable clearly rides several of Kingsley's hobby-horses on social, religious and scientific issues.

WATSON, H[enry] B[rereton] Marriott (1863–1921). Watson was born in Melbourne, Australia, the son of a clergyman. At nine, his family moved to New Zealand where he had his education. In 1885 he came to England, taking up journalism as his profession in 1887. He was an assistant editor on *Black And White* and the *Pall Mall Gazette* and collaborated with James Barrie* on the play *Richard Savage*. Watson wrote numerous novels, including: *Marahuna* (1888), a wild romance about a mysterious girl picked up by a sailor in the Pacific; *Lady Faint Heart* (1890); *Diogenes Of London* (1893); *Galloping Dick* (1896), a highwayman tale; *The Adventurers* (1898); *Chloris Of The Island* (1900), a historical* tale of the early nineteenth century. Watson had an affair with Graham [Rosamund] Tomson, poetess wife of the artist Arthur Tomson, whom he subsequently married. BL 43. *WW*. Wol. Sad. RLF.

WATSON, John ('Ian Maclaren', 1850–1907). Thoroughly Scottish by descent, Watson was never the less born in Manningtree, on the Essex coast. His father was a Civil Servant, who was appointed Receiver-General for Taxes in Scotland, where the family duly moved in 1854. The young Watson went to school in Stirling and Perth, eventually entering university at Edinburgh in 1866. He graduated four years later. Always destined for the Church, he trained at New College, Edinburgh (1870–74) prior to becoming a Presbyterian minister in Scotland. His first ministry was at Logiealmond in Perthshire, the 'Drumtochty' of his later fiction. He remained there three years, moving down to Sefton Park Presbyterian Church in Liverpool in 1880. Watson was successful in his profession, and was noted as a particularly powerful preacher. In this capacity, he toured the USA three times, dying there on his last trip at Mount Pleasant in Iowa. His remains were brought back to be buried in Liverpool. In the intervals of his ministry (enforced by bad health) and the writing of theology, Watson turned his hand to sketches and longer fictions, nostalgically reflective of an idealised rural Scottish life: *Beside The Bonnie Brier Bush** (1894); *The Days Of Auld Lang Syne* (1895); *Kate Carnegie* (1897). These sentimental tributes to his country were very popular and were regarded as among the finest products of the kailyard* school. As did J. M. Barrie*, Watson took his mother's maiden name ('Maclaren') as his *nom de plume*. Watson produced one long, continuous novel, *Graham Of Claverhouse*, which was published posthumously in 1908. BL 7. *DNB*.

WATTS-DUNTON, [Walter] Theodore (1832–1914). The author called himself Watts until 1897, when he added his mother's maiden name, Dunton. Theodore Watts was born at St Ives, Huntingdon, the eldest son of a solicitor. After going to school in Cambridge (where he seems to have been drawn to science) he was articled to his father. As a solicitor, Watts-Dunton came to London late in life (around 1870), where his inclination to write was stimulated. He contributed criticism to a number of papers, notably the *Athenaeum**, with which he was to have a lifelong association. Watts-Dunton seems to have been strongly influenced by the acquaintance of the two great British authorities on gypsy life, George Borrow* and Francis Hindes Groome*. As a coming man of letters he became acquainted with Rossetti and Swinburne, taking both their chaotic personal affairs in hand. Rossetti died in 1882, but Swinburne continued to live with Watts-Dunton at his home, the 'Pines' in Putney, for thirty years until the poet's death in 1909. He acted as friend, agent, guardian and nurse, sacrificing his own career in the process. This custodial relationship was not even affected by Watts-Dunton's marrying Clara Reich at the age of seventy-three in 1905. His first novel, *Aylwin**, a gypsy romance, was also a late-life thing, being published in 1898. (In fact, the work had been written many years before and had even been set up in type as early as 1885.) It reveals a soft-centred romanticism, which Watts-Dunton's otherwise orderly life would seem to belie. His other complete novel, *Vesprie Towers*, was published posthumously in 1916. *Carniola*, a Hungarian novel, was incomplete at the time of his death. All three works show the influence of Meredith*. BL 3. *DNB*. RM. *NCBEL*.

WAUGH, Edwin (1817–90). Waugh was born in Rochdale, the son of a shoemaker who died in 1826. Waugh's mother carried on the business, but with great financial difficulty. The young Edwin consequently educated himself, while working (after 1829) for a local bookseller. Waugh was later apprenticed as a printer, but on finishing his time could find no work. In 1847 (after travelling round the country) he settled again in Lancashire, where he had an appointment in the local educational service. Meanwhile he was publishing descriptive and vernacular pieces in the *Manchester Examiner*. In collected form these enjoyed some success as *Sketches Of Lancashire Life And Localities* (1855). Waugh's success spread beyond the county border with his sentimental dialect song written against the evils of drink, 'Come Whoam To The Childer An' Me'. In sheet form, the composition sold in the millions, boosted by its appeal to the powerful Victorian temperance movement. Waugh came down to London, where he gave public readings. In 1876, however, his health collapsed and he fell on hard times. He was awarded a Civil List pension of £90 by Gladstone in 1882. A typical sketch cum short story of Waugh's is 'Johnny O'Wobbler's And Th' Two-Wheeled Dragon, A Velocipede Story' (1869). His longer work is collected as *Besom Ben Stories* in various volumes from 1865 onwards. BL 19. *DNB. NCBEL. RLF.*

The Way Of All Flesh, Samuel Butler, 1903, 1 vol, Richards. (The novel was written between 1873 and 1884, but held back to avoid hurting living persons. It was published only after the author's death in 1902.) Butler's devastating denunciation of the Victorian family, the usual object of veneration in the period. The narrative covers three generations of the Pontifexes (so called from the parents' habit of laying down the law). George Pontifex, a successful and patriarchal printer of evangelical views, has a son, Theobald, whom he forces to go into the Church. Ordained, the dull-spirited Theobald is captured by Christina Allaby (who plays at cards with her sisters for the eligible young clergyman). The couple set up a conventional middle-class household. The Pontifex son, Ernest (born 1835, like Butler), is a quiet and unhappy child who is unmercifully tyrannised over at home by his father. Even unhappier and more humiliating are his experiences at Roughborough School. He is, however, saved from being utterly crushed by a warm-hearted spinster aunt, Alethea, and her friend Overton. Alethea Pontifex brings out Ernest's interest in music and the making of musical instruments. But, browbeaten by Theobald, the young man follows the conventional path through Cambridge and into the Anglican Church (in which he does not believe). In London, Ernest is cheated out of his inheritance. Worse, he mistakes a decent young lady for a prostitute and, driven by twenty-three years of evangelical repression, sexually assaults her. He goes to prison for six months. In one sense it is ruin; in another liberation from the stifling middle classes and, above all, the institution of the family. On his release, Ernest falls in with one of his family's former servants, whom he marries. But she turns out to be a doltish drunkard and it is with relief that he discovers that her marriage to him was in fact bigamous. With Overton's advice and Alethea's wealth, Ernest eventually becomes a philosophical man of letters and a happy recluse, free of all family connections. The novel is the most savagely comprehensive critique of Victorian ideology to be found in fiction.

The Way We Live Now, Anthony Trollope, 1875, 2 vols, Chapman and Hall. (Serialised in monthly numbers, February 1874–September 1875, with illustrations by L. G. Fawkes.) With this novel the aged Trollope raised his lash and let it fall on a society gone decadent, as he thought. In its satirical design, the novel attacks an all-pervading 'dishonesty'. The dishonesty of the literary world is shown in Lady Carbury's career in authorship. Good reviews of bad books are paid for with sexual favours, and not worth the paper they are printed on. Dishonesty among the younger set is shown at the Bear Garden Club, where Sir Felix Carbury and his cronies pay their gambling debts with worthless paper IOUs. Dishonesty on a grand commercial scale is magnificently portrayed in the career of Augustus Melmotte, the financier. At the suggestion of Hamilton K. Fisker (a sharp American huckster) Melmotte floats a gigantic American railway scheme. The English public, their parliamentary representatives, the City of London and the aristocracy are all taken in by the new Napoleon of commerce (who may be French, Jewish American or stateless) and his paper empire. Melmotte is chosen to host a banquet for the visiting Emperor of China. He is elected MP for Westminster and as the new Tory member is conducted into the House by Disraeli* himself (whom Trollope particularly disliked). The bubble bursts, Melmotte is ruined and commits suicide. Trollope weaves a multiple love plot in with his satire. The caddish Sir Felix is beloved by Melmotte's daughter but drunkenly bungles his elopement with her. His attempts to seduce the country girl, Ruby Ruggles, earn him a deserved beating-up from her aggrieved swain, John Crumb. Felix's amiable sister, Hetta, is torn between the love of her gentlemanly Suffolk cousin Roger (squire of Carbury Manor, and the original hero of the novel, as Trollope designed it) and Paul Montague, a handsome young man dangerously involved with Melmotte. On his part, Paul is entangled with Winifred Hurtle, a 'wild cat' American who has pursued him from San Francisco. In the final working out Paul wins Hetta, and is adopted as heir by Roger. *The Way We Live Now* is one of the longest of Trollope's forty-seven novels, and rich in sub-plot. Roger is in a religious dilemma between the Catholic and Anglican churches (Trollope originally intended to make more of this). And there is a particularly interesting narrative centred around the courtship of the aristocratic Georgiana Longestaffe by the vulgar (but essentially decent) Jewish financier, Brehgert. Trollope was inspired to write *The Way We Live Now* by the financial scandals which rocked England in the early 1870s. It is (with William Black's* *Sunrise*) one of the last memorable novels to come out in 'Dickensian*' monthly numbers.

WEDGWOOD, Frances Julia ('Snow', 'Florence Dawson', 1833–1913). Snow (so called after the weather conditions in Clapham at the time of her birth) was a great-granddaughter of Josiah Wedgwood and born into an intellectual milieu which also included the Darwins. Physically handicapped by deafness, she was severely repressed by the evangelical atmosphere of her upbringing. Throughout life, she was to make passionate and unhappy attachments to dominant men, older than herself. One of the first was to the Scottish theologian Thomas Erskine (1788–1870), whose amanuensis she became. More painfully, she attached herself to the poet Robert Browning, after the death of his wife in 1861. She offered him intelligent criticism of his poetry (especially *The Ring And The Book*) and the relationship was passionate, at least on her side. But he jilted her. At the age of twenty-five Snow Wedgwood embarked on fiction. In autumn 1855 (while assisting Mrs Gaskell* with the Brontë* letters) she began what was to become the novel *Framleigh Hall*. The work was accepted by Hurst and Blackett*, with the usual proviso that the villain be killed off, rather than the hero. The work came out in three volumes in January 1858, anonymously ('by J.W.'). It was well-reviewed and went into a second edition in six months. The story has some strong Eton scenes (showing

Henry Kingsley's* influence) and a Napoleonic War setting. Snow's father, Hensleigh Wedgwood, insisted on editing her second novel, *An Old Debt*, which came out in 1859 (the same year as his *Dictionary Of English Etymology* and her relative Darwin's *Origin Of Species*). This is a tighter more sensational* novel, set in the present. Published as by 'Florence Dawson', it too went into reprint editions on the strength of its appeal to women readers. At this point, the baleful prohibition of her father stopped Wedgwood's promising career in fiction, and she reverted to pious and philosophical writing. Her culminating achievement was a eulogy of self-sacrifice, *The Moral Ideal* (1888), and a life of Josiah Wedgwood, published posthumously in 1915. BL 2. Wol.

WEDMORE, [Sir] Frederick (1844–1921). Wedmore was born at Clifton and educated there and at Paris and Lausanne on the Continent. At the age of nineteen he became a journalist in Bristol and later moved on to London, where he specialised in art criticism for the newspapers, writing for the *Standard* and the *Academy** where he was a strong advocate of French painting. In 1885, he visited America and lectured on art at Harvard. His fiction includes: *The Two Lives Of Wilfrid Harris* (1868); *A Snapt Gold Ring* (1871); *Two Girls* (1873); *The Collapse Of The Penitent* (1900). Wedmore, who was knighted in 1912, also wrote poetry. In *Who's Who* the only fiction Wedmore admits to is the collection of short stories: *Pastorals Of France* (1877). BL 6. *WW*. Wol.

The Weir Of Hermiston, Robert Louis Stevenson, 1896, 1 vol, Chatto. (Serialised in *Cosmopolis**, January–April 1896.) Stevenson's last, fragmentary work of fiction and his most intense study of the father–son relationship which obsessed him. Archie Weir is the only and motherless child of Lord Justice Clerk Hermiston, a Scottish hanging judge with a bitter vernacular turn of phrase. Archie is disgusted with his father's judicial savagery and shouts out at a hanging that it is 'God-defying murder'. He discontinues his law studies. For his impudence he is sent away to the village of Hermiston, in the Scottish Borders, to be a 'laird' on his mother's former estate. There he falls in love with a local girl, Kirstie, the niece and namesake of his loyal housekeeper. Kirstie has four brothers called the 'Black Elliotts' who are legendary for having revenged themselves on the murderer of their father. Archie's affair with Kirstie is betrayed by a false friend, Frank Innes, and he vows not to dishonour her. At this tantalising point, the story was broken off by Stevenson's death. It was to continue with Archie's killing Frank, his being sentenced to death by his own father, his being rescued by the Black Elliotts, his escape to America with Kirstie. The novel is entirely overshadowed by the grim portrait of Lord Hermiston, the punishing father, a man who 'resolutely went up the great, bare staircase of his duty'.

The Well-Beloved, Thomas Hardy, 1897, 1 vol, Osgood, McIlvaine. (Serialised in the *Illustrated London News**, October–December 1892.) The story is most memorable for its evocation of Portland, the tongue of land off Dorset, connected to the shore by a stony causeway. (Portland is here called the 'Isle of Slingers'.) Jocelyn Pierston, a sculptor brought up on the island as the son of a stone merchant, devotes his life to the pursuit of ideal female beauty (the well-beloved). He sees it first in an island woman, Avice

Caro, to whom he becomes engaged. He jilts her for Marcia Bencombe, the daughter of a rival stone merchant. A misunderstanding drives Marcia and Jocelyn apart. As he ages, he glimpses his ideal of the well-beloved once more in Avice's daughter. But she, Jocelyn discovers, is already secretly married. Finally, aged sixty, he proposes to Avice's granddaughter (also called Avice Caro). He fails to capture any of the incarnations of his ideal and accepts time's victory over beauty by marrying the now aged and widowed Marcia. The plot has the implausibility and perfect symmetry of a fable.

WELLS, H[erbert] G[eorge] (1866-1946). Only a small portion of Wells's prodigious literary activity is located in the Victorian era. But it represents an achievement equivalent to the whole literary career of lesser authors. He was born the son of a lady's maid and a professional cricketer (and less successfully, a small tradesman). In his own autobiographical account, Wells stresses books as the means by which he first escaped, and then transcended the class into which he was born. An important episode in his family life was the appointment of his mother as housekeeper of Up Park Manor in 1880. A year later, the young Wells was apprenticed to a pharmacist. This was unsuccessful. So too, was his brief period as a draper's assistant, 1881-83. (The escape from the menial drudgery of retail service inspires his later histories of Kipps, Polly and Hoopdriver.) In 1884, Wells had a scholarship to study at the Normal School of Science in London. His three years there were formative. Especially influential was his encounter with T. H. Huxley, who inspired Wells with the evolutionary view of the universe and the biologism that was, in one way or another, to condition all his fiction of ideas and particularly his scientific romances. After 1887, Wells had a series of health breakdowns, and was forced to give up teaching (a brief sub-career, which he commemorates poignantly in *Love And Mr Lewisham*, 1900). In the late 1880s, he began publishing essays. But his début in authorship effectively begins in 1891, when Frank Harris* published him in the *Fortnightly**. In 1891, Wells married a cousin, only to divorce and remarry in 1895. In the same year, he published *The Time Machine**, and became a celebrity overnight. He was almost at once on friendly terms with the leaders of the London literary world. In the five years that remained of the century, he turned out an astonishingly rich and imaginative body of 'scientific romance', laying the foundation for what was to become twentieth-century science fiction*. Among other classics of the genre, Wells wrote: *The Island Of Dr Moreau** (1896); *The Invisible Man** (1897); *The War Of The Worlds** (1898) and a host of short stories and novellas. The dystopian *When The Sleeper Wakes** (1899) prefigures his move in the twentieth century to grand political and historical themes. But *The First Men In The Moon* (1901) effectively combines Wells's wry humour (which seems to derive from the cockney* school) with a hard science fiction scenario as does *The Food Of The Gods* (1904). Bernard Bergonzi has argued persuasively that the more purely entertaining romance of the nineteenth century represents the best of Wells's achievement. Wells wrote vigorously in a bewildering range of modes and styles up to his last, testamentary work, *Mind At The End Of Its Tether* (1945). BL 34. *DNB*. RM. *NCBEL*. Wol.

Wessex. Thomas Hardy's* antique term for the south-western counties (particularly Dorset) in which most of his novels are set. The region is intricately mapped out with a systematic set of fictitious names, e.g. Budmouth for Weymouth; Casterbridge for Dorchester; Ivell for Yeovil; Wintoncester for Winchester. The thin pseudonyms are quite transparent allowing the novels both geographical authenticity and fictional licence.

WESTALL, William [Bury] (1834–1903). Westall led an interesting life, some small flavour of which infuses his largely pot-boiling efforts in romantic fiction. He was born near Blackburn in Lancashire, into a mill-owning family and after attending Liverpool High School himself worked in the textile business until he was thirty-six, when he retired. His first marriage was in 1855, and in 1863 he married his deceased wife's sister, in Neuchâtel. His knowledge of the industrial North is reflected in his first successful novel, *The Old Factory* (1881). Westall had, in fact, been publishing fiction since 1876 but without any effect on the reading public. On leaving Lancashire in 1870, he worked abroad as a foreign correspondent for *The Times* and the *Daily News*. He also edited the *Swiss Times* in Geneva, an experience he records in one of his better novels, *Her Two Millions**** (1887). In Switzerland Westall mixed with Prince Kropotkin and other political exiles, and in later life, he travelled to North and South America. Apart from exotic locations, little of this experience rubs off on to his numerous novels which include: *Red Ryvington* (1882); *The Phantom City, A Volcanic Romance* (1886); *Captain Trafalgar, A Story Of The Mexican Gulf* (1887), translated from the French of André Laurie; *Nigel Fortescue, An Andean Romance* (1887); *Birch Dene** ** (1889); *Strange Crimes* (1890); *Trust Money* (1892); *Red Bridal* (1899), a story of the Napoleonic War. *For Honour And Life* (1894) is a typical Westall work, set in the late eighteenth century and narrated autobiographically by a 'Lancashire lad' of Swiss origins. The hero is brought up in Giggleswick where his father manages a textile mill. But he gives up this work to join the Swiss Guards in Paris at the period of the Revolution. Routine adventures and romance ensue. Westall returned to England late in life, dying in Sussex. BL 30. *DNB*. Wol. RLF.

Westward Ho!, Charles Kingsley, 1855, 3 vols, Macmillan. (The full title of the work is: *Westward Ho! Or The Voyages And Adventures Of Sir Amyas Leigh, Knight, Of Burrough In The County Of Devon, In The Reign Of Her Most Glorious Majesty Queen Elizabeth. Rendered Into English By CK*.) The hero of the novel is Amyas Leigh, a brutal young berserker. We follow him from school to his first expedition round the world with Sir Francis Drake. His brother Frank is, by contrast, the scholar; physically delicate, but intellectual. Both brothers are opposed to their subtle and treacherous cousin, the Jesuit (as he is to become) Eustace Leigh. All three men, indeed all the young male population of Bideford, love Rose Salterne, for whom they form the Brotherhood of the Rose. None will take advantage of another's absence. Amyas participates in the bloody eviction of the Spaniards from Ireland in 1580. (There is a particularly nasty massacre of Spanish prisoners of which the narrator notes: 'the hint was severe, but it was sufficient. Many years passed before a Spaniard set foot again in Ireland.' The novel was dedicated to 'Rajah' Brooke, recently censured in Parliament for his excesses against natives in Sarawak.) A Spanish officer is taken prisoner, and held at Bideford awaiting ransom. He seduces and elopes with Rose. Amyas and others of the brotherhood follow in their ship, the *Rose*. They track down the couple to America. There ensue various (and colourfully described) adventures on the seas and in the jungle. Frank and Rose, betrayed by Eustace, die at the hands of the Inquisition. Amyas rescues, among other Indians, Ayancanora, who later turns out to be the illegitimate daughter of an earlier British adventurer, and the ward of the hero's bloodthirsty companion, Salvation Yeo. Amyas returns to England in 1588, and sails to fight the Armada in his new ship, the *Vengeance*. He searches for Guzman (the seducer of Rose) like a man possessed. When the Spaniard is driven on to the rocks, Amyas curses God for denying him revenge, is struck by lightning and blinded. (Yeo, meanwhile, is killed.) He returns, chastened, to the loving care of Ayancanora.

WEYMAN, Stanley J[ohn] (1855–1928). Weyman was born in Ludlow, the second son of a solicitor. He went to Shrewsbury School and later to Christ Church, Oxford, graduating with a second-class degree in history in 1877. He subsequently studied law and was called to the Bar in 1881. He evidently was only moderately successful in the years up to 1889 that he practised. On the advice of James Payn*, editor of *Cornhill**, Weyman began writing historical* fiction early in the decade. *The House Of The Wolf*, a Dumas-like romance about the St Bartholomew massacre set in sixteenth-century France, was serialised in 1883. Although this is the pattern of most of his later work, Weyman's career did not take off until the 1890s. His costume romances include: *A Gentleman Of France* (1893); *The Man In Black* (1894); *The Red Cockade* (1895); *Count Hannibal* (1901). Many of his French historical romps were successfully dramatised. Weyman also had aspirations to be a Trollopian*, domestic* writer with such works as *The New Rector* (1891). He married in 1895, had no children and lived the last thirty years of his life at Ruthin, Denbighshire, where he was a JP. Together with Stevenson*, Besant* and Quiller Couch* he is one of the late Victorian exponents of the so-called New Romance. BL 25. *DNB*. *NCBEL*. Wol.

The Wheels Of Chance, H. G. Wells, 1896, 1 vol, Macmillan. (Subtitled 'A Holiday Adventure' it was serialised in *To-Day*, 1896). A precursor of Wells's comic 'guttersnipe' novels, which culminate in *Kipps* (1905) and *The History Of Mr Polly* (1910). The hero of *The Wheels Of Chance* is Hoopdriver, a draper's drudge at Antrobus's shop in Putney High Street. He has a bicycling holiday, a tremendous liberation in his painfully narrow life. Hoopdriver encounters adventures on the road the most exciting of which involve love with Jessie, a middle-class girl he meets. He eventually descends to fisticuffs with a rival, the caddish art critic Bechamel. He has a glimpse of what a full life might be, but takes realistic stock of himself and when his fortnight's holiday is up, returns to the draper's shop despite Jessie's offer to wait for him. Wells mixes pathos and comedy well, and invests his incorrigibly underbred hero with quaint dignity.

When The Sleeper Wakes, H. G. Wells, 1899, 1 vol, Nelson. (Serialised in the *Graphic*, 1898–99.) Wells's first dystopia, and arguably the first fully worked-out fable of progress gone wrong in English literature. He called it 'a fantasia of possibility'. After 200 years, thirty-three-year-old Graham, the sleeper (a kind of Rip Van Winkle), awakes from catalepsy to find himself the richest man in the world, and the cult-object of capitalism.

The explanation is logical. The sleeper, by his longevity, is a one-man dynasty; he has been able to consolidate the wealth which death customarily disperses. The world of the future into which Graham wakes is frozen into Marxian contradiction. There are the capitalists and the proletariat whose revolutionary potential has been nullified by a technology they cannot resist. The totalitarian super state-cum-corporation is ruled by Ostrog, with whom the hero has a number of long expository conversations. Graham (who was in his own time a socialist) leads an abortive uprising of the serfs, and dies in air combat. (The 'aeronautics' of this novel, written four years before the Wright brothers flew, are remarkably prophetic; Wells developed them further in *The War In The Air*, 1908.) The general tendency of the romance is to refute Edward Bellamy's optimistic *Looking Backward* and the socialist utopian visions of William Morris*. Wells put out a revised, shortened and more cheerful version of the tale in 1910, as *The Sleeper Awakes*.

WHITE, Roma ('Blanche Oram', 1866–1930). Roma White was born at Bury in Lancashire. She worked as a journalist, on the *Woman* magazine, winning in 1890 a scholarship offered by the *Review Of Reviews* for would-be women journalists under the age of twenty-seven. In 1897 she married Charles Winder. White's fiction includes: *The Changeling Of Brandlesome* (1896); *A Stolen Mask* (1896); *The Island Of Seven Shadows* (1899). She lived most of her life in Lancashire. Her pseudonym is a play on Blanche ('White') Oram ('Roma'). BL 5. *WW*.

WHITE, William Hale ('Mark Rutherford', 1831–1913). White was born in Bedford, then a country town, the son of a bookseller and printer. His father William White, a dissenter steeped in the writing of Cobbett, was a well-known figure in the town and its nonconformist community, being a deacon of the Bunyan meeting and a Sunday school superintendent. William White later became a doorkeeper at the House of Commons and was an author in his own right. Hale White was 'converted' at seventeen, and trained to become an Independent minister. He was, however, expelled from New College, St John's Wood, London, for unorthodox biblical opinions in 1852. A spiritual awakening which he experienced on reading Wordsworth's *Lyrical Ballads* in 1851 evidently had much to do with his inability to complete his training. (The crisis is closely traced in *The Autobiography Of Mark Rutherford*.) Thereafter, Hale White was a lay preacher. In the early 1850s he worked with the publisher John Chapman, through whom he met George Eliot* (a strong influence on his later writing). Like Eliot he was to become a student of Spinoza and his ethical system. In 1854, he entered the Civil Service as a clerk in the Registrar-General's office at Somerset House. He rose modestly in this line of work, moving to the Accountant-General's office in the Admiralty in 1858 and retiring at sixty in 1892 with a pension of £500. Hale White married twice; first in 1856 to Harriet Arthur, a musician by whom he had six children; secondly (Harriet having died in 1891) to Dorothy Smith, the daughter of a London magistrate. In 1861, he began contributing weekly articles on Parliament for various provincial newspapers. Over the next twenty years, little of note happened to him. He wrote a pamphlet in favour of the extension of the franchise in 1866, and met his idol, Thomas Carlyle (who strongly opposed the second Reform Act), in 1868. Over the period 1879–80 he wrote articles on Shelley and Whitman. Hale White's literary reputation rests on a series of highly autobiographical fictions anatomising the nonconformist sensibility, which he began to bring out in his fifties. Principal among these works are *The Autobiography Of Mark Rutherford* (1881) and its sequel *Mark Rutherford's Deliverance** (1885). Ostensibly edited by 'Reuben Shapcott', these are clearly transcripts of Hale White's own experience, remarkable for the limpid clarity of their expression. *The Revolution In Tanner's Lane** (1887) is a historical*, as opposed to an introspective, analysis of nineteenth-century dissenting conscience. *Miriam's Schooling** (1890) and *Catharine Furze** (1893) are slighter tales, both dealing with the provincial life the author recalled from his childhood in Bedford. His last work of fiction was *Clara Hopgood* (1896), a study of two sisters, Clara and Madge, the second of whom defiantly refuses to marry the man whose child she is carrying. The novel (which has clear connections with the new woman* school of fiction) attracted inevitable accusations of immorality. In his later years, Hale White cultivated his roles of amateur scholar (especially in English Romantic poetry), student of philosophy (especially Spinoza) and astronomer (after 1889, when he bought his first telescope). He spent his retirement in Groombridge, Kent, where he died two years after his second marriage. His son, William Hale White, went on to become a noted surgeon. BL 7. *DNB*. RM. *NCBEL*. Wol. Sad.

The White Company, Arthur Conan Doyle, 1891, 3 vols, Smith, Elder. (Serialised in *Cornhill**, January–December 1891.) A fourteenth-century historical* romance, centred on a famous company of English mercenaries. The story begins with twenty-year-old Alleyne Edricson released into the world from the Abbey of Beaulieu. He has a year to decide whether to pursue a religious or a secular life. A bemused Alleyne makes his way to Minstead, where his brother is socman (or steward). On his arrival, he rescues a noble lady from being ravished by a brute whom he discovers to be his brother. He and Lady Maude escape. Her father, he discovers, is Sir Nigel Loring, a warrior recruiting for the White Company. Alleyne is deeply impressed with the mild-seeming but redoubtable Sir Nigel, and throws in his lot with him. The White Company have various adventures on the battlefields of France and Spain. Alleyne distinguishes himself bringing a message through enemy lines. Sir Nigel is captured by the Spanish enemy (later he returns to England). Alleyne inherits his now deceased brother's estate, marries Maude and eventually becomes a trusted adviser to King Edward. The romance is told in Doyle's usual galloping manner.

WHITEHEAD, Charles (1804–62). Whitehead was born in London, the son of a successful wine merchant. After leaving school, he entered business as a clerk. As a young man of the Romantic period he wrote poetry that quickly attracted attention (notably 'The Solitary', 1831). Notoriety was sparked off by *The Autobiography Of Jack Ketch* (1834), a burlesque which he and his brother wrote anonymously. A couple of years later, on the strength of *Jack Ketch*'s fame, it was he whom Chapman and Hall* first had in mind for the project that eventually turned out to be *The Pickwick Papers**. From 1840 to 1850, Whitehead seems to have lived a spectacularly dissipated existence. He wrote a quantity of novels over the same period. *Richard Savage* (1842) is a historical* novel illustrated by John Leech*

(being first run through *Bentley's Miscellany** as a serial) and based on Dr Johnson's memorial of his doomed friend. The work is autobiographical in narrative form and highly melodramatic in plot. Whitehead's novel is grim in tone, but was much admired, by Charles Dickens* and Dante G. Rossetti among others. It has plausibly been suggested as an influence on Thackeray's* *Henry Esmond** (1852). Whitehead's other works (mostly historical) are: *The Earl Of Essex* (1843); *Jasper Brooke* (1845); *The Wife's Tragedy* (1845); *Smiles And Tears* (1847), collected stories; *The Orphan* (1852); *The Spanish Marriage* (1859). Whitehead's career had a sorry conclusion. In 1857, vainly hoping to start life again, he went to Australia. He died there, after three years, a pauper. BL 7. *DNB. NCBEL.* Wol. RLF.

WHITEING, Richard ('Whyte Thorne', 1840–1928). Whiteing was born in London, the only child of a clerk in the Inland Revenue service at Somerset House. His mother dying early, the boy's upbringing was disturbed, and he spent most of it with foster parents. For seven years, he was apprenticed to Benjamin Wyon the engraver. In the early 1860s, he set up for himself without much success. Meanwhile, he was educating himself. In 1866, he gave up seal engraving and turned to journalism for his living. He subsequently had a successful career as a foreign and North American correspondent, spending many years in Paris. He retired from journalism in 1899. Whiteing's first novel (published as 'Whyte Thorne') was *The Democracy* (1876). It was followed by *The Island* (1888), a utopian idyll of life on Pitcairn Island. This inspired a sequel, *No. 5 John Street* (1899), in which the hero comes over as the representative of Pitcairn to the Queen's Diamond Jubilee. His problem is that he has to make do on £1 a day (payable in yams). This means staying in an East End lodging house. The novel is the sprightly record of low-life London that he sees there. Whiteing received a Civil List pension in 1910, and in 1915 published his autobiography, *My Harvest*. BL 10. *DNB.* Wol. RLF.

WHYTE-MELVILLE, George John (1821–78). Whyte-Melville is probably remembered as the greatest of the hunting novelists, together with Trollope* and Surtees*. His parents were Scottish, and he was born in Fifeshire. Eton-educated, he entered the army with a commission in the 93rd Highlanders in 1839, exchanging into the Coldstream Guards in 1846. In 1847, he married a daughter of Lord Bateman (very unhappily, as it was to turn out). Whyte-Melville resigned his commission in 1849, but rejoined to fight in the Crimea in 1855 as a major of Turkish irregular cavalry. In this capacity, he saw action. In *The Interpreter* (1858) he vividly recollects the Siege of Sebastopol. Descriptions of 'the nightly butchery of the trenches', the troops' disgust with bungling generals and the satire on home-front blimpishness anticipates the best literature of the Great War. (Whyte-Melville's first-hand account contrasts with the chauvinistic blustering of the muscular* school of fiction typified by the oafish G. A. Lawrence*.) After the peace, Whyte-Melville settled first in Northamptonshire then Gloucestershire, devoting himself to hunting, golf and writing. His first novel, *Digby Grand, An Autobiography* (1853) was first serialised in *Fraser's Magazine** and, as an updating of Bulwer-Lytton's* anatomy of a gentleman *Pelham* (1828), closely follows the lineaments of the author's own career. Digby, the son and heir of Sir Peregrine Grand of Haverley Hall, leaves Eton with a commission in the 101st Foot. After service in North America, young Captain Digby devotes himself to dissipation in London, with the dangerous Mrs Margery Man-Trap. Having come of age and into his inheritance, the hero finally settles down to squirearchical respectability with his wife and hounds. Whyte-Melville gained fame with *Holmby House, A Tale Of Old Northamptonshire* (1860), a rattling and artless historical* romance, with Cromwell and King Charles as principal characters. His other perennially popular novel has been *The Gladiators, A Tale Of Rome And Judaea* (1863), the story of a pugnacious young Briton enslaved by the Romans. He wrote twenty-six novels in all, which divide evenly into dramas of contemporary life and sub-*Quentin Durward* period romances. They include: *Cerise** (1866); *Contraband* (1871); *Uncle John** (1874); *Katerfelto* (1875), a tale of Exmoor in the eighteenth century, with some vivid stag-hunting scenes; *Sister Louise* (1876). *Kate Coventry* (1856), the autobiography of a horsey young lady, anticipates the archly prattling Rhoda Broughton* narrator-heroine. The spirit in which Whyte-Melville wrote was amateur and modest. He did not live by his pen, and turned his writing income over to philanthropic causes being particularly interested in the provision of reading rooms for grooms and stable-boys. Sadleir, however, is too harsh in terming him 'Ouida* in breeches' and asserting 'it is impossible to regard him in the role of novelist as anything but absurd'. Whyte-Melville's old-fashioned chivalry is quixotically naïve, and often charming. And of all the Victorian novelists, he writes best about the curious English mania for equine sports. He died, appropriately, on the hunting field, riding 'an old favourite horse, the Shah'. He was a stalwart Chapman and Hall* author, reflecting that house's preference, under Fred Chapman, for morally uncomplicated, 'manly' fiction. On the side, Whyte-Melville wrote and published some translations of Horace's verse in 1850. BL 26. *DNB*. RM. *NCBEL*. Wol. Sad.

The Widow Barnaby, Frances Milton Trollope, 1839, 3 vols, Bentley. Rogue literature was in vogue at the end of the 1830s, and Mrs Trollope joined in with her vigorously comic portrait of Widow Barnaby, a study in dominant femininity to rival Thackeray's* Catherine* and Mrs Gore's* Mrs Armytage*. Born Martha Compton, we follow the heroine's unscrupulous campaign to get herself a husband. After various adventures, she settles on the elderly apothecary, Mr Barnaby, who dutifully dies leaving her £400 a year. Using this as her stake, the now middle-aged widow, blowsy but indomitable, continues her career of social climbing by marriage. This carries over into two sequels: *The Widow Married* (1840) and *The Barnabys In America* (1843). The last of the trilogy profitably recycles Mrs Trollope's *Domestic Manners Of The Americans* (1832) as the amiable widow (now married to the card-sharper Major Allen, her third husband) swindles her way through the New World. As Helen Heineman notes, in her biography of Mrs Trollope: 'the superiority of women had been her concern since *Domestic Manners*. Surely Martha Barnaby is her apotheosis of the new woman.' She might also be labelled a Victorian Widow of Bath. The three books were among the most popular of the author's thirty-five novels.

WIGRAM, William Knox ('A Barrister', 1825–85). Wigram was born in Dulwich, Surrey, the son of the distinguished lawyer and politician, Sir

James Wigram (1793–1866). He was educated at Cambridge University. Subsequently he himself was called to the Bar in 1852, going on to pursue a successful career as a barrister in practice while writing at the same time works of legal theory. Wigram wrote a Bentley* novel, *Five Hundred Pounds Reward* (1867), 'by a Barrister'. He also contributed to *Bentley's Miscellany** the doggerel narrative, *Twelve Wonderful Tales In Rhyme* (1870). BL 1. Wol.

WILDE, Oscar [Fingal O'Flahertie Wills] (1854–1900). Wilde was born in Dublin, the second son of an ocular surgeon (knighted for his services to medicine in 1864). On his mother's side, Oscar was related to the novelist Charles Maturin, author of *Melmoth The Wanderer* (1820). The family circumstances of the Wildes were comfortable and civilised. After attending the Portora Royal School, Enniskillen (in the steps of his two-years-older brother, Willie) Oscar won a scholarship to Trinity College, Dublin in 1871 where among other prizes he won the Berkeley Gold Medal for Greek. As a .classics scholar, Wilde won a further scholarship to Magdalen College, Oxford in 1874. There as the crown of a brilliant student career, he won the Newdigate Prize for poetry and took a first-class degree in Greats in 1878. At Oxford, Wilde came under the dominant influence of Ruskin* (then Slade Professor of Art, and a socialist) and of Walter Pater*, the leading theorist of what was to be known as aestheticism. Already, Wilde had established his personality as a dandy and wit. His mannerisms brought him considerable publicity in London, where in 1879 he took up the role of literary man about town, sharing rooms with the artist and fellow Oxonian, Frank Miles. Wilde's *Poems* were published in 1881. In the same year he was a notorious enough dandy to be satirised in Gilbert and Sullivan's opera *Patience* as 'Reginald Bunthorne'. The following year he undertook a successful lecture tour of North America, leaving behind him a trail of well-recorded epigrams and witticisms. (For instance, to the US customs officer: 'I have nothing to declare but my genius'.) On his return, early in 1883, Wilde spent some time in Paris, where he met such advanced literary figures as Verlaine and Zola. In 1884, Wilde married Constance Lloyd, the daughter of an Irish barrister, and by 1886 the couple had two sons. Money was a problem at this stage of the author's life and in 1887 he became editor of the *Woman's World.* He held the post for two years, and wrote the short fiction published as *The Happy Prince And Other Stories* (1888) and *Lord Arthur Savile's Crime And Other Tales* (1891). In 1890, his powerful novella, *The Picture Of Dorian Gray** was serialised in abbreviated form in *Lippincott's Monthly Magazine.* The story was published in expanded book form in Britain the following year. A volume of criticism, *Intentions*, was published in 1891 as was his influential polemic, *The Soul Of Man Under Socialism.* In the same wonderful year, Wilde wrote his poetic drama, *Salome*, the performance of which was forbidden by the Lord Chamberlain. The work was issued in book form by John Lane* in 1894, illustrated sumptuously (if indecently by the standards of the age) by Aubrey Beardsley*. In 1892, Wilde began his short and brilliant career as a popular dramatist with *Lady Windermere's Fan*, whose stage triumph brought him fame and £7,000. It was followed by *A Woman Of No Importance* (1893); *An Ideal Husband* (1895); *The Importance Of Being Earnest* (1895). But in 1895, at the height of his fame, Wilde's career collapsed when (following an unsuccessful libel suit of his own against the Marquis of Queensberry) he was sentenced to two years' hard labour for sodomy, arising from his connection with the young Lord Alfred Douglas. On his release in May 1897, Wilde fled to France under the incognito 'Sebastian Melmoth', dying prematurely in Paris. His testament, *De Profundis*, written in Reading gaol, was not published in its full form until 1960. The mawkish 'Ballad Of Reading Gaol' appeared in 1898. Wilde's disgrace and persecution had an enduring effect on English literary culture whose tentative flirtations with decadence*, aestheticism and post-Romanticism were promptly discontinued. BL 4. *DNB*. RM. *NCBEL*.

WILKINS, William [Henry] ('W. H. De Winton', 1860–1905). Wilkins was born the son of a Somerset farmer. He was brought up with a view to a career in the Church. But after leaving Cambridge University (where he had been Vice-President of the Union in 1885) he served for a while as private secretary to the Earl of Dunraven, then Under-Secretary of State for the Colonies. Wilkins clearly knew Africa well, and probably travelled to the Continent at this period of his life. He subsequently edited the manuscript remains of the explorer, Sir Richard F. Burton. He went on to work on various journals and produced sundry volumes of biography and history (the Hanoverians were one of his specialities). He also turned out a quantity of miscellaneous fiction, including: *The Forbidden Sacrifice* (1893); *The Green Bay Tree* (1894), a 'Tale Of Today' written in collaboration with Herbert Vivian under the epigraph *difficile est satiram non scribere*; *The Holy Estate* (1895), a study in morals, written in collaboration with Frank Thatcher; *The Alien Invasion* (1899). BL 2. *WW*. Wol.

WILKS, John (d. 1846). The son of a namesake father (1765?–1854) who was an attorney and radical MP for Boston (1830–37), John Wilks is remembered as a notorious fraud. He earned the nickname 'Bubble Wilks' because of the many dishonest companies he set up, with which to cheat speculators. Like his father, an attorney, Wilks was Whig member for Sudbury (1826–28), being forced to resign his seat after accusations of forgery. He was later Paris correspondent for the *Standard*, and was forced to leave the country after charges of spreading false rumours on the *Bourse*. His last recorded venture was a fraudulent Clerical Registry Office. Wilks is supposed to have written one novel, *The Tory Baronet, Or Tories, Whigs And Radicals* (1841), 'By One Who Knows Them'. BL 1. *DNB*. Wol.

WILLS, Charles James (1842–1912). Wills was born in Chichester, and went on to study medicine at the universities of London and Aberdeen, qualifying as MD and MRCS. In 1882, at the age of forty, he turned to literature for his living. Having spent some time as a doctor in Persia, he began his new career with travel books, following with such novels as: *The Pit Town Coronet* (1888); *Was He Justified?* (1891); *John Squire's Secret* (1891); *An Easy Going Fellow* (1896). He collaborated with John Davidson* on *Laura Ruthven's Widowhood* (1893). Wills combined his travel and fictional styles of writing in the popular *Behind An Eastern Veil* (1894), which narrates certain 'events occurring in the experience of a lady who had a unique opportunity of observing the inner life of ladies in the upper class of Persia'. BL 9. *WW*. Wol.

Windsor Castle, William Harrison Ainsworth; 1843, 3 vols, Colburn. (The novel was first run through *Ainsworth's Magazine**, August 1842–December 1843. Over 1843–44, Henry Colburn* reissued the work in one volume, and in eleven monthly parts.) This novel represents the most extraordinary collaboration between author and illustrator in the Victorian period. Ainsworth's original intention was to have the work illustrated by Tony Johannot, and he went to Paris to recruit the distinguished French artist. In the event, Johannot only supplied the first four illustrations to the novel (very detailed and naturalistic). George Cruikshank* provided the subsequent fourteen full-plate illustrations. They are very fine: particularly striking are Cruikshank's nocturnal designs, such as the lightning-illumined Herne appearing before Henry VIII on the Castle terrace. The text of the novel also threads through numerous photographically accurate woodcuts by W. A. Delamotte*. These provide an exhaustive guided tour of the Castle and the grounds. The main story line is little more than a pretext for these artists' work. Historically, it follows the intrigues which lead to Catherine of Aragon's downfall (and Wolsey with her). Her successor Anne Boleyn is, in her turn, discarded and the narrative closes with her execution. More interesting, is the thematic dualism between Castle and Forest. The latter's demonic monarch is 'Herne the Hunter' (a mythic figure Ainsworth borrowed from *The Merry Wives Of Windsor*). The antlered Herne haunts Henry, appearing to him whenever some deed of blood is imminent. Extracted from the illustrations which justify it, Ainsworth's novel is beset by the usual failings. He must bring in historically famous figures, wherever he can. A lengthy sub-plot dealing with Sir Thomas Wyat's love for a forester's granddaughter, in fact Wolsey's daughter*, is completely redundant. And the novel's dialogue is stilted beyond parody.

WINGFIELD, the Hon. Lewis [Strange] (1842–91). Wingfield was born in London, the youngest son of the sixth Viscount Powerscourt. He was educated at Eton and Bonn. He gave up an intended career in the army at the request of his mother, who feared for his health. Nevertheless, Wingfield's subsequent career was remarkably adventurous. In 1865 he was for a while on the London stage. As the *DNB* notes: 'Besides making many whimsical experiments, such as going to the Derby as a negro minstrel, spending nights in workhouses and pauper lodgings, becoming an attendant in a madhouse and in a prison, he travelled in various parts of the East and was one of the first Englishmen to journey to the interior of China.' (See his *The Lovely Wang*, 1887.) Wingfield was in Paris during the siege by the Prussians in 1870, communicating with *The Times* by balloon. For a while he was a painter, and later a theatrical costume designer on which subject he wrote a book. Among much else, Wingfield wrote fiction including: *Slippery Ground* (1876); *Lady Grizel* (1878), an eighteenth-century romance; *In Her Majesty's Keeping* (1880), a story of prison life on Dartmoor; *Abigail Rowe* (1883); *Barbara Philpot* (1885); *The Maid Of Honour* (1891), a French Revolution tale. Wingfield's health never recovered from a tour with the British army in the Sudan in 1884. He died in London, remembered as an extraordinary Victorian jack of all trades. BL 11. *DNB*. Wol. Sad.

WISEMAN, Cardinal [Nicholas Patrick Stephen] (1802–65). Wiseman was born at Seville, Spain, where his father was an Irish merchant. Wiseman went to school in Waterford after which he attended Ushaw College, near Durham. (At this period, he evidently wrote part of an unpublished novel, called 'Fabius'.) Wiseman finished his studies at the English College in Rome, where he was to stay as a priest for twenty years and where he met many of the visiting British great men of the day (e.g. Gladstone, Macaulay, Froude*). In 1836, he returned to England to be head of St Mary's College and devoted himself to mobilising Catholics in the country. With the re-establishment of the Catholic hierarchy, the Pope created him successively Bishop, Cardinal and finally in 1850 Archbishop of Westminster. In the early 1850s, with the Anglican panic about 'Catholic Aggression', Wiseman was one of the most hated and reviled men in the country. To counteract anti-Catholic propaganda, he resolved to write a novel, *Fabiola** (1854), a 'Tale Of The Catacombs'. The work was terrifically successful, with all readers of all religious denominations. Wiseman was also instrumental in persuading J. H. Newman* to write *Callista** for the same series as *Fabiola*. BL 1. *DNB*.

Wives And Daughters, Mrs Elizabeth Gaskell, 1866, 2 vols, Smith, Elder. (Serialised in *Cornhill Magazine**, August 1864–January 1866 with illustrations by George Du Maurier*, subtitled 'An Everyday Story'.) Mrs Gaskell's last novel: substantially complete but unfinished at the time of her death in November 1865. In design, the narrative is the author's most ambitious. The central character (around whom wives and daughters are arrayed) is Mr Gibson, the town doctor of Hollingford in the 1830s. A widower, he has a daughter Molly who is lively, independent, pretty and wholly devoted to her father. Having filled the role of housekeeper to Gibson, she resents his marrying Mrs Clare Kirkpatrick, a former governess in the household of the local landowner, Lord Cumnor. Mrs Kirkpatrick is, in fact, shallow and vain; although not entirely unlikeable. She has a daughter of her own by another marriage, Cynthia, a proud and beautiful girl lacking Molly's warmth of character. Love complications ensue. Cynthia has earlier become sexually compromised with Lord Cumnor's agent, Preston, who possesses some indiscreet letters from her. On her part, Molly becomes involved with Roger Hamley, the son of the local squire. Roger has always been overshadowed by his brother, Osborne. But Osborne fails at Cambridge, secretly marries a French governess and dies, leaving a new-born child and a disgraced reputation. Meanwhile, the more robust Roger distinguishes himself as a science student at university. His irascible father gradually comes to see his worth. At the same time, Roger, after an infatuation with Cynthia, finally comes to see Molly as the worthier woman and the novel was evidently to end with their marriage. With Molly's help, Cynthia disentangles herself from Preston's clutches and finally wins a respectable husband.

The Woman In White, Wilkie Collins, 1860, 3 vols, Sampson Low. (Serialised in *All The Year Round**, November 1859–August 1860.) The pioneer sensation* novel and one of the most popular and stylistically influential novels of the century. Technically, the narrative's most innovative feature is Collins's putting it together largely in the pseudo-documentary form of written testimony, diary entries, sworn evidence; a device which creates a striking effect of authenticity. Through the help of an Italian refugee friend, Professor Pesca, the hero Walter Hartright secures a position as drawing master at Limmeridge House in the north of England. Before leaving London, Walter meets a strange woman in white in a lonely part of Hampstead. She is clearly distracted, and seems to have escaped from a lunatic asylum. Ominously, she knows Limmeridge and its occupants and says some mysterious things about the place. On arrival at his new place of work, Walter discovers that his pupils are two cousins: the energetic and plain Marian Halcombe and the beautiful Laura Fairlie. Both are in the custody of a hypochondriac uncle, Frederick Fairlie. Laura uncannily resembles the Woman in White (whom he meets again at Limmeridge graveyard). Inevitably, Walter falls in love with Laura. But they cannot marry. She is promised to a blackguardly nobleman, Sir Percival Glyde, of Blackwater Park. Aided by the sinisterly fat Count Fosco (a 'Napoleon of crime') it is Glyde's intention to steal Laura's fortune. Walter goes off to the jungles of Central America to forget Laura. After her marriage to Glyde, an epic duel develops between Marian and Fosco. In a complicated twist of plot, Fosco and Glyde take Laura to London and switch her with the woman in white (in fact Anne Catherick, a half-sister). Anne is dying, and it is their intention to inherit Laura's fortune by thus simulating her death. Marian, who has been ill (the result of a soaking while eavesdropping on the villains outside a window), rescues Laura from the asylum where she is held. In a dramatic encounter, Walter is reunited with his love over what he supposes to be her gravestone. In alliance, Laura, Marian and Walter set out to confound the villains. Glyde is burned to death, trying to falsify the parish records which show him to be illegitimate. Fosco, with the help of Pesca, is betrayed to an Italian secret society which eventually assassinates him in Paris. And, by looking at death certificates, the heroic trio eventually prove that Anne could not have been Laura. At the end of the novel, Laura is an heiress again. She and Walter marry and live happily ever after with Marian as their inseparable companion.

The Woman Who Did, Grant Allen, 1895, 1 vol, John Lane. (No. VIII in Lane's *Keynotes** series.) The most notorious of the new woman* novels, and by far the most successful work Allen managed in a long and busy career. The book went through nineteen editions in a year, and brought the author £1,000 per annum for the rest of his life. (The catchy and sexually suggestive title spawned innumerable jests.) The heroine, Herminia Barton, Girton-educated and the daughter of the Dean of Dunwich, is determined to free herself from the traps of marriage. She accordingly has a rational love affair with Alan Merrick, an artist bohemian enough personally but the son of a Harley Street gout specialist of conventional views. Alan and Herminia set up house together, and for six months are blissfully happy. But he dies of typhoid in Italy where they have gone for the birth of their child. Herminia returns to an unforgiving and bourgeois England where decent society shuns her and her bastard daughter, Dolores. She refuses all help from her family and declines an offer of marriage from a fellow Fabian, Harvey Kynaston. Instead, she earns a precarious living writing and determines to bring Dolores up freer even than she has been. With cruel irony, the daughter grows up a wholly conventional woman who returns to her odious paternal grandfather so as to facilitate her engagement. A spiritually exhausted Herminia poisons herself with a vial of prussic acid.

The narrative concludes defiantly, 'Herminia Barton's stainless soul had ceased to exist for ever'.

WOOD, Lady [Emma Caroline] ('C. Sylvester', née Michell, 1802–79). Emma Michell was born in Portugal, the youngest daughter of Sampson Michell, an admiral in the Portuguese navy. She was taken to England in 1807 and in 1820 married a baronet, the Rev. Sir John Page Wood, later Rector of St Peter's at Cornhill in the City of London. He died in 1866, and as a widow Lady Wood wrote a number of novels including: *Rosewarne* (1866, by 'C. Sylvester'); *Sorrow On The Sea* (1868); *On Credit* (1870); *Wild Weather* (1872); *Youth On The Prow* (1879). Some of her fiction (e.g. *Seadrift*, 1871) has a nautical* tang. And there is probably an autobiographical element in the portrait of Myra Leith, the unhappy heroine of *Ruling The Roast* (1874), who unwisely marries the oafish clergyman son of an earl. BL 11. Boase. Wol.

WOOD, Mrs Henry [Ellen] (née Price, 1814–87). Ellen Price was born in Worcester, where her father, a cultivated and musical man, manufactured gloves. (The locality and the industry are reflected in the 'Helstonleigh' sections of the author's later fiction.) The Price household was comfortable and strongly Anglican. Ellen spent most of her childhood with her grandmother and while still a girl developed severe curvature of the spine. She was bedridden for four years and the disorder left her a semi-invalid for the rest of her life. In 1836, Ellen Price married a prominent banker and former consular official, Henry Wood (whose name she always subsequently adopted in her writing). The couple lived abroad (mainly in France) until 1856, when they returned to Norwood, south London to live in a rented house. There were several children and Henry Wood seems at this period to have lost the family fortune, obliging his wife to earn money. Mrs Wood had been publishing short stories and sketches since the early 1850s. Her first novel, *Danesbury House** (1860), was written in twenty-eight days for the prize offered by the Scottish Temperance League. It won her £100. By this date, she was known both to William Harrison Ainsworth* the editor and Richard Bentley* the publisher. The latter, on the recommendation of the former, published *East Lynne** in 1861 giving the still novice author the unusually high price of £600 for the copyright. Wood's ripe melodrama was a terrific hit with the reading public, especially those who patronised the libraries. By 1876 Bentley had printed 65,000 copies of the work. Wood followed up with the equally melodramatic *Mrs Halliburton's Troubles* (1862), the story of a widow who brings up her young brood successfully, despite poverty and in contrast to the wealthy Dare family whose lawyer head has cheated her out of her inheritance. The novel expresses strongly the author's view that moral trials create moral strength. *The Channings** (1862) also has two contrasting families at its centre: the Channings (virtuous) and the Yorkes (worldly). As is usual with Wood's fiction, these novels have a crime and detective* interest woven into the moral narrative (murder in *Mrs Halliburton's Troubles*, theft of a £20 note in *The Channings*). *A Life's Secret* (1867) is one of the bigamy* novels fashionable in the 1860s but is also notable for a sub-plot dealing with a strike at the firm of Hunter and Hunter, in which Wood's Conservative political views are given full play. *The Shadow Of Ashlydyat* (1863) is more of a ghost* story than anything the author had previously written, the title referring to a mysterious shadow that appears whenever any misfortune is about to befall the Godolphin family. The work was the author's favourite, although such gothic* themes did not usually suit her. Henry Wood died in 1866 and the following year his widow (now living in some style in St John's Wood) took over editorship of the *Argosy*, the journal in which most of her later fiction appeared, including after 1868, her various series of 'Johnny Ludlow' papers which recall her childhood in rural Worcester. The stories were published in three volumes in 1874. The various episodes, connected by the person of the narrator-hero, follow Ludlow's growth from boyhood up. Particularly attractive is the picture of his friendship with the local squire's son, Tod. These papers are generally regarded as Wood's finest work, lacking as they do any melodrama, piety or depictions of high life. At this period of her life she was furiously busy, bringing out fifteen novels in the seven years after *East Lynne*. Between 1868 and 1890, she was to bring out eleven full-length new novels for serialisation in *Argosy*, keeping the otherwise undistinguished journal afloat. Wood's other fiction includes: *Lord Oakburn's Daughters* (1864); *Anne Hereford* (1868); *Bessy Wells* (1875); *Court Netherleigh* (1881). Mrs Wood lived her later life in Hampstead. Her son, Charles Wood, took over editorship of the *Argosy* in 1887, and wrote a memorial of his mother, published in 1894. BL 39. *DNB*. RM. *NCBEL*. Wol. Sad.

The Woodlanders, Thomas Hardy, 1887, 3 vols, Macmillan. (Serialised in *Macmillan's Magazine*, May 1886–April 1887.) A story set in the forest areas of Wessex. Having been dispossessed of his family property, Giles Winterborne, a woodlander, has gone into the travelling cider business. He is loved by a peasant girl, Marty South, but does not love her in return; Marty's one attraction is her magnificent head of hair, which poverty obliges her to sell. Giles loves Grace Melbury, the daughter of a timber merchant. Grace has been brought up as a lady and has seen a world outside Wessex. Consequently, she accedes to her father's wish that instead of the unfortunate Giles she should marry the fashionable young doctor, Edred Fitzpiers. Fitzpiers has already seduced a local girl, Suke Damson, and allows himself to be seduced by a rich widow, Felice Charmond, whom he has treated after an accident in her carriage. He deserts Grace, who vainly hopes for release by divorce under the new 1857 law. When Fitzpiers returns from abroad, Grace goes to Giles in his small hut in the woods. Out of respect, Giles sleeps outside, and dies of exposure. Grace and Marty are united over his grave. Grace is eventually reconciled to Fitzpiers.

The Wooing O't, Mrs Hector Alexander, 1873, 3 vols, Bentley. (Serialised in *Temple Bar*, June 1872–October 1873.) One of the more plausible of Victorian Cinderella stories. Set in the 1850s, it follows the career of Margaret ('Maggie') Grey. Maggie is an orphan. She is first encountered unhappily lodging in London with her sharp-tongued aunt and her amiable but ineffectual Uncle John, who runs a chemist's shop. Maggie is offered the post of companion to a woman of the world, Mrs Berry, at £12 a year. This brings her to Paris, where she catches the attention of the heir to an earl, Lord Torchester. But to everyone's amazement (notably Mrs Berry's), she refuses the young lord's proposal. The second half of the story is taken up with Maggie's long wooing by Torchester's cousin, Geoffrey Trafford.

Trafford is financially ruined, becomes a lawyer and marries Maggie instead of the heiress Miss Grantham. Mrs Berry concludes: 'If ever a girl was born with a silver spoon in her mouth, you are that girl'.

WORBOISE, Emma Jane (1825–87). Emma Worboise was born in Birmingham, the daughter of a landowner in the city. She was precocious, and at the age of twenty had a mass of unpublished manuscripts. Her first novel, *Alice Cunningham* appeared in 1846. At some point she married Etherington Guyton. Worboise was an ardent Christian, writing hymns and editing the *Christian World* from 1866 until her death. She wrote a large quantity of improving fictions, including: *Labour And Wait* (1867); *Heart's-Ease In The Family* (1874); *Sissie* (1882). A complete edition of her fiction was brought out by the publisher James Clarke in forty-one volumes, 1882–91. BL 52. *DNB*. Wol.

Workers In The Dawn, George Gissing, 1880, 3 vols, Remington. The author's first novel, published at his own expense. The story follows the wretched career of a would-be friend of the people, Arthur Golding. An orphan, Arthur has an unsatisfactory and doomed affair with a clergyman's daughter, Helen Norman. More interesting (because closely autobiographical) is Arthur's involvement with a young prostitute, Carrie Mitchell. Arthur discovers her dying in the London streets. He takes pity on her, and eventually marries her. But his attempts to raise her to decency fail. She reverts to whoring and brandy-drinking. Eventually, unable to break the shackle of marriage, Arthur flees to America, and finally hurls himself in despair into the Niagara Falls, crying 'Helen! Helen!'. The work has the melodramatic excesses of a first novel which Gissing later brought under better control.

Working-Class Fiction. Relatively little fiction was actually written by the working-class novelist, and even what was written tended to be addressed to a middle-class readership (see, for instance, Thomas Cooper*). There was, however, a quantity of fiction about the Victorian working classes (see the social problem* novel), and a vast amount of fiction produced well-meaningly for the working classes (see RTS*, SPCK*). But throughout the Victorian period, the working-class population constituted a separate readership connected only tenuously to the middle-class mainstream. This readership up to the 1840s was largely catered for by chap-books. And throughout the period, its serious needs were met by the impressive quantity of self-improving literature supplied by pioneers like Charles Knight. But in the 1840s, publishers like Edward Lloyd* and G. W. M. Reynolds* began to churn out fiction for the semi-literate masses. A thriving market in 1d. serials evolved, featuring the work of prolific writers like Malcolm Rymer (or Errym*; see his *Varney The Vampyre*, 1846); Thomas Peckett Prest* (probably the author of *The String Of Pearls*, 1846, the grisly saga of Sweeney Todd, demon barber) and Pierce Egan* the Younger. Ainsworth's* and Dickens's* works were ruthlessly plagiarised and crudified (see Reynolds's *Pickwick Abroad*, 1838). And in 1845, the *London Journal* was launched, to be followed by Reynolds's weekly publications (e.g. his *Miscellany*, 1846–49) and his lurid *Mysteries Of London* (1846–48) which reportedly clocked up sales as high as half a million an issue. 1840s popular fiction drew heavily on the gothic* tradition, although in Reynolds's work (particularly his anti-royalist *Mysteries Of The Court Of London*, 1849–56) a radical sentiment is often present. But in general, fiction for the masses was extravagantly escapist and apolitical. In the 1850s, the working-class reader is gradually absorbed into the middle class orbit.

The World's Desire, H. Rider Haggard and Andrew Lang, 1890, 1 vol, Longman. (Serialised in *The New Review*, April–December 1890.) An ingenious revision of Homer's *Odyssey*. Odysseus returns from his unchronicled 'second wandering' to Ithaca and finds his family dead and his country ravaged by plague. Aphrodite tells him that Helen still lives, and he travels to Egypt (currently suffering the biblical plagues) to find her. His search is frustrated by a beautiful sorceress, Queen Meriaman, who loves him. He becomes Eperitus, captain of the Pharaoh's guard. The hero eventually discovers Helen, in the guise of Hathor, a goddess of love, 'the world's desire'. They are united in death after Odysseus is slain in battle by his son (by Circe), Telegonus. The work combines Lang's scholarship with the romantic imagination of Haggard.

WRAXALL, Sir [Frederic Charles] Lascelles (1828–65). Wraxall was born in Boulogne, the son of an officer in the Royal Artillery. He was educated at Shrewsbury School, left Oxford without a degree and from 1846 to 1855 lived on the Continent. During the Crimean War, he served with a Turkish contingent. After hostilities, in 1858, he edited the *Naval And Military Gazette*. In 1863, he inherited a baronetcy from his uncle. Wraxall published military theory, biography and history. He was the authorised translator of Victor Hugo's *Les Misérables* (1862) and contributed to many magazines. He also wrote a number of action novels, many with a historical* setting. They include: *Wild Oats* (1858); *Camp Life* (1860), a work which recollects the author's experiences in the Crimea; *Only A Woman* (1860); *Married In Haste* (1863); *The Backwoodsman* (1864); *Goldenhair* (1865), a tale of the Pilgrim fathers in New England; *Mercedes* (1865). Wraxall died in Vienna. BL 9. *DNB*. Wol. RLF.

The Wreck of The Grosvenor, W. Clark Russell, 1877, 3 vols, Sampson Low. The most popular mid-Victorian melodrama of adventure and heroism at sea. The *Grosvenor*, a 'small full-rigged ship of 500 tons', sets out from England for Valparaiso, loaded with pianofortes and manned by a surly crew, mutinous over their putrid rations. The second mate, Mr Royle (who tells the story), is the only man they trust. At sea, the *Grosvenor* picks up some survivors from a wreck including a beautiful young girl, Mary Robertson. Royle has to defy his tyrannical captain to carry out the rescue and is clapped in irons. During the subsequent mutiny by the ship's crew, all the officers except Royle are killed. Resourcefully, he manages to dupe the mutineeers so that only he, Mary and two loyal sailors are left on board. After a storm, a shipwreck and another rescue, they find themselves safely aboard a Scottish steamer. On shore they marry and live happily ever after on Mary's fortune. The novel has gripping descriptions of peril at sea and is particularly powerful in depicting the inhumanity of vessels to each other on the high seas. As Russell noted in a preface, the novel 'found its first and best welcome in the United States'.

Wuthering Heights, Ellis Bell (i.e. Emily Brontë), 1847, 3 vols, Newby. The twentieth century's favourite nineteenth-century novel. The narration is complex. It begins as the journal of Mr Lockwood, who has taken over the tenancy of Thrushcross Grange, in Yorkshire. Lockwood goes over to Wuthering Heights, where his misanthropic landlord, Mr Heathcliff, lives. Following this visit, Lockwood learns from his housekeeper Nelly Dean the strange history of the Earnshaw family. Some forty years before, old Mr Earnshaw came back from Liverpool with a gypsy child, later called Heathcliff. Heathcliff and Earnshaw's daughter Catherine grew up wild. But on old Earnshaw's death, his son Hindley victimised Heathcliff, degrading him to the level of a groom. Catherine, meanwhile, was taken up by the genteel Linton family at Thrushcross Grange. Conceding her to his rival, Edgar Linton, Heathcliff ran away. Some years later, mysteriously rich, Heathcliff returned to take his revenge. Pandering to Hindley's weakness for cards and drink, Heathcliff became master of Wuthering Heights. Meanwhile, he came between Catherine and Edgar Linton, provoking the crisis which led to her death in childbirth. Heathcliff, by eloping with Isabella Linton (whom he subsequently brutally abused), continued his vengeance on the Lintons. He completed it, by forcibly marrying his degenerate son to Edgar's daughter (also called Catherine). The climax of the story recounts Heatchliff's haunting by the ghost of his lover, Catherine, and his death from starvation. Young Catherine (a widow) civilises and marries Hindley's son Hareton. Brontë's story is extraordinarily powerful, particularly in its depictions of the older Heathcliff and Catherine, and in its moorland setting.

Y

YATES, Edmund Hodgson (1831–94). Yates was born in Edinburgh where his parents, both theatrical people, were on tour. Yates's mother was a well-known actress and his father later the manager of the Adelphi Theatre in London. Edmund was sent to school in Highgate, and spent a year in Germany before joining the General Post Office as a clerk in 1847. Yates's advance in the service was rapid. By 1862, he was head of the missing letters department and he remained in Post Office employment until 1872, despite a vast amount of literary work, play-writing and editing on the side. From his twentieth year (when Ainsworth* printed one of his poems in his magazine), Yates contributed to various journals (the *Court Journal*, the *Illustrated London News**, *Bentley's Miscellany**, inter alia), belonged to any number of clubs (including the Garrick and Fielding) and was a leading member of the bohemian set which attached itself in a discipleship relation to Dickens*. Yates's domestic life was, however, bourgeois enough and in 1853 he married Louise Wilkinson, one of the daughters of the Wilkinson's Sword Company. The couple had four sons in six years. (Dickens stood as godfather to one, and the novelist Frank Smedley* to another.) From 1854 to 1860, Yates was the drama critic of the *Daily News*. Yates went on to found his own short-lived magazines in the late 1850s. More successfully, he was the *Illustrated Times*'s gossip columnist ('The Lounger at the Clubs'), and in 1858 became the first editor of the weekly, *Town Talk*. It was in this last journal that he attacked Thackeray* and found himself the centre of the furious quarrel that ensued. Despite Dickens's support, Yates was expelled from the Garrick Club for conduct unbecoming a gentleman, a disgrace from which he bounced back remarkably well. Yates also wrote successful pieces for the theatre. In 1860, he took over the editorship of *Temple Bar** and in 1867 progressed to *Tinsley's Magazine**, leaving his bohemian mark on both journals (although his parting from William Tinsley* after two years was acrimonious). In 1873 he became the European correspondent of the *New York Herald* at a munificent salary of £1,200 a year. From 1879 to 1884, he was the editor of *Time*. Yates gave lectures and 'entertainments' (on the Dickens and Albert Smith* pattern) in America and in 1874, founded a successful society magazine, the *World*. The periodical was immensely popular and at its zenith at the end of the 1870s was earning its proprietor an estimated £10,000 a year. A man of wealth and style, Yates could afford such luxuries as a steam yacht and fine houses in London, the country and Brighton. A libellous piece by one of his journalists (whom Yates refused to name) in the *World* about the Earl of Lonsdale and a young lady led to him spending seven weeks in prison in 1885. Yates's health was poor at this stage of his life (and won him early release from Holloway), and he died at the Savoy Hotel at the early age of sixty-three having had a heart attack the previous night at the Garrick Theatre. It may be said that he went out in more style than most Victorian novelists. Yates published his entertaining *Recollections And Experiences* in 1884. Yates published his first story, 'A Fearful Night' in *Household Words** in May 1856. The numerous volumes of fiction which followed are never less than lively and began with *After Office Hours* (1861), a collection of short pieces mainly reprinted from *Household Words*. *Broken To Harness* (1865) was a full-length novel, hastily written for serialisation in *Temple Bar*. The portrait of a sporting lady, Kate Mellon, who kills herself breaking a horse, the narrative also introduces fashionable divorce complications. *Broken To Harness* was a great hit and Yates followed up with *Running The Gauntlet* (1865), which begins with a London theatrical setting and in a series of sensational* complications moves to Germany. Yates's fiction is marked by chaotic, fast-moving plots which feature crime, sexual intrigue and cosmopolitan, up-to-the-minute settings. *Land At Last* (1866) is a *vie de bohème* novel which centres on two children of the Earl and countess of Beauport. The elder, Arthur, is a cripple; the younger, Lionel, a forger. His other fiction includes: *Black Sheep!** (1867), a crime novel which Yates successfully dramatised; *The Rock Ahead* (1868); *The Silent Witness* (1875). The bulk of his fiction appeared in the 1860s (nine novels between 1865 and 1870). With everything else, it was a gruelling rate of production and the *DNB* refers to a widely circulated belief that Mrs Cashel Hoey* secretly collaborated on four of Yates's novels (including *Land At Last* and *Black Sheep!*) and actually wrote the whole of *A Righted Wrong* (1870), a work which carries only Yates's name on its title page. P. D. Edwards who has recently looked into the matter largely discounts the surreptitious collaboration theory, tracking it down to malicious allegations originating with Tinsley. A byword for literary energy and versatility during his lifetime, Yates was described by T. H. Escott after his death as, 'in harmony with, and a favourable type of, the epoch in which he lived'. He was also, for various reasons, probably the most unpopular literary man in London. BL 17. *DNB*. RM. *NCBEL*. Wol.

Yeast, A Problem, Charles Kingsley, 1851, 1 vol, Parker. (Serialised in *Fraser's Magazine**, July–December 1848.) In the late 1840s, Charles Kingsley was associated with the Christian Socialist movement. Among other writing and political activity for the cause over this period, he produced two novels: *Yeast* and *Alton Locke** (1850). *Yeast* was Kingsley's first effort in fiction. Lancelot Smith (the name, like Tom Brown's, is democratic) is a rich young man, just down from Cambridge. Hunting near the country estate of Squire Lavington he meets and falls instantly in love with one of the squire's daughters, Argemone, who is beautiful, High-Church, haughty, bookish. (Her sister, Honoria is, by contrast, sensitive and philanthropic.) Falling from his horse, Lancelot is lucky enough to convalesce in the house of his beloved. Via the Cornish gamekeeper, Tregarva, Lancelot is introduced to the incendiary doctrines of Carlyle, and first-hand experience of rural distress. (Kingsley here drew on his own parish at Eversley, where he had recently been appointed Rector.) The most vivid chapter in the novel is 'The Village Revel' in which Smith witnesses the brutish degradation of 'Merry England'. (Kingsley was principally attacking the romanticised vision of the country propagated by the 'Young England*' Tories.) Tregarva is dismissed, when his employer finds him to be the author of a violently subversive poem about wicked squires. Smith, as catastrophically, loses his expectations, and finds himself a poor man. He and Tregarva join forces with a socialist–utopian mission in mind. They are inspired by the arrival of the visionary prophet Barnakill (i.e. F. D. Maurice, the avatar of Christian Socialism). Argemone dies, having nobly exposed herself as nurse in a typhus epidemic. (Kingsley never loses an opportunity in his fiction to urge sanitary reform.) Tregarva and Lancelot undertake a pilgrimage to the Orient, from whence they will return as England's saviours. The story has a number of subplots. One concerns Colonel Bracebridge, who seduces a country maid and commits suicide when she kills their bastard child. Another polemical subplot (greatly expanded in 1851) has to do with Lancelot's repudiation of his Catholic convert cousin, Luke. *Fraser's Magazine* was subtitled 'For Town And Country' and catered for the English squirearchy. They were not charmed with the novel, and Kingsley was constrained by Parker to cut his rambling narrative short. It was allowed to expand again in book form.

A Yellow Aster, Iota (i.e. Kathleen Mannington Caffyn), 1894, 1 vol, Hutchinson. One of the most popular of the new woman* novels. The rich and intellectual Warings bring up their children, Gwen and Dacre, as stern agnostics. The boy escapes to Eton but Gwen is exposed to the full blast of her parents' arid creed. In order to strengthen her atheism, they arrange for her to have religion outlined to her by the local rector, Mr Fellowes. In fact, he contrives to fan the latent spirituality in the girl. But he predicts that there will be an explosion when she finally learns to respond to the fullness of life. The crisis occurs after her marriage to the aristocratic Humphrey Strange and the birth of a baby boy. She cannot love her husband and the couple separate. But in a climactic reunion, as Humphrey lies at death's door from strain, the couple are reconciled. The novel ends with the three

Stranges in a group: 'she simply held up her face to be kissed, while the baby clutched one of her fingers and one of his father's.' The slangy, free-talking heroine affronted some contemporary reviewers.

The Yellow Book (1894–97). The main organ of 1890s aestheticism. The magazine, an 'Illustrated Quarterly', was published by Elkin Mathews and John Lane* (after October 1894 by Lane alone) and edited by Henry Harland*. For the first four of its thirteen volumes the *Yellow Book* had Aubrey Beardsley* as its art editor. The publication departed in a number of ways from the orthodox Victorian literary magazine. Each edition was book-length (around 300 pages) and cost 5s. The tone of the contributions was consciously advanced and intended to affront the bourgeois; and the editors and publishers laboured to produce 'a beautiful piece of bookmaking'. In fact, the contents of the *Yellow Book* were less outrageous than promised, featuring contributions from Ella D'Arcy* (a sub-editor); John Davidson*; Henry James; George Gissing*; H. G. Wells*; Richard Le Gallienne*. The scandal of Wilde's* trials led to the dismissal of Beardsley (a suspicious figure in the public mind), and eventually to the going-under of the whole journal in April 1897. *BLM.*

Yellowbacks. Novels for railway* reading. The term was originally applied to the cheap 2s. or half-crown reprints of novels (mainly) which Chapman and Hall* provided for W. H. Smith's* to distribute via their station bookstalls in the late 1850s. Other publishers followed the trail blazed by Chapman and Hall (notably Chatto*). The volumes were distinguished by their portable, small octavo format and by their glossy, illustrated board covers (of which a principal designer was Edmund Evans). Michael Sadleir first drew attention in the 1930s to these yellowbacks as interesting products of the Victorian book trade.

YONGE, Charlotte Mary (1823–1901). The best of the Tractarian (or 'Oxford movement') novelists and a formidable woman of letters, with over 150 books to her credit. Yonge was born (and eventually died) in Otterbourne, near Winchester. Her family were old gentry, with some aristocratic fringes. Her father (a dominant influence in Charlotte's life) was a firm-minded churchman and a local magistrate. There were two children, the other being a brother seven years younger. Yonge became a Sunday School teacher at the age of seven and stuck to the task until she was seventy-eight. She was largely educated by her father 'who believed in higher education for women but deprecated any liberty for them'. The formative event in her young-girlhood was the arrival in 1835 of John Keble (thirty years her senior) as vicar in the adjoining parish of Hursley. Keble, an associate of Newman's*, had left Oriel College, Oxford, to make himself practically useful in the Christian ministry. Charlotte was confirmed in 1838; and the sacrament was one of the most momentous experiences of her life. (She commemorates it in *The Castle Builders, Or The Deferred Confirmation*, 1854.) Keble urged Charlotte (who had revealed strikingly precocious literary talents) to use fiction for the propagation of religious, and more particularly Tractarian, instruction. But he equally warned her against the overt preaching which marred many writers with a religious purpose. He edited her work in manuscript rigorously. And before she entered print, a conclave of the Yonge family decided it would be wrong to make profit from fiction, unless it were turned over to a good cause. Yonge's first novel was *Abbey Church, Or Self Control And Self Conceit* (1844). The main event in the novel is the consecration of a new village church (as had recently happened in Otterbourne). Yonge's first great success came with *The Heir Of Redclyffe**, in 1853. This work was turned down by John Murray* (who disliked fiction) and eventually accepted by J. W. Parker* without any expectation that it was to be one of the bestsellers of the century. Thematically, the novel reconciles Byronism (represented in the fascinating hero, Guy Morville) and High Church concepts of Christian self-sacrifice. It was found universally moving, even by the Victorian intelligentsia. William Morris* was inspired by the novel; Rossetti admired it; thousands of soldiers in the Crimea consoled themselves with this story of how the wild young hero is domesticated, dying piously with nothing but philanthropic goodwill towards all men in his heart. The novel earned hugely for its author. True to her family decision, she donated the profits to Bishop Selwyn to buy a schooner for the Melanesian mission. As 'The Author of *The Heir Of Redclyffe*' Yonge went on to produce a stream of novels for adults and juveniles. The best regarded was *The Daisy Chain** (1856), a saga of the May family. *The Pillars Of The House** (1873) was another crowded family story. The Mays reappear in *The Trial* (1863), a sequel which somewhat awkwardly makes concessions to the sensation* novel. Yonge's extremely readable historical* tales for children were much reprinted. Most popular were *The Little Duke, Or Richard The Fearless* (1854, a work set in tenth-century Normandy) and, pre-eminently, *The Dove In The Eagle's Nest** (1866, a work set in fifteenth-century Germany). In 1851, Yonge became editor of the *Monthly Packet**. She was to hold the post thirty-nine years. As her preface put it: 'it has been said that everyone forms their own character between the ages of fifteen and five-and-twenty, and this Magazine is meant to be in some degree a help to those who are thus forming it.' Yonge's life was passed within strictly parochial boundaries and she never married. But her strong maternal instincts were given an outlet in the series of stories she wrote for very young children in her 'Aunt Charlotte' persona. At the same time, she could write one of the most intelligent novels about the problems of Victorian female adolescence in *The Clever Woman Of The Family** (1865). Nor did she flinch from her own singleness in such works as *Hopes And Fears, Or Scenes From The Life Of A Spinster** (1860). Her novels are fluently written, and enjoin virtue without bullying the reader. 'She made goodness attractive', one critic observed. Yonge was in no doubt as to the use she made of her talent: 'I have always viewed myself as a sort of instrument for popularising church views.' She never made the mistake of ruining her popularity by churchiness although the Anglican Church was clearly the most important thing in her life. Her father died in 1854, and she lived with her mother until she died in 1868. Her only brother died in 1892, and her last years seem to have been lonely, although work on her magazine and literary activities brought her into friendly contact with such congenial writers as Christabel Coleridge*, Miss Peard* and Mrs Humphry Ward*. She only once left England's shores, for a short trip to Normandy in 1869. BL 106. *DNB*. RM. *NCBEL*. Wol. Sad.

Young England. A romantic variant of established Toryism, popularised by Disraeli* in the early 1840s. The main tenet was that feudalism represented the high-point of Britain's greatness. They particularly disdained the revolution of 1688 (the so-called 'Dutch' settlement). Young England condemned utilitarianism, supported Bolingbroke, Puseyism and the Tracts. Their Bible was Digby's *The Broad Stone Of Honour, Or The True Sense And Practice Of Chivalry* (1822). In support of the doctrine, Disraeli wrote a 'Young England' trilogy· *Coningsby** (1844); *Sybil** (1845); *Tancred** (1847). As a political force, Young England broke up in 1845 when Disraeli voted against an increased grant to the Catholic seminary at Maynooth (and the 'old faith'). G. M. Young acidly notes in *Portrait Of An Age*: 'Young England was a sincere if boyish gesture of goodwill, and to play King Richard to somebody else's Wat Tyler has always been a Tory fancy'.

Z

ZANGWILL, Israel (1864–1926). 'The Dickens* of the Ghetto'. The son of European immigrants, Zangwill was born in Whitechapel, London. Zangwill's father, a small business man, had fled from Russia in 1848. His mother was a Jewish refugee from Poland. Israel first went to school at Bristol and as a child showed remarkable gifts. In 1872, the family returned to London where Israel attended the Jews' Free School in Whitechapel. Aged ten, the boy was writing stories of school life. At sixteen he won a short story competition in addition to numerous educational scholarships. He eventually graduated from London University in 1884 with the highest honours in Languages and Philosophy. By this time, Zangwill had rejected the extreme religious orthodoxy of his father while retaining a fanatic loyalty to his own Judaism. He gave up a career in schoolteaching in 1888 and devoted himself to writing. His first published novel was *The Premier And The Painter* (1888), written with Louis Cowen. A fantasy, the idea of the story owes something to Mark Twain's *The Prince And The Pauper*. In 1890, Zangwill founded the comic paper, *Ariel*, which he edited until 1892. In its pages he published various short stories, collected as *The Bachelors' Club* (1891) and *The Old Maid's Club* (1892). At this period, Zangwill was commissioned by the Jewish Publication Society of America to write a novel about his people. *Children Of The Ghetto** (1892), written in his realistic mode, was instantly successful. Zangwill followed with *Ghetto Tragedies* (1893) and *Dreamers Of The Ghetto* (1898). Over this period, he was also writing lighter pieces for the *Idler**. In 1896, Zangwill met Theodor Herzl, then in London from Hungary to argue for a Zionist state in Palestine. Zangwill became an ardent convert, and at Herzl's death in 1904 he took over leadership of the international Zionist movement and was a proponent of the so-called 'Uganda plan' for an African homeland for Jews. Later, his devotion to active Zionism was dissipated in a general philanthropic benevolence. After 1900, Zangwill mainly wrote plays for the British and American stage, of which the most famous was *The Melting Pot* (1908).

His last years were clouded by poor health and political disillusionment. (He gave a notorious speech in New York in 1923, declaring Zionism to be dead.) Zangwill's Victorian fiction includes: *The King Of The Schnorrers* (1894), a loose-knit narrative dealing with the conflicts of Ashkenazy and Sephardic Jews in late-eighteenth-century London, first published in the *Idler*; *The Master** (1895), an 'art novel'; *The Mantle Of Elijah* (1900), a political novel. In 1903, Zangwill married a Gentile, Edith Ayrton (daughter of the physicist William Ayrton) who was also a novelist. His brother, Louis Zangwill (b. 1869), wrote fiction under the pseudonym 'ZZ'. (IZ) BL 14. *DNB*. R.M. *NCBEL*. Wol. Sad.

Zanoni, E. G. E. L. Bulwer-Lytton, 1842, 3 vols, Saunders and Otley. Drawing on Maturin's *Melmoth The Wanderer* (1820), the hero of this novel, Zanoni, is supposed to have the elixir of life. 'The Stranger', as he is called, first appears in Naples. Rumours follow him. Old men claim to have seen him, decades ago, no different physically from what he now is. Zanoni saves the life of a young Englishman, Clarence Glyndon, but later becomes his rival in love for the opera singer, Viola Pisani. Mysteriously, Zanoni instructs Glyndon to take Viola away from Naples and marry her. But the Englishman renounces his claims on her, in order to learn the secrets of Zanoni from his fellow Illuminatus, Mejnour. Zanoni, meanwhile, marries Viola himself and they go off to a Greek isle, where she bears a child. Viola intrudes into her husband's secret chamber, and discovers his awful secret. She runs away with Glyndon to Paris. It is now 1794, and the French capital is in the grip of the Terror. Zanoni, pursuing his loved ones, is captured, and gives up his immortal life on the guillotine to save Viola. The similarity between this novel and Dickens's* French Revolution work, *A Tale Of Two Cities**, has often been noted. Bulwer-Lytton (an adept in supernatural lore) claimed that the idea for the novel came to him in a dream.

Zoe, Geraldine Endsor Jewsbury, 1845, 3 vols, Chapman and Hall. (Subtitled 'The History Of Two Lives'.) Geraldine Jewsbury's first novel (begun in 1841). The novel has an eighteenth-century setting, initially in rural Warwickshire. Zoe Gifford (née Cleveland), 'the heretic wife', is the offspring of an English officer and a beautiful Greek mother whom he rescued from pirates in the Aegean. Her mother dies and Zoe is brought up by a clergyman uncle in England who gives her a boy's education. Zoe marries Mr Gifford, 'a Catholic gentleman with a large estate in Devonshire'. Gifford is a widower, and older than his vivacious young wife, who welcomes the prospect of freedom from spinsterhood (in this she anticipates Dorothea in *Middlemarch**). She mixes in salon society with Dr Johnson, Boswell, Fanny Burney, *et al.* Her portrait is painted by Reynolds. Through her husband's faith, she also comes into contact with a Jesuit priest, Everhard Burrows. Everhard is the son of a Catholic English squire, and his unusual early experiences (some in journal form) make up the bulk of the opening sections of the narrative. They fall in love, and Everhard rescues Zoe from a fire. His passion is itself ignited: 'he who in his whole life had never touched a woman, now had a whole life of passion melted into that moment. He crushed her into his arms with ferocious love.' But this 'madness' cannot be. He resigns his priesthood, and wanders over Europe, eventually becoming a philosopher.

Zoe's husband meanwhile dies, and she has a passionate (but unconsummated) affair with Mirabeau. He returns to France; she is free; her two sons are growing up; Everhard finally returns to Gifford Castle, and finding Zoe not there writes her a passionate love letter. She hurries to him, only to find him already dead of a broken heart. Zoe lives on, wearily. 'Life', as the narrator concludes, 'is no holiday game'. Jewsbury's novel is energetic and digressive, and its heterodoxy on sexual and religious matters shocked reviewers. Bulwer-Lytton* was more sagacious, observing that 'at last an honest woman speaks out, right or wrong, to the world'. Zoe was at first intended to be written in collaboration with Jane Carlyle and Elizabeth Paulet. Jane subsequently advised on the unfolding narrative, but did not write. Mrs Paulet gave up, but in 1865 she salvaged some of her original ideas for a three-volume novel, Dharma, Or Three Phases Of Love, an ill-planned but lively contemporary feminist novel which makes an interesting comparison with Zoe.

APPENDIX A
Proper Names and Pseudonyms

Asterisks indicate entries

Adams-Acton*, Marion — Jeanie Hering

Allen*, Grant — Cecil Power

Allen*, Grant — J. Arbuthnot Wilson

Allen*, Grant — Olive Pratt Rayner

Allison*, William — Blinkhoolie

Austin*, Alfred — Oswald Boyle

Baker*, Louie A. — Alien

Banim*, John — the O'Hara Family

Banim*, Michael — the O'Hara Family

Barber*, Margaret F. — Michael Fairless

Barclay*, Florence L. — Brandon Roy

Barker*, Matthew H. — The Old Sailor

Barr*, Robert — Luke Sharp

Barrett*, Alfred W. — R. Andom

Barry*, William F. — Canon Barry

Battersby, Henry F. — Francis Prevost*

Bayly*, Ada E. — Edna Lyall

Becke*, George L. — Louis Becke

Blouet, Leon P. — Max O'Rell*

Blundell*, Francis M. — M. E. Francis

Booth*, Eliza M. von — Rita

Boulger*, Dorothy H. — Theo Gift

Bradley*, Edward — Cuthbert Bede

Brierley*, Benjamin — Ab o' the Yate

Bright, Mary C. — George Egerton*

Brontë*, Anne — Acton Bell

Brontë*, Charlotte — Currer Bell

Brontë*, Emily — Ellis Bell

Brooke*, Emma F. — E. Fairfax Byrrne

Brooks*, Charles W. — Shirley Brooks

Brown*, George D. — George Douglas

Brown*, George D. — Kennedy King

Browne, Hablôt K. — Phiz*

Brown[e], Thomas A. — Rolf Boldrewood*

Buxton*, Bertha — Auntie Bee

Caffyn, Kathleen M. — Iota*

Caird*, Mona — G. Noel Hatton

Campbell*, Gertrude E. — G. E.
  Brunefille

Chapman*, Mary F. — Francis Meredith

Chapman*, Mary F. — J. C. Ayrton

Chesney*, George T. — A Volunteer

Chichester*, Frederick R. — Lord B******

Chorley*, Henry F. — Paul Bell

Christie*, Alexander — Lindsay Anderson

Clarke*, Charles A. — Teddy Ashton

Close*, John — Poet Close

Cochrane*, Alexander B. — Alexander
  Cochrane-Baillie

Collins*, Edward J. — Mortimer Collins

Cook, Charles H. — John Bickerdyke*

Cookson, Hubert M. — H. Crackanthorpe*

Cooper*, Thomas — Adam Hornbook

Cornish*, Farncis W. — Francis
  Warre-Cornish

Couch*, Arthur T. — Q

Couvreur*, Jessie C. — Tasma

Craigie, Pearl M. — John Oliver Hobbes*

Crawfurd*, Oswald — John Dangerfield

Cuffe, William U. — W. Desart*

Currie*, Mary M. — Violet Fane

Davis, James — Owen Hall*

Dawson*, Alec J. — Howard Kerr

De La Ramée, Marie Louise — Ouida*

Index of Proper Names and Pseudonyms

APPENDIX B
Maiden and Married Names

Asterisks indicate entries

Alison, Alice M. — Caird*

Armstrong, Annie E. — Challice*

Arnold, Mary A. — Ward*

Ashford*, Daisy — Norman (2)Devlin

Austen, Catherine — Hubback*

Bacon, Louisa M. — Barwell*

Bagot, Harriet F. — Thynne*

Beauchamp, Mary A. — Von Arnim
   (2)Russell*

Blood, Gertrude E. — Campbell*

Bonham, Elizabeth L. — De La Pasture*
   (2)Clifford

Boole, Ethel L. — Voynich*

Botham, Mary — Howitt*

Braddon*, Mary E. — Maxwell

Bradley, Mabel C. — Birchenough*

Bridges, Frances L. — Marshall [St
   Aubyn*]

Brontë*, Charlotte — Nicholls

Browne, Charlotte E. — Tonna*

Butt, Beatrice M. — Allhusen*

Byerley, Katharine — Thomson*

Caldwell*, Anne — Marsh

Cambridge*, Ada — Cross

Campbell, Charlotte S. — Bury*

Casey, Elizabeth O'B. — Blackburne*

Charlesworth, Florence L. — Barclay*

Clarke, Frances E. — McFall [Grand*]

Clayton*, Eleanor C. — Needham

Collier, Margaret I. — Galletti Di
   Cadilhac*

Collinson, Julia C. — Stretton*

Colquhoun, Lucy B. — Walford*

Connor, Marie — Leighton*

Cowan, Charlotte E. — Riddell*

Cox, Mrs Harry — [Bennett-]Edwards*

Craig*, Isa — Knox

Craik*, Georgiana M. — May

Crawford, Mary — Fraser*

Davis, Julia — Frankau*

Dawson, Louie A. — Baker*

De La Ferronays, Pauline M. — Craven*

Douglas*, Gertrude G. — Stock

Douglas, Christina, J. — Davies*

Douglas, Florence C. — Dixie*

Dowie*, Ménie M. — Norman
   (2)Fitzgerald

Duncan, Elizabeth C. — Grey*

Duncan, Sara J. — Cotes*

Dunne, Mary C. – Clairmonte (2)Bright
   [Egerton*]

Edmonston, Jessie M. — Saxby*

Eliot*, George — Lewes

Elton, Jane O. — Brookfield*

Esterre, Elsa — Keeling*

Evans, Anne A. — Puddicombe*

Farrer*, Henrietta L. — Lear

Farwell, Eveline L. — Forbes*

Fielding, Anna M. — Hall*

Fletcher, Elizabeth S. — Watson
   [Cromarty*]

Foulks, Theodora E. — Lynch*

Fowler*, Ellen T. — Felkin

Fraser, Lydia F. — Miller*

694

Index of Maiden and Married Names

Index of Maiden and Married Names